International Human Rights Law
CASES, MATERIALS, COMMENTARY

How do you keep students motivated when their perception of a subject conflicts with the reality of its academic study? International human rights law, unquestionably an exciting field, is also complex and demanding. With his breakthrough textbook, De Schutter focuses on international human rights law as a global legal system, rather than as a collection of different (though related) rights, giving it relevance and immediacy. Drawing on cases and materials from a wide range of sources, he shows how human rights law is used as a tool to address contemporary issues such as counterterrorism and global poverty. Materials are organized thematically, allowing readers to make comparisons and connections between different legal treaties and systems. Students can also easily assess how human rights are protected under domestic and international laws. The law is placed in context throughout, ensuring full understanding of why laws exist and how they work.

OLIVIER DE SCHUTTER is the UN Special Rapporteur on the right to food. A professor at the University of Louvain (UCL) and at the College of Europe and a Member of the Global Law School Faculty at New York University, he has been Visiting Professor at a number of institutions, most recently at Columbia University. From 2002 to 2006, he chaired the EU Network of Independent Experts on Fundamental Rights, a high-level group of experts which advised the European Union institutions on fundamental rights issues. He has acted on a number of occasions as expert for the Council of Europe and for the European Union. Since 2004, and until his appointment as the UN Special Rapporteur on the right to food, he has been the General Secretary of the International Federation of Human Rights (FIDH) on the issue of globalization and human rights.

International Human Rights Law

CASES, MATERIALS, COMMENTARY

Olivier De Schutter

CAMBRIDGE
UNIVERSITY PRESS

CAMBRIDGE UNIVERSITY PRESS

Cambridge, New York, Melbourne, Madrid, Cape Town, Singapore,
São Paulo, Delhi, Tokyo, Mexico City

Cambridge University Press
The Edinburgh Building, Cambridge CB2 8RU, UK

Published in the United States of America by Cambridge University Press, New York

www.cambridge.org
Information on this title: www.cambridge.org/9780521764872

First published 2010
Reprinted 2011

Printed in the United Kingdom at the University Press, Cambridge

A catalogue record for this publication is available from the British Library

ISBN 978-0-521-76487-2 Hardback
ISBN 978-0-521-74866-7 Paperback

Contents

PART II THE SUBSTANTIVE OBLIGATIONS

Table of Cases

EUROPEAN COMMISSION AND COURT OF HUMAN RIGHTS (ALPHABETICAL)

EUROPEAN COMMITTEE OF SOCIAL RIGHTS

EUROPEAN COURT OF JUSTICE (NUMERICAL)

COURT OF FIRST INSTANCE (GENERAL COURT OF THE EU)

EUROPEAN COURT OF JUSTICE (ALPHABETICAL)

EUROPEAN FREE TRADE ASSOCIATION (EFTA) COURT

HUMAN RIGHTS COMMITTEE

INTER-AMERICAN COMMISSION ON HUMAN RIGHTS

INTER-AMERICAN COURT OF HUMAN RIGHTS

INTERNATIONAL COURT OF JUSTICE

INTERNATIONAL CRIMINAL TRIBUNAL FOR THE FORMER YUGOSLAVIA

PERMANENT COURT OF INTERNATIONAL JUSTICE

ARBITRATION TRIBUNALS

CANADA

CHINA

COLOMBIA

DENMARK

FRANCE

GERMANY

INDIA

UNITED STATES

Table of Treaties and Conventions

DECLARATIONS

RULES OF PROCEDURE 9.21

STATUTES

Table of Comments and Recommendations of Various International Committees

Introduction

PRESENTATION

This course book offers a trajectory through the regime of international human rights law – its rules, institutions, and processes. It does not confine itself to the international dimension, however. Although human rights have migrated to international law since the Second World War, they live in a permanent nostalgia for where they come from: the liberal constitutions of the late eighteenth and nineteenth centuries, when they emerged as the Enlightenment's most visible response to the tyranny of monarchs and to the weight of tradition and prejudice. And as we shall see, the colonization of international law by human rights perfectly illustrates the formation of a 'self-contained regime' – one of those regimes that international lawyers are sometimes tempted to ignore, because they know they cannot be domesticated entirely.

The choice of materials seeks to reflect this hybrid character of human rights. The book collects cases, diplomatic documents, or comments. It places these materials into perspective, and it seeks to provide the reader with a robust analytical structure, which should help improve understanding of how they fit within a broader framework. A consistent effort has been made, both in the selection of texts and in the commentary, to highlight the specificity of human rights. For although human rights may have escaped the confines of the territory of domestic constitutions, they have not dissolved fully into international law and in fact, they resist assimilation. International human rights bodies and domestic courts are in constant dialogue with each other. International human rights courts are under the permanent temptation to mutate into constitutional courts. The domestic judge in turn tends to aggrandize his or her power in the name of bringing home values that are universal and rules that are supranational – but, by invoking international law, the domestic judge also transforms it into something else, that is better suited to the regulation of the relationships between the State and the individual or between individuals, than to the relationships among States. All this combines to form a unique human rights grammar which this book seeks to bring to light. Because this grammar is best illustrated by comparing international jurisprudence with the treatment of human rights arguments before national authorities – in particular judicial authorities – I have extensively relied on comparative material to illustrate the theoretical framework proposed. Thus, while most of the cases presented originate from the Human Rights Committee, from other UN human rights treaty bodies, and from regional courts (particularly the European Court of Human Rights and the Inter-American Court of Human Rights), a significant proportion also originates from the United Kingdom House of Lords (since 1 October 2009 transmuted into the Supreme Court of the United Kingdom), the Canadian Supreme Court, the United States Supreme Court, the South African Constitutional Court, and some other domestic jurisdictions. All these courts contribute to the development of the common law of human rights, and although its focus is on the international dimension, it is this common law that the book is really about.

The book is divided in three parts. Part I is an introduction to the sources of the international law of human rights and to some problems of interpretation that arise as a result of the 'self-contained' character of the human rights regime. Chapter 1 briefly reviews the main stages of the emergence of human rights in international law (whether at universal or at regional level), and it describes the unique characteristics of human rights treaties. Chapter 2 discusses the questions of attribution in the law of State responsibility, in relation to the concepts of 'jurisdiction', 'national territory', and 'effective control'.

Part II describes the substantive obligations of States under international human rights law. Instead of examining the content of States' obligation right by right, the five chapters of this part address, respectively: the obligation to respect human rights (chapter 3); the obligation to protect human rights, and the application of human rights in 'private' relationships (chapter 4); the obligation to fulfil human rights and the progressive realization of rights (chapter 5); derogations in times of emergency (chapter 6); and the prohibition of discrimination (chapter 7). This division is neither functional, as in certain casebooks inspired by the Realist approach; nor does it follow the traditional opposition between civil and political rights on the one hand, and social, economic and cultural rights on the other; nor finally, is it faithful to the separate treatment of each right we find in the treaties themselves. Rather, the choice of this structure was dictated by my overall aim in preparing this volume: to provide the reader with the conceptual tools that will allow him or her to study the development of the case law and the extension of treaty obligations, both of which will continue to evolve at an accelerated pace in the future. On issues such as the obligation of the State to protect human rights from private initiative, the invocation of human rights in relationships between private parties, waiver of rights, or the various meanings of non-discrimination and equality of treatment, my goal has been at once modest and ambitious: modest, in that I have no pretense of being systematic in my treatment of the subject; and yet ambitious, because I hope to provide the reader with a framework for thinking through these issues. The materials selected serve to illustrate this framework, and they are arranged accordingly.

Part III is about institutions or, as stated in the title of this part, 'mechanisms of protection'. It is composed of four chapters, dealing respectively with the protection of human rights at domestic level, through both judicial and non-judicial means (chapter 8); the UN human rights treaties system (chapter 9); the UN Charter-based mechanisms of protection (chapter 10); and the regional systems of protection, in the Council of Europe, the Organization of American States, and the African Union (chapter 11).

Throughout the text, I have inserted a number of 'boxes'. Their length ranges from a paragraph or two to a few pages. These boxes offer a brief discussion of certain specific issues, such as ethnic profiling, the role of the European Committee on Social Rights in the protection of social rights, or the regime of positive (or affirmative) action in EU law, that were considered to be too detailed to form part of the main text. The boxes can be skipped by the reader who is not interested, since they are not essential to the main argument. At the end of most sections or, at least, in closing each chapter, I also have inserted a set of 'questions for discussion', that should serve to stimulate class-room debate. Although they presuppose that the reader is familiar with the materials presented in the section or the chapter concerned, these 'questions' are not merely rehearsing the content of the materials, and they are not meant to test whether the understanding of the materials is correct; rather, they intend to raise new issues, not explored in detail in the main text, or to provoke a critical discussion about the positions presented in the main text. It is very possible in my experience to teach a full course in international human rights based almost entirely on these questions since, taken together, they cover the full range of the subjects examined in the book.

WHAT THE BOOK IS ABOUT

By the time human rights emerged as a part of international law in 1945, they already had a long history. As legal entitlements, they had originated in the liberal constitutions of the late eighteenth, and especially nineteenth centuries. International law did not follow suit immediately. And it did so, initially, only piece by piece, and hesitatingly. But it may be useful to recall certain antecedents to human rights as understood here, in order to make clear what relationships exist between those first attempts to 'humanize' international law – to borrow the formula of Theodor Meron ('The Humanization of Humanitarian Law', *American Journal of International Law*, 94 (2000), 239) – and the human rights that are the topic of this book.

International humanitarian law

Many authors see international humanitarian law as the first important precursor to international human rights law. While international humanitarian law has its roots in customary international law, it was first codified in treaty form with the adoption of the Geneva Convention of 22 August 1864 for the Amelioration of the Condition of the Wounded in Armies in the Field (18 Martens Nouveau Recueil (ser. 1) 607, 129 Consol. T.S. 361). But this instrument, like the ones that followed, still related to situations of armed conflict, a matter pre-eminently suitable for international law as the law regulating relations between States. And it is not before 1949, through the Fourth Geneva Convention relative to the protection of civilians (Convention (IV) relative to the Protection of Civilian Persons in Time of War, signed in Geneva, 12 August 1949, 75 U.N.T.S. 287), that the regulation of armed conflict sought to move beyond the battlefield, and to address what may be called the human rights of civilians during armed conflict.

There is, today, a renewed interest for the interactions between international humanitarian law and human rights law (see, e.g. R. Arnold and N. Quénivet (eds.), *International Humanitarian Law and Human Rights Law* (Leiden: Martinus Nijhoff, 2008); H.-J. Heintze, 'On the Relationship between Human Rights Law Protection and International Humanitarian Law', *International Review of the Red Cross*, 856 (2004), 789; R. Q. Quentin-Baxter, 'Human Rights and Humanitarian Law-Confluence or Conflict?', *Australian Yearbook of International Law*, 9 (1985), 94; L. C. Green, 'Human Rights and the Law of Armed Conflict' in L. C. Green (ed.), *Essays on the Modern Law of War*, second edn (Ardsley, NY: Transnational Publishers, 1999), p. 435; A. Orakhelashvili, 'The Interaction between Human Rights and Humanitarian Law: Fragmentation, Conflict, Parallelism, of Convergence?', *European Journal of International Law*, 19, No. 1 (2008), 161).

It is clear, of course, that both international humanitarian law and human rights law are based on the same ideals of preserving the dignity of the human being – they both have a 'humanitarian character', to use an expression familiar in international jurisprudence. And it is equally clear that, in situations of armed conflict, both these branches of international law can apply simultaneously. Indeed, because of this partial overlap, these two branches of international law may have to be made consistent with one another in ways which sometimes may be seen as compromising the integrity of human rights law. This was the case in the famous Advisory Opinion of the International Court of Justice on the *Legality of the Threat or Use of Nuclear Weapons*, where the Court took the view that Article 6 of the International Covenant on Civil and Political Rights (ICCPR), that guarantees the right to life, should be read in accordance with 'the applicable *lex specialis*, namely, the law applicable in armed conflict which is designed to regulate the conduct of hostilities', so that 'whether a particular loss of life, through the use of a certain weapon in warfare, is to be considered an arbitrary deprivation of life contrary to Article 6 of the Covenant, can only be decided by reference to the law applicable in armed conflict and not deduced from the terms of the Covenant itself' (I.C.J. Reports 1996, 240, para. 25).

This position has been criticized for creating the impression that, where international humanitarian law is applicable, the applicability of international human rights law would somehow be suspended, since it should be treated as *lex generalis* giving way to the *lex specialis*. That critique seems excessive. The treatment by the World Court of the relationship of the two branches of law would only seem to apply to the right to life of combatants, and it would be wrong to generalize, from that specific example, to how international humanitarian law and international human rights law should interact in general. Nevertheless, the temptation to treat both as mutually exclusive remains present, and this should come as no surprise. International humanitarian law and international human rights law emerged as answers to different sets of issues, and they were initially intended to apply to different situations. They influence each other in various ways, of course – although in fact the 'humanization of humanitarian law' (the influence exercised by human rights on international humanitarian law) is probably more significant than the subversion of international human rights by the logic of international humanitarian law. But these two branches of international law confront us nevertheless with different paradigms, which justifies that we treat them separately for the purposes of study.

Diplomatic protection

Another, at least as important influence on the origins of international human rights law, is the exercise of diplomatic protection by States whose nationals have their rights violated in another State. But here again, there are significant differences. Diplomatic protection is clearly instituted in the interest of States, and not for the benefit of the individuals aggrieved themselves: the prejudice caused to the foreigner only may give rise to international responsibility because it is considered to constitute a damage to the State of the nationality of the person concerned. Indeed, the State remains in principle entirely free to extend diplomatic protection or refuse it. There is no obligation under international law for the State to extend diplomatic protection to its nationals: thus, diplomatic protection is not premised on the idea that individuals have rights under international law, although it does presuppose the existence of minimum standards of treatment for aliens and an obligation for each State, who owes in that respect a duty to other States, to comply with those standards.

Of course, here again, there is a tendency for human rights considerations to permeate diplomatic protection, and there exists a lively discussion as to whether, as a result of the rise of human rights, diplomatic protection has become somewhat obsolete (see C. F. Amerasinghe, *Diplomatic Protection* (Oxford University Press, 2008), chapter 16; E. Milano, 'Diplomatic Protection and Human Rights before the International Court of Justice: Re-fashioning tradition?', *Netherlands Yearbook of International Law*, 35 (2004), 85–142). But the two sets of rules still respond to distinct logics, and it is hardly an exaggeration to say that human rights defined themselves, in part, as against the logic of diplomatic protection: the object and purpose of human rights, the Inter-American Court of Human Rights famously stated, 'is the protection of the basic rights of individual human beings *irrespective of their nationality, both against the State of their nationality and all other contracting States*' (Inter-American Court of Human Rights, *The Effect of Reservations on the Entry Into Force of the American Convention on Human Rights (Arts. 74 and 75)*, Advisory Opinion OC-2/82, 24 September 1982, Inter-Am. Ct. H.R. (Ser. A) No. 2 (1982), at para. 29).

The rights of minorities

Two other important developments followed the First World War. The peace treaties concluded then included a number of provisions aiming to protect the rights of minorities, and the Permanent Court of International Justice had the opportunity to identify certain common principles underlying the clauses relating to the protection of minorities in the Advisory Opinion it delivered on the *Minority Schools in Albania*: as it stated there, 'the idea underlying the treaties for the protection of minorities is to secure for certain elements incorporated in a State, the population of which differs from them in race, language or religion, the possibility of living peaceably alongside that population and cooperating amicably with it, while at the same time preserving the characteristics which distinguish them from the majority, and satisfying the ensuing special needs' (Permanent Court of International Justice, *Minority Schools in Albania (Greece v. Albania)*, Advisory Opinion, 1935, P.C.I.J., Ser. A./B., No. 64, p. 4 at p. 17). This, the Court continued, explained that the peace treaties containing clauses in favour of the protection of minorities sought to ensure both that 'nationals belonging to racial, religious or linguistic minorities shall be placed in every respect on a footing of perfect equality with the other nationals of the State', and that the protected minorities would enjoy 'suitable means for the preservation of their racial peculiarities, their traditions and their national characteristics' (*ibid.*).

Quite apart even from the question whether the peace treaties concluded after the First World War still were binding after the Second World War, the idea prevailed in 1945–6 that the protection of minorities had failed to pacify the relationships between States (particularly States where national minorities are located and their kin-States), and that it would become unnecessary in the light of the emergence of an international protection of human rights (see A. W. B. Simpson, *Human Rights and the End of Empire* (Oxford University Press, 2001), pp. 227–34). However, as we shall see in chapter 7 (section 5), there exists since the 1990s an increasing convergence between minority rights and human rights. Minority rights, it is now acknowledged, are human rights. New instruments have been adopted to protect minority rights as such – in particular, the Framework Convention on the Protection of National Minorities, of 1 February 1995 and the European Charter for European or Minority Languages, of 5 November 1992, both adopted within the Council of Europe. Remarkably, these instruments follow the model of classical human rights instruments, rather than that of the earlier treaties on minorities: the lesson has apparently been learnt that, in the absence of mechanisms of protection, the most generous clauses on the protection of minority rights will remain a dead letter. In addition, an increasingly voluminous body of jurisprudence has emerged from human rights bodies that protects minorities through human rights such as the right to respect for private life, freedom of religion, the right to education, or the right to property, either alone or in combination with the requirement of non-discrimination. It would hardly be an exaggeration to say that human rights have legitimized and made politically acceptable a revival of minority rights – that minority rights have re-entered the field of international law through the channel of human rights protection (on this revival, see in particular Y. Dinstein and M. Tabory, *The Protection of Minorities and Human Rights* (Leiden: Martinus Nijhoff, 1992); J. Rehman, *The Weaknesses in the International Protection of Minority Rights* (The Hague: Kluwer Law International, 2000); P. Thornberry, *International Law and the Rights of Minorities* (Oxford: Clarendon Press, 1991)).

Indeed, it is the extension of human rights that has encouraged an increasingly generous reading of 'minorities' protected under international law. Minorities are traditionally (although still controversially) defined as a group of persons who reside on the territory of a State and are citizens thereof, display distinctive ethnic, cultural, religious or linguistic characteristics, are smaller in number than the rest of the population of that State or of a region of that State, and are motivated by a concern to preserve together that which constitutes their common identity, including their culture, their traditions, their religion or their language (see, e.g. Recommendation 1201(1993) adopted by the Parliamentary Assembly of the Council of Europe, proposing the adoption of an additional protocol on the rights of national minorities to the European Convention on Human Rights; F. Capotorti, *Study on the Rights of Persons belonging to Ethnic, Religious and Linguistic Minorities* (New York: United Nations, 1991), para. 568; J. Deschênes, 'Proposal concerning the Definition of the Term "Minority"', E/CN.4/Sub.2/1985/31, 14 May 1985). But there has been a tendency, particularly within the Human Rights Committee (in its interpretation of Article 27 of the International Covenant on Civil and Political Rights) and within the Advisory Committee established under the Framework Convention for the Protection of National Minorities, to broaden the scope of the provisions protecting minority rights, so as to ensure that 'minority rights' benefit all those under the jurisdiction of the State, who present certain distinct characteristics (see further on this issue, chapter 7, section 5.2., b)). This evolution would result in defining minority rights as human rights, thus in principle to be enjoyed by all, whether or not they are found to belong to a 'minority' under the classical definition of this term. This tendency has been strongly opposed by certain States. Germany, for example, argues that 'the objective of the Framework Convention [for the protection of national minorities] is to protect national minorities; it is not a general human rights instrument for all groups of the population which differ from the majority population in one or several respects (ancestry, race, language, culture, homeland, origin, nationality, creed, religious or political beliefs, sexual preferences, etc.). Rather, the members of the latter groups are protected by the general human rights and if they are nationals by the guaranteed civil rights' (Germany, Third State Report, ACFC/SR/III(2009)003, 2009, para. 8). One is led to ask, though, why this opposition is so vehement, if indeed, those groups – the 'non-minorities' who differ through one or more characteristics from the majority – anyway are protected under human rights that, as we shall see, largely ensure the same protection of diversity within increasingly multicultural societies. The convergence is such, between minority rights and human rights, that the former have largely lost their subversive character: it is their distinctiveness that they are now in danger of losing.

International labour rights

A last antecedent to international human rights deserves a mention. In 1919, the International Labour Organization (ILO) was set up in order to promote the development of international labour standards. As expressed in the Preamble of the ILO Constitution, it was built on the basis that 'universal and lasting peace can be established only if it is based upon social justice', and that 'the failure of any nation to adopt humane conditions of labour is an obstacle in the way of other nations which desire to improve the conditions in their own countries'. The text of the ILO Constitution has been amended on a number of occasions since, and it has also been complemented by the Declaration concerning the Aims and Purposes of the International Labour Organization (Declaration of Philadelphia), adopted on 10 May 1944. But the basic purpose of the Organization has remained the same throughout its almost one century of existence. In many ways, the instruments adopted within the ILO, although focused on the rights of workers, served as models to the elaboration of the modern international human rights treaties (on the relationship between labour rights and human rights, see further P. Alston (ed.), *Labour Rights as Human Rights* (Oxford University Press, 2005); and L. A. Compa and S. F. Diamond (eds.), *Human Rights, Labor Rights, and International Trade* (University of Pennsylvania Press, 1996)). They differ, however, not only by their origins, but also by the economic motive behind their adoption – to avoid unfair competition through the lowering of labour standards – and by the fact that labour rights are centred on the sphere of employment.

The focus of this book

While these different bodies of law have been pursuing the same objectives, to a large extent, as international human rights law, they have been doing so through other legal techniques and institutional mechanisms. This book discusses international human rights as they have emerged as a part of international law since the Second World War. References will be made to international humanitarian law, diplomatic protection, the protection of minorities, or international labour rights, only to the extent that they intersect with the protection of general international human rights. To repeat, the structure of the book and the analytical framework it proposes are largely based on the conviction that, as a branch of international law, international human rights possesses a logic of its own, as a result of the hybridization of domestic constitutional law and of general international law. It is this logic which the book seeks to introduce and it is with this view that the materials have been selected.

ACKNOWLEDGMENTS

In closing, I would like to acknowledge a large number of debts. This casebook originated in a syllabus I prepared, then in a most primitive form, when I first taught a human rights class at New York University School of Law, as a member of the Global Law School Faculty in 2004–5, at the invitation of Philip Alston. It developed incrementally as I taught this subject in different institutions, including the University of Louvain, my home institution, and Columbia University. My first debt is towards the students who were foolish enough to sit these courses, and whose questions served greatly to enrich the presentation of the materials. Either within the EU Network of Independent Experts on Fundamental Rights or within the group of 'special procedures' of the UN Human Rights Council, which I joined in May 2008 as the Special Rapporteur on the right to food, I have also been fortunate to work closely with committed human rights defenders who are also important scholars and who were, and still are, a great source of inspiration. Among them are Catarina de Albuquerque, Philip Alston, Emmanuel Decaux, Morten Kjaerum, Rick Lawson, Manfred Nowak, Martin Scheinin, Dean Spielmann, Linos-Alexandre Sicilianos, Françoise Tulkens and Ineta Ziemele. I am also grateful to Matthias Sant'Ana for having assisted me in identifying the relevant materials from the Inter-American human rights system. As to those whose work inspired my own, it would be impossible to cite them all: I hope I will be forgiven therefore for not citing any, out of fear of forgetting one.

Brussels and New York

OLIVIER DE SCHUTTER

PART I

The Sources

1

The Emergence of
International Human Rights

INTRODUCTION

Human rights have a logic of their own. This stems from the fact that they have originated in domestic constitutional documents before becoming part of the corpus of international law, and that they regulate the relationships between the State and individuals under their jurisdiction, rather than simply relationships between States. In order to present this logic, this chapter provides an overview of how human rights came to emerge in international law; it discusses the sources of international human rights law; and it locates human rights within general international law. Sections 1 and 2 offer a brief review of the main developments that have occurred at universal and regional levels, leading to the contemporary regime of international human rights. The description of the evolution of the human rights regime, while forming an indispensable background, is left deliberately superficial for the moment. The following chapters shall provide ample opportunity to explore the most controverial issues which have arisen over the course of the emergence of the human rights regime. And the interesting questions arising about the sources of international human rights – such as the role of the emergence of a *jus commune* in human rights law, the status of human rights in customary international law, or the position of human rights in general international law – are explored in further depth in sections 3 and 4 of this chapter. The readers already familiar with the basic instruments of international human rights should move directly to those sections.

Sections 3 and 4 examine the new dilemmas brought about by the rise of international human rights and the strengthening of the institutions of the human rights regime. A first source of tension results from the development of a *jus commune* in the field of international human rights, particularly since the 1990s. This refers to the fact that international and national courts increasingly refer to one another, seeking inspiration in one another's case law, and progressively building a common understanding of the values which – whatever the precise legal source in which they are embodied – they seek to uphold. This movement reinforces the tendency for human rights law to develop as a self-contained regime of international law, to the extent that the relevance of general principles of international law in the implementation of international human rights is increasingly questioned. Section 3 analyses the emergence of this *jus commune* of human rights, by looking at its manifestations and some of its potential consequences.

Section 4 seeks to locate the place of human rights in general international law. It examines the extent to which general public international law imposes respect for human rights (section 4.1.); whether human rights have a hierarchically superior status in public international law (section 4.2.); whether they impose obligations which States owe to the international community as a whole (section 4.3.); and the place of human rights treaties in the law of treaties as part of general international law (section 4.4.). It also considers the debate on the validity of reservations to human rights treaties, which provides an illustration of the tension between the view that human rights treaties are specific, and the view that they should be subordinated to the general rules of the law of treaties (section 4.5.).

The first question – whether human rights may be derived from customary international law or the general principles of law, rather than only from the treaties which codify them in conventional form – may have far-reaching implications, even now that most of the main human rights treaties have been ratified by a large majority of States: since such treaties are only binding on their signatories – States – we need to identify the sources of international human rights law in general international law in order to hold non-State actors accountable to these rights. The second question requires an examination of the *jus cogens* nature of human rights prescriptions, the consequences of which extend beyond the law of treaties to issues of State responsibility. The third question is relevant, in particular, to the much-debated issue of the *erga omnes* character of human rights norms: while it is uncontested that a State may exercise diplomatic protection where its nationals have their rights violated by another State, it is less clear whether, beyond that specific situation, States have a legal interest in seeking to ensure compliance of other States with their human rights obligations. All these issues may be related to the more fundamental question of whether human rights treaties are specific, and should be treated apart from the rules applicable to other, classical intergovernmental agreements – a question for which the issue of reservations provides an adequate illustration.

1 THE UNIVERSAL LEVEL: THE UNITED NATIONS AND HUMAN RIGHTS

The Charter of the United Nations was adopted on 26 June 1945. It referred to human rights and fundamental freedoms as one of the aims of the Organization, mentioning specifically the right to self-determination of peoples and non-discrimination as belonging to the internationally recognized human rights (see P. G. Lauren, 'First Principles of Racial Equality: the History and Politics and Diplomacy of Human Rights Provisions in the United Nations Charter', 5 *Human Rights Quarterly* (1983), 1; A. Cassese, 'The General Assembly: Historical Perspective 1945–1989' in P. Alston (ed.), *The United Nations and Human Rights: a Critical Appraisal*, second edn (Oxford

University Press, 2004), p. 25). It was understood at the time that the protection of human rights would also enclose the protection of individual members of minorities who, therefore, would no longer need a specific system, as they enjoyed under the League of Nations. The following provisions of the UN Charter are most relevant to the protection of human rights:

Charter of the United Nations, signed in San Francisco, 26 June 1945:

[Preamble]
We the Peoples of the United Nations, determined ... to reaffirm faith in fundamental human rights, in the dignity and worth of the human person, in the equal rights of men and women and of nations large and small, ...

Chapter I. Purposes and Principles

Article 1
The Purposes of the United Nations are: ...
2. To develop friendly relations among nations based on respect for the principle of equal rights and self-determination of peoples, and to take other appropriate measures to strengthen universal peace;
3. To achieve international co-operation in solving international problems of an economic, social, cultural, or humanitarian character, and in promoting and encouraging respect for human rights and for fundamental freedoms for all without distinction as to race, sex, language, or religion; ...

Chapter IX. International Economic and Social Co-operation

Article 55
With a view to the creation of conditions of stability and well-being which are necessary for peaceful and friendly relations among nations based on respect for the principle of equal rights and self-determination of peoples, the United Nations shall promote:
1. higher standards of living, full employment, and conditions of economic and social progress and development;
2. solutions of international economic, social, health, and related problems; and international cultural and educational co-operation; and
3. universal respect for, and observance of, human rights and fundamental freedoms for all without distinction as to race, sex, language, or religion.

Article 56
All Members pledge themselves to take joint and separate action in co-operation with the Organization for the achievement of the purposes set forth in Article 55.

Chapter X. The Economic and Social Council

Article 61
1. The Economic and Social Council shall consist of fifty-four Members of the United Nations elected by the General Assembly ...

Article 62

1. The Economic and Social Council may make or initiate studies and reports with respect to international economic, social, cultural, educational, health, and related matters and may make recommendations with respect to any such matters to the General Assembly to the Members of the United Nations, and to the specialized agencies concerned.
2. It may make recommendations for the purpose of promoting respect for, and observance of, human rights and fundamental freedoms for all.
3. It may prepare draft conventions for submission to the General Assembly, with respect to matters falling within its competence.
4. It may call, in accordance with the rules prescribed by the United Nations, international conferences on matters falling within its competence.

Article 68

The Economic and Social Council shall set up commissions in economic and social fields and for the promotion of human rights, and such other commissions as may be required for the performance of its functions.

During the negotiations which led to the adoption of the UN Charter, the Foreign Affairs Minister of Panama, Ricardo J. Alfaro, with the support of Cuba, had proposed the inclusion of the 'Statement of Essential Human Rights' produced in 1944 within the American Law Institute, an organization of judges, practitioners, and academics dedicated to the improvement of the rule of law, in whose work Alfaro had participated. The proposal was not retained. Thus, although it includes a number of references to 'human rights and fundamental freedoms' as well as to the principles of non-discrimination and self-determination of peoples, the UN Charter does not contain a catalogue of human rights. However, in order to make progress towards this objective, the Economic and Social Council (Ecosoc), the organ of the UN tasked to promote international co-operation in the area of social and economic development, was mandated under Article 68 of the Charter to create commissions on thematic issues, including human rights.

The Ecosoc first convened in London in January and February 1946. It then established the Commission on Human Rights in a nuclear form, comprising nine members under the chairmanship of Eleanor Roosevelt. The Nuclear Commission thus constituted met first between 29 April and 20 May 1946. At the end of its first session, it made a recommendation that work should begin, as soon as possible, on the drafting of an international Bill of Rights: although, at the first session of the UN General Assembly held in January–February and May–June 1946, the Minister for Foreign Affairs of Panama again proposed to adopt by resolution the draft bill elaborated within the American Law Institute, his proposal had been opposed by Eleanor Roosevelt, on behalf of the United States, in part because the draft had in fact never been adopted by the American Law Institute and would have met opposition from the domestic constituency of the United States (A. W. B. Simpson, *Human Rights and the*

End of Empire (Oxford University Press, 2001), p. 323). So the work was left to be done by the Commission on Human Rights. The Nuclear Commission also proposed that the definitive Commission be established in the form of independent experts, rather than governmental delegates. They were also in favour of it having a strong monitoring role, and not merely a role in drafting legal texts for consideration by the Ecosoc and the General Assembly (see, for more details, P. Alston, 'The Commission on Human Rights' in P. Alston (ed.), *The United Nations and Human Rights: a Critical Appraisal*, second edn (Oxford University Press, 2004), p. 126).

The Nuclear Commission was not followed on these last two points when, in June 1946, the Ecosoc discussed its proposals. The Ecosoc established the Commission on Human Rights as one of its first two 'functional commissions' set up to assist it in its work (Ecosoc Resolution 9(II) of 21 June 1946). But instead of independent experts, the Commission on Human Rights was composed of the representatives of eighteen States, including the five permanent members of the Security Council (China, France, the Soviet Union, the United Kingdom and the United States). It later grew in successive phases, in order to remain representative of the United Nations membership, which significantly expanded and diversified following the decolonization of the 1950s and 1960s. It had fifty-three members in 2006, at the time it was replaced by the Human Rights Council. And until the adoption of Resolutions 1235 (XLII) in 1967 and 1503 (XLVIII) in 1970, the Commission primarily functioned as a drafting forum for the setting of standards, without an effective monitoring role.

Alongside the Commission on Human Rights, the Commission on the Status of Women was established by Ecosoc Resolution 11(II) of 21 June 1946, with the aim of preparing recommendations and reports to the Ecosoc on promoting women's rights in political, economic, civil, social and educational fields. Initially, only a Sub-Commission on the Status of Women had been envisaged, subordinate to the Commission on Human Rights: the enhancement of the status of this body was a victory for women's rights. In addition, Ecosoc Resolution 9(II) of 21 June 1946 created the Sub-Commission on Prevention of Discrimination and Protection of Minorities (renamed in 1999 the Sub-Commission on the Promotion and Protection of Human Rights), as a group of independent experts in charge of undertaking studies and making recommendations to the Commission on Human Rights on important issues of human rights promotion. In 2006, at the time it was replaced when the new Human Rights Council was set up, the Sub-Commission on the Promotion and Protection of Human Rights was composed of twenty-six experts, each with a single alternate.

The first task performed within the Commission on Human Rights was to agree on the text of a Declaration of Rights. It did so within a remarkably short period of time, and was able to adopt a draft at its third session of 24 May–18 June 1948. On 10 December 1948, following agreement achieved within the Ecosoc, the UN General Assembly adopted the Universal Declaration of Human Rights (UDHR) (GA Res. 217, UN GAOR, 3d sess., UN Doc. A/810 (1948)). The UDHR was adopted by forty-eight votes to none, with eight abstentions. The abstentions were cast by South Africa, which had just inaugurated its 'apartheid' policy and thus opposed the affirmation of equality without distinction as to race; Saudi Arabia, which opposed the freedom to change one's religion; as well as the USSR and its satellite States which then already formed what was referred to during the Cold War as the 'Soviet Block', who considered that the Declaration could be used as a pretext for interfering with the domestic affairs of the Member States of the United Nations (for detailed histories of the drafting process, see M. A. Glendon, *A World Made New. Eleanor Roosevelt and the Universal Declaration of Human Rights* (New York: Random House, 2001); J. P. Humphrey, *Human Rights and the United Nations: a Great Adventure* (Dobbs Ferry, NY: Transnational Publishers, 1984); and J. Morsink, *The Universal Declaration of Human Rights: Origins, Drafting, and Intent* (University of Philadelphia Press, 1999); for a study on the philosophical underpinnings of the Declaration in the views of the drafters, see J. Morsink, *Inherent Human Rights: Philosophical Roots of the Universal Declaration* (University of Pennsylvania Press: Pennsylvania Studies in Human Rights, 2009)). The adoption of the UDHR took the form of a non-binding resolution. Nevertheless, a majority of the doctrine takes the view today that, whatever the intent of the governments which voted on the Declaration, the rights stipulated in the UDHR now have acquired the status of customary international law or should be considered as part of the 'general principles of law recognized by civilized nations' mentioned in Article 38(1)(c) of the Statute of the International Court of Justice as a source of international law. This issue is explored in greater depth in section 4.1. of this chapter.

The Universal Declaration of Human Rights was later implemented in the form of binding international treaties open to the ratification of the Member States of the United Nations. The initial idea was to have the Declaration as such transformed into a binding legal instrument, proposed to the ratification of the States. Having one single universal covenant was considered to present one major advantage: it would offer a clear recognition of the fact that all the rights of the Declaration were interconnected and interdependent. Within the Ecosoc, however, the delegates gradually came to consider that civil and political rights, on the one hand, and economic and social rights, on the other hand, called for different methods of implementation. Civil and political rights could be monitored by independent experts and were of immediate applicability since they primarily required from States that they abstain from interfering with the rights of the individual. In contrast, economic and social rights (to which cultural rights were assimilated) called for progressive measures of implementation, since they required legislative action in order to become fully justiciable. They also called for budgetary commitments, and therefore their implementation depended on the resources available to each State and on international co-operation. The General Assembly was finally convinced by these arguments. In 1952, following the position of the Ecosoc, it decided to implement the UDHR by elaborating two separate covenants, each corresponding to one category of rights (A/RES/6/543, 4 February 1952). While both sets of rights were considered of equal importance and while all agreed on the interdependence and indivisibility of all rights, the view that prevailed was that these sets of rights were sufficiently different from one another to warrant separate treatment, and to be implemented through different legal techniques (see, in the context of this discussion, A. Eide, 'Economic, Social and Cultural Rights as Human Rights' in A. Eide, C. Krause and A. Rosas (eds.), *Economic, Social and Cultural Rights. A Textbook*, second edn (Dordrecht: Martinus Nijhoff, 2001), p. 9). The discussion on whether the distinction thus established between the two categories of rights is justified continued well through the 1990s, and it may be said that it was only – provisionally – closed with the adoption, on 10 December 2008, of the Optional Protocol to the International Covenant on Economic, Social and Cultural Rights (for an exposition of the arguments against assimilating both sets of rights, see E. W. Vierdag, 'The Legal Nature of the Rights Granted by the International Covenant on Economic, Social and Cultural Rights' in *Netherlands Yearbook of International Law*, 9 (1978), 69, and M. Bossuyt, 'La distinction juridique entre les droits civils et politiques et les droits économiques, sociaux et culturels', *Revue des droits de l'homme*, 8 (1975), 783, and for a riposte, G. J. H. Van Hoof, 'The Legal Nature of Economic, Social and Cultural Rights: a Rebuttal of Some Traditional Views' in P. Alston and K. Tomasevski (eds.), *The Right to Food* (Dordrecht: Martinus Nijhoff, 1984), p. 97: this is further discussed in chapter 8, section 1.2., on the justiciability of economic, social and cultural rights).

Still, even once the UN General Assembly had taken the decision that work should be done towards the adoption of two separate treaties, fourteen more years of negotiations were required before the two covenants could be adopted, simultaneously, on 16 December 1966. By then, a vote had already intervened on the International Convention on the Elimination of All Forms of Racial Discrimination (ICERD), adopted on 21 December 1965 after three years of negotiations. The adoption of the International Covenant on Civil and Political Rights (ICCPR) and of the International Covenant on Economic, Social and Cultural Rights (ICESCR), following that of the ICERD, launched a period of intense treaty-making activity. Nine treaties are often referred to as the 'core human rights treaties', because they present certain common characteristics. They are all based on the Universal Declaration on Human Rights, the values of which they seek to protect and develop. All but one set up bodies of independent experts in order to monitor them, and progressively to clarify the obligations of States which these treaties define: the only exception is the International Covenant on Economic, Social and Cultural Rights, which only provides for a role of the Ecosoc in such monitoring – although this was largely compensated by the establishment of the Committee on Economic, Social and Cultural Rights, through a resolution (1985/17, of 28 May 1985) of the Economic and Social Council. All of these treaties are based primarily on a reporting procedure by States, which undertake to provide information on a regular basis on the measures they take in order to comply with their obligations. The mechanisms set up under these treaties is explored in greater detail in chapter 9. The treaties are the following:

Treaty	Additional protocols	Entry into force	Membership (on 26 August 2009)
International Convention on the Elimination of All Forms of Racial Discrimination (A/RES/20/2106, 21 December 1965) (660 U.N.T.S. 195)		4 January 1969	173 parties
International Covenant on Economic, Social and Cultural Rights (A/RES/21/2200A, 16 December 1966) (993 U.N.T.S. 3)	Optional Protocol to the International Covenant on Economic, Social and Cultural Rights (A/RES/63/117, 10 December 2008)	3 January 1976	160 parties
International Covenant on Civil and Political Rights (A/RES/21/2200A, 16 December 1966) (999 U.N.T.S. 171)	Optional Protocol to the International Covenant on Civil and Political Rights (16 December 1966) (999 U.N.T.S. 171) Second Optional Protocol to the International Covenant on Civil and Political Rights, aiming at the abolition of the death penalty (A/RES/44/128, 15 December 1989) (1642 U.N.T.S. 414)	23 March 1976	164 parties
Convention on the Elimination of All Forms of Discrimination against Women (A/RES/34/180, 18 December 1979) (1249 U.N.T.S. 13)	Optional Protocol to the Convention on the Elimination of All Forms of Discrimination against Women (A/RES/54/4, 6 October 1999) (2131 U.N.T.S. 83)	3 September 1981	186 parties
Convention against Torture and Other Cruel, Inhuman or Degrading Treatment or Punishment (10 December 1984) (1465 U.N.T.S. 85)	Optional Protocol to the Convention against Torture and Other Cruel, Inhuman or Degrading Treatment or Punishment (A/RES/57/199, 18 December 2002)	26 June 1987	146 parties
Convention on the Rights of the Child (A/RES/44/25, 20 November 1989) (1577 UNTS 3)	Optional Protocol to the Convention on the Rights of the Child on the involvement of children in armed conflict; and Optional Protocol to the Convention on the Rights of the Child on the Sale of Children, Child Prostitution and Child Pornography (A/RES/54/263, 25 May 2000)	2 September 1990	193 parties

Treaty	Additional protocols	Entry into force	Membership (on 26 August 2009)
International Convention on the Protection of the Rights of All Migrant Workers and Members of their Families (A/RES/45/158, 18 December 1990)		1 July 2003	42 parties
Convention on the Rights of Persons with Disabilities (A/RES/61/106, 13 December 2006)	Optional Protocol to the Convention on the Rights of Persons with Disabilities (A/RES/61/106, 13 December 2006)	3 May 2008	65 parties
International Convention for the Protection of All Persons from Enforced Disappearance (A/RES/61/177, 20 December 2006)		Not yet in force	13 parties

These nine core human rights treaties are not the only ones adopted within the framework of the United Nations in the field of human rights. Mention should also be made, for instance, of the Convention on the Prevention and Punishment of the Crime of Genocide (78 U.N.T.S. 277), adopted on 9 December 1948 by the UN General Assembly, although without any part being played in its elaboration by the Commission on Human Rights. Like other, similar instruments, such as the Convention on the Non-Applicability of Statutory Limitations to War Crimes and Crimes against Humanity (adopted on 26 November 1968 (754 U.N.T.S. 73)) or the International Convention on the Suppression and Punishment of the Crime of Apartheid (adopted on 30 November 1973 (1015 U.N.T.S. 243)), the 1948 Genocide Convention differs from the core human rights treaties, however, in that it is not monitored by a body of independent experts equipped to build a jurisprudence that gives meaning to its clauses, and thus to contribute to the general development of human rights.

For this reason in particular, the emphasis in this book will be on the core human rights treaties and on the developing law of human rights emanating from their control mechanisms, rather than on these other contributions of the UN to human rights, however important they may be. In addition, even within the core human rights treaties, a certain emphasis has been placed on three instruments, probably the most important whether measured by the scope of the situations they cover or by the output of the monitoring bodies: these are the two covenants adopted in 1966, as a codification into treaty form of the Universal Declaration on Human Rights (on the International Covenant on Civil and Political Rights (ICCPR), see M. Bossuyt, *Guide to the 'Travaux Préparatoires' of the International Covenant on Civil and Political Rights* (Dordrecht: Martinus Nijhoff, 1987); S. Joseph *et al.*, *The International Covenant on Civil and Political Rights*, second edn (Oxford University Press, 2004); K. A. Young, *The Law and Process of the UN*

Human Rights Committee (Ardsley, NY: Transnational Publishers, 2002); D. McGoldrick, *The Human Rights Committee. Its Role in the Development of the International Covenant on Civil and Political Rights*, second edn (Oxford: Clarendon Press, 1994); I. Boerefijn, *The Reporting Procedure under the Covenant on Civil and Political Rights. Practice and Procedures of the Human Rights Committee* (Antwerp-Oxford: Intersentia-Hart, 1999); M. Nowak, *UN Covenant on Civil and Political Rights – CCPR Commentary*, second edn (Kehl am Rhein: N. P. Engel Verlag, 2005); on the International Covenant on Economic, Social and Cultural Rights, see in particular, K. Arambulo, *Strengthening the Supervision of the International Covenant on Economic, Social and Cultural Rights. Theoretical and Procedural Aspects* (Antwerp-Oxford: Intersentia-Hart, 1999); M. Craven, *The International Covenant on Economic, Social and Cultural Rights: a Perspective on its Development* (Oxford: Clarendon Press, 1995); and A. Eide, C. Krause and A. Rosas (eds.), *Economic, Social and Cultural Rights. A Textbook*, second edn (Dordrecht: Martinus Nijhoff, 2001)); and the Convention on the Rights of the Child, adopted in 1989 and soon to become the most universally ratified human rights instrument, with 193 States parties at the time of writing: only the United States and Somalia among the members of the UN are not parties to the treaty (on the Convention on the Rights of the Child, see A. Alen *et al.* (eds.), *The UN Children's Rights Convention: Theory Meets Practice* (Antwerp-Oxford: Intersentia-Hart, 2007); P. Alston, St. Parker and J. Seymour (eds.), *Children, Rights and the Law* (Oxford: Clarendon Press, 1992); A. Glenn Mower, Jr., *The Convention on the Rights of the Child. International Law Support for Children* (Westport, Conn.: Greenwood Press, 1997); L. LeBlanc, *The Convention on the Rights of the Child. United Nations Lawmaking on Human Rights* (Lincoln, Nebras.: University of Nebraska Press, 1995)).

2 THE REGIONAL LEVEL

The modesty with which human rights were addressed within the UN encouraged regional organizations to set up their own system for the protection of human rights. Both the Council of Europe and the Organization of American States moved swiftly in this direction. The Organization of African Unity (now renamed the African Union) also established its own mechanism, although later and under a less ambitious form. A brief overview follows. The description here remains deliberately general and superficial: its only purpose is to recall the framework within which human rights developed in regional settings following the Second World War. In addition, the human rights protection mechanisms set up in these respective organizations are the subject of chapter 11, where they are presented in greater detail in their procedural aspects.

2.1 The Council of Europe and human rights

The Statute of the Council of Europe was adopted on 5 May 1949, and it came into force on 3 August 1949. The initial signatories were Belgium, Denmark, France, Ireland, Italy, Luxembourg, the Netherlands, Norway, Sweden and the United Kingdom. They were soon followed by Germany, Greece, Iceland, and Turkey, all of which joined the organization in 1949 or 1950. Austria joined in 1956, Cyprus in 1961, Switzerland in 1963, Malta in 1965, Portugal in 1976, Spain in 1977, Liechtenstein in 1978, San Marino in 1988, and Finland in 1989. But it was with the accession of newly democratized Eastern and Central European States, in the 1990s, that the organization underwent its deepest transformation (see the Information Report on the Enlargement of the Council of Europe (16 June 1992), Doc. 6629 of the Parliamentary Assembly of the Council of Europe). In addition to Andorra, which joined in 1994, the Council of Europe expanded from twenty-three members in 1990 to thirty-eight members in 1995, beginning with Hungary and Poland respectively in 1990 and 1991, and with seven States joining in 1992–3 (Bulgaria, the Czech Republic, Estonia, Lithuania, Romania, Slovakia and Slovenia). In 1996, together with Croatia, the Federation of Russia became a member; seven other States, including Armenia and Azerbaidjan, were added in 1999 and later. The organization now numbers forty-seven members.

The Statute defines as a condition for membership that '[e]very member of the Council of Europe must accept the principles of the rule of law and of the enjoyment by all persons within its jurisdiction of human rights and fundamental freedoms, and collaborate sincerely and effectively in the realisation of the aim of the Council' (Art. 3). Indeed, even prior to the signing of the Statute, it was understood that the organization's first task should be to adopt a Charter on Human Rights, since that was one of the primary aims of the European Movement at the origin of the establishment of the Council of Europe. The negotiations were launched in August 1949, and were finalized by September 1950, allowing the Convention for the Protection of Human Rights and Fundamental Freedoms (ECHR) – the official name of what is usually referred to as the European Convention on Human Rights – to be signed on 4 November 1950; it entered into force on 3 September 1953. The speed at which the negotiations proceeded was truly remarkable, considering the ambitious nature of the text: for the first time, an international jurisdiction, the European Court of Human Rights, was being set up, empowered to receive files submitted by the European Commission on Human Rights for its consideration, on the basis of individual applications by victims of human rights violations. Of course, the jurisdiction of the Court was initially optional, and individuals did not have direct access to the Court: it was the European Commission on Human Rights that, after an examination of the admissibility of the application, presented the case against the State, unless it chose to direct the case for consideration to the Committee of Ministers of the Council of Europe (see further chapter 11, section 1). Still, under the standards of the time, this constituted a major revolution, as important in significance as had been, only two years earlier, the adoption of the Universal Declaration of Human Rights.

The ratification of the Convention is now considered a condition for membership of the Council of Europe. This has not always been the case: France, for instance, although it is among the founding States of the Council of Europe which it hosts, only ratified the European Convention on Human Rights in 1974. The rule linking membership of the Council of Europe to accession to the ECHR appropriately reflects the pre-eminent role played by this instrument on the European continent. This, however, should not lead to underestimate the other instruments adopted within the organization for the promotion of human rights. Shortly after the ECHR entered into force, it was deemed necessary to pursue work on the implementation of the economic and social rights of the Universal Declaration of Human Rights which, due to their focus on civil and political rights, the drafters of the Convention had essentially neglected. After six years of negotiations, the European Social Charter was signed by thirteen Member States of the Council of Europe in Turin, on 18 October 1961 (CETS No. 35; 529 U.N.T.S. 89), and it entered into force a few years later, on 26 February 1965. Although it is an impressive catalogue of social rights laid out in great detail, the European Social Charter has been almost dormant until the early 1990s, when it was felt necessary to revive it in a context in which the European Communities (now the European Union) were increasingly active in the field of social rights, and in which the shift towards market economy in the Central and Eastern European States seemed to call for a strengthened protection of social rights as a counterweight to large-scale deregulation. These were the main arguments in favour of the 'revitalization' of the Charter, which was formally launched by the Ministerial Conference on Human Rights held in Rome in November 1990 (see further box 11.1., chapter 11).

Although the European Convention on Human Rights and the European Social Charter clearly are the most important human rights instruments adopted within the Council of Europe, other, often innovative systems have been put in place, to improve the monitoring of the conditions in which persons are being held in detention (European Convention for the Prevention of Torture and Inhuman or Degrading Treatment or Punishment (C.E.T.S., No. 126), signed on 26 November 1987), to protect the rights of minorities (European Charter for Regional or Minority Languages (C.E.T.S., No. 148), signed on 5 November 1992; and Framework Convention for the Protection of National Minorities (C.E.T.S., No. 157), signed on 1 February 1995), or to protect the dignity of the person against the misuse of biology and medicine (Convention for the Protection of Human Rights and Dignity of the Human Being with regard to the Application of Biology and Medicine: Convention on Human Rights and Biomedicine (C.E.T.S., No. 164), signed on 4 April 1997). In its standard-setting capacity, the Council of Europe has also played an important role in promoting a common approach to certain subjects, such as the protection of the environment through the criminal law, the fight against corruption, or the fight against trafficking of human beings, that present a more indirect relationship to human rights. At the same time, the leading role of the Council of Europe on the European continent is sometimes seen as being threatened by the increasingly important role played by the European Union (EU) in this area, particularly as the competences of the EU have developed over time to include, at present, a large number of domains that are directly related to civil liberties or social rights (see box 1.1.).

2.2 The Organization of American States and human rights

The role of the Organization of American States in the promotion and protection of human rights presents striking similarities with that of the Council of Europe. In 1948

Box 1.1.

The rise of fundamental rights in the European Union

The original treaties establishing the European Communities in 1951 (European Coal and Steel Community) and 1957 (European Atomic Energy Community and European Economic Community) contained no reference to human rights, apart from certain provisions on free movement of workers (including a prohibition of discrimination on grounds of nationality) and on equal pay between men and women, whose primary purpose remained linked to the needs of economic integration. In the late 1960s, however, the Court of Justice of the European Communities (European Court of Justice or ECJ) gradually sought to include fundamental rights among the general principles of European Community law which, on the basis of Article 164 EEC (later Art. 220 EC), it was competent to ensure respect for in the scope of application of the treaties. This case law was developed as a means to reassure the national courts of the EU Member States that the supremacy of European Community law would not oblige these national courts to set aside guarantees relating to human rights set out in the national constitutions. Following a first series of cases where the European Court of Justice firmly resisted the suggestion that the Community would be bound to respect the fundamental rights guaranteed by the constitutions of the Member States (Case 1/58, *Stork* v. *High Authority* [1959] E.C.R. 17 at 25–6; Joined Cases 36, 37, 38 and 40/59, *Geitling* v. *High Authority* [1960] E.C.R. 423 at 438–9; Case 40/64, *Sgarlata* v. *Commission* [1965] E.C.R. 215 at 227), and yet affirmed that the national jurisdictions of the Member States should accept the supremacy of EC law (Case 6/64, *Costa* v. *Enel* [1964] E.C.R. 585), the German Federal Constitutional Court (*Bundesverfassungsgericht*) and the Italian Constitutional Court (*Corte costituzionale*) reacted by stating that they would not accept this supremacy where this would oblige them to renounce upholding the provisions relating to fundamental rights in their respective national constitutions, in situations where the implementation of EC law would conflict with those guarantees (see Gerhard Bebr, 'A Critical Review of Recent Case Law of National Courts', *Common Market Law Review* (1974) 408). The resistance it faced led the European Court of Justice to accept that 'fundamental human rights' are 'enshrined in the general principles of Community law and protected by the Court' (Case 29/69, *Stauder* v. *City of Ulm* [1969] E.C.R. 419). The Court announced that it would henceforth identify those fundamental rights by referring to the common constitutional traditions of the Member States, although 'the protection of such rights, whilst inspired by the constitutional traditions common to the Member States, must be ensured within the framework of the structure and objectives of the Community' (Case 11/70, *Internationale Handelsgesellschaft* v. *Einfuhr- und Vorratsstelle Getreide* [1970] E.C.R. 1125).

Since that founding period, the European Court of Justice has sought to ensure respect for fundamental rights, as part of the general principles of law, either as regards the acts adopted by the institutions of the European Union, or as regards any acts adopted by the national authorities of the Member States to the extent that they intervene in the scope of application of EU/EC law, for instance when they take measures to implement EU legislation or when they invoke exceptions allowed by the treaties or the case law of the European Court of Justice (see, among many others, the following cases or opinions: Case C-260/89, *ERT* [1991] E.C.R. I-2925, paragraph 41; Opinion 2/94 [1996] E.C.R. I-1759, paragraph 33; Case C-274/99 P, *Connolly* v.

Commission [2001] E.C.R. I–1611, paragraph 37; Case C-94/00, *Roquette Frères* [2002] E.C.R. I-9011, paragraph 25; Case C-112/00, *Schmidberger* [2003] E.C.R. I-5659, paragraph 71; and Case C-36/02, *Omega* [2004] E.C.R. I-9609, paragraph 33).

This case law was constitutionalized in the Treaty on the European Union, that established the EU in 1992 as a single institutional framework for the European Communities and for co-operation in areas of justice and home affairs and in foreign and security policy. Article 6(3) of the EU Treaty reads: 'The Union shall respect fundamental rights, as guaranteed by the European Convention for the Protection of Human Rights and Fundamental Freedoms signed in Rome on 4 November 1950 and as they result from the constitutional traditions common to the Member States, as general principles of Community law.' The explicit mention in this provision of the European Convention on Human Rights is of course no accident. The ECHR is recognized a 'special significance' in this case law: it is *de facto* treated by the European Court of Justice as if it were binding on the EU, and the ECJ systematically seeks to align itself on the interpretation of the European Court of Human Rights. However, other treaties, such as the International Covenant on Civil and Political Rights or the Convention on the Rights of the Child, also have been relied upon by the Court of Justice (on the selective use of international human rights law by the ECJ, see I. de J. Butler and O. De Schutter, 'Binding the EU to International Human Rights Law', *Yearbook of European Law*, 27 (2008), 277).

The dependency of the case law of the European Court of Justice in the field of fundamental rights on the protection afforded to these rights in the national constitutions of the EU Member States has remained a significant factor to this day. Indeed, in its 'Solange' ('so long as') decision of 1974, the German Federal Constitutional Court insisted that, despite the 1969–70 judgments of the European Court of Justice in the cases of *Stauder* and *Internationale Handelsgesellschaft*, it did not consider that it was bound to accept unconditionally the supremacy of EC law, as long as the European Community did not possess a catalogue of rights offering the same legal certainty as the German Constitution (*Grundgesetz*) (BVerfG, judgment of 29 May 1974, [1974] 2 C.M.L.R. 551). Later, following the confirmation of the case law of the European Court of Justice and the political support it received from the then nine EC Member States (Joint Declaration of the Council, of the European Parliament and of the Commission on human rights, O.J. 1977 C103/1), the German Federal Constitutional Court somewhat relaxed its approach, agreeing to abstain from controlling the compatibility with fundamental rights of EC law it was asked to implement, as long as the level of protection of fundamental rights within the European Community would remain satisfactory (BVerfG, judgment of 22 October 1986, 2 BvR 197/83, 73 BVerfGE 339 [1987] 3 C.M.L.R. 225 ('*Solange II*' judgment)). This position was confirmed in the 'Maastricht' judgment delivered on 12 October 1993, (2 BvR 2134/92 and 2159/92, 89 BVerfGE [1993] 1 C.M.L.R. 57). Other supreme courts in the EU Member States have adopted the same attitude (e.g. the Danish Supreme Court, see *Hanne Norup Carlsen and others* v. *Prime Minister Poul Nyrup Rasmussen* [1999] 3 C.M.L.R. 854). Finally in a judgment of 7 June 2000, the German Federal Constitutional Court again slightly amended its view, agreeing to establish a presumption of compatibility of EU law with the requirements of fundamental rights: it is therefore up to the applicant, or to the court referring a case to the Constitutional Court, to bring forward elements justifying that this presumption will be reversed (BVerfG, 2 BvL 1/97). This background explains why the European Court of Justice has consistently sought to achieve a high level of protection of fundamental rights in the EU legal order, on the basis of a comparison between the constitutional traditions of the EU Member States and seeking inspiration from the international human rights instruments they are parties to.

The sequence briefly described above also explains why, during the first semester of 1999 (as Germany was presiding over the European Union), the idea was proposed that the European Union prepare a Charter of Fundamental Rights codifying and making visible to the citizen the *acquis* of the Union in this field. The proposal to adopt such a catalogue of fundamental rights was in part a reaction to the doubts expressed by the German Federal Constitutional Court about the solidity and irreversibility of this *acquis*. The adoption of a Charter of Rights, it was thought, would provide European integration with precisely this important building block, the absence of which the Constitutional Court had deplored in its first 'Solange' judgment of 1974, and which surfaced again in the 1986 and 1993 decisions it delivered on this issue. It would thus strengthen the legitimacy of further steps towards European integration, and justify further integration in the eyes of national constitutional or supreme courts.

Following the political decision to prepare a catalogue of rights for the EU, which was adopted at the Cologne European Council of June 1999, discussions on the content of the Charter of Fundamental Rights took place between December 1999 and September 2000. On 7 December 2000, the Charter of Fundamental Rights of the European Union was proclaimed at the Nice European Council (O.J. 2000 C364/1). It lists both civil and political rights and economic and social rights, and it also includes certain rights specifically linked to the citizenship of the Union and economic freedoms protected under the European treaties. Inspired by the fundamental rights recognized by the European Court of Justice among the general principles of law it ensures respect for, and by the international human rights instruments binding upon the EU Member States, the Charter is now the single most authoritative restatement of the *acquis* of the Union in the field of fundamental rights. Its main impact is not as a legal document, however – indeed, the Charter had no binding force when it was initially proclaimed, and only with the most recent reforms of the European treaties did it acquire formal legal authority (the Reform Treaty, signed at Lisbon on 13 December 2007 in force since 1 December 2009, contains a reference to the Charter, thus confirming its status as a legally binding instrument for the institutions of the Union and for the Member States when they implement Union law: see Article 6(1) of the Treaty on European Union as amended by the Treaty of Lisbon amending the Treaty on European Union and the Treaty establishing the European Community, signed at Lisbon, 13 December 2007 (OJ 2007 C306/1) (referring to the EU Charter of Fundamental Rights in the revised form it has been proclaimed on 12 December 2007 (OJ 2007 C303/1)). Rather, the influence of the Charter has primarily been felt in the transformation it brought about in the culture and the practice of the European institutions: for the European Parliament and the European Commission, in particular, it has become routine to invoke fundamental rights in drafting or discussing policies and laws, now that there exists a document, prepared under conditions which guarantee it a high degree of legitimacy, listing the said rights.

the Pan American Union was renamed the Organization of American States (OAS), a 'regional arrangement' within the new United Nations world architecture (see generally on this organization, A. V. W. Thomas and A. J. Thomas, *The Organization of American States* (Dallas: Southern Methodist University Press, 1963)). At the time, it had twenty-one members, including the United States. The membership expanded gradually. A number of small English-speaking island nations of the Caribbean joined in the 1960s, after they achieved independence; Canada acceded in 1990. The OAS today comprises thirty-six Member States: Antigua and Barbuda, Argentina, the Bahamas, Barbados, Belize, Bolivia, Brazil, Canada, Chile, Colombia, Costa Rica, Cuba (although its participation in the OAS was suspended between 1962 and 2009, because of an alleged incompatibility between its adoption of Marxism-Leninism and the principles and purposes of the OAS Charter), Dominica, the Dominican Republic, Ecuador, El Salvador, Grenada, Guatemala, Guyana, Haiti, Honduras (whose participation was suspended after the *coup d'état* of June 2009), Jamaica, Mexico, Nicaragua, Panama, Paraguay, Peru, Saint Lucia, Saint Vincent and the Grenadines, St Kitts and Nevis, Suriname, Trinidad and Tobago, United States, Uruguay and Venezuela.

In April 1948, at the same time that it established the OAS, the Ninth International Conference of American States held in Bogotá, Colombia, adopted the American Declaration on the Rights and Duties of Man. The Declaration was initially not intended to be a binding instrument. In 1959, however, in part in reaction to the Cuban revolution, the Inter-American Commission on Human Rights was established by a resolution of the Fifth Meeting of Consultation of Ministers for Foreign Affairs. The resolution was adopted on the basis of Article 5(j) (now Article 3(l)) of the OAS Charter, in which the Member States 'reaffirm' and 'proclaim' as a principle of the Organization 'the fundamental rights of the individual without distinction as to race, nationality, creed or sex'. When the Statute of the Inter-American Commission on Human Rights was adopted the following year, it defined the 'human rights' the Commission was to 'further respect' as the rights contained in the American Declaration on the Rights and Duties of Man.

Prior to the adoption of the American Convention in 1969 (see below), the Commission applied the American Declaration to all Member States of the OAS. By becoming a Member State of the OAS, a State implicitly recognized the competence of the Commission to receive individual petitions alleging human rights violations attributable to the Member States. Today the Commission continues to apply the American Declaration, as a default instrument, to those States that have not yet become parties to the American Convention. It thus considers that it is competent to examine violations of the rights set forth by the Declaration, however, once the Convention has entered into force in relation to a State, it is the Convention and not the Declaration that becomes the specific source of law to be applied, as long as the petition alleges violation of substantially identical rights enshrined in both instruments and a continuing situation is not involved (see, e.g. IACHR, Annual Report 2000, *Amílcar Ménendez et al.* v. *Argentina*, Case 11.670, Report No. 3/01, OEA/Ser.L/V/II.111 Doc. 20 rev. at 95, para. 41).

The American Convention on Human Rights (ACHR) itself was adopted in San José, Costa Rica, on 22 November 1969, although it did not enter into force until 18 July 1978. It is the most important human rights instrument in the inter-American system. Largely inspired by the European Convention on Human Rights (as it then was, in its original version of 1950) (see for comparisons J. Frowein, 'The European and the American Conventions on Human Rights: a Comparison', *Human Rights Law Journal*, 1 (1980), 44; T. Buergenthal, 'The American and European Conventions on Human Rights: Similarities and Differences', *American Universities Law Review*, 40 (1980), 155), it created the Inter-American Court of Human Rights, which has its seat in San José, Costa Rica. With the exception of Cuba, which was not participating in the OAS at the time the ACHR was adopted, every Spanish-speaking Member State of the OAS, as well as Brazil, has ratified the American Convention and accepted the compulsory jurisdiction of the Court. Of the thirty-six Member States of the OAS, twenty-four are States parties to the American Convention, as of 1 July 2009. These are: Argentina, Barbados, Bolivia, Brazil, Chile, Colombia, Costa Rica, Dominica, Dominican Republic, Ecuador, El Salvador, Grenada, Guatemala, Haiti, Honduras, Jamaica, Mexico, Nicaragua, Panama, Paraguay, Peru, Suriname, Uruguay and Venezuela. Trinidad and Tobago was a State party but denounced the American Convention on 26 May 1998, as a result of the decision adopted by the Judicial Committee of the Privy Council in *Pratt and Morgan* v. *Attorney General for Jamaica* [1994] 2. A.C. 1 (see box 1.5.). Ten other Member States of the OAS have not ratified the Convention: Antigua and Barbuda, the Bahamas, Belize, Canada, Cuba, Dominica, Guyana, St Kitts and Nevis, St Vincent and the Grenadines, and the United States. As its membership indicates, the system of the ACHR has largely succeeded in establishing its credibility within the Latin American context. In contrast, most of the English-speaking Member States have not yet become States parties to the American Convention, including, notably, the United States and Canada (although the United States signed the ACHR in 1977). Of the English-speaking Member States of the OAS, only Barbados, Grenada and Jamaica are States parties to the American Convention, but of these three only Barbados accepted the compulsory jurisdiction of the Court, in 2000. The mechanisms of the Inter-American Commission and Court of Human Rights are described in greater detail in chapter 11 (section 2).

The 1948 American Declaration on the Rights and Duties of Man and the 1969 American Convention on Human Rights are not the only instruments adopted within the OAS that contribute to the promotion and protection of human rights, however. The Convention itself was complemented in 1988 by an Additional Protocol in the area of Economic, Social and Cultural Rights, called the San Salvador Protocol after the city in which it was signed. It had fourteen States parties on 1 July 2009. While the Additional Protocol provides that only the rights stated in Article 8 a) (trade union rights) and Article 13 (right to education) may lead to the filing of individual petitions before the Inter-American Commission or Court of Human Rights, a reporting system is established for all the economic, social and cultural rights codified in the Additional Protocol. In 1990, another Protocol to the ACHR was adopted, this time to abolish the death penalty. Separate from the ACHR, the Inter-American Convention to Prevent and Punish Torture was adopted in 1985, entering into force two years later. On 1 July 2009 it had seventeen parties to it. It mirrors in many respects the 1984 UN Convention against Torture and Cruel, Inhuman or Degrading Treatment or Punishment. A Convention on the Forced Disappearance of Persons was adopted in 1994, and entered into force in 1996. It had thirteen States parties on 1 July 2009. Under the Convention, the States parties undertake to punish those persons who commit or attempt to commit the crime of forced disappearance of persons and their accomplices and accessories, and to co-operate with one another in helping to prevent, punish, and eliminate the forced disappearance of persons; the Convention lists the measures States should take in order to render this prohibition effective.

2.3 The African Union and human rights

The trajectory followed by the Organization of African Unity (OAU) – now the African Union – was slightly different. The Charter founding the OAU, signed in Addis-Abeba on 25 May 1963, stated that one of the objectives of the new organization was to 'promote international cooperation, having due regard to the Charter of the United Nations and the Universal Declaration of Human Rights' (Art. 2(1), e)). That reference was mainly symbolic: in fact, the principle of non-interference in domestic affairs was much more highly valued, as the OAU members had only recently obtained their independence and were particularly sensitive to affirming their sovereignty. Only later would human rights be put on the agenda of the organization, when certain dictatorships fell in 1979 and democratic movements gained visibility throughout the continent. The African (Banjul) Charter on Human and Peoples' Rights was adopted on 27 June 1981, and it entered into force on 21 October 1986 (OAU Doc. CAB/LEG/67/3 rev. 5, 21 I.L.M. 58 (1982)). It had fifty-three States parties on 1 July 2009. Initially, the African Charter was monitored exclusively by the African Commission on Human and Peoples' Rights. The system was further strengthened by the entry in force, in 2004, of the 1998 Protocol to the African Charter on the Establishment of an African Court on Human and Peoples' Rights, although it is too early still to evaluate the effectiveness of this reform (see further chapter 11, section 3). In addition, a Protocol to the African Charter on the Rights of Women in Africa was adopted on 11 July 2003 in Maputo and entered into force in 2005.

In the Preamble of the African Charter, the OAU members state that they are 'taking into consideration the virtues of their historical tradition and the values of African civilization which should inspire and characterize their reflection on the concept of human and peoples' rights'. Indeed, the Charter presents a number of specificities that, to a certain extent, distinguish it from the other comparable human rights instruments (see J. Matringe, *Tradition et modernité dans la Charte africaine des droits de l'homme et des peuples* (Brussels: Bruylant, 1996); F. Ouguergouz, *La Charte africaine des droits de l'homme et des peuples: une approche juridique entre tradition et modernité* (Geneva: IUHEI and Paris: P.U.F., 1993); and F. Viljoen, 'The African Regional Human

Rights System' in C. Krause and M. Scheinin (eds.), *International Protection of Human Rights: a Textbook* (Abo Akademi University Institute for Human Rights, 2009), p. 503, at pp. 518–25). Thus, the African Charter lists a number of social and economic rights, that are treated as equivalent, as regards their justiciability, to civil and political rights (see, for instance, the *Ogoniland* case, discussed in chapter 3, section 1). It also insists on duties, alongside rights, on the basis that 'the enjoyment of rights and freedoms also implies the performance of duties on the part of everyone' (Preamble, 7th Recital). However, whether this really distinguishes the African Charter from other, equivalent instruments, is doubtful. In practice, the 'duties' component means that States parties should take measures that ensure that individuals are imposed obligations that allow the rights of others to be effectively enjoyed. While the wording may differ, the substance is not truly distinct from what follows from the obligation to protect human rights imposed on States parties to other international human rights instruments (on the obligation to protect, see chapter 4; on the specificity of the African Charter as regards the notion of 'duties', see M. wa Mutua, 'The Banjul Charter and the African Cultural Fingerprint: an Evaluation of the Language of Duties', *Virginia Journal of International Law*, 35 (1995), 339).

Perhaps the most significant characteristic of the African Charter is the importance it affords to the collective rights of peoples, in addition to the human rights of the individual. The African Charter thus recognizes the right of peoples to existence, to self-determination (including the right to dispose of their natural resources), to development, to international peace and security, and to a generally satisfactory environment. Such rights are not unique to the African Charter, of course: international human rights law recognizes the right to self-determination of peoples in the UN Charter and in Article 1 of both Covenants adopted in 1966 to implement the Universal Declaration of Human Rights (see chapter 7, section 5.1.); and the right to development has been affirmed in the 1986 Declaration on the Right to Development adopted by the UN General Assembly (see chapter 2, section 2.4.). What is remarkable, rather, is that these rights – sometimes referred to as 'third generation' rights both because they are rights of peoples and because they are, for the most part, dependent on international solidarity for their realization – are treated in the Charter on a par with other 'first' and 'second' generation rights, leading the African Commission on Human and Peoples' Rights to sometimes bold and innovative interpretations that go beyond what has been achieved at universal level.

The achievements of the OAU in the field of human and peoples' rights are not limited to the adoption and implementation of the Banjul Charter. On 11 July 1990, the African Charter on the Rights and Welfare of the Child was adopted, in order to ensure the transposition, in the African regional context, of the 1989 UN Convention on the Rights of the Child (OAU Doc. CAB/LEG/24.9/49 (1990)). The African Children's Rights Charter sets up a monitoring body, the African Children's Rights Committee, which has the power to examine state reports, as well as to receive individual communications and to launch investigations. The system entered into force on 29 November 1999. It currently has forty-five States parties.

As the African Charter on Human and Peoples' Rights progressively established its credibility through the 1990s, the OAU mutated into the African Union. Article 4 of the African Union Constitutive Act adopted in Lomé on 11 July 2002 enumerates the principles on which the AU is founded. These include 'the right of the Union to intervene in a Member State pursuant to a decision of the Assembly in respect of grave circumstances, namely: war crimes, genocide and crimes against humanity', 'promotion of gender equality', and 'respect for democratic principles, human rights, the rule

---

Box 1.2. **Human rights in South-East Asia: the ASEAN Intergovernmental Commission on Human Rights**

At its Ministerial Meeting of 20 July 2009, the Association of South-East Asian Nations (ASEAN) agreed on the establishment of the ASEAN Intergovernmental Commission on Human Rights (AICHR). This remains a very modest step towards implementing human rights effectively in the region. The AICHR is an intergovernmental body, composed of the representatives of the ASEAN Member States, with purely consultative powers: they may neither receive complaints, nor take decisions, nor conduct investigations. The tasks of the AICHR are promotional in nature: it should contribute to capacity-building, promote awareness, provide advisory services, prepare studies, and favour dialogue between the Members. According to the Terms of Reference adopted on 20 July 2009, five sets of principles should guide the action of the AICHR. A first set of principles are 'respect for the independence, sovereignty, equality, territorial integrity and national identity of all ASEAN Member States'; 'non-interference in the internal affairs of ASEAN Member States' and 'respect for the right of every Member State to lead its national existence free from external interference, subversion and coercion'; 'adherence to the rule of law, good governance, the principles of democracy and constitutional government'; 'respect for fundamental freedoms, the promotion and protection of human rights, and the promotion of social justice'; 'upholding the Charter of the United Nations and international law, including international humanitarian law, subscribed to by ASEAN Member States'; and 'respect for different cultures, languages and religions of the peoples of ASEAN, while emphasising their common values in the spirit of unity in diversity'. The other sets of principles are first, 'respect for international human rights principles, including universality, indivisibility, interdependence and interrelatedness of all human rights and fundamental freedoms, as well as impartiality, objectivity, non-selectivity, non-discrimination, and avoidance of double standards and politicisation'; second, the 'recognition that the primary responsibility to promote and protect human rights and fundamental freedoms rests with each Member State'; third, 'pursuance of a constructive and non-confrontational approach and cooperation to enhance promotion and protection of human rights'; and fourth, 'adoption of an evolutionary approach that would contribute to the development of human rights norms and standards in ASEAN'. In sum, the AICHR is a human rights council at regional level, but with neither special procedures that can ensure an independent monitoring of compliance with human rights standards, nor a peer review of the performances of States in the field of human rights (on the mechanisms at the disposal of the UN Human Rights Council, see chapter 10).

of law and good governance' (paras. (h), (l) and (m), respectively). While the standing and visibility of human rights in the structure of the African Union thus has been enhanced – and rebalanced against the principle of non-interference with domestic affairs – it remains to be seen which concrete implications shall be drawn.

3 THE EMERGING *JUS COMMUNE* OF HUMAN RIGHTS

Since the 1990s, a movement towards the building of a transnational *jus commune* of human rights has become increasingly visible. The formation of this common law is the result of increasingly frequent cross-references between various international and domestic courts interpreting provisions which, although found in different treaties or domestic constitutions, are similarly worded and have their common inspiration in the Universal Declaration on Human Rights (see S. Choudhry, 'Globalization in Search of Justification: Toward a Theory of Comparative Constitutional Interpretation', *Indiana Law Journal*, 74 (1999) 819; S. H. Cleveland, 'Our International Constitution', *Yale Journal of International Law*, 31 (2006) 1; L. Henkin, 'The International Judicial Dialogue: When Domestic Constitutional Courts Join the Conversation', *Harvard Law Review*, 114 (2001) 2049; C. McCrudden, 'A Common Law of Human Rights?: Transnational Judicial Conversations on Constitutional Rights', *Oxford Journal of Legal Studies*, 20 (2000) 499–532; A.-M. Slaughter, 'Judicial Globalization', *Virginia Journal of International Law*, 40 (2000) 1103; A.-M. Slaughter, 'A Global Community of Courts', *Harvard International Law Journal*, 44 (2003) 191). A number of factors have encouraged this development. The single most important factor still has to do with the content and origins of the legal rules themselves. The Universal Declaration of Human Rights was derived from a comparison between the liberal constitutions of the Western nations. The initial draft, prepared by the Human Rights Division of the UN Secretariat under the supervision of its first director, the Canadian international law expert John P. Humphrey, 'may not have included every conceivable right, but it provided the drafting committee with a distillation of nearly two hundred years of efforts to articulate the most basic human values in terms of rights. It contained the first-generation political and civil rights found in the British, French, and American revolutionary declarations of the seventeenth and eighteenth centuries: protections of life, liberty, and property; and freedoms of speech, religion, and assembly. It also included the second-generation economic and social rights found in late-nineteenth- and early-twentieth-century constitutions such as those of Sweden, Norway, the Soviet Union, and several Latin American countries: rights to work, education, and basic subsistence. Each draft article was followed by an extensive annotation detailing its relationship to rights instruments then in force in the UN's member states, already numbering fifty-five and rising' (M.-A. Glendon, *A World Made New. Eleanor Roosevelt and the Universal Declaration of Human Rights* (New York: Random House, 2001) pp. 57–8).

Whether they are adopted at the universal or at the regional levels, all human rights treaties are derived from the UDHR, from which they borrow, sometimes quite literally, much of their language. It is therefore quite natural for international courts or quasi-judicial bodies, whether they belong to regional or to universal systems, to cite one another, and to entertain a dialogue with national courts applying human rights recognized in constitutional instruments, where the wording is similar or identical. In addition, with the development of an international human rights jurisprudence, which brings life into the sometimes vague provisions of international human rights instruments which are thereby made more concrete, the impact of international human rights law on the practice of national courts has increased, a phenomenon which the growing recognition of the direct applicability of international human rights treaties before national authorities further increased (on the influence of the case law, including views adopted on individual communications, general comments, and concluding observations, of the UN human rights treaty bodies, see Committee on International Human Rights Law and Practice of the International Law Association, *Final Report on the Impact of the Work of the United Nations Human Rights Treaty Bodies on National Courts and Tribunals*, adopted at the 2004 Berlin Conference; and H. Niemi, *National Implementation of Findings by United Nations Human Rights Treaty Bodies. A Comparative Study* (Institute for Human Rights, Abo Akademi University, December 2003) (examining the national implementation of UN treaty body findings, including final views, concluding observations, and general comments, in Australia, Canada, the Czech Republic, Finland, Spain and Sweden); on the impact of the case law of the European Court of Human Rights on the national courts of the Member States of the Council of Europe, see J. Polakiewicz, 'The Status of the Convention in National Law' in R. Blackburn and J. Polakiewicz (eds.), *Fundamental Rights in Europe. The ECHR and its Member States, 1950–2000* (Oxford University Press, 2001), at pp. 31–53).

Other factors still have further encouraged this movement towards the building of a *jus commune* in the field of international human rights. The internet and the proliferation of legal databases have immensely facilitated the task of seeking information about the practices followed by other jurisdictions, from which inspiration may be sought. Non-governmental organizations have been increasingly present as *amici curiae* before certain human rights courts, both at regional and at national level, and they have been particularly eager to present those jurisdictions with comparative law materials, identifying the best practices available as a benchmark for all courts to achieve, and encouraging national courts to use international law to develop their own powers (see O. De Schutter, 'L'émergence de la société civile dans le droit international: le rôle des associations devant la Cour européenne des droits de l'homme', *Journal européen du droit international/European Journal of International Law*, 7 (1996), 372–410). Entering this global interjurisdictional conversation may be attractive to judges, finally, because by doing so, they gain in legitimacy, and they can emancipate themselves from the straightjacket of the texts which they are to interpret.

Exceptionally, courts may be directed to take into account the fact that the human rights provisions they are applying stem from a broader conversation in which both international and national bodies take part. For instance, the Commission and Court in charge of monitoring the African Charter on Human and Peoples' Rights are directed to 'draw inspiration from international law on human and people's rights, particularly from ... the Charter of the United Nations, the Charter of the Organization of African Unity, the Universal Declaration of Human Rights, other instruments adopted by the United Nations and by African countries in the field of human and peoples' rights as well as from the provisions of various instruments adopted within the Specialized Agencies of the United Nations of which the parties to the present Charter are members' (African Charter on Human and People's Rights, Art. 60). This has led the African Commission of Human and Peoples' Rights to seek inspiration, primarily, from the European human rights system, and constitutes a powerful counter-weight to the tendency to emphasize the unique nature of the values of the African Charter. Similarly, section 35(1) of the interim South African Constitution provides that 'In interpreting the provisions of [the Bill of Rights contained in a chapter of the Constitution] a court of law shall promote the values which underlie an open and democratic society based on freedom and equality and shall, where applicable, have regard to public international law applicable to the protection of the rights entrenched in this Chapter, and may have regard to comparable foreign case law.' In the case of *S* v. *Makwanyane and another* presented to the Constitutional Court, Chaskalson P made the following comment about this provision:

Constitutional Court of South Africa, *S* v. *Makwanyane and another* 1995 (3) S.A. 391 (CC), 1995 (6) B.C.L.R. 665 (CC):

[P]ublic international law would include non-binding as well as binding law. They may both be used under the section as tools of interpretation. International agreements and customary international law accordingly provide a framework within which [the Bill of Rights included in the South African Constitution] can be evaluated and understood, and for that purpose, decisions of tribunals dealing with comparable instruments, such as the United Nations Committee on Human Rights, the Inter-American Commission on Human Rights, the Inter-American Court of Human Rights, the European Commission on Human Rights, and the European Court of Human Rights, and, in appropriate cases, reports of specialised agencies such as the International Labour Organisation, may provide guidance as to the correct interpretation of particular provisions of [the Bill of Rights].

Most often, however, the reference to human rights as recognized in general international law, particularly as embodied in the Universal Declaration of Human Rights, is made *sua sponte* by the organs concerned, which may find in such a reference a source of legitimacy for the interpretation they propound. In this process, judicial interpretation is increasingly detached from the text to be interpreted; instead, it resembles a conversation between jurisdictions, which are collectively engaged in the task of giving meaning to generally worded human rights provisions whose significance can only be discovered in the course of implementation in a variety of settings. This development has sometimes been controversial. Reliance on foreign human rights norms or judgments seems to presuppose a universalistic view of human rights, in which the solutions which are correct in one jurisdiction should be replicated elsewhere, rather than a relativistic one, in which the broad principles of human rights should be applied differently depending on the specific context of each society. In addition, the development of a *jus commune* of human rights seems to revive the idea of human rights as natural law, detached from the positivist view of law as the set of norms that is recognized as valid in a specific jurisdiction as a result of institutional processes. Finally, and perhaps most obviously, this development favours judicial activism, at the expense of fidelity to the intent of the authors of the text – whether the human rights treaty or the domestic bill of rights – to be interpreted. This, it has been argued, may ultimately threaten the effectiveness of human rights protection, because it undermines the legitimacy of the positions adopted by human rights bodies interpreting specific treaties. In the context of the American Convention on Human Rights, for instance:

Gerald L. Neuman, 'Import, Export, and Regional Consent in the Inter-American Court of Human Rights', *European Journal of International Law*, 19, No. 1 (2008), 101 at 115:

Ignoring the role of the states [by interpreting the ACHR broadly, in line with universal trends, without seeking to ensure that the interpretation conforms with the evolving consensus among the OAS Member States] raises issues both of legitimation and of effectiveness. The character of a positive human rights treaty entails the involvement of states (jointly) in the design of the system, including the choice of rights to be protected and the means of enforcement. The OAS states went to considerable effort to negotiate and adopt their own regional human rights treaty. They did not reduce the treaty to a local enforcement mechanism for the global Covenants, and they did not simply delegate to the Court the task of adopting whatever standards it chooses from a future corpus of soft law texts. Ongoing partnership between the Court and the member states bolsters the Court's authority to define state obligations. The 'humanization' of international law has not proceeded so far as to make international human rights tribunals self-legitimating on the basis of their direct relationship with individual human rights. Moreover, accepting state influence on the evolution of human rights norms is important for the effectiveness of the system, a major factor in institutional interpretation. Making a human right more 'effective' does not necessarily mean giving the right a broader meaning. It means making the enjoyment of the right more of a reality, and that may require defining the positive content of the right in a manner that facilitates its implementation at a particular historical moment within the particular region ... When states within the region participate in the progressive evolution of a right, their actions make national enforcement more feasible and provide insights into the methods of implementation that may succeed. States will also be more likely to assist the Court in influencing a fellow member state to comply with standards to which they themselves already subscribe.

In order to assess the conflicting claims about the merits and dangers of judicial comparativism in this area, it is necessary, however, to distinguish carefully between the different uses of foreign judgments before human rights courts. Consider the following typology proposed by McCrudden:

Christopher McCrudden, 'Judicial Comparativism and Human Rights',
***Oxford Legal Studies Research Paper** No. 29/2007, also published as a
chapter in E. Örücü and D. Nelken (eds.), **Comparative Law: a Handbook,***
(Oxford: Hart Publishing, 2007), p. 371 at pp. 378–9:

There are four uses of this type that are frequently not sufficiently distinguished. The first is
where a court in jurisdiction 'X' quotes from a court in jurisdiction 'Y' a particular phrase or way
of describing an issue that appears to the judge particularly apposite or elegant. Some judges in
some jurisdictions have had a way with words that is deemed by other judges to be particularly
worth quoting. This can be termed the 'rhetorical' use of 'foreign' material and is akin to using
quotations from Shakespeare or the Bible. The second is where a court in jurisdiction 'X' cites
'foreign' material such as a judicial decision in jurisdiction 'Y' as part of the evidence to support
an empirical conclusion that a particular approach is or is not workable in practice, or has
particular unintended effects. The fact that it is a judicial opinion that is part of the evidence is,
essentially, neither here nor there; it is merely a convenient source of the empirical information ...
[The] third and fourth uses are the most controversial [because they treat foreign judgments as
having some persuasive authority]. Both involve the use of a judicial decision in jurisdiction 'Y', or
some other legal norm, that is not legally binding in jurisdiction 'X' (such as an unratified human
rights convention), as part of a judicial decision regarding what is the legal position in jurisdiction
'X'. In both, the 'foreign' material is part of a normative argument, in a judicial context that is, in
any event, often controversial. But there are significant differences within that general category.
One use (our third approach) involves the citation of a 'foreign' material as establishing a reason
(however attenuated) why a human rights claim against a governmental entity should not
succeed. Another (our fourth approach), and probably the most controversial, involves the use of
'foreign' material in a similar context where it establishes a reason (however attenuated) why a
rights claim should succeed.

One underestimated aspect of the emergence of this *jus commune* is that human rights
have been autonomized from international law. The conversation of which this *jus
commune* is a product has increasingly involved national constitutional courts, established outside international law, and whose interpretation of the human rights norms
they are to apply, in most cases, take no account of the broader principles of general international law, even where the human rights they apply originate in international law. As a result, human rights have established themselves as a separate
regime of international law, but one which increasingly borrows its methodology,
including its methods of interpretation, to domestic constitutional law. Both for this
reason and because they have developed their own specialized institutions, human
rights therefore provide a good illustration of the problem of fragmentation of international law into a number of self-contained regimes, each with their own norms and
dispute-settlement mechanisms, and relatively autonomous both *vis-à-vis* each other
and *vis-à-vis* general international law (on this debate, see in particular, B. Simma,
'Self-Contained Regimes', *Netherlands Yearbook of International Law*, 16 (1985), 111;
and the Report of the Study Group of the International Law Commission (chaired by

Martti Koskenniemi), *Fragmentation of International Law: Difficulties Arising from the Diversification and Expansion of International Law*, U.N. doc. A/CN.4/L.702, 18 July 2006 (also reproduced in the Report on the work of the fifty-eighth session (1 May–9 June and 3 July–11 August 2006) of the International Law Commission to the UN General Assembly, Official Records, sixty-first session, Supplement No. 10 (A/61/10), chapter 12)). In practice, this autonomization of international human rights law, accelerated by the formation of a *jus commune* as a result of the conversation between judicial and non-judicial bodies applying human rights law, has favoured a certain activism of the specialized courts of expert bodies concerned. The example of the binding nature of interim measures indicated by human rights bodies illustrates this (see box 1.3.).

Unavoidably, risks of instrumentalization are present in this development. For example, this aspect of the jurisprudence of the European Court of Human Rights has been described as follows:

James G. Merrill, *The Development of International Law by the European Court of Human Rights*, second edn (Manchester University Press, 1993), p. 218:

Although the task of the [European Court of Human Rights] is to interpret the Convention, light can often be shed on its meaning by comparing it with other treaties, and the Court has made extensive use of this assistance. The situations in which it has done so, and which provide further evidence of its resourcefulness in developing the law, fall into three types. [1] When a provision needing interpretation was inspired by an earlier instrument dealing with the subject, the Court has naturally turned to the other treaty for guidance. [2] When, on the other hand, the Convention omits certain rights guaranteed in another treaty, the Court may refer to the other treaty to justify an interpretation holding that a right is not protected. [3] Finally, in cases falling into neither of the preceding categories, the Court may refer to another treaty to show that a particular interpretation is in harmony with other obligations in the human rights field.

The second attitude ([2]) is illustrated in the case law of the European Court of Human Rights by cases such as *Kosiek* v. *Germany*, in which the Court concludes that the ECHR cannot be read as including a right of everyone to equal access to public service in his or her country since, in contrast to the Universal Declaration of Human Rights (Art. 21 para. 2) and the International Covenant on Civil and Political Rights (Art. 25), neither the European Convention nor any of its Protocols sets forth a right of everyone to equal access to public service in his country, and that the omission of such a right was deliberate when Protocol No. 7 was drafted (Eur. Ct. HR (plenary), *Kosiek* v. *Germany*, judgment of 28 August 1986, para. 34); or by the refusal of the Court in the 1986 case of *Johnston* v. *Ireland* to recognize a right to the dissolution of marriage in the ECHR, since, in contrast to Article 16 of the Universal Declaration on Human Rights, Article 12 ECHR does not refer to the dissolution of marriage, an omission which the Court considers to be deliberate (Eur. Ct. HR, *Johnston* v. *Ireland*, judgment of 18 December 1986, at paras. 52–3). But this method of interpretation is clearly not immune from a certain selectivity: in

Box 1.3.

The binding nature of interim measures indicated by human rights bodies

Should the provisional measures adopted by human rights bodies or courts be treated as obligatory for the parties to whom they are addressed? The controversy about this issue illustrates how the idea of a *jus commune* of human rights can encourage an activist attitude by human rights bodies. While they set up judicial or quasi-judicial bodies which may receive individual communications or applications from victims of human rights violations, the major international human rights treaties are silent about the possibility of these bodies granting provisional measures, protecting the alleged victims until a decision is made on the merits of their complaint. However, the idea has gradually emerged that this power of human rights bodies is inherent in their jurisdiction, and that it should be recognized in the name of an effective protection of human rights.

This development was inaugurated under the 1984 Convention against Torture and Other Cruel, Inhuman or Degrading Treatment or Punishment. When, acting in accordance with Article 18(2) of the Convention, the Committee against Torture adopted its Rules of Procedure, it included a Rule 108 §9 enabling it to adopt provisional measures in proceedings brought by individuals alleging a violation of the Convention against Torture. In the case of *Cecilia Rosana Núñez Chipana* v. *Venezuela*, it took the view that non-compliance with such provisional measures should be considered a violation of the Convention, as 'the State party, in ratifying the Convention and voluntarily accepting the Committee's competence [to examine individual communications] under article 22, undertook to cooperate with it in good faith in applying the procedure. Compliance with the provisional measures called for by the Committee in cases it considers reasonable is essential in order to protect the person in question from irreparable harm, which could, moreover, nullify the end result of the proceedings before the Committee' (Committee against Torture, *Cecilia Rosana Núñez Chipana* v. *Venezuela*, final views of 10 November 1998 Communication No. 110/1998 (CAT/C/21/D/110/1998)). The Human Rights Committee followed this lead. Under Rule 86 of its rules of procedure, which the Human Rights Committee adopts in accordance with Article 39(2) of the ICCPR, the Human Rights Committee 'may, prior to forwarding its views on the communication to the State party concerned, inform that State of its views as to whether interim measures may be desirable to avoid irreparable damage to the victim of the alleged violation'. The Human Rights Committee considered unanimously in its final views of 19 October 2000 adopted in the case of *Dante Piandiong, Jesus Morallos and Archie Bulan* v. *The Philippines*, that a refusal of a State to comply with such measures, 'especially by irreversible measures such as the execution of the alleged victim or his/her deportation from the country, undermines the protection of Covenant rights through the Optional Protocol [providing for the possibility of individual complaints filed by alleged victims of violations of the ICCPR]' (Human Rights Committee, final views adopted on the Communication n°869/1999 (U.N. doc. CCPR/C/70/D/869/1999), *Annual Rep.* I, p. 181). It has repeated this statement since (see, e.g. Human Rights Committee, *Weiss* v. *Austria*, communication No. 1086/02, final views of 8 May 2003 (CCPR/C/77/D/1086/2002)), confirming its view that the States parties to the Covenant could be under an obligation to comply with the interim measures indicated by the Committee, despite the fact that the power to adopt such interim measures was not attributed to the Committee under the text of the Covenant itself.

In a judgment of 4 February 2005, the European Court of Human Rights considered for the first time in a final judgment that a refusal by a State party to the European Convention on Human Rights to comply with an interim measure indicated by a Chamber of the Court or its President on the basis of Article 39 of the Rules of the Court constitutes a violation of Article 34 of the Convention, which imposes an obligation on the Contracting Parties 'not to hinder in any way the effective exercise' of the right to individual application (European Court of Human Rights (Grand Chamber), judgment of 5 February 2005 in the case of *Mamatkulov and Askarov* v. *Turkey*, Appl. Nos. 46827/99 and 46951/99). This represented a shift in attitude from the part of the Court. In its previous case law, while finding that there existed a general practice of States parties to the Convention to comply with such interim measures, the Court fell short from identifying the emergence of a rule of a customary nature in the application of the European Convention on Human Rights. Instead, it held: 'The practice of Contracting Parties in this area shows that there has been almost total compliance with Rule 36 indications [indications given by the European Commission of Human Rights or its President that, in the interest of the proceedings, the parties should refrain from adopting certain measures, based on Rule 36 of the Rules of Procedure of the European Commission of Human Rights]. Subsequent practice could be taken as establishing the agreement of Contracting States regarding the interpretation of a Convention provision (see, mutatis mutandis, [the *Soering* v. *United Kingdom*, judgment of 7 July 1989], Series A No. 161, 40–41, §103, and Article 31 §3 (b) of the Vienna Convention of 23 May 1969 on the Law of Treaties) but not to create new rights and obligations which were not included in the Convention at the outset ... In any event, as reflected in the various recommendations of the Council of Europe bodies [calling upon the States parties to the Convention to agree to recognizing the Court has a power to adopt provisional measures of a binding character], *the practice of complying with Rule 36 indications cannot have been based on a belief that these indications gave rise to a binding obligation* ... It was rather a matter of good faith co-operation with the Commission in cases where this was considered reasonable and practicable' (*Cruz Varas* v. *Sweden*, judgment of 20 March 1991, Series A No. 201, at para. 100 (emphasis added)) (for comments, see, e.g. R. Bernhardt, 'Interim Measures of Protection under the European Convention on Human Rights', in R. Bernhardt (ed.), *Interim Measures Indicated by International Courts* (Berlin: Springer Verlag, 1994), p. 102; R. St. J. Mcdonald, 'Interim Measures in International Law, with Special Reference to the European System for the Protection of Human Rights', 52(3–4) *Zeitschrift für ausländisches öffentliches Recht und Völkerrecht* 703 (1992)).

There was good reason for the Court to be cautious. The Rules of the Court are adopted by the plenary Court under Article 26 of the European Convention on Human Rights. They are thus not agreed upon by the States parties to the Convention. Their status therefore differs markedly from that of Article 41 of the Statute of the International Court of Justice, which the International Court of Justice interpreted in the *LaGrand (Germany* v. *United States)*, judgment of 27 June 2001 as imposing on the States parties to a dispute before the Court an obligation to comply with the provisional measures indicated under that provision, despite the vague character of the wording of that provision (Art. 41 of the Statute of the International Court of Justice provides: '1. The Court shall have the power to indicate, if it considers that circumstances so require, any provisional measures which ought to be taken to preserve the respective rights of either party. 2. Pending the final decision, notice of the measures suggested shall forthwith be given to the parties and to the Security Council'). Nor may Article 39 of the Rules adopted by the European Court of Human Rights be considered equivalent to Article 63(2) of the American Convention on Human Rights, which provides explicitly for a power of the Inter-American Court of Human Rights to adopt provisional measures 'in cases of extreme gravity and urgency, and when necessary to avoid irreparable damage to persons'. Both the Statute of the International Court of Justice and the American Convention on Human Rights are international treaties to whose terms the States parties have agreed. No equivalent clause exists in the European Convention on Human Rights. However, in *Mamatkulov and Askarov* v. *Turkey*, the Court considered that the precedents set by the Committee against Torture and the Human Rights Committee authorized it to consider, like these expert bodies, that the obligatory character of interim measures should be considered as a condition of the effectiveness of the protection provided to the individual by a system of individual communications. The episode offers a clear example of human rights bodies developing a doctrine, motivated perhaps by the need to ensure an effective protection of human rights, but which is difficult to reconcile with an orthodox (some might say conservative) view of international law. That this development was made possible by a number of human rights bodies moving in the same direction and, in part, legitimizing their interpretative inventivity by referring to one another's case law, seems hardly contestable.

the case of *Burghartz* v. *Switerland*, the Court noted: 'Unlike some other international instruments, such as the International Covenant on Civil and Political Rights (Article 24 para. 2), the Convention on the Rights of the Child of 20 November 1989 (Articles 7 and 8) or the American Convention on Human Rights (Article 18), Article 8 of the Convention does not contain any explicit provisions on names. As a means of personal identification and of linking to a family, a person's name nonetheless concerns his or her private and family life [and thus deserves protection under Art. 8 ECHR]' (Eur. Ct. HR, *Burghartz* v. *Switzerland*, judgment of 22 February 1994, para. 24). We can safely assume that the European Court of Human Rights has agreed to include the protection of the name of the individual in Article 8 of the European Convention on Human Rights, despite the absence of an explicit reference to the name in that provision, because other international human rights instruments do contain such a reference and ensure such a protection: once the 'right to the name' (whatever its specific implications) is recognized under at least some human rights treaties, reading it into the Convention is easier to justify. This seems to illustrate rather the third of the three attitudes ([3]) distinguished by Merrill, in which the Court draws on the existing corpus of international human rights law to develop the interpretation of the ECHR in line with the content of other human rights instruments, since all these instruments have their common source of inspiration in the Universal Declaration of Human Rights.

Or consider the reasoning followed by the European Committee of Social Rights, to justify setting aside the appendix to the European Social Charter which explicitly states that the Charter only benefits nationals of the Contracting parties:

European Committee on Social Rights, *International Federation for Human Rights (FIDH)* v. France, Collective Complaint No. 14/2003, decision on the merits of 8 September 2004:

[Paragraph 1 of the Appendix to the Revised European Social Charter provides that a wide range of social rights protected under the Charter, including the right to social and medical assistance (Art. 13 para. 1) and the right to the protection of the child (Art. 17), at stake in this case, cover foreigners 'only in so far as they are nationals of other Parties lawfully resident or working regularly within the territory of the Party concerned'. The complaining non-governmental organization nevertheless considered that the Revised European Social Charter had been violated by France, since French law excluded the provision of medical assistance to children of undocumented migrants on French territory, except as regards treatment for emergencies and life threatening conditions. The Committee set aside the limitation imposed on the scope of application *ratione personae* of the Charter:]

26. The present complaint raises issues of primary importance in the interpretation of the Charter. In this respect, the Committee makes it clear that, when it has to interpret the Charter, it does so on the basis of the 1969 Vienna Convention on the Law of Treaties. Article 31§1 of the said Convention states: 'A treaty shall be interpreted in good faith in accordance with the ordinary meaning to be given to the terms of the treaty in their context and in the light of its object and purpose.'

27. The Charter was envisaged as a human rights instrument to complement the European Convention on Human Rights. It is a living instrument dedicated to certain values which inspired it: dignity, autonomy, equality and solidarity. The rights guaranteed are not ends in themselves but they complete the rights enshrined in the European Convention of Human Rights.

28. Indeed, according to the Vienna Declaration of 1993, all human rights are 'universal, indivisible and interdependent and interrelated' (para. 5). The Committee is therefore mindful of the complex interaction between both sets of rights.

29. Thus, the Charter must be interpreted so as to give life and meaning to fundamental social rights. It follows inter alia that restrictions on rights are to be read restrictively, i.e. understood in such a manner as to preserve intact the essence of the right and to achieve the overall purpose of the Charter.

30. As concerns the present complaint, the Committee has to decide how the restriction in the Appendix ought to be read given the primary purpose of the Charter as defined above. The restriction attaches to a wide variety of social rights in Articles 1–17 and impacts on them differently. In the circumstances of this particular case, it treads on a right of fundamental importance to the individual since it is connected to the right to life itself and goes to the very dignity of the human being. Furthermore, the restriction in this instance impacts adversely on children who are exposed to the risk of no medical treatment.

31. Human dignity is the fundamental value and indeed the core of positive European human rights law – whether under the European Social Charter or under the European Convention of Human Rights and health care is a prerequisite for the preservation of human dignity.

32. The Committee holds that legislation or practice which denies entitlement to medical assistance to foreign nationals, within the territory of a State Party, even if they are there illegally, is contrary to the Charter.

This example and that of interim protection granted by human rights bodies (see box 1.3.) are both episodes in which the reference to case law from other courts or quasi-judicial bodies, or to the corpus of international human rights law, has served to expand the power of the courts or bodies tasked with the function of monitoring. In other cases, such references serve to economize judicial resources, by borrowing solutions from other jurisdictions which those jurisdictions are presumed to have carefully weighed, and which can be trusted in developing appropriate solutions. Or they may be a means to ensure that advanced democracies shall move together in the same direction, without excessive differences in approach to similar issues. Consider the following examples:

United States Supreme Court, *Lawrence et al. v. Texas*, 539 U.S. 558 (2003):

[The case has its source in the conviction for deviate sexual intercourse of Lawrence and Gardner, two adult men who were found engaging in a private, consensual sexual act, in violation of a Texas statute forbidding two persons of the same sex to engage in certain intimate sexual conduct. Although, in *Bowers* v. *Hardwick*, 478 U.S. 186 (1986), a similar statute had been considered not to be in violation of the Due Process Clause of the Fourteenth Amendment to the United States Federal Constitution, the Court here reconsiders this holding, which, it is now led to conclude, was wrongly decided. Instead, the Court now finds, the liberty protected by the United States Constitution allows homosexual persons the right to choose to enter into relationships in the confines of their homes and their own private lives and still retain their dignity as free persons. The excerpts below illustrate the role played by the reference to the jurisprudence of the European Court of Human Rights in the reasoning of the United States Supreme Court.]

Justice Kennedy delivered the opinion of the Court.

It must be acknowledged ... that the Court in Bowers was making the broader point that for centuries there have been powerful voices to condemn homosexual conduct as immoral. The condemnation has been shaped by religious beliefs, conceptions of right and acceptable behavior, and respect for the traditional family. For many persons these are not trivial concerns but profound and deep convictions accepted as ethical and moral principles to which they aspire and which thus determine the course of their lives. These considerations do not answer the question before us, however. The issue is whether the majority may use the power of the State to enforce these views on the whole society through operation of the criminal law. 'Our obligation is to define the liberty of all, not to mandate our own moral code.' *Planned Parenthood of Southeastern Pa.* v. *Casey*, 505 U.S. 833, 850 (1992) ...

Chief Justice Burger joined the opinion for the Court in Bowers and further explained his views as follows: 'Decisions of individuals relating to homosexual conduct have been subject to state intervention throughout the history of Western civilization. Condemnation of those practices is firmly rooted in Judeao-Christian moral and ethical standards.' 478 U.S., at 196 ...

The sweeping references by Chief Justice Burger to the history of Western civilization and to Judeo-Christian moral and ethical standards did not take account of other authorities pointing in an opposite direction. A committee advising the British Parliament recommended in 1957 repeal of laws punishing homosexual conduct. The Wolfenden Report: Report of the Committee on Homosexual Offenses and Prostitution (1963). Parliament enacted the substance of those recommendations 10 years later. Sexual Offences Act 1967, §1.

Of even more importance, almost five years before Bowers was decided the European Court of Human Rights considered a case with parallels to Bowers and to today's case. An adult male resident in Northern Ireland alleged he was a practicing homosexual who desired to engage in consensual homosexual conduct. The laws of Northern Ireland forbade him that right. He alleged that he had been questioned, his home had been searched, and he feared criminal prosecution. The court held that the laws proscribing the conduct were invalid under the European Convention on Human Rights. *Dudgeon* v. *United Kingdom*, 45 Eur. Ct. H.R. (1981) §52. Authoritative in all countries that are members of the Council of Europe (21 nations then, 45 nations now), the decision is at odds with the premise in Bowers that the claim put forward was insubstantial in our Western civilization.

In our own constitutional system the deficiencies in Bowers became even more apparent in the years following its announcement. The 25 States with laws prohibiting the relevant conduct referenced in the Bowers decision are reduced now to 13, of which 4 enforce their laws only against homosexual conduct. In those States where sodomy is still proscribed, whether for same-sex or heterosexual conduct, there is a pattern of nonenforcement with respect to consenting adults acting in private. The State of Texas admitted in 1994 that as of that date it had not prosecuted anyone under those circumstances ...

Bowers was not correct when it was decided, and it is not correct today. It ought not to remain binding precedent. *Bowers* v. *Hardwick* should be and now is overruled.

The present case does not involve minors. It does not involve persons who might be injured or coerced or who are situated in relationships where consent might not easily be refused. It does not involve public conduct or prostitution. It does not involve whether the government must give formal recognition to any relationship that homosexual persons seek to enter. The case does involve two adults who, with full and mutual consent from each other, engaged in sexual practices common to a homosexual lifestyle. The petitioners are entitled to respect for their private lives. The State cannot demean their existence or control their destiny by making their private sexual conduct a crime. Their right to liberty under the Due Process Clause gives them the full right to engage in their conduct without intervention of the government. 'It is a promise of the Constitution that there is a realm of personal liberty which the government may not enter.' Casey, *supra*, at 847. The Texas statute furthers no legitimate state interest which can justify its intrusion into the personal and private life of the individual.

Had those who drew and ratified the Due Process Clauses of the Fifth Amendment or the Fourteenth Amendment known the components of liberty in its manifold possibilities, they might have been more specific. They did not presume to have this insight. They knew times can blind us to certain truths and later generations can see that laws once thought necessary and proper in fact serve only to oppress. As the Constitution endures, persons in every generation can invoke its principles in their own search for greater freedom.

The following cases relate to assisted suicide and whether this constitutes an unreasonable restriction to the liberty of the individual. They too illustrate the reliance on comparative law in order to adjudicate human rights claims.

United States Supreme Court, *Washington* v. *Glucksberg*, 521 U.S. 702, 117 S.Ct. 2258 (1997):

[At issue in this case was the criminalization of assisted suicide in the State of Washington. The State made '[p]romoting a suicide attempt' a felony, and provided: 'A person is guilty of [that crime] when he knowingly causes or aids another person to attempt suicide.' Petitioners before the Court sought a declaration that the ban on physician-assisted suicides is, on its face, unconstitutional. They argued that the Fourteenth Amendment's Due Process Clause protected a liberty interest extending to a personal choice by a mentally competent, terminally ill adult to commit physician assisted suicide. The Supreme Court disagreed. It found that the asserted right to commit suicide and to be assisted in doing so had no trace in the United States' traditions, given the country's consistent, almost universal, and continuing rejection of the right, even for terminally ill, mentally competent adults. Rehnquist, C.J. delivered the opinion for a unanimous Court. Referring to the concern of the State of Washington that 'permitting assisted suicide will start it down the path to voluntary and perhaps even involuntary euthanasia', the Court noted:]

This concern is further supported by evidence about the practice of euthanasia in the Netherlands. The Dutch government's own study revealed that in 1990, there were 2,300 cases of voluntary euthanasia (defined as 'the deliberate termination of another's life at his request'), 400 cases of assisted suicide, and more than 1,000 cases of euthanasia without an explicit request. In addition to these latter 1,000 cases, the study found an additional 4,941 cases where physicians administered lethal morphine overdoses without the patients' explicit consent. Physician Assisted Suicide and Euthanasia in the Netherlands: A Report of Chairman Charles T. Canady, at 12–13 (citing Dutch study). This study suggests that, despite the existence of various reporting procedures, euthanasia in the Netherlands has not been limited to competent, terminally ill adults who are enduring physical suffering, and that regulation of the practice may not have prevented abuses in cases involving vulnerable persons, including severely disabled neonates and elderly persons suffering from dementia. Id., at 16–21; see generally C. Gomez, Regulating Death: Euthanasia and the Case of the Netherlands (1991); H. Hendin, Seduced By Death: Doctors, Patients, and the Dutch Cure (1997). The New York Task Force, citing the Dutch experience, observed that 'assisted suicide and euthanasia are closely linked', New York Task Force 145, and concluded that the 'risk of ... abuse is neither speculative nor distant,' id., at 134.

The issue of assisted suicide was presented before European courts in the case of Dianne Pretty. Ms Pretty was suffering from a progressive neuro-degenerative disease of motor cells within the central nervous system, for which there was no treatment available.

Because of the weakness affecting the voluntary muscles of the body, she was unable to commit suicide herself, although she considered that her situation was intolerable, as she was essentially paralysed from the neck downwards, was tube-fed, and would soon die in undignified conditions. However, in English law it was a crime to assist another to commit suicide (section 2(1) of the Suicide Act 1961), and Ms Pretty had failed to obtain from the Director of Public Prosecutions an undertaking not to prosecute her husband should he assist her to commit suicide in accordance with her wishes (for a fuller examination of this case, see chapter 4, section 2.4.). In their successive judgments on this case, both the House of Lords in the United Kingdom and the European Court of Human Rights rejected the claims of Ms Pretty based on the European Convention on Human Rights. Both also referred to the judgment of the Supreme Court of Canada in *Rodriguez v. Attorney General of Canada* [1993] 3 S.C.R. 519. The appellant in that case, Sue Rodriguez, suffered from a disease similar to that afflicting Ms Pretty. Invoking section 7 of the Canadian Charter of Rights and Freedoms (which states that 'Everyone has the right to life, liberty and security of the person and the right not to be deprived thereof except in accordance with the principles of fundamental justice'), she had sought an order which would have allowed a qualified medical practitioner to assist her to commit suicide at a time of her choosing. While suicide in Canada was not a crime, section 241(b) of the Criminal Code was effectively identical to section 2(1) of the English 1961 Act: it contained a blanket prohibition of assistance to suicide. Ms Rodriguez failed in her claim that such prohibition was unconstitutional. The majority of the Supreme Court took the view that the prohibition in section 241(b) fulfils the government's objective of protecting the vulnerable, and that it reflects the policy of the state that human life should not be depreciated by allowing life to be taken, which itself stems from the recognition of the sanctity of life – the fact that, in Dworkin's terms, human life is seen to have a deep intrinsic value of its own (R. Dworkin, *Life's Dominion: an Argument about Abortion, Euthanasia, and Individual Freedom* (New York: Alfred Knopf, 1993)). The Supreme Court also noted that a blanket prohibition on assisted suicide similar to that in section 241(b) seemed to be the norm among Western democracies, and that such a prohibition has never been adjudged to be unconstitutional or contrary to fundamental human rights. The following excerpts illustrate the role of comparative jurisprudence in achieving a consensus on the issue of assisted suicide, and in maintaining the distinction between passive and active forms of intervention in the dying process:

Supreme Court of Canada, *Rodriguez* v. *British Columbia (Attorney General)* [1993] 3 S.C.R. 519 (opinion for a plurality of the Court by Sopinka J):

A brief review of the legislative situation in other Western democracies demonstrates that in general, the approach taken is very similar to that which currently exists in Canada. Nowhere is assisted suicide expressly permitted, and most countries have provisions expressly dealing with assisted suicide which are at least as restrictive as our s. 241 [citing provisions from criminal legislation in Austria, Italy, and Spain].

The relevant provision of the Suicide Act, 1961 of the United Kingdom punishes a 'person who aids, abets, counsels or procures the suicide of another or an attempt by another, to commit suicide', and this form of prohibition is echoed in the criminal statutes of all state and territorial jurisdictions in Australia (M. Otlowski, "Mercy Killing Cases in the Australian Criminal Justice System" (1993) 17 Crim. L.J. 10). The U.K. provision is apparently the only prohibition on assisted suicide which has been subjected to judicial scrutiny for its impact on human rights prior to the present case. In the Application No. 10083/82, *R.* v. *United Kingdom*, July 4, 1983, D.R. 33, p. 270, the European Commission of Human Rights considered whether s. 2 of the Suicide Act, 1961 violated either the right to privacy in Article 8 or freedom of expression in Article 10 of the Convention for the Protection of Human Rights and Fundamental Freedoms. The applicant, who was a member of a voluntary euthanasia association, had been convicted of several counts of conspiracy to aid and abet a suicide for his actions in placing persons with a desire to kill themselves in touch with his co-accused who then assisted them in committing suicide. The European Commission held (at pp. 271–72) that the acts of aiding, abetting, counselling or procuring suicide were 'excluded from the concept of privacy by virtue of their trespass on the public interest of protecting life, as reflected in the criminal provisions of the 1961 Act', and upheld the applicant's conviction for the offence. Further, the Commission upheld the restriction on the applicant's freedom of expression, recognizing (at p. 272): 'the State's legitimate interest in this area in taking measures to protect, against criminal behaviour, the life of its citizens particularly those who belong to especially vulnerable categories by reason of their age or infirmity. It recognises the right of the State under the Convention to guard against the inevitable criminal abuses that would occur, in the absence of legislation, against the aiding and abetting of suicide.'

Although the factual scenario in that decision was somewhat different from the one at bar, it is significant that neither the European Commission of Human Rights nor any other judicial tribunal has ever held that a state is prohibited on constitutional or human rights grounds from criminalizing assisted suicide.

Some European countries have mitigated prohibitions on assisted suicide which might render assistance in a case similar to that before us legal in those countries. In the Netherlands, although assisted suicide and voluntary active euthanasia are officially illegal, prosecutions will not be laid so long as there is compliance with medically established guidelines. Critics of the Dutch approach point to evidence suggesting that involuntary active euthanasia (which is not permitted by the guidelines) is being practised to an increasing degree. This worrisome trend supports the view that a relaxation of the absolute prohibition takes us down 'the slippery slope'. Certain other European countries, such as Switzerland and Denmark, emphasize the motive of the assistor in suicide, such that the Swiss Penal Code, art. 115, criminalizes only those who incite or assist a suicide for a selfish motive, and the Danish Penal Code, art. 240, while punishing all assistance, imposes a greater penalty upon those who act out of self-interest. In France, while no provision of the Penal Code addresses specifically the issue of assisted suicide, failure to seek to prevent someone from committing suicide may still lead to criminal sanctions under art. 63, para. 2 (omission to provide assistance to a person in danger) or art. 319 (involuntary homicide by negligence or carelessness) of that Code. Moreover, the Loi no 87–1133 du 31 décembre 1987 introduced two new articles to the Penal Code, arts. 318–1 and 318–2, which criminalize the provocation of suicide. This offence, which requires a form of incitement over and above merely aiding in the commission of a suicide, was adopted in response to the macabre impact of the book Suicide, mode d'emploi (1982).

Similarly, a few American jurisdictions take into account whether the accused caused the victim to commit suicide by coercion, force, duress or deception in deciding whether the charge should be murder, manslaughter or assisted suicide (Connecticut, Maine and Pennsylvania) or whether the person is guilty of even assisted suicide (Puerto Rico and Indiana). See C. D. Shaffer, 'Criminal Liability for Assisting Suicide' (1986), 86 Colum. L. Rev. 348, at pp. 351–53, nn. 25–26, 35–36. As is the case in Europe and the Commonwealth, however, the vast majority of those American states which have statutory provisions dealing specifically with assisted suicide have no intent or malice requirement beyond the intent to further the suicide, and those states which do not deal with the matter statutorily appear to have common law authority outlawing assisted suicide (Shaffer, supra, at p. 352; and M. M. Penrose, 'Assisted Suicide: A Tough Pill to Swallow' (1993), 20 Pepp. L. Rev. 689, at pp. 700–701). It is notable, also, that recent movements in two American states to legalize physician–assisted suicide in circumstances similar to those at bar have been defeated by the electorate in those states. On November 5, 1991, Washington State voters defeated Initiative 119, which would have legalized physician-assisted suicide where two doctors certified the patient would die within six months and two disinterested witnesses certified that the patient's choice was voluntary. One year later, Proposition 161, which would have legalized assisted suicide in California and which incorporated stricter safeguards than did Initiative 119, was defeated by California voters (usually thought to be the most accepting of such legal innovations) by the same margin as resulted in Washington – 54 to 46 percent. In both states, the defeat of the proposed legislation seems to have been due primarily to concerns as to whether the legislation incorporated adequate safeguards against abuse (Penrose, supra, at pp. 708–14). I note that, at least in the case of California, the conditions to be met were more onerous than those set out by McEachern C.J.B.C. in the court below and by my colleagues the Chief Justice and McLachlin J.

Overall, then, it appears that a blanket prohibition on assisted suicide similar to that in s. 241 is the norm among Western democracies, and such a prohibition has never been adjudged to be unconstitutional or contrary to fundamental human rights. Recent attempts to alter the status quo in our neighbour to the south have been defeated by the electorate, suggesting that despite a recognition that a blanket prohibition causes suffering in certain cases, the societal concern with preserving life and protecting the vulnerable rendered the blanket prohibition preferable to a law which might not adequately prevent abuse.

House of Lords (United Kingdom), *R. (on the Application of Mrs Dianne Pretty (Appellant)) v. Director of Public Prosecutions (Respondent) and Secretary of State for the Home Department (Interested Party)*, judgment of 29 November 2001 [2001] UKHL 61, leading judgment by Lord Bingham of Cornhill:

23. It is evident that all save one of the judges of the Canadian Supreme Court were willing to recognise section 7 of the Canadian charter as conferring a right to personal autonomy extending even to decisions on life and death. Mrs Pretty understandably places reliance in particular on the judgment of McLachlin J. [who expressed a dissenting opinion], in which two other members of the court concurred. But a majority of the court regarded that right as outweighed on the facts by the principles of fundamental justice. The judgments were moreover

directed to a provision with no close analogy in the European Convention. In the European Convention the right to liberty and security of the person appears only in article 5(1), on which no reliance is or could be placed in the present case. Article 8 contains no reference to personal liberty or security. It is directed to the protection of privacy, including the protection of physical and psychological integrity: *X and Y* v. *Netherlands* [judgment of 26 March 1985]. But article 8 is expressed in terms directed to protection of personal autonomy while individuals are living their lives, and there is nothing to suggest that the article has reference to the choice to live no longer.

European Court of Human Rights (4th sect.), *Pretty* v. *United Kingdom* (Appl. No. 2346/02), judgment of 29 April 2002, para. 66:

In the case of *Rodriguez* v. *Attorney General of Canada* ([1994] 2 L.R.C. 136), which concerned a not dissimilar situation to the present, the majority opinion of the Supreme Court considered that the prohibition on the appellant in that case from receiving assistance in suicide contributed to her distress and prevented her from managing her death. This deprived her of autonomy and required justification under principles of fundamental justice. Although the Canadian court was considering a provision of the Canadian Charter framed in different terms from those of Article 8 of the Convention, comparable concerns arose regarding the principle of personal autonomy in the sense of the right to make choices about one's own body.

1.1. Questions for discussion: the role of comparative jurisprudence in human rights adjudication

1. What are the advantages and the dangers associated with an increased use of judgments or materials from other jurisdictions in human rights litigation? Are certain uses of comparative jurisprudence legitimate, while others are not?
2. If there is a need to distinguish between different functions of comparative jurisprudence in human rights litigation, is the typology proposed by Ch. McCrudden complete? Can you think of uses of foreign materials that are not captured by this typology?
3. Is there a risk of selectivity in the reference to foreign jurisprudence? Consider the use of foreign examples in the 1993 case of *Rodriguez* v. *Attorney General of Canada* decided by the Supreme Court of Canada. Why are examples from Europe or from the United States primarily referred to? Within Europe itself, why do certain countries seem to matter most in shaping a consensus? Is there a principled way to guide the reference to foreign jurisprudence, for instance the notion of 'Western democracies'?
4. Should the courts making use of comparative jurisprudence adopt a static or a dynamic approach to the material examined? Should they seek to identify some sort of mathematical average between jurisdictions, or should they instead seek to pay attention to the tendency identified in most recent changes?

5. Are the House of Lords and the European Court of Human Rights in disagreement about the relevance of the 1993 case of *Rodriguez* v. *Attorney General of Canada* decided by the Supreme Court of Canada, or do they differ, rather, on the interpretation to be given to that case?

4 HUMAN RIGHTS LAW AS PART OF INTERNATIONAL LAW

This section discusses the relationship of human rights law to general international law. It first examines the extent to which human rights are protected under general international law, beyond the specific treaties embodying them (section 4.1.). Whether they base their argument on the customary nature of the rights enumerated in the Universal Declaration of Human Rights, on the status of human rights as general principles of law, or on the recognition by the UN Charter of human rights and fundamental freedoms as objectives all the Members of the United Nations have to co-operate in achieving, most authors consider that human rights treaties are the embodiment, in treaty form, of obligations which are already imposed on States. This does not extend, of course, to the monitoring mechanisms which such treaties may include. But, insofar as the substantive rights are concerned, human rights treaties would simply codify already existing obligations: they would not create entirely new obligations for their States parties.

Next, this section examines the status of human rights norms in the hierarchy of international law (section 4.2.). Because of the combination of Articles 55 and 56 of the UN Charter and Article 103 of the Charter, and due to the *jus cogens* nature of at least certain of the internationally recognized human rights, human rights treaties may be considered to be hierarchically superior to other norms of international law, whether they have their source in treaties, in custom, or in general principles of law – all three of which are sources of international law, according to Article 38(1) of the Statute of the International Court of Justice. In addition, serious breaches of peremptory norms of international law – i.e. 'a gross or systematic failure by the responsible State to fulfil the obligation' forming part of *jus cogens* – entail specific obligations on other States to contribute to a cessation of the violation.

Third, human rights norms present certain characteristics which distinguish them from other rules of international law. Whether they are based on custom or on other sources of international law, and whether or not they have the nature of *jus cogens* norms, human rights are often considered to impose obligations *erga omnes* – obligations, that is, towards all the States of the international community (section 4.3.). In addition, human rights treaties are not concluded in order to grant reciprocal advantages to the contracting States: their object, rather, is to protect individuals under the jurisdiction of each State, and this may result in the Vienna Convention on the Law of Treaties being inadequate, in certain respects, as regards human rights treaties (section 4.4.). However, while there exists substantial agreement on these general propositions, both their precise significance and the consequences they entail remain disputed.

Finally, the issue of reservations to human rights treaties is included in this section, as it provides a good illustration of the unsettled relationship of international human rights law to general international law (section 4.5.).

4.1 Human rights beyond treaties

(a) Human rights in the UN Charter

Whether or not they have ratified the relevant treaties which have proliferated since the 1950s at international and regional levels, all States are bound to respect internationally recognized human rights. The Universal Declaration of Human Rights may be seen in this respect as simply clarifying the meaning of the provisions of the UN Charter which refer to human rights as a purpose to be achieved by the Organization and by its Member States. In particular, Article 55 of the Charter imposes on the United Nations a duty to promote 'universal respect for, and observance of, human rights and fundamental freedoms for all without distinction as to race, sex, language or religion'; under Article 56, all Members of the United Nations 'pledge themselves to take joint and separate action in cooperation with the Organization for the achievement of the purposes set forth in Article 55'.

Scholars have sometimes questioned whether these provisions in fact imposed legal obligations, or simply defined in general terms a programme of action for the organization (see, e.g. M. O. Hudson, 'Integrity of International Instruments', *American Journal of International Law*, 42 (1948), 105–8; H. Kelsen, *The Law of the United Nations* (London: The London Institute of World Affairs, 1950), pp. 29–32; in favour of seeing in these provisions of the UN Charter the source of legal obligations, see in particular H. Lauterpacht, *International Law and Human Rights* (New York; Frederick Praeger, Inc., 1950), at pp. 147–9). The sceptical views, however, were often confusing the question whether the Charter's provisions were self-executing, with the question whether they were legally binding; and they were premised on the indeterminate character of the content of the 'human rights and fundamental freedoms' referred to in the Charter, which the Universal Declaration of Human Rights precisely sought to make explicit. The International Court of Justice seems to have definitively put an end to the controversy when it delivered its Advisory Opinion on the *Legal Consequences for States of the Continued Presence of South Africa in Namibia (South West Africa), notwithstanding Security Council Resolution 276 (1970)*, where it stated that 'to establish ..., and to enforce, distinctions, exclusions, restrictions and limitations exclusively based on grounds of race, colour, descent or national or ethnic origin which constitute a denial of fundamental human rights is a flagrant violation of the purposes and principles of the Charter' (I.C.J. Reports 1971, 16). Although the statement was made in relation to the obligations of South Africa as a mandatory power in South West Africa, there is no reason to restrict it to this hypothesis: instead, it would seem to follow from the Opinion that the UN Charter imposes on all States that they comply, at a minimum, with a core set of human rights, which the Charter refers to without listing them exhaustively (see E. Schwelb, 'The International Court of Justice and the Human Rights Clauses of the Charter', *American Journal of International Law*, 66, No. 2 (1972), 337–51, esp. 348–9).

Even if we accept that the UN Charter imposes compliance with human rights to all the Member States of the Organization, it still is only addressed, in principle, to States and the institutions of the UN, rather than to all subjects of international law. However, at the same time that they were codified in international treaties, human rights have also been recognized as binding upon all subjects of international law as part of general international law, either because they are part of customary international law, or because they constitute general principles of law.

(b) Human rights as part of customary international law
The growing consensus is that most, if not all, of the rights enumerated in the Universal Declaration of Human Rights have acquired a customary status in international law (see in particular L. Henkin, *The Age of Rights* (New York: Columbia University, 1990), p. 19; N. S. Rodley, 'Human Rights and Humanitarian Intervention: the Case Law of the World Court', *International and Comparative Law Quarterly*, 38 (1989), at 321, esp. 333; T. Meron, *Human Rights and Humanitarian Norms as Customary Law* (Oxford: Clarendon Press, 1989); L. B. Sohn, 'The Human Rights Law of the Charter', *Texas International Law Journal*, 12 (1977), 129 at 132–4; H. Hannum, 'The Status of the Universal Declaration of Human Rights in National and International Law', *Georgia Journal of International and Comparative Law*, 25 (1995–1996), 287). Custom in principle requires, to be established, both consistent identifiable state practice, and evidence of a belief that this practice is rendered obligatory by the existence of a rule of law requiring it (*opinio juris sive necessitatis*). The classic definition is that adopted by the International Court of Justice in the *North Sea Continental Shelf Cases (Federal Republic of Germany* v. *Denmark* and *Federal Republic of Germany* v. *Netherlands)* (I.C.J. Reports 1969, 44, para. 77): 'Not only must the acts concerned amount to settled practice, but they must also be such or be carried out in such a way, as to be evidence of a belief that this practice is rendered obligatory by the existence of a rule of law requiring it. The need for such a belief, i.e. the existence of a subjective element, is implicit in the very notion of the *opinio juris sive necessitatis*. The states concerned must therefore feel that they are conforming to what amounts to their legal obligation. The frequency or even habitual character of the acts is not in itself enough.'

It has been argued, however, that, in the field of human rights, evidence of custom could be based on the resolutions of the UN General Assembly and statements made within other international organizations, demonstrating a clear commitment of the international community towards certain values, while inconsistent State practice on the other hand would not be an obstacle to the identification of such custom. For instance, the fact that the universal periodic review performed by the UN Human Rights Council takes as a reference, in the review of each State, not only the Charter of the United Nations, but also the Universal Declaration of Human Rights, as well as the human rights instruments to which a State is party (appendix to the Human Rights Council Resolution 5/1 'Institution-building of the United Nations Human Rights Council' (18 June 2007): see further chapter 10), provides as least an indication of the expectation of the international community that all States should comply with a basic corpus of human rights as contained in the UDHR, whichever treaties they have ratified. Some authors have gone so far as to suggest that State 'practice', for the purposes of custom determination in the field of human rights, is composed of official declarations and participation in the negotiation of human rights instruments, as well as of incorporation of human rights within the national legal orders. Consider for instance the attitude adopted by the 1987 *Restatement (Third) of the Foreign Relations Law of the United States* (for an exposé of the background assumptions underlying this position, see the Hague Academy course of Oscar Schachter: O. Schachter, 'International Law in Theory and Practice: General Course in Public International Law', *Recueil des cours*, 178 (1982–V), 2 at 333–42), or the position expressed by Theodor Meron:

American Law Institute, *Restatement (Third) of the Foreign Relations Law of the United States* (St. Paul, Minn.: American Law Institute Publishers, 1987):

[§701, n. 2] Practice accepted as building customary human rights law includes: virtually universal adherence to the United Nations Charter and its human rights provisions, and virtually universal and frequently reiterated acceptance of the Universal Declaration of Human Rights even if only in principle; virtually universal participation of states in the preparation and adoption of international agreements recognizing human rights principles generally, or particular rights; the adoption of human rights principles by states in regional organizations in Europe, Latin America, and Africa ...; general support by states for United Nations resolutions declaring, recognizing, invoking, and applying international human rights principles as international law; action by states to conform their national law or practice to standards or principles declared by international bodies, and the incorporation of human rights provisions, directly or by reference, in national constitutions and law; invocation of human rights principles in national policy, in diplomatic practice, in international organization activities and actions; and other diplomatic communications or action by states reflecting the view that certain practices violate international human rights law, including condemnation and other adverse state reactions to violations by other states.

 [Applying this criterion, the *Restatement* concludes in §702 that:] A state violates international law if, as a matter of state policy, it practices, encourages, or condones (a) genocide, (b) slavery or slave trade, (c) the murder or causing the disappearance of individuals, (d) torture or other cruel, inhuman or degrading treatment or punishment, (e) prolonged arbitrary detention, (f) systematic racial discrimination, or (g) a consistent pattern of gross violations of internationally recognized human rights.

Theodor Meron, *Human Rights and Humanitarian Norms as Customary Law* (Oxford: Clarendon Press, 1989), p. 93:

[T]he initial inquiry must aim at the determination whether, at a minimum, the definition of the core norm claiming customary law status and preferably the contours of the norm have been widely accepted. In this context my own preferred indicators evincing customary human rights are, first, the degree to which a statement of a particular right in one human rights instrument, especially a human rights treaty, has been repeated in other human rights instruments, and second, the confirmation of the right in national practice, primarily through the incorporation of the right in national laws ... It is, of course, to be expected that those rights which are most crucial to the protection of human dignity and of the universally accepted values of humanity, and whose violation triggers broad condemnation by the international community, will require a lesser amount of confirmatory evidence.

Essentially two arguments have been put forward in favour of this position. First, it can be said that the 'practice' of a State towards its own population (the rights of which it is the purpose of the international human rights regime to protect) would be difficult if not impossible to ascertain for practical reasons (violations committed by a State within its borders frequently go unnoticed), so that customary international law could only be determined, not by reference to how States actually behave, but by the justifications they provide for the way they behave: in this view, 'even massive abuses do not militate against assuming a customary rule as long as the responsible author state seeks to hide and conceal its objectionable conduct instead of justifying it by invoking legal reasons' (C. Tomuschat, *Human Rights Between Idealism and Realism* (Oxford University Press, 2003), p. 34). Second, this view about the identification of practice as building customary human rights law is also related to the fact that States have no subjective interest in other States complying with their human rights obligations, except in those rare instances where the rights of the nationals of the first States are at stake. As a result, there is little State practice on the basis of which to identify the formation of a custom, since most instances of human rights violations do not give rise to protests by other States of the international community (O. Schachter, 'International Law in Theory and Practice: General Course in Public International Law', *Recueil des cours*, 178 (1982–V), at 334).

Thus, a 'modern' view of custom has gained some acceptance in the field of human rights (for a discussion, see M. Akehurst, 'Custom as a Source of International Law', *British Yearbook of International Law* (1974–5), 1 *et seq.*; L. Henkin, 'Human Rights and State 'Sovereignty'', 25 *Georgia Journal of International Law* 37 (1995–1996)). This view presents itself as a substitute to the classical view as reflected in Article 38(1) of the Statute of the International Court of Justice. In the 'modern' approach, State 'practice' in the usual sense of 'behaviour' is less determinative than authoritative statements made by governments or intergovernmental bodies. This turn is favoured in part by a general identity crisis of custom as a source of international law. It has been encouraged by well-intentioned authors, eager to provide human rights law with a standing in customary law which would compensate for what was perceived in the 1970s and 1980s as the lack of enthusiasm of States in the ratification of human rights treaties. However, this 'modern' view results in distorting the classical notion of custom in such a way that the notion is barely even recognizable under its new disguise. Philip Alston and Bruno Simma have also argued that it may be ideologically biased towards the recognition of certain particular human rights as forming part of customary international law. The result of the 'new' approach, it turns out, which emphasizes deduction from statements instead of induction from State behaviour, is that those civil and political rights which are recognized in United States constitutional law and which the United States invokes against other States are included, while other rights, equally essential and whose status is identical within the international bill of rights, are excluded. These authors therefore suggest that a certain 'sub-conscious chauvinism' may be at work, for instance, in the list of human rights recognized as customary international law in the *Restatement*. They ask whether 'any theory of human rights law which singles out race but not gender discrimination, which condemns arbitrary imprisonment but not capital punishment for crimes committed by juveniles or death by starvation and which finds no place for a right of access to primary health care, is not flawed in terms both of the theory of human rights and of United Nations doctrine' (B. Simma and P. Alston, 'The Sources of Human Rights Law: Custom, *Jus Cogens*, and General Principles', 12 *Australian Yearbook of International Law* 82 (1988–1989), at 94–5).

The dissatisfaction with the substitution of a 'modern' view of custom to the 'traditional' view has led, in turn, to two reactions. One part of the doctrine has sought to accommodate the competing claims of the 'traditional' and the 'modern' views of custom. Thus for instance, Frederic Kirgis has put the requirements of State practice and *opinio juris*, which compete for influencing the emergence of custom, on a sliding scale: whereas, at one end of the scale, highly consistent State practice should suffice to establish the existence of *opinio juris*, conversely and at the other end, strong indications that there exists a consensus among States about the unacceptability of certain forms of behaviour may establish custom, even if State practice is inconsistent (F. Kirgis, 'Custom on a Sliding Scale', *American Journal of International Law*, 81 (1987), 146; see also, for other attempts in this direction, J. Tasioulas, 'In Defence of Relative Normativity: Communitarian Values and the Nicaragua Case', *Oxford Journal of Legal Studies*, 16 (1996), 85, and A. E. Roberts, 'Traditional and Modern Approaches to Customary International Law: a Reconciliation', *American Journal of International Law*, 95 (2001), 757). But, alternatively, we may turn to other arguments in order to ground human rights law in general international law. The most promising avenue in this direction, and the one preferred by P. Alston and B. Simma, is to identify human rights as general principles of international law.

(c) Human rights as general principles of law

This means of recognizing the Universal Declaration of Human Rights as a source of legal obligations is encouraged by the approach adopted by the International Court of Justice itself. The Court has refrained from stating that the Declaration as such, in the totality of its articles, should be considered as customary international law. But it did refer to the Declaration on a number of occasions, albeit always with respect to a specific right and without always clarifying the source of the authority of the Declaration. For instance, alluding to the prohibition of arbitrary arrest or detention stipulated in Article 9 of the Universal Declaration of Human Rights, it stated in the *Tehran Hostages* case that 'Wrongfully to deprive human beings of their freedom and to subject them to physical constraint in conditions of hardship is in itself manifestly incompatible with the principles of the Charter of the United Nations, as well as with the fundamental principles enunciated in the Universal Declaration of Human Rights' (*United States Diplomatic and Consular Staff in Tehran (United States* v. *Iran) (merits)* (I.C.J. Reports 1980, at 42). The language referring to such 'fundamental principles' is not new. Already in the *Corfu Channel* case, the Court mentioned 'obligations ... based ... on certain general and well-recognized principles', among which it mentioned what it labelled 'elementary considerations of humanity' (*Corfu Channel Case (United Kingdom of Great Britain and Northern Ireland-Albania)* (I.C.J. Reports 1949, 4 at 22)). In the Advisory Opinion it delivered on the issue of *Reservations to the Convention on the Prevention and Punishment of the Crime of Genocide*, it referred to 'the principles underlying the Convention' as 'principles which are recognized by civilized nations as binding on States, even without any conventional obligation' (*Reservations to the Convention on the Prevention and Punishment of the Crime of Genocide*, Advisory Opinion, I.C.J. Reports 1951, 19 (28 May 1951)). Almost identical language may be found in later cases. In its Advisory Opinion on the *Legality of Threat or Use of Nuclear Weapons*, referring to the *Corfu Channel* dictum, the Court stated that 'it is undoubtedly because a great many rules of humanitarian law applicable in armed conflict are so fundamental to the respect of the human person and "elementary considerations of humanity"...., that the Hague and Geneva Conventions have enjoyed a broad accession. Further these fundamental rules are to be observed by all States whether or not they have ratified the conventions that contain them, because they constitute intransgressible principles of international customary law' (I.C.J. Reports 1996, 226, at 257 (para. 79)). Similarly, in the case concerning *Military and Paramilitary Activities in and against Nicaragua (Nicaragua* v. *United States of America)*, the Court had mentioned the 'fundamental general principles of humanitarian law' as the source of obligations for the defendant State (I.C.J. Reports 1986, 14, at 113–14). The *Case Concerning East Timor (Portugal* v. *Australia)* similarly referred to the 'principle' of self-determination as 'one of the essential principles of contemporary international law' (I.C.J. Reports 1995, 90, at 102 (para. 29)).

Although these statements refer, for the most part, to otherwise unspecified 'principles of international law' rather than to the 'general principles of law recognized by civilized nations' mentioned by Article 38(1)(c) of the Statute of the International Court of Justice, they nevertheless have been interpreted as implying that human rights should qualify among the latter principles, and thus as forming part of general international law (see B. Simma and P. Alston, 'The Sources of Human Rights Law: Custom, *Jus Cogens*, and General Principles', cited above, at 102–8; T. Meron, *Human Rights and Humanitarian Norms as Customary Law* (Oxford: Clarendon Press,

1989), at p. 88). Indeed, enthusiastic as they are about the grounding of international human rights law in customary international law, the reporters of the *Restatement (Third) of the Foreign Relations of the United States* note that 'there is a willingness to conclude that prohibitions [against human rights violations] common to the constitutions or laws of many states are general principles that have been absorbed into international law' (para. 701, n. 1). This conclusion also may be seen to follow from the fact that the Universal Declaration of Human Rights has been implemented, or even sometimes almost literally reproduced, in a large number of bill of rights in the world (H. Hannum, 'The Status of the Universal Declaration of Human Rights in National and International Law', *Georgia Journal of International and Comparative Law*, 25 (1995–1996), 287, at 351–2).

(d) The significance of human rights as part of general international law

Does it matter that international human rights have their source both in general public international law, and in specific treaties concluded at universal or regional level? The expansion of the membership of States in international human rights treaties particularly in the 1990s – the Convention on the Rights of the Child has achieved almost universal ratification, and treaties such as the two 1966 Covenants or the International Convention for the Elimination of All Forms of Discrimination against Women have also been very widely ratified – may have created the impression that the controversy about how solid the foundations of human rights law are in general international law, as opposed to treaty law, is not worth the efforts of legal doctrine today, as it might have been in the 1980s. We should resist this impression, however. First, we are far from having achieved universal ratification for all human rights treaties. Second, ratifications by States may be accompanied by reservations about specific rights or about the scope of application of the treaty: grounding the guarantees of the treaty in customary international law or in other sources of general international law may serve to overcome such restrictions. Third, it is increasingly acknowledged that States are not the only addressees of human rights law. As subjects of international law, international organizations are bound by general international law (see further on this issue chapter 2, section 4), and some authors believe this could be extended to transnational corporations (see chapter 4, section 1.2.): in order to impose human rights obligations on such private non-State actors, these obligations must have their source elsewhere than in treaties, which as a rule only States may ratify.

The view that human rights treaties merely embody, in treaty form, pre-existing obligations of States – which have their source in customary international law or in the general principles of law, and which are not at the disposal of States – also has guided the approach of human rights bodies on the question of the denunciation of human rights treaties and of State succession, especially after the dismantling of the former Soviet Union or of the former Federal Republic of Yugoslavia, and the separation of Czechoslovakia into two distinct entities. Box 1.4. discusses this issue.

Box 1.4. **The continuity of human rights obligations**

On 5 March 1993, the Commission on Human Rights adopted Resolution 1993/23, entitled 'Succession of States in respect of International Human Rights Treaties', in which it encouraged successor States to confirm officially that they continued to be bound by obligations under relevant international human rights treaties and urged those that had not yet done so to ratify or to accede to those international human rights treaties to which the predecessor States had not been parties. It also adopted Resolution 1994/16 of 25 February 1994, in which it emphasized the special nature of the treaties aimed at the protection of human rights and reiterated its call to successor States which had not yet done so to confirm that they continued to be bound by obligations under international human rights treaties. Probably emboldened by these resolutions, the Human Rights Committee expressed the following views on the question of denunciation of the International Covenant on Civil and Political Rights, as well as on the question of State succession:

Human Rights Committee, General Comment No. 26, *Continuity of Obligations* (8 December 1997) (CCPR/C/21/Rev.1/Add. 8/Rev.1):

1. The International Covenant on Civil and Political Rights does not contain any provision regarding its termination and does not provide for denunciation or withdrawal. Consequently, the possibility of termination, denunciation or withdrawal must be considered in the light of applicable rules of customary international law which are reflected in the Vienna Convention on the Law of Treaties. On this basis, the Covenant is not subject to denunciation or withdrawal unless it is established that the parties intended to admit the possibility of denunciation or withdrawal or a right to do so is implied from the nature of the treaty.

2. That the parties to the Covenant did not admit the possibility of denunciation and that it was not a mere oversight on their part to omit reference to denunciation is demonstrated by the fact that article 41(2) of the Covenant does permit a State party to withdraw its acceptance of the competence of the Committee to examine inter-State communications by filing an appropriate notice to that effect while there is no such provision for denunciation of or withdrawal from the Covenant itself. Moreover, the Optional Protocol to the Covenant, negotiated and adopted contemporaneously with it, permits States parties to denounce it. Additionally, by way of comparison, the International Convention on the Elimination of All Forms of Racial Discrimination, which was adopted one year prior to the Covenant, expressly permits denunciation. It can therefore be concluded that the drafters of the Covenant deliberately intended to exclude the possibility of denunciation. The same conclusion applies to the Second Optional Protocol in the drafting of which a denunciation clause was deliberately omitted.

3. Furthermore, it is clear that the Covenant is not the type of treaty which, by its nature, implies a right of denunciation. Together with the simultaneously prepared and adopted International Covenant on Economic, Social and Cultural Rights, the Covenant codifies in treaty form the

universal human rights enshrined in the Universal Declaration of Human Rights, the three instruments together often being referred to as the 'International Bill of Human Rights'. As such, the Covenant does not have a temporary character typical of treaties where a right of denunciation is deemed to be admitted, notwithstanding the absence of a specific provision to that effect.

4. The rights enshrined in the Covenant belong to the people living in the territory of the State party. The Human Rights Committee has consistently taken the view, as evidenced by its long-standing practice, that once the people are accorded the protection of the rights under the Covenant, such protection devolves with territory and continues to belong to them, notwith-standing change in government of the State party, including dismemberment in more than one State or State succession or any subsequent action of the State party designed to divest them of the rights guaranteed by the Covenant.

5. The Committee is therefore firmly of the view that international law does not permit a State which has ratified or acceded or succeeded to the Covenant to denounce it or withdraw from it.

This position expressed in General Comment No. 26 is clearly based on the view that human rights treaties are specific among international treaties (in favour of this view, see M. Kamminga, 'State Succession in Respect of Human Rights Treaties', *European Journal of International Law*, 7 (1996) 469, at 482–3; R. Higgins, 'The International Court of Justice and Human Rights' in K. Wellens (ed.), *International Law: Theory and Practice. Essays in Honour of Eric Suy* (Leiden: Martinus Nijhoff, 1998), p. 691, at pp. 696–7; see also the separate opinion of Judge Weeramantry to the 11 July 1996 judgment of the International Court of Justice in the case of the *Application of the Convention on the Prevention and Punishment of the Crime of Genocide (Bosnia and Herzegovina* v. *Serbia and Montenegro)*, I.C.J. Reports 1996, 595). But it seems to contradict the rule established under customary international law for other inter-national law treaties in cases of succession of States, where the solution generally favoured is that succeeding States may choose whether or not to be bound by the treaties to which the predecessor State had acceded (see, for example, *Restatement (Third) of the Foreign Relations Law of the United States (1987)*, para. 210(3), Reporters' Note 4; I. Brownlie, *Principles of Public International Law*, fifth edn (Oxford University Press, 1998), p. 663; A. Cassese, *International Law*, second edn (Oxford University Press, 2005), p. 78; M. Shaw, *International Law*, fifth edn (Cambridge University Press, 2003), p. 875; M. Koskenniemi and P. M. Eisemann (eds.), *State Succession: Codification Tested Against the Facts* (The Hague: Hague Academy of International Law, Martinus Nijhoff, 2000). Even the 1978 Vienna Convention on Succession of States in respect of Treaties, which is not generally considered to faithfully represent customary inter-national law, does not anticipate automatic succession to treaties, at least as regards newly independent States. And, indeed, the General Comment of the Human Rights Committee on the continuity of obligations has been taken issue with, including from within the Committee itself.

Vienna Convention on Succession of States in respect of Treaties (23 August 1978) (excerpts):

Article 16. Position in respect of the treaties of the predecessor State
A newly independent State [defined by the Convention as 'a successor State the territory of which immediately before the date of the succession of States was a dependent territory for the international relations of which the predecessor State was responsible'] is not bound to maintain in force, or to become a party to, any treaty by reason only of the fact that at the date of the succession of States the treaty was in force in respect of the territory to which the succession of States relates.

Article 34. Succession of States in cases of separation of parts of a State
1. When a part or parts of the territory of a State separate to form one or more States, whether or not the predecessor State continues to exist: (a) any treaty in force at the date of the succession of States in respect of the entire territory of the predecessor State continues in force in respect of each successor State so formed; (b) any treaty in force at the date of the succession of States in respect only of that part of the territory of the predecessor State which has become a successor State continues in force in respect of that successor State alone.
2. Paragraph 1 does not apply if: (a) the States concerned otherwise agree; or (b) it appears from the treaty or is otherwise established that the application of the treaty in respect of the successor State would be incompatible with the object and purpose of the treaty or would radically change the conditions for its operation.

Human Rights Committee, *Kuok Koi* v. *Portugal*, Communication No. 925/2000 (final views of 22 October 2001) (CCPR/C/73/D/925/2000) (individual opinion of Mr Nisuke Ando):

Personally, I agree with the Committee's view [as expressed in para. 4 of General Comment No. 26 on the *Continuity of Obligations under the International Covenant on Civil and Political Rights*] as a matter of policy statement, but I cannot agree with it as a statement of a rule of customary international law. As far as State practice with respect to the Covenant is concerned, only in the cases of the dismemberment of the former Yugoslavia and that of Czechoslovakia, each of the newly born States in Central and Eastern Europe except Kazakhstan [which consistently refused to accept that it succeeded automatically to the human rights treaties concluded formerly by the Soviet Union] indicated that it 'succeeds to' the Covenant. All the other seceding or separating States indicated that they 'accede to' the Covenant, which implies that they are not succeeding to the former States' Covenant obligations but are newly acceding to the Covenant obligations on their own. The corresponding State practice with respect to the Optional Protocol makes it clear that only the Czech Republic and Slovakia 'expressly' succeeded to the Optional Protocol obligations. Certainly the State practice shows that there is no 'automatic' devolution of the Covenant obligations, to say nothing of the Optional Protocol obligations, to any State. A State needs to make an 'express' indication as to whether or not it accepts obligations under the Covenant and/or the Optional Protocol. Absent such an indication, it should not be assumed that the State has accepted the obligations.

1.2. Questions for discussion: custom and general principles of law as sources of human rights

1. Are there dangers associated with adapting the classic definition of custom as a source of international law to the specificity of human rights, considering especially the fact that the indivisibility, interdependence and equal importance of all human rights – including both civil and political and economic, social and cultural rights – have been regularly reaffirmed in various UN resolutions and at successive world conferences on human rights?

2. Should human rights, as part of general international law, be identified preferably as part of customary international law, or as part of general principles of law? Or does the best approach consist in seeing human rights – as listed in the Universal Declaration of Human Rights – as imposed under the UN Charter, particularly under Articles 55 and 56?

3. Does it follow from the fact that respect for human rights is obligatory for States, whichever the human rights treaties they have ratified, that States parties to a human rights treaty should not be allowed to denounce it unless the said treaty explicitly provides for this possibility? Does it follow that any successor State is bound by the human rights treaties concluded by the State to which it succeeds, even when it is a newly independent State? Consider that, as recalled by the International Court of Justice, '[t]he fact that the [principles of customary and international law], recognized as such, have been codified or embodied in multilateral conventions does not mean that they cease to exist and to apply as principles of customary law, even as regards countries that are parties to such conventions' (case concerning *Military and Paramilitary Activities in and against Nicaragua (Nicaragua v. United States)* I.C.J. Reports 1984, 424, para. 73 (judgment of 26 November 1984 on the jurisdiction of the Court and on the admissibility of the application)), so that 'customary international law continues to exist and to apply, separately from international treaty law, even where the two categories of law have an identical content' (concerning *Military and Paramilitary Activities in and against Nicaragua (Nicaragua v. United States)* I.C.J. Reports 1986, 14, para. 179 (judgment of 27 June 1986 on the merits)).

4.2. Human rights in the hierarchy of international law

It has sometimes been argued that human rights norms occupy a superior position in international law due to their specific status. The case of the *Sawhoyamaxa Indigenous Community* presented to the Inter-American Court of Human Rights provides a useful starting point. In this case, the State alleged it could not give effect to the indigenous community's right to property over their ancestral lands because, among other reasons, these lands now belonged to a German investor, protected by a bilateral investment treaty. The Court answered:

Inter-American Court of Human Rights, case of *The Sawhoyamaxa Indigenous Community* v. *Paraguay* (judgment of 29 March 2006, Series C No. 146).

137. ... [The] Court has ascertained that the arguments put forth by the State to justify non-enforcement of the indigenous people's property rights have not sufficed to release it from international responsibility. The State has put forth three arguments: 1) that claimed lands have been conveyed from one owner to another 'for a long time' and are duly registered; 2) that said lands are being been adequately exploited, and 3) that the owner's right 'is protected under a bilateral agreement between Paraguay and Germany[,] which ... has become part of the law of the land.' ...

140. ... [W]ith regard to the third argument put forth by the State, the Court has not been furnished with the aforementioned treaty between Germany and Paraguay, but, according to the State, said convention allows for capital investments made by a contracting party to be condemned or nationalized for a 'public purpose or interest', which could justify land restitution to indigenous people. Moreover, the Court considers that the enforcement of bilateral commercial treaties negates vindication of non-compliance with state obligations under the American Convention; on the contrary, their enforcement should always be compatible with the American Convention, which is a multilateral treaty on human rights that stands in a class of its own and that generates rights for individual human beings and does not depend entirely on reciprocity among States.

141. Based on the foregoing, the Court dismisses the three arguments of the State described above and finds them insufficient to justify non-enforcement of the right to property of the Sawhoyamaxa Community.

This position implies, albeit implicitly, that human rights treaties – due to their specific nature as having a 'normative' character, which distinguishes them from treaties which are merely an exchange of rights and obligations between States – occupy a superior position in international law, and that any treaties conflicting with them should therefore be set aside in situations of conflict. Which weight should we recognize to such an assertion?

(a) The arguments in favour of hierarchy

Two arguments are traditionally put forward in order to justify the view that human rights occupy a hierarchically superior position among the norms of international law (see generally I. Seiderman, *Hierarchy in International Law. The Human Rights Dimension* (Antwerp-Oxford: Intersentia-Hart, 2001)). First, Article 103 of the UN Charter provides that 'In the event of a conflict between the obligations of the Members of the United Nations under the present Charter and their obligations under any other international agreement, their obligations under the present Charter shall prevail.' Since one of the purposes of the UN Charter is to achieve international co-operation in promoting and encouraging respect for human rights and for fundamental freedoms for all without discrimination (Art. 1(3)), and since Article 56 of the Charter clearly imposes obligations both on the organization itself and on its Member States to contribute to the fulfilment of this objective, it would follow, then, that any international obligation conflicting with the obligation to promote and protect human rights should be set aside, in order for this latter objective to be given priority.

Second, although the norms of international law (custom, treaties, and the 'general principles of law recognized by civilized nations', as expressed in the list of sources of international law by Art. 38(1) of the Statute of the International Court of Justice) are otherwise not hierarchically ordered according to their various sources, certain norms are specific in that they embody a form of international public policy. In the context of the law of treaties, the Vienna Convention on the Law of Treaties states that any treaty which, at the time of its conclusion, is in violation of a peremptory norm of general international law (also referred to as belonging to *jus cogens*), is to be considered void. A peremptory norm of general international law is defined as 'a norm accepted and recognized by the international community of States as a whole as a norm from which no derogation is permitted and which can be modified only by a subsequent norm of general international law having the same character' (Art. 53; Art. 64 of the Vienna Convention on the Law of Treaties adds that 'If a new peremptory norm of general international law emerges, any existing treaty which is in conflict with that norm becomes void and terminates'). The existing judicial practice shows that such *jus cogens* norms are those which ensure the safeguard of two fundamental interests of the international community: those of its primary subjects, the States, whose essential prerogatives are preserved by the recognition of their equal sovereignty and by the prohibition of the use of force in conditions other than those authorized by the UN Charter; and those of the international community in the preservation of certain fundamental human rights (P.-M. Dupuy, 'L'unité de l'ordre juridique international. Cours général de droit international public', *Recueil des cours*, 297 (2002), at 303).

In theory, the sanctions attached to the hierarchical principle will differ according to whether it is based on Article 103 of the Charter or on the nature of the superior norms recognized as *jus cogens*: whereas a treaty found to be in violation of a *jus cogens* norm becomes void, a treaty incompatible with obligations flowing from membership in the United Nations does not disappear, but shall not be applied to the extent of such an incompatibility (see the Report of the Study Group of the International Law Commission, *Fragmentation of International Law: Difficulties Arising from the Diversification and Expansion of International Law*, cited above, para. 41). However, the logics under which each of these mechanisms operate are not systematically opposed to one another: where a treaty is not *per se* in violation of a *jus cogens* requirement but may lead to certain decisions being adopted which result in such a violation, only those decisions shall have to be considered invalid, while the treaty itself will remain in force (compare J. Combacau, 'Logique de la validité contre logique d'opposabilité dans la Convention de Vienne sur le droit des traités' in *Mélanges M. Virally* (Paris: Pedone, 1991), pp. 195–203). As noted by the International Law Commission in the course of the discussion of the Draft Articles on State Responsibility: 'one might envisage a conflict arising on a subsequent occasion between a treaty obligation, apparently lawful on its face and innocent in its purpose, and a peremptory norm. If such a case were to arise it would be too much to invalidate the treaty as a whole merely because its application in the given case was not foreseen' (*Official Records of the General Assembly, Fifty-sixth Session, Supplement 10* (A/56/10), commentary to Art. 40 of the Draft Articles on State Responsibility, para. (3); also reproduced in J. Crawford (ed.), *The International Law Commission's Articles on State Responsibility. Introduction, Text and Commentaries*, (Cambridge University Press, 2002), at p. 187).

Should the two mechanisms be ranked according to an order of priority? It has been stated that a conflict between the primacy asserted by Article 103 of the UN Charter – which extends to the decisions adopted by the Security Council acting under the Charter (International Court of Justice, Order of 14 April 1992 (provisional measures), *Questions of Interpretation and Application of the 1971 Montreal Convention arising from the Aerial Incident at Lockerbie (Libyan Arab Jamahiriya v. United States of America)*, I.C.J. Reports 1992, 15, para. 39) – and *jus cogens* norms was difficult to contemplate. The Study Group of the International Law Commission on the fragmentation of international law for instance remarks that: 'The United Nations Charter has been universally accepted by States and thus a conflict between *jus cogens* norms and Charter obligations is difficult to contemplate. In any case, according to Article 24(2) of the Charter, the Security Council shall act in accordance with the Purposes and Principles of the United Nations which include norms that have been subsequently treated as *jus cogens*' (Report of the Study Group of the International Law Commission, *Fragmentation of International Law: Difficulties arising from the Diversification and Expansion of International Law*, cited above, at p. 24, para. 40 of the conclusions). This view is, unfortunately, too optimistic, for times such as ours when the UN Security Council may use its powers in ways which may lead to violations of internationally recognized human rights. When such conflicts do occur – as they do in fact – they should be resolved in favour of the primacy of *jus cogens* even over the UN Charter or measures adopted in accordance with the Charter. Article 103 of the UN Charter, after all, has the status of a provision included in a treaty establishing an international organization, whatever the unique character of this organization:

International Court of Justice, Order of 8 April 1993 on the request for the indication of provisional measures in the case of the *Application of the Convention on the Prevention and Punishment of the Crime of Genocide (Bosnia and Herzegovina v. Serbia and Montenegro)*, separate opinion of Judge *ad hoc* Elihu Lauterpacht (I.C.J. Reports 1993, 440, para. 100):

The concept of *jus cogens* operates as a concept superior to both customary international law and treaty. The relief which Article 103 of the Charter may give the Security Council in case of conflict between one of its decisions and an operative treaty obligation cannot – as a matter of simple hierarchy of norms – extend to a conflict between a Security Council resolution and *jus cogens.* Indeed, one only has to state the opposite proposition thus – that a Security Council resolution may even require participation in genocide – for its unacceptability to be apparent.

This is also the reasoning followed by the Court of First Instance of the European Communities (now renamed the EU's General Court) when it was asked to annul Regulation (EC) No. 881/2002 imposing certain specific restrictive measures directed against certain persons and entities associated with Usama bin Laden, the Al-Qaeda network and the Taliban, implementing UN Security Council Resolution 1390 (2002).

Court of First Instance of the European Communities, Case T–315/01, *Yassin Abdullah Kadi* **v.** *Council of the EU and Commission of the European Communities,* **judgment of 21 September 2005:**

226 [Although the resolutions of the Security Council at issue fall, in principle, outside the ambit of the Court's judicial review and although the Court has no authority to call in question, even indirectly, their lawfulness in the light of EU law, nonetheless] the Court is empowered to check, indirectly, the lawfulness of the resolutions of the Security Council in question with regard to *jus cogens,* understood as a body of higher rules of public international law binding on all subjects of international law, including the bodies of the United Nations, and from which no derogation is possible.

227 In this connection, it must be noted that the Vienna Convention on the Law of Treaties, which consolidates the customary international law and Article 5 of which provides that it is to apply 'to any treaty which is the constituent instrument of an international organisation and to any treaty adopted within an international organisation', provides in Article 53 for a treaty to be void if it conflicts with a peremptory norm of general international law (*jus cogens*), defined as 'a norm accepted and recognised by the international community of States as a whole as a norm from which no derogation is permitted and which can be modified only by a subsequent norm of general international law having the same character'. Similarly, Article 64 of the Vienna Convention provides that: 'If a new peremptory norm of general international law emerges, any existing treaty which is in conflict with that norm becomes void and terminates.'

228 Furthermore, the Charter of the United Nations itself presupposes the existence of mandatory principles of international law, in particular, the protection of the fundamental rights of the human person. In the preamble to the Charter, the peoples of the United Nations declared themselves determined to 'reaffirm faith in fundamental human rights, in the dignity and worth of the human person'. In addition, it is apparent from Chapter I of the Charter, headed 'Purposes and Principles', that one of the purposes of the United Nations is to encourage respect for human rights and for fundamental freedoms.

229 Those principles are binding on the Members of the United Nations as well as on its bodies. Thus, under Article 24(2) of the Charter of the United Nations, the Security Council, in discharging its duties under its primary responsibility for the maintenance of international peace and security, is to act 'in accordance with the Purposes and Principles of the United Nations'. The Security Council's powers of sanction in the exercise of that responsibility must therefore be wielded in compliance with international law, particularly with the purposes and principles of the United Nations.

230 International law thus permits the inference that there exists one limit to the principle that resolutions of the Security Council have binding effect: namely, that they must observe the fundamental peremptory provisions of *jus cogens*. If they fail to do so, however improbable that may be, they would bind neither the Member States of the United Nations nor, in consequence, the Community.

231 The indirect judicial review carried out by the Court in connection with an action for annulment of a Community act adopted, where no discretion whatsoever may be exercised, with a view to putting into effect a resolution of the Security Council may therefore, highly exceptionally, extend to determining whether the superior rules of international law falling within the ambit of *jus cogens* have been observed, in particular, the mandatory provisions concerning the universal protection of human rights, from which neither the Member States nor the bodies of the United Nations may derogate because they constitute 'intransgressible principles of international customary law' (Advisory Opinion of the International Court of Justice of 8 July 1996, *The Legality of the Threat or Use of Nuclear Weapons*, Reports 1996, p. 226, paragraph 79).

The Court of First Instance of the European Communities went on to examine whether the fact that there is no judicial remedy available to the organizations or individuals against which restrictive measures are taken, against the sanctions decided by the Sanctions Committee established under the authority of the Security Council, is in violation of *jus cogens* norms. It concluded that it is not, based on the consideration that the right of access to the courts is subject to certain limitations which, in this case, appear to be imposed for legitimate objectives and remain proportionate to the ends pursued. This question was not addressed again in subsequent proceedings before the European Court of Justice, since this Court took the view, based on its understanding of its role as defined in the European Treaties, that it has no competence to review the lawfulness of a resolution adopted by an international body such as the UN Security Council, even if that review were to be limited to examination of the compatibility of that resolution with *jus cogens*. Rather, its role was to review the lawfulness of the implementing Community measure, in particular as regards the fundamental rights included among the general principles of Community law. On the basis of such a review, the European Court of Justice arrived at the conclusion that Regulation No. 881/2002 must be annulled so far as concerns the appellants, by reason of the breach of principles applicable in the procedure followed when the restrictive measures introduced by that regulation were adopted (Joined Cases C-402/05 P and C-415/05 P, judgment of 3 September 2008).

(b) Human rights as *jus cogens* norms

Reliance on the notion of *jus cogens* norms is made difficult, however, by two factors. First, the list of human rights included among norms of that nature remains ill defined. Norms which have the status of *jus cogens* are to be identified on the basis of the evolution of the understanding of the international community – the element of State practice plays here a far less significant role than for the emergence of custom. This list is therefore in constant evolution, and it would be both erroneous and counter-productive to seek to provide an authoritative classification. There is a consensus, however, about the *jus cogens* nature of a number of prohibitions formulated in international human rights law (for an extensive discussion, see I. Seiderman, *Hierarchy in International Law. The Human Rights Dimension* (Antwerp-Oxford: Intersentia-Hart, 2001), at pp. 66–105). These include at a minimum the prohibition of aggression, slavery and the slave trade, genocide (International Court of Justice, case of the *Armed Activities on the Territory of the Congo (New Application: 2002) (Democratic Republic of the Congo v. Rwanda)*, judgment of 3 February 2006 (Jurisdiction of the Court and Admissibility of the Application), para. 64), racial discrimination, apartheid and torture (see the references provided below in para. 153 of the judgment of 10 December 1998 delivered by the International Criminal Tribunal for former Yugoslavia (ICTY), Trial Chamber, in the case of *Prosecutor* v. *Anto Furundzija*, judgment of 10 December 1998), as well as basic rules of international humanitarian law applicable in armed conflict, and the right to self-determination (*Official Records of the General Assembly, Fifty-sixth Session, Supplement 10* (A/56/10), commentary to article 40 of the draft articles on State Responsibility prepared by the International Law Commission, paras. (4)–(6) (also reproduced in J. Crawford (ed.), *The International Law Commission's Articles on State Responsibility. Introduction, Text and Commentaries* (Cambridge University Press, 2003), at p. 188)). Other candidates for future recognition as peremptory norms of international law are the application of the death penalty to juveniles (if not the precise age of majority for purposes of capital punishment) (see Inter-American Commission on Human Rights, Resolution No. 3/87, Case 9647 [1987] *Inter-American Yearbook on Human Rights* 260) and the prohibition of refoulement, i.e. of returning a person to a territory where she runs a risk of torture or of being ill-treated: it is, indeed, well established that even where an extradition treaty would in principle allow for, or prescribe, the extradition of a person to another State, the extraditing State is prohibited from doing so in the presence of such a risk, the Institute of International Law noting in this respect that 'extradition treaties should not be enforced if enforcement would violate a human rights norm external to the treaty', and that 'the notion that there are certain higher norms in the field of human rights which take precedence over extradition treaties owes its origin to the notion of *jus cogens*' (*Yearbook of the Institute of International Law*, 60 (1983), p. 214, at pp. 223–4; see I. Seiderman, *Hierarchy in International Law* (Antwerp-Oxford: Intersentia-Hart, 2001), at pp. 101–5).

However, apart from the evolving nature of this list of norms having acquired *jus cogens* status, there are certain doctrinal uncertainties concerning the recognition criteria of such norms. It remains controversial, in particular, whether the emergence of peremptory norms could be regional, rather than universal and resulting from the consent of the international community as a whole. The Vienna Convention on the Law of Treaties seems to refer only to *jus cogens* of a universal nature. But this may be too restrictive: certain values may be central to a group of States of a particular region, and this may lead to the invalidation of treaties concluded by the States of that region which conflict with the said norm (see G. Gaja, '*Jus Cogens* beyond the Vienna Convention', *Recueil des cours*, 172–III (1981), 271 *et seq.*, at 284; F. Domb,

'*Jus Cogens* and Human Rights', *Israel Yearbook of Human Rights*, 6 (1976), 104, at 110; J. Sztucki, *Jus Cogens and the Vienna Convention on the Law of Treaties: a Critical Appraisal* (Vienna, New York: Springer, 1974), at pp. 107–8). For instance, in his concurring opinion to the judgment delivered on 7 July 1989 by the European Court of Human Rights in *Soering* v. *United Kingdom*, Judge De Meyer made the following comment about the second sentence of Article 2 §1 of the Convention, which states that 'no one shall be deprived of his life intentionally save in the execution of a sentence of a court following his conviction of a crime for which this penalty is provided by law', thereby recognizing that the imposition of the death penalty may be acceptable:

European Court of Human Rights, *Soering* v. *United Kingdom*, judgment of 7 July 1989, concurring opinion of Judge De Meyer:

The second sentence of Article 2 §1 of the Convention was adopted, nearly forty years ago, in particular historical circumstances, shortly after the Second World War. In so far as it still may seem to permit, under certain conditions, capital punishment in time of peace, it does not reflect the contemporary situation, and is now overridden by the development of legal conscience and practice.

Such punishment is not consistent with the present state of European civilisation.

De facto, it no longer exists in any State Party to the Convention.

Its unlawfulness was recognised by the Committee of Ministers of the Council of Europe when it adopted in December 1982, and opened for signature in April 1983, the Sixth Protocol to the Convention, which to date has been signed by sixteen, and ratified by thirteen, Contracting States.

No State Party to the Convention can in that context, even if it has not yet ratified the Sixth Protocol, be allowed to extradite any person if that person thereby incurs the risk of being put to death in the requesting State.

Extraditing somebody in such circumstances would be repugnant to European standards of justice, and contrary to the public order of Europe.

The recognition criteria for *jus cogens* norms are sufficiently vague to allow for the list of human rights norms having this status to be permanently adapted. For instance, the Inter-American Court of Human Rights has asserted that the general principle of equality – understood as the obligation to implement human rights without discrimination – has reached the status of a peremptory norm of international law, because of its close link to human dignity and because of its universal recognition:

Inter-American Court of Human Rights, Advisory Opinion OC–18/03 of 17 September 2003, requested by the United Mexican States on the *Juridical Condition and Rights of the Undocumented Migrants*:

97. The Court now proceeds to consider whether [the principle of equality and non-discrimination] is a *jus cogens* principle ...

100. In particular, when referring to the obligation to respect and ensure human rights, regardless of which of those rights are recognized by each State in domestic or international norms, the Court considers it clear that all States, as members of the international community, must comply with these obligations without any discrimination; this is intrinsically related to the right to equal protection before the law, which, in turn, derives 'directly from the oneness of the human family and is linked to the essential dignity of the individual'. The principle of equality before the law and non-discrimination permeates every act of the powers of the State, in all their manifestations, related to respecting and ensuring human rights. Indeed, this principle may be considered peremptory under general international law, inasmuch as it applies to all States, whether or not they are party to a specific international treaty, and gives rise to effects with regard to third parties, including individuals. This implies that the State, both internationally and in its domestic legal system, and by means of the acts of any of its powers or of third parties who act under its tolerance, acquiescence or negligence, cannot behave in a way that is contrary to the principle of equality and non-discrimination, to the detriment of a determined group of persons.

101. Accordingly, this Court considers that the principle of equality before the law, equal protection before the law and non-discrimination belongs to *jus cogens*, because the whole legal structure of national and international public order rests on it and it is a fundamental principle that permeates all laws. Nowadays, no legal act that is in conflict with this fundamental principle is acceptable, and discriminatory treatment of any person, owing to gender, race, color, language, religion or belief, political or other opinion, national, ethnic or social origin, nationality, age, economic situation, property, civil status, birth or any other status is unacceptable. This principle (equality and non-discrimination) forms part of general international law. At the existing stage of the development of international law, the fundamental principle of equality and non-discrimination has entered the realm of *jus cogens*.

Uncertainty about the list of human rights which have acquired the status of peremptory norms of international law is further increased by the tendency of a number of commentators to base the inclusion of at least certain basic rights in the list of *jus cogens* prescriptions on statements by international courts – particularly the International Court of Justice – which do not mention *jus cogens*, although they do identify certain obligations as having an *erga omnes* character. Thus, in the *Barcelona Traction* Case, the International Court of Justice famously remarked in an *obiter dictum* that:

International Court of Justice, case concerning the *Barcelona Traction, Light and Power Company, Limited (Belgium* v. *Spain)*, Second phase (judgment), judgment of 5 February 1970, I.C.J. Reports 1970, 3 at 32 (paras. 33–4):

An essential distinction should be drawn between the obligation of a State towards the international community as a whole, and those arising vis-à-vis another State ... By their very nature, the former are the concern of all States. In view of the importance of the rights involved, all states can be held to have a legal interest in their protection; they are obligations *erga omnes*. Such obligations derive, for example, in contemporary international law, from the outlawing of acts of agression, and of genocide, as also from the principles and rules concerning the basic rights of the human person, including protection from slavery and racial discrimination. Some of the corresponding rights of protection have entered into the body of general international law; others are conferred by international instruments of a universal or quasi-universal character.

International Court of Justice, case concerning *East Timor (Portugal* v. *Australia),* judgment of 30 June 1995, I.C.J. Reports 1995, 90 at 102 (para. 29):

Portugal's assertion that the right of peoples to self-determination, as it evolved from the Charter and from United Nations practice, has an *erga omnes* character, is irreproachable. The principle of self-determination of peoples has been recognized by the United Nations Charter and in the jurisprudence of the Court.

Although, as already mentioned, it seems beyond dispute that the rules referred to (if not all the 'principles and rules concerning the basic rights of the human person', at least the prohibition of aggression, of genocide, of slavery, of racial discrimination, and of the denial of the right of peoples to self-determination) have now acquired the status of *jus cogens* norms, these statements by the World Court in fact only pertain to their *erga omnes* character, implying that they are obligations owed to all States and which all States have a legal interest in seeking to enforce. But these notions are not interchangeable. They refer to different consequences: while the *jus cogens* character of a norm implies that it is hierarchically superior to any other norm of international law which does not possess the same character, the *erga omnes* nature of an obligation simply means that all States may be recognized as having a legal interest in the obligation being complied with. And, while all peremptory norms of international law also are owed to the community of States as a whole and thus are *erga omnes*, the reverse is not true, as 'not all *erga omnes* obligations are established by peremptory norms of general international law' (Report of the Study Group of the International Law Commission, *Fragmentation of International Law: Difficulties arising from the Diversification and Expansion of International Law*, cited above, para. 38).

A second obstacle to relying more systematically on *jus cogens* is that the consequences attached to the classification of certain human rights among *jus cogens* norms remain debated. Articles 53 and 64 of the Vienna Convention on the Law of Treaties prescribe that treaties which contradict peremptory norms of international law are void. But the Vienna Convention of course only refers to the consequences in the law of treaties of such a conflict. Unless we accept to take these provisions as mere tautologies (of the form 'no derogation shall be permitted to a norm accepted and recognized by the international community of States as a whole as a norm from which no derogation is permitted'), the *jus cogens* nature of a norm must be seen as based on something else than on the sense of the international community that no derogation is to be allowed to those norms; and therefore, other consequences may follow, from the recognition that rules of that nature occupy a higher rank among the norms of international law – and indeed, as will be seen in paragraph (c) below in this section, it is recognized that serious breaches of peremptory norms of international law entail certain specific consequences in the area of State responsibility. It has been stated, for instance, that human rights prescriptions which figure among the *jus cogens* norms oblige States not only to respect, protect and fulfil the rights in question, but also to take measures ensuring that those rights will not be infringed, and that a State should be held in violation of its obligations whenever such measures are not adopted, *even if the violation does not materialize*: given the importance of the basic rights forming part of *jus cogens*, in other terms, State responsibility results not only from actual breaches, but also from merely *potential* breaches which result from State action or inaction. In addition, legal acts adopted by States seeking to legitimize or authorize a violation of *jus cogens* – for example, amnesty laws where acts of torture have been committed, or unilateral measures resulting in a violation of the right to self-determination – should not be recognized or given effect to by any other State. Third, where *jus cogens* violations are concerned, due both to the *erga omnes* character of the corresponding obligations and to their universal condemnation, the traditional restrictions to the extraterritorial jurisdiction of States may have to be disregarded: in particular, any State should have jurisdiction to prosecute and punish individuals responsible for *jus cogens* violations which are found on its territory, even where the violations have been committed outside the national territory and present no other connecting factor to the State exercising such extraterritorial jurisdiction. The following cases discuss certain of these implications of *jus cogens* norms.

International Criminal Tribunal for former Yugoslavia (ICTY), Trial Chamber, *Prosecutor* v. *Anto Furundzija*, judgment of 10 December 1998, paras. 147–57:

147. There exists today universal revulsion against torture: as a USA Court put it in *Filartiga* v. *Peña-Irala*, 'the torturer has become, like the pirate and the slave trader before him, hostis humani generis, an enemy of all mankind' (*Filartiga* v. *Pena-Irala*, 630 F. 2d 876 (2d Cir. 1980)). This revulsion, as well as the importance States attach to the eradication of torture, has led to the cluster of treaty and customary rules on torture acquiring a particularly high status in the international normative system, a status similar to that of principles such as those prohibiting genocide, slavery, racial discrimination, aggression, the acquisition of territory by force and the forcible suppression of the right of peoples to self-determination. The prohibition against torture exhibits three important features, which are probably held in common with the other general principles protecting fundamental human rights.

(a) The prohibition even covers potential breaches

148. Firstly, given the importance that the international community attaches to the protection of individuals from torture, the prohibition against torture is particularly stringent and sweeping. States are obliged not only to prohibit and punish torture, but also to forestall its occurrence: it is insufficient merely to intervene after the infliction of torture, when the physical or moral integrity of human beings has already been irremediably harmed. Consequently, States are bound to put in

place all those measures that may pre-empt the perpetration of torture. As was authoritatively held by the European Court of Human Rights in *Soering* [where the Court stated, in its *Soering v. United Kingdom* judgment of 7 July 1989: 'It is not normally for the Convention institutions to pronounce on the existence or otherwise of potential violations of the Convention. However, where an applicant claims that a decision to extradite him, if implemented, be contrary to Article 3 [prohibiting torture and inhuman or degrading treatment] by reason of its foreseeable consequences in the requesting country, a departure from this principle is necessary, in view of the serious and irreparable nature of the alleged suffering risked, in order to ensure the effectiveness of the safeguard provided by that Article' (para. 90)], international law intends to bar not only actual breaches but also potential breaches of the prohibition against torture (as well as any inhuman and degrading treatment). It follows that international rules prohibit not only torture but also (i) the failure to adopt the national measures necessary for implementing the prohibition and (ii) the maintenance in force or passage of laws which are contrary to the prohibition.

149. Let us consider these two aspects separately. Normally States, when they undertake international obligations through treaties or customary rules, adopt all the legislative and administrative measures necessary for implementing such obligations. However, subject to obvious exceptions, failure to pass the required implementing legislation has only a potential effect: the wrongful fact occurs only when administrative or judicial measures are taken which, being contrary to international rules due to the lack of implementing legislation, generate State responsibility. By contrast, in the case of torture, the requirement that States expeditiously institute national implementing measures is an integral part of the international obligation to prohibit this practice. Consequently, States must immediately set in motion all those procedures and measures that may make it possible, within their municipal legal system, to forestall any act of torture or expeditiously put an end to any torture that is occurring.

150. Another facet of the same legal effect must be emphasised. Normally, the maintenance or passage of national legislation inconsistent with international rules generates State responsibility and consequently gives rise to a corresponding claim for cessation and reparation (lato sensu) only when such legislation is concretely applied [see Mariposa Development Company and others, Decision, US-Panama General Claims Commission, 27 June 1933, UN Reports of International Arbitral Awards, Vol. VI, pp. 340–1; *German Settlers in Upper Silesia*, Advisory Opinion of 10 September 1923, PCIJ, Series B, No. 6, pp. 19–20, 35–8; the arbitral award of 1922 in the *Affaire de l'impôt sur les benefices de guerre*, in UN Reports of International Arbitral Awards, vol. I, pp. 302–5]. By contrast, in the case of torture, the mere fact of keeping in force or passing legislation contrary to the international prohibition of torture generates international State responsibility. The value of freedom from torture is so great that it becomes imperative to preclude any national legislative act authorising or condoning torture or at any rate capable of bringing about this effect.

(b) The prohibition imposes obligations *erga omnes*

151. Furthermore, the prohibition of torture imposes upon States obligations *erga omnes*, that is, obligations owed towards all the other members of the international community, each of which then has a correlative right. In addition, the violation of such an obligation simultaneously constitutes a breach of the correlative right of all members of the international community and gives rise to a claim for compliance accruing to each and every member, which then has the right to insist on fulfilment of the obligation or in any case to call for the breach to be discontinued.

152. Where there exist international bodies charged with impartially monitoring compliance with treaty provisions on torture, these bodies enjoy priority over individual States in establishing whether a certain State has taken all the necessary measures to prevent and punish torture and, if they have not, in calling upon that State to fulfil its international obligations. The existence of such international mechanisms makes it possible for compliance with international law to be ensured in a neutral and impartial manner.

(c) The prohibition has acquired the status of *jus cogens*

153. While the *erga omnes* nature just mentioned appertains to the area of international enforcement (*lato sensu*), the other major feature of the principle proscribing torture relates to the hierarchy of rules in the international normative order. Because of the importance of the values it protects, this principle has evolved into a peremptory norm or *jus cogens*, that is, a norm that enjoys a higher rank in the international hierarchy than treaty law and even 'ordinary' customary rules [see also the *General Comment No. 24: Issues relating to Reservations made upon Ratification or Accession to the Covenant [on Civil and Political Rights] or the Optional Protocol thereto, or in relation to Declarations under Article 41 of the Covenant*, issued on 4 November 1994 by the United Nations Human Rights Committee, para. 10 ('the prohibition of torture has the status of a peremptory norm'). In 1986, the United Nations Special Rapporteur, P. Kooijmans, in his report to the Commission on Human Rights, took a similar view (E/CN. 4/1986/15, p. 1, para 3). That the international proscription of torture has turned into *jus cogens* has been among others held by US courts in *Siderman de Blake* v. *Republic of Argentina*, 965 F. 2d 699 (9th Cir. 1992), cert. denied, *Republic of Argentina* v. *de Blake*, 507 U.S. 1017, 123L. Ed. 2d 444, 113 S. Ct. 1812 (1993); *Committee of US Citizens Living in Nicaragua* v. *Reagan*, 859 F. 2d 929, 949 (D.C. Cir. 1988); *Xuncax et al.* v. *Gramajo*, 886 F. Supp. 162 (D. Mass. 1995); *Cabiri* v. *Assasie-Gyimah*, 921 F. Supp. 1189, 1196 (S.D.N.Y. 1996); and *In re Estate of Ferdinand E. Marcos*, 978 F. 2d 493 (9th Cir. 1992), cert. denied, *Marcos Manto* v. *Thajane*, 508 U.S. 972, 125L. Ed. 2d 661, 113 S. Ct. 2960 (1993)]. The most conspicuous consequence of this higher rank is that the principle at issue cannot be derogated from by States through international treaties or local or special customs or even general customary rules not endowed with the same normative force.

154. Clearly, the *jus cogens* nature of the prohibition against torture articulates the notion that the prohibition has now become one of the most fundamental standards of the international community. Furthermore, this prohibition is designed to produce a deterrent effect, in that it signals to all members of the international community and the individuals over whom they wield authority that the prohibition of torture is an absolute value from which nobody must deviate.

155. The fact that torture is prohibited by a peremptory norm of international law has other effects at the inter-state and individual levels. At the inter-state level, it serves to internationally de-legitimise any legislative, administrative or judicial act authorising torture. It would be senseless to argue, on the one hand, that on account of the *jus cogens* value of the prohibition against torture, treaties or customary rules providing for torture would be null and void *ab initio* [Art. 53 Vienna Convention on the Law of Treaties, 23 May 1969], and then be unmindful of a State say, taking national measures authorising or condoning torture or absolving its perpetrators through an amnesty law. [As for amnesty laws, it bears mentioning that in 1994 the United Nations Human Rights Committee, in its General Comment No. 20 on Art. 7 of the ICCPR stated the following: 'The Committee has noted that some States have granted amnesty in respect of acts of torture. Amnesties are generally incompatible with the duty of States to

investigate such acts; to guarantee freedom from such acts within their jurisdiction; and to ensure that they do not occur in the future. States may not deprive individuals of the right to an effective remedy, including compensation and such full rehabilitation as may be possible.']
If such a situation were to arise, the national measures, violating the general principle and any relevant treaty provision, would produce the legal effects discussed above and in addition would not be accorded international legal recognition. Proceedings could be initiated by potential victims if they had *locus standi* before a competent international or national judicial body with a view to asking it to hold the national measure to be internationally unlawful; or the victim could bring a civil suit for damage in a foreign court, which would therefore be asked *inter alia* to disregard the legal value of the national authorising act. What is even more important is that perpetrators of torture acting upon or benefiting from those national measures may nevertheless be held criminally responsible for torture, whether in a foreign State, or in their own State under a subsequent regime. In short, in spite of possible national authorisation by legislative or judicial bodies to violate the principle banning torture, individuals remain bound to comply with that principle. As the International Military Tribunal at Nuremberg put it: 'individuals have international duties which transcend the national obligations of obedience imposed by the individual State' [I.M.T., 1 (1946), p. 223].

156. Furthermore, at the individual level, that is, that of criminal liability, it would seem that one of the consequences of the *jus cogens* character bestowed by the international community upon the prohibition of torture is that every State is entitled to investigate, prosecute and punish or extradite individuals accused of torture, who are present in a territory under its jurisdiction. Indeed, it would be inconsistent on the one hand to prohibit torture to such an extent as to restrict the normally unfettered treaty-making power of sovereign States, and on the other hand bar States from prosecuting and punishing those torturers who have engaged in this odious practice abroad. This legal basis for States' universal jurisdiction over torture bears out and strengthens the legal foundation for such jurisdiction found by other courts in the inherently universal character of the crime. It has been held that international crimes being universally condemned wherever they occur, every State has the right to prosecute and punish the authors of such crimes. As stated in general terms by the Supreme Court of Israel in *Eichmann*, and echoed by a USA court in *Demjanjuk*, 'it is the universal character of the crimes in question i.e. international crimes which vests in every State the authority to try and punish those who participated in their commission' [*Attorney General of the Government of Israel* v. *Adolf Eichmann*, 36 I.L.R. 298; *In the Matter of the Extradition of John Demjanjuk*, 612].

157. It would seem that other consequences include the fact that torture may not be covered by a statute of limitations, and must not be excluded from extradition under any political offence exemption.

House of Lords (United Kingdom), *R.* v. *Bow Street Metropolitan Stipendiary Magistrate and others, ex parte Pinochet Ugarte (No. 3)*, judgment of 24 March 1999 [2000] A.C. 147:

[In this case, the House of Lords held that the former President of Chile, Senator Pinochet, could be extradited to Spain in respect of charges which concerned conduct that was criminal in the

United Kingdom at the time when it was allegedly committed. The majority of the Law Lords considered that extraterritorial torture did not become a crime in the United Kingdom until section 134 of the Criminal Justice Act 1988 came into effect. As regards the crimes of torture committed outside the United Kingdom after that date, the argument was submitted by the defence of Pinochet that, since under Part II of the State Immunity Act 1978 a former head of State enjoyed immunity from the criminal jurisdiction of the United Kingdom for acts done in his official capacity, Mr Pinochet should benefit such immunity. The Law Lords rejected this argument. Instead, they took the view that torture was an international crime and prohibited by *jus cogens*, and therefore such immunity could not be invoked.]

Lord Browne-Wilkinson (leading judgment) (excerpts):

In general, a state only exercises criminal jurisdiction over offences which occur within its geographical boundaries. If a person who is alleged to have committed a crime in Spain is found in the United Kingdom, Spain can apply to the United Kingdom to extradite him to Spain. The power to extradite from the United Kingdom for an 'extradition crime' is now contained in the Extradition Act 1989. That Act defines what constitutes an 'extradition crime'. For the purposes of the present case, the most important requirement is that the conduct complained of must constitute a crime under the law both of Spain and of the United Kingdom. This is known as the double criminality rule.

Since the Nazi atrocities and the Nuremberg trials, international law has recognised a number of offences as being international crimes. Individual states have taken jurisdiction to try some international crimes even in cases where such crimes were not committed within the geographical boundaries of such states. The most important of such international crimes for present purposes is torture which is regulated by the International Convention Against Torture and other Cruel, Inhuman or Degrading Treatment or Punishment, 1984. The obligations placed on the United Kingdom by that Convention ... were incorporated into the law of the United Kingdom by section 134 of the Criminal Justice Act 1988. That Act came into force on 29 September 1988. Section 134 created a new crime under United Kingdom law, the crime of torture. As required by the Torture Convention 'all' torture wherever committed world-wide was made criminal under United Kingdom law and triable in the United Kingdom. No one has suggested that before section 134 came into effect torture committed outside the United Kingdom was a crime under United Kingdom law. Nor is it suggested that section 134 was retrospective so as to make torture committed outside the United Kingdom before 29 September 1988 a United Kingdom crime. Since torture outside the United Kingdom was not a crime under UK law until 29 September 1988, the principle of double criminality which requires an Act to be a crime under both the law of Spain and of the United Kingdom cannot be satisfied in relation to conduct before that date if the principle of double criminality requires the conduct to be criminal under United Kingdom law at the date it was committed ...

[In] my view only a limited number of the charges relied upon to extradite Senator Pinochet constitute extradition crimes since most of the conduct relied upon occurred long before 1988. In particular, I do not consider that torture committed outside the United Kingdom before 29 September 1988 was a crime under UK law. It follows that the main question discussed at the earlier stages of this case – is a former head of state entitled to sovereign immunity from arrest or prosecution in the UK for acts of torture – applies to far fewer charges. But the question of state immunity remains a point of crucial importance since, in my view, there is certain conduct of Senator Pinochet (albeit a small amount) which does constitute an extradition crime and would enable the Home Secretary (if he thought fit) to extradite Senator Pinochet to Spain unless he is entitled to state immunity. Accordingly, having identified which of the crimes alleged is an extradition crime, I will then go on to consider whether Senator Pinochet is entitled to immunity in respect of those crimes ...

I must ... consider whether, in relation to these two surviving categories of charge [torture and conspiracy to torture after 29 September 1988], Senator Pinochet enjoys sovereign immunity. But first it is necessary to consider the modern law of torture.

Torture

Apart from the law of piracy, the concept of personal liability under international law for international crimes is of comparatively modern growth. The traditional subjects of international law are states not human beings. But consequent upon the war crime trials after the 1939–45 World War, the international community came to recognise that there could be criminal liability under international law for a class of crimes such as war crimes and crimes against humanity. Although there may be legitimate doubts as to the legality of the Charter of the Nuremberg Tribunal, in my judgment those doubts were stilled by the Affirmation of the Principles of International Law recognised by the Charter of Nuremberg Tribunal adopted by the United Nations General Assembly on 11 December 1946. That Affirmation affirmed the principles of international law recognised by the Charter of the Nuremberg Tribunal and the judgment of the Tribunal and directed the Committee on the codification of international law to treat as a matter of primary importance plans for the formulation of the principles recognised in the Charter of the Nuremberg Tribunal. At least from that date onwards the concept of personal liability for a crime in international law must have been part of international law. In the early years state torture was one of the elements of a war crime. In consequence torture, and various other crimes against humanity, were linked to war or at least to hostilities of some kind. But in the course of time this linkage with war fell away and torture, divorced from war or hostilities, became an international crime on its own: see Oppenheim's *International Law* (Jennings and Watts edition) vol. 1, 996; note 6 to Article 18 of the I.L.C. Draft Code of Crimes Against Peace; *Prosecutor* v. *Furundzija Tribunal for Former Yugoslavia*, Case No. 17-95-17/1-T. Ever since 1945, torture on a large scale has featured as one of the crimes against humanity: see, for example, UN General Assembly Resolutions 3059, 3452 and 3453 passed in 1973 and 1975; Statutes of the International Criminal Tribunals for former Yugoslavia (Article 5) and Rwanda (Article 3).

Moreover, the Republic of Chile accepted before your Lordships that the international law prohibiting torture has the character of *jus cogens* or a peremptory norm, i.e. one of those rules of international law which have a particular status [quoting from Furundzija].

The *jus cogens* nature of the international crime of torture justifies states in taking universal jurisdiction over torture wherever committed. International law provides that offences *jus cogens* may be punished by any state because the offenders are 'common enemies of all mankind and all nations have an equal interest in their apprehension and prosecution': *Demjanjuk* v. *Petrovsky* (1985) 603 F. Supp. 1468; 776 F. 2d. 571.

... [L]ong before the Torture Convention of 1984 state torture was an international crime in the highest sense. But there was no tribunal or court to punish international crimes of torture. Local courts could take jurisdiction: see *Demjanjuk* (supra); *Attorney General of Israel* v. *Eichmann* (1962) 36 I.L.R.S. But the objective was to ensure a general jurisdiction so that the torturer was not safe wherever he went. For example, in this case it is alleged that during the Pinochet regime torture was an official, although unacknowledged, weapon of government and that, when the regime was about to end, it passed legislation designed to afford an amnesty to those who had engaged in institutionalised torture. If these allegations are true, the fact that the local court had jurisdiction to deal with the international crime of torture was nothing to the point so long as the totalitarian regime remained in power: a totalitarian regime will not permit adjudication by its own courts on its own shortcomings. Hence the demand for some international machinery to repress state torture which is not dependent upon the local courts where the torture was committed. In the event, over 110 states (including Chile, Spain and the United Kingdom) became state parties to the Torture Convention. But it is far from clear that none of them practised state torture. What was needed therefore was an international system which could punish those who were guilty of torture and which did not permit the evasion of punishment by the torturer moving from one state to another. The Torture Convention was agreed not in order to create an international crime which had not previously existed but to provide an international system under which the international criminal – the torturer – could find no safe haven. Burgers and Danelius (respectively the chairman of the United Nations Working Group on the 1984 Torture Convention and the draftsmen of its first draft) say, at p. 131, that it was 'an essential purpose [of the Convention] to ensure that a torturer does not escape the consequences of his act by going to another country' [J. Herman Burgers and Hans Danelius, *The United Nations Convention against Torture. A Handbook on the Convention against Torture and Other Cruel, Inhuman or Degrading Treatment or Punishment* (Leiden: Martinus Nijhoff, 1988)].

The Torture Convention
Article 1 of the Convention defines torture as the intentional infliction of severe pain and of suffering with a view to achieving a wide range of purposes 'when such pain or suffering is inflicted by or at the instigation of or with the consent or acquiesence of a public official or other person acting in an official capacity.' Article 2(1) requires each state party to prohibit torture on territory within its own jurisdiction and Article 4 requires each state party to ensure that 'all' acts of torture are offences under its criminal law. Article 2(3) outlaws any defence of superior orders. Under Article 5(1) each state party has to establish its jurisdiction over torture (a) when committed within territory under its jurisdiction (b) when the alleged offender is a national of that state, and (c) in certain circumstances, when the victim is a national of that state. Under Article 5(2) a state party has to take jurisdiction over any alleged offender who is found within its territory. Article 6 contains provisions for a state in whose territory an alleged torturer is found to detain him, inquire into the position and notify the states referred to in Article 5(1) and to indicate whether it intends to exercise jurisdiction. Under Article 7 the state in whose territory the alleged torturer is found shall, if he is not extradited to any of the states mentioned in Article 5(1), submit him to its authorities for the purpose of prosecution. Under Article 8(1) torture is to be treated as an extraditable offence and under Article 8(4) torture shall, for the purposes of extradition, be treated as having been committed not only in the place where it occurred but also in the state mentioned in Article 5(1) ...

Universal jurisdiction

There was considerable argument before your Lordships concerning the extent of the jurisdiction to prosecute torturers conferred on states other than those mentioned in Article 5(1). I do not find it necessary to seek an answer to all the points raised. It is enough that it is clear that in all circumstances, if the Article 5(1) states do not choose to seek extradition or to prosecute the offender, other states must do so. The purpose of the Convention was to introduce the principle *aut dedere aut punire* – either you extradite or you punish: Burgers and Danelius p. 131. Throughout the negotiation of the Convention certain countries wished to make the exercise of jurisdiction under Article 5(2) dependent upon the state assuming jurisdiction having refused extradition to an Article 5(1) state. However, at a session in 1984 all objections to the principle of *aut dedere aut punire* were withdrawn. 'The inclusion of universal jurisdiction in the draft Convention was no longer opposed by any delegation': Working Group on the Draft Convention U.N. Doc. E/CN. 4/1984/72, para. 26. If there is no prosecution by, or extradition to, an Article 5(1) state, the state where the alleged offender is found (which will have already taken him into custody under Article 6) must exercise the jurisdiction under Article 5(2) by prosecuting him under Article 7(1).

I gather the following important points from the Torture Convention:

(1) Torture within the meaning of the Convention can only be committed by 'a public official or other person acting in an official capacity', but these words include a head of state. A single act of official torture is 'torture' within the Convention;

(2) Superior orders provide no defence;

(3) If the states with the most obvious jurisdiction (the Article 5(1) states) do not seek to extradite, the state where the alleged torturer is found must prosecute or, apparently, extradite to another country, i.e. there is universal jurisdiction.

(4) There is no express provision dealing with state immunity of heads of state, ambassadors or other officials.

(5) Since Chile, Spain and the United Kingdom are all parties to the Convention, they are bound under treaty by its provisions whether or not such provisions would apply in the absence of treaty obligation. Chile ratified the Convention with effect from 30 October 1988 and the United Kingdom with effect from 8 December 1988.

State immunity

This is the point around which most of the argument turned. It is of considerable general importance internationally since, if Senator Pinochet is not entitled to immunity in relation to the acts of torture alleged to have occurred after 29 September 1988, it will be the first time so far as counsel have discovered when a local domestic court has refused to afford immunity to a head of state or former head of state on the grounds that there can be no immunity against prosecution for certain international crimes.

Given the importance of the point, it is surprising how narrow is the area of dispute. There is general agreement between the parties as to the rules of statutory immunity and the rationale which underlies them. The issue is whether international law grants state immunity in relation to the international crime of torture and, if so, whether the Republic of Chile is entitled to claim such immunity even though Chile, Spain and the United Kingdom are all parties to the Torture Convention and therefore 'contractually' bound to give effect to its provisions from 8 December 1988 at the latest.

It is a basic principle of international law that one sovereign state (the forum state) does not adjudicate on the conduct of a foreign state. The foreign state is entitled to procedural immunity from the processes of the forum state. This immunity extends to both criminal and civil liability. State immunity probably grew from the historical immunity of the person of the monarch. In any event, such personal immunity of the head of state persists to the present day: the head of state is entitled to the same immunity as the state itself. The diplomatic representative of the foreign state in the forum state is also afforded the same immunity in recognition of the dignity of the state which he represents. This immunity enjoyed by a head of state in power and an ambassador in post is a complete immunity attaching to the person of the head of state or ambassador and rendering him immune from all actions or prosecutions whether or not they relate to matters done for the benefit of the state. Such immunity is said to be granted *ratione personae*.

What then when ... the head of state is deposed? ... In my judgment at common law a former head of state ... loses immunity *ratione personae* on ceasing to be head of state: see Watts, 'The Legal Position in International Law of Heads of States, Heads of Government and Foreign Ministers' [*Recueil des cours*, 247 (1994–III), 40, at 88] p. 88 and the cases there cited. He can be sued on his private obligations: *Ex-King Farouk of Egypt* v. *Christian Dior* (1957) 24 I.L.R. 228; *Jimenez* v. *Aristeguieta* (1962) 311 F. 2d 547. As ex head of state he cannot be sued in respect of acts performed whilst head of state in his public capacity: *Hatch* v. *Baez* [1876] 7 Hun. 596. Thus, at common law, ... the former head of state ... enjoy[s] immunity for acts done in performance of [his] functions whilst in office.

... Accordingly, in my judgment, Senator Pinochet as former head of state enjoys immunity *ratione materiae* in relation to acts done by him as head of state as part of his official functions as head of state.

The question then which has to be answered is whether the alleged organisation of state torture by Senator Pinochet (if proved) would constitute an act committed by Senator Pinochet as part of his official functions as head of state. It is not enough to say that it cannot be part of the functions of the head of state to commit a crime. Actions which are criminal under the local law can still have been done officially and therefore give rise to immunity ratione materiae. The case needs to be analysed more closely.

Can it be said that the commission of a crime which is an international crime against humanity and *jus cogens* is an act done in an official capacity on behalf of the state? I believe there to be strong ground for saying that the implementation of torture as defined by the Torture Convention cannot be a state function ... I have doubts whether, before the coming into force of the Torture Convention, the existence of the international crime of torture as jus cogens was enough to justify the conclusion that the organisation of state torture could not rank for immunity purposes as performance of an official function. At that stage there was no international tribunal to punish torture and no general jurisdiction to permit or require its punishment in domestic courts. Not until there was some form of universal jurisdiction for the punishment of the crime of torture could it really be talked about as a fully constituted international crime. But in my judgment the Torture Convention did provide what was missing: a worldwide universal jurisdiction. Further, it required all member states to ban and outlaw torture: Article 2. How can it be for international law purposes an official function to do something which international law itself prohibits and criminalises? Thirdly, an essential feature of the international crime of torture is that it must be committed 'by or with the acquiesence of a public official or other person acting in an official capacity'. As a result all defendants in torture cases will be state officials. Yet, if the former head of state has immunity, the man most responsible will escape liability while his inferiors (the chiefs of police, junior army officers) who carried out his orders will be liable. I find it impossible to accept that this was the intention.

Finally, and to my mind decisively, if the implementation of a torture regime is a public function giving rise to immunity ratione materiae, this produces bizarre results. Immunity *ratione materiae* applies not only to ex-heads of state and ex-ambassadors but to all state officials who have been involved in carrying out the functions of the state. Such immunity is necessary in order to prevent state immunity being circumvented by prosecuting or suing the official who, for example, actually carried out the torture when a claim against the head of state would be precluded by the doctrine of immunity. If that applied to the present case, and if the implementation of the torture regime is to be treated as official business sufficient to found an immunity for the former head of state, it must also be official business sufficient to justify immunity for his inferiors who actually did the torturing. Under the Convention the international crime of torture can only be committed by an official or someone in an official capacity. They would all be entitled to immunity. It would follow that there can be no case outside Chile in which a successful prosecution for torture can be brought unless the State of Chile is prepared to waive its right to its officials immunity. Therefore the whole elaborate structure of universal jurisdiction over torture committed by officials is rendered abortive and one of the main objectives of the Torture Convention – to provide a system under which there is no safe haven for torturers – will have been frustrated. In my judgment all these factors together demonstrate that the notion of continued immunity for ex-heads of state is inconsistent with the provisions of the Torture Convention.

For these reasons in my judgment if, as alleged, Senator Pinochet organised and authorised torture after 8 December 1988, he was not acting in any capacity which gives rise to immunity *ratione materiae* because such actions were contrary to international law, Chile had agreed to outlaw such conduct and Chile had agreed with the other parties to the Torture Convention that all signatory states should have jurisdiction to try official torture (as defined in the Convention) even if such torture were committed in Chile ...

For these reasons, I would allow the appeal so as to permit the extradition proceedings to proceed on the allegation that torture in pursuance of a conspiracy to commit torture, including the single act of torture which is alleged in charge 30, was being committed by Senator Pinochet after 8 December 1988 when he lost his immunity.

There exists a large literature surrounding the *Pinochet* case, including a number of important book-length publications (see, e.g. D. M. Ackerman, *Pinochet Extradition Case: Selected Legal Issues* (Washington DC: Congressional Research Service, 1999); H. Ahlbrecht and K. Ambos (eds.), *Der Fall Pinochet (S). Auslieferung Wegen Staatsverstärkter Kriminalität?* (Baden-Baden: Nomos Verlagsgesellschaft, 1999); S. Brett (ed.), *When Tyrants Tremble: the Pinochet Case* (New York: Human Rights Watch, October 1999); R. Brody and M. Ratner (eds.), *The Pinochet Papers: the Case of Augusto Pinochet in Spain and Britain* (The Hague: Kluwer Law International, 2000); H. Fischer, C. Kress, and S. R. Luder (eds.), *International and National Prosecution of Crimes under International Law: Current Developments* (Berlin: Berlin Verlag Arno

Spitz, 2001); M. Lattimer and P. Sands (eds.), *Justice for Crimes against Humanity* (Oxford: Hart Publishing, 2003); S. Macedo, *Universal Jurisdiction: National Courts and the Prosecution of Serious Crimes under International Law* (Philadelphia: University of Pennsylvania Press, 2004)). The case was widely seen as heralding a new era in international human rights, one in which national courts would be assuming new and far-reaching responsibilities in the prosecution of human rights violations, by relying both on the notion that human rights, due to their *jus cogens* status, could justify setting aside conflicting norms of international law that impose obstacles to such prosecution, and on the tool of extra-territorial (or in some cases universal) jurisdiction, allowing prosecutions against non-nationals for serious violations of international law committed abroad.

The question of the relationship between – on the one hand – the prosecution of human rights violations or the filing of civil claims by victims of such violations, and – on the other hand – international rules relating to immunity, was also discussed in other contexts. In the following case, the Grand Chamber of the European Court of Human Rights arrives at the conclusion that, although the prohibition of torture is of overriding importance and may be considered to have acquired the status of *jus cogens*, it does not follow that foreign States are not entitled to immunity in respect of civil claims for damages for alleged torture committed outside the forum State. The decision was adopted by a very narrow margin, nine votes against eight. Among the eight judges who dissented were a number of specialists of international law, who considered that the reasoning of the majority did not effectively recognize the primacy of *jus cogens* on any other norms of international law.

European Court of Human Rights (GC), *Al–Adsani* v. *United Kingdom* (Appl. No. 35763/97), judgment of 21 November 2001:

[The applicant, a dual British/Kuwaiti national, went to Kuwait in 1991 as a pilot to serve as a member of the Kuwaiti Air Force and, after the Iraqi invasion, he remained behind as a member of the resistance movement. During that period he came into possession of sex videotapes involving a Sheikh related to the Emir of Kuwait. By some means these tapes entered general circulation, for which the applicant was held responsible by the Sheikh. After the Iraqi armed forces were expelled from Kuwait, in May 1991, the Sheikh and others on two separate occasions took him at gunpoint in a government car and he was beaten and tortured. On 17 May 1991, the applicant returned to the United Kingdom, where he spent six weeks in a hospital recovering from the various ill-treatments inflicted upon him. On 29 August 1992 the applicant instituted civil proceedings in England for compensation against the Sheikh and the State of Kuwait in respect of injury to his physical and mental health caused by torture in Kuwait in May 1991 and threats against his life and well-being made after his return to the United Kingdom on 17 May 1991. The action failed, however, because as a sovereign foreign State, Kuwait could claim immunity of jurisdiction under the State Immunity Act 1978. Article 15 of the 1972 European Convention on State Immunity (Basle Convention), to which the United Kingdom is a party, provides that a Contracting State shall be entitled to immunity if the

proceedings do not fall within one of the exceptions exceptions stated in the Convention;
Article 11 of the Basle Convention excludes State immunity for proceedings which relate to
redress for injury to the person or damage to tangible property, if the facts which occasioned the
injury or damage occurred in the territory of the State of forum, and if the author of the injury
or damage was present in that territory at the time when those facts occurred: this exception
is replicated in section 5 of the 1978 State Immunity Act. In its judgment of 21 November 2001,
the majority of the Court takes the view that a) any positive obligation imposed on the basis
of Article 3 ECHR, either to prevent violations of this provision or to provide a remedy when a
violation does take place, does not extend to such violations which may have been committed
outside the jurisdiction of the United Kingdom; and that b) the right of access to a court (under
Art. 6 ECHR) may be limited where this is justified by the need to grant sovereign immunity
to a State in civil proceedings, in accordance with the generally recognized rules of public
international law on State immunity.]

**[The alleged violation of Article 3 of the Convention (prohibiting torture and inhuman or
degrading treatments or punishments)]**
40. The applicant does not contend that the alleged torture took place within the jurisdiction of
the United Kingdom or that the United Kingdom authorities had any causal connection with its
occurrence. In these circumstances, it cannot be said that the High Contracting Party was under
a duty to provide a civil remedy to the applicant in respect of torture allegedly carried out by
the Kuwaiti authorities.

41. It follows that there has been no violation of Article 3 of the Convention in the present
case.

[The alleged violation of Article 6 of the Convention (right to a fair trial)]
53. The right of access to a court [implicit in the guarantees of Art. 6 of the Convention (right to a
fair trial): see the *Golder* v. *United Kingdom* judgment of 21 February 1975, Series A No. 18, 13–18,
§§28–36] is not [...] absolute, but may be subject to limitations; these are permitted by implication
since the right of access by its very nature calls for regulation by the State. In this respect, the
Contracting States enjoy a certain margin of appreciation, although the final decision as to the
observance of the Convention's requirements rests with the Court. It must be satisfied that the
limitations applied do not restrict or reduce the access left to the individual in such a way or to
such an extent that the very essence of the right is impaired. Furthermore, a limitation will not be
compatible with Article 6 §1 if it does not pursue a legitimate aim and if there is no reasonable
relationship of proportionality between the means employed and the aim sought to be achieved
(see *Waite and Kennedy* v. *Germany* [GC], No. 26083/94, §59, ECHR 1999–I).

54. The Court must first examine whether the limitation pursued a legitimate aim. It notes
in this connection that sovereign immunity is a concept of international law, developed out of
the principle *par in parem non habet imperium*, by virtue of which one State shall not be subject
to the jurisdiction of another State. The Court considers that the grant of sovereign immunity
to a State in civil proceedings pursues the legitimate aim of complying with international law
to promote comity and good relations between States through the respect of another State's
sovereignty.

55. The Court must next assess whether the restriction was proportionate to the aim
pursued. It reiterates that the Convention has to be interpreted in the light of the rules set out

in the Vienna Convention on the Law of Treaties of 23 May 1969, and that Article 31 §3 (c) of that treaty indicates that account is to be taken of 'any relevant rules of international law applicable in the relations between the parties'. The Convention, including Article 6, cannot be interpreted in a vacuum. The Court must be mindful of the Convention's special character as a human rights treaty, and it must also take the relevant rules of international law into account (see, *mutatis mutandis*, *Loizidou* v. *Turkey* (merits), judgment of 18 December 1996, *Reports* 1996–VI, 2231, §43). The Convention should so far as possible be interpreted in harmony with other rules of international law of which it forms part, including those relating to the grant of State immunity.

56. It follows that measures taken by a High Contracting Party which reflect generally recognised rules of public international law on State immunity cannot in principle be regarded as imposing a disproportionate restriction on the right of access to a court as embodied in Article 6 §1. Just as the right of access to a court is an inherent part of the fair trial guarantee in that Article, so some restrictions on access must likewise be regarded as inherent, an example being those limitations generally accepted by the community of nations as part of the doctrine of State immunity.

57. The Court notes that the 1978 Act, applied by the English courts so as to afford immunity to Kuwait, complies with the relevant provisions of the 1972 Basle Convention, which, while placing a number of limitations on the scope of State immunity as it was traditionally understood, preserves it in respect of civil proceedings for damages for personal injury unless the injury was caused in the territory of the forum State. Except insofar as it affects claims for damages for torture, the applicant does not deny that the above provision reflects a generally accepted rule of international law. He asserts, however, that his claim related to torture, and contends that the prohibition of torture has acquired the status of a *jus cogens* norm in international law, taking precedence over treaty law and other rules of international law.

58. Following the decision to uphold Kuwait's claim to immunity, the domestic courts were never required to examine evidence relating to the applicant's allegations, which have, therefore, never been proved. However, for the purposes of the present judgment, the Court accepts that the ill-treatment alleged by the applicant against Kuwait in his pleadings in the domestic courts, namely, repeated beatings by prison guards over a period of several days with the aim of extracting a confession ..., can properly be categorised as torture within the meaning of Article 3 of the Convention ...

59. Within the Convention system it has long been recognised that the right under Article 3 not to be subjected to torture or to inhuman or degrading treatment or punishment enshrines one of the fundamental values of democratic society. It is an absolute right, permitting of no exception in any circumstances ... Of all the categories of ill-treatment prohibited by Article 3, 'torture' has a special stigma, attaching only to deliberate inhuman treatment causing very serious and cruel suffering ...

60. Other areas of public international law bear witness to a growing recognition of the overriding importance of the prohibition of torture. Thus, torture is forbidden by Article 5 of the Universal Declaration of Human Rights and Article 7 of the International Covenant on Civil and Political Rights. The United Nations Convention against Torture and Other Cruel, Inhuman and Degrading Treatment or Punishment requires, by Article 2, that each State Party should take effective legislative, administrative, judicial or other measures to prevent torture in any territory

under its jurisdiction, and, by Article 4, that all acts of torture should be made offences under the State Party's criminal law ... In addition, there have been a number of judicial statements to the effect that the prohibition of torture has attained the status of a peremptory norm or *jus cogens*. For example, in its judgment of 10 December 1998 in *Furundzija* ..., the International Criminal Tribunal for the Former Yugoslavia referred, *inter alia*, to the foregoing body of treaty rules and held that '[b]ecause of the importance of the values it protects, this principle [proscribing torture] has evolved into a peremptory norm or *jus cogens*, that is, a norm that enjoys a higher rank in the international hierarchy than treaty law and even "ordinary" customary rules'. Similar statements have been made in other cases before that tribunal and in national courts, including the House of Lords in the case of *ex parte Pinochet (No. 3)* ...

61. While the Court accepts, on the basis of these authorities, that the prohibition of torture has achieved the status of a peremptory norm in international law, it observes that the present case concerns not, as in *Furundzija* and *Pinochet*, the criminal liability of an individual for alleged acts of torture, but the immunity of a State in a civil suit for damages in respect of acts of torture within the territory of that State. Notwithstanding the special character of the prohibition of torture in international law, the Court is unable to discern in the international instruments, judicial authorities or other materials before it any firm basis for concluding that, as a matter of international law, a State no longer enjoys immunity from civil suit in the courts of another State where acts of torture are alleged. In particular, the Court observes that none of the primary international instruments referred to (Article 5 of the Universal Declaration of Human Rights, Article 7 of the International Covenant on Civil and Political Rights and Articles 2 and 4 of the UN Convention) relates to civil proceedings or to State immunity.

62. It is true that in its Report on Jurisdictional Immunities of States and their Property ... the working group of the International Law Commission noted, as a recent development in State practice and legislation on the subject of immunities of States, the argument increasingly put forward that immunity should be denied in the case of death or personal injury resulting from acts of a State in violation of human rights norms having the character of *jus cogens*, particularly the prohibition on torture. However, as the working group itself acknowledged, while national courts had in some cases shown some sympathy for the argument that States were not entitled to plead immunity where there had been a violation of human rights norms with the character of *jus cogens*, in most cases (including those cited by the applicant in the domestic proceedings and before the Court) the plea of sovereign immunity had succeeded.

63. The ILC working group went on to note developments, since those decisions, in support of the argument that a State may not plead immunity in respect of human rights violations: first, the exception to immunity adopted by the United States in the amendment to the Foreign Sovereign Immunities Act (FSIA) which had been applied by the United States courts in two cases [this exception, introduced by section 221 of the Anti-Terrorism and Effective Death Penalty Act of 1996, applies in respect of a claim for damages for personal injury or death caused by an act of torture, extra-judicial killing, aircraft sabotage or hostage-taking, against a State designated by the Secretary of State as a sponsor of terrorism, where the claimant or victim was a national of the United States at the time the act occurred]; secondly, the *ex parte Pinochet (No. 3)* judgment in which the House of Lords 'emphasised the limits of immunity in respect of gross human rights violations by State officials'. The Court does not, however, find that either of these developments provides it with a firm basis on which to conclude that the immunity of States *ratione personae* is no longer enjoyed in respect of civil liability for claims of acts of

torture, let alone that it was not enjoyed in 1996 at the time of the Court of Appeal's judgment in the present case.

64. As to the amendment to the FSIA, the very fact that the amendment was needed would seem to confirm that the general rule of international law remained that immunity attached even in respect of claims of acts of official torture. Moreover, the amendment is circumscribed in its scope: the offending State must be designated as a State sponsor of acts of terrorism, and the claimant must be a national of the United States. The effect of the FSIA is further limited in that after judgment has been obtained, the property of a foreign State is immune from attachment or execution unless one of the statutory exceptions applies ...

65. As to the *ex parte Pinochet (No. 3)* judgment ..., the Court notes that the majority of the House of Lords held that, after the UN Convention and even before, the international prohibition against official torture had the character of *jus cogens* or a peremptory norm and that no immunity was enjoyed by a torturer from one Torture Convention State from the criminal jurisdiction of another. But, as the working group of the ILC itself acknowledged, that case concerned the immunity *ratione materiae* from criminal jurisdiction of a former head of State, who was at the material time physically within the United Kingdom. As the judgments in the case made clear, the conclusion of the House of Lords did not in any way affect the immunity *ratione personae* of foreign sovereign States from the civil jurisdiction in respect of such acts (see in particular, the judgment of Lord Millett ...). In so holding, the House of Lords cited with approval the judgments of the Court of Appeal in *Al-Adsani* itself.

66. The Court, while noting the growing recognition of the overriding importance of the prohibition of torture, does not accordingly find it established that there is yet acceptance in international law of the proposition that States are not entitled to immunity in respect of civil claims for damages for alleged torture committed outside the forum State. The 1978 Act, which grants immunity to States in respect of personal injury claims unless the damage was caused within the United Kingdom, is not inconsistent with those limitations generally accepted by the community of nations as part of the doctrine of State immunity.

67. In these circumstances, the application by the English courts of the provisions of the 1978 Act to uphold Kuwait's claim to immunity cannot be said to have amounted to an unjustified restriction on the applicant's access to a court.

[The Court decided by nine votes to eight that Article 6 §1 ECHR has not been violated. A joint dissenting opinion was filed by Mr Rozakis and Mr Caflisch joined by Mr Wildhaber, Mr Costa, Mr Cabral Barreto and Mrs Vajić. Two separate dissenting opinions were filed, in addition, by Mr Ferrari Bravo and Mr Loucaides. Excerpts of the first dissenting opinion follow.]

Joint dissenting opinion filed by Mr Rozakis and Mr Caflisch joined by Mr Wildhaber, Mr Costa, Mr Cabral Barreto and Mrs Vajić:

By accepting that the rule on prohibition of torture is a rule of *jus cogens*, the majority recognise that it is hierarchically higher than any other rule of international law, be it general or particular, customary or conventional, with the exception, of course, of other *jus cogens* norms. For the basic characteristic of a *jus cogens* rule is that, as a source of law in the now vertical international legal system, it overrides any other rule which does not have the same status. In the event of a conflict between a *jus cogens* rule and any other rule of international law, the former prevails. The consequence of such prevalence is that the conflicting rule is null and void, or, in any event, does not produce legal effects which are in contradiction with the content of the peremptory rule.

The Court's majority do not seem, on the other hand, to deny that the rules on State immunity; customary or conventional, do not belong to the category of *jus cogens*; and rightly so, because it is clear that the rules of State immunity, deriving from both customary and conventional international law, have never been considered by the international community as rules with a hierarchically higher status. It is common knowledge that, in many instances, States have, through their own initiative, waived their rights of immunity; that in many instances they have contracted out of them, or have renounced them. These instances clearly demonstrate that the rules on State immunity do not enjoy a higher status, since *jus cogens* rules, protecting as they do the '*ordre public*', that is the basic values of the international community, cannot be subject to unilateral or contractual forms of derogation from their imperative contents.

The acceptance therefore of the *jus cogens* nature of the prohibition of torture entails that a State allegedly violating it cannot invoke hierarchically lower rules (in this case, those on State immunity) to avoid the consequences of the illegality of its actions. In the circumstances of this case, Kuwait cannot validly hide behind the rules on State immunity to avoid proceedings for a serious claim of torture made before a foreign jurisdiction; and the courts of that jurisdiction (the United Kingdom) cannot accept a plea of immunity, or invoke it *ex officio*, to refuse an applicant adjudication of a torture case. Due to the interplay of the *jus cogens* rule on prohibition of torture and the rules on State immunity, the procedural bar of State immunity is automatically lifted, because those rules, as they conflict with a hierarchically higher rule, do not produce any legal effect. In the same vein, national law which is designed to give domestic effect to the international rules on State immunity cannot be invoked as creating a jurisdictional bar, but must be interpreted in accordance with and in the light of the imperative precepts of *jus cogens*.

The majority, while accepting that the rule on the prohibition of torture is a *jus cogens* norm, refuse to draw the consequences of such acceptance.

In the following case, the dissenting opinion of ad hoc judge Van den Wyngaert relies on the *jus cogens* character of war crimes and crimes against humanity to conclude that the rule according immunity from criminal jurisdiction and inviolability to incumbent Ministers for Foreign Affairs should be set aside in favour of allowing for prosecution to take place where such crimes are concerned. Her reasoning echoes to a large extent that of the House of Lords in the *Pinochet* case and that of the dissenting opinion appended to the judgment of the European Court of Human Rights in *Al-Adsani*.

International Court of Justice, case concerning the *Arrest Warrant of 11 April 2000 (Democratic Republic of Congo* v. *Belgium)*, I.C.J. Reports 2002, 3 (judgment of 14 February 2002):

[The DRC filed an application against Belgium following the issuance of an international arrest on 11 April 2000 by a Belgian investigating judge against the then Minister for Foreign Affairs in office of the Democratic Republic of the Congo, Mr Abdulaye Yerodia Ndombasi. The application contended that Belgium had violated the 'principle that a State may not exercise its authority on the territory of another State', the 'principle of sovereign equality among all Members of the United Nations, as laid down in Article 2, paragraph 1, of the Charter of the United Nations', as well as 'the diplomatic immunity of the Minister for Foreign Affairs of a sovereign State, as recognized by the jurisprudence of the Court and following from Article 41, paragraph 2, of the Vienna Convention of 18 April 1961 on Diplomatic Relations'. The arrest warrant delivered by the Belgian investigating judge charged him, as perpetrator or co-perpetrator, with offences constituting grave breaches of the Geneva Conventions of 1949 and of the Additional Protocols thereto, and with crimes against humanity. These crimes were punishable in Belgium under the Law of 16 June 1993 concerning the Punishment of Grave Breaches of the International Geneva Conventions of 12 August 1949 and of Protocols I and II of 8 June 1977 Additional Thereto, as amended by the Law of 10 February 1999 concerning the Punishment of Serious Violations of International Humanitarian Law, which provides for a universal jurisdiction of Belgian courts to prosecute certain international crimes.

The International Court of Justice concluded by thirteen votes to three that 'the issue against Mr Abdulaye Yerodia Ndombasi of the arrest warrant of 11 April 2000, and its international circulation, constituted violations of a legal obligation of the Kingdom of Belgium towards the Democratic Republic of the Congo, in that they failed to respect the immunity from criminal jurisdiction and the inviolability which the incumbent Minister for Foreign Affairs of the Democratic Republic of the Congo enjoyed under international law'. Without reaching the issue of whether Belgium was authorized to apply an extraterritorial legislation, the Court took the view, first, that 'the functions of a Minister for Foreign Affairs are such that, throughout the duration of his or her office, he or she when abroad enjoys full immunity from criminal jurisdiction and inviolability. That immunity and that inviolability protect the individual concerned against any act of authority of another State would hinder him her in the performance of his or her duties' (para. 54). It then found, having 'carefully examined State practice, including national legislation and those few decisions of national higher courts, such as the House of Lords or the French Court of Cassation', that it was 'unable to deduce from this practice that there exists under customary international law any form of exception to the rule according immunity from criminal jurisdiction and inviolability to incumbent Ministers for Foreign Affairs, where they are suspected of having committed war crimes or crimes against humanity' (para. 58).]

Dissenting opinion of Judge Van den Wyngaert, judge *ad hoc* (para. 28):

The Court ... adopts a formalistic reasoning, examining whether there is, under customary international law, an international crimes exception to the – wrongly postulated – rule of immunity for incumbent Ministers under customary international law (judgment, para. 58). By adopting this approach, the Court implicitly establishes a hierarchy between the rules on immunity (protecting incumbent former Ministers) and the rules on international accountability (calling for the investigation of charges against incumbent Foreign Ministers charged with war crimes and crimes against humanity).

By elevating the former rules to the level of customary international law in the first part of its reasoning, and finding that the latter have failed to reach the same status in the second part of its reasoning, the Court does not need to give further consideration to the status of the principle of international accountability under international law. As a result, the Court does not further examine the status of the principle of international accountability. Other courts, for example the House of Lords in the *Pinochet* case [see above] and the European Court of Human Rights in the *Al-Adsani* case [see above], have given more thought and consideration to the balancing of the relative normative status of international *jus cogens* crimes and immunities.

Questions concerning international accountability for war crimes and crimes against humanity and that were not addressed by the International Court of Justice include the following. Can international accountability for such crimes be considered to be a general principle of law in the sense of Article 38 of the Court's Statute? Should the Court, in reaching its conclusion that there is no international crimes exception to immunities under international law, not have given more consideration to the factor that war crimes and crimes against humanity have, by many, been considered to be customary international law crimes (see: American Law Institute, *Restatement of the Law Third. The Foreign Relations Law of the United States* (St Paul, Minn.: American Law Institute Publishers, 1987), vol. 1, para. 404, Comment; M. C. Bassiouni, *Crimes against Humanity in International Criminal Law* (The Hague, Kluwer Law International, 1999); T. Meron, *Human Rights and Humanitarian Norms as Customary Law* (Oxford: Clarendon Press, 1989); T. Meron, 'International Criminalization of Internal Atrocities', *American Journal of International Law* 89 (1995), 558; A. H. J. Swart, *De berechting van internationale misdrijven* (Deventer: Gouda Quint, 1996), p. 7; ICTY, Decision on the Defence Motion for Interlocutory Appeal on Jurisdiction, 2 October 1995, *Tadic*, paras. 96–127 and 134 (common Art. 3))? Should it not have considered the proposition of writers who suggest that war crimes and crimes against humanity are *jus cogens* crimes (M. C. Bassiouni, 'International Crimes: *Jus Cogens* and *Obligatio Erga Omnes*', *Law and Contemporary Problems*, 59 4 (1996), 63–74; M. C. Bassiouni, *Crimes against Humanity in International Criminal Law* (The Hague: Kluwer Law International, 1999), pp. 210–17; C. J. R. Dugard, *Opinion In: Re Bouterse*, para. 4.5.5, to be consulted at: www.icj.org/objectives/opinion.htm; K. C. Randall, 'Universal Jurisdiction under International Law', *Texas Law Review*, 66 (1988), 829–32; ICTY, judgment, 10 December 1998, *Furundzija*, para. 153 (torture)), which, if it were correct, would only enhance the contrast between the status of the rules punishing these crimes and the rules protecting suspects on the ground of immunities for incumbent Foreign Ministers, which are probably not part of *jus cogens*?

1.3. Question for discussion: human rights as *jus cogens* norms and the normative hierarchy theory

Both the dissenting opinion of ad hoc Judge Van den Wyngaeert and the dissent expressed in the *Al-Adsani* v. *United Kingdom* case are based on the idea that rules regarding immunity should be set aside in order to recognize the primacy of human rights norms that have acquired the status of *jus cogens*. Indeed, although *Al-Adsani* v. *United Kingdom* was heavily debated among the members of the European Court of Human Rights, other cases presented to the Court that raised a question of immunity were far less controversial, because at stake were ECHR rights other than the right not to be subjected to torture or inhuman or degrading treatment or punishment (for a discussion of this range of cases, see M. Kloth, 'Immunities and the Right of Access to Court under the European Convention on Human Rights', *European Law Review*, 27 (2002), 33). Yet, if the Court in *Al-Adsani* had arrived at the conclusion that the ECHR was violated by the United Kingdom, would this have opened the floodgates for a large number of claims unrelated to torture or inhuman or degrading treatment or punishment? Would the position adopted by the dissenting judges in *Al-Adsani* be practical? Consider the following view:

Lee M. Caplan, 'State Immunity, Human Rights, and *Jus Cogens*: a Critique of the Normative Hierarchy Theory', *American Journal of International Law*, 97 (2003), 741 at 773:

The undefined character of *jus cogens*, coupled with the general applicability of the normative hierarchy theory, which invests all peremptory norms with immunity-stripping potential, may present problems for the courts. Requiring application of the theory beyond cases of genocide, slavery and torture would place national courts in an awkward position. The theory not only would deprive the forum state of its right to regulate access to its own courts, but also would oblige them to determine whether a particular norm of international law had attained the status of *jus cogens*, a task that international legal scholars have grappled with for decades with only limited success. Further, the normative hierarchy theory logically requires courts to treat all violations of peremptory norms uniformly, even violations of norms that do not implicate human rights but are arguably *jus cogens*, such as *pacta sunt servanda*. In addition, allowing the courts to determine the parameters of *jus cogens* through application of the normative hierarchy theory may undermine the principle of separation of powers, in some case inappropriately transferring foreign-policymaking power from the political branches of government to the judiciary. Finally, ... adoption of the normative hierarchy theory could be the first step on a slippery slope that begins with state immunity from jurisdiction but could quickly extend to state immunity from execution against sovereign property and ultimately threaten the 'orderly international co-operation' between states.

(c) Serious breaches of *jus cogens* norms

The International Law Commission's Articles on Responsibility of States for internationally wrongful acts provide that a 'serious breach' by a State of an obligation arising under a peremptory norm of general international law – i.e. 'a gross or systematic failure by the responsible State to fulfil the obligation' – imposes on all States an obligation to co-operate in order to put an end to such a breach; an obligation not to recognize as lawful a situation created by such a breach; and an obligation not to 'render aid or assistance in maintaining that situation' (Arts. 40 and 41 of the ILC's Articles on Responsibility of States for internationally wrongful acts, *Official Records of the General Assembly, Fifty-sixth Session, Supplement 10* (A/56/10)). This seems to be the position expressed by the International Court of Justice in the Advisory Opinion it delivered on 9 July 2004 on the question of the legal consequences of the construction of a wall in the Occupied Palestinian Territory (for a reminder of the circumstances in which the Advisory Opinion was delivered, see chapter 2, section 1). After having found that the construction of the wall on Palestinian territory amounts to a violation of the right of the Palestinian peoples to self-determination, the Court states the following:

> **International Court of Justice,** *Legal Consequences of the Construction of a Wall in the Occupied Palestinian Territory*, **Advisory Opinion of 9 July 2004, I.C.J. Reports 2004, 136 at 199:**
>
> 159. Given the character and the importance of the rights and obligations involved, the Court is of the view that all States are under an obligation not to recognize the illegal situation resulting from the construction of the wall in the Occupied Palestinian Territory, including in and around East Jerusalem. They are also under an obligation not to render aid or assistance in maintaining the situation created by such construction. It is also for all States, while respecting the United Nations Charter and international law, to see to it that any impediment, resulting from the construction of the wall, to the exercise by the Palestinian people of its right to self-determination is brought to an end. In addition, all the States parties to the Geneva Convention relative to the Protection of Civilian Persons in Time of War of 12 August 1949 are under an obligation, while respecting the United Nations Charter and international law, to ensure compliance by Israel with international humanitarian law as embodied in that Convention.
>
> 160. Finally, the Court is of the view that the United Nations, and especially the General Assembly and the Security Council, should consider what further action is required to bring to an end the illegal situation resulting from the construction of the wall and the associated régime, taking due account of the present Advisory Opinion.

1.4. Questions for discussion: treating human rights as *jus cogens* norms

1. There remain controversies both about the list of human rights that have acquired the status of *jus cogens*, and about the consequences that follow such characterization. Are the two questions linked? Should the list of norms considered to be peremptory norms of international law vary, depending on the precise consequence that one seeks to attach to this qualification? For instance, could there be a long list of human rights norms treated as *jus cogens* for the purpose of finding void any treaty conflicting with such norms, but a shorter list of norms which could justify setting aside rules relating to immunity where such rules appear to create obstacles to their full implementation?

2. What do the cases above teach us about how a norm – such as, in these cases, the prohibition of torture – evolves into one which is considered to have acquired the status of *jus cogens*? Has

the prohibition of torture evolved into a norm 'accepted and recognised by the international community of States as a whole as a norm from which no derogation is permitted', as defined in Article 53 of the Vienna Convention on the Law of Treaties, or is this rather the result of judicial law-making? Is there anything specific to the prohibition of torture, distinguishing it from other human rights norms, that would justify treating it, like a few other such norms, as *jus cogens*, while excluding other human rights norms from this qualification?

3. In the case of *Al-Adsani* v. *United Kingdom*, how would you characterize the disagreement between the majority of the European Court of Human Rights and the dissenting judges? Does this disagreement stem from a difference in opinion as regards the consequences to be drawn from the *jus cogens* character of the prohibition of torture? Or is it rather that the issue presented to the Court was framed differently by the majority and by the dissenting judges?

4. If indeed the prohibition of torture has the status of a *jus cogens* norm, this means, at a minimum, that any treaty conflicting with this prohibition will be treated as void: this would be the case, for instance, of a treaty through which two States would mutually undertake to extradite individuals suspected of having committed certain crimes even though they may be subjected to torture in the State requesting the extradition. But the cases above illustrate that the consequences of the *jus cogens* character of the prohibition of torture reach much further. What are the limits to such an extension? Does the *jus cogens* character of a norm justify setting aside all other rules of international law that may be an obstacle to its effective implementation, for example rules relating to the limits of State jurisdiction or to immunities? May a State ignore all such rules, in the name of seeking to improve compliance with a norm having a *jus cogens* status?

4.3 The *erga omnes* character of human rights obligations

Human rights treaties do not have as their primary goal the exchange of reciprocal rights and obligations between the contracting States (see further section 4.4. below). In contrast to diplomatic protection – which one State has a right to exercise in favour of its nationals under the jurisdiction of another State – the respect for human rights in one State therefore is of interest to no other State in particular. It is perhaps paradoxical therefore that such respect is of interest to the international community as a whole, allowing each State to pursue remedies against the State alleged to have violated its obligations under the human rights recognized under customary international law or as general principles of law. Article 48(1)(b) of the International Law Commission's Articles on the Responsibility of States for internationally wrongful acts (invocation of responsibility by a State other than an injured State), provides that 'Any State other than an injured State is entitled to invoke the responsibility of another State ... if ... the obligation breached is owed to the international community as a whole.' Any State therefore 'may claim from the responsible State: (a) Cessation of the internationally wrongful act, and assurances and guarantees of non-repetition ...; and (b) Performance of the obligation of reparation ..., in the interest of the injured State or of the beneficiaries of the obligation breached'. As noted above, the International Court of Justice has mentioned, among the obligations which are *erga omnes* (owed to the international community as a whole), not only the prohibition of acts of aggression and of genocide, but also the right to self-determination; the rules of humanitarian international law applicable in armed conflict; and even 'the principles and rules concerning the basic rights of the human person, including protection from slavery and racial discrimination' (Case concerning the *Barcelona Traction, Light and Power Company, Limited (Belgium* v. *Spain)*, Second phase (judgment of 5 February 1970), I.C.J. Reports 1970, 3, 32 (paras. 33–34): see above, section 4.2., b)).

International Court of Justice, *Legal Consequences cf the Construction of a Wall in the Occupied Palestinian Territory*, Advisory Opinion of 9 July 2004, I.C.J. Reports 2004, 136, at 199:

155. The Court would observe that the obligations violated by Israel include certain obligations *erga omnes*. As the Court indicated in the *Barcelona Traction* case, such obligations are by their very nature 'the concern of all States' and, 'In view of the importance of the rights involved, all States can be held to have a legal interest in their protection' *(Barcelona Traction, Light and Power Company, Limited, Second Phase, Judgment,* I.C.J. Reports 1970, 32, para. 33). The obligations *erga omnes* violated by Israel are the obligation to respect the right of the Palestinian people to self-determination, and certain of its obligations under international humanitarian law.

156. As regards the first of these, the Court has already observed ... that in the *East Timor* case, it described as 'irreproachable' the assertion that 'the right of peoples to self-determination, as it evolved from the Charter and from United Nations practice, has an *erga omnes* character' (I.C.J. Reports 1995, 102, para. 29). The Court would also recall that under the terms of General Assembly resolution 2625 (XXV), ... 'Every State has the duty to promote, through joint and separate action, realization of the principle of equal rights and self-determination of peoples, in accordance with the provisions of the Charter, and to render assistance to the United Nations in carrying out the responsibilities entrusted to it by the Charter regarding the implementation of the principle ...'

157. With regard to international humanitarian law, the Court recalls that in its Advisory Opinion on the *Legality of the Threat or Use of Nuclear Weapons* it stated that 'a great many rules of humanitarian law applicable in armed conflict are so fundamental to the respect of the human person and "elementary considerations of humanity" ...', that they are 'to be observed by all States whether or not they have ratified the conventions that contain them, because they constitute intransgressible principles of international customary law' (I.C.J. Reports 1996 (I), 257, para. 79). In the Court's view, these rules incorporate obligations which are essentially of an *erga omnes* character.

Whether all human rights obligations recognized in general public international law are 'owed to the international community as a whole' remains debated. It would be incorrect to limit the range of rights imposing *erga omnes* obligations to those which have the status of *jus cogens*, which constitutes a narrower category, as stated by G. Arangio-Ruiz: '... the concept of *erga omnes* obligation is not characterized by the importance of the interest protected by the norms – this aspect being typical of *jus cogens* – but rather by the "legal indivisibility" of the content of the obligation, namely by the fact that the rule in question provides for obligations which bind simultaneously each and every addressee with respect to all others. This legal structure is typical not only of peremptory norms, but also of other norms of general international law and of a number of multilateral treaty rules (*erga omnes partes* obligations)' (Fourth Report on State Responsibility, A/CN.4/444/Add. 1, at 31 (1992)). Neither should too much weight be attached to the adjective 'basic' before the expression 'rights of the human person' in the *dictum* of the *Barcelona Traction* Case, since such an expression is generic and should be seen as a mere paraphrase to designate the notion of human rights as 'fundamental' in the guarantees they provide. On the other hand, although some authors have taken the view that all human rights internationally recognized should be considered as imposing *erga omnes* obligations (F. Ermacora, in B. Simma *et al.* (eds.), *The Charter of the United Nations: a Commentary* (Oxford University Press, 1995), at pp. 152–3; I. Seiderman, *Hierarchy in International Law. The Human Rights Dimension* (Antwerp-Oxford: Intersentia-Hart, 2001), chapter IV), this would seem to be contradicted by the judgment delivered by the International Court of Justice in the *Barcelona Traction* Case itself. While recognizing that human rights include protection against denial of justice, the Court then added:

> **International Court of Justice, case concerning the *Barcelona Traction, Light and Power Company, Limited (Belgium v. Spain)*, Second phase (judgment), I.C.J. Reports 1970 3, 47 (para. 91):**
>
> However, on the universal level, the instruments which embody human rights do not confer on States the capacity to protect the victims of infringements of such rights irrespective of their nationality. It is therefore still on the regional level that a solution to this problem has had to be sought; thus, within the Council of Europe, of which Spain is not a member [at the time of the judgment], the problem of admissibility encountered by the claim in the present case has been resolved by the European Convention on Human Rights, which entitles each State which is a party to the Convention to lodge a complaint against any other contracting State for violation of the Convention, irrespective of the nationality of the victim.

This statement would be in complete contradiction with para. 34 of the same judgment referring to 'the principles and rules concerning the basic rights of the human person' as imposing *erga omnes* obligations if there were no distinction between core human rights which do impose such obligations, and other rights of the individual, which may only be protected in inter-State proceedings through the traditional channel of diplomatic protection: the right of the shareholders to the protection of the investments made through the establishment of a company with a separate legal personality, which were at stake in *Barcelona Traction* litigation, clearly belongs to the second category. It is true that Section 703(2) of the 1987 *Restatement* of the American Law Institute does provide that all human rights recognized in customary international law impose obligations *erga omnes*: 'Any State may pursue international remedies against any other state for a violation of the customary law of human rights rights', it notes, since 'the customary law of human rights are *erga omnes*'. The comment attached to this clause explains that, as regards human rights recognized in customary international law, 'the international obligation runs equally to all other states, with no state a victim of the violation more than any other. Any state, therefore, may make a claim against the violating state.' However, the list of rights concerned, as we have seen (section 4.1., b)), is in fact quite limited, and certainly does not encompass the full range of the rights listed in the international bill of rights.

The effect of obligations being *erga omnes* concerns the question of standing: all States have a legal interest in using any available remedies in order to ensure that the obligations are complied with. However, in order for remedies to be used against the infringing State, the forum must have jurisdiction over the issue. For instance, while a number of international and regional human rights instruments provide for the possibility of inter-State complaints, these typically require a declaration of acceptance by the defending State, and are subject to a condition of reciprocity (for details, see chapter 9). Article 41 of the International Covenant on Civil and Political Rights thus provides that any State party to this instrument 'may at any time declare ... that it recognizes the competence of the Committee to receive and consider communications to the effect that a State Party claims that another State Party is not fulfilling its obligations under the present Covenant. Communications under this article may be received and considered only if submitted by a State Party which has made a declaration recognizing in regard to itself the competence of the Committee. No communication shall be received by the Committee if it concerns a State Party which has not made such a declaration.' The Human Rights Committee would not be authorized, under the pretext that the civil and political rights enumerated in the ICCPR impose obligations *erga omnes*, to ignore the limits to its jurisdiction which are imposed by this provision, for instance in order to deal with a communication presented by a State which has not itself accepted inter-state communications to be directed against it.

The *erga omnes* character of human rights obligations sometimes has been linked to the fact that human rights are a recognized exception to the principle of non-interference with the domestic affairs of States, as expressed in Article 2(7) of the UN Charter. Consider for instance the Resolution adopted on 13 September 1989 by the International Law Institute, which concerns all measures – 'diplomatic, economic and other' – which may be adopted by any State, where human rights are violated in another State:

International Law Institute, 'The Protection of Human Rights and the Principle of Non-Intervention in Internal Affairs of States', *Institut de Droit International Annuaire,* **63 (1989), 338:**

The Institute of International Law, ...

Considering [that] the protection of human rights as a guarantee of the physical and moral integrity and of the fundamental freedom of every person has been given expression in both the constitutional systems of States and in the international legal system, especially in the charters and constituent instruments of international organizations;

That the members of the United Nations have undertaken to ensure, in co-operation with the Organization, universal respect for and observance of human rights and fundamental freedoms, and that the General Assembly, recognizing that a common understanding of these rights and freedoms is of the highest importance for the full realization of this undertaking, has adopted and proclaimed the Universal Declaration of Human Rights on 10 December 1948;

That frequent gross violations of human rights, including those affecting ethnic, religious and linguistic minorities, cause legitimate and increasing outrage to public opinion and impel many States and international organizations to have recourse to various measures to ensure that human rights are respected;

That these reactions, as well as international doctrine and jurisprudence, bear witness that human rights, having been given international protection, are no longer matters essentially within the domestic jurisdiction of States;

That it is nonetheless important, in the interest of maintaining peace and friendly relations between sovereign States as well as in the interest of protecting human rights, to define more precisely the conditions and limitations imposed by international law on the measures that may be taken by States and international organizations in response to violations of human rights

Adopts the following Resolution:

Article 1. Human rights are a direct expression of the dignity of the human person. The obligation of States to ensure their observance derives from the recognition of this dignity as proclaimed in the Charter of the United Nations and in the Universal Declaration of Human Rights.

This international obligation, as expressed by the International Court of Justice, is 'erga omnes'; it is incumbent upon every State in relation to the international community as a whole, and every State has a legal interest in the protection of human rights. The obligation further implies a duty of solidarity among all States to ensure as rapidly as possible the effective protection of human rights throughout the world.

Article 2. A State acting in breach of its obligations in the sphere of human rights cannot evade its international responsibility by claiming that such matters are essentially within its domestic jurisdiction.

Without prejudice to the functions and powers which the Charter attributes to the organs of the United Nations in case of violation of the obligations assumed by the members of the Organization, States, acting individually or collectively, are entitled to take diplomatic, economic and other measures towards any other State which has violated the obligation set forth in Article 1, provided such measures are permitted under international law and do not involve the use of armed force in violation of the Charter of the United Nations. These measures cannot be considered an unlawful intervention in the internal affairs of that State.

Violations justifying recourse to the measures referred to above shall be viewed in the light of their gravity and of all the relevant circumstances. Measures designed to ensure the collective protection of human rights are particularly justified when taken in response to especially grave violations of these rights, notably large-scale or systematic violations, as well as those infringing rights that cannot be derogated from in any circumstances.

Article 3. Diplomatic representations as well as purely verbal expressions of concern or disapproval regarding any violations of human rights are lawful in all circumstances.

Article 4. All measures, individual or collective, designed to ensure the protection of human rights shall meet the following conditions:

(1) except in case of extreme urgency, the State perpetrating the violation shall be formally requested to desist before the measures are taken;
(2) measures taken shall be proportionate to the gravity of the violation;
(3) measures taken shall be limited to the State perpetrating the violation;
(4) the States having recourse to measures shall take into account the interests of individuals and of third States, as well as the effect of such measures on the standard of living of the population concerned.

Article 5. An offer by a State, a group of States, an international organization or an impartial humanitarian body such as the International Committee of the Red Cross, of food or medical supplies to another State in whose territory the life or health of the population is seriously threatened cannot be considered an unlawful intervention in the internal affairs of that State. However, such offers of assistance shall not, particularly by virtue of the means used to implement them, take a form suggestive of a threat of armed intervention or any other measure of intimidation; assistance shall be granted and distributed without discrimination.

States in whose territories these emergency situations exist should not arbitrarily reject such offers of humanitarian assistance.

Article 6. The provisions of this Resolution apply without prejudice to the procedures prescribed in matters of human rights by the terms of or pursuant to the constitutive instruments and the conventions of the United Nations and of specialized agencies or regional organizations.

Article 7. It is highly desirable to strengthen international methods and procedures, in particular methods and procedures of international organizations, intended to prevent, punish and eliminate violations of human rights.

4.4 Human rights treaties as non-contractual in nature

Human rights treaties have an 'objective' character in that they are not reducible to bilateral exchanges of advantages between the contracting States (on the specificity of human rights treaties from this point of view, see E. Schwelb, 'The Law of Treaties and Human Rights', *Archiv des Völkerrechts*, 16 1 (1973), reprinted in W. M. Reisman and B. Weston (eds.), *Toward World Order and Human Dignity: Essays in Honor of Myres S. McDougal* (New York: Free Press, 1976), at p. 262; or M. Craven, 'Legal Differentiation and the Concept of the Human Rights Treaty in International Law', *European Journal of International Law*, 11, No. 3 (2000), 489–519). The principle has been put concisely by the Human Rights Committee: 'Such treaties, and the [International Covenant on Civil and Political Rights] specifically, are not a web of inter-State exchanges of mutual obligations. They concern the endowment of individuals with rights' (Human Rights Committee, General Comment No. 24 (1994), *Issues relating to Reservations made upon Ratification or Accession to the Covenant or the Optional Protocols thereto, or in relation to Declarations under Article 41 of the Covenant*, at para. 17). The idea is not a new one. Consider the following statements:

International Court of Justice, *Reservations to the Convention on the Prevention and Punishment of the Crime of Genocide*, Advisory Opinion, I.C.J. Reports 1951, 19 (28 May 1951):

[The 1948 Convention on the Prevention and Punishment of the Crime of Genocide] was manifestly adopted for a purely humanitarian and civilizing purpose. It is indeed difficult to imagine a convention that might have this dual character to a greater degree, since its object on the one hand is to safeguard the very existence of certain human groups and on the other to confirm and endorse the most elementary principles of morality. In such a convention the contracting States do not have any interests of their own; they merely have, one and all, a common interest, namely, the accomplishment of those high purposes which are the raison d'être of the convention. Consequently, in a convention of this type one cannot speak of individual advantages or disadvantages to States, or of the maintenance of a perfect contractual balance between rights and duties.

European Commission on Human Rights, *Austria v. Italy (the 'Pfunders' Case)*, Appl. No. 788/60, *European Convention on Human Rights Yearbook*, 4 (1961), 116 at 140:

[The] purpose of the High Contracting Parties in concluding the [European Convention on Human Rights] was not to concede to each other reciprocal rights and obligations in pursuance of their individual national interests but to realize the aims and ideals of the Council of Europe ... and to establish a common public order of the free democracies of Europe with the object of safeguarding their common heritage of political traditions, ideas, freedom and the rule of law. [Thus,] the obligations undertaken by the High Contracting Parties in the European Convention are essentially of an objective character, being designed rather to protect the fundamental rights of individual human beings from infringements by any of the High Contracting Parties than to create subjective and reciprocal rights for the High Contracting Parties themselves.

Inter-American Court of Human Rights, *The Effect of Reservations on the Entry into Force of the American Convention on Human Rights (Arts. 74 and 75)*, Advisory Opinion OC-2/82, 24 September 1982, Inter-American Court of Human Rights (Series A) No. 2 (1982) at para. 29:

[M]odern human rights treaties in general, and the American Convention in particular, are not multilateral treaties of the traditional type concluded to accomplish the reciprocal exchange of rights for the mutual benefit of the contracting States. Their object and purpose is the protection of the basic rights of individual human beings irrespective of their nationality, both against the State of their nationality and all other contracting States. In concluding these human rights treaties, the States can be deemed to submit themselves to a legal order within which they, for the common good, assume various obligations, not in relation to other States, but towards all individuals within their jurisdiction.

The Vienna Convention on the Law of Treaties recognizes the specificity of human rights treaties by stating in Article 60(5) that the principle according to which the material breach of a treaty by one party authorizes the other party to terminate or suspend the agreement does not apply to 'provisions relating to the protection of the human person contained in treaties of a humanitarian character, in particular to provisions prohibiting any form of reprisals against persons protected by such treaties'. The reason for this is obvious: the rule allowing termination or suspension of a treaty in cases of material breach is based on the idea of reciprocity, where the obligations imposed on one party are set for the benefit of the other parties to the treaty. But the beneficiaries of human rights treaties are not the other parties: they are the population under the jurisdiction of the States concerned. It would not only be unjustifiable for State A to take the population under its jurisdiction as hostages (threatening to violate their rights if State B violates the rights of its own peoples); this would also be totally ineffective as a means of dissuading States from breaching their obligations: why would State B care about the sake of the population under the jurisdiction of State A, if that population is led to suffer as a result of counter-measures adopted by that State? See further on this, R. Higgins, 'Human Rights: Some Questions of Integrity' (mistakenly titled 'The United Nations: Still a Force for Peace' due to an editorial error), *Modern Law Review*, 52, No. 1 (1989), 1–21 at 11.

An important consequence of this specific character of human rights treaties is the role which monitoring bodies, or courts, are to play in the supervision of human rights treaties. This role shall be particularly important under such treaties since the other States parties can hardly be counted upon to exercise the kind of horizontal control which, in usual treaties, provides the required disciplining function. This is illustrated, for instance, by the relatively few objections raised to the reservations filed by States upon entering a human rights treaty, or by the striking underuse by States of mechanisms allowing for inter-State complaints, both at the universal level and even, with some exceptions, at the regional level. It is therefore fitting that, in international human rights law, the function of international judicial or quasi-judicial bodies has been so prominent, in comparison to the classical (diplomatic) means of treaty supervision and interpretation. The controversies surrounding the question of reservations to human rights treaties provide an excellent illustration of this. It is to these controversies that we now turn.

4.5 Reservations to human rights treaties

A reservation is 'a unilateral statement, however phrased or named, made by a State, when signing, ratifying, accepting, approving or acceding to a treaty, whereby it purports to exclude or to modify the legal effect of certain provisions of the treaty in their application to that State' (Article 2 §1(d) of the Vienna Convention on the Law of Treaties of 23 May 1969). What matters is the intention of the State, rather than the form of the instrument, as noted by the Human Rights Committee: 'If a statement, irrespective of its name or title, purports to exclude or modify the legal effect of a treaty in its application to the State, it constitutes a reservation. Conversely, if a so-called reservation merely offers a State's understanding of a provision but does not exclude or modify that provision in its application to that State, it is, in reality, not a reservation' (General Comment No. 24, *Issues relating to Reservations made upon Ratification or Accession to the Covenant or the Optional Protocols thereto, or in relation to Declarations under Article 41 of the Covenant*, 4 November 1994, para. 4). The question whether reservations to multilateral human rights treaties should be treated under the same regime as reservations to classical treaties is one to which the International Court of Justice made an important contribution when it delivered its Advisory Opinion on the reservations to the Genocide Convention (a). The Vienna Convention on the Law of Treaties subsequently confirmed the solution proposed by the International Court of Justice. However, it has been recognized, both by the Inter-American Court of Human Rights and by the European Court of Human Rights, that human rights treaties were specific and that the general rules regarding reservations to multilateral treaties might therefore not apply to those instruments (b). These positions have led to a considerable discussion in doctrine (see, e.g. B. Simma, 'Reservations to Human Rights Treaties – Some Recent Developments', in Gerhard Hafner *et al.* (eds.), *Liber Amicorum Professor Ignaz Seidl-Hohenveldern* (The Hague: Kluwer Law International, 1998), pp. 659–82; J. P. Gardner and C. Chinkin (eds.), *Human Rights as General Norms and a State's Right to Opt out: Reservations and Objections to Human Rights Conventions* (London: British Institute of International and Comparative Law, 1997), p. 207; and R. Baratta and I. Ziemele (eds.), *Reservations to Human Rights Treaties and the Vienna Convention Regime: Conflict, Harmony or Reconciliation* (Leiden: Martinus Nijhoff, 2004), p. 319). When the Human Rights Committee transposed the doctrine regarding the specificity of human rights treaties in the context of the International Covenant on Civil and Political Rights, this was resisted by States, who denounced this position as exceeding the competence of the Committee under the ICCPR (c).

(a) The regime of reservations in international law

We may take as departure point the Advisory Opinion adopted by the International Court of Justice in response to the request of the UN General Assembly, which sought the opinion of the Court on the following questions relating to the 1948 Convention on the Prevention and Punishment of the Crime of Genocide. In the event of a State ratifying or acceding to the Convention subject to a reservation made either on ratification or on accession, or on signature followed by ratification, the General Assembly asked: 'I. Can the reserving State be regarded as being a party to the Convention while still maintaining its reservation if the reservation is objected to by one or more of the parties to the Convention but not by others? II. If the answer to Question I is in the affirmative, what is the effect of the reservation as between the reserving State and: (a) The parties which object to the reservation? (b) Those which accept it? III. What would be the legal effect as regards the answer to Question I if an objection to a reservation is made: (a) By a signatory which has not yet ratified? (b) By a State entitled to sign or accede but which has not yet done so?' The following excerpts concern the first of these questions:

International Court of Justice, *Reservations to the Convention on the Prevention and Punishment of the Crime of Genocide*, Advisory Opinion, I.C.J. Reports 1951, 19 (28 May 1951):

It is well established that in its treaty relations a State cannot be bound without its consent, and that consequently no reservation can be effective against any State without its agreement thereto. It is also a generally recognized principle that a multilateral convention is the result of an agreement freely concluded upon its clauses and that consequently none of the contracting parties is entitled to frustrate or impair, by means of unilateral decisions or particular agreements, the purpose and raison d'etre of the convention. To this principle was linked the notion of the integrity of the convention as adopted, a notion which in its traditional concept involved the proposition that no reservation was valid unless it was accepted by all the contracting parties without exception, as would have been the case if it had been stated during the negotiations.

This concept, which is directly inspired by the notion of contract, is of undisputed value as a principle. However, as regards the Genocide Convention, it is proper to refer to a variety of circumstances which would lead to a more flexible application of this principle. Among these circumstances may be noted the clearly universal character of the United Nations under whose auspices the Convention was concluded, and the very wide degree of participation envisaged by Article XI of the Convention. Extensive participation in conventions of this type has already given rise to greater flexibility in the international practice concerning multilateral conventions. More general resort to reservations, very great allowance made for tacit assent to reservations, the existence of practices which go so far as to admit that the author of reservations which have been rejected by certain contracting parties is nevertheless to be regarded as a party to the convention in relation to those contracting parties that have accepted the reservations-all these factors are manifestations of a new need for flexibility in the operation of multilateral conventions.

It must also be pointed out that although the Genocide Convention was finally approved unanimously, it is nevertheless the result of a series of majority votes. The majority principle, while facilitating the conclusion of multilateral conventions, may also make it necessary for certain States to make reservations. This observation is confirmed by the great number of reservations which have been made of recent years to multilateral conventions.

In this state of international practice, it could certainly not be inferred from the absence of an article providing for reservations in a multilateral convention that the contracting States are prohibited from making certain reservations. Account should also be taken of the fact that the absence of such an article or even the decision not to insert such an article can be explained by the desire not to invite a multiplicity of reservations. The character of a multilateral convention, its purpose, provisions, mode of preparation and adoption, are factors which must be considered in determining, in the absence of any express provision on the subject, the possibility of making reservations, as well as their validity and effect.

Although it was decided during the preparatory work not to insert a special article on reservations, it is none the less true that the faculty for States to make reservations was contemplated at successive stages of the drafting of the Convention ...

Furthermore, the faculty to make reservations to the Convention appears to be implicitly admitted by the very terms of Question I.

The Court recognizes that an understanding was reached within the General Assembly on the faculty to make reservations to the Genocide Convention and that it is permitted to conclude therefrom that States becoming parties to the Convention gave their assent thereto. It must now determine what kind of reservations may be made and what kind of objections may be taken to them.

The solution of these problems must be found in the special characteristics of the Genocide Convention. The origins and character of that Convention, the objects pursued by the General Assembly and the contracting parties, the relations which exist between the provisions of the Convention, inter se, and between those provisions and these objects, furnish elements of interpretation of the will of the General Assembly and the parties. The origins of the Convention show that it was the intention of the United Nations to condemn and punish genocide as 'a crime under international law' involving a denial of the right of existence of entire human groups, a denial which shocks the conscience of mankind and results in great losses to humanity, and which is contrary to moral law and to the spirit and aims of the United Nations (Resolution 96 (I) of the General Assembly, December 11th 1946). The first consequence arising from this conception is that the principles underlying the Convention are principles which are recognized by civilized nations as binding on States, even without any conventional obligation. A second consequence is the universal character both of the condemnation of genocide and of the co-operation required 'in order to liberate mankind from such an odious scourge' (Preamble to the Convention). The Genocide Convention was therefore intended by the General Assembly and by the contracting parties to be definitely universal in scope. It was in fact approved on December 9th, 1948, by a resolution which was unanimously adopted by fifty-six States.

The objects of such a convention must also be considered. The Convention was manifestly adopted for a purely humanitarian and civilizing purpose. It is indeed difficult to imagine a convention that might have this dual character to a greater degree, since its object on the one hand is to safeguard the very existence of certain human groups and on the other to confirm and endorse the most elementary principles of morality. In such a convention the contracting States do not have any interests of their own; they merely have, one and all, a common interest, namely, the accomplishment of those high purposes which are the raison d'etre of the convention. Consequently, in a convention of this type one cannot speak of individual advantages or disadvantages to States, or of the maintenance of a perfect contractual balance between rights and duties. The high ideals which inspired the Convention provide, by virtue of the common will of the parties, the foundation and measure of all its provisions.

The foregoing considerations, when applied to the question of reservations, and more particularly to the effects of objections to reservations, lead to the following conclusions.

The object and purpose of the Genocide Convention imply that it was the intention of the General Assembly and of the States which adopted it that as many States as possible should participate. The complete exclusion from the Convention of one or more States would not only restrict the scope of its application, but would detract from the authority of the moral and humanitarian principles which are its basis. It is inconceivable that the contracting parties readily contemplated that an objection to a minor reservation should produce such a result. But even less could the contracting parties have intended to sacrifice the very object of the Convention in favour of a vain desire to secure as many participants as possible. The object and purpose of the Convention thus limit both the freedom of making reservations and that of objecting to them. It follows that it is the compatibility of a reservation with the object and purpose of the Convention that must furnish the criterion for the attitude of a State in making the reservation on accession as well as for the appraisal by a State in objecting to the reservation. Such is the rule of conduct which must guide every State in the appraisal which it must make, individually and from its own standpoint, of the admissibility of any reservation.

Any other view would lead either to the acceptance of reservations which frustrate the purposes which the General Assembly and the contracting parties had in mind, or to recognition that the parties to the Convention have the power of excluding from it the author of a reservation, even a minor one, which may be quite compatible with those purposes.

It has nevertheless been argued that any State entitled to become a party to the Genocide Convention may do so while making any reservation it chooses by virtue of its sovereignty. The Court cannot share this view. It is obvious that so extreme an application of the idea of State sovereignty could lead to a complete disregard of the object and purpose of the Convention.

On the other hand, it has been argued that there exists a rule of international law subjecting the effect of a reservation to the express or tacit assent of all the contracting parties. This theory rests essentially on a contractual conception of the absolute integrity of the convention as adopted. This view, however, cannot prevail if, having regard to the character of the convention, its purpose and its mode of adoption, it can be established that the parties intended to derogate from that rule by admitting the faculty to make reservations thereto.

It does not appear, moreover, that the conception of the absolute integrity of a convention has been transformed into a rule of international law. The considerable part which tacit assent has always played in estimating the effect which is to be given to reservations scarcely permits one to state that such a rule exists, determining with sufficient precision the effect of objections made to reservations. In fact, the examples of objections made to reservations appear to be too rare in international practice to have given rise to such a rule. It cannot be recognized that the report which was adopted on the subject by the Council of the League of Nations on June 17th, 1927, has had this effect. At best, the recommendation made on that date by the Council constitutes the point of departure of an administrative practice which, after being observed by the Secretariat of the League of Nations, imposed itself, so to speak, in the ordinary course of things on the Secretary-General of the United Nations in his capacity of depositary of conventions concluded under the auspices of the League. But it cannot be concluded that the legal problem of the effect of objections to reservations has in this way been solved. The opinion of the Secretary-General of the United Nations himself is embodied in the following passage of his report of September 21st, 1950: 'While it is universally recognized that the consent of the other governments concerned must be sought before they can be bound by the terms of a reservation, there has not been unanimity either as to the procedure to be followed by a depositary in obtaining the necessary consent or as to the legal effect of a State's objecting to a reservation.'

It may, however, be asked whether the General Assembly of the United Nations, in approving the Genocide Convention, had in mind the practice according to which the Secretary-General, in exercising his functions as a depositary, did not regard a reservation as definitively accepted until it had been established that none of the other contracting States objected to it. If this were the case, it might be argued that the implied intention of the contracting parties was to make the effectiveness of any reservation to the Genocide Convention conditional on the assent of all the parties.

The Court does not consider that this view corresponds to reality. It must be pointed out, first of all, that the existence of an administrative practice does not in itself constitute a decisive factor in ascertaining what views the contracting States to the Genocide Convention may have had concerning the rights and duties resulting therefrom. It must also be pointed out that there existed among the American States members both of the United Nations and of the Organization of American States, a different practice which goes so far as to permit a reserving State to become a party irrespective of the nature of the reservations or of the objections raised by other contracting States. The preparatory work of the Convention contains nothing to justify the statement that the contracting States implicitly had any definite practice in mind. Nor is there any such indication in the subsequent attitude of the contracting States: neither the reservations made by certain States nor the position adopted by other States towards those reservations permit the conclusion that assent to one or the other of these practices had been given. Finally, it is not without interest to note, in view of the preference generally said to attach to an established practice, that the debate on reservations to multilateral treaties which took place in the Sixth Committee at the fifth session of the General Assembly reveals a profound divergence of views, some delegations being attached to the idea of the absolute integrity of the Convention, others favouring a more flexible practice which would bring about the participation of as many States as possible.

It results from the foregoing considerations that Question I, on account of its abstract character, cannot be given an absolute answer. The appraisal of a reservation and the effect of objections that might be made to it depend upon the particular circumstances of each individual case.

The Advisory Opinion of the International Court of Justice on the *Reservations to the Convention on the Prevention and Punishment of the Crime of Genocide* sparked an important literature (see, e.g. W. W. Bishop, 'Reservations to the Convention on Genocide. International Court of Justice, Advisory Opinion, May 28, 1951', *American Journal of International Law*, 45 (1951), 579–90; Sir G. Fitzmaurice, 'The Law and Procedure of the International Court of Justice 1951–4: Treaty Interpretation and Other Treaty Points', *British Yearbook of International Law*, 33 (1957), 202–93, esp. 272–93; H. Lauterpacht, 'Some Possible Solutions to the Problem of Reservations to Treaties' in *The Grotius Society Transactions for the Year 1953*, 39 (1954), 97–118; P.-H. Imbert, *Les réserves aux traités multilatéraux. Evolution du droit et de la pratique depuis l'avis consultatif donné par la Cour internationale de justice le 28 mai 1951* (Paris: Pedone, 1979)). When the Vienna Convention on the Law of Treaties was drafted, Articles 19–23 relating to reservations clearly sought to echo the Court's views:

Vienna Convention on the Law of Treaties

Article 19 Formulation of reservations

A State may, when signing, ratifying, accepting, approving or acceding to a treaty, formulate a reservation unless:

(a) the reservation is prohibited by the treaty;

(b) the treaty provides that only specified reservations, which do not include the reservation in question, may be made; or

(c) in cases not falling under sub-paragraphs (a) and (b), the reservation is incompatible with the object and purpose of the treaty.

Article 20 Acceptance of and objection to reservations

1. A reservation expressly authorized by a treaty does not require any subsequent acceptance by the other contracting States unless the treaty so provides.

2. When it appears from the limited number of the negotiating States and the object and purpose of a treaty that the application of the treaty in its entirety between all the parties is an essential condition of the consent of each one to be bound by the treaty, a reservation requires acceptance by all the parties.

3. When a treaty is a constituent instrument of an international organization and unless it otherwise provides, a reservation requires the acceptance of the competent organ of that organization.

4. In cases not falling under the preceding paragraphs and unless the treaty otherwise provides:

    (a) acceptance by another contracting State of a reservation constitutes the reserving State a party to the treaty in relation to that other State if or when the treaty is in force for those States;

    (b) an objection by another contracting State to a reservation does not preclude the entry into force of the treaty as between the objecting and reserving States unless a contrary intention is definitely expressed by the objecting State;

    (c) an act expressing a State's consent to be bound by the treaty and containing a reservation is effective as soon as at least one other contracting State has accepted the reservation.

5. For the purposes of paragraphs 2 and 4 and unless the treaty otherwise provides, a reservation is considered to have been accepted by a State if it shall have raised no objection to the reservation by the end of a period of twelve months after it was notified of the reservation or by the date on which it expressed its consent to be bound by the treaty, whichever is later.

Article 21 Legal effects of reservations and of objections to reservations

1. A reservation established with regard to another party in accordance with articles 19, 20 and 23:

    (a) modifies for the reserving State in its relations with that other party the provisions of the treaty to which the reservation relates to the extent of the reservation; and

    (b) modifies those provisions to the same extent for that other party in its relations with the reserving State.

2. The reservation does not modify the provisions of the treaty for the other parties to the treaty inter se.

3. When a State objecting to a reservation has not opposed the entry into force of the treaty between itself and the reserving State, the provisions to which the reservation relates do not apply as between the two States to the extent of the reservation.

Article 22 Withdrawal of reservations and of objections to reservations

1. Unless the treaty otherwise provides, a reservation may be withdrawn at any time and the consent of a State which has accepted the reservation is not required for its withdrawal.
2. Unless the treaty otherwise provides, an objection to a reservation may be withdrawn at any time.
3. Unless the treaty otherwise provides, or it is otherwise agreed:

   (a) the withdrawal of a reservation becomes operative in relation to another contracting State only when notice of it has been received by that State;
   (b) the withdrawal of an objection to a reservation becomes operative only when notice of it has been received by the State which formulated the reservation.

Article 23 Procedure regarding reservations

1. A reservation, an express acceptance of a reservation and an objection to a reservation must be formulated in writing and communicated to the contracting States and other States entitled to become parties to the treaty.
2. If formulated when signing the treaty subject to ratification, acceptance or approval, a reservation must be formally confirmed by the reserving State when expressing its consent to be bound by the treaty. In such a case the reservation shall be considered as having been made on the date of its confirmation.
3. An express acceptance of, or an objection to, a reservation made previously to confirmation of the reservation does not itself require confirmation.
4. The withdrawal of a reservation or of an objection to a reservation must be formulated in writing.

(b) Reservations in the Inter-American and European systems

The position of the Inter-American Court of Human Rights
Article 75 of the American Convention on Human Rights allows for reservations provided they are 'in conformity with the provisions of the Vienna Convention on the Law of Treaties [of 1969]'. The explicit reference to the Vienna Convention would suggest a strict adherence to the general regime of reservations for multilateral treaties. The Inter-American Commission of Human Rights requested an Advisory Opinion of the Court concerning the consequences of reservations on the entry into force of the Convention. In its application, the Commission noted that under the general regime – and particularly under the provisions of Article 20(4)(c) and (5) of the Vienna Convention – a treaty's entry into force could depend on the acceptance of the reservation by other States. In deciding that this was not the case, the Court relied on the special nature of human rights treaties:

Inter-American Court of Human Rights, Advisory Opinion OC–2/82 of 24 September 1982 on the effect of reservations on the entry into force of the American Convention on Human Rights (Arts. 74 and 75), Series A, No. 2:

26. Having concluded that States ratifying or adhering to the Convention may do so with any reservations that are not incompatible with its object and purpose, the Court must now determine which provisions of Article 20 of the Vienna Convention apply to reservations made to the Convention. The result of this inquiry will of necessity also provide the answer to the question posed by the Commission. This is so because, if under the Vienna Convention reservations to the Convention are not deemed to require acceptance by the other States Parties, then for the here relevant purposes Article 74 of the Convention applies and a State ratifying or adhering to it with or without a reservation is deemed to be a State Party as of the date of the deposit of the instrument of ratification or adherence. [Vienna Convention, Art. 20 (1)] On the other hand, if acceptance of the reservation is required under the Vienna Convention, a reserving State would be deemed to become a State Party only on the date when at least one other State Party has accepted the reservation either expressly or by implication. [Vienna Convention, Art. 20(4)(c) and (5)] ...

28. In deciding whether the Convention envisages the application of paragraph 1 or paragraph 4 of Article 20 of the Vienna Convention, the Court notes that the principles enunciated in Article 20(4) reflect the needs of traditional multilateral international agreements which have as their object the reciprocal exchange, for the mutual benefit of the States Parties, of bargained for rights and obligations. In this context, and given the vastly increased number of States comprising the international community today, the system established by Article 20(4) makes considerable sense ...

29. The Court must emphasize, however, that modern human rights treaties in general, and the American Convention in particular, are not multilateral treaties of the traditional type concluded to accomplish the reciprocal exchange of rights for the mutual benefit of the contracting States. Their object and purpose is the protection of the basic rights of individual human beings irrespective of their nationality, both against the State of their nationality and all other contracting States. In concluding these human rights treaties, the States can be deemed to submit themselves to a legal order within which they, for the common good, assume various obligations, not in relation to other States, but towards all individuals within their jurisdiction ...

31. These views about the distinct character of humanitarian treaties and the consequences to be drawn therefrom apply with even greater force to the American Convention whose first two preambular paragraphs read as follows:

'Reaffirming their intention to consolidate in this hemisphere, within the framework of democratic institutions, a system of personal liberty and social justice based on respect for the essential rights of man;

Recognizing that the essential rights of man are not derived from one's being a national of a certain state, but are based upon attributes of the human personality, and that they therefore justify international protection in the form of a convention reinforcing or complementing the protection provided by the domestic law of the American states.'

32. It must be emphasized also that the Convention, unlike other international human rights treaties, including the European Convention, confers on private parties the right to file a petition

with the Commission against any State as soon as it has ratified the Convention. (Convention, Art. 44.) By contrast, before one State may institute proceedings against another State, each of them must have accepted the Commision's jurisdiction to deal with inter-State communications. (Convention, Art. 45.) This structure indicates the overriding importance the Convention attaches to the commitments of the States Parties vis-à-vis individuals, which can be readily implemented without the intervention of any other State.

33. Viewed in this light and considering that the Convention was designed to protect the basic rights of individual human beings irrespective of their nationality, against States of their own nationality or any other State Party, the Convention must be seen for what in reality it is: a multilateral legal instrument of framework enabling States to make binding unilateral commitments not to violate the human rights of individuals within their jurisdiction.

34. In this context, it would be manifestly unreasonable to conclude that the reference in Article 75 to the Vienna Convention compels the application of the legal regime established by Article 20(4), which makes the entry into force of a ratification with a reservation dependent upon its acceptance by another State. A treaty which attaches such great importance to the protection of the individual that it makes the right of individual petition mandatory as of the moment of ratification, can hardly be deemed to have intended to delay the treaty's entry into force until at least one other State is prepared to accept the reserving State as a party. Given the institutional and normative framework of the Convention, no useful purpose would be served by such a delay.

35. Accordingly, for the purpose of the present analysis, the reference in Article 75 to the Vienna Convention makes sense only if it is understood as an express authorization designed to enable States to make whatever reservations they deem appropriate, provided the reservations are not incompatible with the object and purpose of the treaty. As such, they can be said to be governed by Article 20(1) of the Vienna Convention and, consequently, do not require acceptance by any other State Party.

The Inter-American Court also discussed the issue of reservations in the case of *Hilaire* v. *Trinidad and Tobago*. That case was filed before the Inter-American Court by the Inter-American Commission on Human Rights one day before the denunciation by Trinidad and Tobago of the American Convention on Human Rights – a result of the ruling of the Judicial Committee of the Privy Council in *Pratt and Morgan* v. *Attorney General for Jamaica* (Privy Council Appeal No. 10/1993, 2 November 1994) (see below, box 1.5.) – took effect. In its application, the Inter-American Commission sought a statement from the Court to the effect that the mandatory death penalty was incompatible with the American Convention. In its ruling on preliminary objections, the Inter-American Court considered whether a reservation made to the recognition of compulsory jurisdiction of the Court was compatible with the object and purpose of the treaty. In accepting the jurisdiction of the Court, Trinidad and Tobago had declared that '[a]s regards Article 62 of the Convention, the Government of the Republic of Trinidad and Tobago, recognizes the compulsory jurisdiction of the Inter-American Court of Human Rights, as stated in the said article, only to such extent that recognition is consistent with the relevant sections of the Constitution of the Republic of

Trinidad and Tobago; and provided that Judgment of the Court does not infringe, create or abolish any existing rights or duties of any private citizen'. Article 62(2) of the American Convention allows States to accept the jurisdiction of the Court on the 'condition of reciprocity, for a specified period, or for specific cases'. The reservation made by Trinidad and Tobago went considerably further, and in fact amounted to making the exercise of jurisdiction by the Court conditional upon its compatibility to that State's internal legal order.

Inter-American Court of Human Rights, case of *Hilaire* v. *Trinidad and Tobago*, Preliminary Objections, judgment of 1 September 2001, Series C, No. 80:

82. Interpreting the Convention in accordance with its object and purpose, the Court must act in a manner that preserves the integrity of the mechanism provided for in Article 62(1) of the Convention. It would be unacceptable to subordinate the said mechanism to restrictions that would render the system for the protection of human rights established in the Convention and, as a result, the Court's jurisdictional role, inoperative ...

86. [The] purported 'reservation' contains two parts. The first intends to limit the recognition of the Court's compulsory jurisdiction in the sense that said recognition is only valid to the extent that it is 'consistent with the relevant sections' of the Constitution of Trinidad and Tobago. These expressions can lead to numerous interpretations. Nonetheless, it is clear to the Court that they cannot be given a scope that would impede this Tribunal's ability to judge whether the State had or had not violated a provision of the Convention. The second part of the purported restriction relates to the State's 'recognition' of the Court's compulsory jurisdiction so that its judgments do not 'infringe, create or abolish any existing rights or duties of any private citizen' (*sic*). Again, though the precise meaning of this condition is unclear, without a doubt it cannot be utilized with the purpose of suppressing the jurisdiction of the Court to hear and decide an application related to an alleged violation of the State's conventional obligations ...

88. The Court observes that the instrument of acceptance of the Court's compulsory jurisdiction on the part of Trinidad and Tobago is not consistent with the hypothesis stipulated in Article 62(2) of the American Convention. It is general in scope, which completely subordinates the application of the American Convention to the internal legislation of Trinidad and Tobago as decided by its courts. This implies that the instrument of acceptance is manifestly incompatible with the object and purpose of the Convention. As a result, the said article does not contain a provision that allows Trinidad and Tobago to formulate the 'restriction' it made ...

92. The declaration formulated by the State of Trinidad and Tobago would allow it to decide in each specific case the extent of its own acceptance of the Court's compulsory jurisdiction to the detriment of this Tribunal's compulsory functions. In addition, it would give the State the discretional power to decide which matters the Court could hear, thus depriving the exercise of the Court's compulsory jurisdiction of all efficacy.

93. Moreover, accepting the said declaration in the manner proposed by the State would lead to a situation in which the Court would have the State's Constitution as its first point of reference, and the American Convention only as a subsidiary parameter, a situation which would cause a fragmentation of the international legal order for the protection of human rights, and which would render illusory the object and purpose of the Convention.

94. The American Convention and the other human rights treaties are inspired by a set of higher common values (centered around the protection of the human being), are endowed with specific supervisory mechanisms, are applied as a collective guarantee, embody essentially objective obligations, and have a special character that sets them apart from other treaties. The latter govern mutual interests between and among the States parties and are applied by them, with all the juridical consequences that follow there from for the international and domestic systems ...

98. For the foregoing reasons, the Court considers that Trinidad and Tobago cannot prevail in the limitation included in its instrument of acceptance of the optional clause of the mandatory jurisdiction of the Inter-American Court of Human Rights in virtue of what has been established in Article 62 of the American Convention, because this limitation is incompatible with the object and purpose of the Convention. Consequently, the Court considers that it must dismiss the second and third arguments in the preliminary objection submitted by the State insofar as they refer to the Court's jurisdiction.

The position of the European Court of Human Rights

The views expressed by the Inter-American Court of Human Rights imply both that certain reservations may be invalid, since they would run counter to the object and purpose of the American Convention on Human Rights or to the recognition of the compulsory jurisdiction of the Court, and that it is for the Inter-American Court itself, rather than for the other States parties by the classic mechanism of objections, to decide on the validity of any reservations which any State may have expressed upon ratification or notification of its acceptance of the jurisdiction of the Court. The European Court of Human Rights was even more explicit in the *Belilos* v. *Switzerland* case of 1988 (Eur. Ct. H.R. (plen.), *Belilos* v. *Switzerland*, judgment of 29 April 1988, Series A No. 132). This judgment sparked a number of comments on the doctrine, because it constituted an implicit, albeit unmistakeable, departure from an understanding of the European Convention on Human Rights as a treaty of a traditional kind (see I. Cameron and F. Horn, 'Reservations to the European Convention: the *Belilos* Case', *German Yearbook of International Law*, 33 (1990), 69; S. Marks, 'Reservations Unhinged: the *Belilos* Case before the European Court of Human Rights', *International and Comparative Law Quarterly*, 39 (1990), 300; H. J. Bourguigon, 'The *Belilos* Case: New Lights on Reservations to Multilateral Treaties', *Virginia Journal of International Law*, 29 (1989), 347). In contrast to what is generally the case for multilateral treaties, States parties to human rights instruments generally omit to object to any reservations made by States upon acceding to such instruments, since a human rights treaty does not primarily grant them rights or advantages: rather, as we have seen, such a treaty has an 'objective' character, stipulating rights for the benefit of persons under the jurisdiction of the States parties (see above, section 4.4.). In addition, human rights treaties are often seen as merely embodying, in treaty form, obligations of States which are pre-existing, whether they have their source in customary international law or in the general principles of law, and which are not at the disposal of States (see above, section 4.1.). These characteristics of human rights treaties may explain the attitude of the European Court of Human Rights in *Belilos* which, after it found the Swiss reservation to Article 6 §1 of the Convention to be invalid, considered that it should be 'severed' from the main undertakings of Switzerland under the Convention.

The context was the following. Upon ratifying the European Convention on Human Rights on 28 November 1974, Switzerland made the following declaration on the interpretation of Article 6 para. 1: 'The Swiss Federal Council considers that the guarantee of fair trial in Article 6, paragraph 1 of the Convention, in the determination of civil rights and obligations or any criminal charge against the person in question is intended solely to ensure ultimate control by the judiciary over the acts or decisions of the public authorities relating to such rights or obligations or the determination of such a charge.' In the *Belilos* case, the Court was called upon to examine this reservation under then Article 64 of the Convention (now 57), which states:

1. Any State may, when signing the Convention or when depositing its instrument of ratification, make a reservation in respect of any particular provision of the Convention to the extent that any law then in force in its territory is not in conformity with the provision. Reservations of a general character shall not be permitted under this Article.
2. Any reservation made under this Article shall contain a brief statement of the law concerned.

The Court considered that it had jurisdiction to examine the validity of the Switzerland's reservation to the ratification of the Convention, citing in this regard Articles 19, 45 and 49 of the Convention, which relate to the powers of the Court (para. 50 of the judgment). It found that the reservation did not comply with the conditions imposed under Article 64 (now 57) of the Convention. The wording of the Swiss declaration, the Court noted, did 'not make it possible for the scope of the undertaking by Switzerland to be ascertained exactly, in particular as to which categories of dispute are included and as to whether or not the "ultimate control by the judiciary" takes in the facts of the case. They can therefore be interpreted in different ways, whereas Article 64 §1 requires precision and clarity. In short, they fall foul of the rule that reservations must not be of a general character' (para. 55); in addition, Switzerland has not included in its reservation a 'brief statement of the law concerned' as required by Article 64 para. 2 (now 57 para. 2) of the Convention, whereas the purpose of this provision, said the Court, 'is to provide a guarantee – in particular for the other Contracting Parties and the Convention institutions – that a reservation does not go beyond the provisions expressly excluded by the State concerned. This is not a purely formal requirement but a condition of substance. The omission in the instant case therefore cannot be justified even by important practical difficulties' (para. 59). The Court concluded that it could go on to proceed with the examination of whether Article 6 para. 1 ECHR had been violated (para. 60):

[T]he declaration in question does not satisfy two of the requirements of Article 64 of the Convention, with the result that it must be held to be invalid. At the same time, it is beyond doubt that Switzerland is, and regards itself as, bound by the Convention irrespective of the validity of the declaration. Moreover, the Swiss Government recognised the Court's competence to determine the latter issue, which they argued before it. The Government's preliminary objection must therefore be rejected.

(c) From regional to universal human rights treaties: the doctrine of the Human Rights Committee

The position adopted by the European Court of Human Rights in *Belilos* inspired the Human Rights Committee when it was confronted with the wide-ranging reservations appended by the United States to their accession to the International Covenant on Civil and Political Rights:

Reservations, understandings, and declarations entered by the United States upon ratifying the International Covenant on Civil and Political Rights (8 June 1992):

Reservations:

(1) That article 20 [of the Covenant, providing in particular that 'any advocacy of national, racial or religious hatred that constitutes incitement to discrimination, hostility or violence shall be prohibited by law'] does not authorize or require legislation or other action by the United States that would restrict the right of free speech and association protected by the Constitution and laws of the United States.

(2) That the United States reserves the right, subject to its Constitutional constraints, to impose capital punishment on any person (other than a pregnant woman) duly convicted under existing or future laws permitting the imposition of capital punishment, including such punishment for crimes committed by persons below eighteen years of age. [As stated in the initial report submitted by the United States to the Human Rights Committee, this reservation has been adopted in consideration of the fact that 'approximately half the states have adopted legislation permitting juveniles aged 16 and older to be prosecuted as adults when they commit the most egregious offences, and because the Supreme Court has upheld the constitutionality of such laws' (CCPR/C/81/Add. 4, 24 August 1994, para. 148)].

(3) That the United States considers itself bound by article 7 to the extent that 'cruel, inhuman or degrading treatment or punishment' means the cruel and unusual treatment or punishment prohibited by the Fifth, Eighth, and/or Fourteenth Amendments to the Constitution of the United States. [Again, the initial report submitted by the United States to the Human Rights Committee states: 'As such proceedings and practices have repeatedly withstood judicial review of their constitutionality in the United States, it was determined to be appropriate for the United States to condition its acceptance of the United Nations Convention against Torture and Other Cruel,

Inhuman or Degrading Treatment or Punishment on a formal reservation to the effect that the United States considers itself bound to the extent that "cruel, inhuman treatment or punishment" means the cruel and unusual treatment or punishment prohibited by the Fifth, Eighth and/or Fourteenth Amendments to the Constitution of the United States. For the same reasons, and to ensure uniformity of interpretation as to the obligations of the United States under the Covenant and the Torture Convention on this point, the United States took the [reservation above] to the Covenant' (CCPR/C/81/Add. 4, 24 August 1994, para. 148)].

(4) That because US law generally applies to an offender the penalty in force at the time the offence was committed, the United States does not adhere to the third clause of paragraph 1 of article 15 [according to which: 'If, subsequent to the commission of the offence, provision is made by law for the imposition of the lighter penalty, the offender shall benefit thereby'].

(5) That the policy and practice of the United States are generally in compliance with and supportive of the Covenant's provisions regarding treatment of juveniles in the criminal justice system. Nevertheless, the United States reserves the right, in exceptional circumstances, to treat juveniles as adults, notwithstanding paragraphs 2(b) and 3 of article 10 and paragraph 4 of article 14. The United States further reserves to these provisions with respect to States with respect to individuals who volunteer for military service prior to age 18.

Understandings [(5), which relates to the responsibility of the federal government for the measures to be adopted by states and local authorities, has been omitted here: see chapter 2, box 2.1.]:

(1) That the Constitution and laws of the United States guarantee all persons equal protection of the law and provide extensive protections against discrimination. The United States understands distinctions based upon race, colour, sex, language, religion, political or other opinion, national or social origin, property, birth or any other status – as those terms are used in article 2, paragraph 1 and article 26 – to be permitted when such distinctions are, at minimum, rationally related to a legitimate governmental objective. The United States further understands the prohibition in paragraph 1 of article 4 upon discrimination, in time of public emergency, based 'solely' on the status of race, colour, sex, language, religion or social origin, not to bar distinctions that may have a disproportionate effect upon persons of a particular status.

(2) That the United States understands the right to compensation referred to in articles 9(5) and 14(6) to require the provision of effective and enforceable mechanisms by which a victim of an unlawful arrest or detention or a miscarriage of justice may seek and, where justified, obtain compensation from either the responsible individual or the appropriate governmental entity. Entitlement to compensation may be subject to the reasonable requirements of domestic law.

(3) That the United States understands the reference to 'exceptional circumstances' in paragraph 2(a) of article 10 to permit the imprisonment of an accused person with

convicted persons where appropriate in light of an individual's overall dangerousness, and to permit accused persons to waive their right to segregation from convicted persons. The United States further understands that paragraph 3 of article 10 does not diminish the goals of punishment, deterrence, and incapacitation as additional legitimate purposes for a penitentiary system.

(4) That the United States understands that subparagraphs 3(b) and (d) of article 14 do not require the provision of a criminal defendant's counsel of choice when the defendant is provided with court-appointed counsel on grounds of indigence, when the defendant is financially able to retain alternative counsel, or when imprisonment is not imposed. The United States further understands that paragraph 3(e) does not prohibit a requirement that the defendant make a showing that any witness whose attendance he seeks to compel is necessary for his defense. The United States understands the prohibition upon double jeopardy in paragraph 7 to apply only when the judgment of acquittal has been rendered by a court of the same governmental unit, whether the Federal Government or a constituent unit, as is seeking a new trial for the same cause ...

Declarations:

(1) That the United States declares that the provisions of articles 1 through 27 of the Covenant are not self-executing.

(2) That it is the view of the United States that States Party to the Covenant should wherever possible refrain from imposing any restrictions or limitations on the exercise of the rights recognized and protected by the Covenant, even when such restrictions and limitations are permissible under the terms of the Covenant. For the United States, article 5, paragraph 2, which provides that fundamental human rights existing in any State Party may not be diminished on the pretext that the Covenant recognizes them to a lesser extent, has particular relevance to article 19, paragraph 3 which would permit certain restrictions on the freedom of expression. The United States declares that it will continue to adhere to the requirements and constraints of its Constitution in respect to all such restrictions and limitations.

(3) That the United States declares that the right referred to in article 47 [right of all peoples to enjoy and utilize fully and freely their natural wealth and resources] may be exercised only in accordance with international law.

In reaction, the Human Rights Committee adopted a General Comment on the issue of reservations to the International Covenant on Civil and Political Rights (for a discussion, see C. J. Redgwell, 'Reservations to Treaties and Human Rights Committee General Comment No. 24(52)', *International and Comparative Law Quarterly*, 46 (1997), 390–412; on the question whether the specificity of human rights treaties justifies the approach of the Human Rights Committee, see R. Baratta, 'Should Invalid Reservations to Human Rights Treaties be Disregarded?', *European Journal of International Law*, 11 (2000), 413; K. Korkelia, 'New Challenges to the Regime of Reservations under the International Covenant on Civil and Political Rights', *European Journal of International Law*, 13 (2002), 437).

Human Rights Committee, General Comment No. 24, *Issues Relating to Reservations made upon Ratification or Accession to the Covenant or the Optional Protocols thereto, or in Relation to Declarations under Article 41 of the Covenant*, 4 November 1994 (CCPR/C/21/Rev.1/Add. 6):

[General approach of the Committee]

6. The absence of a prohibition on reservations [in the text of the Covenant] does not mean that any reservation is permitted. The matter of reservations under the Covenant and the first Optional Protocol is governed by international law. Article 19(3) of the Vienna Convention on the Law of Treaties provides relevant guidance. It stipulates that where a reservation is not prohibited by the treaty or falls within the specified permitted categories, a State may make a reservation provided it is not incompatible with the object and purpose of the treaty. Even though, unlike some other human rights treaties, the Covenant does not incorporate a specific reference to the object and purpose test, that test governs the matter of interpretation and acceptability of reservations.

[The object and purpose of the Covenant]

7. In an instrument which articulates very many civil and political rights, each of the many articles, and indeed their interplay, secures the objectives of the Covenant. The object and purpose of the Covenant is to create legally binding standards for human rights by defining certain civil and political rights and placing them in a framework of obligations which are legally binding for those States which ratify; and to provide an efficacious supervisory machinery for the obligations undertaken.

8. Reservations that offend peremptory norms would not be compatible with the object and purpose of the Covenant. Although treaties that are mere exchanges of obligations between States allow them to reserve *inter se* application of rules of general international law, it is otherwise in human rights treaties, which are for the benefit of persons within their jurisdiction. Accordingly, provisions in the Covenant that represent customary international law (and *a fortiori* when they have the character of peremptory norms) may not be the subject of reservations. Accordingly, a State may not reserve the right to engage in slavery, to torture, to subject persons to cruel, inhuman or degrading treatment or punishment, to arbitrarily deprive persons of their lives, to arbitrarily arrest and detain persons, to deny freedom of thought, conscience and religion, to presume a person guilty unless he proves his innocence, to execute pregnant women or children, to permit the advocacy of national, racial or religious hatred, to deny to persons of marriageable age the right to marry, or to deny to minorities the right to enjoy their own culture, profess their own religion, or use their own language. And while reservations to particular clauses of article 14 may be acceptable, a general reservation to the right to a fair trial would not be.

9. Applying more generally the object and purpose test to the Covenant, the Committee notes that, for example, reservation to article 1 denying peoples the right to determine their own political status and to pursue their economic, social and cultural development, would be incompatible with the object and purpose of the Covenant. Equally, a reservation to the obligation to respect and ensure the rights, and to do so on a non-discriminatory basis (article 2(1)) would not be acceptable. Nor may a State reserve an entitlement not to take the necessary steps at the domestic level to give effect to the rights of the Covenant (article 2(2)).

10. The Committee has further examined whether categories of reservations may offend the 'object and purpose' test. In particular, it falls for consideration as to whether reservations to the non-derogable provisions of the Covenant are compatible with its object and purpose. While there is no hierarchy of importance of rights under the Covenant, the operation of certain rights may not be suspended, even in times of national emergency. This underlines the great importance of non-derogable rights. But not all rights of profound importance, such as articles 9 and 27 of the Covenant, have in fact been made non-derogable. One reason for certain rights being made non-derogable is because their suspension is irrelevant to the legitimate control of the state of national emergency (for example, no imprisonment for debt, in article 11). Another reason is that derogation may indeed be impossible (as, for example, freedom of conscience). At the same time, some provisions are non-derogable exactly because without them there would be no rule of law. A reservation to the provisions of article 4 itself, which precisely stipulates the balance to be struck between the interests of the State and the rights of the individual in times of emergency, would fall in this category. And some non-derogable rights, which in any event cannot be reserved because of their status as peremptory norms, are also of this character – the prohibition of torture and arbitrary deprivation of life are examples. While there is no automatic correlation between reservations to non-derogable provisions, and reservations which offend against the object and purpose of the Covenant, a State has a heavy onus to justify such a reservation.

11. The Covenant consists not just of the specified rights, but of important supportive guarantees. These guarantees provide the necessary framework for securing the rights in the Covenant and are thus essential to its object and purpose. Some operate at the national level and some at the international level. Reservations designed to remove these guarantees are thus not acceptable. Thus, a State could not make a reservation to article 2, paragraph 3, of the Covenant, indicating that it intends to provide no remedies for human rights violations. Guarantees such as these are an integral part of the structure of the Covenant and underpin its efficacy. The Covenant also envisages, for the better attainment of its stated objectives, a monitoring role for the Committee. Reservations that purport to evade that essential element in the design of the Covenant, which is also directed to securing the enjoyment of the rights, are also incompatible with its object and purpose. A State may not reserve the right not to present a report and have it considered by the Committee. The Committee's role under the Covenant, whether under article 40 or under the Optional Protocols, necessarily entails interpreting the provisions of the Covenant and the development of a jurisprudence. Accordingly, a reservation that rejects the Committee's competence to interpret the requirements of any provisions of the Covenant would also be contrary to the object and purpose of that treaty.

12. The intention of the Covenant is that the rights contained therein should be ensured to all those under a State party's jurisdiction. To this end certain attendant requirements are likely to be necessary. Domestic laws may need to be altered properly to reflect the requirements of the Covenant; and mechanisms at the domestic level will be needed to allow the Covenant rights to be enforceable at the local level. Reservations often reveal a tendency of States not to want to change a particular law. And sometimes that tendency is elevated to a general policy. Of particular concern are widely formulated reservations which essentially render ineffective all Covenant rights which would require any change in national law to ensure compliance with Covenant obligations. No real international rights or obligations have thus been accepted.

And when there is an absence of provisions to ensure that Covenant rights may be sued on in domestic courts, and, further, a failure to allow individual complaints to be brought to the Committee under the first Optional Protocol, all the essential elements of the Covenant guarantees have been removed.

13. The issue arises as to whether reservations are permissible under the first Optional Protocol [the text of which is silent on the issue of reservations] and, if so, whether any such reservation might be contrary to the object and purpose of the Covenant or of the first Optional Protocol itself. It is clear that the first Optional Protocol is itself an international treaty, distinct from the Covenant but closely related to it. Its object and purpose is to recognize the competence of the Committee to receive and consider communications from individuals who claim to be victims of a violation by a State party of any of the rights in the Covenant. States accept the substantive rights of individuals by reference to the Covenant, and not the first Optional Protocol. The function of the first Optional Protocol is to allow claims in respect of those rights to be tested before the Committee. Accordingly, a reservation to an obligation of a State to respect and ensure a right contained in the Covenant, made under the first Optional Protocol when it has not previously been made in respect of the same rights under the Covenant, does not affect the State's duty to comply with its substantive obligation. A reservation cannot be made to the Covenant through the vehicle of the Optional Protocol but such a reservation would operate to ensure that the State's compliance with that obligation may not be tested by the Committee under the first Optional Protocol. And because the object and purpose of the first Optional Protocol is to allow the rights obligatory for a State under the Covenant to be tested before the Committee, a reservation that seeks to preclude this would be contrary to the object and purpose of the first Optional Protocol, even if not of the Covenant. A reservation to a substantive obligation made for the first time under the first Optional Protocol would seem to reflect an intention by the State concerned to prevent the Committee from expressing its views relating to a particular article of the Covenant in an individual case.

14. The Committee considers that reservations relating to the required procedures under the first Optional Protocol would not be compatible with its object and purpose. The Committee must control its own procedures as specified by the Optional Protocol and its rules of procedure. Reservations have, however, purported to limit the competence of the Committee to acts and events occurring after entry into force for the State concerned of the first Optional Protocol. In the view of the Committee this is not a reservation but, most usually, a statement consistent with its normal competence *ratione temporis*. At the same time, the Committee has insisted upon its competence, even in the face of such statements or observations, when events or acts occurring before the date of entry into force of the first Optional Protocol have continued to have an effect on the rights of a victim subsequent to that date. Reservations have been entered which effectively add an additional ground of inadmissibility under article 5, paragraph 2, by precluding examination of a communication when the same matter has already been examined by another comparable procedure. In so far as the most basic obligation has been to secure independent third party review of the human rights of individuals, the Committee has, where the legal right and the subject-matter are identical under the Covenant and under another international instrument, viewed such a reservation as not violating the object and purpose of the first Optional Protocol ...

[The competence of the Committee to determine the validity of the reservations made to the Covenant or to an additional protocol, and the consequences attached to a finding of invalidity]

16. The Committee finds it important to address which body has the legal authority to make determinations as to whether specific reservations are compatible with the object and purpose of the Covenant. As for international treaties in general, the International Court of Justice has indicated in the Reservations to the Genocide Convention Case (1951) that a State which objected to a reservation on the grounds of incompatibility with the object and purpose of a treaty could, through objecting, regard the treaty as not in effect as between itself and the reserving State. Article 20, paragraph 4, of the Vienna Convention on the Law of Treaties 1969 contains provisions most relevant to the present case on acceptance of and objection to reservations. This provides for the possibility of a State to object to a reservation made by another State. Article 21 deals with the legal effects of objections by States to reservations made by other States. Essentially, a reservation precludes the operation, as between the reserving and other States, of the provision reserved; and an objection thereto leads to the reservation being in operation as between the reserving and objecting State only to the extent that it has not been objected to.

17. As indicated above, it is the Vienna Convention on the Law of Treaties that provides the definition of reservations and also the application of the object and purpose test in the absence of other specific provisions. But the Committee believes that its provisions on the role of State objections in relation to reservations are inappropriate to address the problem of reservations to human rights treaties. Such treaties, and the Covenant specifically, are not a web of inter-State exchanges of mutual obligations. They concern the endowment of individuals with rights. The principle of inter-State reciprocity has no place, save perhaps in the limited context of reservations to declarations on the Committee's competence under article 41 [inter-state communications]. And because the operation of the classic rules on reservations is so inadequate for the Covenant, States have often not seen any legal interest in or need to object to reservations. The absence of protest by States cannot imply that a reservation is either compatible or incompatible with the object and purpose of the Covenant. Objections have been occasional, made by some States but not others, and on grounds not always specified; when an objection is made, it often does not specify a legal consequence, or sometimes even indicates that the objecting party none the less does not regard the Covenant as not in effect as between the parties concerned. In short, the pattern is so unclear that it is not safe to assume that a non-objecting State thinks that a particular reservation is acceptable. In the view of the Committee, because of the special characteristics of the Covenant as a human rights treaty, it is open to question what effect objections have between States *inter se*. However, an objection to a reservation made by States may provide some guidance to the Committee in its interpretation as to its compatibility with the object and purpose of the Covenant.

18. It necessarily falls to the Committee to determine whether a specific reservation is compatible with the object and purpose of the Covenant. This is in part because, as indicated above, it is an inappropriate task for States parties in relation to human rights treaties, and in part because it is a task that the Committee cannot avoid in the performance of its functions. In order to know the scope of its duty to examine a State's compliance under article 40 or a

communication under the first Optional Protocol, the Committee has necessarily to take a view on the compatibility of a reservation with the object and purpose of the Covenant and with general international law. Because of the special character of a human rights treaty, the compatibility of a reservation with the object and purpose of the Covenant must be established objectively, by reference to legal principles, and the Committee is particularly well placed to perform this task. The normal consequence of an unacceptable reservation is not that the Covenant will not be in effect at all for a reserving party. Rather, such a reservation will generally be severable, in the sense that the Covenant will be operative for the reserving party without benefit of the reservation.

[Requirements of specificity and transparency of reservations]

19. Reservations must be specific and transparent, so that the Committee, those under the jurisdiction of the reserving State and other States parties may be clear as to what obligations of human rights compliance have or have not been undertaken. Reservations may thus not be general, but must refer to a particular provision of the Covenant and indicate in precise terms its scope in relation thereto. When considering the compatibility of possible reservations with the object and purpose of the Covenant, States should also take into consideration the overall effect of a group of reservations, as well as the effect of each reservation on the integrity of the Covenant, which remains an essential consideration. States should not enter so many reservations that they are in effect accepting a limited number of human rights obligations, and not the Covenant as such. So that reservations do not lead to a perpetual non-attainment of international human rights standards, reservations should not systematically reduce the obligations undertaken only to those presently existing in less demanding standards of domestic law. Nor should interpretative declarations or reservations seek to remove an autonomous meaning to Covenant obligations, by pronouncing them to be identical, or to be accepted only in so far as they are identical, with existing provisions of domestic law. States should not seek through reservations or interpretative declarations to determine that the meaning of a provision of the Covenant is the same as that given by an organ of any other international treaty body.

20. States should institute procedures to ensure that each and every proposed reservation is compatible with the object and purpose of the Covenant. It is desirable for a State entering a reservation to indicate in precise terms the domestic legislation or practices which it believes to be incompatible with the Covenant obligation reserved; and to explain the time period it requires to render its own laws and practices compatible with the Covenant, or why it is unable to render its own laws and practices compatible with the Covenant. States should also ensure that the necessity for maintaining reservations is periodically reviewed, taking into account any observations and recommendations made by the Committee during examination of their reports. Reservations should be withdrawn at the earliest possible moment. Reports to the Committee should contain information on what action has been taken to review, reconsider or withdraw reservations.

Probably the most important affirmations of the general comment were that the Human Rights Committee had the power to decide on the validity of a reservation to the ICCPR, and that an invalid reservation could be detached from the main commitment to the ICCPR as expressed by its ratification. This position was heavily contested (see, in particular, Observations by France on General Comment 24, 4 *International Human Rights*

Reports, 4 (1997), 6; Observations by the United Kingdom on General Comment 24, 3 *International Human Rights Reports*, 3 (1996), 261; Observations by the United States on General Comment 24, *International Human Rights Reports*, 3 (1996), 265). In 1997, the International Law Commission (ILC) considered the question of the unity or diversity of the juridical regime for reservations. Stating to be 'aware of the discussion currently taking place in other forums on the subject of reservations to normative multilateral treaties, and particularly treaties concerning human rights', the ILC proposed the following conclusions:

International Law Commission, The unity or diversity of the juridical regime for reservations, Preliminary Conclusions of 1997:

1. The Commission reiterates its view that articles 19 to 23 of the Vienna Conventions on the Law of Treaties of 1969 and 1986 govern the regime of reservations to treaties and that, in particular, the object and purpose of the treaty is the most important of the criteria for determining the admissibility of reservations;
2. The Commission considers that, because of its flexibility, this regime is suited to the requirements of all treaties, of whatever object or nature, and achieves a satisfactory balance between the objectives of preservation of the integrity of the text of the treaty and universality of participation in the treaty;
3. The Commission considers that these objectives apply equally in the case of reservations to normative multilateral treaties, including treaties in the area of human rights and that, consequently, the general rules enunciated in the above-mentioned Vienna Conventions govern reservations to such instruments;
4. The Commission nevertheless considers that the establishment of monitoring bodies by many human rights treaties gave rise to legal questions that were not envisaged at the time of the drafting of those treaties, connected with appreciation of the admissibility of reservations formulated by States;
5. The Commission also considers that where these treaties are silent on the subject, the monitoring bodies established thereby are competent to comment upon and express recommendations with regard, *inter alia*, to the admissibility of reservations by States, in order to carry out the functions assigned to them;
6. The Commission stresses that this competence of the monitoring bodies does not exclude or otherwise affect the traditional modalities of control by the contracting parties, on the one hand, in accordance with the above-mentioned provisions of the Vienna Conventions of 1969 and 1986 and, where appropriate by the organs for settling any dispute that may arise concerning the interpretation or application of the treaties;
7. The Commission suggests providing specific clauses in normative multilateral treaties, including in particular human rights treaties, or elaborating protocols to existing treaties if States seek to confer competence on the monitoring body to appreciate or determine the admissibility of a reservation;
8. The Commission notes that the legal force of the findings made by monitoring bodies in the exercise of their power to deal with reservations cannot exceed that resulting from the powers given to them for the performance of their general monitoring role;

9. The Commission calls upon States to cooperate with monitoring bodies and give due consideration to any recommendations that they may make or to comply with their determination if such bodies were to be granted competence to that effect in the future;

10. The Commission notes also that, in the event of inadmissibility of a reservation, it is the reserving State that has the responsibility for taking action. This action may consist, for example, in the State either modifying its reservation so as to eliminate the inadmissibility, or withdrawing its reservation, or forgoing becoming a party to the treaty;

11. The Commission expresses the hope that the above conclusions will help to clarify the reservations regime applicable to normative multilateral treaties, particularly in the area of human rights;

12. The Commission emphasizes that the above conclusions are without prejudice to the practices and rules developed by monitoring bodies within regional contexts.

The Human Rights Committee was not deterred. Following the adoption of these 'Preliminary Conclusions' of the International Law Commission, the Chair of the Human Rights Committee, Ms Christine Chanet, wrote a letter to the Chair of the International Law Commission as well as to the Special Rapporteur on the issue of reservations to treaties, expressing her disagreement (UN Doc. A/53/40, vol. I, p. 95). Upon examining the initial report of the United States of America under the International Covenant on Civil and Political Rights, the Human Rights Committee listed among its 'principal subjects of concern' the following:

Concluding Observations of the Human Rights Committee: United States of America, 3 October 1995 (CCPR/C/79/Add. 50)):

279. The Committee regrets the extent of the State party's reservations, declarations and understandings to the Covenant. It believes that, taken together, they intended to ensure that the United States has accepted only what is already the law of the United States. The Committee is also particularly concerned at reservations to article 6, paragraph 5, and article 7 of the Covenant, which it believes to be incompatible with the object and purpose of the Covenant.

In its most recent Concluding Observations regarding the United States, the Human Rights Committee 'welcomes the Supreme Court's decision in *Roper* v. *Simmons* [543 U.S. 551] (2005), which held that the Eighth and Fourteenth Amendments forbid imposition of the death penalty on offenders who were under the age of 18 when their crimes were committed. In this regard, the Committee reiterates the recommendation made in its previous concluding observations, encouraging the State party to withdraw its reservation to article 6(5) of the Covenant' (CCPR/C/USA/CO/3/Rev.1, 18 December 2006).

In expressing the view in its 1997 preliminary conclusions that 'in the event of inadmissibility of a reservation, it is the reserving State that has the responsibility for taking action' (para. 10), the International Law Commission clearly questions what may be called the 'severability thesis' held both by the European Court of Human Rights and subsequently by the Human Rights Committee – i.e. allowing the treaty to be binding on a State party even though the reservation attached by that State to its ratification might be invalid. It has been remarked, however, that this thesis could in fact better respect the requirements of State consent, since the costs involved by the opposite, 'non-severability' thesis – obliging the State to withdraw from the treaty, and to re-enter without the reservation attached – might on average impose higher reputational costs on States:

Ryan Goodman, 'Human Rights Treaties, Invalid Reservations, and State Consent', *American Journal of International Law*, 96 (2002), 531 at 556:

The record of state treaty practice strongly suggests that error costs derived from a nonseverance presumption exceed those from a presumption favoring severance. In most of the cases, states have consented to having aspects of their legal system modified by international legal developments. In the strongest cases of this kind – newly established democracies – states often prefer locking as much of their domestic fates as practicable into international structures. An adjudicator's erroneous expulsion of a state from a treaty risks significant costs along two dimensions: international (e.g. a sovereignty impact from the state's expulsion against its will, reputational costs to the state's international standing, loss of a leadership or participatory role in the regime) and domestic (e.g. the unhinging of a wide array of judicially enforceable civil and political rights protections, facilitation of illiberal rollbacks). The result would probably involve significant transaction costs in the process of reratifying the agreement.

On the other hand, erroneous severance by the adjudicator, maintaining the state's membership in the treaty, would also risk significant, but seemingly more limited, costs: international (e.g. a sovereignty impact from the state's being held against its will) and domestic (e.g. the creation of legal obligations the state was not prepared to accept; the potential infringement of 'counter-rights', such as limiting freedom of speech in the name of regulating hate speech). In this situation, however, the state has a relatively easy recourse: withdrawal. This back-end solution helps prevent such errors from producing severe impacts. There are potential reputational costs to withdrawal, but these should be balanced against the fact that the state would have preferred expulsion in the first place.

Box 1.5. **The denunciation by Trinidad and Tobago of the ICCPR and the American Convention on Human Rights**

The position of the Human Rights Committee as expressed in its General Comment No. 24 was reaffirmed after Trinidad and Tobago decided to denounce the Optional Protocol on 26 May 1998, and then immediately re-entered this instrument on 26 August 1998, the day when the denunciation became effective. That denunciation, as well as the denunciation by Trinidad and Tobago of the American Convention on Human Rights, also notified on 26 May 1998, were alleged to be the only means the State concerned had at its disposal in order to comply with the ruling of the Judicial Committee of the Privy Council in *Pratt and Morgan* v. *Attorney General for Jamaica* (Privy Council Appeal No. 10/1993, 2 November 1994). This ruling determined that capital sentence appeals should be heard within a reasonable delay (twelve months from conviction), and that it should be possible for the international human rights bodies, such as the United Nations Human Rights Committee and the Inter-American Commission on Human Rights, to dispose of complaints submitted to them in death penalty cases at most within eighteen months, or the detention following conviction to the death penalty could be considered inhuman or degrading treatment. As the possibility of appeals before the Inter-American Commission and Court could exceed this delay by a large margin – the Inter-American Commission of Human Rights could not provide assurances that, in death penalty cases, the petitions would be expedited in order to meet the time-frame requirements set by the Judicial Committee of the Privy Council – the State considered itself obliged to denounce the American Convention on Human Rights. For similar reasons, Trinidad and Tobago alleged it had to denounce the Optional Protocol to the International Covenant on Civil and Political Rights.

When re-entering the Optional Protocol to the ICCPR, Trinidad and Tobago included a reservation under the terms of which it 're-accedes to the Optional Protocol to the International Covenant on Civil and Political Rights with a Reservation to article 1 thereof to the effect that the Human Rights Committee shall not be competent to receive and consider communications relating to any prisoner who is under sentence of death in respect of any matter relating to his prosecution, his detention, his trial, his conviction, his sentence or the carrying out of the death sentence on him and any matter connected therewith'.

A further decision of the Judicial Committee of the Privy Council was announced in March 1999. According to this decision, the execution of any death sentences should be stayed until the Human Rights Committee or the Inter-American Commission and Court of Human Rights have been provided an opportunity to examine the merits of communications filed with them (Judicial Committee of the Privy Council, *Thomas and Hilaire* v. *Attorney General and others*, Privy Council Appeal No. 60 of 1998, appeal from the Court of Appeal of Trinidad and Tobago, 17 March 1999). The decision was based essentially on the reasoning that 'The appellants are contending that their trials were unfair, and hope in due course to obtain binding rulings from the [Inter-American Court of Human Rights] that their convictions should be quashed or their sentences should be commuted. For the Government to carry out the sentences of death before the petitions have been heard would deny the appellants their constitutional right to due process.' This decision also introduced an exception to the time-limits for the execution of the death penalty introduced in *Pratt and Morgan* v. *Attorney General for Jamaica* [1994] 2 A.C. 1 at 33: the Judicial Committee noted 'the delay occasioned by the slowness of the international bodies in dealing with such petitions', but they took the view that such delays 'should not prevent the death sentence from being carried out. Where, therefore, more than 18 months elapses between the date on which a condemned man lodges a petition to an international body and its final determination, [they] would regard it as appropriate to add the excess to the period of 18 months allowed for in *Pratt*.'

Despite these justifications, the reservation attached by Trinidad and Tobago when it re-entered the Optional Protocol to the International Covenant on Civil and Political Rights prompted a number of objections from the EU Member States. And in *Kennedy* v. *Trinidad and Tobago*, following a communication submitted by a person sentenced to the death penalty, the Human Rights Committee decided that the reservation cited above was incompatible with the object and purpose of the Optional Protocol, and that accordingly the Committee was not precluded from considering the communication under the Optional Protocol; on 2 November 1999, it therefore declared the communication admissible. Trinidad and Tobago took the view that 'in registering the communication and purporting to impose interim measures under rule 86 of the Committee's rules of procedure, the Committee has exceeded its jurisdiction, and the State party therefore considers the actions of the Committee in respect of this communication to be void and of no binding effect'. On 27 March 2000, with effect on 27 June 2000, Trinidad and Tobago denounced the Optional Protocol to the ICCPR a second time. The Human Rights Committee nevertheless examined the merits of the communication, on which it adopted a decision on 26 March 2002 (see *Kennedy* v. *Trinidad and Tobago*, Communication No. 845/1998, CCPR/C/74/D/845/1998 (2002)). The Committee noted that the communication was submitted for consideration before Trinidad and Tobago's denunciation of the Optional Protocol became effective on 27 June 2000 and that, in accordance with article 12(2) of the Optional Protocol, it therefore continued to be subject to the application of the Optional Protocol. It found that the case revealed a number of violations of the Covenant and that, therefore, the State party was under an obligation to provide the author of the communication with an effective remedy, including compensation and consideration of early release.

1.5. Questions for discussion: reservations to human rights treaties

1. Arguably, the intention of the International Court of Justice in adopting its Advisory Opinion of 1951 on the reservations to the Convention on the Prevention and Punishment of the Crime of Genocide, was to achieve a compromise between two conflicting objectives: (1) to make accession to the Convention attractive even for States which felt they might not be able immediately to comply with all the obligations imposed by that instrument, and (2) to impose certain limits as to which reservations are acceptable, based on whether or not they are compatible with the object and purpose of the treaty. Has the Court succeeded? Was the position of the Court

guided primarily by the humanitarian character of the Genocide Convention, or by the fact that it was a multilateral treaty seeking to achieve as wide a ratification as possible?

2. Does the Vienna Convention on the Law of Treaties express correctly the position of the International Court of Justice in its Advisory Opinion on the reservations to the Convention on the Prevention and Punishment of the Crime of Genocide? Are the articles of the Vienna Convention on reservations adapted to the needs of human rights treaties?

3. The 1965 International Convention for the Elimination of All Forms of Racial Discrimination provides that 'A reservation incompatible with the object and purpose of this Convention shall not be permitted, nor shall a reservation the effect of which would inhibit the operation of any of the bodies established by this Convention be allowed. A reservation shall be considered incompatible or inhibitive if at least two thirds of the States Parties to this Convention object to it' (Art. 20(2)). Is this solution more appropriate than the one adopted for the International Covenant on Civil and Political Rights by the Human Rights Committee?

4. In its General Comment No. 24, the Human Rights Committee takes the view that 'provisions in the Covenant that represent customary international law (and *a fortiori* when they have the character of peremptory norms) may not be the subject of reservations' (para. 8). Is this statement compatible with the principle recalled by the International Court of Justice – and already referred to above – that 'customary international law continues to exist and to apply, separately from international treaty law, even where the two categories of law have an identical content' (case concerning *Military and Paramilitary Activities in and against Nicaragua (Nicaragua v. United States)* [1986] I.C.J. Reports 14, para. 179 (judgment of 27 June 1986 on the merits))? Is a State entering a reservation related to a guarantee codified in the International Covenant on Civil and Political Rights where this guarantee is part of customary international law 'reserving the right' to violate this guarantee, or is it merely excluding the possibility for the Committee to monitor compliance with that obligation?

5. In general international law, the compatibility of the reservation to a multilateral treaty with its object and purpose is based on the recorded objections to the said reservation expressed by other parties to the multilateral treaty. The shift away from these objections and towards the independent evaluation role of judicial or non-judicial bodies is justified, as regards human rights treaties, by the fact that States parties to multilateral human rights treaties generally show little interest in sanctioning non-compliance with those treaties by other parties. However, is this distrust also justified where objections are in fact expressed? Should such objections be determinative, when they are formulated by a sufficiently representative number of parties? In other terms, should human rights monitoring bodies be bound to conclude that a reservation cannot be accepted, where it has led to a large number of objections being raised?

6. Once a reservation is found to be invalid, how should we balance the respective merits of the 'severability' and 'non-severability' theses, as regards the consequences of such finding? Is the option of withdrawal from a treaty always realistic, politically and legally, for a State whose reservation expressed upon acceding to a multilateral human rights treaty is found invalid?

2

State Responsibility and 'Jurisdiction'

INTRODUCTION

This chapter examines the relevance of the notions of 'national territory' and of 'jurisdiction' to the determination of situations in which the international responsibility of States may be engaged. This has become one of the most debated issues in international human rights doctrine (see, among many others, the essays collected in F. Coomans and M. Kamminga (eds.), *Extraterritorial Application of Human Rights Treaties* (Antwerp-Oxford: Intersentia-Hart, 2004); M. J. Dennis, 'Application of Human Rights Treaties Extraterritorially in Times of Armed Conflict and Military Occupation', *American Journal of International Law*, 99 (2005), 119; T. Meron, 'Extraterritoriality of Human Rights Treaties', *American Journal of International Law*, 89 (1995), 78; O. De Schutter, 'Globalization and Jurisdiction: Lessons from the European Convention on Human Rights', *Baltic Yearbook of International Law*, 6 (2006), 183–245). The main question addressed in much of the literature is whether the notion of 'jurisdiction' (taken separately or in combination with that of 'territory') designates a condition for a finding of State responsibility which is distinct from that of attribution, or whether instead the two notions – 'jurisdiction' and 'attribution' – are in fact synonymous and thus interchangeable. And this is indeed the question this chapter focuses upon, although breaking it down into a set of sub-questions corresponding to the different situations in which the question of State responsibility can be raised.

The various human rights treaties differ in their formulations as to the requirements of 'jurisdiction' or of 'territory', in order to define their scope of application. Under Article 2 para. 1 ICCPR, 'Each State Party to the present Covenant undertakes to respect and to ensure to all individuals within its territory and subject to its jurisdiction' the rights recognized in the Covenant. Article 2 para. 1 of the 1984 Convention against Torture and Other Cruel, Inhuman or Degrading Treatment or Punishment provides that 'Each State Party shall take effective legislative, administrative, judicial or other measures to prevent acts of torture in any territory under its jurisdiction.' Similarly, under Article 2 para. 1 of the 1989 Convention on the Rights of the Child, 'States Parties shall respect and ensure the rights set forth in the present Convention to each child within their jurisdiction.' Certain other UN instruments, although silent on the question of 'jurisdiction', contain a 'federal clause' which implicitly refers to the fact that they impose obligations which are primarily territorial: for instance, Article 4 para. 5 of the Convention on the Rights of Persons with Disabilities provides that it shall extend 'to all parts of federal states without any limitations or exceptions'. By contrast, the International Covenant on Economic, Social and Cultural Rights (ICESCR) does not make reference to any notion of 'jurisdiction', 'competence', or 'territory', apparently implying that its obligations apply irrespective of the place where the alleged violation takes place: although, in its Advisory Opinion of 9 July 2004, the International Court of Justice considered that it could explain this silence 'by the fact that this Covenant guarantees rights which are essentially territorial' (*Legal Consequences of the Construction of a Wall in the Occupied Palestinian Territory*, I.C.J. Reports 2004, 136 at para. 112), this assertion is made without any justification grounded either on the text of the Covenant or on its *travaux préparatoires*.

In general, the regional human rights instruments also provide that they will impose obligations on States owed to all persons under their jurisdiction. Although the African Charter on Human and Peoples' Rights makes no reference either to jurisdiction or to territory, Article 1 of the European Convention on Human Rights provides that the States Parties shall 'secure to everyone within their jurisdiction' the rights and freedoms recognized under that instrument. Similarly, Article 1 para. 1 of the American Convention on Human Rights states that: 'The States Parties to this Convention undertake to respect the rights and freedoms recognized herein and to ensure to all persons subject to their jurisdiction the free and full exercise of those rights and freedoms'.

This chapter examines the interrelationship between the notion of 'jurisdiction', as a condition for engaging State responsibility, and the notions of 'territory' and 'effective control' which are sometimes treated, albeit wrongly, as synonymous. First, section 1 examines the question of whether the human rights obligations of States follow them when they occupy foreign territory, whether legally or in violation of international law. It then asks whether the obligations of States extend to all situations arising on their national territory, even in cases where certain portions of the territory are not under the effective control of the State concerned. Section 2 examines, instead, which extra-territorial obligations may be imposed on States. This latter question, in turn, requires that we distinguish between (a) the responsibility of States for the activities of State agents operating outside the national borders; (b) the responsibility of States for the failure to protect human rights beyond the national territory; and (c) the obligations of international assistance and co-operation imposed under certain human rights treaties, particularly in order to impose on developed States to assist developing States in the realization of economic and social rights on their territory. Section 3 considers the specific questions of international responsibility that may arise when States co-operate internationally, and when the alleged violation of human rights results from their joint action.

1 NATIONAL TERRITORY AND 'EFFECTIVE CONTROL'

1.1 Occupied foreign territory

Even where it should play a central role in determining the scope of the 'jurisdiction' of a State for the purpose of defining the extent of its human rights obligations, the notion of 'national territory' should not necessarily be construed as limited to the territory which falls under the sovereignty of that State, as recognized under international law. The 'jurisdiction' of a State may extend beyond its national territory, where that State exercises effective control, for instance following a military invasion, of other portions of territory. It should not matter whether such occupation is, under international law, legal or illegal. Referring in this regard to the position of the International Court of Justice, the European Court of Human Rights has remarked that 'international law recognises the legitimacy of certain legal arrangements and transactions in such a situation, for instance as regards the registration of births, deaths and marriages', 'the effects of which can be ignored only to the detriment of the inhabitants of the [t]erritory' (Eur. Ct. H.R., *Loizidou* v. *Turkey*, judgment of 18 December 1996 (preliminary objections and merits), para. 45, referring to International Court of Justice, Advisory Opinion on *Legal Consequences for States of the Continued Presence of South Africa in Namibia (South West Africa) Notwithstanding Security Council Resolution 276 (1970)*, I.C.J. Reports 1970 16 at 56, para. 125). For similar reasons, the human rights obligations of the State illegally occupying foreign territories should extend to such territories under occupation: any other solution would result in depriving the population under occupation from the protection of human rights instruments, for the sole reason that the occupation is illegal under international law, which would be highly paradoxical.

European Court of Human Rights, *Loizidou* v. *Turkey*, judgment of 23 March 1995 (preliminary objections), Series A, No. 310:

[The applicant, a Cypriot national, is the owner of plots of land located in northern Cyprus, in an area occupied by the Turkish forces since their invasion of northern Cyprus on 20 July 1974, and now administered by the 'Turkish Republic of Northern Cyprus' (TRNC), a puppet regime not recognized by the international community. The applicant and the Cypriot Government maintained that ever since the Turkish occupation of northern Cyprus the applicant has been denied access to her property and has, consequently, lost all control over it: she has thus been prevented in the past, and is still prevented, by Turkish forces from returning to her land and 'peacefully enjoying' her property. In their submission this constituted a continued and unjustified interference with her right to the peaceful enjoyment of property in breach of Article 1 of Protocol No. 1 as well as a continuing violation of the right to respect for her home under Article 8 of the Convention. In a first judgment of 23 March 1995 on the preliminary objections raised by Turkey, the Court held that her application was 'capable of falling within' Article 1 of the Convention (at paras. 56–64), and that Turkey's territorial reservations were invalid (at paras. 65–89). In its judgment on the merits, delivered on 18 December 1996, the Court addresses the question whether the acts complained of are imputable to Turkey.]

62. [The] Court recalls that, although Article 1 sets limits on the reach of the Convention, the concept of 'jurisdiction' under the provision is not restricted to the national territory of the High Contracting Parties. According to its established case law, for example, the Court has held that the extradition or expulsion of a person by a Contracting State may give rise to an issue under Article 3, and hence engage the responsibility of that State under the Convention [Eur. Ct. H.R., *Soering* v. *United Kingdom*, judgment of 7 July 1989 (see below, section 3.1. of this chapter)]. In addition, the responsibility of Contracting Parties can be involved because of acts of their authorities, whether performed within or outside national boundaries, which produce effects outside their own territory [Eur. Ct. H.R., *Drozd and Janousek* v. *France and Spain*, judgment of 26 June 1992, para 91]. Bearing in mind the object and purpose of the Convention, the responsibility of a Contracting Party may also arise when as a consequence of military action – whether lawful or unlawful – it exercises effective control of an area outside its national territory. The obligation to secure, in such an area, the rights and freedoms set out in the Convention, derives from the fact of such control whether it be exercised directly, through its armed forces, or through a subordinate local administration.

63. In this connection the respondent Government have acknowledged that the applicant's loss of control of her property stems from the occupation of the northern part of Cyprus by Turkish troops and the establishment there of the 'TRNC' [the 'Turkish Republic of Northern Cyprus']. Furthermore, it has not been disputed that the applicant was prevented by Turkish troops from gaining access to her property.

64. It follows that such acts are capable of falling within Turkish 'jurisdiction' within the meaning of Article 1 of the Convention. Whether the matters complained of are imputable to Turkey and give rise to State responsibility are thus questions which fall to be determined by the Court at the merits phase.

European Court of Human Rights, *Loizidou* v. *Turkey*, judgment of 18 December 1996 (preliminary objections and merits), paras. 49–57:

49. The applicant insisted ... that the present case was exceptional in that the authorities alleged to have interfered with the right to the peaceful enjoyment of possessions are not those of the sole legitimate Government of the territory in which the property is situated. That particularity entailed that, in order to determine whether Turkey is responsible for the alleged violation of her rights under Article 1 of Protocol No. 1 with respect to her possessions in northern Cyprus, the Court should take into account the principles of State responsibility under international law. In this context Mrs Loizidou repeated her criticism that the Commission had focused too much on the direct involvement of Turkish officials in the impugned continuous denial of access. Whilst evidence of direct involvement of Turkish officials in violations of the Convention is relevant, it is not a legal condition of responsibility under public international law.

She went on to contend that the concept of State responsibility rested on a realistic notion of accountability. A State was responsible in respect of events in the area for which it is internationally responsible, even if the conduct or events were outside its actual control. Thus, even acts of officials which are *ultra vires* may generate State responsibility.

According to international law, in the applicant's submission, the State which is recognised as accountable in respect of a particular territory remained accountable even if the territory is administered by a local administration. This was the legal position whether the local administration is illegal, in that it is the consequence of an illegal use of force, or whether it is lawful, as in the case of a protected State or other dependency. A State cannot by delegation avoid responsibility for breaches of its duties under international law, especially not for breaches of its duties under the Convention which, as illustrated by the wording of Article 1 of the Convention, involve a guarantee to secure Convention rights.

Mrs Loizidou maintained that the creation of the 'TRNC' was legally invalid and no State, except Turkey, or international organisation has recognised it. Since the Republic of Cyprus obviously cannot be held accountable for the part of the island occupied by Turkey, it must be Turkey which is so accountable. Otherwise the northern part of Cyprus would constitute a vacuum as regards responsibility for violations of human rights, the acceptance of which would be contrary to the principle of effectiveness which underlies the Convention. In any case there is overwhelming evidence that Turkey has effective overall control over events in the occupied area. She added that the fact that the Court, at the preliminary objections phase of the present case, had found Turkey to have jurisdiction created a strong presumption of Turkish responsibility for violations occurring in the occupied area.

50. According to the Cypriot Government, Turkey is in effective military and political control of northern Cyprus. It cannot escape from its duties under international law by pretending to hand over the administration of northern Cyprus to an unlawful 'puppet' regime.

51. The Turkish Government denied that they had jurisdiction in northern Cyprus within the meaning of Article 1 of the Convention. In the first place they recalled the earlier case law of the Commission which limited the jurisdiction of Turkey 'to the border area and not to the whole of northern Cyprus under the control of the Turkish Cypriot authorities' (see the Commission's decisions on the admissibility of applications nos. 6780/74, 6950/75 and 8007/77). In the second place, the presumption of control and responsibility argued for by the applicants was rebuttable. In this respect it was highly significant that the Commission in the *Chrysostomos and Papachrysostomou* v. *Turkey* report of 8 July 1993 found that the applicants' arrest, detention and trial in northern Cyprus were not 'acts' imputable to Turkey. Moreover, the Commission found no indication of control exercised by the Turkish authorities over the prison administration or the administration of justice by Turkish Cypriot authorities in the applicant's case ...

In addition, the Turkish Government contended that the question of jurisdiction in Article 1 of the Convention is not identical with the question of State responsibility under international law. Article 1 was not couched in terms of State responsibility. In their submission this provision required proof that the act complained of was actually committed by an authority of the defendant State or occurred under its direct control and that this authority at the time of the alleged violation exercised effective jurisdiction over the applicant.

Furthermore they argued that seen from this angle, Turkey had not in this case exercised effective control and jurisdiction over the applicant since at the critical date of 22 January 1990 [when Turkey declared that it recognized the compulsory jurisdiction of the European Court of Human Rights for all matters relating to its exercise of its jurisdiction in the meaning of Article 1 ECHR] the authorities of the Turkish Cypriot community, constitutionally organised within the 'TRNC' and in no way exercising jurisdiction on behalf of Turkey, were in control of the property rights of the applicant.

In this context they again emphasised that the 'TRNC' is a democratic and constitutional State which is politically independent of all other sovereign States including Turkey. The administration in northern Cyprus has been set up by the Turkish Cypriot people in the exercise of its right to self-determination and not by Turkey. Moreover, the Turkish forces in northern Cyprus are there for the protection of the Turkish Cypriots and with the consent of the ruling authority of the 'TRNC'. Neither the Turkish forces nor the Turkish Government in any way exercise governmental authority in northern Cyprus. Furthermore, in assessing the independence of the 'TRNC' it must also be borne in mind that there are political parties as well as democratic elections in northern Cyprus and that the Constitution was drafted by a constituent assembly and adopted by way of referendum.

52. As regards the question of imputability, the Court recalls in the first place that in its *Loizidou* v. *Turkey* judgment of 23 March 1995 (preliminary objections), Series A no. 310 (pp. 23–24, para. 62) it stressed that under its established case law the concept of 'jurisdiction' under Article 1 of the Convention is not restricted to the national territory of the Contracting States. Accordingly, the responsibility of Contracting States can be involved by acts and omissions of their authorities which produce effects outside their own territory. Of particular significance to the present case the Court held, in conformity with the relevant principles of international law governing State responsibility, that the responsibility of a Contracting Party could also arise when as a consequence of military action – whether lawful or unlawful – it exercises effective control of an area outside its national territory. The obligation to secure, in such an area, the rights and freedoms set out in the Convention, derives from the fact of such control whether it be exercised directly, through its armed forces, or through a subordinate local administration (see the above-mentioned *Loizidou* judgment (preliminary objections), *ibid.*).

53. In the second place, the Court emphasises that it will concentrate on the issues raised in the present case, without, however, losing sight of the general context.

54. It is important for the Court's assessment of the imputability issue that the Turkish Government have acknowledged that the applicant's loss of control of her property stems from the occupation of the northern part of Cyprus by Turkish troops and the establishment there of the 'TRNC' (see the above-mentioned preliminary objections judgment, p. 24, para. 63). Furthermore, it has not been disputed that the applicant has on several occasions been prevented by Turkish troops from gaining access to her property ...However, throughout the proceedings the Turkish Government have denied State responsibility for the matters complained of, maintaining that its armed forces are acting exclusively in conjunction with and on behalf of the allegedly independent and autonomous 'TRNC' authorities ...

56. ... It is not necessary to determine whether, as the applicant and the Government of Cyprus have suggested, Turkey actually exercises detailed control over the policies and actions of the authorities of the 'TRNC'. It is obvious from the large number of troops engaged in active duties in northern Cyprus ... that her army exercises effective overall control over that part of the island. Such control, according to the relevant test and in the circumstances of the case, entails her responsibility for the policies and actions of the 'TRNC' ... Those affected by such policies or actions therefore come within the 'jurisdiction' of Turkey for the purposes of Article 1 of the Convention. Her obligation to secure to the applicant the rights and freedoms set out in the Convention therefore extends to the northern part of Cyprus.

In view of this conclusion the Court need not pronounce itself on the arguments which have been adduced by those appearing before it concerning the alleged lawfulness or unlawfulness under international law of Turkey's military intervention in the island in 1974 since, as noted above, the establishment of State responsibility under the Convention does not require such an enquiry (see para. 52 above). It suffices to recall in this context its finding that the international community considers that the Republic of Cyprus is the sole legitimate Government of the island and has consistently refused to accept the legitimacy of the 'TRNC' as a State within the meaning of international law ...

57. It follows from the above considerations that the continuous denial of the applicant's access to her property in northern Cyprus and the ensuing loss of all control over the property is a matter which falls within Turkey's 'jurisdiction' within the meaning of Article 1 and is thus imputable to Turkey.

Thus, what is determinative for the existence of 'jurisdiction' is effective control, rather than the formal existence of sovereignty. This view has been shared, broadly, by the UN human rights treaty bodies. For instance, in its Concluding Observations/ Comments on Israel, the Human Rights Committee noted that 'the provisions of the Covenant apply to the benefit of the population of the Occupied Territories, for all conduct by the State party's authorities or agents in those territories that affect the enjoyment of rights enshrined in the Covenant and fall within the ambit of State responsibility of Israel under the principles of public international law' (see Concluding Observations/Comments on Israel (1999) (UN Doc. CCPR/C/79/Add. 93), para. 10; Concluding Observations/Comments on Israel (2003) (UN Doc. CCPR/CO/78/ISR), para. 11). The same position is adopted under the International Covenant on Economic, Social and Cultural Rights by the Committee on Economic, Social and Cultural Rights, which expresses the view that 'the State party's obligations under the Covenant apply to all territories and populations under its effective control' (Concluding Observations of the Committee on Economic, Social and Cultural Rights: Israel, 23 May 2003 (E/C.12/1/ Add. 90), at para. 31). This has been spectacularly endorsed by the International Court of Justice:

International Court of Justice, *Legal Consequences of the Construction of a Wall in the Occupied Palestinian Territory*, Advisory Opinion (9 July 2004), I.C.J. Reports 2004, 136, paras. 107–13:

[By Resolution ES-10/14 adopted on 8 December 2003, the General Assembly of the United Nations requested from the International Court of Justice, in accordance with Article 96 of the Charter of the United Nations and pursuant to Article 65 of the Statute of the Court, urgently to render an Advisory Opinion on the following question: 'What are the legal consequences arising from the construction of the wall being built by Israel, the occupying Power, in the Occupied Palestinian Territory, including in and around East Jerusalem, as described in the report of the Secretary-General, considering the rules and principles of international law, including the Fourth Geneva Convention of 1949, and relevant Security Council and General Assembly resolutions?' Part of the opinion relates to the obligations of Israel under the International Covenant on Civil and Political Rights, the International Covenant on Economic, Social and Cultural Rights, and the United Nations Convention on the Rights of the Child. However, Israel denies that the ICCPR and the ICESCR, both of which it has ratified, are applicable to the occupied Palestinian territory. The portions of the Advisory Opinion extracted below express the view of the Court on this issue.]

107. It remains to be determined whether the two international Covenants and the Convention on the Rights of the Child are applicable only on the territories of the States parties thereto or whether they are also applicable outside those territories and, if so, in what circumstances.

108. The scope of application of the International Covenant on Civil and Political Rights is defined by Article 2, paragraph 1, thereof, which provides: 'Each State Party to the present Covenant undertakes to respect and to ensure to all individuals within its territory and subject to its jurisdiction the rights recognized in the present Covenant, without distinction of any kind, such as race, colour, sex, language, religion, political or other opinion, national or social origin, property, birth or other status.'

This provision can be interpreted as covering only individuals who are both present within a State's territory and subject to that State's jurisdiction. It can also be construed as covering both individuals present within a State's territory and those outside that territory but subject to that State's jurisdiction. The Court will thus seek to determine the meaning to be given to this text.

109. The Court would observe that, while the jurisdiction of States is primarily territorial, it may sometimes be exercised outside the national territory. Considering the object and purpose of the International Covenant on Civil and Political Rights, it would seem natural that, even when such is the case, States parties to the Covenant should be bound to comply with its provisions. The constant practice of the Human Rights Committee is consistent with this. Thus, the Committee has found the Covenant applicable where the State exercises its jurisdiction on foreign territory. It has ruled on the legality of acts by Uruguay in cases of arrests carried out by Uruguayan agents in Brazil or Argentina (case No. 52/79, *López Burgos* v. *Uruguay*; case No. 56/79, *Lilian Celiberti de Casariego* v. *Uruguay*). It decided to the same effect in the case of the confiscation of a passport by a Uruguayan consulate in Germany (case No. 106/81, *Montero* v. *Uruguay*).

The *travaux préparatoires* of the Covenant confirm the Committee's interpretation of Article 2 of that instrument. These show that, in adopting the wording chosen, the drafters of the Covenant did not intend to allow States to escape from their obligations when they exercise jurisdiction outside their national territory. They only intended to prevent persons residing abroad from asserting, *vis-à-vis* their State of origin, rights that do not fall within the competence of that State, but of that of the State of residence (see the discussion of the preliminary draft in the Commission on Human Rights, E/CN.4/SR.194, para. 46; and United Nations, *Official Records of the General Assembly, Tenth Session, Annexes*, A/2929, Part II, chap. V, para. 4 (1955)).

110. The Court takes note in this connection of the position taken by Israel, in relation to the applicability of the Covenant, in its communications to the Human Rights Committee, and of the view of the Committee. In 1998, Israel stated that, when preparing its report to the Committee, it had had to face the question 'whether individuals resident in the occupied territories were indeed subject to Israel's jurisdiction' for purposes of the application of the Covenant (CCPR/C/SR.1675, para. 21). Israel took the position that 'the Covenant and similar instruments did not apply directly to the current situation in the occupied territories' (*ibid.*, para. 27).

The Committee, in its concluding observations after examination of the report, expressed concern at Israel's attitude and pointed 'to the long-standing presence of Israel in [the occupied] territories, Israel's ambiguous attitude towards their future status, as well as the exercise of effective jurisdiction by Israeli security forces therein' (CCPR/C/79/Add. 93, para. 10). In 2003 in face of Israel's consistent position, to the effect that 'the Covenant does not apply beyond its own territory, notably in the West Bank and Gaza ...', the Committee reached the following conclusion: 'in the current circumstances, the provisions of the Covenant apply to the benefit of the population of the Occupied Territories, for all conduct by the State party's authorities or agents in those territories that affect the enjoyment of rights enshrined in the Covenant and fall within the ambit of State responsibility of Israel under the principles of public international law' (CCPR/CO/78/ISR, para. 11).

111. In conclusion, the Court considers that the International Covenant on Civil and Political Rights is applicable in respect of acts done by a State in the exercise of its jurisdiction outside its own territory.

112. The International Covenant on Economic, Social and Cultural Rights contains no provision on its scope of application. This may be explicable by the fact that this Covenant guarantees rights which are essentially territorial. However, it is not to be excluded that it applies both to territories over which a State party has sovereignty and to those over which that State exercises territorial jurisdiction. Thus Article 14 makes provision for transitional measures in the case of any State which 'at the time of becoming a Party, has not been able to secure in its metropolitan territory or other territories under its jurisdiction compulsory primary education, free of charge'.

It is not without relevance to recall in this regard the position taken by Israel in its reports to the Committee on Economic, Social and Cultural Rights. In its initial report to the Committee of 4 December 1998, Israel provided 'statistics indicating the enjoyment of the rights enshrined in the Covenant by Israeli settlers in the occupied Territories'. The Committee noted that, according to Israel, 'the Palestinian population within the same jurisdictional areas were excluded from both the report and the protection of the Covenant' (E/C.12/1/Add. 27, para. 8). The Committee expressed its concern in this regard, to which Israel replied in a further report of 19 October 2001 that it has 'consistently maintained that the Covenant does not apply to areas that are not subject to its sovereign territory and jurisdiction' (a formula inspired by the language of the International Covenant on Civil and Political Rights). This position, continued Israel, is 'based on the well-established distinction between human rights and humanitarian law under international law'. It added: 'the Committee's mandate cannot relate to events in the West Bank and the Gaza Strip, inasmuch as they are part and parcel of the context of armed conflict as distinct from a relationship of human rights' (E/1990/6/Add. 32, para. 5). In view of these observations, the Committee reiterated its concern about Israel's position and reaffirmed 'its view that the State party's obligations under the Covenant apply to all territories and populations under its effective control' (E/C.12/1/Add. 90, paras. 15 and 31).

For the reasons explained in paragraph 106 above, the Court cannot accept Israel's view. It would also observe that the territories occupied by Israel have for over 37 years been subject to its territorial jurisdiction as the occupying Power. In the exercise of the powers available to it on this basis, Israel is bound by the provisions of the International Covenant on Economic, Social and Cultural Rights. Furthermore, it is under an obligation not to raise any obstacle to the exercise of such rights in those fields where competence has been transferred to Palestinian authorities.

113. As regards the Convention on the Rights of the Child of 20 November 1989, that instrument contains an Article 2 according to which 'States Parties shall respect and ensure the rights set forth in the ... Convention to each child within their jurisdiction ...' That Convention is therefore applicable within the Occupied Palestinian Territory.

2.1. **Question for discussion: extending the applicability of human rights treaties to territories occupied in violation of international law**

1. Is there any risk in extending the applicability of human rights treaties to all territories occupied by a State party, even in violation of international law? Could this have the paradoxical effect of reinforcing the camp of those, within the occupying State concerned, who wish the occupation to become permanent and the control over the occupied territory more complete (see for instance the *Al-Skeini* case discussed below, in section 2.1. of this chapter)? Is there any way to mitigate this potential impact? Would it be more advisable to treat 'jurisdiction', rather than in an all-or-nothing fashion, along a sliding scale, with the scope of human rights obligations being more or less extended, depending on the degree of military occupation and, for instance, on the question of whether or not the Occupying Power also manages the educational or health systems? Or should a distinction be made between the imposition of obligations to respect human rights, and the imposition of obligations to protect and to fulfill human rights (for these different categories of State obligations, see chapter 3, section 1)?

2. In *Loizidou*, what seems to be the main reason for extending the applicability of the European Convention on Human Rights to the northern part of Cyprus, occupied by the Turkish armed forces since 1974? If the main concern is that the population in that part of the island would be deprived of the protection of the ECHR which it enjoyed before the Turkish invasion, does it mean, *a contrario*, that if the occupied territory had been located outside the territory of the Member States of the Council of Europe, the ECHR should not have been found applicable? Consider in this respect the discussion in section 2.1. of this chapter, and particularly the characterization, in the decision adopted by the European Court of Human Rights in the *Bankovic* case, of the ECHR as operating 'in an essentially regional context and notably in the legal space (*espace juridique*) of the Contracting States' (para. 80).

1.2 The inability of the State to control all the national territory

It has been recalled that, where a State exercised on a foreign territory a form of control comparable to that of a territorial sovereign, assuming the governmental powers generally associated therewith, the situations occurring on that territory should be considered to fall under its 'jurisdiction' in the meaning of Article 1 ECHR or of other equivalent provisions of other human rights treaties. In their partly dissenting opinion to the judgment of the European Court of Human Rights in *Ilascu and others* v. *Moldova and Russia*, Judge Sir Nicolas Bratza, joined by Judges Rozakis, Hedigan, Thomassen and Pantîru, applying this logic *a contrario*, take the view that 'the presumption that persons within the territory of a State are within its "jurisdiction" for Convention purposes is a rebuttable one and, exceptionally, the responsibility of a State will not be engaged in respect of acts in breach of the Convention which occur within its territory' (judgment of 8 July 2004; for a more detailed discussion of this case, see also below, section 2.2.). In both situations, 'jurisdiction' thus would derive from control (on the idea that responsibility follows control in the law of State responsibility, see C. Eagleton, 'International Organization and the Law of Responsibility', *Recueil des cours*, 76 (1950), 385). Far from being determinative, then, the fact that a particular event occurs on the national territory only would serve to establish a *presumption of control*: 'jurisdiction' should extend to the situations effectively under the control of the State, and in which the State may ensure the protection of the full range of the rights protected under the Convention; but it should be limited, conversely, where a State is *de facto* unable to exercise its governmental powers on some portions of the national territory.

Indeed, this was the position adopted by the European Court of Human Rights in the 2001 case of *Cyprus* v. *Turkey*, where the Court justified reiterating its conclusion that northern Cyprus was under the 'jurisdiction' of Turkey 'having regard to the ... *continuing inability [of the Government of Cyprus] to exercise their Convention obligations in northern Cyprus*, [so that] any other finding would result in a regrettable vacuum in the system of human-rights protection in the territory in question by removing from individuals there the benefit of the Convention's fundamental safeguards and their right to call a High Contracting Party to account for violation of their rights in proceedings before the Court' (Eur. Ct. H.R. (GC), *Cyprus* v. *Turkey* (Appl. No. 25781/94), judgment of 10 May 2001, §78, E.C.H.R. 2001–IV (emphasis added)). That statement seemed to imply, first, that the 'jurisdiction' of a State party to the Convention could not be considered to extend to the whole of the national territory if, on certain portions of that territory, the State is unable in fact to exercise its control in order to effectively guarantee the rights and freedoms set forth in the Convention; second, that the notion of 'jurisdiction' is an all-or-nothing concept, in the sense that any single event falls under the jurisdiction either of State A or of State B, depending on which State effectively could have controlled the event and, therefore, may be held internationally responsible for not having ensured compliance with the rights and freedoms recognized under the Convention. However, this view seems to be challenged by the judgment delivered by the European Court of Human Rights in the case of *Ilascu and others* v. *Moldova and Russia*. Although the Court finds that 'the Moldovan Government, the only legitimate government of the Republic of Moldova under international law, *does not exercise authority over part of its territory*, namely that part which is under the effective control of the [Moldavian Republic of Transdniestria]' [emphasis added], the Court does not conclude therefrom that – it being impossible for Moldova to exercise its jurisdiction on the said territory – this State may not be held responsible for what occurs in the region concerned. Instead, the Court considers that '*even in the absence of effective control over the Transdniestrian region*, Moldova still has a positive obligation under Article 1 of the Convention to take the diplomatic, economic, judicial or other measures that it is in its power to take and are in accordance with international law to secure to the applicants the rights guaranteed by the Convention' (paras. 330–1) [emphasis added]. In the approach the Court took to the Cypriot cases, jurisdiction was an all-or-nothing concept, which therefore could constitute a threshold question to be answered before examining whether the alleged violation may be attributed to the State and whether the State has violated its obligations under the Convention. In *Ilascu and others*, jurisdiction appears as a relative concept, a matter of degree determining the scope of the obligations of the State concerned:

European Court of Human Rights (GC), *Ilascu and others* v. *Moldova and Russia* (Appl. No. 48787/99), judgment of 8 July 2004, para. 333:

[W]here a Contracting State is prevented from exercising its authority over the whole of its territory by a constraining *de facto* situation, such as obtains when a separatist regime is set up, whether or not this is accompanied by military occupation by another State, it does not thereby cease to have jurisdiction within the meaning of Article 1 of the Convention over that part of its territory temporarily subject to a local authority sustained by rebel forces or by another State.

Nevertheless such a factual situation *reduces the scope of that jurisdiction* [emphasis added] in that the undertaking given by the State under Article 1 must be considered by the Court only in the light of the Contracting State's positive obligations towards persons within its territory. The State in question must endeavour, with all the legal and diplomatic means available to it *vis-à-vis* foreign States and international organisations, to continue to guarantee the enjoyment of the rights and freedoms guaranteed by the Convention.

It will be useful to contrast the *Ilascu and others* judgment with the attitude of the Court in its *Assanidze* v. *Georgia* judgment, delivered by the Grand Chamber only three months earlier. The applicant in this case had been held in custody in the Ajarian Autonomous Republic in Georgia since 1993, after having been arrested and convicted for allegedly illegal financial dealings. Although the Georgian President had granted him a pardon in 1999 suspending the remaining two years of his sentence, he had remained in detention. Indeed, soon after the presidential decree granting the pardon had been adopted, the Ajarian High Court had declared the pardon null and void, and the judgments of the Georgian Supreme Court quashing that latter judgment had been ignored by the local authorities in the Ajarian Autonomous Republic. After the applicant was again convicted on another ground in 2000 by the Ajarian High Court, the Supreme Court of Georgia acquitted him. That acquittal judgment also was never executed, however. Despite all the best efforts of the General Prosecutor's Office of Georgia, the Public Defender, the Georgian Ministry of Justice and the Legal Affairs Committee of the Georgian Parliament, and even the President of the Republic of Georgia, seeking the immediate release of Mr Assanidzé, the local authorities concerned in the Ajarian Autonomous Republic refused to comply, apparently believing that he has been conspiring against the President of the Autonomous Republic.

When the question whether Mr Assanidzé was being subjected to arbitrary detention in violation of Article 5(1) ECHR was presented to the European Court of Human Rights, the Georgian Government 'accepted that the Ajarian Autonomous Republic was an integral part of Georgia and that the matters complained of were within the jurisdiction of the Georgian Republic', and it moreover insisted that 'Georgian law was duly applied in the [Ajarian Autonomous Republic] and that, apart from the present case, with its strong political overtones, there was no problem of judicial cooperation between the central authorities and the local Ajarian authorities' (paras. 133–4 of the judgment). The Court took the view that the events complained of by the applicant fell under the 'jurisdiction' of the Georgian State:

European Court of Human Rights (GC), *Assanidze* v. *Georgia* (Appl. No. 71503/01) judgment of 8 April 2004, at paras. 139–42:

139. The Ajarian Autonomous Republic is indisputably an integral part of the territory of Georgia and subject to its competence and control. In other words, there is a presumption of competence. The Court must now determine whether there is valid evidence to rebut that presumption.

140. In that connection, the Court notes, firstly, that Georgia has ratified the Convention for the whole of its territory. Furthermore, it is common ground that the Ajarian Autonomous Republic has no separatist aspirations and that no other State exercises effective overall control there (see, by converse implication, *Ilascu, Lesco, Ivantoc and Petrov-Popa* v. *Moldova and the Russian Federation* [GC], No. 48787/99, decision of 4 July 2001; and *Loizidou* v. *Turkey* (preliminary objections) [judgment of 23 March 1995, Series A No. 310]). On ratifying the Convention, Georgia did not make any specific reservation under Article 57 of the Convention with regard to the Ajarian Autonomous Republic or to difficulties in exercising its jurisdiction over that territory. Such a reservation would in any event have been ineffective, as the case law precludes territorial exclusions (*Matthews* v. *United Kingdom* [GC], No. 24833/94, ECHR 1999-I, §29) other than in the instance referred to in Article 56 §1 of the Convention (dependent territories).

141. Unlike the American Convention on Human Rights of 22 November 1969 (Article 28), the European Convention does not contain a 'federal clause' limiting the obligations of the federal State for events occurring on the territory of the states forming part of the federation. Moreover, since Georgia is not a federal State, the Ajarian Autonomous Republic is not part of a federation. It forms an entity which – like others (the Autonomous Republic of Abkhazia and, before 1991, the Autonomous District of South Ossetia) – must have an autonomous status ..., which is a different matter. Besides, even if an implied federal clause similar in content to that of Article 28 of the American Convention were found to exist in the European Convention (which is impossible in practice), it could not be construed as releasing the federal State from all responsibility, since it requires the federal State to 'immediately take suitable measures, in accordance with its constitution ..., to the end that the [states forming part of the federation] may adopt appropriate provisions for the fulfillment of [the] Convention'.

142. Thus, the presumption referred to in paragraph 139 above is seen to be correct. Indeed, for reasons of legal policy – the need to maintain equality between the State Parties and to ensure the effectiveness of the Convention – it could not be otherwise. But for the presumption, the applicability of the Convention could be selectively restricted to parts only of the territory of certain State Parties, thus rendering the notion of effective human-rights protection underpinning the entire Convention meaningless while, at the same time, allowing discrimination between the State Parties, that is to say beween those which accepted the application of the Convention over the whole of their territory and those which did not.

Box 2.1. **The 'federal clause' of the American Convention on Human Rights and the implementation of human rights instruments in States with a federal structure**

In the *Assanidze* v. *Georgia* judgment of 8 April 2004, the European Court of Human Rights refers to Article 28 of the American Convention on Human Rights (ACHR), which states in its relevant part (Art. 28 §3 is omitted):

Article 28. Federal Clause

1. Where a State Party is constituted as a federal state, the national government of such State Party shall implement all the provisions of the Convention over whose subject matter it exercises legislative and judicial jurisdiction.

2. With respect to the provisions over whose subject matter the constituent units of the federal state have jurisdiction, the national government shall immediately take suitable measures, in accordance with its constitution and its laws, to the end that the competent authorities of the constituent units may adopt appropriate provisions for the fulfillment of this Convention.

This 'federal clause' was inserted into the ACHR at the insistence of the US delegation to the San Jose Conference. The United States saw this clause as a means to ensure that the implementation of the ACHR would remain compatible with the existing allocation of competences between the Union and the States. As the US delegation explained to the Secretary of State following the Conference, the federal clause would ensure that the ACHR 'does not obligate the US Government to *exercise* jurisdiction over subject matter over which it would not exercise authority in the absence of the Convention. The US is merely obligated to take suitable measures to the end that state and local authorities may adopt provisions for the fulfillment of this Convention. Suitable measures could consist of recommendations to the states, for example. The determination of what measures are suitable is a matter of internal decision. The Convention does not require enactment of legislation bringing new subject matter within the federal ambit' (*Report of the United States Delegation to the Inter-American Conference on Protection of Human Rights, San Jose, Costa Rica, 9–22 November 1969*, Department of State, 1970, at p. 37). The United States were guided by a similar intent when, upon ratifying the ICCPR, they included the following 'understanding', which in practice should be treated as a reservation:

Reservations, understandings, and declarations entered by the United States upon ratifying the International Covenant on Civil and Political Rights (8 June 1992):

That the United States understands that this Covenant shall be implemented by the Federal Government to the extent that it exercises legislative and judicial jurisdiction over the matters covered therein, and otherwise by the state and local governments; to the extent that state and local governments exercise jurisdiction over such matters, the Federal Government shall take measures appropriate to the Federal system to the end that the competent authorities of the state or local governments may take appropriate measures for the fulfillment of the Covenant.

However, neither the federal clause inserted into the ACHR nor, for that matter, the 'understanding' appended to the ratification by the United States of the ICCPR, may affect the law of international responsibility, that clearly attributes to the State itself (represented by the central government) any acts or omissions of the constituent entities, without it being allowable for the central government to invoke the allocation of competences under the domestic legislation to limit the scope of its international obligations. This is the position overwhelmingly defended in legal opinion (see, e.g. H. Gross Espiell, 'La Convention américaine et la Convention européenne des droits de l'homme – Analyse comparative', *Recueil des cours*, VI, 218 (1989), at 383–7; T. Buergenthal, 'El Sistema Interamericano para la Protección de los Derechos Humanos', *Anuario Juridico Interamericano 1981*, (Washington: OAS, 1982), 127–8):

Inter-American Court of Human Rights, Case of *Garrido and Baigorria* v. *Argentina*, judgment of 27 August 1998 (Reparations and Costs), Series C No. 39, paras. 45–6:
45. Argentina invoked the federal clause or made reference to the federal structure of the State on three different occasions in this dispute. First, when the merits of the matter were being examined, the State argued that, by virtue of the federal clause, any responsibility in the instant case was imputable to the Province of Mendoza, not to the State. Argentina then backed away from this argument and expressly acknowledged its international responsibility at the hearing of February 1, 1996. The State invoked the federal clause a second time when negotiating the May 31, 1996 reparations agreement. At the time, the Province of Mendoza was party to the agreement, not the Argentine Republic, even though the latter had already acknowledged its international responsibility. The Court, however, held that the agreement did not constitute an agreement between the parties since it was not signed by the Argentine Republic, which was the party in the case. Finally, at the January 20, 1998 hearing, Argentina argued that it would have difficulties adopting certain measures given the federal structure of the State.

46. When a federal state's constituent units have jurisdiction over human rights matters, Article 28 of the Convention makes provision for said federal state becoming a party to the Convention. However, from the time of its approval and ratification of the Convention, Argentina has conducted itself as if the federal State had jurisdiction over human rights matters. Hence, it can hardly argue the contrary now, as this would imply a breach of the principle of estoppel. As for the 'difficulties' invoked by the State at the January 20, 1998 hearing, the Court should note that the case law, which has stood unchanged for more than a century, holds that a State cannot plead its federal structure to avoid complying with an international obligation (*cf.* arbitral award of July 26. VII. 1875 in the *Montijo* case, La Pradelle-Politis, *Recueil des arbitrages internationaux*, Paris, 1954, t. III, p. 675; decision of the France-Mexico Mixed Claims Commission of 7.VI.1929 in the *Hyacinthe Pellat* case, *UN Report of International Arbitral Awards*, vol. V, p. 536).

As noted by Hennebel, although this interpretation does not seem in conformity with the intent guiding the insertion of Article 28 in the ACHR, it nevertheless avoids two major difficulties: it ensures that the bodies of the Inter-American human rights system do not have to decide whether the federal government or State or local governments are competent, under the allocation of competences provided for in the domestic constitutional system, for taking the measures required for the implementation of the Convention; and it ensures that the State will not be allowed to invoke its domestic constitution in order to limit the scope of its international responsibility (L. Hennebel, *La Convention américaine des droits de l'homme. Mécanismes de protection et étendue des droits et libertés* (Brussels: Bruylant, 2007), p. 107; see also, for a general study of the implementation of the ACHR by States with a federal structure, A. E. Dulitzky, 'La Convención Americana sobre Derechos Humanos y los Estados Federales: algunas reflexiones', in V. Bazán (ed.), *Defensa de la Constitución. Garantismo y controles. Libro en reconocimiento al Dr German J. Bidart Campos* (Buenos Aires: Ediar, 2003), p. 157). The approach of the Inter-American Court of Human Rights is, of course, consistent with the requirements of international law. As recalled by the Committee on the Rights of the Child:

Committee on the Rights of the Child, General Comment No. 5 (2003), General Measures of Implementation of the Convention on the Rights of the Child (Arts. 4, 42 and 44, para. 6) (CRC/GC/2003/5, 27 November 2003):
[Decentralization, federalization and delegation]
[D]ecentralization of power, through devolution and delegation of government, does not in any way reduce the direct responsibility of the State party's Government to fulfil its obligations to all children within its jurisdiction, regardless of the State structure.

The Committee reiterates that in all circumstances the State which ratified or acceded to the Convention remains responsible for ensuring the full implementation of the Convention throughout the territories under its jurisdiction. In any process of devolution, States parties have to make sure that the devolved authorities do have the necessary financial, human and other resources effectively to discharge responsibilities for the implementation of the Convention. The Governments of States parties must retain powers to require full compliance with the Convention by devolved administrations or local authorities and must establish permanent monitoring mechanisms to ensure that the Convention is respected and applied for all children within its jurisdiction without discrimination. Further, there must be safeguards to ensure that decentralization or devolution does not lead to discrimination in the enjoyment of rights by children in different regions.

The Inter-American Commission and Court of Human Rights have been confronted with situations where the State claimed that it was unable effectively to control more or less substantial portions of the national territory, and that it should therefore not be held responsible for the failure to protect human rights in those areas. In the case of the *Ituango Massacres* v. *Colombia* (judgment of 1 July 2006, Series C, No. 148), the Government presented testimony according to which the territory in which the massacres – carried out by paramilitaries – had taken place could not be effectively controlled by the local army battalion, due to its excessive area (para. 111, c)). The Court did not make any findings of fact on this point, but considered proven that 'paramilitary groups perpetrated successive armed incursions, murdering defenseless civilians' and that the 'State's responsibility for these acts, which occurred in the context of a pattern of similar massacres, arises from the acts of omission, acquiescence and collaboration by members of the law enforcement bodies based in this municipality' (para. 132).

The Inter-American Commission, under its broader mandate to monitor the situation of human rights in the Americas (see chapter 11, section 2.1.), has regularly included a section in its annual reports on the situation of human rights in selected countries. This is carried out as a follow-up activity on previous special reports on the situation of human rights in a given country, assessing compliance with recommendations. Four criteria are used by the Commission to determine which countries are to be the object of this reporting: (i) the lack of fair and regular elections in the country; (ii) the adoption of emergency powers and the suspension of rights; (iii) the existence of serious accusations that the State is engaged in mass and gross violations of human rights; and (iv) the fact that a State is in a transition phase, moving from any of the above situations. In its consideration of the situation of human rights in Colombia, the Commission was confronted with the fact that the Colombian State did not exercise full *de facto* control over parts of its territory or over all the actors in the internal armed conflict:

Inter-American Commission of Human Rights, Annual Report 1996, OEA/Ser.L/V/ II.95, Doc. 7 rev., 14 March 1997

CHAPTER V
HUMAN RIGHTS DEVELOPMENTS IN THE REGION
COLOMBIA

VII. Paramilitaries

46. The Commission has received credible information from individuals and organizations in the private and public sectors indicating that elements of the Colombian armed forces support and collaborate with the paramilitary groups in carrying out their abusive activities ... The Commission considers to be extremely important the information indicating that state agents participate in the activities of the paramilitaries. That information will be carefully analyzed by the Commission.

47. Nor has the Colombian State acted adequately to control the paramilitary groups. A cloak of impunity has almost completely protected those groups and the members of the security forces allegedly involved with them. The problems described in relation to the military justice system and the excessively broad interpretation of the crimes which should be heard in that system contribute to the problem ...

VIII. The activities of irregular armed groups

53. The extremely difficult conditions caused by the various guerrilla movements in Colombia continued in 1996. These groups committed numerous violent acts, many of which constitute violations of humanitarian law norms applicable to the internal armed conflict in Colombia. These acts included killings outside of armed conflict, kidnapping for ransom, indiscriminate use of land mines and oil pipeline bombings. Guerrillas often carried out extrajudicial executions and other abuses against civilians on the grounds that their victims were either informants for the military or collaborators of the paramilitary groups. The two largest guerrilla groups, the Armed Revolutionary Forces of Colombia ('FARC') and the National Liberation Army ('ELN'), commanded an estimated 10,000 to 15,000 guerrillas organized in various fronts ...

55. Although the Commission does not have the competence under the American Convention to address individual cases alleging violations of rights protected in the Convention which do not involve State responsibility, the Commission has repeatedly condemned the abuses committed by the guerrilla groups in Colombia ...

XII. Conclusions

80. The Commission fully comprehends that Colombia faces extremely difficult circumstances at this time and that the State of Colombia is not directly responsible for all of the harm caused to its citizens. However, the State of Colombia is responsible for human rights abuses committed by its agents using their position of authority, even when those agents act outside the sphere of their authority or violate internal law, as well as for comparable acts committed by private persons which are tolerated or acquiesced in by the State. The Commission also notes that the State may also incur international responsibility for the illicit acts of private individuals or groups when the State fails to adopt the necessary measures to prevent the acts and/or where it fails to properly investigate and sanction those responsible for committing the acts and to provide adequate compensation to the victims ...

XIII. Recommendations

83. The Colombian State should take all appropriate measures to ensure that the right to life and other fundamental guarantees of all of its citizens are respected. The State should take actions to prevent its agents from committing abuses and should provide for training of its agents in the proper observance of the norms relating to human rights and humanitarian law. In addition, the Commission calls on the State to combat, dismantle and disarm all paramilitary and other proscribed self-defense groups. Finally, the State should investigate and sanction all persons responsible for committing violations of rights.

The position of irregular armed groups was discussed further in the third report on the situation of Human Rights in Colombia:

Inter-American Commission of Human Rights, Report on the Human Rights Situation in Colombia of 26 February 1999 (OEA/ Ser.L/V/II.102, Doc. 9 rev. 1), chapter IV, 'Violence and Violations of International Human Rights and Humanitarian Law'

B. Legal framework for the analysis
1. Role and competence of the Commission
3. Under the individual petition procedure set forth in its Statute and the American Convention on Human Rights, the Commission's jurisdiction extends only to situations where the international responsibility of a member State is at issue. Thus, the IACHR is authorized to receive, investigate and decide cases lodged against member States for the acts or omissions of their agents and organs that allegedly violate the human rights guaranteed in the American Convention or the American Declaration of the Rights and Duties of Man (the 'Declaration'). The Commission's jurisdiction also encompasses cases of transgressions of these same rights by private persons or groups who are, in effect, State agents or when such transgressions by private actors are acquiesced in, tolerated, or condoned by the State.

4. The Commission as well as the Court have also consistently pointed out that the State has a duty under the American Convention and the Declaration to prevent and to investigate acts of violence committed by private parties and to prosecute and punish the perpetrators accordingly.

The Commission thus may process individual cases alleging the failure of a State to comply with this duty. At the same time, the Commission recognizes that in situations of civil strife the State cannot always prevent, much less be held responsible for, the harm to individuals and destruction of private property occasioned by the hostile acts of its armed opponents.

5. As noted in its two previous country reports on Colombia, OAS member States opted deliberately not to give the Commission jurisdiction to investigate or hear individual complaints concerning illicit acts of private persons or groups for which the State is not internationally responsible. If it were to act on such complaints, the Commission would be in flagrant breach of its mandate, and, by according these persons or groups the same treatment and status that a State receives as a party to a complaint, it would infringe the sovereign rights and prerogatives of the State concerned ...

8. The Commission has been equally clear that when organized private groups take up arms to overthrow an elected government, the State has a right under domestic and international law to use legal and appropriate military force to put down such insurrection in order to defend its citizenry and the constitutional order. However, during such situations of internal hostilities, the Commission has received from Colombia and other OAS member States numerous complaints alleging serious violations of the fundamental rights guaranteed in the American Convention and Declaration arising out of the conduct of military operations by State security forces and its other agents.

2.2. Questions for discussion: 'jurisdiction' and the scope of the obligation to protect human rights

1. According to Article 50 of the International Covenant on Civil and Political Rights, the provisions of the Covenant 'shall extend to all parts of federal States without any limitations or exceptions' (on the circumstances of the introduction of this rule, see M. Sorensen, 'Federal States and the International Protection of Human Rights', *American Journal of International Law*, 46 (1952), 207). Does this lead to an approach fundamentally different from that of the American Convention on Human Rights, taking into account the 'federal clause' inserted into this instrument?

2. The examples of guerillas or paramilitary groups, sometimes occupying part of the national territory, and which the Government alleges it is unable to control, illustrates the continuity between (1) the question of 'jurisdiction' and the relationship of 'jurisdiction' to national territory, and (2) the question of the scope of the obligation of the State to exercise due diligence in seeking to protect the human rights of individuals under its jurisdiction (on this obligation, see chapter 4). Are these different framings interchangeable? Is it the same thing to assert that a State's jurisdiction does not extend to situations which are outside its control (for instance, when a secessionist government is established, or when a guerilla controls part of the territory), and to assert that a State is unable effectively to protect human rights in certain situations, for example because its military cannot be present all over a large territory, or because of budgetary constraints? If not, where exactly does the difference reside between these two arguments?

2 EXTRATERRITORIAL OBLIGATIONS UNDER INTERNATIONAL HUMAN RIGHTS LAW

This section examines whether there are situations in which a State may be under an obligation to comply with human rights outside its national territory. Three scenarios are distinguished. In the first scenario, a State exercises executive powers outside its borders, by sending State agents abroad, either with the assent of the territorially sovereign State, or without such assent (section 2.1.). In the second scenario, a State may be able to influence situations located outside its national territory, for instance by adopting extraterritorial legislation or by empowering its courts to hear claims related to such situations: the question arises whether there are circumstances in which an obligation may be imposed on the State to take such action, in order to discharge a duty to protect human rights (section 2.2.). Finally, in the third scenario, one State is asked to assist another State, or the efforts of the international community, in improving the situation of human rights elsewhere, particularly where a lack of budgetary resources or the absence of technology transfers create an obstacle to development (section 2.3.). In a very broad meaning of the expression, all three scenarios raise the question of whether or not international human rights entail 'extraterritorial' obligations. But depending on the scenario we explore, the answers will differ markedly.

2.1 The responsibility of States for the activities of State agents operating outside the national borders

A State may be found responsible for the acts of its agents, which are in violation of its international obligations. This rule of attribution has prevailed, in general, over a narrow understanding of the applicability *ratione loci* of the human rights treaties, which would restrict their application to the national territory of the State concerned.

Human Rights Committee, General Comment No. 31, *The Nature of the General Legal Obligation Imposed on States Parties to the Covenant*, CCPR/C/21/Rev.1/ Add. 13, adopted on 29 March 2004 (2,187th meeting), para. 10:

10. States Parties are required by article 2, paragraph 1, to respect and to ensure the Covenant rights to all persons who may be within their territory and to all persons subject to their jurisdiction. This means that a State party must respect and ensure the rights laid down in the Covenant to anyone within the power or effective control of that State Party, even if not situated within the territory of the State Party. As indicated in General Comment 15 ... (1986), the enjoyment of Covenant rights is not limited to citizens of States Parties but must also be available to all individuals, regardless of nationality or statelessness, such as asylum seekers, refugees, migrant workers and other persons, who may find themselves in the territory or subject to the jurisdiction of the State Party. This principle also applies to those within the power or effective control of the forces of a State Party acting outside its territory, regardless of the circumstances in which such power or effective control was obtained, such as forces constituting a national contingent of a State Party assigned to an international peace-keeping or peace-enforcement operation.

This position had first been announced by the Human Rights Committee in the twin cases of *Lopez Burgos* v. *Uruguay* (Communication No. 52/1979 (final views 29 July 1981 (thirteenth session)), at para. 12.3, and of *Celeberti de Casariego* v. *Uruguay* (Communication No. 56/1979 (final views of 29 July 1981 (thirteenth session)), at para. 10.3. In the first of these cases, Mr Lopez Burgos, a trade-union leader in Uruguay, had been detained between December 1974 and May 1975 before being forced into exile by the harassment of the Uruguayan authorities. He was accepted as a refugee in Argentina in September 1975. On 13 July 1976, according to the communication, he was kidnapped in Buenos Aires by members of the 'Uruguayan security and intelligence forces' who were aided by Argentine para-military groups, and was secretly detained in Buenos Aires for about two weeks. Together with several other Uruguayan nationals, he was then illegally and clandestinely transported to Uruguay, where he was detained incommunicado by the special security forces at a secret prison for three months. During his detention of approximately four months both in Argentina and Uruguay, he was continuously subjected to physical and mental torture and other cruel, inhuman or degrading treatment.

Human Rights Committee, *Sergio Euben Lopez Burgos* v. *Uruguay*, Communication No. 52/79 (6 June 1979), Supp. No. 40 (A/36/40) at 176 (1981) (final views of 29 July 1981):

12.1 The Human Rights Committee ... observes that although the arrest and initial detention and mistreatment of Lopez Burgos allegedly took place on foreign territory, the Committee is not barred either by virtue of article 1 of the Optional Protocol ('... individuals subject to its jurisdiction ...') or by virtue of article 2 (1) of the Covenant ('... individuals within its territory and subject to its jurisdiction ...') from considering these allegations, together with the claim of subsequent abduction into Uruguayan territory, inasmuch as these acts were perpetrated by Uruguayan agents acting on foreign soil.

12.2 The reference in article 1 of the Optional Protocol to 'individuals subject to its jurisdiction' does not affect the above conclusion because the reference in that article is not to the place where the violation occurred, but rather to the relationship between the individual and the State in relation to a violation of any of the rights set forth in the Covenant, wherever they occurred.

12.3 Article 2(1) of the Covenant places an obligation upon a State party to respect and to ensure rights 'to all individuals within its territory and subject to its jurisdiction', but it does not imply that the State party concerned cannot be held accountable for violations of rights under the Covenant which its agents commit upon the territory of another State, whether with the acquiescence of the Government of that State or in opposition to it. According to article 5(1) of the Covenant: '1. Nothing in the present Covenant may be interpreted as implying for any State, group or person any right to engage in any activity or perform any act aimed at the destruction of any of the rights and freedoms recognized herein or at their limitation to a greater extent than is provided for in the present Covenant.'

In line with this, it would be unconscionable to so interpret the responsibility under article 2 of the Covenant as to permit a State party to perpetrate violations of the Covenant on the territory of another State, which violations it could not perpetrate on its own territory.

The same position is adopted within the Inter-American human rights system. Two instances deserve particular mention in this regard. In the *Haitian Interdiction* case (*Case 10.675* v. *United States*, Reports No. 28/93 (decision on admissibility) of 13 October 1993 and 51/96 (decision on the merits) of 13 March 1997), the Inter-American Commission was confronted by the US policy of intercepting Haitian boat people in the high seas and returning them to Haiti. One of the crucial issues regarding the legality of the interdiction was whether or not fundamental rights obligations – including due process, non-discrimination and the right to seek asylum – applied to persons prior to their effective entry into the territory of the United States. On 21 June 1993, the US Supreme Court had ruled, in the case of *Sale, Acting Commissioner, Immigration and Naturalization Service, et al.* v. *Haitian Centers Council, INC., et. al.* (509 U.S. 155 (1993)) that neither US law nor Article 33 of the 1951 Geneva Convention on the Status of Refugees prevented the Government from returning refugees interdicted by the US Navy beyond the territorial waters of the United States. In the merits phase, the Inter-American Commission of Human Rights expressed its disagreement with the Supreme Court's ruling that the non-refoulement provision of the Geneva Convention had no extraterritorial effects (para. 157). Moreover it concluded that by interdicting the asylum-seekers in high seas, the United States had denied them the possibility of seeking asylum in other foreign countries.

Inter-American Commission of Human Rights, *Case 10.675* v. *United States* *(Haitian Interdiction case),* **Report No 51/96 of 13 March 1997:**

151. It is convenient to begin with an analysis of Article XXVII of the American Declaration. Article XXVII of the American Declaration is entitled 'Right of Asylum'. This Article outlines two criteria which are cumulative and both of which must be satisfied in order for the right to exist. The first criterion is that the right to seek and receive asylum on foreign territory must be in 'accordance with the laws of each country', that is the country in which asylum is sought. The second criterion is that the right to seek asylum in foreign territory must be 'in accordance with international agreements'.

152. The *travaux préparatoires* show that the first draft in the Article did not have the phrase 'in accordance with the laws of each country'. That phrase was added in the Sixth Session of the Sixth Commission's of the Inter-American Juridical Committee at the Ninth International Conference of American States in Bogota in 1948, and discussed in the Seventh Session of the Sixth Commission, to preserve the states sovereignty in questions of asylum.

153. The effect of the dual cumulative criteria in Article XXVII is that if the right is established in international but not in domestic law, it is not a right which is recognized by Article XXVII of the Declaration ...

155. The Commission will now address the question of the application of the two criteria and will deal first with the criterion of conformity with 'international agreements'. The relevant international agreement is the Convention Relating to the Status of Refugees 1951 and the 1967 Protocol Relating to the Status of Refugees to which the United States is a party. The Convention establishes certain criteria for the qualification of a person as a 'refugee'. The Commission believes that international law has developed to a level at which there is recognition of a right

of a person seeking refuge to a hearing in order to determine whether that person meets the criteria in the Convention.

156. An important provision of the 1951 Convention is Article 33(1) which provides that: 'No Contracting State shall expel or return ("refouler") a refugee in any manner whatsoever to the frontiers of territories where his life or freedom would be threatened on account of his race, religion, nationality, membership of a particular social group or political opinion.' The Supreme Court of the United States, in the case of *Sale, Acting Commissioner, Immigration and Naturalization Service, et al.* v. *Haitian Centers Council, INC., et al.*, No. 92–344, decided June 21, 1993, construed this provision as not being applicable in a situation where a person is returned from the high seas to the territory from which he or she fled. Specifically, the Supreme Court held that the principle of non-refoulement in Article 33 did not apply to the Haitians interdicted on the high seas and not in the United States' territory.

157. The Commission does not agree with this finding. The Commission shares the view advanced by the United Nations High Commissioner for Refugees in its *amicus curiae* brief in its argument before the Supreme Court, that Article 33 had no geographical limitations.

158. However, the finding by the Commission that the United States Government has breached its treaty obligations in respect of Article 33 does not resolve the issue as to whether the United States Government is in breach of Article XXVII of the American Declaration because the cumulative effect of the dual criteria in that Article is that, for the right to seek and receive asylum in foreign territory to exist, it must not only be in accordance with international agreements, but in accordance with the domestic laws of the country in which refuge is sought.

159. After several judicial hearings in respect of the Haitian boat people the United States' domestic law in this matter was finally settled by the Supreme Court in the case of *Sale, Acting Commissioner, Immigration and Naturalization Service, et al.* v. *Haitian Centers Council, INC., et al.*, No. 92–344, decided June 21, 1993. In its reply of January 19, 1995, to the Commission's specific question on the meaning of the phrase 'in accordance with the laws of each country', the United States Government stated that: '... United States law on the question of the "right to asylum" of Haitians is perfectly clear: Haitians interdicted by the United States at sea are not entitled to enter the United States or to avoid repatriation to Haiti, even if they are refugees under the standards of the 1951 Refugee Convention or the standards of US law.' ...

161. The Commission has also noted that the petitioners ... in response to the Commission's question on the meaning of Article XXVII stated that: 'Even if it is true, as the United States Supreme Court decided, that the President possesses inherent constitutional authority to turn back from the United States Government's gates any alien, such a power does not authorize the interdiction and summary return of refugees who are far from, and by no means necessarily heading to the United States. The United States Government's interdiction program had the effect of prohibiting the Haitians from gaining entry into The Bahamas, Jamaica, Cuba, Mexico, the Cayman Islands, or any other country in which they might seek safe haven. It has never been established how many of the interdicted Haitians were headed for the United States. The Justice Department's own Office of Legal Counsel stated in 1981, "experience suggests that" only "two thirds of the [Haitian] vessels are headed toward the United States" ...'

162. It is noted that Article XXVII provides for a right to seek and receive asylum in 'foreign territory'. A question however arises, whether the action of the United States in interdicting Haitians on the high seas is not in breach of their right under Article XXVII of the American Declaration to seek and receive asylum in some foreign territory other than the United States.

This statement from the petitioners has not been contested or contradicted by the United States. The Commission has noted that subsequent to the coup ousting President Aristide from office on September 30, 1991, during the interdiction period, Hatian refugees exercised their right to seek and receive asylum in other foreign territories, such as the Dominican Republic, Jamaica, Bahamas, Cuba, (provided asylum to 3,851 Haitians during 1992) Venezuela, Suriname, Honduras, the Turks and Caico Islands and other Latin American countries.

163. The Commission finds that the United States summarily interdicted and repatriated Haitian refugees to Haiti without making an adequate determination of their status, and without granting them a hearing to ascertain whether they qualified as 'refugees'. The Commission also finds that the dual criteria test of the right to 'seek' and 'receive' asylum as provided by Articles XXVII in 'foreign territory' (in accordance with the laws of each country and with international agreements) of the American Declaration has been satisfied. Therefore, the Commission finds that the United States breached Article XXVII of the American Declaration.

The second case followed the invasion of Grenada by US troops. In *Coard* v. *United States*, the Inter-American Commission on Human Rights was concerned with a case in which citizens of Grenada complained that they had been illegally detained and mistreated by the US forces who invaded the island. The Commission held that the United States was exercising extra-territorial jurisdiction for the purposes of the American Declaration of the Rights and Duties of Man (when read alongside Article 1 of the American Convention on Human Rights which contains positive obligations on the part of States Parties to all persons 'subject to their jurisdiction'). It said:

Inter-American Commission of Human Rights, *Coard* v. *United States*, Report No 109/9 of 29 September 1999 (DC 215–6):

37. While the extraterritorial application of the American Declaration has not been placed at issue by the parties, the Commission finds it pertinent to note that, under certain circumstances, the exercise of its jurisdiction over acts with an extraterritorial locus will not only be consistent with but required by the norms which pertain. The fundamental rights of the individual are proclaimed in the Americas on the basis of the principles of equality and non-discrimination – 'without distinction as to race, nationality, creed or sex'. Given that individual rights inhere simply by virtue of a person's humanity, each American State is obliged to uphold the protected rights of any person subject to its jurisdiction. While this most commonly refers to persons within a State's territory, it may, under given circumstances, refer to conduct with an extraterritorial locus where the person concerned is present in the territory of one State, but subject to the control of another State – usually through the acts of the latter's agents abroad. In principle, the inquiry turns not on the presumed victim's nationality or presence within a particular geographic area, but on whether, under the specific circumstances, the State observed the rights of a person subject to its authority and control.

In effect, this position equates the question of whether an individual is under the jurisdiction of the State with the question of attribution: an individual may be said to be under the jurisdiction of the State, in this view, to the extent that this individual has been directly affected by the act or the omission of the State. But others would see the question of 'jurisdiction' as defining the scope of the State's obligations, and thus as having to be treated as distinct from the question of attribution, as part of the broader inquiry as to whether the State has breached its international obligation. According to this second view, whether or not the alleged victim of the violation was under the jurisdiction of the defending State when the violation was committed thus precedes the two questions which Article 2 of the International Law Commission's Articles on State Responsibility defines as the two constituent elements of an internationally wrongful act of a State, i.e. first, whether the measure complained of (an act or an omission) may be attributed to that State and second, whether that measure constitutes a breach of an international obligation of that State. In this view, far from being a substitute for a particular situation falling under the 'jurisdiction' of the State, the question of imputability only is raised at a second stage, after it has been determined that the event occurred under that State's 'jurisdiction'. 'Jurisdiction' and 'imputability' therefore appear as separate and independent conditions for the existence of State responsibility.

While cases such as *Lopez Burgos* or *Coard* seem to point towards the first view, this understanding has sometimes been challenged. Consider the two following cases by the European Court of Human Rights:

European Court of Human Rights (GC), *Bankovic and others* v. Bel*gium and 16 Other States* (Appl. No. 52207/99), decision (inadmissibility) of 12 December 2001, paras. 54–81:

[The applicants were victims or family members of victims of the bombing by the NATO forces of the Serbian Radio and Television (RTS) buildings in Belgrade, on 23 April 1999, as part of the air strikes campaign launched on 24 March 1999 against former Yugoslavia (Operation Allied Force). They invoke the following provisions of the Convention: Article 2 (the right to life), Article 10 (freedom of expression) and Article 13 (the right to an effective remedy). As regards the question of whether the victims were under the 'jurisdiction' of the defending States for the purposes of Article 1 of the European Convention on Human Rights, they argued that 'the extent of the positive obligation under Article 1 of the Convention to secure Convention rights would be proportionate to the level of control in fact exercised'. The Court disagreed:]

54. The Court notes that the real connection between the applicants and the respondent States is the impugned act which, wherever decided, was performed, or had effects, outside of the territory of those States ('the extra-territorial act'). It considers that the essential question to be examined therefore is whether the applicants and their deceased relatives were, as a result of that extra-territorial act, capable of falling within the jurisdiction of the respondent States (*Drozd and Janousek* v. *France and Spain*, judgment of 26 June 1992, Series A No. 240, §91, the ... *Loizidou* judgments (*preliminary objections* and *merits*) [of 23 March 1995 and 18 December 1996], at §64 and §56 respectively, and the *Cyprus* v. *Turkey* judgment of 10 May 2001... at §80).

(a) The applicable rules of interpretation

55. The Court recalls that the Convention must be interpreted in the light of the rules set out in the Vienna Convention 1969 (*Golder* v. *United Kingdom* judgment of 21 February 1975, Series A No. 18, §29).

56. It will, therefore, seek to ascertain the ordinary meaning to be given to the phrase 'within their jurisdiction' in its context and in the light of the object and purpose of the Convention (Article 31 §1 of the Vienna Convention 1969 and, amongst other authorities, *Johnston and others* v. *Ireland*, judgment of 18 December 1986, Series A No. 112, §51). The Court will also consider 'any subsequent practice in the application of the treaty which establishes the agreement of the parties regarding its interpretation' (Article 31 §3(b) of the Vienna Convention 1969 and the above-cited *Loizidou* judgment (*preliminary objections*), at §73).

57. Moreover, Article 31 §3(c) indicates that account is to be taken of 'any relevant rules of international law applicable in the relations between the parties'. More generally, the Court recalls that the principles underlying the Convention cannot be interpreted and applied in a vacuum. The Court must also take into account any relevant rules of international law when examining questions concerning its jurisdiction and, consequently, determine State responsibility in conformity with the governing principles of international law, although it must remain mindful of the Convention's special character as a human rights treaty (*Loizidou* judgment (*merits*) [of 18 December 1996], at §§43 and 52). The Convention should be interpreted as far as possible in harmony with other principles of international law of which it forms part (*Al-Adsani* v. *United Kingdom*, [GC], [judgment of 21 November 2001] No. 35763/97, §60 ...).

58. It is further recalled that the *travaux préparatoires* can also be consulted with a view to confirming any meaning resulting from the application of Article 31 of the Vienna Convention 1969 or to determining the meaning when the interpretation under Article 31 of the Vienna Convention 1969 leaves the meaning 'ambiguous or obscure' or leads to a result which is 'manifestly absurd or unreasonable' (Article 32) ...

(b) The meaning of the words 'within their jurisdiction'

59. As to the 'ordinary meaning' of the relevant term in Article 1 of the Convention, the Court is satisfied that, from the standpoint of public international law, the jurisdictional competence of a State is primarily territorial. While international law does not exclude a State's exercise of jurisdiction extra-territorially, the suggested bases of such jurisdiction (including nationality, flag, diplomatic and consular relations, effect, protection, passive personality and universality) are, as a general rule, defined and limited by the sovereign territorial rights of the other relevant States (Mann, 'The Doctrine of Jurisdiction in International Law', RdC, 1964, Vol. 1; Mann, 'The Doctrine of Jurisdiction in International Law, Twenty Years Later', RdC, 1984, Vol. 1; Bernhardt, *Encyclopaedia of Public International Law*, Edition 1997, Vol. 3, pp. 55–59 'Jurisdiction of States' and Edition 1995, Vol. 2, pp. 337–343 'Extra-territorial Effects of Administrative, Judicial and Legislative Acts'; Oppenheim's *International Law*, 9th Edition 1992 (Jennings and Watts), Vol. 1, §137; P. M. Dupuy, *Droit International Public*, 4th Edition 1998, p. 61; and Brownlie, *Principles of International Law*, 5th Edition 1998, pp. 287, 301 and 312–314).

60. Accordingly, for example, a State's competence to exercise jurisdiction over its own nationals abroad is subordinate to that State's and other States' territorial competence (Higgins, *Problems and Process* (1994), at p. 73; and Nguyen Quoc Dinh, *Droit International Public*, 6th Edition 1999 (Daillier and Pellet), p. 500). In addition, a State may not actually exercise jurisdiction on the territory of another without the latter's consent, invitation or acquiescence,

unless the former is an occupying State in which case it can be found to exercise jurisdiction in that territory, at least in certain respects (Bernhardt, cited above, Vol. 3 at p. 59 and Vol. 2 at pp. 338–340; Oppenheim, cited above, at §137; P. M. Dupuy, cited above, at pp. 64–65; Brownlie, cited above, at p. 313; Cassese, *International Law*, 2001, p. 89; and, most recently, the *Report on the Preferential Treatment of National Minorities by their Kin-States* adopted by the Venice Commission at its 48th Plenary Meeting, Venice, 19–20 October 2001).

61. The Court is of the view, therefore, that Article 1 of the Convention must be considered to reflect this ordinary and essentially territorial notion of jurisdiction, other bases of jurisdiction being exceptional and requiring special justification in the particular circumstances of each case (see, *mutatis mutandis* and in general, Select Committee of Experts on Extraterritorial Criminal Jurisdiction, European Committee on Crime Problems, Council of Europe, *Extraterritorial Criminal Jurisdiction*, Report published in 1990, at pp. 8–30).

62. The Court finds State practice in the application of the Convention since its ratification to be indicative of a lack of any apprehension on the part of the Contracting States of their extra-territorial responsibility in contexts similar to the present case. Although there have been a number of military missions involving Contracting States acting extra-territorially since their ratification of the Convention (*inter alia*, in the Gulf, in Bosnia and Herzegovina and in the FRY [Federal Republic of Yugoslavia]), no State has indicated a belief that its extra-territorial actions involved an exercise of jurisdiction within the meaning of Article 1 of the Convention by making a derogation pursuant to Article 15 of the Convention. The existing derogations were lodged by Turkey and the United Kingdom in respect of certain internal conflicts (in south-east Turkey and Northern Ireland, respectively) and the Court does not find any basis upon which to accept the applicants' suggestion that Article 15 covers all 'war' and 'public emergency' situations generally, whether obtaining inside or outside the territory of the Contracting State. Indeed, Article 15 itself is to be read subject to the 'jurisdiction' limitation enumerated in Article 1 of the Convention.

63. Finally, the Court finds clear confirmation of this essentially territorial notion of jurisdiction in the *travaux préparatoires* which demonstrate that the Expert Intergovernmental Committee replaced the words 'all persons residing within their territories' with a reference to persons 'within their jurisdiction' with a view to expanding the Convention's application to others who may not reside, in a legal sense, but who are, nevertheless, on the territory of the Contracting States ...

64. It is true that the notion of the Convention being a living instrument to be interpreted in light of present-day conditions is firmly rooted in the Court's case law. The Court has applied that approach not only to the Convention's substantive provisions (for example, the *Soering* judgment cited above, at §102 [Eur. Ct. H.R., *Soering* v. *United Kingdom* judgment of 7 July 1989 (see below, section 3.1. of this chapter)]; the *Dudgeon* v. *United Kingdom* judgment of 22 October 1981, Series A No. 45; the *X, Y and Z* v. *United Kingdom* judgment of 22 April 1997, *Reports* 1997-II; *V.* v. *United Kingdom* [GC], No. 24888/94, §72, E.C.H.R. 1999-IX; and *Matthews* v. *United Kingdom* [GC], No. 24833/94, §39, E.C.H.R. 1999-I) but more relevantly to its interpretation of former Articles 25 and 46 concerning the recognition by a Contracting State of the competence of the Convention organs (the above-cited *Loizidou* judgment (*preliminary objections*), at §71). The Court concluded in the latter judgment that former Articles 25 and 46 of the Convention could not be interpreted solely in accordance with the intentions of their authors expressed more than forty years previously to the extent that, even if it had been established that the

restrictions at issue [to the territorial scope of applicability of the European Convention on Human Rights stipulated in a reservation made by Turkey] were considered permissible under Articles 25 and 46 when the Convention was adopted by a minority of the then Contracting Parties, such evidence 'could not be decisive'.

65. However, the scope of Article 1, at issue in the present case, is determinative of the very scope of the Contracting Parties' positive obligations and, as such, of the scope and reach of the entire Convention system of human rights' protection as opposed to the question, under discussion in the Loizidou case (*preliminary objections*), of the competence of the Convention organs to examine a case. In any event, the extracts from the *travaux préparatoires* detailed above constitute a clear indication of the intended meaning of Article 1 of the Convention which cannot be ignored. The Court would emphasise that it is not interpreting Article 1 'solely' in accordance with the *travaux préparatoires* or finding those *travaux* 'decisive'; rather this preparatory material constitutes clear confirmatory evidence of the ordinary meaning of Article 1 of the Convention as already identified by the Court (Article 32 of the Vienna Convention 1969).

66. Accordingly, and as the Court stated in the *Soering* case: 'Article 1 sets a limit, notably territorial, on the reach of the Convention. In particular, the engagement undertaken by a Contracting State is confined to "securing" ("*reconnaître*" in the French text) the listed rights and freedoms to persons within its own "jurisdiction". Further, the Convention does not govern the actions of States not Parties to it, nor does it purport to be a means of requiring the Contracting States to impose Convention standards on other States.'

(c) Extra-territorial acts recognised as constituting an exercise of jurisdiction

67. In keeping with the essentially territorial notion of jurisdiction, the Court has accepted only in exceptional cases that acts of the Contracting States performed, or producing effects, outside their territories can constitute an exercise of jurisdiction by them within the meaning of Article 1 of the Convention.

68. Reference has been made in the Court's case law, as an example of jurisdiction 'not restricted to the national territory' of the respondent State (the *Loizidou* judgment (*preliminary objections*), at §62), to situations where the extradition or expulsion of a person by a Contracting State may give rise to an issue under Articles 2 and/or 3 (or, exceptionally, under Articles 5 and or 6) and hence engage the responsibility of that State under the Convention (the above-cited *Soering* case, at §91, *Cruz Varas and others* v. *Sweden* judgment of 20 March 1991, Series A No. 201, §§69 and 70, and the *Vilvarajah and others* v. *United Kingdom* judgment of 30 October 1991, Series A No. 215, §103).

However, the Court notes that liability is incurred in such cases by an action of the respondent State concerning a person while he or she is on its territory, clearly within its jurisdiction, and that such cases do not concern the actual exercise of a State's competence or jurisdiction abroad (see also, the above-cited *Al-Adsani* judgment, at §39).

69. In addition, a further example noted at paragraph 62 of the *Loizidou* judgment (*preliminary objections*) was the *Drozd and Janousek* case where, citing a number of admissibility decisions by the Commission, the Court accepted that the responsibility of Contracting Parties (France and Spain) could, in principle, be engaged because of acts of their authorities (judges) which produced effects or were performed outside their own territory (*Drozd and Janousek* judgment of 26 June 1992 [see para. 54 above], at §91). In that case, the impugned acts could not, in the circumstances, be attributed to the respondent States because the judges in question

were not acting in their capacity as French or Spanish judges and as the Andorran courts functioned independently of the respondent States.

70. Moreover, in that first *Loizidou* judgment (*preliminary objections*), the Court found that, bearing in mind the object and purpose of the Convention, the responsibility of a Contracting Party was capable of being engaged when as a consequence of military action (lawful or unlawful) it exercised effective control of an area outside its national territory. The obligation to secure, in such an area, the Convention rights and freedoms was found to derive from the fact of such control whether it was exercised directly, through the respondent State's armed forces, or through a subordinate local administration. The Court concluded that the acts of which the applicant complained were capable of falling within Turkish jurisdiction within the meaning of Article 1 of the Convention.

On the merits, the Court found that it was not necessary to determine whether Turkey actually exercised detailed control over the policies and actions of the authorities of the 'Turkish Republic of Northern Cyprus' ('TRNC'). It was obvious from the large number of troops engaged in active duties in northern Cyprus that Turkey's army exercised 'effective overall control over that part of the island'. Such control, according to the relevant test and in the circumstances of the case, was found to entail the responsibility of Turkey for the policies and actions of the 'TRNC'. The Court concluded that those affected by such policies or actions therefore came within the 'jurisdiction' of Turkey for the purposes of Article 1 of the Convention. Turkey's obligation to secure the rights and freedoms set out in the Convention was found therefore to extend to northern Cyprus.

In its subsequent *Cyprus* v. *Turkey* judgment [of 10 May 2001], the Court added that since Turkey had such 'effective control', its responsibility could not be confined to the acts of its own agents therein but was engaged by the acts of the local administration which survived by virtue of Turkish support. Turkey's 'jurisdiction' under Article 1 was therefore considered to extend to securing the entire range of substantive Convention rights in northern Cyprus.

71. In sum, the case law of the Court demonstrates that its recognition of the exercise of extra-territorial jurisdiction by a Contracting State is exceptional: it has done so when the respondent State, through the effective control of the relevant territory and its inhabitants abroad as a consequence of military occupation or through the consent, invitation or acquiescence of the Government of that territory, exercises all or some of the public powers normally to be exercised by that Government.

72. In line with this approach, the Court has recently found that the participation of a State in the defence of proceedings against it in another State does not, without more, amount to an exercise of extra-territorial jurisdiction (*McElhinney* v. *Ireland and United Kingdom* (dec.), No. 31253/96, p. 7, 9 February 2000, unpublished). The Court said: 'In so far as the applicant complains under Article 6 ... about the stance taken by the Government of the United Kingdom in the Irish proceedings, the Court does not consider it necessary to address in the abstract the question of whether the actions of a Government as a litigant before the courts of another Contracting State can engage their responsibility under Article 6 ... The Court considers that, in the particular circumstances of the case, the fact that the United Kingdom Government raised the defence of sovereign immunity before the Irish courts, where the applicant had decided to sue, does not suffice to bring him within the jurisdiction of the United Kingdom within the meaning of Article 1 of the Convention.'

73. Additionally, the Court notes that other recognised instances of the extra-territorial exercise of jurisdiction by a State include cases involving the activities of its diplomatic or

consular agents abroad and on board craft and vessels registered in, or flying the flag of, that State. In these specific situations, customary international law and treaty provisions have recognised the extra-territorial exercise of jurisdiction by the relevant State.

(d) Were the present applicants therefore capable of coming within the 'jurisdiction' of the respondent States?

74. The applicants maintain that the bombing of RTS by the respondent States constitutes yet a further example of an extra-territorial act which can be accommodated by the notion of 'jurisdiction' in Article 1 of the Convention, and are thereby proposing a further specification of the ordinary meaning of the term 'jurisdiction' in Article 1 of the Convention. The Court must be satisfied that equally exceptional circumstances exist in the present case which could amount to the extra-territorial exercise of jurisdiction by a Contracting State.

75. In the first place, the applicants suggest a specific application of the 'effective control' criteria developed in the northern Cyprus cases. They claim that the positive obligation under Article 1 extends to securing the Convention rights in a manner proportionate to the level of control exercised in any given extra-territorial situation. The Governments contend that this amounts to a 'cause-and-effect' notion of jurisdiction not contemplated by or appropriate to Article 1 of the Convention. The Court considers that the applicants' submission is tantamount to arguing that anyone adversely affected by an act imputable to a Contracting State, wherever in the world that act may have been committed or its consequences felt, is thereby brought within the jurisdiction of that State for the purpose of Article 1 of the Convention.

The Court is inclined to agree with the Governments' submission that the text of Article 1 does not accommodate such an approach to 'jurisdiction'. Admittedly, the applicants accept that jurisdiction, and any consequent State Convention responsibility, would be limited in the circumstances to the commission and consequences of that particular act. However, the Court is of the view that the wording of Article 1 does not provide any support for the applicants' suggestion that the positive obligation in Article 1 to secure 'the rights and freedoms defined in Section I of this Convention' can be divided and tailored in accordance with the particular circumstances of the extra-territorial act in question and, it considers its view in this respect supported by the text of Article 19 of the Convention. Indeed the applicants' approach does not explain the application of the words 'within their jurisdiction' in Article 1 and it even goes so far as to render those words superfluous and devoid of any purpose. Had the drafters of the Convention wished to ensure jurisdiction as extensive as that advocated by the applicants, they could have adopted a text the same as or similar to the contemporaneous Articles 1 of the four Geneva Conventions of 1949.

Furthermore, the applicants' notion of jurisdiction equates the determination of whether an individual falls within the jurisdiction of a Contracting State with the question of whether that person can be considered to be a victim of a violation of rights guaranteed by the Convention. These are separate and distinct admissibility conditions, each of which has to be satisfied in the afore-mentioned order, before an individual can invoke the Convention provisions against a Contracting State.

76. Secondly, the applicants' alternative suggestion is that the limited scope of the airspace control only circumscribed the scope of the respondent States' positive obligation to protect the applicants and did not exclude it. The Court finds this to be essentially the same argument as their principal proposition and rejects it for the same reasons.

77. Thirdly, the applicants make a further alternative argument in favour of the respondent States' jurisdiction based on a comparison with the *Soering* case (cited above). The Court does not find this convincing given the fundamental differences between that case and the present as already noted at paragraph 68 above.

78. Fourthly, the Court does not find it necessary to pronounce on the specific meaning to be attributed in various contexts to the allegedly similar jurisdiction provisions in the international instruments to which the applicants refer because it is not convinced by the applicants' specific submissions in these respects (see §48 above). It notes that Article 2 of the American Declaration on the Rights and Duties of Man 1948 referred to in the above-cited *Coard* Report of the Inter-American Commission of Human Rights (§23 above), contains no explicit limitation of jurisdiction. In addition, and as to Article 2 §1 the CCPR 1966 (§26 above), as early as 1950 the drafters had definitively and specifically confined its territorial scope and it is difficult to suggest that exceptional recognition by the Human Rights Committee of certain instances of extra-territorial jurisdiction (and the applicants give one example only) displaces in any way the territorial jurisdiction expressly conferred by that Article of the CCPR 1966 or explains the precise meaning of 'jurisdiction' in Article 1 of its Optional Protocol 1966 (§27 above). While the text of Article 1 of the American Convention on Human Rights 1978 (§24 above) contains a jurisdiction condition similar to Article 1 of the European Convention, no relevant case law on the former provision was cited before this Court by the applicants.

79. Fifthly and more generally, the applicants maintain that any failure to accept that they fell within the jurisdiction of the respondent States would defeat the *ordre public* mission of the Convention and leave a regrettable vacuum in the Convention system of human rights' protection.

80. The Court's obligation, in this respect, is to have regard to the special character of the Convention as a constitutional instrument of *European* public order for the protection of individual human beings and its role, as set out in Article 19 of the Convention, is to ensure the observance of *the engagements undertaken* by the Contracting Parties (the *Loizidou* judgment (*preliminary objections*), [of 23 March 1995] at §93). It is therefore difficult to contend that a failure to accept the extra-territorial jurisdiction of the respondent States would fall foul of the Convention's *ordre public* objective, which itself underlines the essentially regional vocation of the Convention system, or of Article 19 of the Convention which does not shed any particular light on the territorial ambit of that system.

It is true that, in its above-cited *Cyprus* v. *Turkey* judgment (at §78), the Court was conscious of the need to avoid 'a regrettable vacuum in the system of human-rights protection' in northern Cyprus. However, and as noted by the Governments, that comment related to an entirely different situation to the present: the inhabitants of northern Cyprus would have found themselves excluded from the benefits of the Convention safeguards and system which they had previously enjoyed, by Turkey's 'effective control' of the territory and by the accompanying inability of the Cypriot Government, as a Contracting State, to fulfil the obligations it had undertaken under the Convention.

In short, the Convention is a multi-lateral treaty operating, subject to Article 56 of the Convention [Article 56 para. 1 enables a Contracting State to declare that the Convention shall extend to all or any of the territories for whose international relations that State is responsible], in an essentially regional context and notably in the legal space (*espace juridique*) of the Contracting States. The FRY clearly does not fall within this legal space. The Convention was not designed to be applied throughout the world, even in respect of the conduct of Contracting States. Accordingly, the desirability of avoiding a gap or vacuum in human rights' protection has so far been relied on by the Court in favour of establishing jurisdiction only when the territory in question was one that, but for the specific circumstances, would normally be covered by the Convention.

81. Finally, the applicants relied, in particular, on the admissibility decisions of the Court in the above-cited *Issa* and *Öcalan* cases. It is true that the Court has declared both of these cases admissible and that they include certain complaints about alleged actions by Turkish agents outside Turkish territory. However, in neither of those cases was the issue of jurisdiction raised by the respondent Government or addressed in the admissibility decisions and in any event the merits of those cases remain to be decided. Similarly, no jurisdiction objection is recorded in the decision leading to the inadmissibility of the *Xhavara* case to which the applicants also referred (cited above); at any rate, the applicants do not dispute the Governments' evidence about the sharing by prior written agreement of jurisdiction between Albania and Italy. The *Ilascu* case, also referred to by the applicants, [see below, section 2.2.] concerns allegations that Russian forces control part of the territory of Moldova, an issue to be decided definitively on the merits of that case. Accordingly, these cases do not provide any support for the applicants' interpretation of the jurisdiction of Contracting States within the meaning of Article 1 of the Convention.

A later case, *Issa and others* v. *Turkey*, implicitly overrules *Bankovic* insofar as this latter decision seemed to imply that a State party to the Convention could not be held responsible for the consequences of acts going beyond the jurisdiction it might legitimately exercise under public international law, unless it occupies foreign territory where it exercises *de facto* governmental powers.

European Court of Human Rights (2nd sect.), *Issa and others* v. *Turkey* (Appl. No. 31821/96), judgment of 16 November 2004, paras. 71–5:

[Six Iraqi nationals, acting on their own behalf and on behalf of deceased relatives, alleged the unlawful arrest, detention, ill-treatment and subsequent killing of their relatives in the course of a military operation conducted by the Turkish army in northern Iraq in April 1995.]

71. [Under the principles established in the case law of the Court,] a State may ... be held accountable for violation of the Convention rights and freedoms of persons who are in the territory of another State but who are found to be under the former State's authority and control through its agents operating – whether lawfully or unlawfully – in the latter State ... Accountability in such situations stems from the fact that Article 1 of the Convention cannot be interpreted so as to allow a State party to perpetrate violations of the Convention on the territory of another State, which it could not perpetrate on its own territory.

[The Court considered, however, that the conditions for the applicants' relatives to be under the 'jurisdiction' of Turkey in this sense were not satisfied. It distinguished the situation in *Issa* from that in *Loizidou*:]

75. ... [N]otwithstanding the large number of troops involved in the aforementioned military operations, it does not appear that Turkey exercised effective overall control of the entire area of northern Iraq. This situation is therefore in contrast to the one which obtained in northern

Cyprus in the *Loizidou* v. *Turkey* and *Cyprus* v. *Turkey* cases ... In the latter cases, the Court found that the respondent Government's armed forces totalled more than 30,000 personnel (which is, admittedly, no less than the number alleged by the applicants in the instant case ... but with the difference that the troops in northern Cyprus were present over a very much longer period of time) and were stationed throughout the whole of the territory of northern Cyprus. Moreover, that area was constantly patrolled and had check points on all main lines of communication between the northern and southern parts of the island.

This, however, did not necessarily exclude the imputability to Turkey of the acts complained of in *Issa and others*. Indeed, the Court proceeded to examine whether the allegation that the Turkish troops could be held responsible for the abductions and killings of the Iraqi shepherds whose relatives had brought the application before the Court could be proven. The Turkish troops not exercising a *de facto* control over the northern part of Iraq comparable to that exercised by Turkey on the northern part of the Island of Cyprus, such an imputability could not be presumed. It had to be verified whether at the relevant time Turkish troops conducted operations in the area where the killings took place, or whether other elements could be seen as evidence that those killings could be attributed to them. The Court arrived at the conclusion that 'it has not been established to the required standard of proof that the Turkish armed forces conducted operations in the area in question, and, more precisely, ... where, according to the applicants' statements, the victims were at that time'; therefore 'the Court is not satisfied that the applicants' relatives were within the "jurisdiction" of the respondent State for the purposes of Article 1 of the Convention' (paras. 81–2).

The relationship between *Bankovic* and *Issa* formed a central aspect of the judgment delivered on 14 December 2004 by the English High Court of Justice (Divisional Court), when it examined the claims of relatives of Iraqi citizens who had died in Iraq at a time and within geographical areas where the United Kingdom was recognized as an occupying power. Five claimants were killed in incidents with British troops. A sixth applicant died while in the custody of British troops in a military prison. The claimants alleged violations of Article 2 of the Convention, which guarantees the right to life, and – in the case of the sixth applicant – of Article 3, which prohibits torture and inhuman or degrading treatment, as they considered that the deaths had not led to effective enquiries. Both these provisions were made applicable before British courts by virtue of the Human Rights Act 1998. The High Court concluded that the 'jurisdiction' of the United Kingdom did not extend to the total territory occupied by the British armed forces in Iraq, even though that territory may be said to be under its effective control. It based itself mainly on *Bankovic*, which it considered the leading authority on the interpretation of Article 1 ECHR after an extensive review of the case law of the European Court of Human Rights. It arrived at the following conclusions:

High Court of Justice (Divisional Court) (United Kingdom), *R. (on the Application of Mazin Jumaa Gatteh Al Skeini and others) v. Secretary of State for Defence* [2004] EWHC 2911 (Admin), [2004] W.L.R. 1401:

269. [Article 1] jurisdiction does not extend to a broad, world-wide extra-territorial personal jurisdiction arising from the exercise of authority by party states' agents anywhere in the world, but only to an extra-territorial jurisdiction which is exceptional and limited and to be found in specific cases recognised in international law ...

270. [Such instances] are ones where, albeit the alleged violation of Convention standards takes place outside the home territory of the respondent state, it occurs by reason of the exercise of state authority in or from a location which has a form of discrete quasi-territorial quality, or where the state agent's presence in a foreign state is consented to by that state and protected by international law: such as diplomatic or consular premises, or vessels or aircraft registered in the respondent state. Such a rationalisation could also encompass courts located in a foreign state but, by international treaty, manned by the respondent state's judges acting as such.

[The claims of the first five claimants failed on that basis. However, the Court did recognize that the situation of the sixth claimant, Mr Mousa, warranted a different conclusion. Its reasoning is summarized in the following passage:]

281. It follows [from the analysis of the case law of the European Commission and Court of Human Rights] that, since Iraq is not within the regional sphere of the Convention, the complaints before us do not fall within the article 1 jurisdiction of the United Kingdom under the heading of the extra-territorial doctrine of the 'effective control of an area' exception as found in the cases of northern Cyprus and Moldova.

282. That conclusion makes it unnecessary for us to consider Mr Greenwood's subsidiary submission [as counsel to the United Kingdom Government] that, even if that doctrine could apply in theory to Iraq, and despite the United Kingdom being recognised as an occupying power for the purposes of the Hague Regulations and Fourth Geneva Convention, nevertheless it did not have such control of the relevant provinces where the deaths complained about took place as to amount to 'effective control' of that area within the meaning of that doctrine. Mr Greenwood contrasts the total military and civil control in northern Cyprus and secessionist MRT with the dangerous and volatile situation in Basra and Maysan provinces, where the British (among other national forces of the coalition) were relatively few in number, and where civil government remained in the hands of the Iraqi authorities under the aegis of the US dominated CPA (Coalition Provisional Authority). In this connection we remind ourselves that UN Security Council resolution 1483 of 22 May 2003 *inter alia* reaffirmed the sovereignty and territorial integrity of Iraq, recognised the role of the CPA and of the USA and the UK as 'occupying powers under unified command' and looked forward to the formation of an Iraqi Interim Administration; that on 13 July 2003 the Iraqi Governing Council was formed, which was recognised by UN Security Council resolution 1500 of 14 August 2003; and that UN Security Council resolution 1511 of 16 October 2003, acting under chapter VII of the UN Charter, determined that the Iraqi Governing Council embodied the sovereignty of the state of Iraq during the transitional period.

283. We also remind ourselves that the status of northern Cyprus and MRT as being within the effective control of Turkey and Russia respectively was ultimately decided by the Court only after a full consideration of the facts on the merits of those respective cases and in circumstances where, upon a consideration of those facts, such effective control was plainly established (see,

for instance, *Loizidou* v. *Turkey* (1997) at para 56, cited in *Bankovic* at para 70, and *Ilascu* v. *Moldova and Russia* at paras 379–394). It is therefore perhaps fortunate that, on the view we have taken as to the principle involved in the matter of this exceptional doctrine, it has not been necessary at this preliminary stage to attempt to resolve this factual issue. If it was only a question of whether, on the materials presented to us, and on the assumption that the case of Iraq was like the cases of northern Cyprus and of MRT, these complaints were capable of falling within the jurisdiction of the United Kingdom, we could perhaps conclude that they were. But a definitive decision is something different.

284. There remains the question whether the deaths with which we are concerned can come within the other recognised exception as resulting from the extra-territorial activity of state agents. On the view which we have taken of this exception as narrowly based, not extending to a broad personal extra-territorial jurisdiction, we conclude that it is necessary to consider the first five claimants and the sixth claimant separately. This was not the way in which Mr Singh [counsel for the claimants] argued the matter: indeed, in answer to a specific question from the court as to whether he made any distinction, even on an alternative basis, between the first five and the sixth claimants, he assured the court that he did not. Even so, it seems to us that we are nevertheless obliged to give separate consideration to these respective cases. This is because, on our analysis of the jurisprudence, the case of deaths as a result of military operations in the field, such as those complained of by the first five claimants, selected as reflecting various broadly representative examples of such misfortunes, do not seem to us to come within any possible variation of the examples of acts by state authorities in or from embassies, consulates, vessels, aircraft, (or, we would suggest, courts or prisons) to which the authorities repeatedly refer.

285. In such circumstances it seems to us that to broaden the exception currently under discussion into one which extends extra-territorial jurisdiction to the situations concerned in the case of the first five claimants would be illegitimate in two respects: it would drive a coach and horses through the narrow exceptions illustrated by such limited examples, and it would side-step the limitations we have found to exist under the broader (albeit still exceptional) doctrine of 'effective control of an area'. Although article 2 claims are of course a matter of particular and heightened concern, if jurisdiction existed in these five cases, there would be nothing to stop jurisdiction arising, or potentially arising, across the whole range of rights and freedoms protected by the Convention.

286. The sixth case of Mr Baha Mousa, however, as it seems to us, is different. He was not just a victim, under however unfortunate circumstances, of military operations. He was not, as we understand the matter, a prisoner of war. He was, *prima facie* at any rate, a civilian employee. He was arrested by British forces on suspicion of involvement with weapons hidden in the hotel where he worked as a receptionist, on suspicion therefore of involvement in terrorism. He was taken into custody in a British military base. There he met his death, it is alleged by beatings at the hands of his prison guards. The death certificate referred to 'cardio respiratory arrest: asphyxia'.

287. In the circumstances the burden lies on the British military prison authorities to explain how he came to lose his life while in British custody. It seems to us that it is not at all straining the examples of extra-territorial jurisdiction discussed in the jurisprudence considered above to hold that a British military prison, operating in Iraq with the consent of the Iraqi sovereign authorities, and containing arrested suspects, falls within even a narrowly limited exception exemplified by embassies, consulates, vessels and aircraft, and in the case of *Hess* v. *United*

Kingdom, a prison [*Hess* v. *United Kingdom* ((1975) 2 *Decisions and Reports* 72) concerned the detention of Rudolf Hess, the Nazi war criminal then held under a sentence of life imprisonment, handed down at Nuremberg, in the allied military prison in Spandau. That prison was under the control of the four allied powers, the United States, France, the United Kingdom and the USSR, but was located in the British sector of (West) Berlin. It would seem that it was only the veto of the USSR which prevented the release of Hess, who since October 1966 had been the sole remaining Nazi prisoner in Spandau. The Commission ruled the application inadmissible *ratione personae* on the ground (*inter alia*) that, since the prison was under the joint responsibility of the four powers, and not of the United Kingdom alone, its administration did not come 'within the jurisdiction' of the United Kingdom for the purposes of Article 1. It would seem, however, that if the prison had been in the United Kingdom's sole administration, then jurisdiction might have been established. See further on this case this chapter, below, section 4.1.]. We can see no reason in international law considerations, nor in principle, why in such circumstances the United Kingdom should not be answerable to a complaint, otherwise admissible, brought under articles 2 and/or 3 of the Convention.

288. We would therefore hold that the first five cases do not fall within the jurisdiction of the United Kingdom or the scope of the Convention for the purposes of its article 1, but that that of Mr Mousa does.

The judgment of the High Court of Justice went on to decide that the inadequacies in the enquiries which took place following the death of Mr Mousa justify a finding of a violation of the procedural requirements of Articles 2 and 3 of the Convention. This judgment was substantially affirmed, on appeal, by the Court of Appeal (Civil Division), in a judgment of 21 December 2005 reproduced below. The leading judgment by Lord Justice Brooke distinguishes between two grounds on which the ECHR can be applied extra-territorially: one is when a State party to the Convention is in effective control of a portion of the territory of another State party (ECA, effective control of an area); another is when 'an agent of a contracting state exercises authority through the activities of its diplomatic or consular agents abroad or on board craft and vessels registered in or flying the flag of the state, [in which case] that state is similarly obliged to secure those rights and freedoms to persons affected by that exercise of authority', what is referred to as 'State agent authority' (SAA) (para. 48). Lord Justice Brooke finds that 'Mr Mousa came within the control and authority of the UK from the time he was arrested at the hotel and thereby lost his freedom at the hands of British troops' (para. 108). In contrast, none of the five other applicants was 'under the control and authority of British troops at the time when they were killed' (para. 110), therefore the 'State agent authority' doctrine is inapplicable to them, and the ECHR would only be applicable if the ECA doctrine could apply, i.e. if the United Kingdom were 'in effective control of the area in which [the complainant] is situated with the consent, invitation or acquiescence of the host state or in circumstances that amount to a military occupation' (para. 111). The conditions are not present for the Convention to apply extra-territorially on this basis, however:

Court of Appeal (Civil Division), *R. (on the Application of Mazin Mumaa Galteh Al-Skeini and others)* v. *Secretary of State for Defence* [2005] EWCA Civ 1609 (leading judgment by Lord Justice Brooke):

124. In my judgment it is quite impossible to hold that the UK, although an occupying power for the purposes of the Hague Regulations and Geneva IV, was in effective control of Basrah City for the purposes of ECHR jurisprudence at the material time. If it had been, it would have been obliged, pursuant to the *Bankovic* judgment, to secure to everyone in Basrah City the rights and freedoms guaranteed by the ECHR. One only has to state that proposition to see how utterly unreal it is. The UK possessed no executive, legislative or judicial authority in Basrah City, other than the limited authority given to its military forces, and as an occupying power it was bound to respect the laws in force in Iraq unless absolutely prevented (see Article 43 of the Hague Regulations ...). It could not be equated with a civil power: it was simply there to maintain security, and to support the civil administration in Iraq in a number of different ways ...

125. It would indeed have been contrary to the Coalition's policy to maintain a much more substantial military force in Basrah City when its over-arching policy was to encourage the Iraqis to govern themselves. To build up an alternative power base capable of delivering all the rights and performing all the obligations required of a contracting state under the ECHR at the very time when the IGC had been formed, with CPA [Coalition Provisional Authority] encouragement, as a step towards the formation by the people of Iraq of an internationally recognized representative Government ..., would have run right against the grain of the Coalition's policies.

126. And it is in any event very much open to question whether an effort by an occupying power in a predominantly Muslim country to inculcate what the ECtHR has described (in *Golder* v. *UK* (1975) 1 E.H.R.R. 524 at para 34) as 'the common spiritual heritage of the member states of the country of Europe' during its temporary sojourn in that country would have been consistent with the Coalition's goal, which was to transfer responsibility to representative Iraqi authorities as early as possible ...

127. In the interests of completeness, I should make it clear that I reject the arguments by the claimants to the effect that occupation for the purposes of the Hague Regulations must necessarily be equated with effective control of the occupied area for ECHR purposes. Mr Rabinder Singh [counsel for the appellants] referred to passages in Oppenheim, *International Law*, Vol 2 (1952) at paras 166, 169 and 170 which set out the obligations of an occupying power in wide and general terms. It is a feature of Strasbourg jurisprudence that the Court will examine the facts of each particular case to see if the requisite control is in fact exercised (see *Loizidou* v. *Turkey* (Preliminary Objections) at [62] ...), and the status of the British military forces in Basrah City was markedly different from that featured in the text on which Mr Singh relies.

128. Mr Singh suggests that the consequences of the Secretary of State's argument would be that a state could send a sufficiency of troops to an occupied area, whether within the European region or beyond it, to assert the rights of belligerent occupation but avoid otherwise applicable human rights standards by reducing to a minimum the number of troops. If the territory in question is within the European region, its citizens will enjoy the rights and protections afforded by the ECHR, and it will be a question of fact in each case as to which state is responsible for their violation. If the territory in question is outside the European region, this conclusion is an inevitable consequence of the fact that there is not yet in place an enforceable human rights convention covering the whole world. And although the protections afforded to civilian populations under humanitarian treaties are not nearly so valuable as those afforded by the ECHR, it would be facile to suggest that they do not exist at all.

In a judgment of 13 June 2007, delivered on the crossed appeals of both parties to the litigation, the House of Lords took the view – based on its interpretation of the Human Rights Act (HRA) 1998, and without prejudice of the extra-territorial applicability of the European Convention on Human Rights – that the protection of the HRA does not extend beyond the territory of the United Kingdom:

> **House of Lords (United Kingdom), *Al-Skeini and others (Respondents)* v.**
> ***Secretary of State for Defence (Appellant), Al-Skeini and others (Appellants)* v.**
> ***Secretary of State for Defence (Respondent)* (consolidated Appeals) [2007] UKHL**
> **26, lead judgment by Lord Bingham of Cornhill:**
>
> 24. ... It cannot of course be supposed that in 1997–1998 Parliament foresaw the prospect of British forces being engaged in peacekeeping duties in Iraq. But there can be relatively few, if any, years between 1953 and 1997 in which British forces were not engaged in hostilities or peacekeeping activities in some part of the world, and it must have been appreciated that such involvement would recur. This makes it the more unlikely, in my opinion, that Parliament could, without any express provision to that effect, have intended to rebut the presumption of territorial application so as to authorise the bringing of claims, under the Act, based on the conduct of British forces outside the UK and outside any other contracting state. Differing from the courts below, I regard the statutory presumption of territorial application as a strong one, which has not been rebutted.

2.3. Questions for discussion: applying human rights instruments to State agents acting abroad

1. When, in 1981, the Human Rights Committee adopted its decision in the *Lopez Burgos* case, it explained that it would be unacceptable to 'permit a State party to perpetrate violations of the Covenant on the territory of another State, which violations it could not perpetrate on its own territory'.

   Lopez Burgos is not isolated, illustrating the fear thus expressed by the Committee. Since the forcible abduction of Adolf Eichmann from Argentina in order to ensure that he would be tried in Israel under the Nazi Collaborators (Punishment) Law adopted by the State of Israel, international law offers a number of examples in which States' secret services have been acting on foreign territory, whether with or without the consent of the territorially competent State (on the *Eichmann* case, see *Attorney General of the Government of Israel* v. *Adolf Eichmann*, District Court of Jerusalem (1961), reprinted in 36 I.L.R. 18, at 26 (judgment of 11 December 1961); *Attorney General of Israel* v. *Eichmann*, Israel Supreme Court (1962), reprinted in 36 I.L.R. 28; and the comments by C. Oliver, *American Journal of International Law*, 56, No. 3 (July 1962), 805–45; and J. Fawcett, 'The *Eichmann* Case', *British Yearbook of International Law*, 38 (1962), 181). For instance, in *Ramirez Sanchez* v. *France*, the European Commission of Human Rights considered that the terrorist 'Carlos' abducted from Sudan and surrendered to the French authorities, was 'under the authority, and therefore the jurisdiction', of France upon the moment of his surrender, for the purposes of the applicability of Article 5 ECHR which guarantees the right to liberty and security, even though this authority was exercised in a foreign country (European Commission on Human Rights, *Illich Sanchez Ramirez* v. *France*, 24 June 1996 (inadmissibility decision), No. 28780/95). In the case of *Öçalan* v. *Turkey*, the applicant, the leader in exile of the Workers' Party of Kurdistan (PKK), had been brought by the Kenyan authorities to an aircraft in the international transit area of Nairobi Airport, in which Turkish officials were waiting for him, and from where he was brought to Turkey in order to face trial. The European Court of Human Rights considered that, in such a situation, a person brought under the effective authority of officials of a State party to the Convention is 'within the jurisdiction' of that State for the purposes of Article 1 of the Convention: it distinguished *Bankovic* by emphasizing that, in *Öçalan*, 'the applicant was physically forced to return to Turkey by Turkish officials and was subject to their authority and control following his arrest and return to Turkey' (Eur. Ct. H.R. (GC), *Öçalan* v. *Turkey* (Appl. No. 46221/99), 12 May 2005, para. 91).

Similarly, cases such as *Xhavara and others* v. *Albania and Italy* presented to the European Court of Human Rights, following the deaths of a number of Albanians seeking to enter Italy illegally by boat, after that boat was intercepted and sank (Eur. Ct. H.R., *Xhavara and others* v. *Albania and Italy*, Appl. No. 39473/98 (inadmissibility decision of 11 January 2001)), or the '*Prague Airport*' case presented to the UK House of Lords (*R.* v. *Immigration Officer at Prague Airport and another (Respondents), ex parte European Roma Rights Centre and others (Appellants)* [2004] UKHL 55: see chapter 7, section 2.1.), present certain analogies to the *Haitian Interdiction* case, showing that such a case is not entirely exceptional. On the other hand however, it may be argued that, when a State acts extra-territorially, it usually faces the limit to its powers that stem from the obligation to respect the sovereignty of the territorially competent State: situations such as the clandestine activities of secret services without the consent of the territorial State or acts on high seas are exceptions. Could it be argued therefore that, save in such exceptional circumstances, the human rights of individuals should be defined by the obligations of the State on whose territory they are located, rather than by those of the State under the 'effective control' of the agents of which they find themselves? Would such a solution be workable? Would it better respect the sovereignty of the territorially competent State?

2. In the *Al-Skeini* litigation, the UK Court of Appeal presents 'effective control of an area' (ECA) and 'State agent authority' (SAA) as two separate grounds on which the extra-territorial applicability of the European Convention on Human Rights could be based. Is this approach convincing? Should such doctrines function in an all-or-nothing fashion – the Convention being applicable either in full, or being applicable not at all – or should the scope of obligations imposed on the States parties be made to depend on the *degree* of control exercised?

3. In *Al-Skeini*, the lower courts in the United Kingdom restricted the scope of the ECA doctrine to the territories which are part of the Council of Europe, and they restricted the SAA doctrine to situations where State agents exercise authority lawfully on the territory of a State other than their own, rather than in violation of international law. Both these restrictions are intended to defer to the decision of the European Court of Human Rights in *Bankovic*. But are they justified? Should they be removed? What would be the consequences of removing these restrictions?

2.2 The obligation of States to protect human rights beyond the national territory

The previous section examined whether States are under an obligation to respect their human rights obligations when acting through their agents outside their national territory. This question was answered in the affirmative, although the precise conditions which must be fulfilled in order for any situation to be considered to be under the 'jurisdiction' of the State concerned remain somewhat contested. In this section, we examine whether States may have a duty to protect human rights outside their national territory. The focus thus shifts from enforcement extra-territorial jurisdiction – agents of the executive acting abroad – to prescriptive and adjudicative extra-territorial jurisdiction: the question is, indeed, whether States should adopt legislation with extra-territorial effect, or allow their national courts to hear claims about situations occurring abroad, in order to discharge their obligation to protect human rights abroad. In practice, prescriptive and adjudicative extra-territorial jurisdiction often go hand in hand: when States adopt legislation with an extra-territorial scope of application, they generally allow their domestic courts to adjudicate on claims based on that legislation.

The contemporary, mainstream view is that there exists no general obligation imposed on States, under international human rights law, to exercise extra-territorial jurisdiction (understood here as a combination of adjudicative and prescriptive jurisdiction) in order to contribute to the protection and promotion of internationally recognized human rights outside their national territory. In principle, the international responsibility of a State may not be engaged by the conduct of actors not belonging to the State apparatus unless they are in fact acting under the instructions of, or under the direction or control of, that State in carrying out the conduct (see further on this chapter 4). However, the private-public distinction on which this rule of attribution is based is mooted (though not contradicted) by the imposition under international human rights law of positive obligations on States, since such obligations imply that the State must accept responsibility not only for the acts its organs have adopted, but also for the omissions of these organs, where such omissions result in an insufficient protection of private persons whose rights or freedoms are violated by the acts of other non-State actors. Yet, such positive obligations hitherto have been affirmed only in situations falling under the 'jurisdiction' of the State, i.e. in situations on which the State exercises effective control: outside the national territory, it is not presumed that the State exercises such control, and only in exceptional circumstances will it be considered that the power its organs exercise on persons or property located abroad amounts to that state having 'jurisdiction' in a sense which would justify the extension of the positive obligations derived from any international human rights instruments binding upon the State. Thus, in the current state of development of international law, a clear obligation for States to control private actors operating outside their national territory, in order to ensure that these actors will not violate the human rights of others, has not crystallized yet. This is the case even as regards those private actors having the nationality of the State concerned, and whose behaviour therefore a State may decisively influence and on whom it may impose certain obligations in conformity with international law.

Yet, in a number of general comments, the Committee on Economic, Social and Cultural Rights took the view that the States parties to the International Covenant on Economic, Social and Cultural Rights should respect the enjoyment of the rights stipulated in the Covenant in other countries, *inter alia*, by preventing third parties from violating the right in other countries, 'if they are able to influence these third parties by way of legal or political means, in accordance with the Charter of the United Nations and applicable international law' (General Comment No. 14 (2000), *The Right to the Highest Attainable Standard of Health (Art. 12 of the International Covenant on Economic, Social and Cultural Rights)*, E/C.12/2000/4 (2000), para. 39; General Comment No. 15 (2002), *The Right to Water (Arts. 11 and 12 of the International Covenant on Economic, Social and Cultural Rights)*, E/C.12/2002/11 (26 November 2002), para. 31). This position is supported by an emerging scholarship insisting that the extra-territorial obligations imposed under the ICESCR entail, at a minimum, that States parties should refrain from the adoption of measures that could negatively affect the enjoyment of such rights abroad, and that they should control the activities of private actors, particularly transnational corporations which they recognize as having their 'nationality', in order to ensure that such corporations do not violate these rights, directly or indirectly, in foreign jurisdictions (see W. Vandenhole, 'Completing the UN Complaint Mechanisms for Human Rights Violations Step by Step', *Netherlands Quarterly of Human Rights*, 21, No. 3, 2003, 423–62 at 445–6; M. Craven, *The International Covenant on Economic, Social and Cultural Rights: a Perspective on Its Development* (Oxford University Press, 1995), at pp. 147–50; S. Skogly, *Beyond National Borders: States' Human Rights Obligations in International Cooperation* (Antwerp-Oxford: Intersentia-Hart, 2006), esp. chapter 3, 'Extraterritorial Human Rights Obligations'; M. Sepúlveda, 'Obligations of "International Assistance and Co-operation" in an Optional Protocol to the International Covenant on Economic, Social and Cultural Rights', *Netherlands Quarterly of Human Rights,* 24, No. 2 (2006), 271–303 at 282; see also *The Right to Food*, Report submitted by the Special Rapporteur on the right to food, Jean Ziegler, in accordance with Commission on Human Rights Resolution 2002/25, E/CN.4/2003/54 (10 January 2003), para. 29).

The arguments in favour of imposing extra-territorial obligations to protect human rights are based on the interpretation of Articles 55 and 56 of the UN Charter and on the wording of the International Covenant on Economic, Social and Cultural Rights itself: not only is the Covenant not explicitly restricted in its territorial scope of application, it also refers to 'international assistance and co-operation' for the realization of economic, social and cultural rights, thereby pointing to the need for international solidarity in the realization of these rights. But this position is based, in addition, on three considerations.

First, the imposition of extra-territorial obligations to protect on the home States of private actors, may be seen as a necessary complement to the extension of the rights of these actors under international law, particularly through multilateral, regional or bilateral free trade or investment agreements. For instance, M. Sornarajah argues that 'developed States owe a duty of control to the international community and do in fact have the means of legal control over the conduct abroad of multinational corporations', and he sees the imposition of such an obligation as the logical counterpart of the extensive protections afforded to foreign investors under both general international law and conventional international law (M. Sornarajah, *The International Law on Foreign Investment*, second edn (Cambridge University Press, 2004), chapter 4, esp. p. 169). Consider also the summary of the problem offered in 2008 by the Special Representative of the UN Secretary-General on the issue of human rights and transnational corporations and other business enterprises, John Ruggie, in his 2008 Report to the Human Rights Council:

> ***Protect, Respect and Remedy: a Framework for Business and Human Rights,* Report by the Special Representative of the Secretary-General on the issue of human rights and transnational corporations and other business enterprises, John Ruggie (A/HRC/8/5, 7 April 2008), paras. 34–5:**
>
> 34. To attract foreign investment, host States offer protection through bilateral investment treaties and host government agreements. They promise to treat investors fairly, equitably, and without discrimination, and to make no unilateral changes to investment conditions. But investor protections have expanded with little regard to States' duties to protect, skewing the balance between the two. Consequently, host States can find it difficult to strengthen domestic social and environmental standards, including those related to human rights, without fear of foreign investor challenge, which can take place under binding international arbitration.
>
> 35. This imbalance creates potential difficulties for all types of countries. Agreements between host governments and companies sometimes include promises to 'freeze' the existing regulatory regime for the project's duration, which can be a half-century for major infrastructure and extractive industries projects. During the investment's lifetime, even social and environmental regulatory changes that are applied equally to domestic companies can be challenged by foreign investors claiming exemption or compensation.

In order to make up for this imbalance, the home States of private actors operating transnationally may have to contribute to policing the activities of these actors, in order for the obligations imposed on them in the State in which they operate to be truly effective. Mr El Hadji Guissé, a Special Rapporteur of the UN Commission on Human Rights, has remarked that '[t]he violations committed by the transnational corporations in their mainly transboundary activities do not come within the competence of a single State and, to prevent contradictions and inadequacies in the remedies and sanctions decided upon by States individually or as a group, these violations should form the subject of special attention. The States and the international community should combine their efforts so as to contain such activities by the establishment of legal standards capable of achieving that objective' (*The Realization of Economic, Social and Cultural Rights, Final Report on the Question of the Impunity of Perpetrators of Human Rights Violations (Economic, Social and Cultural Rights)*, prepared by Mr El Hadji Guissé, Special Rapporteur, pursuant to Sub-Commission Resolution 1996/24, E/CN.4/Sub.2/1997/8, 27 June 1997, para. 131).

Second, the imposition of an obligation to protect human rights beyond national borders may be seen as one specific manifestation of a broader duty of States not to allow their territory to be used by private actors in order to cause damage to another State. In his dissenting opinion to the Advisory Opinion of the International Court of Justice on the *Legality of Threat or Use of Nuclear Weapons*, Judge Weeramantry referred in these terms to the principle that 'damage must not be caused to other nations':

International Court of Justice, *Legality of the Threat or Use of Nuclear Weapons, Advisory Opinion*, I.C.J. Reports 1996, 240, dissenting opinion of Judge Weeramantry:

[This principle] is well entrenched in international law and goes as far back as the *Trail Smelter* case *(Reports of International Arbitral Awards,* 1938, Vol. III, p. 1905) and perhaps beyond (see also *Corfu Channel, Merits, Judgment,* I.C.J. Reports 1949, p. 4). This basic principle, that no nation is entitled by its own activities to cause damage to the environment of any other nation, appears as Principle 2 of the Rio Declaration on the Environment, 1992: 'States have, in accordance with the Charter of the United Nations and the principles of international law, the sovereign right to exploit their own resources pursuant to their own environmental and developmental policies, and the responsibility to ensure that activities within their jurisdiction or control do not cause damage to the environment of other States or of areas beyond the limits of national jurisdiction.' *(Report of the United Nations Conference on Environment and Development* (AICONF. 151/26/Rev. I), Vol. 1, Ann. 1, p. 3.). Other international instruments that embody this principle are the Stockholm Declaration on the Human Environment (1972, Principle 21) and the 1986 Noumea Convention, Article 4(6) of which States: 'Nothing in this Convention shall affect the sovereign right of States to exploit, develop and manage their own natural resources pursuant to their own policies, taking into account their duty to protect and preserve the environment. Each Party shall ensure that activities within its jurisdiction or control do not cause damage to the environment of other States or of areas beyond the limits of its national jurisdiction.' (Hohmann, *Basic Documents of International Environmental Law,* vol. 2 (1992), p. 1063.)

Judge Weeramantry considered that the claim to which the Court was confronted in that case – according to New Zealand, nuclear tests should be prohibited where this could risk having an impact on that country's population – should be decided 'in the context of such a deeply entrenched principle, grounded in common sense, case law, international conventions, and customary international law'. There is nothing that prohibits extending this principle, beyond environmental law, to human rights law. On the contrary, the Committee on Economic, Social and Cultural Rights mentioned, in the context of the right to water, that '[a]ny activities undertaken within the State party's jurisdiction should not deprive another country of the ability to realize the right to water for persons in its jurisdiction' (General Comment No. 15 (2002), *The Right to Water (Arts. 11 and 12 of the International Covenant on Economic, Social and Cultural Rights)*, UN Doc. E/C.12/2002/11 (26 November 2002), paras. 31 and 35–6).

Third, apart from the human rights obligations directly imposed on the home State of private actors operating across borders, there is a need to take into account the human rights obligations of the State in which these private actors operate, and the correlative obligation of the home State, under general international law, not to create obstacles to the fulfillment of these obligations. Consider, for instance, the wording chosen by the Committee on Economic, Social and Cultural Rights when it adopted a general comment on the relationship between economic sanctions and respect for economic, social and cultural rights. The core message of that General Comment was that States imposing sanctions should not lead to jeopardizing the economic, social and cultural rights of the population in the targeted State, since this would constitute a violation of their obligations under the International Covenant on Economic, Social and Cultural Rights and, indeed, since the Universal Declaration on Human Rights may be considered as binding under general international law, whether or not the States concerned have ratified the Covenant:

Committee on Economic, Social and Cultural Rights, General Comment No. 8 (1997), *The Relationship between Economic Sanctions and Respect for Economic, Social and Cultural Rights* (E/1998/22), para. 51:

While this obligation of every State is derived from the commitment in the Charter of the United Nations to promote respect for all human rights, it should also be recalled that every permanent member of the Security Council has signed the Covenant, although two (China [which in fact ratified the ICESCR on 27 June 2001, thus after the adoption of the General Comment] and the United States) have yet to ratify it. Most of the non–permanent members at any given time are parties. Each of these States has undertaken, in conformity with article 2, paragraph 1, of the Covenant to 'take steps, individually and through international assistance and co-operation, especially economic and technical, to the maximum of its available resources, with a view to achieving progressively the full realization of the rights recognized in the present Covenant by all appropriate means ...' When the affected State is also a State party, it is doubly incumbent upon other States to respect and take account of the relevant obligations. To the extent that sanctions are imposed on States which are not parties to the Covenant, the same principles would in any event apply given the status of the economic, social and cultural rights of vulnerable groups as part of general international law, as evidenced, for example, by the near–universal ratification of the Convention on the Rights of the Child and the status of the Universal Declaration of Human Rights.

The notion that an obligation would be 'doubly' incumbent upon a State may be a source of confusion. On its face, the use of this expression would seem to betray a certain hesitation among the members of the Committee about whether the obligations of the States adopting sanctions have their source in the international undertakings of those States, or instead in the rights recognized to the population in the targeted State. The reality, however, is that it can be both, and both at the same time. Of course, all that matters, where sanctions adopted by one State have an impact on the population of another State, are the obligations of the first State under international law, which may or may not include the obligation not to violate the rights of populations outside its borders. And the General Comment clearly implies not only that a State party to the ICESCR is under an obligation not to violate the rights stipulated in the Covenant in other countries, but also that such an obligation could be violated by that State voting in favour of adopting or upholding economic sanctions which have a severe impact on the realization of economic and social rights in the targeted country. But this does not mean that the obligations of the targeted State towards its own population are irrelevant to the determination of the question whether or not the State adopting sanctions has violated its own obligations. For, *in addition*, States parties to the ICESCR may be violating their international obligations by coercing other States into violating their own obligations under either the Covenant or under other rules of international law. This is what Article 18 of the International Law Commission's 2001 articles on Responsibility of States for internationally wrongful acts refers to under the heading 'Coercion of another State': 'A State which coerces another State to commit an act is internationally responsible for that act if: (a) The act would, but for the coercion, be an internationally wrongful act of the coerced State; and (b) The coercing State does so with knowledge of the circumstances of the act.'

However important these arguments in favour of the recognition of extra-territorial obligations to protect, the attitude of human rights bodies remains cautious. The Committee on Economic, Social and Cultural Rights has been the most explicit in stating its expectation that States parties to the Covenant on Economic, Social and Cultural Rights should control private actors whose behaviour they may influence. In 2007 the Committee on the Elimination of Racial Discrimination called on Canada to 'take appropriate legislative or administrative measures to prevent acts of transnational corporations registered in Canada which negatively impact on the enjoyment of rights of indigenous peoples in territories outside Canada. In particular, the Committee recommends that the State party explore ways to hold transnational corporations registered in Canada accountable' (Concluding Observations/Comments: Canada, CERD/C/CAN/CO/18 (25 May 2007), para. 17). But judicial bodies have been far less open to claims that States would be in violation of their human rights obligations by not exercising due diligence control over the behaviour of private actors operating beyond their national territory. One exception, albeit in very specific circumstances, is the case of *Ilascu and others* v. *Moldova and Russia* presented to the European Court of Human Rights:

European Court of Human Rights (GC), *Ilascu and others* v. *Moldova and Russia* (Appl. No. 48787/99), judgment of 8 July 2004, paras. 311–18:

[The 'Moldavian Republic of Transdniestria' is a region of Moldova which proclaimed its independence in 1991 but is not recognized by the international community. It has been consistently supported, first by the USSR when the Republic of Moldova proclaimed its independence in August 1991, and later by the Federation of Russia, the successor State to the USSR; indeed, the Fourteenth Army of the USSR, previously deployed in Moldova with its headquarters in Chisinau, had retreated from most of Moldova but remained present in Transdniestria, and actively co-operated with the separatists since. After the end of the conflict between Moldova and the separatist republic in 1991–2, senior officers of the former Fourteenth Army participated in public life in Transdniestria, and soldiers of the former Fourteenth Army took part in the elections in Transdniestria, military parades of the Transdniestrian forces and other public events. Strong links, both economic and legal – for instance in the field of judicial co-operation – were established between the Moldavian Republic of Transdniestria and the Federation of Russia. The four applicants, Moldovan nationals who were arrested in June 1992 and had been condemned by a Transdniestrian court to imprisonment terms or, in the case of Mr Ilascu, to death, alleged in particular that the court which had convicted them was not competent for the purposes of Article 6 of the Convention, that they had not had a fair trial, that their detention in Transdniestria was not lawful, in breach of Article 5, and that their conditions of detention contravened Articles 3 and 8 of the Convention. The applicants argued that the Moldovan authorities were responsible under the Convention for the alleged violations, since they had not taken any appropriate steps to put an end to them. They further asserted that the Russian Federation shared responsibility since the territory of Transdniestria was and is under *de facto* Russian control on account of the Russian troops and military equipment stationed there, and because of the support allegedly given to the separatist regime by the Russian Federation.]

311. It follows from Article 1 that member States must answer for any infringement of the rights and freedoms protected by the Convention committed against individuals placed under their 'jurisdiction'.

The exercise of jurisdiction is a necessary condition for a Contracting State to be able to be held responsible for acts or omissions imputable to it which give rise to an allegation of the infringement of rights and freedoms set forth in the Convention.

312. The Court refers to its case law to the effect that the concept of 'jurisdiction' for the purposes of Article 1 of the Convention must be considered to reflect the term's meaning in public international law (see *Gentilhomme, Schaff-Benhadji and Zerouki* v. *France*, judgment of 14 May 2002, §20; *Banković and others* v. *Belgium and 16 Other Contracting States* (dec.), No. 52207/99, §§59–61, ECHR 2001–XII; and *Assanidze* v. *Georgia*, ECHR 2004– ..., §137).

From the standpoint of public international law, the words 'within their jurisdiction' in Article 1 of the Convention must be understood to mean that a State's jurisdictional competence is primarily territorial (see the *Banković* decision, cited above, §59*)*, but also that jurisdiction is presumed to be exercised normally throughout the State's territory.

This presumption may be limited in exceptional circumstances, particularly where a State is prevented from exercising its authority in part of its territory. That may be as a result of military occupation by the armed forces of another State which effectively controls the territory concerned (see *Loizidou* v. *Turkey* (*Preliminary Objections*) judgment of 23 March 1995, Series A No. 310, and *Cyprus* v. *Turkey* [GC], No. 25781/94, ECHR 2001–IV, §§76–80, as cited in the above-mentioned *Banković* decision, §§70–71), acts of war or rebellion, or the acts of a foreign State supporting the installation of a separatist State within the territory of the State concerned.

313. In order to be able to conclude that such an exceptional situation exists, the Court must examine on the one hand all the objective facts capable of limiting the effective exercise of a

State's authority over its territory, and on the other the State's own conduct. The undertakings given by a Contracting State under Article 1 of the Convention include, in addition to the duty to refrain from interfering with enjoyment of the rights and freedoms guaranteed, positive obligations to take appropriate steps to ensure respect for those rights and freedoms within its territory (see, among other authorities, *Z.* v. *United Kingdom* [GC], No. 29392/95, §73, ECHR 2001–V).

Those obligations remain even where the exercise of the State's authority is limited in part of its territory, so that it has a duty to take all the appropriate measures which it is still within its power to take.

314. Moreover, the Court observes that, although in the *Banković* case it emphasised the preponderance of the territorial principle in the application of the Convention (decision cited above, §80), it also acknowledged that the concept of 'jurisdiction' within the meaning of Article 1 of the Convention is not necessarily restricted to the national territory of the High Contracting Parties (see *Loizidou* v. *Turkey* (*Merits*), judgment of 18 December 1996, *Reports of Judgments and Decisions* 1996–VI, pp. 2234–2235, §52).

The Court has accepted that in exceptional circumstances the acts of Contracting States performed outside their territory or which produce effects there may amount to exercise by them of their jurisdiction within the meaning of Article 1 of the Convention.

According to the relevant principles of international law, a State's responsibility may be engaged where, as a consequence of military action – whether lawful or unlawful – it in practice exercises effective control of an area situated outside its national territory. The obligation to secure, in such an area, the rights and freedoms set out in the Convention derives from the fact of such control, whether it be exercised directly, through its armed forces, or through a subordinate local administration (*ibid.*).

315. It is not necessary to determine whether a Contracting Party actually exercises detailed control over the policies and actions of the authorities in the area situated outside its national territory, since even overall control of the area may engage the responsibility of the Contracting Party concerned (*ibid.*, pp. 2235–2236, §56).

316. Where a Contracting State exercises overall control over an area outside its national territory its responsibility is not confined to the acts of its soldiers or officials in that area but also extends to acts of the local administration which survives there by virtue of its military and other support (see *Cyprus* v. *Turkey* [GC], cited above, §77).

317. A State's responsibility may also be engaged on account of acts which have sufficiently proximate repercussions on rights guaranteed by the Convention, even if those repercussions occur outside its jurisdiction. Thus, with reference to extradition to a non-Contracting State, the Court has held that a Contracting State would be acting in a manner incompatible with the underlying values of the Convention, 'that common heritage of political traditions, ideals, freedom and the rule of law' to which the Preamble refers, if it were knowingly to hand over a fugitive to another State where there are substantial grounds for believing that the person concerned faces a real risk of being subjected to torture or to inhuman or degrading treatment or punishment (see *Soering* v. *United Kingdom*, judgment of 7 July 1989, Series A No. 161, p. 35, §§88–91 [see below, section 3.1. of this chapter]).

318. In addition, the acquiescence or connivance of the authorities of a Contracting State in the acts of private individuals which violate the Convention rights of other individuals within its jurisdiction may engage the State's responsibility under the Convention (see *Cyprus* v. *Turkey*, cited above, §81). That is particularly true in the case of recognition by the State in question of the acts of self-proclaimed authorities which are not recognised by the international community.

Applying those principles to the facts of the case, the Court arrived at the conclusion that the Moldavian Republic of Transdniestria, 'set up in 1991–1992 with the support of the Russian Federation, vested with organs of power and its own administration, remains under the effective authority, *or at the very least under the decisive influence*, of the Russian Federation, and in any event that *it survives by virtue of the military, economic, financial and political support given to it by the Russian Federation*', and that therefore the applicants must be considered to come within the 'jurisdiction' of the Russian Federation for the purposes of Article 1 of the Convention (see paras. 391–4).

Box 2.2. | **The example of the US Alien Torts Claims Act**

Perhaps the most spectacular example of the exercise of extraterritorial jurisdiction in protection of human rights is the revival since 1980 of the Alien Tort Claims Act (ATCA) in the United States. This statute has allowed foreign victims of serious human rights abuses committed by any person over which the US federal courts can exercise personal jurisdiction – including corporations having sufficiently close links to the United States, either because they are incorporated in the United States, or because they have a continuous business relationship to the United States – to seek damages before the United States federal courts.

The Alien Tort Claims Act, a part of the First Judiciary Act 1789, provides that '[t]he district courts shall have original jurisdiction of any civil action by an alien for a tort only, committed in violation of the law of nations or a treaty of the United States'. (28 U.S.C. §1350). For almost two centuries, this clause remained confined to relatively marginal situations. It was first revived in a case involving a Paraguayan police officer, alleged to have tortured a Paraguayan national in his home country, but found by the family of the victim to be on US territory: the Second Circuit Court accepted that it could exercise jurisdiction, on the basis that 'deliberate torture perpetrated under color of official authority violates universally accepted norms of international law of human rights' (*Filartiga* v. *Peña-Irala*, 630 F.2d 876 (2d Cir. 1980)). The ATCA has since been relied upon in a large number of cases related to human rights claims (see, e.g. *Tel-Oren* v. *Libyan Arab Republic*, 233 U.S. App. D.C. 384, 726 F.2d 774 (D.C. Cir. 1984); *In re Estate of Ferdinand E. Marcos Human Rights Litigation*, 978 F.2d 493 (9th Cir. 1992); *Xuncax* v. *Gramajo*, 886 F.Supp 162 (D Mass, 1995); *Kadic* v. *Karadzic*, 70 F.3d 232, 238 (2d Cir. 1995)), including some cases concerning corporations as defendants (see in particular *John Doe I* v. *Unocal Corp.*, 395 F.3d 932, 945–946 (9th Cir. 2002) (complicity of Unocal, a California-based oil company, with human rights abuses committed by the Burmese military)). When, in 2004, the US Supreme Court was provided a first opportunity to influence this development and to examine the exact scope of the powers conferred upon US federal courts by the Alien Tort Claims Act, it took the view that, when confronted with such suits, the federal courts should 'require any claim based on the present-day law of nations to rest on a norm of international character accepted by the civilized world and defined with a specificity comparable to the features of the 18th-century paradigms [violation of safe conducts, infringement of the rights of ambassadors, and piracy]' which Congress had in mind when adopting the First Judiciary Act 1789 (*Sosa* v. *Alvarez-Machain*, 542 U.S. 692 (2004)). This significantly narrows down the potential of the ATCA which, in the future, shall only offer a potential remedy to victims of the most serious violations of human rights.

2.4. Questions for discussion: the scope of the extra-territorial obligation to protect human rights

1. Once it is agreed that human rights obligations extending beyond States' national territory may be imposed, is there any reason in principle to accept such an extension where State agents are acting on foreign territory, but to deny it where prescriptive or adjudicative extraterritoriality is concerned – i.e. where the claim is that the legislator should adopt extra-territorial regulations, or that the courts should have the power to adjudicate claims about situations arising outside the national territory? Which arguments could justify thus limiting the scope of extra-territorial human rights obligations?

2. May the reluctance of courts to imposing obligations to protect human rights beyond national borders be explained by a perception that the exercise of prescriptive or adjudicative extra-territoriality constitutes a threat to the sovereignty of the foreign State? For a State to assert jurisdiction over certain situations located outside its national territory, there must be a reasonable link between the State and the situation concerned. It has been argued, however, that 'one potentially crucial factor to be weighed into the test of reasonableness is that the exercise of extraterritorial jurisdiction in order to contribute to the protection of human rights in the host State of the foreign investment does not fall under the category of forms of extraterritorial jurisdiction which primarily benefit the State thus extending the reach of its national laws. Rather, ... extraterritorial jurisdiction exercised in order to contribute to the protection of internationally recognized human rights belongs to the category of forms of extraterritorial jurisdiction which may be justified in the name of international solidarity: whatever the reasons are for the territorial State not effectively protecting human rights, the exercise of extraterritorial jurisdiction by other States, in particular the home State of the multinational enterprise, in order to ensure such a protection, may be seen as a means to facilitate the compliance of the host State with its international obligations under the international law of human rights. This distinction between the two broadly defined justifications for extraterritorial jurisdiction is essential ... In contrast with situations where States exercise extraterritorial juridiction in order to promote their own, sovereign interests, where extraterritorial jurisdiction promotes solidarity between States, it should be considered as valid in principle, although as a matter of course any risks of conflict with the territorial State should be avoided to the fullest extent possible even is such cases' (O. De Schutter, 'Extraterritorial Jurisdiction as a Tool for Improving the Human Rights Accountability of Transnational Corporations', background paper to the seminar organized in collaboration with the Office of the UN High Commissioner for Human Rights in Brussels on 3–4 November 2006 within the mandate of the Special Representative to the

UN Secretary-General on the issue of human rights and transnational corporations and other enterprises). How relevant is that distinction?

3. How real is the risk that, under the guise of complying with extra-territorial obligations to protect human rights, States will in fact be tempted to enforce their policy preferences, for instance imposing economic sanctions on States whose policies they dislike, and for reasons therefore unconnected with a genuine concern for human rights protection abroad? Consider for instance the measures adopted by the United States targeting persons doing business in Cuba. In 1996, as part of a broader campaign to seek international sanctions against the Castro Government in Cuba, and to encourage a transition government leading to a democratically elected government in Cuba, the United States adopted the Cuban Liberty and Democratic Solidarity (Libertad) Act, better known as the Helms-Burton Act. One provision of the Act allows US nationals who have been expropriated following the 1959 revolution to seek damages against any natural or legal person having 'trafficked' such 'confiscated property'; another provision orders the Secretary of State to deny any visa to individuals found to have trafficked confiscated property, as well as to any 'corporate officer, principal, or shareholder with a controlling interest of an entity which has been involved in the confiscation of property or trafficking in confiscated property, a claim to which is owned by a United States national' (Cuban Liberty and Democratic Solidarity (Libertad) Act of 1996 (Codified in Title 22, Sections 6021–91 of the US Code) P.L. 104–14). The Helms-Burton Act has largely been denounced as an illegitimate exercise by the United States of its extra-territorial jurisdiction, to the extent that sanctions were threatened also against non-US citizens and companies for doing business in Cuba (see A. F. Löwenfeld, 'Congress and Cuba: the Helms-Burton Act', *American Journal of International Law*, 90 (1996), 419–34, and the rejoinder to this critique by B. M. Clagett, 'Title III of the Helms-Burton Act is Consistent with International Law', *American Journal of International Law*, 90 (1996), 434–40; A. Reinisch, 'A Few Public International Law Comments on the "Cuban Liberty and Democratic Solidarity (Libertad) Act" of 1996', *European Journal of International Law*, 7, No. 4 (1996), 55). Based on this example, is there a risk that the development of extra-territorial obligations to protect human rights will encourage instances of instrumentalization of human rights by States? Compare the Helms-Burton Act with the Alien Tort Claims Act (see box 2.2.). What substantially differentiates the two legislations from one another?

2.3 The obligation of international assistance and co-operation

Article 2(1) of the International Covenant on Economic, Social and Cultural Rights provides that the States parties to the Covenant undertake to 'take steps, individually *and through international assistance and co-operation*, especially economic and technical', to the maximum of their available resources, 'with a view to achieving progressively the full realization of the rights' recognized in the Covenant. The notion of international co-operation also is mentioned in relation to the right to an adequate standard of living in Article 11(1) of the Covenant, according to which 'States Parties will take appropriate steps to ensure the realization of this right, recognizing to this effect the essential importance of international co-operation based on free consent'. Under

Part IV of the Covenant, which relates to the measures of implementation, two provisions relate to international assistance and co-operation. Article 22 states that the Economic and Social Council may bring to the attention of other UN bodies and agencies concerned with furnishing technical assistance any information arising out of the reports submitted by States under the Covenant which 'may assist such bodies in deciding, each within its field of competence, on the advisability of international measures likely to contribute to the effective progressive implementation of the present Covenant'. Article 23 specifies the different forms international action for the achievement of the rights recognized in the Covenant may take: such international action 'includes such methods as the conclusion of conventions, the adoption of recommendations, the furnishing of technical assistance and the holding of regional meetings and technical meetings for the purpose of consultation and study organized in conjunction with the Governments concerned'.

The preparatory works show that, in adopting these provisions relating to international assistance and co-operation, the drafters of the International Covenant on Economic, Social and Cultural Rights did not wish to impose an obligation on any State to provide such assistance or co-operation at any specified level (Ph. Alston and G. Quinn, 'The Nature and Scope of States Parties' Obligations under the International Covenant on Economic, Social and Cultural Rights', *Human Rights Quarterly*, 9 (1987), 156 at 186–92). However, this is not to say that the reference made in Article 2(1) of the Covenant to international assistance and co-operation produces no useful effect. Taking as its departure point both Article 56 of the UN Charter, which imposes on all the Members of the United Nations to 'take joint and separate action in co-operation with the Organisation', *inter alia*, in order to achieve universal respect for, and observance of, human rights and fundamental freedoms for all, and paragraph 34 of the Vienna Declaration and Programme of Action adopted at the Vienna World Conference on Human Rights of 14–25 June 1993 – which refers to the '[i]ncreased efforts [which] should be made to assist countries which so request to create the conditions whereby each individual can enjoy universal human rights and fundamental freedoms' (UN Doc. A/CONF.157/23, 12 July 1993), the UN Committee on Economic, Social and Cultural Rights has identified certain obligations the States parties to the Covenant owe to populations under the jurisdiction of other States:

Committee on Economic, Social and Cultural Rights, General Comment No. 12 (1999), *The Right to Adequate Food (Art. 11 of the International Covenant on Economic, Social and Cultural Rights)*, E/C.12/1999/5, para. 38:

States have a joint and individual responsibility, in accordance with the Charter of the United Nations, to co-operate in providing disaster relief and humanitarian assistance in times of emergency, including assistance to refugees and internally displaced persons. Each State should contribute to this task in accordance with its ability. The role of the World Food Programme (WFP) and the Office of the United Nations High Commissioner for Refugees (UNHCR), and increasingly that of UNICEF and FAO is of particular importance in this respect and should be strengthened. Priority in food aid should be given to the most vulnerable populations.

Committee on Economic, Social and Cultural Rights, General Comment No. 14 (2000), *The Right to the Highest Attainable Standard of Health (Art. 12 of the International Covenant on Economic, Social and Cultural Rights)*, E/C.12/2000/4, para. 39:

Depending on the availability of resources, States [in particular States in a position to assist developing countries in fulfilling their core and other obligations under the Covenant] should facilitate access to essential health facilities, goods and services in other countries, wherever possible and provide the necessary aid when required.

The monitoring of States under the ICESCR could constitute an opportunity to iden-tify the needs of that State in terms of development co-operation, or of other forms of co-operation from other States – bilaterally or through international agencies – on the basis of an assessment of the factors which impede the full realization of economic and social rights on the territory of the State concerned. The potential of the Covenant remains significantly underdeveloped in this respect, however, as already noted by the Committee on Economic, Social and Cultural Rights in 1990:

Committee on Economic, Social, and Cultural Rights, General Comment No. 2, *International Technical Assistance Measures (Art. 22 of the Covenant)* (1990) (E/1990/23):

1. Article 22 of the Covenant establishes a mechanism by which the Economic and Social Council may bring to the attention of relevant United Nations bodies any matters arising out of reports submitted under the Covenant 'which may assist such bodies in deciding, each within its field of competence, on the advisability of international measures likely to contribute to the effective progressive implementation of the ... Covenant'. While the primary responsibility under article 22 is vested in the Council, it is clearly appropriate for the Committee on Economic, Social and Cultural Rights to play an active role in advising and assisting the Council in this regard.

2. Recommendations in accordance with article 22 may be made to any 'organs of the United Nations, their subsidiary organs and specialized agencies concerned with furnishing technical assistance'. The Committee considers that this provision should be interpreted so as to include virtually all United Nations organs and agencies involved in any aspect of international development co-operation. It would therefore be appropriate for recommendations in accordance with article 22 to be addressed, *inter alia*, to the Secretary-General, subsidiary organs of the Council such as the Commission on Human Rights, the Commission on Social Development and the Commission on the Status of Women, other bodies such as UNDP, UNICEF and CDP, agencies such as the World Bank and IMF, and any of the other specialized agencies such as ILO, FAO, UNESCO and WHO.

3. Article 22 could lead either to recommendations of a general policy nature or to more narrowly focused recommendations relating to a specific situation. In the former context, the principal role of the Committee would seem to be to encourage greater attention to efforts to promote economic, social and cultural rights within the framework of international

development cooperation activities undertaken by, or with the assistance of, the United Nations and its agencies ...

4. As a preliminary practical matter, the Committee notes that its own endeavours would be assisted, and the relevant agencies would also be better informed, if they were to take a greater interest in the work of the Committee. While recognizing that such an interest can be demonstrated in a variety of ways, the Committee observes that attendance by representatives of the appropriate United Nations bodies at its first four sessions has, with the notable exceptions of ILO, UNESCO and WHO, been very low. Similarly, pertinent materials and written information had been received from only a very limited number of agencies. The Committee considers that a deeper understanding of the relevance of economic, social and cultural rights in the context of international development co-operation activities would be considerably facilitated through greater interaction between the Committee and the appropriate agencies. At the very least, the day of general discussion on a specific issue, which the Committee undertakes at each of its sessions, provides an ideal context in which a potentially productive exchange of views can be undertaken.

5. On the broader issues of the promotion of respect for human rights in the context of development activities, the Committee has so far seen only rather limited evidence of specific efforts by United Nations bodies. It notes with satisfaction in this regard the initiative taken jointly by the Centre for Human Rights and UNDP in writing to United Nations Resident Representatives and other field-based officials, inviting their 'suggestions and advice, in particular with respect to possible forms of co-operation in ongoing projects [identified] as having a human rights dimension or in new ones in response to a specific Government's request'. The Committee has also been informed of long-standing efforts undertaken by ILO to link its own human rights and other international labour standards to its technical co-operation activities.

6. With respect to such activities, two general principles are important. The first is that the two sets of human rights are indivisible and interdependent. This means that efforts to promote one set of rights should also take full account of the other. United Nations agencies involved in the promotion of economic, social and cultural rights should do their utmost to ensure that their activities are fully consistent with the enjoyment of civil and political rights. In negative terms this means that the international agencies should scrupulously avoid involvement in projects which, for example, involve the use of forced labour in contravention of international standards, or promote or reinforce discrimination against individuals or groups contrary to the provisions of the Covenant, or involve large-scale evictions or displacement of persons without the provision of all appropriate protection and compensation. In positive terms, it means that, wherever possible, the agencies should act as advocates of projects and approaches which contribute not only to economic growth or other broadly defined objectives, but also to enhanced enjoyment of the full range of human rights.

7. The second principle of general relevance is that development co-operation activities do not automatically contribute to the promotion of respect for economic, social and cultural rights. Many activities undertaken in the name of 'development' have subsequently been recognized as ill-conceived and even counter-productive in human rights terms. In order to reduce the incidence of such problems, the whole range of issues dealt with in the Covenant should, wherever possible and appropriate, be given specific and careful consideration.

8. Despite the importance of seeking to integrate human rights concerns into development activities, it is true that proposals for such integration can too easily remain at a level of generality. Thus, in an effort to encourage the operationalization of the principle contained in article 22 of the Covenant, the Committee wishes to draw attention to the following specific measures which merit consideration by the relevant bodies:

   (a) As a matter of principle, the appropriate United Nations organs and agencies should specifically recognize the intimate relationship which should be established between development activities and efforts to promote respect for human rights in general, and economic, social and cultural rights in particular ...;

   (b) Consideration should be given by United Nations agencies to the proposal, made by the Secretary-General in a report of 1979 ['The international dimensions of the right to development as a human right in relation with other human rights based on international co-operation, including the right to peace, taking into account the requirements of the new international economic order and the fundamental human needs' (E/CN.4/1334, para. 314)] that a 'human rights impact statement' be required to be prepared in connection with all major development co-operation activities;

   (c) The training or briefing given to project and other personnel employed by United Nations agencies should include a component dealing with human rights standards and principles;

   (d) Every effort should be made, at each phase of a development project, to ensure that the rights contained in the Covenants are duly taken into account. This would apply, for example, in the initial assessment of the priority needs of a particular country, in the identification of particular projects, in project design, in the implementation of the project, and in its final evaluation.

9. A matter which has been of particular concern to the Committee in the examination of the reports of States parties is the adverse impact of the debt burden and of the relevant adjustment measures on the enjoyment of economic, social and cultural rights in many countries. The Committee recognizes that adjustment programmes will often be unavoidable and that these will frequently involve a major element of austerity. Under such circumstances, however, endeavours to protect the most basic economic, social and cultural rights become more, rather than less, urgent. States parties to the Covenant, as well as the relevant United Nations agencies, should thus make a particular effort to ensure that such protection is, to the maximum extent possible, built-in to programmes and policies designed to promote adjustment. Such an approach, which is sometimes referred to as 'adjustment with a human face' or as promoting 'the human dimension of development' requires that the goal of protecting the rights of the poor and vulnerable should become a basic objective of economic adjustment. Similarly, international measures to deal with the debt crisis should take full account of the need to protect economic, social and cultural rights through, *inter alia*, international co-operation. In many situations, this might point to the need for major debt relief initiatives.

10. Finally, the Committee wishes to draw attention to the important opportunity provided to States parties, in accordance with article 22 of the Covenant, to identify in their reports any particular needs they might have for technical assistance or development co-operation.

This General Comment is grounded, for the most part, on the need to seize the process of State reporting to the Committee on Economic, Social and Cultural Rights as an opportunity for the identification of the needs of technical assistance and development co-operation. This idea is also central to the establishment of the Universal Periodic Review, as will be seen in chapter 10. But two other ideas are also put forward in the General Comment. One is that development and human rights should be mutually supportive, strengthening each other rather than competing against one another, or even worse – undermining each other. Another idea is that there may be a need to crystallize into a legal obligation imposed on developed countries, the assistance needs of developing countries. Both ideas are also present in the following paragraphs of the General Comment adopted by the Committee on the Rights of the Child on the general measures of implementation of the Convention on the Rights of the Child:

Committee on the Rights of the Child, General Comment No. 5 (2003), General Measures of Implementation of the Convention on the Rights of the Child (Arts. 4, 42 and 44, para. 6) (CRC/GC/2003/5, 27 November 2003), paras. 60–4:

60. Article 4 emphasizes that implementation of the Convention is a co-operative exercise for the States of the world. This article and others in the Convention highlight the need for international co-operation. The Charter of the United Nations (Arts. 55 and 56) identifies the overall purposes of international economic and social co-operation, and members pledge themselves under the Charter 'to take joint and separate action in co-operation with the Organisation' to achieve these purposes. In the United Nations Millennium Declaration and at other global meetings, including the United Nations General Assembly special session on children, States have pledged themselves, in particular, to international co-operation to eliminate poverty.

61. The Committee advises States parties that the Convention should form the framework for international development assistance related directly or indirectly to children and that programmes of donor States should be rights-based. The Committee urges States to meet internationally agreed targets, including the United Nations target for international development assistance of 0.7 per cent of gross domestic product. This goal was reiterated along with other targets in the Monterrey Consensus, arising from the 2002 International Conference on Financing for Development. The Committee encourages States parties that receive international aid and assistance to allocate a substantive part of that aid specifically to children. The Committee expects States parties to be able to identify on a yearly basis the amount and proportion of international support earmarked for the implementation of children's rights.

62. The Committee endorses the aims of the 20/20 initiative, to achieve universal access to basic social services of good quality on a sustainable basis, as a shared responsibility of developing and donor States. The Committee notes that international meetings held to review progress have concluded that many States are going to have difficulty meeting fundamental economic and social rights unless additional resources are allocated and efficiency in resource allocation is increased. The Committee takes note of and encourages efforts being made to reduce poverty in the most heavily indebted countries through the Poverty Reduction Strategy Paper (PRSP). As the central, country-led strategy for achieving the millennium development goals, PRSPs must include a strong focus on children's rights. The Committee urges Governments,

donors and civil society to ensure that children are a prominent priority in the development of PRSPs and sectorwide approaches to development (SWAps). Both PRSPs and SWAps should reflect children's rights principles, with a holistic, child-centred approach recognizing children as holders of rights and the incorporation of development goals and objectives which are relevant to children.

63. The Committee encourages States to provide and to use, as appropriate, technical assistance in the process of implementing the Convention. The United Nations Children's Fund (UNICEF), the Office of the High Commissioner for Human Rights (OHCHR) and other United Nations and United Nations–related agencies can provide technical assistance with many aspects of implementation. States parties are encouraged to identify their interest in technical assistance in their reports under the Convention.

64. In their promotion of international co-operation and technical assistance, all United Nations and United Nations-related agencies should be guided by the Convention and should mainstream children's rights throughout their activities. They should seek to ensure within their influence that international co-operation is targeted at supporting States to fulfil their obligations under the Convention. Similarly the World Bank Group, the International Monetary Fund and World Trade Organisation should ensure that their activities related to international co-operation and economic development give primary consideration to the best interests of children and promote full implementation of the Convention.

2.4 Human rights and development

Both the idea that human rights and development should be mutually supportive and the idea that there may exist an obligation of mutual assistance and co-operation, as a correlative to a right to development, have made considerable progress in the 1980s and throughout the 1990s. On the one hand, the notion of development has been redefined, particularly under the influence of the economist Amartya K. Sen and of the founder of the Human Development Reports of the United Nations Development Programme, Mahbubul Haq, in order to overcome the risk of development and human rights growing increasingly apart from each other. The construction of development and human rights as mutually supportive remains incomplete, however, as illustrated by the debate on the relationship of the Millennium Development Goals to human rights. On the other hand, attempts have been made to give concrete content to the 'right to development' proclaimed in 1986 by the United Nations General Assembly, but which remains insufficiently operational. This section briefly addresses these questions. While the relationship with the question of 'jurisdiction' as usually understood – i.e. the scope of the human rights obligations imposed on States, particularly the geographical scope – may seem tenuous, this section does ask whether there exists a 'global responsibility' for human rights, and what the implications are of seeing development co-operation as a means of realizing human rights (for useful collections of essays related to this issue, see P. Alston and M. Robinson (eds.), *Human Rights and Development: Towards Mutual*

Reinforcement (Oxford University Press, 2005); B. Andreassen and S. Marks (eds.), *Development as a Human Right* (Cambridge, Mass.: Harvard University Press, 2006); for contributions linking the issue of extraterritorial obligations to development, see M. E. Salomon, *Global Responsibility for Human Rights* (Oxford University Press, 2007) and M. E. Salomon, A. Tostensen and W. Vandenhole (eds.), *Casting the Net Wider: Human Rights, Development and New Duty – Bearers* (Mortsel, Belgium: Intersentia, 2007)).

Amartya K. Sen, *Development as Freedom* (New York: Alfred A. Knopf, 1999), pp. 18–19 and 36–8:

There are two distinct reasons for the crucial importance of individual freedom in the concept of development, related respectively to *evaluation* and *effectiveness*. First, in the normative approach used here, substantive individual freedoms are taken to be critical. The success of a society is to be evaluated, in this view, primarily by the substantive freedoms that the members of that society enjoy. This evaluative position differs from the informational focus of more traditional normative approaches, which focus on other variables, such as utility, or procedural liberty, or real income ... The second reason for taking substantive freedom to be so crucial is that freedom is not only the basis of the evaluation of success and failure, but it is also a principal determinant of individual initiative and social effectiveness. Greater freedom enhances the ability of people to help themselves and also to influence the world, and these matters are central to the process of development ... In this approach, expansion of freedom is viewed as both (1) the *primary end* and (2) the *principal means* of development. They can be called respectively the 'constitutive role' and the 'instrumental role' of freedom in development. The constitutive role of freedom relates to the importance of substantive freedom in enriching human life. The substantive freedoms include elementary capabilities like being able to avoid such deprivations as starvation, undernourishment, escapable morbidity and premature mortality, as well as the freedoms that are associated with being literate and numerate, enjoying political participation and uncensored speech and so on. In this constitutive perspective, development involves expansion of these and other basic freedoms ... The instrumental role of freedom concerns the way different kinds of rights, opportunities, and entitlements contribute to the expansion of human freedom in general, and thus to promoting development ... The effectiveness of freedom as an instrument lies in the fact that different kinds of freedom interrelate with one another, and freedom of one type may greatly help in advancing freedom of other types ... [Instrumental freedoms such as (1) political freedoms, (2) economic facilities, (3) social opportunities, (4) transparency guarantees, and (5) protective security] tend to contribute to the general capability of a person to live more freely, but they also serve to complement one another. While development analysis must, on the one hand, be concerned with the objectives and aims that make the instrumental freedoms consequentially important, it must also take note of the empirical linkages that tie the distinct types of freedom together, strengthening their joint importance. Indeed, these connections are central to a fuller understanding of the instrumental role of freedom. The claim that freedom is not only the primary objective of development but also its principal means relates particularly to these linkages.

The view of development promoted by Sen challenged the dominant use of economic growth, measured through the level of GDP per capita, as a proxy for development. This view influenced the introduction in 1990, by the United Nations Development Programme (UNDP), of the human development index (HDI) as an alternative means of evaluating development. The UNDP selected three basic dimensions of development to be the main focus of its analysis of development: longevity, as a proxy for health; adult literacy, and later mean years of school enrollment, as proxies for education and learning; and per capita income, or 'command over resources needed for a decent living'. The HDI, an indicator combining these three components, relied on a multidimensional definition of development, redefined as 'a process of enlarging people's choices'. The 1990 Human Development Report established that broader scope of choice was only available to people who could lead long and healthy lives, acquire knowledge and have 'access to resources needed for a decent standard of living'. Income was an inappropriate yardstick for development for three main reasons: first, information on average income did not reveal the composition of wealth or its beneficiaries; second, people 'often value achievements that do not show up at all, or not immediately, in higher measured income or growth figures'; and finally, there was no automatic empirical link between income growth and the expansion of choice (i.e. there are high-income countries which afford relatively low levels of choice – as expressed in longevity, or level of education – and, conversely, there are low-income countries in which choices are relatively broad). Therefore, 'development must ... be more than just the expansion of income and wealth. Its focus must be people' (UNDP, *Human Development Report 1990* (Oxford University Press, 1990), pp. 9–10).

Although this represented an important advance in comparison to definitions of development that equate it with economic growth, the link between development and human rights remained implicit in this new measure of development. In contrast, such a link is explicit in the Declaration on the Right to Development adopted in 1986 by the UN General Assembly:

Declaration on the Right to Development (adopted by General Assembly Resolution 41/128 of 4 December 1986):

The General Assembly,

Bearing in mind the purposes and principles of the Charter of the United Nations relating to the achievement of international co-operation in solving international problems of an economic, social, cultural or humanitarian nature, and in promoting and encouraging respect for human rights and fundamental freedoms for all without distinction as to race, sex, language or religion,

Recognizing that development is a comprehensive economic, social, cultural and political process, which aims at the constant improvement of the well-being of the entire population and of all individuals on the basis of their active, free and meaningful participation in development and in the fair distribution of benefits resulting therefrom,

Considering that under the provisions of the Universal Declaration of Human Rights everyone is entitled to a social and international order in which the rights and freedoms set forth in that Declaration can be fully realized,

Recalling the provisions of the International Covenant on Economic, Social and Cultural Rights and of the International Covenant on Civil and Political Rights, ...

Recalling the right of peoples to self-determination, by virtue of which they have the right freely to determine their political status and to pursue their economic, social and cultural development,

Recalling also the right of peoples to exercise, subject to the relevant provisions of both International Covenants on Human Rights, full and complete sovereignty over all their natural wealth and resources,

Mindful of the obligation of States under the Charter to promote universal respect for and observance of human rights and fundamental freedoms for all without distinction of any kind such as race, colour, sex, language, religion, political or other opinion, national or social origin, property, birth or other status,

Considering that the elimination of the massive and flagrant violations of the human rights of the peoples and individuals affected by situations such as those resulting from colonialism, neo-colonialism, apartheid, all forms of racism and racial discrimination, foreign domination and occupation, aggression and threats against national sovereignty, national unity and territorial integrity and threats of war would contribute to the establishment of circumstances propitious to the development of a great part of mankind,

Concerned at the existence of serious obstacles to development, as well as to the complete fulfilment of human beings and of peoples, constituted, *inter alia*, by the denial of civil, political, economic, social and cultural rights, and considering that all human rights and fundamental freedoms are indivisible and interdependent and that, in order to promote development, equal attention and urgent consideration should be given to the implementation, promotion and protection of civil, political, economic, social and cultural rights and that, accordingly, the promotion of, respect for and enjoyment of certain human rights and fundamental freedoms cannot justify the denial of other human rights and fundamental freedoms,

Considering that international peace and security are essential elements for the realization of the right to development,

Reaffirming that there is a close relationship between disarmament and development and that progress in the field of disarmament would considerably promote progress in the field of development and that resources released through disarmament measures should be devoted to the economic and social development and well-being of all peoples and, in particular, those of the developing countries,

Recognizing that the human person is the central subject of the development process and that development policy should therefore make the human being the main participant and beneficiary of development,

Recognizing that the creation of conditions favourable to the development of peoples and individuals is the primary responsibility of their States,

Aware that efforts at the international level to promote and protect human rights should be accompanied by efforts to establish a new international economic order,

Confirming that the right to development is an inalienable human right and that equality of opportunity for development is a prerogative both of nations and of individuals who make up nations,

Proclaims the following Declaration on the Right to Development:

Article 1

1. The right to development is an inalienable human right by virtue of which every human person and all peoples are entitled to participate in, contribute to, and enjoy economic,

social, cultural and political development, in which all human rights and fundamental freedoms can be fully realized.

2. The human right to development also implies the full realization of the right of peoples to self-determination, which includes, subject to the relevant provisions of both International Covenants on Human Rights, the exercise of their inalienable right to full sovereignty over all their natural wealth and resources.

Article 2

1. The human person is the central subject of development and should be the active participant and beneficiary of the right to development.
2. All human beings have a responsibility for development, individually and collectively, taking into account the need for full respect for their human rights and fundamental freedoms as well as their duties to the community, which alone can ensure the free and complete fulfilment of the human being, and they should therefore promote and protect an appropriate political, social and economic order for development.
3. States have the right and the duty to formulate appropriate national development policies that aim at the constant improvement of the well-being of the entire population and of all individuals, on the basis of their active, free and meaningful participation in development and in the fair distribution of the benefits resulting therefrom.

Article 3

1. States have the primary responsibility for the creation of national and international conditions favourable to the realization of the right to development.
2. The realization of the right to development requires full respect for the principles of international law concerning friendly relations and co-operation among States in accordance with the Charter of the United Nations.
3. States have the duty to co-operate with each other in ensuring development and eliminating obstacles to development. States should realize their rights and fulfil their duties in such a manner as to promote a new international economic order based on sovereign equality, interdependence, mutual interest and co-operation among all States, as well as to encourage the observance and realization of human rights.

Article 4

1. States have the duty to take steps, individually and collectively, to formulate international development policies with a view to facilitating the full realization of the right to development.
2. Sustained action is required to promote more rapid development of developing countries. As a complement to the efforts of developing countries, effective international co-operation is essential in providing these countries with appropriate means and facilities to foster their comprehensive development.

Article 5

States shall take resolute steps to eliminate the massive and flagrant violations of the human rights of peoples and human beings affected by situations such as those resulting from apartheid, all forms of racism and racial discrimination, colonialism, foreign domination and occupation, aggression, foreign interference and threats against national sovereignty, national unity and territorial integrity, threats of war and refusal to recognize the fundamental right of peoples to self-determination.

Article 6

1. All States should co-operate with a view to promoting, encouraging and strengthening universal respect for and observance of all human rights and fundamental freedoms for all without any distinction as to race, sex, language or religion.
2. All human rights and fundamental freedoms are indivisible and interdependent; equal attention and urgent consideration should be given to the implementation, promotion and protection of civil, political, economic, social and cultural rights.
3. States should take steps to eliminate obstacles to development resulting from failure to observe civil and political rights, as well as economic social and cultural rights.

Article 7

All States should promote the establishment, maintenance and strengthening of international peace and security and, to that end, should do their utmost to achieve general and complete disarmament under effective international control, as well as to ensure that the resources released by effective disarmament measures are used for comprehensive development, in particular that of the developing countries.

Article 8

1. States should undertake, at the national level, all necessary measures for the realization of the right to development and shall ensure, *inter alia*, equality of opportunity for all in their access to basic resources, education, health services, food, housing, employment and the fair distribution of income. Effective measures should be undertaken to ensure that women have an active role in the development process. Appropriate economic and social reforms should be carried out with a view to eradicating all social injustices.
2. States should encourage popular participation in all spheres as an important factor in development and in the full realization of all human rights.

Article 9

1. All the aspects of the right to development set forth in the present Declaration are indivisible and interdependent and each of them should be considered in the context of the whole.
2. Nothing in the present Declaration shall be construed as being contrary to the purposes and principles of the United Nations, or as implying that any State, group or person has a right to engage in any activity or to perform any act aimed at the violation of the rights set forth in the Universal Declaration of Human Rights and in the International Covenants on Human Rights.

Article 10

Steps should be taken to ensure the full exercise and progressive enhancement of the right to development, including the formulation, adoption and implementation of policy, legislative and other measures at the national and international levels.

The Declaration on the right to development sees development as a process through which all human rights and fundamental freedoms can be fully realized. In practice, however, development agencies have been slow at recognizing the operational character of human rights – i.e. the positive contribution human rights could make to guiding their activities and the process of development itself. A new and significant attempt was made by the UNDP in the 2000 Human Development Report, which explored at length the relationship between human rights and human development. The report emphasized in particular how human rights could reinforce and support human development in two ways: first, by guiding the process of development towards the realization of human rights, in line with the 1986 Declaration on the Right to Development; and second, by reconceptualizing human needs as rights, thus transforming the relationship between governments and populations to one between duty-bearers and rights-holders. Indeed, whereas human development goals were valued both as useful as means of development in an instrumental perspective and as desirable for their own sake as ends of development, they still remained short of being considered entitlements from a *legal* perspective. This, the 2000 Human Development Report saw as a missed opportunity. The notion that realizing certain development goals is a *duty* rather than an *option* modifies both the nature of the goal, and the allocation of responsibility among social actors (state, corporations, civil society and individuals). Human rights provide a new analytical tool: capability deprivation, often a multi-causal phenomenon, when seen through the lens of human rights, can be analysed in terms of attribution of responsibility. By affirming that a development goal is an entitlement, human rights language empowers actors to make claims against duty-bearers and forces them to act against all types of capability-constraining obstacles, from lack of resources to discriminatory social practices. Moreover, a human rights approach to development calls for an analysis of both the ends and the *process* of development, and particularly sets limits to, or otherwise guides, the policies that can be carried out in the pursuit of development goals. The principles of accountability, participation, non-discrimination, and empowerment, are particularly relevant in this regard. A final contribution of a human rights approach to development thinking is that human rights assessment focuses not only on progress made so far in the fulfillment of rights, but also on the 'extent to which the gains are socially protected against potential threats': they constitute safeguards against the risk of policy reversals (UNDP, *Human Development Report 2000* (Oxford University Press, 2000), p. 23).

These considerations also played a central role in the discussion concerning the relationship between the Millennium Development Goals (MDGs) and human rights. The MDGs were derived from the Millennium Declaration adopted by the UN General Assembly in September 2000, at a World Summit attended by 147 heads of State or government. The eight MDGs relate to (1) the eradication of extreme poverty and hunger; (2) the achievement of universal primary education; (3) the promotion of gender equality and the empowerment of women; (4) the reduction of child mortality; (5) the improvement of maternal health; (6) combating HIV/AIDS, malaria, and other diseases; (7) environmental sustainability; and (8) the establishment of a global partnership for development. Eighteen time-bound targets and forty-eight indicators have been agreed upon in order to improve monitoring of progress towards the achievement of these goals, and a series of institutional initiatives, including the development of national MDG reports in each developing country, have been taken in order to ensure that progress is made towards fulfilling these objectives. Although Millennium Human Rights Goals have also been agreed upon, they have attracted far less attention, they are less operational, and they have not been the same focus of attention, than the MDGs; nor have they led to similar degrees of resource mobilization. Attempts have been made to build human rights into the MDG process:

The Millennium Development Goals and economic, social and cultural rights. A Joint Statement by the UN Committee on Economic, Social and Cultural Rights and the UN Commission on Human Rights' Special Rapporteurs on Economic, Social and Cultural Rights (29 November 2002), paras. 3–4:

We believe that chances for attaining Millennium Development Goals will improve if all UN agencies and governments adopt a comprehensive human rights approach to realizing the MDGs, including in the formulation of the corresponding indicators.

The Committee on Economic, Social and Cultural Rights (CESCR) and Commission on Human Rights' Special Rapporteurs on Economic, Social and Cultural Rights believe that human rights, including economic, social and cultural rights help to realize any strategy to meet the MDGs for example by:

(i) providing a compelling normative framework, underpinned by universally recognized human values and reinforced by legal obligations, for the formulation of national and international development policies towards achieving the MDGs;

(ii) raising the level of empowerment and participation of individuals;

(iii) Affirming the accountability of various stakeholders, including international organisations and NGOs, donors and transnational corporations, *vis-à-vis* people affected by problems related to poverty, hunger, education, gender inequality, health, housing and safe drinking water; and

(iv) reinforcing the twin principles of global equity and shared responsibility which are the very foundation for the Millennium Declaration.

Philip Alston, 'Ships Passing in the Night: the Current State of the Human Rights and Development Debate Seen Through the Lens of the Millennium Development Goals', *Human Rights Quarterly*, 27 (2005), 755 at 813 and 826–7:

Institutionalized arrangements for monitoring processes and outcomes and for establishing some form of accountability are indispensable in any human rights context and they are equally relevant and necessary in relation to MDGs. Such a dimension is necessary to ensure that the MDG initiative is more than just another bureaucratic scheme that will come and go just as its predecessors have. In the MDG context this would require the setting of explicit targets or benchmarks and then detailed annual or biannual reporting on the progress achieved in relation to those targets. Where the benchmark has not been met, a re-examination of the relevant policies would be triggered. The reporting would also need to be disaggregated to the extent possible, to take account of elements such as gender, regional disparities, and the situation of the most disadvantaged groups in the society in question (who should be identified in the benchmarking process). There is ... an important role for international human rights mechanisms in this regard, but the first line of support should be at the national level. Thus, in every state in which a national human rights institution exists, the institution should be given an explicit mandate to review and report on the realization of MDG targets at regular intervals ...

[Actors of the human rights community share a responsibility for the lack of integration of the MDG and human rights agendas.] In the future, human rights proponents need to prioritize, stop expecting a paradigm shift, and tailor their prescriptions more carefully to address particular situations. The key elements in a new approach to ensuring effective complementarity between human rights and the MDGs should be: (i) overt recognition of the relevance of human rights obligations; (ii) ensuring an appropriate legal framework; (iii) encouraging community participation but doing so in a realistic and targeted way; and (iv) promoting MDG accountability mechanisms. All of these elements should, however, avoid being too prescriptive. Instead, what is needed is faith in the dynamism and self-starting nature of the rights framework once it is brought inside the gates of the development enterprise.

United Nations Development Program (UNDP), The Application of a Human Rights-Based Approach to Development Programming – What is the Added Value? (1998) (excerpt):

A human rights-based approach not only defines and identifies the subjects of development but it also translates people's needs into rights, and recognises the human person as the active subject and claim-holder. It further identifies the duties and obligations of those, against whom a claim can be brought, to ensure that needs are met. Thus, the concept of claim-holders and duty-bearers introduces another important element of the rights approach namely, accountability, which in current development strategies is not adequately addressed. Increased focus on promoting accountability, using the human rights obligations as the vehicle, holds the key to improved effectiveness and transparency of action and as such offers the potential 'added-value' flowing from the application of a rights-based approach. Accountability derives from the duties and obligations of States that are required to take steps, for example, through legislation, policies and programmes, that aim to respect, protect, promote and fulfil the human rights of all people within their jurisdiction. It should be underscored that this does not imply conditionalities but rather encourages action through co-operation and constructive dialogue in the development process.

Consider also the following proposal for strengthening the human rights dimension of development co-operation, both in clarifying the nature of the obligations donor States owe to developing States, and in defining how development co-operation should be made more accountable towards the ultimate beneficiaries, who should also become active participants in the process of development, as stated in the Declaration on the right to development:

The Role of development Co-operation and Food Aid in Realizing the Right to Adequate Food: Moving from Charity to Obligation, Report of the Special Rapporteur on the right to food, Mr Olivier De Schutter (A/HRC/10/005, 6 February 2009):

2. Development co-operation is one aspect of a broader obligation of international assistance and co-operation which may include, but is not limited to, the transfer of resources. In recent

years, development co-operation has been criticized from a number of different angles. Some have dismissed it as excessively donor-driven and top-down, and therefore as insufficiently informed by the views of the ultimate beneficiaries. The tendency of donors – whether Governments, intergovernmental agencies or private non-governmental organisations – to impose various demands on recipients without co-ordination has also been seen as imposing a heavy burden on the partner Government's administrative capacities, leading to suboptimal results. Others have denounced the mismanagement of aid by recipient Governments, noting that poor governance often resulted in aid not being used effectively. On 2 March 2005, the Paris Declaration on Aid Effectiveness was adopted as an attempt to improve the quality of aid. It has been endorsed by 122 Governments and the European Commission, 27 international organisations including six regional development banks, the World Bank and the Organisation for Economic Co-operation and Development (OECD), and a number of non-governmental organisations. The commitments contained in the Paris Declaration focus on the five principles of ownership, alignment, harmonization, managing for results and mutual accountability. These principles mark a shift from donor-driven to needs-driven aid strategies, and emphasize the need for evaluating the performance of both donors, particularly as regards harmonization and predictability of aid, and their partners ... [The] Paris Declaration could be further concretized if placed under a human rights framework, and particularly by taking into account the human right to adequate food ...

5. ... By co-operating internationally, ... donor States are not only meeting basic human needs. They are also contributing to realize the human right to adequate food. This has potentially three implications. First, there is the question of whether States are under an obligation to provide international assistance, including food aid, in certain circumstances, or at certain levels. Second, the way international assistance is delivered must take into account that it should contribute to implement the right to food: the principles of participation, transparency, accountability and non-discrimination, as well as access to remedies, must therefore be taken into account in the implementation of development co-operation policies and in the delivery of food aid. Third, the effectiveness of the aid provided should be regularly evaluated by measuring the contribution of the existing policies to the realization of the right to adequate food.

6. Whether in the field of development co-operation or in the field of food aid, their contributions are argued by donor countries to be made on a purely voluntary basis. However, donors cannot ignore their obligations under human rights law in the implementation of their policies in these fields. There are also situations where they may be under a duty to help, particularly when they have made commitments to this effect, and where reneging on those commitments would violate the principle of predictability for the recipient State.

[Defining obligations to provide aid]
7. Millennium Development Goal 8 is to develop a global partnership for development, a goal to which increased levels of donor country commitments to official development assistance can contribute ... Despite repeated commitments, again reaffirmed in the Millennium Declaration, in the Monterrey Consensus [Final Outcome of the International Conference on Financing for Development, adopted on 22 March 2002 in Monterrey, Mexico, A/CONF.198/3], in the Food and Agriculture Organisation of the United Nations (FAO) Voluntary Guidelines to support the progressive realization of the right to adequate food in the context of national food security ('FAO Guidelines') [see below, chapter 5], and in the 2008 Doha Declaration on Financing for Development, developed countries have mostly failed to meet the targets for ODA of

0.7 per cent of GDP to developing countries and 0.15 per cent to 0.2 per cent of GDP to least developed countries.

8. The Charter of the United Nations imposes in general terms an obligation on all its Members to 'take joint and separate action in cooperation with the Organisation', *inter alia*, for the achievement of human rights (see Arts. 55 and 56). Neither the International Covenant on Economic, Social and Cultural Rights, nor other human rights instruments, define precise levels at which States should provide aid. That, however, is not equivalent to saying that there is no such obligation; it is to say, rather, that this obligation is still 'imperfect', in need of being further clarified [A. Sen, 'Human Rights and Development' in B. Andreassen and St. Marks, *Development as a Human Right* (Cambridge, Mass.: Harvard University Press, 2006), chapter 2]. According to the Committee on Economic, Social and Cultural Rights, 'States parties [to the Covenant] should take steps to respect the enjoyment of the right to food in other countries, to protect that right, to facilitate access to food *and to provide the necessary aid when required*.' In the General Comment it devoted in 2000 to the right to the highest attainable standard of health, the Committee similarly noted that 'Depending on the availability of resources, States [in particular States in a position to assist developing countries in fulfilling their core and other obligations under the Covenant] should facilitate access to essential health facilities, goods and services in other countries, wherever possible *and provide the necessary aid when required*.' A consensus seems to emerge, at a minimum, on three requirements.

9. First, the Covenant imposes an obligation on all States parties to 'move as expeditiously and effectively as possible' towards the full realization of all human rights, including the right to adequate food. Moreover, 'any deliberately retrogressive measures in that regard would require the most careful consideration and would need to be fully justified by reference to the totality of the rights provided for in the Covenant and in the context of the full use of the maximum available resources' [E/1991/23, para. 9]. Therefore, at a minimum, developed countries should make measurable progress towards contributing to the full realization of human rights by supporting the efforts of governments in developing countries, and they should not diminish pre-existing levels of aid calculated as ODA in percentage of the GDP. Any regression in the level of aid provided that is not fully justified should be treated, presumptively, as a violation of States' obligations under international law.

10. Second, the assistance provided should be non-discriminatory. Even if it remains based on the voluntary decisions of each donor Government, the aid provided should not be determined by the political, strategic, commercial or historically rooted interests of the donors, but by an objective assessment of the identified needs in developing countries. This is required if aid is to be effective ... It also follows from the recognition of the fact that development co-operation is a means of fulfilling human rights, particularly the right to food. The implication is that aid should be informed by an adequate mapping of needs – including, in particular, the existence in certain countries of food insecurity and vulnerability ...

11. Third, the amount of aid provided to recipient countries remains volatile and unpredictable, changing from one year to the next and from one country to another. This does not allow recipient countries to plan their development over a number of years and creates the risk of aid being suspended or interrupted for politically motivated reasons, without such measures being based on objective and transparently applied considerations. Where such decisions result in negative impacts on the enjoyment of human rights, particularly on the right to food, they require careful consideration of the donor State's obligations. Donor States must therefore follow

up on the commitments they make to provide certain levels of aid at a specific time and in a given year. Such commitments give rise to legitimate expectations for the recipient State, which cannot be disappointed without an adequate justification being provided by the donor State.

[Implementing development co-operation in a human rights framework]
26. Until a few years ago, international aid was seen as a unilateral undertaking, by a donor country, to provide assistance to a recipient country, whether through bilateral or through multilateral channels. Now, strategies which were donor-driven are increasingly needs-driven, and expected to be aligned with strategies developed at the level of the partner country. A human rights framework requires that we deepen the principles of ownership, alignment and mutual accountability, by shifting our attention to the role of national parliaments, civil society organisations, and the ultimate beneficiaries of aid – the rights-holders – in the implementation and evaluation of foreign aid. It is this triangulation, away from a purely bilateral relationship between Governments, which the adoption of a human rights framework requires.

27. The current reform process of international aid is based on the principles of ownership, alignment, harmonization, managing for results, and mutual evaluation, which are made explicit in the Paris Declaration on Aid Effectiveness. An explicit endorsement of a human rights framework for the implementation of these principles could make them more concrete and operational. At a general level, human rights-based approaches to development co-operation recognize people 'as key actors in their own development, rather than passive recipients of commodities and services': they emphasize participation as both a means and a goal; they seek to empower, and thus should combine top-down and bottom-up approaches; both outcomes and processes should be monitored and evaluated, following the adoption of measurable goals and targets in programming; all stakeholders should be involved in analysis; and the programmes should focus on marginalized, disadvantaged, and excluded groups, and aim at reducing disparity [United Nations Development Group, The Human Rights Based Approach to Development Co-operation – Towards a Common Understanding among UN Agencies (2003)]. The human right to adequate food in particular should be guiding countries' choices of development strategies, and provide an objective benchmark to evaluate the effectiveness of development efforts, thus improving the accountability of both donors and partners.

28. Specifically, the implementation of the principles of national ownership and alignment would be greatly facilitated if the recipient State were to define its national priorities according to a national strategy for the realization of the right to food, whether it is formally integrated into broader poverty-reduction strategy documents or not. The Committee on Economic, Social and Cultural Rights has insisted on the need for States to work towards the adoption of a national strategy to ensure food and nutrition security for all, based on human rights principles that define the objectives, and the formulation of policies and corresponding benchmarks (E/C.12/1999/5, para. 21). Guideline 3 of the FAO Guidelines provides useful indications about how States could adopt a national human rights-based strategy for the realization of the right to adequate food, emphasizing in particular the need to allow for monitoring of progress and accountability, and to develop such strategies through participatory processes.

29. One of the commitments of the States adhering to the Paris Declaration on Aid Effectiveness is to enhance partner countries' accountability to their citizens and parliaments for their development policies, strategies and performance (paras. 3 (iii), and 14). This objective has been further reaffirmed by the Accra Summit on Aid Effectiveness of 2–4 September 2008 and in the 2008 Doha Declaration on Financing for Development. The elaboration, through participatory

processes, of a national strategy for the realization of the right to food provides a concrete means to improve the accountability of national governments and their responsiveness to the needs of their populations. The Accra Agenda for Action provides that developing countries and donors will 'ensure that their respective development policies and programmes are designed and implemented in ways consistent with their agreed international commitments on gender equality, human rights, disability and environmental sustainability' (para. 13(d)). Grounding development assistance on the human right to food would contribute to this agenda. Since development co-operation programmes would fit into a national strategy for the realization of the right to food defined at national level, the recipient Government would improve its bargaining position in aid negotiations. Since this national strategy would involve national parliaments and civil society organisations, development policies would be democratized. And since it would set benchmarks and allocate responsibilities, it would increase accountability in their implementation.

The principles of progressive realization, non-discrimination (or needs-based development co-operation), and predictability, are put forward in the Report above as a means to overcome the dichotomy between an understanding of development co-operation as 'charity' (i.e. as purely voluntary), and one which sees development co-operation as an 'obligation' (i.e. to transfer resources at certain defined levels). An interesting proposal made by Arjun Sengupta, the former independent expert on the right to development, also in order to overcome this dichotomy, is that of 'development compacts': developing countries would commit to fulfil and protect human rights, in particular by the adoption and implementation of a rights-based development programme and by setting up appropriate institutions, against the promise of the international community – including the United Nations system, the international financial institutions, and developed States – to support that process. Specifically, Sengupta proposed that the Development Assistance Committee of the Organization for Economic Co-operation and Development (OECD) could organize a 'support group' to scrutinize, review and approve the national development policies of the developing country; identify financial burden sharing and specific responsibilities and duties of the parties to the compact; and monitor the implementation of the compact. A new financing facility could also be established in order to ensure that resources are made available to finance the programmes which have been approved. Thus conceived, development compacts are 'a mechanism for ensuring that all stakeholders recognize the mutuality of obligations, so that the obligations of developing countries to carry out rights-based programmes are matched by reciprocal obligations of the international community to co-operate to enable the implementation of the programmes. The purpose of development compacts is to assure the developing countries that if they fulfil their obligations, the programme for realizing the right to development will not be disrupted owing to lack of financing' (*Fifth Report of the Independent Expert on the Right to Development*, E/CN.4/2002/WG.18/6, para. 14). Such development compacts thus clarify, by mutual agreement, the content of the obligations that correspond to the right to development, both for developing countries and for developed countries that are in a position to assist (see also A. Sengupta, 'On the

Theory and Practice of the Right to Development', *Human Rights Quarterly*, 24, No. 4 (2002), 837–89; and A. Sengupta, A. Negi and M. Basu (eds.), *Reflections on the Right to Development* (London: Sage Publications, 2005)).

Finally, it is vital to emphasize that neither the right to development, nor the obligation of international assistance and co-operation, are exclusively or even primarily about the transfer of resources from wealthy States to poorer States. This is first because the right to development can be given concrete meaning, and be considered justiciable, when considered in its 'do no harm' component: even if the obligation to assist is considered, at yet, to constitute an 'imperfect' obligation insofar as resource transfers are considered, at a minimum, it does require that States abstain from taking measures that could create obstacles to the realization of the right to development, for example by plundering the natural resources of another State or by allowing the revenues from the exploitation of natural resources to be diverted from the development needs of the population (indeed, these are the consequences derived by the African Commission on Human and Peoples' Rights from Article 22 of the African Charter, that recognizes the right to development: see Communication 227/1999, *Democratic Republic of Congo* v. *Burundi, Rwanda and Uganda* (2004) A.H.R.L.R. 19 (ACHPR 2004) (20th Activity Report); and Communication 155/96, *The Social and Economic Rights Action Center and the Center for Economic and Social Rights* v. *Nigeria* (2001) A.H.R.L.R. 60 (ACHPR 2001) (15th Annual Activity Report), presented in chapter 3, section 1).

But a second reason to be distrustful about assimilating the right to development to the transfer of resources from rich countries to poor countries is because such a view exemplifies a typically 'humanitarian' approach to the question of development – one that insists on alleviating poverty, rather than on combating the structural causes of poverty. It is for taking such an approach that the Millennium Development Goals have been heavily criticized, both by certain economists and by certain jurists. Erik Reinert, a Norwegian economist, thus notes that '[t]he pursuit of the MDGs seems to indicate that the United Nations institutions, following several failed development decades, have abandoned the effort to treat the causes of poverty, and have instead concentrated on attacking the symptoms of poverty ... Instead of attacking the sources of poverty from the inside of the production system ... the symptoms are addressed by throwing money at them from the outside' (E. S. Reinert, *How Rich Countries Got Rich ... and Why Poor Countries Stay Poor* (London: Constable, 2007), p. 240). This echoes the critique by Margot Salomon:

Margot E. Salomon, 'Poverty, Privilege and International Law: the Millennium Development Goals and the Guise of Humanitarianism', *German Yearbook of International Law*, 51 (2009), 39–73 at 72:

International law's sting, that which is said to distinguish it from other social scientific approaches to addressing poverty, is the principle of accountability. Yet there has been little accountability to the poor and impoverished, to the hungry, and to those without access to the basic necessities of life struggling on the other side of this small planet. Accountability remains all but absent in the wake of the financial crisis as poor people in poor countries pay the heaviest price for a disaster they had no hand in creating, and we can anticipate that climate change will apportion its retribution similarly. The MDGs are not being achieved because they exist as a discrete humanitarian project rooted in the idea of collective good and shared responsibility, appended to the far grander economic project resting on a belief in individualized gain and minimal regulation. As a result, the MDGs were not set up to challenge structural inequality, nor to present economic alternatives, nor were they given any teeth with which to confront the demands of poverty reduction.

It is thus important to anchor the right to development, as does the Declaration on the Right to Development, into Article 28 of the Universal Declaration of Human Rights, which states that everyone is entitled to 'a social and international order in which the rights and freedoms set forth in that Declaration can be fully realized'. The implication is that all international agreements – including in particular in areas such as trade and investment – should be evaluated, in order to ensure that they will contribute to the full realization of human rights and to development as defined by the Declaration on the Right to Development. It is also this more ambitious view of the right to development that was approved at the Vienna World Conference on Human Rights:

Vienna Declaration and Programme of Action (World Conference on Human Rights, 14–25 June 1993), paras. 10–12:

10. As stated in the Declaration on the Right to Development, the human person is the central subject of development.

While development facilitates the enjoyment of all human rights, the lack of development may not be invoked to justify the abridgement of internationally recognized human rights.

States should co-operate with each other in ensuring development and eliminating obstacles to development. The international community should promote an effective international co-operation for the realization of the right to development and the elimination of obstacles to development.

Lasting progress towards the implementation of the right to development requires effective development policies at the national level, as well as equitable economic relations and a favourable economic environment at the international level.

11. The right to development should be fulfilled so as to meet equitably the developmental and environmental needs of present and future generations ...

12. The World Conference on Human Rights calls upon the international community to make all efforts to help alleviate the external debt burden of developing countries, in order to supplement the efforts of the Governments of such countries to attain the full realization of the economic, social and cultural rights of their people.

2.5. Questions for discussion: international co-operation and the right to development

1. What are the commonalities and differences between Sen's concept of 'development as freedom' and the human rights-based approaches to development, as put forward, for instance, in the context of the discussion on the Millennium Development Goals? Are these views identical, albeit expressed in different terminologies? Are they compatible and complementary? Or are they incompatible?

2. One of the main critics of the 'big push' idea underlying the Millennium Development Goals is the economist William Easterly. Easterly argues against the idea that lack of development essentially is attributable to a 'poverty trap', itself the result of insufficient savings and thus insufficient ability to invest in the future: 'Rather than worrying about how much investment is "needed" to sustain a given growth rate, we should concentrate on strengthening incentives to invest in the future and let the various forms of investment play out how they may ... Giving aid on the basis of the financing gap creates perverse incentives for the recipient ... The financing gap is larger, and aid larger, the lower the saving of the recipient. This creates incentives against the recipient's marshaling its own resources for development' (W. Easterly, *The Elusive Quest for Growth* (Cambridge, Mass.: MIT Press, 2001), p. 44). He also contrasts the role of 'planners' with that of 'searchers', the former imposing solutions top-down on the basis of their understanding of the needs of developing countries, and the latter identifying bottom-up projects that work best in specific local contexts (W. Easterly, *The White Man's Burden: Why the West's Efforts to Aid the Rest have done so much Ill and so Little Good* (Oxford University Press, 2006)). Are Sen's ideas about the instrumental role of freedoms in achieving development, and the human rights-based approaches to development (that put forward the principles of accountability, non-discrimination, participation and empowerment), appropriate answers to the concerns expressed by Easterly?

3. There are three obstacles, it could be argued, to making the right to development operational. One is the problem of causality: lack of development in any particular region or country cannot be attributed solely to policies or measures adopted by one actor or set of actors, but are instead the result of a combination of causes, making assertions of responsibility problematic. Another is what some have referred to as the 'paradox of the many hands': since the international community as a whole is responsible for the lack of development, no State in particular bears responsibility. A third is the apparently limitless character of the obligation of assistance and co-operation: it appears difficult to define the precise levels at which resources should be transferred from rich States to developing States, in order to fulfil the right to development. Are the 'development compacts' proposed by Sengupta an adequate answer to these obstacles? Should the obligations corresponding to the right to development be defined through a new international agreement? Should other solutions be explored?

3 THE RESPONSIBILITY OF STATES IN INTER-STATE CO-OPERATION

Specific problems of imputability arise in circumstances where a State has acted in collaboration with other States, either in their bilateral relations, or in the establishment of an international organization to which certain powers are delegated. This section reviews situations where States co-operate with one another, and where their collaborative action results in a violation of an international obligation of at least one of the States concerned. Section 4 examines the specific case of international organizations. This latter situation is both more complex, since a distinct subject of the international legal order has been created with its own rights and obligations under international law; and in certain ways more simple, since, if none of the States participating in the establishment of the organization or in its decision-making may be held responsible under international law, there remains the possibility that the responsibility of the organization itself will be engaged.

3.1 Deportation cases

A first typical case where human rights violations may result from the collaborative conduct by States, is where an individual is removed by one State to another, where he or she faces the risk of violations in the receiving State. Article 3 of the 1984 Convention against Torture and Other Cruel, Inhuman or Degrading Treatment or Punishment stipulates:

1. No State Party shall expel, return ('*refouler*') or extradite a person to another State where there are substantial grounds for believing that he would be in danger of being subjected to torture.
2. For the purpose of determining whether there are such grounds, the competent authorities shall take into account all relevant considerations including, where applicable, the existence in the State concerned of a consistent pattern of gross, flagrant or mass violations of human rights.

The prohibition against *refoulement* was then developed in the case law at both the regional and universal levels. While this prohibition is explored further in greater detail as an illustration of the nature of the protection benefiting rights of an 'absolute' character (see chapter 3, section 2.2.), the examples set out in this section aim to introduce the specific difficulties encountered where the measure which is alleged to constitute a violation is part of a larger operation involving more than one State.

European Court of Human Rights (plen.), *Soering* v. *United Kingdom*, judgment of 7 July 1989, Series A, No. 161:

[At the time of the application, the applicant, Mr Jens Soering, a German national, was detained in prison in England pending extradition to the United States to face charges of murder in the

Commonwealth of Virginia. Indeed, on 11 August 1986 the Government of the United States had requested the applicant's and Miss Haysom's extradition under the terms of the Extradition Treaty of 1972 between the United States and the United Kingdom. Both Jens Soering and his girlfriend had been indicted on charges of murdering the parents of the latter, and they had fled the United States when they were arrested in England in connection with a cheque fraud. Later – in March 1987 – Germany too requested the extradition of Jens Soering, since the German courts had jurisdiction to try the applicant. Mr Soering lodged an application (No. 14038/88) with the European Commission of Human Rights on 8 July 1988. In his application Mr Soering stated his belief that there was a serious likelihood that he would be sentenced to death if extradited to the United States. He maintained that in the circumstances and, in particular, having regard to the 'death row phenomenon', he would thereby be subjected to inhuman and degrading treatment and punishment contrary to Article 3 of the Convention. In his further submission his extradition to the United States would constitute a violation of Article 6(3)(c) of the Convention because of the absence of legal aid in the State of Virginia to pursue various appeals. Finally, he claimed that, in breach of Article 13, he had no effective remedy under UK law in respect of his complaint under Article 3. Interim measures were granted by the President of the Commission, which were subsequently prolonged by the Commission on several occasions until the reference of the case to the Court.]

80. The applicant alleged that the decision by the Secretary of State for the Home Department to surrender him to the authorities of the United States of America would, if implemented, give rise to a breach by the United Kingdom of Article 3 of the Convention, which provides: 'No one shall be subjected to torture or to inhuman or degrading treatment or punishment.'

A. Applicability of Article 3 in cases of extradition

81. The alleged breach derives from the applicant's exposure to the so-called 'death row phenomenon'. This phenomenon may be described as consisting in a combination of circumstances to which the applicant would be exposed if, after having been extradited to Virginia to face a capital murder charge, he were sentenced to death.

82. In its report ... the Commission reaffirmed 'its case law that a person's deportation or extradition may give rise to an issue under Article 3 of the Convention where there are serious reasons to believe that the individual will be subjected, in the receiving State, to treatment contrary to that Article' ... The applicant likewise submitted that Article 3 not only prohibits the Contracting States from causing inhuman or degrading treatment or punishment to occur within their jurisdiction but also embodies an associated obligation not to put a person in a position where he will or may suffer such treatment or punishment at the hands of other States. For the applicant, at least as far as Article 3 is concerned, an individual may not be surrendered out of the protective zone of the Convention without the certainty that the safeguards which he would enjoy are as effective as the Convention standard.

83. The United Kingdom Government, on the other hand, contended that Article 3 should not be interpreted so as to impose responsibility on a Contracting State for acts which occur outside its jurisdiction. In particular, in their submission, extradition does not involve the responsibility of the extraditing State for inhuman or degrading treatment or punishment which the extradited person may suffer outside the State's jurisdiction. To begin with, they maintained, it would be straining the language of Article 3 intolerably to hold that by surrendering a fugitive criminal the extraditing State has 'subjected' him to any treatment or punishment that he will receive following conviction and sentence in the receiving State. Further arguments advanced against

the approach of the Commission were that it interferes with international treaty rights; it leads to a conflict with the norms of international judicial process, in that it in effect involves adjudication on the internal affairs of foreign States not Parties to the Convention or to the proceedings before the Convention institutions; it entails grave difficulties of evaluation and proof in requiring the examination of alien systems of law and of conditions in foreign States; the practice of national courts and the international community cannot reasonably be invoked to support it; it causes a serious risk of harm in the Contracting State which is obliged to harbour the protected person, and leaves criminals untried, at large and unpunished.

In the alternative, the United Kingdom Government submitted that the application of Article 3 in extradition cases should be limited to those occasions in which the treatment or punishment abroad is certain, imminent and serious. In their view, the fact that by definition the matters complained of are only anticipated, together with the common and legitimate interest of all States in bringing fugitive criminals to justice, requires a very high degree of risk, proved beyond reasonable doubt, that ill-treatment will actually occur.

84. The Court will approach the matter on the basis of the following considerations.

85. As results from Article 5 §1(f), which permits 'the lawful ... detention of a person against whom action is being taken with a view to ... extradition', no right not to be extradited is as such protected by the Convention. Nevertheless, in so far as a measure of extradition has consequences adversely affecting the enjoyment of a Convention right, it may, assuming that the consequences are not too remote, attract the obligations of a Contracting State under the relevant Convention guarantee (see, *mutatis mutandis*, the *Abdulaziz, Cabales and Balkandali* judgment of 25 May 1985, Series A No. 94, pp. 31–32, §§59–60 – in relation to rights in the field of immigration). What is at issue in the present case is whether Article 3 can be applicable when the adverse consequences of extradition are, or may be, suffered outside the jurisdiction of the extraditing State as a result of treatment or punishment administered in the receiving State.

86. Article 1 of the Convention, which provides that 'the High Contracting Parties shall secure to everyone within their jurisdiction the rights and freedoms defined in Section I', sets a limit, notably territorial, on the reach of the Convention. In particular, the engagement undertaken by a Contracting State is confined to 'securing' ('*reconnaître*' in the French text) the listed rights and freedoms to persons within its own 'jurisdiction'. Further, the Convention does not govern the actions of States not Parties to it, nor does it purport to be a means of requiring the Contracting States to impose Convention standards on other States. Article 1 cannot be read as justifying a general principle to the effect that, notwithstanding its extradition obligations, a Contracting State may not surrender an individual unless satisfied that the conditions awaiting him in the country of destination are in full accord with each of the safeguards of the Convention. Indeed, as the United Kingdom Government stressed, the beneficial purpose of extradition in preventing fugitive offenders from evading justice cannot be ignored in determining the scope of application of the Convention and of Article 3 in particular.

In the instant case it is common ground that the United Kingdom has no power over the practices and arrangements of the Virginia authorities which are the subject of the applicant's complaints. It is also true that in other international instruments cited by the United Kingdom Government – for example the 1951 United Nations Convention relating to the Status of Refugees (Article 33), the 1957 European Convention on Extradition (Article 11) and the 1984 United Nations Convention against Torture and Other Cruel, Inhuman and Degrading Treatment or Punishment (Article 3) – the problems of removing a person to another jurisdiction where unwanted consequences may follow are addressed expressly and specifically.

These considerations cannot, however, absolve the Contracting Parties from responsibility under Article 3 for all and any foreseeable consequences of extradition suffered outside their jurisdiction.

87. In interpreting the Convention regard must be had to its special character as a treaty for the collective enforcement of human rights and fundamental freedoms (see the *Ireland* v. *United Kingdom* judgment of 18 January 1978, Series A No. 25, p. 90, §239). Thus, the object and purpose of the Convention as an instrument for the protection of individual human beings require that its provisions be interpreted and applied so as to make its safeguards practical and effective (see, *inter alia*, the *Artico* judgment of 13 May 1980, Series A No. 37, p. 16, §33). In addition, any interpretation of the rights and freedoms guaranteed has to be consistent with 'the general spirit of the Convention, an instrument designed to maintain and promote the ideals and values of a democratic society' (see the *Kjeldsen, Busk Madsen and Pedersen* judgment of 7 December 1976, Series A No. 23, p. 27, §53).

88. Article 3 makes no provision for exceptions and no derogation from it is permissible under Article 15 in time of war or other national emergency. This absolute prohibition of torture and of inhuman or degrading treatment or punishment under the terms of the Convention shows that Article 3 enshrines one of the fundamental values of the democratic societies making up the Council of Europe. It is also to be found in similar terms in other international instruments such as the 1966 International Covenant on Civil and Political Rights and the 1969 American Convention on Human Rights and is generally recognised as an internationally accepted standard.

The question remains whether the extradition of a fugitive to another State where he would be subjected or be likely to be subjected to torture or to inhuman or degrading treatment or punishment would itself engage the responsibility of a Contracting State under Article 3. That the abhorrence of torture has such implications is recognised in Article 3 of the United Nations Convention Against Torture and Other Cruel, Inhuman or Degrading Treatment or Punishment, which provides that 'no State Party shall ... extradite a person where there are substantial grounds for believing that he would be in danger of being subjected to torture'. The fact that a specialised treaty should spell out in detail a specific obligation attaching to the prohibition of torture does not mean that an essentially similar obligation is not already inherent in the general terms of Article 3 of the European Convention. It would hardly be compatible with the underlying values of the Convention, that 'common heritage of political traditions, ideals, freedom and the rule of law' to which the Preamble refers, were a Contracting State knowingly to surrender a fugitive to another State where there were substantial grounds for believing that he would be in danger of being subjected to torture, however heinous the crime allegedly committed. Extradition in such circumstances, while not explicitly referred to in the brief and general wording of Article 3, would plainly be contrary to the spirit and intendment of the Article, and in the Court's view this inherent obligation not to extradite also extends to cases in which the fugitive would be faced in the receiving State by a real risk of exposure to inhuman or degrading treatment or punishment proscribed by that Article.

89. What amounts to 'inhuman or degrading treatment or punishment' depends on all the circumstances of the case ... Furthermore, inherent in the whole of the Convention is a search for a fair balance between the demands of the general interest of the community and the

requirements of the protection of the individual's fundamental rights. As movement about the world becomes easier and crime takes on a larger international dimension, it is increasingly in the interest of all nations that suspected offenders who flee abroad should be brought to justice. Conversely, the establishment of safe havens for fugitives would not only result in danger for the State obliged to harbour the protected person but also tend to undermine the foundations of extradition. These considerations must also be included among the factors to be taken into account in the interpretation and application of the notions of inhuman and degrading treatment or punishment in extradition cases.

90. It is not normally for the Convention institutions to pronounce on the existence or otherwise of potential violations of the Convention. However, where an applicant claims that a decision to extradite him would, if implemented, be contrary to Article 3 by reason of its foreseeable consequences in the requesting country, a departure from this principle is necessary, in view of the serious and irreparable nature of the alleged suffering risked, in order to ensure the effectiveness of the safeguard provided by that Article ...

91. In sum, the decision by a Contracting State to extradite a fugitive may give rise to an issue under Article 3, and hence engage the responsibility of that State under the Convention, where substantial grounds have been shown for believing that the person concerned, if extradited, faces a real risk of being subjected to torture or to inhuman or degrading treatment or punishment in the requesting country. The establishment of such responsibility inevitably involves an assessment of conditions in the requesting country against the standards of Article 3 of the Convention. Nonetheless, there is no question of adjudicating on or establishing the responsibility of the receiving country, whether under general international law, under the Convention or otherwise. In so far as any liability under the Convention is or may be incurred, it is liability incurred by the extraditing Contracting State by reason of its having taken action which has as a direct consequence the exposure of an individual to proscribed ill-treatment.

B. Application of Article 3 in the particular circumstances of the present case

92. The extradition procedure against the applicant in the United Kingdom has been completed, the Secretary of State having signed a warrant ordering his surrender to the United States authorities ...; this decision, albeit as yet not implemented, directly affects him. It therefore has to be determined on the above principles whether the foreseeable consequences of Mr Soering's return to the United States are such as to attract the application of Article 3. This inquiry must concentrate firstly on whether Mr Soering runs a real risk of being sentenced to death in Virginia, since the source of the alleged inhuman and degrading treatment or punishment, namely the 'death row phenomenon', lies in the imposition of the death penalty. Only in the event of an affirmative answer to this question need the Court examine whether exposure to the 'death row phenomenon' in the circumstances of the applicant's case would involve treatment or punishment incompatible with Article 3.

Whether the applicant runs a real risk of a death sentence and hence of exposure to the 'death row phenomenon'

93. The United Kingdom Government ... did not accept that the risk of a death sentence attains a sufficient level of likelihood to bring Article 3 into play. Their reasons were fourfold.

Firstly, as illustrated by his interview with the German prosecutor where he appeared to deny any intention to kill ..., the applicant has not acknowledged his guilt of capital murder as such.

Secondly, only a prima facie case has so far been made out against him. In particular, in the United Kingdom Government's view the psychiatric evidence ... is equivocal as to whether Mr Soering was suffering from a disease of the mind sufficient to amount to a defence of insanity under Virginia law ...

Thirdly, even if Mr Soering is convicted of capital murder, it cannot be assumed that in the general exercise of their discretion the jury will recommend, the judge will confirm and the Supreme Court of Virginia will uphold the imposition of the death penalty ... The United Kingdom Government referred to the presence of important mitigating factors, such as the applicant's age and mental condition at the time of commission of the offence and his lack of previous criminal activity, which would have to be taken into account by the jury and then by the judge in the separate sentencing proceedings ...

Fourthly, the assurance received from the United States must at the very least significantly reduce the risk of a capital sentence either being imposed or carried out ...

At the public hearing the Attorney General nevertheless made clear his Government's understanding that if Mr Soering were extradited to the United States there was 'some risk', which was 'more than merely negligible', that the death penalty would be imposed ...

96. [The] various elements arguing for or against the imposition of a death sentence [in the State of Virginia] have to be viewed in the light of the attitude of the prosecuting authorities.

97. The Commonwealth's Attorney for Bedford County, Mr Updike, who is responsible for conducting the prosecution against the applicant, has certified that 'should Jens Soering be convicted of the offence of capital murder as charged ... a representation will be made in the name of the United Kingdom to the judge at the time of sentencing that it is the wish of the United Kingdom that the death penalty should not be imposed or carried out' ... The Court notes ... that this undertaking is far from reflecting the wording of Article IV of the 1972 Extradition Treaty between the United Kingdom and the United States, which speaks of 'assurances satisfactory to the requested Party that the death penalty will not be carried out' ... However, the offence charged, being a State and not a Federal offence, comes within the jurisdiction of the Commonwealth of Virginia; it appears as a consequence that no direction could or can be given to the Commonwealth's Attorney by any State or Federal authority to promise more; the Virginia courts as judicial bodies cannot bind themselves in advance as to what decisions they may arrive at on the evidence; and the Governor of Virginia does not, as a matter of policy, promise that he will later exercise his executive power to commute a death penalty ...

This being so, Mr Updike's undertaking may well have been the best 'assurance' that the United Kingdom could have obtained from the United States Federal Government in the particular circumstances. According to the statement made to Parliament in 1987 by a Home Office Minister, acceptance of undertakings in such terms 'means that the United Kingdom authorities render up a fugitive or are prepared to send a citizen to face an American court on the clear understanding that the death penalty will not be carried out ... It would be a fundamental blow to the extradition arrangements between our two countries if the death penalty were carried out on an individual who had been returned under those circumstances' ... Nonetheless, the effectiveness of such an undertaking has not yet been put to the test.

98. The applicant contended that representations concerning the wishes of a foreign government would not be admissible as a matter of law under the Virginia Code or, if admissible, of any influence on the sentencing judge.

Whatever the position under Virginia law and practice ..., and notwithstanding the diplomatic context of the extradition relations between the United Kingdom and the United States, objectively it cannot be said that the undertaking to inform the judge at the sentencing stage of the wishes of the United Kingdom eliminates the risk of the death penalty being imposed. In the independent exercise of his discretion the Commonwealth's Attorney has himself decided to seek and to persist in seeking the death penalty because the evidence, in his determination, supports such action ... If the national authority with responsibility for prosecuting the offence takes such a firm stance, it is hardly open to the Court to hold that there are no substantial grounds for believing that the applicant faces a real risk of being sentenced to death and hence experiencing the 'death row phenomenon'.

99. The Court's conclusion is therefore that the likelihood of the feared exposure of the applicant to the 'death row phenomenon' has been shown to be such as to bring Article 3 into play ...

111. ... in the Court's view, having regard to the very long period of time spent on death row in such extreme conditions, with the ever present and mounting anguish of awaiting execution of the death penalty, and to the personal circumstances of the applicant, especially his age and mental state at the time of the offence, the applicant's extradition to the United States would expose him to a real risk of treatment going beyond the threshold set by Article 3. A further consideration of relevance is that in the particular instance the legitimate purpose of extradition could be achieved by another means which would not involve suffering of such exceptional intensity or duration.

Accordingly, the Secretary of State's decision to extradite the applicant to the United States would, if implemented, give rise to a breach of Article 3.

Interestingly, the European Court of Human Rights has refused to consider that the fact that a receiving State was bound by the European Convention on Human Rights necessarily excluded a responsibility of the sending State, where there are circumstances which may give rise to fear that there exists a substantial risk of torture or ill-treatment in a third State, to which the individual could be removed by the receiving State.

European Court of Human Rights (3d sect.), *T.I.* v. *United Kingdom* (Appl. No. 43844/98), decision (inadmissibility) of 7 March 2000:

[After having fled Sri Lanka, where he feared persecution in the hands of pro-governmental groups as well as by the the Tamil Tigers (LTTE, a Tamil terrorist organization), T.I. arrived in Germany, where he claimed asylum on 13 February 1996. The claim failed, since the local courts considered that the actions of the LTTE could not be attributed to the State and that the applicant would be sufficiently safe from political persecution if he returned to the south of Sri Lanka. Without exhausting the appeals in Germany, T.I. then left for the United Kingdom, where he filed another asylum claim in September 1997. On 15 January 1998, the UK Government requested that Germany accept responsibility for the applicant's asylum request pursuant to the Dublin Convention. The Dublin Convention (the Convention Determining the State Responsible for Examining Applications for Asylum Lodged in one of the Member States of the European

Communities, 15 June 1990) provides for measures to ensure that applicants for asylum have their applications examined by one of the EU Member States and that applicants for asylum are not referred successively from one Member State to another. Articles 4–8 set out the criteria for determining the single Member State responsible for examining an application for asylum. Pursuant to Article 7, the responsibility for examining an application for asylum is incumbent upon the Member State responsible for controlling the entry of the alien into the territory of the Member States. The United Kingdom and Germany are both signatory States. In accordance with its obligations under the Dublin Convention, on 26 January 1998, Germany agreed to take T.I. back. On 28 January 1998, the Secretary of State issued a certificate under section 2 of the Asylum and Immigration Act 1996 and directed the applicant's removal to Germany. He refused to examine the substance of the applicant's asylum claim. After his appeals before the UK courts failed, T.I. filed an application with the European Court of Human Rights. He complained that the United Kingdom's conduct in ordering his removal to Germany, from where he will be summarily removed to Sri Lanka, violated Articles 2, 3, 8 and 13 of the Convention. He submitted in particular that there are substantial grounds for believing that, if returned to Sri Lanka, there was a real risk of facing treatment contrary to Article 3 of the Convention at the hands of the security forces, the LTTE and the pro-Government Tamil militant organizations. He noted that the German authorities only treated as relevant the acts of the State and that they did not consider excesses by individual State officials as State acts. The Court's answer follows:]

The Court reiterates in the first place that Contracting States have the right, as a matter of well-established international law and subject to their treaty obligations including the Convention, to control the entry, residence and expulsion of aliens. It also notes that the right to political asylum is not contained in either the Convention or its protocols (see the *Vilvarajah and others* v. *United Kingdom* judgment of 30 October 1991, Series A No. 215, p. 34, §102). It is however well-established in its case law that the fundamentally important prohibition against torture and inhuman and degrading treatment under Article 3, read in conjunction with Article 1 of the Convention to 'secure to everyone within their jurisdiction the rights and freedoms defined in [the] Convention', imposes an obligation on Contracting States not to expel a person to a country where substantial grounds have been shown for believing that he would face a real risk of being subjected to treatment contrary to Article 3 (see, amongst other authorities, the *Ahmed* v. *Austria* judgment of 17 December 1996, *Reports* 1996–VI, p. 2206, §§39–40).

The Court's case law further indicates that the existence of this obligation is not dependent on whether the source of the risk of the treatment stems from factors which involve the responsibility, direct or indirect, of the authorities of the receiving country. Having regard to the absolute character of the right guaranteed, Article 3 may extend to situations where the danger emanates from persons or groups of persons who are not public officials, or from the consequences to health from the effects of serious illness (see *H.L.R.* v. *France* judgment of 29 April 1997, *Reports* 1997–III, §40, *D* v. *United Kingdom* judgment of 2 May 1997, *Reports* 1997–III, §49). In any such contexts, the Court must subject all the circumstances surrounding the case to a rigorous scrutiny.

In the present case, the applicant is threatened with removal to Germany, where a deportation order was previously issued to remove him to Sri Lanka. It is accepted by all parties that the applicant is not, as such, threatened with any treatment contrary to Article 3 in Germany. His removal to Germany is however one link in a possible chain of events which might result in his return to Sri Lanka where it is alleged that he would face the real risk of such treatment.

The Court finds that the indirect removal in this case to an intermediary country, which is also a Contracting State, does not affect the responsibility of the United Kingdom to ensure that the applicant is not, as a result of its decision to expel, exposed to treatment contrary to Article 3 of the Convention. Nor can the United Kingdom rely automatically in that context on the arrangements made in the Dublin Convention concerning the attribution of responsibility between European countries for deciding asylum claims. Where States establish international organisations, or *mutatis mutandis* international agreements, to pursue co-operation in certain fields of activities, there may be implications for the protection of fundamental rights. It would be incompatible with the purpose and object of the Convention if Contracting States were thereby absolved from their responsibility under the Convention in relation to the field of activity covered by such attribution (see e.g. *Waite and Kennedy* v. *Germany* judgment of 18 February 1999, *Reports* 1999, §67). The Court notes the comments of the UNHCR that, while the Dublin Convention may pursue laudable objectives, its effectiveness may be undermined in practice by the differing approaches adopted by Contracting States to the scope of protection offered.

On the facts however, the Court arrived at the conclusion that the fears expressed by Mr T.I. were not substantiated. It was not established in its view that there was a real risk that Germany would expel the applicant to Sri Lanka in breach of Article 3 of the Convention. Consequently, the United Kingdom had not failed in their obligations under this provision by taking the decision to remove the applicant to Germany.

A similar approach was adopted by the Human Rights Committee under the International Covenant on Civil and Political Rights (ICCPR). But the methodology followed by the Committee did undergo a certain evolution. In 1993, in *Kindler* v. *Canada*, the Human Rights Committee had taken the view that, although Canada had abolished the death penalty on its territory, it was not in violation with Article 6 ICCPR when extraditing Mr Kindler to the United States, where he faced the imposition of the death penalty. Canada would be in violation of Article 6 of the Covenant if it decided to reintroduce the death penalty under its jurisdiction. However, the Committee reasoned that the question whether Mr Kindler's rights under Article 6 of the Covenant would be violated by extraditing him to the United States should be answered taking into account the situation of the death penalty in the United States, where it was not abolished and where, therefore, the imposition of the death penalty remains acceptable under the Covenant. The Committee thus considered that '[w]hile States must be mindful of the possibilities for the protection of life when exercising their discretion in the application of extradition treaties, the Committee does not find that the terms of article 6 of the Covenant necessarily require Canada to refuse to extradite or to seek assurances. The Committee notes that the extradition of Mr Kindler would have violated Canada's obligations under article 6 of the Covenant, if the decision to extradite without assurances would have been taken arbitrarily or summarily. The evidence before the Committee reveals, however, that the Minister of Justice reached a decision after hearing argument in favour of seeking assurances. The Committee further takes note of the reasons given by Canada not to seek assurances in Mr Kindler's case, in particular, the absence of exceptional circumstances, the availability of due process, and the importance of not providing a safe haven for those accused of or found guilty of murder' (Communication No. 470/1990, final views adopted on 30 July 1993, para. 14.6.). This approach was abandoned ten years later, in the case of *Judge* v. *Canada*:

Human Rights Committee, *Judge* v. *Canada*, Communication No. 829/1998, final views of 20 October 2003 (CCPR/C/78/D/829/1998 (2003)).

[The author of the communication is Mr Roger Judge, a citizen of the United States. At the time of the submission, he was detained in Québec, Canada. Mr Judge had been convicted on 15 April 1987 in Philadelphia, Pennsylvania, on two counts of first-degree murder and possession of an instrument of crime, and had subsequently been sentenced to death by electric chair. He escaped from prison on 14 June 1987 and fled to Canada. He was deported to the United States on 7 August 1998, on the day the communication was submitted on his behalf to the Human Rights Committee.]

Question 1. As Canada has abolished the death penalty, did it violate the author's right to life under article 6, his right not to be subjected to torture or to cruel, inhuman or degrading treatment or punishment under article 7, or his right to an effective remedy under article 2, paragraph 3, of the Covenant by deporting him to a State in which he was under sentence of death without ensuring that that sentence would not be carried out?

10.2 In considering Canada's obligations, as a State party which has abolished the death penalty, in removing persons to another country where they are under sentence of death, the Committee recalls its previous jurisprudence in *Kindler* v. *Canada*, that it does not consider that the deportation of a person from a country which has abolished the death penalty to a country where he/she is under sentence of death amounts *per se* to a violation of article 6 of the Covenant. The Committee's rationale in this decision was based on an interpretation of the Covenant which read article 6, paragraph 1, together with article 6, paragraph 2, which does not prohibit the imposition of the death penalty for the most serious crimes. It considered that as Canada itself had not imposed the death penalty but had extradited the author to the United States to face capital punishment, a State which had not abolished the death penalty, the extradition itself would not amount to a violation by Canada unless there was a real risk that the author's rights under the Covenant would be violated in the United States. On the issue of assurances, the Committee found that the terms of article 6 did not necessarily require Canada to refuse to extradite or to seek assurances but that such a request should at least be considered by the removing State.

10.3 While recognizing that the Committee should ensure both consistency and coherence of its jurisprudence, it notes that there may be exceptional situations in which a review of the scope of application of the rights protected in the Covenant is required, such as where an alleged violation involves that most fundamental of rights – the right to life – and in particular if there have been notable factual and legal developments and changes in international opinion in respect of the issue raised. The Committee is mindful of the fact that the abovementioned jurisprudence was established some 10 years ago, and that since that time there has been a broadening international consensus in favour of abolition of the death penalty, and in States which have retained the death penalty, a broadening consensus not to carry it out. Significantly, the Committee notes that since *Kindler* the State party itself has recognized the need to amend its own domestic law to secure the protection of those extradited from Canada under sentence of death in the receiving State, in the case of *United States* v. *Burns* [[2001] 1 S.C.R. 283: see also on this case the references in *Suresh* v. *Canada (Minister of Citizenship and Immigration)* [2002] 1 S.C.R. 3, discussed in chapter 3, section 2.2.]. There, the Supreme Court of Canada held that the government must seek assurances, in all but exceptional cases, that the death penalty will not be applied prior to extraditing an individual to a State where he/she faces capital punishment. It is pertinent to note that under the terms of this judgment, 'Other abolitionist countries do not, in general, extradite without assurances.' The Committee considers that the Covenant should be interpreted as a living instrument and the rights protected under it should be applied in context and in the light of present-day conditions.

10.4 In reviewing its application of article 6, the Committee notes that, as required by the Vienna Convention on the Law of Treaties, a treaty should be interpreted in good faith and in accordance with the ordinary meaning to be given to the terms of the treaty in their context and in the light of its object and purpose. Paragraph 1 of article 6, which states that 'Every human being has the inherent right to life …', is a general rule: its purpose is to protect life. States parties that have abolished the death penalty have an obligation under this paragraph to so protect in all circumstances. Paragraphs 2 to 6 of article 6 are evidently included to avoid a reading of the first paragraph of article 6, according to which that paragraph could be understood as abolishing the death penalty as such. This construction of the article is reinforced by the opening words of paragraph 2 ('In countries which have not abolished the death penalty …') and by paragraph 6 ('Nothing in this article shall be invoked to delay or to prevent the abolition of capital punishment by any State Party to the present Covenant.'). In effect, paragraphs 2 to 6 have the dual function of creating an exception to the right to life in respect of the death penalty and laying down limits on the scope of that exception. Only the death penalty pronounced when certain elements are present can benefit from the exception. Among these limitations are that found in the opening words of paragraph 2, namely, that only States parties that 'have not abolished the death penalty' can avail themselves of the exceptions created in paragraphs 2 to 6. For countries that have abolished the death penalty, there is an obligation not to expose a person to the real risk of its application. Thus, they may not remove, either by deportation or extradition, individuals from their jurisdiction if it may be reasonably anticipated that they will be sentenced to death, without ensuring that the death sentence would not be carried out.

10.5 The Committee acknowledges that by interpreting paragraphs 1 and 2 of article 6 in this way, abolitionist and retentionist States parties are treated differently. But it considers that this is an inevitable consequence of the wording of the provision itself, which, as becomes clear from the *Travaux Préparatoires*, sought to appease very divergent views on the issue of the death penalty, in an effort at compromise among the drafters of the provision. The Committee notes that it was expressed in the *Travaux* that, on the one hand, one of the main principles of the Covenant should be abolition, but on the other, it was pointed out that capital punishment existed in certain countries and that abolition would create difficulties for such countries. The death penalty was seen by many delegates and bodies participating in the drafting process as an 'anomaly' or a 'necessary evil'. It would appear logical, therefore, to interpret the rule in article 6, paragraph 1, in a wide sense, whereas paragraph 2, which addresses the death penalty, should be interpreted narrowly.

10.6 For these reasons, the Committee considers that Canada, as a State party which has abolished the death penalty, irrespective of whether it has not yet ratified the Second Optional

Protocol to the Covenant Aiming at the Abolition of the Death Penalty, violated the author's right to life under article 6, paragraph 1, by deporting him to the United States, where he is under sentence of death, without ensuring that the death penalty would not be carried out. The Committee recognizes that Canada did not itself impose the death penalty on the author. But by deporting him to a country where he was under sentence of death, Canada established the crucial link in the causal chain that would make possible the execution of the author.

10.7 As to the State party's claim that its conduct must be assessed in the light of the law applicable at the time when the alleged treaty violation took place, the Committee considers that the protection of human rights evolves and that the meaning of Covenant rights should in principle be interpreted by reference to the time of examination and not, as the State party has submitted, by reference to the time the alleged violation took place. The Committee also notes that prior to the author's deportation to the United States the Committee's position was evolving in respect of a State party that had abolished capital punishment (and was a State party to the Second Optional Protocol to the International Covenant on Human Rights, aiming at the abolition of the death penalty), from whether capital punishment would subsequent to removal to another State be applied in violation of the Covenant to whether there was a real risk of capital punishment as such (Communication No. 692/1996, *A.R.J.* v. *Australia*, Views adopted on 28 July 1997 and Communication No. 706/1996, *G.T.* v. *Australia*, Views adopted on 4 November 1997). Furthermore, the State party's concern regarding possible retroactivity involved in the present approach has no bearing on the separate issues to be addressed under question 2 below.

Question 2. The State party had conceded that the author was deported to the United States before he could exercise his right to appeal the rejection of his application for a stay of his deportation before the Quebec Court of Appeal. As a consequence the author was not able to pursue any further remedies that might be available. By deporting the author to a State in which he was under sentence of death before he could exercise all his rights to challenge that deportation, did the State party violate his rights under articles 6, 7 and 2, paragraph 3 of the Covenant?

10.8 As to whether the State party violated the author's rights under articles 6, and 2, paragraph 3, by deporting him to the United States where he is under sentence of death, before he could exercise his right to appeal the rejection of his application for a stay of deportation before the Quebec Court of Appeal and, accordingly, could not pursue further available remedies, the Committee notes that the State party removed the author from its jurisdiction within hours after the decision of the Superior Court of Quebec, in what appears to have been an attempt to prevent him from exercising his right of appeal to the Court of Appeal. It is unclear from the submissions before the Committee to what extent the Court of Appeal could have examined the author's case, but the State party itself concedes that as the author's petition was dismissed by the Superior Court for procedural and substantive reasons ..., the Court of Appeal could have reviewed the judgment on the merits.

10.9 The Committee recalls its decision in *A.R.J.* v. *Australia*, a deportation case where it did not find a violation of article 6 by the returning state as it was not foreseeable that he would be sentenced to death and 'because the judicial and immigration instances seized of the case heard extensive arguments' as to a possible violation of article 6. In the instant case, the Committee finds that, by preventing the author from exercising an appeal available to him under domestic law, the State party failed to demonstrate that the author's contention that his deportation to a country where he faces execution would violate his right to life, was sufficiently considered. The

State party makes available an appellate system designed to safeguard any petitioner's, including the author's, rights and in particular the most fundamental of rights – the right to life. Bearing in mind that the State party has abolished capital punishment, the decision to deport the author to a state where he is under sentence of death without affording him the opportunity to avail himself of an available appeal, was taken arbitrarily and in violation of article 6, together with article 2, paragraph 3, of the Covenant.

10.10. Having found a violation of article 6, paragraph 1 alone and, read together with article 2, paragraph 3 of the Covenant, the Committee does not consider it necessary to address whether the same facts amount to a violation of article 7 of the Covenant.

The Human Rights Committee returned to this case law in its most recent General Comment on Article 7 ICCPR. It will be noted, however, that certain controversies continue to exist concerning the degree of certainty which must exist about the risks incurred by the individual upon being returned to a country where he/she fears for his/her life or security (see *Cox* v. *Canada*, Communication No. 539/1993 (final views of 31 October 1994) (CCPR/C/52/D/539/1993 (1994)), discussed in chapter 9):

Human Rights Committee, General Comment No. 20, *Article 7 (Prohibition of Torture, or Other Cruel, Inhuman or Degrading Treatment or Punishment)* (1992), para. 9:

In the view of the Committee, States parties must not expose individuals to the danger of torture or cruel, inhuman or degrading treatment or punishment upon return to another country by way of their extradition, expulsion or refoulement. States parties should indicate in their reports what measures they have adopted to that end.

The vast majority of cases presented to the Committee against Torture (CAT) in individual communications concern deportation cases, where an individual expelled, extradited, or denied entry (*refouled*) fears that he/she will be subject to torture in the country of destination. The CAT summarized the factors to be taken into account in the assessment of such claims:

Committee against Torture, General Comment No. 1, *Implementation of Article 3 of the Convention in the Context of Article 22* (Refoulement *and Communications)* (1996):

In view of the requirements of article 22, paragraph 4, of the Convention against Torture and Other Cruel, Inhuman or Degrading Treatment or Punishment that the Committee against Torture 'shall consider communications received under article 22 in the light of all information made available to it by or on behalf of the individual and by the State party concerned',

In view of the need arising as a consequence of the application of rule 111, paragraph 3, of the rules of procedure of the Committee (CAT/C/3/Rev.2), and,

In view of the need for guidelines for the implementation of article 3 under the procedure foreseen in article 22 of the Convention

The Committee against Torture, at its nineteenth session, 317th meeting, held on 21 November 1997, adopted the following general comment for the guidance of States parties and authors of communications:

1. Article 3 is confined in its application to cases where there are substantial grounds for believing that the author would be in danger of being subjected to torture as defined in article 1 of the Convention.
2. The Committee is of the view that the phrase 'another State' in article 3 refers to the State to which the individual concerned is being expelled, returned or extradited, as well as to any State to which the author may subsequently be expelled, returned or extradited.
3. Pursuant to article 1, the criterion, mentioned in article 3, paragraph 2, of 'a consistent pattern or gross, flagrant or mass violations of human rights' refers only to violations by or at the instigation of or with the consent or acquiescence of a public official or other person acting in an official capacity.

Admissibility

4. The Committee is of the opinion that it is the responsibility of the author to establish a prima facie case for the purpose of admissibility of his or her communication under article 22 of the Convention by fulfilling each of the requirements of rule 107 of the rules of procedure of the Committee.

Merits

5. With respect to the application of article 3 of the Convention to the merits of a case, the burden is upon the author to present an arguable case. This means that there must be a factual basis for the author's position sufficient to require a response from the State party.
6. Bearing in mind that the State party and the Committee are obliged to assess whether there are substantial grounds for believing that the author would be in danger of being subjected to torture were he/she to be expelled, returned or extradited, the risk of torture must be assessed on grounds that go beyond mere theory or suspicion. However, the risk does not have to meet the test of being highly probable.
7. The author must establish that he/she would be in danger of being tortured and that the grounds for so believing are substantial in the way described, and that such danger is personal and present. All pertinent information may be introduced by either party to bear on this matter.
8. The following information, while not exhaustive, would be pertinent:
   (a) Is the State concerned one in which there is evidence of a consistent pattern of gross, flagrant or mass violations of human rights (see article 3, paragraph 2)?
   (b) Has the author been tortured or maltreated by or at the instigation of or with the consent of acquiescence of a public official or other person acting in an official capacity in the past? If so, was this the recent past?
   (c) Is there medical or other independent evidence to support a claim by the author that he/she has been tortured or maltreated in the past? Has the torture had after-effects?
   (d) Has the situation referred to in (a) above changed? Has the internal situation in respect of human rights altered?
   (e) Has the author engaged in political or other activity within or outside the State concerned which would appear to make him/her particularly vulnerable to the risk of being placed in danger of torture were he/she to be expelled, returned or extradited to the State in question?

(f) Is there any evidence as to the credibility of the author?

(g) Are there factual inconsistencies in the claim of the author? If so, are they relevant?

9. Bearing in mind that the Committee against Torture is not an appellate, a quasi-judicial or an administrative body, but rather a monitoring body created by the States parties themselves with declaratory powers only, it follows that: (a) Considerable weight will be given, in exercising the Committee's jurisdiction pursuant to article 3 of the Convention, to findings of fact that are made by organs of the State party concerned; but (b) The Committee is not bound by such findings and instead has the power, provided by article 22, paragraph 4, of the Convention, of free assessment of the facts based upon the full set of circumstances in every case.

2.6. Questions for discussion: the nature of State responsibility in deportation cases and beyond

1. Is the shift in the position of the Human Rights Committee, from Kindler v. Canada in 1993 to Judge v. Canada in 2003, justified? Consider Article 16 of the International Law Commission's 2001 Draft Articles on Responsibility of States for Internationally Wrongful Acts (entitled 'Aid or Assistance in the Commission of an Internationally Wrongful Act'), which reads: 'A State which aids or assists another State in the commission of an internationally wrongful act by the latter is internationally responsible for doing so if: (a) That State does so with knowledge of the circumstances of the internationally wrongful act; and (b) The act would be internationally wrongful if committed by that State.' Is the question raised by the deportation cases reviewed in this section one of complicity, as understood in this provision of the ILC's Draft Articles?

2. The case law inaugurated by the European Court of Human Rights in *T. I.* v. *United Kingdom* may be evolving. In the case of *K. R. S.* v. *United Kingdom*, the European Court of Human Rights had initially requested the United Kingdom, under rule 39 of its Rules of Procedure, not to return the applicant, an Iranian national, to Greece. The Court made this request after the United Nations High Commissioner for Refugees (UNHCR) had recommended that parties to the Dublin Regulation – implementing into EU law the Dublin Convention (Council Regulation (EC) No 343/2003 of 18 February 2003 establishing the criteria and mechanisms for determining the Member State responsible for examining an asylum application lodged in one of the Member States by a third-country national, OJ 2003 L50) – refrain from returning asylum seekers to Greece, as it believed that the prevailing situation in Greece called into question whether 'Dublin returnees' would have access to an effective remedy as foreseen by Article 13 of the Convention. Following further exchanges with the UK authorities, the Court nevertheless concluded later that the application of *K. R. S.* should be held inadmissible. While recognizing the weight which was to be given to this evaluation by the UNHCR, the European Court of Human Rights noted that the applicant in the case before it was an Iranian national, and that 'Greece does not currently remove people to Iran ... so it cannot be said that there is a risk that the applicant would be removed there upon arrival in Greece'. The Court also noted

that 'the Dublin Regulation, under which such a removal would be effected, is one of a number of measures agreed in the field of asylum policy at the European level and must be considered alongside Member States' additional obligations under Council Directive 2005/85/EC and Council Directive 2003/9/EC to adhere to minimum standards in asylum procedures and to provide minimum standards for the reception of asylum seekers. The presumption must be that Greece will abide by its obligations under those Directives.' The Court finally concluded that 'in the absence of any proof to the contrary, it must be presumed that Greece will comply with [its obligations under the ECHR and in particular with interim measures ordered under rule 39 of the Rules of Court] in respect of returnees including the applicant' (Eur. Ct. H.R. (4th sect.), *K. R. S.* v. *United Kingdom* (Appl. No. 32733/08), decision of 2 December 2008). Do you agree? How strong should the presumption be that a State will in fact comply with its obligations under existing instruments that are binding upon that State?

3. In *Judge* v. *Canada*, the Human Rights Committee concluded that Canada had violated its obligations under the Covenant because it 'established the crucial link in the causal chain that would make possible the execution of the author'. What are the limits of this reasoning? How relevant is it that the violation alleged in that case concerned 'the most fundamental of rights – the right to life', as noted by the Committee? Would a State be in violation of the Covenant by returning a person under its jurisdiction to a country where his rights to defence would not be fully complied with in a criminal trial? Or by sending back a LGBT person to a country where she would be facing harassment for her sexual orientation? Consider in this respect the inadmissibility decision of the European Court of Human Rights in *Fashkami* v. *United Kingdom* (Appl. No. 17341/03, decision of 22 June 2004), where – in a case in which a gay person of Iranian nationality alleged that he could not be returned to Iran, since 'the existence of a criminal law criminalising adult consensual homosexual acts violated Article 8' – the Court observes 'that its case law has found responsibility attaching to Contracting States in respect of expelling persons who are at risk of treatment contrary to Articles 2 and 3 of the Convention. This is based on the fundamental importance of these provisions, whose guarantees it is imperative to render effective in practice ... Such compelling considerations do not automatically apply under the other provisions of the Convention. On a purely pragmatic basis, it cannot be required that an expelling Contracting State only return an alien to a country which is in full and effective enforcement of all the rights and freedoms set out in the Convention.'

4. The probability of the rights of the individual being violated in the country of return may be difficult to assess. For instance, does the notoriety of the individual concerned protect him from serious violations of his rights by the authorities, or do they put him at a special risk? Is the existence of a 'consistent pattern of gross, flagrant or mass violations of human rights', as referred to in Article 3, para. 2, of the Convention against Torture, sufficient evidence of the risk to the individual, or should circumstances specific to the individual be adduced, in addition, before he/she can assert protection from expulsion, extradition or refoulement under the relevant human rights instruments?

5. Could reasonings held in *Soering* and *Judge* be transposed to cases other than deportation cases? For instance, would a State be in violation of its human rights obligations if it provided evidence allowing a foreign court to convict a defendant in violation of due process rights? Would it be in violation of its obligations if it transferred personal data without ensuring that such data will be processed in accordance with the rules pertaining to the processing of personal data? If so, does this amount for States bound by such obligations to imposing human rights norms they have chosen to comply with on other States, not committed to upholding the same standards? Is this an excessive restriction on the possibilities of inter-State co-operation, precisely at a moment when such co-operation is particularly important given the transnational dimension of a number of issues, including crime and migrations?

3.2 The execution of foreign judgments

Deportation cases are not the only ones where the collaborative conduct by States may result in human rights violations. Another typical instance where this may happen is in the context of international judicial co-operation, where the courts in one State are requested to recognize and executed a judgment delivered by foreign courts, which – either because of procedural deficiencies or because of the outcome – may have been adopted in violation of human rights binding on the State of execution. Consider the following examples:

European Court of Human Rights (2nd sect.), *Pellegrini* v. *Italy* (Appl. No. 30882/96), judgment of 20 July 2001:

[In 1962 the applicant, Ms Pellegrini, married Mr A. Gigliozzi in a religious ceremony which was also valid in the eyes of the law (*matrimonio concordatario*). On 23 February 1987 Ms Pellegrini petitioned the Rome District Court for judicial separation. In a judgment dated 2 October 1990 the District Court granted her petition and also ordered Mr Gigliozzi to pay the applicant maintenance (*mantenimento*) of 300,000 Italian lira per month. In the meantime, on 20 November 1987, Ms Pellegrini was summoned to appear before the Lazio Regional Ecclesiastical Court of the Rome Vicariate on 1 December 1987, since on 6 November 1987 her husband had sought to have the marriage annulled on the ground of consanguinity (the applicant's mother and Mr Gigliozzi's father being cousins). In a judgment delivered on 10 December 1987 and deposited with the registry on the same day, the Ecclesiastical Court annulled the marriage on the ground of consanguinity. The court had followed a summary procedure (*praetermissis solemnitatibus processus ordinarii*) under Article 1688 of the Code of Canon Law. That procedure is followed where, once the parties have been summoned to appear and the *defensor vinculis* (defender of the institution of marriage) has intervened, it is clear from an agreed document that there is a ground for annulling the marriage. Ms Pellegrini appealed against the judgment of the Ecclesiastical Court, complaining of a number of procedural defects. However, in a judgment of 13 April 1988, the Roman Rota upheld the decision annulling the marriage on the ground of consanguinity.

On 23 November 1988 the Rota informed the applicant and her ex-husband that its judgment, which had become enforceable by a decision of the superior ecclesiastical review body, had been referred to the Florence Court of Appeal for a declaration that it could be enforced under Italian law (*delibazione*). This is in accordance with Article 8 §2 of the Concordat between Italy and the Vatican, according to which a judgment of the ecclesiastical courts annulling a marriage, which has become enforceable by a decision of the superior ecclesiastical review body, may be made enforceable in Italy at the request of one of the parties by a judgment of the relevant court of appeal. This provision also states that the Court of Appeal should verify that 'in the nullity proceedings the defence rights of the parties have been recognised in a manner compatible with the fundamental principles of Italian law'. In a judgment of 8 November 1991, the Florence Court of Appeal declared the judgment of 13 April 1988 enforceable. The Court found that the opportunity given to the applicant on 1 December 1987 to answer questions had been sufficient to ensure that the adversarial principle had been complied with and that, moreover, she had freely chosen to bring the proceedings before the Rota and had been able to exercise her defence rights in those proceedings 'irrespective of the special features of proceedings under canon law'. Ms Pellegrini appealed the judgment. However, the Italian Court of Cassation dismissed the appeal in a judgment of 10 March 1995. It held, first of all, that the adversarial principle had been complied with in the proceedings before the ecclesiastical courts; moreover, there was case law authority to support the view that while the assistance of a lawyer was not a requirement under canon law, it was not forbidden: the applicant could therefore have taken advantage of that possibility. The court also held that the fact that the applicant had had a very short time in which to prepare her defence in November 1987 did not amount to an infringement of her defence rights because she had not indicated why she had needed more time.

Ms Pellegrini complained before the European Court of Human Rights of a violation of Article 6 of the Convention on the ground that the Italian courts declared the decision of the ecclesiastical courts annulling her marriage enforceable following proceedings in which her defence rights had been breached.]

40. The Court notes at the outset that the applicant's marriage was annulled by a decision of the Vatican courts which was declared enforceable by the Italian courts. The Vatican has not ratified the Convention and, furthermore, the application was lodged against Italy. The Court's task therefore consists not in examining whether the proceedings before the ecclesiastical courts complied with Article 6 of the Convention, but whether the Italian courts, before authorising enforcement of the decision annulling the marriage, duly satisfied themselves that the relevant proceedings fulfilled the guarantees of Article 6. A review of that kind is required where a decision in respect of which enforcement is requested emanates from the courts of a country which does not apply the Convention. Such a review is especially necessary where the implications of a declaration of enforceability are of capital importance for the parties.

41. The Court must examine the reasons given by the Florence Court of Appeal and the Court of Cassation for dismissing the applicant's complaints about the proceedings before the ecclesiastical courts.

42. The applicant had complained of an infringement of the adversarial principle. She had not been informed in detail of her ex-husband's application to have the marriage annulled and had not had access to the case file. She was therefore unaware, in particular, of the contents of the statements made by the three witnesses who had apparently given evidence in favour of her ex-husband and of the observations of the *defensor vinculis*. Furthermore, she was not assisted by a lawyer.

43. The Florence Court of Appeal held that the circumstances in which the applicant had appeared before the Ecclesiastical Court and the fact that she had subsequently lodged an appeal against that court's judgment were sufficient to conclude that she had had the benefit of an adversarial trial. The Court of Cassation held that, in the main, ecclesiastical court proceedings complied with the adversarial principle.

44. The Court is not satisfied by these reasons. The Italian courts do not appear to have attached importance to the fact that the applicant had not had the possibility of examining the evidence produced by her ex-husband and by the 'so-called witnesses'. However, the Court reiterates in that connection that the right to adversarial proceedings, which is one of the elements of a fair hearing within the meaning of Article 6 §1, means that each party to a trial, be it criminal or civil, must in principle have the opportunity to have knowledge of and comment on all evidence adduced or observations filed with a view to influencing the court's decision (see, *mutatis mutandis*, *Lobo Machado* v. *Portugal*, and *Vermeulen* v. *Belgium*, judgments of 20 February 1996, *Reports of Judgments and Decisions* 1996–I, pp. 206–07, §31, and p. 234, §33, respectively, and *Mantovanelli* v. *France*, judgment of 18 March 1997, p. 436, §33).

45. It is irrelevant that, in the Government's opinion, as the nullity of the marriage derived from an objective and undisputed fact the applicant would not in any event have been able to challenge it. It is for the parties to a dispute alone to decide whether a document produced by the other party or by witnesses calls for their comments. What is particularly at stake here is litigants' confidence in the workings of justice, which is based on, *inter alia*, the knowledge that they have had the opportunity to express their views on every document in the file (see, *mutatis mutandis*, *F.R.* v. *Switzerland*, No. 37292/97, §39, 28 June 2001, unreported).

46. The position is no different with regard to the assistance of a lawyer. Since such assistance was possible, according to the Court of Cassation, even in the context of the summary procedure before the Ecclesiastical Court, the applicant should have been put in a position enabling her to secure the assistance of a lawyer if she wished. The Court is not satisfied by the Court of Cassation's argument that the applicant should have been familiar with the case law on the subject: the ecclesiastical courts could have presumed that the applicant, who was not assisted by a lawyer, was unaware of that case law. In the Court's opinion, given that the applicant had been summoned to appear before the Ecclesiastical Court without knowing what the case was about, that court had a duty to inform her that she could seek the assistance of a lawyer before she attended for questioning.

47. In these circumstances the Court considers that the Italian courts breached their duty of satisfying themselves, before authorising enforcement of the Roman Rota's judgment, that the applicant had had a fair trial in the proceedings under canon law.

48. There has therefore been a violation of Article 6 §1 of the Convention.

European Court of Human Rights (1st sect.), *Lindberg* v. *Sweden* (Appl. No. 48198/99), decision (inadmissibility) of 15 January 2004:

[The applicant, Mr Lindberg, a Norwegian national living in Sweden, had been on board the seal hunting vessel *M/S Harmoni* as a seal hunting inspector for the Norwegian Ministry of Fisheries for the 1988 season. He served on board the *Harmoni* from 12 March to 11 April 1988.

Thereafter, and until 20 July 1988, a Norwegian newspaper, *Bladet Tromsø*, published twenty-six articles on Mr Lindberg's inspection, including his entire inspection report (of 30 June 1988). Following the wide publicity made around the report, the nineteen crew members of *Harmoni* brought, mostly with success, a series of defamation proceedings against the applicant and a number of media corporations and companies, including *Bladet Tromsø* and its former ~~editor~~. The defamation case against *Bladet Tromsø* and its former editor were the subject-matter ~~of~~ an application (No. 21980/93) lodged under the European Convention on Human Rights. In its *Bladet Tromsø and Stensaas* v. *Norway* judgment of 20 May 1999 ([GC], No. 21980/93, E.C.H.R. 1999–III), the Court, by thirteen votes to four, found that there had been a violation of Article 10 of the Convention with regard to the newspaper and the former editor.

Here, Mr Lindberg complains about the Swedish courts' refusal to prevent the enforcement in Sweden (where he lived) of a judgment of 25 August 1990 (delivered by the Sarpsborg City Court) in defamation proceedings against him on account of similar or comparable allegations. In that judgment, the Sarpsborg City Court declared five statements in the inspection report of Mr Lindberg null and void under Article 253 §1 of the Penal Code (since they were considered defamatory), as well as two other statements made by him in television programmes. It further prohibited the applicant from making accessible to the relevant public film footage, where the plaintiffs could be identified, and ordered him to pay to each of them NOK 10,000 in compensation for non-pecuniary damage, plus NOK 3,000 in respect of profits he had obtained through illegal publication of the film, as well as legal costs. Invoking that the 25 August 1990 judgment violated his right to freedom of expression under Article 10 of the Convention, Mr Lindberg opposed the execution of the judgment by the Swedish courts. The European Court of Human Rights summarizes thus the proceedings before the Swedish courts: '... the Vänersborg City Court (*tingsrätt*), by a decision (*beslut*) of 22 February 1996, rejected the applicant's claim. It noted that the impugned matter predated the entry into force of the 1988 Lugano Convention (on Jurisdiction and the Enforcement of Judgments in Civil and Commercial Matters) for Sweden and Norway (respectively on 2 January and 1 May 1993), so it fell to be considered under Act 1977:595 regarding the Recognition and Enforcement of Nordic Judgments in the area of Private Law, section 8 §1 No. 6 of which provided that a judgment which was obviously incompatible with the Swedish public order should not be recognised or implemented in Sweden. According to the preparatory works this provision should be applied with great caution. In practice it had only been applied in narrowly defined and exceptional circumstances, when there was question of principles fundamental to the Swedish legal system and provisions protecting the interests of a weaker party. In this respect the City Court observed that the principle of exclusive responsibility on the part of the publisher of an allegation in a periodical or a film was a very important part of the Swedish constitutional protection of free speech. That principle did not exist in the Norwegian legal system, under which several persons might incur liability with respect to the contents of a periodical or a television programme. However, this difference between the Swedish and the Norwegian law, albeit decisive in part for the outcome before the Sarpsborg City Court, did not amount to an exceptional circumstance warranting the application of the public order provision in the 1977 Act. Accordingly, there was no obstacle to recognition and enforcement of the Sarpsborg City Court's judgment of 25 August 1990. Nor could that judgment be said to breach the Convention.'

This position was upheld by the Court of Appeal and by the Swedish Supreme Court. The Supreme Court stated that: 'an examination ought to be made of [the applicant's] submission that the Sarpsborg City Court's judgment must not be executed on the grounds that it violates Article 10 in the Convention. It can, however, not be a question of undertaking a complete review of the City Court's judgment. Such a scheme would cause an excessive burden to the international co-operation aimed at facilitating the execution of judgments in countries other than that where the judgment was delivered. It is also apparent that a court in the State of origin is normally better placed than an authority in the State of enforcement to make certain assessments, for example evidentiary matters and the application of the national law of the State of origin. Normally the proceedings in that State have been complete and afforded the parties an opportunity to adduce evidence and legal arguments in support for their case. This can be presumed to be the case especially with respect to States which have ratified the Convention. In the relations among the Convention States themselves it should normally suffice for the authority in the country of execution to pursue a rather summary assessment in verifying whether the judgment is in conformity with the Convention. However, should there, for example on a claim by a party, emerge circumstances that would make it questionable whether the judgment fulfils the requirements in the Convention, a closer scrutiny must be carried out.'

The position of the European Court of Human Rights is expressed below:]

The applicant complains under Article 13 of the Convention, in conjunction with Article 10, that the Swedish Supreme Court had failed to carry out a proper review of his claim that the Norwegian City Court's judgment of 25 August 1990 violated his rights under Article 10 of the Convention.

The applicant further submitted that the Swedish recognition and enforcement of the Norwegian judgment also entailed a violation of Article 10 of the Convention taken on its own.

... [I]n so far as the applicant claims that the outcome of the main proceedings in Norway was incompatible with Article 10 of the Convention, the proper venue of redress for him would have been to pursue an application to Strasbourg against Norway in accordance with the formal conditions under the Convention. He did in fact seek to bring an application (No. 26604/95) under Article 10 of the Convention, but failed to observe the six months' time limit and so, on 26 February 1997, the former Commission declared the application inadmissible as being out of time. Thus, the Court's assessment of the existence of an arguable claim in the present case may not directly address the main libel case in Norway but is limited to the ensuing enforcement proceedings in Sweden. A contrary approach would give an applicant the undue possibility of having reopened matters already finally settled, at the risk of upsetting the coherence of the division of roles between national review bodies and the European Court, making up the system of collective enforcement under the Convention.

Accordingly, ... the Court does not find that the applicant could pray in aid the *Bladet Tromsø and Stensaas* judgment to underpin his argument that the Swedish authorities recognition and enforcement of the Norwegian judgment in his case violated Article 10 of the Convention. On a whole, the Court finds it questionable whether the applicant could at all be said to have an arguable claim for the purposes of Article 13 with respect to his claim that the Swedish authorities' co-operation was inconsistent with Article 10 of the Convention. However, for the reasons set out below it does not need to decide this question and will proceed on the assumption that Article 13 is applicable.

Turning, then, to the issue whether the applicant was afforded an effective remedy in Sweden against the Swedish authorities' recognition and enforcement of the Norwegian judgment, the Court cannot but note that the Swedish courts, at three levels of jurisdiction, reviewed the applicant's appeal against enforcement. The only question is whether the scope of review carried out was sufficient to provide the applicant an effective remedy for the purposes of Article 13 of the Convention.

Comparable issues have previously been examined in the context of co-operation between States inside and outside the Convention territory, notably in the plenary *Drozd and Janousek* v. *France and Spain* judgment of 26 June 1992 (Series A No. 240) and the *Iribarne Pérez* v. *France* judgment of 24 October 1995 (Series A No. 325–B). Both cases concerned complaints about the enforcement in a Contracting State of a judgment by a court of a non-Contracting State (in Andorra – before joining the Council of Europe) reached in proceedings claimed to be at variance with due process. The Court attached decisive weight to whether the impugned conviction was the result of a 'flagrant denial of justice' (see *Drozd and Janousek*, §110; and *Iribarne Pérez*, § 31; see also *Pellegrini* v. *Italy*, No. 30882/96, E.C.H.R. 2001–VIII, even though no express mention was made of the said criterion in that judgment).

However, the Court does not deem it necessary for the purposes of its examination of the present case to determine the general issue concerning what standard should apply where the enforcing State as well as the State whose court gave the contested decision is a Contracting Party to the Convention and where the subject-matter is one of substance (i.e. here, the freedom of expression) rather than procedure. In the particular circumstances it suffices to note that the Swedish courts found that the requested enforcement (in respect of the award of compensation and costs made in the Norwegian judgment) was neither prevented by Swedish public order or any other obstacles under Swedish law. The Court, bearing in mind its findings above as to whether the applicant had an arguable claim, does not find that there were any compelling reasons against enforcement. That being so, the Court is clearly satisfied that the Swedish courts reviewed the substance of the applicant's complaint against the requested enforcement of the Norwegian judgment, to a sufficient degree to provide him an effective remedy for the purposes of Article 13 of the Convention.

It follows that this part of the application is manifestly ill-founded ...

The applicant further alleged that the Swedish recognition and enforcement of the Norwegian judgment entailed in addition a violation of Article 10 of the Convention taken on its own.

However, the Court sees no reason to doubt that the interference with the applicant's Article 10 rights by the Swedish authorities' enforcement of the Norwegian judgment was 'prescribed by law' and pursued legitimate aims, namely 'the protection of the reputation or rights of others' and 'maintaining the authority of the judiciary'. Moreover, bearing in mind its reasoning and conclusions above in relation to Article 13, the Court finds that the interference resulting from the decision to enforce the judgment was clearly 'necessary' within the meaning of the second paragraph of Article 10. The application discloses no appearance of violation of Article 10 of the Convention.

2.7. Questions for discussion: human rights requirements and mutual trust in international judicial co-operation

1. Are *Pellegrini* and *Lindberg* in contradiction with one another? What is the difference that may justify a distinction being made between these cases? In particular, is justifiable to require

from the Italian courts that they verify whether the Vatican courts have adopted their deci- sions in accordance with the requirements of Article 6 of the Convention, and not to impose the same requirements on the Swedish courts enforcing judgments adopted in Norway, despite the fact that these judgments were found, in the *Bladet Tromsø and Stensaas* v. *Norway* judgment adopted on 20 May 1999 by the European Court of Human Rights, to be in violation of freedom of expression? Or were other differences between *Pellegrini* and *Lindberg* more relevant?

2. Should *Lindberg* be taken as authority for the view that, where a State party to the European Convention on Human Rights is requested to execute a foreign judgment delivered by a court of another State party, it may presume the compatibility of that judgment with the requirements of the Convention, and thus exercise only a minimal scrutiny on the content of the judgment as well as on the respect with the procedural requirements of Article 6 ECHR, where this provision is applicable? Is this compatible with the decision in *T.I.* v. *United Kingdom*? Does it imply that States parties to the Convention may agree, among themselves, to enter into forms of judicial co-operation based on mutual trust, on the presumption that they comply with the require- ments of the Convention?

4 THE RESPONSIBILITY OF STATES FOR THE ACTS OF THE INTERNATIONAL ORGANIZATIONS

4.1 The general regime

By concluding a treaty establishing an intergovernmental organization, States may transfer to this organization certain powers which the organization may then exercise in violation of human rights its Member States have agreed to uphold. But the organ- ization is recognized as a separate international legal personality, for the purposes of exercising those attributed powers. As a result, its acts are in principle not attribut- able to its Member States. Although this situation is obviously not satisfactory, human rights bodies have sometimes considered it was the inevitable result of the growth of international co-operation. Consider the following cases:

European Commission of Human Rights, *Ilse Hess* v. *United Kingdom* (Appl. No. 6231/73), 2 DR 73; 18 Yearbook of the European Convention of Human Rights 174 (1975)

[The applicant is the wife of Rudolf Hess, a close collaborator of Hitler, who was condemned to life imprisonment in 1946 by the International Military Tribunal of Nuremberg after being found guilty of conspiracy to wage aggressive war and crimes against peace. He was transferred on 18 July 1947 to the Allied Military Prison in Berlin-Spandau, located in the British sector of Berlin and guarded in monthly turns by the United States, France, the United Kingdom and the Union of Soviet Socialist Republics. Since 1966, when the last other prisoners were released, Rudolf Hess was in solitary confinement in a prison which could hold 600 prisoners. The applicant argues that this situation amounts to a violation of Articles 3 and 8 of the European Convention on Human

Rights. She argues that the Convention on Human Rights also applies to the interpretation of the Agreement of 8 August 1945 concluded in London between the Governments of the United Kingdom, the United States of America, France and the Union of Soviet Socialist Republics. She states that her husband has served long enough and claims that the Commission should press the United Kingdom (at the time of the application, the only one of these four States to be bound by the ECHR) to step up its efforts to secure renegotiation of the Four Power Agreement over Berlin in order to obtain the release of Rudolf Hess; or, alternatively, release him when it is next responsible for his custody.]

For the purposes of determining the obligations of the United Kingdom under Art. 1 of the Convention, the Commission recalls that Spandau Allied Prison was established by the Allied Kommandatura Berlin in compliance with a directive of the Control Council. This followed from the assumption in 1945 of supreme authority by the Four Powers with respect to Germany. The supreme authority over the prison was vested in the Allied Kommandatura. The executive authority consists of four governors acting by unanimous decisions. Each of the governors is the delegate and the representative of one of the Four Powers.

The rights and obligations arising out of the agreements between the Four Powers concerning Spandau Prison continued to be in force after the withdrawal of the Soviet Union from the Kommandatura. This fact is not disputed by any of the parties. In regard to the administration of the prison, the Commission notes that changes therein can only be made by the unanimous decision of the representatives of the Four Powers in Germany or by the unanimous decision of the Four Governors. Administration and supervision is at all times quadripartite, including the day to day 'civil administration' of the prison and the responsibility for providing the military guard ...

The Commission concludes that the responsibility for the prison at Spandau, and for the continued imprisonment of Rudolf Hess, is exercised on a Four Power basis and that the United Kingdom acts only as a partner in the joint responsibility which it shares with the three other Powers.

The Commission is of the opinion that the joint authority cannot be divided into four separate jurisdictions and that therefore the United Kingdom's participation in the exercise of the joint authority and consequently in the administration and supervision of Spandau Prison is not a matter 'within the jurisdiction' of the United Kingdom, within the meaning of Art. 1 of the Convention.

The conclusion by the respondent Government of an agreement concerning Spandau prison of the kind in question in this case could raise an issue under the Convention if it were entered into when the Convention was already in force for the respondent Government. The agreement concerning the prison, however, came into force in 1945. Moreover, a unilateral withdrawal from such an agreement is not valid under international law.

Human Rights Committee, *H. v. d.P.* v. *Netherlands*, Communication No. 217/1986 (CCPR/C/OP/2 at 70) (1990) (final views (inadmissibility) of 8 April 1987):

[The author of the communication is a national of the Netherlands. Previously an industrial engineer in the Netherlands, he was subsequently employed as a substantive patent examiner at the European Patent Office (EPO) in Munich, Germany. A few months after having accepted a post at the AI, step 2 level in the EPO, he came to the conclusion that he had been appointed at a discriminatorily low level and he felt that the preponderance of citizens of the Federal Republic of Germany in the higher grades was the result of the discriminatory practices of the organization. His internal appeals were rejected, however. He filed an application with the European Commission of Human Rights, which on 15 May 1986 declared his application inadmissible *ratione materiae* on the grounds that litigation concerning the modalities of employment as a civil servant, on either the national or international level, fell outside the scope of the European Convention on Human Rights. The author then turned to the Human Rights Committee, which he considered competent to consider the case, since five States parties (France, Italy, Luxembourg, the Netherlands and Sweden) to the European Patent Convention are also parties to the Optional Protocol to the International Covenant on Civil and Political Rights.]

3.1. Before considering any claims contained in a communication, the Human Rights Committee shall, in accordance with rule 87 of its provisional rules of procedure, decide whether or not it is admissible under the Optional Protocol to the Covenant.

3.2. The Human Rights Committee observes in this connection that it can only receive and consider communications in respect of claims that come under the jurisdiction of a State party to the Covenant. The author's grievances, however, concern the recruitment policies of an international organisation, which cannot, in any way, be construed as coming within the jurisdiction of the Netherlands or of any other State party to the International Covenant on Civil and Political Rights and the Optional Protocol thereto. Accordingly, the author has no claim under the Optional Protocol.

More recently, the case law has evolved in order to ensure that States parties to human rights treaties would not circumvent their pre-existing obligations by establishing international organizations to which certain powers are attributed. A first step in this direction are the judgments delivered by the European Court of Human Rights in the cases of *Matthews*, *Beer and Regan*, and *Waite and Kennedy*.

European Court of Human Rights (GC), *Matthews* v. *United Kingdom* (Appl. No. 24833/94), judgment of 18 February 1999, paras. 31–3:

[The applicant, Ms Denise Matthews, was denied the right to take part in the June 1994 elections of the European Parliament. Previously an assembly with purely advisory powers, the European Parliament has received significant supplementary powers with the entry into force, on 1 November 1993, of the Treaty on the European Union signed in Maastricht. This makes Article 3 of Protocol No. 1 to the Convention, under which the States parties to the Convention 'undertake to hold free elections at reasonable intervals by secret ballot, under conditions which will ensure the free expression of the opinion of the people in the choice of the legislature', applicable to the elections to the European Parliament – now considered to have become a 'legislature' in the meaning of that provision. However, the elections to the European Parliament are regulated by Council Decision 76/787 (the Council Decision), signed by the President of the Council of the European Communities and the then Member States' foreign ministers, which was adopted pursuant to a provision of the EEC Treaty (Art. 138(3)) requiring the Council to 'lay down the appropriate provisions, which it [was to] recommend to Member States for adoption in accordance with their respective constitutional requirements'. The specific provisions concerning the modalities of European elections were set out in an Act Concerning the Election of the Representatives of the European Parliament by Direct Universal Suffrage of 20 September 1976 (the 1976 Act), signed by the respective foreign ministers, which was attached to the Council Decision. Annex II to the 1976 Act, which forms an integral part thereof, states that 'The United Kingdom will apply the provisions of this Act only in respect of the United Kingdom.' Residents of Gibraltar are thus excluded from the right to participate in elections to the European Parliament.]

31. The Court must ... consider whether, notwithstanding the nature of the elections to the European Parliament as an organ of the EC, the United Kingdom can be held responsible under Article 1 of the Convention for the absence of elections to the European Parliament in Gibraltar, that is, whether the United Kingdom is required to 'secure' elections to the European Parliament notwithstanding the Community character of those elections.

32. The Court observes that acts of the EC as such cannot be challenged before the Court because the EC is not a Contracting Party. The Convention does not exclude the transfer of competences to international organisations provided that Convention rights continue to be 'secured'. Member States' responsibility therefore continues even after such a transfer.

33. In the present case, the alleged violation of the Convention flows from an annex to the 1976 Act, entered into by the United Kingdom, together with the extension to the European Parliament's competences brought about by the Maastricht Treaty. The Council Decision and the 1976 Act ..., and the Maastricht Treaty, with its changes to the EEC Treaty, all constituted international instruments which were freely entered into by the United Kingdom. Indeed, the 1976 Act cannot be challenged before the European Court of Justice for the very reason that it is not a 'normal' act of the Community, but is a treaty within the Community legal order. The Maastricht Treaty, too, is not an act of the Community, but a treaty by which a revision of the EEC Treaty was brought about. The United Kingdom, together with all the other parties to the Maastricht Treaty, is responsible *ratione materiae* under Article 1 of the Convention and, in particular, under Article 3 of Protocol No. 1, for the consequences of that Treaty.

In their joint dissenting opinion, judges Sir John Freeland and Jungwiert took the view that there is 'a certain incongruity in the branding of the United Kingdom as a violator of obligations under Article 3 of Protocol No. 1 when the exclusion from the franchise effected multilaterally by the 1976 Decision and Act – in particular, Annex II – was at that time wholly consistent with those obligations (because on no view could the Assembly, as it was then known, be regarded as a legislature); when at no subsequent time has it been possible for the United Kingdom unilaterally to secure the modification of the position so as to include Gibraltar within the franchise; and when such a modification would require the agreement of all the member States (including a member State in dispute with the United Kingdom about sovereignty over Gibraltar)' (para. 8).

European Court of Human Rights (GC), *Beer and Regan* v. *Germany* **(Appl. No. 28934/95), judgment of 18 February 1999, paras. 49, 53–4, 57–60, 62–3.**

[Both applicants were put at the disposal of the European Space Agency (ESA) by private companies who employed them. In October and November 1993, they instituted proceedings before the Darmstadt Labour Court (*Arbeitsgericht*) against the ESA, arguing that, pursuant to the German Provision of Labour (Temporary Staff) Act (*Arbeitnehmerüberlassungsgesetz*), they had acquired the status of employees of ESA. The ESA however relied on its immunity from jurisdiction under Article XV para. 2 and Annex 1 of the Convention for the Establishment of a European Space Agency (ESA Convention) of 30 May 1975 (*United Nations Treaty Series* 1983, vol. 1297, I – No. 21524). The applicants contended that they had not had a fair hearing by a tribunal on the question of whether, pursuant to the German Provision of Labour (Temporary Staff) Act, a contractual relationship existed between them and ESA. They alleged that there had been a violation of Article 6 para. 1 of the Convention, which guarantees the right to access of a court for the determination of claims concerning civil rights and obligations.]

49. The Court recalls that the right of access to the courts secured by Article 6 §1 of the Convention is not absolute, but may be subject to limitations; these are permitted by implication since the right of access by its very nature calls for regulation by the State. In this respect, the Contracting States enjoy a certain margin of appreciation, although the final decision as to the observance of the Convention's requirements rests with the Court. It must be satisfied that the limitations applied do not restrict or reduce the access left to the individual in such a way or to such an extent that the very essence of the right is impaired. Furthermore, a limitation will not be compatible with Article 6 §1 if it does not pursue a legitimate aim and if there is not a reasonable relationship of proportionality between the means employed and the aim sought to be achieved ...

53. ... the Court points out that the attribution of privileges and immunities to international organisations is an essential means of ensuring the proper functioning of such organisations free from unilateral interference by individual governments. The immunity from jurisdiction commonly accorded by States to international organisations under the organisations' constituent instruments or supplementary agreements is a long-standing practice established in the interest of the good working of these organisations. The importance of this practice is enhanced by a trend towards extending and strengthening international cooperation in all domains of modern society.

Against this background, the Court finds that the rule of immunity from jurisdiction, which the German courts applied to ESA in the present case, has a legitimate objective.

54. As to the issue of proportionality, the Court must assess the contested limitation placed on Article 6 in the light of the particular circumstances of the case ...

57. The Court is of the opinion that where States establish international organisations in order to pursue or strengthen their co-operation in certain fields of activities, and where they attribute to these organisations certain competences and accord them immunities, there may be implications as to the protection of fundamental rights. It would be incompatible with the purpose and object of the Convention, however, if the Contracting States were thereby absolved from their responsibility under the Convention in relation to the field of activity covered by such attribution. It should be recalled that the Convention is intended to guarantee not theoretical or illusory rights, but rights that are practical and effective. This is particularly true for the right of access to the courts in view of the prominent place held in a democratic society by the right to

a fair trial (see, as a recent authority, the *Aït-Mouhoub* v. *France* judgment of 28 October 1998, *Reports* 1998–VIII, p. 3227, §52, referring to the *Airey* v. *Ireland* judgment of 9 October 1979, Series A No. 32, pp. 12–13, §24).

58. For the Court, a material factor in determining whether granting ESA immunity from German jurisdiction is permissible under the Convention is whether the applicants had available to them reasonable alternative means to protect effectively their rights under the Convention.

59. The ESA Convention, together with its Annex I, expressly provides for various modes of settlement of private-law disputes, in staff matters as well as in other litigation ... Since the applicants argued an employment relationship with ESA, they could and should have had recourse to the ESA Appeals Board. In accordance with Regulation 33 §1 of the ESA Staff Regulations, the ESA Appeals Board, which is 'independent of the Agency', has jurisdiction 'to hear disputes relating to any explicit or implicit decision taken by the Agency and arising between it and a staff member' ...

60. Moreover, it is in principle open to temporary workers to seek redress from the firms that have employed them and hired them out. Relying on general labour regulations or, more particularly, on the German Provision of Labour (Temporary Staff) Act, temporary workers can file claims in damages against such firms. In such court proceedings, a judicial clarification of the nature of the labour relationship can be obtained. The fact that any such claims under the Provision of Labour (Temporary Staff) Act are subject to a condition of good faith ... does not generally deprive this kind of litigation of reasonable prospects of success ...

62. The Court shares the Commission's conclusion that, bearing in mind the legitimate aim of immunities of international organisations ..., the test of proportionality cannot be applied in such a way as to compel an international organisation to submit itself to national litigation in relation to employment conditions prescribed under national labour law. To read Article 6 §1 of the Convention and its guarantee of access to court as necessarily requiring the application of national legislation in such matters would, in the Court's view, thwart the proper functioning of international organisations and run counter to the current trend towards extending and strengthening international co-operation.

63. In view of all these circumstances, the Court finds that, in giving effect to the immunity from jurisdiction of ESA ..., the German courts did not exceed their margin of appreciation. Taking into account in particular the alternative means of legal process available to the applicants, it cannot be said that the limitation on their access to the German courts with regard to ESA impaired the essence of their 'right to a court' or was disproportionate for the purposes of Article 6 §1 of the Convention.

Paragraphs 32 and 33 of the judgment delivered by the European Court of Human Rights in the case of *Matthews* could be read to suggest that the EU Member States could only be held responsible for the consequences of measures originating in the European Union where such measures cannot be reviewed by the European Court of Justice. However, the judgment delivered by the European Court of Human Rights on 30 June 2005 in the case of *Bosphorus Hava Yolları Turizm ve Ticaret Anonim Şirketi* v. *Ireland* widens the range of situations in which States parties to the European Convention on Human Rights may be found responsible for the adoption or the implementation of measures adopted within the EU.

European Court of Human Rights (GC), *Bosphorus Hava Yolları Turizm* v. *Ticaret Anonim Şirketi v. Ireland* **(Appl. No. 45036/98), judgment of 30 June 2005, paras. 150–8:**

[In April 1992, the applicant company, an airline company chartered in Turkey, had leased two aircraft from Yugoslav Airlines (JAT), the national airline of the former Yugoslavia. However, from 1991 onwards the United Nations adopted a series of sanctions against the former Federal Republic of Yugoslavia (Serbia and Montenegro) (FRY) designed to address the armed conflict and human rights violations taking place in the former Yugoslavia. On 17 April 1993 the UN Security Council adopted Resolution 820 (1993), which provided that States should impound, *inter alia*, all aircraft in their territories 'in which a majority or controlling interest is held by a person or undertaking' in or operating from the FRY. That Resolution was implemented in the European Community by EC Regulation 990/93 which entered into force on 28 April 1993. After one of the applicant's leased aircraft arrived in Dublin for maintenance on 17 May 1993, it was stopped from departing after the maintenance work had been completed. In the course of the ensuing judicial proceedings before the Irish courts, the European Court of Justice was asked to interpret EC Regulation 990/93. In a judgment of 30 July 1996, it concluded that Article 8 of the said Regulation did apply and that, therefore, the impounding of the aircraft was an obligation imposed under EC law on the Irish authorities. It considered the argument of the applicant company that the impounding was in violation of its right to peaceful enjoyment of his possessions and its freedom to pursue a commercial activity, but it rejected that argument, considering that 'As compared with an objective of general interest so fundamental for the international community, which consists in putting an end to the state of war in the region and to the massive violations of human rights and humanitarian international law in the Republic of Bosnia-Herzegovina, the impounding of the aircraft in question, which is owned by an undertaking based in or operating from the [FRY], cannot be regarded as inappropriate or disproportionate.'

Before the European Court of Human Rights, the applicant company alleges a violation of Article 1 of Protocol No. 1 to the ECHR, which guarantees the right to property. In its submissions to the Court, before which it appeared as *amicus curiae*, the European Commission (Commission of the European Communities) noted that the application concerned in substance a State's responsibility for Community acts. In the view of the European Commission, this question had to be answered by reference to the 1990 decision of the European Commission on Human Rights in the '*M. & Co.*' case (Appl. No. 13258/87, decision of 9 February 1990, *Decisions and Reports* (D.R.) 64, p. 138) and its 1994 decision in the case of *Heinz* v. *Contracting Parties also Parties to the European Patent Convention* (Appl. No. 21090/92, decision of 10 January 1994, D.R. 76–A, p. 125). Those decisions suggested that while a State retained some Convention responsibility after it had ceded powers to an international organization, that responsibility was fulfilled once there was proper provision in that organization's structure for effective protection of fundamental rights at a level at least 'equivalent' to that of the Convention. Thereafter, any Convention responsibility, over and above the need to establish equivalent protection, would only arise when the State exercised a discretion accorded to it by the international organizations. The European Court of Human Rights essentially agreed with that position:]

150. The Court considers ... that the general interest pursued by the impugned action was compliance with legal obligations flowing from the Irish State's membership of the EC. It is, moreover, a legitimate interest of considerable weight. The Convention has to be interpreted in

the light of any relevant rules and principles of international law applicable in relations between the Contracting Parties (Article 31 §3(c) of the Vienna Convention on the Law of Treaties of 23 May 1969 and *Al-Adsani* v. *United Kingdom* [GC], No. 35763/97, §55, E.C.H.R. 2001–XI), which principles include that of *pacta sunt servanda*. The Court has also long recognised the growing importance of international co-operation and of the consequent need to secure the proper functioning of international organisations (the above-cited cases of *Waite and Kennedy*, at §§63 and 72 and *Al-Adsani*, §54. See also Article 234 (now Article 307) of the EC Treaty). Such considerations are critical for a supranational organisation such as the EC [which produces rules binding on the Member States: *Costa* v. *Ente Nazionale per l'Energia Electtrica* (ENEL), Case 6/64, [1964] E.C.R. 585] ...

151. The question is therefore whether, and if so to what extent, that important general interest of compliance with EC obligations can justify the impugned interference by the State with the applicant's property rights.

152. The Convention does not, on the one hand, prohibit Contracting Parties from transferring sovereign power to an international (including a supranational) organisation in order to pursue co-operation in certain fields of activity (the *M. & Co.* decision, at p. 144 and *Matthews* at §32, both cited above). Moreover, even as the holder of such transferred sovereign power, that organisation is not itself held responsible under the Convention for proceedings before, or decisions of, its organs as long as it is not a Contracting Party (see *CFDT* v. *European Communities*, No. 8030/77, Commission decision of 10 July 1978, D.R. 13, p. 231; *Dufay* v. *European Communities*, No. 13539/88, Commission decision of 19 January 1989; the above-cited *M. & Co.* case, at p. 144 and the above-cited *Matthews* judgment, at §32).

153. On the other hand, it has also been accepted that a Contracting Party is responsible under Article 1 of the Convention for all acts and omissions of its organs regardless of whether the act or omission in question was a consequence of domestic law or of the necessity to comply with international legal obligations. Article 1 makes no distinction as to the type of rule or measure concerned and does not exclude any part of a Contracting Party's 'jurisdiction' from scrutiny under the Convention (*United Communist Party of Turkey and others* v. *Turkey* judgment of 30 January 1998, Reports, 1998–I, §29).

154. In reconciling both these positions and thereby establishing the extent to which State action can be justified by its compliance with obligations flowing from its membership of an international organisation to which it has transferred part of its sovereignty, the Court has recognised that absolving Contracting States completely from their Convention responsibility in the areas covered by such a transfer would be incompatible with the purpose and object of the Convention: the guarantees of the Convention could be limited or excluded at will thereby depriving it of its peremptory character and undermining the practical and effective nature of its safeguards (*M. & Co.* at p. 145 and *Waite and Kennedy*, at §67). The State is considered to retain Convention liability in respect of treaty commitments subsequent to the entry into force of the Convention (*mutatis mutandis*, the above-cited *Matthews* v. *United Kingdom* judgment, at §§29 and 32–34, and *Prince Hans–Adam II of Liechtenstein* v. *Germany* [GC], No. 42527/98, §47, E.C.H.R. 2001–VIII).

155. In the Court's view, State action taken in compliance with such legal obligations is justified as long as the relevant organisation is considered to protect fundamental rights, as regards both the substantive guarantees offered and the mechanisms controlling their observance, in a manner which can be considered at least equivalent to that for which the

Convention provides (see the above-cited *M. & Co.* decision, at p. 145, an approach with which the parties and the European Commission agreed). By 'equivalent' the Court means 'comparable': any requirement that the organisation's protection be 'identical' could run counter to the interest of international co-operation pursued ... However, any such finding of equivalence could not be final and would be susceptible to review in the light of any relevant change in fundamental rights' protection.

156. If such equivalent protection is considered to be provided by the organisation, the presumption will be that a State has not departed from the requirements of the Convention when it does no more than implement legal obligations flowing from its membership of the organisation.

However, any such presumption can be rebutted if, in the circumstances of a particular case, it is considered that the protection of Convention rights was manifestly deficient. In such cases, the interest of international co-operation would be outweighed by the Convention's role as a 'constitutional instrument of European public order' in the field of human rights (*Loizidou* v. *Turkey (preliminary objections)*, judgment of 23 March 1995, Series A No. 310, §75).

157. It remains the case that a State would be fully responsible under the Convention for all acts falling outside its strict international legal obligations ... The *Matthews* case can ... be distinguished: the acts for which the United Kingdom was found responsible were 'international instruments which were freely entered into' by it (§33 of that judgment) ...

158. Since the impugned act constituted solely compliance by Ireland with its legal obligations flowing from membership of the EC ..., the Court will now examine whether a presumption arises that Ireland complied with its Convention requirements in fulfilling such obligations and whether any such presumption has been rebutted in the circumstances of the present case.

[Taking into account the protection of fundamental rights in the legal order of the European Union, the European Court of Human Rights arrives at the conclusion that 'the protection of fundamental rights by EC law can be considered to be, and to have been at the relevant time, "equivalent" (within the meaning of para. 155 above) to that of the Convention system. Consequently, the presumption arises that Ireland did not depart from the requirements of the Convention when it implemented legal obligations flowing from its membership of the EC' (para. 165). It moreover considered that 'there was no dysfunction of the mechanisms of control of the observance of Convention rights [and that] therefore, it cannot be said that the protection of the applicant's Convention rights was manifestly deficient with the consequence that the relevant presumption of Convention compliance by the respondent State has not been rebutted' (para. 166). It concluded that the impoundment of the aircraft did not give rise to a violation of Article 1 of Protocol No. 1 to the Convention.]

When, in August 2001, it adopted its Articles on the responsibility of States for internationally wrongful acts, the International Law Commission had deliberately left open the question of the responsibility of States for the acts of international organisations. These Articles were 'without prejudice to any question of the responsibility of ... any State for the conduct of an international organisation' (Art. 57). This question however is under consideration by the International Law Commission in its ongoing work on the responsibility of international organizations. The inclusion of the following provisions is envisaged (see Report of the International Law Commission on the work of its fifty-eighth session, 1 May–9 June and 3 July–11 August 2006, I.L.C. Report, A/61/10 (2006), chapter VI, paras. 77–91):

International Law Commission, Draft Articles on the Responsibility of International Organisations (2006):

Article 25. Aid or assistance by a State in the commission of an internationally wrongful act by an international organisation

A State which aids or assists an international organisation in the commission of an internationally wrongful act by the latter is internationally responsible for doing so if:

(a) That State does so with knowledge of the circumstances of the internationally wrongful act; and

(b) The act would be internationally wrongful if committed by that State.

Article 26. Direction and control exercised by a State over the commission of an internationally wrongful act by an international organisation

A State which directs and controls an international organisation in the commission of an internationally wrongful act by the latter is internationally responsible for that act if:

(a) That State does so with knowledge of the circumstances of the internationally wrongful act; and

(b) The act would be internationally wrongful if committed by that State.

Article 27. Coercion of an international organisation by a State

A State which coerces an international organisation to commit an act is internationally responsible for that act if:

(a) The act would, but for the coercion, be an internationally wrongful act of that international organisation; and

(b) That State does so with knowledge of the circumstances of the act.

Article 28. International responsibility in case of provision of competence to an international organisation

1. A State member of an international organisation incurs international responsibility if it circumvents one of its international obligations by providing the organisation with competence in relation to that obligation, and the organisation commits an act that, if committed by that State, would have constituted a breach of that obligation.

2. Paragraph 1 applies whether or not the act in question is internationally wrongful for the international organisation.

Article 29. Responsibility of a State member of an international organisation for the internationally wrongful act of that organisation

1. Without prejudice to draft articles 25 to 28, a State member of an international organisation is responsible for an internationally wrongful act of that organisation if:

(a) It has accepted responsibility for that act; or

(b) It has led the injured party to rely on its responsibility.

2. The international responsibility of a State which is entailed in accordance with paragraph 1 is presumed to be subsidiary.

Article 30. Effect of this chapter

This chapter is without prejudice to international responsibility, under other provisions of these draft articles, of the international organisation which commits the act in question, or of any other international organisation.

The Commentaries to certain of these provisions deserve to be mentioned here. The Commentary to Article 25 states in part: 'A State aiding or assisting an international organisation in the commission of an internationally wrongful act may or may not be a member of that organisation. Should the State be a member, the influence that may amount to aid or assistance could not simply consist in participation in the decision-making process of the organisation according to the pertinent rules of the organisation. However, it cannot be totally ruled out that aid or assistance could result from conduct taken by the State within the framework of the organisation. This could entail some difficulties in ascertaining whether aid or assistance has taken place in borderline cases. The factual context such as the size of membership and the nature of the involvement will probably be decisive.' Similar comments are made in respect of Articles 26 and 27 of the draft Articles. As to the Commentary to Article 28, it states in part that: 'the existence of a specific intention of circumvention is not required and responsibility cannot be avoided by showing the absence of an intention to circumvent the international obligation. The use of the term "circumvention" is meant to exclude that international responsibility arises when the act of the international organisation, which would constitute a breach of an international obligation if taken by the State, has to be regarded as an unwitting result of providing the international organisation with competence. On the other hand, the term "circumvention" does not refer only to cases in which the member State may be said to be abusing its rights.'

While they seek to codify the existing emerging customary law in the area of the responsibility of international organizations (and of States in relation to wrongful acts adopted by international organizations), these rules are not entirely satisfactory. They leave open an important gap: where States have transferred competences to an international organization without it being reasonably possible to anticipate that those competences will be exercised by the organization in a way which would constitute a breach of their international obligations if they had adopted such acts directly – and, in particular, where such transferral of competences has been accompanied by certain safeguards, intended to ensure that the organization will comply with such international obligations in the exercise of its powers – they will not be held responsible for such acts, even if they took part in the decision-making within the organization. Thus, to the extent that the international organization either is not under the same international obligations as its Member States (in particular, in the event that the Member States have ratified certain international human rights treaties to which the international organization itself is not a party), or cannot be subjected to enforcement mechanisms similar to those which can be invoked against States, situations may arise where the international organization will adopt measures which have an impact similar to that of measures which, if they were adopted by its Member States, would constitute a breach of their international obligations, and for which nevertheless neither the Member States, nor the international organization itself, will be responsible under international law.

It is in order to overcome these difficulties that the following proposal has been made:

Jean d'Aspremont, 'Abuse of the Legal Personality of International Organisations and the Responsibility of Member States', *International Organisations Law Review* **(2007), 91–119 at 102 and 109–10:**

When member states effectively and overwhelmingly control the decision-making process of an international organisation, ... the legal personality of that organisation can no longer constitute a shield behind which member states can evade a responsibility that they would have incurred if they had themselves committed the contested action ...

The influence over the decision-making process turns abusive when one or a few member states overrule(s) the whole process, thereby stifling any adverse opinion that could be expressed ... [However,] the exercise of overwhelming control requires resort to types of pressure that are not expressly provided for by the constitutive treaty of the organisation concerned. In other words, if a member state overrules the decision-making process of an organisation thanks to the procedural rights that it has been granted under the constitutive treaty of the organisation, this cannot be considered overwhelming control.

The exercise of such 'overwhelming control' would constitute a form of abuse of the separate legal personality of the organization, since the autonomy of the organization, which is at the core of the attribution of a legal personality, would be reduced to a mere fiction. The extension of State responsibility to such situations would go beyond the hypothesis known as coercion of an international organization, since it would not be required that the State have knowledge about the illegal character of the act in question. In addition, the substantive obligations violated would be those of the State exercising overwhelming control, rather than those of the international organization itself, a difference which may prove crucial in the field of human rights where a number of obligations are treaty-based and therefore apply only to States parties to those treaties, rather than to all subjects of international law.

Such an extension of the law of State responsibility is not sufficient, however, to fill in the gap referred to. Indeed, since the hypothesis of 'overwhelming control' would not seem to include situations where a State simply exercises its voting rights as part of the normal decision-making process of the organization, it would still be possible for a State or a group of States to transfer certain powers to an intergovernmental organization, which this organization would have to exercise on the basis of its own, internal decision-making procedures, and for such a transferral to lead to the adoption of acts which, if they had been adopted by the Member States themselves, would have been in violation of their international obligations, without this engaging the responsibility of the Member States concerned. Of course, the provision of competences to the international organization may itself engage the responsibility of the Member States, however this will not be the case where the violation resulting from the exercise by the organization of the powers it has been entrusted is simply 'an unwitting result of providing the international organization with competence', as expressed by the International Law Commission's Rapporteur on this issue. But the reality is that in many cases, especially where whole areas of competence are being transferred to international organizations, such violations cannot be predicted in advance. This is especially so as regards human rights obligations, which are evolutive by nature, since they are grounded in covenants whose general and vague language is progressively filled in by expert bodies or courts which interpret these obligations in concrete settings.

Another proposal, then, would be to adopt a 'holistic' approach to the question of the responsibility of Member States for the acts of an international organization to which they have transferred certain powers which the organization may then use in violation of their pre-existing human rights obligations. Such an approach would refuse to distinguish between the three modalities of participation of the State in the life of the international organization (the setting up of the organization and the transferral of certain competences; participation in the decision-making within the organization; and the implementation of any decisions of the organization which the Member States are to comply with). The responsibility of States, in this view, would result from the fact that this sequence of events has led to a violation of their human rights obligations, even if this could not have been anticipated in the transferral of powers to the organization, if the State concerned has merely taken part in the decision-making of the organization without abusing its rights by seeking to exercise 'overwhelming control' over the organization, and if it then merely implements the decisions adopted by the organization. This would allow for the possibility that, whereas the State will not be internationally responsible for any of these steps separately, it will nevertheless be responsible for the result of the full sequence.

Box 2.3.	Alternatives to Member States' responsibility for human rights violations committed by international organizations

This section explores whether the Member States of an intergovernmental organization (IO) may be held accountable for human rights violations stemming from the acts adopted by the organization. But there are other ways to ensure that any such violations resulting from the transfer of powers to an IO do not remain unpunished (see generally on this issue, A. Reinisch, 'Securing the Accountability of International Organizations', *Global Governance*, 7 (2001), 131; A. Reinisch, 'Governance without Accountability', *German Yearbook of International Law* (2001), 270; H. G. Schermers, 'Liability of International Organizations', *Leiden Journal of International Law*, 1 (1988), 3; W. E. Holder, 'Can International Organizations be Controlled? Accountability and Responsibility', *American Society of International Law Proceedings*, 97 (2003), 231).

1. First, as subjects of international law, international organizations are 'bound by any obligations incumbent upon them under general rules of international law, under their constitutions or under international agreements to which they are parties' (International Court of Justice, *Interpretation of the Agreement of 25 March 1951 between the WHO and Egypt*, Advisory Opinion (20 December 1980), I.C.J. Reports 1980, 73 at 89–90 (para. 37)). For the moment, most human rights treaties are not open to the participation of international organizations. An evolution may be discerned in this respect, however: the recent Convention on the Rights of Persons

with Disabilities provides for the signature and expression of consent to be bound by regional integration organizations (see Art. 44 of the Convention, and Art. 12 of the Optional Protocol to the Convention), in order to facilitate accession by the European Union which has been attributed legislative powers by the EU Member States in certain of the domains covered by the Convention. In addition, human rights obligations have their source in general international law as well as in human rights treaties (see chapter 1, section 4.1.).

To the extent IOs are imposed human rights obligations under general international law, national courts may in principle provide a forum for the victims of the measures they adopt. The main obstacle this avenue will be facing resides in the immunity of jurisdiction generally recognized to international organizations before domestic courts (see J.-F. Lalive, 'L'immunité de juridiction des Etats et des organizations internationales', *Recueil des cours de l'Académie de droit international*, 84 (1953–III), 205–396; A. S. Muller, *International Organizations and their Host States: Aspects of Their Legal Relationship* (The Hague: Kluwer Law International, Martinus Nijhoff, 1995), esp. chapter 5 on immunity of jurisdiction; M. Singer, 'Jurisdictional Immunity of International Organizations: Human Rights and Functional Necessity Concerns', *Virginia Journal of International Law*, 36 (1995), 53; E. Gaillard and I. Pingel-Lenuzza, 'International Organizations and Immunity from Jurisdiction: to Restrict or to Bypass', *International and Comparative Law Quarterly*, 51 (2002), 1). August Reinisch confirms the importance of this argument in his empirical study of the practice of national courts when facing suits against international organizations, and he documents other 'avoidance techniques' resorted to by national courts to avoid entertaining claims against IOs, including the lack of recognition of the legal personality of international organizations; the refusal to attribute a particular act to the organization, in particular because it has been adopted *ultra vires*; doctrines of act of state, political questions, or other doctrines of non-justiciability; lack of jurisdiction of the forum court; absence of case or controversy; or abuse of right by the plaintiff (A. Reinisch, *International Organizations before National Courts* (Cambridge University Press, 2000), p. 127 *et seq.*).

The obstacle resulting from immunity of jurisdiction is not necessarily insuperable. Certain international organizations have renounced benefiting from such immunity in their constitutive instruments. This is the case, in particular, for two member organizations of the World Bank Group (the International Bank for Reconstruction and Development (IBRD) and the International Development Agency (IDA)), which provide for the possibility of legal action being brought against the institution 'only in a court of competent jurisdiction in the territories of a member' in which the Bank has offices (Art. VII, section 3 of the Articles of Agreement of the IBRD; and Art. VIII, section 3 of the IDA Agreement). Although the resulting waiver of immunity has sometimes been interpreted very restrictively in order to ensure that it will remain compatible with the fulfilment by the IBRD of its functions, a suit based on alleged violations of human rights universally recognized should not be treated as having a disruptive effect on its activities such as to justify upholding the immunity rule (compare *Mendaro* v. *World Bank*, 717 F.2d 610, 614–15 (D.C. Cir. 1983), where the US Court of Appeal for the District of Columbia Circuit held that the justification for granting immunity to international organizations was to enable them to pursue their functions more effectively, in particular, to operate freely from unilateral control by a Member State over their activities within its territory, leading it to offer a very restrictive interpretation of the waiver of immunity contained in the Agreement establishing the IBRD in the context of a sexual harassment suit based on Title VII of the 1964 Civil Rights Act against the IBRD by a former employee: see the comment by M. Leigh, *American Journal of International Law*, 78, No. 1 (1984), 221–3). National courts have also considered that immunity of jurisdiction should only be granted when it is expressly invoked by the defendant international organisation – that, in other terms, the waiver could be implicit.

Even beyond the rather exceptional case where, explicitly or tacitly, the international organization concerned waives its right to immunity of jurisdiction, it should be asked whether the blanket invocation of its immunity by the international organization may be reconciled with the requirements of the right of access to a court, as recognized in international human rights law (see M. Singer, 'Jurisdictional Immunity of International Organisations: Human Rights and Functional Necessity Concerns', *Virginia Journal of International Law*, 36 (1995), 53–165 (arguing, at 91–5, that the international responsibility of a Member State of the international organization could be engaged for granting immunity to the international organization in the absence of an adequate alternative remedy); and K. Wellens, *Remedies against International Organizations* (Cambridge University Press, 2002), at p. 214). As we have seen earlier in this section, while the European Court of Human Rights has adopted the view that the application by national courts of the doctrine on immunity of jurisdiction of an international organization does not necessarily constitute a violation of Article 6 para. 1 of the European Convention on Human Rights, this was based on the consideration that 'the applicants had available to them reasonable alternative means to protect effectively their rights under the Convention' (Eur. Ct. H.R. (GC), *Beer and Regan* v. *Germany* (Appl. No. 28934/95), judgment of 18 February 1999, para. 58; Eur. Ct. H.R. (GC), *Waite and Kennedy* v. *Germany* (Appl. No. 26083/94), judgment of 18 February 1999, para. 73).

2. A second possibility is self-regulation. Initiatives through which international organizations voluntarily choose to develop procedures which aim to ensure that they will comply with human rights (or with certain standards related to human rights but better adapted to their specific areas of activity) have proliferated in recent years. Certain mechanisms omit any reference to external forms of control or pre-existing standards. Thus, the World Bank and the International Monetary Fund have developed a set of operational policies, rather comparable to internal codes of conduct regulating their activities, which integrate human rights considerations. In addition, institutional mechanisms have been set up for monitoring compliance. Both the World Bank and the IMF have set up internal evaluation units to enhance accountability and improve the effectiveness of the strategies of these institutions. These units are 'independent' in the sense that they are not part of the administrative hierarchy of the organizations: they are the Independent Evaluation Group (IEG) for the IBRD/IDA, IFC and MIGA; and the Independent Evaluation Office (IEO) for the Fund (see P. G. Grasso, S. S. Wasty and R. V. Weaving, *World Bank Operations Evaluation Department – the First 30 Years* (Washington, D.C.: The International Bank for Reconstruction and Development/The World Bank, 2003)). In addition, alleged breaches of the aforementioned operational policies may be examined the World Bank's Inspection Panel (for IBRD and IDA operations) or Compliance and Accountability Ombudsman (CAO) (for the IFC and MIGA) (see in particular, L. Boisson de Chazournes, 'The Bretton Woods

Institutions and Human Rights: Converging Tendencies' in W. Benedek, K. De Feyter, and F. Marrella (eds.), *Economic Globalization and Human Rights* (Cambridge University Press, 2007), pp. 210–42; D. Bradlow, 'The World Bank, the IMF and Human Rights', 6 *Transnational Law and Contemporary Problems* 63 (1996); R. Dañino, 'The Legal Aspects of the World Bank's Work on Human Rights' in P. Alston and M. Robinson (eds.), *Human Rights and Development. Towards Mutual Reinforcement* (Oxford University Press, 2005)), p. 509; M. Darrow, *Between Light and Shadow: the World Bank, the International Monetary Fund and International Human Rights Law* (Oxford: Hart Publishing, 2003); S. Skogly, *The Human Rights Obligations of the World Bank and the International Monetary Fund* (London: Cavendish, 2001)). These mechanisms remain internal to the operations of the international financial institutions, however. And human rights considerations, if relevant at all to the evaluation of the operations of the international financial institutions, are so only indirectly – not because of a recognition that they would constitute binding obligations on these institutions, but because they are integrated in their operational policies or in the terms of reference of the evaluation mechanisms which have been set up.

3. In other cases, international agencies have chosen to submit to existing monitoring mechanisms, although they were not originally a party to the intergovernmental agreements establishing these mechanisms. This has been the case in particular in Kosovo, after it was placed under the administration of the United Nations following the 1999 conflict. Section 2 of Regulation 1999/1 adopted by the United Nations Interim Administration Mission in Kosovo (UNMIK) provides that in the discharge of its functions, UNMIK shall comply with international human rights standards. On 23 August 2004, the UNMIK and the Council of Europe concluded an Agreement whereby UNMIK accepted not only to comply with the substantive provisions of the Council of Europe Framework Convention for the Protection of National Minorities, but also to be bound by the provisions on the monitoring of the implementation of the FCNM by UNMIK in Kosovo. A similar agreement was concluded between the UNMIK and the Council of Europe on technical arrangements related to the 1987 European Convention for the Prevention of Torture and Inhuman or Degrading Treatment or Punishment, allowing the European Committee for the Prevention of Torture and Inhuman or Degrading Treatment or Punishment (CPT), by means of visits, to examine the treatment of persons deprived of their liberty in Kosovo with a view to ensure their protection and to prevent risks of torture or ill treatment. In 2006, an exchange of letters was concluded between the Secretaries-General of the Council of Europe and the North Atlantic Treaty Organisation (NATO), allowing the CPT to exercise its monitoring functions also as regards detention facilities managed by the NATO troops under K-FOR.

2.8. Questions for discussion: ensuring accountability in transfers of powers to intergovernmental organizations

1. Consider the joint dissenting opinion of Judges Sir John Freeland and Jungwiert to the judgment adopted by the European Court of Human Rights in the case of *Matthews* v. *United Kingdom*. As these judges predicted, the implementation of the judgment was particularly difficult, because

the United Kingdom alone could not in principle decide to comply with the judgment of the European Court of Human Rights. While the European Parliament (Representation) Act 2003 (EPRA 2003) finally did provide for the enfranchisement of the Gibraltar electorate for the purposes of European Parliamentary elections as of 2004, this action was taken unilaterally after a failure to secure the unanimous agreement of the Council to an amendment to the EC Act on Direct Elections of 1976 to provide for its application to Gibraltar. Indeed, Spain considered that, by extending the right to vote in European Parliament elections, as provided for by the EPRA 2003, to persons who are not UK nationals for the purposes of Community law, the United Kingdom had violated its obligations under Community law. It decided to file a direct action against the United Kingdom before the European Court of Justice. The Court rejected this claim in a judgment of 12 September 2006 (Case C-145/04, *Kingdom of Spain* v. *United Kingdom of Great Britain and Northern Ireland*). It took the view that the EU Member States are allowed to grant the right to vote and to stand as a candidate for elections to the European Parliament 'to certain persons who have close links to them, other than their own nationals or citizens of the Union resident in their territory'. Although Spain argued that the United Kingdom would be in breach of Annex I to the 1976 Act Concerning the Election of the Representatives of the European Parliament by Direct Universal Suffrage and of the Declaration of 18 February 2002, the European Court of Justice considered that, in the light of the judgment of the European Court of Human Rights in *Matthews* v. *United Kingdom*, 'the United Kingdom cannot be criticised for adopting the legislation necessary for the holding of such elections under conditions equivalent, with the necessary changes, to those laid down by the legislation applicable in the United Kingdom' (para. 95). Does this epilogue validate the fears expressed by Judges Sir John Freeland and Jungwiert? These judges consider that 'at no subsequent time [following the adoption of the 1976 Act] has it been possible for the United Kingdom unilaterally to secure the modification of the position so as to include Gibraltar within the franchise'. What could have been expected from the United Kingdom, which they failed to do, in order to secure the right to vote of the residents of Gibraltar?

2. In order to ensure that the conferral of powers to intergovernmental organizations does not lead to accountability gaps and to conflicting obligations being imposed on States – stemming respectively from their pre-existing obligations and from their membership of, and participation in the life of, the IO – Dan Sarooshi proposes that States setting up IOs should 'decide to "delegate" and not "transfer" their powers to an organisation so that they will not be bound to comply with decisions taken by the organization when exercising conferred powers'. This proposal is based on the distinction between *delegations of powers* to international organizations and *transfers of powers*. In the former case, according to this distinction, States retain the right to exercise powers on a unilateral basis; they are not bound to comply with any measure adopted by the organization on the basis of the delegation of powers; and they may put an end, in principle, to the conferral of powers. In the latter case, by contrast, States are bound to comply with obligations flowing from the exercise by the organization of the powers which it has transferred (D. Sarooshi, *International Organizations and their Exercise of Sovereign Powers* (Oxford University Press, 2005), chapter 5, section II (pp. 58–64)). Is this a viable solution? Should States be prohibited from 'transferring' powers to IOs, in order to ensure that no attribution of powers

to IOs will result in States circumventing their international obligations? Sarooshi notes that 'the World Health Organisation, the Universal Postal Union, and the International Civil Aviation Organisation are given powers such that an organ of the organization can adopt binding regulations by majority decision, but in such cases the Member States have an express right to contract out of, or make reservations to, the application of a specific regulation to them, usually before it enters into force' (p. 59). Could these models be generalized?

3. How attractive are the alternatives to asserting a responsibility of its Member States for the acts adopted by an international organization in violation of human rights (see box 2.3.)? Consider the following arguments against seeing the direct responsibility of international organizations as an adequate substitute for the responsibility of its Member States: 'first, the human rights obligations of its member States may not correspond to those of the international organisation itself (in particular insofar as the international organisation will not be subjected to the monitoring mechanisms provided for in human rights treaties), so that the international responsibility resulting from the attribution of an international legal personality to the organisation should not be seen as a substitute for the compliance by its member States with their international obligations; second, the principle of the continuity of States' obligations imposed by human rights treaties is opposed to the idea that such obligations may be lessened, or set aside, by the transferral of powers to an international organisation; and third, since human rights treaties create obligations of an objective character, rather than institute a web of mutual rights and obligations between the States parties, it will generally not be in the interest of any State taking part in the negotiation of multilateral treaties establishing international organisations or in the decision-making procedures within those organisations to raise the issue of the compatibility with the human rights obligations of the acts adopted within that organisation'. Are these arguments convincing? Which counter-arguments could be invoked?

4. If, despite the objections recalled above, the option of a direct responsibility of the international organization appears preferable, what are the obstacles to the development of such a responsibility?

4.2 The specific character of the UN Charter and of UN Security Council Resolutions

Following the end of the conflict in Kosovo (March-June 1999), UN Security Council Resolution 1244 of 10 June 1999 decided on the deployment, under UN auspices, of an interim administration for Kosovo (UNMIK), as well as for the establishment of a security presence (KFOR) by 'Member States and relevant international institutions', 'under UN auspices', with 'substantial NATO participation' but under the 'unified command and control' of COMKFOR from NATO. KFOR contingents, whose troops came from thirty-five NATO and non-NATO countries, were grouped into four multinational brigades, each responsible for one geographic sector. KFOR was mandated to exercise complete military control in Kosovo. UNMIK was to provide an interim international administration and the authority vested in it by the UN Security Council was considered to comprise all legislative and executive power as well as the authority to administer the judiciary (as confirmed by the First UNMIK Regulation (UNMIK Regulation 1999/1)). Although there was no formal or hierarchical relationship between the two presences, civil through UNMIK and military through KFOR, UNMIK and KFOR were to co-ordinate closely.

This was the background for two cases in which the issue of the responsibility of the States participating in the UNMIK or in the KFOR arose under the European Convention on Human Rights. In the case of *A. and B. Behrami* v. *France*, an application had been filed by the father of two children, one of whom was killed and the other seriously disabled in March 2000 when playing with undetonated cluster bomb units (CBUs) which had been dropped during the bombardment by NATO in 1999 in the municipality of Mitrovica, in an area placed under the authority of a multinational brigade (MNB) led by France. The investigation into the incident by the UNMIK police highlighted that UNMIK could not access the site without KFOR agreement and that, while KFOR had been aware of the unexploded CBUs for months, these had not been considered a high priority, although the detonation site had been marked out by KFOR the day after the incident took place. The complaint filed with the French Troop Contributing Nation Claims Office (TCNCO) was rejected on the ground that the UNSC Resolution 1244 had required KFOR to supervise mine-clearing operations until UNMIK could take over and that such operations had been the responsibility of the UN since 5 July 1999. However, when the UN were requested by the European Court of Human Rights to intervene as a third party in the *Behrami* case, they submitted that, while de-mining fell within the mandate of UNMIK, the absence of the necessary CBU location information from KFOR meant that the impugned inaction could not be attributed to UNMIK. Before the Court, Agim Behami complained under Article 2 ECHR that the incident took place because of the failure of French KFOR troops to mark and/or defuse the un-detonated CBUs which those troops knew to be present on that site.

In the companion case of *R. Saramati* v. *France, Germany and Norway*, Mr Saramati was detained on remand upon decision of KFOR, between 24 April 2001 and the decision to release him adopted by the Supreme Court on 4 June 2001. He was subsequently again arrested on 13 July 2001 by the UNMIK police, in the sector assigned to MNB Southeast, of which the lead nation was Germany. The detention was decided by order of the Commander of KFOR (COMKFOR), who was a Norwegian officer at the material time, after Mr Saramati had reported to the UNMIK police in Prizren, in order to collect belongings confiscated from him upon his previous arrest. At each trial hearing from 17 September 2001 to 23 January 2002, Mr Saramati's representatives requested his release. The Trial Court consistently responded that, although the Supreme Court had ruled against the continuation of the detention of Mr Saramati in June 2001, his detention was entirely the responsibility of KFOR. On 23 January 2002, Mr Saramati was convicted of attempted murder. He was detained until 9 October 2002, when the Supreme Court of Kosovo quashed Mr Saramati's conviction and sent his case for re-trial, and ordered his release. In answer to a letter from Mr Saramati's representatives taking issue with the legality of his detention, the KFOR Legal Adviser advised that

KFOR had the authority to detain under the UNSC Resolution 1244 any individual insofar as it was necessary 'to maintain a safe and secure environment' and to protect KFOR troops.

Mr Saramati complained under Article 5 ECHR alone, and in conjunction with Article 13 of the Convention, about his extra-judicial detention by KFOR between 13 July 2001 and 23 January 2002. He also complained under Article 6 para. 1 that he did not have access to court and about a breach of the respondent States' positive obligation to guarantee the Convention rights of those residing in Kosovo.

Following an analysis of the respective mandates of the KFOR and the UNMIK as defined in UNSC Resolution 1244, the European Court of Human Rights takes the view that issuing detention orders fell within the security mandate of KFOR and that the supervision of de-mining fell within UNMIK's mandate. It then asks, in the remainder of the decision, whether the action (the allegedly arbitrary detention) and the inaction (the failure to de-mine) complained of can be attributed to the United Nations (paras. 128–43). Having answered in the affirmative to this question as regards both the action of the KFOR (para. 141) and the inaction of the UNMIK (para. 143), the Court then addresses the question whether it is competent, *ratione personae*, to decide on the applications submitted (paras. 144–52).

European Court of Human Rights (GC), *A. and B. Behrami* v. *France* and *R. Saramati* v. *France, Germany and Norway* (Appl. Nos. 71412/01 and 78166/01), decision (inadmissibility) of 2 May 2007, paras. 144–52:

144. It is therefore the case that the impugned action and inaction are, in principle, attributable to the UN. It is, moreover, clear that the UN has a legal personality separate from that of its member states (*The Reparations case*, I.C.J. Reports 1949) and that that organisation is not a Contracting Party to the Convention.

145. In its *Bosphorus* judgment ([see above, section 4.1.], §§152–153), the Court held that, while a State was not prohibited by the Convention from transferring sovereign power to an international organisation in order to pursue co-operation in certain fields of activity, the State remained responsible under Article 1 of the Convention for all acts and omissions of its organs, regardless of whether they were a consequence of the necessity to comply with international legal obligations, Article 1 making no distinction as to the rule or measure concerned and not excluding any part of a State's 'jurisdiction' from scrutiny under the Convention. The Court went on, however, to hold that where such State action was taken in compliance with international legal obligations flowing from its membership of an international organisation and where the relevant organisation protected fundamental rights in a manner which could be considered at least equivalent to that which the Convention provides, a presumption arose that the State had not departed from the requirements of the Convention. Such presumption could be rebutted, if in the circumstances of a particular case, it was considered that the protection of Convention rights was manifestly deficient: in such a case, the interest of international co-operation would be outweighed by the Convention's role as a 'constitutional instrument of European public order' in the field of human rights (*ibid.*, §§155–156).

146. The question arises in the present case whether the Court is competent *ratione personae* to review the acts of the respondent States carried out on behalf of the UN and, more generally,

as to the relationship between the Convention and the UN acting under Chapter VII of its Charter.

147. The Court first observes that nine of the twelve original signatory parties to the Convention in 1950 had been members of the UN since 1945 (including the two Respondent States), that the great majority of the current Contracting Parties joined the UN before they signed the Convention and that currently all Contracting Parties are members of the UN. Indeed, one of the aims of this Convention (see its Preamble) is the collective enforcement of rights in the Universal Declaration of Human Rights of the General Assembly of the UN. More generally, ... the Convention has to be interpreted in the light of any relevant rules and principles of international law applicable in relations between its Contracting Parties. The Court has therefore had regard to two complementary provisions of the Charter, Articles 25 and 103, as interpreted by the International Court of Justice ... [Article 103 implies that the Charter obligations of UN member states prevail over conflicting obligations from another international treaty, regardless of whether the latter treaty was concluded before or after the UN Charter or was only a regional arrangement; Article 25 of the UN Charter states: 'The Members of the United Nations agree to accept and carry out the decisions of the [UNSC] in accordance with the present Charter', and implies that UN member states' obligations under a UNSC Resolution prevail over obligations arising under any other international agreement: see on these provisions chapter 1, section 4.2., a)]].

148. Of even greater significance is the imperative nature of the principle aim of the UN and, consequently, of the powers accorded to the UNSC under Chapter VII to fulfil that aim. In particular, it is evident from the Preamble, Articles 1, 2 and 24 as well as Chapter VII of the Charter that the primary objective of the UN is the maintenance of international peace and security. While it is equally clear that ensuring respect for human rights represents an important contribution to achieving international peace (see the Preamble to the Convention), the fact remains that the UNSC has primary responsibility, as well as extensive means under Chapter VII, to fulfil this objective, notably through the use of coercive measures. The responsibility of the UNSC in this respect is unique and has evolved as a counterpart to the prohibition, now customary international law, on the unilateral use of force ...

149. In the present case, Chapter VII allowed the UNSC to adopt coercive measures in reaction to an identified conflict considered to threaten peace, namely UNSC Resolution 1244 establishing UNMIK and KFOR.

Since operations established by UNSC Resolutions under Chapter VII of the UN Charter are fundamental to the mission of the UN to secure international peace and security and since they rely for their effectiveness on support from member states, the Convention cannot be interpreted in a manner which would subject the acts and omissions of Contracting Parties which are covered by UNSC Resolutions and occur prior to or in the course of such missions, to the scrutiny of the Court. To do so would be to interfere with the fulfilment of the UN's key mission in this field including, as argued by certain parties, with the effective conduct of its operations. It would also be tantamount to imposing conditions on the implementation of a UNSC Resolution which were not provided for in the text of the Resolution itself. This reasoning equally applies to voluntary acts of the respondent States such as the vote of a permanent member of the UNSC in favour of the relevant Chapter VII Resolution and the contribution of troops to the security mission: such acts may not have amounted to obligations flowing from membership of the UN but they remained crucial to the effective fulfilment by the UNSC of its Chapter VII mandate and, consequently, by the UN of its imperative peace and security aim.

150. The applicants argued that the substantive and procedural protection of fundamental rights provided by KFOR was in any event not 'equivalent' to that under the Convention within the meaning of the Court's *Bosphorus* judgment, with the consequence that the presumption of Convention compliance on the part of the respondent States was rebutted.

151. The Court, however, considers that the circumstances of the present cases are essentially different from those with which the Court was concerned in the *Bosphorus* case. In its judgment in that case, the Court noted that the impugned act (seizure of the applicant's leased aircraft) had been carried out by the respondent State authorities, on its territory and following a decision by one of its Ministers (§135 of that judgment). The Court did not therefore consider that any question arose as to its competence, notably *ratione personae*, *vis-à-vis* the respondent State despite the fact that the source of the impugned seizure was an EC Council Regulation which, in turn, applied a UNSC Resolution. In the present cases, the impugned acts and omissions of KFOR and UNMIK cannot be attributed to the respondent States and, moreover, did not take place on the territory of those States or by virtue of a decision of their authorities. The present cases are therefore clearly distinguishable from the *Bosphorus* case in terms both of the responsibility of the respondent States under Article 1 and of the Court's competence *ratione personae*.

There exists, in any event, a fundamental distinction between the nature of the international organisation and of the international co-operation with which the Court was there concerned and those in the present cases. As the Court has found above, UNMIK was a subsidiary organ of the UN created under Chapter VII and KFOR was exercising powers lawfully delegated under Chapter VII of the Charter by the UNSC. As such, their actions were directly attributable to the UN, an organisation of universal jurisdiction fulfilling its imperative collective security objective.

152. In these circumstances, the Court concludes that the applicants' complaints must be declared incompatible *ratione personae* with the provisions of the Convention.

2.9. Questions for discussion: the primacy of the UN Charter and UN Security Council Resolutions and the absence of jurisdiction *ratione personae* of the European Court of Human Rights

1. In order to arrive at its first conclusion that the acts or omissions allegedly violating the ECHR rights of the applicants are imputable to the United Nations rather than to the States having contributed troops to the UN, the Court in *Behrami* refers to Article 5 of the draft Articles on the Responsibility of International Organizations as adopted in 2004 during the fifty-sixth session of the ILC. This provision is entitled 'Conduct of Organs or Agents Placed at the Disposal of an International Organization by a State or Another International Organization', and reads: 'The conduct of an organ of a State or an organ or agent of an international organization that is placed at the disposal of another international organization shall be considered under international law an act of the latter organization if the organization exercises effective control over that conduct.' The Court seems to consider that it is rule particularly well suited to address peace-keeping operations of the UN. However, this raises at least two questions. First, is there a risk of abuse in this rule of attribution? Could this rule be used by States in order to circumvent

their human rights obligations? Second, is this provision appropriate in situations where the UN Security Council has merely authorized peace-keeping operations, conducted by certain States who retain authority and control over their troops, and are bound only by the end result prescribed – a solution which States appear to have most often preferred in recent years (see S. Chesterman, *You, the People – the United Nations, Transitional Administration and State-Building* (Oxford University Press, 2004), p. 241)?

2. Having identified the United Nations as the organization to which the acts or omissions complained of are attributable, the Court then asks whether it is competent to 'review the acts of the respondent States carried out on behalf of the UN'. Are the reasons put forward by the European Court of Human Rights for distinguishing *Behrami* from *Bosphorus* on this point relevant and convincing?

3. It has been remarked that the Court in *Behrami* focuses on the question of imputability, rather than on the question of whether the applicants were under the 'jurisdiction' of the defendant States, although this latter route could have led to the same conclusion based on a less contestable reasoning (A. Sari, 'Jurisdiction and International Responsibility in Peace Support Operations: the *Behrami* and *Saramati* Cases', *Human Rights Law Review* (2008), 159). Do you agree?

4. Recall the discussion in chapter 1, section 4.2. above. Is the solution adopted by the Court in *Behrami* consistent with the position of human rights in the hierarchy of international law, and particularly with the *jus cogens* status of at least a core set of human rights?

PART II

The Substantive Obligations

3

The Typology of States' Obligations and the Obligation to Respect Human Rights

INTRODUCTION

Part II seeks to introduce the substantive content of international human rights. It includes five chapters. Chapters 3, 4 and 5 discuss the three levels of obligations imposed on States: to respect, to protect and to fulfil human rights. Chapter 6 describes under which conditions rights may be derogated from in times of emergency. Chapter 7 examines the non-discrimination requirement, which cuts across the different obligations imposed on States, and is a core principle of human rights law, with a number of different ramifications.

Although this chapter focuses on the obligation of States to respect human rights, it first explores the origins of the distinction between the three levels of States' obligations, since it is on this distinction that chapters 3–5 are based. Section 1 describes the respect /protect/fulfil framework, and it then relates this framework to the '4-As' scheme (availability, accessibility, adequacy and adaptability), which is also widely used in order to clarify the implications for States of ensuring compliance with social and economic rights. While the respect/protect/fulfil framework has its basis in discussions around the normative content of the right to food, and the 4-As scheme originated in work around the right to education, both typologies have been used beyond these rights, although the usefulness of expanding their reach is still debated, particularly as regard civil and political rights.

Sections 2 and 3 examine the obligation to respect human rights, focusing respectively on rights of an 'absolute' character and other rights, which may be subject to certain limitations. Most human rights protected under international or domestic law fall under this second category. Such rights may be restricted, provided three conditions are satisfied: the objectives justifying such restrictions must be legitimate; the restriction must be prescribed by law; and the restriction must not be disproportionate, i.e. it should not go beyond what is necessary for the fulfilment of the said objective. Some rights, however, are of an absolute character. These rights may not be subjected to restrictions: even if strong and legitimate reasons could be put forward to do so, no limitation to these rights is allowed. Section 2 seeks to illustrate certain of the difficulties posed by this category or rights. Section 3 then examines the regime of rights which may be subject to limitations: it describes in detail the requirements of each of the conditions under which such limitations may be allowed; and it illustrates these requirements by reviewing how the issue of restrictions to religious freedom through vestimentary codes has been approach by various human rights bodies.

1 THE TYPOLOGY OF STATES' OBLIGATIONS

1.1 Obligations to respect, to protect and to fulfil

A major conceptual breakthrough took place in the mid 1980s, when Asbjorn Eide, as the Rapporteur to the then UN Sub-Commission on Prevention of Discrimination and Protection of Minorities, proposed that four 'layers' of State obligations could be discerned, defined as an obligation to respect, an obligation to protect, an obligation to ensure, and an obligation to promote (*The Right to Adequate Food as a Human Right*, Report prepared by Mr A. Eide, E/CN.4/Sub.2/1983/25 (1983)). Later, this was revised to become a tripartite division of the human rights obligations of States, distinguishing between the obligation to respect, to protect, and to fulfil human rights (*The Right to Adequate Food as a Human Right*, Report prepared by Mr A. Eide, E/CN.4/Sub.2/1987/23 (1987)). Simultaneously to Eide, the political philosopher Henry Shue had noted in 1980 that 'there are no distinctions between rights. The useful distinctions are among duties, and there are no one-to-one pairings between kinds of duties and kinds of rights.' Shue offered a distinction between the duty to avoid depriving; the duty to protect people from deprivation by other people; and the duty to provide for the security (or subsistence) of those unable to provide for their own – i.e. the duty to aid the deprived. He thus offered a 'tripartite typology of duties', noting: 'For all its own simplicity, it goes considerably beyond the usual assumption that for every right there is a single correlative duty, and suggests instead that for every basic right – and many other rights as well – there are three types of duties, all of which must be performed if the basic right is to be fully honored but not all of which must necessarily be performed by the same individuals or institutions' (H. Shue, *Basic Rights, Subsistence, Affluence, and US Foreign Policy* (Princeton, N.J.: Princeton University Press, 1980), at p. 52). Shue proposed, more precisely, that States have three sets of duties:

I. To avoid depriving.
II. To protect from deprivation (1) by enforcing duty (I) and (2) by designing institutions that avoid the creation of strong incentives to violate duty (I).
III. To aid the deprived (1) who are one's special responsibility; (2) who are victims or social failures in the performance of duties (I), (II–(1)), and (II–(2)); and (3) who are victims of natural disasters.

These typologies are not precisely interchangeable. As noted by Shue, placing the 'duty of aid' in the list, following an obligation to respect and an obligation to protect, may convey better that we owe a duty to victims of violations:

Henry Shue, 'The Interdependence of Duties', in Philip Alston and Katarina Tomasevski (eds.), *The Right to Food* (The Hague: SIM, Martinus Nijhoff, 1985), pp. 83–95 at p. 86:

What is distinctive about the duty to aid is that it is what is owed to victims – to people whose rights have already been violated. The duty of aid is ... largely a duty of recovery – recovery from failures in the performance of the duties to respect and protect. (This is not true of duty III–(3) in the original typology – it is 'pure' assistance, with no basis in fault or failure, since it is a response to purely natural disasters, of which there are relatively few).

... Think briefly of a different kind of right, say, the right to physical security. Suppose the current situation in a certain region is that landowners always send thugs to beat up sharecroppers who complain about the terms of their tenancy, and it has long been like this in the region. A plausible description, especially if some of the sharecroppers have never enjoyed physical security against beatings, is that their right to physical security needs to be fulfilled or promoted. But another perfectly reasonable description of the situation is that the sharecroppers have been deprived of their physical security and therefore need assistance ... The description in terms of filfillment and promotion suggests that the rest of us would be going beyond duties to respect and to protect if we acted upon duties to fulfill and promote. The rights of some people need to be 'fulfilled' or 'promoted', however, because other people have already failed to perform duties to respect and protect. Rather than going beyond respect and protection, we are having to go back and make up for failures in respect and protection. This is more clearly conveyed by saying that we are assisting the deprived. If our assistance enables them to enjoy adequate food, physical security, or whatever else they have been deprived of, their right will in fact have been fulfilled.

Despite what, according to Shue, might be seen as its weakness – in that the obligation to 'fulfil' does not recognize the rights-holders as people whose rights have been violated in the first place – the tripartite typology of Eide has been adopted, since the early 1990s, in the doctrinal analysis of economic and social rights. The following documents show the development of the typology in the field of economic, social and cultural rights:

The Maastricht Guidelines on Violations of Economic, Social and Cultural Rights (1997) (adopted by a group of academic experts meeting in Maastricht 22–26 January 1997), para. 6:

Like civil and political rights, economic, social and cultural rights impose three different types of obligations on States: the obligations to respect, protect and fulfil. Failure to perform any one of these three obligations constitutes a violation of such rights. The obligation to *respect* requires States to refrain from interfering with the enjoyment of economic, social and cultural rights. Thus, the right to housing is violated if the State engages in arbitrary forced evictions. The obligation to *protect* requires States to prevent violations of such rights by third parties. Thus, the failure to ensure that private employers comply with basic labour standards may amount to a violation of the right to work or the right to just and favourable conditions of work. The obligation to *fulfil* requires States to take appropriate legislative, administrative, budgetary, judicial and other measures towards the full realization of such rights. Thus, the failure of States to provide essential primary health care to those in need may amount to a violation.

Committee on Economic, Social and Cultural Rights, General Comment No. 12, *The Right to Adequate Food* (Art. 11) (E/C.12/1999/5, 12 May 1999), paras. 14–20:

14. The nature of the legal obligations of States parties are set out in .article 2 of the Covenant and has been dealt with in the Committee's General Comment No. 3 (1990). The principal obligation is to take steps to achieve progressively the full realization of the right to adequate food. This imposes an obligation to move as expeditiously as possible towards that goal. Every State is obliged to ensure for everyone under its jurisdiction access to the minimum essential food which is sufficient, nutritionally adequate and safe, to ensure their freedom from hunger.

15. The right to adequate food, like any other human right, imposes three types or levels of obligations on States parties: the obligations to respect, to protect and to fulfil. In turn, the obligation to fulfil incorporates both an obligation to facilitate and an obligation to provide. The obligation to respect existing access to adequate food requires States parties not to take any measures that result in preventing such access. The obligation to protect requires measures by the State to ensure that enterprises or individuals do not deprive individuals of their access to adequate food. The obligation to fulfil (facilitate) means the State must pro-actively engage in activities intended to strengthen people's access to and utilization of resources and means to ensure their livelihood, including food security. Finally, whenever an individual or group is unable, for reasons beyond their control, to enjoy the right to adequate food by the means at their disposal, States have the obligation to fulfil (provide) that right directly. This obligation also applies for persons who are victims of natural or other disasters.

16. Some measures at these different levels of obligations of States parties are of a more immediate nature, while other measures are more of a long-term character, to achieve progressively the full realization of the right to food.

17. Violations of the Covenant occur when a State fails to ensure the satisfaction of, at the very least, the minimum essential level required to be free from hunger. In determining which actions or omissions amount to a violation of the right to food, it is important to distinguish the inability from the unwillingness of a State party to comply. Should a State party argue that resource constraints make it impossible to provide access to food for those who are unable by themselves to secure such access, the State has to demonstrate that every effort has been made to use all the resources at its disposal in an effort to satisfy, as a matter of priority, those minimum obligations. This follows from .Article 2.1 of the Covenant, which obliges a State party

to take the necessary steps to the maximum of its available resources, as previously pointed out by the Committee in its General Comment No. 3, paragraph 10. A State claiming that it is unable to carry out its obligation for reasons beyond its control therefore has the burden of proving that this is the case and that it has unsuccessfully sought to obtain international support to ensure the availability and accessibility of the necessary food.

18. Furthermore, any discrimination in access to food, as well as to means and entitlements for its procurement, on the grounds of race, colour, sex, language, age, religion, political or other opinion, national or social origin, property, birth or other status with the purpose or effect of nullifying or impairing the equal enjoyment or exercise of economic, social and cultural rights constitutes a violation of the Covenant.

19. Violations of the right to food can occur through the direct action of States or other entities insufficiently regulated by States. These include: the formal repeal or suspension of legislation necessary for the continued enjoyment of the right to food; denial of access to food to particular individuals or groups, whether the discrimination is based on legislation or is pro-active; the prevention of access to humanitarian food aid in internal conflicts or other emergency situations; adoption of legislation or policies which are manifestly incompatible with pre-existing legal obligations relating to the right to food; and failure to regulate activities of individuals or groups so as to prevent them from violating the right to food of others, or the failure of a State to take into account its international legal obligations regarding the right to food when entering into agreements with other States or with international organizations.

20. While only States are parties to the Covenant and are thus ultimately accountable for compliance with it, all members of society – individuals, families, local communities, non-governmental organizations, civil society organizations, as well as the private business sector – have responsibilities in the realization of the right to adequate food. The State should provide an environment that facilitates implementation of these responsibilities. The private business sector – national and transnational – should pursue its activities within the framework of a code of conduct conducive to respect of the right to adequate food, agreed upon jointly with the Government and civil society.

The Right to Adequate Food and to be Free from Hunger. Updated Study on the Right to Food, submitted by Mr Asbjørn Eide in accordance with Sub-Commission decision 1998/106 (E/CN.4/Sub.2/1999, 28 June 1999):

52. My 1987 study was intended as a contribution to the clarification of the nature and levels of State obligations under economic and social rights. Drawing on my earlier work, I introduced an analytical framework under which State obligations can be assessed on three levels: the obligation to respect, the obligation to protect, and the obligation to assist and fulfil human rights. The framework proved very useful, and has since been taken widely into use. In my progress report in 1998 I explained my previously elaborated framework in greater detail, as follows (para. 9):

(a) Since State obligations must be seen in the light of the assumption that human beings, families or wider groups seek to find their own solutions to their needs, States should, at the primary level, respect the resources owned by the individual, her or his freedom to find a job of preference, to make optimal use of her/his own knowledge and the freedom to take the necessary actions and use the necessary resources – alone or in association with others – to satisfy his or her own needs. The State cannot, however, passively leave it at that. Third parties are likely to interfere negatively with the possibilities that individuals or groups otherwise might have had to solve their own needs;

(b) At a secondary level, therefore, State obligations require active protection against other, more assertive or aggressive subjects – more powerful economic interests, such as protection against fraud, against unethical behaviour in trade and contractual relations, against the marketing and dumping of hazardous or dangerous products. This protective function of the State is widely used and is the most important aspect of State obligations with regard to economic, social and cultural rights, similar to the role of the State as protector of civil and political rights;

(c) At the tertiary level, the State has the obligation to facilitate opportunities by which the rights listed can be enjoyed. It takes many forms, some of which are spelled out in the relevant instruments. For example, with regard to the right to food, the State shall, under the International Covenant (art. 11 (2)), take steps to 'improve measures of production, conservation and distribution of food by making full use of technical and scientific knowledge and by developing or reforming agrarian systems'.

(d) At the fourth and final level, the State has the obligation to fulfil the rights of those who otherwise cannot enjoy their economic, social and cultural rights. This fourth level obligation increases in importance with increasing rates of urbanization and the decline of group or family responsibilities. Obligations towards the elderly and disabled, which in traditional agricultural society were taken care of by the family, must increasingly be borne by the State and thus by the national society as a whole.

The following case illustrates how the typology which Shue and Eide developed independently from each other may facilitate the task of judicial or quasi-judicial bodies in adjudicating economic and social rights:

African Commission on Human and Peoples' Rights, *The Social and Economic Rights Action Center and the Center for Economic and Social Rights* v. *Nigeria*, Comm. No. 155/96 (2001) A.H.R.L.R. 60 (ACHPR 2001) (15th Annual Activity Report):

[The Communication alleges that the Military Government of Nigeria has been directly involved in oil production through the State oil company, the Nigerian National Petroleum Company (NNPC), the majority shareholder in a consortium with Shell Petroleum Development Corporation (SPDC), and that these operations have caused environmental degradation and health problems resulting from the contamination of the environment among the Ogoni People. The Complainants allege that the Nigerian Government violated the right to health and the right to clean environment as recognized under Articles 16 and 24 of the African Charter of Human and Peoples' Rights. This, the Complainants allege, the Government has done by directly participating in the contamination of air, water and soil and thereby harming the health of the Ogoni population; by failing to protect the Ogoni population from the harm caused by the NNPC Shell Consortium but instead using its security forces to facilitate the damage; and by failing to provide or permit studies of potential or actual environmental and health risks caused by the oil operations. The African Commission on Human and Peoples' Rights approached the issue following the tripartite typology referred to above:]

44. Internationally accepted ideas of the various obligations engendered by human rights indicate that all rights – both civil and political rights and social and economic – generate at least four levels of duties for a State that undertakes to adhere to a rights regime, namely the duty to respect, protect, promote, and fulfil these rights. These obligations universally apply to all rights and entail a combination of negative and positive duties. As a human rights instrument, the African Charter is not alien to these concepts and the order in which they are dealt with here is chosen as a matter of convenience and in no way should it imply the priority accorded to them. Each layer of obligation is equally relevant to the rights in question.

45. At a primary level, the obligation to respect entails that the State should refrain from interfering in the enjoyment of all fundamental rights; it should respect right-holders, their freedoms, autonomy, resources, and liberty of their action. With respect to socio economic rights, this means that the State is obliged to respect the free use of resources owned or at the disposal of the individual alone or in any form of association with others, including the household or the family, for the purpose of rights-related needs. And with regard to a collective group, the resources belonging to it should be respected, as it has to use the same resources to satisfy its needs.

46. At a secondary level, the State is obliged to protect right-holders against other subjects by legislation and provision of effective remedies. This obligation requires the State to take measures to protect beneficiaries of the protected rights against political, economic and social interferences. Protection generally entails the creation and maintenance of an atmosphere or framework by an effective interplay of laws and regulations so that individuals will be able to freely realize their rights and freedoms. This is very much intertwined with the tertiary obligation of the State to promote the enjoyment of all human rights. The State should make sure that individuals are able to exercise their rights and freedoms, for example, by promoting tolerance, raising awareness, and even building infrastructures.

47. The last layer of obligation requires the State to fulfil the rights and freedoms it freely undertook under the various human rights regimes. It is more of a positive expectation on the part of the State to move its machinery towards the actual realization of the rights. This is also very much intertwined with the duty to promote mentioned in the preceding paragraph. It could consist in the direct provision of basic needs such as food or resources that can be used for food (direct food aid or social security).

48. Thus States are generally burdened with the above set of duties when they commit themselves under human rights instruments. Emphasizing the all embracing nature of their obligations, the International Covenant on Economic, Social, and Cultural Rights, for instance, under Article 2(1), stipulates exemplarily that States 'undertake to take steps ... by all appropriate means, including particularly the adoption of legislative measures'. Depending on the type of rights under consideration, the level of emphasis in the application of these duties varies. But sometimes, the need to meaningfully enjoy some of the rights demands a concerted action from the State in terms of more than one of the said duties.

The tripartite typology of States' obligations has been widely seen as allowing a concretization of economic, social and cultural rights, and therefore as encouraging their justiciability. The limits to such an approach, however, have also been pointed out, particularly as regards the issue of justiciability (see I. E. Koch, 'Dichotomies, Trichotomies or Waves of Duties?', *Human Rights Law Review*, 5, No. 1 (2005), 81–103; and I. E. Koch, 'The Justiciability of Indivisible Rights', *Nordic Journal of International Law*, 72, No. 1 (2003), 3–39). In addition, attaching distinct legal regimes to the obligation to respect on the one hand – where violations are committed directly by State agents – and the obligation to protect on the other hand – where the direct source of the violation are private persons, and where the responsibility of the State arises only due to its lack of due diligence – may be questionable since the privatization of a number of functions which traditionally have been assumed by the State has blurred the distinction between the core State functions and the market.

It seems clear nevertheless that this typology has facilitated the justiciability of social and economic rights both before international or regional and before national courts (for more on the justiciability of economic and social rights before domestic courts, see chapter 8). Consider again, for instance, the reasoning of the African Commission on Human and Peoples' Rights in the case of *The Social and Economic Rights Action Center and the Center for Economic and Social Rights* v. *Nigeria*, where the rights to housing, to food, and to life are addressed:

African Commission on Human and Peoples' Rights, *The Social and Economic Rights Action Center and the Center for Economic and Social Rights* v. *Nigeria*, Comm. No. 155/96 (2001) A.H.R.L.R. 60 (ACHPR 2001) (15th Annual Activity Report):

[The right to housing]
59. The Complainants also assert that the Military Government of Nigeria massively and systematically violated the right to adequate housing of members of the Ogoni community under Article 14 and implicitly recognised by Articles 16 and 18(1) of the African Charter.

Article 14 of the Charter reads: 'The right to property shall be guaranteed. It may only be encroached upon in the interest of public need or in the general interest of the community and in accordance with the provisions of appropriate laws.'

Article 18(1) provides: 'The family shall be the natural unit and basis of society. It shall be protected by the State ...'

60. Although the right to housing or shelter is not explicitly provided for under the African Charter, the corollary of the combination of the provisions protecting the right to enjoy the best attainable state of mental and physical health, cited under Article 16 above, the right to property, and the protection accorded to the family forbids the wanton destruction of shelter because when housing is destroyed, property, health, and family life are adversely affected. It is thus noted that the combined effect of Articles 14, 16 and 18(1) reads into the Charter a right to shelter or housing which the Nigerian Government has apparently violated.

61. At a very minimum, the right to shelter obliges the Nigerian Government not to destroy the housing of its citizens and not to obstruct efforts by individuals or communities to rebuild lost homes. The State's obligation to respect housing rights requires it, and thereby all of its organs and agents, to abstain from carrying out, sponsoring or tolerating any practice, policy or legal measure violating the integrity of the individual or infringing upon his or her freedom to use those material or other resources available to them in a way they find most appropriate to satisfy individual, family, household or community housing needs. [S. Leckie, 'The Right to Housing', in A. Eide, C. Krause and A. Rosas (eds.), *Economic, Social and Cultural Rights* (Leiden: Martinus Nijhoff, 1995)]. Its obligations to protect obliges it to prevent the violation of any individual's right to housing by any other individual or non-state actors like landlords, property developers, and land owners, and where such infringements occur, it should act to preclude further deprivations as well as guaranteeing access to legal remedies [*ibid.*]. The right to shelter even goes further than a roof over one's head. It extends to embody the individual's right to be let alone and to live in peace – whether under a roof or not.

62. The protection of the rights guaranteed in Articles 14, 16 and 18 (1) leads to the same conclusion. As regards the earlier right, and in the case of the Ogoni People, the Government of Nigeria has failed to fulfil these two minimum obligations. The Government has destroyed Ogoni houses and villages and then, through its security forces, obstructed, harassed, beaten and, in some cases, shot and killed innocent citizens who have attempted to return to rebuild their ruined homes. These actions constitute massive violations of the right to shelter, in violation of Articles 14, 16, and 18(1) of the African Charter.

63. The particular violation by the Nigerian Government of the right to adequate housing as implicitly protected in the Charter also encompasses the right to protection against forced evictions. The African Commission draws inspiration from the definition of the term 'forced evictions' by the Committee on Economic Social and Cultural Rights which defines this term as 'the permanent removal against their will of individuals, families and/or communities from the homes and/or which they occupy, without the provision of, and access to, appropriate forms of legal or other protection' [General Comment No.7, *The Right to Adequate Housing* (1997) (Art. 11.1): Forced Evictions]. Wherever and whenever they occur, forced evictions are extremely traumatic. They cause physical, psychological and emotional distress; they entail losses of means of economic sustenance and increase impoverishment. They can also cause physical injury and in some cases sporadic deaths … Evictions break up families and increase existing levels of homelessness. [General Comment No. 7, *The Right to Adequate Housing* (1997) (Art. 11.1): Forced Evictions]. In this regard, General Comment No. 4 of the Committee on Economic, Social and Cultural Rights on *The Right to Adequate Housing* (1991) states that 'all persons should possess a degree of security of tenure which guarantees legal protection against forced eviction, harassment and other threats' (E/1992/23, annex III. Paragraph 8(a)). The conduct of the Nigerian Government clearly demonstrates a violation of this right enjoyed by the Ogonis as a collective right.

[The right to food]

64. The Communication argues that the right to food is implicit in the African Charter, in such provisions as the right to life (Art. 4), the right to health (Art. 16) and the right to economic, social and cultural development (Art. 22). By its violation of these rights, the Nigerian

Government trampled upon not only the explicitly protected rights but also upon the right to food implicitly guaranteed.

65. The right to food is inseparably linked to the dignity of human beings and is therefore essential for the enjoyment and fulfilment of such other rights as health, education, work and political participation. The African Charter and international law require and bind Nigeria to protect and improve existing food sources and to ensure access to adequate food for all citizens. Without touching on the duty to improve food production and to guarantee access, the minimum core of the right to food requires that the Nigerian Government should not destroy or contaminate food sources. It should not allow private parties to destroy or contaminate food sources, and prevent peoples' efforts to feed themselves.

66. The Government's treatment of the Ogonis has violated all three minimum duties of the right to food. The Government has destroyed food sources through its security forces and State Oil Company; has allowed private oil companies to destroy food sources; and, through terror, has created significant obstacles to Ogoni communities trying to feed themselves. The Nigerian Government has again fallen short of what is expected of it as under the provisions of the African Charter and international human rights standards, and hence, is in violation of the right to food of the Ogonis.

[The right to life]

67. The Complainants also allege that the Nigerian Government has violated Article 4 of the Charter which guarantees the inviolability of human beings and everyone's right to life and integrity of the person respected. Given the wide spread violations perpetrated by the Government of Nigeria and by private actors (be it following its clear blessing or not), the most fundamental of all human rights, the right to life has been violated. The Security forces were given the green light to decisively deal with the Ogonis, which was illustrated by the wide spread terrorisations and killings. The pollution and environmental degradation to a level humanly unacceptable has made living in the Ogoni land a nightmare. The survival of the Ogonis depended on their land and farms that were destroyed by the direct involvement of the Government. These and similar brutalities not only persecuted individuals in Ogoniland but also the whole of the Ogoni Community as a whole. They affected the life of the Ogoni Society as a whole. The Commission conducted a mission to Nigeria from the 7th–14th March 1997 and witnessed first hand the deplorable situation in Ogoni land including the environmental degradation.

68. The uniqueness of the African situation and the special qualities of the African Charter on Human and Peoples' Rights imposes upon the African Commission an important task. International law and human rights must be responsive to African circumstances. Clearly, collective rights, environmental rights, and economic and social rights are essential elements of human rights in Africa. The African Commission will apply any of the diverse rights contained in the African Charter. It welcomes this opportunity to make clear that there is no right in the African Charter that cannot be made effective. As indicated in the preceding paragraphs, however, the Nigerian Government did not live up to the minimum expectations of the African Charter.

69. The Commission does not wish to fault governments that are labouring under difficult circumstances to improve the lives of their people. The situation of the people of Ogoniland, however, requires, in the view of the Commission, a reconsideration of the Government's attitude to the allegations contained in the instant communication. The intervention of multinational

corporations may be a potentially positive force for development if the State and the people concerned are ever mindful of the common good and the sacred rights of individuals and communities.

As illustrated by this case, the clarification by the Committee on Economic, Social, and Cultural Rights of the normative content of the ICESCR, in particular through the adoption of General Comments, has been particularly effective in encouraging the adjudication of the social and economic rights enshrined in this instrument. This explanatory task has been greatly facilitated by the adoption by the Committee of the tripartite typology of obligations, and it has been influential beyond the right to food where it has its origin. Consider for instance the paragraphs addressing the 'general legal obligations' of States under Article 13 of the ICESCR, which guarantees the right to education:

Committee on Economic, Social and Cultural Rights, General Comment No. 13, *The Right to Education (Art. 13 of the Covenant)* (twenty-first session, 1999) (UN Doc. E/C.12/1999/10, 8 December 1999)

43. While the Covenant provides for progressive realization and acknowledges the constraints due to the limits of available resources, it also imposes on States parties various obligations which are of immediate effect.

States parties have immediate obligations in relation to the right to education, such as the 'guarantee' that the right 'will be exercised without discrimination of any kind' (art. 2(2)) and the obligation 'to take steps' (art. 2(1)) towards the full realization of article 13.

Such steps must be 'deliberate, concrete and targeted' towards the full realization of the right to education.

44. The realization of the right to education over time, that is 'progressively', should not be interpreted as depriving States parties' obligations of all meaningful content. Progressive realization means that States parties have a specific and continuing obligation 'to move as expeditiously and effectively as possible' towards the full realization of article 13.

45. There is a strong presumption of impermissibility of any retrogressive measures taken in relation to the right to education, as well as other rights enunciated in the Covenant. If any deliberately retrogressive measures are taken, the State party has the burden of proving that they have been introduced after the most careful consideration of all alternatives and that they are fully justified by reference to the totality of the rights provided for in the Covenant and in the context of the full use of the State party's maximum available resources.

46. The right to education, like all human rights, imposes three types or levels of obligations on States parties: the obligations to respect, protect and fulfil. In turn, the obligation to fulfil incorporates both an obligation to facilitate and an obligation to provide.

47. The obligation to respect requires States parties to avoid measures that hinder or prevent the enjoyment of the right to education. The obligation to protect requires States parties to take measures that prevent third parties from interfering with the enjoyment of the right to

education. The obligation to fulfil (facilitate) requires States to take positive measures that enable and assist individuals and communities to enjoy the right to education. Finally, States parties have an obligation to fulfil (provide) the right to education. As a general rule, States parties are obliged to fulfil (provide) a specific right in the Covenant when an individual or group is unable, for reasons beyond their control, to realize the right themselves by the means at their disposal. However, the extent of this obligation is always subject to the text of the Covenant.

48. In this respect, two features of article 13 require emphasis. First, it is clear that article 13 regards States as having principal responsibility for the direct provision of education in most circumstances; States parties recognize, for example, that the 'development of a system of schools at all levels shall be actively pursued' (art. 13(2)(e)). Secondly, given the differential wording of article 13(2) in relation to primary, secondary, higher and fundamental education, the parameters of a State party's obligation to fulfil (provide) are not the same for all levels of education. Accordingly, in light of the text of the Covenant, States parties have an enhanced obligation to fulfil (provide) regarding the right to education, but the extent of this obligation is not uniform for all levels of education. The Committee observes that this interpretation of the obligation to fulfil (provide) in relation to article 13 coincides with the law and practice of numerous States parties.

Whether the tripartite typology of States' obligations constitutes a useful tool not only for the implementation of economic and social rights, but also for civil and political rights, remains a matter of debate. In the following excerpts, the authors of the 2003 Draft Principles and Guidelines for a Human Rights Approach to Poverty Reduction Strategies clearly believe such an extension is both feasible and desirable. Paul Hunt, Manfred Nowak and Siddiq Osmani prepared this document at the request of the Committee on Economic, Social and Cultural Rights, in order to explore and articulate a human rights approach to poverty reduction. As illustrated in the following excerpt, they seek to provide all human rights with a common conceptual framework describing the entailed obligations.

Office of the High Commissioner for Human Rights, Principles and Guidelines for a Human Rights Approach to Poverty Reduction Strategies (2005), paras. 47–8:

47. Poverty is so deeply entrenched in many societies that it is unrealistic to hope that even with the best of intentions it can be eliminated in a very short time. Equally, one must accept the reality that in a context of scarce resources it may not be possible to fulfil all human rights immediately. However, the fact that the realization of some human rights is constrained by the scarcity of resources does not relieve States of their international human rights obligations to take reasonable and appropriate steps, to the maximum of available resources, to ensure the realization of rights.

48. All human rights – economic, civil, social, political and cultural – impose negative as well as positive obligations on States, as is captured in the distinction between the duties to respect, protect and fulfil. *The duty to respect* requires the duty-bearer to refrain from interfering with the enjoyment of any human right. *The duty to protect* requires the duty-bearer to take measures to prevent violations of any human right by third parties. *The duty to fulfil* requires the duty-bearer to adopt appropriate legislative, administrative and other measures towards the full realization of human rights. Resource implications of the obligations to *respect* and *protect* are generally less significant than those of implementing the obligations to *fulfil*, for which more proactive and resource-intensive measures may be required. Consequently, resource constraints may not affect a State's ability to respect and protect human rights to the same extent as its ability to fulfil human rights.

3.1. Question for discussion: the typology of duties and the categories of rights

Is the tripartite typology of duties proposed by Eide suitable for all human rights? In particular, what are the advantages and disadvantages of using this typology in order to clarify the obligations of States to guarantee civil and political rights? Does the use of this typology imply the risk of relieving States from their immediate obligation to ensure respect for civil and political rights? Conversely, does it obfuscate the fact that the State can never simply 'abstain' from interfering with a right, since the right cannot exist without State action?

In answering these questions, consider the view expressed by Stephen Holmes and Cass R. Sunstein in *The Cost of Rights. Why Liberty Depends on Taxes* (New York and London: W. W. Norton, 1999), pp. 44 and 48: ' "Where there is a right, there is a remedy" ... This simple point goes a long way toward disclosing the inadequacy of the negative rights/positive rights distinction. What it shows is that all legally enforced rights are necessarily positive rights ... The financing of basic rights through tax revenues helps us see clearly that rights are public goods: taxpayer-funded and government-managed social services designed to improve collective and individual well-being. All rights are positive rights.'

1.2 Availability, accessibility, acceptability, and adaptability

The tripartite distinction between the obligation to respect, to protect and to fulfil is not the only analytical tool which has been used in order to clarify the content of States' obligations, particularly in the field of social and economic rights entailing certain obligations to ensure that individuals have the resources which allow them access to certain social goods such as housing, education, or health services. In its general comment on the right to education as guaranteed under Article 13 of the International Covenant on Economic, Social and Cultural Rights, the Committee on Economic, Social and Cultural Rights states (in para. 6) that:

Committee on Economic, Social and Cultural Rights, General Comment No. 13,
The Right to Education (Art. 13 of the Covenant) **(E/C.12/1999/10) (1999):**

6. While the precise and appropriate application of the terms will depend upon the conditions prevailing in a particular State party, education in all its forms and at all levels shall exhibit the following interrelated and essential features:

(a) Availability – functioning educational institutions and programmes have to be available in sufficient quantity within the jurisdiction of the State party. What they require to function depends upon numerous factors, including the developmental context within which they operate; for example, all institutions and programmes are likely to require buildings or other protection from the elements, sanitation facilities for both sexes, safe drinking water, trained teachers receiving domestically competitive salaries, teaching materials, and so on; while some will also require facilities such as a library, computer facilities and information technology;

(b) Accessibility – educational institutions and programmes have to be accessible to everyone, without discrimination, within the jurisdiction of the State party. Accessibility has three overlapping dimensions:

Non-discrimination – education must be accessible to all, especially the most vulnerable groups, in law and fact, without discrimination on any of the prohibited grounds ...;
Physical accessibility – education has to be within safe physical reach, either by attendance at some reasonably convenient geographic location (e.g. a neighbourhood school) or via modern technology (e.g. access to a 'distance learning' programme);
Economic accessibility – education has to be affordable to all. This dimension of accessibility is subject to the differential wording of article 13(2) in relation to primary, secondary and higher education: whereas primary education shall be available 'free to all', States parties are required to progressively introduce free secondary and higher education;

(c) Acceptability – the form and substance of education, including curricula and teaching methods, have to be acceptable (e.g. relevant, culturally appropriate and of good quality) to students and, in appropriate cases, parents; this is subject to the educational objectives required by article 13(1) and such minimum educational standards as may be approved by the State (see art. 13(3) and (4));

(d) Adaptability – education has to be flexible so it can adapt to the needs of changing societies and communities and respond to the needs of students within their diverse social and cultural settings.

This typology was initially developed by the former UN Special Rapporteur on the Right to Education, Katarina Tomasevski (1998–2004) (see Preliminary Report of the Special Rapporteur on the Right to Education, Ms. Katarina Tomasevski, submitted in accordance with Commission on Human Rights Resolution 1998/33, E/CN.4/1999/49, 13 January 1999, paras. 42–74). But the '4-As' scheme is also derived, in part, from previous general comments of the Committee. In 1991, in its General Comment on *The Right to Adequate Housing*, the Committee already had indicated:

Committee on Economic, Social and Cultural Rights, General Comment No. 4,
The Right to Adequate Housing (Art. 11(1) of the Covenant) **(sixth session, 1991) (E/1992/23):**

8. [The] concept of adequacy is particularly significant in relation to the right to housing since it serves to underline a number of factors which must be taken into account in determining whether particular forms of shelter can be considered to constitute 'adequate housing' for the purposes of the Covenant. While adequacy is determined in part by social, economic, cultural, climatic, ecological and other factors, the Committee believes that it is nevertheless possible to identify certain aspects of the right that must be taken into account for this purpose in any particular context. They include the following:

(a) Legal security of tenure. Tenure takes a variety of forms, including rental (public and private) accommodation, co-operative housing, lease, owner-occupation, emergency housing and informal settlements, including occupation of land or property. Notwithstanding the type of tenure, all persons should possess a degree of security of tenure which guarantees legal protection against forced eviction, harassment and other threats. States parties should consequently take immediate measures aimed at conferring legal security of tenure upon those persons and households currently lacking such protection, in genuine consultation with affected persons and groups;

(b) Availability of services, materials, facilities and infrastructure. An adequate house must contain certain facilities essential for health, security, comfort and nutrition. All beneficiaries of the right to adequate housing should have sustainable access to natural and common resources, safe drinking water, energy for cooking, heating and lighting, sanitation and washing facilities, means of food storage, refuse disposal, site drainage and emergency services;

(c) Affordability. Personal or household financial costs associated with housing should be at such a level that the attainment and satisfaction of other basic needs are not threatened or compromised. Steps should be taken by States parties to ensure that the percentage of housing-related costs is, in general, commensurate with income levels. States parties should establish housing subsidies for those unable to obtain affordable housing, as well as forms and levels of housing finance which adequately reflect housing needs. In accordance with the principle of affordability, tenants should be protected by appropriate means against unreasonable rent levels or rent increases. In societies where natural materials constitute the chief sources of building materials for housing, steps should be taken by States parties to ensure the availability of such materials;

(d) Habitability. Adequate housing must be habitable, in terms of providing the inhabitants with adequate space and protecting them from cold, damp, heat, rain, wind or other threats to health, structural hazards, and disease vectors. The physical safety of occupants must be guaranteed as well. The Committee encourages States parties to comprehensively apply the Health Principles of Housing prepared by [the World Health Organization (WHO)] which view housing as the environmental factor most frequently associated with conditions for disease in epidemiological analyses; i.e. inadequate and deficient housing and living conditions are invariably associated with higher mortality and morbidity rates;

(e) Accessibility. Adequate housing must be accessible to those entitled to it. Disadvantaged groups must be accorded full and sustainable access to adequate housing resources. Thus, such disadvantaged groups as the elderly, children, the physically disabled, the terminally ill, HIV-positive individuals, persons with persistent medical problems, the mentally ill, victims of natural disasters, people living in disaster-prone areas and other groups should be ensured some degree of priority consideration in the housing sphere. Both housing law and policy should take fully into account the special housing needs of these groups. Within many States parties increasing access to land by landless or impoverished segments of the society should constitute a central policy goal. Discernible governmental obligations need to be developed aiming to substantiate the right of all to a secure place to live in peace and dignity, including access to land as an entitlement;

(f) Location. Adequate housing must be in a location which allows access to employment options, health-care services, schools, child-care centres and other social facilities. This is true both in large cities and in rural areas where the temporal and financial costs of getting to and from the place of work can place excessive demands upon the budgets of poor households. Similarly, housing should not be built on polluted sites nor in immediate proximity to pollution sources that threaten the right to health of the inhabitants;

(g) Cultural adequacy. The way housing is constructed, the building materials used and the policies supporting these must appropriately enable the expression of cultural identity and diversity of housing. Activities geared towards development or modernization in the housing sphere should ensure that the cultural dimensions of housing are not sacrificed, and that, inter alia, modern technological facilities, as appropriate are also ensured.

3.2. Questions for discussion: the '4-As' typology

1. Is the '4-As' scheme applicable across all social and economic rights listed in the International Covenant on Economic, Social and Cultural Rights? And is it useful beyond those rights, in the area of civil and political rights?

2. How is the '4-As' scheme to be combined with the respect/protect/fulfil framework? If we combine the two frameworks with the matrix below, is the implication that the obligation of the State to respect is also always necessarily subject to progressive realization, since it includes the requirement to ensure that the good or service which the individual should have access to is available in sufficient quantities – for example, schools or hospitals covering all parts of the national territory, or a police force which ensures physical security in all areas?

The '4-As' scheme can be combined with the above differentiation between the obligations of the State to respect, protect and fulfil human rights. Indeed, the '4-As' describe the characteristics of the good or service that the individual right-holder has a right to; the respect/protect/fulfil framework describes the different obligations of the State either not to interfere with the enjoyment of that good or service, or to regulate private actors, or to facilitate access to that good or service by market mechanisms, or in certain cases to provide it. The following matrix expresses both these dimensions combined:

	Availability	Accessibility (non-discrimination, physical and economic accessibility)	Acceptability	Adaptability
Obligation to respect (not to interfere with existing enjoyment)				
Obligation to protect (to regulate private parties)				
Obligation to fulfil by facilitating market mechanisms				
Obligation to fulfil by providing the good or service				

2 RIGHTS OF AN 'ABSOLUTE' CHARACTER

This section discusses the specific regime of rights of an 'absolute' character. Rights which are 'absolute' must be respected at all times, and may not be restricted even for compelling reasons. This is the case, for example, of Article 7 ICCPR, which prohibits torture, or other cruel, inhuman or degrading treatment or punishment, and which allows of no limitation. The cases below illustrate situations where the absolute character of the prohibition met with resistance, in particular in the context of the fight against terrorism.

2.1 The absolute character of the prohibition of torture in 'ticking bomb' situations

It has been repeatedly asserted that '[t]he use of torture or of inhuman or degrading treatment or punishment, is absolutely prohibited, in all circumstances, and in particular during the arrest, questioning and detention of a person suspected of or convicted of terrorist activities, irrespective of the nature of the acts that the person is suspected of or for which he/she was convicted.' (Guidelines of the Committee of Ministers of the Council of Europe on Human Rights and the Fight against Terrorism, adopted by the Committee of Ministers of the Council of Europe at its 804th meeting (11 July 2002), Guideline IV). Consider, however, the following case (for a commentary, see A. Reichman and T. Kahana, 'Israel and the Recognition of Torture: Domestic and International Aspects', in C. Scott (ed.), *Torture as Tort* (Oxford: Hart Publishing, 2001), pp. 631–58):

Supreme Court of Israel, sitting as the High Court of Justice, *Public Committee Against Torture in Israel* v. *The State of Israel and the General Security Service*, HCJ 5100/94, judgment of 6 September 1999

[In its investigations, the General Security Service (GSS) makes use of methods that include subjecting suspects to moderate physical pressure. The means are employed under the authority of directives. These directives allow for the use of moderate physical pressure if such pressure is immediately necessary to save human life. Petitioners challenge the legality of these methods. In this judgment, the Court holds that the GSS did not have the authority to employ certain methods challenged by the petitioners. The Court also holds that the 'necessity defense', found in the Israeli Penal Law, could not serve *ex ante* to allow GSS investigators to employ such interrogation practices. The Court's decision does not negate the possibility that the 'necessity defense' would be available *post factum* to GSS investigators – either in the choice made by the Attorney General in deciding whether to prosecute, or according to the discretion of the court if criminal charges were brought against them.]

23. It is not necessary for us to engage in an in-depth inquiry into the 'law of interrogation' for the purposes of the petitions before us. These laws vary, depending on the context. For instance, the law of interrogation is different in the context of an investigator's potential criminal liability, and in the context of admitting evidence obtained by questionable means. Here we deal with the 'law of interrogation' as a power of an administrative authority. The 'law of interrogation' by its very nature, is intrinsically linked to the circumstances of each case. This having been said, a number of general principles are nonetheless worth noting.

First, a reasonable investigation is necessarily one free of torture, free of cruel, inhuman treatment, and free of any degrading conduct whatsoever. There is a prohibition on the use of 'brutal or inhuman means' in the course of an investigation ... Human dignity also includes the dignity of the suspect being interrogated ... This conclusion is in accord with international treaties, to which Israel is a signatory, which prohibit the use of torture, 'cruel, inhuman treatment' and 'degrading treatment' ... These prohibitions are 'absolute'. There are no exceptions to them and there is no room for balancing. Indeed, violence directed at a suspect's body or spirit does not constitute a reasonable investigation practice. The use of violence during investigations can lead to the investigator being held criminally liable ...

Second, a reasonable investigation is likely to cause discomfort. It may result in insufficient sleep. The conditions under which it is conducted risk being unpleasant. Of course, it is possible to conduct an effective investigation without resorting to violence. Within the confines of the law, it is permitted to resort to various sophisticated techniques. Such techniques – accepted in the most progressive of societies – can be effective in achieving their goals. In the end result, the legality of an investigation is deduced from the propriety of its purpose and from its methods. Thus, for instance, sleep deprivation for a prolonged period, or sleep deprivation at night when this is not necessary to the investigation time-wise, may be deemed disproportionate ...

33. We have arrived at the conclusion that GSS personnel who have received permission to conduct interrogations, as per the Criminal Procedure Statute [Testimony], are authorized to do so. This authority – like that of the police investigator – does not include most of the physical means of interrogation in the petition before us. Can the authority to employ these methods be anchored in a legal source beyond the authority to conduct an interrogation? This question was answered by the state in the affirmative. As noted, our law does not contain an explicit

authorization permitting the GSS to employ physical means. An authorization of this nature can, however, in the State's opinion, be obtained in specific cases by virtue of the criminal law defense of 'necessity', as provided in section 34(1) of the Penal Law. The statute provides: 'A person will not bear criminal liability for committing any act immediately necessary for the purpose of saving the life, liberty, body or property, of either himself or his fellow person, from substantial danger of serious harm, in response to particular circumstances during a specific time, and absent alternative means for avoiding the harm.'

The State's position is that by virtue of this defense against criminal liability, GSS investigators are authorized to apply physical means – such as shaking – in the appropriate circumstances and in the absence of other alternatives, in order to prevent serious harm to human life or limb. The State maintains that an act committed under conditions of 'necessity' does not constitute a crime. Instead, the State sees such acts as worth committing in order to prevent serious harm to human life or limb. These are actions that society has an interest in encouraging, which should be seen as proper under the circumstances. In this, society is choosing the lesser evil. Not only is it legitimately permitted to engage in fighting terrorism, it is our moral duty to employ the means necessary for this purpose. This duty is particularly incumbent on the State authorities – and, for our purposes, on the GSS investigators – who carry the burden of safeguarding the public peace. As this is the case, there is no obstacle preventing the investigators' superiors from instructing and guiding them as to when the conditions of the 'necessity' defense are fulfilled. This, the State contends, implies the legality of the use of physical means in GSS interrogations.

In the course of their argument, the State presented the 'ticking bomb' argument. A given suspect is arrested by the GSS. He holds information regarding the location of a bomb that was set and will imminently explode. There is no way to diffuse the bomb without this information. If the information is obtained, the bomb may be neutralized. If the bomb is not neutralized, scores will be killed and injured. Is a GSS investigator authorized to employ physical means in order to obtain this information? The State answers in the affirmative. The use of physical means should not constitute a criminal offence, and their use should be sanctioned, according to the state, by the 'necessity' defense.

34. We are prepared to assume, although this matter is open to debate, that the 'necessity defense' is available to all, including an investigator, during an interrogation, acting in the capacity of the state ... Likewise, we are prepared to accept – although this matter is equally contentious – that the 'necessity defense' can arise in instances of 'ticking bombs', and that the phrase 'immediate need' in the statute refers to the imminent nature of the act rather than that of the danger. Hence, the imminence criteria is satisfied even if the bomb is set to explode in a few days, or even in a few weeks, provided the danger is certain to materialize and there is no alternative means of preventing it ... In other words, there exists a concrete level of imminent danger of the explosion's occurrence ...

Consequently we are prepared to presume, as was held by the Report of the Commission of Inquiry, that if a GSS investigator – who applied physical interrogation methods for the purpose of saving human life – is criminally indicted, the 'necessity defense' is likely to be open to him in the appropriate circumstances ... A long list of arguments, from the fields of ethics and political science, may be raised in support of and against the use of the 'necessity defense' ... This matter, however, has already been decided under Israeli law. Israeli penal law recognizes the 'necessity defense'.

35. Indeed, we are prepared to accept that, in the appropriate circumstances, GSS investigators may avail themselves of the 'necessity defense' if criminally indicted. This, however, is not the issue before this Court. We are not dealing with the criminal liability of a GSS investigator who employed physical interrogation methods under circumstances of 'necessity'. Nor are we addressing the issue of the admissibility or probative value of evidence obtained as a result of a GSS investigator's application of physical means against a suspect. We are dealing with a different question. The question before us is whether it is possible, *ex ante*, to establish permanent directives setting out the physical interrogation means that may be used under conditions of 'necessity'. Moreover, we must decide whether the 'necessity defense' can constitute a basis for the authority of a GSS investigator to investigate, in the performance of his duty. According to the State, it is possible to imply from the 'necessity defense' – available *post factum* to an investigator indicted of a criminal offence – the *ex ante* legal authorization to allow the investigator to use physical interrogation methods. Is this position correct?

36. In the Court's opinion, the authority to establish directives respecting the use of physical means during the course of a GSS interrogation cannot be implied from the 'necessity defense'. The 'necessity defense' does not constitute a source of authority, which would allow GSS investigators to make use physical means during the course of interrogations. The reasoning underlying our position is anchored in the nature of the 'necessity defense'. The defense deals with cases involving an individual reacting to a given set of facts. It is an improvised reaction to an unpredictable event ... Thus, the very nature of the defense does not allow it to serve as the source of authorization. Authorization of administrative authority is based on establishing general, forward looking criteria, as noted by Professor Enker: 'Necessity is an after-the-fact judgment based on a narrow set of considerations in which we are concerned with the immediate consequences, not far-reaching and long-range consequences, on the basis of a clearly established order of priorities of both means and ultimate values ... The defense of necessity does not define a code of primary normative behavior. Necessity is certainly not a basis for establishing a broad detailed code of behavior such as how one should go about conducting intelligence interrogations in security matters, when one may or may not use force, how much force may be used and the like' (see A. Enker, 'The Use of Physical Force in Interrogations and the Necessity Defense' in *Israel and International Human Rights Law: The Issue of Torture* 61, 62 (1995)).

In a similar vein, Kremnitzer and Segev [M. Kremnitzer and R. Segev, 'The Petition of Force in the Course of GSS Interrogations – a Lesser Evil?', *Mishpat U'Memshal*, 4 (1989), 667 at 707] note: 'The basic rationale underlying the necessity defense is the impossibility of establishing accurate rules of behavior in advance, appropriate in concrete emergency situations, whose circumstances are varied and unexpected. From this it follows, that the necessity defense is not well suited for the regulation of a general situation, the circumstances of which are known and may repeat themselves. In such cases, there is no reason for not setting out the rules of behavior in advance, in order that their content be determined in a thought out and well-planned manner, which would allow them to apply in a uniform manner to all'.

The 'necessity defense' has the effect of allowing one who acts under the circumstances of 'necessity' to escape criminal liability. The 'necessity defense' does not possess any additional normative value. It can not authorize the use of physical means to allow investigators to execute their duties in circumstances of necessity. The very fact that a particular act does not constitute a criminal act – due to the 'necessity defense' – does not in itself authorize the act and the concomitant infringement of human rights. The rule of law, both as a formal and as a substantive principle, requires that an infringement of human rights be prescribed by statute. The lifting of criminal responsibility does not imply authorization to infringe a human right. It shall be noted that the Commission of Inquiry did not conclude that the 'necessity defense' is the source of authority for employing physical means by GSS investigators during the course of their interrogations. All that the Commission of Inquiry determined was that, if an investigator finds himself in a situation of 'necessity', forcing him to choose the 'lesser evil' – harming the suspect for the purpose of saving human lives – the 'necessity defense' shall be available to him. Indeed, the Commission of Inquiry noted that, 'the law itself must ensure a proper framework governing the actions of the security service with respect to the interrogation of hostile terrorist activities and the related problems particular to it'. *Ibid.* at 328.

37. In other words, general directives governing the use of physical means during interrogations must be rooted in an authorization prescribed by law and not in defenses to criminal liability. The principle of 'necessity' cannot serve as a basis of authority ... If the State wishes to enable GSS investigators to utilize physical means in interrogations, it must enact legislation for this purpose. This authorization would also free the investigator applying the physical means from criminal liability. This release would not flow from the 'necessity defense', but rather from the 'justification' defense. This defense is provided for in section 34(13) of the Penal Law, which states: 'A person shall not bear criminal liability for an act committed in one of the following cases: (1) He was obliged or authorized by law to commit it.'

This 'justification' defense to criminal liability is rooted in an area outside the criminal law. This 'external' law serves as a defense to criminal liability. This defense does not rest upon 'necessity', which is 'internal' to the Penal Law itself. Thus, for instance, where the question of when an officer is authorized to apply deadly force in the course of detention arises, the answer is found in the laws of detention, which is external to the Penal Law. If a man is killed as a result of this application of force, the 'justification' defense will likely come into play ... The 'necessity' defense cannot constitute the basis for rules regarding an interrogation. It cannot constitute a source of authority on which the individual investigator can rely on for the purpose of applying physical means in an investigation. The power to enact rules and to act according to them requires legislative authorization. In such legislation, the legislature, if it so desires, may express its views on the social, ethical and political problems of authorizing the use of physical means in an interrogation. Naturally, such considerations did not come before the legislature when the 'necessity' defense was enacted ... The 'necessity' defense is not the appropriate place for laying out these considerations ...

Granting GSS investigators the authority to apply physical force during the interrogation of suspects suspected of involvement in hostile terrorist activities, thereby harming the suspect's dignity and liberty, raises basic questions of law and society, of ethics and policy, and of the rule of law and security. These questions and the corresponding answers must be determined by the legislative branch ...

38. We conclude, therefore, that, according to the existing state of the law, neither the government nor the heads of the security services have the authority to establish directives regarding the use of physical means during the interrogation of suspects suspected of hostile terrorist activities, beyond the general rules which can be inferred from the very concept of

an interrogation itself. Similarly, the individual GSS investigator – like any police officer – does not possess the authority to employ physical means that infringe a suspect's liberty during the interrogation, unless these means are inherent to the very essence of an interrogation and are both fair and reasonable.

An investigator who employs these methods exceeds his authority. His responsibility shall be fixed according to law. His potential criminal liability shall be examined in the context of the 'necessity defense'. Provided the conditions of the defense are met by the circumstances of the case, the investigator may find refuge under its wings. Just as the existence of the 'necessity defense' does not bestow authority, the lack of authority does not negate the applicability of the necessity defense or of other defenses from criminal liability. The Attorney General can establish guidelines regarding circumstances in which investigators shall not stand trial, if they claim to have acted from 'necessity'. A statutory provision is necessary to authorize the use of physical means during the course of an interrogation, beyond what is permitted by the ordinary 'law of investigation', and in order to provide the individual GSS investigator with the authority to employ these methods. The 'necessity defense' cannot serve as a basis for such authority.

2.2 The absolute character of the prohibition of torture in the context of deportation proceedings

(a) The principle

Article 3 of the 1984 Convention against Torture and Other Cruel, Inhuman or Degrading Treatment or Punishment, provides that '1. No State Party shall expel, return ("refouler") or extradite a person to another State where there are substantial grounds for believing that he would be in danger of being subjected to torture. 2. For the purpose of determining whether there are such grounds, the competent authorities shall take into account all relevant considerations including, where applicable, the existence in the State concerned of a consistent pattern of gross, flagrant or mass violations of human rights.' As we have seen in chapter 2 (section 3.1.), a similar absolute prohibition is imposed under Article 3 of the European Convention on Human Rights and under Article 7 of the International Covenant on Civil and Political Rights. Although this norm has only been affirmed in international human rights since the 1980s, its roots are in fact older, and they are already present, in part, in Articles 32 and 33 of the Geneva Convention on the Status of Refugees, of 28 July 1951. Article 32 allows the expulsion of a refugee on grounds of national security or public order. Article 33 provides: '1. No Contracting State shall expel or return a refugee in any manner whatsoever to the frontiers of territories where his life or freedom would be threatened on account of his race, religion, nationality, membership of a particular social group or political opinion. 2. The benefit of the present provision may not, however, be claimed by a refugee whom there are reasonable grounds for regarding as a danger to the security of the country in which he is, or who, having been convicted by a final judgment of a particularly serious crime, constitutes a danger to the community of that country.'

The following case restates the principle of the absolute prohibition of refoulement in international human rights law, in terms that go beyond the protection provided for under the Geneva Convention:

European Court of Human Rights, *Chahal and others* v. *United Kingdom*, judgment of 15 November 1996:

[The first applicant, Karamjit Singh Chahal, is an Indian citizen who entered the United Kingdom illegally in 1971 in search of employment. In 1974 he applied to the Home Office to regularize his stay and on 10 December 1974 was granted indefinite leave to remain under the terms of an amnesty for illegal entrants who arrived before 1 January 1973. In early 1984, upon returning to India, he was arrested by the Punjab police. He was taken into detention and held for twenty-one days, during which time he was, he contended, kept handcuffed in insanitary conditions, beaten to unconsciousness, electrocuted on various parts of his body and subjected to a mock execution. He was subsequently released without charge. On his return to the United Kingdom he engaged in political activities within the Sikh community. In October 1985 he was detained under the Prevention of Terrorism (Temporary Provisions) Act 1984 (PTA) on suspicion of involvement in a conspiracy to assassinate the Indian Prime Minister, Mr Rajiv Gandhi, during an official visit to the United Kingdom. He was released for lack of evidence. He was subsequently interrogated and arrested on a number of occasions, in connection with his political activities in the United Kingdom. Finally, on 14 August 1990 the Home Secretary (Mr Hurd) decided that Mr Chahal ought to be deported because his continued presence in the United Kingdom was unconducive to the public good for reasons of national security and other reasons of a political nature, namely the international fight against terrorism. On 16 August 1990 he was therefore placed into detention for the purposes of deportation in Bedford Prison. Mr Chahal claimed, however, that if returned to India he had a well-founded fear of persecution within the terms of the United Nations 1951 Convention on the Status of Refugees. He applied for asylum. The request was refused in March 1991. As to the risks of ill-treatment in India, the Home Secretary did not consider that Mr Chahal's experiences in India in 1984 had any continued relevance, since that had been a time of particularly high tension in Punjab.

The asylum refusal was quashed by the High Court on 2 December 1991 and referred back to the Home Secretary. The Court found that the reasoning behind it was inadequate, principally because the Home Secretary had neglected to explain whether he believed the evidence provided by NGOs relating to the situation in Punjab and, if not, the reasons for such disbelief. A fresh decision to refuse asylum was adopted in June 1992. The Home Secretary (Mr Clarke) considered that the breakdown of law and order in Punjab was due to the activities of Sikh terrorists and was not evidence of persecution within the terms of the 1951 Convention. Furthermore, relying upon Articles 32 and 33 of that Convention, he expressed the view that, even if Mr Chahal were at risk of persecution, he would not be entitled to the protection of the 1951 Convention because of the threat he posed to national security.

An appeal before the Court of Appeal was dismissed on 22 October 1993 (*R.* v. *Secretary of State for the Home Department, ex parte Chahal* [1994] *Immigration Appeal Reports* 107). The Court held that the combined effect of the 1951 Convention and the Immigration Rules was to require the Home Secretary to weigh the threat to Mr Chahal's life or freedom if he were deported against the danger to national security if he were permitted to stay. In the words of

Lord Justice Nolan: 'The proposition that, in deciding whether the deportation of an individual would be in the public good, the Secretary of State should wholly ignore the fact that the individual has established a well-founded fear of persecution in the country to which he is to be sent seems to me to be surprising and unacceptable. Of course there may very well be occasions when the individual poses such a threat to this country and its inhabitants that considerations of his personal safety and well-being become virtually irrelevant. Nonetheless one would expect that the Secretary of State would balance the risks to this country against the risks to the individual, albeit that the scales might properly be weighted in favour of the former.' In the view of the Court of Appeal, the Home Secretary did take into account the evidence that the applicant might be persecuted and it was not possible for the court to judge whether his decision to deport was irrational or perverse because it did not have access to the evidence relating to the national security risk posed by Mr Chahal. In the absence of evidence of irrationality or perversity, it was impossible under English law to set aside the Home Secretary's decision. Leave to appeal from that decision was denied.

The excerpts below relate to the claim that by deporting Mr Chahal to India, the United Kingdom would be committing a breach of Article 3 of the European Convention on Human Rights.]

75. The Court notes that the deportation order against the first applicant was made on the ground that his continued presence in the United Kingdom was unconducive to the public good for reasons of national security, including the fight against terrorism. The parties differed as to whether, and if so to what extent, the fact that the applicant might represent a danger to the security of the United Kingdom affected that State's obligations under Article 3.

76. Although the Government's primary contention was that no real risk of ill-treatment had been established, they also emphasised that the reason for the intended deportation was national security. In this connection they submitted, first, that the guarantees afforded by Article 3 were not absolute in cases where a Contracting State proposed to remove an individual from its territory. Instead, in such cases, which required an uncertain prediction of future events in the receiving State, various factors should be taken into account, including the danger posed by the person in question to the security of the host nation. Thus, there was an implied limitation to Article 3 entitling a Contracting State to expel an individual to a receiving State even where a real risk of ill-treatment existed, if such removal was required on national security grounds. The Government based this submission in the first place on the possibility of implied limitations as recognised in the Court's case law, particularly paragraphs 88 and 89 of its above-mentioned *Soering* judgment [see chapter 2, section 3.1.] In support, they furthermore referred to the principle under international law that the right of an alien to asylum is subject to qualifications, as is provided for, *inter alia*, by Articles 32 and 33 of the United Nations 1951 Convention on the Status of Refugees.

In the alternative, the threat posed by an individual to the national security of the Contracting State was a factor to be weighed in the balance when considering the issues under Article 3. This approach took into account that in these cases there are varying degrees of risk of ill-treatment. The greater the risk of ill-treatment, the less weight should be accorded to the threat to national security. But where there existed a substantial doubt with regard to the risk of ill-treatment, the threat to national security could weigh heavily in the balance to be struck between protecting the rights of the individual and the general interests of the community. This was the case here: it was at least open to substantial doubt whether the alleged risk of ill-treatment would materialise; consequently, the fact that Mr Chahal constituted a serious threat to the security of the United Kingdom justified his deportation.

77. The applicant denied that he represented any threat to the national security of the United Kingdom, and contended that, in any case, national security considerations could not justify exposing an individual to the risk of ill-treatment abroad any more than they could justify administering torture to him directly.

78. The Commission ... rejected the Government's arguments. It ... expressed the opinion that the guarantees afforded by Article 3 were absolute in character, admitting of no exception.

At the hearing before the Court, the Commission's Delegate suggested that the passages in the Court's *Soering* judgment upon which the Government relied (see paragraph 76 above) might be taken as authority for the view that, in a case where there were serious doubts as to the likelihood of a person being subjected to treatment or punishment contrary to Article 3, the benefit of that doubt could be given to the deporting State whose national interests were threatened by his continued presence. However, the national interests of the State could not be invoked to override the interests of the individual where substantial grounds had been shown for believing that he would be subjected to ill-treatment if expelled.

79. Article 3 enshrines one of the most fundamental values of democratic society ... The Court is well aware of the immense difficulties faced by States in modern times in protecting their communities from terrorist violence. However, even in these circumstances, the Convention prohibits in absolute terms torture or inhuman or degrading treatment or punishment, irrespective of the victim's conduct. Unlike most of the substantive clauses of the Convention and of Protocols Nos. 1 and 4, Article 3 makes no provision for exceptions and no derogation from it is permissible under Article 15 even in the event of a public emergency threatening the life of the nation (see the *Ireland* v. *United Kingdom* judgment of 18 January 1978, Series A No. 25, p. 65, para. 163, and also the *Tomasi* v. *France* judgment of 27 August 1992, Series A No. 241-A, p. 42, para. 115).

80. The prohibition provided by Article 3 against ill-treatment is equally absolute in expulsion cases. Thus, whenever substantial grounds have been shown for believing that an individual would face a real risk of being subjected to treatment contrary to Article 3 if removed to another State, the responsibility of the Contracting State to safeguard him or her against such treatment is engaged in the event of expulsion (see the above-mentioned *Vilvarajah and others* judgment, p. 34, para. 103). In these circumstances, the activities of the individual in question, however undesirable or dangerous, cannot be a material consideration. The protection afforded by Article 3 is thus wider than that provided by Articles 32 and 33 of the United Nations 1951 Convention on the Status of Refugees ...

81. Paragraph 88 of the Court's above-mentioned *Soering* judgment, which concerned extradition to the United States, clearly and forcefully expresses the above view. It should not be inferred from the Court's remarks concerning the risk of undermining the foundations of extradition, as set out in paragraph 89 of the same judgment, that there is any room for balancing the risk of ill-treatment against the reasons for expulsion in determining whether a State's responsibility under Article 3 is engaged.

82. It follows from the above that it is not necessary for the Court to enter into a consideration of the Government's untested, but no doubt bona fide, allegations about the first applicant's terrorist activities and the threat posed by him to national security.

[Applying these principles to the circumstances of the case, the Court arrives at the conclusion that, taking into account in particular 'the attested involvement of the Punjab police in killings and abductions outside their State and the allegations of serious human rights violations which continue to be levelled at members of the Indian security forces elsewhere', there is a real risk of Mr Chahal being subjected to treatment contrary to Article 3 if he is returned to India (paras. 83–107 of the judgment). This part of the judgment was adopted by twelve votes to seven.]

Joint partly dissenting opinion, by judges Gölcüklü, Matscher, Sir John Freeland, Mr Baka, Mifsud Bonnici, Gotchev and Levits:

We agree with the majority that national security considerations could not be invoked to justify ill-treatment at the hands of a Contracting State within its own jurisdiction, and that in that sense the protection afforded by Article 3 is absolute in character. But in our view the situation is different where, as in the present case, only the extra-territorial (or indirect) application of the Article is at stake. There, a Contracting State which is contemplating the removal of someone from its jurisdiction to that of another State may legitimately strike a fair balance between, on the one hand, the nature of the threat to its national security interests if the person concerned were to remain and, on the other, the extent of the potential risk of ill-treatment of that person in the State of destination. Where, on the evidence, there exists a substantial doubt as to the likelihood that ill-treatment in the latter State would indeed eventuate, the threat to national security may weigh heavily in the balance. Correspondingly, the greater the risk of ill-treatment, the less weight should be accorded to the security threat.

3.3. Questions for discussion: the scope of the absolute prohibition of torture

1. If the presence of Chahal truly represents a threat to the national security of the United Kingdom should he be allowed to remain on the national territory, then could it be said that the *Chahal* judgment in fact does not recognize the absolute character of the right to life (see on this situation the scope of the obligation to protect, chapter 4)?

2. Is the opinion expressed by the seven judges who filed a joint dissenting opinion in *Chahal* in fact contradicting the reasoning followed by the majority? If there is a difference of opinion between the majority and the dissenting opinion, then where exactly does it lie?

3. What similarities and differences exist between the question of *refoulement* and a 'ticking-bomb' scenario, such as the one explored in the preceding section? Does it matter whether the risk of ill-treatment is uncertain in one case, and certain in the other?

4. Does it matter whether the risk of ill-treatment is merely foreseeable in one case (*refoulement*), while it is intended in another case (torture inflicted in a 'ticking-bomb' situation)? Does this make any difference? Western ethics has traditionally distinguished the two. In this ethical tradition, 'it is permissible to allow a bad consequence to result from one's actions, even if it is foreseen as certain to follow, provided certain conditions are satisfied. Those conditions are identified by the principle of "double effect". According to this ethical principle, it is permissible to produce a bad consequence if: (1) the act one is engaged in is not itself bad; (2) the bad consequence is not a means to the good consequence; (3) the bad consequence is foreseen but

not intended; and (4) there is a sufficiently serious reason for allowing the bad consequence to occur' (J. Keown, *Euthanasia, Ethics and Public Policy. An Argument against Legalisation* (Cambridge University Press, 2002), p. 20 (reference omitted)). Can this argument be transposed here?

The absolute character of the prohibition imposed in *Chahal* has been recently questioned by certain States parties to the Convention, particularly where other, equally absolute rights, were seen by these States to compete with the protection from torture or ill-treatment. In the case of *Ramzy* v. *Netherlands* (Appl. No. 25424/05), the Governments of Lithuania, Portugal, Slovakia and the United Kingdom, were given leave to intervene in support of the Dutch Government's position, as is possible under Article 36 para. 3 ECHR. As summarized in the admissibility decision adopted by the Court in this case, these Governments argue that the principle stated in the *Chahal* case – according to which 'in view of the absolute nature of the prohibition of treatment contrary to Article 3 of the Convention, the risk of such treatment could not be weighed against the reasons (including the protection of national security) put forward by the respondent State to justify expulsion' – was causing difficulties for the Contracting States by preventing them in practice from enforcing expulsion measures, 'due to its rigidity':

European Court of Human Rights (3rd sect.), *Ramzy* v. *Netherlands* **(Appl. No. 25424/05), admissibility decision of 28 May 2008, paras. 126–30:**

126. The Governments observed in that connection that whilst Contracting States could obtain diplomatic assurances that an applicant would not be subjected to treatment contrary to the Convention, the Court had held in the above-mentioned *Chahal* case that Article 3 required examination of whether such assurances would achieve sufficient practical protection. As had been shown by the opinions of the majority and the minority of the Court in that case, identical assurances could be interpreted differently. Furthermore, it was unlikely that any State other than the one of which the applicant was a national would be prepared to receive into its territory a person suspected of terrorist activities. In addition, the possibility of having recourse to criminal sanctions against the suspect did not provide sufficient protection for the community. The individual concerned might not commit any offence (or else, before a terrorist attack, only minor ones) and it could prove difficult to establish his involvement in terrorism beyond reasonable doubt, since it was frequently impossible to use confidential sources or information supplied by intelligence services. Other measures, such as detention pending expulsion, placing the suspect under surveillance or restricting his freedom of movement provided only partial protection.

127. Terrorism seriously endangered the right to life, which was the necessary precondition for enjoyment of all other fundamental rights. According to a well-established principle of international law, States could use immigration legislation to protect themselves from external threats to their national security. The Convention did not guarantee the right to political asylum.

This was governed by the 1951 Convention relating to the Status of Refugees, which explicitly provided that there was no entitlement to asylum where there was a risk for national security or where the asylum seeker had been responsible for acts contrary to the principles of the United Nations. Moreover, Article 5 §1(f) of the Convention authorised the arrest of a person 'against whom action is being taken with a view to deportation ...', and thus recognised the right of States to deport aliens.

128. It was true that the protection against torture and inhuman or degrading treatment or punishment provided by Article 3 of the Convention was absolute. However, in the event of expulsion, the treatment in question would be inflicted not by the signatory State but by the authorities of another State. The signatory State was then bound by a positive obligation of protection against torture implicitly derived from Article 3. Yet in the field of implied positive obligations the Court had accepted that the applicant's rights must be weighed against the interests of the community as a whole.

129. In expulsion cases the degree of risk in the receiving country depended on a speculative assessment. The level required to accept the existence of the risk was relatively low and difficult to apply consistently. Moreover, Article 3 of the Convention prohibited not only extremely serious forms of treatment, such as torture, but also conduct covered by the relatively general concept of 'degrading treatment'. And the nature of the threat presented by an individual to the signatory State also varied significantly.

130. In the light of the foregoing considerations, the intervening Governments argued that, in cases concerning the threat created by international terrorism, the approach followed by the Court in the *Chahal* case (which did not reflect a universally recognised moral imperative and was in contradiction with the intentions of the original signatories of the Convention) had to be altered and clarified. In the first place, the threat presented by the person to be deported must be a factor to be assessed in relation to the possibility and the nature of the potential ill-treatment. That would make it possible to take into consideration all the particular circumstances of each case and weigh the rights secured to the applicant by Article 3 of the Convention against those secured to all other members of the community by Article 2. Secondly, national-security considerations had to influence the standard of proof required of the applicant. In other words, if the respondent State adduced evidence that there was a threat to national security, stronger evidence had to be adduced to prove that the applicant would be at risk of ill-treatment in the receiving country. In particular, the individual concerned had to prove that it was 'more likely than not' that he would be subjected to treatment prohibited by Article 3. That interpretation was compatible with the wording of Article 3 of the United Nations Convention against Torture, which had been based on the case law of the Court itself, and took account of the fact that in expulsion cases it was necessary to assess a possible future risk.

In the case of *Nassim Saadi* v. *Italy*, the United Kingdom Government also joined as an intervening third party, formulating essentially the same argument against the principle established by the *Chahal* case. On 28 February 2008, the Grand Chamber of the European Court of Human Rights delivered its judgment in that case. It held unanimously that if the decision to deport the applicant to Tunisia were to be enforced, there would be a violation of Article 3 of the European Convention on Human Rights (prohibition of torture and inhuman or degrading treatment). The judgment reaffirms the absolute nature of the prohibition of deportation where there is a 'substantial risk' of torture or ill-treatment being committed, refusing to weigh the risk that a person might be subjected to ill-treatment against his dangerousness to the community if not sent back.

European Court of Human Rights (GC), *Saadi* v. *Italy* **(Appl. No. 37201/06), judgment of 28 February 2008, paras. 137–40:**

137. The Court notes first of all that States face immense difficulties in modern times in protecting their communities from terrorist violence ... It cannot therefore underestimate the scale of the danger of terrorism today and the threat it presents to the community. That must not, however, call into question the absolute nature of Article 3.

138. Accordingly, the Court cannot accept the argument of the United Kingdom Government, supported by the respondent Government, that a distinction must be drawn under Article 3 between treatment inflicted directly by a signatory State and treatment that might be inflicted by the authorities of another State, and that protection against this latter form of ill-treatment should be weighed against the interests of the community as a whole ... Since protection against the treatment prohibited by Article 3 is absolute, that provision imposes an obligation not to extradite or expel any person who, in the receiving country, would run the real risk of being subjected to such treatment. As the Court has repeatedly held, there can be no derogation from that rule ... It must therefore reaffirm the principle ... that it is not possible to weigh the risk of ill-treatment against the reasons put forward for the expulsion in order to determine whether the responsibility of a State is engaged under Article 3, even where such treatment is inflicted by another State. In that connection, the conduct of the person concerned, however undesirable or dangerous, cannot be taken into account, with the consequence that the protection afforded by Article 3 is broader than that provided for in Articles 32 and 33 of the 1951 United Nations Convention relating to the Status of Refugees ... Moreover, that conclusion is in line with points IV and XII of the guidelines of the Committee of Ministers of the Council of Europe on human rights and the fight against terrorism ...

139. The Court considers that the argument based on the balancing of the risk of harm if the person is sent back against the dangerousness he or she represents to the community if not sent back is misconceived. The concepts of 'risk' and 'dangerousness' in this context do not lend themselves to a balancing test because they are notions that can only be assessed independently of each other. Either the evidence adduced before the Court reveals that there is a substantial risk if the person is sent back or it does not. The prospect that he may pose a serious threat to the community if not returned does not reduce in any way the degree of risk of ill treatment that the person may be subject to on return. For that reason it would be incorrect to require a higher standard of proof, as submitted by the intervener, where the person is considered to represent a serious danger to the community, since assessment of the level of risk is independent of such a test.

140. With regard to the second branch of the United Kingdom Government's arguments, to the effect that where an applicant presents a threat to national security, stronger evidence must be adduced to prove that there is a risk of ill-treatment ..., the Court observes that such an approach is not compatible with the absolute nature of the protection afforded by Article 3 either. It amounts to asserting that, in the absence of evidence meeting a higher standard,

protection of national security justifies accepting more readily a risk of ill-treatment for the individual. The Court therefore sees no reason to modify the relevant standard of proof, as suggested by the third-party intervener, by requiring in cases like the present that it be proved that subjection to ill-treatment is 'more likely than not'. On the contrary, it reaffirms that for a planned forcible expulsion to be in breach of the Convention it is necessary – and sufficient – for substantial grounds to have been shown for believing that there is a real risk that the person concerned will be subjected in the receiving country to treatment prohibited by Article 3.

This position appears not to be shared by all supreme courts. The Supreme Court of Canada for instance has adopted the following view:

Supreme Court of Canada, *Suresh* v. *Canada (Minister of Citizenship and Immigration)* [2002] 1 S.C.R. 3, 2002 SCC 1

[The appellant is a Convention refugee from Sri Lanka who has applied for landed immigrant status. In 1995, the Canadian Government detained him and commenced deportation proceedings on security grounds, based on the opinion of the Canadian Security Intelligence Service that he was a member and fund-raiser of the Liberation Tigers of Tamil Eelam, an organization alleged to be engaged in terrorist activity in Sri Lanka. The Federal Court, Trial Division upheld as reasonable the deportation certificate under s. 40.1 of the Immigration Act and, following a deportation hearing, an adjudicator held that the appellant should be deported. The Minister of Citizenship and Immigration, after notifying the appellant that she was considering issuing an opinion declaring him to be a danger to the security of Canada under s. 53(1)(b) of the Act, issued such an opinion on the basis of an immigration officer's memorandum and concluded that he should be deported. Although the appellant had presented written submissions and documentary evidence to the Minister, he had not been provided with a copy of the immigration officer's memorandum, nor was he provided with an opportunity to respond to it orally or in writing. The appellant applied for judicial review, alleging that: (1) the Minister's decision was unreasonable; (2) the procedures under the Act were unfair; and (3) the Act infringed ss. 7, 2(b) and (d) of the Canadian Charter of Rights and Freedoms. The application for judicial review was dismissed on all grounds. The Federal Court of Appeal upheld that decision.

In the following judgment, the Supreme Court concludes that the appeal should be allowed, and that the appellant is entitled to a new deportation hearing. However, it also takes the view that, while deportation to torture may deprive a refugee of the right to liberty, security and perhaps life protected by s. 7 of the Charter, in determining whether this deprivation is in accordance with the principles of fundamental justice, Canada's interest in combating terrorism must be balanced against the refugee's interest in not being deported to torture. Section 7 of the Charter provides that 'Everyone has the right to life, liberty and security of the person and the right not to be deprived thereof except in accordance with the principles of fundamental justice.' Section 1 of the Charter states: 'The Canadian Charter of Rights and Freedoms guarantees the rights and freedoms set out in it subject only to such reasonable limits prescribed by law as can be demonstrably justified in a free and democratic society'.]

1   In this appeal we hold that Suresh is entitled to a new deportation hearing under the
     Immigration Act, R.S.C. 1985, c. I–2. Suresh came to Canada from Sri Lanka in 1990. He was
     recognized as a Convention refugee in 1991 and applied for landed immigrant status. In 1995
     the government detained him and started proceedings to deport him to Sri Lanka on grounds
     he was a member and fundraiser for the Liberation Tigers of Tamil Eelam (LTTE), an organiza-
     tion alleged to engage in terrorist activity in Sri Lanka. Suresh challenged the order for his
     deportation on various grounds of substance and procedure. In these reasons we examine the
     Immigration Act and the Canadian Charter of Rights and Freedoms, and find that deportation
     to face torture is generally unconstitutional and that some of the procedures followed in
     Suresh's case did not meet the required constitutional standards. We therefore conclude that
     Suresh is entitled to a new hearing.

2   The appeal requires us to consider a number of issues: the standard to be applied in review-
     ing a ministerial decision to deport; whether the Charter precludes deportation to a country
     where the refugee faces torture or death; whether deportation on the basis of mere mem-
     bership in an alleged terrorist organization unjustifiably infringes the Charter rights of free
     expression and free association; whether 'terrorism' and 'danger to the security of Canada'
     are unconstitutionally vague; and whether the deportation scheme contains adequate pro-
     cedural safeguards to ensure that refugees are not expelled to a risk of torture or death.

3   The issues engage concerns and values fundamental to Canada and indeed the world. On the
     one hand stands the manifest evil of terrorism and the random and arbitrary taking of inno-
     cent lives, rippling out in an ever-widening spiral of loss and fear. Governments, expressing
     the will of the governed, need the legal tools to effectively meet this challenge.

4   On the other hand stands the need to ensure that those legal tools do not undermine values
     that are fundamental to our democratic society – liberty, the rule of law, and the principles
     of fundamental justice – values that lie at the heart of the Canadian constitutional order
     and the international instruments that Canada has signed. In the end, it would be a Pyrrhic
     victory if terrorism were defeated at the cost of sacrificing our commitment to those values.
     Parliament's challenge is to draft laws that effectively combat terrorism and conform to the
     requirements of our Constitution and our international commitments.

5   We conclude that to deport a refugee to face a substantial risk of torture would generally
     violate s. 7 of the Charter. The Minister of Citizenship and Immigration must exercise her
     discretion to deport under the Immigration Act accordingly. Properly applied, the legislation
     conforms to the Charter. We reject the arguments that the terms 'danger to the security of
     Canada' and 'terrorism' are unconstitutionally vague and that ss. 19 and 53(1)(b) of the Act
     violate the Charter guarantees of free expression and free association, and conclude that the
     Act's impugned procedures, properly followed, are constitutional. We believe these findings
     leave ample scope to Parliament to adopt new laws and devise new approaches to the press-
     ing problem of terrorism.

6   Applying these conclusions, we find that the appellant Suresh made a prima facie case show-
     ing a substantial risk of torture if deported to Sri Lanka, and that his hearing did not provide
     the procedural safeguards required to protect his right not to be expelled to a risk of torture
     or death. This means that the case must be remanded to the Minister for reconsideration.
     The immediate result is that Suresh will remain in Canada until his new hearing is complete.
     Parliament's scheme read in light of the Canadian Constitution requires no less ...

42 Suresh opposes his deportation to Sri Lanka on the ground, among others, that on return he faces a substantial risk of torture ...

43 Section 53 of the Immigration Act permits deportation 'to a country where the person's life or freedom would be threatened'. The question is whether such deportation violates s. 7 of the Charter. Torture is defined in Article 1 of the CAT as including the unlawful use of psychological or physical techniques to intentionally inflict severe pain and suffering on another, when such pain or suffering is inflicted by or with the consent of public officials ...

44 Section 7 of the Charter guarantees '[e]veryone ... the right to life, liberty and security of the person and the right not to be deprived thereof except in accordance with the principles of fundamental justice'. It is conceded that 'everyone' includes refugees and that deportation to torture may deprive a refugee of liberty, security and perhaps life. The only question is whether this deprivation is in accordance with the principles of fundamental justice. If it is not, s. 7 is violated and, barring justification of the violation under s. 1 of the Charter, deportation to torture is unconstitutional.

45 The principles of fundamental justice are to be found in 'the basic tenets of our legal system' [*United States* v. *Burns* [2001] 1 S.C.R. 283, 2001 SCC 7, at para. 70]. 'They do not lie in the realm of general public policy but in the inherent domain of the judiciary as guardian of the justice system': *Re B.C. Motor Vehicle Act* [1985] 2 S.C.R. 486, at p. 503. The relevant principles of fundamental justice are determined by a contextual approach that 'takes into account the nature of the decision to be made' [*Kindler* v. *Canada (Minister of Justice)* [1991] 2 S.C.R. 779], at p. 848, per McLachlin J. (as she then was). The approach is essentially one of balancing. As we said in *Burns*, '[i]t is inherent in the ... balancing process that the outcome may well vary from case to case depending on the mix of contextual factors put into the balance' (para. 65). Deportation to torture, for example, requires us to consider a variety of factors, including the circumstances or conditions of the potential deportee, the danger that the deportee presents to Canadians or the country's security, and the threat of terrorism to Canada. In contexts in which the most significant considerations are general ones, it is likely that the balance will be struck the same way in most cases. It would be impossible to say in advance, however, that the balance will necessarily be struck the same way in every case.

46 The inquiry into the principles of fundamental justice is informed not only by Canadian experience and jurisprudence, but also by international law, including *jus cogens*. This takes into account Canada's international obligations and values as expressed in '[t]he various sources of international human rights law – declarations, covenants, conventions, judicial and quasi-judicial decisions of international tribunals, [and] customary norms': *Burns*, at paras. 79–81 ...

47 Determining whether deportation to torture violates the principles of fundamental justice requires us to balance Canada's interest in combatting terrorism and the Convention refugee's interest in not being deported to torture. Canada has a legitimate and compelling interest in combatting terrorism. But it is also committed to fundamental justice. The notion of proportionality is fundamental to our constitutional system. Thus we must ask whether the government's proposed response is reasonable in relation to the threat. In the past, we have held that some responses are so extreme that they are *per se* disproportionate to any legitimate government interest: see *Burns, supra*. We must ask whether deporting a refugee to torture would be such a response.

48 With these thoughts in mind, we turn to the question of whether the government may, consistent with the principles of fundamental justice, expel a suspected terrorist to face torture

elsewhere: first from the Canadian perspective; then from the perspective of the international norms that inform s. 7.

(i) The Canadian Perspective

49 The inquiry at this stage is whether, viewed from a Canadian perspective, returning a refugee to the risk of torture because of security concerns violates the principles of fundamental justice where the deportation is effected for reasons of national security. A variety of phrases have been used to describe conduct that would violate fundamental justice. The most frequent is conduct that would ' "shoc[k]" the Canadian conscience' (see *Kindler, supra*, at p. 852, and *Burns, supra*, at para. 60). Without resorting to opinion polls, which may vary with the mood of the moment, is the conduct fundamentally unacceptable to our notions of fair practice and justice?

50 It can be confidently stated that Canadians do not accept torture as fair or compatible with justice. Torture finds no condonation in our Criminal Code; indeed the Code prohibits it (see, for example, s. 269.1). The Canadian people, speaking through their elected representatives, have rejected all forms of state-sanctioned torture. Our courts ensure that confessions cannot be obtained by threats or force. The last vestiges of the death penalty were abolished in 1998 and Canada has not executed anyone since 1962: see An Act to amend the National Defence Act and to make consequential amendments to other Acts, S.C. 1998, c. 35. In *Burns*, the then Minister of Justice, in his decision on the order to extradite the respondents Burns and Rafay, emphasized that 'in Canada, Parliament has decided that capital punishment is not an appropriate penalty for crimes committed here, and I am firmly committed to that position' (para. 76). While we would hesitate to draw a direct equation between government policy or public opinion at any particular moment and the principles of fundamental justice, the fact that successive governments and Parliaments have refused to inflict torture and the death penalty surely reflects a fundamental Canadian belief about the appropriate limits of a criminal justice system.

51 When Canada adopted the Charter in 1982, it affirmed the opposition of the Canadian people to government-sanctioned torture by proscribing cruel and unusual treatment or punishment in s. 12. A punishment is cruel and unusual if it 'is so excessive as to outrage standards of decency': see *R. v. Smith* [1987] 1 S.C.R. 1045, at pp. 1072–73, per Lamer J. (as he then was). It must be so inherently repugnant that it could never be an appropriate punishment, however egregious the offence. Torture falls into this category. The prospect of torture induces fear and its consequences may be devastating, irreversible, indeed, fatal. Torture may be meted out indiscriminately or arbitrarily for no particular offence. Torture has as its end the denial of a person's humanity; this end is outside the legitimate domain of a criminal justice system: see, generally, E. Scarry, *The Body in Pain: The Making and Unmaking of the World* (1985), at pp. 27–59. Torture is an instrument of terror and not of justice. As Lamer J. stated in *Smith, supra*, at pp. 1073–74, 'some punishments or treatments will always be grossly disproportionate and will always outrage our standards of decency: for example, the infliction of corporal punishment'. As such, torture is seen in Canada as fundamentally unjust.

52 We may thus conclude that Canadians reject government-sanctioned torture in the domestic context. However, this appeal focuses on the prospect of Canada expelling a person to face torture in another country. This raises the question whether s. 7 is implicated at all. On one theory, our inquiry need be concerned only with the Minister's act of deporting and not with the possible consequences that the expelled refugee may face upon arriving in the destination country. If our s. 7 analysis is confined to what occurs on Canadian soil as a necessary and

immediate result of the Minister's decision, torture does not enter the picture. If, on the other hand, our analysis must take into account what may happen to the refugee in the destination country, we surely cannot ignore the possibility of grievous consequences such as torture and death, if a risk of those consequences is established.

53 We discussed this issue at some length in *Burns*. In that case, the United States sought the extradition of two Canadian citizens to face aggravated first degree murder charges in the state of Washington. The respondents Burns and Rafay contested the extradition on the grounds that the Minister of Justice had not sought assurances that the death penalty would not be imposed. We rejected the respondents' argument that extradition in such circumstances would violate their s. 12 right not to be subjected to cruel and unusual treatment or punishment, finding that the nexus between the extradition order and the mere possibility of capital punishment was too remote to engage s. 12. We agreed, however, with the respondents' argument under s. 7, writing that '[s]ection 7 is concerned not only with the act of extraditing, but also the *potential* consequences of the act of extradition' (para. 60 (emphasis in original)). We cited, in particular, *Canada* v. *Schmidt* [1987] 1 S.C.R. 500, at p. 522, in which La Forest J. recognized that 'in some circumstances the manner in which the foreign state will deal with the fugitive on surrender, whether that course of conduct is justifiable or not under the law of that country, may be such that it would violate the principles of fundamental justice to surrender an accused under those circumstances'. In that case, La Forest J. referred specifically to the possibility that a country seeking extradition might torture the accused on return.

54 While the instant case arises in the context of deportation and not extradition, we see no reason that the principle enunciated in *Burns* should not apply with equal force here. In *Burns*, nothing in our s. 7 analysis turned on the fact that the case arose in the context of extradition rather than *refoulement*. Rather, the governing principle was a general one – namely, that the guarantee of fundamental justice applies even to deprivations of life, liberty or security effected by actors other than our government, if there is a sufficient causal connection between our government's participation and the deprivation ultimately effected. We reaffirm that principle here. At least where Canada's participation is a necessary precondition for the deprivation and where the deprivation is an entirely foreseeable consequence of Canada's participation, the government does not avoid the guarantee of fundamental justice merely because the deprivation in question would be effected by someone else's hand.

55 We therefore disagree with the Federal Court of Appeal's suggestion that, in expelling a refugee to a risk of torture, Canada acts only as an 'involuntary intermediary' (para. 120). Without Canada's action, there would be no risk of torture. Accordingly, we cannot pretend that Canada is merely a passive participant. That is not to say, of course, that any action by Canada that results in a person being tortured or put to death would violate s. 7. There is always the question, as there is in this case, of whether there is a sufficient connection between Canada's action and the deprivation of life, liberty, or security.

56 While this Court has never directly addressed the issue of whether deportation to torture would be inconsistent with fundamental justice, we have indicated on several occasions that extraditing a person to face torture would be inconsistent with fundamental justice ...

58 Canadian jurisprudence does not suggest that Canada may never deport a person to face treatment elsewhere that would be unconstitutional if imposed by Canada directly, on Canadian soil. To repeat, the appropriate approach is essentially one of balancing. The outcome will depend

not only on considerations inherent in the general context but also on considerations related to the circumstances and condition of the particular person whom the government seeks to expel. On the one hand stands the state's genuine interest in combatting terrorism, preventing Canada from becoming a safe haven for terrorists, and protecting public security. On the other hand stands Canada's constitutional commitment to liberty and fair process. This said, Canadian jurisprudence suggests that this balance will usually come down against expelling a person to face torture elsewhere.

(ii) The International Perspective

59 We have examined the argument that from the perspective of Canadian law to deport a Convention refugee to torture violates the principles of fundamental justice. However, that does not end the inquiry. The provisions of the Immigration Act dealing with deportation must be considered in their international context ... Similarly, the principles of fundamental justice expressed in s. 7 of the Charter and the limits on rights that may be justified under s. 1 of the Charter cannot be considered in isolation from the international norms which they reflect. A complete understanding of the Act and the Charter requires consideration of the international perspective.

60 International treaty norms are not, strictly speaking, binding in Canada unless they have been incorporated into Canadian law by enactment. However, in seeking the meaning of the Canadian Constitution, the courts may be informed by international law. Our concern is not with Canada's international obligations qua obligations; rather, our concern is with the principles of fundamental justice. We look to international law as evidence of these principles and not as controlling in itself.

61 It has been submitted by the intervener, Amnesty International, that the absolute prohibition on torture is a peremptory norm of customary international law, or *jus cogens* ...

62 In the case at bar, there are three compelling indicia that the prohibition of torture is a peremptory norm. First, there is the great number of multilateral instruments that explicitly prohibit torture ...

63 Second, Amnesty International submitted that no state has ever legalized torture or admitted to its deliberate practice and that governments accused of practising torture regularly deny their involvement, placing responsibility on individual state agents or groups outside the government's control. Therefore, it argues that the weight of these domestic practices is further evidence of a universal acceptance of the prohibition on torture ...

64 Last, a number of international authorities state that the prohibition on torture is an established peremptory norm ...

65 Although this Court is not being asked to pronounce on the status of the prohibition on torture in international law, the fact that such a principle is included in numerous multilateral instruments, that it does not form part of any known domestic administrative practice, and that it is considered by many academics to be an emerging, if not established peremptory norm, suggests that it cannot be easily derogated from. With this in mind, we now turn to the interpretation of the conflicting instruments at issue in this case.

66 Deportation to torture is prohibited by both the ICCPR, which Canada ratified in 1976, and the CAT [Convention against Torture and Other Cruel, Inhuman or Degrading Treatment or Punishment], which Canada ratified in 1987 ... While the provisions of the ICCPR do not themselves specifically address the permissibility of a state's expelling a person to face torture

elsewhere, General Comment 20 to the ICCPR makes clear that Article 7 is intended to cover that scenario, explaining that '... States parties must not expose individuals to the danger of torture ... upon return to another country by way of their extradition, expulsion or *refoulement*' (para. 9) ...

69 Robertson J.A., however, held that the CAT's clear proscription of deportation to torture must defer to Article 33(2) of the Refugee Convention, which permits a country to return (*refouler*) a refugee who is a danger to the country's security ...

70 Article 33 of the Refugee Convention appears on its face to stand in opposition to the categorical rejection of deportation to torture in the CAT. Robertson J.A., faced with this apparent contradiction, attempted to read the two conventions in a way that minimized the contradiction, holding that the anti-deportation provisions of the CAT were not binding, but derogable.

71 We are not convinced that the contradiction can be resolved in this way. It is not apparent to us that the clear prohibitions on torture in the CAT were intended to be derogable. First, the absence of an express prohibition against derogation in Article 3 of the CAT together with the 'without prejudice' language of Article 16 do not seem to permit derogation. Nor does it follow from the assertion in Article 2(2) of CAT that '[n]o exceptional circumstances ... may be invoked as a justification of torture', that the absence of such a clause in the Article 3 *refoulement* provision permits acts leading to torture in exceptional circumstances. Moreover, the history of Article 16 of the CAT suggests that it was intended to leave the door open to other legal instruments providing greater protection, not to serve as the means for reducing protection. During the deliberations of the Working Group that drafted the CAT, Article 16 was characterized as a 'saving clause affirming the continued validity of other instruments prohibiting punishments or cruel, inhuman, or degrading treatment': Convention against Torture, *travaux préparatoires*, UN Doc. E/CN.4/1408, at p. 66. This undermines the suggestion that Article 16 can be used as a means of narrowing the scope of protection that the CAT was intended to provide.

72 In our view, the prohibition in the ICCPR and the CAT on returning a refugee to face a risk of torture reflects the prevailing international norm. Article 33 of the Refugee Convention protects, in a limited way, refugees from threats to life and freedom from all sources. By contrast, the CAT protects everyone, without derogation, from state-sponsored torture. Moreover, the Refugee Convention itself expresses a 'profound concern for refugees' and its principal purpose is to 'assure refugees the widest possible exercise of ... fundamental rights and freedoms' (Preamble). This negates the suggestion that the provisions of the Refugee Convention should be used to deny rights that other legal instruments make universally available to everyone.

73 Recognition of the dominant status of the CAT in international law is consistent with the position taken by the UN Committee against Torture, which has applied Article 3(1) even to individuals who have terrorist associations. (The CAT provides for the creation of a Committee against Torture to monitor compliance with the treaty: see CAT, Part II, Articles 17–24.) More particularly, the Committee against Torture has advised that Canada should '[c]omply fully with article 3(1) ... whether or not the individual is a serious criminal or security risk': see Committee against Torture, Conclusions and Recommendations of the Committee against Torture: Canada, UN Doc. CAT/C/XXV/Concl.4, at para. 6(a).

74 Finally, we note that the Supreme Court of Israel sitting as the High Court of Justice and the House of Lords have rejected torture as a legitimate tool to use in combatting terrorism and

protecting national security: H.C. 6536/95, *Hat'm Abu Zayda* v. *Israel General Security Service*, 38 I.L.M. 1471 (1999); *Secretary of State for the Home Department* v. *Rehman* [2001] 3 W.L.R. 877, at para. 54, per Lord Hoffmann.

75 We conclude that the better view is that international law rejects deportation to torture, even where national security interests are at stake. This is the norm which best informs the content of the principles of fundamental justice under s. 7 of the Charter.

(iii) Application to Section 53(1)(b) of the Immigration Act

76 The Canadian rejection of torture is reflected in the international conventions to which Canada is a party. The Canadian and international perspectives in turn inform our constitutional norms. The rejection of state action leading to torture generally, and deportation to torture specifically, is virtually categoric. Indeed, both domestic and international jurisprudence suggest that torture is so abhorrent that it will almost always be disproportionate to interests on the other side of the balance, even security interests. This suggests that, barring extraordinary circumstances, deportation to torture will generally violate the principles of fundamental justice protected by s. 7 of the Charter. To paraphrase Lord Hoffmann in *Rehman, supra*, at para. 54, states must find some other way of ensuring national security.

77 The Minister is obliged to exercise the discretion conferred upon her by the Immigration Act in accordance with the Constitution. This requires the Minister to balance the relevant factors in the case before her. As stated in *Rehman, supra*, at para. 56, per Lord Hoffmann: 'The question of whether the risk to national security is sufficient to justify the appellant's deportation cannot be answered by taking each allegation seriatim and deciding whether it has been established to some standard of proof. It is a question of evaluation and judgment, in which it is necessary to take into account not only the degree of probability of prejudice to national security but also the importance of the security interest at stake and the serious consequences of deportation for the deportee.'

Similarly, Lord Slynn of Hadley stated, at para. 16: 'Whether there is ... a real possibility [of an adverse effect on the United Kingdom even if it is not direct or immediate] is a matter which has to be weighed up by the Secretary of State and balanced against the possible injustice to th[e] individual if a deportation order is made.'

In Canada, the balance struck by the Minister must conform to the principles of fundamental justice under s. 7 of the Charter. It follows that insofar as the Immigration Act leaves open the possibility of deportation to torture, the Minister should generally decline to deport refugees where on the evidence there is a substantial risk of torture.

78 We do not exclude the possibility that in exceptional circumstances, deportation to face torture might be justified, either as a consequence of the balancing process mandated by s. 7 of the Charter or under s. 1. (A violation of s. 7 will be saved by s. 1 'only in cases arising out of exceptional conditions, such as natural disasters, the outbreak of war, epidemics and the like': see *Re B.C. Motor Vehicle Act, supra*, at p. 518; and *New Brunswick (Minister of Health and Community Services)* v. *G. (J.)* [1999] 3 S.C.R. 46, at para. 99.) Insofar as Canada is unable to deport a person where there are substantial grounds to believe he or she would be tortured on return, this is not because Article 3 of the CAT directly constrains the actions of the Canadian government, but because the fundamental justice balance under s. 7 of the Charter generally precludes deportation to torture when applied on a case-by-case basis. We may predict that it will rarely be struck in favour of expulsion where there is a serious risk of torture. However, as

the matter is one of balance, precise prediction is elusive. The ambit of an exceptional discretion to deport to torture, if any, must await future cases.

79 In these circumstances, s. 53(1)(b) does not violate s. 7 of the Charter. What is at issue is not the legislation, but the Minister's obligation to exercise the discretion s. 53 confers in a constitutional manner.

Predictably, this decision led to strong reactions from the UN human rights treaty bodies. The Human Rights Committee expressed its concern about Canada's policy according to which 'in exceptional circumstances, persons can be deported to a country where they would face the risk of torture or cruel, inhuman or degrading treatment', a position which the Committee said 'amounts to a grave breach' of Article 7 of the International Covenant on Civil and Political Rights:

Human Rights Committee, Concluding Observations: Canada (UN Doc. CCPR/C/CAN/CO/5, 20 April 2006), para. 15:

The State party should recognize the absolute nature of the prohibition of torture, cruel, inhuman or degrading treatment, which in no circumstances can be derogated from. Such treatments can never be justified on the basis of a balance to be found between society's interest and the individual's rights under article 7 of the Covenant. No person, without any exception, even those suspected of presenting a danger to national security or the safety of any person, and even during a state of emergency, may be deported to a country where he/she runs the risk of being subjected to torture or cruel, inhuman or degrading treatment. The State party should clearly enact this principle into its law.

(b) Diplomatic assurances

In recent years, one contentious issue in this area has been the tendency of States to rely on assurances given by States of return about the treatment which the persons removed will receive, in order to effectuate removals in circumstances which otherwise – in the absence of such 'diplomatic assurances' – would not be acceptable (on diplomatic assurances, see generally G. Noll, 'Diplomatic Assurances and the Silence of Human Rights Law', *Melbourne Journal of International Law*, 7 (2006), 104; M. Jones, 'Lies, Damned Lies and Diplomatic Assurances: the Misuse of Diplomatic Assurances in Removal Proceedings', *European Journal of Migration and Law*, 8 (2006), 9; or, by the UN Special Rapporteur against torture, M. Nowak, 'Challenges to the Absolute Nature of the Prohibition of Torture and Ill-Treatment', *Netherlands Quarterly of Human Rights*, 23 (2005), 674).

The human rights bodies or independent experts generally take the view that such 'diplomatic assurances' cannot be a substitute for a verification, on a case-to-case basis, that the person returned will not be subjected to a real risk of torture, to other forms of inhuman or degrading treatment or punishment or to the death penalty, and that the security of that person will not be threatened. For instance, on 20 May 2005 the UN Committee against Torture (CAT) ruled that Sweden had violated the unconditional ban on torture in public international law by expelling a terrorism suspect, Ahmed Agiza, to Egypt. The Swedish Government had based its decision to proceed with the expulsion in December 2001 on a so-called 'diplomatic assurances' of fair treatment from the Egyptian authorities upon his return. The Committee nevertheless came to the conclusion that Sweden had violated Article 3 of the Convention against Torture and Cruel, Inhuman or Degrading Treatment or Punishment. In the view of CAT, the applicant had credibly alleged that he would be under a risk of torture after his forcible return to Egypt. The Committee stressed that assurances of the kind that has been given to the Swedish authorities could not protect Agiza from the risk of torture he faced upon return: 'the procurement of diplomatic assurances, which, moreover, provided no mechanism for their enforcement, did not suffice to protect against this manifest risk' (CAT/C/34/D/233/2003, 20 May 2005, p. 34). The Committee against Torture also pointed out that it 'should have been known, to the State party's authorities at the time of the complainant's removal that Egypt resorted to consistent and widespread use of torture against detainees, and that the risk of such treatment was particularly high in the case of detainees held for political and security reasons'. This position is shared by the UN Special Rapporteur on the question of torture, who summarizes his position as follows:

Report of the Special Rapporteur on the question of torture, Manfred Nowak, submitted to the sixty-second session of the Commission on Human Rights, E/CN.4/2006/6 23 December 2005, para. 31:

(a) The principle of non-refoulement (CAT, art. 3; ECHR, art. 3; International Covenant on Civil and Political Rights (ICCPR), art. 7) is an absolute obligation deriving from the absolute and non-derogable nature of the prohibition of torture;

(b) Diplomatic assurances are sought from countries with a proven record of systematic torture, i.e. the very fact that such diplomatic assurances are sought is an acknowledgement that the requested State, in the opinion of the requesting State, is practising torture. In most cases, those individuals in relation to whom diplomatic assurances are being sought belong to a high-risk group ('Islamic fundamentalists');

(c) It is often the case that the requesting and the requested States are parties to CAT, ICCPR and other treaties absolutely prohibiting torture. Rather than using all their diplomatic and legal powers as States parties to hold other States parties accountable for their violations, requesting States, by means of diplomatic assurances, seek only an exception from the practice of torture for a few individuals, which leads to double standards *vis-à-vis* other detainees in those countries;

(d) Diplomatic assurances are not legally binding. It is therefore unclear why States that violate binding obligations under treaty and customary international law should comply with non-binding assurances. Another important question in this regard is whether the authority providing such diplomatic assurances has the power to enforce them *vis-à-vis* its own security forces;

(e) Post-return monitoring mechanisms are no guarantee against torture – even the best monitoring mechanisms (e.g. ICRC and CPT) are not 'watertight' safeguards against torture;

(f) The individual concerned has no recourse if assurances are violated;

(g) In most cases, diplomatic assurances do not contain any sanctions in case they are violated, i.e. there is no accountability of the requested or requesting State, and therefore the perpetrators of torture are not brought to justice;

(h) Both States have a common interest in denying that returned persons were subjected to torture. Therefore, where States have identified independent organizations to undertake monitoring functions under the agreement, these interests may translate into undue political pressure upon these monitoring bodies, particularly where one is funded by the sending and/or receiving State.

In the following case, however, the House of Lords upholds earlier rulings of the Special Immigration Appeals Commission (SIAC), an immigration court that hears appeals against national security deportations. The judgment allows the Government to deport two Algerians and a Jordanian national, Omar Othman (known as Abu Qatada), in reliance on 'diplomatic assurances' against torture from the Governments of Algeria and Jordan respectively. On the issue of diplomatic assurances, the leading opinion (by Lord Phillips of Worth Matravers) states the following:

House of Lords (United Kingdom), *R.B. and U. (Algeria)* **v.** *Secretary of State for the Home Department* **and** *Secretary of State for the Home Department* **v.** *O.O. (Jordan)* **[2009] UKHL 10 (on appeal from [2007] EWCA Civ 808 and [2008] EWCA Civ 290):**

107. The Secretary of State accepted that neither Algeria, in the case of RB and U, nor Jordan, in the case of Mr Othman, was a country to which the appellants could safely have been returned had the United Kingdom not received assurances from the respective Governments as to the way in which they would be treated. In the case of RB and U SIAC held that, having particular regard to the assurances that had been given, the individual appellants would not face a real risk of treatment of a kind covered by article 3 (I shall refer to this hereafter as inhuman treatment) if returned to his own country. Before the Court of Appeal RB and U sought to challenge this finding, but the court held that it had no jurisdiction to reconsider it as the finding was one of fact, not law. Nonetheless the Court of Appeal considered the merits of the challenge and expressed the view that the criticism of SIAC's decision was unfounded.

108. The picture in relation to Mr Othman is more complex. The assurances in his case, which were contained in a Memorandum of Understanding (MOU) covered all human rights but dealt specifically with treatment if detained, promptness of judicial process and fairness of any trial. SIAC's judgment extends to some 130 pages in length. SIAC referred repeatedly to the influence of the MOU and found this significant, but it does not seem that this was critical to reducing the risk of inhuman treatment to an acceptable level, for SIAC expressed the following conclusion in relation to the effectiveness of the MOU:

'It is in this context that we examine the effect of the MOU and the monitoring provisions. First, the conclusions which we have reached about the treatment which the Appellant would experience on return, and the lack of a real risk of a breach of Article 3 at that stage, are reinforced by their existence. We expect the MOU to have some influence on the way in which the legal procedures pre-trial are carried out. The MOU and monitoring reinforce our conclusions about other risks, although we have not relied on them as the crucial components which make what would otherwise be a real risk of a breach of Article 3 into something less.'

109. Mr Othman sought to challenge before the Court of Appeal the reliance that SIAC had placed on the assurances given by Jordan that he would not be subjected to inhuman treatment. The court followed the decision in *RB and U* in holding that SIAC's decision was not open to attack as a matter of principle and also summarily dismissed the suggestion that SIAC's decision was irrational.

110. Before the House counsel for RB and U submitted that it was irrational and unlawful for SIAC to rely on assurances for two independent reasons: first because Algeria had not been prepared to agree to independent monitoring of the manner in which the appellants would be treated; secondly because, on their true construction, the assurances did not promise that the appellants would not be subjected to inhuman treatment. Counsel for Mr Othman submitted that, as a matter of principle, assurances could not be relied upon where there was a pattern of human rights violations in the receiving State coupled with a culture of impunity for the State agents in the security service and the persons who perpetrated these violations. It was further submitted that in all the circumstances SIAC's reliance on the assurances that had been given was irrational.

111. These submissions were supported by all three interveners [three non-governmental organizations, Justice, Human Rights Watch, and Liberty, intervened in support of the appellants]. They advanced a further argument of principle. They submitted that once it was accepted that there was a continuing risk of inhuman treatment in a country, assurances could not be relied upon unless their effect was to remove all risk of ill-treatment. I propose to deal at the outset with the submissions that there are principles of law that govern whether reliance can be placed on assurances in relation to safety on return.

112. The starting point is *Chahal*. In that case the ECtHR referred to the relevant test for ascertaining whether expulsion will violate article 3, namely whether there are substantial grounds for believing that the person in question, if expelled, will face a real risk of being subjected to treatment contrary to article 3. In contending that there was no such risk the United Kingdom had relied on the fact that they had sought and received assurances from the Indian Government. The court referred to the fact that despite the efforts of the Government and the courts the violation of human rights by the security forces remained prevalent and commented that it was not persuaded that the assurances 'would provide Mr Chahal with an adequate guarantee of safety'. The court did not specify what it meant by an 'adequate guarantee'. Counsel for the appellants equated the phrase to an absolute guarantee. Counsel for the Secretary of State submitted that it was enough if the guarantee removed the substantial grounds that might otherwise exist for believing that there was a real risk of inhuman treatment. In *Mamatkulov* v. *Turkey* (2005) 41 EHRR 494 [see Box 1.3., chapter 1] the ECtHR was not satisfied that Turkey had violated article 3 in permitting the extradition of the applicant to Uzbekistan and, in reaching that conclusion, had regard to the fact that the Government of Uzbekistan had given assurances

against ill-treatment. In this case the existence of assurances was treated by the court as part of the matrix that had to be considered when deciding whether there were substantial grounds for believing in the existence of a real risk of inhuman treatment. The ECtHR applied a similar approach in *Shamayev* v. *Georgia and Russia* (application 36378/02 judgment of 12 April 2005) [see below in this section] as did the United Nations Committee Against Torture in *Hanan Attia* v. *Sweden* (17 November 2003, Communication No. 199/2002).

113. Counsel for RB and U relied on *Saadi* v. *Italy* [see above in this section, a], where at para 129 the ECtHR spoke of the requirement of the deporting Government to 'dispel any doubts' about the safety of the deportee. They also referred to two recent claims against Russia where the court spoke of the need for diplomatic assurances to 'ensure adequate protection against the risk of ill-treatment where reliable sources had reported practices resorted to or tolerated by the authorities which were manifestly contrary to the principles of the Convention' – *Ismoilov and others* v. *Russia* (application no 2947/06) paragraph 127 and *Ryabikin* v. *Russia* (application no 8320/04) paragraph 119.

114. I do not consider that these decisions establish a principle that assurances must eliminate all risk of inhuman treatment before they can be relied upon. It is obvious that if a State seeks to rely on assurances that are given by a country with a record for disregarding fundamental human rights it will need to show that there is good reason to treat the assurances as providing a reliable guarantee that the deportee will not be subjected to such treatment. If, however, after consideration of all the relevant circumstances of which assurances form part, there are no substantial grounds for believing that a deportee will be at real risk of inhuman treatment, there will be no basis for holding that deportation will violate article 3.

115. That said, there is an abundance of material that supports the proposition that assurances should be treated with scepticism if they are given by a country where inhuman treatment by State agents is endemic. This comes close to the 'Catch 22' proposition that if you need to ask for assurances you cannot rely on them. If a State is unwilling or unable to comply with the obligations of international law in relation to the avoidance and prevention of inhuman treatment, how can it be trusted to be willing or able to give effect to an undertaking that an individual deportee will not be subject to such treatment?

116. Much of the material to which I have referred is summarised in the decision of de Montigny J, sitting in the Federal Court of Canada, in *Sing* v. *Canada (Minister of Citizenship and Immigration)* 2007 FC 361. He referred to the joint report of Amnesty International, Human Rights Watch and the International Commission of Jurists of December 2 2005; Tribunal Record, vol 1, pages 179–223, which stated that diplomatic assurances were not an effective safeguard against torture, and to the report to the UN General Assembly of September 1 2004 of the UN Special Rapporteur on Torture (UN Document A/59/324). The latter urged the importance of verification of assurances, including effective monitoring, something that is particularly difficult as a person in detention may be understandably reluctant to complain to a monitor of torture or inhuman treatment. These are matters that counsel for the appellants urged before your Lordships.

117. *Sing* was a claim for judicial review and, when considering the standard of review, Montigny J remarked that the evaluation of the reliability of a diplomatic assurance was a question of fact reviewable on the standard of patent unreasonableness. He referred to the

following passage in the judgment of the Supreme Court in *Suresh* v. *Canada (Minister of Citizenship and Immigration)* [2002] 1 SCR 3 at paragraph 39:

'As mentioned earlier, whether there is a substantial risk of torture if Suresh is deported is a threshold question. The threshold question here is in large part a fact-driven inquiry. It requires consideration of the human rights record of the home state, the personal risk faced by the claimant, any assurances that the claimant will not be tortured and their worth and, in that respect, the ability of the home state to control its own security forces, and more. It may also involve a reassessment of the refugee's initial claim and a determination of whether a third country is willing to accept the refugee. Such issues are largely outside the realm of expertise of reviewing courts and possess a negligible legal dimension.'

This passage expresses my reaction to the suggestion that SIAC's conclusions in relation to assurances give rise to issues of law. The only ground upon which those conclusions can be attacked on an appeal restricted to questions of law is irrationality.

Was SIAC's decision in relation to RB and U irrational?

118. In considering this question it is right to bear in mind the material to which I have referred that emphasises the reasons why assurances are unlikely to be reliable. With article 3 rights in issue SIAC could be expected to scrutinise with great care the Secretary of State's contention that assurances from the Algerian Government sufficed to remove the substantial grounds that would otherwise exist for believing that the appellants would be at real risk of inhuman treatment if sent back to Algeria. It is also right, however, to bear in mind the following comments of Baroness Hale in relation to an appeal on questions of law from an expert Tribunal – in that case the Asylum and Immigration Tribunal – in *AH (Sudan)* v. *Secretary of State for the Home Department (UNHCR intervening)* [2007] UKHL 49; [2008] 1 AC 678:

'This is an expert tribunal charged with administering a complex area of law in challenging circumstances. [T]he ordinary courts should approach appeals from [such expert tribunals] with an appropriate degree of caution; it is probable that in understanding and applying the law in their specialised field the tribunal will have got it right: see *Cooke* v. *Secretary of State for Social Security* [2002] 3 All ER 279, para 16. They and they alone are the judges of the facts. It is not enough that their decision on those facts may seem harsh to people who have not heard and read the evidence and arguments which they have heard and read. Their decisions should be respected unless it is quite clear that they have misdirected themselves in law. Appellate courts should not rush to find such misdirections simply because they might have reached a different conclusion on the facts or expressed themselves differently.'

119. That passage was cited by the Court of Appeal when rejecting an appeal by the Secretary of State from the decision of SIAC in *AS and DD (Libya)* v. *Secretary of State for the Home Department (Liberty intervening)* [2008] EWCA Civ 289. SIAC had allowed appeals by AS and DD against deportation to Libya for reasons of national security. The ground of appeal that succeeded was that there were substantial grounds for believing that they faced a real risk of inhuman treatment if sent back to Libya. The Secretary of State had sought, unsuccessfully, to rely upon assurances in a memorandum of understanding concluded between the United Kingdom and Libya. A witness, whose experience and integrity SIAC commended, had

given evidence that it was 'well nigh unthinkable' that Libya would break that undertaking. Notwithstanding this SIAC concluded that the memorandum of understanding was not sufficiently reliable. Applying the approach of the ECtHR in *Saadi* the Court of Appeal held that:

'Consistently with that approach, it was for SIAC to examine whether the assurances given by Libya, in their practical application, were a sufficient guarantee that the respondents would be protected against torture. The weight to be given to the assurances depended upon the facts of this particular case. It can thus be seen that the exercise upon which SIAC was embarking was an investigation of fact, leading to a conclusion of fact. In our judgment, if SIAC made any error (and we do not divine one), it was an error of fact and not an error of law.'

120. In *AS and DD* SIAC applied with care the test originally laid down in Chahal. Are RB and U correct to contend that the results that SIAC reached in their cases were irrational? The weight to be attached to assurances was a question that different divisions of SIAC had to consider four times in relation to Algeria, once in respect of *Y*, once in respect of *RB*, once in respect of *G* and once in respect of *U*. The later decisions built on the earlier ones and in the final case of *U* SIAC had regard to the experience of four Algerians who had been repatriated to Algeria.

121. When considering RB and U's appeals the Court of Appeal considered the individual attacks that had been made on SIAC's findings of fact and found them without merit. I have none the less considered SIAC's decisions to see whether, having regard to the obligation on the Secretary of State to show good reason for treating Algeria's assurances as reliable, SIAC's conclusions are irrational.

122. The foundation of SIAC's decisions in relation to RB and U is to be found in their judgment, delivered by Ouseley J, in the case of *Y* on 24 August 2006 (Appeal No. SC/36/2005). This judgment extended to 416 paragraphs and it dealt in detail with the obtaining of assurances by the British Government. The context in which these were obtained was the desire of the Government to establish a means of returning terrorist suspects to their countries of origin without violation of the requirements of Article 3 of the Convention. In the case of Algeria this led to negotiations at the highest level, including discussions between the Prime Minister and President Bouteflika of Algeria. These negotiations ultimately resulted in assurances being given in relation to Y and also the assurances given in respect of RB and U that I set out earlier in this opinion. As I have already observed, the phrase 'diplomatic assurances' does not accurately reflect assurances obtained in such circumstances. That phrase more adequately describes routine assurances offered as a matter of course by State authorities seeking extradition, such as those considered by the ECtHR in *Ismoilov and Ryabikin*.

123. I have described earlier in this opinion the consideration given by SIAC to the reliance that could be placed on the Algerian assurances. This had particular regard to the general conditions in Algeria at the time that the assurances were given, the attitude of the Algerian authorities to the observance of human rights, the degree of control exercised by the Algerian authorities over the DRS, the internal security service, and the manner in which the performance of the assurances could be verified. SIAC paid careful regard to all relevant matters and applied to them the proper test of whether they amounted to substantial grounds for believing that RB and U would be at real risk of inhuman treatment if returned to Algeria.

124. SIAC gave consideration to the reasons why Algeria was not prepared to agree to monitoring and concluded that this was not indicative of bad faith and that there were

alternative ways of ascertaining whether there was compliance with the assurances. These conclusions were not irrational. The contention that the assurances did not, on their true construction, protect against inhuman treatment was not well founded.

125. For these reasons the irrationality challenge to SIAC's conclusions does not succeed. I would reject the appeals brought by RB and U.

Was SIAC's decision in relation to Mr Othman's article 3 challenge irrational?
126. The attack made by counsel for Mr Othman on SIAC's conclusions in relation to article 3 was essentially founded on the weight that SIAC had given to the assurances in the MOU. Just as in the case of Algeria, these assurances were agreed in principle at the highest level in discussions between the Prime Minister and the King of Jordan and between the Foreign Secretary and the Jordanian Foreign Minister. SIAC considered in depth the way that Mr Othman was likely to be treated before his trial, during the trial process and after it. The conclusion reached was that there were not substantial grounds for believing that there was a real risk that Mr Othman would be subjected to inhuman treatment. The MOU was not critical to this conclusion. SIAC commented that the political realities in Jordan and the bilateral diplomatic relationship mattered more than the terminology of the assurances. The former matters, and the fact that Mr Othman would have a high public profile, were the most significant factors in SIAC's assessment of article 3 risk. Study of SIAC's lengthy and detailed reasoning discloses no irrationality.

The European Court of Human Rights appears to accept that diplomatic assurances may be relevant to the evaluation of the seriousness of the risk taken in returning a person to a country where that person alleges he or she will be subjected to forms of treatment contrary to Article 3 ECHR, or will be sentenced to death. In fact, it may even be said that the practice of the Court itself is to accept diplomatic assurances. In the case of *Shamayev and others* v. *Georgia and Russia* for instance, the Court was asked to decide whether the extradition from Georgia to Russia of a number of individuals accused of committing terrorist acts in Chechenya would be in violation of Article 3 ECHR. When it received the application, the Court decided to indicate to the Georgian Government, in application of Rule 39 of its Rules of Procedure, that it would be in the interests of the parties and the proper conduct of the proceedings before the Court not to extradite the eleven applicants to Russia until it had an opportunity to examine the application in the light of the information which the Georgian Government would provide. The Court invited Georgia to submit information on the measures that the Russian Government intended to take in their regard should the extradition go ahead. The interim measure was lifted after the Russian Government gave undertakings to the Court in connection with the applicants, promising in particular that the death penalty would not be applied to them; that their safety and health would be protected; and that they would be guaranteed unhindered access to the Court and free correspondence with it. The Court approaches as follows the weight to be given to such assurances:

European Court of Human Rights, *Shamayev and others* v. *Georgia and Russia* (Appl. No. 36378/02), judgment of 12 April 2005, paras. 343–53:

343. As to the assurances, the Court notes that they were submitted in respect of each of the applicants ... by the Acting Procurator-General, the highest prosecuting authority in criminal cases in Russia. The parties do not dispute that the Georgian Procurator-General also obtained verbal assurances from his Russian colleagues ... In the above-mentioned letters of guarantee, the Acting Russian Procurator-General formally assured the Georgian authorities that the applicants would not be sentenced to death and pointed out that, in any case, application of the death penalty had been forbidden in Russia since the 1996 moratorium. The letter of 27 September 2002 also included specific assurances, ruling out 'torture [and] treatment or punishment that was cruel, inhuman or contrary to human dignity'.

344. In assessing the credibility which the Georgian authorities could have attributed to those assurances, the Court considers it important that they were issued by the Procurator-General, who, within the Russian system, supervises the activities of all prosecutors in the Russian Federation, who, in turn, argue the prosecution case before the courts ... It is also appropriate to note that the prosecution authorities fulfil a supervisory role in respect of the rights of prisoners in the Russian Federation, and that this role includes, *inter alia*, the right to visit and supervise places of detention without hindrance ...

345. In fact, the Court finds nothing in the evidence submitted by the parties and obtained by its delegation in Tbilisi which could reasonably have given the Georgian authorities grounds to doubt the credibility of the guarantees provided by the Russian Procurator-General during the decision-making process. However, the merits of the Georgian authorities' reasoning and the reliability of the assurances in question must also be assessed in the light of the information and evidence obtained subsequent to the applicants' extradition, to which the Court attaches considerable importance.

346. It notes, firstly, that the Georgian authorities clearly agreed only to the extradition of those applicants whose identity could be substantiated ... and who had been in possession of Russian passports at the time of their arrest ...

348. The Court also takes into consideration the photographs of the extradited applicants and of their cells, together with the video recording made in the SIZO in town B and various medical certificates submitted by the Russian Government ... Even if, in certain respects, ... those documents are to be treated with caution, it does not appear that the extradited applicants have been detained in conditions which are contrary to Article 3 or that they have been subjected to treatment prohibited by that provision. In this regard, it is also appropriate to note that Mr Khadjiev and Mr Aziev, the only applicants to have been in correspondence with the Court following their extradition ..., have not complained at any time that they have been subjected to ill-treatment in Russia. Nor have they submitted any information about previous convictions in that country.

349. However, the Court does not overlook the fact that, following their extradition, with the exception of a few written exchanges with the Court, the applicants were deprived of an opportunity to express their version of the facts of the case freely and to inform the Court about their situation in Russia ... In those circumstances, the applicants themselves cannot be entirely blamed for not providing sufficient evidence after their extradition.

350. Nevertheless, it remains the case that the applicants' representatives, in alleging the existence of a risk to the applicants in Russia, have also failed to submit sufficient information as to the objective likelihood of the personal risk run by their clients as a result of extradition. The documents and reports from various international bodies to which they referred provide detailed but general information on acts of violence committed by the Russian Federation's armed forces against civilians in the Chechen Republic ... However, they do not establish that extradition would have imposed a personal threat on the extradited applicants (see *Čonka and others v. Belgium* (dec.), no. 51564/99, 13 March 2001, and also, *mutatis mutandis, H.L.R.* v. *France* [judgment of 29 April 1997], §42).

351. The applicants' representatives never referred to the manner in which the death sentence is executed in Russia, the conditions of detention while awaiting execution or other circumstances capable of bringing this punishment within the scope of Article 3 ... At no point did they indicate whether the applicants had previously been subjected to treatment that was contrary to this provision, nor did they refer to the applicants' personal experiences in connection with their ethnic origin or their previous political or military experience in the Chechen Republic. The lawyers merely referred to the general context of the armed conflict which is raging in this region and the extreme violence from which their clients all wished to flee. Supposing that the applicants did fight against federal troops within the context of that conflict, the Court has no information about their role and position within their community prior to August 2002, which prevents it from assessing the likelihood of personal risk arising from the applicants' previous history. It notes that the applicants heard by it in Tbilisi had all submitted that neither they nor the extradited applicants had been carrying weapons when they crossed the border ... Some of them even claimed to have been leading a peaceful civilian life in Chechnya or in the border regions of Georgia adjacent to Chechnya ... However, it does not appear from the judicial decisions in Georgia that this was really the case ... Whatever the truth, there is nothing in the evidence before it which enables the Court to consider the applicants as warlords, political figures or individuals who were well-known for other reasons in their country (contrast *Chahal*, cited above, p. 1861, §106), all factors which could have served to render tangible or increase the personal risk hanging over the applicants after they had been handed over to the Russian authorities.

352. Thus, in the absence of other specific information, the evidence submitted to the Court by the applicants' representatives concerning the general context of the conflict in the Chechen Republic does not establish that the applicants' personal situation was likely to expose them to the risk of treatment contrary to Article 3 of the Convention. The Court does not rule out the possibility that the applicants ran the risk of ill-treatment, although they submitted no evidence of previous experience in this connection (contrast *Hilal* v. *United Kingdom*, no. 45276/99, §64, ECHR 2001-II, and *Vilvarajah and others* [judgment of 26 September 1991] §§10, 22 and 33). A mere possibility of ill-treatment in such circumstances, however, is not in itself sufficient to give rise to a breach of Article 3 ..., especially as the Georgian authorities had obtained assurances from their Russian counterparts against even that possibility.

353. In consequence, the Court concludes that, in the light of the evidence in its possession, the facts of the case do not support 'beyond any reasonable doubt' the assertion that, at the time when the Georgian authorities took the decision, there were real or well-founded grounds

to believe that extradition would expose the applicants to a real and personal risk of inhuman or degrading treatment, within the meaning of Article 3 of the Convention. There has accordingly been no violation of that provision by Georgia.

3.4. Question for discussion: diplomatic assurances

Are there any conditions under which diplomatic assurances should be considered to render acceptable, under international human rights law, the return of certain foreigners to their country of origin or to a third country, in circumstances where such return would not be allowed in the absence of such assurances? Imagine a case in which a removal is made possible thanks to diplomatic assurances being obtained from the authorities of return, but where (a) the final decision to remove a person following the reception of these assurances can be challenged before an independent court, prior to its execution; (b) an independent monitoring system is established, allowing the person concerned to return to the State from which he/she is refouled if it appears that the commitments made by the authorities of the State where that person is removed are not complied with. Would this be acceptable? Could such a system be plausibly set up?

3 THE REGIME OF RIGHTS WHICH MAY BE RESTRICTED

3.1 The acceptability of limitations on human rights

Rights of an absolute character are the exception. In general, limitations may be imposed on human rights, provided three conditions are satisfied. First, any interference with a right should be prescribed by law (condition of legality). Second, it must be justified by the pursuance of a legitimate aim (condition of legitimacy). Third, the interference must be limited to what is necessary for the fulfilment of that aim, which means that it must be appropriate to pursuing the objective, and that it may not go beyond what is required in order to effectively achieve that aim – or, at a minimum, that all the interests involved should be carefully balanced against one another (condition of proportionality). The principles to which restrictions to rights should conform have been summarized thus by a group of eminent international law experts:

UN Sub-Commission on Prevention of Discrimination and Protection of Minorities, Siracusa Principles on the Limitation and Derogation of Provisions in the International Covenant on Civil and Political Rights, Annex, E/CN.4/1984/4 (1984) (also reproduced in *Human Rights Quarterly*, 7 (1985), 1–57):

A. General Interpretative Principles Relating to the Justification of Limitations

1. No limitations or grounds for applying them to rights guaranteed by the Covenant are permitted other than those contained in the terms of the Covenant itself.

2. The scope of a limitation referred to in the Covenant shall not be interpreted so as to jeopardize the essence of the right concerned.
3. All limitation clauses shall be interpreted strictly and in favor of the rights at issue.
4. All limitations shall be interpreted in the light and context of the particular right concerned.
5. All limitations on a right recognized by the Covenant shall be provided for by law and be compatible with the objects and purposes of the Covenant.
6. No limitation referred to in the Covenant shall be applied for any purpose other than that for which it has been prescribed.
7. No limitation shall be applied in an arbitrary manner.
8. Every limitation imposed shall be subject to the possibility of challenge to and remedy against its abusive application.
9. No limitation on a right recognized by the Covenant shall discriminate contrary to Article 2, paragraph 1.
10. Whenever a limitation is required in the terms of the Covenant to be 'necessary', this term implies that the limitation:

    (a) is based on one of the grounds justifying limitations recognized by the relevant article of the Covenant,
    (b) responds to a pressing public or social need,
    (c) pursues a legitimate aim, and
    (d) is proportionate to that aim.

Any assessment as to the necessity of a limitation shall be made on objective considerations.

11. In applying a limitation, a state shall use no more restrictive means than are required for the achievement of the purpose of the limitation.
12. The burden of justifying a limitation upon a right guaranteed under the Covenant lies with the state.
13. The requirement expressed in Article 12 of the Covenant, that any restrictions be consistent with other rights recognized in the Covenant, is implicit in limitations to the other rights recognized in the Covenant.
14. The limitation clauses of the Covenant shall not be interpreted to restrict the exercise of any human rights protected to a greater extent by other international obligations binding upon the state.

Article 18 ICCPR provides that 'Freedom to manifest one's religion or beliefs may be subject only to such limitations as are prescribed by law and are necessary to protect public safety, order, health, or morals or the fundamental rights and freedoms of others'; a similar formulation may be found in Article 12 para. 3 ICCPR as regards the right to liberty of movement and freedom to choose his residence, and the right to leave any country, which rights 'shall not be subject to any restrictions except those which are provided by law, are necessary to protect national security, public order (*ordre public*), public health or morals or the rights and freedoms of others, and are consistent with the other rights recognized in the present Covenant'. Even where the Covenant is less explicit, the same requirements have been identified by the Human

Rights Committee in other provisions of this instrument. For instance, whereas Article 17 ICCPR merely provides for the right of every person to be protected against 'arbitrary or unlawful interference with his privacy, family, home or correspondence as well as against unlawful attacks on his honour and reputation', this has been read by the Committee to include the following requirements:

Human Rights Committee, General Comment No. 16, *The Right to Respect of Privacy, Family, Home and Correspondence, and Protection of Honour and Reputation* (Art. 17) (8 April 1988):

3. The term 'unlawful' means that no interference can take place except in cases envisaged by the law. Interference authorized by States can only take place on the basis of law, which itself must comply with the provisions, aims and objectives of the Covenant.

4. The expression 'arbitrary interference' is also relevant to the protection of the right provided for in article 17. In the Committee's view the expression 'arbitrary interference' can also extend to interference provided for under the law. The introduction of the concept of arbitrariness is intended to guarantee that even interference provided for by law should be in accordance with the provisions, aims and objectives of the Covenant and should be, in any event, reasonable in the particular circumstances ...

7. As all persons live in society, the protection of privacy is necessarily relative. However, the competent public authorities should only be able to call for such information relating to an individual's private life the knowledge of which is essential in the interests of society as understood under the Covenant. Accordingly, the Committee recommends that States should indicate in their reports the laws and regulations that govern authorized interferences with private life.

8. Even with regard to interferences that conform to the Covenant, relevant legislation must specify in detail the precise circumstances in which such interferences may be permitted. A decision to make use of such authorized interference must be made only by the authority designated under the law, and on a case-by-case basis. Compliance with article 17 requires that the integrity and confidentiality of correspondence should be guaranteed de jure and de facto. Correspondence should be delivered to the addressee without interception and without being opened or otherwise read. Surveillance, whether electronic or otherwise, interceptions of telephonic, telegraphic and other forms of communication, wire-tapping and recording of conversations should be prohibited. Searches of a person's home should be restricted to a search for necessary evidence and should not be allowed to amount to harassment. So far as personal and body search is concerned, effective measures should ensure that such searches are carried out in a manner consistent with the dignity of the person who is being searched. Persons being subjected to body search by State officials, or medical personnel acting at the request of the State, should only be examined by persons of the same sex.

The requirements thus formulated in the specific context of the International Covenant on Civil and Political Rights in fact may be generalized to all human rights treaties, whose regimes of limitations follow a same basic structure. For instance, Article 30 of the American Convention on Human Rights states:

The restrictions that, pursuant to this Convention, may be placed on the enjoyment or exercise of the rights or freedoms recognized herein may not be applied except in accordance with laws enacted for reasons of general interest and in accordance with the purpose for which such restrictions have been established.

These requirements are by no means limited to interferences with civil and political rights. In concluding the International Covenant on Economic, Social and Cultural Rights, the States Parties recognized that, 'in the enjoyment of those rights provided by the State in conformity with the present Covenant, the State may subject such rights only to such limitations as are determined by law only in so far as this may be compatible with the nature of these rights and solely for the purpose of promoting the general welfare in a democratic society' (Art. 4 ICESCR):

Limburg Principles on the Implementation of the International Covenant on Economic, Social and Cultural Rights adopted in Maastricht on 2–6 June 1986:

46. Article 4 was primarily intended to be protective of the rights of individuals rather than permissive of the imposition of limitations by the State.

47. The article was not meant to introduce limitations on rights affecting the subsistence or survival of the individual or integrity of the person.

'determined by law'

48. No limitation on the exercise of economic, social and cultural rights shall be made unless provided for by national law of general application which is consistent with the Covenant and is in force at the time the limitation is applied.

49. Laws imposing limitations on the exercise of economic, social and cultural rights shall not be arbitrary or unreasonable or discriminatory.

50. Legal rules limiting the exercise of economic, social and cultural rights shall be clear and accessible to everyone.

51. Adequate safeguards and effective remedies shall be provided by law against illegal or abusive imposition on application of limitations on economic, social and cultural rights.

'promoting the general welfare'

52. This term shall be construed to mean furthering the well-being of the people as a whole.

'in a democratic society'

53. The expression 'in a democratic society' shall be interpreted as imposing a further restriction on the application of limitations.

54. The burden is upon a State imposing limitations to demonstrate that the limitations do not impair the democratic functioning of the society.

55. While there is no single model of a democratic society, a society which recognizes and respects the human rights set forth in the United Nations Charter and the Universal Declaration of Human Rights may be viewed as meeting this definition.

'compatible with the nature of these rights'

56. The restriction 'compatible with the nature of these rights' requires that a limitation shall not be interpreted or applied so as to jeopardize the essence of the right concerned.

While the different human rights expert bodies or courts have applied this test in a variety of ways, and while their approach is not in all respects uniform, the basic grammar used in order to examine the acceptability of restrictions being imposed to fundamental rights is essentially the same throughout all jurisdictions. A typical formulation is provided by the Human Rights Committee in the following General Comment:

Human Rights Committee, General Comment No. 27, *Freedom of Movement* (Art. 12) (2 November 1999) (CCPR/C/21/Rev.1/Add. 9):

11. Article 12, paragraph 3, provides for exceptional circumstances in which rights under paragraphs 1 and 2 may be restricted. This provision authorizes the State to restrict these rights only to protect national security, public order (*ordre public*), public health or morals and the rights and freedoms of others. To be permissible, restrictions must be provided by law, must be necessary in a democratic society for the protection of these purposes and must be consistent with all other rights recognized in the Covenant ...

12. The law itself has to establish the conditions under which the rights may be limited. State reports should therefore specify the legal norms upon which restrictions are founded. Restrictions which are not provided for in the law or are not in conformity with the requirements of article 12, paragraph 3, would violate the rights guaranteed by paragraphs 1 and 2.

13. In adopting laws providing for restrictions permitted by article 12, paragraph 3, States should always be guided by the principle that the restrictions must not impair the essence of the right (cf. art. 5, para. 1); the relation between right and restriction, between norm and exception, must not be reversed. The laws authorizing the application of restrictions should use precise criteria and may not confer unfettered discretion on those charged with their execution.

14. Article 12, paragraph 3, clearly indicates that it is not sufficient that the restrictions serve the permissible purposes; they must also be necessary to protect them. Restrictive measures must conform to the principle of proportionality; they must be appropriate to achieve their protective function; they must be the least intrusive instrument amongst those which might achieve the desired result; and they must be proportionate to the interest to be protected.

15. The principle of proportionality has to be respected not only in the law that frames the restrictions, but also by the administrative and judicial authorities in applying the law. States should ensure that any proceedings relating to the exercise or restriction of these rights are expeditious and that reasons for the application of restrictive measures are provided.

16. States have often failed to show that the application of their laws restricting the rights enshrined in article 12, paragraphs 1 and 2, are in conformity with all requirements referred to in article 12, paragraph 3. The application of restrictions in any individual case must be based on clear legal grounds and meet the test of necessity and the requirements of proportionality. These conditions would not be met, for example, if an individual were prevented from leaving a country merely on the ground that he or she is the holder of 'State secrets', or if an individual were prevented from travelling internally without a specific permit. On the other hand, the conditions could be met by restrictions on access to military zones on national security grounds, or limitations on the freedom to settle in areas inhabited by indigenous or minorities communities.

The next sections offer certain clarifications on the three conditions which apply to restrictions to fundamental rights: legality (section 3.2.), legitimacy (section 3.3), and proportionality (section 3.4.). In order to illustrate the regime applicable to restrictions of rights, we then turn to a number of cases – respectively from the European Court of Human Rights, from the Human Rights Committee, and from the Canadian Supreme Court – which concern the imposition of vestimentary codes which, in different circumstances, were denounced as resulting in a violation of freedom of religion (section 3.5.).

3.2 The condition of legality

As we have seen, the condition of legality requires that the relevant legislation, on the basis of which the restriction is imposed, must specify in detail the precise circumstances in which such interferences may be permitted. The Inter-American Court of Human Rights has developed a particularly demanding interpretation of the requirement according to which any restriction or suspension of rights should be established according to the principle of legality. It takes the following view:

> **Inter-American Court of Human Rights, *The Word 'Laws' in Article 30 of the American Convention on Human Rights*, Advisory Opinion OC–06/86, of 9 May 1986, paras. 22 and 24:**
>
> In order to guarantee human rights, it is ... essential that state actions affecting basic rights not be left to the discretion of the government but, rather, that they be surrounded by a set of guarantees designed to ensure that the inviolable attributes of the individual not be impaired. Perhaps the most important of these guarantees is that restrictions to basic rights only be established by a law passed by the Legislature in accordance with the Constitution ...
>
> Such a procedure not only clothes these acts with the assent of the people through its representatives, but also allows minority groups to express their disagreement, propose different initiatives, participate in the shaping of the political will, or influence public opinion so as to prevent the majority from acting arbitrarily. [The law thus enacted] must [not only be] formally proclaimed but there must also be a system that will effectively ensure their application and an effective control of the manner in which the organs exercise their powers.

Similar requirements are not imposed under other international instruments. Far more common is the understanding of the principle of legality adopted under the Siracusa Principles on the Limitation and Derogation of Provisions in the International Covenant on Civil and Political Rights, which state that the expression 'prescribed by law' in that treaty must be seen as imposing a requirement of transparency and accessibility, and as a protection from arbitrariness. 'Law', in that sense, is understood in the material, rather than in the formal sense:

UN Sub-Commission on Prevention of Discrimination and Protection of Minorities, Siracusa Principles on the Limitation and Derogation of Provisions in the International Covenant on Civil and Political Rights, Annex, E/CN.4/1984/4 (1984):

15. No limitation on the exercise of human rights shall be made unless provided for by national law of general application which is consistent with the Covenant and is in force at the time the limitation is applied.

16. Laws imposing limitations on the exercise of human rights shall not be arbitrary or unreasonable.

17. Legal rules limiting the exercise of human rights shall be clear and accessible to everyone.

18. Adequate safeguards and effective remedies shall be provided by law against illegal or abusive imposition or application of limitations on human rights.

This is also in substance the position adopted by the Human Rights Committee:

Human Rights Committee, *Pinkney* v. *Canada*, Communication No. 27/1978, final views of 29 October 1981 (CCPR/C/OP/1 at 95):

31. Mr Pinkney [serving a prison sentence in Canada] complains that while detained at the Lower Mainland Regional Correction Centre he was prevented from communicating with outside officials and was thereby subjected to arbitrary or unlawful interference with his correspondence contrary to article 17(1) of the Covenant. In its submission of 22 July 1981 the State party gives the following explanation of the practice with regard to the control of prisoners' correspondence at the Correction Centre:

Mr Pinkney, as a person awaiting trial, was entitled under section 1.21(c) of the Gaol Rules and Regulations, 1961, British Columbia Regulations 73/61, in force at the time of his detention to the 'provision of writing material for communicating by letter with (his) friends or for conducting correspondence or preparing notes in connexion with (his) defence'. The Government of Canada does not deny that letters sent by Mr Pinkney were subject to control and could even be censored. Section 2.40(b) of the Gaol Rules and Regulations, 1961 is clear on that point:

2.40(b) Every letter to or from a prisoner shall (except as hereinafter provided in these regulations in the case of certain communications to or from a legal adviser) be read by the Warden or by a responsible officer deputed by him for the purpose, and it is within the discretion of the Warden to stop or censor any letter, or any part of a letter, on the ground that its contents are objectionable or that the letter is of excessive length.

Section 42 of the Correctional Centre Rules and Regulations, British Columbia Regulation 284/78, which came into force on 6 July 1978 provides that:

42(1) A director or a person authorized by the director may examine all correspondence other than privileged correspondence between an inmate and another person where he is of the opinion that the correspondence may threaten the management, operation, discipline or security of the correctional centre.

(2) Where in the opinion of the director, or a person authorized by the director, correspondence contains matter that threatens the management, operation, discipline or security of the correctional centre, the director or person authorized by the director may censor that matter.

(3) The director may withhold money, or drugs, weapons, or any other object which may threaten the management, operation, discipline, or security of a correctional centre, or an object in contravention of the rules established for the correctional centre by the director contained in correspondence, and where this is done the director shall

(a) Advise the inmate,
(b) In so far as the money or object is not held as evidence for the prosecution of an offence against an enactment of the province or of Canada, place the money or object in safe-keeping and give it to the inmate on his release from the correctional centre, and
(c) Carry out his duties under this section in a manner that, in so far as is reasonable, respects the privacy of the inmate and person corresponding with the inmate.

(4) An inmate may receive books or periodicals sent to him directly from the publisher.
(5) Every inmate may send as many letters per week as he sees fit.

32. Although these rules were only enacted subsequent to Mr Pinkney's departure from the Lower Mainland Regional Correction Centre, in practice they were being applied when he was detained in that institution. This means that privileged correspondence, defined in section 1 of the regulations as meaning 'correspondence addressed by an inmate to a Member of Parliament, Members of the Legislative Assembly, barrister or solicitor, commissioner of corrections, regional director of corrections, chaplain, or the director of inspection and standards', were not examined or subject to any control or censorship. As for non-privileged correspondence, it was only subject to censorship if it contained matter that threatened the management, operation, discipline, or security of the correctional centre. At the time when Mr Pinkney was detained therein, the procedure governing prisoners' correspondence did not allow for a general restriction on the right to communicate with government officials. Mr Pinkney was not denied this right. To seek to restrict his communication with various government officials while at the same time allowing his access to his lawyers would seem a futile gesture since through his lawyers, he could put his case to the various government officials whom he was allegedly prevented from contacting ...

34. No specific evidence has been submitted by Mr Pinkney to establish that his correspondence was subjected to control or censorship which was not in accordance with the practice described by the State party. However, article 17 of the Covenant provides not only that 'No one shall be subjected to arbitrary or unlawful interference with his correspondence' but also that 'Everyone has the right to the protection of the law against such interference.' At the time when Mr Pinkney was detained at the Lower Mainland Regional Correction Centre the only law in force governing the control and censorship of prisoners' correspondence appears to have been section 2.40(b) of the Gaol Rules and Regulations, 1961. A legislative provision in the very general terms of this section did not, in the opinion of the Committee, in itself provide satisfactory legal safeguards against arbitrary application, though, as the Committee has already found, there is no evidence to establish that Mr Pinkney was himself the victim of a violation of the Covenant as a result. The Committee also observes that section 42 of the Correctional Centre Rules and Regulations that came into force on 6 July 1978 has now made the relevant law considerably more specific in its terms.

In United States constitutional law, a criminal provision that is vague can be found invalid on its face 'for either of two independent reasons. First, it may fail to provide the kind of notice that will enable ordinary people to understand what conduct it prohibits; second, it may authorize and even encourage arbitrary and discriminatory enforcement' (*City of Chicago* v. *Morales et al.*, 527 U.S. 41 (1999) (finding a loitering ordinance unconstitutionally vague); see also, for a very explicit statement in this regard, *Grayned* v. *City of Rockford*, 408 U.S. 104 at 108–9 (1972)). These are also the two values that are protected by the requirement of legality in international human rights law. Vagueness can lead the individual to abstain from exercising certain freedoms, out of fear that he or she might be subject to certain penalties or sanctions, when the conduct that is prohibited is not defined with sufficient clarity. It creates, in other terms, a 'chilling effect' on the exercise of these freedoms. In addition, vagueness creates a risk of arbitrariness and, hence, discrimination, in the enforcement of the law, in violation of the principle of equality before the law (on this principle, see chapter 7, section 2.1.).

However, the requirement of legality in the interference with human rights has not been interpreted uniformly throughout all situations in which it was invoked. The European Court of Human Rights for instance, has occasionally insisted on the 'quality of the law' providing for a restriction to the individual right, thus adding a new set of requirements concerning the guarantees provided by the legal framework. This is illustrated by the two following cases, which concern respectively the right to respect for private life and freedom of association:

European Court of Human Rights (GC), *Rotaru* v. *Romania* (Appl. No. 28341/95), judgment of 4 May 2000:

[In 1989, after the communist regime had been overthrown in Romania, Legislative Decree No. 118/1990 was passed, granting certain rights to those who had been persecuted by the communist regime and who had not engaged in Fascist activities. In accordance with this legislation, the applicant sought to have a prison sentence that had been imposed in a 1948 judgment for political activities taken into account in the calculation of his length of service at work. He also sought payment of the corresponding retirement entitlements. However, in the course of those proceedings, the Ministry of the Interior submitted to the Court a letter of 19 December 1990 that it had received from the Romanian Intelligence Service (RIS), stating that Aurel Rotaru had been a member of the Romanian extreme-right legionnaire movement and that he had no criminal record and, contrary to what he maintained, was not imprisoned during the period he mentioned. This, Mr Rotaru considered to be defamatory, and he sued for damages. The Romanian courts found that the information that the applicant had been a legionnaire was false. The claim for damages was dismissed, however, on the ground that the RIS could not be held to have been negligent as it was merely the depositary of the impugned information, and that in the absence of negligence the rules on tortious liability did not apply. Before the European Court of Human Rights, Mr Rotaru complained that the RIS held and could at any moment make use of information about his private life, some of which was false and defamatory. He alleged a violation of Article 8 of the Convention, which guarantees the right to respect for private life.]

52. The Court reiterates its settled case law, according to which the expression 'in accordance with the law' not only requires that the impugned measure should have some basis in domestic law, but also refers to the quality of the law in question, requiring that it should be accessible to the person concerned and foreseeable as to its effects ...

53. In the instant case the Court notes that Article 6 of Legislative Decree No. 118/1990, which the Government relied on as the basis for the impugned measure, allows any individual to prove that he satisfies the requirements for having certain rights conferred on him, by means of official documents issued by the relevant authorities or any other material of evidential value. However, the provision does not lay down the manner in which such evidence may be obtained and does not confer on the RIS any power to gather, store or release information about a person's private life.

The Court must therefore determine whether Law No. 14/1992 on the organisation and operation of the RIS, which was likewise relied on by the Government, can provide the legal basis for these measures. In this connection, it notes that the law in question authorises the RIS to gather, store and make use of information affecting national security. The Court has doubts as to the relevance to national security of the information held on the applicant. Nevertheless, it reiterates that it is primarily for the national authorities, notably the courts, to interpret and apply domestic law ... and notes that in its judgment of 25 November 1997 the Bucharest Court of Appeal confirmed that it was lawful for the RIS to hold this information as depositary of the archives of the former security services.

That being so, the Court may conclude that the storing of information about the applicant's private life had a basis in Romanian law.

54. As to the accessibility of the law, the Court regards that requirement as having been satisfied, seeing that Law No. 14/1992 was published in Romania's Official Gazette on 3 March 1992.

55. As regards the requirement of foreseeability, the Court reiterates that a rule is 'foreseeable' if it is formulated with sufficient precision to enable any individual – if need be with appropriate advice – to regulate his conduct. The Court has stressed the importance of this concept with regard to secret surveillance in the following terms (see the *Malone* v. *United Kingdom* judgment of 2 August 1984, Series A No. 82, p. 32, §67 ...):

'The Court would reiterate its opinion that the phrase 'in accordance with the law' does not merely refer back to domestic law but also relates to the quality of the 'law', requiring it to be compatible with the rule of law, which is expressly mentioned in the preamble to the Convention ... The phrase thus implies – and this follows from the object and purpose of Article 8 – that there must be a measure of legal protection in domestic law against arbitrary interferences by public authorities with the rights safeguarded by paragraph 1 ... Especially where a power of the executive is exercised in secret, the risks of arbitrariness are evident ...

... Since the implementation in practice of measures of secret surveillance of communications is not open to scrutiny by the individuals concerned or the public at large, it would be contrary to the rule of law for the legal discretion granted to the executive to be expressed in terms of an unfettered power. Consequently, the law must indicate the scope of any such discretion conferred on the competent authorities and the manner of its exercise with sufficient clarity, having regard to the legitimate aim of the measure in question, to give the individual adequate protection against arbitrary interference.'

56. The 'quality' of the legal rules relied on in this case must therefore be scrutinised, with a view, in particular, to ascertaining whether domestic law laid down with sufficient precision the circumstances in which the RIS could store and make use of information relating to the applicant's private life.

57. The Court notes in this connection that section 8 of Law No. 14/1992 provides that information affecting national security may be gathered, recorded and archived in secret files.

No provision of domestic law, however, lays down any limits on the exercise of those powers. Thus, for instance, the aforesaid Law does not define the kind of information that may be recorded, the categories of people against whom surveillance measures such as gathering and keeping information may be taken, the circumstances in which such measures may be taken or the procedure to be followed. Similarly, the Law does not lay down limits on the age of information held or the length of time for which it may be kept.

Section 45 of the Law empowers the RIS to take over for storage and use the archives that belonged to the former intelligence services operating on Romanian territory and allows inspection of RIS documents with the Director's consent.

The Court notes that this section contains no explicit, detailed provision concerning the persons authorised to consult the files, the nature of the files, the procedure to be followed or the use that may be made of the information thus obtained.

58. It also notes that although section 2 of the Law empowers the relevant authorities to permit interferences necessary to prevent and counteract threats to national security, the ground allowing such interferences is not laid down with sufficient precision.

59. The Court must also be satisfied that there exist adequate and effective safeguards against abuse, since a system of secret surveillance designed to protect national security entails the risk of undermining or even destroying democracy on the ground of defending it ...

In order for systems of secret surveillance to be compatible with Article 8 of the Convention, they must contain safeguards established by law which apply to the supervision of the relevant services' activities. Supervision procedures must follow the values of a democratic society as faithfully as possible, in particular the rule of law, which is expressly referred to in the Preamble to the Convention. The rule of law implies, *inter alia*, that interference by the executive authorities with an individual's rights should be subject to effective supervision, which should normally be carried out by the judiciary, at least in the last resort, since judicial control affords the best guarantees of independence, impartiality and a proper procedure ...

60. In the instant case the Court notes that the Romanian system for gathering and archiving information does not provide such safeguards, no supervision procedure being provided by Law No. 14/1992, whether while the measure ordered is in force or afterwards.

61. That being so, the Court considers that domestic law does not indicate with reasonable clarity the scope and manner of exercise of the relevant discretion conferred on the public authorities.

62. The Court concludes that the holding and use by the RIS of information on the applicant's private life were not 'in accordance with the law', a fact that suffices to constitute a violation of Article 8. Furthermore, in the instant case that fact prevents the Court from reviewing the legitimacy of the aim pursued by the measures ordered and determining whether they were – assuming the aim to have been legitimate – 'necessary in a democratic society'.

63. There has consequently been a violation of Article 8.

Box 3.1. **The right to respect for private life and the processing of personal data**

It is noteworthy that the *Rotaru* judgment concerns information related to public demonstrations in which the author had allegedly taken part, or to writings he was initially said to have authored, rather than to elements belonging to his 'private life'. Indeed, the judgment delivered by the European Court of Human Rights in this case is the first in which Article 8 ECHR, which guarantees the right to respect for private life, is explicitly applied to the processing of personal data, *whether or not such data relate to the private life of the individual*. Historically, the two guarantees have developed separately, and they initially pursued two quite different objectives. In its original definition, the right to respect for private life seeks to protect a sphere of intimacy for individuals and families: it has been described famously as 'the claim of individuals, groups, or institutions to determine for themselves when, how, and to what extent information about them is communicated to others' (A. F. Westin, *Privacy and Freedom* (New York: Atheneum, 1967), p. 1). It was this dimension of privacy that Samuel D. Warren and Louis D. Brandeis sought to define as protected under the common law doctrine of torts in their seminal article of 1890, where they wrote: 'Recent inventions and business methods call attention to the next step which must be taken for the protection of the person, and for securing to the individual what Judge Cooley calls the right "to be let alone". Instantaneous photographs and newspaper enterprise have invaded the sacred precincts of private and domestic life; and numerous mechanical devices threaten to make good the prediction that "what is whispered in the closet shall be proclaimed from the house-tops" ' (S. D. Warren and L. D. Brandeis, 'The Right to Privacy', *Harvard Law Review*, 4 (1890), 193)

But the emergence of computerization and databanks in the 1970s has led to new threats to the freedom of individuals, quite different from these – although they too were anticipated, in part, by Westin. The systematic processing of information related to the individual – whether or not that information relates to his/her private life – may encourage decisions based on automatic processes; it may lead to the establishment of 'profiles'; and thus, to systematic stereotyping. Originally, the new threats to individual freedom that stemmed from the power of computers to process information were seen as distinct from infringements into the 'privacy' of individuals, understood as the information they had a right not to divulge. For instance, the Council of Europe adopted a Convention for the Protection of Individuals with regard to Automatic Processing of Personal Data (CETS, No. 108), signed on 28 January 1981, which was based on the recognition that it was 'desirable to *extend* the safeguards for everyone's rights and fundamental freedoms, and in particular the right to the respect for privacy, taking account of the increasing flow across frontiers of personal data undergoing automatic processing' (Preamble – emphasis added). Article 8 ECHR was not considered to be sufficient in this regard, since it was interpreted, both by the Court and by commentators, as only shielding individuals from the risks of unwanted intrusion into a sphere of intimacy. In contrast, 'personal data', the automated processing of which was seen to call for regulation, is 'any information relating to an identified or identifiable individual' (Art. 1 of the Convention for the Protection of Individuals with regard to Automatic Processing of Personal Data), whether such information relates to the 'private life' of the individual (i.e. which he/she could reasonably expect not to be in the public domain), or whether it relates to his/her 'public' life: for instance, birthdates, addresses, social security numbers, but also bibliographies or the list of public events in which an individual took part, are all 'personal data' that cannot be processed without certain principles being complied with.

At the time of its adoption in 1981, the Convention for the Protection of Individuals with regard to Automatic Processing of Personal Data was the most advanced international instrument in this area – although it was inspired primarily by the French law of 1978 'Informatique et libertés' (loi No. 78–17 relative à l'informatique, aux fichiers et aux libertés, 6 January 1978). The Council of Europe Convention established the main principles that have since been structuring the protection of the individual *vis-à-vis* the processing of personal data. These principles relate, first, to the quality of the data: data may only be processed if they are obtained and processed fairly and lawfully (it is here that the protection of privacy *vis-à-vis* the processing of personal data intersects with the traditional protection of privacy as intimacy – data obtained in violation of privacy rights cannot be processed); they must be stored for specified and legitimate purposes and not used in a way incompatible with those purposes; they must be adequate, relevant and not excessive in relation to the purposes for which they are stored; they must be accurate and, where necessary, kept up to date; and they must be preserved in a form which permits identification of the data subjects for no longer than is required for the purpose for which those data are stored. In addition, the Convention provides that 'special categories' of personal data (those revealing racial origin, political opinions or religious or other beliefs, those concerning health or sexual life, or those related to criminal convictions) require specific safeguards. The Convention also guarantees certain rights of the data subject, such as the right to be informed about the existence of an automated personal data file, its main purposes, as well as the identity of the controller of the file, and the right to have data rectified or erased if they have not been processed in accordance with the principles of the Convention. Most of these principles have inspired the United Nations Guidelines for the Regulation of Computerized Personal Data Files, adopted by General Assembly Resolution 45/95 of 14 December 1990.

European Court of Human Rights (GC), *Gorzelik and others* v. *Poland* (Appl. No. 44158/98), judgment of 17 February 2004:

[The applicants, who describe themselves as 'Silesians', decided together with 190 other persons to form an association called 'Union of People of Silesian Nationality'. They sought to have their association registered in accordance with section 8(2) of the Law on Associations of 7 April 1989. The Polish authorities refused this, however, on the grounds that the memorandum of association used such terms as 'Silesian nation' and 'Silesian national minority', whereas such a national minority was denied to exist. In rejecting the final appeal of the applicants, the Polish Supreme Court noted in particular: '"National minority" is a legal term (see Article 35 of the Constitution of 2 February 1997), although it is not defined either in Polish law or in the conventions relied on in the appeal on points of law. However, the explanatory report to the [Council of Europe Framework Convention for the Protection of National Minorities] states plainly that the individual's subjective choice of a nation is inseparably linked to objective criteria relevant to his or her national identity. That means that a subjective declaration of belonging to a specific national group implies prior social acceptance of the existence of the national group in question ... An individual has the right to choose his or her nation but this ... does not in itself lead to the establishment of a new, distinct nation or national minority. There was, and still is, a common perception that a Silesian ethnic group does exist; however, this group has never been regarded as a national group and has not claimed to be regarded as such. Registration of the association, which in paragraph 30 of its memorandum of association states that it is an organisation of a [specific] national minority, would be in breach of the law because it would result in a non-existent "national minority" taking advantage of privileges conferred on [genuine] national minorities. This concerns, in particular, the privileges granted by the 1993 Elections Act.' Before the European Court of Human Rights, the applicants subsequently alleged a violation of their freedom of association. One of the questions submitted to the Court was whether, despite the absence of a definition of the notion of 'national minority', this criterion could be relied upon by the Polish authorities in order to refuse to register an association.]

64. The Court reiterates that the expression 'prescribed by law' requires firstly that the impugned measure should have a basis in domestic law. It also refers to the quality of the law in question, requiring that it be accessible to the persons concerned and formulated with sufficient precision to enable them – if need be, with appropriate advice – to foresee, to a degree that is reasonable in the circumstances, the consequences which a given action may entail and to regulate their conduct.

However, it is a logical consequence of the principle that laws must be of general application that the wording of statutes is not always precise. The need to avoid excessive rigidity and to keep pace with changing circumstances means that many laws are inevitably couched in terms which, to a greater or lesser extent, are vague. The interpretation and application of such enactments depend on practice (see *Rekvényi* v. *Hungary* [GC], No. 25390/94, §34, ECHR 1999-III, and, as a recent authority, *Refah Partisi (the Welfare Party) and others* v. *Turkey* [GC], Nos. 41340/98, 41342/98, 41343/98 and 41344/98, §57, ECHR 2003–II, with further references).

65. The scope of the notion of foreseeability depends to a considerable degree on the content of the instrument in question, the field it is designed to cover and the number and status of those to whom it is addressed.

It must also be borne in mind that, however clearly drafted a legal provision may be, its application involves an inevitable element of judicial interpretation, since there will always be a need for clarification of doubtful points and for adaptation to particular circumstances. A margin of doubt in relation to borderline facts does not by itself make a legal provision unforeseeable in its application. Nor does the mere fact that such a provision is capable of more than one construction mean that it fails to meet the requirement of 'foreseeability' for the purposes of the Convention. The role of adjudication vested in the courts is precisely to dissipate such interpretational doubts as remain, taking into account the changes in everyday practice (see *Refah Partisi (the Welfare Party) and others* and *Rekvényi*, cited above).

66. Turning to the circumstances of the present case, the Court observes that the applicants' arguments as to the alleged unforeseeablity of Polish law do not concern the legal provisions on which the refusal to register their association was actually based, namely Article 32 of the Constitution and various provisions of the Law on associations and the Civil Code ...

The Court notes in this respect that the Law on associations gives the courts the power to register associations (section 8) and in this context to verify, *inter alia*, the conformity with the law of the memorandum of association (section 16), including the power to refuse registration if it is found that the conditions of the Law on associations have not been met (section 14) ...

In the present case the Polish courts refused registration because they considered that the applicants' association could not legitimately describe itself as an 'organisation of a national minority', a description which would give it access to the electoral privileges conferred under section 5 of the 1993 Elections Act ..., as the Silesian people did not constitute a 'national minority' under Polish law.

The applicants essentially criticised the absence of any definition of a national minority or any procedure whereby such a minority could obtain recognition under domestic law. They contended that that lacuna in the law made it impossible for them to foresee what criteria they were required to fulfil to have their association registered and left an unlimited discretionary power in that sphere to the authorities ...

67. It is not for the Court to express a view on the appropriateness of methods chosen by the legislature of a respondent State to regulate a given field. Its task is confined to determining whether the methods adopted and the effects they entail are in conformity with the Convention.

With regard to the applicants' argument that Polish law did not provide any definition of a 'national minority', the Court observes firstly, that ... such a definition would be very difficult to formulate. In particular, the notion is not defined in any international treaty, including the Council of Europe Framework Convention (see ... for example, Article 27 of the United Nations International Covenant on Civil and Political Rights, Article 39 of the United Nations Convention on the Rights of the Child and the 1992 United Nations Declaration on the Rights of Persons Belonging to National or Ethnic, Religious and Linguistic Minorities).

Likewise, practice regarding official recognition by States of national, ethnic or other minorities within their population varies from country to country or even within countries. The choice as to what form such recognition should take and whether it should be implemented through international treaties or bilateral agreements or incorporated into the Constitution or a special statute must, by the nature of things, be left largely to the State concerned, as it will depend on particular national circumstances.

68. While it appears to be a commonly shared European view that, as laid down in the preamble to the Framework Convention, 'the upheavals of European history have shown that the protection of national minorities is essential to stability, democratic security and peace on this continent' and that respect for them is a condition *sine qua non* for a democratic society, it cannot be said that the Contracting States are obliged by international law to adopt a particular concept of 'national minority' in their legislation or to introduce a procedure for the official recognition of minority groups.

69. In Poland the rules applicable to national or ethnic minorities are not to be found in a single document, but are divided between a variety of instruments, including the Constitution, electoral law and international agreements. The constitutional guarantees are afforded to both

national and ethnic minorities. The Constitution makes no distinction between national and ethnic minorities as regards their religious, linguistic and cultural identities, the preservation, maintenance and development of their language, customs, traditions and culture, or the establishment of educational and cultural institutions ... In contrast, electoral law introduces special privileges only in favour of 'registered organisations of national minorities' ... It does not give any indication as to the criteria a 'national minority' must fulfil in order to have its organisation registered.

However, the Court considers that the lack of an express definition of the concept of 'national minority' in the domestic legislation does not mean that the Polish State was in breach of its duty to frame law in sufficiently precise terms. Nor does it find any breach on account of the fact that the Polish State chose to recognise minorities through bilateral agreements with neighbouring countries rather than under a specific internal procedure. The Court recognises that, for the reasons explained above, in the area under consideration it may be difficult to frame laws with a high degree of precision. It may well even be undesirable to formulate rigid rules. The Polish State cannot, therefore, be criticised for using only a general statutory categorisation of minorities and leaving interpretation and application of those notions to practice.

70. Consequently, the Court does not consider that leaving to the authorities a discretion to determine the applicable criteria with regard to the concept of 'registered associations of national minorities' underlying section 5 of the 1993 Elections Act was, as the applicants alleged, tantamount to granting them an unlimited and arbitrary power of appreciation. As regards the registration procedure, it was both inevitable and consistent with the adjudicative role vested in them for the national courts to be left with the task of interpreting the notion of 'national minority', as distinguished from 'ethnic minority' within the meaning of the Constitution, and assessing whether the applicants' association qualified as an 'organisation of a national minority' ...

71. In reviewing the relevant principles, the [Polish courts] took into consideration all the statutory provisions applicable to associations and national minorities as well as social factors and other legal factors, including all the legal consequences that registering the applicants' association in the form they proposed might entail ...

Contrary to what the applicants have alleged, those courts do not appear to have needlessly transformed the registration procedure into a dispute over the concept of Silesian nationality. Rather, it was the statement in paragraph 30 of the memorandum of association that made it necessary to consider that issue in the proceedings ... The applicants must have been aware, when that paragraph was drafted, that the courts would have no alternative but to interpret the notion of 'national minority' as it applied in their case.

Having regard to the foregoing, the Court is satisfied that the Polish law applicable in the present case was formulated with sufficient precision, for the purposes of paragraph 2 of Article 11 of the Convention, to enable the applicants to regulate their conduct.

The following case is also instructive, for two reasons. First, it illustrates how the requirement of legality may apply to interferences committed by private parties – in this case, a private employer monitoring communications by its employee. Second, it shows the added value of this requirement. In the absence of clear and accessible regulations stipulating under which conditions interferences may take place, individuals may be reluctant to exercise their freedoms, since they cannot know in advance when such freedoms may be restricted and which sanctions may be imposed on them; this produces the 'chilling effect' referred to above, which the requirement of legality seeks to avoid.

European Court of Human Rights (4th sect.), *Copland* v. *United Kingdom* (Appl. No. 62617/00), judgment of 3 April 2007:

[The applicant was employed since 1991 by Carmarthenshire College. During her employment, and up to November 1999, the applicant's telephone, e-mail and internet usage were subjected to monitoring at the Deputy Principal (DP)'s instigation. According to the Government, this monitoring took place in order to ascertain whether the applicant was making excessive use of College facilities for personal purposes. The Government stated that the monitoring of telephone usage consisted of analysis of the College telephone bills showing telephone numbers called, the dates and times of the calls and their length and cost. The applicant also believed that there had been detailed and comprehensive logging of the length of calls, the number of calls received and made and the telephone numbers of individuals calling her. She stated that on at least one occasion the DP became aware of the name of an individual with whom she had exchanged incoming and outgoing telephone calls. The applicant's internet usage was also monitored by the DP. This monitoring took the form of analysing the web sites visited, the times and dates of the visits to the web sites and their duration. At the relevant time there was no general right to privacy in English law. The Regulation of Investigatory Powers Act 2000 provided for the regulation of, *inter alia*, interception of communications. The Telecommunications (Lawful Business Practice) Regulations 2000 were promulgated under the 2000 Act and came into force on 24 October 2000. The Regulations set out the circumstances in which employers could record or monitor employees' communications (such as e-mail or telephone) without the consent of either the employee or the other party to the communication. Employers were required to take reasonable steps to inform employees that their communications might be intercepted.]

45. The Court recalls that it is well established in the case law that the term 'in accordance with the law' implies – and this follows from the object and purpose of Article 8 – that there must be a measure of legal protection in domestic law against arbitrary interferences by public authorities with the rights safeguarded by Article 8 §1. This is all the more so in areas such as the monitoring in question, in view of the lack of public scrutiny and the risk of misuse of power ...

46. This expression not only requires compliance with domestic law, but also relates to the quality of that law, requiring it to be compatible with the rule of law (see, *inter alia, Khan* v. *United Kingdom*, judgment of 12 May 2000, *Reports of Judgments and Decisions* 2000–V, §26; *P.G. and J.H.* v. *United Kingdom*, No. 44787/98, ECHR 2001–IX, §44). In order to fulfil the requirement of foreseeability, the law must be sufficiently clear in its terms to give individuals an adequate indication as to the circumstances in which and the conditions on which the authorities are empowered to resort to any such measures (see *Halford*, [judgment of 25 June 1997] §49 and *Malone*, [judgment of 2 August 1984] §67).

47. The Court is not convinced by the Government's submission that the College was authorised under its statutory powers to do 'anything necessary or expedient' for the purposes of providing higher and further education, and finds the argument unpersuasive. Moreover, the Government do not seek to argue that any provisions existed at the relevant time, either in general domestic law or in the governing instruments of the College, regulating the circumstances in which employers could monitor the use of telephone, e-mail and the internet by employees. Furthermore, it is clear that the Telecommunications (Lawful Business Practice) Regulations 2000 (adopted under the Regulation of Investigatory Powers Act 2000) which make such provision were not in force at the relevant time.

48. Accordingly, as there was no domestic law regulating monitoring at the relevant time, the interference in this case was not 'in accordance with the law' as required by Article 8 §2 of the Convention. The Court would not exclude that the monitoring of an employee's use of a telephone, e-mail or internet at the place of work may be considered 'necessary in a democratic society' in certain situations in pursuit of a legitimate aim. However, having regard to its above conclusion, it is not necessary to pronounce on that matter in the instant case.

49. There has therefore been a violation of Article 8 in this regard.

3.5. Questions for discussion: the function of the requirement of legality

1. Is there any added value to the requirement imposed by the Inter-American Court of Human Rights, that any restriction to human rights be imposed by a law adopted through parliamentary procedures? Is this superfluous, since any such restriction in any case must comply with the principle of proportionality? Are there any disadvantages associated with this requirement?

2. How do you interpret the insistance of the European Court of Human Rights, in the 2000 case of *Rotaru* v. *Romania*, on the 'quality of the law' restricting the right to respect for private life? Is this judicial law-making? Could it be defended on the grounds that it imports, within Article 8 ECHR, certain of the requirements of the 1981 Convention for the Protection of Individuals with regard to Automatic Processing of Personal Data, also adopted within the framework of the Council of Europe (see box 3.1.)?

3. Should the requirement that the law (in the material sense) restricting a fundamental right of the individual be sufficiently precise, apply equally across all human rights? Or are the risks associated with insufficiently precise wording more or less important, depending on the nature of the right which is regulated? Could you explain the different attitude of the European Court of Human Rights in *Rotaru* and in *Gorzelik* by the nature of the respective rights at stake in these cases?

4. Does the requirement of legality raise specific questions in the context of relationships between private parties? For example, should it influence the way rights may be restricted through private contracts? How could it apply to situations where two freedoms are in conflict with one another, and where the relationships between individuals are thus characterized, not as the right of A corresponding to a duty of B, but as two opposing 'privileges', in the terminology of W. N. Hohfeld (W. N. Hohfeld in W. W. Cook (ed.), *Fundamental Legal Conceptions* (New Haven,

Conn.: Yale University Press, 1919)? Imagine for example that the freedom of expression of A is being nullified, neither by State censorship nor by any contractual obligation owed, for instance, to her employer, but by the use others make of their freedom of expression, opposing the ideas of A.

3.3 The condition of legitimacy

The 1984 Siracusa Principles on the Limitation and Derogation of Provisions in the International Covenant on Civil and Political Rights include a detailed discussion of the different aims which may justify a restriction being imposed on the rights of the Covenant, thus limiting the freedom of States to impose such restrictions simply for reasons of expediency:

UN Sub-Commission on Prevention of Discrimination and Protection of Minorities, Siracusa Principles on the Limitation and Derogation of Provisions in the International Covenant on Civil and Political Rights, Annex, E/CN.4/1984/4 (1984):

B. Interpretative Principles Relating to Specific Limitation Clauses

...

iii. 'public order (ordre public)' 22. The expression 'public order (ordre public)' as used in the Covenant may be defined as the sum of rules which ensure the functioning of society or the set of fundamental principles on which society is founded. Respect for human rights is part of public order (ordre public).

23. Public order (ordre public) shall be interpreted in the context of the purpose of the particular human right which is limited on this ground.

24. State organs or agents responsible for the maintenance of public order (ordre public) shall be subject to controls in the exercise of their power through the parliament, courts, or other competent independent bodies.

iv. 'public health' 25. Public health may be invoked as a ground for limiting certain rights in order to allow a state to take measures dealing with a serious threat to the health of the population or individual members of the population. These measures must be specifically aimed at preventing disease or injury or providing care for the sick and injured.

26. Due regard shall be had to the international health regulations of the World Health Organization.

v. 'public morals' 27. Since public morality varies over time and from one culture to another, a state which invokes public morality as a ground for restricting human rights, while enjoying a certain margin of discretion, shall demonstrate that the limitation in question is essential to the maintenance of respect for fundamental values of the community.

28. The margin of discretion left to states does not apply to the rule of non-discrimination as defined in the Covenant.

vi. 'national security' 29. National security may be invoked to justify measures limiting certain rights only when they are taken to protect the existence of the nation or its territorial integrity or political independence against force or threat of force.

30. National security cannot be invoked as a reason for imposing limitations to prevent merely local or relatively isolated threats to law and order.

31. National security cannot be used as a pretext for imposing vague or arbitrary limitations and may only be invoked when there exists adequate safeguards and effective remedies against abuse.

32. The systematic violation of human rights undermines true national security and may jeopardize international peace and security. A state responsible for such violation shall not invoke national security as a justification for measures aimed at suppressing opposition to such violation or at perpetrating repressive practices against its population.

vii. 'public safety' 33. Public safety means protection against danger to the safety of persons, to their life or physical integrity, or serious damage to their property.

34. The need to protect public safety can justify limitations provided by law. It cannot be used for imposing vague or arbitrary limitations and may only be invoked when there exist adequate safeguards and effective remedies against abuse.

viii. 'rights and freedoms of others' or the 'rights or reputations of others' 35. The scope of the rights and freedoms of others that may act as a limitation upon rights in the Covenant extends beyond the rights and freedoms recognized in the Covenant.

36. When a conflict exists between a right protected in the Covenant and one which is not, recognition and consideration should be given to the fact that the Covenant seeks to protect the most fundamental rights and freedoms. In this context especial weight should be afforded to rights not subject to limitations in the Covenant.

37. A limitation to a human right based upon the reputation of others shall not be used to protect the state and its officials from public opinion or criticism.

ix. 'restrictions on public trial' 38. All trials shall be public unless the Court determines in accordance with law that:

(a) the press or the public should be excluded from all or part of a trial on the basis of specific findings announced in open court showing that the interest of the private lives of the parties or their families or of juveniles so requires; or

(b) the exclusion is strictly necessary to avoid publicity prejudicial to the fairness of the trial or endangering public morals, public order (ordre public), or national security in a democratic society.

The condition of legitimacy should in principle allow supervisory bodies to scrutinize the motives behind particular restrictions being imposed on fundamental rights, and to screen out, in particular, illegitimate motives, such as where restrictions are animated by prejudice against certain groups. However, due probably to the open-ended formulations by which the admissible aims are described, these bodies have generally exercised a rather minimal degree of scrutiny on the aims pursued by such restrictions. It is remarkable, for instance, that when it was confronted by a policy in the UK armed forces excluding homosexuals from the army's ranks, the European Court of

Human Rights contented itself with observing that 'the essential justification offered by the Government for the policy and for the consequent investigations and discharges is the maintenance of the morale of service personnel and, consequently, of the fighting power and the operational effectiveness of the armed forces ... The Court finds no reason to doubt that the policy was designed with a view to ensuring the operational effectiveness of the armed forces or that investigations were, in principle, intended to establish whether the person concerned was a homosexual to whom the policy was applicable. To this extent, therefore, the Court considers that the resulting interferences can be said to have pursued the legitimate aims of "the interests of national security" and "the prevention of disorder"' (Eur. Ct. H.R. (3d sect.), *Smith and Grady* v. *United Kingdom* (Applications Nos. 33985/96 and 33986/96), judgment of 27 September 1999, para. 74). The reality was that, as implicitly acknowledged by the Court itself, the alleged 'threat to the fighting power and operational effectiveness of the armed forces [which would result from the acceptance of homosexuals in the armed forces] were founded solely upon the negative attitudes of heterosexual personnel towards those of homosexual orientation', and that such attitudes should not constitute an adequate justification for restrictions to the right to respect for private life of the individuals concerned. Indeed, as the Court emphasized when examining the necessity of the impugned measures: 'these attitudes, even if sincerely felt by those who expressed them, ranged from stereotypical expressions of hostility to those of homosexual orientation, to vague expressions of unease about the presence of homosexual colleagues. To the extent that they represent a predisposed bias on the part of a heterosexual majority against a homosexual minority, these negative attitudes cannot, of themselves, be considered by the Court to amount to sufficient justification for the interferences with the applicants' rights outlined above any more than similar negative attitudes towards those of a different race, origin or colour' (para. 97).

The determination of the objective pursued by the restriction to a fundamental right may be decisive for the examination of the question whether the interference may be considered 'disproportionate' or – as in the terminology of the European Convention on Human Rights – 'necessary in a democratic society' (a requirement examined in greater detail below, in section 3.4.). Consider the following case:

European Court of Human Rights (plen.), *Open Door and Dublin Well Woman* v. *Ireland*, judgment of 29 October 1992, Series A No. 246–A:

[The applicants in this case are two non-profit organizations: (a) Open Door Counselling Ltd, engaged, *inter alia*, in counselling pregnant women in Dublin and in other parts of Ireland; and (b) Dublin Well Woman Centre Ltd, providing similar services at two clinics in Dublin; as well as four individuals: (c) Bonnie Maher and Ann Downes, who worked as trained counsellors for Dublin Well Woman; (d) Mrs X, born in 1950 and Ms Maeve Geraghty, born in 1970, who join in the Dublin Well Woman application as women of child-bearing age. The applicants complained of an injunction imposed by the Irish courts on Open Door and Dublin Well Woman to restrain them from providing certain information to pregnant women concerning abortion facilities outside the jurisdiction of Ireland. The two associations concerned provided non-directive counselling, understood as 'counselling which neither included advice nor was judgmental but … was a service essentially directed to eliciting from the client her own appreciation of her problem and her own considered choice for its solution' (as according to the description offered by Mr Justice Finlay CJ the Supreme Court of Ireland (judgment of 16 March 1988 [1988] *Irish Reports* 618 at 621)). The injunction followed a private action brought by the Society for the Protection of Unborn Children (Ireland) Ltd (SPUC). It was based on Article 40.3.3° of the Irish Constitution (the Eighth Amendment), which came into force in 1983 following a referendum, and which protects the life of the unborn child. Under this provision: 'The State acknowledges the right to life of the unborn and, with due regard to the equal right to life of the mother, guarantees in its laws to respect, and, as far as practicable, by its laws to defend and vindicate that right.' In their applications, the applicants complained in particular that the injunction in question constituted an unjustified interference with their right to impart or receive information, in violation of Article 10 of the European Convention on Human Rights. Article 10 ECHR guarantees freedom of expression, including 'freedom to hold opinions and to receive and impart information and ideas without interference by public authority and regardless of frontiers' Article 10 para. 2 ECHR states: 'The exercise of these freedoms, since it carries with it duties and responsibilities, may be subject to such formalities, conditions, restrictions or penalties as are prescribed by law and are necessary in a democratic society, in the interests of national security, territorial integrity or public safety, for the prevention of disorder or crime, for the protection of health or morals, for the protection of the reputation or rights of others, for preventing the disclosure of information received in confidence, or for maintaining the authority and impartiality of the judiciary.' Before the Court, the applicants alleged that the Supreme Court injunction, restraining them from assisting pregnant women to travel abroad to obtain abortions, infringed the rights of the two applicant associations and the two counsellors to impart information, as well as the rights of Mrs X and Ms Geraghty to receive information.]

[Did the restriction have aims that were legitimate under Article 10 para. 2?] 61. The Government submitted that the relevant provisions of Irish law are intended for the protection of the rights of others – in this instance the unborn –, for the protection of morals and, where appropriate, for the prevention of crime.

62. The applicants disagreed, contending *inter alia* that, in view of the use of the term 'everyone' in Article 10 para. 1 and throughout the Convention, it would be illogical to interpret the 'rights of others' in Article 10 para. 2 as encompassing the unborn.

63. The Court cannot accept that the restrictions at issue pursued the aim of the prevention of crime since … neither the provision of the information in question nor the obtaining of an abortion outside the jurisdiction involved any criminal offence. However, it is evident that the protection afforded under Irish law to the right to life of the unborn is based on profound moral values concerning the nature of life which were reflected in the stance of the majority of the Irish people against abortion as expressed in the 1983 referendum … The restriction thus pursued the legitimate aim of the protection of morals of which the protection in Ireland of the right to life of the unborn is one aspect. It is not necessary in the light of this conclusion to decide whether the term 'others' under Article 10 para. 2 extends to the unborn.

[Was the restriction necessary in a democratic society?] 64. The Government submitted that the Court's approach to the assessment of the 'necessity' of the restraint should be guided by the fact that the protection of the rights of the unborn in Ireland could be derived from Articles 2, 17 and 60 of the Convention. They further contended that the 'proportionality' test was inadequate where the rights of the unborn were at issue. The Court will examine these issues in turn.

1. Article 2 65. The Government maintained that the injunction was necessary in a democratic society for the protection of the right to life of the unborn and that Article 10 should be interpreted *inter alia* against the background of Article 2 of the Convention which, they argued, also protected unborn life. The view that abortion was morally wrong was the deeply held view of the majority of the people in Ireland and it was not the proper function of the Court to seek to impose a different viewpoint.

66. The Court observes at the outset that in the present case it is not called upon to examine whether a right to abortion is guaranteed under the Convention or whether the foetus is encompassed by the right to life as contained in Article 2. The applicants have not claimed that the Convention contains a right to abortion, as such, their complaint being limited to that part of the injunction which restricts their freedom to impart and receive information concerning abortion abroad ...

Thus the only issue to be addressed is whether the restrictions on the freedom to impart and receive information contained in the relevant part of the injunction are necessary in a democratic society for the legitimate aim of the protection of morals as explained above (see paragraph 63). It follows from this approach that the Government's argument based on Article 2 of the Convention does not fall to be examined in the present case ...

2. Proportionality 67. The Government stressed the limited nature of the Supreme Court's injunction which only restrained the provision of certain information ... There was no limitation on discussion in Ireland about abortion generally or the right of women to travel abroad to obtain one. They further contended that the Convention test as regards the proportionality of the restriction was inadequate where a question concerning the extinction of life was at stake. The right to life could not, like other rights, be measured according to a graduated scale. It was either respected or it was not. Accordingly, the traditional approach of weighing competing rights and interests in the balance was inappropriate where the destruction of unborn life was concerned. Since life was a primary value which was antecedent to and a prerequisite for the enjoyment of every other right, its protection might involve the infringement of other rights such as freedom of expression in a manner which might not be acceptable in the defence of rights of a lesser nature.

The Government also emphasised that, in granting the injunction, the Supreme Court was merely sustaining the logic of Article 40.3.3° of the Constitution. The determination by the Irish courts that the provision of information by the relevant applicants assisted in the destruction of unborn life was not open to review by the Convention institutions.

68. The Court cannot agree that the State's discretion in the field of the protection of morals is unfettered and unreviewable (see, *mutatis mutandis*, for a similar argument, the *Norris* v. *Ireland* judgment of 26 October 1988, Series A No. 142, p. 20, para. 45).

It acknowledges that the national authorities enjoy a wide margin of appreciation in matters of morals, particularly in an area such as the present which touches on matters of belief concerning the nature of human life. As the Court has observed before, it is not possible to find in the legal and social orders of the Contracting States a uniform European conception of morals, and the State authorities are, in principle, in a better position than the international judge to give an opinion on the exact content of the requirements of morals as well as on the 'necessity' of a 'restriction' or 'penalty' intended to meet them (see, *inter alia*, the *Handyside* v. *United Kingdom* judgment of 7 December 1976, Series A No. 24, p. 22, para. 48, and the *Müller and others* v. *Switzerland* judgment of 24 May 1988, Series A No. 133, p. 22, para. 35).

However this power of appreciation is not unlimited. It is for the Court, in this field also, to supervise whether a restriction is compatible with the Convention.

69. As regards the application of the 'proportionality' test, the logical consequence of the Government's argument is that measures taken by the national authorities to protect the right to life of the unborn or to uphold the constitutional guarantee on the subject would be automatically justified under the Convention where infringement of a right of a lesser stature was alleged. It is, in principle, open to the national authorities to take such action as they consider necessary to respect the rule of law or to give effect to constitutional rights. However, they must do so in a manner which is compatible with their obligations under the Convention and subject to review by the Convention institutions. To accept the Government's pleading on this point would amount to an abdication of the Court's responsibility under Article 19 'to ensure the observance of the engagements undertaken by the High Contracting Parties ...'.

70. Accordingly, the Court must examine the question of 'necessity' in the light of the principles developed in its case law (see, *inter alia*, *The Observer and Guardian* v. *United Kingdom* judgment of 26 November 1991, Series A No. 216, pp. 29–30, para. 59). It must determine whether there existed a pressing social need for the measures in question and, in particular, whether the restriction complained of was 'proportionate to the legitimate aim pursued' (*ibid.*).

71. In this context, it is appropriate to recall that freedom of expression is also applicable to 'information' or 'ideas' that offend, shock or disturb the State or any sector of the population. Such are the demands of that pluralism, tolerance and broadmindedness without which there is no 'democratic society' (see, *inter alia*, the above-mentioned *Handyside* judgment, Series A No. 24, p. 23, para. 49).

72. While the relevant restriction, as observed by the Government, is limited to the provision of information, it is recalled that it is not a criminal offence under Irish law for a pregnant woman to travel abroad in order to have an abortion. Furthermore, the injunction limited the freedom to receive and impart information with respect to services which are lawful in other Convention countries and may be crucial to a woman's health and well-being. Limitations on information concerning activities which, notwithstanding their moral implications, have been and continue to be tolerated by national authorities, call for careful scrutiny by the Convention institutions as to their conformity with the tenets of a democratic society.

73. The Court is first struck by the absolute nature of the Supreme Court injunction which imposed a 'perpetual' restraint on the provision of information to pregnant women concerning abortion facilities abroad, regardless of age or state of health or their reasons for seeking counselling on the termination of pregnancy. The sweeping nature of this restriction has since been highlighted by the case of the *Attorney General* v. *X and others* and by the concession made

by the Government at the oral hearing that the injunction no longer applied to women who, in the circumstances as defined in the Supreme Court's judgment in that case, were now free to have an abortion in Ireland or abroad ...

74. On that ground alone the restriction appears overbroad and disproportionate. Moreover, this assessment is confirmed by other factors.

75. In the first place, it is to be noted that the corporate applicants were engaged in the counselling of pregnant women in the course of which counsellors neither advocated nor encouraged abortion, but confined themselves to an explanation of the available options ... The decision as to whether or not to act on the information so provided was that of the woman concerned. There can be little doubt that following such counselling there were women who decided against a termination of pregnancy. Accordingly, the link between the provision of information and the destruction of unborn life is not as definite as contended. Such counselling had in fact been tolerated by the State authorities even after the passing of the Eighth Amendment in 1983 until the Supreme Court's judgment in the present case. Furthermore, the information that was provided by the relevant applicants concerning abortion facilities abroad was not made available to the public at large.

76. It has not been seriously contested by the Government that information concerning abortion facilities abroad can be obtained from other sources in Ireland such as magazines and telephone directories ... or by persons with contacts in Great Britain. Accordingly, information that the injunction sought to restrict was already available elsewhere although in a manner which was not supervised by qualified personnel and thus less protective of women's health. Furthermore, the injunction appears to have been largely ineffective in protecting the right to life of the unborn since it did not prevent large numbers of Irish women from continuing to obtain abortions in Great Britain ...

77. In addition, the available evidence, which has not been disputed by the Government, suggests that the injunction has created a risk to the health of those women who are now seeking abortions at a later stage in their pregnancy, due to lack of proper counselling, and who are not availing themselves of customary medical supervision after the abortion has taken place ... Moreover, the injunction may have had more adverse effects on women who were not sufficiently resourceful or had not the necessary level of education to have access to alternative sources of information (see paragraph 76 above). These are certainly legitimate factors to take into consideration in assessing the proportionality of the restriction ...

4. Conclusion 80. In the light of the above, the Court concludes that the restraint imposed on the applicants from receiving or imparting information was disproportionate to the aims pursued. Accordingly there has been a breach of Article 10.

3.6. Questions for discussion: policy choices and 'legitimate ends' pursued in the restriction of rights

1. Human rights treaties either list exhaustively the legitimate grounds which may justify imposing restrictions on the rights they codify, or they use broader and vaguer expressions such as 'general welfare' or 'general interest'. Whichever the wording used, the general purpose of imposing

this condition is that the human rights of the individual may not be restricted merely because this corresponds to the preferences of the majority. Not only may such preferences not embody prejudices against a certain category of persons; in addition, they must be related to some objective which it is legitimate (and rational) for the majority to pursue. How should the legitimacy of the ends pursued by the majority be assessed? In assessing the legitimacy of the aims pursued, are courts necessarily crossing the line between applying the law and imposing their own policy preferences? Which objective benchmarks do they have in exercising this control?

2. There is a range of possibilities between clearly irrational choices (or choices which are tainted by an element of prejudice against a disadvantaged or politically disempowered group) at one end, and choices that are justified in the name of the overall realization of human rights, at the other end. Should all choices which cannot be justified against the full range of human rights (i.e. as serving the realization of other human rights) be dismissed as illegitimate and, thus, the restrictions based on such choices be counted as violations? Consider for instance land-use policies that restrict the possibilities for the Roma/Gypsies having maintained a traditional nomadic lifestyle to circulate across the territory in caravans (see in this respect the case of *Chapman* v. *United Kingdom* before the European Court of Human Rights, discussed in chapter 7, section 5.2., b)). If the only purpose of land-use policies is an aesthetic one – which corresponds to the tastes of a majority of the population, but has no further instrumental purpose – is this a legitimate objective?

3. Most of the restrictions imposed on human rights are the result of decisions adopted through democratic processes, typically by elected parliamentary assemblies. Some may be adopted by the executive, with less democratic control. Some still may be the result of judicial decisions, and are thus insulated, by design, from democratic accountability. Should the legitimacy of the objectives pursued by these different branches of government be assessed differently? Would it be justified to take into consideration the process through which the measure imposing a restriction has been adopted, in addressing the question of legitimacy?

4. Echoing the notion of 'compelling state interest' used in US constitutional law, the European Court of Human Rights sometimes refers to the need for the restriction imposed on the rights and freedoms of the Convention to correspond to a 'pressing social need'. What does this terminology add to our understanding of the requirement of legitimacy?

3.4 The condition of proportionality

(a) The general principle

In order for an interference with a protected right to be justified, the measure creating the interference (i) must be appropriate to the fulfilment of the legitimate aim pursued (a condition referred to as 'appropriateness' or 'rational connection'); and (ii) it must not go beyond what is strictly required by the need to achieve that aim, i.e. it must be necessary to attain the objective justifying the interference (condition of 'necessity' or 'minimal impairment'). However, this second condition is sometimes described instead as requiring that the balance of interests has been respected. This alternative test – a balancing of interests, instead of a 'strict necessity' test – will in particular be preferred where the aim pursued by the restriction was the protection of other fundamental rights, so that two values, of presumptively equal weight, come into conflict. Occasionally too, instead of being relaxed, the necessity test will be reinforced by the additional requirement that the aim pursued has a sufficient weight justifying the restriction.

A violation of the requirement of proportionality may have its source in the fact that the authorities have not acted with the requisite caution in interfering with the right of the individual. In the following cases, for instance, house searches which took place created an unnecessary trauma, which the authorities could easily have avoided:

Human Rights Committee, *Rojas García* v. *Colombia*, Communication No. 687/1996, final views of 3 April 2001 (CCPR/C/71/D/687/1996 (2001)):

[On 5 January 1993 at 2 a.m. a group of armed men, wearing civilian clothes, from the Public Prosecutor's office, forcibly entered the author's house through the roof, apparently in the belief that in the house were murderers of the local mayor. The group carried out a room-by-room search of the premises, terrifying and verbally abusing the members of the author's family, including small children. One of the officials fired a gunshot in the course of the search. It appeared later that the search hit the wrong house (No. 2–44 in the street instead of No. 2–36).]

10.3 The Committee must first determine whether the specific circumstances of the raid on the Rojas García family's house (hooded men entering through the roof at 2 a.m.) constitute a violation of article 17 of the Covenant. By submission of 28 December 1999, the State party reiterates that the raid on the Rojas García family's house was carried out according to the letter of the law, in accordance with article 343 of the Code of Criminal Procedure. The Committee does not enter into the question of the legality of the raid; however, it considers that, under article 17 of the Covenant, it is necessary for any interference in the home not only to be lawful, but also not to be arbitrary. The Committee considers, in accordance with its General Comment No. 16 [see above, section 3.1. in this chapter] that the concept of arbitrariness in article 17 is intended to guarantee that even interference provided for by law should be in accordance with the provisions, aims and objectives of the Covenant and should be, in any event, reasonable in the particular circumstances. It further considers that the State party's arguments fail to justify the conduct described. Consequently, the Committee concludes that there has been a violation of article 17, paragraph 1, insofar as there was arbitrary interference in the home of the Rojas García family.

European Court of Human Rights (4th sect.), *Keegan* v. *United Kingdom* (Appl. No. 28867/03), judgment of 18 July 2006 (final on 8 October 2006), paras. 29–36:

[The applicants are a family whose house was raided on 21 October 1999, at 7 a.m., by police officers who were briefed that the previous tenant of the house was linked to a number of robberies in the neighborhood. The police knew that the robberies had involved the use of firearms. The police used a metal ram to make a hole in the door. The noise of the battering ram awoke and frightened the applicants. The search led to no result. The subsequent proceedings against the Chief Constable of Merseyside Police for the tort of maliciously procuring a search warrant, unlawful entry and false imprisonment, failed, although the Keegan family alleged that they had been caused terror, distress and psychiatric harm. Medical reports indicated that the applicants were suffering from varying degrees of post-traumatic stress disorder. The English courts found on the facts that the police, who were investigating serious and violent offences, had not acted with reckless indifference to the lawfulness of their acts, which element was necessary for the tort of maliciously procuring a search warrant. They held that the entry was made subject to a lawful search warrant and also under the powers of section 17 of the Police and Criminal Evidence Act 1984, which allowed entry without warrant where intending to arrest a person for an arrestable offence. They found that the method of forcible entry was justified as the police had foremost in their minds the potential danger from the use of firearms by the suspect robber and in particular that the sergeant had no cause to suspect that innocent people were the only ones on the premises.]

29. It is not disputed that the forcible entry by the police into the applicants' home interfered with their right to respect for their home under Article 8 paragraph 1 of the Convention and that it was 'in accordance with the law' on a domestic level and pursued a legitimate aim, the prevention of disorder and crime, as required by the second paragraph of Article 8. What remains to be determined is whether the interference was justified under the remaining requirement of paragraph 2, namely whether it was 'necessary in a democratic society' to achieve that aim.

30. According to the Court's settled case law, the notion of necessity implies that the interference corresponds to a 'pressing social need' and, in particular that it is proportionate to the legitimate aim pursued (see e.g. *Olsson* v. *Sweden*, judgment of 24 March 1988, Series A No. 130, §67). The Court must accordingly ascertain whether, in the circumstances of the case, the entry of the applicants' home struck a fair balance between the relevant interests, namely their right to respect for their home balance, on the one hand, and the prevention of disorder and crime on the other (see *McLeod* v. *United Kingdom*, judgment of 23 September 1998, *Reports of Judgments and Decisions* 1998–VIII, §53).

31. While a certain margin of appreciation is left to the Contracting States, the exceptions provided for in paragraph 2 of Article 8 are to be interpreted narrowly and the need for measures in a given case must be convincingly established (see *Funke* v. *France*, judgment of 25 February 1993, Series A No. 256–A, §55). The Court will assess in particular whether the reasons adduced to justify such measures were relevant and sufficient and whether there were adequate and effective safeguards against abuse (see e.g. *Buck* v. *Germany*, judgment of 28 April 2005, §§44–45).

32. Turning to the present case, the Court recalls that domestic law and practice regulates the conditions under which the police may obtain entry to private premises, either with or without a warrant. In the event, the police obtained a warrant from a Justice of the Peace, giving information under oath that they had reason to believe the proceeds of a robbery were at the address which had been used by one of the suspected robbers. No doubt was cast, in the domestic proceedings or before the Court, on the genuineness of the belief of the officers who obtained the warrant or those who executed it. If this belief had been correct, the Court does not doubt that the entry would have been found to have been justified.

33. However, the applicants had been living at the address for about six months and they had no connection whatsoever with any suspect or offence. As the County Court judge noted, it is difficult to conceive that enquiries were not made by the police to verify the residents of the address which the suspected robber had been known to give and that if such enquiries had been properly made (via the local authority or utility companies) they would not have revealed the change in occupation. The loss of the police notes renders it impossible to deduce whether it was a failure to make the proper enquiries or a failure to transmit or properly record the information obtained that led to the mistake that was made. In any event, as found by the domestic courts, although the police did not act with malice and indeed with the best of intentions, there was no reasonable basis for their action in breaking down the applicants' door early one morning while they were in bed. Put in Convention terms, there might have been relevant reasons, but, as in the circumstances they were based on a misconception which could, and should, have been avoided with proper precautions, they cannot be regarded as sufficient (see, *mutatis mutandis*, *McLeod*, cited above, where the police did not take steps to verify whether the applicant's ex-husband had the right to enter her house, notwithstanding his genuine belief, and did not wait until her return).

34. The fact that the police did not act maliciously is not decisive under the Convention which is geared to protecting against abuse of power, however motivated or caused (see, *mutatis mutandis*, *McLeod*, cited above, where the police suspected a breach of the peace might occur). The Court cannot agree that a limitation of actions for damages to cases of malice is necessary to protect the police in their vital functions of investigating crime. The exercise of powers to interfere with home and private life must be confined within reasonable bounds to minimise the impact of such measures on the personal sphere of the individual guaranteed under Article 8 which is pertinent to security and well-being (see, e.g. *Buckley* v. *United Kingdom*, judgment of 25 September 1996, *Reports* 1996–IV, §76). In a case where basic steps to verify the connection between the address and the offence under investigation were not effectively carried out, the resulting police action, which caused the applicants considerable fear and alarm, cannot be regarded as proportionate.

35. As argued by the applicants, this finding does not imply that any search, which turns out to be unsuccessful, would fail the proportionality test, only that a failure to take reasonable and available precautions may do so.

36. The Court accordingly concludes that the balance has not been properly struck in the present case and that there has been a violation of Article 8 of the Convention.

(b) The importance of procedures for weighing all relevant interests

It is noteworthy that, increasingly, the procedures followed in the course of the adoption of a measure alleged to constitute a disporportionate interference with a protected right are considered decisive in the assessment of the question of proportionality. In the case of *Hatton and others* v. *United Kingdom*, the applicants challenged before the European Court of Human Rights the implementation in 1993 of the new scheme for regulating night flights at Heathrow. The scheme replaced the earlier system of movement limitations with a regime which gave aircraft operators a choice, through a quota count, as to whether to fly fewer noisier aircraft, or more less noisy types. The 1993 scheme accepted the conclusions of the 1992 sleep study that found that, for the large majority of people living near airports, there was no risk of substantial sleep disturbance due to aircraft noise, and that only a small percentage of individuals (some 2–3 per cent) were more sensitive than others. On this basis, disturbances caused by aircraft noise were regarded as negligible in relation to overall normal disturbance rates. It was agreed, nevertheless, that the new scheme was susceptible of adversely affecting the quality of the applicants' private life and the scope for their enjoying the amenities of their respective homes, and thus their rights protected by Article 8 of the Convention. The Court described the problem it faced thus:

European Court of Human Rights (GC), *Hatton and others* v. *United Kingdom* (Appl. No. 36022/97), judgment of 8 July 2003:

103. The Court is thus faced with conflicting views as to the margin of appreciation to be applied: on the one hand, the Government claim a wide margin on the ground that the case concerns matters of general policy, and, on the other hand, the applicants' claim that where the ability to sleep is affected, the margin is narrow because of the 'intimate' nature of the right protected. This conflict of views on the margin of appreciation can be resolved only by reference to the context of a particular case.

104. In connection with the procedural element of the Court's review of cases involving environmental issues, the Court is required to consider all the procedural aspects, including the type of policy or decision involved, the extent to which the views of individuals (including the applicants) were taken into account throughout the decision-making procedure, and the procedural safeguards available.

[Turning to this second dimension, the Court notes as follows:]

128. On the procedural aspect of the case, the Court notes that a governmental decision-making process concerning complex issues of environmental and economic policy such as in the present case must necessarily involve appropriate investigations and studies in order to allow them to strike a fair balance between the various conflicting interests at stake. However, this does not mean that decisions can only be taken if comprehensive and measurable data are available in relation to each and every aspect of the matter to be decided. In this respect it is relevant that the authorities have consistently monitored the situation, and that the 1993 Scheme was the latest in a series of restrictions on night flights which stretched back to 1962. The position concerning research into sleep disturbance and night flights is far from static, and it was the government's policy to announce restrictions on night flights for a maximum of five years at a time, each new scheme taking into account the research and other developments of the previous period. The 1993 Scheme had thus been preceded by a series of investigations and studies carried out over a long period of time. The particular new measures introduced by that scheme were announced to the public by way of a Consultation Paper which referred to the results of a study carried out for the Department of Transport, and which included a study of aircraft noise and sleep disturbance. It stated that the quota was to be set so as not to allow a worsening of noise at night, and ideally to improve the situation. This paper was published in January 1993 and sent to bodies representing the aviation industry and people living near airports. The applicants and persons in a similar situation thus had access to the Consultation

Paper, and it would have been open to them to make any representations they felt appropriate. Had any representations not been taken into account, they could have challenged subsequent decisions, or the scheme itself, in the courts. Moreover, the applicants are, or have been, members of HACAN [an association of inhabitants of the Heathrow Airport region], and were thus particularly well-placed to make representations.

129. In these circumstances the Court does not find that, in substance, the authorities overstepped their margin of appreciation by failing to strike a fair balance between the right of the individuals affected by those regulations to respect for their private life and home and the conflicting interests of others and of the community as a whole, nor does it find that there have been fundamental procedural flaws in the preparation of the 1993 regulations on limitations for night flights.

This does not constitute an isolated example. In the case of *Chapman* v. *United Kingdom* for instance – a case more fully presented in chapter 7, section 5.2. (Eur. Ct. H.R. (GC), *Chapman* v. *United Kingdom* (Appl. No. 27238/95), judgment of 18 January 2001) – the applicant, Ms Sally Chapman, was a Gypsy by birth, who had been travelling constantly with her family during her youth, and continued to live in caravans with her husband and children after her marriage. After she finally decided to leave the itinerant life and bought a piece of land with the intention of living on it in a mobile home, she was denied the permission to station caravans on the land due to land planning requirements: the area was located within a 'Green Belt' in which, for environmental reasons, the stationing of caravans was not allowed. The European Court of Human Rights agreed that 'the applicant's occupation of her caravan is an integral part of her ethnic identity as a Gypsy, reflecting the long tradition of that minority of following a travelling lifestyle', and that therefore '[m]easures affecting the applicant's stationing of her caravans ... have an impact going beyond the right to respect for her home. They also affect her ability to maintain her identity as a Gypsy and to lead her private and family life in accordance with that tradition' (para. 73). Nevertheless, the Court concluded that Article 8 of the European Convention on Human Rights had not been violated, since the national authorities had not exceeded their margin of appreciation in seeking to achieve a balance between environmental concerns and right to respect for private life. The care with which such balance was sought at national level appears to have decisively influenced the Court, which notes in para. 114 that 'proper regard was had to the applicant's predicament both under the terms of the regulatory framework, which contained adequate procedural safeguards protecting her interests under Article 8 and by the responsible planning authorities when exercising their discretion in relation to the particular circumstances of her case. The decisions were reached by those authorities after weighing in the balance the various competing interests. It is not for this Court to sit in appeal on the merits of those decisions, which were based on reasons which were relevant and sufficient, for the purposes of Article 8, to justify the interferences with the exercise of the applicant's rights.'

At the same time, the imposition of procedural safeguards, such as were prescribed in the case of *Hatton and others* and such as were taken into consideration by the Court in *Chapman*, should not be separated from the obligation to comply with the substantive requirements of the Convention. This is well illustrated by the controversy that surrounded the *Denbigh High School* case in the United Kingdom. Shabina Begum, a Muslim girl, who was 14 years old at the material time, was excluded from the Denbigh High School in Luton after she insisted on wearing a long coat-like garment known as a *jilbab*, in violation of the dress codes imposed by the school. She felt that this was in violation of her freedom of religion, as recognized under Article 9 ECHR, and that it violated her right not to be denied education under Article 2 of the First Additional Protocol to the Convention. Her contentions were initially rejected by the Administrative Court, but they were subsequently upheld on appeal (see [2004] EWHC 1389 (Admin) (Bennett J.), [2004] E.L.R. 374, followed by the decision of the Court of Appeal (Brooke, Mummery and Scott Baker L.JJ.) [2005] EWCA Civ 199, [2005] 1 W.L.R. 3372 (judgment of 2 March 2005)). The Court of Appeal's decision, however, was based on the consideration that the decision-making procedure by the direction of the school had been inadequate. The leading judgment by Brooke L.J. took the view that, since the premiss of the decision by the school should be that freedom of religion and the right to education should allow Shabina Begum access to the school, the school authorities should have explained why the exclusion was justified in the light of those principles. Remarkably, the judgment emphasized that it should not be taken to mean that it would be impossible for the school to justify its stance if it were to reconsider its uniform policy in the light of the judgment and decide not to alter it in any significant respect; and indeed, in paragraph 81 of the judgment, the Court of Appeal explicitly provides guidance on the matters the school would need to consider. This approach was criticized by legal commentators as introducing a new kind of formalism, signifying a retreat of the courts from substance to procedure and an abandonment of the kind of scrutiny required by the principle of proportionality prescribed under the Convention (G. Davies, 'Banning the Jilbab: Reflections on Restricting Religious Clothing in the Light of the Court of Appeal in *SB v Denbigh High School*', *European Constitutional Law Review*, 1–3 (2005) 511).

The House of Lords agreed with these critiques. In his leading judgment for the House of Lords, Lord Bingham of Cornhill put forward three reasons why the Court of Appeal had erred in adopting a purely procedural approach to the issue it was presented with.

House of Lords (United Kingdom), *R. (on the application of Begum (by her litigation friend, Rahman)) (Respondent) v. Headteacher and Governors of Denbigh High School (Appellants)*, (judgment of 22 March 2006) [2006] UKHL 15, leading judgment per Lord Bingham of Cornhill:

29. I am persuaded that the Court of Appeal's approach to this procedural question was mistaken, for three main reasons. First, the purpose of the Human Rights Act 1998 [providing

that the UK courts would apply the European Convention on Human Rights] was not to enlarge the rights or remedies of those in the United Kingdom whose Convention rights have been violated but to enable those rights and remedies to be asserted and enforced by the domestic courts of this country and not only by recourse to Strasbourg ... But the focus at Strasbourg is not and has never been on whether a challenged decision or action is the product of a defective decision-making process, but on whether, in the case under consideration, the applicant's Convention rights have been violated. In considering the exercise of discretion by a national authority the court may consider whether the applicant had a fair opportunity to put his case, and to challenge an adverse decision, the aspect addressed by the court in the passage from its judgment in *Chapman* [on the case of *Chapman v. the United Kingdom*, see above in this section]. But the House has been referred to no case in which the Strasbourg Court has found a violation of Convention right on the strength of failure by a national authority to follow the sort of reasoning process laid down by the Court of Appeal. This pragmatic approach is fully reflected in the 1998 Act. The unlawfulness proscribed by section 6(1) is acting in a way which is incompatible with a Convention right, not relying on a defective process of reasoning, and action may be brought under section 7(1) only by a person who is a victim of an unlawful act.

30. Secondly, it is clear that the court's approach to an issue of proportionality under the Convention must go beyond that traditionally adopted to judicial review in a domestic setting ... There is no shift to a merits review, but the intensity of review is greater than [the 'manifestly irrational' test that] was previously appropriate, and greater even than the heightened scrutiny test adopted by the Court of Appeal in *R. v. Ministry of Defence, Ex p Smith* [1996] Q.B. 517, 554. The domestic court must now make a value judgment, an evaluation, by reference to the circumstances prevailing at the relevant time ... Proportionality must be judged objectively, by the court ... As Davies observed in his article cited above, 'The retreat to procedure is of course a way of avoiding difficult questions.' But it is in my view clear that the court must confront these questions, however difficult. The school's action cannot properly be condemned as disproportionate, with an acknowledgement that on reconsideration the same action could very well be maintained and properly so.

31. Thirdly, ... I consider that the Court of Appeal's approach would introduce 'a new formalism' and be 'a recipe for judicialisation on an unprecedented scale'. The Court of Appeal's decision-making prescription would be admirable guidance to a lower court or legal tribunal, but cannot be required of a head teacher and governors, even with a solicitor to help them. If, in such a case, it appears that such a body has conscientiously paid attention to all human rights considerations, no doubt a challenger's task will be the harder. But what matters in any case is the practical outcome, not the quality of the decision-making process that led to it.

32. It is therefore necessary to consider the proportionality of the school's interference with the respondent's right to manifest her religious belief by wearing the jilbab to the school. In doing so we have the valuable guidance of the Grand Chamber of the Strasbourg court in [the case of *Leyla Sahin v. Turkey*, paras. 104–11: see below, section 3.5. in this chapter]. The court there recognises the high importance of the rights protected by article 9; the need in some situations to restrict freedom to manifest religious belief; the value of religious harmony and tolerance between opposing or competing groups and of pluralism and broadmindedness; the need for compromise and balance; the role of the state in deciding what is necessary to protect

the rights and freedoms of others; the variation of practice and tradition among member states; and the permissibility in some contexts of restricting the wearing of religious dress.

33. The respondent criticised the school for permitting the headscarf while refusing to permit the jilbab, for refusing permission to wear the jilbab when some other schools permitted it and for adhering to their own view of what Islamic dress required. None of these criticisms can in my opinion be sustained. The headscarf was permitted in 1993, following detailed consideration of the uniform policy, in response to requests by several girls. There was no evidence that this was opposed. But there was no pressure at any time, save by the respondent, to wear the jilbab, and that has been opposed. Different schools have different uniform policies, no doubt influenced by the composition of their pupil bodies and a range of other matters. Each school has to decide what uniform, if any, will best serve its wider educational purposes. The school did not reject the respondent's request out of hand: it took advice, and was told that its existing policy conformed with the requirements of mainstream Muslim opinion.

34. On the agreed facts, the school was in my opinion fully justified in acting as it did. It had taken immense pains to devise a uniform policy which respected Muslim beliefs but did so in an inclusive, unthreatening and uncompetitive way. The rules laid down were as far from being mindless as uniform rules could ever be. The school had enjoyed a period of harmony and success to which the uniform policy was thought to contribute. On further enquiry it still appeared that the rules were acceptable to mainstream Muslim opinion. It was feared that acceding to the respondent's request would or might have significant adverse repercussions. It would in my opinion be irresponsible of any court, lacking the experience, background and detailed knowledge of the head teacher, staff and governors, to overrule their judgment on a matter as sensitive as this. The power of decision has been given to them for the compelling reason that they are best placed to exercise it, and I see no reason to disturb their decision. After the conclusion of argument the House was referred to the recent decision of the Supreme Court of Canada in *Multani* v. *Commission scolaire Marguerite-Bourgeoys* [2006] SCC 6 [see below, section 3.5. in this chapter]. That was a case decided, on quite different facts, under the Canadian Charter of Rights and Freedoms. It does not cause me to alter the conclusion I have expressed.

This opinion may in fact exaggerate the difference between the approach of the Court of Appeal on the one hand, and that of the House of Lords on the other hand. The Court of Appeal insisted on the school authorities complying with certain procedural requirements in the course of devising their policy. But although it condemns this shift to procedure and away from the substantial requirements of the Convention, the House of Lords does insist on 'detailed consideration of the uniform policy' which preceded the introduction of the uniform policy; it emphasizes that the school 'took advice' about the compatibility of this policy with Muslim opinion; and that the uniform policy is not 'mindless'. Such insistence on procedural requirements is in fact entirely predictable, once it is agreed that such decisions should be adopted at the local level, on the basis of considerations related to the specific context in which they are taken: it then becomes imperative to impose certain conditions on the decision-making process of local authorities.

(c) The importance of contextual assessments

The requirement to take all reasonable measures that could accommodate specific needs on a case-by-case basis may become increasingly relevant in the evaluation of the condition of proportionality, for the same reasons it matters in the evaluation of compliance with the requirement of non-discrimination (see chapter 7, section 3.2.). While certain measures may be justified as both appropriate and necessary to the achievement of certain legitimate objectives when considered at a *general* level, they may appear less so when it is asked whether, in the *specific* instance in which the implementation of the measure is alleged to result in a violation of the rights of the individual, certain exceptions could have been introduced to the general rule. While this question is discussed in the section below in further detail on the basis of the cases of *Leyla Sahin* and *Multani*, respectively decided by the European Court of Human Rights and by the Supreme Court of Canada, it is appropriate to provide here an illustration of the usefulness of this notion by referring to the judgment of the Supreme Court of Canada in the case of *Rodriguez* v. *Attorney General of Canada* [1993] 3 S.C.R. 519. This case was already briefly addressed above (chapter 1, section 3). In his dissent, Lamer, C.J. took the view that the prohibition of assistance to suicide under section 241(b) of the Criminal Code resulted in a discrimination against persons with disabilities, in violation of section 15(1) of the Canadian Charter of Rights and Freedoms. He reasoned that unlike persons capable of causing their own deaths, persons with disabilities who are or will become unable to end their lives without assistance are deprived of the option of choosing suicide. This resulted in a violation of the equality clause of the Canadian Charter. In the course of explaining this position, he noted:

Supreme Court of Canada, *Rodriguez* v. *Attorney General of Canada* [1993] 3 S.C.R. 519, Lamer C.J. dissenting:

It was argued that if assisted suicide were permitted even in limited circumstances, then there would be reason to fear that homicide of the terminally ill and persons with physical disabilities could be readily disguised as assisted suicide and that, as a result, the most vulnerable people would be left most exposed to this grave threat ...

The principal fear is that the decriminalization of assisted suicide will increase the risk of persons with physical disabilities being manipulated by others. This 'slippery slope' argument appeared to be the central justification behind the Law Reform Commission of Canada's recommendation not to repeal this provision ...

While I share a deep concern over the subtle and overt pressures that may be brought to bear on such persons if assisted suicide is decriminalized, even in limited circumstances, I do not think legislation that deprives a disadvantaged group of the right to equality can be justified solely on such speculative grounds, no matter how well intentioned. Similar dangers to the ones outlined above have surrounded the decriminalization of attempted suicide as well. It is impossible to know the degree of pressure or intimidation a physically able person may have been under when deciding to commit suicide. The truth is that we simply do not and cannot know the range of implications that allowing some form of assisted suicide will have for persons with physical disabilities. What we do know and cannot ignore is the anguish of those in the position of Ms Rodriguez. Respecting the consent of those in her position may necessarily imply running the risk that the consent will have been obtained improperly. The proper role of the legal system in these circumstances is to provide safeguards to ensure that the consent in question is as independent and informed as is reasonably possible.

The fear of a 'slippery slope' cannot, in my view, justify the over-inclusive reach of the *Criminal Code* to encompass not only people who may be vulnerable to the pressure of others but also persons with no evidence of vulnerability, and, in the case of the appellant, persons where there is positive evidence of freely determined consent. Sue Rodriguez is and will remain mentally competent. She has testified at trial to the fact that she alone, in consultation with her physicians, wishes to control the decision-making regarding the timing and circumstances of her death. I see no reason to disbelieve her, nor has the Crown suggested that she is being wrongfully influenced by anyone. Ms Rodriguez has also emphasized that she remains and wishes to remain free *not* to avail herself of the opportunity to end her own life should that be her eventual choice. The issue here is whether Parliament is justified in denying her the ability to make this choice lawfully, as could any physically able person.

While s. 241(*b*) restricts the equality rights of all those people who are physically unable to commit suicide without assistance, the choice for a mentally competent but physically disabled person who additionally suffers from a terminal illness is, I think, different from the choice of an individual whose disability is not life-threatening; in other words, for Ms Rodriguez, tragically, the choice is not whether to live as she is or to die, but rather when and how to experience a death that is inexorably impending. I do not, however, by observing this distinction, mean to suggest that the terminally ill are immune from vulnerability, or that they are less likely to be influenced by the intervention of others whatever their motives. Indeed, there is substantial evidence that people in this position may be susceptible to certain types of vulnerability that others are not. Further, it should not be assumed that a person with a physical disability who chooses suicide is doing so only as a result of the incapacity. It must be acknowledged that mentally competent people who commit suicide do so for a wide variety of motives, irrespective of their physical condition or life expectancy.

The law, in its present form, takes no account of the particular risks and interests that may be at issue in these differing contexts ... However, I fail to see how preventing against abuse in one context must result in denying self-determination in another. I remain unpersuaded by the government's apparent contention that it is not possible to design legislation that is somewhere in between complete decriminalization and absolute prohibition.

In my view, there is a range of options from which Parliament may choose in seeking to safeguard the interests of the vulnerable and still ensure the equal right to self-determination of persons with physical disabilities ... I find that an absolute prohibition that is indifferent to the individual or the circumstances in question cannot satisfy the constitutional duty on the government to impair the rights of persons with physical disabilities as little as reasonably possible. Section 241(*b*) cannot survive the minimal impairment component of the proportionality test.

| Box 3.2. | Competing versions of the necessity/proportionality test and the problems of 'balancing' |

Although it is fair to say that most human rights cases ultimately are decided on the basis of the question whether the restriction which is challenged is proportionate to the legitimate object-ive pursued, the methodology relied upon by human rights bodies often remains vague and ad hoc. A 'strict necessity' test would oblige the author of the measure to choose, from the various ways through which the objective could be achieved, the least restrictive alternative, i.e. the route that imposes on the right or freedom at stake the minimal impairment. But this version of the proportionality requirement essentially negates the margin of appreciation for the author of the measure, and it leads the judge (or the quasi-judicial body performing such a test) to second-guess the wisdom of the solutions chosen, in a way that may be questionable, particu-larly insofar as the impunged measure has been adopted through democratic means.

As a result, most human rights bodies prefer to rely on a vaguer, but more flexible 'balancing of interests', in which the weight of the various public and private interests involved is evaluated and the reasonableness of the measure tested against the interference it causes with the rights or freedoms of the individual. However, the difficulties with this method are equally considerable:

1. When national security concerns are weighed against the right to respect for private life, or the economic well-being of the country is measured against the right to property, there arises the problem known by legal theorists as the problem of incommensurability (see, *inter alia*, R. Chang (ed.), *Incommensurability, Incomparability and Practical Reason* (Cambridge, Mass.: Harvard University Press, 1997)). The very image of having to 'weigh' one right against another value or interest presupposes that there would exist some common scale according to which their respective importance (or 'weight') could be measured. But this, as famously remarked by Justice Scalia, 'is more like judging whether a particular line is longer than a particular rock is heavy' (*Bendix Autolite Cort.* v. *Midwesco Enterprises, Inc., et al.*, 486 U.S. 888 at 897 (1988) (Scalia, J., diss.)).

2. In addition, there may be the temptation for the judge, in his/her eagerness to proceed with such a balancing objectively – to the point even of striving towards mathematical exactitude – to confuse the balancing of fundamental rights with the cost-benefit analysis in use in the evaluation of public policies. This in turn may lead to undervalue the 'worth' of rights which are not susceptible of economic measurement or which the right-holders, due to their vul-nerable position, may be ready to waive against a relatively modest compensation, while, in contrast, interests to which economic value can be attached, or which are invoked by actors who can demonstrate the 'worth' these interests present to them or to the collectivity, will be overvalued. More specifically, there are three difficulties involved with such a balancing test developing into a cost-benefit analysis. First, both 'revealed preference' and 'hypothetical markets' methods, which are used in cost-benefit analyis in order to value interests (or rights), fail to take into account that the willingness of the individual to pay for a certain advan-tage is a function, not only of the importance of that advantage to that individual (the extent to which that advantage may contribute to the self-fulfilment of that individual), but also to

his/her ability to pay (or the economic necessities and other priorities for the individual with limited resources) (on the difference between actual consent and hypothetical consent and the resulting critique of the willingness-to-pay approaches in cost-benefit analysis, see H. M. Hurd, 'Justifiably Punishing the Justified', *Michigan Law Review*, 90 (1992), 2203 *et seq.* at 2305; and M. Adler, 'Incommensurability and Cost-Benefit Analysis', *University of Pennsylvania Law Review, 146* (1998), 1371 *et seq.*). Second, such valuations, whether they are 'contingent valuations' based on surveys of the 'willingness to pay' in the absence of markets or whether they are based on the preferences exhibited by economic agents through the choices they make in the market, have been demonstrated to be strongly baseline-dependent, in the sense that the position already occupied by any individual will shape his/her estimation of the value of any regulatory benefits or sacrifices (see E. Hoffman and M. L. Spitzer, 'Willingness to Pay vs. Willingness to Accept: Legal and Economic Implications', *Washington University Law Quarterly*, 71 (1993), 59 *et seq.*; M. Adler, 'Incommensurability and Cost-Benefit Analysis', cited above, at 1396–8). A third, related, difficulty is that we value not only our position in absolute terms, but also relative to the position of others (see R. H. Frank and C. R. Sunstein, 'Cost-Benefit Analysis and Relative Position', *University of Chicago Law Review*, 68 (2001), 323 *et seq.*).

3. The balancing test is typically performed in a procedural setting in which one of the interests in conflict is endorsed by the State, facing the interest of the individual in the preservation of his/her right or freedom. But the State is presumed to embody a broad collective interest whose weight, in comparison to that of the individual right-holder, will necessarily appear considerable, at least until we realize that this individual might well be representative, in his/her claims, of far wider societal interests, which the State may have paid insufficient consideration to. 'When it comes to weighing or valuing claims or demands, we must be careful to compare them on the same plane. If we put one as an individual interest and the other as a social interest we may decide the question in advance of our very way of putting it' (R. Pound, 'A Survey of Social Interests', *Harvard Law Review*, 57 (1943) (study initially written in 1921), 1 *et seq.* at 2). This is also the danger which C. Fried and L. Frantz first pointed at when, in 1959, the balancing test first made its appearance in the First Amendment case law of the US Supreme Court (*Barenblatt* v. *United States*, 360 U.S. 109 at 126 (1959) ('Whether First Amendment rights are asserted to bar governmental interrogation resolution of the issue always involves a balancing by the courts of the competing private and public interests at stake in the particular circumstances shown'): see C. Fried, 'Two Concepts of Interests: Some Reflections on the Supreme Court's Balancing Test', *Harvard Law Review*, 76 (1963), 755 *et seq.*; L. Frantz, 'Is the First Amendment Law? A Reply to Professor Mendelson', *California Law Review*, 51 (1963), 729 at 747–9).

4. A final difficulty is in the obligation for the judge to circulate, uncomfortably, between purely ad hoc balancing, seeking to define, in the specific circumstances of each case, which of the two rights in conflict should be recognized more weight in the balance, on the one hand; and 'definitional' balancing on the other hand, according to which the judge provides certain reasons for choosing one right over the other and, therefore, imports into his/her reasoning considerations not limited to the specific case at hand, but including anticipated future

cases where the same conflict might recur (see M. Nimmer, 'The Right to Speak from Times to Time: First Amendment Theory Applied to Libel and Misapplied to Privacy', *California Law Review*, 56 (1968), 935 *et seq.* at 942; J. H. Ely, 'Flag Desecration: a Case Study in the Roles of Categorization and Balancing in First Amendment Analysis', *Harvard Law Review*, 88 (1975), 1482 *et seq.* at 1500–2; L. Henkin, 'Infallibility Under Law: Constitutional Balancing', *Columbia Law Review*, 78 (1978), 1022 *et seq.* at 1027–8; T. A. Aleinikoff, 'Constitutional Law in the Age of Balancing', *Yale Law Journal*, 96 (1987), 943 at 948; K. M. Sullivan, 'Post-Liberal Judging: the Roles of Categorization and Balancing', *University of Colorado Law Review*, 63 (1992), 293). At the most superficial level, the dilemma between ad hoc and definitional balancing is between two judicial attitudes, one in which the judge seeks to identify the solution most adequate for the case at hand and the equity of which the parties will recognize – this is the judge as arbitrator – and another in which the judge is to clarify the requirements of the law, thus contributing for the future to legal certainty and to developing principles for the solution of future like cases – this is the judge as law-giver, or at least, as *expositor* of the law – (see P. McFadden, 'The Balancing Test', *Boston College Law Review*, 29 (1988), 585 *et seq.* at 642–51). At a deeper level, the dilemma relates to the fundamental question whether the act of balancing really may be reconciled with the definition of the judicial function itself, as consisting in the application, to certain facts, of certain pre-existing rules and principles, in order to arrive at a conclusion justified on the basis of such rules and principles. Which rules or principles guide the act of balancing itself? If such rules or principles exist, why should they not be expressed and made explicit? If they cannot be made explicit, what is the nature of the constraints facing the judge having to provide a reasoning justifying his or her conclusions?

3.7. Questions for discussion: the necessity test, balancing, and dilemmas facing human rights bodies

1. It has sometimes been argued that 'balancing' should simply be seen as any other rule applied by courts: as has been remarked by V. Luizzi, '[w]hen courts balance interests, they are, in effect, bringing their activity under a rule – that in certain cases, courts are to resolve the dispute by balancing the interests of the parties' (V. Luizzi, 'Balancing of Interests in Courts', *Jurimetrics Journal*, 20, No. 4 (1980), 373 *et seq.* at 402). Is this argument – that 'balancing' is, after all, a mode of decision-making like any other, a 'rule' followed by the judge – an answer to the concern that such a 'rule' may be unpredictable in its outcome, and thus does not allow those affected to plan their activities accordingly? If, as suggested by Luizzi, courts are in fact applying a rule when performing a balancing test, to which extent should we require from them that they make explicit the criteria they use in balancing, both in the interest of legal certainty and in order to improve the accountability of judicial decision-making?

2. If neither the 'strict necessity' test nor the 'balancing' test are fully adequate or easy to reconcile with the judicial function (see box 3.2.), what are the alternatives? Should human rights

bodies prefer a more procedural approach, focused on the process through which a particular measure interfering with human rights has been adopted, rather than on its substantive content? Which elements should characterize such a procedural approach, (a) when the measure is of a general nature, such as a land planning policy or a regulation applicable to a range of situations, and (b) when the measure is of an individual nature, such as the decision to remove a child from his/her family or to prohibit a particular public demonstration?

3. One of the difficulties of balancing individual rights or freedoms against wider societal interests is that the framing of the issue – the individual interest being pitted against the collective interest represented by the State – may prejudge the outcome of the test (see box 3.2.). Is the requirement of reasonable accommodation an answer to this concern? Could this requirement be described as imposing on the author of a general measure interfering with the right of the individual that the measure be justified not only in the generality of cases to which the measure applies, but also with respect to the specific situation of the individual?

3.5 Case study: restrictions to freedom of religion in vestimentary codes

In order to illustrate the above principles and, in particular, the difficulties facing courts or human rights expert bodies when asked to balance individuals rights against the general interests of the community, this section explores in depth the question of the prohibition of the wearing of religious symbols. The positions adopted by various judicial or quasi-judicial bodies, or by independent experts, are presented here in chronological fashion, particularly since these decisions or statements often refer to each other.

This series of cases begins with *Dahlab* v. *Switzerland*, presented to the European Court of Human Rights in 1998, but which the Court dismissed in 2001. The applicant was appointed as a primary school teacher by the Geneva Cantonal Government on 1 September 1990. She subsequently abandoned the Catholic faith and converted to Islam in March 1991. On 19 October 1991 she married an Algerian national. She began wearing an Islamic headscarf in class towards the end of the 1990–1 school year, her stated intention being to observe a precept laid down in the Koran whereby women are enjoined to draw their veils over themselves in the presence of men and male adolescents. In May 1995 the schools inspector for the Vernier district informed the Canton of Geneva Directorate General for Primary Education that the applicant regularly wore an Islamic headscarf at school; the inspector added that she had never had any comments from parents on the subject. In July 1996, however, the Director General requested the applicant to stop wearing the headscarf while carrying out her professional duties, as such conduct was incompatible with section 6 of the 1940 Public Education Act, which provides that the public education system 'shall ensure that the political and religious beliefs of pupils and parents are respected'. After she was formally prohibited from wearing a headscarf during her professional duties, Ms Dahlab challenged the decision, but her appeals were dismissed: the Federal Court upheld the

Geneva Cantonal Government's decision in a judgment of 12 November 1997. In her application to the European Court of Human Rights, Ms Dahlab submitted that the measure prohibiting her from wearing a headscarf in the performance of her teaching duties infringed upon her freedom to manifest her religion, as guaranteed by Article 9 of the Convention. The Court rejected the application as inadmissible because manifestly ill founded.

European Court of Human Rights (2nd sect.), *Lucia Dahlab v. Switzerland* **(Appl. No. 42393/98), decision (inadmissibility) of 15 February 2001:**

[T]he Court notes that the [Swiss] Federal Court held that the measure by which the applicant was prohibited, purely in the context of her activities as a teacher, from wearing a headscarf was justified by the potential interference with the religious beliefs of her pupils, other pupils at the school and the pupils' parents, and by the breach of the principle of denominational neutrality in schools. In that connection, the Federal Court took into account the very nature of the profession of State school teachers, who were both participants in the exercise of educational authority and representatives of the State, and in doing so weighed the protection of the legitimate aim of ensuring the neutrality of the State education system against the freedom to manifest one's religion. It further noted that the impugned measure had left the applicant with a difficult choice, but considered that State school teachers had to tolerate proportionate restrictions on their freedom of religion. In the Federal Court's view, the interference with the applicant's freedom to manifest her religion was justified by the need, in a democratic society, to protect the right of State school pupils to be taught in a context of denominational neutrality. It follows that religious beliefs were fully taken into account in relation to the requirements of protecting the rights and freedoms of others and preserving public order and safety. It is also clear that the decision in issue was based on those requirements and not on any objections to the applicant's religious beliefs.

The Court notes that the applicant, who abandoned the Catholic faith and converted to Islam in 1991, by which time she had already been teaching at the same primary school for more than a year, wore an Islamic headscarf for approximately three years, apparently without any action being taken by the head teacher or the district schools inspector or any comments being made by parents. That implies that during the period in question there were no objections to the content or quality of the teaching provided by the applicant, who does not appear to have sought to gain any kind of advantage from the outward manifestation of her religious beliefs.

The Court accepts that it is very difficult to assess the impact that a powerful external symbol such as the wearing of a headscarf may have on the freedom of conscience and religion of very young children. The applicant's pupils were aged between four and eight, an age at which children wonder about many things and are also more easily influenced than older pupils. In those circumstances, it cannot be denied outright that the wearing of a headscarf might have some kind of proselytising effect, seeing that it appears to be imposed on women by a precept which is laid down in the Koran and which, as the Federal Court noted, is hard to square with the principle of gender equality. It therefore appears difficult to reconcile the wearing of an Islamic headscarf with the message of tolerance, respect for others and, above all, equality and non-discrimination that all teachers in a democratic society must convey to their pupils.

Accordingly, weighing the right of a teacher to manifest her religion against the need to protect pupils by preserving religious harmony, the Court considers that, in the circumstances of the case and having regard, above all, to the tender age of the children for whom the applicant was responsible as a representative of the State, the Geneva authorities did not exceed their margin of appreciation and that the measure they took was therefore not unreasonable.

In the light of the above considerations and those set out by the Federal Court in its judgment of 12 November 1997, the Court is of the opinion that the impugned measure may be considered justified in principle and proportionate to the stated aim of protecting the rights and freedoms of others, public order and public safety. The Court accordingly considers that the measure prohibiting the applicant from wearing a headscarf while teaching was 'necessary in a democratic society'.

It follows that this part of the application is manifestly ill-founded.

Human Rights Committee, *Hudoyberganova* v. *Uzbekistan*, Communication No. 931/2000 (CCPR/C/82/D/931/2000), final views of 18 January 2005:

6.2 The Committee has noted the author's claim that her right to freedom of thought, conscience and religion was violated as she was excluded from University because she refused to remove the headscarf that she wore in accordance with her beliefs. The Committee considers that the freedom to manifest one's religion encompasses the right to wear clothes or attire in public which is in conformity with the individual's faith or religion. Furthermore, it considers that to prevent a person from wearing religious clothing in public or private may constitute a violation of article 18, paragraph 2, which prohibits any coercion that would impair the individual's freedom to have or adopt a religion. As reflected in the Committee's General Comment No. 22 (para. 5), policies or practices that have the same intention or effect as direct coercion, such as those restricting access to education, are inconsistent with article 18, paragraph 2. It recalls, however, that the freedom to manifest one's religion or beliefs is not absolute and may be subject to limitations, which are prescribed by law and are necessary to protect public safety, order, health, or morals, or the fundamental rights and freedoms of others (article 18, paragraph 3, of the Covenant). In the present case, the author's exclusion took place on 15 March 1998, and was based on the provisions of the Institute's new regulations. The Committee notes that the State party has not invoked any specific ground for which the restriction imposed on the author would in its view be necessary in the meaning of article 18, paragraph 3. Instead, the State party has sought to justify the expulsion of the author from University because of her refusal to comply with the ban. Neither the author nor the State party have specified what precise kind of attire the author wore and which was referred to as 'hijab' by both parties. In the particular circumstances of the present case, and without either prejudging the right of a State party to limit expressions of religion and belief in the context of article 18 of the Covenant and duly taking into account the specifics of the context, or prejudging the right of academic institutions to adopt specific regulations relating to their own functioning, the Committee is led to conclude, in the absence of any justification provided by the State party, that there has been a violation of article 18, paragraph 2.

European Court of Human Rights (GC), *Leyla Sahin* **v.** *Turkey* **(Appl. No. 44774/98), judgment of 10 November 2005:**

[After the University of Istanbul issued a circular directing that students with beards and students wearing the Islamic headscarf would be refused admission to lectures, courses and tutorials, the applicant was denied in March 1998 access to a written examination on one of the subjects she was studying because was wearing the Islamic headscarf. The University authorities subsequently refused on the same grounds to enrol her on a course, or to admit her to various lectures and a written examination. Before the Court, Ms Leyla Sahin complained under Article 9 (freedom of religion) that she had been prohibited from wearing the Islamic headscarf at University. She also complained of an unjustified interference with her right to education, within the meaning of Article 2 of Protocol No. 1 and of a violation of Article 14 (non-discrimination), taken together with Article 9, arguing that the prohibition on wearing the Islamic headscarf obliged students to choose between education and religion and discriminated between believers and non-believers.

These complaints are rejected by the Grand Chamber of the European Court of Human Rights, in a decision confirming the judgment delivered on 29 June 2004 by a Chamber of the Court. While agreeing that the circular in issue, adopted on 23 February 1998 by the Vice-Chancellor of the University of Istanbul, which placed restrictions of place and manner on the right to wear the Islamic headscarf in universities, constituted an interference with the applicant's right to manifest her religion, the Court considers that such interference pursues the legitimate aims of protecting the rights and freedoms of others and of protecting the public order. It also considers that the interference is necessary, as it is based in particular on the principles of secularism and equality. The Court agrees with the Turkish Constitutional Court that the principle of secularism, which guides the State in its role of impartial arbiter, also serves to protect the individual not only against arbitrary interference by the State but from external pressure from extremist movements. It considers that upholding that principle may be considered necessary to protect the democratic system in Turkey. The Court also notes the emphasis placed in the Turkish constitutional system on the protection of the rights of women and gender equality. Taking into account the fact that in Turkey, the majority of the population, while professing a strong attachment to the rights of women and a secular way of life, adheres to the Islamic faith, and that there are extremist political movements in Turkey which seek to impose on society as a whole their religious symbols and conception of a society founded on religious precepts, the Court takes the view that imposing limitations on the freedom to wear the headscarf can be regarded as meeting a pressing social need by seeking to achieve those two legitimate aims, especially since that religious symbol has taken on political significance in Turkey in recent years. The Court notes also that practising Muslim students in Turkish universities remain free, within the limits imposed by educational organizational constraints, to manifest their religion in accordance with habitual forms of Muslim observance. In addition, a resolution adopted by Istanbul University on 9 July 1998 shows that various other forms of religious attire were also forbidden on the university premises. While agreeing that any institutions of higher education existing at a given time in a State party to the Convention come within the scope of the first sentence of Article 2 of Protocol No. 1, since the right of access to such institutions is an inherent part of the right to education set out in that provision, the ban on wearing the Islamic headscarf has not impaired the very essence of the applicant's right to education. The Court therefore finds that there had been no violation of Article 2 of Protocol No. 1. Finally, examining the complaint under the non-discrimination clause of Article 14 of the Convention (see further chapter 7 on the requirement of non-discrimination), the Court simply notes that the regulations on the Islamic headscarf are not directed against the applicant's religious affiliation, but pursue, among other things, the legitimate aim of protecting order and the rights and freedoms of others and are manifestly intended to preserve the secular nature of educational institutions. The following excerpts encapsulate the main reasoning of the Court.]

[Whether the restriction was 'prescribed by law']

81. The applicant said that while university authorities, including vice chancellors' offices and deaneries, were unquestionably at liberty to use the powers vested in them by law, the scope of those powers and the limits on them were also defined by law, as were the procedures by which they were to be exercised and the safeguards against abuse of authority. In the instant case, the Vice Chancellor had not possessed the authority or power, either under the laws in force or the Students Disciplinary Procedure Rules, to refuse students 'wearing the headscarf' access to university premises or examination rooms. In addition, the legislature had at no stage sought to issue a general ban on wearing religious signs in schools and universities and there had never been support for such a ban in Parliament, despite the fierce debate to which the Islamic headscarf had given rise. Moreover, the fact that the administrative authorities had not introduced any general regulations providing for the imposition of disciplinary penalties on students wearing the headscarf in institutions of higher education meant that no such ban existed.

82. The applicant considered that the interference with her right had not been foreseeable and was not based on a 'law' within the meaning of the Convention ...

84. The Court reiterates its settled case law that the expression 'prescribed by law' requires firstly that the impugned measure should have a basis in domestic law. It also refers to the quality of the law in question, requiring that it be accessible to the persons concerned and formulated with sufficient precision to enable them – if need be, with appropriate advice – to foresee, to a degree that is reasonable in the circumstances, the consequences which a given action may entail and to regulate their conduct (*Gorzelik and others* v. *Poland* [GC], No. 44158/98, §64 [on this case, see above, section 3.2.]).

85. The Court observes that the applicant's arguments relating to the alleged unforeseeability of Turkish law do not concern the circular of 23 February 1998 on which the ban on students wearing the veil from lectures, courses and tutorials was based. That circular was issued by the Vice Chancellor of Istanbul University, who, as the person in charge in whom the main decision-making powers were vested, was responsible for overseeing and monitoring the administrative and scientific aspects of the functioning of the University. He issued the circular within the statutory framework set out in section 13 of Law No. 2547 ... and in accordance with the regulatory provisions that had been adopted earlier.

86. According to the applicant, however, the circular was not compatible with transitional section 17 of Law No. 2547, as that section did not proscribe the Islamic headscarf and there were no legislative norms in existence capable of constituting a legal basis for a regulatory provision.

87. The Court must therefore consider whether transitional section 17 of Law No. 2547 was capable of constituting a legal basis for the circular. It reiterates in that connection that it is

primarily for the national authorities, notably the courts, to interpret and apply domestic law (see *Kruslin* v. *France*, judgment of 24 April 1990, Series A No. 176–A, p. 21, §29) and notes that in rejecting the argument that the circular was illegal, the administrative courts relied on the settled case law of the Supreme Administrative Court and the Constitutional Court ...

88. Further, as regards the words 'in accordance with the law' and 'prescribed by law' which appear in Articles 8 to 11 of the Convention, the Court observes that it has always understood the term 'law' in its 'substantive' sense, not its 'formal' one; it has included both 'written law', encompassing enactments of lower ranking statutes (*De Wilde, Ooms and Versyp* v. *Belgium*, judgment of 18 June 1971, Series A No. 12, p. 45, §93) and regulatory measures taken by professional regulatory bodies under independent rule-making powers delegated to them by parliament (*Bartold* v. *Germany*, judgment of 25 March 1985, Series A No. 90, p. 21, §46), and unwritten law. 'Law' must be understood to include both statutory law and judge-made 'law' (see, among other authorities, *Sunday Times* v. *United Kingdom* (No. 1), judgment of 26 April 1979, Series A No. 30, p. 30, §47; *Kruslin*, cited above, §29 *in fine*; and *Casado Coca* v. *Spain*, judgment of 24 February 1994, Series A No. 285–A, p. 18, §43). In sum, the 'law' is the provision in force as the competent courts have interpreted it.

89. Accordingly, the question must be examined on the basis not only of the wording of transitional section 17 of Law No. 2547, but also of the relevant case law.

In that connection, as the Constitutional Court noted in its judgment of 9 April 1991 ..., the wording of that section shows that freedom of dress in institutions of higher education is not absolute. Under the terms of that provision, students are free to dress as they wish 'provided that [their choice] does not contravene the laws in force'.

90. The dispute therefore concerns the meaning of the words 'laws in force' in the aforementioned provision.

91. The Court reiterates that the scope of the notion of foreseeability depends to a considerable degree on the content of the instrument in question, the field it is designed to cover and the number and status of those to whom it is addressed. It must also be borne in mind that, however clearly drafted a legal provision may be, its application involves an inevitable element of judicial interpretation, since there will always be a need for clarification of doubtful points and for adaptation to particular circumstances. A margin of doubt in relation to borderline facts does not by itself make a legal provision unforeseeable in its application. Nor does the mere fact that such a provision is capable of more than one construction mean that it fails to meet the requirement of 'foreseeability' for the purposes of the Convention. The role of adjudication vested in the courts is precisely to dissipate such interpretational doubts as remain, taking into account the changes in everyday practice (*Gorzelik and others*, judgment cited above, §65).

92. The Court notes in that connection that in its aforementioned judgment the Constitutional Court found that the words 'laws in force' necessarily included the Constitution. The judgment also made it clear that authorising students to 'cover the neck and hair with a veil or headscarf for reasons of religious conviction' in the universities was contrary to the Constitution ...

93. That decision of the Constitutional Court, which was both binding ... and accessible, as it had been published in the Official Gazette of 31 July 1991, supplemented the letter of transitional section 17 and followed the Constitutional Court's previous case law ... In addition, the Supreme Administrative Court had by then consistently held for a number of years that wearing the Islamic headscarf at university was not compatible with the fundamental principles

of the Republic, since the headscarf was in the process of becoming the symbol of a vision that was contrary to the freedoms of women and those fundamental principles ...

94. As to the applicant's argument that the legislature had at no stage imposed a ban on wearing the headscarf, the Court reiterates that it is not for it to express a view on the appropriateness of the methods chosen by the legislature of a respondent State to regulate a given field. Its task is confined to determining whether the methods adopted and the effects they entail are in conformity with the Convention (*Gorzelik and others*, judgment cited above, §67).

95. Furthermore, the fact that Istanbul University or other universities may not have applied a particular rule – in this instance transitional section 17 of Law No. 2547 read in the light of the relevant case law – rigorously in all cases, preferring to take into account the context and the special features of individual courses, does not by itself make that rule unforeseeable. In the Turkish constitutional system, the university authorities may not under any circumstances place restrictions on fundamental rights without a basis in law (see Article 13 of the Constitution). Their role is confined to establishing the internal rules of the educational institution concerned in accordance with the rule requiring conformity with statute and subject to the administrative courts' powers of review.

96. Further, the Court accepts that it can prove difficult to frame laws with a high degree of precision on matters such as internal university rules, and tight regulation may be inappropriate (see, *mutatis mutandis*, *Gorzelik and others*, judgment cited above, §67).

97. Likewise, it is beyond doubt that regulations on wearing the Islamic headscarf existed at Istanbul University since 1994 at the latest, well before the applicant enrolled there ...

98. In these circumstances, the Court finds that there was a legal basis for the interference in Turkish law, namely transitional section 17 of Law No. 2547 read in the light of the relevant case law of the domestic courts. The law was also accessible and can be considered sufficiently precise in its terms to satisfy the requirement of foreseeability. It would have been clear to the applicant, from the moment she entered Istanbul University, that there were restrictions on wearing the Islamic headscarf on the university premises and, from 23 February 1998, that she was liable to be refused access to lectures and examinations if she continued to do so.

[The Court then finds that the impugned interference primarily pursued the legitimate aims of protecting the rights and freedoms of others and of protecting public order, an issue which was not contested by the parties. It then continues:]

[Whether the restriction was 'necessary in a democratic society']

106. In democratic societies, in which several religions coexist within one and the same population, it may be necessary to place restrictions on freedom to manifest one's religion or belief in order to reconcile the interests of the various groups and ensure that everyone's beliefs are respected ... This follows both from paragraph 2 of Article 9 and the State's positive obligation under Article 1 of the Convention to secure to everyone within its jurisdiction the rights and freedoms defined in the Convention.

107. The Court has frequently emphasised the State's role as the neutral and impartial organiser of the exercise of various religions, faiths and beliefs, and stated that this role is conducive to public order, religious harmony and tolerance in a democratic society. It also considers that the State's duty of neutrality and impartiality is incompatible with any power on the State's part to assess the legitimacy of religious beliefs or the ways in which those beliefs

are expressed (see *Manoussakis and others* v. *Greece*, judgment of 26 September 1996, *Reports* 1996–IV, p. 1365, §47; *Hassan and Chauch* v. *Bulgaria* [GC], No. 30985/96, §78, ECHR 2000–XI; *Refah Partisi and others*, [judgment of 13 February 2003], §91) and that it requires the State to ensure mutual tolerance between opposing groups (*United Communist Party of Turkey and others* v. *Turkey*, judgment of 30 January 1998, *Reports* 1998–I, §57). Accordingly, the role of the authorities in such circumstances is not to remove the cause of tension by eliminating pluralism, but to ensure that the competing groups tolerate each other (*Serif* v. *Greece*, No. 38178/97, §53, ECHR 1999–IX).

108. Pluralism, tolerance and broadmindedness are hallmarks of a 'democratic society'. Although individual interests must on occasion be subordinated to those of a group, democracy does not simply mean that the views of a majority must always prevail: a balance must be achieved which ensures the fair and proper treatment of people from minorities and avoids any abuse of a dominant position (see, *mutatis mutandis*, *Young, James and Webster* v. *United Kingdom*, judgment of 13 August 1981, Series A No. 44, p. 25, §63; and *Chassagnou and others* v. *France* [GC], Nos. 25088/94, 28331/95 and 28443/95, §112, ECHR 1999–III). Pluralism and democracy must also be based on dialogue and a spirit of compromise necessarily entailing various concessions on the part of individuals or groups of individuals which are justified in order to maintain and promote the ideals and values of a democratic society (see, *mutatis mutandis*, *United Communist Party of Turkey and others*, judgment cited above, pp. 21–22, §45; and *Refah Partisi and others*, judgment cited above §99). Where these 'rights and freedoms' are themselves among those guaranteed by the Convention or its Protocols, it must be accepted that the need to protect them may lead States to restrict other rights or freedoms likewise set forth in the Convention. It is precisely this constant search for a balance between the fundamental rights of each individual which constitutes the foundation of a 'democratic society' (*Chassagnou and others*, judgment cited above, §113).

109. Where questions concerning the relationship between State and religions are at stake, on which opinion in a democratic society may reasonably differ widely, the role of the national decision-making body must be given special importance (see, *mutatis mutandis*, ... *Wingrove* v. *United Kingdom* judgment of 25 November 1996, *Reports* 1996–V, p. 1958, §58). This will notably be the case when it comes to regulating the wearing of religious symbols in educational institutions, especially (as the comparative-law materials illustrate ...) in view of the diversity of the approaches taken by national authorities on the issue. It is not possible to discern throughout Europe a uniform conception of the significance of religion in society (*Otto-Preminger-Institut* v. *Austria*, judgment of 20 September 1994, Series A No. 295–A, p. 19, §50) and the meaning or impact of the public expression of a religious belief will differ according to time and context (see, among other authorities, *Dahlab* v. *Switzerland* (dec.) No. 42393/98, ECHR 2001–V [see above in this section]). Rules in this sphere will consequently vary from one country to another according to national traditions and the requirements imposed by the need to protect the rights and freedoms of others and to maintain public order (see, *mutatis mutandis*, *Wingrove*, judgment cited above, p. 1957, §57). Accordingly, the choice of the extent and form such regulations should take must inevitably be left up to a point to the State concerned, as it will depend on the domestic context concerned (see, *mutatis mutandis*, *Gorzelik*, judgment cited above, §67; and *Murphy* v. *Ireland* [judgment of 10 July 2003], No. 44179/98, §73 ...).

110. This margin of appreciation goes hand in hand with a European supervision embracing both the law and the decisions applying it. The Court's task is to determine whether the

measures taken at national level were justified in principle and proportionate (*Manoussakis and others*, judgment cited above, §44). In delimiting the extent of the margin of appreciation in the present case the Court must have regard to what is at stake, namely the need to protect the rights and freedoms of others, to preserve public order and to secure civil peace and true religious pluralism, which is vital to the survival of a democratic society (see, *mutatis mutandis*, *Kokkinakis*, judgment [of 25 May 1983, Series A No. 260–A], §31; *Manoussakis and others*, judgment cited above, p. 1364, §44; and *Casado Coca*, judgment cited above, §55).

111. The Court also notes that in the decisions of *Karaduman* v. *Turkey* (No. 16278/90, Commission decision of 3 May 1993, DR 74, p. 93) and *Dahlab* v. *Switzerland* (No. 42393/98, ECHR 2001–V) the Convention institutions found that in a democratic society the State was entitled to place restrictions on the wearing of the Islamic headscarf if it was incompatible with the pursued aim of protecting the rights and freedoms of others, public order and public safety. In the *Karaduman* case, measures taken in universities to prevent certain fundamentalist religious movements from exerting pressure on students who did not practise their religion or who belonged to another religion were found to be justified under Article 9 §2 of the Convention. Consequently, it is established that institutions of higher education may regulate the manifestation of the rites and symbols of a religion by imposing restrictions as to the place and manner of such manifestation with the aim of ensuring peaceful co-existence between students of various faiths and thus protecting public order and the beliefs of others (see, among other authorities, *Refah Partisi and others*, cited above, §95). In the *Dahlab* case, which concerned the teacher of a class of small children, the Court stressed among other matters the 'powerful external symbol' which her wearing a headscarf represented and questioned whether it might have some kind of proselytising effect, seeing that it appeared to be imposed on women by a religious precept that was hard to reconcile with the principle of gender equality. It also noted that wearing the Islamic headscarf could not easily be reconciled with the message of tolerance, respect for others and, above all, equality and non-discrimination that all teachers in a democratic society should convey to their pupils.

112. The interference in issue caused by the circular of 23 February 1998 imposing restrictions as to place and manner on the rights of students such as Ms Şahin to wear the Islamic headscarf on university premises was, according to the Turkish courts ..., based in particular on the two principles of secularism and equality.

113. In its judgment of 7 March 1989, the Constitutional Court stated that secularism, as the guarantor of democratic values, was the meeting point of liberty and equality. The principle prevented the State from manifesting a preference for a particular religion or belief; it thereby guided the State in its role of impartial arbiter, and necessarily entailed freedom of religion and conscience. It also served to protect the individual not only against arbitrary interference by the State but from external pressure from extremist movements. The Constitutional Court added that freedom to manifest one's religion could be restricted in order to defend those values and principles ...

114. As the Chamber rightly stated [in the judgment of 29 June 2004] (see paragraph 106 of its judgment), the Court considers this notion of secularism to be consistent with the values underpinning the Convention. It finds that upholding that principle, which is undoubtedly one of the fundamental principles of the Turkish State which are in harmony with the rule of law and respect for human rights, may be considered necessary to protect the democratic system in Turkey. An attitude which fails to respect that principle will not necessarily be accepted as being

covered by the freedom to manifest one's religion and will not enjoy the protection of Article 9 of the Convention (see *Refah Partisi and others*, judgment cited above, §93).

115. After examining the parties' arguments, the Grand Chamber sees no good reason to depart from the approach taken by the Chamber (see paragraphs 107–109 of the Chamber judgment) as follows: '... The Court ... notes the emphasis placed in the Turkish constitutional system on the protection of the rights of women ... Gender equality – recognised by the European Court as one of the key principles underlying the Convention and a goal to be achieved by member States of the Council of Europe (see, among other authorities, *Abdulaziz, Cabales and Balkandali* v. *United Kingdom*, judgment of 28 May 1985, Series A No. 77, p. 38, §78; *Schuler-Zgraggen* v. *Switzerland*, judgment of 24 June 1993, Series A No. 263, pp. 21–22, §67; *Burgharz* v. *Switzerland*, judgment of 22 February 1994, Series A No. 280–B, p. 29, §27; *Van Raalte* v. *Netherlands*, judgment of 21 February 1997, *Reports* 1997–I, p. 186, §39, *in fine*; and *Petrovic* v. *Austria*, judgment of 27 March 1998, *Reports* 1998–II, p. 587, §37) – was also found by the Turkish Constitutional Court to be a principle implicit in the values underlying the Constitution ... In addition, like the Constitutional Court ..., the Court considers that, when examining the question of the Islamic headscarf in the Turkish context, there must be borne in mind the impact which wearing such a symbol, which is presented or perceived as a compulsory religious duty, may have on those who choose not to wear it. As has already been noted (see *Karaduman*, decision cited above; and *Refah Partisi and others*, cited above, §95), the issues at stake include the protection of the 'rights and freedoms of others' and the 'maintenance of public order' in a country in which the majority of the population, while professing a strong attachment to the rights of women and a secular way of life, adhere to the Islamic faith. Imposing limitations on freedom in this sphere may, therefore, be regarded as meeting a pressing social need by seeking to achieve those two legitimate aims, especially since, as the Turkish courts stated ..., this religious symbol has taken on political significance in Turkey in recent years ... The Court does not lose sight of the fact that there are extremist political movements in Turkey which seek to impose on society as a whole their religious symbols and conception of a society founded on religious precepts ... It has previously said that each Contracting State may, in accordance with the Convention provisions, take a stance against such political movements, based on its historical experience (*Refah Partisi and others*, cited above, §124). The regulations concerned have to be viewed in that context and constitute a measure intended to achieve the legitimate aims referred to above and thereby to preserve pluralism in the university.'

116. Having regard to the above background, it is the principle of secularism, as elucidated by the Constitutional Court ..., which is the paramount consideration underlying the ban on the wearing of religious symbols in universities. In such a context, where the values of pluralism, respect for the rights of others and, in particular, equality before the law of men and women are being taught and applied in practice, it is understandable that the relevant authorities should wish to preserve the secular nature of the institution concerned and so consider it contrary to such values to allow religious attire, including, as in the present case, the Islamic headscarf, to be worn.

117. The Court must now determine whether in the instant case there was a reasonable relationship of proportionality between the means employed and the legitimate objectives pursued by the interference.

118. [The Court] notes at the outset that it is common ground that practising Muslim students in Turkish universities are free, within the limits imposed by educational organisational constraints, to manifest their religion in accordance with habitual forms of Muslim observance. In addition, the resolution adopted by Istanbul University on 9 July 1998 shows that various other forms of religious attire are also forbidden on the university premises ...

119. It should also be noted that when the issue of whether students should be allowed to wear the Islamic headscarf surfaced at Istanbul University in 1994 in relation to the medical courses, the Vice Chancellor reminded them of the reasons for the rules on dress. Arguing that calls for permission to wear the Islamic headscarf in all parts of the university premises were misconceived and pointing to the public-order constraints applicable to medical courses, he asked the students to abide by the rules, which were consistent with both the legislation and the case law of the higher courts ...

120. Furthermore, the process whereby the regulations that led to the decision of 9 July 1998 were implemented took several years and was accompanied by a wide debate within Turkish society and the teaching profession ... The two highest courts, the Supreme Administrative Court and the Constitutional Court, have managed to establish settled case law on this issue ... It is quite clear that throughout that decision-making process the university authorities sought to adapt to the evolving situation in a way that would not bar access to the university to students wearing the veil, through continued dialogue with those concerned, while at the same time ensuring that order was maintained and in particular that the requirements imposed by the nature of the course in question were complied with.

121. In that connection, the Court does not accept the applicant's submission that the fact that there were no disciplinary penalties for failing to comply with the dress code effectively meant that no rules existed ... As to how compliance with the internal rules should have been secured, it is not for the Court to substitute its view for that of the university authorities. By reason of their direct and continuous contact with the education community, the university authorities are in principle better placed than an international court to evaluate local needs and conditions or the requirements of a particular course (see, *mutatis mutandis*, *Valsamis* v. *Greece*, judgment of 18 December 1996, *Reports* 1996–VI, p. 2325, §32). Besides, having found that the regulations pursued a legitimate aim, it is not open to the Court to apply the criterion of proportionality in a way that would make the notion of an institution's 'internal rules' devoid of purpose. Article 9 does not always guarantee the right to behave in a manner governed by a religious belief (*Pichon and Sajous* v. *France* (dec.), No. 49853/99, ECHR 2001–X) and does not confer on people who do so the right to disregard rules that have proved to be justified (see the opinion of the Commission, §51, contained in its report of 6 July 1995 appended to the *Valsamis* judgment cited above, p. 2337).

122. In the light of the foregoing and having regard to the Contracting States' margin of appreciation in this sphere, the Court finds that the interference in issue was justified in principle and proportionate to the aim pursued.

123. Consequently, there has been no breach of Article 9 of the Convention.

The UN Special Rapporteur on freedom of religion or belief, Ms Asma Jahangir, also provided useful comments on this issue. Following a mission to France in 2005, she expressed her concern at certain consequences of the Law of 15 March 2004 on the wearing of religious symbols in public schools, particularly as regards the radicalization of Muslim communities and, generally, the feeling of exclusion of these communities. She also proposed a set of criteria, in order to assist governments in assessing whether the regulations in place on the wearing of religious symbols comply with the requirements of freedom of religion.

Report submitted by Asma Jahangir, Special Rapporteur on freedom of religion or belief: Mission to France (18–29 September 2005), E/CN.4/2006/5/Add. 4 (8 March 2006):

IV. Religious symbols in public schools

47. Since the beginning of the school year 2004/05, in application of Law 2004–228 of 15 March 2004 on '*laïcité*', and conspicuous religious symbols in public schools (Loi no 2004–228 du 15 mars 2004 encadrant, en application du principe de laïcité, le port de signes ou de tenues manifestant une appartenance religieuse dans les écoles, collèges et lycées publics), the wearing of conspicuous religious symbols is prohibited in public schools.

A. Background 48. Until March 2004, there was no legislation related to the wearing of religious symbols in schools. In 1989, the State Council (*Conseil d'Etat*), referring to the right to freedom of expression and the right to publicly manifest one's religion or beliefs, decided that the wearing of symbols intended to show a child's affiliation to a religion in public schools was not necessarily considered incompatible with the principle of the separation of Church and State. It would only constitute a breach of this principle, and therefore be considered illegal, if it was accompanied by proof of proselytizing behaviour or provocation. It distinguished between an 'ostentatious (*ostentatoire*) religious symbol' and the 'ostentatious wearing of a religious symbol'.

49. School administrations found this regime complex and difficult to implement on a case-by-case basis, in the absence of any legislation. Accordingly, educational professionals advocated for the adoption of a law on the issue.

50. As a result, in December 2003, a special commission was appointed by the President and headed by the national ombudsman, Bernard Stasi, to analyse the application of the principle of *laïcité* in France. Among other recommendations, the Commission recommended that a law be drafted banning conspicuous religious symbols (including large Christian crosses, Jewish skullcaps and Islamic headscarves) in State schools.

51. Law 2004–228, which amended the Education Act, was adopted by a large majority in the National Assembly and across party lines. In its article 1, it provides that in public elementary schools, middle schools (*collèges*) and secondary schools (*lycées*), wearing symbols or clothing by which students ostentatiously show a religious identity is prohibited. School rules are to stipulate that any disciplinary procedure must be preceded by dialogue with the student.

52. The assessment of whether a religious symbol constitutes a conspicuous sign is left to the head of the school establishment, a power that is said to have led in some cases to abuse, including in cases where some of the heads decided to ban all manner of head coverings, with even the slightest religious connotation.

B. The reasons behind and arguments supporting the law 53. According to many interlocutors, the reasons behind this legislation go beyond the application of the principle of the separation of Church and State. This legislation is also illustrative of the relationship between the French State and religion, in particular certain practices of the Muslim community.

54. The French religious landscape has dramatically changed since 1905, in part as a result of the immigration of a large amount of people from Muslim backgrounds. Throughout the years, the population of Muslim background has significantly increased and, in many places, has settled in some of the so-called *banlieues* or housing estates. The *banlieues* are the suburbs surrounding France's larger cities, such as Paris and Marseilles. The population of the *banlieues* is often characterized by poverty, high unemployment rates among young people, growing extremism among Muslim youth and an increasing feeling of alienation from French society at large.

55. On 4 October 2002, Sohane Benziane was burnt alive, reportedly for reasons related to her refusal to wear the headscarf. This tragic incident was at the origin of the creation of movements such as *Ni putes, ni soumises* ... [Associations defending women's rights] mainly claim that most young women of Muslim background wear the headscarf because they are forced to do so by their family and, in particular, by the male members. They emphasize the individual character of the right to freedom of religion and consider that the exercise of this right, which would include the right to wear the headscarf, should be based on free and individual choice.

56. The associations argue that an increasing proportion of young French citizens of Muslim background want to emancipate themselves from the religion to which they are associated. They are of the opinion that Law 2004–228 has provided them with a legitimate means of reaching this goal.

57. The National Assembly and the Government reportedly considered that this law would constitute a means of protecting young women who were not willing to abide by certain so-called religious norms, including the wearing of the headscarf. The banning of religious symbols at school would enable those young female children to freely choose the way they conduct their lives.

58. Many supporters of the law have also argued that the school is a place where children should learn about the elements that unify them rather than the elements that differentiate them. In this context, they argue that differentiating between pupils on the basis of religion has resulted in some pupils refusing to participate in classes such as biology or swimming classes.

59. The Special Rapporteur noted the inconsistency in the position of certain interlocutors from women's organizations who argued that Islam does not, as such, require women to wear a headscarf whilst at the same time arguing that the law should be applied to the headscarf because it was, in fact, being worn as a religious symbol.

60. Finally, at a meeting with members of staff of the office of the Minister of National Education, the Special Rapporteur was told that the wearing of religious symbols in schools hurt the freedom of conscience of the other children. She was concerned about the intolerant nature of such arguments.

C. Consequences of the implementation of the law 61. It is claimed by the Government that the implementation of the law has actually proved less problematic than expected and most interlocutors have agreed with this conclusion. According to the Minister of National Education, 47 children have been expelled from schools, including three Sikh pupils who had refused to remove their under-turban. French tribunals have usually upheld these expulsions.

62. It is however difficult to assess the number of pupils who have chosen not to abandon their religious signs. In addition to dismissals, some have removed themselves from the school system by abstaining from registering with a school. Others aged above 16 are no longer obliged to attend school. A few have left France or have registered with private schools, which allowed them to keep wearing their symbols. Finally, a few have enrolled with distance learning systems (*Centre national d'enseignement à distance*).

63. When assessing the indirect consequences of the law, opinions are much more divided. Although the scope of the new law applies equally to all religious symbols, its application disproportionately affects young Muslim women wearing the headscarf. A large number of these women told the Special Rapporteur about the difficulties they had endured because they had freely chosen to wear the headscarf. Many had been intimidated or humiliated for expressing their personal opinion on the question. Even in cases where young girls were obliged to wear headscarves by their families, the law is said to have provoked particularly painful situations within the families. Some girls who did not wear the headscarf before the law have decided to wear it when they leave the school as a form of protest. Some informed the Special Rapporteur that they felt torn between loyalty to their religious community and their commitment to women's rights.

64. The adoption of the law is also said to have radicalized a fraction of the Muslim youth and has been systematically used in the *banlieues* and Mosques to disseminate a message of religious radicalism. Some critics of the new law argue that it may have been among the different elements explaining the widespread violence and riots that erupted all around France's *banlieues* in early November 2005.

65. While CFCM [*Conseil français du culte musulman*] was unable to reach a unified position on Law 2004–228 UOIF [*union des organisations islamiques de France*] openly denounced the adoption of the law, although it did ask Muslim girls to comply with it.

66. Another religious minority that has been seriously affected by the adoption of the law is the Sikh community. Their members reported to the Special Rapporteur that displaying religious symbols was an essential part of their faith. They described the painful experiences they endured when their children had to cut their hair, as a result of the rigid application of the law by some educational institutions.

67. The law also appears to have sent the wrong message to a certain portion of the population which has come to believe that the wearing of religious symbols per se, and in particular headscarves, is generally unlawful. As a result of the new law, a portion of the population has come to associate the headscarf solely with gender inequality and oppression. The Special Rapporteur was informed about instances where women were refused access to shops or were insulted in the street because they wore the headscarf. For the same reasons, some women were dismissed from their employment, while others found it difficult to find employment.

68. More generally, some interlocutors criticized the law because, in their opinion it was meant to solve a problem of a more social than religious nature. They consider that the law has had a negative impact on social cohesion and that, instead of prohibiting religious symbols, the school system should teach the peaceful cohabitation of communities and universal values.

D. Human rights law 69. With regard to the compatibility of Law 2004–228 with human rights law and, in particular, the right to freedom of religion or belief, the Special Rapporteur notes that the law constitutes a limitation of the right to manifest a religion or a belief ...

70. Paragraph 3 of article 18 of the International Covenant on Civil and Political Rights provides for certain such limitations under restrictive conditions. General comment No. 22 (1993) of the Human Rights Committee emphasizes that paragraph 3 of article 18 '... is to be strictly interpreted: restrictions are not allowed on grounds not specified there, even if they would be allowed as restrictions to other rights protected in the Covenant, such as national security. Limitations may be applied only for those purposes for which they were prescribed and must be directly related and proportionate to the specific need on which they are predicated. Restrictions may not be imposed for discriminatory purposes or applied in a discriminatory manner ...' (para. 8). So far, there has not been an assessment of the compatibility of this legislation with relevant international standards protecting the right to freedom of religion or belief by a judicial or quasi–judicial international human rights body.

71. However, besides a strict assessment of compatibility with the right to freedom of religion or belief, the law has been the object of careful consideration by the United Nations treaty bodies. The Committee on the Rights of the Child, in its concluding observations on the second periodic report of France, expressed its concern that 'the new legislation (Law No. 2004–228 of 15 March 2004) on wearing religious signs in public schools may be counterproductive, by neglecting the principle of the best interests of the child and the right of the child to access to education ... the Committee recommends that the State party ... consider alternative means, including mediation, of ensuring the secular character of public schools, while guaranteeing that individual rights are not infringed upon and that children are not excluded or marginalized from the school system ... The dress code in schools may be better addressed within the public schools themselves, encouraging participation of children' (CRC/C/15/Add. 4, paras. 25–26).

72. In its concluding observations on the fifteenth and sixteenth periodic reports of France, the Committee on the Elimination of Racial Discrimination 'recommend[ed] to the State party that it should continue to monitor the implementation of the Act of 15 March 2004 closely, to ensure that it has no discriminatory effects and that the procedures followed in its implementation always place emphasis on dialogue, to prevent it from denying any pupil the right to education and to ensure that everyone can always exercise that right' (CERD/C/FRA/CO/16, para 18).

IX. Conclusions and Recommendations

98. Law 2004–228 of 15 March 2004 on the wearing of conspicuous religious symbols in public schools is widely supported by the political apparatus as well as by the population. Although the law is intended to apply equally to all persons, the Special Rapporteur is of the opinion that it has mainly affected certain religious minorities, and notably, people of a Muslim background. The Special Rapporteur believes that the wide political support for the law has conveyed a demoralizing message to religious minorities in France.

99. The law is appropriate insofar as it is intended, in accordance with the principle of the best interests of the child, to protect the autonomy of minors who may be pressured or forced to wear a headscarf or other religious symbols. However, the law denies the right of those minors who have freely chosen to wear a religious symbol to school as part of their religious belief.

100. The Special Rapporteur is of the opinion that the direct and, in particular, the indirect consequences of this law may not have been thoroughly considered. Although many interlocutors at the governmental level are satisfied with the results of the implementation of the law, she noticed that the figures are often disputed, including because the criteria used for the assessment vary. Moreover, the Special Rapporteur considers that aside from statistics, the issue is one of principle.

101. The concerns of the Special Rapporteur are more serious with regard to the indirect consequences of Law 2004–228 in the longer term. The implementation of the law by educational institutions has led, in a number of cases, to abuses that have provoked humiliation, in particular amongst young Muslim women. According to many sources, such humiliation can only lead to the radicalization of the persons affected and those associated with them. Moreover, the stigmatization of the headscarf has provoked instances of religious intolerance when women wear it outside school, at university or in the workplace. Although the law was aimed at regulating symbols related to all religions, it appears to mainly target girls from a Muslim background wearing the headscarf.

102. The Special Rapporteur encourages the Government to closely monitor the way educational institutions are implementing the law, in order to avoid the feelings of humiliation that were reported to her during her visit. She also recommends a flexible implementation of the law which would accommodate the schoolchildren for whom the display of religious symbols constitutes an essential part of their faith.

103. In all circumstances, the Government should uphold the principle of the best interests of the child and guarantee the fundamental right of access to education, as has been recommended by several United Nations treaty-monitoring bodies.

104. Moreover, the Government should take appropriate measures to better inform school authorities, and more generally the French population, about the exact nature and purpose of the law. It should be made clear that the wearing or display of religious symbols is an essential part of the right to manifest one's religion or belief that can only be limited under restrictive conditions. The Government should also promptly provide redress in any situation where persons have been the victim of discrimination or other act of religious intolerance because of their religious symbols, including by prosecuting the perpetrators of such acts in the relevant cases.

Report submitted by Asma Jahangir, the Special Rapporteur on freedom of religion or belief, E/CN.4/2006/5 (9 January 2006), paras. 36–72:

III. Religious symbols

A. Factual aspects 36. When dealing with the issue of religious symbols, two aspects of the question need to be taken into account. On the one hand, many individuals in various parts of the world are prevented from identifying themselves through the display of religious symbols, while on the other hand the reports and activities of the mandate have revealed the practice in some countries of requiring people to identify themselves through the display of religious symbols, including religious dress in public. The Special Rapporteur refers to the former as positive freedom of religion or belief, and to the latter as negative freedom of religion. The following paragraphs examine, from an international human rights perspective, both positive and negative freedom of religion or belief of individuals with regard to the wearing of religious symbols such as garments and ornaments. A different, albeit related, issue is the display of religious symbols in public locations such as courthouses, polling stations, classrooms, public squares, etc. Some aspects of these situations have been the subject of several national legal judgements at the highest level, but the question will not be covered in this section.

37. A comparative analysis of the factual aspects reveals a set of regulations or prohibitions on wearing religious symbols in more than 25 countries all over the world. Several religions are affected and religious symbols remain a subject of controversy in a number of countries. Examples of affected believers and their religious garments or ornaments include Muslims wearing headscarves, Jews wearing yarmulkes, Christians wearing crucifixes, collars and nuns' habits, Hindus displaying a bindi, Buddhists wearing saffron robes, Sikhs wearing turbans or kirpans as well as followers of Bhagwan (Osho) wearing reddish-coloured clothing. There are different levels of regulation or prohibition on the wearing of religious symbols including constitutional provisions, legislative acts at the national level, regulations and mandatory directives of regional or local authorities, rules in public or private organizations or institutions (e.g. school rules) and court judgements. The intensity of possible adverse effects for individuals who do not abide by the regulations or prohibitions also depends on the respective field of application. Pupils in primary and secondary schools run the risk of being expelled from the public school system, whereas teachers are in danger of reprimands, suspension and, ultimately, dismissal from their jobs. At the university level, students also run the risk of being expelled or of not being awarded their degrees unless they abide by prescriptions concerning religious symbols. University lecturers are likely not to be employed in the first place. In the work environment in general there is a risk of reprimands, suspension and dismissal directly connected to the wearing of religious symbols. This may affect both employees in private enterprises and civil servants, as well as members of Parliament and military personnel. When certain dress codes are applicable for ID photographs, e.g. on permanent resident cards, visas, passports and driving licences, individuals run the risk of not receiving the official ID or of being forced to wear the required head covering on ID photographs for deportation purposes. In public, individuals may either be prevented (positive aspect of freedom of religion or belief) or coerced to wear religious symbols that they consider not essential to their convictions (negative freedom of religion or belief).

38. The obligation to wear religious dress in public in certain countries was particularly criticized by Special Rapporteur Amor, who stated that 'women are among those who suffer most because of severe restrictions on their education and employment, and the obligation to wear what is described as Islamic dress' (E/CN.4/1998/6, para. 60). There were reports of punishment by whipping and/or a fine (A/51/542/Add. 2, para. 51) and a growing number of women being attacked in the streets (E/CN.4/2003/66/Add. 1, para. 59), or even killed after being threatened for failing to wear religious symbols (E/CN.4/1995/91, p. 36). After in situ visits, Special Rapporteur Amor addressed possible solutions by urging that dress should not be the subject of political regulation and by calling for flexible and tolerant attitudes in this regard. At the same time he emphasized that traditions and customs were worthy of respect (E/CN.4/1996/95/Add. 2, para. 97 and A/51/542/Add. 2, para. 140). In his thematic studies he also referred to the different possible meanings of religious symbols (E/CN.4/2002/73/Add. 2, paras. 101–102) and in particular to the situation of pupils in the public school system (A/CONF.189/PC.2/22, paras. 56–59).

39. Furthermore, in resolution 1464 (2005) on 'Women and religion in Europe', the Parliamentary Assembly of the Council of Europe has recently called on its member States to 'ensure that freedom of religion and respect for culture and tradition are not accepted as pretexts to justify violations of women's rights, including when underage girls are forced to submit to religious codes (including dress codes)' (Parliamentary Assembly of the Council of Europe, resolution 1464 (2005), para. 7.4, adopted on 4 October 2005).

B. Legal framework at the international level 40. As mentioned in the Special Rapporteur's previous annual report (E/CN.4/2005/61, para. 65), most international judicial or quasi-judicial bodies consider the display of religious symbols as a manifestation of religion or belief (*forum externum*) rather than being part of internal conviction (*forum internum*), which is not subject to limitation. Several universal and regional human rights instruments refer to the freedom 'to manifest his religion or belief in worship, *observance*, *practice* and teaching' (emphasis added). The Declaration on the Elimination of All Forms of Intolerance and of Discrimination Based on Religion or Belief more specifically enumerates the freedom to 'make, acquire and use to an adequate extent the necessary articles and materials related to rites or customs of a religion or belief' (Article 6(c) of the 1981 Declaration) According to the Human Rights Committee's general comment No. 22 on article 18 of the Covenant, '[t]he observance and practice of religion or belief may include not only ceremonial acts but also such customs as ... the wearing of distinctive clothing or head coverings' (para. 4).

41. It is not clear whether the wearing of religious symbols falls under the category of 'practice' or 'observance'. In listing the features that required protection, the Committee does not seem to distinguish clearly between these two categories. However, some commentators have suggested that observance refers to 'prescriptions that are inevitably connected with a religion or belief and protects both the right to perform certain acts and the right to refrain from doing certain things', whereas practice concerns manifestations which are 'not prescribed, but only authorized by a religion or belief'. Such a distinction between compulsory prescriptions and mere authorizations may ultimately lead to problems when trying to determine who should be competent to consider this aspect of the individual's freedom of religion or belief. During the elaboration of general comment No. 22, Human Rights Committee member Rosalyn Higgins stated that '... it was not the Committee's responsibility to decide what should constitute a manifestation of religion'. She resolutely opposed the idea that 'States could have complete latitude to decide what was and what was not a genuine religious belief. The contents of a religion should be defined by the worshippers themselves' (See the Human Rights Committee discussion on 24 July 1992, Summary Records of the 1166th meeting of the forty-fifth session, para. 48). A certain appearance or exhibition of a symbol may or may not be linked to any religious sentiment or belief. It would therefore be most inappropriate for the State to determine whether the symbol in question was indeed a manifestation of religious belief. The Special Rapporteur therefore shares the approach of the Human Rights Committee in dealing with the wearing of religious symbols under the headings of 'practice and observance' together.

42. The controversy under international human rights law tends to centre on possible limitations on the freedom to manifest one's religion or belief, e.g. according to article 29(2) of the Universal Declaration on Human Rights, article 18(3) of the International Covenant on Civil and Political Rights, article 1(3) of the Declaration, article 9(2) of the European Convention on Human Rights (ECHR) and article 12(3) of the American Convention on Human Rights (AmCHR).

Generally speaking, these clauses only accept such limitations as are prescribed or determined by law and are necessary – in a democratic society – to protect public safety, order, health, or morals or the fundamental rights and freedoms of others. The list of permissible reasons for intervention notably does not include additional grounds stipulated for different human rights, e.g. national security or the reputations of others. Furthermore, article 4(2) of the Covenant and article 27(2) of the American Convention on Human Rights prescribe that, even in time of public emergency or war, no derogation from the freedom of conscience and religion is permissible. That this right is non-derogable again underlines the importance of the freedom of religion or belief.

C. International case law 43. When discussing the wording of its general comment No. 22, the Human Rights Committee also took account of the 'need to avoid rivalry or provocation' (id., para. 27 (Human Rights Committee member Mr Sadi)) with regard to the wearing of clothing in accordance with religious practice. The following cases illustrate typical contentious situations and the respective findings of the relevant international judicial or quasi-judicial body. Two cases before the Human Rights Committee as well as concluding observations of the Committee on the Rights of the Child appear to be pertinent to the issue of religious symbols. Furthermore, there are a number of precedents, including the most recent Grand Chamber decision of 10 November 2005, in the case law of the European Court of Human Rights and of the European Commission on Human Rights.

44. Communication No. 931/2000, *Hudoyberganova* v. *Uzbekistan* [see above in this section] concerned a female Muslim student of the Tashkent State Institute for Eastern Languages who allegedly had been suspended for wearing a headscarf. On 5 November 2004, the majority of the Human Rights Committee concluded, in the absence of any justification provided by the State party, that there had been a violation of article 18, paragraph 2, of the Covenant. It also confirmed that 'the freedom to manifest one's religion encompasses the right to wear clothes or attire in public which is in conformity with the individual's faith or religion. Furthermore, it considers that to prevent a person from wearing religious clothing in public or private may constitute a violation of article 18, paragraph 2, which prohibits any coercion that would impair the individual's freedom to have or adopt a religion' (CCPR/C/82/D/931/2000, para. 6.2). Three Committee members, however, decided to append individual opinions, referring to the uncertain state of the record and to more complex causes for Ms Hudoyberganova's exclusion from the institute, based on her own statements.

45. In communication No. 208/1986, *Bhinder* v. *Canada* [discussed in greater detail in chapter 7, section 3.1.] the Human Rights Committee held on 9 November 1989 that the requirement for Sikhs to wear safety headgear during work was justified under article 18(3) of the Covenant, without further specifying which of the grounds for limitation it thought to be in question. In addition, the Committee did not find de facto discrimination against persons of the Sikh religion violating article 26 of the Covenant because the legislation was to be 'regarded as reasonable and directed towards objective purposes that are compatible with the Covenant' (CCPR/C/37/D/208/1986, para. 6.2.).

46. The Committee on the Rights of the Child in its concluding observations on the second periodic report of France was concerned at the alleged rise in discrimination, including that based on religion, and that the new legislation on wearing religious symbols and clothing in public schools may neglect the principle of the best interests of the child and the right of the

child to access to education. It recommended that the State party 'consider alternative means, including mediation, of ensuring the secular character of public schools, while guaranteeing that individual rights are not infringed upon and that children are not excluded or marginalized from the school system and other settings as a result of such legislation. The dress code of schools may be better addressed within the public schools themselves, encouraging participation of children.' The Committee further recommended that 'the State party continue to closely monitor the situation of girls being expelled from schools as a result of the new legislation and ensure that they enjoy the right of access to education' (CRC/C/15/Add. 240, paras. 25–26).

47. At the regional level, the European Court of Human Rights and, previously, the European Commission on Human Rights appear to be more inclined to allow States to limit individuals' positive freedom of religion or belief. The Court case *Şahin* v. *Turkey* concerned the refusal of admission to lectures and examinations at Istanbul University for students whose heads were covered [see above in this section]. Both the Court Chamber and the recent Grand Chamber judgements held the notion of secularism to be consistent with the values underpinning the European Convention on Human Rights. With regard to article 9 of ECHR, 'the Court considered that, when examining the question of the Islamic headscarf in the Turkish context, there had to be borne in mind the impact which wearing such a symbol, which was presented or perceived as a compulsory religious duty, may have on those who chose not to wear it' (*Şahin* v. *Turkey*, application No. 44774/98, ECtHR Chamber judgement of 29 June 2004, para. 108 and ECtHR Grand Chamber judgement of 10 November 2005, para. 115). In her dissenting opinion, however, Judge Tulkens disagreed with the manner in which the principles of secularism and equality were applied by the majority of the Grand Chamber. She underlined that not mere worries, but only 'indisputable facts and reasons whose legitimacy is beyond doubt' were capable of justifying interference with a right guaranteed by the Convention.

48. In the case *Dahlab* v. *Switzerland*, the application of a teacher in a primary school who had been prohibited from wearing a headscarf in the performance of her professional duties was dismissed by the European Court of Human Rights at the admissibility stage [see above in this section]. The Court held that a teacher, wearing a 'powerful external symbol' such as the headscarf might have some kind of proselytizing effect on young children, who were in this case aged between 4 and 8 years. Thus, the Court concurred with the view of the Swiss Federal Court that the prohibition of wearing a headscarf in the context of the applicant's activities as a teacher was 'justified by the potential interference with the religious beliefs of her pupils, other pupils at the school and the pupils' parents, and by the breach of the principle of denominational neutrality in schools' (*Dahlab* v. *Switzerland*, application No. 42393/98, ECtHR decision of 15 February 2001(ECHR 2001–V at p. 462)).

49. The protection of the beliefs of others and of public order was also stressed in the case *Refah Partisi (the Welfare Party) and others* v. *Turkey*, where the Grand Chamber of the European Court stated that 'measures taken in universities to prevent certain fundamentalist religious movements from exerting pressure on students who do not practise that religion or on those who belong to another religion may be justified under article 9 [paragraph] 2 of the Convention' (*Refah Partisi (the Welfare Party) and others* v. *Turkey*, applications Nos. 41340/98, 41342/98, 41343/98 and 41344/98, ECtHR Grand Chamber judgement of 13 February 2003, para. 95. See also the ECtHR Chamber judgement of 31 July 2001, para. 51).

50. The European Commission on Human Rights also dealt with two applications, *Karaduman* v. *Turkey* (No. 16278/90) and *Bulut* v. *Turkey* (No. 18783/91), concerning the university's refusal to issue a diploma because the photographs that the applicants had submitted for their identity documents portrayed them with their heads covered. In its decisions of 3 May 1993, the Commission did not regard the rejection to be an interference with the applicants' freedom of religion or belief as secular universities may regulate manifestation of religious rites and symbols with the aim of ensuring harmonious coexistence between students of various faiths and thus protecting public order and the beliefs of others.

D. Development of a set of general criteria to balance competing human rights 51. In general, contentious situations should be evaluated on a case-by-case basis, e.g. by weighing the right of a teacher to manifest his or her religion against the need to protect pupils by preserving religious harmony according to the circumstances of a given case. However, developing a set of general criteria to balance competing human rights seems to be desirable in order to give some guidance in terms of the applicable international human rights standards and their scope. In a manner similar to the guideline developed in 2004 by the Office for Democratic Institutions and Human Rights (ODIHR) of the OSCE, the aim of these general criteria is to assist national and international bodies in their analyses and reviews of laws and draft legislation pertaining to the freedom of religion or belief. The Special Rapporteur invites Governments that intend to regulate the wearing of religious symbols to consider seeking advisory services from the Office of the High Commissioner for Human Rights.

52. When developing such a set of general criteria, the competing human rights and public interests put forward in national and international forums need to be borne in mind. Freedom of religion or belief may be invoked both in terms of the positive freedom of persons who wish to wear or display a religious symbol and in terms of the negative freedom of persons who do not want to be confronted with or coerced into it. Another competing human right may be the equal right of men and women to the enjoyment of all civil and political rights, as well as the principle of the right to be protected from discrimination of any kind, including on the basis of race, colour, sex, religion, political or other opinion, national or social origin, property, birth or other status. The right of everyone to education may be invoked by pupils who have been expelled for wearing religious symbols in accordance with their religion or belief. Furthermore, the rights of parents or legal guardians to organize life within the family in accordance with their religion or belief and bearing in mind the moral education which they believe should inform the child's upbringing (see article 5(1) of the Declaration) may also be at stake. On the other hand, the State may try to invoke the 'denominational neutrality of the school system' and the desire to '[preserve] religious harmony in schools' (see the Swiss Federal Court in the *Dahlab* case). According to the individual opinion by Human Rights Committee member Ruth Wedgwood in the *Hudoyberganova* case 'a State may be allowed to restrict forms of dress that directly interfere with effective pedagogy'. Furthermore, the recent European Court Grand Chamber judgement in the *Şahin* case referred to the need to 'preserve public order and to secure civil peace and true religious pluralism, which is vital to the survival of a democratic society'.

53. However, any limitation must be based on the grounds of public safety, order, health, or morals, or the fundamental rights and freedoms of others, it must respond to a pressing public or social need, it must pursue a legitimate aim and it must be proportionate to that aim.

Furthermore, the burden of justifying a limitation upon the freedom to manifest one's religion or belief lies with the State. Consequently, a prohibition of wearing religious symbols which is based on mere speculation or presumption rather than on demonstrable facts is regarded as a violation of the individual's religious freedom (See Board of Experts of the International Religious Liberty Association, Guiding Principles Regarding Student Rights to Wear or Display Religious Symbols (15 November 2005), Principles Nos. 6 and 7, available at www.irla.org/documents/reports/symbols.html).

54. With regard to the scope of permissible limitation clauses, the Human Rights Committee's general comment No. 22 emphasizes that article 18 (3) of the Covenant 'is to be strictly interpreted: restrictions are not allowed on grounds not specified there, even if they would be allowed as restrictions to other rights protected in the Covenant, such as national security. Limitations may be applied only for those purposes for which they were prescribed and must be directly related and proportionate to the specific need on which they are predicated. Restrictions may not be imposed for discriminatory purposes or applied in a discriminatory manner (para. 8).'

55. On the basis of the above-mentioned factual aspects, the legal framework and international case law, the Special Rapporteur has endeavoured to develop a set of general criteria in order to evaluate – from a human rights law perspective – restrictions and prohibitions on wearing religious symbols. The following 'aggravating indicators' show legislative and administrative actions which typically are incompatible with international human rights law whereas the subsequent 'neutral indicators' by themselves do not tend to contravene these standards:

(a) Aggravating indicators:

- The limitation amounts to the nullification of the individual's freedom to manifest his or her religion or belief;
- The restriction is intended to or leads to either overt discrimination or camouflaged differentiation depending on the religion or belief involved;
- Limitations on the freedom to manifest a religion or belief for the purpose of protecting morals are based on principles deriving exclusively from a single tradition;
- Exceptions to the prohibition of wearing religious symbols are, either expressly or tacitly, tailored to the predominant or incumbent religion or belief;
- In practice, State agencies apply an imposed restriction in a discriminatory manner or with a discriminatory purpose, e.g. by arbitrarily targeting certain communities or groups, such as women;
- No due account is taken of specific features of religions or beliefs, e.g. a religion which prescribes wearing religious dress seems to be more deeply affected by a wholesale ban than a different religion or belief which places no particular emphasis on this issue;
- Use of coercive methods and sanctions applied to individuals who do not wish to wear a religious dress or a specific symbol seen as sanctioned by religion. This would include legal provisions or State policies allowing individuals, including parents, to use undue pressure, threats or violence to abide by such rules;

(b) Neutral indicators:

- The language of the restriction or prohibition clause is worded in a neutral and all-embracing way;

- The application of the ban does not reveal inconsistencies or biases *vis-à-vis* certain religious or other minorities or vulnerable groups;
- As photographs on ID cards require by definition that the wearer might properly be identified, proportionate restrictions on permitted headgear for ID photographs appear to be legitimate, if reasonable accommodation of the individual's religious manifestation are foreseen by the State;
- The interference is crucial to protect the rights of women, religious minorities or vulnerable groups;
- Accommodating different situations according to the perceived vulnerability of the persons involved might in certain situations also be considered legitimate, e.g. in order to protect underage schoolchildren and the liberty of parents or legal guardians to ensure the religious and moral education of their children in conformity with their own convictions.

56. In seeking to accommodate different categories of individual details of permissible limitations will be controversial. In general schoolchildren are generally considered vulnerable in view of their age, immaturity and the compulsory nature of education. In addition, parental rights are also put forward as justification for limiting teachers' positive freedom to manifest their religion or belief. In all actions concerning children, the best interests of the child shall be the primary consideration. University students, however, have normally reached the age of majority and are generally considered to be less easily influenced than schoolchildren, and parental rights are usually no longer involved.

57. The above-mentioned controversy over the peculiarities of certain institutional settings was already alluded to in 1959 by Arcot Krishnaswami, then Special Rapporteur of the Sub-Commission on Prevention of Discrimination and Protection of Minorities, in his seminal study of discrimination in the matter of religious rights and practices: 'A prohibition of the wearing of religious apparel in certain institutions, such as public schools, may be motivated by the desire to preserve the non-denominational character of these institutions. It would therefore be difficult to formulate a rule of general application as to the right to wear religious apparel, even though it is desirable that persons whose faith prescribes such apparel should not be unreasonably prevented from wearing it.' (E/CN.4/Sub.2/200/Rev.1, p. 33).

58. Where a policy decision has been taken at the national level to interfere with the freedom to manifest one's religion or belief with regard to wearing religious symbols issues of commensurability need to be thoroughly respected both by the administration and during possible legal review. For this purpose, the following questions should be answered in the affirmative:

- Was the interference, which must be capable of protecting the legitimate interest that has been put at risk, appropriate?
- Is the chosen measure the least restrictive of the right or freedom concerned?
- Was the measure proportionate, i.e. balancing of the competing interests?
- Would the chosen measure be likely to promote religious tolerance?
- Does the outcome of the measure avoid stigmatizing any particular religious community?

59. When dealing with the prohibition of religious symbols, two general questions should always be borne in mind: What is the significance of wearing a religious symbol and its relationship with competing public interests, and especially with the principles of secularism and equality? Who is

to decide ultimately on these issues, e.g. should it be up to the individuals themselves, religious authorities, the national administration and courts, or international human rights mechanisms? While acknowledging that the doctrine of 'margin of appreciation' may accommodate ethnic, cultural or religious peculiarities, this approach should not lead to questioning the international consensus that '[a]ll human rights are universal, indivisible and interdependent and interrelated', as proclaimed in the Vienna Declaration and Programme of Action adopted by the World Conference on Human Rights in 1993.

60. The fundamental objective should be to safeguard both the positive freedom of religion or belief as manifested in observance and practice by voluntarily wearing or displaying religious symbols, and also the negative freedom from being forced to wear or display religious symbols. At the same time, the competing human rights need to be balanced and public interest limitations should be applied restrictively. The Special Rapporteur fully agrees with European Court Judge Tulkens' closing remarks: 'Above all, the message that needs to be repeated over and over again is that the best means of preventing and combating fanaticism and extremism is to uphold human rights' (dissenting opinion of Judge Tulkens in the ECtHR Grand Chamber judgement of 10 November 2005 in the case of *Şahin* v. *Turkey*, para. 20).

Finally, the *Multani* case decided by the Canadian Supreme Court highlights the usefulness of relying on the notion of 'reasonable accommodation' in making decisions about the proportionality of restrictions to rights such as freedom of religion (see also, for a discussion of the notion of reasonable accommodation in equal treatment cases, chapter 7, section 3.2.). When such restrictions are based on considerations of a general nature, such considerations may not apply in specific, individual instances, where a solution better taking into account specific circumstances might be identified. This explains the reference made in the *Multani* judgment to the case of *Eldridge* v. *British Columbia* [1997] 3 S.C.R. 624. In that case, the appellants were born deaf and their preferred means of communication was sign language. They argued that it followed from the requirement of equality that they should be provided sign language interpreters as an insured benefit under the Medical Services Plan. They relied on s. 15(1) of the Canadian Charter of Rights and Freedoms, which provides: 'Every individual is equal before and under the law and has the right to the equal protection and equal benefit of the law without discrimination and, in particular, without discrimination based on race, national or ethnic origin, colour, religion, sex, age or mental or physical disability.' Having failed to obtain a declaration to that effect in the Supreme Court of British Columbia, they then appealed to the Supreme Court of Canada, contending that the absence of interpreters impairs their ability to communicate with their doctors and other health-care providers, and thus increases the risk of misdiagnosis and ineffective treatment. The Canadian Supreme Court agreed, noting: 'The principle that discrimination can accrue from a failure to take positive steps to ensure that disadvantaged groups benefit equally from services offered to the general public is widely accepted in the human rights field ... It is also a cornerstone of human rights jurisprudence, of course, that the duty to take positive action to ensure that members of disadvantaged groups benefit equally from services offered to the general public is subject to the principle of reasonable accommodation. The obligation to make reasonable accommodation for those adversely affected by a facially neutral policy or rule extends only to the point of "undue hardship"' (paras. 78–9). This notion played a central role in *Multani*, which related to the wearing of the kirpan, a religious object that resembles a dagger and must be made of metal, on the school's premises:

Supreme Court of Canada, *Multani v. Commission scolaire Marguerite-Bourgeoys* [2006] 1 S.C.R. 256, 2006 SCC 6:

[Gurbaj Singh Multani (G) and his father Balvir Singh Multani (B) are orthodox Sikhs. G believes that his religion requires him to wear a kirpan at all times. In 2001, the school board authorized G to wear his kirpan to school provided that he complied with certain conditions to ensure that it was sealed inside his clothing. G and his parents agreed to this arrangement. However, the governing board of the school refused to ratify the agreement on the basis that wearing a kirpan at the school violated art. 5 of the school's *Code de vie* (code of conduct), which prohibited the carrying of weapons. The school board's council of commissioners upheld that decision and notified G and his parents that a symbolic kirpan in the form of a pendant or one in another form made of a material rendering it harmless would be acceptable in the place of a real kirpan. B then filed in the Superior Court a motion for a declaratory judgment to the effect that the council of commissioners' decision was of no force or effect. The Superior Court granted the motion, declared the decision to be null, and authorized G to wear his kirpan under certain conditions (judgment of Grenier J. [2002] Q.J. No. 1131 (QL)). The Court of Appeal set aside the Superior Court's judgment ((Pelletier and Rochon JJ.A. and Lemelin J. (ad hoc)) [2004] R.J.Q. 824, 241 D.L.R. (4th) 336, 12 Admin. L.R. (4th) 233, [2004] Q.J. No. 1904 (QL)). After deciding that the applicable standard of review was reasonableness simpliciter, the Court of Appeal restored the council of commissioners' decision. It concluded that the decision in question infringed G's freedom of religion under s. 2(a) of the Canadian Charter of Rights and Freedoms (Canadian Charter) and s. 3 of Quebec's Charter of human rights and freedoms (Quebec Charter), but that the infringement was justified for the purposes of s. 1 of the Canadian Charter ('The Canadian Charter of Rights and Freedoms guarantees the rights and freedoms set out in it subject only to such reasonable limits prescribed by law as can be demonstrably justified in a free and democratic society') and s. 9.1 of the Quebec Charter. On appeal, the Supreme Court strikes down the order of the Quebec school authority prohibiting the wearing of a kirpan to school as a violation of freedom of religion under s. 2(a) of the Canadian Charter of Rights and Freedoms. The Supreme Court takes the view that the order could not be saved under s. 1 of the Charter.]

Per McLachlin C.J. and Bastarache, Binnie, Fish and Charron JJ. [LeBel J. filed a separate opinion, essentially concurring with that of the majority. It is not reproduced here.]:

24 The parties have been unable to agree on the most appropriate analytical approach. The appellant considers it clear that the council of commissioners' decision infringes his son's freedom of religion protected by s. 2(*a*) of the *Canadian Charter*. In response to the respondents' submissions, he maintains that only a limit that meets the test for the application of s. 1 of the *Canadian Charter* can be justified. The Attorney General of Quebec concedes that the prohibition against the appellant's son wearing his kirpan to school infringes the son's freedom of religion,

but submits that, regardless of the conditions ordered by the Superior Court, the prohibition is a fair limit on freedom of religion, which is not an absolute right.

25 According to the CSMB [Commission scolaire Marguerite-Bourgeoys], freedom of religion has not been infringed, because it has internal limits. The CSMB considers that, in the instant case, the freedom of religion guaranteed by s. 2(*a*) must be limited by imperatives of public order, safety, and health, as well as by the rights and freedoms of others. In support of this contention, it relies primarily on *Trinity Western University* v. *British Columbia College of Teachers* [2001] 1 S.C.R. 772, 2001 SCC 31, in which the Court defined the scope of the rights in issue (freedom of religion and the right to equality) in order to resolve any potential conflict. The CSMB is of the view that, in the case at bar, delineating the rights in issue in this way would preserve Gurbaj Singh's freedom of religion while, as in *Trinity Western University*, circumscribing his freedom to act in accordance with his beliefs. According to this line of reasoning, the outcome of this appeal would be decided at the stage of determining whether freedom of religion has been infringed rather than at the stage of reconciling the rights of the parties under s. 1 of the *Canadian Charter*.

26 This Court has clearly recognized that freedom of religion can be limited when a person's freedom to act in accordance with his or her beliefs may cause harm to or interfere with the rights of others (see *R.* v. *Big M Drug Mart Ltd* [1985] 1 S.C.R. 295, at p. 337, and *Syndicat Northcrest* v. *Amselem* [2004] 2 S.C.R. 551, 2004 SCC 47, at para. 62). However, the Court has on numerous occasions stressed the advantages of reconciling competing rights by means of a s. 1 analysis. For example, in *B. (R.)* v. *Children's Aid Society of Metropolitan Toronto* [1995] 1 S.C.R. 315, the claimants, who were Jehovah's Witnesses, contested an order that authorized the administration of a blood transfusion to their daughter. While acknowledging that freedom of religion could be limited in the best interests of the child, La Forest J., writing for the majority of the Court, stated the following, at paras. 109–10: 'This Court has consistently refrained from formulating internal limits to the scope of freedom of religion in cases where the constitutionality of a legislative scheme was raised; it rather opted to balance the competing rights under s. 1 of the *Charter* ... In my view, it appears sounder to leave to the state the burden of justifying the restrictions it has chosen. Any ambiguity or hesitation should be resolved in favour of individual rights. Not only is this consistent with the broad and liberal interpretation of rights favoured by this Court, but s. 1 is a much more flexible tool with which to balance competing rights than s. 2(*a*) ...'

27 *Ross* [v. *New Brunswick School District No. 15* [1996] 1 S.C.R. 825] provides another example of this. In that case, the Court recognized a teacher's right to act on the basis of antisemitic views that compromised the right of students to a school environment free of discrimination, but opted to limit the teacher's freedom of religion pursuant to s. 1 of the *Canadian Charter* (at paras. 74–75): 'This mode of approach is analytically preferable because it gives the broadest possible scope to judicial review under the *Charter* ..., and provides a more comprehensive method of assessing the relevant conflicting values ...

... That approach seems to me compelling in the present case where the respondent's claim is to a serious infringement of his rights of expression and of religion in a context requiring a detailed contextual analysis. In these circumstances, there can be no doubt that the detailed s. 1 analytical approach developed by this Court provides a more practical and comprehensive mechanism, involving review of a whole range of factors for the assessment of competing interests and the imposition of restrictions upon individual rights and freedoms.'

28 It is important to distinguish these decisions from the ones in which the Court did not conduct a s. 1 analysis because there was no conflict of fundamental rights. For example, in *Trinity Western University*, the Court, asked to resolve a potential conflict between religious freedoms and equality rights, concluded that a proper delineation of the rights involved would make it possible to avoid any conflict in that case. Likewise, in *Amselem*, a case concerning the *Quebec Charter,* the Court refused to pit freedom of religion against the right to peaceful enjoyment and free disposition of property, because the impact on the latter was considered 'at best, minimal' (para. 64). Logically, where there is not an apparent infringement of more than one fundamental right, no reconciliation is necessary at the initial stage.

29 In the case at bar, the Court does not at the outset have to reconcile two constitutional rights, as only freedom of religion is in issue here. Furthermore, since the decision genuinely affects both parties and was made by an administrative body exercising statutory powers, a contextual analysis under s. 1 will enable us to balance the relevant competing values in a more comprehensive manner.

30 This Court has frequently stated, and rightly so, that freedom of religion is not absolute and that it can conflict with other constitutional rights. However, since the test governing limits on rights was developed in *Oakes*, the Court has never called into question the principle that rights are reconciled through the constitutional justification required by s. 1 of the *Canadian Charter*. In this regard, the significance of *Big M Drug Mart*, which predated *Oakes*, was considered in *B. (R.)*, at paras. 110–11; see also *R. v. Keegstra* [1990] 3 S.C.R. 697, at pp. 733–34. In *Dagenais v. Canadian Broadcasting Corp.* [1994] 3 S.C.R. 835, the Court, in formulating the common law test applicable to publication bans, was concerned with the need to 'develop the principles of the common law in a manner consistent with the fundamental values enshrined in the Constitution' (p. 878). For this purpose, since the media's freedom of expression had to be reconciled with the accused's right to a fair trial, the Court held that a common law standard that 'clearly reflects the substance of the *Oakes* test' was the most appropriate one (p. 878).

31 Thus, the central issue in the instant case is best suited to a s. 1 analysis. But before proceeding with this analysis, I will explain why the contested decision clearly infringes freedom of religion.

6. Infringement of Freedom of Religion

32 This Court has on numerous occasions stressed the importance of freedom of religion. For the purposes of this case, it is sufficient to reproduce the following statement from *Big M Drug Mart*, at pp. 336–37 and 351: 'The essence of the concept of freedom of religion is the right to entertain such religious beliefs as a person chooses, the right to declare religious beliefs openly and without fear of hindrance or reprisal, and the right to manifest religious belief by worship and practice or by teaching and dissemination. But the concept means more than that … Freedom means that, subject to such limitations as are necessary to protect public safety, order, health, or morals or the fundamental rights and freedoms of others, no one is to be forced to act in a way contrary to his beliefs or his conscience … With the *Charter*, it has become the right of every Canadian to work out for himself or herself what his or her religious obligations, if any, should be and it is not for the state to dictate otherwise.'

33 It was explained in *Amselem* [*Syndicat Northcrest v. Anselem* [2004] 2 S.C.R. 551], at para. 46, that freedom of religion consists of the freedom to undertake practices and harbour beliefs, having a nexus with religion, in which an individual demonstrates he or she sincerely believes or

is sincerely undertaking in order to connect with the divine or as a function of his or her spiritual faith, *irrespective of whether a particular practice or belief is required by official religious dogma or is in conformity with the position of religious officials* [emphasis added].

34 In *Amselem*, the Court ruled that, in order to establish that his or her freedom of religion has been infringed, the claimant must demonstrate (1) that he or she sincerely believes in a practice or belief that has a nexus with religion, and (2) that the impugned conduct of a third party interferes, in a manner that is non-trivial or not insubstantial, with his or her ability to act in accordance with that practice or belief.

35 The fact that different people practise the same religion in different ways does not affect the validity of the case of a person alleging that his or her freedom of religion has been infringed. What an individual must do is show that he or she sincerely believes that a certain belief or practice is required by his or her religion. The religious belief must be asserted in good faith and must not be fictitious, capricious or an artifice (*Amselem*, at para. 52). In assessing the sincerity of the belief, a court must take into account, *inter alia*, the credibility of the testimony of the person asserting the particular belief and the consistency of the belief with his or her other current religious practices (*Amselem*, at para. 53).

36 In the case at bar, Gurbaj Singh must therefore show that he sincerely believes that his faith requires him at all times to wear a kirpan made of metal. Evidence to this effect was introduced and was not contradicted. No one contests the fact that the orthodox Sikh religion requires its adherents to wear a kirpan at all times …

37 Much of the CSMB's argument is based on its submission that 'the kirpan is essentially a dagger, a weapon designed to kill, intimidate or threaten others'. With respect, while the kirpan undeniably has characteristics of a bladed weapon capable of wounding or killing a person, this submission disregards the fact that, for orthodox Sikhs, the kirpan is above all a religious symbol. Chaplain Manjit Singh mentions in his affidavit that the word 'kirpan' comes from 'kirpa', meaning 'mercy' and 'kindness', and 'aan', meaning 'honour'. There is no denying that this religious object could be used wrongly to wound or even kill someone, but the question at this stage of the analysis cannot be answered definitively by considering only the physical characteristics of the kirpan. Since the question of the physical makeup of the kirpan and the risks the kirpan could pose to the school board's students involves the reconciliation of conflicting values, I will return to it when I address justification under s. 1 of the *Canadian Charter*. In order to demonstrate an infringement of his freedom of religion, Gurbaj Singh does not have to establish that the kirpan is not a weapon. He need only show that his personal and subjective belief in the religious significance of the kirpan is sincere.

38 Gurbaj Singh says that he sincerely believes he must adhere to this practice in order to comply with the requirements of his religion. Grenier J. of the Superior Court declared (at para. 6) – and the Court of Appeal reached the same conclusion (at para. 70) – that Gurbaj Singh's belief was sincere. Gurbaj Singh's affidavit supports this conclusion, and none of the parties have contested the sincerity of his belief.

39 Furthermore, Gurbaj Singh's refusal to wear a replica made of a material other than metal is not capricious. He genuinely believes that he would not be complying with the requirements of his religion were he to wear a plastic or wooden kirpan. The fact that other Sikhs accept such a compromise is not relevant, since as Lemelin J. mentioned at para. 68 of her decision, '[w]e must recognize that people who profess the same religion may adhere to the dogma and practices of that religion to varying degrees of rigour'.

40 Finally, the interference with Gurbaj Singh's freedom of religion is neither trivial nor insignificant. Forced to choose between leaving his kirpan at home and leaving the public school system, Gurbaj Singh decided to follow his religious convictions and is now attending a private school. The prohibition against wearing his kirpan to school has therefore deprived him of his right to attend a public school.

41 Thus, there can be no doubt that the council of commissioners' decision prohibiting Gurbaj Singh from wearing his kirpan to Sainte-Catherine-Labouré school infringes his freedom of religion. This limit must therefore be justified under s. 1 of the *Canadian Charter*.

7. Section 1 of the Canadian Charter

42 As I mentioned above, the council of commissioners made its decision pursuant to its discretion under s. 12 of the *Education Act*. The decision prohibiting the wearing of a kirpan at the school thus constitutes a limit prescribed by a rule of law within the meaning of s. 1 of the *Canadian Charter* and must accordingly be justified in accordance with that section: 'The *Canadian Charter of Rights and Freedoms* guarantees the rights and freedoms set out in it subject only to such reasonable limits prescribed by law as can be demonstrably justified in a free and democratic society.'

43 The onus is on the respondents to prove that, on a balance of probabilities, the infringement is reasonable and can be demonstrably justified in a free and democratic society. To this end, two requirements must be met. First, the legislative objective being pursued must be sufficiently important to warrant limiting a constitutional right. Next, the means chosen by the state authority must be proportional to the objective in question: *Oakes*; *R. v. Edwards Books and Art Ltd.* [1986] 2 S.C.R. 713.

7.1 Importance of the Objective 44 As stated by the Court of Appeal, the council of commissioners' decision 'was motivated by [a pressing and substantial] objective, namely, to ensure an environment conducive to the development and learning of the students. This requires [the CSMB] to ensure the safety of the students and the staff. This duty is at the core of the mandate entrusted to educational institutions' (para. 77). The appellant concedes that this objective is laudable and that it passes the first stage of the test. The respondents also submitted fairly detailed evidence consisting of affidavits from various stakeholders in the educational community explaining the importance of safety in schools and the upsurge in problems relating to weapons and violence in schools.

45 Clearly, the objective of ensuring safety in schools is sufficiently important to warrant overriding a constitutionally protected right or freedom. It remains to be determined what level of safety the governing board was seeking to achieve by prohibiting the carrying of weapons and dangerous objects, and what degree of risk would accordingly be tolerated. As in *British Columbia (Superintendent of Motor Vehicles)* v. *British Columbia (Council of Human Rights)* [1999] 3 S.C.R. 868, at para. 25, the possibilities range from a desire to ensure absolute safety to a total lack of concern for safety. Between these two extremes lies a concern to ensure a reasonable level of safety.

46 Although the parties did not present argument on the level of safety sought by the governing board, the issue was addressed by the intervener Canadian Human Rights Commission, which correctly stated that the standard that seems to be applied in schools is reasonable safety, not absolute safety. The application of a standard of absolute safety could result in the installation of metal detectors in schools, the prohibition of all potentially dangerous objects

(such as scissors, compasses, baseball bats and table knives in the cafeteria) and permanent expulsion from the public school system of any student exhibiting violent behaviour. Apart from the fact that such a standard would be impossible to attain, it would compromise the objective of providing universal access to the public school system.

47 On the other hand, when the governing board approved the article in question of the *Code de vie*, it was not seeking to establish a minimum standard of safety. As can be seen from the affidavits of certain stakeholders from the educational community, violence and weapons are not tolerated in schools, and students exhibiting violent or dangerous behaviour are punished. Such measures show that the objective is to attain a certain level of safety beyond a minimum threshold.

48 I therefore conclude that the level of safety chosen by the governing council and confirmed by the council of commissioners was reasonable safety. The objective of ensuring a reasonable level of safety in schools is without question a pressing and substantial one.

7.2 Proportionality

7.2.1 Rational Connection 49 The first stage of the proportionality analysis consists in determining whether the council of commissioners' decision was rendered in furtherance of the objective. The decision must have a rational connection with the objective. In the instant case, prohibiting Gurbaj Singh from wearing his kirpan to school was intended to further this objective. Despite the profound religious significance of the kirpan for Gurbaj Singh, it also has the characteristics of a bladed weapon and could therefore cause injury. The council of commissioners' decision therefore has a rational connection with the objective of ensuring a reasonable level of safety in schools. Moreover, it is relevant that the appellant has never contested the rationality of the *Code de vie*'s rule prohibiting weapons in school.

7.2.2 Minimal Impairment 50 The second stage of the proportionality analysis is often central to the debate as to whether the infringement of a right protected by the *Canadian Charter* can be justified. The limit, which must minimally impair the right or freedom that has been infringed, need not necessarily be the least intrusive solution. In *RJR-MacDonald Inc.* v. *Canada (Attorney General)* [1995] 3 S.C.R. 199, at para. 160, this Court defined the test as follows: 'The impairment must be "minimal", that is, the law must be carefully tailored so that rights are impaired no more than necessary. The tailoring process seldom admits of perfection and the courts must accord some leeway to the legislator. If the law falls within a range of reasonable alternatives, the courts will not find it overbroad merely because they can conceive of an alternative which might better tailor objective to infringement ...'

51 The approach to the question must be the same where what is in issue is not legislation, but a decision rendered pursuant to a statutory discretion. Thus, it must be determined whether the decision to establish an absolute prohibition against wearing a kirpan 'falls within a range of reasonable alternatives'.

52 In considering this aspect of the proportionality analysis, Lemelin J. expressed the view that '[t]he duty to accommodate this student is a corollary of the minimal impairment [test]' (para. 92). In other words, she could not conceive of the possibility of a justification being sufficient for the purposes of s. 1 if reasonable accommodation is possible (para. 75). This correspondence of the concept of reasonable accommodation with the proportionality analysis is not without precedent. In *Eldridge*, [*Eldridge* v. *British Columbia* [1997] 3 S.C.R. 624 (in which

the Court had concluded that sign-language interpreters should be available to deaf patients in hospitals)] at para. 79, this Court stated that, in cases concerning s. 15(1) of the *Canadian Charter*, 'reasonable accommodation' was equivalent to the concept of 'reasonable limits' provided for in s. 1 of the *Canadian Charter*.

53 In my view, this correspondence between the legal principles is logical. In relation to discrimination, the courts have held that there is a duty to make reasonable accommodation for individuals who are adversely affected by a policy or rule that is neutral on its face, and that this duty extends only to the point at which it causes undue hardship to the party who must perform it. Although it is not necessary to review all the cases on the subject, the analogy with the duty of reasonable accommodation seems to me to be helpful to explain the burden resulting from the minimal impairment test with respect to a particular individual, as in the case at bar ... Professor José Woehrling correctly explained the relationship between the duty to accommodate or adapt and the *Oakes* analysis in the following passage: 'Anyone seeking to disregard the duty to accommodate must show that it is necessary, in order to achieve a legitimate and important legislative objective, to apply the standard in its entirety, without the exceptions sought by the claimant. More specifically, in the context of s. 1 of the *Canadian Charter*, it is necessary, in applying the test from *R.* v. *Oakes*, to show, in succession, that applying the standard in its entirety constitutes a rational means of achieving the legislative objective, that no other means are available that would be less intrusive in relation to the rights in question (minimal impairment test), and that there is proportionality between the measure's salutary and limiting effects. At a conceptual level, the minimal impairment test, which is central to the section 1 analysis, corresponds in large part with the undue hardship defence against the duty of reasonable accommodation in the context of human rights legislation. This is clear from the Supreme Court's judgment in *Edwards Books*, in which the application of the minimal impairment test led the Court to ask whether the Ontario legislature, in prohibiting stores from opening on Sundays and allowing certain exceptions for stores that were closed on Saturdays, had done enough to accommodate merchants who, for religious reasons, had to observe a day of rest on a day other than Sunday' (J. Woehrling, 'L'obligation d'accommodement raisonnable et l'adaptation de la société à la diversité religieuse', *McGill Law Journal*, 43 (1998) 325 at 360)

54 The council of commissioners' decision establishes an absolute prohibition against Gurbaj Singh wearing his kirpan to school. The respondents contend that this prohibition is necessary, because the presence of the kirpan at the school poses numerous risks for the school's pupils and staff. It is important to note that Gurbaj Singh has never claimed a right to wear his kirpan to school without restrictions. Rather, he says that he is prepared to wear his kirpan under the above-mentioned conditions imposed by Grenier J. of the Superior Court. Thus, the issue is whether the respondents have succeeded in demonstrating that an absolute prohibition is justified.

55 According to the CSMB, to allow the kirpan to be worn to school entails the risks that it could be used for violent purposes by the person wearing it or by another student who takes it away from him, that it could lead to a proliferation of weapons at the school, and that its presence could have a negative impact on the school environment. In support of this last point, the CSMB submits that the kirpan is a symbol of violence and that it sends the message that the use of force is the way to assert rights and resolve conflicts, in addition to undermining the perception of safety and compromising the spirit of fairness that should prevail in schools, in that its presence suggests the existence of a double standard. Let us look at those arguments.

7.2.2.1 Safety in Schools 56 According to the respondents, the presence of kirpans in schools, even under certain conditions, creates a risk that they will be used for violent purposes, either by those who wear them or by other students who might take hold of them by force.

57 The evidence shows that Gurbaj Singh does not have behavioural problems and has never resorted to violence at school. The risk that this particular student would use his kirpan for violent purposes seems highly unlikely to me. In fact, the CSMB has never argued that there was a risk of his doing so.

58 As for the risk of another student taking his kirpan away from him, it also seems to me to be quite low, especially if the kirpan is worn under conditions such as were imposed by Grenier J. of the Superior Court. In the instant case, if the kirpan were worn in accordance with those conditions, any student wanting to take it away from Gurbaj Singh would first have to physically restrain him, then search through his clothes, remove the sheath from his guthra, and try to unstitch or tear open the cloth enclosing the sheath in order to get to the kirpan. There is no question that a student who wanted to commit an act of violence could find another way to obtain a weapon, such as bringing one in from outside the school. Furthermore, there are many objects in schools that could be used to commit violent acts and that are much more easily obtained by students, such as scissors, pencils and baseball bats.

59 ... The Court does not believe that the safety of the environment would be compromised. In argument, it was stated that in the last 100 years, not a single case of kirpan-related violence has been reported. Moreover, in a school setting, there are usually all sorts of instruments that could be used as weapons during a violent incident, including compasses, drawing implements and sports equipment, such as baseball bats (*Multani (Tuteur de)* v. *Commission scolaire Marguerite-Bourgeois* [2002] Q.J. No. 619 (QL) (Sup. Ct.), at para. 28) ...

62 The respondents maintain that freedom of religion can be limited even in the absence of evidence of a real risk of significant harm, since it is not necessary to wait for the harm to occur before correcting the situation ...

67 ... I agree that it is not necessary to wait for harm to be done before acting, but the existence of concerns relating to safety must be unequivocally established for the infringement of a constitutional right to be justified. Given the evidence in the record, it is my opinion that the respondents' argument in support of an absolute prohibition – namely that kirpans are inherently dangerous – must fail.

7.2.2.2 Proliferation of Weapons in Schools 68 The respondents also contend that allowing Gurbaj Singh to wear his kirpan to school could have a ripple effect. They submit that other students who learn that orthodox Sikhs may wear their kirpans will feel the need to arm themselves so that they can defend themselves if attacked by a student wearing a kirpan.

69 This argument is essentially based on the one discussed above, namely that kirpans in school pose a safety risk to other students, forcing them to arm themselves in turn in order to defend themselves. For the reasons given above, I am of the view that the evidence does not support this argument. It is purely speculative and cannot be accepted in the instant case: see *Eldridge*, at para. 89. Moreover, this argument merges with the next one, which relates more specifically to the risk of poisoning the school environment. I will therefore continue with the analysis.

7.2.2.3 Negative Impact on the School Environment 70 The respondents submit that the presence of kirpans in schools will contribute to a poisoning of the school environment. They maintain that the kirpan is a symbol of violence and that it sends the message that using force is the way to assert rights and resolve conflict, compromises the perception of safety in schools and establishes a double standard.

71 The argument that the wearing of kirpans should be prohibited because the kirpan is a symbol of violence and because it sends the message that using force is necessary to assert rights and resolve conflict must fail. Not only is this assertion contradicted by the evidence regarding the symbolic nature of the kirpan, it is also disrespectful to believers in the Sikh religion and does not take into account Canadian values based on multiculturalism.

72 As for the submissions based on the other students' perception regarding safety and on feelings of unfairness that they might experience, these appear to stem from the affidavit of psychoeducator Denis Leclerc, who gave his opinion concerning a study in which he took part that involved, *inter alia*, questioning students and staff from 14 high schools belonging to the CSMB about the socio-educational environment in schools. The results of the study seem to show that there is a mixed or negative perception regarding safety in schools. It should be noted that this study did not directly address kirpans, but was instead a general examination of the situation in schools in terms of safety. Mr Leclerc is of the opinion that the presence of kirpans in schools would heighten this impression that the schools are unsafe. He also believes that allowing Gurbaj Singh to wear a kirpan would engender a feeling of unfairness among the students, who would perceive this permission as special treatment. He mentions, for example, that some students still consider the right of Muslim women to wear the chador to be unfair, because they themselves are not allowed to wear caps or scarves ...

74 With respect for the view of the Court of Appeal, I cannot accept Denis Leclerc's position. Among other concerns, the example he presents concerning the chador is particularly revealing. To equate a religious obligation such as wearing the chador with the desire of certain students to wear caps is indicative of a simplistic view of freedom of religion that is incompatible with the *Canadian Charter*. Moreover, his opinion seems to be based on the firm belief that the kirpan is, by its true nature, a weapon. The CSMB itself vigorously defends this same position ... These assertions strip the kirpan of any religious significance and leave no room for accommodation ...

76 Religious tolerance is a very important value of Canadian society. If some students consider it unfair that Gurbaj Singh may wear his kirpan to school while they are not allowed to have knives in their possession, it is incumbent on the schools to discharge their obligation to instil in their students this value that is, as I will explain in the next section, at the very foundation of our democracy.

77 In my opinion, the respondents have failed to demonstrate that it would be reasonable to conclude that an absolute prohibition against wearing a kirpan minimally impairs Gurbaj Singh's rights.

7.2.3 Effects of the Measure 78 Since we have found that the council of commissioners' decision is not a reasonable limit on religious freedom, it is not strictly necessary to weigh the deleterious effects of this measure against its salutary effects. I do believe, however, like the intervener Canadian Civil Liberties Association, that it is important to consider some effects that could result from an absolute prohibition. An absolute prohibition would stifle the promotion of values such as multiculturalism, diversity, and the development of an educational culture respectful of the rights of others. This Court has on numerous occasions reiterated the importance of these values ...

79 A total prohibition against wearing a kirpan to school undermines the value of this religious symbol and sends students the message that some religious practices do not merit the same protection as others. On the other hand, accommodating Gurbaj Singh and allowing him to wear his kirpan under certain conditions demonstrates the importance that our society attaches to protecting freedom of religion and to showing respect for its minorities. The deleterious effects of a total prohibition thus outweigh its salutary effects.

[Not all justices of the Supreme Court agreed. Two justices – Deschamps and Abella JJ. – considered instead that recourse to a constitutional law justification is not appropriate where, as in this case, what must be assessed is the propriety of an administrative body's decision relating to human rights. Whereas a constitutional justification analysis must be carried out when reviewing the validity or enforceability of a norm such as a law, regulation or other similar rule of general application, the administrative law approach must be retained for reviewing decisions and orders made by administrative bodies. Therefore, while they arrive at the same conclusion – that the appeal should be upheld – they do so for quite distinct reasons, based on administrative law reasons rather than on constitutional law justifications. Their opinion is interesting in that it shows the ambiguities which result from extending the scope of the expression 'law' to individual decisions, when this expression is used to refer to the form through which a restriction to a constitutionally protected right must be justified. The opinion also leads to question the level – individual or, on the contrary, collective – at which the test of proportionality ought to be performed. Excerpts of their opinion follow:]

Meaning of the Expression 'Law' in Section 1 of the Canadian Charter 112 An administrative body determines an individual's rights in relation to a particular issue. A decision or order made by such a body is not a law or regulation, but is instead the result of a process provided for by statute and by the principles of administrative law in a given case. A law or regulation, on the other hand, is enacted or made by the legislature or by a body to which powers are delegated. The norm so established is not limited to a specific case. It is general in scope. Establishing a norm and resolving a dispute are not usually considered equivalent processes. At first glance, therefore, equating a decision or order with a law, as Lamer J. does in *Slaight*, seems anomalous. [In *Slaight Communications Inc.* v. *Davidson* [1989] 1 S.C.R. 1038, Lamer J. had explained (at pp. 1079–80) that 'where the legislation pursuant to which an administrative body has made a contested decision confers a discretion (in the instant case, the choice of means to keep schools safe) and does not confer, either expressly or by implication, the power to limit the rights and freedoms guaranteed by the *Canadian Charter*, the decision should, if there is an infringement, be subjected to the test set out in s. 1 of the *Canadian Charter* to ascertain whether it constitutes a reasonable limit that can be demonstrably justified in a free and democratic society. If it is not justified, the administrative body has exceeded its authority in making the contested decision.' In *Multani*, the majority considered that this doctrine applied since the council of commissioners' decision may be said to infringes Gurbaj Singh's freedom of religion (para. 23).]

113 ... [The] expression 'law' (*règle de droit*) used in s. 1 of the *Canadian Charter* naturally refers to a norm or rule of general application: 'The *Canadian Charter of Rights and Freedoms* guarantees the rights and freedoms set out in it subject only to such reasonable limits prescribed by law as can be demonstrably justified in a free and democratic society' ...

115 ... Professors Brun and Tremblay define 'law' as follows (H. Brun and G. Tremblay, *Droit constitutionnel* (4th ed. 2002), at p. 944): 'A law, within the meaning of s. 1, is an "intelligible legal standard". The notion of a legal standard relates to the unilaterally coercive and legally enforceable character of the act in question.' These authors express surprise at the unified approach suggested in *Slaight* (at p. 945): 'It would appear that an order of a court or tribunal is also a law within the meaning of s. 1. The Supreme Court has applied the reasonableness test under s. 1 to such orders on several occasions. This means that limits on rights can arise out of individualized legal standards, which is surprising. Such orders are of course law, but to have s. 1 apply to them without reservation means that litigants may often be unable to determine the status of their fundamental rights in advance, as in the case of limits resulting from general norms, such as statutes and regulations. We would have thought that limits on rights could not result from individualized orders unless the legislation conferring authority for those orders envisaged such a possibility ...

117 E. Mendes, 'The Crucible of the Charter: Judicial Principles v. Judicial Deference in the Context of Section', in G.-A. Beaudoin and E. Mendes, eds., *Canadian Charter of Rights and Freedoms* (4th ed. 2005), 165, attempts to reconcile the various approaches the Court has taken in dealing with the expression 'law' (at pp. 172–73): 'An analysis that could reconcile the various cases in this area is one which argues that the courts have distinguished between arbitrary action that is exercised without legal authority and discretion that is constrained by intelligible legal standards and they have held that the latter will meet the "prescribed by law" requirement. However, in *Irwin Toy*, the Supreme Court held that it would not find that a law provided an intelligible standard if it was vague. The "void for vagueness" doctrine comes from the rule of law principle that a law must provide sufficient guidance for others to determine its meaning ... Put another way, the phrase "prescribed by law" requires that "the legislature [provide] an intelligible standard according to which the judiciary must do its work."'

118 To include administrative decisions in the concept of 'law' therefore implies that it is necessary in every case to begin by assessing the validity of the statutory or regulatory provision on which the decision is based. This indicates that the expression 'law' is used first and foremost in its normative sense. Professor Mendes does not seem totally convinced that it is helpful to apply s. 1 of the *Canadian Charter* to assess a decision (at p. 173): 'One could argue that this is a form of double deference: first, to the legislature to allow them to enact provisions which, although vague, are not beyond the ability of the judiciary to interpret. Second, there is a form of self-deference that the judiciary can turn such legislated vagueness into sufficient precision and certainty to satisfy the requirements of section 1. Depending how consistent the courts are in interpreting the vastly open-textured terms of section 1, this form of self-deference may or may not be justified.'

119 The fact that justification is based on the collective interest also suggests that the expression 'law' should be limited to rules of general application. In *R. v. Oakes* [1986] 1 S.C.R. 103, Dickson C.J. wrote the following (at p. 136): 'The rights and freedoms guaranteed by the *Charter* are not, however, absolute. It may become necessary to limit rights and freedoms in circumstances where their exercise would be inimical to *the realization of collective goals of fundamental importance*' (emphasis added).

120 To suggest that the decisions of administrative bodies must be justifiable under the *Oakes* test implies that the decision makers in question must incorporate this analysis into their decision-making process. This requirement makes the decision-making process formalistic and distracts the reviewing court from the objective of the analysis, which relates instead to the substance of the decision and consists of determining whether it is correct or reasonable.

121 An administrative decision maker should not have to justify its decision under the *Oakes* test, which is based on an analysis of societal interests and is better suited, conceptually and literally, to the concept of 'prescribed by law'. That test is based on the duty of the executive and legislative branches of government to account to the courts for any rules they establish that infringe protected rights. The *Oakes* test was developed to assess legislative policies. The duty to account imposed – conceptually and in practice – on the legislative and executive branches is not easily applied to administrative tribunals ...

125 We accordingly believe that the expression 'law' should not include the decisions of administrative bodies. Such decisions should be reviewed in accordance with the principles of administrative law, which will both allow claimants and administrative bodies to know in advance which rules govern disputes and help prevent any blurring of roles ...

Reasonable Accommodation 129 The apparent overlap between the concepts of minimal impairment and reasonable accommodation is another striking example of the need to preserve the distinctiveness of the administrative law approach ... We agree that these concepts have a number of similarities, but in our view they belong to two different analytical categories ...

131 The process required by the duty of reasonable accommodation takes into account the specific details of the circumstances of the parties and allows for dialogue between them. This dialogue enables them to reconcile their positions and find common ground tailored to their own needs.

132 The approach is different, however, in the case of minimal impairment when it is considered in the context of the broad impact of the result of the constitutional justification analysis. The justification of the infringement is based on societal interests, not on the needs of the individual parties. An administrative law analysis is microcosmic, whereas a constitutional law analysis is generally macrocosmic. The values involved may be different. We believe that there is an advantage to keeping these approaches separate.

133 Furthermore, although the minimal impairment test under s. 1 of the *Canadian Charter* is similar to the undue hardship test in human rights law, the perspectives in the two cases are different, as is the evidence that can support the analysis. Assessing the scope of a law sometimes requires that social facts or the potential consequences of applying the law be taken into account, whereas determining whether there is undue hardship requires evidence of hardship in a particular case.

134 These separate streams – public versus individual – should be kept distinct. A lack of coherence in the analysis can only be detrimental to the exercise of human rights. Reasonable accommodation and undue hardship belong to the sphere of administrative law and human rights legislation, whereas the assessment of minimal impairment is part of a constitutional analysis with wider societal implications.

3.8. **Questions for discussion: restrictions to freedom of religion in vestimentary codes**

1. Would the notion of reasonable accommodation, if it were taken into account more fully in the case law of the European Court of Human Rights, have led to a different outcome in the case of *Leyla Sahin* v. *Turkey*? How could such a notion be implemented in practice, in a situation such as that the Court was presented with in that case?

   Is the reference to the criteria set forth by the UN Special Rapporteur on freedom of religion and belief useful in order to arrive at a satisfactory solution? Consider in particular her insistance on the fact that 'freedom of religion or belief may be invoked both in terms of the positive freedom of persons who wish to wear or display a religious symbol and in terms of the negative freedom of persons who do not want to be confronted with or coerced into it'. Is the implication that, in each specific case, the respective weight of each of these freedoms should be evaluated, depending on the social context, the family situation of the individual concerned, etc?

2. In *Leyla Sahin* v. *Turkey*, the European Court of Human Rights emphasizes the importance of gender equality, as one of the two main justifications for the prohibition of the wearing of the hijab in Turkish public universities. However, the result of such prohibition may be, in practice, that students belonging to certain Muslim families will be relegated to private institutions, with fewer or no contacts with other student bodies. Did the Court underestimate this risk?

3. How relevant is *Leyla Sahin* v. *Turkey* to the evaluation of a situation such as that created by the Law of 15 March 2004 adopted in France? To which extent was the outcome reached by the Court in the case of *Leyla Sahin* dependent on the specific situation of Turkey, where the Muslim religion is largely dominant and where there exists a strong social pressure towards conforming with the prescriptions of the Muslim faith?

4. Both *Leyla Sahin* and *Multani* seem to betray a hesitation between the two approaches which could be taken in order to assess the proportionality of the interference with freedom of religion resulting from the application of a dress code prohibiting certain religious symbols: one approach is to examine whether the general regulatory framework is proportionate to the aims pursued, and to accept that in certain cases the application of the framework will impose restrictions on the freedom to manifest one's religion; another approach is to examine whether this application itself leads to undue hardship in individual cases.

   (a) Should such proportionality be assessed as regards the general rule concerned, or should the individual measure, applying the general rule to the specific individual, also be justified?

   (b) If the latter, how could the principle of legality be complied with, since, per definition, it may be impossible to anticipate whether specific exemptions might benefit the individual concerned, where his/her particular situation could lead to identify particular accommodation measures, tailored to meet his/her needs? If, indeed, the requirement of proportionality ultimately calls for the necessity of the restriction of a right to be evaluated on a strictly individual basis, taking into account the possibility of accommodating the specific needs of the individual concerned, this may require us to rethink the classical understanding of the condition of legality: in order for this condition to be fulfilled, would it be sufficient to ensure that each restriction be decided according to procedures established in advance and allowing for all relevant views to the considered in making the decision, even though the outcome of such a decisional process may not always be predictable? Is this an adequate substitute to the idea that any restriction to human rights should be 'accessible to the persons concerned and formulated with sufficient precision to enable them – if need be, with appropriate advice – to foresee, to a degree that is reasonable in the circumstances, the consequences which a given action may entail and to regulate their conduct', as stated by the European Court of Human Rights?

4

The Application of Human Rights in Private Relationships and the Obligation to Protect

INTRODUCTION

States must not only abstain from violating the rights of individuals under their juris-diction, by ensuring that State agents do not commit such infringements. They must also intervene where acts committed by private parties, whether individuals, groups or legal persons, threaten to violate those rights. Where there are indications that an individual is at risk of having his/her rights violated, or where a situation exists which gives rise to such a risk, preventive measures must be taken, in order to ensure, to the fullest extent possible, that these risks do not materialize. And when the measures they adopt fail, and violations are caused by the conduct of non-State actors, State authori-ties may not remain passive: they are under an obligation to provide effective remedies to the individual whose rights have been violated, in order to ensure that he/she will be compensated, and in certain cases, that the wrongdoer will be sanctioned through administrative or criminal penalties.

This chapter is focused on this obligation to protect. This obligation arises where the State is confronted with acts of private actors which may lead to human rights being violated: an obligation is then imposed on the State to prevent such violations from occuring, and to provide remedies where the preventive measures have failed. But it seems necessary, as a preliminary matter, carefully to circumscribe the notion of the obligation to protect, in order to avoid confusing it with situations which present a superficial similarity to those that give rise to such an obligation. Section 1 recalls that, under certain, rather restrictive conditions, the State may be directly attributed the acts of private parties. Where this is the case, it is the classical obligation to respect which is at stake; there is no question of extending the obligation of the State to an obligation to protect, since, per hypothesis, the act of the private individual will be treated as an act of the State itself.

Section 2 then describes the obligation to protect in more detail. In principle, inter-national human rights instruments only prescribe the result to be achieved, leaving it to the State to choose the means through which to provide this protection (section 2.1.). In addition, the 'result' itself – the prevention of human rights violations which may have their source in private initiatives – is not to be understood in absolute terms. The obligation to protect is defined as an obligation to take all reasonable measures that might have prevented the event from occurring: it is thus an obligation of means, rather than an obligation of result. In order to engage the responsibility of the State, it is therefore not enough that the event which should have been prevented did occur: it must be shown, *in addition*, that the State could have taken certain measures which might have succeeded to prevent the event, and yet failed to take such measures (section 2.2.).

Sections 2.3. to 2.5. review what might be called the 'limiting factors' to the obligation to protection, i.e. the arguments the State may invoke in order to justify remaining passive. These are in particular (a) the fact that, in a free society, human conduct remains in part unpredictable by authorities; (b) the budgetary constraints facing States; and (c) the obligation for States to respect other, conflicting human rights. In addition, where alleged violations have their source in contractual relationships, (d) respect for the contractual freedom of parties, one of which has agreed to a restriction to his/her right, may play a role. Finally, since individual right-holders may inflict harm upon themselves, the question arises whether (e) the autonomy of the individual who chose to waive his/her right, by means other than by the conclusion of a contract, deserves to be respected and may create an obstacle to the protection provided by the State. Because of the complex and controversial nature of these issues, specific developments focus on two of these limiting factors: section 2.4. addresses human rights in contractual relationships and the question of waiver of rights; section 2.5. discusses the situations of conflicting rights which may occur when, in order to discharge its obligation to protect certain human rights, the State intervenes in private relationships to restrict other, competing human rights.

I regret that, in these sub-sections, I have borrowed my illustrations primarily from the case law of the European Court of Human Rights. I have thus been unable to comply with the rule I have otherwise sought to impose upon myself, which is to seek to highlight the identical nature of the questions (if not necessarily always of the answers) confronting different human rights bodies, under the various human rights instruments. However, what I have sought here – even more so than in other chapters – is to propose a sound analytical framework, enabling the reader to relate the further developments of the case law to the framework offered, in order to enrich and criticize it. The origin of the materials that illustrate the framework matter less, in my mind, than whether or not the conceptual apparatus is useful and promotes further study.

1 THE IMPUTABILITY TO THE STATE OF THE CONDUCT OF NON-STATE ACTORS AND THE OBLIGATION TO PROTECT

The obligation to protect may arise in situations where the rights of the individual are threatened as the result of private initiatives. The State is not allowed to remain passive in such a circumstance: it must adopt measures, both preventive and remedial, in order to avoid the violation from occurring, or to provide remedies to the individual if the preventive measures fail. In that sense, violations of human rights originating in private relationships may reveal a failure of the State to discharge its obligation to protect. This should not be confused with situations where the acts of non-State actors, as such, are imputed to the State, and are thus considered to be those of the State itself.

1.1 The attribution to the State of acts committed by private entities

In general international law, States may only exceptionally be imputed acts committed by private persons. According to the International Law Commission's 2001 Articles on Responsibility of States for Internationally Wrongful Acts, while any organ of the State may engage the responsibility of the State (Art. 4), the act of a person who is not an organ of the State will be attributed to the State only if (a) that person is empowered by the law of that State to exercise elements of the governmental authority and has acted in that capacity in the particular instance (Art. 5); or (b) that person has in fact acted on the instructions of, or under the direction or control of, the State in carrying out the conduct (Art. 8); or (c) the State has acknowledged and adopted the conduct in question as its own (Art. 11).

International Law Commission, Articles on Responsibility of States for Internationally Wrongful Acts, Report of the International Law Commission on the Work of Its Fifty-third Session, 2001 (A/56/10):

Article 4 Conduct of organs of a State
1. The conduct of any State organ shall be considered an act of that State under international law, whether the organ exercises legislative, executive, judicial or any other functions, whatever position it holds in the organization of the State, and whatever its character as an organ of the central government or of a territorial unit of the State.
2. An organ includes any person or entity which has that status in accordance with the internal law of the State.

Article 5 Conduct of persons or entities exercising elements of governmental authority
The conduct of a person or entity which is not an organ of the State under article 4 but which is empowered by the law of that State to exercise elements of the governmental authority shall be considered an act of the State under international law, provided the person or entity is acting in that capacity in the particular instance.

Article 8 Conduct directed or controlled by a State
The conduct of a person or group of persons shall be considered an act of a State under international law if the person or group of persons is in fact acting on the instructions of, or under the direction or control of, that State in carrying out the conduct.

Article 11 Conduct acknowledged and adopted by a State as its own
Conduct which is not attributable to a State under the preceding articles shall nevertheless be considered an act of that State under international law if and to the extent that the State acknowledges and adopts the conduct in question as its own.

In practice, it is the situation where the conduct of a private party is directed or controlled by a State, and thus may be attributed to that State, which has been most controversial. Article 8 of the ILC's Articles, which is reproduced above, reflects the position adopted by the International Court of Justice in the 1986 *Nicaragua* case. There, the Court refused to impute to the United States the violations of human rights and of humanitarian law committed by the *contras*, a guerilla combating the Nicaraguan Sandinista Government, despite the fact that they were trained and financed by US agencies:

International Court of Justice, case of *Military and Paramilitary Activities in and against Nicaragua (Nicaragua v. United States of America) (merits)*, judgment of 27 June 1986, I.C.J. Reports 1986, 14:

106. In the light of the evidence and material available to it, the Court is not satisfied that all the operations launched by the contra force, at every stage of the conflict, reflected strategy and tactics wholly devised by the United States. However, it is in the Court's view established that the support of the United States authorities for the activities of the contras took various forms over the years, such as logistic support, the supply of information on the location and movements of the Sandinista troops, the use of sophisticated methods of communication, the deployment of field broadcasting networks, radar coverage, etc. The Court finds it clear that a number of military and paramilitary operations by this force were decided and planned, if not actually by United States advisers, then at least in close collaboration with them, and on the basis of the intelligence and logistic support which the United States was able to offer, particularly the supply aircraft provided to the contras by the United States.

107. To sum up, despite the secrecy which surrounded it, at least initially, the financial support given by the Government of the United States to the military and paramilitary activities of the contras in Nicaragua is a fully established fact. The legislative and executive bodies of the respondent State have moreover, subsequent to the controversy which has been sparked off in the United States, openly admitted the nature, volume and frequency of this support. Indeed, they clearly take responsibility for it, this government aid having now become the major element of United States foreign policy in the region. As to the ways in which such financial support has been translated into practical assistance, the Court has been able to reach a general finding.

108. Despite the large quantity of documentary evidence and testimony which it has examined, the Court has not been able to satisfy itself that the respondent State 'created' the contra force in Nicaragua. It seems certain that members of the former Somoza National Guard, together with civilian opponents to the Sandinista regime, withdrew from Nicaragua soon after that regime was installed in Managua, and sought to continue their struggle against it, even if in a disorganized way and with limited and ineffectual resources, before the Respondent took advantage of the existence of these opponents and incorporated this fact into its policies *vis-à-vis* the regime of the Applicant. Nor does the evidence warrant a finding that the United States gave 'direct and critical combat support', at least if that form of words is taken to mean that this support was tantamount to direct intervention by the United States combat forces, or that all contra operations reflected strategy and tactics wholly devised by the United States. On the other hand, the Court holds it established that the United States authorities largely financed, trained, equipped, armed and organized the FDN [Fuerza Democratica Nicaraguense, an armed opposition group to the Sandinista Government of Nicaragua].

109. What the Court has to determine at this point is whether or not the relationship of the contras to the United States Government was so much one of dependence on the one side and control on the other that it would be right to equate the contras, for legal purposes, with an organ of the United States Government, or as acting on behalf of that Government ... Yet despite the heavy subsides and other support provided to them by the United States, there is no clear evidence of the United States having actually exercised such a degree of control in all fields as to justify treating the contras as acting on its behalf.

110. So far as the potential control constituted by the possibility of cessation of United States military aid is concerned, it may be noted that after 1 October 1984 such aid was no longer authorized, though the sharing of intelligence, and the provision of 'humanitarian assistance' ... may continue. Yet, according to Nicaragua's own case, and according to press reports, contra activity has continued. In sum, the evidence available to the Court indicates that the various forms of assistance provided to the contras by the United States have been crucial to the pursuit of their activities, but is insufficient to demonstrate their complete dependence on United States aid. On the other hand, it indicates that in the initial years of United States assistance the contra force was so dependent. However, whether the United States Government at any stage devised the strategy and directed the tactics of the contras depends on the extent to which the United States made use of the potential for control inherent in that dependence. The Court already indicated that it has insufficient evidence to reach a finding on this point. It is a fortiori unable to determine that the contra force may be equated for legal purposes with the forces of the United States. This conclusion, however, does not of course suffice to resolve the entire question of the responsibility incurred by the United States through its assistance to the contras.

111. In the view of the Court it is established that the contra force has, at least at one period, been so dependent on the United States that it could not conduct its crucial or most significant military and paramilitary activities without the multi-faceted support of the United States. This finding is fundamental in the present case. Nevertheless, adequate direct proof that all or the great majority of contra activities during that period received this support has not been, and indeed probably could not be, advanced in every respect. It will suffice the Court to stress that a degree of control by the United States Government, as described above, is inherent in the position in which the contra force finds itself in relation to that Government.

112. To show the existence of this control, the Applicant argued before the Court that the political leaders of the contra force had been selected, installed and paid by the United States; it also argued that the purpose herein was both to guarantee United States control over this force, and to excite sympathy for the Government's policy within Congress and among the public in the United States. According to the affidavit of Mr Chamorro, who was directly concerned, when the FDN was formed 'the name of the organization, the members of the political junta, and the members of the general staff were all chosen or approved by the CIA'; later the CIA asked that a particular person be made head of the political directorate of the FDN, and this was done. However, the question of the selection, installation and payment of the leaders of the contra force is merely one aspect among others of the degree of dependency of that force. This partial dependency on the United States authorities, the exact extent of which the Court cannot establish, may certainly be inferred *inter alia* from the fact that the leaders were selected by the United States. But it may also be inferred from other factors, some of which have been examined by the Court, such as the organization, training and equipping of the force, the planning of operations, the choosing of targets and the operational support provided.

113. The question of the degree of control of the contras by the United States Government is relevant to the claim of Nicaragua attributing responsibility to the United States for activities of the contras whereby the United States has, it is alleged, violated an obligation of international law not to kill, wound or kidnap citizens of Nicaragua. The activities in question are said to represent a tactic which includes 'the spreading of terror and danger to non-combatants as an end in itself with no attempt to observe humanitarian standards and no reference to the concept of military necessity'. In support of this, Nicaragua has catalogued numerous incidents, attributed to 'CIA-trained mercenaries' or 'mercenary forces', of kidnapping, assassination, torture, rape, killing of prisoners, and killing of civilians not dictated by military necessity ...

114. In this respect, the Court notes that according to Nicaragua, the contras are no more than bands of mercenaries which have been recruited, organized, paid and commanded by the Government of the United States. This would mean that they have no real autonomy in relation to that Government. Consequently, any offences which they have committed would be imputable to the Government of the United States, like those of any other forces placed under the latter's command. In the view of Nicaragua, 'stricto sensu, the military and paramilitary attacks launched by the United States against Nicaragua do not constitute a case of civil strife. They are essentially the acts of the United States.' If such a finding of the imputability of the acts of the contras to the United States were to be made, no question would arise of mere complicity in those acts, or of incitement of the contras to commit them.

115. The Court has taken the view (paragraph 110 above) that United States participation, even if preponderant or decisive, in the financing, organizing, training, supplying and equipping of the contras, the selection of its military or paramilitary targets, and the planning of the whole of its operation, is still insufficient in itself, on the basis of the evidence in the possession of the Court, for the purpose of attributing to the United States the acts committed by the contras in the course of their military or paramilitary operations in Nicaragua. All the forms of United States participation mentioned above, and even the general control by the respondent State over a force with a high degree of dependency on it, would not in themselves mean, without further evidence, that the United States directed or enforced the perpetration of the acts contrary to human rights and humanitarian law alleged by the applicant State. Such acts could well be committed by members of the contras without the control of the United States. For this conduct to give rise to legal responsibility of the United States, it would in principle have to be proved that that State had effective control of the military or paramilitary operations in the course of which the alleged violations were committed.

116. The Court does not consider that the assistance given by the United States to the contras warrants the conclusion that these forces are subject to the United States to such an extent that any acts they have committed are imputable to that State. It takes the view that the contras remain responsible for their acts, and that the United States is not responsible for the acts of the contras, but for its own conduct *vis-à-vis* Nicaragua, including conduct related to the acts of the contras. What the Court has to investigate is not the complaints relating to alleged violations of humanitarian law by the contras, regarded by Nicaragua as imputable to the United States, but rather unlawful acts for which the United States may be responsible directly in connection with the activities of the contras. The lawfulness or otherwise of such acts of the United States is a question different from the violations of humanitarian law of which the contras may or may not have been guilty. It is for this reason that the Court does not have to determine whether the violations of humanitarian law attributed to the contras were in fact committed by them. At the

same time, the question whether the United States Government was, or must have been, aware at the relevant time that allegations of breaches of humanitarian law were being made against the contras is relevant to an assessment of the lawfulness of the action of the United States.

In *Prosecutor* v. *Tadic*, the International Criminal Tribunal for the former Yugoslavia (ICTY) examined what degree of State control was required under international law over organized military groups in order to decide whether certain provisions of international humanitarian law applicable to international armed conflicts could be invoked. In formulating its standard, it took into account the UN Security Council Resolutions and debates surrounding the raids of South Africa into Zambia in order to destroy bases of the South West Africa People's Organization (SWAPO) in 1976, the Israeli incursions into Lebanon in June 1982, the South African raid in Lesotho in December 1982, and of course the judgment of the International Court of Justice in the *Nicaragua* case. It arrived at this conclusion:

International Criminal Tribunal for the former Yugoslavia, *Prosecutor* v. *Tadic*, Case No. IT–94–1–A, Judgment of 15 July 1999, para. 120:

[I]t would seem that for such control to come about, it is not sufficient for the group to be financially or even militarily assisted by a State ... [I]t must be proved that the State wields overall control over the group, not only by equipping and financing the group, but also by coordinating or helping in the general planning of its military activity. Only then can the State be held internationally accountable for any misconduct of the group. However, it is not necessary that, in addition, the State should also issue, either to the head or to members of the group, instructions for the commission of specific acts contrary to international law.

This could have been seen as relaxing the standard required by the *Nicaragua* case, although the context was entirely different, and although at issue was the individual responsibility of an individual and not the international responsibility of a State. The International Law Commission (ILC), in any case, remained unconvinced: Article 8 of the Draft Articles on Responsibility of States for Internationally Wrongful Acts simply reiterates the classical *Nicaragua* doctrine. The position of the ILC was subsequently confirmed by the International Court of Justice (ICJ), although with an important nuance. The circumstances were as follows. In March 1993, the Government of Bosnia and Herzegovina had filed an application instituting proceedings against the Federal Republic of Yugoslavia (FRY) (later Serbia and Montenegro, and now the Republic of Serbia) alleging violations of the Convention on the Prevention and Punishment of the Crime of Genocide, adopted by the General Assembly of the United Nations on 9 December 1948. One of the arguments of Bosnia and Herzegovina was that certain paramilitary groups involved in the operation in Srebenica where Bosnian Serb forces killed over 7,000 Bosnian Muslim men following the takeover of the 'safe area' in July

1995, even if they were not *de jure* organs of the defendant State (at the time, the FRY), nevertheless had to be considered '*de facto* organs' of the FRY, 'so that all of their acts, and specifically the massacres at Srebrenica, must be considered attributable to the FRY, just as if they had been organs of that State under its internal law; reality must prevail over appearances' (para. 390). In its judgment of 26 February 2007, the Court responds as follows:

International Court of Justice, case concerning the *Application of the Convention on the Prevention and Punishment of the Crime of Genocide (Bosnia and Herzegovina* v. *Serbia and Montenegro) (merits)*, judgment of 26 February 2007, I.C.J. Reports 2007, paras. 391–7 and 400–6:

391. The first issue raised by this argument is whether it is possible in principle to attribute to a State conduct of persons – or groups of persons – who, while they do not have the legal status of State organs, in fact act under such strict control by the State that they must be treated as its organs for purposes of the necessary attribution leading to the State's responsibility for an internationally wrongful act. The Court has in fact already addressed this question, and given an answer to it in principle, in its Judgment of 27 June 1986 in the case concerning *Military and Paramilitary Activities in and against Nicaragua (Nicaragua v. United States of America)* (Merits, Judgment, I.C.J. Reports 1986, pp. 62–64). In paragraph 109 of that Judgment the Court stated that it had to 'determine ... whether or not the relationship of the contras to the United States Government was so much one of dependence on the one side and control on the other that it would be right to equate the contras, for legal purposes, with an organ of the United States Government, or as acting on behalf of that Government' (p. 62). Then, examining the facts in the light of the information in its possession, the Court observed that 'there is no clear evidence of the United States having actually exercised such a degree of control in all fields as to justify treating the contras as acting on its behalf' (para. 109), and went on to conclude that 'the evidence available to the Court ... is insufficient to demonstrate [the contras'] complete dependence on United States aid', so that the Court was 'unable to determine that the contra force may be equated for legal purposes with the forces of the United States' (pp. 62–63, para. 110).

392. The passages quoted show that, according to the Court's jurisprudence, persons, groups of persons or entities may, for purposes of international responsibility, be equated with State organs even if that status does not follow from internal law, provided that in fact the persons, groups or entities act in 'complete dependence' on the State, of which they are ultimately merely the instrument. In such a case, it is appropriate to look beyond legal status alone, in order to grasp the reality of the relationship between the person taking action, and the State to which he is so closely attached as to appear to be nothing more than its agent: any other solution would allow States to escape their international responsibility by choosing to act through persons or entities whose supposed independence would be purely fictitious.

393. However, so to equate persons or entities with State organs when they do not have that status under internal law must be exceptional, for it requires proof of a particularly great degree of State control over them, a relationship which the Court's Judgment quoted above expressly described as 'complete dependence'. It remains to be determined in the present case whether, at the time in question, the persons or entities that committed the acts of genocide at Srebrenica had such ties with the FRY that they can be deemed to have been completely dependent on it;

it is only if this condition is met that they can be equated with organs of the Respondent for the purposes of its international responsibility.

394. The Court can only answer this question in the negative. At the relevant time, July 1995, neither the Republika Srpska nor the VRS [Army of the Republika Srpska (Bosnian Serbs)] could be regarded as mere instruments through which the FRY was acting, and as lacking any real autonomy. While the political, military and logistical relations between the federal authorities in Belgrade and the authorities in Pale, between the Yugoslav army and the VRS, had been strong and close in previous years ... and these ties undoubtedly remained powerful, they were, at least at the relevant time, not such that the Bosnian Serbs' political and military organizations should be equated with organs of the FRY. It is even true that differences over strategic options emerged at the time between Yugoslav authorities and Bosnian Serb leaders; at the very least, these are evidence that the latter had some qualified, but real, margin of independence. Nor, notwithstanding the very important support given by the Respondent to the Republika Srpska, without which it could not have 'conduct[ed] its crucial or most significant military and paramilitary activities' (I.C.J. Reports 1986, p. 63, para. 111), did this signify a total dependence of the Republika Srpska upon the Respondent.

[The Court concludes that the acts of genocide at Srebrenica cannot be attributed to the FRY, since these acts have been committed neither by its organs nor by persons or entities wholly dependent upon it. The FRY's international responsibility therefore cannot be engaged on this basis alone. The ICJ then turns to the question whether such attribution can be made on the basis of direction or control, as envisaged in Article 8 of the ILC's Articles on State Responsibility for Internationally Wrongful Acts. The Court first emphasizes that this is a question different from the one dealt with above:]

397. ... An affirmative answer to [the question whether, in the Srebrenica events, the perpetrators of genocide were acting on the instructions of the FRY, or under its direction or control] would in no way imply that the perpetrators should be characterized as organs of the FRY, or equated with such organs. It would merely mean that the FRY's international responsibility would be incurred owing to the conduct of those of its own organs which gave the instructions or exercised the control resulting in the commission of acts in breach of its international obligations. In other words, it is no longer a question of ascertaining whether the persons who directly committed the genocide were acting as organs of the FRY, or could be equated with those organs – this question having already been answered in the negative. What must be determined is whether FRY organs – incontestably having that status under the FRY's internal law – originated the genocide by issuing instructions to the perpetrators or exercising direction or control, and whether, as a result, the conduct of organs of the Respondent, having been the cause of the commission of acts in breach of its international obligations, constituted a violation of those obligations.

[Referring both to Article 8 of the ILC's Articles on Responsibility of States for Internationally Wrongful Acts, which it considers to embody customary international law, and to para. 115 of its 1986 judgment in the case of *Military and Paramilitary Activities in and against Nicaragua (Nicaragua v. United States of America) (merits)*, the Court adopts the following view:]

400. The test thus formulated [in the case of *Military and Paramilitary Activities in and against Nicaragua (Nicaragua v. United States of America) (merits)*] differs in two respects from the test – described above – to determine whether a person or entity may be equated with a State organ even if not having that status under internal law. First, in this context it is not necessary

to show that the persons who performed the acts alleged to have violated international law were in general in a relationship of 'complete dependence' on the respondent State; it has to be proved that they acted in accordance with that State's instructions or under its 'effective control'. It must however be shown that this 'effective control' was exercised, or that the State's instructions were given, in respect of each operation in which the alleged violations occurred, not generally in respect of the overall actions taken by the persons or groups of persons having committed the violations ...

402. The Court notes however that the Applicant has ... questioned the validity of applying, in the present case, the criterion adopted in the *Military and Paramilitary Activities* Judgment. It has drawn attention to the Judgment of the ICTY Appeals Chamber in the *Tadić* case (IT-94-1-A, Judgment, 15 July 1999). In that case the Chamber did not follow the jurisprudence of the Court in the *Military and Paramilitary Activities* case: it held that the appropriate criterion, applicable in its view both to the characterization of the armed conflict in Bosnia and Herzegovina as international, and to imputing the acts committed by Bosnian Serbs to the FRY under the law of State responsibility, was that of the 'overall control' exercised over the Bosnian Serbs by the FRY; and further that that criterion was satisfied in the case (on this point, *ibid.*, para. 145). In other words, the Appeals Chamber took the view that acts committed by Bosnian Serbs could give rise to international responsibility of the FRY on the basis of the overall control exercised by the FRY over the Republika Srpska and the VRS, without there being any need to prove that each operation during which acts were committed in breach of international law was carried out on the FRY's instructions, or under its effective control.

403. The Court has given careful consideration to the Appeals Chamber's reasoning in support of the foregoing conclusion, but finds itself unable to subscribe to the Chamber's view. First, the Court observes that the ICTY was not called upon in the *Tadić* case, nor is it in general called upon, to rule on questions of State responsibility, since its jurisdiction is criminal and extends over persons only. Thus, in that Judgment the Tribunal addressed an issue which was not indispensable for the exercise of its jurisdiction. As stated above, the Court attaches the utmost importance to the factual and legal findings made by the ICTY in ruling on the criminal liability of the accused before it and, in the present case, the Court takes fullest account of the ICTY's trial and appellate judgments dealing with the events underlying the dispute. The situation is not the same for positions adopted by the ICTY on issues of general international law which do not lie within the specific purview of its jurisdiction and, moreover, the resolution of which is not always necessary for deciding the criminal cases before it.

404. This is the case of the doctrine laid down in the *Tadić* Judgment. Insofar as the 'overall control' test is employed to determine whether or not an armed conflict is international, which was the sole question which the Appeals Chamber was called upon to decide, it may well be that the test is applicable and suitable; the Court does not however think it appropriate to take a position on the point in the present case, as there is no need to resolve it for purposes of the present Judgment. On the other hand, the ICTY presented the 'overall control' test as equally applicable under the law of State responsibility for the purpose of determining – as the Court is required to do in the present case – when a State is responsible for acts committed by paramilitary units, armed forces which are not among its official organs. In this context, the argument in favour of that test is unpersuasive.

405. It should first be observed that logic does not require the same test to be adopted in resolving the two issues, which are very different in nature: the degree and nature of a State's

involvement in an armed conflict on another State's territory which is required for the conflict to be characterized as international, can very well, and without logical inconsistency, differ from the degree and nature of involvement required to give rise to that State's responsibility for a specific act committed in the course of the conflict.

406. It must next be noted that the 'overall control' test has the major drawback of broadening the scope of State responsibility well beyond the fundamental principle governing the law of international responsibility: a State is responsible only for its own conduct, that is to say the conduct of persons acting, on whatever basis, on its behalf. That is true of acts carried out by its official organs, and also by persons or entities which are not formally recognized as official organs under internal law but which must nevertheless be equated with State organs because they are in a relationship of complete dependence on the State. Apart from these cases, a State's responsibility can be incurred for acts committed by persons or groups of persons – neither State organs nor to be equated with such organs – only if, assuming those acts to be internationally wrongful, they are attributable to it under the rule of customary international law reflected in Article 8 [of the ILC's Articles on State Responsibility]. This is so where an organ of the State gave the instructions or provided the direction pursuant to which the perpetrators of the wrongful act acted or where it exercised effective control over the action during which the wrong was committed. In this regard the 'overall control' test is unsuitable, for it stretches too far, almost to breaking point, the connection which must exist between the conduct of a State's organs and its international responsibility.

In sum, the International Court of Justice considers that there are two situations where the acts of non-State actors may be attributed to a State: such an attribution is justified either (a) when the non-State actor is under the 'complete dependence' of the State, so that it has in fact no autonomous will of its own; or (b) when the non-State entity is acting on the instructions of the State, or is under its direction or control in the adoption of the act which is alleged to engage the responsibility of the State. As such, 'overall control' by the State would therefore not be sufficient to engage its responsibility. This position, however, should not lead to obfuscate that positive obligations imposed on the State under international human rights law might in fact extend such responsibility, not by attributing to the State acts adopted by the private entity, but by imposing on the State a duty to exercise control on that entity. It is here that the obligation to protect in fact adds a layer to the responsibility of the State in human rights cases: in addition to having to *respect* human rights in all the acts it adopts, directly through its organs or through entities whose conduct it may be imputed, the State may be obliged to *protect* human rights, whereby remaining passive, State organs would be allowing infringements upon human rights by private actors to go undeterred and unremedied.

It may be useful in that respect to contrast the position of the ICJ with that of the European Court of Human Rights in the case of *Ilascu and others* v. *Moldova and Russia* (Appl. No. 48787/99, judgment of 8 July 2004; see also on this judgment the discussion in chapter 2, section 2.2., where the background to the case is explained). The Court recalled in that case that, where a State party to the Convention exercises *de facto* control over territory which is not its national territory, situations occuring on that territory fall under its 'jurisdiction' for the purposes of Article 1 ECHR: 'it is not necessary to determine whether a Contracting Party actually exercises detailed control over the policies and actions of the authorities in the area situated outside its national territory, since even overall control of the area may engage the responsibility of the Contracting Party concerned ... Where a Contracting State exercises overall control over an area outside its national territory its responsibility is not confined to the acts of its soldiers or officials in that area but also extends to acts of the local administration which survives there by virtue of its military and other support' (paras. 315–16). The Court arrived at the conclusion that the influence exercised by Russia on the Transdniestrian separatist regime was such that its responsibility could be engaged by the acts adopted by this regime, located on the national territory of Moldova (paras. 379–94). The following excerpts show its reasoning on this point:

European Court of Human Rights (GC), *Ilascu and others* v. *Moldova and Russia* (Appl. No. 48787/99), judgment of 8 July 2004, paras. 379–94:

(a) Before ratification of the Convention by the Russian Federation
379. The Court notes that on 14 November 1991, when the USSR was being broken up, the young Republic of Moldova asserted a right to the equipment and weapons stocks of the USSR's Fourteenth Army which was stationed in its territory ... It also entered into negotiations with the Russian Federation with a view to the withdrawal of that army from its territory.

380. The Court observes that during the Moldovan conflict in 1991–92 forces of the former Fourteenth Army (which owed allegiance to the USSR, the CIS and the Russian Federation in turn) stationed in Transdniestria, an integral part of the territory of the Republic of Moldova, fought with and on behalf of the Transdniestrian separatist forces. Moreover, large quantities of weapons from the stores of the Fourteenth Army (which later became the ROG [Russian Operational Group in the Transdniestrian region of Moldova]) were voluntarily transferred to the separatists, who were also able to seize possession of other weapons unopposed by Russian soldiers ...

The Court notes that from December 1991 onwards the Moldovan authorities systematically complained, to international bodies among others, of what they called 'the acts of aggression' of the former Fourteenth Army against the Republic of Moldova and accused the Russian Federation of supporting the Transdniestrian separatists.

Regard being had to the principle of States' responsibility for abuses of authority, it is of no consequence that, as the Russian Government submitted, the former Fourteenth Army did not participate as such in the military operations between the Moldovan forces and the Transdniestrian insurgents.

381. Throughout the clashes between the Moldovan authorities and the Transdniestrian separatists the leaders of the Russian Federation supported the separatist authorities by their political declarations ... The Russian Federation drafted the main lines of the ceasefire agreement of 21 July 1992, and moreover signed it as a party.

382. In the light of all these circumstances the Court considers that the Russian Federation's responsibility is engaged in respect of the unlawful acts committed by the Transdniestrian separatists, regard being had to the military and political support it gave them to help them set up the separatist regime and the participation of its military personnel in the fighting. In acting

thus the authorities of the Russian Federation contributed both militarily and politically to the creation of a separatist regime in the region of Transdniestria, which is part of the territory of the Republic of Moldova.

The Court next notes that even after the ceasefire agreement of 21 July 1992 the Russian Federation continued to provide military, political and economic support to the separatist regime ..., thus enabling it to survive by strengthening itself and by acquiring a certain amount of autonomy *vis-à-vis* Moldova.

383. The Court further notes that in the context of the events mentioned above the applicants were arrested in June 1992 with the participation of soldiers of the Fourteenth Army (subsequently the ROG). The first three applicants were then detained on Fourteenth Army premises and guarded by Fourteenth Army troops. During their detention these three applicants were interrogated and subjected to treatment which could be considered contrary to Article 3 of the Convention [prohibiting torture and other inhuman or degrading treatments or punishments]. They were then handed over into the charge of the Transdniestrian police.

Similarly, after his arrest by soldiers of the Fourteenth Army, the fourth applicant was handed over to the Transdniestrian separatist police, then detained, interrogated and subjected on police premises to treatment which could be considered contrary to Article 3 of the Convention.

384. The Court considers that on account of the above events the applicants came within the jurisdiction of the Russian Federation within the meaning of Article 1 of the Convention, although at the time when they occurred the Convention was not in force with regard to the Russian Federation.

This is because the events which gave rise to the responsibility of the Russian Federation must be considered to include not only the acts in which the agents of that State participated, like the applicants' arrest and detention, but also their transfer into the hands of the Transdniestrian police and regime, and the subsequent ill-treatment inflicted on them by those police, since in acting in that way the agents of the Russian Federation were fully aware that they were handing them over to an illegal and unconstitutional regime.

In addition, regard being had to the acts the applicants were accused of, the agents of the Russian Government knew, or at least should have known, the fate which awaited them.

385. In the Court's opinion, all of the acts committed by Russian soldiers with regard to the applicants, including their transfer into the charge of the separatist regime, in the context of the Russian authorities' collaboration with that illegal regime, are capable of engaging responsibility for the acts of that regime.

It remains to be determined whether that responsibility remained engaged and whether it was still engaged at the time of the ratification of the Convention by the Russian Federation.

(b) After ratification of the Convention by the Russian Federation

386. With regard to the period after ratification of the Convention, on 5 May 1998, the Court notes the following.

387. The Russian army is still stationed in Moldovan territory in breach of the undertakings to withdraw them completely given by the Russian Federation at the OSCE summits in Istanbul (1999) and Porto (2001). Although the number of Russian troops stationed in Transdniestria has in fact fallen significantly since 1992 ..., the Court notes that the ROG's weapons stocks are still there.

Consequently, in view of the weight of this arsenal ..., the ROG's military importance in the region and its dissuasive influence persist.

388. The Court further observes that by virtue of the agreements between the Russian Federation, on the one hand, and the Moldovan and Transdniestrian authorities respectively, on the other ..., the 'MRT' authorities were supposed to acquire the infrastructure and arsenal of the ROG at the time of its total withdrawal. It should be noted in that connection that the interpretation given by the Russian Government of the term 'local administrative authorities' of the region of Transdniestria, to be found, among other places, in the agreement of 21 October 1994 ... is different from that put forward by the Moldovan Government, a fact which enabled the 'MRT' regime to acquire that infrastructure.

389. As regards military relations, the Court notes that the Moldovan delegation to the Joint Control Commission constantly raised allegations of collusion between the ROG personnel and the Transdniestrian authorities regarding transfers of weapons to the latter. It notes that the ROG personnel denied those allegations in the presence of the delegates, declaring that some equipment could have found its way into the separatists' hands as a result of thefts.

Taking into account the accusations made against the ROG and the dangerous nature of its weapons stocks, the Court finds it hard to understand why the ROG troops do not have effective legal resources to prevent such transfers or thefts, as is apparent from their witness evidence to the delegates.

390. The Court attaches particular importance to the financial support enjoyed by the 'MRT' by virtue of the following agreements it has concluded with the Russian Federation:

- the agreement signed on 20 March 1998 between the Russian Federation and the representative of the 'MRT', which provided for the division between the 'MRT' and the Russian Federation of part of the income from the sale of the ROG's equipment;
- the agreement of 15 June 2001, which concerned joint work with a view to using armaments, military technology and ammunition;
- the Russian Federation's reduction by 100 million US dollars of the debt owed to it by the 'MRT'; and
- the supply of Russian gas to Transdniestria on more advantageous financial terms than those given to the rest of Moldova ...

The Court further notes the information supplied by the applicants and not denied by the Russian Government to the effect that companies and institutions of the Russian Federation normally controlled by the State, or whose policy is subject to State authorisation, operating particularly in the military field, have been able to enter into commercial relations with similar firms in the 'MRT' ...

391. The Court next notes that, both before and after 5 May 1998, in the security zone controlled by the Russian peacekeeping forces, the 'MRT' regime continued to deploy its troops illegally and to manufacture and sell weapons in breach of the agreement of 21 July 1992 ...

392. All of the above proves that the 'MRT', set up in 1991–1992 with the support of the Russian Federation, vested with organs of power and its own administration, remains under the effective authority, or at the very least under the decisive influence, of the Russian Federation, and in any event that it survives by virtue of the military, economic, financial and political support given to it by the Russian Federation.

393. That being so, the Court considers that there is a continuous and uninterrupted link of responsibility on the part of the Russian Federation for the applicants' fate, as the Russian Federation's policy of support for the regime and collaboration with it continued beyond 5 May 1998, and after that date the Russian Federation made no attempt to put an end to the

applicants' situation brought about by its agents, and did not act to prevent the violations allegedly committed after 5 May 1998.

Regard being had to the foregoing, it is of little consequence that since 5 May 1998 the agents of the Russian Federation have not participated directly in the events complained of in the present application.

394. In conclusion, the applicants therefore come within the 'jurisdiction' of the Russian Federation for the purposes of Article 1 of the Convention and its responsibility is engaged with regard to the acts complained of.

1.2 Positive obligations to protect

The private–public distinction on which the rules of attribution discussed above are based is mooted (though not contradicted) by the imposition of positive obligations on the States parties to international human rights instruments: once a situation is found to fall under its 'jurisdiction', the State must accept responsibility not only for the acts its organs have adopted (or for the conduct of private entities which, in exceptional cases, it may be imputed), but also for the omissions of these organs, in situations where such omissions result in an insufficient protection of private persons whose rights or freedoms are violated by the acts of other non-State actors.

(a) Before UN human rights treaty bodies

Under the International Covenant for Civil and Political Rights (ICCPR), the obligation to protect developed, initially, as an answer to the phenomenon of forced disappearances. Indeed, what is typical about forced disappearances is that only in rare cases shall it be possible for the family members of the victim to prove the involvement of State agents: in most cases, the body of the 'disappeared' will not have been found, and no information will have been provided to the family members allowing them to impute to the State a direct responsibility. It was therefore found necessary to identify an obligation of the State to take measures in order to provide effective protection from forced disappearances:

Human Rights Committee, General Comment No. 6, *The Right to Life* (Art. 6), 30 April 1982:

4. States parties should ... take specific and effective measures to prevent the disappearance of individuals, something which unfortunately has become all too frequent and leads too often to arbitrary deprivation of life. Furthermore, States should establish effective facilities and procedures to investigate thoroughly cases of missing and disappeared persons in circumstances which may involve a violation of the right to life.

Human Rights Committee, *Herrera Rubio et al.* v. *Colombia*, Communication No. 161/1983, final views of 2 November 1987 (CCPR/C/OP/2 at 192) (1990):

[The author alleges that on 17 March 1981 he was arrested in Cartagena del Chaira, Colombia, by members of the armed forces, taken to a military camp and subjected to torture in an attempt to extract from him information about a guerrilla movement, although he did not possess such information. After being transferred to another place of detention, he was again tortured, and was told that his parents would be killed if he refused to sign a confession prepared by his captors. He was later transferred to the military barracks of Juananbu in the city of Florencia, where he was again beaten (the name of the responsible officer is given) and threatened with his parents' possible death. He was then taken before Military Tribunal No. 35 and allegedly forced to sign a confession, pleading guilty, *inter alia*, of having kidnapped a man called Vicente Baquero, who later declared that he had never been kidnapped. On 5 April 1981, the author was taken to the prison in Florencia and informed that his parents had been killed. At his request, he was immediately brought again before the military judge, before whom he retracted his 'confession' and denounced the death threats received earlier concerning his parents. His new declaration allegedly disappeared from his dossier. He was finally released in December 1982.

Concerning the death of his parents, the author alleges that on two occasions his father had been taken away by the armed forces and tortured, before being released, in February 1981. On 27 March 1981, at 3 a.m., a group of individuals in military uniforms, identified as members of the 'counterguerrilla', arrived at the home of the author's parents and ordered his father to follow them. When his mother objected, she was also obliged to follow them. The author's brothers reported the disappearance of their parents immediately afterwards to the Tribunal of Doncello. One week later they were called by the authorities of Doncello to identify the bodies of their parents; their father's body was decapitated and his hands tied with a rope.]

10.2. Joaquin Herrera Rubio was arrested on 17 March 1981 by members of the Colombian armed forces on suspicion of being a 'guerrillero'. He claims that he was tortured … by Colombian military authorities who also threatened him that unless he signed a confession his parents would be killed. On 27 March 1981, several individuals wearing military uniforms, identifying themselves as members of the counter-guerrilla, came to the home of the author's parents and led them away by force. One week later the bodies of Jose Herrera and Emma Rubio de Herrera were found in the vicinity. At that time the District of Caqueta is reported to have been the scene of a military counterinsurgency operation, during which most villages in the area were subjected to stringent controls by the armed forces. The State party has shown that a judicial investigation of the killings was carried out from 24 September 1982 to 25 January 1983, and claims that it was established that no member of the armed forces had taken part in the killings. With respect to the author's allegations of torture, the State party contends that they are not credible in view of the fact that three months elapsed from the time of the alleged ill-treatment before the author's complaint was brought to the attention of the Court.

10.3. Whereas the Committee considers that there is reason to believe, in the light of the author's allegations, that Colombian military persons bear responsibility for the deaths of Josh Herrera and Emma Rubio de Herrera, no conclusive evidence has been produced to establish the identity of the murderers. In this connection the Committee refers to its general comment No. 6 (16) concerning article 6 of the Covenant [see above in this section], which provides, *inter alia*, that States parties should take specific and effective measures to prevent the disappearance of individuals and establish effective facilities and procedures to investigate thoroughly, by an appropriate impartial body, cases of missing and disappeared persons in circumstances which may involve a violation of the right to life. The Committee has duly noted the State party's submissions concerning the investigations carried out in this case, which, however, appear to have been inadequate in the light of the State party's obligations under article 2 of the Covenant.

10.4. With regard to the author's allegations of torture, the Committee notes that the author has given a very detailed description of the ill-treatment to which he was subjected and has provided the names of members of the armed forces allegedly responsible. In this connection, the Committee observes that the initial investigations conducted by the State party may have been concluded prematurely and that further investigations were called for in the light of the author's submission of 4 October 1986 and the Working Group's request of 18 December 1986 for more precise information.

10.5. With regard to the burden of proof, the Committee has already established in other cases (for example, Nos. 30/1978 and 85/1981) that this cannot rest alone on the author of the communication, especially considering that the author and the State party do not always have equal access to the evidence and that frequently the State party alone has access to relevant information. In the circumstances, due weight must be given to the author's allegations. It is implicit in article 4, paragraph 2, of the Optional Protocol that the State party has the duty to investigate in good faith all allegations of violation of the Covenant made against it and its authorities, and to furnish to the Committee the information available to it. In no circumstances should a State party fail to investigate fully allegations of ill-treatment when the person or persons allegedly responsible for the ill-treatment are identified by the author of a communication. The State party has in this matter provided no precise information and reports, *inter alia*, on the questioning of military officials accused of maltreatment of prisoners, or on the questioning of their superiors.

11. The Human Rights Committee ... is of the view that the facts as found by the Committee disclose violations of the Covenant with respect to:

- Article 6, because the State party failed to take appropriate measures to prevent the disappearance and subsequent killings of Jose Herrera and Emma Rubio de Herrera and to investigate effectively the responsibility for their murders; and
- Article 7 and article 10, paragraph 1, because Joaquin Herrera Rubio was subjected to torture and ill-treatment during his detention.

The existence of an obligation to protect cuts across the full range of the rights listed in the ICCPR, however:

Human Rights Committee, General Comment No. 31, *Nature of the General Legal Obligation Imposed on States Parties to the Covenant* (CCPR/C/21/Rev.1/Add. 13), 26 May 2004, para. 8:

The article 2, paragraph 1, obligations [according to which 'Each State Party to the ... Covenant undertakes to respect and to ensure to all individuals within its territory and subject to its jurisdiction' the rights recognized in the Covenant] are binding on States [Parties] and do not, as such, have direct horizontal effect as a matter of international law. The Covenant cannot be viewed as a substitute for domestic criminal or civil law. However the positive obligations on States Parties to ensure Covenant rights will only be fully discharged if individuals are protected by the State, not just against violations of Covenant rights by its agents, but also against acts committed by private persons or entities that would impair the enjoyment of Covenant rights in so far as they are amenable to application between private persons or entities. There may be circumstances in which a failure to ensure Covenant rights as required by article 2 would give rise to violations by States Parties of those rights, as a result of States Parties' permitting or failing to take appropriate measures or to exercise due diligence to prevent, punish, investigate or redress the harm caused by such acts by private persons or entities. States are reminded of the interrelationship between the positive obligations imposed under article 2 and the need to provide effective remedies in the event of breach under article 2, paragraph 3. The Covenant itself envisages in some articles certain areas where there are positive obligations on States Parties to address the activities of private persons or entities. For example, the privacy-related guarantees of article 17 must be protected by law. It is also implicit in article 7 that States Parties have to take positive measures to ensure that private persons or entities do not inflict torture or cruel, inhuman or degrading treatment or punishment on others within their power. In fields affecting basic aspects of ordinary life such as work or housing, individuals are to be protected from discrimination within the meaning of article 26.

The 1984 Convention against Torture and Other Cruel, Inhuman or Degrading Treatment or Punishment provides in Article 16: 'Each State Party shall undertake to prevent in any territory under its jurisdiction [acts of cruel, inhuman or degrading treatment or punishment], when such acts are committed by or at the instigation of or with the consent or acquiescence of a public official or other person acting in an official capacity.' Where prevention has failed, Article 12 of the Convention requires a 'prompt and impartial investigation, wherever there is reasonable ground to believe that an act of torture [or acts of cruel, inhuman or degrading treatment or punishment] has been committed in any territory under its jurisdiction'. Article 13 guarantees that the complainant shall have his case promptly and impartially examined by the competent national authorities. While Articles 12 and 13 refer explicitly only to acts of torture, Article 16 extends their guarantees to acts of cruel, inhuman or degrading treatment or punishment, where the latter have been committed by or at the instigation of or with the consent or acquiescence of a public official or other person acting in an official capacity. Although this latter limitation suggests that acts of cruel, inhuman or degrading treatment or punishment in which State agents have no implication whatsoever may not raise an issue under this provision of the CAT, the interpretation of the Committee against Torture in fact equates passivity of the authorities, when circumstances would have dictated that they adopt measures of protection, with 'acquiescence'. It follows from this interpretation that the CAT imposes an obligation to protect from torture or acts of cruel, inhuman or degrading treatment or punishment. The following case provides an illustration.

Committee against Torture, *Hajrizi Dzemajl et al.* v. *Serbia and Montenegro,* Communication No. 161/2000, decision of 21 November 2002 (CAT/C/29/D/161/2000):

[The sixty-five complainants are all of Romani origin and nationals of the Federal Republic of Yugoslavia. On 14 April 1995, after it received a report indicating that two Romani minors had raped a minor ethnic Montenegrin girl, the Danilovgrad Police Department entered and searched a number of houses in the Bozova Glavica Roma settlement and brought into custody all of the young male Romani men present in the settlement. The same day, around midnight, 200 ethnic Montenegrins, led by relatives and neighbours of the raped girl, assembled in front of the police station and publicly demanded that the Municipal Assembly adopt a decision expelling all Roma from Danilovgrad. The crowd shouted slogans addressed to the Roma, threatening to 'exterminate' them and 'burn down' their houses. When the Roma which had been arrested for interrogation were released (except for two men who had confessed to the crime), they were told by the police to leave Danilovgrad immediately with their families because they would be at risk of being lynched by their non-Roma neighbours. The other Romani residents of the settlement were also told by the police that they must evacuate the settlement immediately; they fled in panic. Then, in the morning, a group of non-Roma residents of Danilovgrad entered the Bozova Glavica Roma settlement, hurling stones and breaking windows of houses owned by the complainants. Those Roma who had still not left the settlement hid in one of the houses from which they eventually managed to flee through the fields and woods towards Podgorica. In the afternoon, the non-Roma residents of Danilovgrad attacked the settlement. Houses were burned down. The pogrom lasted for hours. The police remained passive throughout. According to the presentation of the facts by the complainants: 'As the violence and destruction unfolded, police officers did no more than feebly seek to persuade some of the attackers to calm down pending a final decision of the Municipal Assembly with respect to a popular request to evict Roma from the Bozova Glavica settlement.' A few days after the incident, the debris of the Roma settlement were cleared away, so that no trace of the Roma presence in Danilovgrad remained. Only one of the non-Roma residents of Danilovgrad was prosecuted for the attack on the settlement, but the case against him was dropped due to lack of evidence. At the time when the complainants addressed themselves to the Committee against Torture, their civil claims were still pending.]

9.2 As to the legal qualification of the facts that have occurred on 15 April 1995, as they were described by the complainants, the Committee first considers that the burning and destruction of houses constitute, in the circumstances, acts of cruel, inhuman or degrading treatment or punishment. The nature of these acts is further aggravated by the fact that some of the complainants were still hidden in the settlement when the houses were burnt and destroyed, the particular vulnerability of the alleged victims and the fact that the acts were committed with a significant level of racial motivation. Moreover, the Committee considers that the complainants have sufficiently demonstrated that the police (public officials), although they had been informed of the immediate risk that the complainants were facing and had been present at the scene of the events, did not take any appropriate steps in order to protect the complainants, thus implying 'acquiescence' in the sense of article 16 of the Convention. In this respect, the Committee has reiterated on many instances its concerns about 'inaction by police and law-enforcement officials who fail to provide adequate protection against racially motivated attacks when such groups have been threatened' (concluding observations on the initial report of Slovakia, CAT A/56/44 (2001), paragraph 104; see also concluding observations on the second periodic report of the Czech Republic, CAT A/56/44 (2001), paragraph 113 and concluding observations on the second periodic report of Georgia, CAT A/56/44 (2001), paragraph 81). Although the acts referred to by the complainants were not committed by public officials themselves, the Committee considers that they were committed with their acquiescence and constitute therefore a violation of article 16, paragraph 1, of the Convention by the State party.

9.3 Having considered that the facts described by the complainants constitute acts within the meaning of article 16, paragraph 1 of the Convention, the Committee will analyse other alleged violations in the light of that finding.

9.4 Concerning the alleged violation of article 12 of the Convention, the Committee, as it has underlined in previous cases (see *inter alia Encarnacion Blanco Abad* v. *Spain*, Case No. 59/1996, decided on 14 May 1998), is of the opinion that a criminal investigation must seek both to determine the nature and circumstances of the alleged acts and to establish the identity of any person who might have been involved therein. In the present case, the Committee notes that, despite the participation of at least several hundred non-Roma in the events of 15 April 1995 and the presence of a number of police officers both at the time and at the scene of those events, no person nor any member of the police forces has been tried by the courts of the State party. In these circumstances, the Committee is of the view that the investigation conducted by the authorities of the State party did not satisfy the requirements of article 12 of the Convention.

9.5 Concerning the alleged violation of article 13 of the Convention, the Committee considers that the absence of an investigation as described in the previous paragraph also constitutes a violation of article 13 of the Convention. Moreover, the Committee is of the view that the State party's failure to inform the complainants of the results of the investigation by, *inter alia*, not serving on them the decision to discontinue the investigation, effectively prevented them from assuming 'private prosecution' of their case. In the circumstances, the Committee finds that this constitutes a further violation of article 13 of the Convention.

9.6 ... The positive obligations that flow from the first sentence of article 16 of the Convention include an obligation to grant redress and compensate the victims of an act in breach of that provision. The Committee is therefore of the view that the State party has failed to observe its obligations under article 16 of the Convention by failing to enable the complainants to obtain redress and to provide them with fair and adequate compensation.

(b) Before regional courts

The obligation to protect thus affirmed by the Human Rights Committee has been emerging in the international law of human rights, since the mid-1980s. Both the European Court of Human Rights and the Inter-American Court of Human Rights delivered leading judgments on this issue during that period (see, e.g. E. A. Alkema, 'The Third-Party Applicability or "*Drittwirkung*" of the European Convention on Human Rights' in F. Matscher, H. Petzold, and G. J. Wiarda (eds.), *Protecting Human Rights: the European Dimension* (Cologne: Carl Heymans Verlag, 1988), p. 35; A. Clapham, *Human Rights in the Private Sphere* (Oxford: Clarendon Press, 1993); A. Drzemczewski, 'The European Human Rights Convention and Relations between Private Parties', *Netherlands International Law Review*, 2 (1979), 168; A. R. Mowbray, *The Development of Positive*

Obligations under the European Convention on Human Rights by the European Court of Human Rights (Oxford: Hart Publishing, 2004)). Although the notion of positive obligations, used in a broader meaning to refer to the obligation of the State to take certain measures in order to ensure that the rights stipulated in the European Convention on Human Rights are not violated, pre-dated these cases, the first judgments in which the European Court of Human Rights affirmed that the ECHR may require positive measures to be taken, even in the sphere of relations between individuals, were in the cases of *Young, James and Webster* v. *the United Kingdom* and of *X and Y* v. *Netherlands*:

European Court of Human Rights (plenary), *Young, James and Webster* v. *the United Kingdom*, judgment of 13 August 1981, Series A, No. 44:

12. Mr Young, Mr James and Mr Webster are former employees of the British Railways Board ('British Rail'). In 1975, a 'closed shop' agreement was concluded between British Rail and three trade unions, providing that thenceforth membership of one of those unions was a condition of employment. The applicants failed to satisfy this condition and were dismissed in 1976. They alleged that the treatment to which they had been subjected gave rise to violations of Articles 9 [freedom of religion and belief], 10 [freedom of expression], 11 [freedom of association] and 13 [effective remedy] of the Convention.

13. In essence, a closed shop is an undertaking or workplace in which, as a result of an agreement or arrangement between one or more trade unions and one or more employers or employers' associations, employees of a certain class are in practice required to be or become members of a specified union. The employer is not under any legal obligation to consult or obtain the consent of individual employees directly before such an agreement or arrangement is put into effect. Closed shop agreements and arrangements vary considerably in both their form and their content; one distinction that is often drawn is that between the 'pre-entry' shop (the employee must join the union before engaged) and the 'post-entry' shop (he must join within a reasonable time after being engaged), the latter being more common.

In the United Kingdom, the institution of the closed shop is of very long standing. In recent years, closed shop arrangements have become more formalised and the number of employees covered thereby has increased (3.75 million in the 1960's and 5 million in 1980, approximately). Recent surveys suggest that in many cases the obligation to join a specified union does not extend to existing non-union employees ...

29. In 1970, British Rail had concluded a closed shop agreement with the National Union of Railwaymen ('NUR'), the Transport Salaried Staffs' Association ('TSSA') and the Associated Society of Locomotive Engineers and Firemen ('ASLEF'), but, with the enactment of the Industrial Relations Act 1971 [which introduced specific provisions making the operation of the majority of closed shops unlawful, and treating as unfair dismissal the dismissal of employees exercising their right not to be a member of a trade union], it was not put into effect.

The matter was, however, revived in July 1975 when British Rail concluded a further agreement with the same unions [following the repeal of the Industrial Relations Act 1971 by the Trade Union and Labour Relations Act 1974, which removed both the prohibition on closed shops and the employee's right not to belong to a union, although it maintained the protection against unfair dismissal if the employee genuinely objected (i) on grounds of religious belief to being a member of any union whatsoever; or (ii) on any reasonable grounds to being a member of a particular union]. It was provided that as from 1 August 1975 membership of one of those unions was to be a condition of employment for certain categories of staff – including the applicants – and that the terms of the agreement were 'incorporated in and form[ed] part of' each contract of employment. Like other staff of British Rail, Mr Young, Mr James and Mr Webster had, it appears, been supplied when engaged with a written statement containing a provision to the effect that they were subject to such terms and conditions of employment as might from time to time be settled for employees of their category under the machinery of negotiation established between their employer and any trade union or other organisation.

The membership requirement did not apply to 'an existing employee who genuinely objects on grounds of religious belief to being a member of any Trade Union whatsoever or on any reasonable grounds to being a member of a particular Trade Union'. The agreement also set out the procedure for applying for exemption on these grounds and provided for applications to be heard by representatives of the employer and the unions.

30. In July/August 1975, notices were posted at the premises of British Rail, including those where the applicants were then working, drawing the attention of staff to the agreement with the unions and the change in conditions of employment.

A further notice of September 1975 stated that it had been agreed that the exemption on religious grounds would be available only where a denomination specifically proscribed its members from joining unions. The notice added that 'confining exemption only to religious grounds depends upon the passing through Parliament of the Trade Union and Labour Relations (Amendment) Bill' and that staff would be advised further on this point ... The Amendment Act came into force on 25 March 1976.

On the same date, a further agreement between British Rail and the railway unions came into effect. It was in identical terms to the July 1975 agreement, except that the words 'or on any reasonable grounds to being a member of a particular Trade Union' (see paragraph 29 above) were omitted.

31. The applicants and the representative of the Trades Union Congress informed the Court that NUR, TSSA and ASLEF were the only unions actually operating in 1975 in those sectors of the railway industry in which Mr Young, Mr James and Mr Webster worked. According to the Government, other unions did have members in, although they were not recruiting amongst, the relevant grades.

It appears that, prior to the conclusion of the 1975 closed shop agreement, between 6,000 and 8,000 British Rail employees, out of a total staff of 250,000, were not already members of one of the specified unions. In the final event, 54 individuals were dismissed for refusal to comply with the membership requirement.

[Preliminary: responsibility of the respondent State]

48. Mr Young, Mr James and Mr Webster alleged that [the enforcement of TULRA and the Amendment Act, allowing their dismissal from employment when they objected on reasonable grounds to joining a trade union, interfered with their freedom of thought, conscience, expression and association with others. They further complained that no adequate remedies had been available to them.]. Before the substance of the matter is examined, it must be considered whether responsibility can be attributed to the respondent State, the United Kingdom.

The Government conceded that, should the Court find that the termination of the applicants' contracts of employment constituted a relevant interference with their rights under Article 11 and that that interference could properly be regarded as a direct consequence of TULRA and the Amendment Act, the responsibility of the respondent State would be engaged by virtue of the enactment of that legislation ...

49. Under Article 1 of the Convention, each Contracting State 'shall secure to everyone within [its] jurisdiction the rights and freedoms defined in ... [the] Convention'; hence, if a violation of one of those rights and freedoms is the result of non-observance of that obligation in the enactment of domestic legislation, the responsibility of the State for that violation is engaged. Although the proximate cause of the events giving rise to this case was the 1975 agreement between British Rail and the railway unions, it was the domestic law in force at the relevant time that made lawful the treatment of which the applicants complained. The responsibility of the respondent State for any resultant breach of the Convention is thus engaged on this basis. Accordingly, there is no call to examine whether, as the applicants argued, the State might also be responsible on the ground that it should be regarded as employer or that British Rail was under its control.

[The alleged violation of Article 11 ECHR]

54. As a consequence of the agreement concluded in 1975 (see paragraph 29 above), the applicants were faced with the dilemma either of joining NUR (in the case of Mr James) or TSSA or NUR (in the cases of Mr Young and Mr Webster) or of losing jobs for which union membership had not been a requirement when they were first engaged and which two of them had held for several years. Each applicant regarded the membership condition introduced by that agreement as an interference with the freedom of association to which he considered that he was entitled; in addition, Mr Young and Mr Webster had objections to trade union policies and activities coupled, in the case of Mr Young, with objections to the political affiliations of the specified unions ... As a result of their refusal to yield to what they considered to be unjustified pressure, they received notices terminating their employment. Under the legislation in force at the time ..., their dismissal was 'fair' and, hence, could not found a claim for compensation, let alone reinstatement or re-engagement.

55. The situation facing the applicants clearly runs counter to the concept of freedom of association in its negative sense.

Assuming that Article 11 does not guarantee the negative aspect of that freedom on the same footing as the positive aspect, compulsion to join a particular trade union may not always be contrary to the Convention.

However, a threat of dismissal involving loss of livelihood is a most serious form of compulsion and, in the present instance, it was directed against persons engaged by British Rail before the introduction of any obligation to join a particular trade union.

In the Court's opinion, such a form of compulsion, in the circumstances of the case, strikes at the very substance of the freedom guaranteed by Article 11. For this reason alone, there has been an interference with that freedom as regards each of the three applicants.

[The Court concludes that Article 11 ECHR has been violated, since in the view of the Court 'the detriment suffered by Mr Young, Mr James and Mr Webster went further than was required to achieve a proper balance between the conflicting interests of those involved and cannot be regarded as proportionate to the aims being pursued', the interference with the rights of the applicants under Article 11 ECHR was disproportionate.]

European Court of Human Rights, *X and Y* v. *Netherlands*, judgment of 26 March 1985, Series A, No. 91;

[The applicants are Mr X and his daughter, Y. The daughter, born in 1961, is mentally handicapped. She has been living since 1970 in a privately run home for mentally handicapped children. In December 1977, on the day after her sixteenth birthday, Y was sexually abused in the institution by Mr B., the son-in-law of the directress of the institution where Y was staying. When Mr X went to the local police station to file a complaint against the author of the abuse, and to ask for criminal proceedings to be instituted, he was told that since Mr X considered his daughter unable to sign the complaint because of her mental condition, he could do so himself. However, it later appeared that the offence for which there might have been sufficient evidence to justify the launch of a prosecution (acts of indecency committed against a person by abuse of authority: Art. 248 *ter*), required that the victim file a complaint him/herself: under Article 64 para. 1, the legal representative may lodge the complaint on behalf of the victim only if the latter is under the age of sixteen or is placed under guardianship (curateele); this latter institution exists only for persons who have reached the age of majority, namely twenty-one (Art. 378, Book I, of the Civil Code). The applicants argue before the Court that the impossibility of having criminal proceedings instituted against Mr B violated Article 8 of the Convention, which guarantees the right to respect for private life.]

22. There was no dispute as to the applicability of Article 8: the facts underlying the application to the Commission concern a matter of 'private life', a concept which covers the physical and moral integrity of the person, including his or her sexual life.

23. The Court recalls that although the object of Article 8 is essentially that of protecting the individual against arbitrary interference by the public authorities, it does not merely compel the State to abstain from such interference: in addition to this primarily negative undertaking, there may be positive obligations inherent in an effective respect for private or family life (see the *Airey* judgment of 9 October 1979, Series A No. 32, p. 17, para. 32). These obligations may involve the adoption of measures designed to secure respect for private life even in the sphere of the relations of individuals between themselves.

[Necessity for criminal law provisions]

24. The applicants argued that, for a young girl like Miss Y, the requisite degree of protection against the wrongdoing in question would have been provided only by means of the criminal law. In the Government's view, the Convention left it to each State to decide upon the means to be utilised and did not prevent it from opting for civil-law provisions.

The Court ... observes that the choice of the means calculated to secure compliance with Article 8 in the sphere of the relations of individuals between themselves is in principle a matter that falls within the Contracting States' margin of appreciation. In this connection, there are different ways of ensuring 'respect for private life', and the nature of the State's obligation will depend on the particular aspect of private life that is at issue. Recourse to the criminal law is not necessarily the only answer.

25. The Government cited the difficulty encountered by the legislature in laying down criminal-law provisions calculated to afford the best possible protection of the physical integrity of the mentally handicapped: to go too far in this direction might lead to unacceptable paternalism and occasion an inadmissible interference by the State with the individual's right to respect for his or her sexual life.

The Government stated that under Article 1401 of the Civil Code, taken together with Article 1407, it would have been possible to bring before or file with the Netherlands courts, on behalf of Miss Y: an action for damages against Mr B, for pecuniary or non-pecuniary damage; an application for an injunction against Mr B, to prevent repetition of the offence; a similar action or application against the directress of the children's home.

The applicants considered that these civil-law remedies were unsuitable. They submitted that, amongst other things, the absence of any criminal investigation made it harder to furnish evidence on the four matters that had to be established under Article 1401, namely a wrongful act, fault, damage and a causal link between the act and the damage. Furthermore, such proceedings were lengthy and involved difficulties of an emotional nature for the victim, since he or she had to play an active part therein ...

27. The Court finds that the protection afforded by the civil law in the case of wrongdoing of the kind inflicted on Miss Y is insufficient. This is a case where fundamental values and essential aspects of private life are at stake. Effective deterrence is indispensable in this area and it can be achieved only by criminal-law provisions; indeed, it is by such provisions that the matter is normally regulated.

Moreover, as was pointed out by the Commission, this is in fact an area in which the Netherlands has generally opted for a system of protection based on the criminal law. The only gap, so far as the Commission and the Court have been made aware, is as regards persons in the situation of Miss Y; in such cases, this system meets a procedural obstacle which the Netherlands legislature had apparently not foreseen.

[Compatibility of the Netherlands legislation with Article 8]
28. According to the Government, it was the exceptional nature of the facts of the case which disclosed the gap in the law and it could not be said that there had been any failure on the part of the legislature ...

According to the applicants, on the other hand, the current Criminal Code offered insufficient protection ...

29. ... Article 248 *ter* requires a complaint by the actual victim before criminal proceedings can be instituted against someone who has contravened this provision. [In] the case in question criminal proceedings could not be instituted on the basis of Article 248 *ter* ...

30. Thus, [the provisions of the Dutch Criminal Code were insufficient to provide] Miss Y with practical and effective protection. It must therefore be concluded, taking account of the nature of the wrongdoing in question, that she was the victim of a violation of Article 8 of the Convention.

The Inter-American Court of Human Rights has developed an extensive interpretation of the obligations of States under the American Convention on Human Rights (ACHR), establishing a typology that distinguishes the obligation to *respect* the rights and freedoms recognized by the Convention, from that of *ensuring* the exercise of all rights. Both obligations are enshrined in Article 1(1) ACHR, which reads: 'The States Parties to this Convention undertake to respect the rights and freedoms recognized herein and to ensure to all persons subject to their jurisdiction the free and full exercise of those rights and freedoms, without any discrimination for reasons of race, color, sex, language, religion, political or other opinion, national or social origin, economic status, birth, or any other social condition.' Article 2 ACHR provides that: 'Where the exercise of any of the rights or freedoms referred to in Article 1 is not already ensured by legislative or other provisions, the States Parties undertake to adopt, in accordance with their constitutional processes and the provisions of this Convention, such legislative or other measures as may be necessary to give effect to those rights or freedoms.' However, the obligation to ensure the exercise of all rights may go far beyond the obligation to adopt the kind of measures, of a legal or regulatory nature, established by this latter provision.

This was first clearly established in the *Velasquez-Rodriguez* case. The case involved the forced disappearance of Manfredo Velasquez, a Honduran student, in 1981, during a period in which such practices were systematic. The Court concluded that the disappearance had been carried out by military personnel or by persons connected to and tolerated by the military; it thereby found a violation of Articles 7 (personal liberty), 5 (personal integrity) and 4 (right to life). The Court then decided *motu propio* to examine whether the acts also involved a violation of Article 1(1) of the ACHR:

Inter-American Court of Human Rights, case of *Velásquez–Rodríguez* v. *Honduras* (merits), judgment of 29 July 1988, Series C No. 4:

164. Article 1(1) is essential in determining whether a violation of the human rights recognized by the Convention can be imputed to a State Party. In effect, that article charges the States Parties with the fundamental duty to respect and guarantee the rights recognized in the Convention. Any impairment of those rights which can be attributed under the rules of international law to the action or omission of any public authority constitutes an act imputable to the State, which assumes responsibility in the terms provided by the Convention.

165. The first obligation assumed by the States Parties under Article 1(1) is 'to respect the rights and freedoms' recognized by the Convention. The exercise of public authority has certain limits which derive from the fact that human rights are inherent attributes of human dignity and are, therefore, superior to the power of the State ...

166. The second obligation of the States Parties is to 'ensure' the free and full exercise of the rights recognized by the Convention to every person subject to its jurisdiction. This obligation implies the duty of States Parties to organize the governmental apparatus and, in general, all the structures through which public power is exercised, so that they are capable of juridically ensuring the free and full enjoyment of human rights. As a consequence of this obligation, the States must prevent, investigate and punish any violation of the rights recognized by the Convention and, moreover, if possible attempt to restore the right violated and provide compensation as warranted for damages resulting from the violation.

167. The obligation to ensure the free and full exercise of human rights is not fulfilled by the existence of a legal system designed to make it possible to comply with this obligation – it also requires the government to conduct itself so as to effectively ensure the free and full exercise of human rights.

168. The obligation of the States is, thus, much more direct than that contained in Article 2.

169. According to Article 1(1), any exercise of public power that violates the rights recognized by the Convention is illegal. Whenever a State organ, official or public entity violates one of

those rights, this constitutes a failure of the duty to respect the rights and freedoms set forth in the Convention.

170. This conclusion is independent of whether the organ or official has contravened provisions of internal law or overstepped the limits of his authority: under international law a State is responsible for the acts of its agents undertaken in their official capacity and for their omissions, even when those agents act outside the sphere of their authority or violate internal law.

171. This principle suits perfectly the nature of the Convention, which is violated whenever public power is used to infringe the rights recognized therein. If acts of public power that exceed the State's authority or are illegal under its own laws were not considered to compromise that State's obligation under the treaty, the system of protection provided for in the Convention would be illusory.

172. Thus, in principle, any violation of rights recognized by the Convention carried out by an act of public authority or by persons who use their position of authority is imputable to the State. However, this does not define all the circumstances in which a State is obligated to prevent, investigate and punish human rights violations, nor all the cases in which the State might be found responsible for an infringement of those rights. An illegal act which violates human rights and which is initially not directly imputable to a State (for example, because it is the act of a private person or because the person responsible has not been identified) can lead to international responsibility of the State, not because of the act itself, but because of the lack of due diligence to prevent the violation or to respond to it as required by the Convention ...

174. The State has a legal duty to take reasonable steps to prevent human rights violations and to use the means at its disposal to carry out a serious investigation of violations committed within its jurisdiction, to identify those responsible, to impose the appropriate punishment and to ensure the victim adequate compensation.

175. This duty to prevent includes all those means of a legal, political, administrative and cultural nature that promote the protection of human rights and ensure that any violations are considered and treated as illegal acts, which, as such, may lead to the punishment of those responsible and the obligation to indemnify the victims for damages. It is not possible to make a detailed list of all such measures, since they vary with the law and the conditions of each State Party. Of course, while the State is obligated to prevent human rights abuses, the existence of a particular violation does not, in itself, prove the failure to take preventive measures. On the other hand, subjecting a person to official, repressive bodies that practice torture and assassination with impunity is itself a breach of the duty to prevent violations of the rights to life and physical integrity of the person, even if that particular person is not tortured or assassinated, or if those facts cannot be proven in a concrete case.

176. The State is obligated to investigate every situation involving a violation of the rights protected by the Convention. If the State apparatus acts in such a way that the violation goes unpunished and the victim's full enjoyment of such rights is not restored as soon as possible, the State has failed to comply with its duty to ensure the free and full exercise of those rights to the persons within its jurisdiction. The same is true when the State allows private persons or groups to act freely and with impunity to the detriment of the rights recognized by the Convention.

The 'positive obligations' of States under the American Convention have been interpreted broadly, and include such duties as:

- '[to] ensure protection of children against mistreatment, whether in their relations with public authorities, or in relations among individuals or with non-governmental entities' and to 'safeguard the prevailing role of the family in protection of the child; [the State] must also provide assistance to the family by public authorities, by adopting measures that promote family unity' (IACtHR, *Juridical Condition and Human Rights of the Child*. Advisory Opinion OC–17/02 of 28 August 2002, Series A No. 17 at paras. 87–8);

- '[to exercise] due diligence ... to avoid operations [by paramilitary groups against civilian populations] in a zone that had been declared an emergency zone, subject to military operations' (IACtHR, case of the *Pueblo Bello Massacre* v. *Colombia*, merits, reparations and costs, judgment of 31 January 2006, Series C No. 140 at para. 139);

- '[to] undertake as guarantor, to protect and ensure the right to life, [by] generating minimum living conditions that are compatible with the dignity of the human person and of not creating conditions that hinder or impede it. [The] State has the duty to take positive, concrete measures geared toward fulfillment of the right to a decent life, especially in the case of persons who are vulnerable and at risk' (IACtHR, case of the *Yakye Axa Indigenous Community* v. *Paraguay*, merits, reparations and costs, judgment of 17 June 2005, Series C, No. 125, para. 162; see also case of the *Sawhoyamaxa Indigenous Community* v. *Paraguay*, merits, reparations and costs, judgment of 29 March 2006, Series C No. 146, para. 153);

- 'to provide [the individual with publicly-held information], so that the individual may have access to such information or receive an answer that includes a justification when, for any reason permitted by the Convention, the State is allowed to restrict access to the information in a specific case' (IACtHR, case of *Claude-Reyes et al.* v. *Chile*, merits, reparations and costs, judgment of 19 September 2006, Series C, No. 151, para 77).

The following Advisory Opinion is also representative of the approach of the Inter-American Court:

Inter-American Court of Human Rights, *Juridical Condition and Rights of the Undocumented Migrants*, Advisory Opinion OC–18/03 of 17 September 2003, requested by the Union of Mexican States:

[Mexico requested, in substance, whether an American State could establish in its labour legislation a differential treatment between legal residents or citizens on the one hand, undocumented migrant workers, on the other hand, in the enjoyment of their labour rights.]

146. [The] obligation to respect and ensure human rights, which normally has effects on the relations between the State and the individuals subject to its jurisdiction, also has effects on relations between individuals. As regards this Advisory Opinion, the said effects of the obligation to respect human rights in relations between individuals is defined in the context of the private employment relationship, under which the employer must respect the human rights of his workers.

147. The obligation to respect and guarantee the human rights of third parties is also based on the fact that it is the State that determines the laws that regulate the relations between individuals and, thus, private law; hence, it must also ensure that human rights are respected in

these private relationships between third parties; to the contrary, the State may be responsible for the violation of those rights.

148. The State is obliged to respect and ensure the labor human rights of all workers, irrespective of their status as nationals or aliens, and not to tolerate situations of discrimination that prejudice the latter in the employment relationships established between individuals (employer-worker). The State should not allow private employers to violate the rights of workers, or the contractual relationship to violate minimum international standards.

149. This State obligation arises from legislation that protects workers – legislation based on the unequal relationship between both parties – which therefore protects the workers as the more vulnerable party. In this way, States must ensure strict compliance with the labor legislation that provides the best protection for workers, irrespective of their nationality, social, ethnic or racial origin, and their migratory status; therefore they have the obligation to take any necessary administrative, legislative or judicial measures to correct *de jure* discriminatory situations and to eradicate discriminatory practices against migrant workers by a specific employer or group of employers at the local, regional, national or international level.

150. On many occasions migrant workers must resort to State mechanisms for the protection of their rights. Thus, for example, workers in private companies have recourse to the Judiciary to claim the payment of wages, compensation, etc. Also, these workers often use State health services or contribute to the State pension system. In all these cases, the State is involved in the relationship between individuals as a guarantor of fundamental rights, because it is required to provide a specific service.

151. In labor relations, employers must protect and respect the rights of workers, whether these relations occur in the public or private sector. The obligation to respect the human rights of migrant workers has a direct effect on any type of employment relationship, when the State is the employer, when the employer is a third party, and when the employer is a natural or legal person.

152. The State is thus responsible for itself, when it acts as an employer, and for the acts of third parties who act with its tolerance, acquiescence or negligence, or with the support of some State policy or directive that encourages the creation or maintenance of situations of discrimination.

153. In summary, employment relationships between migrant workers and third party employers may give rise to the international responsibility of the State in different ways. First, States are obliged to ensure that, within their territory, all the labor rights stipulated in its laws – rights deriving from international instruments or domestic legislation – are recognized and applied. Likewise, States are internationally responsible when they tolerate actions and practices of third parties that prejudice migrant workers, either because they do not recognize the same rights to them as to national workers or because they recognize the same rights to them but with some type of discrimination.

154. Furthermore, there are cases in which it is the State that violates the human rights of the workers directly. For example, when it denies the right to a pension to a migrant worker who has made the necessary contributions and fulfilled all the conditions that were legally required of workers, or when a worker resorts to the corresponding judicial body to claim his rights and this body does not provide him with due judicial protection or guarantees.

The distinction between situations where the acts of private parties are directly imputable to the State and situations where they merely highlight a failure of the State to discharge its obligation to protect may break down in certain situations. Consider for instance:

European Court of Human Rights (2nd sect.), *M.M.* **v.** *Netherlands* **(Appl. No. 39339/98), judgment of 8 April 2003:**

[The applicant, a criminal defence lawyer, was alleged by the criminal defendant for whom he was acting as a legal counsel to have made sexual advances towards his wife, Mrs S. The police therefore suggested that Mrs S. connect a tape recorder to her telephone in order to allow her to tape incoming conversations with the applicant. Mrs S. recorded three conversations with the applicant, which were transcribed by the police. These transcripts were added to the case-file on the investigation against the applicant, and following press releases about the investigation against the applicant, other women came forward complaining that they too had been abused. M.M. was finally convicted for sexual assault, although the courts did not rely on the recorded telephone conversations as evidence. The applicant alleged that the recording of his telephone conversations with Mrs S. constituted a violation of Article 8 of the Convention.]

36. The question before the Court is whether the 'interference' with the applicant's Article 8 rights – to wit, the recording of telephone conversations which he had with Mrs S. with a view to their use as prosecution evidence against the applicant – is imputable to a 'public authority' or not.

37. It is not in dispute that it was the police who made the suggestion to the Mrs S. to record telephone conversations with the applicant. With the prior permission of the public prosecutor, police officers connected a tape recorder to Mrs S.'s telephone. They suggested that she steer her conversations with the applicant towards the latter's sexual approaches. They instructed Mrs S. in the operation of the tape recorder. They came to her home and collected the recordings. It was left to Mrs S. to entrap the applicant into making statements amounting to admissions of guilt and to activate the tape recorder.

38. It is recalled that in the case of *A.* v. *France* (judgment of 23 November 1993, Series A No. 277–B), a certain private citizen of his own motion reported a conspiracy to commit murder to a police superintendent. He volunteered to call the applicant A., a participant in the conspiracy, and suggested the recording of the telephone conversation in question. The police superintendent '... made a crucial contribution to executing the scheme by making available for a short time his office, his telephone and his tape recorder. Admittedly, he did not inform his superiors of his actions and he had not sought the prior authorisation of an investigating judge, but he was acting in the performance of his duties as a high-ranking police officer. It follows that the public authorities were involved to such an extent that the State's responsibility under the Convention was engaged.' (*loc. cit.*, p. 48, §36)

39. The same considerations apply here. Acting as they did, with the permission of the public prosecutor, the police 'made a crucial contribution to the execution of the scheme', as well as being responsible for its inception. The public prosecutor and the police all acted in the performance of their official duties. The responsibility of the respondent State is therefore engaged.

40. In the present case, which like the *A.* v. *France* case is characterised by the police setting up a private individual to collect evidence in a criminal case, the Court is not persuaded by the Government's argument that it was ultimately Mrs S. who was in control of events. To accept such an argument would be tantamount to allowing investigating authorities to evade their responsibilities under the Convention by the use of private agents.

41. It is not necessary to consider the Government's suggestion that Mrs S. would have been fully entitled to record telephone calls from the applicant without the involvement of public authority and use the recordings as she wished, the issue in this case being precisely the involvement of public authority.

42. There has accordingly been an 'interference by a public authority' with the applicant's right to respect for his 'correspondence'.

43. Such an interference will violate Article 8 of the Convention unless it is 'in accordance with the law', pursues one of the 'legitimate aims' set out in the second paragraph of that Article, and can be considered 'necessary in a democratic society' in pursuit of that aim.

[Applying these principles, the Court finds that, under the Dutch law applicable at the material time, the tapping or interception of telecommunications presupposed, first, a preliminary judicial investigation, and second, an order given by an investigating judge (Articles 125f and 125g §1 of the Code of Criminal Procedure, see para. 22 above). Since neither of these condition was met, the interference with the right to respect for private life, which is imputable to the State, was not 'in accordance with the law'; therefore Article 8 ECHR is violated.]

Box 4.1. **The issue of human rights and transnational corporations**

The discussion above has contrasted two means through which the protection of human rights in the context of private (inter-individual) relationships could be improved. This could be achieved, it has been implied, either by imputing to the State the violations committed by non-State actors; or by extending the scope of the State's obligation to protect. Both options are premised on the idea that international human rights are binding upon the State, which is therefore the primary duty-bearer; and indeed, the existing mechanisms in international human rights law are addressed to the State, and are not directly controlling on private actors. However, a third option could be explored, which would consist in strengthening the ability of international law to address directly the human rights violations committed by non-State actors (P. Alston, 'The 'Not-a-Cat' Syndrome: Can the International Human Rights Regime Accommodate Non-State Actors?' in P. Alston (ed.), *Non-State Actors and Human Rights*, Series of the Collected Courses of the Academy of European Law (Oxford University Press, 2005), p. 3 (arguing that we should not be held hostage to a classical understanding of international law as limited to inter-State relations); and O. De Schutter, 'The Challenge of Imposing Human Rights Norms on Corporate Actors' in O. De Schutter (ed.), *Transnational Corporations and Human Rights* (Oxford: Hart Publishing, 2006), pp. 1–40). National institutions, including national courts, routinely apply international human rights norms directly to the acts of private parties: there should be no obstacle in principle to allow this to develop at the international level, if necessary, in order to overcome the inability or the unwillingness of States to control non-State actors adequately. Indeed, this may be particularly relevant in the context of economic globalization, because of the threat this process may represent to the regulatory capacity of States.

The recent debate about the human rights responsibilities of transnational corporations provides a good illustration of this more structural question. A growing body of doctrine is willing, for well understandable reasons, to consider transnational corporations as subjects of international law – altough this is neither a necessary, nor a sufficient condition for account-ability mechanisms to develop at international level in order to improve the compliance of transnational corporations with the requirements of human rights (see in particular D. Kokkini-latridou and P. de Waart, 'Foreign Investments in Developing Countries – Legal Personality of Multinationals in International Law', *Netherlands Yearbook of International Law*, 14 (1983), 87; P. Malanczuk, 'Multinational Enterprises and Treaty-Making – a Contribution to the Discussion on Non-State Actors and the "Subjects" of International Law' in V. Gowlland-Debaas (ed.), *Multilateral Treaty-Making. The Current Status of Challenges to and Reforms Needed in the International Legislative Process*, Proceedings of the American Society of International Law/ Graduate Institute of International Studies, Forum Geneva, May 16, 1998 (Leiden: Martinus Nijhoff, 2000, p. 35); J. Charney, 'Transnational Corporations and Developing Public International Law', *Duke Law Journal* (1983), 748, esp. at 774–6).

The insistence on an improved control of the activities of transnational corporations ini-tially formed part of the vindication of a 'new international economic order' in the early 1970s, which the recently decolonized States pushed forward during that period (see the resolution adopted by the General Assembly of the United Nations on 1 May 1974, calling for a New International Economic Order (UN Doc. A/Res/3201 (S–VI)); and followed upon, in particular, by GA Resolution 3281(XXIX) of 15 January 1975, UN GAOR Supp. (No. 31), UN Doc. A/9631 (1975), the Charter of Economic Rights and Duties of States). The context then was relatively favour-able to an improved regulation of the activities of transnational corporations: while developed States feared that certain abuses by transnational corporations, or their interference with local political processes, might lead to hostile reactions by developing States, and possibly to the imposition of restrictions on the rights of foreign investors, the 'Group of 77' non-aligned (developing) countries insisted on their permanent sovereignty over natural resources and on the need to improve the supervision of the activities of transnational corporations. On the basis of a report prepared at the request of the Economic and Social Council, a draft Code of Conduct on Transnational Corporations (TNCs) was even prepared until 1992 within the UN Commission on Transnational Corporations (see E/1990/94, 12 June 1990). The Draft Code failed to be adopted, however, because of major disagreements between industrialized and developing countries, in particular, on the reference to international law and on the inclusion in the Code of standards of treatment for TNCs: while the industrialized countries were in favor of a Code protecting TNCs from discriminatory treatment of other behaviour of host States which would be in violation of certain minimum standards, the developing States primarily sought to ensure that TNCs would be better regulated, and in particular would be prohib-ited from interfering either with political independence of the investment-receiving States or with their nationally defined economic objectives (for comments, see W. Spröte, 'Negotiations on a United Nations Code of Conduct on Transnational Corporations', *German Yearbook of International Law*, 33 (1990) 331; P. Muchlinski, 'Attempts to Extend the Accountability of Transnational Corporations: the Role of UNCTAD', in M. T. Kamminga and S. Zia-Zarifi (eds.),

Liability of Multinational Corporations under International Law (The Hague: Kluwer Law International, 2000), pp. 97–117; N. Jägers, *Corporate Human Rights Obligations: in Search of Accountability* (Antwerp-Oxford-New York: Hart-Intersentia, 2002), at pp. 119–24).

It is also during the 1970s that the Organization for Economic Co-operation and Development (OECD) adopted the Guidelines for Multinational Enterprises. These Guidelines were revised on a number of occasions since their initial adoption on 21 June 1976. In 2000, the supervisory mechanism was revitalized and a general obligation on multinational enterprises to 'respect the human rights of those affected by their activities consistent with the host government's international obligations and commitments' was stipulated. Almost simultaneously, the International Labour Organization (ILO) adopted the Tripartite Declaration of Principles concerning Multinational Enterprises and Social Policy (adopted by the Governing Body of the International Labour Organization at its 204th session (November 1977), and revised at the 279th session (November 2000)). The aim of the Tripartite Declaration of Principles is to 'encourage the positive contribution which multinational enterprises can make to economic and social progress and to minimize and resolve the difficulties to which their various operations may give rise, taking into account the United Nations resolutions advocating the Establishment of a New International Economic Order' (para. 2). Yet, although of high moral significance because of its adoption by consensus by the ILO Governing Body at which governments, employers and workers are represented, the Tripartite Declaration remains, like the OECD Guidelines, a non-binding instrument. Both these instruments impose on States certain obligations of a procedural nature: in particular, States must set up national contact points under the OECD Guidelines in order to promote the Guidelines and to receive 'specific instances', or complaints by interested parties in cases of non-compliance by companies; they must report on a quadriennal basis under the ILO Tripartite Declaration on the implementation of the principles listed therein. However, both the ILO Tripartite Declaration and the OECD Guidelines instruments are explicitly presented as non-binding instruments, with respect to the multinational enterprises whose practices they ultimately seek to address, and their effectiveness in bringing about change in the conduct of companies is questionable.

The debate on how to improve the human rights accountability of transnational corporations was relaunched as concerns grew, in the late 1990s, about the impacts of unbridled economic globalization on values such as the environment, human rights, and the rights of workers. At the 1999 Davos World Economic Forum, the UN Secretary-General, K. Annan proposed a Global Compact based on shared values in the areas of human rights, labour, and the environment, and to which anti-corruption has been added in 2004. The ten principles to which participants in the Global Compact adhere are derived from the Universal Declaration of Human Rights, the International Labour Organization's Declaration on Fundamental Principles and Rights at Work, the Rio Declaration on Environment and Development, and the UN Convention Against Corruption. The process is voluntary. It is based on the idea that good practices should be rewarded by being publicized, and that they should be shared in order to promote a mutual learning among businesses. The companies acceding to the Global Compact are to 'embrace, support and enact, within their sphere of influence', the ten (initially nine) principles on which it is based, and they are to report annually on the initiatives they have taken to make those principles part of their operations.

Developments occurred also within the UN Commission on Human Rights. On 14 August 2003, the UN Sub-Commission for the Promotion and Protection of Human Rights approved in Resolution 2003/16 a set of 'Norms on the Human Rights Responsibilities of Transnational Corporations and Other Business Enterprises' (E/CN.4/Sub.2/2003/12/Rev.2 (2003)). The 'Norms' proposed by the Sub-Commission on Human Rights essentially present themselves as a restatement of the human rights obligations imposed on companies under international law. They are based on the idea that 'even though States have the primary responsibility to promote, secure the fulfillment of, respect, ensure respect of and protect human rights, trans-national corporations and other business enterprises, as organs of society, are also responsible for promoting and securing the human rights set forth in the Universal Declaration of Human Rights', and therefore 'transnational corporations and other business enterprises, their officers and persons working for them are also obligated to respect generally recognized responsibilities and norms contained in United Nations treaties and other international instruments' (Preamble, third and fourth Recitals; see, on this initiative, D. Weissbrodt and M. Kruger, 'Current Developments: Norms on the Responsibilities of Transnational Corporations and Other Business Enterprises with Regard to Human Rights', *American Journal of International Law*, 97 (2003), 901).

Although the initiative of the UN Sub-Commission on Human Rights was received with suspicion, and sometimes overt hostility, both by the business community and by a number of governments, it did serve to put the issue on the agenda of the UN Commission on Human Rights. In April 2005, the Commission on Human Rights requested that the UN Secretary-General appoint a Special Representative to identify ways through which the accountability of transnational corporations for human rights violations may be improved. The Special Representative of the Secretary-General, John Ruggie, set aside the 'Norms' of the Sub-Commission, on the basis that they mistakenly equated the human rights responsibilities of companies with those of the State and thus 'would turn transnational corporations into more benign twenty-first century versions of East India companies, undermining the capacity of developing countries to generate independent and democratically controlled institutions capable of acting in the public interest – which to my mind is by far the most effective guarantor of human rights' (Statement of the Special Representative of the Secretary-General on the issue of business and human rights to the Human Rights Council, 25 September 2006). Then, following almost three years of consultations and studies, he proposed a framework resting on the 'differentiated but complementary responsibilities' of the States and corporations. The framework comprises 'three core principles: the State duty to protect against human rights abuses by third parties, including business; the corporate responsibility to respect human rights; and the need for more effective access to remedies' (J. Ruggie, *Protect, Respect and Remedy: a Framework for Business and Human Rights. Report of the Special Representative of the Secretary-General on the Issue of Human Rights and Transnational Corporations and Other Business Enterprises*, A/HRC/8/5, 7 April 2008, para. 9). Hence, while restating that human rights are primarily for the State to protect as required under international human rights law, the framework does not exclude that private companies may have human rights responsibilities: although companies essentially should comply with a 'do no harm' principle, this also entails certain positive duties: 'To discharge the responsibility to respect requires due diligence. This concept describes the steps a company must take to become aware of, prevent and address adverse human rights impacts' (para. 56).

2 MEASURING THE SCOPE OF THE OBLIGATION TO PROTECT

2.1 The principle

The scope of the obligation to protect will vary according to the circumstances. As the cases presented in this section will illustrate, the criterion is ultimately one of 'reasonableness': what matters is whether it is reasonable to expect from the State that it take certain measures, that might prevent the violation of the rights of the individual from occurring. For analytical purposes, it is useful to see the solutions adopted by human rights courts or bodies as located along a spectrum. At one end of the spectrum, the State may be imposed actively to protect the exercise by an individual of his/her freedom, or the enjoyment of his/her right, by defining as a civil tort or as a criminal offence the attempt to interfere with such rights and freedoms, or by otherwise imposing on private actors far-reaching obligations to ensure that the right-holder may effectively exercise his/her right. At the other end of the spectrum however, the State is allowed to remain passive: however much the individual faces opposition in the exercise of his/her freedom, or however much he/she is unable to enjoy his/her right because of other private initiatives, the State may allow these private freedoms to collide with each other.

Even at this latter end, however, the State may not remain entirely passive. At a minimum, it must protect the right-holder from physical assault in the exercise of the freedom or in the enjoyment of the right: as has been remarked by Matthew H. Kramer, 'in almost every situation outside the Hobbesian state of nature, conduct in accordance with a liberty will receive at least a modicum of protection', particularly through the role of the State in guaranteeing the physical security of the person (M. H. Kramer, N. E. Simmonds and H. Steiner, *A Debate Over Rights. Philosophical Enquiries* (Oxford University Press, 1998, reprinted 2000), pp. 11–12). In the case of *Ozgür Gundem* v. *Turkey*, for instance, one of the reasons for the finding of a violation of Article 10 ECHR was that the Turkish authorities had done too little to protect a newspaper holding views allegedly supportive of the Kurdish Workers' Party (PKK) against the threats of violent action addressed to them. Although of course the opinions defended by this newspaper may be contradicted and challenged by others – clashing, in that sense, with the freedom of expression of the journalists – there is an elementary duty on the State not to remain passive in the face of attempts to silence the newspaper by violent means:

European Court of Human Rights (4th sect.), *Özgür Gundem* **v.** *Turkey* **(Appl. No. 23144/93) judgment of 16 March 2000:**

[The Court found that from 1992 to 1994 there were numerous incidents of violence, including killings, assaults and arson attacks, involving the newspaper *Özgür Gündem* and journalists, distributors and other persons associated with it. Despite the fact that the concerns of the newspaper and its fears that it was the victim of a concerted campaign tolerated, if not approved, by State officials, were brought to the attention of the authorities, no measures were taken to investigate this allegation. Nor did the authorities, for the main part, respond by any protective measures.]

42. The Court has long held that, although the essential object of many provisions of the Convention is to protect the individual against arbitrary interference by public authorities, there may in addition be positive obligations inherent in an effective respect of the rights concerned. It has found that such obligations may arise under Article 8 (see, amongst others, the *Gaskin* v. *United Kingdom* judgment of 7 July 1989, Series A No. 160, pp. 17–20, §§42–49) and Article 11 (see the *Plattform 'Ärzte für das Leben'* v. *Austria* judgment of 21 June 1988, Series A No. 139, p. 12, §32). Obligations to take steps to undertake effective investigations have also been found to accrue in the context of Article 2 (see, for example, the *McCann and others* v. *United Kingdom* judgment of 27 September 1995, Series A No. 324, p. 49, §161) and Article 3 (see the *Assenov and others* v. *Bulgaria* judgment of 28 October 1998, *Reports* 1998–VIII, p. 3290, §102), while a positive obligation to take steps to protect life may also exist under Article 2 (see the *Osman* v. *United Kingdom* judgment of 28 October 1998, *Reports* 1998–VIII, pp. 3159–61, §§115–17).

43. The Court recalls the key importance of freedom of expression as one of the preconditions for a functioning democracy. Genuine, effective exercise of this freedom does not depend merely on the State's duty not to interfere, but may require positive measures of protection, even in the sphere of relations between individuals (see *mutatis mutandis*, the *X and Y* v. *Netherlands* judgment of 26 March 1985, Series A No. 91, p. 11, §23). In determining whether or not a positive obligation exists, regard must be had to the fair balance that has to be struck between the general interest of the community and the interests of the individual, the search for which is inherent throughout the Convention. The scope of this obligation will inevitably vary, having regard to the diversity of situations obtaining in Contracting States, the difficulties involved in policing modern societies and the choices which must be made in terms of priorities and resources. Nor must such an obligation be interpreted in such a way as to impose an impossible or disproportionate burden on the authorities (see, among other authorities, the *Rees* v. *United Kingdom* judgment of 17 October 1986, Series A No. 106, p. 15, §37, and the *Osman* v. *United Kingdom* judgment cited above, pp. 3159–60, §116).

44. In the present case, the authorities were aware that Özgür Gündem, and persons associated with it, had been subject to a series of violent acts and that the applicants feared that they were being targeted deliberately in efforts to prevent the publication and distribution of the newspaper. However, the vast majority of the petitions and requests for protection submitted by the newspaper or its staff remained unanswered. The Government have only been able to identify one protective measure concerning the distribution of the newspaper which was taken while the newspaper was still in existence. The steps taken after the bomb attack at the Istanbul office in December 1994 concerned the newspaper's successor. The Court finds, having regard to the seriousness of the attacks and their widespread nature, that the Government cannot rely on the investigations ordered by individual public prosecutors into specific incidents. It is not convinced

by the Government's contention that these investigations provided adequate or effective responses to the applicants' allegations that the attacks were part of a concerted campaign which was supported, or tolerated, by the authorities.

45. The Court has noted the Government's submissions concerning its strongly held conviction that Özgür Gündem and its staff supported the PKK and acted as its propaganda tool. This does not, even if true, provide a justification for failing to take steps effectively to investigate and, where necessary, provide protection against unlawful acts involving violence.

46. The Court concludes that the Government have failed, in the circumstances, to comply with their positive obligation to protect Özgür Gündem in the exercise of its freedom of expression.

The opposition between 'privileges' and 'rights' put forward in the analytical jurisprudence of W. N. Hohfeld usefully captures the contrast between the two extreme situations which have been distinguished above: either the right/freedom of the individual is no more than a 'privilege', to which there corresponds for others no obligation enforceable before courts (the others simply have a 'no-right', i.e. they cannot seek from courts that they prohibit the exercise by the right-holder of his right/freedom); or the right/freedom of the individual leads to impose on others obligations that courts may enforce (the correlative of the 'right' of the individual, in this case, is the 'obligation' imposed on the duty-bearer) (see W. N. Hohfeld in W. W. Cook (ed.), *Fundamental Legal Conceptions as Applied in Judicial Reasoning* (New Haven, Conn.: Yale University Press, 1964, reprinted Greenwood Press, 1978).

It is important however to recognize that, even where the right/freedom of the individual is a true 'right' – protected by courts by imposing on others certain correlative obligations – there is a wide range of possibilities as to which obligations precisely correspond to the right/freedom concerned. Indeed, not only is the scope of the obligation to protect variable across the range of rights, the techniques according to which the State discharges its obligation to protect may also vary widely. In principle, international human rights instruments only prescribe the result to be achieved, leaving it to the State to choose the means through which to provide this protection. States must choose, in particular, how the relationship between the domestic legal order and international law shall influence the means of protecting human rights in private relationships (for a fuller discussion, see chapter 8). Thus, States may choose to empower their courts to apply directly human rights recognized in international treaties in force *vis-à-vis* the State to the cases presented to them, including cases opposing private parties. This option is sometimes referred to as 'direct third-party applicability' of human rights, by reference to the theory of *'unmittelbare Drittwirkung'* originally developed in Germany to justify the reliance, especially in labour disputes, of the fundamental rights of the German Basic Law (see H. C. Nipperdey, *Allgemeiner Teil des bürgerlichen Rechts* (Tübingen: Mohr Siebeck, 1952), vol. I, p. 53 *et seq.*; W. Leisner, *Grundrechte und Privatrecht* (Munich-Berlin: Ch Beck'sche Verlagsbuchhandlung, 1960), 414 pp.; and, for an examination of how the German courts have applied this approach, K. M. Lewan,

'The Significance of Constitutional Rights for Private Law: Theory and Practice in West Germany', *International and Comparative Law Quarterly*, 17 (1968), 571).

What makes this first option sometimes difficult to implement is that the regime applicable to the 'vertical' relationship between the individual and the State may not be transposable, *mutatis mutandis*, to the 'horizontal' relationship between private individuals. This appears clearly from any attempt to refer to the classical conditions imposed on the State when it interferes with human rights, in order to rely on those conditions in disputes between private parties (for a discussion of these conditions, see chapter 3, section 3). Consider first the condition of legitimacy which imposes on the State that it should always justify the restrictive measures it adopts by reference to a legitimate objective. It is of course the duty of the State to act in the public interest; in contrast, individuals pursue a variety of aims, and it would violate an elementary principle of moral pluralism to impose on all individuals that they only act in accordance to some predefined notion of what serves the common good. Hence, the condition according to which restrictions to the rights of the individual may only be justified if they are based on the pursuit of a legitimate aim is of little use in relationships between private parties, except perhaps in certain contexts such as in employment or, more broadly, market relationships, where the roles of each individual (and thus the conditions they may force the other party to accept in their mutual relationships) are defined by the nature of the transaction between them. Consider, second, the condition of legality: again with certain exceptions, such as rules internal to the undertaking set by the employer, or regulations addressed by unions or other associations towards their members, it would not seem realistic to expect that the conditions under which restrictions may be imposed to the rights of the individual as a result of private initiatives be clarified to the same degree as when such restrictions stem from publicly adopted rules. Rather, what may be expected is that the State regulate with a sufficient degree of precision the conditions under which the rights of the individual are protected, and the remedies available to the right-holder when his/her rights have been affected. But this is a requirement imposed on the State: it is not one which can be imposed, as such, on non-State actors, even where they are directly responsible for the interference with the rights of the individual. As to the condition of necessity or proportionality – the third condition imposed on the State seeking to justify an interference with a human right – it may be extended to the acts of private parties through the use of concepts such as abuse of rights or fault in civil liability regimes. However, particularly when a private actor infringes upon the human right of another by exercising a basic freedom – for instance, when freedom of expression impacts on the right to respect for private life, or when the freedom of association exercised by the union in adopting its internal regulations affects the 'negative' freedom of association of its members – it cannot be expected from a private actor, X that it only adopts a conduct that brings about a minimal impairment to the right of other private actors with whom X interacts. The implication is not necessarily that human rights, as they appear stipulated in international treaties as obligations imposed on the State, cannot be relied upon by domestic courts in order to impose obligations on private parties.

But in applying these rights to private relationships, courts may have to be inventive, and the criteria developed by international monitoring bodies may not always provide them with well-suited answers. The direct application of constitutional human rights clauses in private relationships creates similar difficulties: as noted by Aharon Barak, the President of the Supreme Court of Israel (although writing here in his non-judicial capacity), 'where constitutional provisions do not contain limitations clauses regarding the restriction of one person's right arising from the right of another, the obvious result is that judges will have to create judicial limitation clauses. Thus, judges will acquire enormous constitutional power without any concomitant constitutional guidance' (A. Barak, 'Constitutional Human Rights and Private Law' in D. Friedmann and D. Barak-Erez (eds.), *Human Rights in Private Law* (Oxford: Hart Publishing, 2001), p. 13 at p. 17)

Of course, there are other options available to States than the direct application of internationally recognized human rights to inter-individual relationships. A second possibility has already been alluded to. It is for courts to interpret notions of domestic law (such as the notions of 'fault' or 'negligence' in civil liability cases, 'good faith' in contracts, 'abuse of rights' or 'public policy') in order to ensure that these notions embody the requirements of international human rights. This is a technique sometimes referred to as '*mittelbare Drittwirkung*', in order to contrast it with the previous one (see, e.g. A. Barak, 'Constitutional Human Rights and Private Law' in D. Friedmann and D. Barak-Erez (eds.), *Human Rights in Private Law* (Oxford: Hart Publishing, 2001), p. 13 at pp. 21–4; S. Gardbaum, 'The "Horizontal Effect" of Constitutional Rights', *Michigan Law Review*, 102 (2003), 401 *et seq.*). The 1958 *Lüth* decision of the German Federal Constitutional Court provides the classic illustration: in this case, the Constitutional Court took into account Lüth's freedom of expression in order to find that the boycott he had initiated against a film produced by a former collaborator with the Nazis should not be treated as the kind of intentionally caused damage that may give rise to an obligation to compensate, under section 826 of the German Civil Code (BGB) (7 BverfGE (1958)). In practice, there is a continuum between the two first options: because internationally recognized human rights per necessity have to rely on tools of national law in order to be applied by domestic courts – such as, minimally, those regulating evidence, statutory limitations or other procedural issues – the direct application of international human rights is always in at least some respect 'mediated' through domestic law when it is invoked in the framework of private law relationships. Nevertheless, there are cases of more or less 'direct', or 'unmediated', application of international human rights law to private disputes, in which domestic courts essentially base their reasoning on international law, sometimes even setting aside the rules of domestic law that would create obstacles to the full implementation of international human rights: it is then that these courts face the difficulties discussed above when referring to the first of our three options.

Finally, a third possibility is for States to decide to implement their obligations to protect under international human rights instruments by adopting domestic legislation, for instance, by defining the violation of certain human rights as a criminal offence or as giving rise to a specific form of extra-contractual liability. Only in exceptional cases will international law go beyond imposing obligations of result, and identify obligations of conduct imposed on States – i.e. the means through which the protection should be achieved, rather than simply the level of protection to be ensured. For instance, certain interferences with human rights may be of such a serious character that they require sanctions of a criminal nature, rather than only civil remedies:

European Court of Human Rights (GC), *Vo v. France* (Appl. No. 53924/00), judgment of 8 July 2004:

[On 27 November 1991, the applicant, Mrs Thi-Nho Vo, who is of Vietnamese origin, attended Lyons General Hospital for a medical examination scheduled during the sixth month of pregnancy. On the same day another woman, Mrs Thi Thanh Van Vo, was due to have a contraceptive coil removed at the same hospital. When Dr G., who was to remove the coil, called out the name 'Mrs Vo' in the waiting room, it was the applicant who answered. After a brief interview, the doctor noted that the applicant had difficulty in understanding French. Having consulted the medical file, he sought to remove the coil without examining her beforehand. In so doing, he pierced the amniotic sac causing the loss of a substantial amount of amniotic fluid. As a result, the pregnancy had to be terminated on health grounds on 5 December 1991. Ms Vo had lost her unborn child as a result of medical negligence. The applicant and her partner subsequently lodged a criminal complaint, together with an application to join the proceedings as civil parties, alleging unintentional injury to the applicant entailing total unfitness for work for a period not exceeding three months and unintentional homicide of her child. However, the action failed, since the French courts were unwilling to interpret the provisions of the Criminal Code on unintentional homicide as extending to cover fatal injury to an unborn child. The applicant complained of the lack of protection of the unborn child under French criminal law and argued that the State had failed to discharge its obligations under Article 2 of the Convention. She further submitted that the remedy available in the administrative courts was ineffective as it was incapable of securing judicial acknowledgment of the homicide of her child as such. Lastly, the applicant asserted that she had had a choice between instituting criminal and administrative proceedings and that, while her recourse to the criminal courts had, unforeseeably, proved unsuccessful, the possibility of applying to the administrative courts had in the meantime become statute barred.]

74. The applicant complained that she had been unable to secure the conviction of the doctor whose medical negligence had caused her to have to undergo a therapeutic abortion. It has not been disputed that she intended to carry her pregnancy to full term and that her child was in good health. Following the material events, the applicant and her partner lodged a criminal complaint, together with an application to join the proceedings as civil parties, alleging unintentional injury to the applicant and unintentional homicide of the child she was carrying. The courts held that the prosecution of the offence of unintentional injury to the applicant was statute-barred and, quashing the Court of Appeal's judgment on the second point, the Court of Cassation held that, regard being had to the principle that the criminal law was to be strictly construed, a foetus could not be the victim of unintentional homicide. The central question raised by the application is whether the absence of a criminal remedy within the French legal system to punish the unintentional destruction of a foetus constituted a failure on the part of the State to protect by law the right to life within the meaning of Article 2 of the Convention.

1. Existing case law

75. Unlike Article 4 of the American Convention on Human Rights, which provides that the right to life must be protected 'in general, from the moment of conception', Article 2 of the Convention is silent as to the temporal limitations of the right to life and, in particular, does not define 'everyone' ('*toute personne*') whose 'life' is protected by the Convention. The Court has yet to determine the issue of the 'beginning' of 'everyone's right to life' within the meaning of this provision and whether the unborn child has such a right.

To date it has been raised solely in connection with laws on abortion. Abortion does not constitute one of the exceptions expressly listed in paragraph 2 of Article 2, but the Commission has expressed the opinion that it is compatible with the first sentence of Article 2 §1 in the interests of protecting the mother's life and health because 'if one assumes that this provision applies at the initial stage of the pregnancy, the abortion is covered by an implied limitation, protecting the life and health of the woman at that stage, of the "right to life" of the foetus' (see *X* v. *United Kingdom*, [Appl. No. 8416/79, Commission decision of 13 May 1980, Decisions and Reports (D.R.) 19, 244] at p. 253).

76. Having initially refused to examine *in abstracto* the compatibility of abortion laws with Article 2 of the Convention (see *X* v. *Norway*, No. 867/60, Commission decision of 29 May 1961, Collection of Decisions, vol. 6, p. 34, and *X* v. *Austria*, No. 7045/75, Commission decision of 10 December 1976, DR 7, p. 87), the Commission acknowledged in *Brüggemann and Scheuten* [Appl. No. 6959/75, Commission's report of 12 July 1977, D.R. 10, p. 100] that women complaining under Article 8 of the Convention about the Constitutional Court's decision restricting the availability of abortions had standing as victims. It stated on that occasion: '... pregnancy cannot be said to pertain uniquely to the sphere of private life. Whenever a woman is pregnant her private life becomes closely connected with the developing foetus' (*ibid.*, p. 116, §59). However, the Commission did not find it 'necessary to decide, in this context, whether the unborn child is to be considered as "life" in the sense of Article 2 of the Convention, or whether it could be regarded as an entity which under Article 8 §2 could justify an interference "for the protection of others"' (*ibid.*, p. 116, §60). It expressed the opinion that there had been no violation of Article 8 of the Convention because 'not every regulation of the termination of unwanted pregnancies constitutes an interference with the right to respect for the private life of the mother' (*ibid.*, pp. 116–17, §61), while emphasising: 'There is no evidence that it was the intention of the Parties to the Convention to bind themselves in favour of any particular solution' (*ibid.*, pp. 117–18, §64).

77. In *X* v. *United Kingdom* (cited above), the Commission considered an application by a man complaining that his wife had been allowed to have an abortion on health grounds. While it accepted that the potential father could be regarded as the 'victim' of a violation of the right to life, it considered that the term 'everyone' in several Articles of the Convention could not apply prenatally, but observed that 'such application in a rare case – e.g. under Article 6, paragraph 1 – cannot be excluded' (p. 249, §7; for such an application in connection with access to a court, see *Reeve* v. *United Kingdom*, No. 24844/94, Commission decision of 30 November 1994, DR 79–A, p. 146). The Commission added that the general usage of the term 'everyone' ('*toute personne*') and the context in which it was used in Article 2 of the Convention did not include the unborn. As to the term 'life' and, in particular, the beginning of life, the Commission noted a 'divergence of thinking on the question of where life begins' and added: 'While some believe that it starts already with conception, others tend to focus upon the moment of nidation, upon the point that the foetus becomes "viable", or upon live birth' (*X* v. *United Kingdom*, p. 250, §12).

The Commission went on to examine whether Article 2 was 'to be interpreted: as not covering the foetus at all; as recognising a "right to life" of the foetus with certain implied limitations; or as recognising an absolute "right to life" of the foetus' (*ibid.* p. 251, §17). Although it did not express an opinion on the first two options, it categorically ruled out the third interpretation, having regard to the need to protect the mother's life, which was indissociable from that of the unborn child: 'The "life" of the foetus is intimately connected with, and it cannot be regarded in isolation of, the life of the pregnant woman. If Article 2 were held to cover the foetus and its protection under this Article were, in the absence of any express limitation, seen as absolute, an abortion would have to be considered as prohibited even where the continuance of the pregnancy would involve a serious risk to the life of the pregnant woman. This would mean that the "unborn life" of the foetus would be regarded as being of a higher value than the life of the pregnant woman' (*ibid.*, p. 252, §19). The Commission adopted that solution, noting that by 1950 practically all the Contracting Parties had 'permitted abortion when necessary to save the life of the mother' and that in the meantime the national law on termination of pregnancy had 'shown a tendency towards further liberalisation' (*ibid.*, p. 252, §20).

78. In *H*. v. *Norway* [Appl. No. 17004/90, Commission decision of 19 May 1992, D.R. 73, 155], concerning an abortion carried out on non-medical grounds against the father's wishes, the Commission added that Article 2 required the State not only to refrain from taking a person's life intentionally but also to take appropriate steps to safeguard life (p. 167). It considered that it did not have to decide 'whether the foetus may enjoy a certain protection under Article 2, first sentence', but did not exclude the possibility that 'in certain circumstances this may be the case notwithstanding that there is in the Contracting States a considerable divergence of views on whether or to what extent Article 2 protects the unborn life' (*ibid.*). It further noted that in such a delicate area the Contracting States had to have a certain discretion, and concluded that the mother's decision, taken in accordance with Norwegian legislation, had not exceeded that discretion (p. 168).

79. The Court has only rarely had occasion to consider the application of Article 2 to the foetus. In *Open Door and Dublin Well Woman* [judgment of 29 October 1992, Series A No. 246–A: see chapter 3, section 3.3.], the Irish Government relied on the protection of the life of the unborn child to justify their legislation prohibiting the provision of information concerning abortion facilities abroad. The only issue that was resolved was whether the restrictions on the freedom to receive and impart the information in question had been necessary in a democratic society, within the meaning of paragraph 2 of Article 10 of the Convention, to pursue the 'legitimate aim of the protection of morals of which the protection in Ireland of the right to life of the unborn is one aspect' (pp. 27–28, §63), since the Court did not consider it relevant to determine 'whether a right to abortion is guaranteed under the Convention or whether the foetus is encompassed by the right to life as contained in Article 2' (p. 28, §66). Recently, in circumstances similar to those in *H*. v. *Norway* (cited above), where a woman had decided to terminate her pregnancy against the father's wishes, the Court held that it was not required to determine 'whether the foetus may qualify for protection under the first sentence of Article 2 as interpreted [in the case law relating to the positive obligation to protect life]', and continued: 'Even supposing that, in certain circumstances, the foetus might be considered to have rights protected by Article 2 of the Convention, ... in the instant case ... [the] pregnancy was terminated in conformity with section 5 of Law no. 194 of 1978' – a law which struck a fair balance between the woman's interests and the need to ensure protection of the foetus (see *Boso* v. *Italy* [Appl. No. 50490/99, E.C.H.R. 2002–VII]).

80. It follows from this recapitulation of the case law that in the circumstances examined to date by the Convention institutions – that is, in the various laws on abortion – the unborn child is not regarded as a 'person' directly protected by Article 2 of the Convention and that if the unborn do have a 'right' to 'life', it is implicitly limited by the mother's rights and interests. The Convention institutions have not, however, ruled out the possibility that in certain circumstances safeguards may be extended to the unborn child. That is what appears to have been contemplated by the Commission in considering that 'Article 8 §1 cannot be interpreted as meaning that pregnancy and its termination are, as a principle, solely a matter of the private life of the mother' (see *Brüggemann and Scheuten*, cited above, pp. 116–17, §61) and by the Court in the above-mentioned *Boso* decision. It is also clear from an examination of these cases that the issue has always been determined by weighing up various, and sometimes conflicting, rights or freedoms claimed by a woman, a mother or a father in relation to one another or *vis-à-vis* an unborn child.

2. Approach in the instant case

81. The special nature of the instant case raises a new issue. The Court is faced with a woman who intended to carry her pregnancy to term and whose unborn child was expected to be viable, at the very least in good health. Her pregnancy had to be terminated as a result of an error by a doctor and she therefore had to have a therapeutic abortion on account of negligence by a third party. The issue is consequently whether, apart from cases where the mother has requested an abortion, harming a foetus should be treated as a criminal offence in the light of Article 2 of the Convention, with a view to protecting the foetus under that Article. This requires a preliminary examination of whether it is advisable for the Court to intervene in the debate as to who is a person and when life begins, in so far as Article 2 provides that the law must protect 'everyone's right to life'.

82. As is apparent from the above recapitulation of the case law, the interpretation of Article 2 in this connection has been informed by a clear desire to strike a balance, and the Convention institutions' position in relation to the legal, medical, philosophical, ethical or religious dimensions of defining the human being has taken into account the various approaches to the matter at national level. This has been reflected in the consideration given to the diversity of views on the point at which life begins, of legal cultures and of national standards of protection, and the State has been left with considerable discretion in the matter, as the opinion of the European Group on Ethics in Science and New Technologies at the European Commission appositely puts it: 'the ... Community authorities have to address these ethical questions taking into account the moral and philosophical differences, reflected by the extreme diversity of legal rules applicable to human embryo research ... It is not only legally difficult to seek harmonisation of national laws at Community level, but because of lack of consensus, it would be inappropriate to impose one exclusive moral code.'

It follows that the issue of when the right to life begins comes within the margin of appreciation which the Court generally considers that States should enjoy in this sphere, notwithstanding an evolutive interpretation of the Convention, a 'living instrument which must be interpreted in the light of present-day conditions' (see *Tyrer* v. *United Kingdom*, judgment of 25 April 1978, Series A No. 26, pp. 15–16, §31, and subsequent case law). The reasons for that conclusion are, firstly, that the issue of such protection has not been resolved within the majority of the Contracting States themselves, in France in particular, where it is the subject of debate ... and, secondly, that there is no European consensus on the scientific and legal definition of the beginning of life ...

85. Having regard to the foregoing, the Court is convinced that it is neither desirable, nor even possible as matters stand, to answer in the abstract the question whether the unborn child is a person for the purposes of Article 2 of the Convention ('*personne*' in the French text). As to the instant case, it considers it unnecessary to examine whether the abrupt end to the applicant's pregnancy falls within the scope of Article 2, seeing that, even assuming that that provision was applicable, there was no failure on the part of the respondent State to comply with the requirements relating to the preservation of life in the public-health sphere. With regard to that issue, the Court has considered whether the legal protection afforded the applicant by France in respect of the loss of the unborn child she was carrying satisfied the procedural requirements inherent in Article 2 of the Convention.

86. In that connection, it observes that the unborn child's lack of a clear legal status does not necessarily deprive it of all protection under French law. However, in the circumstances of the present case, the life of the foetus was intimately connected with that of the mother and could be protected through her, especially as there was no conflict between the rights of the mother and the father or of the unborn child and the parents, the loss of the foetus having been caused by the unintentional negligence of a third party.

87. In *Boso*, cited above, the Court said that even supposing that the foetus might be considered to have rights protected by Article 2 of the Convention (see paragraph 79 above), Italian law on the voluntary termination of pregnancy struck a fair balance between the woman's interests and the need to ensure protection of the unborn child. In the present case, the dispute concerns the involuntary killing of an unborn child against the mother's wishes, causing her particular suffering. The interests of the mother and the child clearly coincided. The Court must therefore examine, from the standpoint of the effectiveness of existing remedies, the protection which the applicant was afforded in seeking to establish the liability of the doctor concerned for the loss of her child *in utero* and to obtain compensation for the abortion she had to undergo. The applicant argued that only a criminal remedy would have been capable of satisfying the requirements of Article 2 of the Convention. The Court does not share that view, for the following reasons.

88. The Court reiterates that the first sentence of Article 2, which ranks as one of the most fundamental provisions in the Convention and also enshrines one of the basic values of the democratic societies making up the Council of Europe (see *McCann and others* v. *United Kingdom*, judgment of 27 September 1995, Series A No. 324, pp. 45–46, §147), requires the State not only to refrain from the 'intentional' taking of life, but also to take appropriate steps to safeguard the lives of those within its jurisdiction (see, for example, *L.C.B.* v. *United Kingdom*, judgment of 9 June 1998, *Reports of Judgments and Decisions* 1998–III, p. 1403, §36).

89. Those principles apply in the public-health sphere too. The positive obligations require States to make regulations compelling hospitals, whether private or public, to adopt appropriate measures for the protection of patients' lives. They also require an effective independent judicial system to be set up so that the cause of death of patients in the care of the medical profession, whether in the public or the private sector, can be determined and those responsible made accountable (see *Powell* v. *United Kingdom* (dec.), No. 45305/99, ECHR 2000–V, and *Calvelli and Ciglio* ([GC], No. 32967/96, §51, ECHR 2002–I), §49).

90. Although the right to have third parties prosecuted or sentenced for a criminal offence cannot be asserted independently (see *Perez* v. *France* [GC], No. 47287/99, §70, ECHR 2004–I), the Court has stated on a number of occasions that an effective judicial system, as required

by Article 2, may, and under certain circumstances must, include recourse to the criminal law. However, if the infringement of the right to life or to physical integrity is not caused intentionally, the positive obligation imposed by Article 2 to set up an effective judicial system does not necessarily require the provision of a criminal-law remedy in every case. In the specific sphere of medical negligence, 'the obligation may for instance also be satisfied if the legal system affords victims a remedy in the civil courts, either alone or in conjunction with a remedy in the criminal courts, enabling any liability of the doctors concerned to be established and any appropriate civil redress, such as an order for damages and for the publication of the decision, to be obtained. Disciplinary measures may also be envisaged' (see *Calvelli and Ciglio* [judgment of 17 January 2002], §51; *Lazzarini and Ghiacci* v. *Italy* (dec.), No. 53749/00, 7 November 2002; and *Mastromatteo* v. *Italy* [GC], No. 37703/97, §90, ECHR 2002–VIII).

91. In the instant case, in addition to the criminal proceedings which the applicant instituted against the doctor for unintentionally causing her injury – which, admittedly, were terminated because the offence was covered by an amnesty, a fact that did not give rise to any complaint on her part – she had the possibility of bringing an action for damages against the authorities on account of the doctor's alleged negligence (see *Kress* v. *France* [GC], No. 39594/98, §§14 et seq., ECHR 2001–VI). Had she done so, the applicant would have been entitled to have an adversarial hearing on her allegations of negligence (see *Powell*, cited above) and to obtain redress for any damage sustained. A claim for compensation in the administrative courts would have had fair prospects of success and the applicant could have obtained damages from the hospital ...

92. The applicant's submission concerning the fact that the action for damages in the administrative courts was statute-barred cannot succeed in the Court's view. In this connection, it refers to its case law to the effect that the 'right to a court', of which the right of access is one aspect, is not absolute; it is subject to limitations permitted by implication, in particular where the conditions of admissibility of an appeal are concerned, since by its very nature it calls for regulation by the State, which enjoys a certain margin of appreciation in this regard (see, among other authorities, *Brualla Gómez de la Torre* v. *Spain*, judgment of 19 December 1997, *Reports* 1997–VIII, p. 2955, §33). These legitimate restrictions include the imposition of statutory limitation periods, which, as the Court has held in personal injury cases, 'serve several important purposes, namely to ensure legal certainty and finality, protect potential defendants from stale claims which might be difficult to counter and prevent the injustice which might arise if courts were required to decide upon events which took place in the distant past on the basis of evidence which might have become unreliable and incomplete because of the passage of time' (see *Stubbings and others* v. *United Kingdom*, judgment of 22 October 1996, *Reports* 1996–IV, pp. 1502–03, §51).

93. In the instant case, a four-year limitation period does not in itself seem unduly short, particularly in view of the seriousness of the damage suffered by the applicant and her immediate desire to prosecute the doctor. However, the evidence indicates that the applicant deliberately turned to the criminal courts, apparently without ever being informed of the possibility of applying to the administrative courts ...

94. In conclusion, the Court considers that in the circumstances of the case an action for damages in the administrative courts could be regarded as an effective remedy that was available to the applicant. Such an action, which she failed to use, would have enabled her to prove the medical negligence she alleged and to obtain full redress for the damage resulting from the doctor's negligence, and there was therefore no need to institute criminal proceedings in the instant case.

95. The Court accordingly concludes that, even assuming that Article 2 was applicable in the instant case (see paragraph 85 above), there has been no violation of Article 2 of the Convention.

[Although the Court held by fourteen votes to three that there had been no violation of Article 2 of the Convention, two separate opinions and two dissenting opinions were filed by, in total, ten members of the Court. Among them was the dissenting opinion of Judge Ress:]

Dissenting opinion of Judge Ress:

France's positive obligation to protect unborn children against unintentional homicide, that is to say against negligent acts that could cause a child's death, can only be discharged if French law has effective procedures in place to prevent the recurrence of such acts. On this point, I am unable to agree with the opinion expressed by the majority that an action in damages in the administrative courts (on account of the hospital doctor's alleged negligence) afforded the unborn child adequate and effective protection against medical negligence. As Judge Rozakis, joined by Judges Bonello and Strážnická, pointed out in his partly dissenting opinion in *Calvelli and Ciglio* v. *Italy* ([GC], No. 32967/96, E.C.H.R. 2002–I), an action in pecuniary and even non-pecuniary damages will not in all circumstances be capable of protecting against the unintentional taking of life, especially in a case such as the present one in which a mother lost her child as a result of a doctor's negligence. Even though I accepted the outcome in *Calvelli and Ciglio*, which was based on the fact that the applicants had agreed to compensation under a friendly settlement, criminal proceedings were commenced in that case (although they were not continued because prosecution of the offence became time-barred).

It is not retribution that makes protection by the criminal law desirable, but deterrence. In general, it is through the criminal law that society most clearly and strictly conveys messages to its members and identifies values that are most in need of protection. Life, which is one of the values, if not the main value, protected by the Convention (see *Streletz, Kessler and Krenz* v. *Germany* [GC], Nos. 34044/96, 35532/97 and 44801/98, §§92–94, ECHR 2001–II, and *McCann and others* v. *United Kingdom*, judgment of 27 September 1995, Series A No. 324, pp. 45–46, §147), will in principle require the protection of the criminal law if it is to be adequately safeguarded and defended. Financial liability to pay compensation is only a secondary form of protection. In addition, hospitals and doctors are usually insured against such risks, so that the 'pressure' on them is reduced.

One might consider that imposing a disciplinary penalty on a doctor could be regarded as equivalent to imposing a criminal penalty in certain circumstances. Disciplinary measures were viewed as an alternative means of discouraging negligence in *Calvelli and Ciglio* (cited above, §51). However, it is equally clear that, as unpleasant as the consequences may be professionally, a disciplinary penalty does not amount to general condemnation (*Unwerturteil*). Disciplinary penalties depend on conditions that are entirely specific to the profession concerned (the bodies being self-regulating) and in general do not afford the deterrence necessary to protect such an important value as life. Nevertheless, the question has to be asked whether in the present case a disciplinary penalty for such a serious error could have provided sufficient deterrence. Here, though, is where the problem lies, as the authorities at no stage brought disciplinary proceedings against the doctor. For an error as serious as that committed by Dr G., such disciplinary proceedings accompanied by an adequate measure could at least have sent an appropriate signal to the medical profession to prevent the recurrence of such tragic events. I do not think it necessary to say that France requires criminal legislation. However, it does need to take strict disciplinary action in order to meet its obligation to afford effective protection of the life of the unborn child. In my opinion, therefore, there was no effective protection.

Among the factors that may influence the choice of the State as to how to implement its obligation to protect, is the nature of the obligation imposed on private parties as a correlative of the right recognized to the individual. An especially important distinction will be between 'negative' obligations, which merely impose on others that they abstain from interfering with the right/freedom of the right-holder; and 'positive' obligations, that require from others that they take certain steps towards supporting the exercise of the right/freedom by the individual right-holder. While 'negative' obligations can in principle be imposed *erga omnes* (for instance, any person illegally intercepting the communications of others may be civilly liable to the victim), 'positive' obligations require the duty-bearer to be identified. However, even where positive obligations are concerned, courts may rely directly on the provisions of human rights treaties in order to ensure adequate protection of the rights they enunciate:

European Court of Human Rights (2nd sect.), *Verein gegen Tierfabriken (VgT)* v. *Switzerland* (Appl. No. 24699/94), judgment of 28 June 2001:

[Verein gegen Tierfabriken (VgT) is a Swiss association for the protection of animals. As a reaction to various meat industry television commercials, VgT prepared a television commercial, which it sought to have broadcasted on Swiss Radio and Television Company programmes. However, the Commercial Television Company (now Publisuisse) responsible for television advertising, informed VgT that it would not broadcast the commercial in view of its 'clear political character'. This refusal was challenged and failed. The Swiss Courts found that the prohibition of political advertising laid down in section 18(5) of the Federal Radio and Television Act, on which the position of the Commercial Television Company was based, served various purposes, including to 'prevent financially powerful groups from obtaining a competitive political advantage. In the interest of the democratic process it is designed to protect the formation of public opinion from undue commercial influence and to bring about a certain equality of opportunity among the different forces of society'.]

[On the imputability to the respondent State]

44. It is not in dispute between the parties that the Commercial Television Company is a company established under Swiss private law. The issue arises, therefore, whether the company's refusal to broadcast the applicant association's commercial fell within the respondent State's jurisdiction. In this respect, the Court notes in particular the Government's submission according to which the Commercial Television Company, when deciding whether or not to acquire advertising, was acting as a private party enjoying contractual freedom.

45. Under Article 1 of the Convention, each Contracting State 'shall secure to everyone within [its] jurisdiction the rights and freedoms defined in ... [the] Convention'. As the Court stated in *Marckx* v. *Belgium* (judgment of 13 June 1979, Series A No. 31, pp. 14–15, §31; see also *Young, James and Webster* v. *United Kingdom*, judgment of 13 August 1981, Series A No. 44, p. 20, §49), in addition to the primarily negative undertaking of a State to abstain from interference in Convention guarantees, 'there may be positive obligations inherent' in such guarantees. The responsibility of a State may then be engaged as a result of not observing its obligation to enact domestic legislation.

46. The Court does not consider it desirable, let alone necessary, to elaborate a general theory concerning the extent to which the Convention guarantees should be extended to relations between private individuals *inter se*.

47. Suffice it to state that in the instant case the Commercial Television Company and later the Federal Court in its decision of 20 August 1997, when examining the applicant association's request to broadcast the commercial at issue, both relied on section 18 of the Swiss Federal Radio and Television Act, which prohibits 'political advertising'. Domestic law, as interpreted in the last resort by the Federal Court, therefore made lawful the treatment of which the applicant association complained (see Marckx and Young, James and Webster, cited above). In effect, political speech by the applicant association was prohibited. In the circumstances of the case, the Court finds that the responsibility of the respondent State within the meaning of Article 1 of the Convention for any resultant breach of Article 10 may be engaged on this basis.

48. The responsibility of the respondent State having been established, the refusal to broadcast the applicant association's commercial amounted to an 'interference by public authority' in the exercise of the rights guaranteed by Article 10.

[Whether the interference was 'prescribed by law', motivated a 'legitimate aim' set out in Art. 10 para. 2 ECHR, and 'necessary in a democratic society' to achieve that aim]
[Having found that the interference was sufficiently foreseeable and that it pursued the objective of 'the protection of the rights of others' within the meaning of Article 10 para. 2 ECHR, the Court then examines whether the interference is 'necessary' for the fulfilment of that aim.]

72. The Court will consequently examine carefully whether the measure in issue was proportionate to the aim pursued. In that regard, it must balance the applicant association's freedom of expression, on the one hand, with the reasons adduced by the Swiss authorities for the prohibition of political advertising, on the other, namely to protect public opinion from the pressures of powerful financial groups and from undue commercial influence; to provide for a certain equality of opportunity among the different forces of society; to ensure the independence of broadcasters in editorial matters from powerful sponsors; and to support the press.

73. It is true that powerful financial groups can obtain competitive advantages in the area of commercial advertising and may thereby exercise pressure on, and eventually curtail the freedom of, the radio and television stations broadcasting the commercials. Such situations undermine the fundamental role of freedom of expression in a democratic society as enshrined in Article 10 of the Convention, in particular where it serves to impart information and ideas of general interest, which the public is moreover entitled to receive. Such an undertaking cannot be successfully accomplished unless it is grounded in the principle of pluralism of which the State is the ultimate guarantor. This observation is especially valid in relation to audio-visual media, whose programmes are often broadcast very widely (see *Informationsverein Lentia and others* v. *Austria (No. 1)*, judgment of 24 November 1993, Series A No. 276, p. 16, §38).

74. In the present case, the contested measure, namely the prohibition of political advertising as provided in section 18(5) of the Federal Radio and Television Act, was applied only to radio and television broadcasts, and not to other media such as the press. The Federal Court explained

in this respect in its judgment of 20 August 1997 that television had a stronger effect on the public on account of its dissemination and immediacy. In the Court's opinion, however, while the domestic authorities may have had valid reasons for this differential treatment, a prohibition of political advertising which applies only to certain media, and not to others, does not appear to be of a particularly pressing nature.

75. Moreover, it has not been argued that the applicant association itself constituted a powerful financial group which, with its proposed commercial, aimed at endangering the independence of the broadcaster; at unduly influencing public opinion or at endangering equality of opportunity among the different forces of society. Indeed, rather than abusing a competitive advantage, all the applicant association intended to do with its commercial was to participate in an ongoing general debate on animal protection and the rearing of animals. The Court cannot exclude that a prohibition of 'political advertising' may be compatible with the requirements of Article 10 of the Convention in certain situations. Nevertheless, the reasons must be 'relevant' and 'sufficient' in respect of the particular interference with the rights under Article 10. In the present case, the Federal Court, in its judgment of 20 August 1997, discussed at length the general reasons which justified a prohibition of 'political advertising'. In the Court's opinion, however, the domestic authorities have not demonstrated in a 'relevant and sufficient' manner why the grounds generally advanced in support of the prohibition of political advertising also served to justify the interference in the particular circumstances of the applicant association's case.

76. The domestic authorities did not adduce the disturbing nature of any particular sequence, or of any particular words, of the commercial as a ground for refusing to broadcast it. It therefore mattered little that the pictures and words employed in the commercial at issue may have appeared provocative or even disagreeable.

77. In so far as the Government pointed out that there were various other possibilities to broadcast the information at issue, the Court observes that the applicant association, aiming at reaching the entire Swiss public, had no other means than the national television programmes of the Swiss Radio and Television Company at its disposal, since these programmes were the only ones broadcast throughout Switzerland. The Commercial Television Company was the sole instance responsible for the broadcasting of commercials within these national programmes. Private regional television channels and foreign television stations cannot be received throughout Switzerland.

78. The Government have also submitted that admitting the applicant association's claim would be to accept a 'right to broadcast' which in turn would substantially interfere with the rights of the Commercial Television Company to communicate information. Reference was further made to the danger of untimely interruptions in television programmes by means of commercials. The Court recalls that its judgment is essentially declaratory. Its task is to determine whether the Contracting States have achieved the result called for by the Convention. Various possibilities are conceivable as regards the organisation of broadcasting television commercials; the Swiss authorities have entrusted the responsibility in respect of national programmes to one sole private company. It is not the Court's task to indicate which means a State should utilise in order to perform its obligations under the Convention (see *De Cubber* v. *Belgium*, judgment of 26 October 1984, Series A No. 86, p. 20, §35).

79. In the light of the foregoing, the measure in issue cannot be considered as 'necessary in a democratic society'. Consequently, there has been a violation of Article 10 of the Convention.

2.2 An obligation of means

The positive obligation to protect the exercise of rights is not absolute. It constitutes, in terms borrowed from the civil law, an obligation of means, rather than an obligation of result. In the case of *Plattform 'Ärzte für das Leben'*, an association of doctors who were campaigning against abortion and were seeking to bring about reform of the Austrian legislation on the matter held two demonstrations in 1980 and 1982 which were disrupted by counter-demonstrators despite the presence of a large police contingent. They complained that the Austrian authorities had violated the freedom of assembly guaranteed in Article 11 of the European Convention on Human Rights by having failed to take practical steps to ensure that its demonstrations passed off without any trouble. The question before the European Court of Human Rights was whether this was an 'arguable' complaint justifying the applicability of Article 13 of the Convention, which guarantees the right to an effective remedy to all persons who are victims of violations of Convention rights. It concluded that the Austrian authorities did not fail to take reasonable and appropriate measures which could be expected from them:

> **European Court of Human Rights, *Plattform 'Ärzte für das Leben'* v. *Austria* (Appl. No. 10126/82), judgment of 21 June 1988:**
>
> 31. The Court does not have to develop a general theory of the positive obligations which may flow from the Convention, but before ruling on the arguability of the applicant association's claim it has to give an interpretation of Article 11.
>
> 32. A demonstration may annoy or give offence to persons opposed to the ideas or claims that it is seeking to promote. The participants must, however, be able to hold the demonstration without having to fear that they will be subjected to physical violence by their opponents; such a fear would be liable to deter associations or other groups supporting common ideas or interests from openly expressing their opinions on highly controversial issues affecting the community. In a democracy the right to counter-demonstrate cannot extend to inhibiting the exercise of the right to demonstrate.
>
> Genuine, effective freedom of peaceful assembly cannot, therefore, be reduced to a mere duty on the part of the State not to interfere: a purely negative conception would not be compatible with the object and purpose of Article 11. Like Article 8, Article 11 sometimes requires positive measures to be taken, even in the sphere of relations between individuals, if need be (see, *mutatis mutandis*, the *X and Y* v. *Netherlands* judgment of 26 March 1985, Series A No. 91, p. 11, §23 [see above in this section]).
>
> 33. Concurring with the Government and the Commission, the Court finds that Austrian law is concerned to protect demonstrations by such positive action. For example, Articles 284 and 285 of the Criminal Code make it an offence for any person to disperse, prevent or disrupt a meeting that has not been prohibited, and sections 6, 13 and 14(2) of the Assembly Act, which empower the authorities in certain cases to prohibit, bring to an end or disperse by force an assembly, also apply to counter-demonstrations ...
>
> 34. While it is the duty of Contracting States to take reasonable and appropriate measures to enable lawful demonstrations to proceed peacefully, they cannot guarantee this absolutely and they have a wide discretion in the choice of the means to be used (see, *mutatis mutandis*, the

Abdulaziz, Cabales and Balkandali judgment of 28 May 1985, Series A No. 94, pp. 33–34, §67, and the *Rees* judgment of 17 October 1986, Series A No. 106, pp. 14–15, §§35–37). In this area the obligation they enter into under Article 11 of the Convention is an obligation as to measures to be taken and not as to results to be achieved.

2.3 The limits of the obligation to protect

The obligation to protect is clearly not unlimited. It must be understood as an obligation imposed on the State to take all reasonable measures that might have prevented the event from occurring. The mere fact that the event which should have been prevented did occur therefore is not evidence, *per se*, that the State has not discharged its obligation to protect: only if it is demonstrated, *in addition*, that there were certain supplementary measures which the State could have taken but failed to take, although this would not have imposed a disproportionate burden, will the State be considered to be in violation of its obligations. This is illustrated, for instance, by the disjunction between paragraphs 89 and 92, respectively, in the case of *E. and others* v. *United Kingdom* presented below: whereas, in paragraph 89, the European Court of Human Rights notes that the kind of abuse the applicants have been subjected to during their childhood 'falls within the scope of Article 3 of the Convention [European Convention on Human Rights] as inhuman and degrading treatment', in paragraph 92, it notes that 'the question therefore arises whether the [local authority concerned, in particular its social department] was, or ought to have been, aware that the applicants were suffering or at risk of abuse and, if so, whether they took the steps reasonably available to them to protect them from that abuse'. The prejudice to the victim is therefore a necessary, but still an insufficient condition, for a finding of violation by the State of its obligation to protect. For such a finding to be justified, a failure of the State must have contributed to the prejudice being caused.

However, this definition of the scope of the obligation to protect remains excessively vague. It raises in turn two questions, one of procedure, and the other of substance. The procedural question is that of the burden of proof. By definition, when the State is accused of having failed to prevent a particular violation from occuring, it remains a matter of speculation whether or not the intervention by the State would have been effective in ensuring that the violation will not take place. The nature of the evidence which victims must put forward has occasionally been the subject of controversy, as the following two cases illustrate:

European Court of Human Rights (2nd sect.), *E. and others* v. *United Kingdom* (Appl. No. 33218/96), judgment of 26 November 2002:

[The four applicants, E., H., L. and T., born between 1960 and 1965, are the sons and daughters of a woman who cohabited with W.H. after the death of their father in 1965. The family were known to the social services of Dumfries and Galloway Regional Council (designated in the judgment as 'the local authority'). They were principally concerned from 1970 onwards with the mother's severe financial difficulties. In 1977, W.H. was arrested by the police and charged with indecently assaulting two of the applicants. He entered a guilty plea to those charges. The pleas were accepted by the prosecution and the case proceeded on the basis that W.H. had committed one act of indecency against E. between 20 October 1972 and 31 August 1976, and two acts of indecency against L. between 1 January 1975 and 7 January 1977. W.H., however, was not detained pending sentence. Instead, he returned to live at the applicants' home. He was then sentenced to two years' probation, and the understanding was that he was not permitted to live in the family home due to the nature of the offences. Only in 1988 did the applicants report a history of sexual abuse by W.H. in the family. In 1992, the four applicants brought proceedings against the local authority seeking damages on the basis that the local authority had failed to carry out its statutory duties, in particular, that W.H. had breached his probation order by residing at the family home and that the social services had, or ought to have, known this and had failed to report the breach to the court or to take the children into care. They agreed, however, to the dismissal of their action, in the light of the case law of the House of Lords in *X. and others* v. *Bedfordshire County Council* [1995] 3 All E.R. 353. Three of the applicants received compensation from the Criminal Injuries Compensation Board.]

88. Article 3 enshrines one of the most fundamental values of a democratic society. It prohibits in absolute terms torture or inhuman or degrading treatment or punishment. The obligation on High Contracting Parties under Article 1 of the Convention to secure to everyone within their jurisdiction the rights and freedoms defined in the Convention, taken together with Article 3, requires States to take measures designed to ensure that individuals within their jurisdiction are not subjected to torture or inhuman or degrading treatment, including such ill-treatment administered by private individuals (see *A.* v. *United Kingdom*, judgment of 23 September 1998, *Reports of Judgments and Decisions* 1998–VI, p. 2699, §22). These measures should provide effective protection, in particular, of children and other vulnerable persons, and include reasonable steps to prevent ill-treatment of which the authorities had or ought to have had knowledge (*mutatis mutandis*, *Osman* v. *United Kingdom*, judgment of 28 October 1998, *Reports* 1998–VIII, §116). Thus a failure, over four and a half years, to protect children from serious neglect and abuse of which the local authority were aware disclosed a breach of Article 3 of the Convention in the case of *Z. and others* v. *United Kingdom* ([GC] No. 29392/95, ECHR 2001–V, §§74–75).

89. The Court recalls that the four applicants allege that they suffered sexual and physical abuse from W.H. over a long period of time. There is no doubt that the treatment described ... falls within the scope of Article 3 of the Convention as inhuman and degrading treatment ...

92. The question therefore arises whether the local authority (acting through its Social Work Department) was, or ought to have been, aware that the applicants were suffering or at risk of abuse and, if so, whether they took the steps reasonably available to them to protect them from that abuse.

93. The parties appear agreed that it is the period after January 1977 which is in issue ... The parties do disagree whether the authorities should have been aware of the abuse that continued thereafter.

94. The Court recalls that until T. made disclosures of sexual abuse to her social worker in 1988 there is no indication that any of the children in the house made any complaint about W.H.'s ongoing assaults after January 1977. The Government take the view that there was

nothing to alert the social workers that he continued to be a risk and that in the light of knowledge and practice at the time the fact that he had been found in the family home after the conviction in January 1977 would not have been regarded as any significant cause for alarm or have provided sufficient ground for action against him.

95. However, the Court notes that the Government accept that even if it was not a formal condition of his probation it would have been understood that W.H. was no longer permitted to reside in the applicant's home. [The Court lists a number of factors which seem to converge to illustrate the dangerous character of W.H., who had been charged with a series of serious sexual offences against two children of the family indicating a background of repetitive offending.]

96. The Court is satisfied from these elements that the social services should have been aware that the situation in the family disclosed a history of past sexual and physical abuse from W.H. and that, notwithstanding the probation order, he was continuing to have close contact with the family, including the children ...

97. Yet the social services failed to take steps which would have enabled them to discover the exact extent of the problem and, potentially, to prevent further abuse taking place. The Government have accepted that after the initial disclosures the social services should have worked with both E. and L. who had shown significant distress at the situation at home which could have led to further understanding of family dynamics; and, most importantly, that the social services should have referred L. to the Reporter of the Children's Hearing, which could have led to a supervision requirement over one or more of the children who had been living with a known and convicted offender.

98. In addition, the Government have accepted that more should have been done to investigate the possible breach by W.H. of the probation order, that there was a consistent failure to place the full and relevant details of the family situation before the Sheriff's Court or Children's Hearing when the applicant children were the subject of a specific examination in the context of offending and truancy ... and that there was no effective co-operation or exchange of information between the school authorities which were attempting to deal with a persistent truancy problem and the social services who had access to the information about the wider family situation and history. It is also not apparent that E.'s disclosures at the hospital in December 1976 were passed to the social services or that, if they were, they led to any response.

99. The Court recalls that the Government argued that notwithstanding any acknowledged shortcomings it has not been shown that matters would have turned out any differently, in other words, that fuller co-operation and communication between the authorities under the duty to protect the applicants and closer monitoring and supervision of the family would not necessarily have either uncovered the abuse or prevented it. The test under Article 3 however does not require it to be shown that 'but for' the failing or omission of the public authority ill-treatment would not have happened. A failure to take reasonably available measures which could have had a real prospect of altering the outcome or mitigating the harm is sufficient to engage the responsibility of the State.

100. The Court is satisfied that the pattern of lack of investigation, communication and co-operation by the relevant authorities disclosed in this case must be regarded as having had a significant influence on the course of events and that proper and effective management of their responsibilities might, judged reasonably, have been expected to avoid, or at least, minimise the risk or the damage suffered.

European Court of Human Rights (2nd sect.), *Younger* v. *United Kingdom* (Appl. No. 57420/00), decision (inadmissibility) of 7 January 2003:

[The applicant's son, Stuart Gipp, was found hanging from his shoelaces which were attached to the bolt hole of his open cell hatch while he was in custody at Lion Yard Magistrates' Court, Cambridge, on 9 February 1999. He died in hospital at 9.55 a.m. on the following day, aged twenty. He had been arrested on 8 February 1999. Although he had confided in his solicitor that he was a heroin user and was just beginning to experience withdrawal symptoms, he had decided not to call the police surgeon at that time.]

[The] Court concludes that there is no evidence of anything about Stuart Gipp's actions or behaviour that ought to have put the authorities on notice that he was at a real and immediate risk of suicide either at the times at which he requested a doctor or when he revealed that he was a drug user.

The applicant submits, however, that, had the authorities acted with reasonable care – in particular by ensuring that Stuart Gipp was seen by a doctor and/or by the community psychiatric nurse, who was on duty at the court that morning – there is a real possibility that they would have been made aware of Stuart Gipp's vulnerability to the risk of suicide. The Court finds this assertion to be too speculative. While the Court does not regard it as appropriate to apply a 'real possibility' test, which it finds puts the threshold far too low for the purposes of determining whether there has been a violation of Article 2, the Court would reach the same conclusion even on the basis of such a test. It cannot conclude on the available evidence that there was even a real possibility that, had Stuart Gipp been seen by a medical professional at a time prior to his bail application at about 2.50 p.m., the authorities would have become aware that he was at a real and immediate risk of suicide, nor that the calling of a doctor would have made any difference to the tragic outcome of the case. The Court notes that, from 2.50 p.m. onwards, a doctor would have been unavailable, even if called, as SCO [Senior Custody Officer] Davis had been trying to get one to attend another detainee since that time without success at the time at which she spoke to Mr Milsom at 3.50 p.m.

While the Court regards it as most unfortunate that Stuart Gipp was not seen by a medical practitioner in the circumstances of the case, it would be pure speculation to conclude that the summoning of a medical professional would have had the outcome for which the applicant contends.

The substantive question raised by the definition offered above of the obligation to protect is, of course, what 'reasonable' measures should consist in, and which limits attach to the scope of this obligation. A useful departure point is the judgment the European Court of Human Rights delivered in the case of *Osman*:

European Court of Human Rights (GC), *Osman* v. *United Kingdom* (Appl. No. 23452/94), judgment of 28 October 1998, paras. 115–22:

[The applicants are respectively the widow and the son of Mr Ali Osman who was shot dead by Mr Paul Paget-Lewis on 7 March 1988. The second applicant, Ahmet Osman, was a former pupil of Paul Paget-Lewis at Homerton House School. He was wounded in the shooting incident which led to the death of his father. The applicants complain about the failure of the authorities to appreciate and act on what they claim was a series of clear warning signs that Paul Paget-Lewis represented a serious threat to the physical safety of Ahmet Osman and his family.

The background was as follows. In 1986, it appeared that Paul Paget-Lewis had developed an attachment to his pupil, Ahmet Osman. He subsequently harassed a friend of Ahmet Osman, Leslie Green, about whom he spread rumours, and whom he warned against disrupting what he called his 'special relationship' with Ahmet Osman. In March 1987, information concerning Paget-Lewis' conduct towards Ahmet Osman was passed on to the police. Although the police officer contacted did not keep any record of the meetings, and did not make any report concerning the nature and extent of the information that was communicated to him, the Government stressed that all concerned were satisfied that there was no sexual element to Paget-Lewis' attachment to Ahmet and the matter could be dealt with internally by the school. A series of incidents followed. On 14 April 1987, Paget-Lewis changed his name by deed poll to Paul Ahmet Yildirim Osman, leading to fears that he might attempt to abscond with Ahmet Osman to another country. In May 1987, a brick was thrown through a window of the applicants' house. The police were informed and a police officer was sent to the house and completed a crime report. On two occasions in June 1987 the tyres of Ali Osman's car were deliberately burst. Both incidents were reported to the police, but no police records relating to the offences can be found. In June 1987, following the request of the head of the school and a medical examination concluding that he should remain away from Homerton House and be designated temporarily unfit to work, Paget-Lewis informed the school that he would be taking medical leave for the remainder of the school term. He then left Homerton House and did not return again. The incidents of vandalism against the Osman family continued during the following months. In an interview with the police following those incidents, however, Paget-Lewis denied any involvement in the acts of vandalism and criminal damage. No evidence was found implicating him in those incidents. Yet, in December 1987, after threatening statements made by Paget-Lewis before the Inner London Education Authority (ILEA), the police sought to arrest him on suspicion of criminal damage. After this failed, in early January 1988, the police commenced the procedure of laying an information before the Magistrates' Court with a view to prosecuting Paget-Lewis for driving without due care and attention, and Paget-Lewis' name was put on the Police National Computer as being wanted in relation to a collision incident and on suspicion of having committed offences of criminal damage. Between January and March 1988 Paget-Lewis travelled around England hiring cars in his adopted name of Osman and was involved in a number of accidents. He spent time at his home address during this period and continued to receive mail there. Finally, on 7 March 1988 Paget-Lewis shot and killed Ali Osman and seriously wounded Ahmet. He then drove to the home of the principal of Homerton House School where he shot and wounded him and killed his son.

On 28 October 1988 Paget-Lewis was convicted of two charges of manslaughter having pleaded guilty on grounds of diminished responsibility. He was sentenced to be detained in a secure mental hospital without limit of time. The applicants filed proceedings against, *inter alios*, the Commissioner of Police of the Metropolis alleging negligence in that although the police were aware of Paget-Lewis' activities since May 1987 they failed to apprehend or interview him, search his home or charge him with an offence before March 1988. This action failed: on 7 October 1992 the Court of Appeal held that in light of previous authorities no action could lie against the police in negligence in the investigation and suppression of crime on the grounds that public policy required an immunity from suit (*Osman and another* v. *Ferguson and another* [1993] 4 All E.R 344); the House of Lords refused leave to appeal from that judgment. Following this decision, the applicants filed an application relying on Articles 2, 6, 8 and 13 ECHR. They complained that there had been a failure to protect the lives of Ali and Ahmet Osman and to prevent the harassment of their family, and that they had no access to court or effective remedy in respect of that failure. By seventeen votes to three, the European Court of Human Rights found that neither Article 2 ECHR nor Article 8 ECHR had been violated. It held unanimously that Article 6 para. 1 ECHR had been violated, and that no separate issue was raised under Article 13 ECHR. As regards the alleged failure of the UK authorities to protect the rights to life of Ali and Ahmet Osman, the Court reasoned as follows:]

115. The Court notes that the first sentence of Article 2 §1 enjoins the State not only to refrain from the intentional and unlawful taking of life, but also to take appropriate steps to safeguard the lives of those within its jurisdiction (see the *L.C.B.* v. *United Kingdom* judgment of 9 June 1998, *Reports of Judgments and Decisions* 1998–III, p. 1403, §36). It is common ground that the State's obligation in this respect extends beyond its primary duty to secure the right to life by putting in place effective criminal-law provisions to deter the commission of offences against the person backed up by law-enforcement machinery for the prevention, suppression and sanctioning of breaches of such provisions. It is thus accepted by those appearing before the Court that Article 2 of the Convention may also imply in certain well-defined circumstances a positive obligation on the authorities to take preventive operational measures to protect an individual whose life is at risk from the criminal acts of another individual. The scope of this obligation is a matter of dispute between the parties.

116. For the Court, and bearing in mind the difficulties involved in policing modern societies, the unpredictability of human conduct and the operational choices which must be made in terms of priorities and resources, such an obligation must be interpreted in a way which does not impose an impossible or disproportionate burden on the authorities. Accordingly, not every claimed risk to life can entail for the authorities a Convention requirement to take operational measures to prevent that risk from materialising. Another relevant consideration is the need to ensure that the police exercise their powers to control and prevent crime in a manner which fully respects the due process and other guarantees which legitimately place restraints on the scope of their action to investigate crime and bring offenders to justice, including the guarantees contained in Articles 5 [right to liberty and to security] and 8 [right to respect for private and family life, home and correspondance] of the Convention.

In the opinion of the Court where there is an allegation that the authorities have violated their positive obligation to protect the right to life in the context of their above-mentioned duty to prevent and suppress offences against the person (see paragraph 115 above), it must be established to its satisfaction that the authorities knew or ought to have known at the time of the existence of a real and immediate risk to the life of an identified individual or individuals from the criminal acts of a third party and that they failed to take measures within the scope of their powers which, judged reasonably, might have been expected to avoid that risk. The Court does not accept the Government's view that the failure to perceive the risk to life in the circumstances known at the time or to take preventive measures to avoid that risk must be tantamount to gross negligence or wilful disregard of the duty to protect life ... Such a rigid standard must be considered to be incompatible with the requirements of Article 1 of the Convention and the obligations of Contracting States under that Article to secure the practical and effective protection of the rights and freedoms laid down therein, including Article 2 (see, *mutatis mutandis*, the above-mentioned *McCann and others* judgment, p. 45, §146). For the Court, and having regard to the nature of the right protected by Article 2, a right fundamental in the scheme of the Convention, it is sufficient for an applicant to show that the authorities did not do all that could be reasonably expected of them to avoid a real and immediate risk to life of which they have or ought to have knowledge. This is a question which can only be answered in the light of all the circumstances of any particular case ...

117. The Court observes, like the Commission, that the concerns of the school about Paget-Lewis' disturbing attachment to Ahmet Osman can be reasonably considered to have been communicated to the police over the course of the five meetings which took place between 3 March and 4 May 1987 ..., having regard to the fact that Mr Prince's decision to call in the police in the first place was motivated by the allegations which Mrs Green had made against Paget-Lewis and the school's follow-up to those allegations. It may for the same reason be reasonably accepted that the police were informed of all relevant connected matters which had come to light by 4 May 1987 including the graffiti incident, the theft of the school files and Paget-Lewis' change of name.

It is the applicants' contention that by that stage the police should have been alert to the need to investigate further Paget-Lewis' alleged involvement in the graffiti incident and the theft of the school files or to keep a closer watch on him given their awareness of the obsessive nature of his behaviour towards Ahmet Osman and how that behaviour manifested itself. The Court for its part is not persuaded that the police's failure to do so at this stage can be impugned from the standpoint of Article 2 having regard to the state of their knowledge at that time. While Paget-Lewis' attachment to Ahmet Osman could be judged by the police officers who visited the school to be most reprehensible from a professional point of view, there was never any suggestion that Ahmet Osman was at risk sexually from him, less so that his life was in danger. Furthermore, Mr Perkins, the deputy headmaster, alone had reached the conclusion that Paget-Lewis had been responsible for the graffiti in the neighbourhood of the school and the theft of the files. However Paget-Lewis had denied all involvement when interviewed by Mr Perkins and there was nothing to link him with either incident. Accordingly, at that juncture, the police's appreciation of the situation and their decision to treat it as a matter internal to the school cannot be considered unreasonable ...

118. The applicants have attached particular weight to Paget-Lewis' mental condition and in particular to his potential to turn violent and to direct that violence at Ahmet Osman. However, it is to be noted that Paget-Lewis continued to teach at the school up until June 1987. Dr Ferguson examined him on three occasions and was satisfied that he was not mentally ill. On 7 August 1987 he was allowed to resume teaching, although not at Homerton House ... It is most improbable that the decision to lift his suspension from teaching duties would have been made if it had been believed at the time that there was the slightest risk that he constituted a danger to the safety of young people in his charge. The applicants are especially critical of Dr Ferguson's psychiatric assessment of Paget-Lewis. However, that assessment was made on the basis of three separate interviews with Paget-Lewis and if it appeared to a professional psychiatrist that he did not at the time display any signs of mental illness or a propensity to violence it would be unreasonable to have expected the police to have construed the actions of Paget-Lewis as they were reported to them by the school as those of a mentally disturbed and highly dangerous individual.

119. In assessing the level of knowledge which can be imputed to the police at the relevant time, the Court has also had close regard to the series of acts of vandalism against the Osmans' home and property between May and November 1987 … It observes firstly that none of these incidents could be described as life-threatening and secondly that there was no evidence pointing to the involvement of Paget-Lewis. This was also the view of Detective Sergeant Boardman in his report on the case in mid-December 1987 having interviewed the Green and Osman families, visited the school and taken stock of the file … The completeness of Detective Sergeant Boardman's report and the assessment he made in the knowledge of all the allegations made against Paget-Lewis would suggest that even if it were to be assumed that the applicants are correct in their assertions that the police did not keep records of the reported incidents of vandalism and of their meetings with the school and ILEA officials, this failing could not be said to have prevented them from apprehending at an earlier stage any real threat to the lives of the Osman family or that the irrationality of Paget-Lewis' behaviour concealed a deadly disposition. The Court notes in this regard that when the decision was finally taken to arrest Paget-Lewis it was not based on any perceived risk to the lives of the Osman family but on his suspected involvement in acts of minor criminal damage …

120. The Court has also examined carefully the strength of the applicants' arguments that Paget-Lewis on three occasions communicated to the police, either directly or indirectly, his murderous intentions … However, in its view these statements cannot be reasonably considered to imply that the Osman family were the target of his threats and to put the police on notice of such. The applicants rely in particular on Paget-Lewis' threat to 'do a sort of Hungerford' [tragic event in 1987 in which a gunman killed sixteen people before killing himself in Hungerford, United Kingdom] which they allege he uttered at the meeting with ILEA officers on 15 December 1987 … The Government have disputed that these words were said on that occasion, but even taking them at their most favourable to the applicants' case, it would appear more likely that they were uttered with respect to Mr Perkins whom he regarded as principally to blame for being forced to leave his teaching post at Homerton House. Furthermore, the fact that Paget-Lewis is reported to have intimated to the driver of the car with which he collided on 7 December 1987 that he was on the verge of committing some terrible deed … could not reasonably be taken at the time to be a veiled reference to a planned attack on the lives of the Osman family. The Court must also attach weight in this respect to the fact that, even if Paget-Lewis had deliberately rammed the vehicle as alleged, that act of hostility was in all probability directed at Leslie Green, the passenger in the vehicle. Nor have the applicants adduced any further arguments which would enhance the weight to be given to Paget-Lewis' claim that he had told PC Adams that he was in danger of doing something criminally insane … In any event, as with his other cryptic threats, this statement could not reasonably be construed as a threat against the lives of the Osman family.

121. In the view of the Court the applicants have failed to point to any decisive stage in the sequence of the events leading up to the tragic shooting when it could be said that the police knew or ought to have known that the lives of the Osman family were at real and immediate risk from Paget-Lewis. While the applicants have pointed to a series of missed opportunities which would have enabled the police to neutralise the threat posed by Paget-Lewis, for example by searching his home for evidence to link him with the graffiti incident or by having him detained under the Mental Health Act 1983 or by taking more active investigative steps following his disappearance, it cannot be said that these measures, judged reasonably, would in fact have

produced that result or that a domestic court would have convicted him or ordered his detention in a psychiatric hospital on the basis of the evidence adduced before it. As noted earlier (see paragraph 116 above), the police must discharge their duties in a manner which is compatible with the rights and freedoms of individuals. In the circumstances of the present case, they cannot be criticised for attaching weight to the presumption of innocence or failing to use powers of arrest, search and seizure having regard to their reasonably held view that they lacked at relevant times the required standard of suspicion to use those powers or that any action taken would in fact have produced concrete results.

122. For the above reasons, the Court concludes that there has been no violation of Article 2 of the Convention in this case.

In a situation such as that presented to the European Court of Human Rights in the *Osman* case, essentially three factors limit the scope of the obligation to protect. These are: (a) first, what the Court refers to as the 'unpredictability of human conduct', which is one way to describe the degree of risk inevitable in a free society – only in a totalitarian society, it has sometimes been remarked, would the risk of human rights violations be entirely eliminated by State control (see B. Dickson, 'The Horizontal Application of Human Rights Law' in A. Hegarty and S. Leonard (eds.), *Human Rights. An Agenda for the 21st Century* (London: Cavendish Publishing Ltd, 1999), p. 59 *et seq.*). Indeed, the partly dissenting opinion appended to the *Osman* judgment was based on the conviction of three members of the Court – Judge De Meyer, joined by Judges Lopes Rocha and Casadevall – that the majority exaggerated the unpredictable character of the flow of events having led to the murder of Mr Osman: in the view of Judge De Meyer, '[the police] should have taken Mr Paget-Lewis into custody before it was too late in order to have him cared for properly. Instead they let things go until he killed two persons and wounded two others. Mr Paget-Lewis himself asked the police arresting him why they did not stop him before he acted as he did and reminded them that he had given all the warning signs. He was right.' The other factors referred to by the Court in *Osman* as limiting the scope of the obligation to protect are: (b) the budgetary constraints facing States, which face competing claims on limited resources; and (c) the obligation for States to respect other, conflicting human rights.

But the full range of factors that may limit the scope of the State's obligation to protect is in fact wider than the statement of the European Court of Human Rights in *Osman* would seem to suggest. Depending on the particular circumstances of each case, other candidates may be, in particular: (d) respect for the contractual freedom of parties, one of which has agreed to a restriction to his/her right in exchange of another advantage, whether pecuniary or not, to which he or she attaches greater value; or (e) the autonomy of the individual who chose to waive his/her right, by means other than by the conclusion of a contract. Nor is this list meant to be exhaustive. A factor such as (f) respect for the intention expressed, unilaterally, in legal acts such as wills, may also play a role. In the case of *Pla and Puncernau* v. *Andorra*, certain members of the European Court of Human Rights expressed their uneasiness at re-examining the interpretation given by the domestic courts to a discriminatory clause inserted into a testamentary will in order to ensure an interpretation compliant with the Convention:

European Court of Human Rights (4th sect.), *Pla and Puncernau* v. *Andorra* (Appl. No. 69498/01), judgment of 13 July 2004:

[In 1939, Carolina Pujol Oller, Francesc Pla Guash's widow, made a will before a notary, one clause of which settled her estate on her son, Francesc-Xavier, as life tenant with the remainder to a son or grandson of a lawful and canonical marriage. Should those conditions not be met, the testatrix stipulated that her estate had to pass to the children and grandchildren of the remaindermen under the settlement. In 1949 Carolina Pujol Oller died. The beneficiary under the will, Francesc-Xavier Pla Pujol, contracted canonical marriage to Roser Puncernau Pedro. The couple adopted two children. In 1996, when Francesc-Xavier Pla Pujol died, it was found that he had left the assets he had inherited under his mother's will to his wife for life, with the remainder to his adopted son, Antoni. However, two great-grandchildren of Carolina Pujol Oller challenged this. In their view, Antoni Pla Puncernau could not inherit under the will made by the testatrix in 1939, since he was an adopted child. These great-grandchildren brought civil proceedings in the *Tribunal des Batlles*, which dismissed their action. However, the High Court of Justice set the judgment aside on appeal and granted the appellants' claim, and the appeal (*empara*) against that judgment was dismissed by the Constitutional Court. The applicants before the Court are Antoni Pla Puncernau, the first adoptive child of Francesc-Xavier Pla Pujol, and his mother, Roser Puncernau Pedro. They complained that, in determining inheritance rights, the High Court of Justice and the Constitutional Court had breached the applicants' right to respect for their private and family life by unjustifiably discriminating against the first applicant on the ground of his filiation. They submitted that this had resulted in a violation of Article 14 of the Convention taken in conjunction with Article 8.]

53. The Court notes that the Andorran courts gave two different interpretations: the first, given by the *Tribunal des Batlles*, was favourable to the applicants and the second, given by the High Court of Justice, went against them. Both are based on factual and legal elements that were duly evaluated in the light of the particular circumstances of the case ...

56. The Court does not consider it appropriate or even necessary to analyse the legal theory behind the principles on which the domestic courts, and in particular the High Court of Justice of Andorra, based their decision to apply one legal system rather than another, be it Roman law, canon law, Catalan law or Spanish law. That is a sphere which, by definition, falls within the competence of the domestic courts.

57. The Court considers that, contrary to the Government's affirmations, no question relating to the testatrix's free will is in issue in the present case. Only the interpretation of the testamentary disposition falls to be considered. The Court's task is therefore confined to determining whether, in the circumstances of the case, the first applicant was a victim of discrimination contrary to Article 14 of the Convention.

58. In the present case, the Court observes that the legitimate and canonical nature of the marriage contracted by the first applicant's father is indisputable. The sole remaining question is therefore whether the notion of 'son' in Carolina Pujol Oller's will extended only, as the High Court of Justice maintained, to biological sons. The Court cannot agree with that conclusion of the Andorran appellate court. There is nothing in the will to suggest that the testatrix intended to exclude adopted grandsons. The Court understands that she could have done so but, as she did not, the only possible and logical conclusion is that this was not her intention.

The High Court of Justice's interpretation of the testamentary disposition, which consisted in inferring a negative intention on the part of the testatrix and concluding that since she did not expressly state that she was not excluding adopted sons this meant that she did intend to exclude them, appears over contrived and contrary to the general legal principle that where a statement is unambiguous there is no need to examine the intention of the person who made it (*quum in verbis nulla ambiguitas est, non debet admitti voluntatis queastio*).

59. Admittedly, the Court is not in theory required to settle disputes of a purely private nature. That being said, in exercising the European supervision incumbent on it, it cannot remain passive where a national court's interpretation of a legal act, be it a testamentary disposition, a private contract, a public document, a statutory provision or an administrative practice appears unreasonable, arbitrary or, as in the present case, blatantly inconsistent with the prohibition of discrimination established by Article 14 and more broadly with the principles underlying the Convention (see *Larkos* v. *Cyprus* [GC], No. 29515/95, §§30–31, ECHR 1999–I).

60. In the present case, the High Court of Justice's interpretation of the testamentary disposition in question had the effect of depriving the first applicant of his right to inherit under his grandmother's estate and benefiting his cousin's daughters in this regard ...

Since the testamentary disposition, as worded by Carolina Pujol Oller, made no distinction between biological and adopted children it was not necessary to interpret it in that way. Such an interpretation therefore amounts to the judicial deprivation of an adopted child's inheritance rights.

61. The Court reiterates that a distinction is discriminatory for the purposes of Article 14 if it has no objective and reasonable justification, that is if it does not pursue a legitimate aim or if there is not a 'reasonable relationship of proportionality between the means employed and the aim sought to be realised' (see, *inter alia*, *Fretté* v. *France*, No. 36515/97, §34, ECHR 2002–I). In the present case, the Court does not discern any legitimate aim pursued by the decision in question or any objective and reasonable justification on which the distinction made by the domestic court might be based. In the Court's view, where a child is adopted (under the full adoption procedure, moreover), the child is in the same legal position as a biological child of his or her parents in all respects: relations and consequences connected with his or her family life and the resulting property rights. The Court has stated on many occasions that very weighty reasons need to be put forward before a difference in treatment on the ground of birth out of wedlock can be regarded as compatible with the Convention.

Furthermore, there is nothing to suggest that reasons of public policy required the degree of protection afforded by the Andorran appellate court to the appellants to prevail over that afforded to the first applicant.

62. The Court reiterates that the Convention, which is a dynamic text and entails positive obligations for States, is a living instrument, to be interpreted in the light of present-day conditions and that great importance is attached today in the member States of the Council of Europe to the question of equality between children born in and children born out of wedlock as regards their civil rights ... Thus, even supposing that the testamentary disposition in question did require an interpretation by the domestic courts, that interpretation could not be made exclusively in the light of the social conditions existing when the will was made or at the time of the testatrix's death, namely in 1939 and 1949, particularly where a period of fifty-seven years had elapsed between the date when the will was made and the date on which the estate passed to the heirs. Where such a long period has elapsed, during which profound social, economic and

legal changes have occurred, the courts cannot ignore these new realities. The same is true with regard to wills: any interpretation, if interpretation there must be, should endeavour to ascertain the testator's intention and render the will effective, while bearing in mind that 'the testator cannot be presumed to have meant what he did not say' and without overlooking the importance of interpreting the testamentary disposition in the manner that most closely corresponds to domestic law and to the Convention as interpreted in the Court's case law.

63. Having regard to the foregoing, the Court considers that there has been a violation of Article 14 of the Convention taken in conjunction with Article 8.

Partly dissenting opinion of Judge Sir Nicolas Bratza:

2. As is noted in the judgment, the present case is of an entirely different character from those previously examined by the Court involving allegations of discriminatory treatment in the field of succession and inheritance. In each of the earlier cases, it was the domestic legislation itself which gave rise to the difference of treatment of which complaint was made under the Convention, distinguishing as it did between the rights of succession of legitimate and illegitimate children (see *Marckx* v. *Belgium*, judgment of 13 June 1979, Series A No. 31, p. 24, §54; *Vermeire* v. *Belgium*, judgment of 29 November 1991, Series A No. 214–C, p. 83, §28; and *Inze* v. *Austria*, judgment of 28 October 1987, Series A No. 126, p. 18, §40) or between children born of an adulterous relationship and other children, whether legitimate or not (see *Mazurek* v. *France*, No. 34406/97, §43, ECHR 2000–II). In the present case, no such complaint is made or could be made against Andorra, discrimination on grounds of birth being expressly prohibited by both the Andorran Constitution and the special law on adoption.

3. It is also important to observe that, although the applicants complain of the decisions of the High Court of Justice and the Constitutional Court of Andorra, it is not asserted that the decisions directly interfered with the applicants' Article 8 rights or subjected the first applicant to discriminatory treatment in the enjoyment of his family life by creating distinctions between the biological and adopted members of his family. As appears from the terms of its judgment, in upholding the appeals of the Serra Areny sisters and finding that, as an adopted child of the life tenant under the will of Carolina Pujol Oller, the first applicant was excluded from inheriting under the will, the High Court of Justice of Andorra sought to give effect to the intention of the testatrix herself in the exercise of her right to dispose of her property on her death. The circumstances of the present case are in this respect quite different from those which have frequently been examined by the Court, ... in which it was the decisions of the domestic courts themselves which had restricted, penalised or otherwise interfered with the exercise of the Convention right in question and which required to be justified.

4. The fact that, under the Convention, the legislative or judicial organs of the State are precluded from discriminating between individuals (by, for instance, creating distinctions based on biological or adoptive links between children and parents in the enjoyment of inheritance rights) does not mean that private individuals are similarly precluded from discriminating by drawing such distinctions when disposing of their property. It must in principle be open to a testator, in the exercise of his or her right of property, to choose to whom to leave the property and, by the terms of the will, to differentiate between potential heirs, by (*inter alia*) distinguishing between biological and adoptive children and grandchildren. As pointed out in the opinion of Judge Garlicki [see below], the testator's right of choice finds protection under the Convention, namely in Article 8 and in Article 1 of Protocol No. 1. The State must in principle give effect, through its judicial organs, to such private testamentary disposition and cannot be held

to be in breach of its Convention obligations (including its obligations under Article 14) by doing so, save in exceptional circumstances where the disposition may be said to be repugnant to the fundamental ideals of the Convention or to aim at the destruction of the rights and freedoms set forth therein. This remains true even if there may appear to be no objective and reasonable justification for the distinction made by a testator.

5. In my view, the distinction which was held by the domestic courts to have been intended by the testatrix in the present case between biological and adopted grandchildren cannot be said to be repugnant to the fundamental ideals of the Convention or otherwise destructive of Convention rights and freedoms. Nor do I understand the majority of the Chamber of the Court to suggest to the contrary. It is true that in paragraph 46 of the judgment it is said that an issue of interference with private and family life under the Convention could arise if the national court's assessment of the facts or domestic law were 'blatantly inconsistent with the fundamental principles of the Convention' and in paragraph 59 such inconsistency is found to have existed in the national courts' assessment in the present case. However, I do not read this finding as suggesting that the upholding by a national court of a will which distinguishes between biological and adopted children is of itself to be seen as incompatible with Convention principles. The majority's finding is, as I understand it, based rather on the ground that the High Court's interpretation of the will in the present case and its assessment of the intention of the testatrix were clearly wrong and that accordingly it was that court's decision that, as an adopted grandchild, the first applicant was excluded from inheriting the estate which itself gave rise to a violation of Article 14.

6. The central question thus raised is whether the manner in which the domestic courts interpreted the will of the testatrix or applied the principles of domestic law was such as to permit such a finding. The majority of the Chamber have reiterated in paragraph 46 of the judgment the principles established by the Court's jurisprudence concerning the interpretation and application of domestic law: it is in the first place for the national authorities, and in particular the national courts, to construe and apply domestic law. I would agree with the majority that this principle applies *a fortiori* when the national courts are concerned with resolving disputes between private individuals or interpreting a private testamentary disposition, such courts being better placed than an international court to evaluate, in the light of local legal traditions, the particular context of the legal dispute and the competing rights and interests involved.

This being so, an issue would in my view only arise under the Convention if the Court were satisfied that the interpretation of the will or of the relevant principles of domestic law by the national courts was, to use the terms of the judgment, 'manifestly unreasonable or arbitrary'.

7. Thus far, I am in agreement with the majority's approach. Where I strongly disagree is as to the majority's application of these principles when examining the judgments of the national courts. Far from assessing the judgments according to these strict standards, the majority have to my mind substituted their own view of the proper interpretation of the will for that of the High Court of Justice of Andorra, preferring the construction placed on the will by the *Tribunal des Batlles*. While I can readily accept that one might prefer both the reasoning and the result reached by the first-instance court, I cannot accept that the decision of the appeal court may be characterised as either arbitrary or manifestly unreasonable ...

15. For these reasons, regrettable as the result of the High Court's judgment may seem, I am unable to find that the decision gave rise to a violation of the applicants' rights under Article 14 of the Convention taken in conjunction with Article 8.

Dissenting opinion of Judge Garlicki:

It is with regret that I have to disagree with the majority.

This case relates to two important principles which determine the scope of the Court's jurisdiction: the principle of subsidiarity and the principle of State action.

In respect of the former, I fully subscribe to the arguments developed by Judge Sir Nicolas Bratza that the interpretation of the will or of the relevant principles of domestic law by the national courts cannot be regarded as arbitrary or manifestly erroneous or unreasonable.

In respect of the latter, it should be noted that the case did not involve any direct interference by the national courts with the applicants' Article 8 rights. The courts were confronted with a will which contained a clause discriminating against adopted children *vis-à-vis* biological children. The courts first determined the correct interpretation of the will and, in accordance with that interpretation, gave effect to it. Thus, the real question before our Court is to what extent the Convention enjoys a 'horizontal' effect, that is, an effect prohibiting private parties from taking action which interferes with the rights and liberties of other private parties. Consequently, to what extent is the State under an obligation either to prohibit or to refuse to give effect to such private action?

It seems clear that the authors of the Convention did not intend this instrument to possess a 'third-party effect' (see A. Drzemczewski: 'The European Human Rights Convention and Relations between Private Parties', *Netherlands International Law Review* 1979, No. 2, p. 168). However, under our case law it is obvious that there may be certain positive obligations of the State to adopt measures designed to secure respect for Convention rights, even in the sphere of the relations of individuals between themselves (see *X and Y* v. *Netherlands*, judgment of 26 March 1985, Series A No. 91, p. 11, §23). Such 'indirect third-party effect' has been addressed by the Court in many different areas, such as the right to life (State obligation to carry out an effective investigation in a case of a murder committed by private persons – see, for example, *Menson* v. *United Kingdom*, (dec.), No. 47916/99, ECHR 2003–V), freedom of expression (*Appleby* v. *United Kingdom*, No. 44306/98, ECHR 2003–VI, in which the Court indicated that the State may be obliged to adopt 'positive measures of protection, even in the sphere of relations between individuals', §39), freedom of association (*Young, James and Webster* v. *United Kingdom*, judgment of 13 August 1981, Series A No. 44, representing the first ruling of this kind), freedom of assembly (*Plattform 'Ärzte für das Leben'* v. *Austria*, judgment of 21 June 1988, Series A No. 139) and, above all, the protection of private life (see, for example, *Ignaccolo-Zenide* v. *Romania*, No. 31679/96, ECHR 2000–I, in particular §113).

Nevertheless, it seems equally obvious that the level of protection against a private action cannot be the same as the level of protection against State action. The very fact that, under the Convention, the State may be prohibited from taking certain action (such as introducing inheritance distinctions between children – see *Marckx* v. *Belgium*, judgment of 13 June 1979, Series A No. 31; *Vermeire* v. *Belgium*, judgment of 29 November 1991, Series A No. 214–C; and *Mazurek* v. *France*, No. 34406/97, ECHR 2000–II) does not mean that private persons are similarly precluded from taking such action. In other words, what is prohibited for the State need not necessarily also be prohibited for individuals. Of course, in many areas such prohibition may appear necessary and well-founded. However, it should not be forgotten that every prohibition of private action (or any refusal to judicially enforce such action), while protecting the rights of some persons, unavoidably restricts the rights of other persons. This is particularly visible in regard to 'purely' private-law relations, such as inheritance. The whole idea of a will is to depart from the general system of inheritance, that is, to discriminate between potential heirs. But at the same time, the testator must retain a degree of freedom to dispose of his/her property and this freedom is protected by both Article 8 of the Convention and Article 1 of Protocol No. 1. Thus, in my opinion, the rule should be that the State must give effect to private testamentary dispositions, save in exceptional circumstances where the disposition may be said to be repugnant to the fundamental ideals of the Convention or to aim at the destruction of the rights and freedoms set forth therein. As in respect of all exceptional circumstances, however, their presence must be clearly demonstrated and cannot be assumed.

No exceptional circumstances of the above-mentioned kind existed in the present case. The testatrix had taken a decision, which was perhaps unjust, but cannot, even by present-day standards, be regarded as repugnant to the fundamental ideals of the Convention or otherwise destructive of Convention rights. Thus, the State was under a duty to respect and give effect to her will and was neither allowed nor expected to substitute its own inheritance criteria for what had been decided in the will. Accordingly, the State cannot be held to be in breach of the Convention by giving effect to this will.

2.4 Human rights in contractual relationships and the question of waiver of rights

While all the limiting factors listed above (in the preceding section 2.3.) may potentially restrict the scope of obligation to protect, a fundamental distinction may have to be made between the situations where the right or freedom of the individual is interfered with *in the absence of any choice* of the right-holder – as was the case in the cases of *X and Y* v. *Netherlands* or *Osman* v. *United Kingdom* – and the situations where the right-holder has *chosen* – whether by agreeing to the terms of a contract or otherwise – to submit to a restriction of his/her rights. The latter set of situations may in turn be sub-divided in two categories: while all these situations raise the question whether the right-holder should be allowed to waive his/her human right (or whether, instead, the obligation to protect of the State extends to an obligation to protect the right-holder against him/herself), only where contractual relationships are concerned does the question arise whether private compulsion should be distinguished from compulsion exercised by the State (or should be treated, instead, as equivalent).

The table on the next page offers a simplified typology of the arguments concerning the limits of the obligation to protect of the State.

Section 2.5. discusses how respect for other, competing human rights, may impose limits to the scope of the obligation of the State to protect – an issue which appears, in this typology, in the far right-hand column, as argument (v). This section reviews arguments (iii) and (iv) (in the lower part of this simplified typology), which are exchanged about the weight to be given to the choice expressed by the individual right-holder, whether he/she has agreed by contract to a limitation of his/her right (for instance in the context of employment), or whether he/she chooses, unilaterally, to waive his/her right (a situation for which the cases of voluntary euthanasia or assisted suicide provide useful illustrations).

Situation		Limits of the obligation to protect		
No choice of the individual right-holder		(i) Budgetary constraints (ii) Unpredictability of human conduct in free societies		(v) Respect for other human rights
Choice of the individual right-holder	In contractual relationships	(iii) Deference to the will expressed by the parties to the contract	(iv) Autonomy of the individual waiving his/her right	
	Through unilateral decisions			

Little needs to be said here about the deference which the State should have for contractual agreements that bring about a restriction to the rights of the individual (argument (iii)). Indeed, there seems to exist a general agreement on two basic propositions. First, the kind of compulsion on the right-holder that a private actor may exercise in contractual relationships differs from that which the State may exercise: as noted by Heilbroner, 'there is a qualitative difference between the power of an institution to wield the knout, to brand, mutilate, deport, chain, imprison, or execute those who defy its will, and the power of an institution to withdraw its support, no matter how life-giving that support may be. Even if we imagined that all capital was directed by a single capitalist, the sentence of starvation that could be passed by his refusal to sell his commodities or to buy labor power differs from the sentence of the king who casts his opponents into a dungeon to starve, because the capitalist has no legal right to forbid his victims from moving elsewhere, or from appealing to the state or other authorities against himself' (R. L. Heilbroner, *The Nature and Logic of Capitalism* (New York and London: W.W. Norton & Co., 1985), at pp. 39–40). Second, however, private compulsion may exercise an equally powerful constraint on the free will of the individual right-holder. In situations where the right-holder is in need and where he/she faces few alternatives (or none at all, as in situations of monopoly or monopsony), in particular, the possibility for the private actor with whom the right-holder interacts to withhold certain goods or services (such as food, life-saving medical treatment, or a waged employment) may in fact lead to a form of coercion equivalent to that at the disposal of the State. In addition, even in situations where 'coercion' is not present and where the right-holder seems to have consented 'freely' to certain restrictions, the State would be justified in seeking to remove certain obstacles to the individual making fully rational choices, for instance because of phenomena of addiction or myopia (i.e. the individual placing his short-term desires above his long-term interests).

Since the rise of large-scale private organizations in the early twentieth century, it is understood that the individual is not necessarily more 'free' (whether or not to submit to certain conditions which another actor seeks to impose on him) in interindividual (or 'horizontal') relationships, particularly in the sphere of the market, than he is in the ('vertical') relationships with the State (see, in particular, R. L. Hale, 'Force and the State: a Comparison of Political and Economic Compulsion', *Columbia Law Review*, 35 (1935), 149; R. L. Hale, 'Our Equivocal Constitutional Guarantees', *Columbia Law Review*, 39 (1939), 563). It is therefore fitting that human rights courts have generally considered with suspicion the argument that the State should be allowed not to intervene in private contractual relationships, out of respect for the 'free will' embodied in such contracts. On the contrary, they have generally adopted the view that, while the consent of the individual may be *necessary* to justify certain restrictions to his/her rights, such a consent, as expressed in contractual clauses, should never be considered, as such, a *sufficient* justification. It is significant for instance that, in two cases concerning restrictions to the right to respect for private life of employees, the European Court of Human Rights did not satisfy itself with the consideration that the employees concerned must be presumed to have consented to such restrictions as a condition for their employment, but instead examined whether the said restrictions were justified as 'necessary, in a democratic society' (as required under para. 2 of Art. 8 ECHR) to the achievement of the legitimate aims put forward – in the cases concerned, public safety on a vessel or on a nuclear plant (see Eur. Ct. H.R. (1st sect.), decision of 7 November 2002, *Madsen* v. *Denmark*, Appl. No. 58341/00 (inadmissibility); and Eur. Ct. H.R. (4th sect.), decision of 9 March 2004, *Wretlund* v. *Sweden*, Appl. No. 46210/99 (inadmissibility)). Consider also the following example:

European Court of Human Rights (2nd sect.), *Wilson, National Union of Journalists and others v. United Kingdom* (Appl. Nos. 30668/96, 30671/96 and 30678/96), judgment of 2 July 2002:

[The applicants are employees and unions to which they belong. The individual applicants were invited by their employers to sign a personal contract and lose union rights, or accept a lower pay rise. They allege that the law of the United Kingdom, by allowing the employer to de-recognize trade unions, fails to ensure their rights to protect their interests through trade union membership and to freedom of expression, contrary to Articles 11 and 10 of the Convention. In addition, the individual applicants complain that UK law permitted discrimination by employers against trade union members, contrary to Article 14 of the Convention taken in conjunction with Articles 10 and 11.]

41. The Court observes at the outset that although the essential object of Article 11 is to protect the individual against arbitrary interference by public authorities with the exercise of the rights protected, there may in addition be positive obligations to secure the effective enjoyment of these rights. In the present case, the matters about which the applicants complain – principally, the employers' de-recognition of the unions for collective-bargaining purposes and offers of more favourable conditions of employment to employees agreeing not to be represented by the unions – did not involve direct intervention by the State. The responsibility of the United Kingdom would, however, be engaged if these matters resulted from a failure on its part to secure to the applicants under domestic law the rights set forth in Article 11 of the Convention (see *Gustafsson* v. *Sweden*, judgment of 25 April 1996, *Reports of Judgments and Decisions* 1996–II, pp. 652–53, §45).

42. The Court reiterates that Article 11 §1 presents trade union freedom as one form or a special aspect of freedom of association (see *National Union of Belgian Police* v. *Belgium*, judgment of 27 October 1975, Series A No. 19, pp. 17–18, §38, and *Swedish Engine Drivers' Union* v. *Sweden*, judgment of 6 February 1976, Series A No. 20, pp. 14–15, §39). The words 'for the protection of his interests' in Article 11 §1 are not redundant, and the Convention safeguards freedom to protect the occupational interests of trade union members by trade union action, the conduct and development of which the Contracting States must both permit and make possible. A trade union must thus be free to strive for the protection of its members' interests, and the individual members have a right, in order to protect their interests, that the trade union should be heard (see *National Union of Belgian Police*, cited above, p. 18, §§39–40, and *Swedish Engine Drivers' Union*, cited above, pp. 15–16, §§40–41). Article 11 does not, however, secure any particular treatment of trade unions or their members and leaves each State a free choice of the means to be used to secure the right to be heard (see *National Union of Belgian Police*, cited above, pp. 17–18, §§38–39, and *Swedish Engine Drivers' Union*, cited above, pp. 14–15, §§39–40).

43. The Court notes that, at the time of the events complained of by the applicants, United Kingdom law provided for a wholly voluntary system of collective bargaining, with no legal obligation on employers to recognise trade unions for the purposes of collective bargaining. There was, therefore, no remedy in law by which the applicants could prevent the employers in the present case from de-recognising the unions and refusing to renew the collective-bargaining agreements ...

44. However, the Court has consistently held that although collective bargaining may be one of the ways by which trade unions may be enabled to protect their members' interests, it is not indispensable for the effective enjoyment of trade union freedom. Compulsory collective bargaining would impose on employers an obligation to conduct negotiations with trade unions. The Court has not yet been prepared to hold that the freedom of a trade union to make its voice heard extends to imposing on an employer an obligation to recognise a trade union. The union and its members must however be free, in one way or another, to seek to persuade the employer to listen to what it has to say on behalf of its members. In view of the sensitive character of the social and political issues involved in achieving a proper balance between the competing interests and the wide degree of divergence between the domestic systems in this field, the Contracting States enjoy a wide margin of appreciation as to how trade union freedom may be secured (see *Swedish Engine Drivers' Union*, cited above, pp. 14–15, §39; *Gustafsson*, cited above, pp. 652–53, §45; and *Schettini and Others* v. *Italy* (dec.), No. 29529/95, 9 November 2000).

45. The Court observes that there were other measures available to the applicant trade unions by which they could further their members' interests. In particular, domestic law conferred protection on a trade union which called for or supported strike action 'in contemplation or furtherance of a trade dispute'. The grant of the right to strike, while it may be subject to regulation, represents one of the most important of the means by which the State may secure a trade union's freedom to protect its members' occupational interests (see *Schmidt and Dahlström* v. *Sweden*, judgment of 6 February 1976, Series A No. 21, p. 16, §36 ...). Against this background, the Court does not consider that the absence, under United Kingdom law, of an obligation on employers to enter into collective bargaining gave rise, in itself, to a violation of Article 11 of the Convention.

46. The Court agrees with the Government that the essence of a voluntary system of collective bargaining is that it must be possible for a trade union which is not recognised by an employer to take steps including, if necessary, organising industrial action, with a view to persuading the

employer to enter into collective bargaining with it on those issues which the union believes are important for its members' interests. Furthermore, it is of the essence of the right to join a trade union for the protection of their interests that employees should be free to instruct or permit the union to make representations to their employer or to take action in support of their interests on their behalf. If workers are prevented from so doing, their freedom to belong to a trade union, for the protection of their interests, becomes illusory. It is the role of the State to ensure that trade union members are not prevented or restrained from using their union to represent them in attempts to regulate their relations with their employers.

47. In the present case, it was open to the employers to seek to pre-empt any protest on the part of the unions or their members against the imposition of limits on voluntary collective bargaining, by offering those employees who acquiesced in the termination of collective bargaining substantial pay rises, which were not provided to those who refused to sign contracts accepting the end of union representation. The corollary of this was that United Kingdom law permitted employers to treat less favourably employees who were not prepared to renounce a freedom that was an essential feature of union membership. Such conduct constituted a disincentive or restraint on the use by employees of union membership to protect their interests. However, as the House of Lords' judgment made clear, domestic law did not prohibit the employer from offering an inducement to employees who relinquished the right to union representation, even if the aim and outcome of the exercise was to bring an end to collective bargaining and thus substantially to reduce the authority of the union, as long as the employer did not act with the purpose of preventing or deterring the individual employee simply from being a member of a trade union.

48. Under United Kingdom law at the relevant time it was, therefore, possible for an employer effectively to undermine or frustrate a trade union's ability to strive for the protection of its members' interests. The Court notes that this aspect of domestic law has been the subject of criticism by the Social Charter's Committee of Independent Experts and the ILO's Committee on Freedom of Association ... It considers that, by permitting employers to use financial incentives to induce employees to surrender important union rights, the respondent State has failed in its positive obligation to secure the enjoyment of the rights under Article 11 of the Convention. This failure amounted to a violation of Article 11, as regards both the applicant trade unions and the individual applicants.

The more fundamental question which should be raised, and which argument (iv) in the typology presented earlier in this section obliges us to address, is whether there are situations in which the State is under an obligation to respect the autonomy of the individual right-holder, when he/she deliberately chooses not to be protected by the State and, instead, denounces such a protection as paternalistic (for a discussion of this issue, see O. De Schutter, 'Waiver of Rights and State Paternalism under the European Convention on Human Rights', *Northern Ireland Legal Quarterly*, 51, No. 3 (2000), 481–508). What makes this question a difficult one conceptually is that essentially the same argument (that the individual should be allowed not to be encumbered by the protection provided by the State) is invoked alternatively by the individual right-holder and by the State, depending on the circumstances. The individual right-holder may seek to invoke, against the paternalistic pretense of the State, a right to sacrifice her rights against an advantage to which she attaches greater value, for instance a well-paid employment. She may also consider that waiving her right is part of her individual freedom, that the State ought to respect: by seeking to restrict that freedom, she may add, the State is in fact imposing on all the members of society its own conception of the 'good life', in violation of the requirement of moral pluralism. This is, indeed, the core of the anti-paternalistic argument. As to the State, it may justify its failure to protect the enjoyment of a human right by the freedom exercised by the individual right-holder, and it may be tempted to invoke the existence of a right of the individual not to have imposed an unwanted paternalism as a reason for the public authorities to remain passive in the face of certain risks facing the invididual. Both these arguments invoke the idea that the individual should be free to make certain choices, even though they may not be in her best interests. But in the first situation, the individual right-holder will be denouncing the State for wanting to protect too much; in the second situation, the State will be seeking to justify why it has been protecting so little.

In order to see how these arguments relate to one another, we need to examine more carefully how the legal system can address this tension between the autonomy of the individual and the State's obligation to protect. Focusing on the role of waiver as a limit to the State obligation to protect, three positions can be envisaged. (a) A first possibility is that the State is under an obligation to respect the right of the individual not to be protected. This will be the case where a right to 'autonomy' or 'self-determination' is recognized, imposing an obstacle to the adoption by the State of certain measures of protection. (b) A second possibility is that the State is free to restrict the possibility for the individual to waive his rights: while there is no right to 'autonomy' or 'self-determination' as in the first case, nor is the State under an obligation to extend its protection to the individual who chooses, voluntarily, to sacrifice his right, or to accept certain limitations. (c) Finally, a third possibility is that the State has an obligation to protect the individual from waiving his rights. The State is then duty bound to prohibit the possibility of waiver, and to oppose any choice of the individual which would result in him sacrificing his rights. While the existence of an individual's right to 'autonomy' or 'self-determination' per necessity implies that the State will be prohibited from imposing its protection (since the individual would be allowed to invoke her 'autonomy' against what she would see as a form of paternalism), it does not follow from the absence of such a right to 'autonomy' that the State's obligation to protect must necessarily extend to situations where the individual makes the choice to sacrifice his right: this is only one possibility, the other being that the State may choose whether or not to provide such protection. This range of possibilities is presented in the table on the next page.

Unsurprisingly, where the appropriate solution should be located will depend on the specific circumstances of each case, under each human rights instrument concerned. International human rights law remains short of recognizing an individual's general right to sacrifice their human rights, as part of a free-standing 'right to autonomy' or to 'self-determination'. It may be said in this regard that human rights do not generally follow

Individual as right-holder	State as duty-bearer
(a1) The right-holder may choose to sacrifice his/her right, or to trade it off against other advantages: there is a right to 'autonomy' or to 'self-determination'	(a2) The State is prohibited from imposing on the right-holder a form of paternalism that the right-holder has a right to refuse: this restricts the extent of the State's obligation to protect
(b1) The right-holder has no right to 'autonomy' or to 'self-determination' to invoke against the State; nor does he/she have a right to be protected against his/her choice to waive his/her human rights	(b2) The State may choose to extend its protection to the right-holder, even where this implies opposing the right-holder's choice to waive his/her right; but the State is under no obligation to do so
(c1) The right-holder has a right to be protected by the State, also from the consequences of his/her choices, unless this imposes an unreasonable burden on the State	(c2) The State's obligation to protect extends to situations where individuals waive their rights, although such an obligation to protect should be understood reasonably

the model of the right to property, in that the recognition of an individual's human rights does not entail a correlative recognition of the right of the individual to sell, exchange, or sacrifice the rights they have been granted. On the other hand, certain forms of State paternalism, even when purportedly justified in the name of protecting the human rights of those on whom it is imposed, may constitute an unacceptable restriction to their individual freedom. The 2002 judgment of the European Court of Human Rights in the case of *Pretty* v. *United Kingdom*, presented below (see also chapter 1, section 3), provides a good illustration of the nature of the arguments exchanged at this level of the debate.

Human rights courts have been more explicit when examining claims by the State that the 'free choice' of the individual limits the scope of the obligation to protect imposed on the State. Such claims by the State can be made in one of the three situations distinguished above (although in a slightly different form). They have been generally treated with suspicion: although not dismissed as simply irrelevant – in that sense, human rights bodies do consider that the choices of the individual do matter, and that they may influence the scope of the State's obligation to protect – the conditions which the 'consent' of the individual to the sacrifice of his/her rights must satisfy in order to be taken into consideration have been gradually clarified, to ensure that, to the extent that such consent plays a role in defining the scope of the obligation to protect, it will not be abused. This is illustrated by the important judgment delivered on 13 November 2007 by the Grand Chamber of the European Court of Human Rights in the case of *D.H. and others* v. *Czech Republic* (see further below).

European Court of Human Rights (4th sect.), *Pretty* v. *United Kingdom* (Appl. no. 2346/02), judgment of 29 April 2002:

[The applicant is a 43-year-old woman suffering from motor neurone disease (MND), a progressive neuro-degenerative disease of motor cells within the central nervous system which is associated with progressive muscle weakness affecting the voluntary muscles of the body. No treatment is available. As a result of the progression of the disease, death usually occurs as a result of weakness of the breathing muscles, in association with weakness of the muscles controlling speaking and swallowing, leading to respiratory failure and pneumonia. The life expectancy of Ms Pretty, at the advanced stage of the disease, is very poor. However her intellect and capacity to make decisions are unimpaired. As she is frightened and distressed at the suffering and indignity that she will endure if the disease runs its course, she very strongly wishes to be able to control how and when she dies and thereby be spared that suffering and indignity. However, she is prevented by her disease from ending her life without assistance. It is, however, a crime to assist another to commit suicide (section 2(1) of the Suicide Act 1961). Contacted by her solicitor, the Director of Public Prosecutions (DPP) refused to give an undertaking not to prosecute the applicant's husband should he assist her to commit suicide in accordance with her wishes. Before the Court, the applicant alleges that this results in a violation of a number of rights under the Convention, including Article 2, which guarantees the right to life, Article 3, which prohibits the infliction of inhuman and degrading treatments and punishments, and Article 8, which protects the right to respect for private life.]

[The right to life (Art. 2 of the Convention)]

38. The text of Article 2 expressly regulates the deliberate or intended use of lethal force by State agents. It has been interpreted however as covering not only intentional killing but also the situations where it is permitted to 'use force' which may result, as an unintended outcome, in the deprivation of life (*McCann and others* v. *United Kingdom* [judgment of 27 September 1995, Series A No. 324], §148). The Court has further held that the first sentence of Article 2 §1 enjoins the State not only to refrain from the intentional and unlawful taking of life, but also to take appropriate steps to safeguard the lives of those within its jurisdiction (see the *L.C.B.* v. *United Kingdom* judgment of 9 June 1998, *Reports of Judgments and Decisions* 1998–III, p. 1403, §36). This obligation extends beyond a primary duty to secure the right to life by putting in place effective criminal-law provisions to deter the commission of offences against the person backed up by law-enforcement machinery for the prevention, suppression and sanctioning of breaches of such provisions; it may also imply in certain well-defined circumstances a positive obligation on the authorities to take preventive operational measures to protect an individual whose life is at risk from the criminal acts of another individual (*Osman* v. *United Kingdom* judgment of 28 October 1998, *Reports* 1998–VIII, §115; *Kılıç* v. *Turkey*, No. 22492/93, (Sect. 1) ECHR 2000–III, §§62 and 76). More recently, in the case of *Keenan* v. *United Kingdom*, Article 2 was found to apply to the situation of a mentally ill prisoner who disclosed signs of being a suicide risk (at §91).

39. The consistent emphasis in all the cases before the Court has been the obligation of the State to protect life. The Court is not persuaded that 'the right to life' guaranteed in Article 2 can be interpreted as involving a negative aspect. While, for example, in the context of Article 11 of the Convention, the freedom of association was found to involve not only a right to join an association but a corresponding right not to be forced to join an association, the Court observes that the notion of a freedom implies some measure of choice as to its exercise (see the *Young, James and Webster* v. *United Kingdom* judgment of 13 August 1981, Series A No. 44, §52, and *Sigurður A. Sigurjónsson* v. *Island* judgment of 30 June 1993, Series A No. 264, pp. 15–16, §35). Article 2 of the Convention is phrased in different terms. It is unconcerned with issues to do with the quality of living or what a person chooses to do with his or her life. To the extent that these aspects are recognised as so fundamental to the human condition that they require protection from State interference, they may be reflected in the rights guaranteed by other Articles of the Convention, or in other international human rights instruments. Article 2 cannot, without

a distortion of language, be interpreted as conferring the diametrically opposite right, namely a right to die; nor can it create a right to self-determination in the sense of conferring on an individual the entitlement to choose death rather than life.

40. The Court accordingly finds that no right to die, whether at the hands of a third person or with the assistance of a public authority, can be derived from Article 2 of the Convention. It is confirmed in this view by the recent Recommendation 1418 (1999) of the Parliamentary Assembly of the Council of Europe ...

41. The applicant has argued that a failure to acknowledge a right to die under the Convention would place those countries which do permit assisted suicide in breach of the Convention. It is not for the Court in this case to attempt to assess whether or not the state of law in any other country fails to protect the right to life. As it recognised in the case of *Keenan*, the measures which may reasonably be taken to protect a prisoner from self-harm will be subject to the restraints imposed by other provisions of the Convention, such as Articles 5 and 8 of the Convention, as well as more general principles of personal autonomy (see §91). Similarly, the extent to which a State permits, or seeks to regulate, the possibility for the infliction of harm on individuals at liberty, by their own or another's hand, may raise conflicting considerations of personal freedom and the public interest that can only be resolved on examination of the concrete circumstances of the case (see, *mutatis mutandis*, *Laskey, Jaggard and Brown* v. *United Kingdom* judgment of 19 February 1997, *Reports* 1997–I). However, even if circumstances prevailing in a particular country which permitted assisted suicide were found not to infringe Article 2 of the Convention, that would not assist the applicant in this case, where the very different proposition – that the United Kingdom would be in breach of its obligations under Article 2 if it did not allow assisted suicide – has not been established.

42. The Court finds that there has been no violation of Article 2 of the Convention.

[The right to respect for private life (Art. 8 of the Convention)]
61. As the Court has had previous occasion to remark, the concept of 'private life' is a broad term not susceptible to exhaustive definition. It covers the physical and psychological integrity of a person (*X. and Y.* v. *Netherlands* judgment of 26 March 1985, Series A No. 91, p. 11, §22). It can sometimes embrace aspects of an individual's physical and social identity (*Mikulić* v. *Croatia*, No. 53176/99 [Sect. 1], judgment of 7 February 2002, §53). Elements such as, for example, gender identification, name and sexual orientation and sexual life fall within the personal sphere protected by Article 8 (see e.g. the *B.* v. *France* judgment of 25 March 1992, Series A No. 232–C, §63; the *Burghartz* v. *Switzerland* judgment of 22 February 1994, Series A No. 280–B, §24; the *Dudgeon* v. *United Kingdom* judgment of 22 October 1991, Series A No. 45, §41, and the *Laskey, Jaggard and Brown* v. *United Kingdom* judgment of 19 February 1997, *Reports* 1997–1, §36). Article 8 also protects a right to personal development, and the right to establish and develop relationships with other human beings and the outside world (see, for example, *Burghartz* v. *Switzerland*, Commission's report, *op. cit.*, §47; *Friedl* v. *Austria*, Series A No. 305–B, Commission's report, §45). Though no previous case has established as such any right to self-determination as being contained in Article 8 of the Convention, the Court considers that the notion of personal autonomy is an important principle underlying the interpretation of its guarantees.

62. The Government have argued that the right to private life cannot encapsulate a right to die with assistance, such being a negation of the protection that the Convention was intended to provide. The Court would observe that the ability to conduct one's life in a manner of one's own choosing may also include the opportunity to pursue activities perceived to be of a physically

or morally harmful or dangerous nature for the individual concerned. The extent to which a State can use compulsory powers or the criminal law to protect people from the consequences of their chosen lifestyle has long been a topic of moral and jurisprudential discussion, the fact that the interference is often viewed as trespassing on the private and personal sphere adding to the vigour of the debate. However, even where the conduct poses a danger to health, or arguably, where it is of a life-threatening nature, the case law of the Convention institutions has regarded the State's imposition of compulsory or criminal measures as impinging on the private life of the applicant within the scope of Article 8 §1 and requiring justification in terms of the second paragraph (see, for example, concerning involvement in consensual sado-masochistic activities which amounted to assault and wounding, the above-cited *Laskey, Jaggard and Brown* judgment and concerning refusal of medical treatment, No. 10435/83, Commission decision of 10 December 1984, DR 40, p. 251).

63. While it might be pointed out that death was not the intended consequence of the applicants' conduct in the above situations, the Court does not consider that this can be a decisive factor. In the sphere of medical treatment, the refusal to accept a particular treatment might, inevitably, lead to a fatal outcome, yet the imposition of medical treatment, without the consent of a mentally competent adult patient, would interfere with a person's physical integrity in a manner capable of engaging the rights protected under Article 8 §1 of the Convention. As recognised in domestic case law, a person may claim to exercise a choice to die by declining to consent to treatment which might have the effect of prolonging his life ...

64. In the present case, though medical treatment is not an issue, the applicant is suffering from the devastating effects of a degenerative disease which will cause her condition to deteriorate further and increase her physical and mental suffering. She wishes to mitigate that suffering by exercising a choice to end her life with the assistance of her husband. As stated by Lord Hope, the way she chooses to pass the closing moments of her life is part of the act of living, and she has a right to ask that this too must be respected ...

65. The very essence of the Convention is respect for human dignity and human freedom. Without in any way negating the principle of sanctity of life protected under the Convention, the Court considers that it is under Article 8 that notions of the quality of life take on significance. In an era of growing medical sophistication combined with longer life expectancies, many people are concerned that they should not be forced to linger on in old age or in states of advanced physical or mental decrepitude which conflict with strongly held ideas of self and personal identity ...

67. The applicant in this case is prevented by law from exercising her choice to avoid what she considers will be an undignified and distressing end to her life. The Court is not prepared to exclude that this constitutes an interference with her right to respect for private life as guaranteed under Article 8 §1 of the Convention. It considers below whether this interference conforms with the requirements of the second paragraph of Article 8.

2. Compliance with Article 8 §2 of the Convention

68. An interference with the exercise of an Article 8 right will not be compatible with Article 8 §2 unless it is 'in accordance with the law', has an aim or aims that is or are legitimate under that paragraph and is 'necessary in a democratic society' for the aforesaid aim or aims (see the *Dudgeon* v. *United Kingdom* judgment of 22 October 1981, Series A No. 45, p. 19, §43).

69. The only issue arising from the arguments of the parties is the necessity of any interference, it being common ground that the restriction on assisted suicide in this case was

imposed by law and in pursuit of the legitimate aim of safeguarding life and thereby protecting the rights of others.

70 According to the Court's established case law, the notion of necessity implies that the interference corresponds to a pressing social need and, in particular, that it is proportionate to the legitimate aim pursued; in determining whether an interference is 'necessary in a democratic society', the Court will take into account that a margin of appreciation is left to the national authorities, whose decision remains subject to review by the Court for conformity with the requirements of the Convention. The margin of appreciation to be accorded to the competent national authorities will vary in accordance with the nature of the issues and the importance of the interests at stake.

71. The Court recalls that the margin of appreciation has been found to be narrow as regards interferences in the intimate area of an individual's sexual life (see *Dudgeon* v. *United Kingdom*, *op. cit.*, p. 21, §52; *A.D.T.* v. *United Kingdom* No. 35765/97 (Sect. 3) ECHR 2000–IX, §37). Though the applicant has argued that there must therefore be particularly compelling reasons for the interference in her case, the Court does not find that the matter under consideration in this case can be regarded as of the same nature, or as attracting the same reasoning.

72. The parties' arguments have focussed on the proportionality of the interference as disclosed in the applicant's case. The applicant attacked in particular the blanket nature of the ban on assisted suicide as failing to take into account her situation as a mentally competent adult who knows her own mind, who is free from pressure and who has made a fully informed and voluntary decision, and therefore cannot be regarded as vulnerable and requiring protection. This inflexibility means, in her submission, that she will be compelled to endure the consequences of her incurable and distressing illness, at a very high personal cost.

73. The Court would note that although the Government argued that the applicant, as a person who is both contemplating suicide and severely disabled, must be regarded as vulnerable, this assertion is not supported by the evidence before the domestic courts or by the judgments of the House of Lords which, while emphasising that the law in the United Kingdom was there to protect the vulnerable, did not find that the applicant was in that category.

74. Nonetheless, the Court finds, in agreement with the House of Lords and the majority of the Canadian Supreme Court in the *Rodriguez* case, that States are entitled to regulate through the operation of the general criminal law activities which are detrimental to the life and safety of other individuals (see also the above-mentioned *Laskey, Jaggard and Brown* case, §43). The more serious the harm involved the more heavily will weigh in the balance considerations of public health and safety against the countervailing principle of personal autonomy. The law in issue in this case, section 2 of the 1961 Act, was designed to safeguard life by protecting the weak and vulnerable and especially those who are not in a condition to take informed decisions against acts intended to end life or to assist in ending life. Doubtless the condition of terminally ill individuals will vary. But many will be vulnerable and it is the vulnerability of the class which provides the rationale for the law in question. It is primarily for States to assess the risk and the likely incidence of abuse if the general prohibition on assisted suicides were relaxed or if exceptions were to be created. Clear risks of abuse do exist, notwithstanding arguments as to the possibility of safeguards and protective procedures.

75. The applicant's counsel attempted to persuade the Court that a finding in this case would not create a general precedent or any risk to others. It is true that it is not this Court's role under Article 34 of the Convention to issue opinions in the abstract but to apply the Convention to the

concrete facts of the individual case. However, judgments issued in individual cases establish precedents albeit to a greater or lesser extent and a decision in this case could not, either in theory or practice, be framed in such a way as to prevent application in later cases.

76. The Court does not consider therefore that the blanket nature of the ban on assisted suicide is disproportionate. The Government have stated that flexibility is provided for in individual cases by the fact that consent is needed from the DPP to bring a prosecution and by the fact that a maximum sentence is provided, allowing lesser penalties to be imposed as appropriate. The Select Committee report indicated that between 1981 and 1992 in 22 cases in which 'mercy killing' was an issue, there was only one conviction for murder, with a sentence for life imprisonment, while lesser offences were substituted in the others and most resulted in probation or suspended sentences ... It does not appear to be arbitrary to the Court for the law to reflect the importance of the right to life, by prohibiting assisted suicide while providing for a system of enforcement and adjudication which allows due regard to be given in each particular case to the public interest in bringing a prosecution, as well as to the fair and proper requirements of retribution and deterrence.

77. Nor in the circumstances is there anything disproportionate in the refusal of the DPP to give an advance undertaking that no prosecution would be brought against the applicant's husband. Strong arguments based on the rule of law could be raised against any claim by the executive to exempt individuals or classes of individuals from the operation of the law. In any event, the seriousness of the act for which immunity was claimed was such that the decision of the DPP to refuse the undertaking sought in the present case cannot be said to be arbitrary or unreasonable.

78. The Court concludes that the interference in this case may be justified as 'necessary in a democratic society' for the protection of the rights of others and, accordingly, that there has been no violation of Article 8 of the Convention.

European Court of Human Rights (GC), *D.H. and others* v. *Czech Republic* (Appl. No. 57325/00), judgment of 13 November 2007:

[The applicants are eighteen Czech nationals of Roma origin who were placed in special schools (*zvláštní školy*) for children with learning difficulties considered unable to follow the ordinary school curriculum. Such placements required, *inter alia*, the consent of the child's legal representative. The following excerpts deal with the issue of parental consent. For a fuller treatment of the case, see chapter 7, section 3.1.]

202. As regards parental consent, the Court notes the Government's submission that this was the decisive factor without which the applicants would not have been placed in special schools. In view of the fact that a difference in treatment has been established in the instant case, it follows that any such consent would signify an acceptance of the difference in treatment, even if discriminatory, in other words a waiver of the right not to be discriminated against. However, under the Court's case law, the waiver of a right guaranteed by the Convention – in so far as such a waiver is permissible – must be established in an unequivocal manner, and be given in full knowledge of the facts, that is to say on the basis of informed consent (*Pfeifer and Plankl* v. *Austria*, judgment of 25 February 1992, Series A No. 227, §§37–38) and without constraint (*Deweer* v. *Belgium*, judgment of 27 February 1980, Series A No. 35, §51).

203. In the circumstances of the present case, the Court is not satisfied that the parents of the Roma children, who were members of a disadvantaged community and often poorly educated, were capable of weighing up all the aspects of the situation and the consequences of giving their consent. The Government themselves admitted that consent in this instance had been given by means of a signature on a pre-completed form that contained no information on the available alternatives or the differences between the special-school curriculum and the curriculum followed in other schools. Nor do the domestic authorities appear to have taken any additional measures to ensure that the Roma parents received all the information they needed to make an informed decision or were aware of the consequences that giving their consent would have for their children's futures. It also appears indisputable that the Roma parents were faced with a dilemma: a choice between ordinary schools that were ill-equipped to cater for their children's social and cultural differences and in which their children risked isolation and ostracism and special schools where the majority of the pupils were Roma.

204. In view of the fundamental importance of the prohibition of racial discrimination (see *Nachova and others* [v. *Bulgaria*, judgment of 16 July 2005], §145; and *Timishev* v. *Russia*, Nos. 55762/00 and 55974/00, §56), the Grand Chamber considers that ... no waiver of the right not to be subjected to racial discrimination can be accepted, as it would be counter to an important public interest (see, *mutatis mutandis, Hermi* v. *Italy* [GC], No. 18114/02, §73).

The position of the Court in *D.H. and others v. Czech Republic* concerning the question of waiver appears to have been heavily influenced by the amicus brief submitted to the Court by the International Federation for Human Rights (FIDH), following the leave to intervene granted by the President of the Court. Referring to *Wilson, National Union of Journalists and others v. United Kingdom,* the brief emphasized that 'the freedom left to the individual to waive a right recognized by the Convention may result, for all the individuals confronted to the same choice, in a specific vulnerability, such that the possibility of waiver should not exonerate the State from the obligations imposed by the Convention'. The FIDH noted:

International Federation for Human Rights, Observations submitted to the European Court of Human Rights in the case of *D.H. and others* v. *Czech Republic* (Appl. No. 57325/00), in accordance with Article 44 para. 2 of the Rules of the Court (12 October 2006) [unofficial translation from the French original]:

In a situation such as that presented to the Court in *Wilson, National Union of Journalists and others* v. *United Kingdom*, it is *the freedom left to workers to negotiate individual employment contracts*, including restrictions to the freedom of association rights consented to against benefits not extended to unionized workers, that led the Court to a finding of violation of Article 11 of the Convention. Thus, it is the fact that non-unionized workers waived their freedom of association rights that resulted in a vulnerability for all the workers employed in the same undertaking. The waiver by one worker of his/her freedom of association [thus affects] all the workers, by the incentives it creates and the resulting pressure exercised on these workers ... In *D.H. and others v. Czech Republic*, the 'freedom' of the parents of the applicants to choose whether or not to place their children in special schools or to require that they have access to the general educational system, creates a situation in which the choice of each parent depends on the choices made by all the other parents similarly situated: it is perfectly possible ... that all the parents of Roma children prefer an integrated form of education for their children, but that, given their uncertainty about the choice of the other parents in this same situation, they still prefer the 'security' of special educational establishments, which the Roma parents choose by a large majority, to the risk of placing their child in the general educational system, in which he/she could be isolated and harassed.

[The FIDH therefore urged the Court to take into account the context in which the parents of Roma children were asked to consent to their child being placed in special schools. That context, they recalled, is one of historically perpetuated segregation.] In this circumstance, the choice of the parents of Roma children cannot be analyzed as a choice between integrated education or the placement of children in special schools: the choice is, rather, between (a) placing children in schools where [the children will be treated with hostility and risk being harassed] and (b) placing children in special schools where the Roma children form an overwhelming majority, and where they therefore will not be subject to the same kind of prejudice. It would therefore be incorrect to state that the parents of the applicants have opted for the special educational system, rather than for an integrated system: in reality, they have chosen the lesser of two evils, in the absence of a real possibility to benefit from a truly integrated educational system, in which Roma children would be truly welcome, and in which their specific needs would be taken into account.

[The FIDH referred in this respect to the case of *Green et al.* v. *County School Board of New Kent County et al.*, 391 U.S. 430 (1968). In *Green*, the US Supreme Court found the Equality Clause of the Fourteenth Amendment to the United States Constitution to be violated in a situation where a 'freedom-of-choice' plan adopted to implement the desegregation prescribed by *Brown* v. *Board of Education of Topeka*, 347 U.S. 483 (1954) failed to produce a truly integrated system, because the choices of parents under this plan were tainted by the legacy of racial segregation. They cited P. Gewirtz, 'Choice in Transition: School Desegregation and the Corrective Ideal', *Columbia Law Review*, 86 (1986), 728 at 749, who provided the following explanation: 'because choices are interdependent, ignorance about the simultaneous choices of others is likely to lead both blacks and whites to choose to remain in their separate schools. If ... most blacks will be reluctant to attend a previously white school unless they are convinced that a significant number of other blacks will also attend, and if most whites will be reluctant to attend a previously black school absent other whites, uncertain information is not outcome-neutral. Rather, we can predict a "replication of the status quo" – a segregated pattern.']

Another remarkable aspect of *D.H. and others* is its reference to the 1980 judgment adopted by the European Court of Human Rights in the *Deweer* case. Indeed, this judgment acknowledged with a particular clarity the dangers associated with presenting an individual with an alternative, where the benefits associated with one branch so clearly outweigh the benefits associated with the other that the 'freedom to choose' of the right-holder becomes purely formal, and even fictitious. The *Deweer* case also illustrates what might be referred to as an equivalent to the 'unconstitutional conditions' doctrine in international human rights law (for recent important contributions on this issue in US constitutional law, see in particular R. A. Epstein, 'Foreword – Unconstitutional

Conditions, State Power, and the Limits of Consent', *Harvard Law Review*, 102 (1989), 4; K. M. Sullivan, 'Unconstitutional Conditions', *Harvard Law Review*, 102 (1989), 1413; C. R. Sunstein, 'Why the Unconstitutional Conditions Doctrine is an Anachronism (with Particular Reference to Religion, Speech, and Abortion)', *Boston University Law Review*, 70 (1990), 593; for earlier but influential contributions, see M. Merrill, 'Unconstitutional Conditions', *University of Pennsylvania Law Review*, 77 (1929), 879; R. L. Hale, 'Unconstitutional Conditions and Constitutional Rights', *Columbia Law Review*, 35 (1935), 321). Even when the State makes offers which individuals are free to accept or to refuse, or provides advantages which could be altogether denied, the State is bound to comply with the requirements of human rights: it may therefore not make the acceptance of such offer or the enjoyment of such advantages conditional upon sacrificing certain human rights. In the jurisprudence of the Human Rights Committee, the cases of *Waldman* and *Gauthier* illustrate this. These cases are presented in chapter 7 concerning discrimination (sections 1.1. (*Waldman*), and 2.1. (*Gauthier*)). In the case law of the European Court of Human Rights, cases concerning employment in the public sector (such as *Dahlab*, presented above in chapter 3, section 3.5.) also provide an illustration of this position. The *Deweer* case also is an instructive example:

European Court of Human Rights, *Deweer* v. *Belgium* (Appl. No. 6903/75), judgment of 27 February 1980:

[The applicant is a retail butcher in Louvain. On 18 September 1974, his shop was the subject of a visit by an official in the Economic Inspectorate General. This official found an infringement of the Ministerial Decree of 9 August 1974 'fixing the selling price to the consumer of beef and pig meat'. In addition to imprisonment of one month to five years and a fine of 3,000 to 30,000,000 BF (section 9 para. 1), offenders were liable under this legislation to various criminal and administrative sanctions (sections 2 par. 5, 3, 7, 9 par. 2–6, 10, 11 and 11 *bis*), including the closure of the offender's business. On 30 September, citing the gravity of the facts, the Louvain procureur du Roi (Attorney General) ordered the provisional closure of the applicant's shop within forty-eight hours from notification of the decision. The closure was to come to an end either on the day after the payment of a sum of 10,000 BF by way of friendly settlement or, at the latest, on the date on which judgment was passed on the offence; Mr Deweer had eight days in which to indicate whether he accepted the offer of settlement. While agreeing to the friendly settlement proposed, Mr Deweer wrote to the procureur du Roi: 'I reserve all my rights to take action against the Belgian State before the civil courts, in particular for the restitution of this sum plus damages … I have therefore paid the amount of the friendly settlement for the sole purpose of limiting the damage suffered by me; for the prejudice resulting from the closure of my establishment as from today until the eventual hearing of the case before the criminal court might be far in excess of 10,000 BF and the civil court might then draw certain conclusions from the fact I had not mitigated my loss.' However, following the payment of the sum of 10,000 BF, Mr Deweer did not bring any action before the civil courts for restitution of money paid over without cause and for damages; nor did he apply to the Conseil d'État for a declaration of annulment of the Decree of 9 August 1974. As a result of the payment, no criminal proceedings were brought against Mr Deweer, since payment of the fine by way of settlement had barred any such proceedings.

Mr Deweer claims to be the victim of 'the imposition of a fine paid by way of settlement under constraint of provisional closure of his establishment'. The claim is based on Article 6 par. 1 of the Convention, which states that 'In the determination of his civil rights and obligations or of any criminal charge against him, everyone is entitled to a fair and public hearing within a reasonable time by an independent and impartial tribunal established by law.']

48. Under Article 6 par. 1, Mr Deweer had the right to a fair trial (see the *Golder* judgment of 21 February 1975, Series A No. 18, p. 18, par. 36) before 'an independent and impartial tribunal established by law', incorporating a 'hearing' followed by 'determination of [the] criminal charge against him' ... Before the trial court, the applicant would therefore have been entitled not only to rely ... on his good faith or the additional costs incurred by a butcher buying on the hoof ... but also to plead that the Decree of 9 August 1974 was contrary to the Constitution or incompatible with Community law ... Mr Deweer would in addition have enjoyed the benefit of the guarantees in paragraphs 2 and 3 of Article 6.

49. ... By paying the 10,000 BF which the Louvain procureur du Roi 'required' by way of settlement ..., Mr Deweer waived his right to have his case dealt with by a tribunal.

In the Contracting States' domestic legal systems a waiver of this kind is frequently encountered both in civil matters, notably in the shape of arbitration clauses in contracts, and in criminal matters in the shape, *inter alia*, of fines paid by way of composition. The waiver, which has undeniable advantages for the individual concerned as well as for the administration of justice, does not in principle offend against the Convention ...

Nevertheless, in a democratic society too great an importance attaches to the 'right to a court' ... for its benefit to be forfeited solely by reason of the fact that an individual is a party to a settlement reached in the course of a procedure ancillary to court proceedings. In an area concerning the public order (ordre public) of the member States of the Council of Europe, any measure or decision alleged to be in breach of Article 6 calls for particularly careful review ... Absence of constraint is at all events one of the conditions to be satisfied; this much is dictated by an international instrument founded on freedom and the rule of law (see the above-mentioned *Golder* judgment, pp. 16–17, par. 34) ...

50. ... the Commission expressed the opinion that there was constraint in the present case: it considered that the applicant waived the guarantees of Article 6 par. 1 only 'under the threat of [the] serious prejudice' that the closure of his shop would have caused him.

51. (a) The Government's first submission was as follows: the offer of settlement made to Mr Deweer on 30 September 1974 amounted in law to no more than a 'proposal for a friendly settlement' which he could quite well have rejected; 'in accepting the offer and acting upon it on 2 October', the applicant, 'by paying a relatively modest sum, succeeded in avoiding the risk of receiving a sentence which might have been more severe than this fine paid by way of settlement' and 'which might, if appropriate, have been accompanied by a court order for the closure of the establishment' ...

Furthermore, the Government maintained, the Commission's reasoning is inconsistent. Whereas the procedure followed in the circumstances is stated at paragraph 57 of the report to be in breach of the Convention for the reason that it was tainted with constraint, paragraphs 55 and 59 contain the recognition that settlement of criminal cases is legitimate. In a sense, so the argument continued, that kind of settlement 'always takes place under some form of "constraint" and under the "threat" of more or less "serious" prejudice'; thus, criminal proceedings represent, 'for the majority of those' against whom they are taken 'or likely to be taken, something to be feared' and, in very many instances, 'a sufficiently serious "threat" to encourage [them] ... to forgo' the trial of their case by a court of law.

(b) The Court points out that while the prospect of having to appear in court is certainly liable to prompt a willingness to compromise on the part of many persons 'charged with a criminal offence', the pressure thereby brought to bear is in no way incompatible with the Convention: provided that the requirements of Articles 6 and 7 are observed, the Convention in principle leaves the Contracting States free to designate and prosecute as a criminal offence conduct not constituting the normal exercise of one of the rights it protects ...

Moreover, the applicant was probably scarcely apprehensive about criminal prosecution since it was not unlikely that prosecution would result in an acquittal ... The 'constraint' complained of by the applicant was to be found in another quarter, namely in the closure order of 30 September 1974.

This order was due to come into effect forty-eight hours after notification of the decision of the procureur du Roi and it could have remained in force until the date on which the competent court passed judgment on the offence ... In the meantime, that is possibly during a period of months, the applicant would have been deprived of the income accruing from his trade; he would nonetheless have incurred the risk of having to continue to pay his staff and of not being able to resume business with all his former customers once his shop reopened ... Mr Deweer would have suffered considerable loss as a consequence.

The Louvain procureur du Roi did admittedly offer Mr Deweer a means of avoiding the danger, namely by paying 10,000 BF in 'friendly settlement' ... This solution certainly represented by far a lesser evil. As the Government rightly pointed out, the sum in question was only slightly above the minimum amount – 3,000 BF – of 'the fine laid down by law', whereas under section 11 par. 1 of the 1945/1971 Act it could have been more than the maximum, namely 30,000,000 BF ... Accordingly, as the Delegates observed, there was a 'flagrant disproportion' between the two alternatives facing the applicant. The 'relative moderation' of the sum demanded in fact tells against the Government's argument since it added to the pressure brought to bear by the closure order. The moderation rendered the pressure so compelling that it is not surprising that Mr Deweer yielded ...

53. The Government finally stressed that 'the Commission admitted' that 'the outright closure' of the shop would have been reconcilable with the Convention, even though 'so radical a solution would certainly have cost the applicant more than 10,000 [Belgian] francs'. From this premise, they described the logic of the reasoning followed in the report as 'curious', submitting that, 'still according to the Commission', the breach of Article 6 stemmed in substance from a 'favour' granted to Mr Deweer, namely the offer of a settlement whereby the procureur du Roi was to adopt a solution milder, more flexible and less burdensome than closure. In this way, claimed the Government, an 'absurd conclusion' was reached.

The Court recalls that it is limiting its examination to the combined use of the two procedures ...; it has no intention of ruling whether a closure order unaccompanied by any offer of settlement would have been compatible with the Convention.

... Besides, in the area of human rights he who can do more cannot necessarily do less. The Convention permits under certain conditions some very serious forms of treatment, such as the death penalty (Article 2 par. 1, second sentence), whilst at the same time prohibiting others which by comparison can be regarded as rather mild, for example 'unlawful' detention for a brief period (Article 5 par. 1) or the expulsion of a national (Article 3 par. 1 of Protocol No. 4). The fact that it is possible to inflict on a person one of the first-mentioned forms of treatment cannot authorise his being subjected to one of the second-mentioned, even if he agrees or acquiesces ...

54. To sum up, Mr Deweer's waiver of a fair trial attended by all the guarantees which are required in the matter by the Convention was tainted by constraint. There has accordingly been breach of Article 6 par. 1 ...

2.5 Respect for conflicting human rights as a limit to the scope of the obligation to protect

In discharging its duty to protect human rights, the State will frequently be led to impose restrictions to other, conflicting human rights (in the specific context of the obligation to protect from discrimination, see also chapter 7, section 2.3.). However, despite a renewed interest in legal theory for the issue of conflicting rights, there is no agreed upon methodology as to how such conflicts should be solved (for important recent contributions on this issue, see R. Alexy, 'Balancing Constitutional Review and Representation', *International Journal of Constitutional Law* (2005), 572–81; R. Alexy, *A Theory of Constitutional Rights* (Oxford University Press, 2002), pp. 47–8; S. Greer, 'Balancing and the European Court of Human Rights: a Contribution to the Habermas-Alexy Debate', *Cambridge Law Journal*, 63(2) (2004), 412–24; for examinations of the practice of courts, see L. Zucca, *Constitutional Dilemmas: Conflicts of Fundamental Legal Rights in Europe and the USA* (Oxford University Press, 2007), and the essays collected in E. Brems (ed.), *Conflicts Between Fundamental Rights* (Antwerp-Oxford-Portland: Intersentia-Hart, 2008)). As we have seen, 'balancing' is questionable as a metaphor, and it is too vague if it is to serve as a methodology in the context of adjudication (see box 3.2., chapter 3). The main alternative options seem to be (a) to affirm a priority of the State's obligation to respect over its obligation to protect, so that the scope of the obligation to protect would be limited by the State's obligation not to impose disproportionate interferences with other human rights; (b) to recognize a broad margin of appreciation to national and non-judicial (i.e. executive and legislative) authorities in addressing situations of conflicting rights, leading to a 'hands-off' attitude of the courts in such situations, particularly if they are international courts; and (c) to develop judicial techniques that can solve conflicts between rights, beyond the vague, and largely empty, reference to the need to 'balance' the rights against one another. This section offers a brief overview of the issues raised under each of these different options.

(a) Affirming the priority of the obligation to respect over the obligation to protect
A first approach is to consider that the obligation to protect should also be secondary to the obligation to respect, the implication being that the conflict should always be settled in favour of a minimum degree of State intervention in inter-individual relationships. As we have seen, the *Osman* judgment, for instance, limits the scope of the positive obligations imposed on the States parties to the European Convention

on Human Rights to the adoption of measures which do not result in disproportionate restrictions being imposed on other protected rights (see para. 116 of the judgment). The tendency to prioritize the obligation to respect over the obligation to protect has been questioned recently in the following terms, in the context of the adoption of counter-terrorism measures:

Stefan Sottiaux, *Terrorism and the Limitations of Rights. The European Convention on Human Rights and the United States Constitution* (Oxford: Hart Publishing, 2008), pp. 8–9:

It would be difficult to maintain that the state's positive obligation to protect the rights of its citizens is less important than its negative obligation to respect those rights. The former duty is as firmly grounded in human rights law as the latter: both stem from the same fundamental legal guarantees. To attach more weight to the state's negative obligation to respect than to its positive obligation to protect would boil down to introducing a hierarchy between the rights occurring on the different sides of the balance, and there is no place in modern human rights law for such a hierarchy. The conflict between liberty and security in the context of terrorism is one between two equally significant human rights values, one of which cannot take precedence over the other. As Richard Posner recently noted, 'One is not to ask whether liberty is more or less important than safety. One is to ask whether a particular security measures harms liberty more or less than it promotes safety' [R. A. Posner, *Not a Suicide Pact. The Constitution in a Time of National Emergency*, Oxford University Press, Oxford, 2006, at pp. 31–32].

(b) Deferring to the evaluation of other authorities

Another tendency of courts in conflicting rights situations has been procedural in nature. Conflicting rights situations are, almost by definition, highly controversial. It is therefore not surprising if human rights courts – particularly international courts – have generally tended to adopt a relatively 'hands-off' approach, deferring to the appreciation made by other branches of government or by the national authorities as to how such situations should be solved. This has been explicit in particular in the jurisprudence of the European Court of Human Rights. The Court suggested in *Chassagnou and others* v. *France* that it would as a matter of principle allow a wide margin of appreciation to be enjoyed by States in situations of conflicting rights (Eur. Ct. H.R. (GC), *Chassagnou and others* v. *France*, judgment of 29 April 1999, §113). In addition, States parties to the European Convention on Human Rights are generally considered to enjoy a broader margin of appreciation where their positive obligations are concerned – since they are to choose the means which achieve the result prescribed by the Convention – than in the area of negative obligations; and cases implying the imposition of positive obligations, i.e. requiring that States intervene in relationships between private parties, are typically cases in which situations of conflicts of rights occur. Finally, the margin of appreciation will be particularly wide in areas where, in the absence of a uniform European conception of the implications of the Convention, the solutions adopted at national level are widely divergent. This has guided the attitude of the Court, for instance, where the protection of the rights of others in relation to attacks on the religious convictions of a segment of the population lead to restrictions being imposed on freedom of expression (Eur. Ct. H.R., *Otto-Preminger-Institut v. Austria*, judgment of 20 September 1994, §49, and Eur. Ct. H.R., *Murphy* v. *Ireland*, judgment of 10 July 2003, §67; Eur. Ct. H.R., *Wingrove* v. *United Kingdom*, judgment of 25 November 1996, §53); or where different aspects of freedom of association conflict with one another (see, e.g. Eur. Ct. H.R., *Gustafsson* v. *Sweden*, judgment of 25 April 1996, §45). All three rationales explaining the reliance on the doctrine of the 'national margin of appreciation' were present in *Odièvre* v. *France*, where the Court was confronted with a conflict between the child's right to know its origins and the mother's interest in keeping her identity secret:

European Court of Human Rights (GC), *Odièvre* v. *France* (Appl. No. 42326/98), judgment of 13 February 2003:

Ms Odièvre was born in 1965 to a mother who requested that the birth be kept secret in a form she completed at the Health and Social Security Department when abandoning her. She was subsequently placed with the Child Welfare Service at the Health and Social Services Department (*Direction de l'action sanitaire et sociale* – the DASS). A full adoption order was made on 10 January 1969 in favour of Mr and Mrs Odièvre. On 27 January 1998 the applicant applied to the Paris *tribunal de grande instance* for an order for the 'release of information about her birth and permission to obtain copies of any documents, birth, death and marriage certificates, civil-status documents and full copies of long-form birth certificates'. She was told that she should address herself to the administrative courts and that, in any case, the application would be denied, since the French Law of 8 January 1993, which confirmed the system of anonymous births which had been traditional in the French legal system also introduced new provisions concerning the secret abandonment of children, and stipulated for the first time that choosing to give birth in secret had an effect on the determination of filiation, as Articles 341 and 341–1 of the Civil Code created an estoppel defence to proceedings to establish maternity: where a child had been secretly abandoned, there was no mother in the legal sense of the word. Following a number of reports about problems emerging from the 1993 legislation, however, the Law of 22 January 2002 was adopted. Without calling into question the right to give birth anonymously, this law allows arrangements to be made for disclosure of identity subject to the mother's and the child's express consent being obtained. And it abolishes the parents' right to request confidentiality under Article L. 224–5 of the Social Action and Families Code. The 2002 Law provides for the establishment of a National Council for Access to Information about Personal Origins entrusted with facilitating access to information about personal origins. The Council shall acceed to the request of the child or his representatives to be informed about the identity of his/her natural mother (a) if it already has in its possession an express declaration waiving confidentiality in respect of the mother's identity; (b) if the mother's wishes have been verified and she has not expressly stated that she wishes to keep her identity secret; (c) if one of its members or a person appointed by it has been able to obtain the mother's express consent without interfering with her private life; (d) if the mother has died, provided that she has not expressed a contrary intent following a request for access to information about the child's origins. In such cases, one of the members of the Council or a person appointed by it shall advise the mother's family and offer it assistance.]

41. The applicant complained that France had failed to ensure respect for her private life by its legal system, which totally precluded an action to establish maternity being brought if the natural mother had requested confidentiality and, above all, prohibited the Child Welfare Service or any other body that could give access to such information from communicating identifying data on the mother.

42. In the Court's opinion, people 'have a vital interest, protected by the Convention, in receiving the information necessary to know and to understand their childhood and early development'. With regard to an application by Mr Gaskin for access to the case records held on him by the social services – he was suffering from psychological trauma as a result of ill-treatment to which he said he had been subjected when in State care – the Court stated: '... confidentiality of public records is of importance for receiving objective and reliable information, and ... such confidentiality can also be necessary for the protection of third persons. Under the latter aspect, a system like the British one, which makes access to records dependent on the consent of the contributor, can in principle be considered to be compatible with the obligations under Article 8, taking into account the State's margin of appreciation. The Court considers, however, that under such a system the interests of the individual seeking access to records relating to his private and family life must be secured when a contributor to the records either is not available or improperly refuses consent. Such a system is only in conformity with the principle of proportionality if it provides that an independent authority finally decides whether access has to be granted in cases where a contributor fails to answer or withholds consent.' (*Gaskin*, judgment of 7 July 1989, Series A No. 160, p. 20, §49; see also *M.G.* v. *United Kingdom*, No. 39393/98, §27, 24 September 2002)

In [*Mikulić* v. *Croatia*, judgment of 7 February 2002, Appl. No. 53176/99] the applicant, a 5-year-old girl, complained of the length of a paternity suit which she had brought with her mother and the lack of procedural means available under Croatian law to enable the courts to compel the alleged father to comply with a court order for DNA tests to be carried out. The Court weighed the vital interest of a person in receiving the information necessary to uncover the truth about an important aspect of his or her personal identity against the interest of third parties in refusing to be compelled to make themselves available for medical testing. It found that the State had a duty to establish alternative means to enable an independent authority to determine the paternity claim speedily. It held that there had been a breach of the proportionality principle as regards the interests of the applicant, who had been left in a state of prolonged uncertainty as to her personal identity (§§64–66).

43. The Court observes that Mr Gaskin and Miss Mikulić were in a different situation to the applicant. The issue of access to information about one's origins and the identity of one's natural parents is not of the same nature as that of access to a case record concerning a child in care or to evidence of alleged paternity. The applicant in the present case is an adopted child who is trying to trace another person, her natural mother, by whom she was abandoned at birth and who has expressly requested that information about the birth remain confidential.

44. The expression 'everyone' in Article 8 of the Convention applies to both the child and the mother. On the one hand, people have a right to know their origins, that right being derived from a wide interpretation of the scope of the notion of private life. The child's vital interest in its

personal development is also widely recognised in the general scheme of the Convention (see, among many other authorities, *Johansen* v. *Norway*, judgment of 7 August 1996, *Reports* 1996–III, p. 1008, §78; *Mikulić*, No. 53176/99, §64; and *Kutzner* v. *Germany*, No. 46544/99, §66, ECHR 2002–I). On the other hand, a woman's interest in remaining anonymous in order to protect her health by giving birth in appropriate medical conditions cannot be denied. In the present case, the applicant's mother never went to see the baby at the clinic and appears to have greeted their separation with total indifference ... Nor is it alleged that she subsequently expressed the least desire to meet her daughter. The Court's task is not to judge that conduct, but merely to take note of it. The two private interests with which the Court is confronted in the present case are not easily reconciled; moreover, they do not concern an adult and a child, but two adults, each endowed with her own free will.

In addition to that conflict of interest, the problem of anonymous births cannot be dealt with in isolation from the issue of the protection of third parties, essentially the adoptive parents, the father and the other members of the natural family. The Court notes in that connection that the applicant is now 38 years old, having been adopted at the age of four, and that non-consensual disclosure could entail substantial risks, not only for the mother herself, but also for the adoptive family which brought up the applicant, and her natural father and siblings, each of whom also has a right to respect for his or her private and family life.

45. There is also a general interest at stake, as the French legislature has consistently sought to protect the mother's and child's health during pregnancy and birth and to avoid abortions, in particular illegal abortions, and children being abandoned other than under the proper procedure. The right to respect for life, a higher-ranking value guaranteed by the Convention, is thus one of the aims pursued by the French system.

In these circumstances, the full scope of the question which the Court must answer – does the right to know imply an obligation to divulge? – is to be found in an examination of the law of 22 January 2002, in particular as regards the State's margin of appreciation.

46. The Court reiterates that the choice of the means calculated to secure compliance with Article 8 in the sphere of the relations of individuals between themselves is in principle a matter that falls within the Contracting States' margin of appreciation. In this connection, there are different ways of ensuring 'respect for private life', and the nature of the State's obligation will depend on the particular aspect of private life that is at issue (see *X and Y* v. *Netherlands* [judgment of 26 March 1985, Series A No. 91: see above, section 1.2. in this chapter], p. 12, §24).

47. The Court observes that most of the Contracting States do not have legislation that is comparable to that applicable in France, at least as regards the child's permanent inability to establish parental ties with the natural mother if she continues to keep her identity secret from the child she has brought into the world. However, it notes that some countries do not impose a duty on natural parents to declare their identities on the birth of their children and that there have been cases of child abandonment in various other countries that have given rise to renewed debate about the right to give birth anonymously. In the light not only of the diversity of practice to be found among the legal systems and traditions but also of the fact that various means are being resorted to for abandoning children, the Court concludes that States must be afforded a margin of appreciation to decide which measures are apt to ensure that the rights guaranteed by the Convention are secured to everyone within their jurisdiction.

48. The Court observes that in the present case the applicant was given access to non-identifying information about her mother and natural family that enabled her to trace some of her roots, while ensuring the protection of third-party interests.

49. In addition, while preserving the principle that mothers may give birth anonymously, the system recently set up in France improves the prospect of their agreeing to waive confidentiality, something which, it will be noted in passing, they have always been able to do even before the enactment of the law of 22 January 2002. The new legislation will facilitate searches for information about a person's biological origins, as a National Council for Access to Information about Personal Origins has been set up. That council is an independent body composed of members of the national legal service, representatives of associations having an interest in the subject matter of the law and professional people with good practical knowledge of the issues. The legislation is already in force and the applicant may use it to request disclosure of her mother's identity, subject to the latter's consent being obtained to ensure that her need for protection and the applicant's legitimate request are fairly reconciled. Indeed, though unlikely, the possibility that the applicant will be able to obtain the information she is seeking through the new Council that has been set up by the legislature cannot be excluded.

The French legislation thus seeks to strike a balance and to ensure sufficient proportion between the competing interests. The Court observes in that connection that the States must be allowed to determine the means which they consider to be best suited to achieve the aim of reconciling those interests. Overall, the Court considers that France has not overstepped the margin of appreciation which it must be afforded in view of the complex and sensitive nature of the issue of access to information about one's origins, an issue that concerns the right to know one's personal history, the choices of the natural parents, the existing family ties and the adoptive parents.

Consequently, there has been no violation of Article 8 of the Convention

Joint dissenting opinion of Mr Wildhaber, Sir Nicolas Bratza, Mr Bonello, Mr Loucaides, Mr Cabral Barreto, Mrs Tulkens and Mr Pellonpää:

4. As regards *compliance* with Article 8, this is a situation in which there are competing rights or interests: on the one hand, the child's right to have access to information about its origins and, on the other, the mother's right, for a series of reasons specific to her and concerning her personal autonomy, to keep her identity as the child's mother secret. Other interests may also come into play, such as the need to protect the health of mother and child during pregnancy and at the birth, and the need to prevent abortion or infanticide.

5. In the instant case, while reiterating that Article 8 does not merely compel States to abstain from arbitrary interference but that 'in addition to this primarily negative undertaking, there may be positive obligations inherent in an effective respect for private life' (see paragraph 40 of the judgment), the Court found that the applicant's complaint was not so much that the State had interfered with her rights under the Convention, but that it had not complied with its duty to act. In other words, 'the substance of the [applicant's] complaint is not that the State has acted but that it has failed to act' (see *Airey* v. *Ireland*, judgment of 9 October 1979, Series A No. 32, p. 17, §32). In these circumstances, the Court had to examine whether the State was in breach of its positive obligation under Article 8 of the Convention when it turned down the applicant's request for information about her natural mother's identity. Its task was not therefore to verify whether

the interference with the applicant's right to respect for her private life was proportionate to the aim pursued but to examine whether the obligation imposed on the State was unreasonable having regard to the individual right to be protected, even if there are similarities between the principles applicable in both cases as regards the balance to be struck between the rights of the individual and of the community (see *Keegan* v. *Ireland*, judgment of 26 May 1994, Series A No. 290, p. 19, §49, and *Kroon and others* v. *Netherlands*, judgment of 27 October 1994, Series A No. 297-C, p. 56, §31).

6. In order to decide that issue, the Court must examine whether a fair balance has been struck between the competing interests. It is not, therefore, a question of determining which interest must, in a given case, take absolute precedence over others. In more concrete terms, the Court is not required to examine whether the applicant should, by virtue of her rights under Article 8, have been given access to the information regarding her origins, whatever the consequences and regardless of the importance of the competing interests or, conversely, whether a refusal of the applicant's request for the information in question was justified for the protection of the rights of the mother (or, for instance, for the protection of the rights of others or in the interests of public health). It must perform a 'balancing of interests' test and examine whether in the present case the French system struck a reasonable balance between the competing rights and interests.

7. That is the nub of the problem. As a result of the domestic law and practice, no balancing of interests was possible in the instant case, either in practice or in law. In practice, French law accepted that the mother's decision constituted an absolute defence to any requests for information by the applicant, irrespective of the reasons for or legitimacy of that decision. In all circumstances, the mother's refusal is definitively binding on the child, who has no legal means at its disposal to challenge the mother's unilateral decision. The mother thus has a discretionary right to bring a suffering child into the world and to condemn it to lifelong ignorance. This, therefore, is not a multilateral system that ensures any balance between the competing rights. The effect of the mother's absolute 'right of veto' is that the rights of the child, which are recognised in the general scheme of the Convention (see *Johansen* v. *Norway*, judgment of 7 August 1996, *Reports of Judgments and Decisions* 1996–III, and *Kutzner* v. *Germany*, No. 46544/99, ECHR 2002–I), are entirely neglected and forgotten. In addition, the mother may also by the same means paralyse the rights of third parties, in particular those of the natural father or the brothers and sisters, who may also find themselves deprived of the rights guaranteed by Article 8 of the Convention. In view of these considerations, we cannot be satisfied by the majority's concession that 'the applicant was given access to non-identifying information about her mother and natural family that enabled her to trace some of her roots while ensuring the protection of third-party interests' (see paragraph 48 of the judgment) ...

17. With regard to striking a fair balance between the competing interests, we consider the approach adopted by the Court in *Gaskin* v. *United Kingdom* (judgment of 7 July 1989, Series A No. 160, p. 20, §49), which it followed in *M.G.* v. *United Kingdom* (No. 39393/98, 24 September 2002) to be relevant. 'In the Court's opinion, persons in the situation of the applicant have a vital interest, protected by the Convention, in receiving the information necessary to know and to understand their childhood and early development. On the other hand, it must be borne in mind that confidentiality of public records is of importance for receiving objective and reliable information, and that such confidentiality can also be necessary for the protection of third persons. Under the latter aspect, a system like the British one, which makes access to records dependent on the consent of the contributor, can in principle be considered to be compatible

with the obligations under Article 8, taking into account the State's margin of appreciation. The Court considers, however, that under such a system the interests of the individual seeking access to records relating to his private and family life must be secured when a contributor to the records either is not available or improperly refuses consent. Such a system is only in conformity with the principle of proportionality if it provides that an independent authority finally decides whether access has to be granted in cases where a contributor fails to answer or withholds consent.'

18. If the system of anonymous births is to be retained, an *independent authority* of that type should have the power to decide, on the basis of all the factual and legal aspects of the case and following adversarial argument, whether or not to grant access to the information; such access may in appropriate cases be made conditional, or subject to compliance with a set procedure. In the present situation, in the absence of any machinery enabling the applicant's right to find out her origins to be balanced against competing rights and interests, blind preference was inevitably given to the sole interests of the mother. The applicant's request for information was totally and definitively refused, without any balancing of the competing interests or prospect of a remedy.

The Court arrived at a conclusion of non-violation in *Odièvre*, essentially, on the basis that the French authorities had been aware of the conflicting interests at stake, and had taken sufficient care in balancing these interests against one another. This is a procedural solution, based on institutional considerations linked both to the division of tasks between courts and other branches of government, and to the relationship of an international court to domestic authorities. However, it provides little guidance to those authorities as to how they should arbitrate situations of conflicting rights presented to them.

(c) Developing judicial techniques that can solve conflicts between rights: 'practical concordance' and beyond

One influential proposal on how to adjudicate issues of conflicting rights was put forward by the German constitutional lawyer Konrad Hesse (*Grundzüge des Verfassungsrechts der Bundesrepublik Deutschland*, twentieth edn (Heidelberg: C. F. Müller, 1995), §172). Hesse suggests reliance on the principle of 'practical concordance' in such situations. The notion appears in a number of decisions of the German Federal Constitutional Court (*Bundesverfassungsgericht*) (see T. Marauhn and N. Ruppel, 'Balancing Conflicting Human Rights: Konrad Hesse's Notion of '*praktische Konkordanz*' and the German Federal Constitutional Court' in E. Brems (ed.), *Conflicts Between Fundamental Rights* (Antwerp-Oxford-Portland: Intersentia-Hart, 2008), p. 273). In situations of conflicting rights, the doctrine of 'practical concordance' seeks to avoid, to the fullest extent possible, sacrificing one right against the other. Instead, it posits, a compromise should be sought between the rights in conflict which will respect their respective claims, by 'optimizing' each of the rights against the other. This idea already represents a significant progress from the metaphor of 'balancing': whereas the 'balancing' of one right against another should lead to preferring the right with the highest 'value' (or the most important 'weight'), above the other, the principle of 'practical concordance' instead rejects the very idea that this may be a desirable outcome: in substance, it acknowledges that it is inappropriate to set aside one claim simply because a competing claim appears, in the particular circumstances of a case, to deserve to be recognized more weight. However, 'practical concordance' thus understood may not be going far enough:

Olivier De Schutter and Françoise Tulkens, 'Rights in Conflict: the European Court of Human Rights as a Pragmatic Institution' in E. Brems (ed.), *Conflicts Between Fundamental Rights* (Antwerp-Oxford-Portland: Intersentia–Hart, 2008), pp. 169–216:

Despite the advance it represents, the principle of practical concordance shares with the idea of 'balancing' two characteristics which seem to us potentially contestable. First, it shares with the methodology of 'weighing the scales' the idea that the judge has a privileged access to where the equilibrium is to be found: in the final instance, it will be for the judge to decide whether or not the rights in conflict have been reconciled to the fullest extent possible, without any of the two rights in conflict having been completely sacrificed to the other. Second, and more importantly, it lacks any constructivist dimension: just like the process of 'balancing' does not include the need to search for ways to transform the context in which the conflict has arisen, the idea of a 'practical concordance' does not take into account the need to develop imaginative solutions to limit the conflict and to avoid its recurrence in the future. But it is precisely the development of such solutions which we require: the identification of adequate solutions on an *ad hoc* basis, where conflicts emerge which are presented to the judge, needs to be complemented by the establishment of mechanisms which will allow for a permanent search for devices which will contribute to avoid the repetition of the conflict in the future ...

Practical concordance ... is most useful not as a rule helping us to identify where, on a scale going from the total sacrifice of one right to the total sacrifice of a competing right, we should locate ourselves. Rather, it should be seen as an objective to be achieved by an exercise in institutional imagination. We must ask, not only how the conflict should best be solved where the objective is to minimize the negative impacts on any of the competing rights, but also how the conflict can be avoided altogether, or lessened, by transforming the background conditions which made the conflict possible.

[In this context, the role of courts should be], first, to identify the responsibility of the State authorities in creating and maintaining the background conditions which made the conflict of rights 'inevitable' ...; second, ... to progressively formulate rules which may serve to guide the States parties in the future, where certain regimes are proven to allow for this 'practical concordance' between competing rights to be effective. Moreover, in order to identify which background conditions may explain the conflict between rights, and what it would mean, therefore, to modify such conditions, it may be crucial to compare the situation of conflict emerging in one jurisdiction with similar situations which have occurred in other jurisdictions, and how they were solved in such cases. Such comparisons may help identifying which conditions might be created to either lessen the conflict between rights, or even to remove it altogether, by making the appropriate institutional changes, which will allow these conflicting rights to be reconciled with one another's requirements.

In order to illustrate this position, the authors rely on a number of examples, including the dissenting opinion expressed in her judicial capacity, by one of the authors, in the case of *Odièvre* v. *France* (reproduced above in this section, under b)). Indeed, by insisting on the possibility of setting up an independent authority empowered to decide upon requests emanating from persons born in conditions of anonymity, and to provide access to information about those persons' biological parents on the basis of an examination of all relevant circumstances, the joint dissenting opinion expressed in *Odièvre* in fact suggests it may be possible to move beyond the conflict by an 'exercise in institutional imagination', that may precisely avoid having to 'blindly' sacrifice one right against the other.

Another illustration is sought in *Öllinger* v. *Austria*. In that case, the applicant had notified the Austrian police that he intended to hold a meeting at the Salzburg municipal cemetery in front of the war memorial, on All Saints Day, in order to commemorate the Salzburg Jews killed by the SS during the Second World War. However, the date and place of the meeting coincided with the assembly of a group commemorating the SS soldiers killed in the Second World War, and Mr Öllinger had refused to give an undertaking that his meeting would not disturb that gathering, which he considered illegal. Thus, on the basis that the disturbances which would predictably occur on the site were likely to offend the religious feelings of members of the public visiting the cemetery, the applicant was denied the authorization to hold the commemorative meeting he intended: indeed, since the commemoration meeting held for the SS soldiers during the Second World War was considered by the Salzburg Federal Police Authority to be a popular ceremony, it did not require authorization under the Austrian Assembly Act. The European Court of Human Rights took the view that this was a violation of Mr Öllinger's freedom of assembly:

European Court of Human Rights (1st sect.), *Öllinger* v. *Austria* (Appl. No. 76900/01), judgment of 29 June 2006, paras. 34–50:

34. The Court notes at the outset that the present case is one concerned with competing fundamental rights. The applicant's right to freedom of peaceful assembly and his right to freedom of expression have to be balanced against the other association's right to protection against disturbance of its assembly and the cemetery-goers' right to protection of their freedom to manifest their religion.

35. As regards the right to freedom of peaceful assembly as guaranteed by Article 11, the Court reiterates that it comprises negative and positive obligations on the part of the Contracting State.

36. On the one hand, the State is compelled to abstain from interfering with that right, which also extends to a demonstration that may annoy or give offence to persons opposed to the ideas or claims that it is seeking to promote (see *Stankov and the United Macedonian Organisation Ilinden*, [judgment of 2 October 2001], §86, and *Plattform 'Ärzte für das Leben'* v. *Austria*, judgment of 21 June 1988, Series A No. 139, p. 12, §32). If every probability of tension and heated exchange between opposing groups during a demonstration was to warrant its prohibition, society would be faced with being deprived of the opportunity of hearing differing views (see *Stankov and the United Macedonian Organisation Ilinden*, cited above, §107).

37. On the other hand, States may be required under Article 11 to take positive measures in order to protect a lawful demonstration against counter-demonstrations (see *Plattform 'Ärzte für das Leben'*, cited above, p. 12, §34).

38. Notwithstanding its autonomous role and particular sphere of application, Article 11 of the Convention must also be considered in the light of Article 10. The protection of opinions and the freedom to express them is one of the objectives of freedom of assembly and association enshrined in Article 11 (see *Stankov and the United Macedonian Organisation Ilinden,* cited above, §85). In this connection it must be borne in mind that there is little scope under Article 10 §2 for restrictions on political speech or on debate on questions of public interest (*ibid.*, § 88; see also *Scharsach and News Verlagsgesellschaft* v. *Austria*, No. 39394/98, §30, ECHR 2003–XI).

39. Turning finally to Article 9 of the Convention, the Court has held that, while those who choose to exercise the freedom to manifest their religion cannot reasonably expect to be exempt from all criticism, the responsibility of the State may be engaged where religious beliefs are opposed or denied in a manner which inhibits those who hold such beliefs from exercising their freedom to hold or express them. In such cases the State may be called upon to ensure the peaceful enjoyment of the right guaranteed under Article 9 to the holders of those beliefs (see *Otto-Preminger-Institut* v. *Austria*, judgment of 20 September 1994, Series A No. 295–A, p. 18, §49).

40. In the present case, the Salzburg Federal Police Authority and the Salzburg Public Security Authority considered the prohibition of the applicant's assembly necessary in order to prevent disturbances of the Comradeship IV commemoration meeting, which was considered a popular ceremony not requiring authorisation under the Assembly Act. They had particular regard to the experience of previous protest campaigns by other organisers against the gathering of Comradeship IV, which had provoked vehement discussions, had disturbed other visitors to the cemetery and had made police intervention necessary.

41. The Constitutional Court dismissed this approach as being too narrow. It observed that the prohibition of the intended meeting would not be justified if its sole purpose were the protection of the Comradeship IV commemoration ceremony. It went on to say that the prohibition was nevertheless justified or even required by the State's positive obligation under Article 9 to protect persons manifesting their religion against deliberate disturbance by others. In arriving at that conclusion, the Constitutional Court had particular regard to the fact that All Saints' Day was an important religious holiday on which the population traditionally went to cemeteries to commemorate the dead and that disturbances caused by disputes between members of the assembly organised by the applicant and members of Comradeship IV were likely to occur in the light of the experience of previous years.

42. The Court notes that the domestic authorities had regard to the various competing Convention rights. Its task is to examine whether they achieved a fair balance between them.

43. The applicant's assembly was clearly intended as a counter-demonstration to protest against the gathering of Comradeship IV, an association which undisputedly consists mainly of former members of the SS. The applicant emphasises that the main purpose of his assembly was to remind the public of the crimes committed by the SS and to commemorate the Salzburg Jews murdered by them. The coincidence in time and venue with the commemoration ceremony of Comradeship IV was an essential part of the message he wanted to convey.

44. In the Court's view, the unconditional prohibition of a counter-demonstration is a very far-reaching measure which would require particular justification, all the more so as the

applicant, being a member of parliament, essentially wished to protest against the gathering of Comradeship IV and, thus, to express an opinion on a issue of public interest (see, *mutatis mutandis, Jerusalem* v. *Austria*, No. 26958/95, §36, ECHR 2001–II). The Court finds it striking that the domestic authorities attached no weight to this aspect of the case.

45. It is undisputed that the aim of protecting the gathering of Comradeship IV does not provide sufficient justification for the contested prohibition. This has been clearly pointed out by the Constitutional Court. The Court fully agrees with that position.

46. Therefore, it remains to be examined whether the prohibition was justified to protect the cemetery-goers' right to manifest their religion. The Constitutional Court relied on the solemn nature of All Saints' Day, traditionally dedicated to the commemoration of the dead, and on the disturbances experienced in previous years as a result of disputes between members of Comradeship IV and members of counter-demonstrations.

47. However, the Court notes a number of factors which indicate that the prohibition at issue was disproportionate to the aim pursued. First and foremost, the assembly was in no way directed against the cemetery-goers' beliefs or the manifestation of them. Moreover, the applicant expected only a small number of participants. They envisaged peaceful and silent means of expressing their opinion, namely the carrying of commemorative messages, and had explicitly ruled out the use of chanting or banners. Thus, the intended assembly in itself could not have hurt the feelings of cemetery-goers. Moreover, while the authorities feared that, as in previous years, heated debates might arise, it was not alleged that any incidents of violence had occurred on previous occasions.

48. In these circumstances, the Court is not convinced by the Government's argument that allowing both meetings while taking preventive measures, such as ensuring police presence in order to keep the two assemblies apart, was not a viable alternative which would have preserved the applicant's right to freedom of assembly while at the same time offering a sufficient degree of protection as regards the rights of the cemetery's visitors.

49. Instead, the domestic authorities imposed an unconditional prohibition on the applicant's assembly. The Court therefore finds that they gave too little weight to the applicant's interest in holding the intended assembly and expressing his protest against the meeting of Comradeship IV, while giving too much weight to the interest of cemetery-goers in being protected against some rather limited disturbances.

50. Having regard to these factors, and notwithstanding the margin of appreciation afforded to the State in this area, the Court considers that the Austrian authorities failed to strike a fair balance between the competing interests.

This has elicited the following comment:

Olivier De Schutter and Françoise Tulkens, 'Rights in Conflict: the European Court of Human Rights as a Pragmatic Institution' in E. Brems (ed.), Conflicts Between Fundamental Rights (Antwerp-Oxford-Portland: Intersentia-Hart, 2008), pp. 169–216 at pp. 205–6:

The main problem in the eyes of the Court, we would submit, is not solely that the diverse interests at stake were not recognized an adequate 'weight' [by the Austrian authorities]. It is also that, instead of identifying how the conflict could be avoided – by organizing the separation of the two groups on the premises, by deploying a police force –, the police authorities simply chose to prioritize certain interests above the others, *without seeking to modify the background conditions which may create the conflict in the first place*. They took the conflict they were faced with as 'necessary', where in fact it might have been construed as 'accidental' and as having its source, in part, in the unwillingness of the local authorities to deploy the police forces which would have been required to ensure that the competing claims at stake could have been satisfied simultaneously.

4.1. Questions for discussion: the State duty to apply human rights in private relationships

1. In the light of the regime of the obligation to protect, as described in section 2, what are the real stakes of the discussion in the previous section 1 of this chapter concerning the difference between the imputability to the State of the acts of non-State actors, and the failure of the State to discharge its obligation to protect?

2. An alternative to strengthening the State's obligation to protect, it might be argued, would be to impose on non-State actors direct obligations under international human rights law. In recent years, the desirability of each of these two options has been debated particularly in the context of attempts to strengthen the responsibilities of transnational corporations towards human rights (see box 4.1.). What are the advantages and disadvantages of each approach? Are they mutually exclusive or could they be complementary?

3. In section 2.1., we have contrasted three models through which international human rights could be applied to private relationships: these are (i) by 'direct application', (ii) by 'indirect application', or (iii) by the adoption of domestic legislation through which the human rights are protected from the potential infringements by private initiatives. In his discussion of this issue, A. Barak adopts a different typology, not including the latter model, but including the 'judiciary model'. This model, he writes, 'begins with the assumption that … human rights are protected only against the State'. The State, however, includes the judiciary: 'Accordingly, the judiciary is prohibited from developing the common law or granting relief in a specific case in a way that violates a constitutional human right. Thus, under this model, if A is obligated to B not to sell his products to C on racial grounds and A breaches this obligation, B will not be entitled to a remedy of specific performance or damages against A. The reason for this is that if the court orders A to fulfill his obligations towards B, it will be violating C's right to equality, a right he holds against the State' (A. Barak, 'Constitutional Human Rights and Private Law' in D. Friedmann and D. Barak-Erez (eds.), *Human Rights in Private Law* (Oxford: Hart Publishing, 2001) p. 13 at p. 25). A typical example, albeit in domestic constitutional law, is the case of *Shelley* v. *Kraemer*, 334 U.S. 1 (1948), in which the US Supreme Court considered that the judicial enforcement of racially restrictive covenants would constitute 'State action' for the purposes of applicability of the Equality Clause of the Fourteenth Amendment of the United States Constitution. Hence,

no remedies would be available to parties complaining about the non-execution of such a covenant, although the Court does acknowledge that the provisions of the Bill of Rights appended to the Constitution only protect against the State: '[Since the Fourteenth Amendment] erects no shield against merely private conduct, however discriminatory or unlawful ... the restrictive agreements standing alone cannot be regarded as violative of any rights guaranteed to petitioners by the Fourteenth Amendment. So long as the purposes of those agreements are effectuated by voluntary adherence to their terms, it would appear clear that there has been no action by the state and the provisions of the Amendment would not have been violated.' How different is the 'judiciary model' from the 'direct application' and 'indirect application' models? Is the 'judiciary model' a useful one to consider (Barak himself believes not)? Consider in this respect the case of *Pla and Puncernau*, decided in 2004 by the European Court of Human Rights (section 2.3.). Is this case applying the 'judiciary model', as implied by the dissenting opinions of Judges Sir Nicolas Bratza and Garlicki? Or is it a compromise between this model and one which defers to the autonomy of will of private parties?

4. Consider the following statement of the Canadian Supreme Court about the relationship between the Canadian Charter of Rights and Freedoms and private law: 'Where ... private party "A" sues private party "B" relying on the common law and where no act of government is relied upon to support the action, the Charter will not apply ... [T]his is a distinct issue from the question whether the judiciary ought to apply and develop the principles of the common law in a manner consistent with the fundamental values enshrined in the Constitution. The answer to this question must be in the affirmative. In this sense, then, the Charter is far from irrelevant to private litigants, whose disputes fall to be decided at common law. But this is different from the proposition that one private party owes a constitutional duty to another' (*Retail, Wholesale & Department Store Union, Local 580* v. *Dolphin Delivery* (1987) 33 D.L.R. (4th) 174, 199 (SCC)). To which of the three models contrasted in section 2.1. does this correspond, assuming internationally recognized human rights are treated like the Canadian Charter of Rights and Freedoms in relationship to private law? What are the advantages and disadvantages of this model?

5. Consider the cases of *X and Y* v. *Netherlands* and *Vo* v. *France*, decided respectively in 1985 and in 2004 by the European Court of Human Rights (see section 1.2. and section 2.1. respectively). What are the arguments in favour of or against imposing on States parties to human rights instruments that they protect human rights in private relationships by criminal law sanctions, rather than simply by civil law remedies? Are there arguments against the use of criminal law sanctions?

6. In *E and others* v. *United Kingdom* (presented in section 2.3.) the Court remarks that, under Article 3 ECHR, any failure by the State to 'take reasonably available measures which could have had a real prospect of altering the outcome or mitigating the harm is sufficient to engage the responsibility of the State'. In *Younger*, the Court finds 'too speculative' the argument that the suicide of the son of the applicant could have been averted if he had been able to see a medical practitioner on the morning of the suicide, but at the same time considers that it would not be required from the applicant to prove that the measure would have had a 'real possibility' of changing the outcome. Where should the threshold lie? Is a mere

possibility, even remote, of the measure which the State has failed to adopt changing the outcome, sufficient?

7. In section 2.4., it has been stated that freedom of contract is not generally treated as having a normative status equivalent to a human right – indeed, human rights instruments do not usually refer to freedom of contract, which therefore human rights bodies generally treat as subordinate to considerations based on human dignity and equality. Are there arguments in favour of a different approach, however? Which arguments may be advanced in support of treating the individual's autonomy of will on a par with human rights?

5

The Progressive Realization of Human Rights and the Obligation to Fulfil

INTRODUCTION

The obligation to fulfil requires the State to adopt appropriate legislative, administrative and other measures towards the full realization of human rights. The implication is that the realization of human rights must become the object of a policy aimed at improving them. Not only must policies in place not violate human rights, and take them into account as a transversal concern (a requirement referred to as mainstreaming); in addition, policies must be put in place explicitly in order to make progress towards fulfilling them. Human rights require, in that sense, appropriate policy-making.

This chapter is divided into four sections. Section 1 describes the general principles that should guide States in seeking to achieve the progressive realization of human rights by discharging their obligation to fulfil. The focus is particularly on economic and social rights, but the principles apply equally to civil and political rights, which also require, for their implementation, the provision of resources (whether human, financial, natural, technological, or informational: for a slightly different list, see R. E. Robertson, 'Measuring State Compliance with the Obligation to Devote the "Maximum Available Resources" to Realizing Economic, Social, and Cultural Rights', *Human Rights Quarterly*, 16, No. 4 (1994), 693 at 703–13). Section 2 then examines the usefulness of framework laws and action plans in the realization of human rights, and section 3 discusses the use of indicators and benchmarks in monitoring progress with the objective of full realization.

The tools described in sections 2 and 3 are procedural in nature. The insistence on these tools in much of the recent scholarship in human rights, particularly as regards economic and social rights such as the right to health, to education, or to food, stems from the need to impose concrete obligations on States to 'take steps' towards the progressive realization of rights that, because of the resources required for their implementation, may not be achievable immediately in all their dimensions: since neither the precise level of commitments nor the precise speed at which progress should be made can be determined without taking into account the capacity of each State and the level of development achieved, we should at least (so the reasoning goes) impose on States to set up mechanisms that ensure that they move in the right direction, and that they do so as swiftly as possible. The adoption of national strategies, the transposition of such strategies into framework laws, the setting of quantified and time-bound objectives through the establishment of benchmarks, and the monitoring of progress through indicators, are all instrumental to that purpose. At the same time, however, such tools should not be treated as ends in themselves: they should remain linked to the substantive obligations, i.e. to whether the outcomes of whichever strategies are in place are satisfactory. Section 4 seeks to examine how that link can be maintained.

1 THE PRINCIPLE

The 2006 Principles and Guidelines for a Human Rights Approach to Poverty Reduction Strategies contain a number of useful recommendations about the components of a policy aimed at the full realization of human rights:

Office of the High Commissioner for Human Rights, Principles and Guidelines for a Human Rights Approach to Poverty Reduction Strategies (2006), paras. 49–61:

49. The recognition that the full realization of some human rights may have to occur in a progressive manner, over a period of time due to resource constraints, has two implications for policy. First, it allows for a time dimension in the strategy for human rights fulfilment, making the setting of targets and benchmarks an indispensable element of strategies for human rights fulfilment. Second, it allows for setting priorities among different rights and considering trade-offs among them, since the constraint of resources may not permit a strategy to pursue all rights simultaneously, or with equal vigour.

50. The recognition of a time dimension and the need for considering trade-offs and prioritization are common features of all approaches to policymaking. The distinctiveness of the human rights approach is that it imposes certain conditions on those features that the duty-bearers are required to respect. The conditions on the time dimension are aimed at ensuring that the State does not defer or relax the efforts needed to realize human rights. The conditions on trade-offs and prioritization are aimed at ensuring that all trade-offs conform to the human rights norms.

51. In cases where a right cannot be realized immediately due to resource constraints, the State must begin immediately to take steps to fulfil the rights in question as expeditiously as possible. The human rights approach requires that steps taken by States satisfy the following conditions.

52. First, the State must acknowledge that with a serious commitment to poverty reduction it may be possible to make rapid progress towards the realization of many human rights even within an existing resource constraint. Thus, it may be possible to improve the efficiency of resource use – for example, by scaling down expenditures on unproductive activities and by reducing spending on activities whose benefits go disproportionately to the rich.

53. Second, to the extent that the realization of human rights may be contingent on a gradual expansion in the availability of resources, the State is required, as an immediate step, to develop and implement a time-bound plan of action. The plan must spell out when and how the State hopes to arrive at the realization of rights.

54. Third, as the realization of some human rights may take considerable time, the plan must set benchmarks (i.e. intermediate targets) corresponding to each ultimate target. As a prerequisite of setting targets and benchmarks, the State should identify appropriate indicators, so that the rate of progress can be monitored and, if progress is slow, corrective action can be taken. Indicators should be as disaggregated as possible for each subgroup of the population living in poverty.

55. Fourth, the targets, benchmarks and indicators must be set in a participatory manner, ... so that they reflect the concerns and interests of all segments of the society. At the same time, appropriate accountability mechanisms must be set up, ... so as to ensure that the State commits itself fully to realizing the agreed targets and benchmarks.

56. With regard to trade-offs and prioritization, the human rights approach does not in itself offer any hard and fast rules as to which rights are to be given priority. The act of prioritization has to be context-specific, as circumstances differ from country to country. However, the human rights approach imposes certain conditions on the process and substance of prioritization.

57. The *process* of setting priorities must involve effective participation of all stakeholders, including the poor. Value judgements will inevitably enter into the process of setting priorities, but the rights-based approach demands that they should do so in an inclusive and equitable manner. This implies that the process of resource allocation must permit all segments of society, especially the poor, to express their opinions with regard to priorities. It also implies that just institutional mechanisms must be put in place so that potentially conflicting opinions can be reconciled in a fair and equitable manner.

58. The *substance* of prioritization refers to the basis on which priorities are to be decided and the manner in which resources are to be allocated to the rights that have been accorded priority. The following principles must guide the substance of prioritization.

59. First, no right can be given precedence over others on the grounds of intrinsic merit, because from the human rights perspective all rights are equally valuable. However, strategies to ensure effective protection of all human rights may prioritize certain types of intervention on practical grounds. For example, a country may decide to give priority to a right that has remained especially under-realized compared to others, or to a right whose fulfilment is expected to act as a catalyst towards the fulfilment of other rights, or to a right which a country may feel especially well equipped to deal with in view of its traditions or experience.

60. Second, while prioritization entails trade-offs between rights, in an important way the human rights approach circumscribes the nature of such trade-offs. In particular, the principle of equality and non-discrimination rules out any trade-offs which would result in or exacerbate unequal and discriminatory outcomes, e.g. giving priority to providing health and education services to the more affluent parts of society, rather than to the most disadvantaged and marginalized groups. The human rights approach also cautions against making trade-offs whereby one right suffers a marked decline in its level of realization. Such trade-offs would need to be subject to the most careful consideration and to be fully justified by reference to the totality of human rights. In practice, this puts a restriction on the manner in which resources are allocated in favour of the rights that have been accorded priority at any point in time. Additional resources required in order to realize these rights should, as a rule, not be extracted by reducing the level of resources currently allocated to other rights (unless reduced allocation of resources can be offset by increased efficiency of resource use). Instead, as more resources become available to a country over time, increased share of the incremental resources should be

allocated to those rights previously allocated fewer resources. In other words, trade-offs should normally be made only in the allocation of incremental resources. For example, if a State decides to accord priority to the right to education, it should devote more of its resources to education than to other spheres such as food and housing, rather than reducing the level of resources allocated to other rights in a way that might lead to retrogression of those rights.

61. Third, notwithstanding the recognition that resource constraints negatively affect a State's ability to implement its human rights obligations, the international human rights system specifies some core obligations that require States to ensure, with immediate effect, certain minimum levels of enjoyment of various rights. Core obligations must be treated as binding constraints to the allocation of resources, i.e. no trade-offs are permitted with regard to them. These obligations must be met before allocating resources to other purposes. For example, a State has a core obligation, derived from the rights to life, food and health, to ensure that all individuals within its jurisdiction are free from starvation. Therefore, even if the full enjoyment of the right to food – in all its dimensions – may be achieved only progressively over a period of time, the pain of starvation must be removed immediately.

In what is the most comprehensive description of the obligation to fulfil available to date, the UN Committee on Economic, Social and Cultural Rights stated in its General Comment on the right to water:

Committee on Economic, Social and Cultural Rights, *General Comment No. 15 (2002): The Right to Water (Arts. 11 and 12 of the International Covenant on Economic, Social and Cultural Rights)* **(E/C.12/2002/11, 20 January 2003), paras. 25–9:**

brr bütün pargolarına ayırmak

The obligation to *fulfil* can be disaggregated into the obligations to facilitate, promote and provide. The obligation to facilitate requires the State to take positive measures to assist individuals and communities to enjoy the right. The obligation to promote obliges the State party to take steps to ensure that there is appropriate education concerning the hygienic use of water, protection of water sources and methods to minimize water wastage. States parties are also obliged to fulfil (provide) the right when individuals or a group are unable, for reasons beyond their control, to realize that right themselves by the means at their disposal.

The obligation to fulfil requires States parties to adopt the necessary measures directed towards the full realization of the right to water. The obligation includes, *inter alia*, according sufficient recognition of this right within the national political and legal systems, preferably by way of legislative implementation; adopting a national water strategy and plan of action to realize this right; ensuring that water is affordable for everyone; and facilitating improved and sustainable access to water, particularly in rural and deprived urban areas.

To ensure that water is affordable, States parties must adopt the necessary measures that may include, *inter alia*: (a) use of a range of appropriate low-cost techniques and technologies; (b) appropriate pricing policies such as free or low-cost water; and (c) income supplements. Any payment for water services has to be based on the principle of equity, ensuring that these services, whether privately or publicly provided, are affordable for all, including socially disadvantaged groups. Equity demands that poorer households should not be disproportionately burdened with water expenses as compared to richer households.

States parties should adopt comprehensive and integrated strategies and programmes to ensure that there is sufficient and safe water for present and future generations. Such strategies and programmes may include: (a) reducing depletion of water resources through unsustainable extraction, diversion and damming; (b) reducing and eliminating contamination of watersheds and water-related eco-systems by substances such as radiation, harmful chemicals and human excreta; (c) monitoring water reserves; (d) ensuring that proposed developments do not interfere with access to adequate water; (e) assessing the impacts of actions that may impinge upon water availability and natural-ecosystems watersheds, such as climate changes, desertification and increased soil salinity, deforestation and loss of biodiversity; (f) increasing the efficient use of water by end-users; (g) reducing water wastage in its distribution; (h) response mechanisms for emergency situations; (i) and establishing competent institutions and appropriate institutional arrangements to carry out the strategies and programmes.

Ensuring that everyone has access to adequate sanitation is not only fundamental for human dignity and privacy, but is one of the principal mechanisms for protecting the quality of drinking water supplies and resources. In accordance with the rights to health and adequate housing (see General Comments No. 4 (1991) and 14 (2000)) States parties have an obligation to progressively extend safe sanitation services, particularly to rural and deprived urban areas, taking into account the needs of women and children.

This description highlights adequately two characteristics of the obligation to fulfil. First, it is dynamic: since it aims towards the full realization of the right – and not merely towards avoiding interfering with the right, or towards adopting measures to ensure that private actors will not thus interfere – it is necessarily open-ended and implemented progressively. Second, the implications of the obligation are primarily procedural: what is required from States is that they set up procedures which will monitor the fulfilment of the right; that they adopt action plans or national strategies; and that they ensure, through such devices, that steps are being taken which develop the right further, making it more effective – available, accessible, acceptable and adaptable to changing needs.

One important tool for the implementation of the obligation to fulfil human rights is the adoption of framework legislations or national strategies or action plans. This is discussed in section 2. The development of indicators and the setting of benchmarks also are essential tools for the progressive realization of human rights. Apart from their contribution to public debate, indicators may serve for self-assessment by State authorities. They also facilitate the task of monitoring bodies. And they may help identify instances of discrimination or retrogression in the fulfilment of any particular right. Section 3 describes this in more detail. Section 4 then addresses the question of the relationship of these tools to the substantive obligations of States in the progressive realization of human rights, particularly insofar as they face budgetary constraints and competing priorities and resources.

2 FRAMEWORK LAWS AND ACTION PLANS

2.1 Framework laws

Framework laws transpose into legislative commitments policies that aim at the fulfilment of human rights. This not only improves these policies at the operational level, by clearly allocating responsibilities across different branches of government, by setting precise time-bound targets (benchmarks) to be achieved, and by encouraging permanent evaluation and thus improvement of the measures taken to reach the targets set. It also improves the legitimacy of such policies, if framework laws are adopted through participatory mechanisms or are discussed in parliamentary assemblies. Most importantly, framework laws ensure accountability: at a minimum, they oblige different public authorities to explain their choices, and if they do not take the measures expected from them, to offer a proper justification for any delays or failures to take such measures; at best, they invest individual right-holders with what Amartya Sen has referred to as 'metarights' – rights to have policies adopted that aim at the realizing of rights.

Amartya K. Sen, 'The Right Not to be Hungry' in P. Alston and K. Tomasevski (eds.), *The Right to Food* (Leiden: Martinus Nijhoff, 1984), p. 69 at 70–1:

A metaright to something x can be defined as the right to have policies p(x) that genuinely pursue the objective of making the right to x realisable. As an example, consider the following 'Directive Principle of State Policy' inserted in the Constitution of India when it was adopted in 1950: 'The state shall, in particular, direct its policy towards securing ... that the citizens, men and women equally, have the right to an adequate means of livelihood.' The wording was careful enough to avoid asserting that such a right already exists, but saying only that policy should be directed to making it possible to have that as a right. If this right were accepted, then the effect will not be to make the 'right to adequate means of livelihood' real – even as an abstract, background right – but to give a person the right to demand that policy be directed towards securing the objective of making the right to adequate means a realisable right, even if that objective cannot be immediately achieved. It is a right of a different kind: not to x but to p(x) ...

It is not difficult to see why metarights of this kind have a particular relevance for economic aims such as the removal of poverty or hunger. For many countries where poverty or hunger is widespread, there might not exist any feasible way whatsoever by which freedom from them could be guaranteed for all in the very near future, but policies that would rapidly lead to such freedom do exist. The metaright for freedom from hunger is the right to such a policy, but what lies behind that right is ultimately the objective of achieving that freedom.

In its General Comment No. 15 of 2002 on *The Right to Water*, the Committee on Economic, Social and Cultural Rights notes: 'States parties may find it advantageous to adopt framework legislation to operationalize their right to water strategy. Such legislation should include: (*a*) targets or goals to be attained and the time-frame for their achievement; (*b*) the means by which the purpose could be achieved; (*c*) the intended collaboration with civil society, private sector and international organizations; (*d*) institutional responsibility for the process; (*e*) national mechanisms for its monitoring;

and (*f*) remedies and recourse procedures' (at para. 50). The same recommendation is made, for instance, in General Comment No. 12 (1999) on *The Right to Food*. Arjun Sengupta has summarized the components of such a framework law:

Arjun Sengupta, 'The Right to Food in the Perspective of the Right to Development' in W. B. Eide and U. Kracht (eds.), *Food and Human Rights in Development* (Antwerp–Oxford: Intersentia–Hart, 2007), vol. II, 'Evolving Issues and Emerging Applications', p. 107 at p. 131:

1. The targets for the different levels of achievement of the rights over a period of time, will have to be fixed in terms of the indicators of those rights to be realized in phases. The fixing of these targets must follow from an intensive consultation between the stakeholders, the State Party and the civil society organisation, following the human rights principles of equity, non-discrimination and participation.
2. A programme has to be worked out by the State authorities to realise these rights, using their interdependence and by assignment of the direct and indirect duties to all the agents including the State administration at different levels.
3. Mechanisms have to be established to review and monitor each of these agents' performance in terms of their assigned duties, and for that purpose appropriate legislations may have to be enacted when the duties may be directly related to the outcomes of the targets. For this, institutions may have to be created when the existing institutional arrangements are not adequate for the task.
4. With appropriate legislation, part of these rights and their components can be fully justiciable, with a Court of Law deciding on the extent of responsibilities of the different agents and recommending corrective actions.
5. The institutional mechanisms set up in addition to the administrative procedures should monitor and review the programme in the light of the performance of the different duty-holders, and make recommendations about corrective actions which would be binding on the different agents. Again, such a procedure could be carried out with full participation of all the stakeholders and the civil society organisations at the different levels of implementation of the rights.
6. A procedure must be set up, consistent with human rights standards, to revise the targets periodically in order to secure the rights through progressive realisation.

Writing in the context of the right to food, S. Khoza outlines the benefits of framework legislations as follows:

Sibonile Khoza, 'The Role of Framework Legislation in Realising the Right to Food: Using South Africa as a Case Study of this New Breed of Law' in W. B. Eide and U. Kracht (eds.), *Food and Human Rights in Development* (Antwerp–Oxford: Intersentia–Hart, 2005), vol. I, 'Legal and Institutional Dimensions and Selected Topics', pp. 187–204 at pp. 196–7:

Managing a complex process. Implementing the right to food … involves a complex process. Access to food is multi-dimensional and cross-sectoral in nature requiring legislative and other measures in many sectors pertaining to the right. Framework law provides a useful tool in ensuring comprehensiveness and better coordination in the conception and implementation process of national strategies and policies.

Instructing role players and ensuring accountability. Framework law allocates specific responsibilities to different spheres and departments of government as well as to the public institutions such as Ombudsmen/Public Protectors. This ensures that specific government departments and agents bear express responsibility for implementing the right, and are held accountable for failure to do so.

Reinforcing human rights and democratic principles. The process leading to enacting framework law is grounded on human rights and democratic principles of transparency, participation, accountability and inclusivity. In this regard, it would demand the full participation of a wide range of sectors in addressing the currently inadequate measures, and at the same time, would command the holding of extensive public consultations to allow vigorous debates and submissions on the draft legislation.

Defining purpose and principles of law in respect of the right. Framework law provides for the description of its purpose and the governing principles. It would also provide a detailed description of the nature and scope of the right. It would identify the right-holder and duty-holder in respect of the ... entitlements. It arguably purports to confirm the judicial enforceability of the right and sets the remedial procedures that would enable people to claim their right.

Operationalizing the implementation process. Depending on the approach adopted to include the crucial elements, framework law could be seen as a transformed policy framework. By featuring such operational [elements] as benchmarks, indicators and time-framed targets and goals, framework law provides a systematic approach and viable tool for measuring and monitoring progress towards achieving the progressive realisation of the right.

Tangibly re-affirming government's commitment. By adopting framework legislation, government would be making a firm political and legislative statement that it is committed to realising the constitutional right to food progressively, and would ensure immediate access to basic food needs for those most vulnerable ...

The absence of framework legislation tends to have the opposite effects of maintaining a fragmented, and often weak and inadequate legislative system relating to the implementation of the right to sufficient food at the expense of people's basic needs, human dignity and life. Without such a law, there is also no assured way of measuring progress in and monitoring the implementation of the right.

One example of such a framework law is the Brazilian Law of 15 September 2006 establishing a National Food and Nutritional Security System (SISAN). In 2003, Brazil launched a multisectoral Zero Hunger programme, and it re-established the National Food and Nutritional Security Council (CONSEA), which had briefly functioned in 1993–5 but had been dismantled under the pretext of its mandate being incorporated under a broader poverty eradication strategy. SISAN was set up as a result of the need to improve the co-ordination of the variety of programmes set up under 'Zero Hunger', and to improve the accountability of the agencies responsible for implementing these programmes. It provides that it will be the task of an inter-ministerial taskforce to develop a National Policy and Plan on Food and Nutritional Security, which should include guidelines, objectives, an identification of the resources needed for the implementation, and adequate monitoring and evaluation procedures. This national strategy should be set up in accordance with the guidelines agreed upon in CONSEA, which is composed of civil society organizations (representing two-thirds of its membership) and of governmental representatives (for the remaining third):

[Brazil] Law No. 11.346 of 15 September of 2006 establishing SISAN – National Food and Nutritional Security System – to guarantee the human right to adequate food and nutrition (Official Gazette of 18 September 2006) (unofficial translation):

Chapter 1. General provisions

Art. 1. This Law establishes the definitions, principles, guidelines, objectives, and composition of the National Food and Nutritional Security System – SISAN, through which the government, together with the organized participation of the civil society, shall formulate and implement policies, plans, programs, and actions which seek to guarantee the human right to adequate food.

Art. 2. Adequate food is a basic human right, inherent to human dignity and indispensable to the realization of the rights established by the Federal Constitution. The government shall adopt the policies and actions needed to promote and guarantee food and nutritional security for the population.

§1. The adoption of these policies and actions shall take into account environmental, cultural, economic, regional, and social dimensions.

§2. The government shall respect, protect, promote, provide, inform, monitor, supervise, and evaluate the realization of the human right to adequate food, as well as guarantee the mechanisms for its exigibility.

Art. 3. Food and nutritional security consists in the realization of the human right to regular and permanent access to good quality food, in sufficient quantity, without compromising the fulfillment other basic needs, having as its basis healthy nutritional habits that respect cultural diversity and that are environmentally, culturally, economically and socially sustainable.

Art. 4. Food and nutritional security comprises:

I. Expansion of access to food through its production, particularly via family and traditional farming, food processing, industrialization and commercialization, including international agreements; better food supply and distribution, including of water; job creation and redistribution of wealth;

II. The conservation of biodiversity and the sustainable use of resources;

III. The promotion of health, food, and nutrition for the population, including specific population groups and those more socially vulnerable;

IV. The guarantee of the biological, sanitary, nutritional, and technological qualities of the food, as well as its good use, which stimulates healthy food practices and lifestyles that respect the ethnic and racial diversity of the population;

V. The production of knowledge and the access to information; and

VI. The implementation of public policies and sustainable and participatory strategies of food production, commercialization and consumption, respecting the diverse cultural characteristics of the country.

Art. 5. The realization of the human right to adequate food and the attainment of food and nutritional security require respect for sovereignty, which confers to countries primacy in their decisions regarding the production and consumption of food products.

Art. 6. The Brazilian State shall make an effort to promote technical cooperation with foreign countries, thus contributing to the realization of the human right to adequate food worldwide.

Chapter II. The National Food and Security System

Art. 7. The realization of the human right to adequate food and the attainment of food and nutritional security will be made possible through SISAN, constituted by agencies and entities of the Federal Union, States, the Federal District and of municipalities, and private institutions, profitable or not, related to food and nutritional security and interested in integrating the System, provided that the applicable legislation is respected.

§1. The participation in SISAN to which this article refers shall obey the principles and guidelines of the System and will be defined based on the criteria established by the National Council for Food and Nutritional Security – CONSEA – and by the Inter-Ministerial Chamber for Food and Nutritional Security, to be created by the Federal Executive Power.

§2. The agencies which are responsible for the definition of the criteria to which §1 refers may establish distinct and particular requirements for the private and public sectors.

§3. The private or public agencies and entities which are part of SISAN shall work in an interdependent manner, but their autonomy to make decisions shall be preserved.

§4. The obligation of the State does not exclude the responsibility of those entities of the civil society that are part of SISAN.

Art. 8. SISAN shall be ruled by the following principles:

I. Universality and equity in the access to adequate food, without any kind of discrimination;

II. The preservation of autonomy and respect for the dignity of all;

III. Social participation in the formulation, execution, examination, monitoring, and control of the policies and plans on food and nutritional security in all spheres of the Government; and

IV. Transparency in the programs, actions, and public and private resources, and in the criteria for their concession.

Art. 9. SISAN is based on the following guidelines:

I. Promotion of the inter-sectorality of policies, programs, and governmental and non-governmental actions;

II. Decentralization of actions and articulation, under cooperation, among the spheres of the government;

III. Monitoring of the food and nutrition condition of the population, seeking to subsidize the management cycle of policies for the area in the different spheres of the government;

IV. Conjunction of immediate and direct measures which guarantee access to adequate food, through actions that improve the resources and means of autonomous subsistence of the population;

V. Articulation between budget and management; and

VI. Encouragement of research development and training of human resources.

Art. 10. SISAN seeks to formulate and implement policies and plans on food and nutritional security, motivate the integration of efforts between the government and civil society, as well as promote the examination, monitoring, and evaluation of food and nutritional security in the country.

Art. 11. SISAN is composed by:

I. The National Conference for Food and Nutritional Security, responsible for the recommendation to CONSEA of the guidelines and priorities of the National Policy and Plan on Food and Nutritional Security, as well as for the evaluation of SISAN;

II. CONSEA, which is responsible for the immediate advising of the President of the Republic, is in charge of:

  (a) Arranging for the convocation of the National Conference for Food and Nutritional Security, periodically, not more than four years apart, as well as defining the parameters of its composition, organization, and operation, based on its own regulation;

  (b) Suggesting to the Federal Executive Power, in view of the deliberations of the National Conference for Food and Nutritional Security, the guidelines and priorities of the Nation Policy and Plan on Food and Nutritional Security, including the budgetary requirements for its execution.

  (c) Articulating, examining, and monitoring, in collaboration with other members of the System, the implementation and convergence of actions which are inherent to the National Policy and Plan on Food and Nutritional Security;

  (d) Defining, in collaboration with the Inter-Ministerial Chamber for Food and Nutritional Security, the criteria and procedures of integration into SISAN;

  (e) Instituting permanent mechanisms of articulation with related agencies and entities of food and nutritional security in the States, the Federal District, and municipalities, seeking to promote dialogue and the convergence of the actions which integrate SISAN;

  (f) Mobilizing and supporting entities of civil society in the discussion and implementation of public actions for food and nutritional security;

III. The Inter-Ministerial Chamber for Food and Nutritional Security, composed of Ministers of State and Special Secretaries who are responsible for the portfolios related to the attainment of food and nutritional security, has the following responsibilities, among others:

  (a) To elaborate, in view of the guidelines from CONSEA, the National Policy and Plan on Food and Nutritional Security, suggesting the guidelines, goals, basis of resources and tools to examine, monitor, and evaluate its implementation;

  (b) To coordinate the execution of the Policy and of the Plan;

  (c) To articulate the policies and plans of their related state agencies as well as those of the Federal District;

IV. Agencies and entities of food and nutritional security of the Federal Union, states, Federal District, and municipalities;

V. Private institutions, profitable or not, which are interested in integrating the System and respect the criteria, principles, and guidelines of SISAN.

§1. The National Conference for Food and Nutritional Security will be preceded by state, district, and municipal conferences, which shall be summoned and organized by related agencies and entities in the states, Federal District, and municipalities, from which the delegates to the National Conference will be chosen.

§2. CONSEA shall be composed based on the following criteria:

I. (one third) of governmental representatives constituted by Ministers of State and Special Secretaries responsible for the portfolios related to the attainment of food and nutritional security;

II. (two thirds) of civil society representatives chosen based on appointment criteria approved at the National Conference for Food and Nutritional Security; and

III. observers, including representatives of allied Federal Councils, international bodies, and of the Federal Public Ministry.

§3. CONSEA shall be presided over by one of its members, a civil society representative, appointed by collegiate jury, according to regulations, and chosen by the President of the Republic.

§4. The performance of advisers, and permanent and substitute members of CONSEA shall be considered of relevant public interest and non-remunerated service.

2.2 National strategies and action plans

Framework laws are simply one component of broader national strategies for the fulfilment of human rights, which aim to ensure their progressive realization. The area of the right to food probably offers the best illustration. The implementation of the right to food has been encouraged by the adoption in 2004, within the Council of the UN Organization for Food and Agriculture (FAO), of a set of Voluntary Guidelines which are concrete recommendations about how to operationalize the right to food at domestic level. Guidelines 3 and 7 relate, respectively, to the adoption of national strategies, and to the adoption of an appropriate legal framework:

Council of the FAO, Voluntary Guidelines on the Progressive Realization of the Right to Adequate Food in the Context of National Food Security (23 November 2004):

Guideline 3: Strategies

3.1 States, as appropriate and in consultation with relevant stakeholders and pursuant to their national laws, should consider adopting a national human-rights based strategy for the progressive realization of the right to adequate food in the context of national food security as part of an overarching national development strategy, including poverty reduction strategies, where they exist.

3.2 The elaboration of these strategies should begin with a careful assessment of existing national legislation, policy and administrative measures, current programmes, systematic identification of existing constraints and availability of existing resources. States should formulate the measures necessary to remedy any weakness, and propose an agenda for change and the means for its implementation and evaluation.

3.3 These strategies could include objectives, targets, benchmarks and time frames; and actions to formulate policies, identify and mobilize resources, define institutional mechanisms, allocate responsibilities, coordinate the activities of different actors, and provide for monitoring mechanisms. As appropriate, such strategies could address all aspects of the food system, including the production, processing, distribution, marketing and consumption of safe food. They could also address access to resources and to markets as well as parallel measures in other fields.

These strategies should, in particular, address the needs of vulnerable and disadvantaged groups, as well as special situations such as natural disasters and emergencies.

3.4 Where necessary, States should consider adopting and, as appropriate, reviewing a national poverty reduction strategy that specifically addresses access to adequate food.

3.5 States, individually or in cooperation with relevant international organizations, should consider integrating into their poverty reduction strategy a human rights perspective based on the principle of non-discrimination. In raising the standard of living of those below the poverty line, due regard should be given to the need to ensure equality in practice to those who are traditionally disadvantaged and between women and men.

3.6 In their poverty reduction strategies, States should also give priority to providing basic services for the poorest, and investing in human resources by ensuring access to primary education for all, basic health care, capacity building in good practices, clean drinking-water, adequate sanitation and justice and by supporting programmes in basic literacy, numeracy and good hygiene practices.

3.7 States are encouraged, *inter alia* and in a sustainable manner, to increase productivity and to revitalize the agriculture sector including livestock, forestry and fisheries through special policies and strategies targeted at small-scale and traditional fishers and farmers in rural areas, and the creation of enabling conditions for private sector participation, with emphasis on human capacity development and the removal of constraints to agricultural production, marketing and distribution.

3.8 In developing these strategies, States are encouraged to consult with civil society organizations and other key stakeholders at national and regional levels, including small-scale and traditional farmers, the private sector, women and youth associations, with the aim of promoting their active participation in all aspects of agricultural and food production strategies.

3.9 These strategies should be transparent, inclusive and comprehensive, cut across national policies, programmes and projects, take into account the special needs of girls and women, combine short-term and long-term objectives, and be prepared and implemented in a participatory and accountable manner.

3.10 States should support, including through regional cooperation, the implementation of national strategies for development, in particular for the reduction of poverty and hunger as well as for the progressive realization of the right to adequate food.

Guideline 7: Legal framework

7.1 States are invited to consider, in accordance with their domestic legal and policy frameworks, whether to include provisions in their domestic law, possibly including constitutional or legislative review that facilitates the progressive realization of the right to adequate food in the context of national food security.

7.2 States are invited to consider, in accordance with their domestic legal and policy frameworks, whether to include provisions in their domestic law, which may include their constitutions, bills of rights or legislation, to directly implement the progressive realization of the right to adequate food. Administrative, quasi-judicial and judicial mechanisms to provide adequate, effective and prompt remedies accessible, in particular, to members of vulnerable groups may be envisaged.

7.3 States that have established a right to adequate food under their legal system should inform the general public of all available rights and remedies to which they are entitled.

7.4 States should consider strengthening their domestic law and policies to accord access by women heads of households to poverty reduction and nutrition security programmes and projects.

Recent years have witnessed a growing interest in the adoption of national action plans, or strategies, in the field of human rights, as a means of bridging the gap between generous but vague norms set at international level and practical implementation (see, e.g. Office of the High Commissioner for Human Rights (OHCHR) Professional Training Series No.10, *Handbook on National Human Rights Plans of Action*, UN, 2002; United Nations Development Programme (UNDP), *A Desk Study of National Human Rights Action Plans* (UNDP Oslo Governance Centre, October 2003)). In April 2009, China adopted its first human rights action plan, covering 2009–10. The plan covers a wide range of human rights, including both economic, social and cultural rights, and civil and political rights, and it includes a series of commitments related to the implementation of China's international human rights obligations. The introduction explains the reasons that guided the adoption of the action plan and how it was developed:

National Human Rights Action Plan of China (2009–2010) (Information Office of the State Council of the People's Republic of China and Xinhua News Agency, 13 April 2009):

The Chinese government unswervingly pushes forward the cause of human rights in China, and, in response to the United Nations' call for establishing a national human rights action plan, has instituted the National Human Rights Action Plan of China (2009–2010) on the basis of painstakingly summing up past experience and objectively analyzing the current situation. The plan defines the Chinese government's goals in promoting and protecting human rights, and the specific measures it is taking to this end.

The plan was framed on the following fundamental principles: First, in pursuit of the basic principles prescribed in the Constitution of China, and the essentials of the Universal Declaration of Human Rights and International Covenant on Civil and Political Rights, the plan is aimed at improving laws and regulations upholding human rights and advancing the cause of China's human rights in accordance with the law; second, adhering to the principle that all kinds of human rights are interdependent and inseparable, the plan encourages the coordinated development of economic, social and cultural rights as well as civil and political rights, and the balanced development of individual and collective rights; third, in the light of practicality and China's reality, the plan ensures the feasibility of the proposed goals and measures, and scientifically promotes the development of the cause of human rights in China.

The National Human Rights Action Plan of China (2009–2010) involves broad participation by the relevant government departments and all social sectors. The Chinese government has established the 'joint meeting mechanism for the National Human Rights Action Plan' for the purpose of working out a good plan. The Information Office of the State Council and Ministry of Foreign Affairs, two members of the 'joint meeting mechanism', take the responsibility of convening meetings. Other members include: Legislative Affairs Committee of the Standing Committee of the National People's Congress, Committee for Social and Legal Affairs of the Chinese People's Political Consultative Conference National Committee, Supreme People's Court, Supreme People's Procuratorate, National Development and Reform Commission, Ministry of Education, State Ethnic Affairs Commission, Ministry of Civil Affairs, Ministry of Justice, Ministry of Human Resources and Social Security, Ministry of Health, China Disabled Persons' Federation, and China Society for Human Rights Studies, altogether 53 organizations.

A group of experts from universities and research institutions ... also participated in the drafting and formulation of the plan. In the drafting and formulation process, joint meetings were held on many occasions to conduct thorough discussions with relevant government departments; several symposia were convened with representation from over 20 organizations, such as China Law Society, All-China Lawyers' Association, China Legal Aid Foundation, China Environmental Protection Foundation, Chinese Society of Education, China Women's Development Foundation, China Foundation for Poverty Alleviation, China Foundation for Disabled Persons, and China Foundation for Human Rights Development, to solicit suggestions for revisions through thorough discussions among social and non-governmental organizations, universities and research institutions, and other social sectors.

The National Human Rights Action Plan of China (2009–2010) is a document explaining the policy of the Chinese government with regard to the promotion and protection of human rights during the period 2009–2010, covering the political, economic, social and cultural fields. Governments and government departments at all levels shall make the action plan part of their responsibilities, and proactively implement it in line with the principle of 'each performing its own functions and sharing out the work and responsibilities'. All enterprises, public institutions, social and non-governmental organizations, press and media agencies, and the general public shall give vigorous publicity to this action plan, and expedite its implementation. Initiated by the State Council Information Office and the Ministry of Foreign Affairs, the 'joint meeting mechanism for the National Human Rights Action Plan', comprising legislative and judicial organs and departments under the State Council, is responsible for coordinating the implementation, supervision and assessment of the plan.

Lithuania is one of the relatively few developed countries which has adopted a human rights action plan. This process began in December 1999, initially under the leadership of a working group (the National HURIST Country Team, part of a joint UNDP–OHCHR human rights strengthening programme) established by decree of the Prime Minister of Lithuania in January 2000. This working group was chaired by the Chairman of the Parliamentary Committee on Human Rights. It also included senior public officials, NGO representatives and a UNDP Programme Officer. At the end of 2000, it was decided to hand over the political responsibility for developing the national human rights action plan (NHRAP) to the Parliamentary Committee on Human Rights, although the National HURIST Country Team continued to be involved and had to ensure the involvement of the relevant ministries and government agencies as well as civil society organizations in the development of the NHRAP. The preparation of the NHRAP entered its active phase in September 2001, after the strategy for its development was agreed upon. The Parliament finally approved the national action plan in November 2002. Tomas Baranovas, Programme Officer within the UNDP office in Lithuania in 1999–2003, prepared a report summarizing the conclusions drawn from this experience. He describes the process through which the national action plan was adopted, and the 'lessons learned':

Tomas Baranovas, Development of a National Human Rights Action Plan: the Experience of Lithuania, UNDP Oslo Governance Centre, December 2002:

The UNDP project was implemented in three phases. In the first phase (September 2001–March 2002), priority issues were identified through a participatory process. A baseline study on human rights in Lithuania was also developed and validated at the expert level. During the second phase (March 2002–June 2002), the baseline study on human rights in Lithuania was verified and corrected involving broad participation of the public, including five regional workshops and a national conference. In the third phase (July–October 2002), the National Human Rights Action Plan was drafted on the basis of the conclusions and recommendations of the baseline study on human rights in Lithuania as well as the results of the regional workshops and the national conference. The Action Plan was approved by the Parliament in November 2002. During the three phases, key roles were played by the Parliament, the Project Manager, the National HURIST Country Team and UNDP. Public information and awareness measures included a TV and radio campaign ...

A number of lessons may be drawn from the process of development of a National Human Rights Action Plan in Lithuania:

- The assignment of overall responsibility to an inter-agency working group did not prove to be an effective arrangement due to insufficient concentration of accountability and commitment for the task.
- The shift of political responsibility to the Parliament, which was considered to be 'closer to the people', assisted by an inter-agency working group, proved to be an effective management arrangement. It also ensured national political commitment at the highest level.
- Choosing public opinion as a primary basis for identifying priority human rights issues ensured broad-based public involvement in the process of development of the Action Plan.
- The decrease in intensity of UNDP's involvement in developing the Action Plan helped to strengthen the leadership and commitment of national entities.
- Lithuania's desire for raising its international standing in the area of human rights protection encouraged commitment to the Action Plan.
- Networking with international partners significantly facilitated the process.
- The 15 months allocated to the UNDP project proved to be too short to accommodate the participatory process.
- The linkage with other national development strategies proved to be effective in integrating a human rights approach with other national policies, although tensions between 'the voice of the people', as expressed in the Action Plan, and the 'regular' work of the ministries had to be dealt with.
- The personal commitment of stakeholders played a key role.
- The 1998 UNDP guidelines on Integrating Human Rights with Sustainable Human Development provided a conceptual framework to the process but did not serve as practical guidance because they do not elaborate on the development of NHRAPs.

The Lithuanian National Human Rights Action Plan was developed in a participatory manner, with involvement of the Parliament, government agencies and civil organizations at all stages of the process. Results of public opinion surveys were given a special emphasis. The methodology applied has laid the groundwork for the implementation of the Action Plan and a significant improvement in the human rights situation in Lithuania. It may also be of use to other countries wishing to develop a National Human Rights Action Plan.

The Committee on the Rights of the Child has also stressed the advantages of adopting a national action plan, or a strategy, for the implementation of children's rights. Among the advantages it sees is improved accountability (since governments commit to certain time-bound objectives), improved dissemination about the government's international obligations, and improved co-ordination across different branches of government:

Committee on the Rights of the Child, General Comment No. 5 (2003), *General Measures of Implementation of the Convention on the Rights of the Child* **(Arts. 4, 42 and 44, para. 6) (UN Doc. CRC/GC/2003/5, 27 November 2003), paras. 27–39:**

[Elements for a national strategy for the implementation of the rights of the child]
The Committee believes that effective implementation of the Convention requires visible cross-sectoral coordination to recognize and realize children's rights across Government, between different levels of government and between Government and civil society – including in particular children and young people themselves. Invariably, many different government departments and other governmental or quasi-governmental bodies affect children's lives and children's enjoyment of their rights. Few, if any, government departments have no effect on children's lives, direct or indirect. Rigorous monitoring of implementation is required, which should be built into the process of government at all levels but also independent monitoring by national human rights institutions, NGOs and others.

A. Developing a comprehensive national strategy rooted in the Convention If Government as a whole and at all levels is to promote and respect the rights of the child, it needs to work on the basis of a unifying, comprehensive and rights-based national strategy, rooted in the Convention.

The Committee commends the development of a comprehensive national strategy or national plan of action for children, built on the framework of the Convention. The Committee expects States parties to take account of the recommendations in its concluding observations on their periodic reports when developing and/or reviewing their national strategies. If such a strategy is to be effective, it needs to relate to the situation of all children, and to all the rights in the Convention. It will need to be developed through a process of consultation, including with children and young people and those living and working with them. [M]eaningful consultation with children requires special child-sensitive materials and processes; it is not simply about extending to children access to adult processes.

Particular attention will need to be given to identifying and giving priority to marginalized and disadvantaged groups of children. The non-discrimination principle in the Convention requires that all the rights guaranteed by the Convention should be recognized for all children within the jurisdiction of States ...

To give the strategy authority, it will need to be endorsed at the highest level of government. Also, it needs to be linked to national development planning and included in national budgeting; otherwise, the strategy may remain marginalized outside key decision–making processes.

The strategy must not be simply a list of good intentions; it must include a description of a sustainable process for realizing the rights of children throughout the State; it must go beyond statements of policy and principle, to set real and achievable targets in relation to the full range of economic, social and cultural and civil and political rights for all children. The comprehensive national strategy may be elaborated in sectoral national plans of action – for example for education and health – setting out specific goals, targeted implementation measures and allocation of financial and human resources. The strategy will inevitably set priorities, but it must not neglect or dilute in any way the detailed obligations which States parties have accepted under the Convention. The strategy needs to be adequately resourced, in human and financial terms.

Developing a national strategy is not a one-off task. Once drafted the strategy will need to be widely disseminated throughout Government and to the public, including children (translated into child-friendly versions as well as into appropriate languages and forms). The strategy will need to include arrangements for monitoring and continuous review, for regular updating and for periodic reports to parliament and to the public.

The 'national plans of action' which States were encouraged to develop following the first World Summit for Children, held in 1990, were related to the particular commitments set by nations attending the Summit. In 1993, the Vienna Declaration and Programme of Action, adopted by the World Conference on Human Rights, called on States to integrate the Convention on the Rights of the Child into their national human rights action plans.

The outcome document of the United Nations General Assembly special session on children, in 2002, also commits States 'to develop or strengthen as a matter of urgency if possible by the end of 2003 national and, where appropriate, regional action plans with a set of specific time-bound and measurable goals and targets based on this plan of action ...' The Committee welcomes the commitments made by States to achieve the goals and targets set at the special session on children and identified in the outcome document, *A World Fit for Children*. But the Committee emphasizes that making particular commitments at global meetings does not in any way reduce States parties' legal obligations under the Convention. Similarly, preparing specific plans of action in response to the special session does not reduce the need for a comprehensive implementation strategy for the Convention. States should integrate their response to the 2002 special session and to other relevant global conferences into their overall implementation strategy for the Convention as a whole.

The outcome document also encourages States parties to 'consider including in their reports to the Committee on the Rights of the Child information on measures taken and results achieved in the implementation of the present Plan of Action'. The Committee endorses this proposal; it is committed to monitoring progress towards meeting the commitments made at the special session and will provide further guidance in its revised guidelines for periodic reporting under the Convention.

B. Coordination of implementation of children's rights In examining States parties' reports the Committee has almost invariably found it necessary to encourage further coordination of Government to ensure effective implementation: coordination among central govern-ment departments, among different provinces and regions, between central and other levels of government and between Government and civil society. The purpose of coordination is to ensure respect for all of the Convention's principles and standards for all children within the State jurisdiction; to ensure that the obligations inherent in ratification of or accession to the Convention are not only recognized by those large departments which have a substantial impact on children – education, health or welfare and so on – but right across Government, including for example departments concerned with finance, planning, employment and defence, and at all levels.

The Committee believes that, as a treaty body, it is not advisable for it to attempt to prescribe detailed arrangements appropriate for very different systems of government across States parties. There are many formal and informal ways of achieving effective coordination, including for example inter-ministerial and interdepartmental committees for children. The Committee proposes that States parties, if they have not already done so, should review the machinery of government from the perspective of implementation of the Convention and in particular of the four articles identified as providing general principles ...

Many States parties have with advantage developed a specific department or unit close to the heart of Government, in some cases in the President's or Prime Minister's or Cabinet office, with the objective of coordinating implementation and children's policy. As noted above, the actions of virtually all government departments impact on children's lives. It is not practicable to bring responsibility for all children's services together into a single department, and in any case doing so could have the danger of further marginalizing children in Government. But a special unit, if given high-level authority – reporting directly, for example, to the Prime Minister, the President or a Cabinet Committee on children – can contribute both to the overall purpose of making children more visible in Government and to coordination to ensure respect for children's rights across Government and at all levels of Government. Such a unit can be given responsibility for developing the comprehensive children's strategy and monitoring its implementation, as well as for coordinating reporting under the Convention.

3 INDICATORS AND BENCHMARKS

Human rights indicators are data related to certain institutional or normative developments, to specific events, or to the situation existing within a particular territory or population, that are related to human rights standards (on human rights indicators, see generally G. de Beco, *Non-Judicial Mechanisms for the Implementation of Human Rights in European States* (Brussels: Bruylant, 2009), part III; M. Green, 'What We Talk About When We Talk About Indicators: Current Approaches to Human Rights Assessment', *Human Rights Quarterly*, 23 (2001), 1062; S. Hertel and L. Minkler, 'Economic and Social Rights: the Terrain' in S. Hertel and L. Minkler (eds.), *Economic Rights: Conceptual, Measurement and Policy Issues* (Cambridge University Press, 2007); P. Hunt, *State Obligations, Indicators, Benchmarks and the Right to Education* (Background paper submitted to the Committee on Economic, Social and Cultural Rights), 16 July 1998, E/C. 12/1998/11; T. Landman, 'Measuring Human Rights: Principle, Practice, and Policy', *Human Rights Quarterly*, 26 (2004), 906; T. Landman and E. Carvalho, *Measuring Human Rights* (London: Routledge-Cavendish, 2009); K. Tomasevski, 'Indicators' in A. Eide, C. Krause and A. Rosas (eds.), *Economic, Social and Cultural Rights* (Dordrecht: Martinus Nijhoff, 2001), pp. 389–403). Although they may build on development indicators (measuring the degree of social or economic 'development'), human rights indicators are therefore specific. Paul Hunt, a former UN Special Rapporteur on the right to health, emphasizes for instance that an indicator relating to the right to health 'derives from, reflects and is designed to monitor the realisation, or otherwise, of specific right to health norms, usually with a view to holding a duty bearer to account'; it therefore owes its specific characteristics to '(i) its explicit derivation from specific right to health norms; and (ii) the purpose to which it is put, namely right to health monitoring with a view to holding duty-bearers to account' (*Interim Report of the Special Rapporteur on the Right of Everyone to the Enjoyment of the Highest Attainable Standard of Physical and Mental Health, Mr Paul Hunt*, 10 October 2003, A/58/427, at para. 10; see also the updated set of indicators on the right to health proposed by Paul Hunt in his capacity as Special Rapporteur on the right to health, *Report of the Special Rapporteur on the Right of Everyone to the Enjoyment of the Highest Attainable Standard of Physical and Mental Health, Mr Paul Hunt*, 3 March 2006, E/CN.4/2006/48, Annex; and P. Hunt and G. MacNaughton, 'A Human Rights-Based Approach to Health Indicators' in M. Baderin and R. McCorquodale (eds.), *Economic, Social and Cultural Rights in Action* (Oxford University Press, 2007), pp. 303–30, Annex). Yet, it is also this specificity of human rights indicators that makes them more complex than development indicators, since what needs to be measured is not only the level of deprivation of the right-holder, but also the extent to which the State is complying with its obligations as set out in human rights instruments, by making efforts towards the removal of obstacles to the full enjoyment of the right.

Human rights indicators can measure (a) whether a State has ratified the relevant international instruments, adapted its regulatory framework, and set up the institutional mechanisms, that should improve compliance with the right (*structural indicators*); (b) whether a State has taken the policy measures, and made the necessary budgetary commitments, to ensure effective implementation of the right (*process indicators*); and (c) whether a State is succeeding in its efforts to realize the right (*outcome indicators*). Indicators serve a number of purposes, including (i) guiding the adoption of appropriate policies, aimed at the full realization of human rights – for instance, where outcome indicators reveal that the efforts pursued are not succeeding, requiring that the State reorient its policies to improve their efficacy; (ii) monitoring compliance with the requirement of non-discrimination – which in turn requires that the indicators be broken down by population group and according to gender (see chapter 7, boxes 7.3. and 7.5. and section 4); (iii) improving accountabilty towards rights-holders; and (iv) facilitating monitoring by domestic and international bodies. While initially developed for use in the implementation of economic and social rights, indicators are now also recognized to be a useful tool in the implementation of civil and political rights, as illustrated by the examples in the table presented below.

This section examines the use of indicators in human rights monitoring (section 3.1.), with a particular emphasis on the Committee on Economic, Social and Cultural Rights and the IBSA (indicators – benchmarks – scoping – assessment) procedure for monitoring compliance witht the rights of the International Covenant on Economic, Social and Cultural Rights (section 3.2.), as well as on the use of indicators in the Inter-American system (section 3.3.). In chapter 7 (section 4), indicators are discussed further in the specific context of anti-discrimination policies.

Category of indicator	Structural indicators	Process indicators	Outcome indicators
What does it serve to measure?	Goodwill of the State in establishing an institutional and legal framework	Efforts made by the State in order to move from the framework to implementation	Results achieved: success in achieving objectives
How indicative is it of the State's compliance with its obligations?	Depends on the State	Requires maximum use of available resources	Depends on the State, but also on internal and external factors or constraints
Examples	• Ratification of international instruments • Legal recognition of the right • Empowering courts to monitor compliance • Adoption of a national strategy • Establishment of a national human rights institution	• Financing of policies aimed at implementing the right • Number of complaints filed • Proportion of the population reached by public programmes • Percentage of national budget going to education, health, etc.	• Reported cases of arbitrary deprivation of life • Percentage of undernourished population • Percentage of children attending school at different levels of education

3.1 General considerations on the role of indicators in human rights monitoring

Although they regularly call upon States to develop indicators in order to measure progress in the realization of human rights – particularly economic and social rights and the right to non-discrimination – the use of statistics by UN human rights treaty bodies has been mostly ad hoc and superficial (on the difficulties they encounter in this regard, see A. Chapman, 'The Status of Efforts to Monitor Economic, Social and Cultural Rights' in A. Minkler and S. Hertel (eds.), *Economic Rights: Conceptual, Measurement, and Policy Issues* (Cambridge University Press, 2007), p. 143). The paper below follows a request of the chairpersons of the human rights treaty bodies to the Office of the High Commissioner for Human Rights to assist the treaty bodies in analysing statistical information in States parties' reports. It discusses how indicators could better inform the work of the UN human rights treaty bodies. It identifies a number of associated challenges.

Office of the High Commissioner for Human Rights, Report on Indicators for Monitoring Compliance with International Human Rights Instruments: a Conceptual and Methodological Framework (HRI/MC/2006/7, 11 May 2006):

Introduction
[I]n the context of the ongoing reform of the treaty bodies in general, and the reporting procedure in particular, it has been argued that the use of appropriate quantitative indicators for assessing the implementation of human rights – in what is essentially a qualitative and

quasi-judicial exercise – could contribute to streamlining the process, enhance its transparency, make it more effective, reduce the reporting burden and above all improve follow-up on the recommendations and concluding observations, both at the committee, as well as the country, levels.

3. Indeed, the demand for appropriate indicators is not only for monitoring the implementation of the human rights instruments by States parties, but indicators are also seen as useful tools in reinforcing accountability, in articulating and advancing claims on the duty–bearers and in formulating requisite public policies and programmes for facilitating the realization of human rights. In this attempt to make the reporting, implementation and monitoring of human rights treaties more effective and efficient, there is an understanding that one needs to move away from using general statistics, the relevance of which to such tasks is often indirect and lacks clarity, to using specific indicators that, while embedded in the relevant human rights normative framework, can be easily applied and interpreted by the potential users.

4. While the importance of quantitative indicators is reflected in the human rights normative framework, as well as in the States parties' reporting obligations, the use of such indicators in the reporting and the follow-up procedure of the treaty bodies have been limited. There are conceptual and methodological considerations that explain this. For quantitative indicators to be effective tools in monitoring the implementation of human rights, it is necessary that they be anchored in a conceptual framework that addresses the concerns and goals of that process. The need for an adequate conceptual basis lies in having a rationale for identifying and designing the relevant indicators and not reducing the exercise to a mere listing of possible alternatives. It is also important that such indicators are explicitly and precisely defined, based on an acceptable methodology of data collection and presentation, and are or could be available on a regular basis. Moreover, it is equally important that indicators be suitable to the context where they are applied. In the absence of these considerations being met, it may not be feasible or even acceptable to the States parties to use quantitative indicators in their reporting obligations to the treaty bodies. At the same time, it would be difficult for the committees to demonstrate the relevance and encourage the use of appropriate indicators in the reporting and follow-up process ...

I. Human rights indicators, notion and rationale

7. ... [H]uman rights indicators are specific information on the state of an event, activity or an outcome that can be related to human rights norms and standards; that address and reflect the human rights concerns and principles; and that are used to assess and monitor promotion and protection of human rights. Defined in this manner, there could be some indicators that are uniquely human rights indicators because they owe their existence to certain human rights norms or standards and are generally not used in other contexts. This could be the case, for instance, with an indicator like the reported number of extrajudicial, summary or arbitrary executions, or the number of victims of torture by the police and the paramilitary forces, or the number of children who do not have access to primary education because of discrimination exerted by officials. At the same time, there could be a large number of other indicators such as socio-economic statistics (e.g. UNDP's human development indicators) that could meet (at least implicitly) all the definitional requirements of a human rights indicator as laid out here. In all these cases, to the extent that such indicators relate to the human rights standards and are used for human rights assessment, it would be helpful to consider them as human rights indicators.

Quantitative and qualitative indicators 8. Indicators can be quantitative or qualitative. The first category views indicators narrowly as an equivalent of 'statistics' and the latter, a broader 'topical' usage, covering any information relevant to the observance or enjoyment of a specific right. In this paper the term 'quantitative indicator' is used to designate any kind of indicators that are or can be expressed in quantitative form, such as numbers, percentages or indices. Some commonly used quantitative indicators are enrolment rates for the school-age group of children, indicators on ratification of treaties, proportion of seats held by women in national parliament and reported number of enforced or involuntary disappearances. One also finds a widespread use of 'checklists' or a set of questions as indicators, which sometimes seek to complement or elaborate numerical information on the realization of human rights. In the agencies of the United Nations system and in the human rights community, many experts have often favoured such an interpretation of the word indicator. These two main usages of the word 'indicator' in the human rights community, do not reflect two opposed approaches. Given the complexity of assessing compliance with human rights standards, all relevant qualitative and quantitative information is potentially useful. [Human rights indicators could also be categorized as objective or subjective indicators. This distinction is not necessarily based on the consideration of using, or not using, reliable or replicable methods of data collection for defining the indicators. Instead, it is ideally seen in terms of the information content of the indicators concerned. Thus, objects, facts or events that can, in principle, be directly observed or verified (for example, weight of children and number of reported violent deaths) are categorized as objective indicators. Indicators based on perceptions, opinions, assessment or judgments expressed by individuals are categorized as subjective indicators.] Quantitative indicators can facilitate qualitative evaluations by measuring the magnitude of certain events. Reciprocally, qualitative information can complement the interpretation of quantitative indicators. Indeed, the choice of a particular kind of indicator in any assessment depends, in the first instance, on the requirements and the needs of the user. This paper essentially looks at quantitative indicators that by virtue of their definition, presentation and on account of their data–generating methodologies are particularly suitable for supporting the assessment of States parties' compliance with international human rights treaties.

Indicators in the international legal framework 9. The human rights monitoring mechanisms refer to a wide range of indicators (qualitative and quantitative) that are reflected in the human rights normative framework comprising the various international instruments, their elaborations through general comments, reporting guidelines and concluding observations. While some quantitative indicators are explicitly quoted in the human rights treaties, the general comments adopted by the treaty bodies specify the type and role of these indicators.

10. Quantitative indicators are explicitly quoted in provisions of international human rights treaties. In the International Covenant on Economic, Social and Cultural Rights, for instance, article 12 states that to achieve the full realization of the right to health 'the steps to be taken by the States parties shall include those necessary for the provision for the reduction of the stillbirth–rate and of infant mortality'. Article 10 of the Convention on the Elimination of All Forms of Discrimination against Women (CEDAW), on the right to education contains a provision for 'the reduction of female student drop-out rates' and article 14 of the ICCPR requires that in the case of criminal charges everyone has the right to be tried 'without undue delay'. Such references to quantitative indicators, in this case essentially to officially compiled statistics, contribute to the definition of the content of the concerned human right and help to reinforce its operational aspects.

11. The importance of indicators is also highlighted in general comments adopted by the treaty bodies as well as in their concluding observations on State parties' reports. For instance, the Human Rights Committee (HRC) called for statistics on the number and handling of complaints for victims of maltreatment to support its normative assessment of the realization of the right not to be subjected to torture or to cruel, inhuman or degrading treatment or punishment. In relation to the right to participate in the conduct of public affairs, the same committee asked for statistical information on the percentage of women in publicly elected office, including the legislature, as well as in high-ranking civil service positions and the judiciary. The Committee on Economic, Social and Cultural Rights, the Committee on the Elimination of Racial Discrimination, the Committee on the Elimination of Discrimination against Women and the Committee on the Rights of the Child have been quite systematic on their request for statistics and disaggregated data relevant to the assessment of the compliance with human rights standards. While the Committee against Torture appears, at first sight, to be less involved in indicators and statistics, it has been seeking evidences on patterns of gross human rights violations in countries concerned with the 'refoulement' of individuals.

From indicators to benchmarks 12. Benchmarks are indicators that are constrained by normative or empirical considerations to have a predetermined value. While the normative considerations may be based on international standards or political and social aspirations of the people, the empirical considerations are primarily related to issues of feasibility and resources. For instance, consider the indicator proportion of one-year-olds immunized against vaccine-preventable diseases; using a benchmark on this indicator may require fixing a specific value to the indicator, say, raising it to 90 per cent, or improving the existing coverage by 10 percentage points, so that the efforts of the implementing agency could be focused on attaining that value in the reference period. In the context of the compliance assessment of State parties, the use of a benchmark, as against an indicator, contributes to enhancing the accountability of the State parties by making them commit to a certain performance standard on the issue under assessment. The Committee on Economic, Social and Cultural Rights, in particular, has called for the setting of benchmarks to accelerate the implementation process. In the use of indicators for monitoring the implementation of human rights, the first step should be to have a general agreement on the choice of indicators. This should be followed by setting performance benchmarks on those selected indicators. [See *General Comment No. 14 on the Right to Health* and Eibe Riedel's IBSA framework proposing a four-step procedure covering indicators, benchmarks, scoping and assessment, discussed below in section 3.2.]

II. The conceptual framework
13. In outlining a conceptual framework for human rights indicators there are a number of interrelated aspects to be addressed. First, there is a need to anchor indicators identified for a human right in the normative content of that right, as enumerated in the relevant articles of the treaties and related general comments of the committees. Secondly, it is necessary to reflect cross-cutting human rights norms or principles (such as non-discrimination and equality, indivisibility, accountability, participation and empowerment) in the choice of indicators. Thirdly, the primary focus of human rights assessment (and its value-added) is in measuring the effort that the duty-holder makes in meeting his/her obligations – irrespective of whether it is directed at promoting a right or protecting it. At the same time, it is essential to get a measure of the 'intent or acceptance of' human rights standards by the State party, as well as the consolidation

of its efforts, as reflected in appropriate 'outcome' indicators. While such a focus recognizes an implicit linkage between the intent of a State party, its efforts in meeting those commitments and the consolidated outcomes of those efforts, the linkage may not always translate into a direct causal relationship between indicators for the said three stages in the implementation of a human right. This is because human rights are indivisible and interdependent such that outcomes and the efforts behind the outcomes associated with the realization of one right may, in fact, depend on the promotion and protection of other rights. Moreover, such a focus in measuring the implementation of human rights supports a common approach to assessing and monitoring civil and political rights, as well as economic, social and cultural rights. [The Expert Consultation organized by OHCHR, in Geneva, 29 August 2005, agreed that a common approach to assess and monitor civil and political rights and economic, social and cultural rights was feasible as well as desirable and that such an approach could be built around the use of structural-process-outcome indicators.] Finally, the adopted framework should be able to reflect the obligation of the duty-holder to *respect*, *protect* and *fulfil* human rights. Each of these aspects is discussed here.

Indicators for substantive human rights

Identifying attributes 14. As a starting point, for each human right there is a need to translate the narrative on the legal standard of the right into a limited number of characteristic attributes that facilitate the identification of appropriate indicators for monitoring the implementation of the right. Such a step is prompted first by the analytic convenience of having a structured approach to read the normative content of the right. Often, one finds that the enumeration of the right in the relevant articles and their elaboration in the concerned general comments are quite general and even overlapping, not quite amenable to the process of identifying indicators. By identifying the major attributes of a right, the process of selecting suitable indicators or clusters of indicators is facilitated. Secondly, in identifying the attributes the intention is to take a step closer to operationalizing the human rights standards. Thus, in articulating the attributes one arrives at a categorization with a terminology that is clear and, perhaps, more 'tangible' in facilitating the selection of indicators. Finally, to the extent feasible, for all substantive rights, the attributes have to be based on an exhaustive reading of the legal standard of the right and identified in a mutually exclusive manner.

15. Consider the case of the right to life, following this approach and taking into account primarily article 6 of the ICCPR and general comment No. 6 of the Human Rights Committee on the right to life (1982). Four attributes of the right to life, namely 'arbitrary deprivation of life'; 'disappearances of individuals'; 'health and nutrition' and 'death penalty' were identified. Similarly, in the case of the right to food, based on article 11 of ICESCR and general comment No. 12 of the Committee on Economic, Social and Cultural Rights on the right to adequate food (1999), 'nutrition'; 'food safety and consumer protection'; 'food availability'; and 'food accessibility' were identified as the relevant attributes. [It may be argued, for instance, in case of most economic, social and cultural rights to adopt a generic approach to the identification of attributes based on the notion of 'adequacy', 'accessibility'; 'availability'; 'adaptability' and 'quality'. While such an approach may not be feasible for most civil and political rights, even in case of the economic, social and cultural rights it may not be easy to follow consistently.] Attributes, in case of the right to judicial review of detention, were primarily based on ICCPR, article 9, and general comment No. 8 of the Human Rights Committee on the right to liberty and

security of persons (1982). For the right to health, the attributes were based on ICESCR, article 12, and general comment No. 14 of the Committee on Economic, Social and Cultural Rights on the right to the highest attainable standard of health (2000); general recommendation No. 24 (article 12 of CEDAW on women and health, 1999) of the Committee on the Elimination of Discrimination against Women; general comments No. 3 on HIV/AIDS and the rights of the child (2003) and No. 4 on adolescent health and development in the context of the Convention on the Rights of the Child, (2003) of the Committee on the Rights of the Child. In addition, relevant articles from the Universal Declaration of Human Rights and all conventions, based on the chart of congruence in the substantive provisions of the seven core international human rights treaties, were also used for reading the normative content of these four rights.

Configuring indicators for human rights attributes 16. In the second stage, a configuration of structural, process and outcome indicators is identified for the selected attributes of a human right. A key concern in proposing such a configuration of indicators is to bring to the fore an assessment of steps taken by the State parties in addressing its obligations – from intent to efforts, and on to outcomes of those efforts.

17. *Structural indicators* reflect the ratification/adoption of legal instruments and existence of basic institutional mechanisms deemed necessary for facilitating realization of the human right concerned. They capture the intent or acceptance of human rights standards by the State in undertaking measures for the realization of the human right concerned. Structural indicators have to focus foremost on the nature of domestic law as relevant to the concerned right – whether it incorporates the international standards – and the institutional mechanisms that promote and protect the standards. Structural indicators also need to look at the policy framework and indicated strategies of the State as relevant to the right. Some of the structural indicators may be common to all human rights and there may be others that are more relevant to specific human rights or even to a particular attribute of a human right.

18. *Process indicators* relate State policy instruments to milestones that become outcome indicators, which in turn can be more directly related to the realization of human rights. State policy instruments refer to all such measures including public programmes and specific interventions that a State is willing to take in order to give effect to its intent/acceptance of human rights standards to attain outcomes identified with the realization of a given human right. By defining the process indicators in terms of a concrete cause-and-effect relationship, the accountability of the State to its obligations can be better assessed. At the same time, these indicators help in directly monitoring the progressive fulfilment of the right or the process of protecting the right, as the case may be for the realization of the right concerned. Process indicators are more sensitive to changes than outcome indicators. Hence they are better at capturing progressive realization of the right or in reflecting the efforts of the State parties in protecting the rights.

19. *Outcome indicators* capture attainments, individual and collective, that reflect the status of realization of human rights in a given context. It is not only a more direct measure of the realization of a human right but it also reflects the importance of the indicator in assessing the enjoyment of the right. Since it consolidates over time the impact of various underlying processes (that can be captured by one or more process indicators), an outcome indicator is often a slow-moving indicator, less sensitive to capturing momentary changes than a process indicator. For example, life expectancy or mortality indicators could be a function of the immunization of a population, education or public health awareness of the population, as well as availability and accessibility of individuals to adequate nutrition.

20. In using the framework of structural, process and outcome indicators, the objective is to consistently and comprehensively cover indicators that can reflect the intent and outcome aspect of the realization of human rights. In the final analysis, it may not matter if an indicator is identified as a process or outcome indicator so long as it captures relevant aspect(s) of an attribute of a right or the right in general. Working with such a configuration of indicators simplifies the selection of indicators; it encourages the use of contextually relevant information; it facilitates a more comprehensive coverage of the different attributes or aspects of the realization of the right; and, perhaps, it also minimizes the overall number of indicators required to monitor the realization of the concerned right in any context. Secondly, though there is no one-to-one correspondence between the three categories of indicators and States' obligations to respect, protect and fulfil human rights, an appropriate combination of structural, process and outcome indicators, particularly the process indicators could help in assessing the implementation of the three obligations. [This is particularly so if one is using socio-economic and other administrative data (see para. 24) for inferring the implementation of the three kinds of obligations. For instance, though an outcome indicator may reveal the overall failure of the State party in meeting the three obligations, it may not be able to distinguish which of the three obligations are indeed violated. For example, this could be the case with high-mortality rate. In case of the process indicators it may be easier to identify the specific obligations that are being violated. However, if we consider events-based data on human rights violations (see para. 25) given the nature and methodology for collection of relevant information, it may be the easiest way to derive indicators that capture specifically the violations to respect, protect or fulfil.] Thirdly, process and outcome indicators may not be mutually exclusive. It is possible that a process indicator for one human right can be an outcome indicator in the context of another right. For instance, the proportion of the population below a minimum level of dietary energy consumption may be an outcome indicator for the right to adequate food and a process indicator for the right to life. The guiding concern being that for each right, or rather an attribute of a right, it is important to identify at least one outcome indicator that can be closely related to the realization/enjoyment of that right/attribute. In other words, the selected outcome indicator should sufficiently reflect its importance in the realization of that right. The process indicators are identified in a manner that they reflect the effort of the duty-holders in meeting or making progress in attaining the identified outcome. Having said this, there is an attempt in the illustrated list of indicators to use a consistent approach to differentiate process indicators from outcome indicators. Fourthly, the selection of all indicators has to be primarily guided by the empirical evidence on the use of those indicators. If identified indicators do not fare well on the criteria of empirical relevance, they will not be useful as monitoring tools.

Indicators for cross-cutting norms 21. The indicators that capture the cross-cutting human rights norms or principles do not necessarily relate exclusively to the realization of any specific human right. But they are meant to capture the extent to which the process to implement and realize human rights is, for instance, participatory, inclusionary, empowering, non-discriminatory, accountable or, where required, supported by international cooperation. While some of these cross-cutting norms could guide the process of identifying indicators itself, some could be reflected in the choice of data and its disaggregation in defining an indicator and some others could be reflected in the choice of indicators on specific human rights standards, such as the right to take part in public affairs, or rights related to personal liberty, security and remedy. In reflecting the human rights norms on non-discrimination and equality in the selection of structural, process and outcome indicators, a starting point is to seek disaggregated data by prohibited grounds of discrimination, such as sex, age, disability, ethnicity, religion, language, social, economic, regional or political status of people. Thus, for instance, if the indicator on the proportion of accused persons seeking and receiving legal aid is broken down by ethnic groups, it would be possible to capture some aspect of discrimination faced by ethnic groups or minorities in accessing justice in a given country. In other instances, the norm of effective remedies and procedural guarantees could be addressed as a 'procedural right' that has a bearing on the realization of a specific 'substantive right', hence is defined in reference to that substantive right. Also, compliance with the norm on non-discrimination in the context of the right to education, as a substantive right, could be captured using an indicator like the proportion of the girls in school-age groups enrolled in school to the proportion of the boys in the same age group enrolled in school. More important, in reflecting the norm on non-discrimination and equality, the emphasis is on indicators that capture the nature of access, and not just availability, to such goods and services that allow an individual to realize his/her rights. Similarly, in the case of the human rights norm of participation the attempt could be to reflect whether the vulnerable and marginalized segments of the population in a country have had a voice in the selection of indicators included in the reporting procedure of the State, or the extent to which they have participated in identifying measures that are being taken by the duty-holder in meeting its obligations.

22. At a more aggregate level, one could consider indicators such as the Gini coefficient, which reflects the distribution of household consumption expenditure/income to assess whether the development process in a country is encouraging participation, inclusion and equality in the distribution of returns from development. Indicators on work participation rates and educational attainment of the population, in general, and of specific groups, in particular (for instance, women, minorities and other social groups) could help in providing an assessment of the extent to which the norms on empowerment are being respected and promoted by the duty-bearer. In reflecting the role of international cooperation in the implementation of human rights, particularly for some economic and social rights, indicators on the contribution of donors, as well as the share of aid/technical cooperation in the efforts of the recipient country to implement the concerned right have to be included. Finally, the first steps in the implementation of the cross-cutting norm on accountability are already being taken as one translates the normative content of a right into quantitative indicators. Indeed, the availability of information sensitive to human rights and its collection and dissemination through independent mechanisms using transparent procedures demonstrates the existence of accountability and reinforces it. Moreover, as noted earlier, by identifying a process indicator as a measure that links State effort to a specific 'policy action – milestone relationship', the framework takes an important step in enhancing State accountability in implementing human rights. Ultimately, the reflection of cross-cutting human rights norms in the list of illustrative indicators is to be seen in terms of the configuration of suggested indicators and the totality of the framework, and not necessarily in terms of individual indicators for each of these norms.

III. Methodological framework

23. To be useful in monitoring the implementation of human rights treaties, quantitative indicators have to be explicitly and precisely defined, based on an acceptable methodology of data collection, processing and dissemination, and have to be available on a regular basis. The main methodological issue relates to data sources and generating mechanisms, criteria for

selection of indicators and the amenability of the framework to support contextually relevant indicators.

Sources and data-generating mechanisms

Socio-economic and other administrative statistics 24. Socio-economic statistics (for short) refers to quantitative information compiled and disseminated by the State through its administrative records and statistical surveys, usually in collaboration with national statistical agencies and under the guidance of international and specialized organizations. In the context of the treaty-body system, this category of indicators is of primary importance given the commitment of States, as parties to international human rights instruments, to report on their compliance. Socio-economic statistics enlighten issues not only related to economic, social and cultural rights, but also to civil and political rights, such as issues of the administration of justice and the rule of law (e.g. executions carried out under death penalty statutes; prison populations; and incidence of violent crimes). The use of a standardized methodology in the collection of information, be it through census operations, household surveys or through civil registration systems, and usually with reasonable reliability and validity, makes indicators based on such a methodology vital for the efforts to bring about greater transparency, credibility and accountability in human rights monitoring. However, in the context of human rights assessment, in general and monitoring undertaken by treaty bodies, in particular, it is in most instances essential to make use of information collected by non-governmental sources to supplement socio-economic statistics.

Events-based data on human rights violations 25. Events-based data (for short) consists mainly of data on alleged or reported cases of human rights violations, identified victims and perpetrators. Indicators, such as the alleged incidence of arbitrary deprivations of life, enforced or involuntary disappearances, arbitrary detention and torture, are usually reported by NGOs and are also processed in a standardized manner by United Nations special procedures. In general, such data may underestimate the incidence of violations and may even prevent valid comparisons over time or across regions, yet it may provide relevant indications to the treaty bodies in undertaking their assessment of the human rights situation in a given country. Though recent attempts have shown that this method can also be applied for monitoring the protection of economic, social and cultural rights, it has been mainly and most effectively used only for monitoring the violation of civil and political rights. Moreover, the information that is compiled through the use of events-based data methods often supplements the information captured through socio-economic statistics. In many other instances, particularly when there is a systematic denial or deprivation of human rights, event-based data is a substitute for the socio-economic statistics. It is necessary, therefore, to identify and use indicators based on these methods of information collection in a complementary manner. [There are at least two other data-generating mechanisms, namely household perception and opinion surveys, and data based on expert judgments that have been widely used in human rights assessments. However, both these methods have limitations (such as lack of objectivity and consistency in the data generated over time) that make them less useful in the compliance assessment of State parties with international human rights instruments.]

Criteria for the selection of quantitative indicators 26. The foremost consideration in adopting a methodology for identifying and building human rights indicators, or for that matter any set of indicators, as addressed in the discussion on the conceptual framework, is its relevance and effectiveness in addressing the objective(s) for which the indicators are to be used. Most other methodological requirements follow from this consideration. In the context of the work undertaken by the treaty bodies in monitoring the implementation of human rights, quantitative indicators should ideally be:

Relevant, valid and reliable;

Simple, timely and few in number;

Based on objective information and data-generating mechanisms;

Suitable for temporal and spatial comparison and following relevant international statistical standards; and

Amenable to disaggregation in terms of sex, age and other vulnerable or marginalized population segments.

One other consideration, namely the opportunity cost of the compilation of relevant information on an indicator could be useful in selecting indicators for use in human rights assessments.

27. It is worthwhile to note that, although disaggregated data is essential for addressing human rights concerns, it is not practical or feasible always to undertake disaggregation of data at the desired level. Disaggregation by sex, age, regions or administrative units may, for instance, be less difficult than by ethnicity, as the identification of ethnic groups often involves objective (e.g. language) and subjective (e.g. self-identity) criteria that may evolve over time. The production of any statistical data also has implications for the right to privacy, data protection and confidentiality issues, and will, therefore, require appropriate legal and institutional standards ...

Contextual relevance of indicators 28. The contextual relevance of indicators is a key consideration in the acceptability and use of indicators among potential users engaged in monitoring the implementation of human rights. Countries and regions within countries differ in terms of their social, economic and political attainments. They differ in the level of realization of human rights. These differences are invariably reflected in terms of differences in development priorities. Therefore, it may not be possible to always have a universal set of indicators to assess the realization of human rights. Having said that, it is also true that certain human rights indicators, for example those capturing the realization of some civil and political rights, may well be relevant across all countries and their regions. Others that capture the realization of economic or social rights, such as the right to education or housing, may have to be customized to be of relevance in different countries. But even in the latter case, it would be relevant to monitor the core content of the rights universally. Thus, in designing a set of human rights indicators, like any other set of indicators, there is a need to strike a balance between universally relevant indicators and contextually specific indicators, as both kinds of indicators are needed. The approach outlined in the preceding section permits such a balance between a core set of human rights indicators that may be universally relevant and, at the same time, it presents a framework that encourages a more detailed and focused assessment on certain attributes of the relevant human right, depending on the requirements of a particular situation.

The Committee on the Rights of the Child emphasized in particular the empowering impact of collecting data on children's rights, particularly if this is done through participatory processes:

Committee on the Rights of the Child, *General Comment No. 5 (2003),* *General Measures of Implementation of the Convention on the Rights of the Child* (Arts. 4, 42 and 44, para. 6) (CRC/GC/2003/5, 27 November 2003), paras. 48–50:

F. Data collection and analysis and development of indicators

Collection of sufficient and reliable data on children, disaggregated to enable identification of discrimination and/or disparities in the realization of rights, is an essential part of implementation. The Committee reminds States parties that data collection needs to extend over the whole period of childhood, up to the age of 18 years. It also needs to be coordinated throughout the jurisdiction, ensuring nationally applicable indicators. States should collaborate with appropriate research institutes and aim to build up a complete picture of progress towards implementation, with qualitative as well as quantitative studies. The reporting guidelines for periodic reports call for detailed disaggregated statistical and other information covering all areas of the Convention. It is essential not merely to establish effective systems for data collection, but to ensure that the data collected are evaluated and used to assess progress in implementation, to identify problems and to inform all policy development for children. Evaluation requires the development of indicators related to all rights guaranteed by the Convention.

The Committee commends States parties which have introduced annual publication of comprehensive reports on the state of children's rights throughout their jurisdiction. Publication and wide dissemination of and debate on such reports, including in parliament, can provide a focus for broad public engagement in implementation. Translations, including child-friendly versions, are essential for engaging children and minority groups in the process.

The Committee emphasizes that, in many cases, only children themselves are in a position to indicate whether their rights are being fully recognized and realized. Interviewing children and using children as researchers (with appropriate safeguards) is likely to be an important way of finding out, for example, to what extent their civil rights, including the crucial right set out in article 12, to have their views heard and given due consideration, are respected within the family, in schools and so on.

Indicators are generally considered useful for a number of reasons. As noted by the United Nations Development Program (UNDP) in the *Human Development Report 2000*, indicators can: guide policy-making and evaluation and help monitor progress; help identify unintended impacts of laws, policies and practices; help identify which actors have an impact on the realization of rights and whether these actors comply with their obligations; give early warning about potential violations, prompting preventive action; enhance social consensus on trade-offs to be made in the face of resource constraints; shed light on issues that might otherwise be neglected or silenced (UNDP, *Human Development Report 2000*, chapter 5, 'Using Indicators for Human Rights Accountability'). Yet, the same report also notes that statistics need to be handled with care:

United Nations Development Programme (UNDP), *Human Development Report 2000* (Oxford University Press, 2000), p. 90 (box 5.1.):

The powerful impact of statistics creates four caveats in their use:

- Overuse – Statistics alone cannot capture the full picture of rights and should not be the only focus of assessment. All statistical analysis needs to be embedded in an interpretation drawing on broader political, social and contextual analysis.
- Underuse – Data are rarely voluntarily collected on issues that are incriminating, embarrassing or simply ignored. One European social worker in the 1980s, complaining about the lack of data on homeless people, remarked, 'Everything else is counted – every cow and chicken and piece of butter.' Even when data are collected, they may not be made public for many years – and then there may be political pressure on the media not to publicize the findings.
- Misuse – Data collection is often biased towards institutions and formalized reporting, towards events that occur, not events prevented or suppressed. But lack of data does not always mean fewer occurrences. Structural repression is invisible when fear prevents people from protesting, registering complaints or speaking out.
- Political abuse – Indicators can be manipulated for political purposes to discredit certain countries or actors. And using them as criteria for trade or aid relationships would create new incentives to manipulate reporting.

3.2 The use of indicators by the Committee on Economic, Social and Cultural Rights and the IBSA methodology for monitoring compliance with economic and social rights

An even more ambitious view is that indicators could be used by the Committee on Economic, Social and Cultural Rights to breathe new life into its monitoring of the implementation of the International Covenant on Economic, Social and Cultural Rights, by a process through which each State party would identify its priorities with the Committee, and set well-defined objectives to be achieved by the time of the submission of its next report. The methodology is referred to as 'IBSA' since it involves four steps: (a) the choice of appropriate *indicators*; (b) the choice, at national level, of *benchmarks*, i.e. objectives to be realized within a defined time framework; (c) *scoping*, i.e. the discussion of those benchmarks between the Committee and the State concerned, with a view both to adopting objectives ambitious enough and to being realistic; (d) *assessment*, following the expiration of the time-period concerned, taking as a departure point whether the benchmarks agreed upon have been achieved. Already in its first general comment, the Committee on Economic, Social and Cultural Rights had referred to the usefulness of benchmarks being adopted by States parties to the Covenant, in order to enable monitoring of progress towards time-bound targets (see General Comment No. 1, *Reporting by State Parties* (1989), para. 6). This is also what the Committee on Economic, Social and Cultural Rights refers to, more explicitly, in the following general comments:

Committee on Economic, Social and Cultural Rights, General Comment No. 14 (2000), *The Right to the Highest Attainable Standard of Health (Art. 12 of the International Covenant on Economic, Social and Cultural Rights)* **(E/C.12/2000/4, 11 August 2000), paras. 57–8:**

Right to health indicators and benchmarks

57. National health strategies should identify appropriate right to health indicators and benchmarks. The indicators should be designed to monitor, at the national and international levels, the State party's obligations under article 12. States may obtain guidance on appropriate right to health indicators, which should address different aspects of the right to health, from the ongoing work of WHO and the United Nations Children's Fund (UNICEF) in this field. Right to health indicators require disaggregation on the prohibited grounds of discrimination.

58. Having identified appropriate right to health indicators, States parties are invited to set appropriate national benchmarks in relation to each indicator. During the periodic reporting procedure the Committee will engage in a process of scoping with the State party. Scoping involves the joint consideration by the State party and the Committee of the indicators and national benchmarks which will then provide the targets to be achieved during the next reporting period. In the following five years, the State party will use these national benchmarks to help monitor its implementation of article 12. Thereafter, in the subsequent reporting process, the State party and the Committee will consider whether or not the benchmarks have been achieved, and the reasons for any difficulties that may have been encountered.

Committee on Economic, Social and Cultural Rights, General Comment No. 15 (2002), *The Right to Water (Arts. 11 and 12 of the International Covenant on Economic, Social and Cultural Rights)* **(E/C.12/2002/11, 20 January 2003), paras. 53–4:**

Indicators and benchmarks

53. To assist the monitoring process, right to water indicators should be identified in the national water strategies or plans of action. The indicators should be designed to monitor, at the national and international levels, the State party's obligations under articles 11, paragraph 1, and 12. Indicators should address the different components of adequate water (such as sufficiency, safety and acceptability, affordability and physical accessibility), be disaggregated by the prohibited grounds of discrimination, and cover all persons residing in the State party's territorial jurisdiction or under their control. States parties may obtain guidance on appropriate indicators from the ongoing work of WHO, the Food and Agriculture Organization of the United Nations (FAO), the United Nations Centre for Human Settlements (Habitat), the International Labour Organization (ILO), the United Nations Children's Fund (UNICEF), the United Nations Environment Programme (UNEP), the United Nations Development Programme (UNDP) and the United Nations Commission on Human Rights.

54. Having identified appropriate right to water indicators, States parties are invited to set appropriate national benchmarks in relation to each indicator [see E. Riedel, 'New Bearings to the State Reporting Procedure: Practical Ways to Operationalize Economic, Social and Cultural

Rights – the Example of the Right to Health' in S. von Schorlemer (ed.), *Praxishandbuch UNO. Die Vereinten Nationen im Lichte globaler Herausforderungen* (Heidelberg: Springer Verlag, 2002), pp. 345–58. The Committee notes, for example, the commitment in the 2002 World Summit on Sustainable Development Plan of Implementation to halve, by the year 2015, the proportion of people who are unable to reach or to afford safe drinking water (as outlined in the Millennium Declaration) and the proportion of people who do not have access to basic sanitation.] During the periodic reporting procedure, the Committee will engage in a process of 'scoping' with the State party. Scoping involves the joint consideration by the State party and the Committee of the indicators and national benchmarks which will then provide the targets to be achieved during the next reporting period. In the following five years, the State party will use these national benchmarks to help monitor its implementation of the right to water. Thereafter, in the subsequent reporting process, the State party and the Committee will consider whether or not the benchmarks have been achieved, and the reasons for any difficulties that may have been encountered (see General Comment No.14 (2000), para. 58). Further, when setting benchmarks and preparing their reports, States parties should utilize the extensive information and advisory services of specialized agencies with regard to data collection and disaggregation.

This methodology was first conceptualized in 2002 primarily by Eibe Riedel, a member of the Committee on Economic, Social and Cultural Rights, in a partnership between the University of Mannheim and the international NGO FIAN (Foodfirst Information and Action Network), using the right to adequate food as an example. Riedel provides the following summary of the four steps involved and of the advantages of the approach:

Eibe Riedel, 'The IBSA Procedure as a Tool of Human Rights Monitoring', paper prepared for a joint project between the chair of Professor Riedel and FIAN international (no date):

With regard to the first step, human rights indicators involve the State Party acceptance of relevant indicators as agreed upon through close cooperation with NGOs and relevant specialized agencies that contribute to the effective mainstreaming of human rights in their respective domains.

The next step, national benchmarks, are subsequently set by States Parties which enable a differentiated approach to the vastly differing situations in which most countries find themselves.

The third step, scoping, involves a discussion with the Committee of the State Party established benchmarks, in order to arrive at a consensus about them.

The previous three steps form the basis for the final assessment step that occurs during the dialogue stage between the State Party and the Committee in preparation for the drafting of the latter's Concluding Observations.

The advantage of this four-step IBSA-procedure lies in the truly cooperative and interactive spirit between States Parties, the Committee, specialized agencies, and NGOs wherein a more focussed and meaningful discussion can take place. This new approach is premised on the assumption that article 2(1) of the Covenant places an unequivocal legally binding duty on all States Parties, the intensity of which is balanced against the objective situation in which States Parties find themselves. Here, while all States must strive to realize all Covenant rights, poorer countries' obligations depend on an assessment of their specific country situations. For example, with reference to the Millennium Development Goals (MDG)-indicator 'Proportion of population with access to improved sanitation', while State Party A, belonging to the group of least developed nations, may have to demonstrate that its percentage of population with access to such a sanitation improved from 50% to 60% during a given reporting period, State Party B, belonging to the group of the most highly developed countries may have to demonstrate that its literacy rate improved from 92% to 95% during that same reporting period. At the subsequent State reporting period five years later, if State A, on assessment by the Committee proved to have reached only a 52% level of improved sanitation, 8% short of the benchmarked 60%, certain mitigating factors may be taken into consideration. Here, had State Party A allocated more resources to food care, or a natural disaster beset the nation upsetting State Party resource allocations, the Committee might still be inclined to praise the State Party A for its progress under difficult circumstances. On the other hand, during the same reporting period, had State Party B achieved an 96% improved sanitation in the absence of mitigating factors, although objectively achieving a much more substantial gain than State Party A, the Committee would still be free to criticize State Party B for not fulfilling its set benchmark. Although, at first glance, the aforesaid example may appear to impose a double standard, this is not the case as, in fact, it simply means that in setting benchmarks, realistic targets have to be agreed, and once agreed, are critically assessed at the next reporting stage. In essence, this means that both States Parties A and B owe fulfilment obligations. However, should they fall short of their benchmarked goals, the onus is on each State Party to prove why these targets were not or could not be met.

This exercise involves the prioritization of a constructive dialogue over an adversarial violations approach. Within this context, only in situations where a State Party wilfully violated its Covenant duties, or obligations, would the Committee in fact, recommend effective measures to redress the grievances caused by such violations.

… These benchmarks will be recruited from all the different categories of indicators, that is outcome benchmarks, structural benchmarks and process benchmarks. Particularly well suited for the benchmarking are the outcome indicators with their result-oriented character. On the other hand, it can be doubted that structural and process benchmarks would be helpful for the monitoring process. These doubts are based on the fact that many structural and process indicators are not obligatory by themselves, the state having a margin of discretion as how to realize the esc-rights. But this discretion requires that the state identifies goals (benchmarks) and the legislative intent (structural benchmarks), and the implementation effort (process benchmarks), and the journey is the reward.

… In cases where benchmarked targets are not met, the Committee can examine State Party reasons for such non-fulfilment. In such circumstances, civil strife and natural catastrophes undoubtedly will act as mitigating factors. It will be interesting to differentiate between the three categories of indicators: If the state has failed to meet structural benchmarks (e.g. because it did not implement a scheduled consumer protection law), the state will hardly be able to exculpate itself, as these structural measures are mostly resource-independent. The non-compliance with set process benchmarks, by contrast, will more often be approved by the Committee, as the assessment has to take into consideration the often resource-intensive aspect of these benchmarks. Finally, the Committee has to undertake a critical assessment of the outcome benchmarks. For instance, it may be very difficult to criticize a State's noncompliance of a particular outcome situation, if the state has met its structural and process obligations. A comprehensive assessment also requires to take the factors into account that the state can not or can only influence with a great difficulty.

... The IBSA process thus has a Janus-type appearance: it looks back, in order to assess the past reporting period; it looks forward, in order to target future developments in the fuller realization of rights. Looking back, it may force the State party to candidly assess for itself, why certain targets were not met, or could not be met, and this will enable the State party to set realistic new benchmarks for the next reporting period.

3.3 Indicators in the Inter-American system

On 16 November 1999, the Additional Protocol to the American Convention on Human Rights in the Area of Economic, Social and Cultural Rights (Protocol of San Salvador) (O.A.S. Treaty Series No. 69 (1988)) entered into force. Although the Protocol lists a number of social and economic rights which the States parties undertake to observe, this is subject to a progressivity clause, making the implementation of the rights dependent on the available resources: the parties 'undertake to adopt the necessary measures, both domestically and through international cooperation, especially economic and technical, to the extent allowed by their available resources, and taking into account their degree of development, for the purpose of achieving progressively and pursuant to their internal legislations, the full observance of the rights recognized in this Protocol' (Art. 1). In addition, only the right to form and join trade unions (Art. 8(a)) and the right to education (Art. 13) may be adjudicated through the filing of individual petitions (Art. 19(5)). All the rights listed are the subject of reporting by the States parties to the Protocol, however: the reports submitted by States are transmitted to the Inter-American Economic and Social Council and the Inter-American Council for Education, Science and Culture in order that they be examined, together with information provided by specialized organizations of the Inter-American system. In their annual reports submitted to the OAS General Assembly, the Inter-American Economic and Social Council and the Inter-American Council for Education, Science and Culture include a summary of the information received from the States parties to the Protocol and the specialized organizations concerning the measures adopted in order to ensure respect for the rights acknowledged in the Protocol itself and their general recommendations.

Inter-American Commission on Human Rights (IACHR), Guidelines for Preparation of Progress Indicators in the Area of Economic, Social and Cultural Rights (OEA/Ser/L/V/II.129 Doc. 5, 5 October 2007):

[Article 19 of the Protocol of San Salvador provides that States parties shall submit periodic reports on the progressive measures they have taken to ensure due respect for the rights set forth in the Protocol. The Standards for the preparation of the periodic reports mentioned in Article 19 of the Protocol of San Salvador, adopted by the General Assembly of the OAS (Res. AG/ RES. 2074 XXXV-O/05 of 7 June 2005), provide for the drawing up of 'guidelines and rules' for the design of reports in accordance with a system of progress indicators. This is in conformity with the idea that 'particular attention has been given to the principle of progressiveness of economic, social, and cultural rights (ESCR), understood as the adoption of public policy that recognizes ESCR as human rights, whose full realization, generally speaking, cannot be rapidly achieved and which, therefore, require a process in which each country moves at a different pace toward achieving the goal. Except as warranted in extreme cases, this principle regards regressive measures as invalid and excludes inaction.']

28. In addition to quantitative indicators, the IACHR considers it important that the evaluation include a number of qualitative indicators, which this document refers to as qualitative signs of progress. Qualitative dimensions are included in the proposed model for the purposes of description and interpretation. Qualitative signs of progress differ from quantitative indicators in that they do not start from a predetermined category or from an established (statistical) measurement scale, but examine the interpretation of a situation by the social actor and the meaning that they attribute to the phenomenon under evaluation, which are critical for interpreting the facts. Accordingly, these dimensions can be included in the evaluation process and, though less visible, are, nevertheless, absolutely essential for monitoring purposes. Thus, with respect to the right to health, an indicator is the number of doctors per inhabitant, and a qualitative sign of progress is public perception of the health system's accessibility.

29. The IACHR has defined three types of indicators and qualitative signs of progress based on the indicators model proposed in the framework of the UN in the aforementioned 'Report on Indicators for Monitoring Compliance with International Human Rights Instruments'. These categories of indicators and signs are: i) structural; ii) process-related; and, iii) outcome-related.

30. Structural indicators seek to determine what measures the State would be able to adopt to implement the rights contained in the Protocol. Put another way, they collect information in order to evaluate how the State's institutional apparatus and legal system are organized to perform the obligations under the Protocol: if it has in place – or has adopted – measures, legal standards, strategies, plans, programs, or policies, or created public agencies to implement those rights. Although structural indicators merely inquire about the existence or not of measures, they can sometimes include information that is relevant for understanding some of their main characteristics, such as, for example, whether or not standards are in operation, or the rank or jurisdiction of a particular government agency or institution.

31. Process indicators seek to measure the quality and extent of state efforts to implement rights by measuring the scope, coverage, and content of strategies, plans, programs, or policies, or other specific activities and interventions designed to accomplish the goals necessary for the realization of a given right. These indicators help to monitor directly the application of public policies in terms of progressive realization of rights. Process indicators can also offer information on shifts in the quality or coverage of social services or programs over a given time. Whereas structural indicators do not normally need a reference base (they usually elicit a yes/no answer), process indicators depend on reference bases or goals that are usually figures or percentages, and, therefore, will have a more dynamic and evolutionary component than structural indicators.

32. Outcome indicators seek to measure the actual impact of government strategies, programs, and interventions. To some extent they are an indication of how those government

measures impact on the aspects that determine how effective a right recognized in the Protocol is. Thus, they offer a quantitatively verifiable and comparable measurement of the performance of the State in terms of the progressive realization of rights. An improvement in outcome indicators may be a sign of the adequacy of the measures adopted and of progressive improvements towards full realization of rights. However, to form a definitive opinion in this respect, a review of the specific measures adopted is necessary; a decline in outcome indicators may be due to circumstances not attributable to the actions of the State, while an improvement may be caused by fortuitous factors. Accordingly, particular attention should be given to process indicators.

33. Since time consolidates the effects of various underlying processes (which can be measured by one or more process indicators), outcome indicators are usually slow indicators and less sensitive to momentary changes than process indicators ...

34. In order to improve the possibility of analysis and better organize information collected in the process, we suggest dividing it into three categories: i) incorporation of the right; ii) state capabilities; and, iii) financial context and budgetary commitment.

35. The first category is the incorporation of the right in the legal system, in the institutional apparatus, and in public policy. The idea is to collect relevant information on how the right recognized in the Protocol is incorporated in the domestic law books and in public policy and practice. On one hand is the level of the provisions that recognize it, as well as their effectiveness and statutory rank. The right may be recognized in the Constitution, in laws, in jurisprudence or in government programs or practices. The idea, too, is to collect information on the scope of that recognition, that is the degree of precision with which the basic obligations of the State or minimum enforceable standards are defined; also, an indication as to the persons who are individually or collectively possessed of that right; the conditions for its exercise, for example, if it is considered an effective right and can be demanded directly from the government authorities and, as appropriate, enforced by the courts, or if it is not directly enforceable. Finally, what guarantees or appeal procedures are available in the event of a violation of the respective obligations?

36. Another aspect that is important to explore is what social services or policies has the State established for implementation or realization of the rights contained in Protocol? Sometimes programs or services create benefits of a welfare nature and do not recognize the existence of rights. The extent to which a right is a part of the logic and meaning of public policy is an aspect usually measured through process indicators.

37. An example of a structural indicator of the incorporation of a right is, if the right has been included in the Constitution, is it effective or not? A process indicator on the incorporation of a right is if relevant jurisprudence exist on its enforceability; or the scope and coverage of public policies enacted as implementation measures for that right.

38. The second category has to do with state capabilities. This category describes a technical-instrumental and distributive aspect of government resources within the state apparatus. That is, it entails a review of how and according to what parameters government (and its various branches and departments) deals with different socially problematized issues; in particular, how it establishes its goals and development strategies; and under what parameters the implementation of the rights contained in the Protocol is inscribed therein. It entails reviewing the rules of play within the state apparatus, interagency relations, task allocation, financial capacity, and the skills of the human resources that must carry out the allotted tasks. To provide an example, a structural indicator of state capacity is the existence of specific government

agencies for the protection or implementation of a social right. A structural indicator may also be used to examine competencies and functions. A process indicator on state capacity endeavors to determine the scope and coverage of the programs and services implemented by those agencies. A process indicator on state capacity could also measure changes in the quality and scope of those interventions over a period of time.

39. The purpose of including state capabilities as a category in the indicators is to collect information on core aspects that serve to evaluate the extent to which the political will of the State is materialized. Their inclusion also serves to verify if the conditions are in place for effectively implementing, through public policy, a rights-based approach in the framework of the existing state structure. The aim of including this category is also to have a more accurate idea of the problems that the State faces for fulfilling its obligations, by making it possible in the evaluation to identify problems to do with policy decision-making as distinct from public administration problems.

40. An important aspect for measuring state capabilities is the existence of oversight, monitoring, and evaluation agencies for social services and programs within the state structure, as well as the capacity of the State to implement policies to combat corruption and patronage in the use of funds allocated to the social sector. The idea is also to collect information on the accessibility of social programs and services organized by the State by examining, for example, physical access, disclosure, and cultural pertinence.

41. Another aspect that the proposed indicators on state capabilities are designed to capture has to do with fragmentation in the different levels of the government administration and in different social services. The provision of goods and services connected with social rights overall is administered by different levels of government. Decentralization of social services and policies can allow a greater measure of flexibility and adaptation to regional realities and local needs. That said, it can also entail numerous coordination problems. The problem stems, therefore, from a lack of clarity in the definition and distribution of areas of responsibility among different government agencies and, on occasion, among different governments at the national, regional, provincial, and local level. [The study on access to social rights adopted by the European Committee for Social Cohesion identifies a number of the main 'fragmentation' problems connected with health and other social rights: (i) lack of co-ordination among different political spheres; (ii) insufficient information about responsibilities and functions at the national, regional, and local levels (this is the case with social and welfare services and can also occur in the areas of health, employment, and housing services); (iii) insufficient independence permitted to local administrations in the use of resources, as well as insufficient participation in decision-making, implementation, and resource-mobilization processes; (iv) monitoring and implementation of policies at the national level inadequate to ensure equitable nationwide provision: see European Committee for Social Cohesion, 'Access to Social Rights in Europe', Strasbourg, May 2002.] Added to the foregoing is the customary fragmentation in social services themselves due to deficient coordination and lack of communication among agencies as well as the absence of comprehensive policies and adequate record-keeping.

42. In a similar vein, another category to include in the measurement and evaluation process is the basic financial context, which has to do with the actual amount of state funds available for public social spending and how it is distributed, whether it be measured in the usual manner (as a percentage of gross domestic product for each social sector) or by means of an alternative mechanism. In that connection, included in the same category is budgetary commitment, which

makes it possible to assess the importance that the State accords to the right in question. This information also complements the measurement of state capabilities. The importance of measuring this category stems from the fact that if a State institutes a public spending policy that entails a cutback in the area of social infrastructure (for instance, health care and sanitation), apart from acting as a regressive measure, it will have the effect of transferring the costs of care directly to families, and within the family to women.

43. However many categories are included and no matter how many conceptual aspects their analysis might seek to uncover, it will never be possible to encompass all of the issues that shape the effectiveness of a right. Therefore, it is advisable to limit the number of categories to those that are most relevant to the right under consideration and that match the compliance goals set. For that reason, it is advisable to review the availability of information for measurement. This is not a minor consideration given the difficulties in the region as regards access to information sources.

44. In conclusion, the information requested from the State on each right contained in the Protocol would be organized under a model composed of quantitative indicators and qualitative signs of progress arranged according to three types of indicators (structural, process, and outcome indicators), which would provide information on three conceptual categories (incorporation of the right, state capabilities, and financial context and budgetary commitment).

4 MEASURING THE OBLIGATION OF PROGRESSIVE REALIZATION

The tools described in this chapter – national strategies and action plans, framework laws, indicators and benchmarks – ultimately should serve to ensure that States comply with their obligation to fulfil human rights. As we have seen in section 1, the obligation to fulfil includes an obligation to facilitate (by pro-actively removing obstacles to the full enjoyment of the right by individuals), an obligation to promote (by providing individuals with the necessary information that ensures that they will be able to enjoy the right), and an obligation to provide (by delivering goods and services to individuals in situations where they are unable to provide for themselves). To the extent that the States face constraints, particularly budgetary constraints, in discharging this obligation, the right is subject to progressive realization. This is acknowledged by Article 2 para. 1 of the International Covenant on Economic, Social and Cultural Rights, according to which each State party 'undertakes to take steps, individually and through international assistance and co-operation, especially economic and technical, to the maximum of its available resources, with a view to achieving progressively the full realization of the rights recognized in the present Covenant by all appropriate means, including particularly the adoption of legislative measures'.

However, as noted by the Committee on Economic, Social and Cultural Rights, progressive realization should by no means be treated as a licence to remain passive:

Committee on Economic, Social and Cultural Rights, General Comment No. 3, *The Nature of States Parties' Obligations* (Art. 2, para. 1, of the Covenant) (E/1991/23) (1990):

1. [W]hile the Covenant provides for progressive realization and acknowledges the constraints due to the limits of available resources, it also imposes various obligations which are of immediate effect. Of these, two are of particular importance in understanding the precise nature of States parties' obligations. One of these ... is the 'undertaking to guarantee' that relevant rights 'will be exercised without discrimination ...'

2. The other is the undertaking in article 2 (1) 'to take steps', which in itself, is not qualified or limited by other considerations. The full meaning of the phrase can also be gauged by noting some of the different language versions. In English the undertaking is 'to take steps', in French it is 'to act' ('s'engage à agir') and in Spanish it is 'to adopt measures' ('a adoptar medidas'). Thus while the full realization of the relevant rights may be achieved progressively, steps towards that goal must be taken within a reasonably short time after the Covenant's entry into force for the States concerned. Such steps should be deliberate, concrete and targeted as clearly as possible towards meeting the obligations recognized in the Covenant ...

9. ... The concept of progressive realization constitutes a recognition of the fact that full realization of all economic, social and cultural rights will generally not be able to be achieved in a short period of time. In this sense the obligation differs significantly from that contained in article 2 of the International Covenant on Civil and Political Rights which embodies an immediate obligation to respect and ensure all of the relevant rights. Nevertheless, the fact that realization over time, or in other words progressively, is foreseen under the Covenant should not be misinterpreted as depriving the obligation of all meaningful content. It is on the one hand a necessary flexibility device, reflecting the realities of the real world and the difficulties involved for any country in ensuring full realization of economic, social and cultural rights. On the other hand, the phrase must be read in the light of the overall objective, indeed the raison d'être, of the Covenant which is to establish clear obligations for States parties in respect of the full realization of the rights in question. It thus imposes an obligation to move as expeditiously and effectively as possible towards that goal. Moreover, any deliberately retrogressive measures in that regard would require the most careful consideration and would need to be fully justified by reference to the totality of the rights provided for in the Covenant and in the context of the full use of the maximum available resources.

Nevertheless, uncertainty remains as to which efforts precisely may be expected from States facing a variety of constraints, including limited resources (see R. E. Robertson, 'Measuring State Compliance with the Obligation to Devote the "Maximum Available Resources" to Realizing Economic, Social, and Cultural Rights', *Human Rights Quarterly*, 16 (1994), 693–714). Indeed, some authors have taken the view that the idea of monitoring 'progressive realization' should be abandoned altogether, Audrey Chapman proposing that we instead substitute to this approach a 'violations approach', ensuring that States (a) do not take measures that infringe upon human rights, (b) do not maintain or adopt discriminatory policies, and (c) comply with the core content of each right (A. R. Chapman, '"Violations Approach" for Monitoring the International Covenant on

Economic, Social and Cultural Rights', *Human Rights Quarterly*, 18(1) (1996), 23–66; see further chapter 8, section 1.2.).

The Limburg Principles on the Implementation of the International Covenant on Economic, Social and Cultural Rights were elaborated by a group of international law experts in 1986, soon after the Committee on Economic, Social and Cultural Rights was established under Resolution 17/1985 of the Economic and Social Council. These experts gave the following indications concerning the obligation to progressively implement the rights of the Covenant, 'to the maximum of available resources' of each State:

Limburg Principles on the Implementation of the International Covenant on Economic, Social and Cultural Rights (1986):

16. All States parties have an obligation to begin immediately to take steps towards full realization of the rights contained in the Covenant.

17. At the national level States parties shall use all appropriate means, including legislative, administrative, judicial, economic, social and educational measures, consistent with the nature of the rights in order to fulfil their obligations under the Covenant.

18. Legislative measures alone are not sufficient to fulfil the obligations of the Covenant. It should be noted, however, that article 2.1 would often require legislative action to be taken in cases where existing legislation is in violation of the obligations assumed under the Covenant.

19. States parties shall provide for effective remedies including, where appropriate, judicial remedies.

20. The appropriateness of the means to be applied in a particular State shall be determined by that State party, and shall be subject to review by the United Nations Economic and Social Council, with the assistance of the Committee. Such review shall be without prejudice to the competence of the other organs established pursuant to the Charter of the United Nations.

21. The obligation 'to achieve progressively the full realization of the rights' requires States parties to move as expeditiously as possible towards the realization of the rights. Under no circumstances shall this be interpreted as implying for States the right to deter indefinitely efforts to ensure full realization. On the contrary all States parties have the obligation to begin immediately to take steps to fulfil their obligations under the Covenant.

22. Some obligations under the Covenant require immediate implementation in full by all States parties, such as the prohibition of discrimination in article 2.2 of the Covenant.

23. The obligation of progressive achievement exists independently of the increase in resources; it requires effective use of resources available.

24. Progressive implementation can be effected not only by increasing resources, but also by the development of societal resources necessary for the realization by every one of the rights recognized in the Covenant.

'to the maximum of its available resources'

25. States parties are obligated, regardless of the level of economic development, to ensure respect for minimum subsistence rights for all.

26. 'Its available resources' refers to both the resources within a State and those available from the international community through international co-operation and assistance.

27. In determining whether adequate measures have been taken for the realization of the rights recognized in the Covenant, attention shall be paid to equitable and effective use of and access to the available resources.

28. In the use of the available resources due priority shall be given to the realization of rights recognized in the Covenant, mindful of the need to assure to everyone the satisfaction of subsistence requirements as well as the provision of essential services.

'individually and through international assistance and co-operation, especially economic and technical'

29. International co-operation and assistance pursuant to the Charter of the United Nations (arts. 55 and 56) and the Covenant shall have in view as a matter of priority the realization of all human rights and fundamental freedoms, economic, social and cultural as well as civil and political.

30. International co-operation and assistance must be directed towards the establishment of a social and international order in which the rights and freedoms set forth in the Covenant can be fully realized (cf. article 28 of the Universal Declaration of Human Rights).

31. Irrespective of differences in their political, economic and social systems, States shall co-operate with one another to promote international social, economic and cultural progress, in particular the economic growth of developing countries, free from discrimination based on such differences.

32. States parties shall take steps by international means to assist and co-operate in the realization of the rights recognized by the Covenant.

33. International co-operation and assistance shall be based on the sovereign equality of States and be aimed at the realization of the rights contained in the Covenant.

34. In undertaking international co-operation and assistance pursuant to article 2.1 the role of international organizations and the contribution of non-governmental organizations shall be kept in mind ...

[Violations of economic, social and cultural rights]

70. A failure by a State party to comply with an obligation contained in the Covenant is, under international law, a violation of the Covenant.

71. In determining what amounts to a failure to comply, it must be borne in mind that the Covenant affords to a State party a margin of discretion in selecting the means for carrying out its objects, and that factors beyond its reasonable control may adversely affect its capacity to implement particular rights.

72. A State party will be in violation of the Covenant, *inter alia*, if:

It fails to take a step which it is required to take by the Covenant;

It fails to remove promptly obstacles which it is under a duty to remove to permit the immediate fulfilment of a right;

It fails to implement without delay a right which it is required by the Covenant to provide immediately;

It wilfully fails to meet a generally accepted international minimum standard of achievement, which is within its powers to meet;

It applies a limitation to a right recognized in the Covenant other than in accordance with the Covenant;

It deliberately retards or halts the progressive realization of a right, unless it is acting within a limitation permitted by the Covenant or it does so due to a lack of available resources or *force majeure*;

It fails to submit reports as required under the Covenant.

The Maastricht Guidelines on Violations of Economic, Social and Cultural Rights were adopted in 1997, by a group of experts aiming to build on the Limburg Principles of 1986 in order to reflect the evolution of international law since that date.

The Maastricht Guidelines on Violations of Economic, Social and Cultural Rights (1997):

Margin of discretion
8. As in the case of civil and political rights, States enjoy a margin of discretion in selecting the means for implementing their respective obligations. State practice and the application of legal norms to concrete cases and situations by international treaty monitoring bodies as well as by domestic courts have contributed to the development of universal minimum standards and the common understanding of the scope, nature and limitation of economic, social and cultural rights. The fact that the full realization of most economic, social and cultural rights can only be achieved progressively, which in fact also applies to most civil and political rights, does not alter the nature of the legal obligation of States which requires that certain steps be taken immediately and others as soon as possible. Therefore, the burden is on the State to demonstrate that it is making measurable progress toward the full realization of the rights in question. The State cannot use the 'progressive realization' provisions in article 2 of the Covenant as a pretext for non-compliance. Nor can the State justify derogations or limitations of rights recognized in the Covenant because of different social, religious and cultural backgrounds.

Minimum core obligations
9. Violations of the Covenant occur when a State fails to satisfy what the Committee on Economic, Social and Cultural Rights has referred to as 'a minimum core obligation to ensure the satisfaction of, at the very least, minimum essential levels of each of the rights ... Thus, for example, a State party in which any significant number of individuals is deprived of essential foodstuffs, of essential primary health care, of basic shelter and housing, or of the most basic forms of education is, prima facie, violating the Covenant.' Such minimum core obligations apply irrespective of the availability of resources of the country concerned or any other factors and difficulties.

Availability of resources
10. In many cases, compliance with such obligations may be undertaken by most States with relative ease, and without significant resource implications. In other cases, however, full realization of the rights may depend upon the availability of adequate financial and material resources. Nonetheless, as established by Limburg Principles 25–28, and confirmed by the developing jurisprudence of the Committee on Economic, Social and Cultural Rights, resource scarcity does not relieve States of certain minimum obligations in respect of the implementation of economic, social and cultural rights.

State policies
11. A violation of economic, social and cultural rights occurs when a State pursues, by action or omission, a policy or practice which deliberately contravenes or ignores obligations of the Covenant, or fails to achieve the required standard of conduct or result. Furthermore, any discrimination on grounds of race, colour, sex, language, religion, political or other opinion, national or social origin, property, birth or other status with the purpose or effect of nullifying or

impairing the equal enjoyment or exercise of economic, social and cultural rights constitutes a violation of the Covenant.

Gender discrimination

12. Discrimination against women in relation to the rights recognized in the Covenant, is understood in the light of the standard of equality for women under the Convention on the Elimination of All Forms of Discrimination against Women. That standard requires the elimination of all forms of discrimination against women including gender discrimination arising out of social, cultural and other structural disadvantages.

Inability to comply

13. In determining which actions or omissions amount to a violation of an economic, social or cultural right, it is important to distinguish the inability from the unwillingness of a State to comply with its treaty obligations. A State claiming that it is unable to carry out its obligations for reasons beyond its control has the burden of proving that this is the case. A temporary closure of an educational institution due to an earthquake, for instance, would be a circumstance beyond the control of the State, while the elimination of a social security scheme without an adequate replacement programme could be an example of unwillingness by the State to fulfil its obligations.

Violations through acts of commission

14. Violations of economic, social and cultural rights can occur through the direct action of States or other entities insufficiently regulated by States. Examples of such violations include:

(a) The formal removal or suspension of legislation necessary for the continued enjoyment of an economic, social and cultural right that is currently enjoyed;

(b) The active denial of such rights to particular individuals or groups, whether through legislated or enforced discrimination;

(c) The active support for measures adopted by third parties which are inconsistent with economic, social and cultural rights;

(d) The adoption of legislation or policies which are manifestly incompatible with pre-existing legal obligations relating to these rights, unless it is done with the purpose and effect of increasing equality and improving the realization of economic, social and cultural rights for the most vulnerable groups;

(e) The adoption of any deliberately retrogressive measure that reduces the extent to which any such right is guaranteed;

(f) The calculated obstruction of, or halt to, the progressive realization of a right protected by the Covenant, unless the State is acting within a limitation permitted by the Covenant or it does so due to a lack of available resources or *force majeure*;

(g) The reduction or diversion of specific public expenditure, when such reduction or diversion results in the non-enjoyment of such rights and is not accompanied by adequate measures to ensure minimum subsistence rights for everyone.

Violations through acts of omission

15. Violations of economic, social and cultural rights can also occur through the omission or failure of States to take necessary measures stemming from legal obligations. Examples of such violations include:

(a) The failure to take appropriate steps as required under the Covenant;

(b) The failure to reform or repeal legislation which is manifestly inconsistent with an obligation of the Covenant;

(c) The failure to enforce legislation or put into effect policies designed to implement provisions of the Covenant;

(d) The failure to regulate activities of individuals or groups so as to prevent them from violating economic, social and cultural rights;

(e) The failure to utilize the maximum of available resources towards the full realization of the Covenant;

(f) The failure to monitor the realization of economic, social and cultural rights, including the development and application of criteria and indicators for assessing compliance;

(g) The failure to remove promptly obstacles which it is under a duty to remove to permit the immediate fulfilment of a right guaranteed by the Covenant;

(h) The failure to implement without delay a right which it is required by the Covenant to provide immediately;

(i) The failure to meet a generally accepted international minimum standard of achievement, which is within its powers to meet;

(j) The failure of a State to take into account its international legal obligations in the field of economic, social and cultural rights when entering into bilateral or multilateral agreements with other States, international organizations or multinational corporations.

The Committee on Economic, Social and Cultural Rights itself has provided little guidance on this issue. It considers that (a) 'a minimum core obligation to ensure the satisfaction of, at the very least, minimum essential levels of each of the rights is incumbent upon every State party' (General Comment No. 3, para. 10); (b) although a State may in principle attribute its failure to meet at least its minimum core obligations to a lack of available resources, 'it must demonstrate that every effort has been made to use all resources that are at its disposition in an effort to satisfy, as a matter of priority, those minimum obligations' (para. 10); (c) 'even where the available resources are demonstrably inadequate, the obligation remains for a State party to strive to ensure the widest possible enjoyment of the relevant rights under the prevailing circumstances' (para. 11); (d) 'the obligations to monitor the extent of the realization, or more especially of the non-realization, of economic, social and cultural rights, and to devise strategies and programmes for their promotion, are not in any way eliminated as a result of resource constraints' (para. 11); (e) 'even in times of severe resources constraints whether caused by a process of adjustment, of economic recession, or by other factors the vulnerable members of society can and indeed must be protected by the adoption of relatively low-cost targeted programmes' (para. 12); finally, (f) since 'the phrase "to the maximum of its available resources" was intended by the drafters of the Covenant to refer to both the resources existing within a State and those available from the international community through international cooperation and assistance, ... international cooperation for development and thus for the realization of economic, social and cultural rights is an obligation of all States [although it] is particularly incumbent upon those States which are in a position to assist others in this regard' (paras. 13–14). These six principles are useful and important, but they remain insufficient to provide guidance to States as to what exactly is expected from them in the progressive realization of rights: at which speed should they proceed? which levels of resources should they commit? how should they arbitrate between the competing demands imposed on them, in a context of limited resources requiring prioritization?

In answering these questions, it is important not to confuse the means with the ends. National strategies and action plans, framework legislation, the setting of benchmarks and indicators to measure progress and improve accountability, are all useful – but they are procedural tools, and they are no substitute for complying with the substantive requirement laid down in the right itself. A State would not be complying with its obligations merely by adopting these instruments, if no progress is made in the everyday lives of the population under its jurisdiction: a violation of its obligations in such circumstances would be revealed by contrasting how much a State achieves as measured through structural indicators (measuring whether a State has set up the appropriate institutions and adapted its regulatory framework), with how well a State performs according to process or outcome indicators (focusing respectively on the policies effectively implemented and the results achieved). For the same reason, a State setting benchmarks and indicators to measure progress towards achieving these benchmarks would not be complying with its international obligations if the targets were set too low, or if, without appropriate justification, it failed to reach them. It is maintaining the link between procedural tools and substantive outcomes that constitutes the main difficulty facing process-based approaches to the definition of the content of the obligation of 'progressive realization' (such as, for instance, the approach proposed by K. G. Young, 'The Minimum Core of Economic and Social Rights: a Concept in Search of Content', *Yale Journal of International Law*, 33 (2008), 113). Indeed, this is why, in the IBSA methodology outlined above (section 3.2.), provision is made for 'scoping', as explained by Eibe Riedel:

Eibe Riedel, 'The IBSA Procedure as a Tool of Human Rights Monitoring', paper prepared for a joint project between the chair of Professor Riedel and FIAN international (no date), pp. 72–3:

As the process of benchmarking is undertaken by individual States Parties, it is highly desirable that a control mechanism exists to ensure that established goals are set neither too high nor too low. If national benchmarks [were] to be set too low, State Parties could avoid being held in breach of their ICESCR obligations, and could go so far as to claim [praise from the Committee on Economic, Social and Cultural Rights] for limited progress of little value. In order to avoid such undesirable consequences, State Party proposed benchmarks should be scoped, an objective that can be reached through a constructive State Party/Committee dialogue that strives towards reaching a consensus concerning said nationally set benchmarks. If the projected benchmarks were found to be overly modest, the Committee could ask for a State Party explanation, and could recommend benchmark reconsideration. As applied to the development of right to food benchmarks, the expertise of specialized agencies, such as the FAO, non-governmental organizations, and national human rights commissions or institutes with special food rights expertise should be engaged to assist in this process. While in most instances, a cooperative spirit prevails between the Committee and the State Party, in extreme cases where benchmark consensus can not be reached, the treaty body might set an elevated benchmark more in line with State Party Covenant obligations. In practice, the constructive dialogue approach of the [Committee on Economic, Social and Cultural Rights] will seek consensus with the State party, to avoid unnecessary conflict.

At the same time, another risk – in some way a reverse of the latter – would be to consider that a failure by the State to meet its international obligations simply follows from the fact that the outcomes are not satisfactory. The lack of resources, or other factors (both internal and external, such as weather-related events, civil strife, or the imposition of economic sanctions by other States), may play a role in explaining that the results are not achieved. Hence, we need to devise methods to take into account these constraints, while not relieving a State from its obligations both to achieve the fullest possible realization of human rights within these constraints, and to put its best efforts into removing these constraints as soon as possible.

A useful attempt in this direction is the causality analysis proposed by Eitan Felner. Felner proposes to use quantitative data, combined with qualitative information, in order to move from outcomes (economic and social rights deprivations and disparities of outcome) (step #1 of the three-steps approach), to the identification of the 'main determinants of these outcomes so as to identify the policy responses that can reasonably be expected of the state' (step #2), and finally (in step #3) to the assessment of the extent to which 'deprivations, disparities and lack of progress can be traced back to failures of government policy' (E. Felner, 'A New Frontier in Economic and Social Rights Advocacy? Turning Quantitative Data into a Tool for Human Rights Accountability', *Sur – International Journal on Human Rights*, 9 (2008), 109–46 at 116). The use of outcome indicators is thus useful, and in particular it serves to identify whether a State complies with the core minimum content of each right, with the requirement of non-discrimination, of whether it is making progress or is instead retrogressing over time. But the information collected through outcome indicators is only a departure point. The following two steps move from the situation of the right-holder to the question whether the State has failed to discharge its human rights obligations:

Eitan Felner, 'A New Frontier in Economic and Social Rights Advocacy? Turning Quantitative Data into a Tool for Human Rights Accountability', *Sur – International Journal on Human Rights*, (2008), 109–46 at 126:

Imagine for instance that during Step #1 of the proposed methodological framework, one finds that in the focus country, a large proportion of girls are dropping out of school, while most boys complete primary school. If in Step #2, one finds that customs and social norms may be influencing parents' decisions not to send girls to school, then in Step #3, one should see whether the government has made efforts to counteract these entrenched social norms that have proven to be useful in other circumstances. This could include legislative reforms such as marriage rights and inheritance, or public awareness campaigns about the benefits of girls' education. But in Step #2, one may find that the primary reason that many parents are not sending their girls to school is not due to cultural or social norms, but rather due to economic reasons. For example, in that country, educated boys can expect to receive more future income than equally educated girls, and poor households without the means to send all their children to school, thus choose to send boys rather than girls. In such a case, during this step, one should assess whether governments have made specific efforts to change labor market circumstances, so that it does not discriminate against women, and so that opportunities and advantages faced by all children at given levels of education and achievement are broadly equal.

Such a causality analysis should make it possible to identify which deprivations of social and economic rights (as measured by outcome indicators) are attributable to a failure of the State to comply with its obligations, and which are instead the result of a lack of capacity of the State. Indeed, the final stage of the analysis (step #3) should enable the identification of 'cases in which the government had the capacity to deal with some of the determinants of specific deprivations and inequalities identified in Step #2, but failed to do so' (at 122). This of course requires what may reasonably be expected from the State to be clarified. Felner proposes a variety of methods to achieve this, including (a) the reference to internationally agreed benchmarks; (b) cross-country comparisons, between countries of the same region or at the same level of development; and (c) budget analysis:

Eitan Felner, 'A New Frontier in Economic and Social Rights Advocacy? Turning Quantitative Data into a Tool for Human Rights Accountability', *Sur – International Journal on Human Rights*, **9 (2008), 109–46 at 123 and 127:**

[Cross-country comparisons could be achieved by] comparing the levels of goods and services in the focus country with those of other countries in the same region. For instance, if the focus country has a much lower proportion of immunization rates, fewer hospital beds per 1,000 people, lower proportion of people with access to an improved water source, lower percentage of textbooks per pupil, or higher pupil-teacher ratio than most of the countries in the region, it would suggest that these levels are insufficient given its level of development, and that the focus country has failed to ensure the availability of these essential services in sufficient quantity. Similar to the cross-country comparisons of outcome indicators made in Step #1, cross-country comparisons over time can also useful for assessing whether the progress the focus country made has been bigger or smaller than that of other countries in same region.

[In order to evaluate whether the State commits sufficient resources to the fulfilment of human rights, Felner proposes what he calls a 'basic framework of expenditure and resource allocation ratios' to analyze expenditure patterns, based on the UNDP's proposals for the evaluation of public funding on human development. He notes that] these ratios could also be a powerful monitoring tool allowing human rights advocates to identify when: a government devotes insufficient resources to an area related to a specific right, such as education, health, food security, etc; a government appears not to raise sufficient revenues to be able to adequately fund the competing needs the state has; within a sector related to ESC rights, a government allocates disproportionately little resources to those budgetary items that should be a priority, in that they could have more impact on ensuring minimum essential levels of rights enjoyment in areas related to core elements of the right to health, education etc (e.g. disproportionate spending on tertiary versus primary education, or on metropolitan hospitals as opposed to rural primary health care services).

There at least three advantages to this approach – apart from the evident fact that it allows monitoring the obligation of progressive realization, thus giving a content to the obligation to fulfil that goes beyond a purely procedural dimension. First, the approach allows for a highly contextualized analysis. Even when the levels of deprivation in certain areas (such as health, education or food) are identical across various countries, different recipes will correspond to their respective conditions. An inductive approach, taking outcomes as a departure point and moving backwards along the causality chain, adequately reflects the need to avoid prescriptive approaches, based on a presumption that there are certain policies valid across time and geography to address social and economic deprivation. Second, the approach rightly does not take lack of resources as a given, which per definition it would not be possible for the State to reverse. For the same reasons, in measuring resources available, GDP per capita is more appropriate (although it remains a very crude indicator) than the public budget, because it is the duty of the State to raise taxes (without increasing inequalities of income) in order to ensure the fulfilment of rights that require resources. Third, the approach does not underestimate the validity of the use of quantitative indicators (measuring socio-economic deprivation) either for the purpose of comparing evolutions at different times (in order to measure whether progress is made or whether a State has been retrogressing), or for the purposes of cross-country comparisons (in order to set an appropriate benchmark for States, based on what other States in a similar situation or from the same region achieve, under similar conditions). These advantages are also present in the 'index of economic and social rights fulfillment' developed by Fukuda-Parr and others (S. Fukuda-Parr, T. Lawson-Remer and S. Randolph, 'An Index of Economic and Social Rights Fulfillment: Concept and Methodology', *Journal of Human Rights*, 8, Issue 3 (2009), 195), in which economic and social rights fulfilment is measured either as a ratio between the extent of rights enjoyment (x), and State resource capacity (y), or on the basis of the position achieved by a country along an Achievement Possibility Frontier (APF), which 'determines the maximum level of achievement possible ... on each ESR indicator at a given per capita income level, based on the highest level of the indicator historically achieved by any country at that per capita GDP level'. While it is not possible here to enter into the methodological debates such use of quantitative methods in measuring the degree of achievement of human rights give rise to, it is clear that these represent some of the most promising efforts in this area, in which important advances can be expected over the next few years.

5.1. Questions for discussion: tools for discharging the obligation to fulfil human rights

1. Are the tools described in this chapter applicable both to economic, social and cultural rights, and to civil and political rights, as implied by the 2006 Principles and Guidelines for a Human Rights Approach to Poverty Reduction Strategies? The view has been expressed that civil and political rights entail for their effective implementation considerable resources and thus may be subject to progressive realization: F. Jhabvala has argued, for instance, that 'ensuring the free exercise of civil and political rights will often involve significant State intervention and the incurring of considerable public expenditure in order to establish a system of courts, to train police and other public officials, and to establish a system of safeguards against potential abuses of rights be State officials themselves' (F. Jhabvala, 'On Human Rights and the Socio-Economic Context', *Netherlands International Law Review* 31 (1984), 149 at 163). Note that this position not only would appear to apply to the 'fulfil' component of States' obligations, but also to the 'respect' and 'protect' components, for the full range of human rights. Do you agree? To which extent should socio-economic conditions be taken into account in assessing whether a State complies with its human rights obligations?

2. Does the 2006 Brazilian Law establishing SISAN seem appropriate to fulfil all the functions identified for a framework law by Arjun Sengupta? Or are elements missing? What should the role of courts be in the implementation of such a framework law?

3. Is there a risk that, with the adoption of a national strategy concerning the realization of one right in particular, or/and the adoption of a framework law relating to that right, other rights get comparatively neglected, and that fewer resources be earmarked for their realization? Would the adoption of a strategy or/and framework law concerning only one right contradict the idea of indivisibility, interdependence, and equal importance of all human rights? Arjun Sengupta takes the view that: 'It is not necessary that the programmes included in [a] framework legislation should cover all rights. But it is important that they encompass a number of rights which are closely interdependent, together with a provision that in the process of realisation of these rights, no other rights are violated. If our concern is mostly with the right to food, it will be useful to combine it with at least the right to health, the right to education, the right to sanitation and clean water, as well as the right to an adequate standard of living and employment established for the food producers and consumers' (A. Sengupta, 'The Right to Food in the Perspective of the Right to Development' in W. B. Eide and U. Kracht (eds.), *Food and Human Rights in Development* (Antwerp-Oxford: Intersentia-Hart, 2007), vol. II, 'Evolving Issues and Emerging Applications', p. 107 at p. 131). Do you agree?

4. The Committee on the Rights of the Child seems to favour the adoption of a national strategy for the realization of children's rights, grounded in the Convention on the Rights of the Child. Is this appropriate? What are the disadvantages of such a strategy, as compared to more global national human rights action plans cutting across all rights?

5. In its 2007 Guidelines addressed to the States parties to the Protocol of San Salvador on economic, social and cultural rights, the Inter-American Commission on Human Rights proposes that States develop separate indicators on: (i) incorporation of the right; (ii) state capabilities;

and (iii) financial context and budgetary commitment. Is this an appropriate way of measuring the obligation to take steps towards progressive realization of economic, social and cultural rights? How should the information on financial context and budgetary commitment be evaluated for such an evaluation to be meaningful?

6. The allocation of resources across different areas (*inter alia*, health, education, housing, agriculture, social protection, public security, communications, national defence) requires trade-offs that are in principle trusted to the democratic process. Is this compatible with the adoption of a national strategy for the realization of a right such as the right to health or the right to education, or even with the adoption of a national human rights action plan cutting across all rights? Is participation of civil society in the drafting of such strategies or action plans a substitute for parliamentary processes? Is giving leadership in the preparation of a national strategy or action plan to the parliament appropriate, as was done in the case of Lithuania? Generally, do national strategies or action plans empower parliament? Do they empower the government, enhancing its ability to impose its agenda in the name of fulfilling human rights? Or do they empower courts? What impact, generally, does the adoption of such strategies or action plans have on the relationship between different branches of government? Does it make any difference whether the strategy or action plan is codified into a framework law? Does it make any difference whether it is set according to a process defined in a framework law, as illustrated by the Brazilian 2006 law establishing SISAN?

7. What differentiates a national human rights action plan from other plans (such as 'five-year action plans') guiding governmental action? Which conditions should be fulfilled for a national human rights action plan to qualify as such?

8. If the full realization of human rights requires international assistance and co-operation and, more generally, an enabling international environment, should the international community agree on 'international strategies', for example, for the realization of the right to food or the right to health? Consider the brief discussion earlier on the Millennium Development Goals in chapter 2, section 2.4. What would make such an international strategy, or action plan, for the realization of human rights at global level, different from the MDGs?

9. How can monitoring compliance with the obligation progressively to realize rights 'to the maximum of available resources' be compatible with democratic self-determination? The 2006 Principles and Guidelines for a Human Rights Approach to Poverty Reduction Strategies suggest that, without necessarily pre-determining which priorities should be set at one particular moment in time, a human rights approach 'cautions against making trade-offs whereby one right suffers a marked decline in its level of realization', which 'puts a restriction on the manner in which resources are allocated in favour of the rights that have been accorded priority at any point in time' since, in principle, any additional resources required in order to realize the rights which are given priority 'should, as a rule, not be extracted by reducing the level of resources currently allocated to other rights (unless reduced allocation of resources can be offset by increased efficiency of resource use)'. Is this an acceptable limit to what may be decided through democratic decision-making? (This issue is explored in greater depth in chapter 8.)

6

Derogations in Time of Public Emergency

INTRODUCTION

A number of human rights instruments contain provisions which allow States to adopt measures suspending the enjoyment of these rights to the extent strictly required by situations of emergency, for instance in the event of an armed conflict, internal or international, or following a natural disaster (see S. R. Chowdhury, *Rule of Law in a State of Emergency: the Paris Minimum Standards of Human Rights Norms in a State of Emergency* (London: Pinter Publishers, 1989); J. Fitzpatrick, *Human Rights in Crisis: the International System for Protecting Rights During States of Emergency* (Philadelphia, Penn.: University of Pennsylvania Press, 1994); J. Oraá, *Human Rights in States of Emergency in International Law* (Oxford: Clarendon Press, 1992); R. Higgins, 'Derogations under Human Rights Treaties', *British Yearbook of International Law*, 48 (1976–77), 281; T. Buergenthal, 'To Respect and Ensure: State Obligations and Permissible Derogations' in L. Henkin (ed.), *The International Bill of Rights: the Covenant on Civil and Political Rights* (New York: Columbia University Press, 1981) 72–91; C. Schreuer, 'Derogation of Human Rights in Situations of Public Emergency', *Yale Journal of World Public Order*, 9 (1982), 113; A.-L. Svensson-McCarthy, *The International Law of Human Rights and States of Exception* (The Hague: Martinus Nijhoff, 1998)).

The relevant provisions of the International Covenant on Civil and Political Rights (ICCPR) (Art. 4), the American Convention on Human Rights (ACHR) (Art. 27) and the European Convention on Human Rights (ECHR) (Art. 15), present clear similarities (for convenience, these clauses are reproduced in box 6.1.). The Paris Minimum Standards of Human Rights Norms in a State of Emergency, the result of work done by experts within the International Law Association in 1976–84 primarily under the leadership of S. R. Chowdhury (see the presentation by R. B. Lillich, 'The Paris Minimum Standards of Human Rights Norms in a State of Emergency', *American Journal of International Law*, 79 (1985), 1072–81) and the Siracusa Principles on the Limitation and Derogation Provisions in the International Covenant on Civil and Political Rights (UN doc. E/CN.4/1985/4 and *Human Rights Quarterly*, 6 (1984), 3), also the result of the work of independent experts, may also guide the interpretation of these clauses.

These provisions list six conditions for a State to be authorized to adopt measures derogating from their obligations under the cited instruments: a public emergency threatening the life of the nation must exist; the measures adopted must be strictly required by the exigencies of the situation; they must not entail a discrimination 'on the ground of race, colour, sex, language, religion, or social origin' (Art. 4(1) ICCPR and Article 27(1) ACHR, although the ECHR is silent on this condition); the measures derogating from these instruments may only be allowed to the extent that they are not inconsistent with the other obligations of the State concerned under international law; the derogation may not justify the suspension of certain guarantees, which are defined as 'non-derogable'; and the derogation must be notified to the other States parties to the instrument concerned.

Box 6.1. **Provisions relating to derogations in human rights instruments**

International Covenant on Civil and Political Rights, Art. 4:

1. In time of public emergency which threatens the life of the nation and the existence of which is officially proclaimed, the States Parties to the present Covenant may take measures derogating from their obligations under the present Covenant to the extent strictly required by the exigencies of the situation, provided that such measures are not inconsistent with their other obligations under international law and do not involve discrimination solely on the ground of race, colour, sex, language, religion or social origin.

2. No derogation from [Art. 6 (right to life), Art. 7 (prohibition of torture or cruel, inhuman or degrading punishment, or of medical or scientific experimentation without consent), Art. 8, paragraphs 1 and 2 (prohibition of slavery, slave trade and servitude), Art. 11 (prohibition of imprisonment because of inability to fulfil a contractual obligation), Art. 15 (the principle of legality in the field of criminal law, i.e. the requirement of both criminal liability and punishment being limited to clear and precise provisions in the law that was in place and applicable at the time the act or omission took place, except in cases where a later law imposes a lighter penalty), Art. 16 (the recognition of everyone as a person before the law), and Art. 18 (freedom of thought, conscience and religion)] may be made under this provision. [The same applies, in relation to States that are parties to the Second Optional Protocol to the Covenant, aiming at the abolition of the death penalty, as prescribed in Art. 6 of that Protocol.]

3. Any State Party to the present Covenant availing itself of the right of derogation shall immediately inform the other States Parties to the present Covenant, through the intermediary of the Secretary-General of the United Nations, of the provisions from which it has derogated and of the reasons by which it was actuated. A further communication shall be made, through the same intermediary, on the date on which it terminates such derogation.

American Convention on Human Rights, Article 27.
Suspension of Guarantees:

1. In time of war, public danger, or other emergency that threatens the independence or security of a State Party, it may take measures derogating from its obligations under the present

Convention to the extent and for the period of time strictly required by the exigencies of the situation, provided that such measures are not inconsistent with its other obligations under international law and do not involve discrimination on the ground of race, color, sex, language, religion, or social origin.

2. The foregoing provision does not authorize any suspension of the following articles: Article 3 (Right to Juridical Personality), Article 4 (Right to Life), Article 5 (Right to Humane Treatment), Article 6 (Freedom from Slavery), Article 9 (Freedom from Ex Post Facto Laws), Article 12 (Freedom of Conscience and Religion), Article 17 (Rights of the Family), Article 18 (Right to a Name), Article 19 (Rights of the Child), Article 20 (Right to Nationality), and Article 23 (Right to Participate in Government), or of the judicial guarantees essential for the protection of such rights.

3. Any State Party availing itself of the right of suspension shall immediately inform the other States Parties, through the Secretary General of the Organization of American States, of the provisions the application of which it has suspended, the reasons that gave rise to the suspension, and the date set for the termination of such suspension.

European Convention on Human Rights, Article 15:

1. In time of war or other public emergency threatening the life of the nation any High Contracting Party may take measures derogating from its obligations under this Convention to the extent strictly required by the exigencies of the situation, provided that such measures are not inconsistent with its other obligations under international law.

2. No derogation from Article 2, except in respect of deaths resulting from lawful acts of war, or from Articles 3, 4 (paragraph 1) and 7 shall be made under this provision.

3. Any High Contracting Party availing itself of this right of derogation shall keep the Secretary-General of the Council of Europe fully informed of the measures which it has taken and the reasons therefor. It shall also inform the Secretary-General of the Council of Europe when such measures have ceased to operate and the provisions of the Convention are again being fully executed.

The function of derogation clauses in the three human rights instruments which include them is not to exonerate the State from complying with human rights in the face of certain emergency situations. Quite to the contrary, these clauses serve to define carefully under which conditions certain guarantees may be (in part) suspended. In other words, as stated by the Siracusa Principles, 'derogation from rights recognized under international law in order to respond to a threat to the life of the nation is not exercised in a legal vacuum. It is authorized by law and as such it is subject to several legal principles of general application' (para. 61). A number of consequences follow:

Siracusa Principles on the Limitation and Derogation Provisions in the International Covenant on Civil and Political Rights (1985), paras. 62–64:

62. A proclamation of a public emergency shall be made in good faith based upon an objective assessment of the situation in order to determine to what extent, if any, it poses a threat to the life of the nation. A proclamation of a public emergency, and consequent derogations from Covenant obligations, that are not made in good faith are violations of international law.

63. The provisions of the Covenant allowing for certain derogations in a public emergency are to be interpreted restrictively.

64. In a public emergency the rule of law shall still prevail. Derogation is an authorized and limited perogative in order to respond adequately to a threat to the life of the nation. The derogating state shall have the burden of justifying its actions under law.

This chapter examines the conditions under which States may rely on the derogation mechanism, and it provides a number of illustrations of how courts have evaluated measures adopted by States seeking to derogate from their human rights obligations. The United Kingdom's derogation to Article 5(1) ECHR, following the terrorist attacks on New York and Washington on 11 September 2001, offers a spectacular example, to which frequent reference will be made. The United Kingdom derogated from Article 5 ECHR in anticipation of the adoption of sections 21–3 of the Anti-terrorism, Crime and Security Act 2001, which provided for the potentially indefinite detention of foreign nationals the Home Secretary suspects of involvement in international terrorism and whom he/she is unable to deport owing to a well-founded fear of persecution in the country of origin and the inability to secure a third country of destination (see box 6.2.). The derogation was ultimately found to be incompatible with the requirements of the ECHR both by the House of Lords in 2004 and by the European Court of Human Rights in 2009, in what is sometimes referred to as the *Belmarsh Detainees* case.

Box 6.2.

Derogation in the context of counter-terrorist measures: the derogation by the United Kingdom to Art. 5(1) ECHR

Following the 11 September 2001 attacks on New York and Washington, the United Kingdom adopted the Anti-terrorism Crime and Security Act 2001, which received Royal Assent on 14 December 2001, and the Human Rights Act 1998 (Designated Derogation) Order 2001 (SI 2001/3644). This Derogation Order, adopted pursuant to section 14 of the Human Rights Act 1998, found that 'There exists a terrorist threat to the United Kingdom from persons suspected of involvement in international terrorism. In particular, there are foreign nationals present in the United Kingdom who are suspected of being concerned in the commission, preparation or instigation of acts of international terrorism, of being members of organisations or groups which are so concerned or of having links with members of such organisations or groups, and who are a threat to the national security of the United Kingdom.' The Derogation Order also recalled the *Chahal* case law of the European Court of Human Rights, imposing an absolute prohibition on deportation of foreign nationals whenever substantial grounds have been shown for believing that the individual concerned would face a real risk of being subjected to treatment contrary to Article 3 ECHR if removed to another State (chapter 3, section 2.2.), implying that there were certain individuals found in the United Kingdom who, while representing a threat to the national security of the United Kingdom, might not be deported in accordance with this case law. The Derogation Order recognized that the extended power in the new legislation to detain a person against whom no action was being taken with a view to deportation might be inconsistent with Article 5(1)(f) ECHR. Indeed, this provision allows for the lawful arrest or detention of a person against whom action is being taken with a view to deportation or extradition, which presupposes that removal from the national territory is a realistic possibility and that it is effectively pursued. The United Kingdom concluded that it was necessary to derogate from the ECHR in this respect. On 18 December 2001, the Secretary-General of the Council of Europe was formally notified, through a 'note verbale', that the United Kingdom intended to derogate from Article 5(1) ECHR. Corresponding steps were taken to derogate from Article 9 of the International Covenant on Civil and Political Rights.

1 FIRST CONDITION: A PUBLIC EMERGENCY WHICH THREATENS THE LIFE OF THE NATION

1.1 What is a public emergency threatening the life of the nation?

In order for a derogation to be admissible, the situation must constitute a 'public emergency which theatens the life of the nation'. In its General Comment No. 29 on Article 4 of the International Covenant on Civil and Political Rights, the Human Rights Committee noted:

Human Rights Committee, General Comment No. 29, *Derogations during a State of Emergency* (Art. 4), (CCPR/C/21/Rev.1/Add. 11) (24 July 2001), para. 3:

Not every disturbance or catastrophe qualifies as a public emergency which threatens the life of the nation, as required by article 4, paragraph 1. During armed conflict, whether international or non-international, rules of international humanitarian law become applicable and help, in addition to the provisions in article 4 and article 5, paragraph 1, of the Covenant, to prevent the abuse of a State's emergency powers. The Covenant requires that even during an armed conflict measures derogating from the Covenant are allowed only if and to the extent that the situation constitutes a threat to the life of the nation. If States parties consider invoking article 4 in other situations than an armed conflict, they should carefully consider the justification and why such a measure is necessary and legitimate in the circumstances. On a number of occasions the Committee has expressed its concern over States parties that appear to have derogated from rights protected by the Covenant, or whose domestic law appears to allow such derogation in situations not covered by article 4.

By reference to Article 4 ICCPR, the Siracusa Principles state the following, under the heading 'Public Emergency which Threatens the Life of the Nation':

Siracusa Principles on the Limitation and Derogation Provisions in the International Covenant on Civil and Political Rights (1985), paras. 39–40:

39. A state party may take measures derogating from its obligations under the International Covenant on Civil and Political Rights pursuant to Article 4 (hereinafter called 'derogation measures') only when faced with a situation of exceptional and actual or imminent danger which threatens the life of the nation. A threat to the life of the nation is one that:

(a) affects the whole of the population and either the whole or part of the territory of the State, and

(b) threatens the physical integrity of the population, the political independence or the territorial integrity of the State or the existence or basic functioning of institutions indispensable to ensure and protect the rights recognised in the Covenant.

40. Internal conflict and unrest that do not constitute a grave and imminent threat to the life of the nation cannot justify derogations under Article 4.

It is doubtful, however, whether Article 4 ICCPR implies a requirement that the danger 'affects *the whole of the population* and either the whole or part of the territory of the State' (emphasis added). In fact, this may be in contradiction with the statement by the Human Rights Committee that derogation measures must be limited in scope, also as regards 'geographical coverage ... of the state of emergency and any measures of derogation resorted to because of the emergency' (see below).

Lawless v. *Ireland*, the first case adjudicated by the European Court of Human Rights, was concerned with very low-level IRA terrorist activity in Ireland and Northern Ireland in 1954–57. The Irish Government derogated from Article 5 ECHR in July 1957 in order to permit detention without charge or trial and the applicant was detained between July and December 1957. Applying Article 15 of the European Convention on Human Rights, the European Court of Human Rights initially noted the following:

European Court of Human Rights, *Lawless* v. *Ireland* (No. 3), judgment of 1 July 1961:

[T]he natural and customary meaning of the words 'other public emergency threatening the life of the nation' is sufficiently clear; they refer to an exceptional situation of crisis or emergency which affects the whole population and constitutes a threat to the organised life of the community of which the State is composed. Having thus established the natural and customary meaning of this conception, the Court must determine whether the facts and circumstances which led the Irish Government to make their Proclamation of 5 July 1957 come within this conception. The Court, after an examination, finds this to be the case; the existence at the time of a 'public emergency threatening the life of the nation' was reasonably deduced by the Irish Government from a combination of several factors, namely: in the first place, the existence in the territory of the Republic of Ireland of a secret army engaged in unconstitutional activities and using violence to attain its purposes; secondly, the fact that this army was also operating outside the territory of the State, thus seriously jeopardising the relations of the Republic of Ireland with its neighbour; thirdly, the steady and alarming increase in terrorist activities from the autumn of 1956 and throughout the first half of 1957.

The requirement that the emergency should affect the whole population was again repeated in the *Greek* case (1969) (12 *Yearbook of the ECHR* 1), when the Government of Greece failed to persuade the European Commission of Human Rights that there had been such a public emergency threatening the life of the nation justifying derogation. In para. 153 of its opinion the Commission said: 'Such a public emergency may then be seen to have, in particular, the following characteristics: (1) It must be actual or imminent. (2) Its effects must involve the whole nation. (3) The continuance of the organised life of the community must be threatened. (4) The crisis or danger must be exceptional, in that the normal measures or restrictions, permitted by the Convention for the maintenance of public safety, health and order, are plainly inadequate.' However, in later cases the European Court of Human Rights adopted a more flexible position. In *Ireland* v. *United Kingdom*, the Court emphasized that the national authorities are in principle better placed than an international court to evaluate which measures are required by the emergence of a particular situation, thus inaugurating a doctrine about the 'margin of appreciation' which has since played a central role in its jurisprudence.

European Court of Human Rights (Plenary), *Ireland* v. *United Kingdom*, judgment of 18 January 1978, Series A No. 25, para. 207:

It falls in the first place to each Contracting State, with its responsibility for 'the life of [its] nation', to determine whether that life is threatened by a 'public emergency' and, if so, how far it is necessary to go in attempting to overcome the emergency. By reason of their direct and continuous contact with the pressing needs of the moment, the national authorities are in principle in a better position than the international judge to decide both on the presence of such an emergency and on the nature and scope of derogations necessary to avert it. In this matter, Article 15(1) leaves those authorities a wide margin of appreciation.

In *Ireland* v. *United Kingdom*, the Court also considered that the 'public emergency' justifying a derogation could affect only part of the national territory, referring in that case to 'a particularly far-reaching and acute danger for the territorial integrity of the United Kingdom, the institutions of the six counties [of Northern Ireland] and the lives of the province's inhabitants' (para. 212).

The question of whether there indeed existed a 'public emergency threatening the life of the nation' was also raised in the context of the derogation measures adopted by the United Kingdom following the 11 September 2001, terrorist attacks (see box 6.2.). In December 2002, the United Kingdom responded as follows to the Concluding Observations of the Human Rights Committee, which the Committee adopted on 29

October 2001 on the United Kingdom's fourth and fifth combined report presented pursuant to Article 40 ICCPR:

Comments by the Government of the United Kingdom of Great Britain and Northern Ireland on the reports of the United Kingdom (CCPR/CO/73/UK) and the Overseas Territories (CCPR/CO/73/UKOT) (CCPR/CO/73/UK/Add. 2 and CCPR/CO/73/UKOT/Add. 2, 4 December 2002):

We believe the measures contained in [the Anti-terrorism Crime and Security Act 2001] both respect and meet the United Kingdom's international human rights obligations.

Terrorism represents a grave and fundamental threat to the national security of the United Kingdom and the safety of its citizens. This is a threat that needs to be addressed without compromising the integrity of those international obligations.

Article 4 of the International Covenant on Civil and Political Rights permits States to derogate under certain conditions from certain of their obligations under the Covenant in time of public emergency which threatens the life of the nation the existence of which is officially proclaimed.

2. Article 4 (1) of the Covenant

(a) Is there a public emergency? We believe that there is a public emergency threatening the life of the nation. On 30 July 2002, the Special Immigration Appeals Commission in the case of *A and others* v. *Secretary of State for the Home Department* found it was 'satisfied that what has been put before us in the open generic statements and the other material in the bundles which are available to the parties does justify the conclusion that there does exist a public emergency threatening the life of the nation within the terms of Article 15 [of the ECHR]. That the risk has been heightened since 11 September is clear, but we do not regard that description as in any way inconsistent with the existence of an emergency within the meaning of Article 15 ECHR. The United Kingdom is a prime target, second only to the United States of America, and the history of events both before and after 11 September 2001 as well as on that fateful day does show that if one attack were to take place it could well occur without warning and be on such a scale as to threaten the life of the nation.'

As regards the closed evidence also before the Special Immigration Appeals Commission, the Commission said: 'We have considered the closed material. Suffice to say that it confirms our view that the emergency is established.'

...

7. Developments since Royal Assent 14 December 2001

(a) Individuals detained Eleven individuals have been detained in total since the Act received Royal Assent. Two of these have since left the United Kingdom voluntarily. The nine remaining in detention have all lodged appeals against the certification and against the decision to deport. All have brought actions challenging the lawfulness of the derogation that underpins the detention power in the Act.

(b) The SIAC hearings These were heard at the end of July and the SIAC judgement on 30 July [2002] recognized that, in the light of the 11 September attacks, there is a public emergency threatening the United Kingdom. SIAC also held that the powers of detention in the Anti-terrorism, Crime and Security Act 2001 are a necessary and proportionate response to that emergency in ECHR terms.

While the UK Special Immigration Appeals Commission (SIAC) found that the detention powers provided under the Anti-terrorism Crime and Security Act 2001 were a necessary and proportionate response to the terrorist threat, it also took the view that the detention powers were discriminatory on grounds of national origin against foreign nationals. The UK Government appealed that holding. On 25 October 2002, the Court of Appeal (Lord Woolf C.J., Brooke and Chadwick L.JJ.) allowed the appeal ([2002] EWCA Civ 1502, [2004] Q.B. 335). The nine detainees in turn appealed to the House of Lords, which delivered its judgment on 16 December 2004. Again, the House of Lords addressed the question of whether there existed a 'public emergency' in the meaning required by Article 15 ECHR or Article 4 ICCPR for derogation powers to be exercised. One of the Lords (Lord Hoffmann) answered in the negative in his opinion, stating: 'This is a nation which has been tested in adversity, which has survived physical destruction and catastrophic loss of life. I do not underestimate the ability of fanatical groups of terrorists to kill and destroy, but they do not threaten the life of the nation. Whether we would survive Hitler hung in the balance, but there is no doubt that we shall survive Al-Qaeda. The Spanish people have not said that what happened in Madrid, hideous crime as it was, threatened the life of their nation. Their legendary pride would not allow it. Terrorist violence, serious as it is, does not threaten our institutions of government or our existence as a civil community.' This view was not shared by the majority:

House of Lords (United Kingdom), A. (F.C.) and others (F.C.) (Appellants) v. Secretary of State for the Home Department (Respondent), X. (F.C.) and another (F.C.) (Appellants) v. Secretary of State for the Home Department (Respondent) [2004] UKHL 56, leading opinion by Lord Bingham of Cornhill:

[Public emergency]
20. The appellants did not seek to play down the catastrophic nature of what had taken place on 11 September 2001 nor the threat posed to western democracies by international terrorism. But they argued that there had been no public emergency threatening the life of the British nation, for three main reasons: if the emergency was not (as in all the decided cases) actual, it must be shown to be imminent, which could not be shown here; the emergency must be of a temporary nature, which again could not be shown here; and the practice of other states, none of which had derogated from the European Convention, strongly suggested that there was no public emergency calling for derogation. All these points call for some explanation.

21. The requirement of imminence is not expressed in article 15 of the European Convention or article 4 of the ICCPR but it has ... been treated by the European Court as a necessary condition of a valid derogation. It is a view shared by the distinguished academic authors of the Siracusa Principles, who in 1985 formulated the rule (applying to the ICCPR): '54. The principle of strict necessity shall be applied in an objective manner. Each measure shall be directed to an actual, clear, present, or imminent danger and may not be imposed merely because of an apprehension of potential danger.'

In submitting that the test of imminence was not met, the appellants pointed to ministerial statements in October 2001 and March 2002: 'There is no immediate intelligence pointing to a specific threat to the United Kingdom, but we remain alert, domestically as well as internationally'; and '[I]t would be wrong to say that we have evidence of a particular threat.'

22. The requirement of temporariness is again not expressed in article 15 or article 4 unless it be inherent in the meaning of 'emergency'. But the UN Human Rights Committee on 24 July 2001, in General Comment No. 29 on article 4 of the ICCPR, observed in para 2 that: 'Measures derogating from the provisions of the Covenant must be of an exceptional and temporary nature.'

This view was also taken by the parliamentary Joint Committee on Human Rights, which in its Eighteenth Report of the Session 2003–2004 (HL paper 158, HC 713, 21 July 2004), in para 4, observed: 'Derogations from human rights obligations are permitted in order to deal with emergencies. They are intended to be temporary. According to the Government and the Security Service, the UK now faces a near-permanent emergency.'

It is indeed true that official spokesmen have declined to suggest when, if ever, the present situation might change.

23. No state other than the United Kingdom has derogated from article 5. In Resolution 1271 adopted on 24 January 2002, the Parliamentary Assembly of the Council of Europe resolved (para. 9) that: 'In their fight against terrorism, Council of Europe members should not provide for any derogations to the European Convention on Human Rights.' It also called on all member states (para. 12) to: 'refrain from using Article 15 of the European Convention on Human Rights (derogation in time of emergency) to limit the rights and liberties guaranteed under its Article 5 (right to liberty and security)' ...

The Committee of Privy Counsellors established pursuant to section 122 of the 2001 Act under the chairmanship of Lord Newton of Braintree, which reported on 18 December 2003 (Anti-terrorism, Crime and Security Act 2001 Review: Report, HC 100) attached significance to this point: '189. The UK is the only country to have found it necessary to derogate from the European Convention on Human Rights. We found this puzzling, as it seems clear that other countries face considerable threats from terrorists within their borders.' It noted that France, Italy and Germany had all been threatened, as well as the UK.

24. The appellants submitted that detailed information pointing to a real and imminent danger to public safety in the United Kingdom had not been shown. In making this submission they were able to rely on a series of reports by the Joint Committee on Human Rights. In its Second Report of the Session 2001–2002 (HL paper 37, HC 372), made on 14 November 2001 when the 2001 Act was a Bill before Parliament, the Joint Committee stated (in para. 30): 'Having considered the Home Secretary's evidence carefully, we recognise that there may be evidence of the existence of a public emergency threatening the life of the nation, although none was shown by him to this Committee.'

It repeated these doubts in para. 4 of its Fifth Report of the Session 2001–2002 (3 December 2001). In para. 20 of its Fifth Report of the Session 2002–2003 (HL paper 59, HC 462, 24 February 2003), following the decisions of SIAC and the Court of Appeal, the Joint Committee noted that SIAC had had sight of closed as well as open material but suggested that each House might wish to seek further information from the Government on the public emergency issue. In its report of 23 February 2004 (Sixth Report of the Session 2003–2004, HL Paper 38, HC 381), the Joint Committee stated, in para. 34: 'Insufficient evidence has been presented to Parliament to make it possible for us to accept that derogation under ECHR Article 15 is strictly required by the exigencies of the situation to deal with a public emergency threatening the life of the nation.'

It adhered to this opinion in paras. 15–19 of its Eighteenth Report of the Session 2003–2004 (HL Paper 158, HC 713), drawing attention (para. 82) to the fact that the UK was the only country out of 45 countries in the Council of Europe which had found it necessary to derogate from article 5. The appellants relied on these doubts when contrasting the British derogation with the conduct of other Council of Europe member states which had not derogated, including even Spain which had actually experienced catastrophic violence inflicted by Al-Qaeda.

25. The Attorney General, representing the Home Secretary, answered these points. He submitted that an emergency could properly be regarded as imminent if an atrocity was credibly threatened by a body such as Al-Qaeda which had demonstrated its capacity and will to carry out such a threat, where the atrocity might be committed without warning at any time. The Government, responsible as it was and is for the safety of the British people, need not wait for disaster to strike before taking necessary steps to prevent it striking. As to the requirement that the emergency be temporary, the Attorney General did not suggest that an emergency could ever become the normal state of affairs, but he did resist the imposition of any artificial temporal limit to an emergency of the present kind ... Little help, it was suggested, could be gained by looking at the practice of other states. It was for each national government, as the guardian of its own people's safety, to make its own judgment on the basis of the facts known to it. Insofar as any difference of practice as between the United Kingdom and other Council of Europe members called for justification, it could be found in this country's prominent role as an enemy of Al-Qaeda and an ally of the United States. The Attorney General also made two more fundamental submissions. First, he submitted that there was no error of law in SIAC's approach to this issue and accordingly, since an appeal against its decision lay only on a point of law, there was no ground upon which any appellate court was entitled to disturb its conclusion. Secondly, he submitted that the judgment on this question was pre-eminently one within the discretionary area of judgment reserved to the Secretary of State and his colleagues, exercising their judgment with the benefit of official advice, and to Parliament.

26. The appellants have in my opinion raised an important and difficult question, as the continuing anxiety of the Joint Committee on Human Rights, the observations of the Commissioner for Human Rights and the warnings of the UN Human Rights Committee make clear. In the result, however, not without misgiving (fortified by reading the opinion of my noble and learned friend Lord Hoffmann), I would resolve this issue against the appellants, for three main reasons.

27. First, it is not shown that SIAC or the Court of Appeal misdirected themselves on this issue. SIAC considered a body of closed material, that is, secret material of a sensitive nature not shown to the parties. The Court of Appeal was not asked to read this material. The Attorney General expressly declined to ask the House to read it. From this I infer that while the closed material no doubt substantiates and strengthens the evidence in the public domain, it does not alter its essential character and effect. But this is in my view beside the point. It is not shown that SIAC misdirected itself in law on this issue, and the view which it accepted was one it could reach on the open evidence in the case.

28. My second reason is a legal one. The European Court decisions in *Ireland* v. *United Kingdom* (1978) 2 EHRR 25; *Brannigan and McBride* v. *United Kingdom* (1993) 17 EHRR 539; *Aksoy* v. *Turkey* (1996) 23 EHRR 553 and *Marshall* v. *United Kingdom* (10 July 2001, Appn. No. 41571/98) seem to me to be, with respect, clearly right. In each case the member state had actually experienced widespread loss of life caused by an armed body dedicated to destroying the territorial integrity of the state. To hold that the article 15 test was not satisfied in such circumstances, if a response beyond that provided by the ordinary course of law was required,

would have been perverse. But these features were not, on the facts found, very clearly present in *Lawless* v. *Ireland* (No 3) (1961) 1 EHRR 15 ... If ... it was open to the Irish Government in Lawless to conclude that there was a public emergency threatening the life of the Irish nation, the British Government could scarcely be faulted for reaching that conclusion in the much more dangerous situation which arose after 11 September.

29. Thirdly, I would accept that great weight should be given to the judgment of the Home Secretary, his colleagues and Parliament on this question, because they were called on to exercise a pre-eminently political judgment. It involved making a factual prediction of what various people around the world might or might not do, and when (if at all) they might do it, and what the consequences might be if they did. Any prediction about the future behaviour of human beings (as opposed to the phases of the moon or high water at London Bridge) is necessarily problematical. Reasonable and informed minds may differ, and a judgment is not shown to be wrong or unreasonable because that which is thought likely to happen does not happen. It would have been irresponsible not to err, if at all, on the side of safety. As will become apparent, I do not accept the full breadth of the Attorney General's argument on what is generally called the deference owed by the courts to the political authorities. It is perhaps preferable to approach this question as one of demarcation of functions or what Liberty in its written case called 'relative institutional competence'. The more purely political (in a broad or narrow sense) a question is, the more appropriate it will be for political resolution and the less likely it is to be an appropriate matter for judicial decision. The smaller, therefore, will be the potential role of the court. It is the function of political and not judicial bodies to resolve political questions. Conversely, the greater the legal content of any issue, the greater the potential role of the court, because under our constitution and subject to the sovereign power of Parliament it is the function of the courts and not of political bodies to resolve legal questions. The present question seems to me to be very much at the political end of the spectrum ...

Nevertheless, in its judgement of 16 December 2004, the House of Lords found that section 23 of the Anti-terrorism, Crime and Security Act 2001 is incompatible with Articles 5 and 14 of the European Convention insofar as it is disproportionate and permits detention of suspected international terrorists in a way that discriminates on the ground of nationality or immigration status (see below). It therefore issued a quashing order in respect of the Human Rights Act 1998 (Designated Derogation) Order 2001, and made a declaration under section 4 of the Human Rights Act 1998. However, this declaration of incompatibility made by the House of Lords was not binding on the parties to the litigation. Except for those who had elected to leave the United Kingdom or were released on bail on conditions amounting to house arrest, those detained under the provisions of the 2001 Act remained in detention, and they were not entitled, under domestic law, to compensation in respect of their detention. As a result, eleven persons detained under the 2001 Act lodged an application to the European Court of Human Rights on 21 January 2005.

On 11 March 2005, part 4 of the 2001 Act was repealed. It was replaced with a regime of control orders provided for by the Prevention of Terrorism Act 2005, imposing various restrictions on individuals, regardless of nationality, reasonably suspected of being involved in terrorism. In accordance with this legislative change, the applicants before the Court who remained in detention were released on 10–11 March 2005 and immediately made subject to control orders under the Prevention of Terrorism Act 2005. On 11 August 2005, following negotiations commenced towards the end of 2003 to seek from the Algerian and Jordanian Governments assurances that the applicants would not be ill-treated if returned, the Government notified its intention to deport to these countries seven of the eleven individuals whose applications were pending before the European Court of Human Rights (six to Algeria and one to Jordan). These applicants were taken into immigration custody pending their removal to Algeria and Jordan: the decision of the House of Lords following the appeals lodged against those procedures is presented in chapter 3 (section 2.2., b)).

The European Court of Human Rights delivered its judgment on 19 February 2009. The following excerpts concern the derogation notified by the UK Government, which the House of Lords had already found invalid in December 2004, prompting the European Court of Human Rights to remark that 'in the unusual circumstances of the present case, where the highest domestic court has examined the issues relating to the State's derogation and concluded that there was a public emergency threatening the life of the nation but that the measures taken in response were not strictly required by the exigencies of the situation, the Court considers that it would be justified in reaching a contrary conclusion only if satisfied that the national court had misinterpreted or misapplied Article 15 or the Court's jurisprudence under that Article or reached a conclusion which was manifestly unreasonable' (para. 174). The position of the Court on the question of whether the United Kingdom was facing a 'public emergency threatening the life of the nation' is the following:

European Court of Human Rights (GC), *A. and others* v. *United Kingdom* (Appl. No. 3455/05), judgment of 19 February 2009:

Whether there was a 'public emergency threatening the life of the nation'

175. The applicants argued that there had been no public emergency threatening the life of the British nation, for three main reasons: first, the emergency was neither actual nor imminent; secondly, it was not of a temporary nature; and, thirdly, the practice of other States, none of which had derogated from the Convention, together with the informed views of other national and international bodies, suggested that the existence of a public emergency had not been established.

176. The Court recalls that in [*Lawless* v. *Ireland* (No. 3), judgment of 1 July 1961, §28], it held that in the context of Article 15 the natural and customary meaning of the words 'other public emergency threatening the life of the nation' was sufficiently clear and that they referred to 'an exceptional situation of crisis or emergency which affects the whole population and constitutes a threat to the organised life of the community of which the State is composed'. In the *Greek Case* (1969) 12 YB 1, §153, the Commission held that, in order to justify a derogation, the emergency should be actual or imminent; that it should affect the whole nation to the extent that the continuance of the organised life of the community was threatened; and that the crisis or danger should be exceptional, in that the normal measures or restrictions, permitted by the

Convention for the maintenance of public safety, health and order, were plainly inadequate. In *Ireland* v. *United Kingdom*, judgment of 18 January 1978, §§205 and 212, the parties were agreed, as were the Commission and the Court, that the Article 15 test was satisfied, since terrorism had for a number of years represented 'a particularly far-reaching and acute danger for the territorial integrity of the United Kingdom, the institutions of the six counties and the lives of the province's inhabitants' ...

177. Before the domestic courts, the Secretary of State adduced evidence to show the existence of a threat of serious terrorist attacks planned against the United Kingdom. Additional closed evidence was adduced before SIAC. All the national judges accepted that the danger was credible (with the exception of Lord Hoffmann, who did not consider that it was of a nature to constitute 'a threat to the life of the nation'). Although when the derogation was made no al'Qaeda attack had taken place within the territory of the United Kingdom, the Court does not consider that the national authorities can be criticised, in the light of the evidence available to them at the time, for fearing that such an attack was 'imminent', in that an atrocity might be committed without warning at any time. The requirement of imminence cannot be interpreted so narrowly as to require a State to wait for disaster to strike before taking measures to deal with it. Moreover, the danger of a terrorist attack was, tragically, shown by the bombings and attempted bombings in London in July 2005 to have been very real. Since the purpose of Article 15 is to permit States to take derogating measures to protect their populations from future risks, the existence of the threat to the life of the nation must be assessed primarily with reference to those facts which were known at the time of the derogation. The Court is not precluded, however, from having regard to information which comes to light subsequently (see, *mutatis mutandis, Vilvarajah and others* v. *United Kingdom*, judgment of 30 October 1991, §107(2), Series A No. 215).

178. While the United Nations Human Rights Committee has observed that measures derogating from the provisions of the ICCPR must be of 'an exceptional and temporary nature' ..., the Court's case law has never, to date, explicitly incorporated the requirement that the emergency be temporary, although the question of the proportionality of the response may be linked to the duration of the emergency. Indeed, the cases cited above, relating to the security situation in Northern Ireland, demonstrate that it is possible for a 'public emergency' within the meaning of Article 15 to continue for many years. The Court does not consider that derogating measures put in place in the immediate aftermath of the al'Qaeda attacks in the United States of America, and reviewed on an annual basis by Parliament, can be said to be invalid on the ground that they were not 'temporary'.

179. The applicants' argument that the life of the nation was not threatened is principally founded on the dissenting opinion of Lord Hoffman, who interpreted the words as requiring a threat to the organised life of the community which went beyond a threat of serious physical damage and loss of life. It had, in his view, to threaten 'our institutions of government or our existence as a civil community' ... However, the Court has in previous cases been prepared to take into account a much broader range of factors in determining the nature and degree of the actual or imminent threat to the 'nation' and has in the past concluded that emergency situations have existed even though the institutions of the State did not appear to be imperilled to the extent envisaged by Lord Hoffman.

180. As previously stated, the national authorities enjoy a wide margin of appreciation under Article 15 in assessing whether the life of their nation is threatened by a public emergency. While

it is striking that the United Kingdom was the only Convention State to have lodged a derogation in response to the danger from al'Qaeda, although other States were also the subject of threats, the Court accepts that it was for each Government, as the guardian of their own people's safety, to make their own assessment on the basis of the facts known to them. Weight must, therefore, attach to the judgment of the United Kingdom's executive and Parliament on this question. In addition, significant weight must be accorded to the views of the national courts, who were better placed to assess the evidence relating to the existence of an emergency.

181. On this first question, the Court accordingly shares the view of the majority of the House of Lords that there was a public emergency threatening the life of the nation.

1.2 The need for an official proclamation of a state of emergency

Article 4 of the International Covenant on Civil and Political Rights adds that the existence of the public emergency justifying the derogation must be 'officially proclaimed'. In its General Comment No. 29, the Human Rights Committee noted that such official proclamation 'is essential for the maintenance of the principles of legality and rule of law at times when they are most needed. When proclaiming a state of emergency with consequences that could entail derogation from any provision of the Covenant, States must act within their constitutional and other provisions of law that govern such proclamation and the exercise of emergency powers; it is the task of the Committee to monitor the laws in question with respect to whether they enable and secure compliance with article 4' (para. 2). It has sometimes been considered that such an official proclamation necessarily has to be done in writing, in the form of an official publication (*Law Society of Lesotho* v. *Minister of Defence and Internal Security*, Supreme Court of Lesotho, [1988] L.R.C. (Const.), 226).

The requirement of an official proclamation of the state of emergency is explicitly stated neither in the European Convention on Human Rights nor in the American Convention on Human Rights. However, in his 2002 opinion on the 2001 UK derogation from Article 5 para. 1 ECHR, Mr Alvaro Gil Robles, the Commissioner for Human Rights of the Council of Europe, took the view that derogations should be subjected to parliamentary scrutiny by the national parliament concerned, and that this had implications both as to the sequence and as to the information to be provided to the parliament:

Opinion of the Council of Europe Commissioner for Human Rights on certain aspects of the United Kingdom 2001 derogation from Art. 5 para. 1 of the European Convention on Human Rights, Opinion 1/2002 of 28 August 2002, CommDH(2002)7, paras. 5–12 and 14–23:

5. The Convention does not expressly require an effective domestic scrutiny of derogations under Article 15, and the Court has not yet had occasion to pronounce on the matter. The requirement is, however, easily discerned.

6. The Court has repeatedly emphasised the close relationship between democracy and the rights guaranteed by the Convention, stating, for instance, that 'democracy appears to be the only political model contemplated by the Convention and, accordingly, the only one compatible with it' [*United Communist Party of Turkey and others* v. *Turkey*, judgment of 30 January 1998, Reports 1998–I, para. 45].

7. The separation of powers, whereby the Government's legislative proposals are subject to the approval of Parliament and, on enactment, review by the courts, is a constitutive element of democratic governance.

8. Effective domestic scrutiny must, accordingly, be of particular importance in respect of measures purporting to derogate from the Convention: parliamentary scrutiny and judicial review represent essential guarantees against the possibility of an arbitrary assessment by the executive and the subsequent implementation of disproportionate measures.

9. It is, furthermore, precisely because the Convention presupposes domestic controls in the form of a preventive parliamentary scrutiny and posterior judicial review that national authorities enjoy a large margin of appreciation in respect of derogations. This is, indeed, the essence of the principle of the subsidiarity of the protection of Convention rights.

10. This opinion is not concerned with the judicial review of derogations.

11. The parliamentary scrutiny of derogations is consistent with the Constitutional norms of several European countries regarding the use of emergency powers. Declarations of different types of emergencies typically require simple or qualified parliamentary majorities, or are subject, along with the related measures, to subsequent parliamentary confirmation.

12. The formal requirement of the parliamentary approval of derogations is not on its own sufficient, however, to guarantee an independent assessment of the existence of an emergency and the necessity of the measures taken to deal with it. It is clear that the effectiveness of the parliamentary scrutiny of derogations depends in large measure on the access of at least some of its members to the information on which the decision to derogate is based.

[Applying the considerations above to evaluate the adequacy of the procedure followed in the United Kingdom with respect to derogations (see box 6.2.), the Commissioner for Human Rights noted:]

14. The Human Rights Act [1998, which incorporates the rights guaranteed by the Convention into United Kingdom domestic law] outlines in sections 14 and 16 the procedure for derogating from Convention rights for the purposes of domestic law. The Secretary of State responsible designates the derogation through a statutory instrument in the form of an Order in Council, which must subsequently be included in Schedule 3 of the Act. The order designating the derogation comes into effect immediately, but expires after a period of 40 days unless both Houses pass a resolution approving it. A designation order may be made in anticipation of a proposed derogation.

15. The Home Secretary first announced proposals to combat the 'the threat from international terrorism' on 15th October 2001. On 11th November 2001 the Human Rights Act 1998 (Designated Derogation) Order 2001 was made by the Home Secretary. It came into effect two days later. The Designated Derogation Order was debated in Parliament on 19th November and approved on 21st November 2001. The first draft of the Anti-terrorism, Crime and Security Bill 2001 was laid before Parliament on 12th November 2001 and received Royal Assent on 13th December 2001. The Secretary-General of the Council of Europe was informed of the United Kingdom's derogation by Note verbale on 18th December 2001.

16. It is clear from the related chronology that the United Kingdom Parliament enjoyed, in principle, two separate occasions on which to scrutinise the derogation in question; firstly, on approving the Derogation Order and, secondly, when passing the derogating provisions of the Anti-terrorism, Crime and Security Bill. (The United Kingdom Parliament exercises no control over the notification of the Secretary General of the Council of Europe of a derogation from the Convention, which, as a treaty obligation, remains a crown prerogative. However, in so far as the United Kingdom Parliament is required to approve the derogating measures themselves this would not appear to be problematic, especially when, as is desirable, the notification of the Secretary-General occurs only after the passage of the relevant Act).

17. It is to be noted that the derogation was designated for the purposes of domestic law in anticipation, not merely, as is provided for by section 14(6) of the Human Rights Act, of the United Kingdom's derogation from its obligations under the Convention, but prior also to the enactment of the legislation necessitating the derogation, in this case, even, before the proposed Bill had been laid before Parliament. Two related problems would appear to arise in respect of this chronology.

18. It is not clear, firstly, that this sequence is consistent with the legal nature of derogations. A derogation is made in respect of certain measures that would otherwise infringe rights guaranteed by the Convention and is constituted by its formal announcement (under the Convention, through notification of the Secretary-General of the Council of Europe) in relation to those measures. Indeed the Court has shown some flexibility with regards to the timing of notifications, accepting delays of up to two weeks following the adoption of the measures in question, suggesting that the derogation comes into force not on notification but on promulgation. This is unsurprising since it is only the measures themselves that can define the scope of the derogation. Indeed, the notification or, for the purposes of domestic law, the designation of a derogation will, on its own, be of no legal consequence. The effect of the procedure adopted in respect of the United Kingdom derogation was, therefore, oddly, to invert the formal requirement; instead of the order sanctioning the measures, the measures confirmed the order.

19. There is, secondly, a risk that this sequence will undermine the effectiveness of the parliamentary scrutiny of the derogation. A designated derogation comes into effect immediately, and, therefore, unless the measures themselves have been examined beforehand, prior to any scrutiny whatsoever. The United Kingdom parliament must, however, subsequently approve the order. Parliament's ability to scrutinise the necessity of the derogation at this stage, might appear, in this case, to have been limited by the fact that the derogating measures had not yet been finalised. Indeed, the first draft of the proposed Bill was laid before Parliament only the day after the designated derogation was made, the House of Commons, having, furthermore, only one week to consider the Bill before being asked to approve the order. It is true that the designated derogation has no effect until the enactment of the attendant measures. However, the practice of designating a derogation prior to the debating of the derogating measures risks not only eliminating an effective scrutiny of the order itself, but also potentially reducing the urgency of a detailed scrutiny of the subsequent measures. This will especially be the case where the derogation order enables the Secretary of State to make a declaration of compatibility in respect of the Bill he wishes to put forward. In effect, two small parliamentary hurdles are substituted for one large one.

20. The Commissioner is of the opinion, therefore, that it would be both more coherent and provide a greater guarantee of effective parliamentary scrutiny if, as a general rule, derogations

were designated for the purposes of domestic law – and the Secretary-General notified – only after the measures requiring them have been promulgated.

21. In the instant case, the Commons' debates of 19th November suggest that its members were well acquainted with the proposed provisions of the Anti-terrorism, Crime and Security Bill, reasonably precise indications of which were, in any case, already available since 15th October. Nor do the debates during the subsequent passage of the Bill reveal an absence of concern over the real necessity of taking the significant step of derogating from Convention rights. What the latter debates do reveal, however, is that several members of Parliament felt insufficiently informed as to the extent of the threat and unable to assess, therefore, whether it constituted a public emergency and whether the relevant provisions of the Bill were strictly required.

22. An effective parliamentary scrutiny presupposes an informed and independent assessment. The information relevant to proposed derogations is likely, however, to be of a sensitive and perhaps publicly undisclosable nature. Whilst it might, under such circumstances, be acceptable to restrict parliamentary access to such information, the failure to disclose any information at all, where it is maintained that such information exists, is manifestly incompatible with the requirement of the democratic control of executive authority which is of particular importance in respect of measures limiting rights guaranteed by the Convention.

23. One mechanism amongst many might be to make the information warranting the derogation available to a specially constituted ad hoc Committee. The Committee, made up, perhaps, of selected representatives from a limited number of concerned parliamentary Committees, could, in turn, report their assessments to both Houses. One might have included, for example, in respect of the derogation in question, the Home Affairs Committee, the Joint Committee on Human Rights and the Joint Committee on Statutory Instruments. It is to be noted in this respect that special parliamentary commissions competent to examine classified information exist in several Council of Europe member States for the control of secret services.

2 SECOND CONDITION: THE NECESSITY REQUIREMENT

Only measures which are strictly required by the exigencies of the situation may be covered by a derogation. Under the International Covenant on Civil and Political Rights, the position of the Human Rights Committee is expressed as follows:

Human Rights Committee, General Comment No. 29, *Derogations during a State of Emergency* (Art. 4), UN Doc. CCPR/C/21/Rev.1/Add. 11 (2001), paras. 4–5:

[The requirement that any measure adopted under cover of a derogation be strictly required by the exigencies of the situation] relates to the duration, geographical coverage and material scope of the state of emergency and any measures of derogation resorted to because of the emergency. Derogation from some Covenant obligations in emergency situations is clearly distinct from restrictions or limitations allowed even in normal times under several provisions of the Covenant [see for instance, Arts. 12 and 19 of the Covenant]. Nevertheless, the obligation to limit any derogations to those strictly required by the exigencies of the situation reflects the principle of proportionality which is common to derogation and limitation powers. Moreover, the mere fact that a permissible derogation from a specific provision may, of itself, be justified by the exigencies of the situation does not obviate the requirement that specific measures taken pursuant to the derogation must also be shown to be required by the exigencies of the situation. In practice, this will ensure that no provision of the Covenant, however validly derogated from will be entirely inapplicable to the behaviour of a State party.

[T]his condition requires that States parties provide careful justification not only for their decision to proclaim a state of emergency but also for any specific measures based on such a proclamation. If States purport to invoke the right to derogate from the Covenant during, for instance, a natural catastrophe, a mass demonstration including instances of violence, or a major industrial accident, they must be able to justify not only that such a situation constitutes a threat to the life of the nation, but also that all their measures derogating from the Covenant are strictly required by the exigencies of the situation. In the opinion of the Committee, the possibility of restricting certain Covenant rights under the terms of, for instance, freedom of movement (article 12) or freedom of assembly (article 21) is generally sufficient during such situations and no derogation from the provisions in question would be justified by the exigencies of the situation.

The implication of this is that, in practice, notifying a derogation will only rarely present a significant advantage for the government concerned: as regards rights which are not absolute, i.e. which may be restricted in the public interest under the usual conditions of legality and necessity (or proportionality), the degree of scrutiny exercised by courts will be essentially similar, whether the measure is adopted under a derogation or whether it is presented as a mere limitation (under non-exceptional circumstances) to the right concerned.

A similar requirement exists under the European Convention on Human Rights. In the case of *Brannigan and McBride* v. *United Kingdom*, the applicants, supported by Liberty and Amnesty International acting as third-party intervenors to the proceedings, requested that the European Court of Human Rights control the validity of the United Kingdom's derogation. The applicants were put into detention in January 1989. This occured shortly after the United Kingdom had notified a derogation to the Convention, following the Court's judgment of 29 November 1988 in the case of *Brogan and others* (judgment of 29 November 1988, Series A No. 145–B). Under the Prevention of Terrorism (Temporary Provisions) Act 1974, a person arrested on reasonable suspicion of involvement in acts of terrorism could be detained by police for an initial period of forty-eight hours and, on the authorization of the Secretary of State for Northern Ireland, for a further period or periods of up to five days. In *Brogan*, the European Court of Human Rights had found this to be in violation of Article 5(3) of the Convention, according to which a person arrested upon suspicion of having committed an offence 'shall be brought promptly before a judge or other officer authorised by law to exercise judicial powers'. The UK derogation was notified on 23 December 1988 under Article 15 of the Convention. The relevant part of declaration made by the United Kingdom read:

Following [the *Brogan and others* judgment], the Secretary of State for the Home Department informed Parliament on 6 December 1988 that, against the background of the terrorist campaign, and the over-riding need to bring terrorists to justice, the Government did not believe that the maximum period of detention should be reduced. He informed Parliament that the Government were examining the matter with a view to responding to the judgment. On 22 December 1988, the Secretary of State further informed Parliament that it remained the Government's wish, if it could be achieved, to find a judicial process under which extended detention might be reviewed and where appropriate authorised by a judge or other judicial officer. But a further period of reflection and consultation was necessary before the Government could bring forward a firm and final view. Since the judgment of 29 November 1988 as well as previously, the Government have found it necessary to continue to exercise, in relation to terrorism connected with the affairs of Northern Ireland, the powers described above enabling further detention without charge, for periods of up to 5 days, on the authority of the Secretary of State, to the extent strictly required by the exigencies of the situation to enable necessary enquiries and investigations properly to be completed in order to decide whether criminal proceedings should be instituted. To the extent that the exercise of these powers may be inconsistent with the obligations imposed by the Convention the Government have availed themselves of the right of derogation conferred by Article 15(1) of the Convention and will continue to do so until further notice.

As regards the necessity requirement, the Court noted the following:

European Court of Human Rights, *Brannigan and McBride* v. *United Kingdom* (Appl. Nos. 14553/89 and 14554/89), judgment of 25 May 1993:

41. The applicants argued that it would be inconsistent with Article 15 para. 2 if, in derogating from safeguards recognised as essential for the protection of non-derogable rights such as Articles 2 and 3, the national authorities were to be afforded a wide margin of appreciation. This was especially so where the emergency was of a quasi-permanent nature such as that existing in Northern Ireland. To do so would also be inconsistent with the *Brogan and others* judgment where the Court had regarded judicial control as one of the fundamental principles of a democratic society and had already – they claimed – extended to the Government a margin of appreciation by taking into account ... the context of terrorism in Northern Ireland ...

43. The Court recalls that it falls to each Contracting State, with its responsibility for 'the life of [its] nation', to determine whether that life is threatened by a 'public emergency' and, if so, how far it is necessary to go in attempting to overcome the emergency. By reason of their direct and continuous contact with the pressing needs of the moment, the national authorities are in principle in a better position than the international judge to decide both on the presence of such an emergency and on the nature and scope of derogations necessary to avert it. Accordingly, in this matter a wide margin of appreciation should be left to the national authorities (see the *Ireland* v. *United Kingdom* judgment of 18 January 1978, Series A No. 25, pp. 78–79, para. 207).

Nevertheless, Contracting Parties do not enjoy an unlimited power of appreciation. It is for the Court to rule on whether *inter alia* the States have gone beyond the 'extent strictly required by the exigencies' of the crisis. The domestic margin of appreciation is thus accompanied by a European supervision (*ibid.*). At the same time, in exercising its supervision the Court must give appropriate weight to such relevant factors as the nature of the rights affected by the derogation, the circumstances leading to, and the duration of, the emergency situation.

44. Although the applicants did not dispute that there existed a public emergency 'threatening the life of the nation', they submitted that the burden rested on the Government to satisfy the Court that such an emergency really existed.

45. It was, however, suggested by Liberty and others in their written submissions that at the relevant time there was no longer any evidence of an exceptional situation of crisis. They maintained that reconsideration of the position could only properly have led to a further derogation if there was a demonstrable deterioration in the situation since August 1984 when the Government withdrew their previous derogation. For the Standing Advisory Commission on Human Rights, on the other hand, there was a public emergency in Northern Ireland at the relevant time of a sufficient magnitude to entitle the Government to derogate.

46. Both the Government and the Commission, referring to the existence of public disturbance in Northern Ireland, maintained that there was such an emergency.

47. Recalling its case law in *Lawless* v. *Ireland* (judgment of 1 July 1961, Series A No. 3, p. 56, para. 28) and *Ireland* v. *United Kingdom* (Series A No. 25, p. 78, para. 205) and making its own assessment, in the light of all the material before it as to the extent and impact of terrorist violence in Northern Ireland and elsewhere in the United Kingdom ..., the Court considers there can be no doubt that such a public emergency existed at the relevant time.

It does not judge it necessary to compare the situation which obtained in 1984 with that which prevailed in December 1988 since a decision to withdraw a derogation is, in principle, a matter within the discretion of the State and since it is clear that the Government believed that the legislation in question was in fact compatible with the Convention (see paragraphs 49–51 below).

Were the measures strictly required by the exigencies of the situation?
(a) General considerations 48. The Court recalls that judicial control of interferences by the executive with the individual's right to liberty provided for by Article 5 is implied by one of the fundamental principles of a democratic society, namely the rule of law (see the above-mentioned *Brogan and others* judgment, Series A No. 145–B, p. 32, para. 58). It further observes that the notice of derogation invoked in the present case was lodged by the respondent Government soon after the judgment in the above-mentioned *Brogan and others* case where the Court had found the Government to be in breach of their obligations under Article 5 para. 3 by not bringing the applicants 'promptly' before a court.

The Court must scrutinise the derogation against this background and taking into account that the power of arrest and detention in question has been in force since 1974. However, it must be observed that the central issue in the present case is not the existence of the power to detain suspected terrorists for up to seven days – indeed a complaint under Article 5 para. 1 was withdrawn by the applicants ... – but rather the exercise of this power without judicial intervention.

(b) Was the derogation a genuine response to an emergency situation? 49. For the applicants, the purported derogation was not a necessary response to any new or altered state of affairs but was the Government's reaction to the decision in *Brogan and others* and was lodged merely to circumvent the consequences of this judgment.

50. The Government and the Commission maintained that, while it was true that this judgment triggered off the derogation, the exigencies of the situation have at all times since 1974 required

the powers of extended detention conferred by the Prevention of Terrorism legislation. It was the view of successive Governments that these powers were consistent with Article 5 para. 3 and that no derogation was necessary. However, both the measures and the derogation were direct responses to the emergency with which the United Kingdom was and continues to be confronted.

51. The Court first observes that the power of arrest and extended detention has been considered necessary by the Government since 1974 in dealing with the threat of terrorism. Following the *Brogan and others* judgment the Government were then faced with the option of either introducing judicial control of the decision to detain under section 12 of the 1984 Act or lodging a derogation from their Convention obligations in this respect. The adoption of the view by the Government that judicial control compatible with Article 5 para. 3 was not feasible because of the special difficulties associated with the investigation and prosecution of terrorist crime rendered derogation inevitable. Accordingly, the power of extended detention without such judicial control and the derogation of 23 December 1988 being clearly linked to the persistence of the emergency situation, there is no indication that the derogation was other than a genuine response.

(c) Was the derogation premature? 52. The applicants maintained that derogation was an interim measure which Article 15 did not provide for since it appeared from the notice of derogation communicated to the Secretary-General of the Council of Europe on 23 December 1988 that the Government had not reached a 'firm or final view' on the need to derogate from Article 5 para. 3 and required a further period of reflection and consultation. Following this period the Secretary of State for the Home Department confirmed the derogation in a statement to Parliament on 14 November 1989 ... Prior to this concluded view Article 15 did not permit derogation. Furthermore, even at this date the Government had not properly examined whether the obligation in Article 5 para. 3 could be satisfied by an 'officer authorised by law to exercise judicial power'.

53. The Government contended that the validity of the derogation was not affected by their examination of the possibility of judicial control of extended detention since, as the Commission had pointed out, it was consistent with the requirements of Article 15 para. 3 to keep derogation measures under constant review.

54. The Court does not accept the applicants' argument that the derogation was premature.

While it is true that Article 15 does not envisage an interim suspension of Convention guarantees pending consideration of the necessity to derogate, it is clear from the notice of derogation that 'against the background of the terrorist campaign, and the over-riding need to bring terrorists to justice, the Government did not believe that the maximum period of detention should be reduced'. However it remained the Government's wish 'to find a judicial process under which extended detention might be reviewed and where appropriate authorised by a judge or other judicial officer' ...

The validity of the derogation cannot be called into question for the sole reason that the Government had decided to examine whether in the future a way could be found of ensuring greater conformity with Convention obligations. Indeed, such a process of continued reflection is not only in keeping with Article 15 para. 3 which requires permanent review of the need for emergency measures but is also implicit in the very notion of proportionality.

(d) Was the absence of judicial control of extended detention justified? 55. The applicants further considered that there was no basis for the Government's assertion that control of extended detention by a judge or other officer authorised by law to exercise judicial power was not possible or that a period of seven days' detention was necessary. They did not accept that the material required to satisfy a court of the justification for extended detention could be more sensitive than that needed in proceedings for habeas corpus. They and the Standing Advisory Commission on Human Rights also pointed out that the courts in Northern Ireland were frequently called on to deal with submissions based on confidential information – for example, in bail applications – and that there were sufficient procedural and evidential safeguards to protect confidentiality. Procedures also existed where judges were required to act on the basis of material which would not be disclosed either to the legal adviser or to his client. This was the case, for example, with claims by the executive to public interest immunity or application by the police to extend detention under the Police and Criminal Evidence (Northern Ireland) Order 1989 ...

56. On this point the Government responded that none of the above procedures involved both the non-disclosure of material to the detainee or his legal adviser and an executive act of the court. The only exception appeared in Schedule 7 to the Prevention of Terrorism (Temporary Provisions) Act 1989 where *inter alia* the court may make an order in relation to the production of, and search for, special material relevant to terrorist investigations. However, paragraph 8 of Schedule 7 provides that, where the disclosure of information to the court would be too sensitive or would prejudice the investigation, the power to make the order is conferred on the Secretary of State and not the court ...

It was also emphasised that the Government had reluctantly concluded that, within the framework of the common-law system, it was not feasible to introduce a system which would be compatible with Article 5 para. 3 but would not weaken the effectiveness of the response to the terrorist threat. Decisions to prolong detention were taken on the basis of information the nature and source of which could not be revealed to a suspect or his legal adviser without risk to individuals assisting the police or the prospect of further valuable intelligence being lost. Moreover, involving the judiciary in the process of granting or approving extensions of detention created a real risk of undermining their independence as they would inevitably be seen as part of the investigation and prosecution process.

In addition, the Government did not accept that the comparison with habeas corpus was a valid one since judicial involvement in the grant or approval of extension would require the disclosure of a considerable amount of additional sensitive information which it would not be necessary to produce in habeas corpus proceedings. In particular, a court would have to be provided with details of the nature and extent of police inquiries following the arrest, including details of witnesses interviewed and information obtained from other sources as well as information about the future course of the police investigation.

Finally, Lords Shackleton and Jellicoe and Viscount Colville in their reports had concluded that arrest and extended detention were indispensable powers in combating terrorism. These reports also found that the training of terrorists in remaining silent under police questioning hampered and protracted the investigation of terrorist offences. In consequence, the police were required to undertake extensive checks and inquiries and to rely to a greater degree than usual on painstaking detective work and forensic examination ...

57. The Commission was of the opinion that the Government had not overstepped their margin of appreciation in this regard.

58. The Court notes the opinions expressed in the various reports reviewing the operation of the Prevention of Terrorism legislation that the difficulties of investigating and prosecuting

terrorist crime give rise to the need for an extended period of detention which would not be subject to judicial control ... Moreover, these special difficulties were recognised in its above-mentioned *Brogan and others* judgment (see Series A No. 145–B, p. 33, para. 61).

It further observes that it remains the view of the respondent Government that it is essential to prevent the disclosure to the detainee and his legal adviser of information on the basis of which decisions on the extension of detention are made and that, in the adversarial system of the common law, the independence of the judiciary would be compromised if judges or other judicial officers were to be involved in the granting or approval of extensions.

The Court also notes that the introduction of a 'judge or other officer authorised by law to exercise judicial power' into the process of extension of periods of detention would not of itself necessarily bring about a situation of compliance with Article 5 para. 3. That provision – like Article 5 para. 4 – must be understood to require the necessity of following a procedure that has a judicial character although that procedure need not necessarily be identical in each of the cases where the intervention of a judge is required ...

59. It is not the Court's role to substitute its view as to what measures were most appropriate or expedient at the relevant time in dealing with an emergency situation for that of the Government which have direct responsibility for establishing the balance between the taking of effective measures to combat terrorism on the one hand, and respecting individual rights on the other (see the above-mentioned *Ireland* v. *United Kingdom* judgment, Series A No. 25, p. 82, para. 214, and the *Klass and others* v. *Germany* judgment of 6 September 1978, Series A No. 28, p. 23, para. 49). In the context of Northern Ireland, where the judiciary is small and vulnerable to terrorist attacks, public confidence in the independence of the judiciary is understandably a matter to which the Government attach great importance.

60. In the light of these considerations it cannot be said that the Government have exceeded their margin of appreciation in deciding, in the prevailing circumstances, against judicial control.

(e) Safeguards against abuse ... 62. Although submissions have been made by the applicants and the organisations concerning the absence of effective safeguards, the Court is satisfied that such safeguards do in fact exist and provide an important measure of protection against arbitrary behaviour and incommunicado detention.

63. In the first place, the remedy of habeas corpus is available to test the lawfulness of the original arrest and detention. There is no dispute that this remedy was open to the applicants had they or their legal advisers chosen to avail themselves of it and that it provides an important measure of protection against arbitrary detention (see the above-mentioned *Brogan and others* judgment, Series A No. 145–B, pp. 34–35, paras. 63–65). The Court recalls, in this context, that the applicants withdrew their complaint of a breach of Article 5 para. 4 of the Convention ...

64. In the second place, detainees have an absolute and legally enforceable right to consult a solicitor after forty-eight hours from the time of arrest. Both of the applicants were, in fact, free to consult a solicitor after this period ...

Moreover, within this period the exercise of this right can only be delayed where there exists reasonable grounds for doing so. It is clear from judgments of the High Court in Northern Ireland that the decision to delay access to a solicitor is susceptible to judicial review and that in such proceedings the burden of establishing reasonable grounds for doing so rests on the authorities. In these cases judicial review has been shown to be a speedy and effective manner of ensuring that access to a solicitor is not arbitrarily withheld ...

It is also not disputed that detainees are entitled to inform a relative or friend about their detention and to have access to a doctor.

65. In addition to the above basic safeguards the operation of the legislation in question has been kept under regular independent review and, until 1989, it was subject to regular renewal.

(f) Conclusion 66. Having regard to the nature of the terrorist threat in Northern Ireland, the limited scope of the derogation and the reasons advanced in support of it, as well as the existence of basic safeguards against abuse, the Court takes the view that the Government have not exceeded their margin of appreciation in considering that the derogation was strictly required by the exigencies of the situation.

In his 2002 opinion on the 2001 UK derogation from Article 5 para. 1 ECHR (see box 6.2.), the Commissioner for Human Rights of the Council of Europe provided the following appreciation of the above-cited derogation entered by the UK Government in December 2001:

Opinion of the Council of Europe Commissioner for Human Rights on certain aspects of the United Kingdom 2001 derogation from Article 5 para. 1 of the European Convention on Human Rights, Opinion 1/2002 of 28 August 2002, CommDH(2002)7, paras. 33–39:

33. Whilst acknowledging the obligation of governments to protect their citizens against the threat of terrorism, the Commissioner is of the opinion that general appeals to an increased risk of terrorist activity post September 11th 2001 cannot, on their own, be sufficient to justify derogating from the Convention. Several European states long faced with recurring terrorist activity have not considered it necessary to derogate from Convention rights. Nor have any found it necessary to do so under the present circumstances. Detailed information pointing to a real and imminent danger to public safety in the United Kingdom will, therefore, have to be shown.

34. Even assuming the existence of a public emergency, it is questionable whether the measures enacted by the United Kingdom are strictly required by the exigencies of the situation.

35. In interpreting the strict necessity requirement, the Court has so far declined to examine the relative effectiveness of competing measures, preferring instead to allow such an assessment to fall within the margin of appreciation enjoyed by national authorities. This does not exclude the possibility, however, that demonstrable availability of more or equally effective non-derogating alternatives will not cast doubt on the necessity of the derogating measures. This might especially be the case where so important right as the right to liberty and security is at stake. It is, at any rate, not clear that the indefinite detention of certain persons suspected of involvement with international terrorism would be more effective than the monitoring of their activity in accordance with standard surveillance procedures.

36. The proportionality of the derogating measures is further brought into question by the definition of international terrorist organisations provided by section 21(3) of the Act. The section would appear to permit the indefinite detention of an individual suspected of having links with an international terrorist organisation irrespective of its presenting a direct threat to public

security in the United Kingdom and perhaps, therefore, of no relation to the emergency originally requiring the legislation under which his Convention rights may be prejudiced.

37. Another anomaly arises in so far as an individual detained on suspicion of links with international terrorist organisations must be released and deported to a safe receiving country should one become available. If the suspicion is well founded, and the terrorist organisation a genuine threat to UK security, such individuals will remain, subject to possible controls by the receiving state, at liberty to plan and pursue, albeit at some distance from the United Kingdom, activity potentially prejudicial to its public security.

38. It would appear, therefore, that the derogating measures of the Anti-terrorism, Crime and Security Act allow both for the detention of those presenting no direct threat to the United Kingdom and for the release of those of whom it is alleged that they do. Such a paradoxical conclusion is hard to reconcile with the strict exigencies of the situation.

39. Whilst detention under the derogating powers of the Anti-terrorism, Crime and Security Act requires that the individual be an undeportable foreigner, it is triggered, ultimately, only on the suspicion of involvement with an international terrorist organisation. Though the reasonableness of the Home Secretary's suspicion is justiciable, it remains the case that the detention is effected without any formal accusation and subject only to a review in which important procedural guarantees are absent. The indefinite detention under such circumstances represents a severe limitation to the enjoyment of the right to liberty and security and gravely prejudices both the presumption of innocence and the right to a fair trial in the determination of ones rights and obligations or of any criminal charge brought against one. It should be recalled that an ill-founded deprivation of liberty is difficult, indeed impossible, to repair adequately.

The views of the UK government on the necessity of the derogation measure adopted in December 2001 are the following:

Comments by the Government of the United Kingdom of Great Britain and Northern Ireland on the reports of the United Kingdom (CCPR/CO/73/UK) and the Overseas Territories (CCPR/CO/73/UKOT) (CCPR/CO/73/UK/Add. 2 and CCPR/CO/73/UKOT/Add. 2, 4 December 2002):

(b) Are the measures strictly required by the exigencies of the situation? We believe that they are. This was something considered by the Special Immigration Appeals Commission [which] considered the argument on behalf of A and others that other, less intrusive, alternative measures were available to the Government. In the course of considering the lawfulness of the United Kingdom's derogation from article 15 of the European Convention on Human Rights and whether the measures taken were strictly required by the exigencies of the situation, the Commission, having considered the arguments, said: 'Bearing that guidance [of the European Court of Human Rights and of the Canadian Supreme Court] and noting and accepting the Government's assertion that there are individuals against whom the provisions (or proposed provisions) identified by the appellants would not be effective, the position is that, even applying the most intrusive scrutiny, we are satisfied that the existence of possible alternative measures does not of itself harm the Government's argument.' The Commission further confirmed that they accepted the submissions on behalf of the Government that the provisions for judicial and democratic supervision contained within the Anti-terrorism, Crime and Security Act are both appropriate and sufficient ...

3. Domestic law powers of detention

The Government has powers under the Immigration Act 1971 ('the 1971 Act') to remove or deport persons on the grounds that their presence in the United Kingdom is not conducive to the public good on national security grounds. Persons can also be arrested and detained under Schedules 2 and 3 to the 1971 Act pending their removal or deportation, including deportation on the grounds that their presence in the United Kingdom is contrary to the public good. The courts in the United Kingdom have ruled that this power of detention only persists for so long as the person's removal remains a real possibility. If there were no such real possibility (for example, because removal would result in torture or inhuman or degrading treatment) the power of detention would fall away. The person would have to be released, and would be at large within the United Kingdom.

4. Article 9(1) of the Covenant

Article 9 provides, amongst other things, that everyone has the right to liberty and security of person, and that no one shall be deprived of his liberty except on such grounds and in accordance with such procedures as are established by law.

It became clear, however, before, during and since the passage of the Anti-terrorism, Crime and Security Act 2001 ('the Act') that the balance between respecting these fundamental civil liberties and safeguarding them from exploitation by those who would destroy them for the wider public is profoundly delicate.

The Government was, and remains, of the view that the only practicable way to protect and maintain this equilibrium was to derogate from article 5(1) of the European Convention on Human Rights and from article 9(1) of the International Covenant on Civil and Political Rights in respect of the detention powers contained in the Act.

The measures in Part 4 of the Act were introduced in particular to deal with the situation where an alien would in normal circumstances be removed or deported from the United Kingdom in the exercise of immigration powers, on grounds that his presence here is contrary to the public good, but where removal or deportation to his country of origin would have given rise to a serious risk of torture or inhuman or degrading treatment. There are cases in which a suspected terrorist, even though not a United Kingdom national, cannot be removed from the United Kingdom. The measures were rigorously considered and scrutinized at the time and were and continue to be judged to be a necessary and proportionate response to the 'public emergency threatening the life of the nation'.

5. The Anti-terrorism, Crime and Security Act 2001

(a) Legislative powers Part 4 of the Act recognizes that a suspected terrorist should not be returned to a country where there is a serious risk that he might be tortured or killed, but at the same time he should not be allowed to be at large in the United Kingdom. Given the public emergency threatening the life of the nation, Part 4 of the Act strikes a balance between the interests of the individual suspected terrorist and the general community. It extends the period for which a suspected terrorist may be detained in the United Kingdom, in cases where his removal is precluded, so as to overcome the limitations discussed above on the powers to detain under the Immigration Act 1971.

Under section 21(1) of the Act, the Secretary of State may issue a certificate in respect of a person if the Secretary of State reasonably: (a) believes that the person's presence in the United Kingdom is a risk to national security; and (b) suspects that the person is a terrorist. Under section 22 of the Act, various immigration measures, for example, making a deportation order, may be taken in relation to a suspected international terrorist, notwithstanding that his actual removal will be incompatible with the United Kingdom's international obligations. By virtue of section 23(1) of the Act, a suspected international terrorist may be detained under the detention powers contained in the Immigration Act 1971 despite the fact that his removal or departure from the United Kingdom is prevented (whether temporarily or indefinitely) by a point of law relating to an international agreement or a practical consideration.

(b) Legislative safeguards This certificate is subject to an appeal to the Special Immigration Appeals Commission, established under the Special Immigration Appeals Commission Act 1997, which has the power to cancel it if it considers that the certificate should not have been issued. In addition, SIAC is obliged to review the certificate after six months after the appeal is finally determined (if there is one) or after the date on which the certificate was issued (if there is no appeal). Subsequent reviews will occur three monthly intervals thereafter (section 26 of the Act). There is the possibility of appeals from SIAC on points of law to the higher courts. SIAC is also able to grant bail, where appropriate, subject to conditions. It is open to a detainee to end his detention at any time by agreeing to leave the United Kingdom.

Sections 21–23 of the Act are temporary provisions which automatically expire after 15 months, subject to renewal for periods not exceeding one year at a time if both Houses of Parliament are in agreement (sect. 29(1)). This ensures periodic review by the legislature, in addition to continuing review by the executive. Further, the detention provisions will end with the final expiry of sections 21–23 of Part 4 of the Act on 10 November 2006 (sect. 29(7)). If, in the Government's assessment, the public emergency no longer exists or the extended power is no longer strictly required by the exigencies of the situation, then the Secretary of State will, by Order under section 29(2), discontinue the provision.

6. Review procedures and sunsets

The operation of the detention powers (sects. 21–23) in the Act are being reviewed specifically by Lord Carlile of Berriew QC, who is also the independent reviewer of the Terrorism Act 2000. He has been appointed by the Secretary of State under section 28 of the Act and is required to conduct a review of the operation of the detention powers not later than 14 months after the passing of the Act. He is required to send a report of his review as soon as is reasonably practicable to the Secretary of State, who is in turn required to lay the report before Parliament as soon as is reasonably practicable.

The provisions of the Act, as a whole, are being reviewed by a Committee of nine Privy Counsellors in accordance with sections 122 and 123. This Committee is obliged to provide a report on their findings and conclusions to the Secretary of State by 14 December 2003.

Although reasoning on the basis of Article 15 ECHR rather than on the basis of Article 4 ICCPR, the House of Lords disagreed when called upon to adjudicate the matter in 2004:

House of Lords (United Kingdom), *A. (F.C.) and others (F.C.) (Appellants)* v. *Secretary of State for the Home Department (Respondent), X. (F.C.) and another (F.C.) (Appellants)* v. *Secretary of State for the Home Department (Respondent)* **[2004] UKHL 56, leading opinion by Lord Bingham of Cornhill:**

30. Article 15 requires that any measures taken by a member state in derogation of its obligations under the Convention should not go beyond what is 'strictly required by the exigencies of the situation'. Thus the Convention imposes a test of strict necessity or, in Convention terminology, proportionality. The appellants founded on the principle adopted by the Privy Council in *de Freitas* v. *Permanent Secretary of Ministry of Agriculture, Fisheries, Lands and Housing* [1999] 1 AC 69, 80. In determining whether a limitation is arbitrary or excessive, the court must ask itself: 'whether: (i) the legislative objective is sufficiently important to justify limiting a fundamental right; (ii) the measures designed to meet the legislative objective are rationally connected to it; and (iii) the means used to impair the right or freedom are no more than is necessary to accomplish the objective'. This approach is close to that laid down by the Supreme Court of Canada in *R* v. *Oakes* [1986] 1 SCR 103, paras 69–70, and in *Libman* v. *Attorney General of Quebec* (1997) 3 BHRC 269, para 38. To some extent these questions are, or may be, interrelated. But the appellants directed the main thrust of their argument to the second and third questions. They submitted that even if it were accepted that the legislative objective of protecting the British people against the risk of catastrophic Al-Qaeda terrorism was sufficiently important to justify limiting the fundamental right to personal freedom of those facing no criminal accusation, the 2001 Act was not designed to meet that objective and was not rationally connected to it. Furthermore, the legislative objective could have been achieved by means which did not, or did not so severely, restrict the fundamental right to personal freedom.

31. The appellants' argument under this head can, I hope fairly, be summarised as involving the following steps:

(1) Part 4 of the 2001 Act reversed the effect of the decisions in *Hardial Singh* [1984] 1 WLR 704 and *Chahal* (1996) 23 EHRR 413 and was apt to address the problems of immigration control caused to the United Kingdom by article 5(1)(f) of the Convention read in the light of those decisions.

(2) The public emergency on which the United Kingdom relied to derogate from the Convention right to personal liberty was the threat to the security of the United Kingdom presented by Al-Qaeda terrorists and their supporters.

(3) While the threat to the security of the United Kingdom derived predominantly and most immediately from foreign nationals, some of whom could not be deported because they would face torture or inhuman or degrading treatment or punishment in their home countries and who could not be deported to any third country willing to receive them, the threat to the United Kingdom did not derive solely from such foreign nationals.

(4) Sections 21 and 23 did not rationally address the threat to the security of the United Kingdom presented by Al-Qaeda terrorists and their supporters because (a) it did not address the threat presented by UK nationals, (b) it permitted foreign nationals suspected of being Al-Qaeda terrorists or their supporters to pursue their activities abroad if there was any country to which they were able to go, and (c) the sections permitted the certification and detention of persons who were not suspected of presenting any threat to the security of the United Kingdom as Al-Qaeda terrorists or supporters.

(5) If the threat presented to the security of the United Kingdom by UK nationals suspected of being Al-Qaeda terrorists or their supporters could be addressed without infringing their right to personal liberty, it is not shown why similar measures could not adequately address the threat presented by foreign nationals.

(6) Since the right to personal liberty is among the most fundamental of the rights protected by the European Convention, any restriction of it must be closely scrutinised by the national court and such scrutiny involves no violation of democratic or constitutional principle.

(7) In the light of such scrutiny, neither the Derogation Order nor sections 21 and 23 of the 2001 Act can be justified.

32. It is unnecessary to linger on the first two steps of this argument, neither of which is controversial and both of which are clearly correct. The third step calls for closer examination. The evidence before SIAC was that the Home Secretary considered 'that the serious threats to the nation emanated predominantly (albeit not exclusively) and more immediately from the category of foreign nationals'. In para 95 of its judgment SIAC held:

'But the evidence before us demonstrates beyond argument that the threat is not so confined. There are many British nationals already identified – mostly in detention abroad – who fall within the definition of "suspected international terrorists", and it was clear from the submissions made to us that in the opinion of the [Home Secretary] there are others at liberty in the United Kingdom who could be similarly defined.'

This finding has not been challenged, and since SIAC is the responsible fact-finding tribunal it is unnecessary to examine the basis of it. There was however evidence before SIAC that 'upwards of a thousand individuals from the UK are estimated on the basis of intelligence to have attended training camps in Afghanistan in the last five years', that some British citizens are said to have planned to return from Afghanistan to the United Kingdom and that 'The backgrounds of those detained show the high level of involvement of British citizens and those otherwise connected with the United Kingdom in the terrorist networks.' It seems plain that the threat to the United Kingdom did not derive solely from foreign nationals or from foreign nationals whom it was unlawful to deport. Later evidence, not before SIAC or the Court of Appeal, supports that conclusion. The Newton Committee recorded the Home Office argument that the threat from Al-Qaeda terrorism was predominantly from foreigners but drew attention (para 193) to 'accumulating evidence that this is not now the case. The British suicide bombers who attacked Tel Aviv in May 2003, Richard Reid ("the Shoe Bomber"), and recent arrests suggest that the threat from UK citizens is real. Almost 30% of Terrorism Act 2000 suspects in the past year have been British. We have been told that, of the people of interest to the authorities because of their suspected involvement in international terrorism, nearly half are British nationals.'

33. The fourth step in the appellants' argument is of obvious importance to it. It is plain that sections 21 and 23 of the 2001 Act do not address the threat presented by UK nationals since they do not provide for the certification and detention of UK nationals. It is beside the point that other sections of the 2001 Act and the 2000 Act do apply to UK nationals, since they are not the subject of derogation, are not the subject of complaint and apply equally to foreign nationals. Yet the threat from UK nationals, if quantitatively smaller, is not said to be qualitatively different from that from foreign nationals. It is also plain that sections 21 and 23 do permit a person certified and detained to leave the United Kingdom and go to any other country willing to receive him, as two of the appellants did when they left for Morocco and France respectively ... Such freedom to leave is wholly explicable in terms of immigration control: if the British authorities

wish to deport a foreign national but cannot deport him to country 'A' because of *Chahal* their purpose is as well served by his voluntary departure for country 'B'. But allowing a suspected international terrorist to leave our shores and depart to another country, perhaps a country as close as France, there to pursue his criminal designs, is hard to reconcile with a belief in his capacity to inflict serious injury to the people and interests of this country. It seems clear from the language of section 21 of the 2001 Act, read with the definition of terrorism in section 1 of the 2000 Act, that section 21 is capable of covering those who have no link at all with Al-Qaeda (they might, for example, be members of the Basque separatist organisation ETA), or who, although supporting the general aims of Al-Qaeda, reject its cult of violence. The Attorney General conceded that sections 21 and 23 could not lawfully be invoked in the case of suspected international terrorists other than those thought to be connected with Al-Qaeda, and undertook that the procedure would not be used in such cases ... The appellants were content to accept the Attorney General's concession and undertaking. It is not however acceptable that interpretation and application of a statutory provision bearing on the liberty of the subject should be governed by implication, concession and undertaking ...

35. The fifth step in the appellants' argument permits of little elaboration. But it seems reasonable to assume that those suspected international terrorists who are UK nationals are not simply ignored by the authorities. When G, one of the appellants, was released from prison by SIAC on bail (*G* v. *Secretary of State for the Home Department* (SC/2/2002, Bail Application SCB/10, 20 May 2004), it was on condition (among other things) that he wear an electronic monitoring tag at all times; that he remain at his premises at all times; that he telephone a named security company five times each day at specified times; that he permit the company to install monitoring equipment at his premises; that he limit entry to his premises to his family, his solicitor, his medical attendants and other approved persons; that he make no contact with any other person; that he have on his premises no computer equipment, mobile telephone or other electronic communications device; that he cancel the existing telephone link to his premises; and that he install a dedicated telephone link permitting contact only with the security company. The appellants suggested that conditions of this kind, strictly enforced, would effectively inhibit terrorist activity. It is hard to see why this would not be so.

36. In urging the fundamental importance of the right to personal freedom, as the sixth step in their proportionality argument, the appellants were able to draw on the long libertarian tradition of English law, dating back to chapter 39 of Magna Carta 1215, given effect in the ancient remedy of habeas corpus, declared in the Petition of Right 1628, upheld in a series of landmark decisions down the centuries and embodied in the substance and procedure of the law to our own day ... In its treatment of article 5 of the European Convention, the European Court also has recognised the prime importance of personal freedom. In *Kurt* v. *Turkey* (1998) 27 EHRR 373, para 122, it referred to 'the fundamental importance of the guarantees contained in Article 5 for securing the right of individuals in a democracy to be free from arbitrary detention at the hands of the authorities' and to the need to interpret narrowly any exception to 'a most basic guarantee of individual freedom' ... The authors of the Siracusa Principles, although acknowledging that the protection against arbitrary detention (article 9 of the ICCPR) might be limited if strictly required by the exigencies of an emergency situation (article 4), were nonetheless of the opinion that some rights could never be denied in any conceivable emergency and, in particular (para 70 (b)), 'no person shall be detained for an indefinite period of time, whether detained pending judicial investigation or trial or detained without charge; ....'

37. ... the Attorney General ... submitted that as it was for Parliament and the executive to assess the threat facing the nation, so it was for those bodies and not the courts to judge the response necessary to protect the security of the public. These were matters of a political character calling for an exercise of political and not judicial judgment. Just as the European Court allowed a generous margin of appreciation to member states, recognising that they were better placed to understand and address local problems, so should national courts recognise, for the same reason, that matters of the kind in issue here fall within the discretionary area of judgment properly belonging to the democratic organs of the state. It was not for the courts to usurp authority properly belonging elsewhere ... This is an important submission, properly made, and it calls for careful consideration.

38. Those conducting the business of democratic government have to make legislative choices which, notably in some fields, are very much a matter for them, particularly when (as is often the case) the interests of one individual or group have to be balanced against those of another individual or group or the interests of the community as a whole ...

39. While any decision made by a representative democratic body must of course command respect, the degree of respect will be conditioned by the nature of the decision ...

40. The Convention regime for the international protection of human rights requires national authorities, including national courts, to exercise their authority to afford effective protection ...

41. Even in a terrorist situation the Convention organs have not been willing to relax their residual supervisory role ... In *Aksoy* v. *Turkey* (1996) 23 EHRR 553, para 76, the Court, clearly referring to national courts as well as the Convention organs, held: 'The Court would stress the importance of Article 5 in the Convention system: it enshrines a fundamental human right, namely the protection of the individual against arbitrary interference by the State with his or her right to liberty. Judicial control of interferences by the executive with the individual's right to liberty is an essential feature of the guarantee embodied in Article 5(3), which is intended to minimise the risk of arbitrariness and to ensure the rule of law' ...

42. It follows from this analysis that the appellants are in my opinion entitled to invite the courts to review, on proportionality grounds, the Derogation Order and the compatibility with the Convention of section 23 and the courts are not effectively precluded by any doctrine of deference from scrutinising the issues raised. It also follows that I do not accept the full breadth of the Attorney General's submissions. I do not in particular accept the distinction which he drew between democratic institutions and the courts. It is of course true that the judges in this country are not elected and are not answerable to Parliament. It is also of course true, as pointed out in para 29 above, that Parliament, the executive and the courts have different functions. But the function of independent judges charged to interpret and apply the law is universally recognised as a cardinal feature of the modern democratic state, a cornerstone of the rule of law itself. The Attorney General is fully entitled to insist on the proper limits of judicial authority, but he is wrong to stigmatise judicial decision-making as in some way undemocratic. It is particularly inappropriate in a case such as the present in which Parliament has expressly legislated in section 6 of the [1998 Human Rights Act] to render unlawful any act of a public authority, including a court, incompatible with a Convention right, has required courts (in section 2) to take account of relevant Strasbourg jurisprudence, has (in section 3) required courts, so far as possible, to give effect to Convention rights and has conferred a right of appeal on derogation issues. The effect is not, of course, to override the sovereign legislative authority of the Queen in Parliament, since if primary legislation is declared to be incompatible the validity of the legislation is unaffected

(section 4(6)) and the remedy lies with the appropriate minister (section 10), who is answerable to Parliament. The 1998 Act gives the courts a very specific, wholly democratic, mandate ...

43. The appellants' proportionality challenge to the Order and section 23 is, in my opinion, sound, for all the reasons they gave and also for those given by the European Commissioner for Human Rights and the Newton Committee. The Attorney General could give no persuasive answer. In a discussion paper Counter-Terrorism Powers: Reconciling Security and Liberty in an Open Society (Cm 6147, February 2004) the Secretary of State replied to one of the Newton Committee's criticisms in this way: '32. It can be argued that as suspected international terrorists their departure for another country could amount to exporting terrorism: a point made in the Newton Report at paragraph 195. But that is a natural consequence of the fact that Part 4 powers are immigration powers: detention is permissible only pending deportation and there is no other power available to detain (other than for the purpose of police enquiries) if a foreign national chooses voluntarily to leave the UK. (Detention in those circumstances is limited to 14 days after which the person must be either charged or released.) Deportation has the advantage moreover of disrupting the activities of the suspected terrorist.'

This answer, however, reflects the central complaint made by the appellants: that the choice of an immigration measure to address a security problem had the inevitable result of failing adequately to address that problem (by allowing non-UK suspected terrorists to leave the country with impunity and leaving British suspected terrorists at large) while imposing the severe penalty of indefinite detention on persons who, even if reasonably suspected of having links with Al-Qaeda, may harbour no hostile intentions towards the United Kingdom. The conclusion that the Order and section 23 are, in Convention terms, disproportionate is in my opinion irresistible ...

It is clear from its judgment delivered on 19 Febuary 2009 in *A. and others* v. *United Kingdom* that this is also the position of the European Court of Human Rights. The relevant excerpts are presented in section 3 below, which discusses the condition of non-discrimination, because the Court rightly considers that one of the reasons why the measures adopted by the United Kingdom are disproportionate is because they unjustifiably make a distinction on grounds of nationality.

The requirement of necessity has been detailed by the Inter-American Court of Human Rights in the following terms:

Inter-American Court of Human Rights, *Habeas Corpus in Emergency Situations (Arts. 27(2), 25(1) and 7(6) American Convention on Human Rights)*, Advisory Opinion OC-8/87 of 30 January 1987, Series A No. 8:

19. The starting point for any legally sound analysis of Article 27 [ACHR] and the function it performs is the fact that it is a provision for exceptional situations only. It applies solely 'in time of war, public danger, or other emergency that threatens the independence or security of a State Party'. And even then, it permits the suspension of certain rights and freedoms only 'to the extent and for the period of time strictly required by the exigencies of the situation'. Such measures must also not violate the State Party's other international legal obligations, nor may they involve 'discrimination on the ground of race, color, sex, language, religion or social origin' ...

22. Since Article 27(1) envisages different situations and since, moreover, the measures that may be taken in any of these emergencies must be tailored to 'the exigencies of the situation', it is clear that what might be permissible in one type of emergency would not be lawful in another. The lawfulness of the measures taken to deal with each of the special situations referred to in Article 27(1) will depend, moreover, upon the character, intensity, pervasiveness, and particular context of the emergency and upon the corresponding proportionality and reasonableness of the measures ...

24. The suspension of guarantees also constitutes an emergency situation in which it is lawful for a government to subject rights and freedoms to certain restrictive measures that, under normal circumstances, would be prohibited or more strictly controlled. This does not mean, however, that the suspension of guarantees implies a temporary suspension of the rule of law, nor does it authorize those in power to act in disregard of the principle of legality by which they are bound at all times. When guarantees are suspended, some legal restraints applicable to the acts of public authorities may differ from those in effect under normal conditions. These restraints may not be considered to be non-existent, however, nor can the government be deemed thereby to have acquired absolute powers that go beyond the circumstances justifying the grant of such exceptional legal measures. The Court has already noted, in this connection, that there exists an inseparable bond between the principle of legality, democratic institutions and the rule of law' ...

38. If, as the Court has already emphasized, the suspension of guarantees may not exceed the limits of that strictly required to deal with the emergency, any action on the part of the public authorities that goes beyond those limits, which must be specified with precision in the decree promulgating the state of emergency, would also be unlawful notwithstanding the existence of the emergency situation.

39. The Court should also point out that since it is improper to suspend guarantees without complying with the conditions referred to in the preceding paragraph, it follows that the specific measures applicable to the rights or freedoms that have been suspended may also not violate these general principles. Such violation would occur, for example, if the measures taken infringed the legal regime of the state of emergency, if they lasted longer than the time limit specified, if they were manifestly irrational, unnecessary or disproportionate, or if, in adopting them, there was a misuse or abuse of power.

The Court could test the notion of necessity/arbitrariness of suspension measures in the *Castillo-Petruzzi et al.* v. *Peru* case. The case concerns the detention, trial and life sentence convictions of three Chilean nationals by a Peruvian 'faceless' military tribunal (*tribunal sin rostro*) under counter-terrorist laws adopted during a state of emergency. In the following passage, only the denial of *habeas corpus* is under discussion:

Inter-American Court of Human Rights, case of *Castillo-Petruzzi et al.* v. *Peru*, merits, reparations and costs, judgment of 30 May 1999, Series C No. 52:

109. In the instant case, the detention occurred amid a terrible disruption of public law and order that escalated in 1992 and 1993 with acts of terrorism that left many victims in their wake. In response to these events, the State adopted emergency measures, one of which was to allow

those suspected of treason to be detained without a lawful court order. As for Peru's allegation that the state of emergency that was declared involved a suspension of Article 7 of the Convention, the Court has repeatedly held that the suspension of guarantees must not exceed the limits strictly required and that 'any action on the part of the public authorities that goes beyond those limits, which must be specified with precision in the decree promulgating the state of emergency, would ... be unlawful'. The limits imposed upon the actions of a State come from 'the general requirement that in any state of emergency there be appropriate means to control the measures taken, so that they are proportionate to the needs and do not exceed the strict limits imposed by the Convention or derived from it'.

110. As to the State's alleged violation of Article 7(5) of the Convention, the Court is of the view that those Peruvian laws that allow the authorities to hold a person suspected of the crime of treason in preventive custody for 15 days, with the possibility of a 15-day extension, without bringing that person before a judicial authority, are contrary to the provision of the Convention to the effect that '[a]ny person detained shall be brought promptly before a judge or other officer authorized by law to exercise judicial power' ...

111. Applying the laws in force to this specific case, the State held Mr Mellado Saavedra, Mrs Pincheira Sáez and Mr Astorga Valdez in custody, without judicial oversight, from October 14, 1993, to November 20, 1993, the date on which they were brought before a military court judge. Mr Castillo Petruzzi, for his part, was detained on October 15, 1993, and brought before the judge in question on November 20 of that year. This Court finds that the period of approximately 36 days that elapsed between the time of detention and the date on which the alleged victims were brought before a judicial authority is excessive and contrary to the provisions of the Convention.

112. The Court therefore finds that the State violated Article 7(5) of the Convention.

3 THIRD CONDITION: THE NON-DISCRIMINATION REQUIREMENT

The condition of non-discrimination is stipulated explicitly only in Article 4 ICCPR and in Article 27 ACHR. According to Article 27 ACHR, the measures derogating from the guarantees of this instrument may not involve discrimination 'on the ground of race, color, sex, language, religion, or social origin'. Article 4 para. 1 ICCPR uses a more ambiguous wording, stating as one of the conditions for the justifiability of any derogation from the Covenant that the measures taken 'do not involve discrimination *solely* on the ground of race, colour, sex, language, religion or social origin' (emphasis added). Some commentators have read this in terms very generous to the State:

Scott Davidson, 'Chapter 8: Equality and Non-Discrimination', in A. Conte, S. Davidson and R. Burchill, *Defining Civil and Political Rights* (London: Ashgate, 2004), p. 161:

The reason for [the wording in the ICCPR] is that very often during war or national emergency it is permissible to discriminate against enemy aliens and their property. Furthermore it would seem justifiable for a state, in the interests of the greater social good, to be able to discriminate against those who hold political opinions which might be injurious to the well-being of society during times of war or national emergency. The drafting of article 4(1) also suggests that there will be occasions on which it is permissible for a state to discriminate against those of a particular race, colour, sex, language, religion or a particular social origin. This view is tenable since the prohibition of the discrimination in question is conditioned by the use of the word 'solely' which seems to indicate that as long as the discrimination is not disproportionate to the end to be achieved, it will be justifiable. Such a situation may occur, for example, where there is civil unrest in a part of a state where the population is of a particular ethnic origin.

In reality, Article 4(1) ICCPR prohibits in clear terms all differences of treatment directly based on the listed grounds. However, what it does not prohibit are measures making differences of treatment on grounds of nationality, national origin or political opinion – none of which grounds is among those listed in Article 4(1) – or measures which are indirectly discriminatory against the members of a group characterized by one of the enumerated grounds – as in the example of a state of emergency declared in a region where a particular ethnic group is predominant (see also, for instance, the first 'understanding' appended by the United States to their ratification of the International Covenant on Civil and Political Rights on 8 June 1992, discussed above in chapter 1, section 4.5.). There is no such thing, however, as a 'discrimination [which] is not disproportionate', since a discrimination is disproportionate by definition – only differences of treatment may not be disproportionate, in which case they are not discriminatory.

In contrast to the ICCPR and to the ACHR, Article 15 ECHR is silent about the condition of non-discrimination. However, any discriminatory measure adopted under a derogation would be invalid, since it would be in violation of the other international obligations of the State concerned. In addition, the non-discrimination requirement may be seen as implicit in the condition of 'necessity'. The decisions of the House of Lords and of the European Court of Human Rights in the *Belmarsh Detainees* cases are illustrative:

House of Lords (United Kingdom), *A. (F.C.) and others (F.C.) (Appellants)* v. *Secretary of State for the Home Department (Respondent), X. (F.C.) and another (F.C.) (Appellants)* v. *Secretary of State for the Home Department (Respondent)* [2004] UKHL 56, leading opinion by Lord Bingham of Cornhill:

Discrimination ...
46. The appellants complained that in providing for the detention of suspected international terrorists who were not UK nationals but not for the detention of suspected international terrorists who were UK nationals, section 23 unlawfully discriminated against them as non-UK nationals in breach of article 14 of the European Convention ...
   54. ... The undoubted aim of the relevant measure, section 23 of the 2001 Act, was to protect the UK against the risk of Al-Qaeda terrorism ... that risk was thought to be presented mainly by non-UK nationals but also and to a significant extent by UK nationals also. The effect of the

measure was to permit the former to be deprived of their liberty but not the latter. The appellants were treated differently because of their nationality or immigration status ...

57. In Resolution 1271 adopted on 24 January 2002, the Parliamentary Assembly of the Council of Europe held that 'The combat against terrorism must be carried out in compliance with national and international law and respecting human rights.' The Committee of Ministers of the Council of Europe on 11 July 2002 adopted 'Guidelines on human rights and the fight against terrorism'. These recognised the obligation to take effective measures against terrorism, but continued: 'All measures taken by States to fight terrorism must respect human rights and the principle of the rule of law, while excluding any form of arbitrariness, as well as any discriminatory or racist treatment.' ...

In its General Policy Recommendations published on 8 June 2004, the European Commission against Racism and Intolerance, a Council of Europe body, considered it the duty of the state to fight against terrorism; stressed that the response should not itself encroach on the values of freedom, democracy, justice, the rule of law, human rights and humanitarian law; stressed that the fight against terrorism should not become a pretext under which racial discrimination was allowed to flourish; noted that the fight against terrorism since 11 September 2001 had in some cases resulted in the adoption of discriminatory legislation, notably on grounds of nationality, national or ethnic origin and religion; stressed the responsibility of member states to ensure that the fight against terrorism did not have a negative impact on any minority group; and recommended them 'to review legislation and regulations adopted in connection with the fight against terrorism to ensure that these do not discriminate directly or indirectly against persons or group of persons, notably on grounds of 'race', colour, language, religion, nationality or national or ethnic origin, and to abrogate any such discriminatory legislation.' ...

66. SIAC concluded that section 23 was discriminatory and so in breach of article 14 of the Convention. It ruled, in paras 94–95 of its judgment: '94. If there is to be an effective derogation from the right to liberty enshrined in Article 5 in respect of suspected international terrorists – and we can see powerful arguments in favour of such a derogation – the derogation ought rationally to extend to all irremovable suspected international terrorists. It would properly be confined to the alien section of the population only if, as [counsel for the appellants] contends, the threat stems exclusively or almost exclusively from that alien section ...

95. But the evidence before us demonstrates beyond argument that the threat is not so confined. There are many British nationals already identified – mostly in detention abroad – who fall within the definition of 'suspected international terrorists', and it was clear from the submissions made to us that in the opinion of the [Secretary of State] there are others at liberty in the United Kingdom who could be similarly defined. In those circumstances we fail to see how the derogation can be regarded as other than discriminatory on the grounds of national origin'.

European Court of Human Rights (GC), *A. and others* v. *United Kingdom* (Appl. No. 3455/05), judgment of 19 February 2009:

Whether the measures were strictly required by the exigencies of the situation
182. Article 15 provides that the State may take measures derogating from its obligations under the Convention only 'to the extent strictly required by the exigencies of the situation'.

... [T]he Court considers that it should in principle follow the judgment of the House of Lords on the question of the proportionality of the applicants' detention, unless it can be shown that the national court misinterpreted the Convention or the Court's case law or reached a conclusion which was manifestly unreasonable. It will consider the Government's challenges to the House of Lords' judgment against this background.

183. The Government contended, first, that the majority of the House of Lords should have afforded a much wider margin of appreciation to the executive and Parliament to decide whether the applicants' detention was necessary. A similar argument was advanced before the House of Lords, where the Attorney General submitted that the assessment of what was needed to protect the public was a matter of political rather than judicial judgment ...

184. When the Court comes to consider a derogation under Article 15, it allows the national authorities a wide margin of appreciation to decide on the nature and scope of the derogating measures necessary to avert the emergency. Nonetheless, it is ultimately for the Court to rule whether the measures were 'strictly required'. In particular, where a derogating measure encroaches upon a fundamental Convention right, such as the right to liberty, the Court must be satisfied that it was a genuine response to the emergency situation, that it was fully justified by the special circumstances of the emergency and that adequate safeguards were provided against abuse ... The doctrine of the margin of appreciation has always been meant as a tool to define relations between the domestic authorities and the Court. It cannot have the same application to the relations between the organs of State at the domestic level. As the House of Lords held, the question of proportionality is ultimately a judicial decision, particularly in a case such as the present where the applicants were deprived of their fundamental right to liberty over a long period of time. In any event, having regard to the careful way in which the House of Lords approached the issues, it cannot be said that inadequate weight was given to the views of the executive or of Parliament.

185. The Government also submitted that the House of Lords erred in examining the legislation in the abstract rather than considering the applicants' concrete cases. However, in the Court's view, the approach under Article 15 is necessarily focussed on the general situation pertaining in the country concerned, in the sense that the court – whether national or international – is required to examine the measures that have been adopted in derogation of the Convention rights in question and to weigh them against the nature of the threat to the nation posed by the emergency. Where, as here, the measures are found to be disproportionate to that threat and to be discriminatory in their effect, there is no need to go further and examine their application in the concrete case of each applicant.

186. The Government's third ground of challenge to the House of Lords' decision was directed principally at the approach taken towards the comparison between non-national and national suspected terrorists. The Court, however, considers that the House of Lords was correct in holding that the impugned powers were not to be seen as immigration measures, where a distinction between nationals and non-nationals would be legitimate, but instead as concerned with national security. Part 4 of the 2001 Act was designed to avert a real and imminent threat of terrorist attack which, on the evidence, was posed by both nationals and non-nationals. The choice by the Government and Parliament of an immigration measure to address what was essentially a security issue had the result of failing adequately to address the problem, while imposing a disproportionate and discriminatory burden of indefinite detention on one group of suspected terrorists. As the House of Lords found, there was no significant difference in the

potential adverse impact of detention without charge on a national or on a non-national who in practice could not leave the country because of fear of torture abroad.

187. Finally, the Government advanced two arguments which the applicants claimed had not been relied on before the national courts. Certainly, there does not appear to be any reference to them in the national courts' judgments or in the open material which has been put before the Court. In these circumstances, even assuming that the principle of subsidiarity does not prevent the Court from examining new grounds, it would require persuasive evidence in support of them.

188. The first of the allegedly new arguments was that it was legitimate for the State, in confining the measures to non-nationals, to take into account the sensitivities of the British Muslim population in order to reduce the chances of recruitment among them by extremists. However, the Government has not placed before the Court any evidence to suggest that British Muslims were significantly more likely to react negatively to the detention without charge of national rather than foreign Muslims reasonably suspected of links to al'Qaeda. In this respect the Court notes that the system of control orders, put in place by the Prevention of Terrorism Act 2005, does not discriminate between national and non-national suspects.

189. The second allegedly new ground relied on by the Government was that the State could better respond to the terrorist threat if it were able to detain its most serious source, namely non-nationals. In this connection, again the Court has not been provided with any evidence which could persuade it to overturn the conclusion of the House of Lords that the difference in treatment was unjustified. Indeed, the Court notes that the national courts, including SIAC, which saw both the open and the closed material, were not convinced that the threat from non-nationals was more serious than that from nationals.

190. In conclusion, therefore, the Court, like the House of Lords, and contrary to the Government's contention, finds that the derogating measures were disproportionate in that they discriminated unjustifiably between nationals and non-nationals. It follows there has been a violation of Article 5 §1 in respect of the first, third, fifth, sixth, seventh, eighth, ninth, tenth and eleventh applicants.

4 FOURTH CONDITION: COMPLIANCE WITH OTHER INTERNATIONAL OBLIGATIONS

The relevant provisions of the ICCPR (Art. 4), of the ECHR (Art. 15), and of the ACHR (Art. 27), all state that the measures derogating from these instruments may only be allowed to the extent that they are not inconsistent with the other obligations of the State concerned under international law. This does not only mean that a measure allowed once a State has notified its intention to derogate from its obligations under those instruments may nevertheless, under international law, be in violation with other obligations of the State, and therefore still not be allowed to the State: rather, it means that, as a condition of acceptability under the derogation provisions themselves, the measures concerned should fully comply with the other obligations of the State under international law. This is important, since a number of widely ratified universal or regional treaties – including the Convention on the Rights of the Child or the International Covenant on Economic, Social and Cultural Rights – do not provide for the possibility of a derogation in times of war or other public emergency. Therefore, any measure presented as covered by a derogation under the ICCPR, the ECHR or the ACHR will not be considered acceptable under these treaties if they do not comply with those other instruments. Moreover, the Human Rights Committee insisted that 'States parties should duly take into account the developments within international law as to human rights standards applicable in emergency situations', mentioning in this regard for instance the Paris Minimum Standards of Human Rights Norms in a State of Emergency (International Law Association, 1984) and the Siracusa Principles on the Limitation and Derogation Provisions in the International Covenant on Civil and Political Rights (Human Rights Committee, General Comment No. 29, *Derogations during a State of Emergency* (Art. 4), UN Doc. CCPR/C/21/Rev.1/Add. 11 (2001), para. 10 and note 6). This significantly restricts the margin of manoeuvre for States acting under these derogation provisions. It also places the Human Rights Committee, the European Court of Human Rights or the Inter-American Court of Human Rights in the awkward situation of having to decide whether a State has complied with other international obligations than those stated in the instrument which these bodies in principle are set up to monitor:

European Court of Human Rights, *Brannigan and McBride* v. *United Kingdom* (Appl. Nos. 14553/89 and 14554/89), judgment of 25 May 1993:

67. The Court recalls that under Article 15 para. 1 measures taken by the State derogating from Convention obligations must not be 'inconsistent with its other obligations under international law' ...

68. In this respect, before the Court the applicants contended for the first time that it was an essential requirement for a valid derogation under Article 4 of the 1966 United Nations International Covenant on Civil and Political Rights ..., to which the United Kingdom is a Party, that a public emergency must have been 'officially proclaimed'. Since such proclamation had never taken place the derogation was inconsistent with the United Kingdom's other obligations under international law. In their view this requirement involved a formal proclamation and not a mere statement in Parliament.

69. For the Government, it was open to question whether an official proclamation was necessary for the purposes of Article 4 of the Covenant, since the emergency existed prior to the ratification of the Covenant by the United Kingdom and has continued to the present day. In any event, the existence of the emergency and the fact of derogation were publicly and formally announced by the Secretary of State for the Home Department to the House of Commons on 22 December 1988. Moreover there had been no suggestion by the United Nations Human Rights Committee that the derogation did not satisfy the formal requirements of Article 4 ...

71. The relevant part of Article 4 of the Covenant states:

'In time of public emergency which threatens the life of the nation and the existence of which is officially proclaimed ...'

72. The Court observes that it is not its role to seek to define authoritatively the meaning of the terms 'officially proclaimed' in Article 4 of the Covenant. Nevertheless it must examine whether there is any plausible basis for the applicant's argument in this respect.

73. In his statement of 22 December 1988 to the House of Commons the Secretary of State for the Home Department explained in detail the reasons underlying the Government's decision to derogate and announced that steps were being taken to give notice of derogation under both Article 15 of the European Convention and Article 4 of the Covenant. He added that there was 'a public emergency within the meaning of these provisions in respect of terrorism connected with the affairs of Northern Ireland in the United Kingdom ...' ...

In the Court's view the above statement, which was formal in character and made public the Government's intentions as regards derogation, was well in keeping with the notion of an official proclamation. It therefore considers that there is no basis for the applicants' arguments in this regard.

5 FIFTH CONDITION: RIGHTS WHICH ARE NOT SUBJECT TO DEROGATION

Certain rights cannot be derogated from, under whichever circumstances (on the question of whether this should be interpreted as signalling a hierarchy within human rights and for a comparison with the notions of core human rights, human rights imposing *erga omnes* obligations, and *jus cogens* norms, see T. Koji, 'Emerging Hierarchy in International Human Rights and Beyond: From the Perspective of Non-derogable Rights', *European Journal of International Law*, 12, No. 5 (2001), 917–41). The most recent of the three human rights instruments providing for the possibility of derogations, the American Convention on Human Rights, contains the longest list of non-derogable rights. Only four rights – the right to life, the prohibition of torture or cruel, inhuman or degrading treatments or punishments, the prohibition of slavery or involuntary servitude, and the prohibition of retroactive criminal law – are excluded from derogation under all three instruments (see box 6.1.). However, the list contained in the relevant provisions in not necessarily finite, as made clear by the Human Rights Committee (see also, for instance, C. Olivier, 'Revisiting General Comment No. 29 of the United Nations Human Rights Committee: About Fair Trial Rights and Derogations in Times of Public Emergency', *Leiden Journal of International Law*, 17, No. 2 (2004), 405–19 (arguing in favour of the non-derogable character of the right to a fair trial, as this right constitutes a guarantee necessary to the effective enjoyment of all human rights, the preservation of legality in a democratic society, and the effectiveness of the principle of separation of powers)):

Human Rights Committee, General Comment No. 29, *Derogations during a State of Emergency* (Art. 4), (CCPR/C/21/Rev.1/Add. 11) (24 July 2001), paras. 11–16:

11. The enumeration of non-derogable provisions in article 4 is related to, but not identical with, the question whether certain human rights obligations bear the nature of peremptory norms of international law. The proclamation of certain provisions of the Covenant as being of a non-derogable nature, in article 4, paragraph 2, is to be seen partly as recognition of the peremptory

nature of some fundamental rights ensured in treaty form in the Covenant (e.g. arts. 6 [right to life] and 7 [prohibition of torture or cruel, inhuman or degrading treatment or punishment]). However, it is apparent that some other provisions of the Covenant were included in the list of non-derogable provisions because it can never become necessary to derogate from these rights during a state of emergency (e.g. arts. 11 [no imprisonment for inability to fulfil a contractual obligation] and 18 [freedom of religion]). Furthermore, the category of peremptory norms extends beyond the list of non-derogable provisions as given in article 4, paragraph 2. States parties may in no circumstances invoke article 4 of the Covenant as justification for acting in violation of humanitarian law or peremptory norms of international law, for instance by taking hostages, by imposing collective punishments, through arbitrary deprivations of liberty or by deviating from fundamental principles of fair trial, including the presumption of innocence.

12. In assessing the scope of legitimate derogation from the Covenant, one criterion can be found in the definition of certain human rights violations as crimes against humanity. If action conducted under the authority of a State constitutes a basis for individual criminal responsibility for a crime against humanity by the persons involved in that action, article 4 of the Covenant cannot be used as justification that a state of emergency exempted the State in question from its responsibility in relation to the same conduct. Therefore, the recent codification of crimes against humanity, for jurisdictional purposes, in the Rome Statute of the International Criminal Court is of relevance in the interpretation of article 4 of the Covenant [see articles 6 (genocide) and 7 (crimes against humanity) of the Statute ... While many of the specific forms of conduct listed in article 7 of the Statute are directly linked to violations against those human rights that are listed as non–derogable provisions in article 4, paragraph 2, of the Covenant, the category of crimes against humanity as defined in that provision covers also violations of some provisions of the Covenant that have not been mentioned in the said provision of the Covenant. For example, certain grave violations of article 27 [rights of minorities] may at the same time constitute genocide under article 6 of the Rome Statute, and article 7, in turn, covers practices that are related to, besides articles 6, 7 and 8 of the Covenant, also articles 9, 12, 26 and 27].

13. In those provisions of the Covenant that are not listed in article 4, paragraph 2, there are elements that in the Committee's opinion cannot be made subject to lawful derogation under article 4.

Some illustrative examples are presented below.

(a) All persons deprived of their liberty shall be treated with humanity and with respect for the inherent dignity of the human person. Although this right, prescribed in article 10 of the Covenant, is not separately mentioned in the list of non-derogable rights in article 4, paragraph 2, the Committee believes that here the Covenant expresses a norm of general international law not subject to derogation. This is supported by the reference to the inherent dignity of the human person in the preamble to the Covenant and by the close connection between articles 7 and 10.

(b) The prohibitions against taking of hostages, abductions or unacknowledged detention are not subject to derogation. The absolute nature of these prohibitions, even in times of emergency, is justified by their status as norms of general international law.

(c) The Committee is of the opinion that the international protection of the rights of persons belonging to minorities includes elements that must be respected in all circumstances. This is reflected in the prohibition against genocide in international law, in the inclusion of a non-discrimination clause in article 4 itself (paragraph 1), as well as in the non-derogable nature of article 18.

(d) As confirmed by the Rome Statute of the International Criminal Court, deportation or forcible transfer of population without grounds permitted under international law, in the form of forced displacement by expulsion or other coercive means from the area in which the persons concerned are lawfully present, constitutes a crime against humanity. The legitimate right to derogate from article 12 of the Covenant during a state of emergency can never be accepted as justifying such measures.

(e) No declaration of a state of emergency made pursuant to article 4, paragraph 1, may be invoked as justification for a State party to engage itself, contrary to article 20, in propaganda for war, or in advocacy of national, racial or religious hatred that would constitute incitement to discrimination, hostility or violence.

14. Article 2, paragraph 3, of the Covenant requires a State party to the Covenant to provide remedies for any violation of the provisions of the Covenant. This clause is not mentioned in the list of non-derogable provisions in article 4, paragraph 2, but it constitutes a treaty obligation inherent in the Covenant as a whole. Even if a State party, during a state of emergency, and to the extent that such measures are strictly required by the exigencies of the situation, may introduce adjustments to the practical functioning of its procedures governing judicial or other remedies, the State party must comply with the fundamental obligation, under article 2, paragraph 3, of the Covenant to provide a remedy that is effective.

15. It is inherent in the protection of rights explicitly recognized as non-derogable in article 4, paragraph 2, that they must be secured by procedural guarantees, including, often, judicial guarantees. The provisions of the Covenant relating to procedural safeguards may never be made subject to measures that would circumvent the protection of non-derogable rights. Article 4 may not be resorted to in a way that would result in derogation from non-derogable rights. Thus, for example, as article 6 of the Covenant is non-derogable in its entirety, any trial leading to the imposition of the death penalty during a state of emergency must conform to the provisions of the Covenant, including all the requirements of articles 14 and 15.

16. Safeguards related to derogation, as embodied in article 4 of the Covenant, are based on the principles of legality and the rule of law inherent in the Covenant as a whole. As certain elements of the right to a fair trial are explicitly guaranteed under international humanitarian law during armed conflict, the Committee finds no justification for derogation from these guarantees during other emergency situations. The Committee is of the opinion that the principles of legality and the rule of law require that fundamental requirements of fair trial must be respected during a state of emergency. Only a court of law may try and convict a person for a criminal offence. The presumption of innocence must be respected. In order to protect non-derogable rights, the right to take proceedings before a court to enable the court to decide without delay on the lawfulness of detention, must not be diminished by a State party's decision to derogate from the Covenant.

As with other human rights instruments, the American Convention on Human Rights establishes a set of rights that cannot be suspended under any circumstances. The ACHR goes further than other human rights treaties by prohibiting the suspension of the 'judicial guarantees essential for the protection of (non-derogable) rights'. The nature of this additional procedural guarantee is developed by the Court as follows:

Inter-American Court of Human Rights, *Habeas Corpus in Emergency Situations (Arts. 27(2), 25(1) and 7(6) American Convention on Human Rights)*, **Advisory Opinion OC–8/87 of January 30, 1987. Series A No. 8:**

21. It is clear that no right guaranteed in the Convention may be suspended unless very strict conditions – those laid down in Article 27(1) – are met. Moreover, even when these conditions are satisfied, Article 27(2) provides that certain categories of rights may not be suspended under any circumstances ...

23. Article 27(2), as has been stated, limits the powers of the State Party to suspend rights and freedoms. It establishes a certain category of specific rights and freedoms from which no derogation is permitted under any circumstances and it includes in that category 'the judicial guarantees essential for the protection of such rights'. Some of these rights refer to the physical integrity of the person, such as the right to juridical personality (Art. 3); the right to life (Art. 4); the right to humane treatment (Art. 5); freedom from slavery (Art. 6) and freedom from ex post facto laws (Art. 9). The list of non-derogable rights and freedoms also includes freedom of conscience and religion (Art. 12); the rights of the family (Art. 17); the right to a name (Art. 18); the rights of the child (Art. 19); the right to nationality (Art. 20) and the right to participate in government (Art. 23) ...

27. As the Court has already noted, in serious emergency situations it is lawful to temporarily suspend certain rights and freedoms whose free exercise must, under normal circumstances, be respected and guaranteed by the State. However, since not all of these rights and freedoms may be suspended even temporarily, it is imperative that 'the judicial guarantees essential for (their) protection' remain in force. Article 27(2) does not link these judicial guarantees to any specific provision of the Convention, which indicates that what is important is that these judicial remedies have the character of being essential to ensure the protection of those rights.

28. The determination as to what judicial remedies are 'essential' for the protection of the rights which may not be suspended will differ depending upon the rights that are at stake. The 'essential' judicial guarantees necessary to guarantee the rights that deal with the physical integrity of the human person must of necessity differ from those that seek to protect the right to a name, for example, which is also non-derogable.

29. It follows from what has been said above that the judicial remedies that must be considered to be essential within the meaning of Article 27(2) are those that ordinarily will effectively guarantee the full exercise of the rights and freedoms protected by that provision and whose denial or restriction would endanger their full enjoyment.

30. The guarantees must be not only essential but also judicial. The expression 'judicial' can only refer to those judicial remedies that are truly capable of protecting these rights. Implicit in this conception is the active involvement of an independent and impartial judicial body having the power to pass on the lawfulness of measures adopted in a state of emergency.

31. The Court must now determine whether, despite the fact that Articles 25 and 7 are not mentioned in Article 27(2), the guarantees contained in Articles 25(1) [right to an effective remedy, or 'amparo'] and 7(6) [right to habeas corpus], which are referred to in the instant advisory opinion request, must be deemed to be among those 'judicial guarantees' that are 'essential' for the protection of the non-derogable rights.

32. ... the procedural institution known as 'amparo', which is a simple and prompt remedy designed for the protection of all of the rights recognized by the constitutions and laws of the

States Parties and by the Convention. Since 'amparo' can be applied to all rights, it is clear that it can also be applied to those that are expressly mentioned in Article 27(2) as rights that are non-derogable in emergency situations.

33. In its classical form, the writ of habeas corpus, as it is incorporated in various legal systems of the Americas, is a judicial remedy designed to protect personal freedom or physical integrity against arbitrary detentions by means of a judicial decree ordering the appropriate authorities to bring the detained person before a judge so that the lawfulness of the detention may be determined and, if appropriate, the release of the detainee be ordered ...

35. In order for habeas corpus to achieve its purpose, which is to obtain a judicial determination of the lawfulness of a detention, it is necessary that the detained person be brought before a competent judge or tribunal with jurisdiction over him. Here habeas corpus performs a vital role in ensuring that a person's life and physical integrity are respected, in preventing his disappearance or the keeping of his whereabouts secret and in protecting him against torture or other cruel, inhumane, or degrading punishment or treatment ...

37. A further question that needs to be asked, and which goes beyond the consideration of habeas corpus as a judicial remedy designed to safeguard the nonderogable rights set out in Article 27(2), is whether the writ may remain in effect as a means of ensuring individual liberty even during states of emergency, despite the fact that Article 7 is not listed among the provisions that may not be suspended in exceptional circumstances.

38. If, as the Court has already emphasized, the suspension of guarantees may not exceed the limits of that strictly required to deal with the emergency, any action on the part of the public authorities that goes beyond those limits, which must be specified with precision in the decree promulgating the state of emergency, would also be unlawful notwithstanding the existence of the emergency situation.

39. The Court should also point out that since it is improper to suspend guarantees without complying with the conditions referred to in the preceding paragraph, it follows that the specific measures applicable to the rights or freedoms that have been suspended may also not violate these general principles. Such violation would occur, for example, if the measures taken infringed the legal regime of the state of emergency, if they lasted longer than the time limit specified, if they were manifestly irrational, unnecessary or disproportionate, or if, in adopting them, there was a misuse or abuse of power.

40. If this is so, it follows that in a system governed by the rule of law it is entirely in order for an autonomous and independent judicial order to exercise control over the lawfulness of such measures by verifying, for example, whether a detention based on the suspension of personal freedom complies with the legislation authorized by the state of emergency. In this context, habeas corpus acquires a new dimension of fundamental importance ...

42. From what has been said before, it follows that writs of habeas corpus and of 'amparo' are among those judicial remedies that are essential for the protection of various rights whose derogation is prohibited by Article 27(2) and that serve, moreover, to preserve legality in a democratic society.

43. The Court must also observe that the Constitutions and legal systems of the States Parties that authorize, expressly or by implication, the suspension of the legal remedies of habeas corpus or of 'amparo' in emergency situations cannot be deemed to be compatible with the international obligations imposed on these States by the Convention.

The Court, in a later advisory opinion, determined that the right to due process contained in Article 8 of the Convention, although not among its non-derogable provisions, was the framework under which the 'essential judicial guarantees' of Articles 7(6) and 25(1) were to be exercised in states of emergency (Inter-American Court H.R., *Judicial Guarantees in States of Emergency (Arts. 27(2), 25 and (8) American Convention on Human Rights)*. Advisory Opinion OC-9/87 of 6 October 1987, Series A No. 9).

6 SIXTH CONDITION: INTERNATIONAL NOTIFICATION

Human Rights Committee, General Comment No. 29, *Derogations during a State of Emergency* (Art. 4), (CCPR/C/21/Rev.1/Add. 11) (24 July 2001), para. 17:

A State party availing itself of the right of derogation must immediately inform the other States parties, through the United Nations Secretary–General, of the provisions it has derogated from and of the reasons for such measures. Such notification is essential not only for the discharge of the Committee's functions, in particular in assessing whether the measures taken by the State party were strictly required by the exigencies of the situation, but also to permit other States parties to monitor compliance with the provisions of the Covenant. In view of the summary character of many of the notifications received in the past, the Committee emphasizes that the notification by States parties should include full information about the measures taken and a clear explanation of the reasons for them, with full documentation attached regarding their law. Additional notifications are required if the State party subsequently takes further measures under article 4, for instance by extending the duration of a state of emergency. The requirement of immediate notification applies equally in relation to the termination of derogation. These obligations have not always been respected: States parties have failed to notify other States parties, through the Secretary-General, of a proclamation of a state of emergency and of the resulting measures of derogation from one or more provisions of the Covenant, and States parties have sometimes neglected to submit a notification of territorial or other changes in the exercise of their emergency powers. Sometimes, the existence of a state of emergency and the question of whether a State party has derogated from provisions of the Covenant have come to the attention of the Committee only incidentally, in the course of the consideration of a State party's report. The Committee emphasizes the obligation of immediate international notification whenever a State party takes measures derogating from its obligations under the Covenant. The duty of the Committee to monitor the law and practice of a State party for compliance with article 4 does not depend on whether that State party has submitted a notification.

Article 27(3) of the American Convention on Human Rights similarly imposes an obligation to notify the Organization of American States (OAS) General Secretary and the Contracting Parties. This is not a mere formality. The case of *Zambrano Vélez et al.* v. *Ecuador* involves a series of extra-judicial killings that occurred in Ecuador in 1993, a period characterized by the suspension of guarantees and the widespread use of military force for police enforcement activities. Although the State of Ecuador accepted its international responsibility for the killings, including a violation of Article 27, the Court decided to clarify the extent of the obligation under the said Article:

Inter-American Court of Human Rights, case of *Zambrano Vélez et al.* v. *Ecuador*, judgment of 4 July 2007, Series C, No. 166 (unofficial translation):

69. ... [I]t has been accepted by the State that, at the moment in which it issued Decree No. 86 of September 3, 1992, the State did not inform the other Contracting Parties of the Convention, by the intermediary of the Secretary-General of the Organization of American States (hereinafter, OAS), of the provisions of the Convention the application of which was suspended, of the reasons that justified the suspension and of the date at which the suspension's effects would be terminated, as required by Article 27(3) of the Convention. In this respect, the Court assesses positively the statement by Ecuador, to the effect that:

... [T]he States of the region must be conscious [of the requirements of] Article 27(3) of the American Convention ... obligation which is often ignored by the states and which, in this case, was ignored by the Equatoran State ...

70. The Court considers that the international obligation owed by the State Parties under Article 27(3) of the American Convention constitutes a mechanism in the framework of the notion of collective guarantee established by this treaty, the objective and finality of which is the protection of the human being. Furthermore, it constitutes a safeguard to prevent the abuse of the exceptional powers of suspension of rights and allows other States Parties to observe whether the extent of these measures complies with the provisions of the Convention. Finally, failure to comply with this duty to inform implies the failure to comply with the obligation contained in Article 27(3). Still regarding this final issue, the State is not excused from the need to justify the existence of a situation of emergency and the conformity of the measures adopted in response to it, in the terms identified previously.

In the absence of a proclamation of emergency powers, or in the absence of the OAS Secretary-General being notified of this suspension, the Inter-American Court has rejected the invocation by the State concerned of arguments of necessity or emergency, including cases involving counter-terrorist activities (see, for instance, case of *Baena Ricardo et al.* v. *Panama*, decision on the merits of 2 February 2001, Series C, No. 72, paras. 92–4).

6.1. Questions for discussion: the State's margin of appreciation and derogation in times of emergency

1. Why does Article 4 of the International Covenant on Civil and Political Rights insist on the need for the state of emergency to be 'officially proclaimed'? Was Mr Alvaro Gil Robles, the Commissioner for Human Rights of the Council of Europe, right in taking the view in August 2002 that despite the absence of a similar requirement in Article 15 ECHR, derogations under this instrument should be subjected to parliamentary scrutiny by the national parliament concerned?

2. How should the 'necessity' requirement imposed on measures derogating from human rights be evaluated by international bodies, whether judicial or non-judicial? Should the degree of scrutiny depend on whether a parliamentary body has been involved in adopting the measures that are taken in order to meet the exigencies of the situation? Should it depend on whether domestic courts have a possibility to control whether these measures meet the test of necessity? How is this linked to the prohibition imposed under the American Convention on Human Rights to suspend 'judicial guarantees essential for the protection of (non-derogable) rights'? Should such a prohibition extend to other human rights instruments?

3. Leaving aside the special case of rights that are absolute and, yet, may be subject to a derogation, why should a State suspend human rights in the face of a situation of emergency, when such rights can be restricted in normal circumstances? Does the derogation clause provide any additional flexibility to the State concerned?

7

The Prohibition of Discrimination

INTRODUCTION

It is one of the purposes of the United Nations to 'promot[e] and encourag[e] respect for human rights and for fundamental freedoms for all without distinction as to race, sex, language, or religion' (Article 1, para. 3 of the UN Charter; see also Article 55(c), in chapter IX on international economic and social co-operation). The Universal Declaration on Human Rights (UDHR) reflects this emphasis on the prohibition of discrimination, by stating that '[a]ll human beings are born free and equal in dignity and rights' (Art. 1, first sentence), and by providing: 'Everyone is entitled to all the rights and freedoms set forth in this Declaration, without distinction of any kind, such as race, colour, sex, language, religion, political or other opinion, national or social origin, property, birth or other status' (Article 2, first para.). Article 7 of the UDHR, which extends the scope of the requirement of non-discrimination beyond the enjoyment of the rights listed in the Declaration, also clearly imposes a positive obligation in this regard on the Member States of the United Nations: 'All are equal before the law and are entitled without any discrimination to equal protection of the law. All are entitled to equal protection against any discrimination in violation of this Declaration and against any incitement to such discrimination.' In addition, a number of rights of the UDHR refer to equal treatment among its different components: for example, Article 10 states that everyone 'is entitled in full equality to a fair and public hearing by an independent and impartial tribunal, in the determination of his rights and obligations and of any criminal charge against him'; under Article 16, men and women 'are entitled to equal rights as to marriage, during marriage and at its dissolution'; the participatory rights listed in Article 21 include the right of everyone to 'equal access to public service in his country' and to 'universal and equal suffrage'; Article 26 para. 2 mentions the right of everyone, without any discrimination, to equal pay for equal work.

Thus, the requirements of equality and non-discrimination have been at the centre of international human rights law since its origins (for general comments on the non-discrimination requirement in international human rights law, in particular as embodied in Article 26 of the International Covenant on Civil and Political

Rights (ICCPR), see Lord Lester of Herne Q.C. and S. Joseph, 'Obligations of Non-Discrimination' in D. Harris and S. Joseph (eds.), *The International Covenant on Civil and Political Rights and United Kingdom Law* (Oxford: Clarendon Press, 1995), p. 563; T. Opsahl, 'Equality in Human Rights Law. With Particular Reference to Article 26 of the International Covenant on Civil and Political Rights' in *Festschrift für Felix Ermacora: Fortschritt im Bewußtsein der Gruhnd- und Menschenrechte* (Kehl am Rhein: N. P. Engel Verlag, 1988), at pp. 51–65; B. Ramcharan, 'Equality and Non-Discrimination' in L. Henkin (ed.), *The International Bill of Rights. The Covenant on Civil and Political Rights* (New York: Columbia University Press, 1981), at pp. 246–68; W. Vandenhole, *Non-Discrimination and Equality in the View of the UN Human Rights Treaty Bodies* (Antwerp-Oxford: Intersentia-Hart, 2005)). This chapter first offers a brief overview of the most important provisions which prohibit discrimination in international human rights law (see box 7.1.). In section 1, it discusses the scope of application of those provisions, i.e. the situations to which they apply. Section 2 then examines the different obligations imposed on States, following the structure of Article 26 ICCPR. Section 3 considers the notion of discrimination itself, and the various forms it may take. The final section relates the non-discrimination requirement to the protection of minority rights and to the right of self-determination, which – notwithstanding the highly distinctive status it has acquired in international human rights law – to a significant extent may be seen as an implication of the principle of non-discrimination. While Article 26 ICCPR, which has the widest scope of application, will constitute the main focus of the discussion in this chapter and inspires the structure of presentation followed, references will also be made to other instruments where they go beyond the requirements of the ICCPR, as well as to the case law of the bodies which have offered authoritative guidance on this issue.

1 THE SCOPE OF THE REQUIREMENT OF NON-DISCRIMINATION

The non-discrimination provisions summarized in box 7.1. fall into two categories. Some of them stipulate that the human rights they codify will be guaranteed to all without discrimination. Such clauses are not independent: they may only be invoked in combination with the other substantive provisions of the treaties concerned. Others, on the contrary, have an independent status: they protect from discrimination in all fields, and not only in the implementation of human rights listed in the instruments in which they appear. This section reviews the debates which the determination of the scope of application of non-discrimination clauses has led to under the International Covenant on Civil and Political Rights, the European Convention on Human Rights, the European Social Charter, and the American Convention on Human Rights.

1.1 The International Covenant on Civil and Political Rights

Like the Universal Declaration on Human Rights, the ICCPR contains separate clauses prohibiting discrimination in the enjoyment of the Covenant rights and generally: the provisions concerned, Articles 2(1) and 26 of the ICCPR, have been reproduced in

Box 7.1.	**Equality and non-discrimination under the main human rights instruments**

The UN Charter and the Universal Declaration on Human Rights already express a consensus on the need to combat discrimination, especially discrimination on grounds of race. Both of the Covenants adopted in 1966 in order to implement the UDHR into legally binding treaties also contain provisions relating to discrimination. Article 2(1) ICCPR provides that '[e]ach State Party to the present Covenant undertakes to respect and to ensure to all individuals within its territory and subject to its jurisdiction the rights recognized in the present Covenant, without distinction of any kind, such as race, colour, sex, language, religion, political or other opinion, national or social origin, property, birth or other status'. This prohibition is further reinforced in the ICCPR by Article 3 (prohibiting sex discrimination), Article 4(1) (prohibiting discrimination in relation to derogations), Article 23(4) (imposing on States parties to 'take appropriate steps to ensure equality of rights and responsibilities of spouses as to marriage, during marriage and at its dissolution'), Article 24 (in relation to the rights of the child), or Article 25 (in relation to rights of political participation). Similarly, under Article 2(2) of the International Covenant on Economic, Social and Culturual Rights (ICESCR), the States Parties 'undertake to guarantee that the rights enunciated in the present Covenant will be exercised without discrimination of any kind as to race, colour, sex, language, religion, political or other opinion, national or social origin, property, birth or other status'. The significance of this provision has been detailed by the Committee on Economic, Social and Cultural Rights in its General Comment No. 20, *Non-Discrimination in Economic, Social and Cultural Rights* (Art. 2, para. 2 of the Covenant) (E/C.12/GC/20, 20 May 2009).

However, only the ICCPR includes a general non-discrimination clause, which may be invoked independently of any other substantive guarantee. Article 26 ICCPR reads: 'All persons are equal before the law and are entitled without any discrimination to the equal protection of the law. In this respect, the law shall prohibit any discrimination and guarantee to all persons equal and effective protection against discrimination on any ground such as race, colour, sex, language, religion, political or other opinion, national or social origin, property, birth or other status.' The Human Rights Committee expanded on the meaning of this requirement in its General Comment No. 18, *Non-discrimination*, which it adopted in 1989 (HRI/GEN/1/Rev.7).

In a context characterized by decolonization and the emergence of the non-aligned movement, this consensus was further strengthened by the adoption of the Convention against Discrimination in Education (adopted by the General Conference of the United Nations Educational, Scientific and Cultural Organization (UNESCO) on 14 December 1960), and of the International Convention on the Elimination of All Forms of Racial Discrimination by UN General Assembly Resolution 2106 (XX) of 21 December 1965. More recently, the UN General Assembly adopted the Convention on the Elimination of All Forms of Discrimination against Women (opened for signature on 18 December 1979) and the Convention on the Rights of Persons with Disabilities (opened for signature on 30 March 2007), which also have non-discrimination as their central concern, albeit for the specific grounds concerned.

Similar non-discrimination provisions exist under regional human rights instruments. Within the Council of Europe, both the European Convention on Human Rights and the European Social Charter contain non-discrimincation clauses. Article 14 of the European Convention on Human Rights provides that: 'The enjoyment of the rights and freedoms set forth in this Convention shall be secured without discrimination on any ground such as sex, race, colour, language, religion, political or other opinion, national or social origin, association with a national minority, property, birth or other status.' Although this provision only applies in combination with other rights recognized under the Convention or under one of its Protocols (it thus does not apply independently from such other rights), an Additional Protocol (No. 12) to the Convention was adopted in 2000, which does include such an independent non-discrimination provision for the States parties. The European Social Charter (ESC) of 1961 does not contain an explicit provision on equal treatment or non-discrimination, with the exception of Article 4(3) which recognizes 'the right of men and women workers to equal pay for work of equal value'. However, the Preamble to the ESC does mention that 'the enjoyment of social rights should be secured without discrimination on grounds of race, colour, sex, religion, political opinion, national extraction or social origin', and the European Committee of Social Rights (ECSR) has accordingly read Article 1(2) of the ESC (according to which States parties undertake to 'protect effectively the right of the worker to earn his living in an occupation freely entered upon') as prohibiting all forms of discrimination in employment (see, e.g. Concl. 2002, pp. 22–8 (France)). In order to comply with para. 2 of Article 1 of the Charter, States which have accepted that provision should therefore 'take legal measures to safeguard the effectiveness of the prohibition of discrimination', ensuring to all the persons covered by the ESC that they will have access to employment and be treated in occupation without discrimination; they also should ensure that the legal framework will be effective, a requirement from which the ECSR has derived a number of supplementary requirements; and they should take policy measures promoting the professional integration of certain target groups. The adoption of the Revised European Social Charter (ESCRev) in 1996 further strengthened the prohibition of discrimination, since Article E was included in Part V of the Revised Charter: like Article 14 ECHR, Article E prohibits any discrimination in the enjoyment of the rights set forth in the ESCRev.

The American Convention on Human Rights contains two provisions concerning non-discrimination: Article 1(1) provides that States must ensure the enjoyment of the convention rights without discrimination, whereas Article 24 provides for equal treatment before the law. In addition, the Inter-American Convention on the Elimination of All Forms of Discrimination Against Persons With Disabilities was adopted on 7 June 1999.

The African Charter on Human and Peoples' Rights of 27 June 1981 contains two non-discrimination provisions. Article 2 provides that 'Every individual shall be entitled to the enjoyment of the rights and freedoms recognized and guaranteed in the present Charter without distinction of any kind such as race, ethnic group, color, sex, language, religion, political or any other opinion, national and social origin, fortune, birth or other status.' Article 3 guarantees that every individual shall be equal before the law (para. 1) and shall be entitled to equal protection of the law (para. 2). In addition, Article 15 embodies the principle of equal pay for equal work.

box 7.1. In its 1989 General Comment on *Non-discrimination*, the Human Rights Committee confirmed that:

Human Rights Committee, General Comment No. 18, *Non-discrimination* (1989) (HRI/GEN/1/Rev.7, at 146):

While article 2 limits the scope of the rights to be protected against discrimination to those provided for in the Covenant, article 26 does not specify such limitations. That is to say, article 26 provides that all persons are equal before the law and are entitled to equal protection of the law without discrimination, and that the law shall guarantee to all persons equal and effective protection against discrimination on any of the enumerated grounds. In the view of the Committee, article 26 does not merely duplicate the guarantee already provided for in article 2 but provides in itself an autonomous right. It prohibits discrimination in law or in fact in any field regulated and protected by public authorities. Article 26 is therefore concerned with the obligations imposed on States parties in regard to their legislation and the application thereof. Thus, when legislation is adopted by a State party, it must comply with the requirement of article 26 that its content should not be discriminatory. In other words, the application of the principle of non-discrimination contained in article 26 is not limited to those rights which are provided for in the Covenant.

Although it was implied by the very wording of the ICCPR (see M. Bossuyt, *L'interdiction de la discrimination dans le droit international des droits de l'homme* (Brussels: Bruylant, 1976), p. 89), this interpretation was only formally adopted by the Human Rights Committee ten years after its entry into force, in two decisions concerning the Netherlands. The *Broeks* case concerned the application of section 13(1) of the Dutch Unemployment Benefits Act (WWG), which, at the material time, laid down that WWV benefits could not be claimed by those married women who were neither breadwinners nor permanently separated from their husbands. As explained by the Human Rights Committee: 'whether a married woman was deemed to be a breadwinner depended, *inter alia*, on the absolute amount of the family's total income and on what proportion of it was contributed by the wife. That the conditions for granting benefits laid down in section 13, subsection 1(1), of WWV applied solely to married women and not to married men is due to the fact that the provision in question corresponded to the then prevailing views in society in general concerning the roles of men and women within marriage and society. Virtually all married men who had jobs could be regarded as their family's breadwinner, so that it was unnecessary to check whether they met this criterion for the granting of benefits upon becoming unemployed.' However, Ms Broeks argued that an unacceptable distinction was thereby made on the grounds of sex and status: if she were a man, married or unmarried, the law in question would not deprive her of unemployment benefits; however, because she is a woman, and was married at the time in question, the law excludes her from continued unemployment benefits. In the following excerpts of the *Broeks* decision, the Human Rights Committee answers, in particular, the Dutch Government's argument that Article 26 ICCPR only prohibits discrimination in the areas not covered under the International Covenant on Economic, Social and Cultural Rights.

Human Rights Committee, *S. W. M. Broeks* v. *Netherlands*, Communication No. 172/1984 (CCPR/C/OP/2 at 196 (1990)), final views adopted on 9 April 1987:

12.1. The State party contends that there is considerable overlapping of the provisions of article 26 with the provisions of article 2 of the International Covenant on Economic, Social and Cultural Rights. The Committee is of the view that the International Covenant on Civil and Political Rights would still apply even if a particular subject-matter is referred to or covered in other international instruments, for example, the International Convention on the Elimination of All Forms of Racial Discrimination, the Convention on the Elimination of All Forms of Discrimination against Women, or, as in the present case, the International Covenant on Economic, Social and Cultural Rights. Notwithstanding the interrelated drafting history of the two Covenants, it remains necessary for the Committee to apply fully the terms of the International Covenant on Civil and Political Rights. The Committee observes in this connection that the provisions of article 2 of the International Covenant on Economic, Social and Cultural Rights do not detract from the full application of article 26 of the International Covenant on Civil and Political Rights.

12.2. The Committee has also examined the contention of the State party that article 26 of the International Covenant on Civil and Political Rights cannot be invoked in respect of a right which is specifically provided for under article 9 of the International Covenant on Economic, Social and Cultural Rights (social security, including social insurance). In so doing, the Committee has perused the relevant *travaux préparatoires* of the International Covenant on Civil and Political Rights, namely, the summary records of the discussions that took place in the Commission on Human Rights in 1948, 1949, 1950 and 1952 and in the Third Committee of the General Assembly in 1961, which provide a 'supplementary means of interpretation' (art. 32 of the Vienna Convention on the Law of Treaties) ... The discussions, at the time of drafting, concerning the question whether the scope of article 26 extended to rights not otherwise guaranteed by the Covenant, were inconclusive and cannot alter the conclusion arrived at by the ordinary means of interpretation referred to in paragraph 12.3 below.

12.3. For the purpose of determining the scope of article 26, the Committee has taken into account the 'ordinary meaning' of each element of the article in its context and in the light of its object and purpose (art. 31 of the Vienna Convention on the Law of Treaties). The Committee begins by noting that article 26 does not merely duplicate the guarantees already provided for in article 2. It derives from the principle of equal protection of the law without discrimination, as contained in article 7 of the Universal Declaration of Human Rights, which prohibits discrimination in law or in practice in any field regulated and protected by public authorities. Article 26 is thus concerned with the obligations imposed on States in regard to their legislation and the application thereof.

12.4. Although article 26 requires that legislation should prohibit discrimination, it does not of itself contain any obligation with respect to the matters that may be provided for by legislation. Thus it does not, for example, require any State to enact legislation to provide for social security. However, when such legislation is adopted in the exercise of a State's sovereign power, then such legislation must comply with article 26 of the Covenant.

12.5. The Committee observes in this connection that what is at issue is not whether or not social security should be progressively established in the Netherlands, but whether the legislation providing for social security violates the prohibition against discrimination contained in article 26 of the International Covenant on Civil and Political Rights and the guarantee given therein to all persons regarding equal and effective protection against discrimination.

13. The right to equality before the law and to equal protection of the law without any discrimination does not make all differences of treatment discriminatory. A differentiation based on reasonable and objective criteria does not amount to prohibited discrimination within the meaning of article 26.

14. It therefore remains for the Committee to determine whether the differentiation in Netherlands law at the time in question and as applied to Mrs Broeks constituted discrimination within the meaning of article 26. The Committee notes that in Netherlands law the provisions of articles 84 and 85 of the Netherlands Civil Code impose equal rights and obligations on both spouses with regard to their joint income. Under section 13, subsection 1(1), of the Unemployment Benefits Act (WWV), a married woman, in order to receive WWV benefits, had to prove that she was a 'breadwinner' – a condition that did not apply to married men. Thus a differentiation which appears on one level to be one of status is in fact one of sex, placing married women at a disadvantage compared with married men. Such a differentiation is not reasonable; and this seems to have been effectively acknowledged even by the State party by the enactment of a change in the law on 29 April 1985, with retroactive effect to 23 December 1984 ...

15. The circumstances in which Mrs Broeks found herself at the material time and the application of the then valid Netherlands law made her a victim of a violation, based on sex, of article 26 of the International Covenant on Civil and Political Rights, because she was denied a social security benefit on an equal footing with men.

16. The Committee notes that the State party had not intended to discriminate against women and further notes with appreciation that the discriminatory provisions in the law applied to Mrs Broeks have, subsequently, been eliminated. Although the State party has thus taken the necessary measures to put an end to the kind of discrimination suffered by Mrs Broeks at the time complained of, the Committee is of the view that the State party should offer Mrs Broeks an appropriate remedy.

Although, in retrospect, this outcome appears entirely predictable, the *Broeks* case and its companion case, *Zwaan-de Vries* (see the decision adopted on the same day in *F. H. Zwaan-de Vries* v. *Netherlands*, Communication No. 182/1984, CCPR/C/29/D/182/1984) were met with great hostility. The Netherlands themselves considered denouncing the Covenant and immediately ratifying it again with a reservation on Article 26, before renouncing the idea (see M. Nowak, *UN Covenant on Civil and Political Rights. CCPR Commentary*, second edn (Kehl am Rhein: N. P. Engel, 2005), at p. 601). Other States, such as Switzerland or Liechtenstein, included such a reservation in their ratification instrument respectively in 1992 and 1998. The principle of the independent application of the non-discrimination clause is nevertheless firmly established in the case law of the Human Rights Committee, which has applied Article 26 ICCPR to a variety of social and economic rights such as retirement benefits (Communication No. 786/97, *J. Vos* v. *Netherlands*, final views of 19 July 1999, CCPR/C/66/D/786/1997 (1999); Communication No. 415/90, *Pauger* v. *Austria*, final views of 16 March 1992, CCPR/C/44/D/415/1990 (1992)), compensation for being dismissed from employment in the public sector (Communication No. 309/1988, *Carlos Orihuela Valenzuela* v. *Peru*, final views of 14 July 1993, *Selection of Decisions*, vol. 5, p. 25), disability benefits (Communication No. 218/1986, *Hendrika S. Vos* v. *Netherlands*, final views of 29 March 1989, Supp. No. 40 (A/44/40), at 232 (1989)), aids to education (Communication No. 191/1985, *Blom* v. *Sweden*, final views of 4 April 1988, Supp. No. 40 (A/43/40), at 211 (1988)), or family benefits (Communication Nos. 406/1990 and 426/1990, *Oulajin and Kaiss* v. *Netherlands*, final views of 23 October 1992, CCPR/C/46/D/406/1990 and 426/1990 (1992)). However, in areas such as taxation or social security, a wide margin of appreciation is granted to the States parties. In the case of *Sprenger* v. *Netherlands*, in which the Committee concluded that the differentiation between married and unmarried persons in the Health Insurance Act did not constitute discrimination prohibited under Article 26 ICCPR, three members of the Committee argued as follows:

Human Rights Committee, *Sprenger* v. *Netherlands*, Communication No. 395/1990, UN Doc. CCPR/C/44/D/395/1990 (1992), individual opinion of Messrs Nisuke Ando, Kurt Herndl and Birame Ndiaye:

While it is clear that article 26 of the Covenant postulates an autonomous right to non-discrimination, we believe that the implementation of this right may take different forms, depending on the nature of the right to which the principle of non-discrimination is applied.

We note, firstly, that the determination whether prohibited discrimination within the meaning of article 26 has occurred depends on complex considerations, particularly in the field of economic, social and cultural rights. Social security legislation, which is intended to achieve aims of social justice, necessarily must make distinctions. While the aims of social justice vary from country to country, they must be compatible with the Covenant. Moreover, whatever distinctions are made must be based on reasonable and objective criteria. For instance, a system of progressive taxation, under which persons with higher incomes fall into a higher tax bracket and pay a greater percentage of their income for taxes, does not entail a violation of article 26 of the Covenant, since the distinction between higher and lower incomes is objective and the purpose of more equitable distribution of wealth is reasonable and compatible with the aims of the Covenant.

Surely, it is also necessary to take into account the reality that the socio-economic and cultural needs of society are constantly evolving, so that legislation – in particular in the field of social security – may well, and often does, lag behind developments. Accordingly, article 26 of the Covenant should not be interpreted as requiring absolute equality or non-discrimination in that field at all times; instead, it should be seen as a general undertaking on the part of the States parties to the Covenant to regularly review their legislation in order to ensure that it corresponds to the changing needs of society. In the field of civil and political rights, a State party is required to respect Covenant rights such as the right to a fair trial, to freedom of expression and freedom of religion, immediately from the date of entry into force of the Covenant, and to do so without discrimination. On the other hand, with regard to rights enshrined in the International Covenant on Economic, Social and Cultural Rights, it is generally understood that States parties may need time for the progressive implementation of these rights and to adapt relevant legislation in stages; moreover, constant efforts are needed to ensure that distinctions that were reasonable and objective at the time of enactment of a social security provision are not rendered unreasonable and discriminatory by the socio-economic evolution of society. Finally, we recognize that legislative review is a complex process entailing consideration of many factors, including limited financial resources, and the potential effects of amendments on other existing legislation.

It has been argued that the extension to all fields of the requirement of non-discrimination, including in particular the area of social security, has a 'creative effect', by obliging the States parties to the Covenant to extend to certain disadvantaged categories advantages which had hitherto been reserved to a privileged segment of the population (M. Bossuyt, *L'interdiction de la discrimination dans le droit international des droits de l'homme* (Brussels: Bruylant, 1976), at p. 219). However, the restriction a stand-alone non-discrimination requirement imposes to the freedom of the State concerned to define at what speed it should progressively realize socio-economic rights should not be exaggerated. While a State may not allocate benefits on the basis of criteria which amount to a discrimination, it may in principle choose to deny those benefits altogether; when it is found to have committed a discrimination, it may deprive the privileged from the advantages which were unjustifiably reserved to them, instead of aligning the situation of the disadvantaged with that of the privileged.

Human Rights Committee, *Arieh Hollis Waldman* v. *Canada*, Communication No. 694/1996 (CCPR/C/67/D/694/1996), final views of 5 November 1999:

[The author of the communication, a Canadian citizen residing in the province of Ontario, is a father of two school-age children and a member of the Jewish faith who enrols his children in a private Jewish day school. In the province of Ontario Roman Catholic schools are the only non-secular schools receiving full and direct public funding. Other religious schools must fund through private sources, including the charging of tuition fees. This situation has its source in a constitutional compromise reached in 1867, at a time when Catholics represented 17 per cent of the population of Ontario, while Protestants represented 82 per cent and all other religions combined represented 0.2 per cent of the population. In order to avoid the new province of Ontario being controlled by a Protestant majority that might exercise its power over education to take away the rights of its Roman Catholic minority, the Roman Catholics were guaranteed their rights to denominational education: section 93 of the 1867 Canadian Constitution contains explicit guarantees of denominational school rights, thus limiting in this respect the exclusive jurisdiction of each province in Canada to enact laws regarding education; in Ontario, the section 93 power is exercised through the Education Act, which provides that every separate school is entitled to full public funding, and defines separate schools as Roman Catholic schools. As a result of this system, Roman Catholic schools are the only religious schools entitled to the same public funding as the public secular schools. Thus, in 1994, Mr Waldman paid $14,050 in tuition fees for his children to attend Bialik Hebrew Day School in Toronto, Ontario, an amount which was reduced by a federal tax credit system to $10,810.89; in addition, the author is required to pay local property taxes to fund a public school system he does not use. In his communication to the Committee, Mr Waldman claims to be a victim of a violation of article 26, and articles 18(1), (4) and 27 taken in conjunction with article 2(1).]

10.2 The issue before the Committee is whether public funding for Roman Catholic schools, but not for schools of the author's religion, which results in him having to meet the full cost of education in a religious school, constitutes a violation of the author's rights under the Covenant.

10.3 The State party has argued that no discrimination has occurred, since the distinction is based on objective and reasonable criteria: the privileged treatment of Roman Catholic schools is enshrined in the Constitution; as Roman Catholic schools are incorporated as a distinct part of the public school system, the differentiation is between private and public schools, not between private Roman Catholic schools and private schools of other denominations; and the aims of the public secular education system are compatible with the Covenant.

10.4 The Committee begins by noting that the fact that a distinction is enshrined in the Constitution does not render it reasonable and objective. In the instant case, the distinction was made in 1867 to protect the Roman Catholics in Ontario. The material before the Committee does not show that members of the Roman Catholic community or any identifiable section of that community are now in a disadvantaged position compared to those members of the Jewish community that wish to secure the education of their children in religious schools. Accordingly, the Committee rejects the State party's argument that the preferential treatment of Roman Catholic schools is nondiscriminatory because of its Constitutional obligation.

10.5 With regard to the State party's argument that it is reasonable to differentiate in the allocation of public funds between private and public schools, the Committee notes that it is not possible for members of religious denominations other than Roman Catholic to have their religious schools incorporated within the public school system. In the instant case, the author has sent his children to a private religious school, not because he wishes a private non–Government dependent education for his children, but because the publicly funded school system makes no provision for his religious denomination, whereas publicly funded religious schools are available to members of the Roman Catholic faith. On the basis of the facts before it, the Committee considers that the differences in treatment between Roman Catholic religious schools, which are publicly funded as a distinct part of the public education system, and schools of the author's religion, which are private by necessity, cannot be considered reasonable and objective.

10.6 The Committee has noted the State party's argument that the aims of the State party's secular public education system are compatible with the principle of nondiscrimination laid down in the Covenant. The Committee does not take issue with this argument but notes, however, that the proclaimed aims of the system do not justify the exclusive funding of Roman Catholic religious schools. It has also noted the author's submission that the public school system in Ontario would have greater resources if the Government would cease funding any religious schools. In this context, the Committee observes that the Covenant does not oblige States parties to fund schools which are established on a religious basis. However, if a State party chooses to provide public funding to religious schools, it should make this funding available without discrimination. This means that providing funding for the schools of one religious group and not for another must be based on reasonable and objective criteria. In the instant case, the Committee concludes that the material before it does not show that the differential treatment between the Roman Catholic faith and the author's religious denomination is based on such criteria. Consequently, there has been a violation of the author's rights under article 26 of the Covenant to equal and effective protection against discrimination.

[In 2006, Canada had still not adopted the measures required by the *Waldman* decision: see Human Rights Committee, Concluding Observations on the fifth periodic report of Canada (CCPR/C/CAN/2004/5) (CCPR/C/CAN/CO/5, 20 April 2006), at para. 21.]

7.1. Question for discussion: is non-discrimination applied to social rights 'legislating social rights from the bench'?

The Committee on Economic, Social and Cultural Rights considers that 'any deliberately retrogressive measures [in the realization of the rights of the ICESCR] would require the most careful consideration and would need to be fully justified by reference to the totality of the rights provided for in the Covenant and in the context of the full use of the maximum available resources' (General Comment No. 3, *The Nature of States Parties' Obligations* (1990), para. 9; see also General Comment No. 13, *The Right to Education* (Art. 13) (1999), para. 45; General Comment No. 14, *The Right to the Highest Attainable Standard of Health* (Art. 12) (2000), para. 32; General Comment No. 15, *The Right to Water* (Arts. 11 and 12 of the Convenant) (2002), para. 19). Is the implication that the independent application of the non-discrimination requirement of Article 26 ICCPR in fact does oblige States parties to the ICCPR to make progress towards the realization of economic and social rights faster than they would have otherwise, following the domestic decision-making processes, resulting in the 'creative effect' feared by M. Bossuyt?

1.2 The European Convention on Human Rights

A similar discussion concerning the scope of the non-discrimination clause has taken place under the ECHR. Article 14 of the European Convention on Human Rights does not create an independent protection from discrimination. It may only be invoked in combination with another substantive provision of the ECHR or of one of its additional Protocols: it is only when discrimination is found to exist *in the enjoyment of the rights and freedoms set forth in the Convention* that it will come into play. This is not to say that Article 14 ECHR has no autonomous function to fulfil in the system of the Convention. On the contrary, it supplements all the other substantive provisions by adding the requirement that they be applied and implemented without discrimination.

European Court of Human Rights, *Case 'Relating to Certain Aspects of the Laws on the Use of Languages in Education in Belgium' v. Belgium ('Belgian Linguistics Case')*, judgment of 23 July 1968, Series A No. 6, pp. 33–4, para. 9:

[Article 2 of Additional Protocol No. 1 to the ECHR states that 'No person shall be denied the right to education.' Although the right to obtain from the public authorities the creation of a particular kind of educational establishment could not be inferred from this provision,] nevertheless, a State which had set up such an establishment could not, in laying down entrance requirements, take discriminatory measures within the meaning of Article 14. [Thus, similarly,] Article 6 of the Convention does not compel States to institute a system of appeal courts. A State which does set up such courts consequently goes beyond its obligations under Article 6. However it would violate that Article, read in conjunction with Article 14, were it to debar certain persons from these remedies without a legitimate reason while making them available to others in respect of the same type of actions. In such cases there would be a violation of a guaranteed right or freedom as it is proclaimed by the relevant Article read in conjunction with Article 14. It is as though the latter formed an integral part of each of the Articles laying down rights and freedoms. No distinctions should be made in this respect according to the nature of these rights and freedoms and of their correlative obligations, and for instance as to whether the respect due to the right concerned implies positive action or mere abstention.

Thus, the application of Article 14 ECHR does not presuppose a breach of another right or freedom of the Convention: a violation of the non-discrimination clause may be found even if, considered independently from that clause, the provision it is combined with is not violated. Nevertheless, in order for Article 14 ECHR to come into play, it is still required for the discrimination to occur 'within the ambit of' one or more other rights of the Convention. The European Court of Human Rights formulates this restriction by stating that 'Article 14 of the Convention complements the other substantive provisions of the Convention and the Protocols. It has no independent existence since it has effect solely in relation to "the enjoyment of the rights and freedoms" safeguarded by those provisions. Although the application of Article 14 does not presuppose a breach of those provisions – and to this extent it is autonomous –, there can be no room for its application unless the facts at issue fall within the ambit of one or more of the latter' (see, e.g. Eur. Ct. H.R., *Abdulaziz, Cabales and Balkandali* v. *United Kingdom*, 28 May 1985, Series A No. 94, p. 35, §71; Eur. Ct. H.R., *Inze* v. *Austria*, judgment of 28 October 1987, Series A No. 126, p. 17, §36; *Karlheinz Schmidt* v. *Germany*, 18 July 1994, Series A No. 291–B, p. 32, §22; Eur. Ct. H.R., *Van Raalte* v. *Netherlands*, judgment of 21 February 1997, *Reports of Judgments and Decisions* 1997–I, p. 184, §33; Eur. Ct. H.R., *Petrovic* v. *Austria*, 27 March 1998, *Reports of Judgments and Decisions* 1998–II, p. 585, §22; Eur. Ct. HR, *Haas* v. *Netherlands* (Appl. No. 36983/97), judgment of 13 January 2004, §41).

In recent years, this condition has been interpreted as allowing the invocation of Article 14 ECHR in two situations: first, when the alleged discrimination occurs in the enjoyment of a right protected under the European Convention on Human Rights; second, when the discrimination is on a ground which corresponds to the exercise of a right protected under the Convention (see R. Wintemute, '"Within the Ambit": How Big *Is* the "Gap" in Article 14 European Convention on Human Rights?', *European Human Rights Law Review* (2004), 366 at 371). The applicability of Article 14 ECHR to this second type of situation has been affirmed by the European Court of Human Rights for the first time in the 2000 case of *Thlimmenos* v. *Greece*, in which the non-discrimination clause was invoked successfully in combination with Article 9 ECHR by a Jehovah's Witness denied access to the profession of chartered accountant because of a past criminal conviction for having refused to serve in the army for religious motives (Eur. Ct. H.R. (GC), *Thlimmenos* v. *Greece* (Appl. No. 34369/97), judgment of 6 April 2000, §42). But Article 14 ECHR may also be presumed to apply (whichever the nature of the disadvantage inflicted or of the advantage which is denied), for example, where the discrimination penalizes persons for having sought to defend their rights before a court (Art. 6 ECHR), for having chosen a sexual orientation or a particular lifestyle or for being in a particular family status (Art. 8 ECHR), for opinions they have expressed (Art. 10 ECHR), for having joined an association or having refused to join an association (Art. 11 ECHR), or for having married or refused to enter into a marital relationship (Art. 12 ECHR).

Despite these limitations to its scope of application, Article 14 ECHR has been successfully invoked in a wide range of situations involving, for instance, the right to social security benefits considered as part of the right to property (Eur. Ct. H.R., *Gaygusuz* v. *Austria*, judgment of 16 September 1996, *Reports of Judgments and Decisions* 1996–IV, p. 1141; Eur. Ct. H.R. (2nd section), *Koua-Poirrez* v. *France* (Appl. No. 40892/98), judgment of 30 September 2003), or the granting of a parental leave allowance, which the Court links to the enjoyment of the right to respect for private and family life (Eur. Ct. H.R., *Petrovic* v. *Austria* (Appl. No. 20458/92), judgment of 27 March 1998, §§26–7), This extension is not without limits, however. For example, most instances of discrimination in access to employment would not be considered to fall under the scope of application of Article 14 ECHR, although in certain extreme cases where across-the-board prohibitions are imposed, the individual's inability to have access to certain professions may constitute an interference with the right to respect for private life (see Eur. Ct. H.R. (2nd sect.), *Sidabras and Dziautas* v. *Lithuania* (Appl. Nos. 55480/00 and 59330/00), judgment of 27 July 2004, §48). And the European Court of Human Rights has considered that public authorities were not obliged under Article 8 ECHR to take measures in order to facilitate the social or professional integration of persons with disabilities, for instance by ensuring the accessibility of private sea resorts (Eur. Ct. H.R., *Botta* v. *Italy*, judgment of 24 February 1998) or public buildings to persons with limited mobility (Eur. Ct. H.R., *Zehlanova and Zehnal* v. *Czech Republic*, decision of 14 May 2002 (Appl. No. 38621/97)) or by providing them with certain equipment which would diminish their dependency on others (Eur. Ct. H.R., *Sentges* v. *Netherlands*, decision of 8 July 2003 (Appl. No. 27677/02)). The Court concluded that, because Article 8 ECHR was inapplicable in such cases, Article 14 ECHR could not be invoked either.

The restricted scope of application of Article 14 ECHR is partly compensated for by the European Court of Human Rights' recognition that where it attains a certain level of severity, discrimination based on race or ethnic origin (see the report adopted on 14 December 1973 by the Commission under former Art. 31 ECHR in *East African Asians* v. *United Kingdom* (*Decisions and Reports* 78–A, p. 62)), sex (see Eur. Ct. H.R., *Abdulaziz, Cabales and Balkandali* v. *United Kingdom,* Series A No. 94, at p. 42, §91), religion (Eur. Ct. H.R. (GC), *Cyprus* v. *Turkey* (Appl. No. 25781/94), judgment of 10 May 2001, §309) or sexual orientation (Eur. Ct. H.R. (3rd sect.), *Smith and Grady* v. *United Kingdom* (Appl. Nos. 33985/96 and 33986/96), judgment of 27 September 1999, §121) may constitute a degrading treatment prohibited in absolute terms (i.e. without the possibility of justification) under Article 3 ECHR. Despite these qualifications, and the possible further extension in the future of the scope of application of Article 14 ECHR in combination especially with Article 8 ECHR and Article 1 of Protocol No. 1 ECHR, the prohibition of discrimination under the ECHR remains limited to 'the enjoyment of the rights and freedoms' recognized in the ECHR. An additional Protocol No. 12 to the ECHR was drafted in order to extend the discrimination protection in the Convention; the Protocol was opened for signature on 4 November 2000 and entered into force on 1 April 2005. Article 1 of Protocol No. 12 to the ECHR contains a general prohibition of discrimination:

1. The enjoyment of any right set forth by law shall be secured without discrimination on any ground such as sex, race, colour, language, religion, political or other opinion, national or social origin, association with a national minority, property, birth or other status.
2. No one shall be discriminated against by any public authority on any ground such as those mentioned in paragraph 1.

Although Article 1 of Protocol No. 12 to the ECHR concerns only the 'enjoyment of any right set forth by law', the protection from discrimination thus afforded by the Protocol goes beyond that afforded by Article 14 ECHR (see generally, J. Schokkenbroek, 'A New European Standard Against Discrimination: Negotiating Protocol No. 12 to the European Convention on Human Rights' in J. Niessen and Isabelle Chopin (eds.), *The Development of Legal Instruments to Combat Racism in a Diverse Europe* (Leiden: Martinus Nijhoff, 2004), pp. 61–79). Social security matters being covered under Article 1 of Additional Protocol No. 1 to the ECHR since *Gaygusuz*, the areas concerned by this extension shall be, in particular, access to public places, access to goods, provision of services, access to nationality, and in certain cases access to employment. Where the discrimination is based on other grounds than the exercise of rights protected under the ECHR, the European Court of Human Rights might rely on Protocol No. 12 in order to extend its jurisdiction to those situations which, presently, are not covered under Article 14 ECHR.

7.2. **Question for discussion: the role of international courts in implementing the principle of equality**

The Member States of the Council of Europe already are bound by a non-discrimination requirement, whether this follows from an equality clause in their domestic constitutions or from their ratification of the International Covenant on Civil and Political Rights. In this respect, the ratification of Protocol No. 12 to the ECHR essentially amounts to transferring, from the domestic courts to the European Court of Human Rights, the task of assessing whether regulations adopted in areas such as taxation, social security, or land planning, are compatible with the prohibition of discrimination. Is this transfer desirable? Which arguments can be presented in favour of such a transfer?

1.3 The European Social Charter

In contrast to the original version of the European Social Charter, the 1996 revised European Social Charter contains a provision (Art. E) specifically prohibiting discrimination in the enjoyment of the rights recognized by the other substantive provisions of the Charter. In its decision on the merits of Collective Complaint No. 13/2002 directed by the non-governmental organization Autism-Europe against France, the European Committee of Social Rights concluded that France had violated Articles 15 para. 1 (obligation to take the necessary measures to provide persons with disabilities with guidance, education and vocational training in the framework of general schemes whenever possible) and 17 para. 1 (right to education by the provision of institutions and services sufficient and adequate) of the revised ESC, either alone or in combination with Article E (non-discrimination), because the proportion of children with autism being educated in either general or specialist schools is much lower than in the case of other children, whether or not disabled, and because of the chronic shortage of care and support facilities for autistic adults. In adopting that decision, the Committee underlined that 'the insertion of Article E into a separate Article in the Revised Charter indicates the heightened importance the drafters paid to the principle of non-discrimination with respect to the achievement of the various substantive rights contained therein'. It considered that this provision should be read per analogy with Article 14 ECHR – the wording of which it replicates – as protecting from discrimination in the enjoyment of the substantive rights of the Charter, on all grounds not limited to those explicitly enumerated in that provision. This decision is presented below in greater detail (see also, for a comment by the Member of the Committee acting as Rapporteur on the case, G. Quinn, 'The European Social Charter and EU Anti-Discrimination Law in the Field of Disability: Two Gravitational Fields with One Common Purpose' in G. de Búrca and B. de Witte (eds.), *Social Rights in Europe* (Oxford University Press, 2005), p. 279 at pp. 293–99).

1.4 The American Convention on Human Rights

As already noted in box 7.1., the ACHR – in line with the ICCPR – contains two provisions concerning non-discrimination: Article 1(1) provides that States must ensure the enjoyment of the convention rights without discrimination, whereas Article 24 provides for equal treatment before the law. The Inter-American Commission and Court have interpreted these two provisions in roughly the same manner as the UN Human Rights Committee (see also the Inter-American Commission's *Report on the Status of Women in the Americas* of 13 October 1998 [OEA/Ser.L/V/II.100 Doc. 17]).

Inter-American Court of Human Rights, *Proposed Amendments of the Naturalization Provisions of the Constitution of Costa Rica*, Advisory Opinion OC–4/84 of January 19, 1984 [Series A No. 4]:

53. Article 1(1) of the Convention, a rule general in scope which applies to all the provisions of the treaty, imposes on the States Parties the obligation to respect and guarantee the free and full exercise of the rights and freedoms recognized therein 'without any discrimination' ...

54. Article 24 of the Convention, in turn, reads as follows: ... All persons are equal before the law. Consequently, they are entitled, without discrimination, to equal protection of the law. Although Articles 24 and 1(1) are conceptually not identical – the Court may perhaps have occasion at some future date to articulate the differences – Article 24 restates to a certain degree the principle established in Article 1(1). In recognizing equality before the law, it prohibits all discriminatory treatment originating in a legal prescription. The prohibition against discrimination so broadly proclaimed in Article 1(1) with regard to the rights and guarantees enumerated in the Convention thus extends to the domestic law of the States Parties, permitting the conclusion that in these provisions the States Parties, by acceding to the Convention, have undertaken to maintain their laws free of discriminatory regulations.

---

2 THE RANGE OF STATES' OBLIGATIONS

Although it is not explicit in this regard, Article 26 ICCPR in fact contains four separate norms, imposing on the States parties both negative and positive obligations. These obligations are that States shall (1) guarantee equality before the law; (2) guarantee the equal protection of the law; (3) prohibit any discrimination; and (4) guarantee to all persons equal and effective protection against discrimination. This latter obligation may impose on States to adopt positive action measures in situations of structural discrimination, where certain social groups are permanently excluded from integration factors such as employment, housing, or education, so that the prohibition of individual discriminatory acts appears insufficient to protect them effectively from marginalization. Taken together, these four norms have been presented as corresponding to the different stages through which the concept of non-discrimination has made progress (T. Opsahl, 'Equality in Human Rights Law. With Particular Reference to

Article 26 of the International Covenant on Civil and Political Rights' in *Festschrift für Felix Ermacora: Fortschritt im Bewußtsein der Gruhnd- und Menschenrechte* (Kehl am Rhein: N.P. Engel Verlag, 1988), at pp. 51–65). They are examined in turn in the following paragraphs. Each norm is illustrated not only through the Human Rights Committee's jurisprudence, but also through the case law of other bodies applying the same norms, while not necessarily relying on the same typology.

2.1 Equality before the law

This norm is addressed to law enforcement authorities, whether they belong to the executive or to the judiciary. It formulates at a general level a requirement which Article 14(1) ICCPR specifies in the context of judicial procedures, where it states that all persons 'shall be equal before the courts and tribunals'. The following case offers an example:

Human Rights Committee, *Kavanagh* v. *Ireland*, Communication No. 819/1998 (CCPR/C/71/D/819/1998), final views of 4 April 2001:

[Article 38(3) of the Irish Constitution provides for the establishment by law of Special Courts for the trial of offences in cases where it may be determined, according to law, that the ordinary courts are 'inadequate to secure the effective administration of justice and the preservation of public peace and order'. On 26 May 1972, the Government exercised its power to make a proclamation pursuant to section 35(2) of the Offences Against the State Act 1939 which led to the establishment of the Special Criminal Court for the trial of certain offences. By virtue of section 47(1) of the Act, a Special Criminal Court has jurisdiction over a 'scheduled offence' (i.e. an offence specified in a list) where the Attorney General 'thinks proper' that a person so charged should be tried before the Special Criminal Court rather than the ordinary courts. The Special Criminal Court also has jurisdiction over non-scheduled offences where the Attorney General certifies, under section 47(2) of the Act, that in his/her opinion the ordinary courts are 'inadequate to secure the effective administration of justice in relation to the trial of such person on such charge'. The Director of Public Prosecutions (DPP) exercises these powers of the Attorney General by delegated authority. In contrast to the ordinary courts of criminal jurisdiction, which employ juries, Special Criminal Courts consist of three judges who reach a decision by majority vote. The Special Criminal Court also utilizes a different procedure from that of the ordinary criminal courts, including that an accused cannot avail himself/herself of preliminary examination procedures concerning the evidence of certain witnesses.]

10.1 The author claims a violation of article 14, paragraph 1, of the Covenant, in that, by subjecting him to a Special Criminal Court which did not afford him a jury trial and the right to examine witnesses at a preliminary stage, he was not afforded a fair trial. The author accepts that neither jury trial nor preliminary examination is in itself required by the Covenant, and that the absence of either or both of these elements does not necessarily render a trial unfair, but he claims that all of the circumstances of his trial before a Special Criminal Court rendered his trial unfair. In the Committee's view, trial before courts other than the ordinary courts is not necessarily, *per se*, a violation of the entitlement to a fair hearing and the facts of the present case do not show that there has been such a violation.

10.2 The author's claim that there has been a violation of the requirement of equality before the courts and tribunals, contained in article 14, paragraph 1, parallels his claim of violation of his right under article 26 to equality before the law and to the equal protection of the law. The [Director of Public Prosecutions'] decision to charge the author before the Special Criminal Court resulted in the author facing an extra-ordinary trial procedure before an extra-ordinarily constituted court. This distinction deprived the author of certain procedures under domestic law, distinguishing the author from others charged with similar offences in the ordinary courts. Within the jurisdiction of the State party, trial by jury in particular is considered an important protection, generally available to accused persons. Under article 26, the State party is therefore required to demonstrate that such a decision to try a person by another procedure was based upon reasonable and objective grounds. In this regard, the Committee notes that the State party's law, in the Offences Against the State Act, sets out a number of specific offences which can be tried before a Special Criminal Court at the DPP's option. It provides also that any other offence may be tried before a Special Criminal Court if the DPP is of the view that the ordinary courts are 'inadequate to secure the effective administration of justice'. The Committee regards it as problematic that, even assuming that a truncated criminal system for certain serious offences is acceptable so long as it is fair, Parliament through legislation set out specific serious offences that were to come within the Special Criminal Court's jurisdiction in the DPP's unfettered discretion ('thinks proper'), and goes on to allow, as in the author's case, any other offences also to be so tried if the DPP considers the ordinary courts inadequate. No reasons are required to be given for the decisions that the Special Criminal Court would be 'proper', or that the ordinary courts are 'inadequate', and no reasons for the decision in the particular case have been provided to the Committee. Moreover, judicial review of the DPP's decisions is effectively restricted to the most exceptional and virtually undemonstrable circumstances.

10.3 The Committee considers that the State party has failed to demonstrate that the decision to try the author before the Special Criminal Court was based upon reasonable and objective grounds. Accordingly, the Committee concludes that the author's right under article 26 to equality before the law and to the equal protection of the law has been violated. In view of this finding with regard to article 26, it is unnecessary in this case to examine the issue of violation of equality 'before the courts and tribunals' contained in article 14, paragraph 1, of the Covenant.

This first implication of Article 26 ICCPR, if read extensively, could have the potential of requiring that any individual decision adopted by the public authorities be justified, since in the absence of such a justification it might be denounced as arbitrary and, thus, discriminatory. Consider the following case:

Human Rights Committee, *Robert W. Gauthier* v. *Canada*, Communication No. 633/1995 (CCPR/C/65/D/633/1995), final views of 5 May 1999:

[Mr Gauthier is the publisher of the National Capital News, a newspaper founded in 1982. He applied for membership in the Parliamentary Press Gallery, a private association that administers the accreditation for access to the precincts of Parliament, but was denied permanent membership. He was provided instead with a temporary pass that gave only limited privileges. Repeated requests for equal access on the same terms as other reporters and publishers were denied. In his communication to the Committee, he claims that the denial of equal access to press facilities in Parliament constitutes a violation of his rights under Article 19 of the Covenant. Since, in its admissibility decision of 10 July 1997, the Committee considered that the case could also raise a question under Articles 22 (freedom of association) and 26 (non-discrimination) of the Covenant, the author subsequently commented under that provision that the difference in treatment between him and journalist members of the Press Gallery was unreasonable, and that he had been arbitrarily denied equal access to media facilities. Although he accepts that the State party may limit access to press facilities in Parliament, he submits that such limits must not be unduly restraining, must be administered fairly, must not infringe on any person's right to freedom of expression and the right to seek and receive information, and must be subject to review.]

13.2 With regard to the author's claims under articles 22 and 26 of the Covenant, the Committee ... considers that the author had not substantiated, for purposes of admissibility, his claim under the said articles. Nor has he further substantiated it, for the same purposes, with his further submissions. In these circumstances, the Committee concludes that the author's communication is inadmissible under article 2 of the Optional Protocol, as far as it relates to articles 22 and 26 of the Covenant. In this regard, the admissibility decision is therefore repealed.

13.3 The issue before the Committee is thus whether the restriction of the author's access to the press facilities in Parliament amounts to a violation of his right under article 19 of the Covenant, to seek, receive and impart information.

13.4 In this connection, the Committee also refers to the right to take part in the conduct of public affairs, as laid down in article 25 of the Covenant, and in particular to General Comment No. 25 (57) which reads in part: 'In order to ensure the full enjoyment of rights protected by article 25, the free communication of information and ideas about public and political issues between citizens, candidates and elected representatives is essential. This implies a free press and other media able to comment on public issues without censorship or restraint and to inform public opinion.' [General Comment No. 25, para. 25, adopted by the Committee on 12 July 1996.] Read together with article 19, this implies that citizens, in particular through the media, should have wide access to information and the opportunity to disseminate information and opinions about the activities of elected bodies and their members. The Committee recognizes, however, that such access should not interfere with or obstruct the carrying out of the functions of elected bodies, and that a State party is thus entitled to limit access. However, any restrictions imposed by the State party must be compatible with the provisions of the Covenant.

13.5 In the present case, the State party has restricted the right to enjoy the publicly funded media facilities of Parliament, including the right to take notes when observing meetings of Parliament, to those media representatives who are members of a private organisation, the Canadian Press Gallery. The author has been denied active (i.e. full) membership of the Press Gallery. On occasion he has held temporary membership which has given him access to some but not all facilities of the organisation. When he does not hold at least temporary membership he does not have access to the media facilities nor can he take notes of Parliamentary proceedings.

The Committee notes that the State party has claimed that the author does not suffer any significant disadvantage because of technological advances which make information about Parliamentary proceedings readily available to the public. The State party argues that he can report on proceedings by relying on broadcasting services, or by observing the proceedings. In view of the importance of access to information about the democratic process, however, the Committee does not accept the State party's argument and is of the opinion that the author's exclusion constitutes a restriction of his right guaranteed under paragraph 2 of article 19 to have access to information. The question is whether or not this restriction is justified under paragraph 3 of article 19. The restricion is, arguably, imposed by law, in that the exclusion of persons from the precinct of Parliament or any part thereof, under the authority of the Speaker, follows from the law of parliamentary privilege.

13.6 The State party argues that the restrictions are justified to achieve a balance between the right to freedom of expresssion and the need to ensure both the effective and dignified operation of Parliament and the safety and security of its members, and that the State party is in the best position to assess the risks and needs involved. As indicated above, the Committee agrees that the protection of Parliamentary procedure can be seen as a legitimate goal of public order and an accreditation system can thus be a justified means of achieving this goal. However, since the accreditation system operates as a restriction of article 19 rights, its operation and application must be shown as necessary and proportionate to the goal in question and not arbitrary. The Committee does not accept that this is a matter exclusively for the State to determine. The relevant criteria for the accreditation scheme should be specific, fair and reasonable, and their application should be transparent. In the instant case, the State party has allowed a private organization to control access to the Parliamentary press facilities, without intervention. The scheme does not ensure that there will be no arbitrary exclusion from access to the Parliamentary media facilities. In the circumstances, the Committee is of the opinion that the accreditation system has not been shown to be a necessary and proportionate restriction of rights within the meaning of article 19, paragraph 3, of the Covenant, in order to ensure the effective operation of Parliament and the safety of its members. The denial of access to the author to the press facilities of Parliament for not being a member of the Canadian Press Gallery Association constitutes therefore a violation of article 19(2) of the Covenant.

13.7 In this connection, the Committee notes that there is no possibility of recourse, either to the Courts or to Parliament, to determine the legality of the exclusion or its necessity for the purposes spelled out in article 19 of the Covenant. The Committee recalls that under article 2, paragraph 3 of the Covenant, States parties have undertaken to ensure that any person whose rights are violated shall have an effective remedy, and that any person claiming such a remedy shall have his right thereto determined by competent authorities. Accordingly, whenever a right recognized by the Covenant is affected by the action of a State agent there must be a procedure established by the State allowing the person whose right has been affected to claim before a competent body that there has been a violation of his rights.

14. The Human Rights Committee, acting under article 5, paragraph 4, of the Optional Protocol to the International Covenant on Civil and Political rights, is of the view that the facts before it disclose a violation of article 19, paragraph 2, of the Covenant.

Individual opinion by members Lord Colville, Elizabeth Evatt, Ms Cecilia Medina Quiroga and Mr Hipólito Solari Yrigoyen (partly dissenting) [A virtually identical position was adopted in his individual opinion (partly dissenting) by Committee member Prafullachandra N. Bhagwati. Therefore five members of the Committee in total were of the opinion that Article 26 ICCPR had been violated in this case.]

In regard to paragraph 13.2 of the Committee's Views, our opinion is that the claims of the author under articles 22 and 26 of the Covenant have been sufficiently substantiated and that there is no basis to [consider these claims as non-admissible].

Article 26 of the Covenant stipulates that all persons are equal before the law. Equality implies that the application of laws and regulations as well as administrative decisions by Government officials should not be arbitrary but should be based on clear coherent grounds, ensuring equality of treatment. To deny the author, who is a journalist and seeks to report on parliamentary proceedings, access to the Parliamentary press facilities without specifically identifying the reasons, was arbitrary. Furthermore, there was no procedure for review. In the circumstances, we are of the opinion that the principle of equality before the law protected by article 26 of the Covenant was violated in the author's case.

In regard to article 22, the author's claim is that requiring membership in the Press Gallery Association as a condition of access to the Parliamentary press facilities violated his rights under article 22. The right to freedom of association implies that in general no one may be forced by the State to join an association. When membership of an association is a requirement to engage in a particular profession or calling, or when sanctions exist on the failure to be a member of an association, the State party should be called on to show that compulsory membership is necessary in a democratic society in pursuit of an interest authorised by the Covenant. In this matter, the Committee's deliberations in paragraph 13.6 of the Views make it clear that the State party has failed to show that the requirement to be a member of a particular organisation is a necessary restriction under paragraph 2 of article 22 in order to limit access to the press gallery in Parliament for the purposes mentioned. The restrictions imposed on the author are therefore in violation of article 22 of the Covenant.

Individual opinion by Committee member David Kretzmer (partly dissenting)

I do not share their view that a violation of article 26 has also been substantiated. In my mind, it is not sufficient, in order to substantiate a violation of article 26, merely to state that no reasons were given for a decision. Furthermore, it seems to me that the author's claim under article 26 is in essence a restatement of his claim under article 19. It amounts to the argument that while others were allowed access to the Press Gallery, the author was denied access. Accepting that this constitutes a violation of article 26 would seem to imply that in almost every case in which one individual's rights under other articles of the Covenant are violated, there will also be a violation of article 26. I therefore join the Committee in the view that the author's claim of a violation of article 26 has not been substantiated. The Committee's decision on admissibility should be revised and the claim under article 26 be held inadmissible.

The result that, as expressed in his dissent, Mr D. Kretzmer wanted to avoid was firmly established under the case law of the Inter-American Court of Human Rights, as ever since the *Velasquez-Rodriguez* case, the Court has found that a violation of any substantive right in the ACHR entails a violation of Article 1(1), the obligation to respect and ensure rights without discrimination (IACtHR, case of *Velasquez-Rodriguez* v. *Honduras*, decision on the merits of 29 July 1988, Series C-04, paras. 162–88).

However, the question of equality before the law has also been addressed explicitly within the ACHR. The Inter-American System has long held that the impartiality and non-discriminatory character of judicial decisions are fundamental requirements of the right to justice (Arts. 8 and 25, combined, read with Art. 1(1)). This issue was raised in the following Advisory Opinion, in which the Court suggests that the prohibition of arbitrary treatment by judicial authorities may require positive measures be taken to counterbalance the vulnerability of the situation of certain criminal defendants.

Inter-American Court of Human Rights, *The Right to Information on Consular Assistance in the Framework of the Guarantees of the Due Process of Law*, Advisory Opinion OC–16/99 of 1 October 1999 (Series A No. 16):

[Mexico had requested an Advisory Opinion by the Court on the issue of whether the 'right to consular assistance' established by Article 36 of the Vienna Convention on Consular Relations of 1963 (596 U.N.T.S. 261) was to be considered an element of the 'due process' guarantees established by both the American Convention and Declaration on Human Rights. This opinion predates the landmark judgment delivered on 27 June 2001 by the International Court of Justice (ICJ) in the *LaGrand* case *(Germany v. United States)*, in which the ICJ held that the Vienna Convention grants rights to individuals on the basis of its plain meaning, and that domestic laws may not limit the rights of the accused under the Convention, but only specify the means by which those rights were to be exercised. Mexico and other States were concerned about the validity of convictions of their nationals involving the use of the death penalty.]

117. In the opinion of this Court, for 'the due process of law' a defendant must be able to exercise his rights and defend his interests effectively and in full procedural equality with other defendants. It is important to recall that the judicial process is a means to ensure, insofar as possible, an equitable resolution of a difference. The body of procedures, of diverse character and generally grouped under the heading of the due process, is all calculated to serve that end. To protect the individual and see justice done, the historical development of the judicial process has introduced new procedural rights. An example of the evolutive nature of judicial process are the rights not to incriminate oneself and to have an attorney present when one speaks. These two rights are already part of the laws and jurisprudence of the more advanced legal systems. And so, the body of judicial guarantees given in Article 14 of the International Covenant on Civil and Political Rights has evolved gradually. It is a body of judicial guarantees to which others of the same character, conferred by various instruments of international law, can and should be added ...

119. To accomplish its objectives, the judicial process must recognize and correct any real disadvantages that those brought before the bar might have, thus observing the principle of equality before the law and the courts and the corollary principle prohibiting discrimination. The presence of real disadvantages necessitates countervailing measures that help to reduce or eliminate the obstacles and deficiencies that impair or diminish an effective defense of one's interests. Absent those countervailing measures, widely recognized in various stages of the proceeding, one could hardly say that those who have the disadvantages enjoy a true opportunity for justice and the benefit of the due process of law equal to those who do not have those disadvantages ...

121. In the case to which this Advisory Opinion refers, the real situation of the foreign nationals facing criminal proceedings must be considered. Their most precious juridical rights, perhaps even their lives, hang in the balance. In such circumstances, it is obvious that notification of one's right to contact the consular agent of one's country will considerably enhance one's chances of defending oneself and the proceedings conducted in the respective cases, including the police investigations, are more likely to be carried out in accord with the law and with respect for the dignity of the human person ...

123. The inclusion of this right in the Vienna Convention on Consular Relations – and the discussions that took place as it was being drafted – are evidence of a shared understanding that the right to information on consular assistance is a means for the defense of the accused that has repercussions – sometimes decisive repercussions – on enforcement of the accused' other procedural rights.

124. In other words, the individual's right to information, conferred in Article 36(1)(b) of the Vienna Convention on Consular Relations, makes it possible for the right to the due process of law upheld in Article 14 of the International Covenant on Civil and Political Rights, to have practical effects in tangible cases; the minimum guarantees established in Article 14 of the International Covenant can be amplified in the light of other international instruments like the Vienna Convention on Consular Relations, which broadens the scope of the protection afforded to those accused.

Another illustration of the requirement of equality before the law is provided by the judgment adopted by the UK House of Lords in a case concerning the screening of Roma at Prague Airport by British immigration officers. These officers were temporarily posted to Prague Airport to 'pre-clear' all passengers before they boarded flights for the United Kingdom, in accordance with an agreement concluded in February 2001 between the Czech Republic and the United Kingdom. While most of the argument in this case was about the applicability to such a situation – where potential asylum-seekers have not left their national territory – of the 1951 Geneva Convention on the Status of Refugees, the excerpts presented here concern the allegation that the Roma seeking to leave Prague were victims of discrimination.

House of Lords (United Kingdom), *R. v. Immigration Officer at Prague Airport and another (Respondents), ex parte European Roma Rights Centre and others (Appellants)* [2004] UKHL 55

Leading judgment, Lord Bingham of Cornhill

1. At issue in this appeal is the lawfulness of procedures adopted by the British authorities and applied to the six individual appellants at Prague Airport in July 2001. All these appellants are Czech nationals of Romani ethnic origin ('Roma'). All required leave to enter the United Kingdom. All were refused it by British immigration officers temporarily stationed at Prague Airport. Three of these appellants stated that they intended to claim asylum on arrival in the UK. Two gave other reasons for wishing to visit the UK but were in fact intending to claim asylum on

arrival. One (HM) gave a reason for wishing to visit the UK which the immigration officer did not accept: she may have been intending to claim asylum on arrival in the UK or she may not. The individual appellants, with the first-named appellant ('the [European Roma Rights] Centre' (ERRC), a non-governmental organisation, based in Budapest, devoted to protection of the rights of Roma in Europe), challenge the procedures applied to the individual appellants as incompatible with the obligations of the UK under the Geneva Convention (1951) and Protocol (1967) relating to the Status of Refugees and under customary international law. They also challenge the procedures as involving unjustifiable discrimination on racial grounds.

[On the question of whether the treatment of the Roma seeking to embark for the United Kingdom at Prague Airport was discrimination, the leading judgment refers to the other opinions expressed by the Lords. Excerpts follow:]

Lord Steyn

32. In this appeal many significant issues have been debated. But surely the most important issue is whether the operation mounted by immigration officers at Prague Airport under the authority of the Home Secretary in 2001 and 2002 discriminated against Roma on grounds of their race. It is unlawful for public authorities, such as the Home Secretary and an immigration officer, to discriminate on racial grounds in carrying out any of their functions. The appellants put forward a case of direct discrimination on the grounds of race under the Race Relations Act 1976. The Home Secretary and the immigration officers strenuously denied that any discrimination had taken place. Mr Howell, who appeared on behalf of the Home Secretary and the immigration officer, invited the House of Lords to regard the allegations as very serious. He submitted that the case of the appellants should be viewed with an initial scepticism that the United Kingdom could have put in place a system of discrimination on the grounds of race. That is how I will approach the matter.

33. The operation at Prague Airport is unique in the history of the immigration service. It was the first time such a procedure had been undertaken. And it has not been repeated. But the decision of the House transcends the particular circumstances of the case: it has implications for the responsibility of government not only for immigration policy but also for race relations policy generally.

34. The essential features of the operation can be stated quite simply. It was designed as a response to an influx of Czech Roma into the United Kingdom. The immigration officers knew that the reason why they were stationed in Prague was to stop asylum seekers travelling to the United Kingdom. They also knew that almost all Czech asylum seekers were Roma, because the Roma are a disadvantaged racial minority in the Czech Republic. Thus there was from the outset a high risk that individuals recognised as Roma would be targeted by specially intrusive and sceptical questioning. There was a striking difference in treatment of Roma and non-Roma at the hands of immigration officers operating at Prague Airport. The statistics show that almost 90% of Roma were refused leave to enter and only 0.2% of non-Roma were refused leave to enter. Roma were 400 times more likely than non-Roma to be refused permission. No attempt was made by the Home Office to explain by the evidence of immigration officers the difference in treatment of Roma and non-Roma. Although the Home Office was from the beginning on notice of the high risk of discrimination on grounds of race, no attempt was made to guard against discrimination.

35. New documents rightly produced by the Home Office during the hearing of the appeal are revealing. One extract is sufficient to show what immigration officers must have understood their functions at Prague Airport to involve: 'The fact that a passenger belongs to one of these ethnic or national groups will be sufficient to justify discrimination – without reference to additional statistical or intelligence information – if an immigration officer considers such discrimination is warranted.'

The immigration officers would have read this document in the light of a formal authorisation by the Secretary of State under section 19D of the Race Relations Act 1976. That authorisation purported to confer on immigration officers the express power to discriminate by reason of a person's ethnic origin against Roma. It is true that the Secretary of State does not rely on the authorisation. But it would have been known to immigration officers sent to Prague. Counsel for the Secretary of State argued that the authorisation was not in law an instruction. I would accept that. But the documents nevertheless reveal how immigration officers would have understood their principal task.

36. Following the principles affirmed by the House of Lords in *Nagarajan* v. *London Regional Transport* [2000] 1 AC 501, there is in law a single issue: why did the immigration officers treat Roma less favourably than non-Roma? In my view the only realistic answer is that they did so because the persons concerned were Roma. They discriminated on the grounds of race. The motive for such discrimination is irrelevant: *Nagarajan* v. *London Regional Transport, supra.*

37. The reasoning of the majority of the Court of Appeal in this case had at first glance the attractiveness of appearing to be in accord with common sense: *R. (European Roma Rights Centre)* v. *Immigration Officer at Prague Airport* [2004] QB 811. Simon Brown LJ said (para 86, 840): 'because of the greater degree of scepticism with which Roma applicants will inevitably be treated, they are more likely to be refused leave to enter than non-Roma applicants. But this is because they are less well placed to persuade the immigration office that they are not lying in order to seek asylum. That is not to say, however, that they are being stereotyped. Rather it is to acknowledge the undoubtedly disadvantaged position of many Roma in the Czech Republic. Of course it would be wrong in any individual case to assume that the Roma applicant is lying, but I decline to hold that the immigration officer cannot properly be warier of that possibility in a Roma's case than in the case of a non-Roma applicant. If a terrorist outrage were committed on our streets today, would the police not be entitled to question more suspiciously those in the vicinity appearing to come from an Islamic background?'

Mantell LJ agreed with this analysis. Laws LJ dissented. In 'Equality: The Neglected Virtue' [2004] EHRLR 142, Mr Rabinder Singh QC convincingly exposed the flaw in the reasoning of the majority. He stated (at p 154): 'It is clear that there was less favourable treatment. It is also clear that it was on racial grounds. As all the judges acknowledged, the reason for the discrimination is immaterial: in particular, the absence of a hostile intent or the presence of a benign motive is immaterial. What the majority view amounts to is, on analysis, an attempt to introduce into the law of direct discrimination the possibility of justification. But Parliament could have provided for that possibility – as it has done in the context of allegations of indirect discrimination – and has chosen not to do so. In so far as the fields of immigration and nationality may be thought to require special treatment, permitting discrimination on certain grounds (ethnic or national origins) but not others (such as colour), again Parliament has catered for that possibility in enabling a minister to give an authorisation. The Government did not want to rely on the authorisation in the Roma case: that was a matter for its tactical choice but the courts should not bend over backwards to save the executive from what may have been its own folly. Their duty, as Laws LJ said, is to apply the will of Parliament as enacted in its laws. Moreover, the danger in the majority's reasoning is that it is capable of application outside the limited areas with which the Court was concerned. For example, it could be applied in the context of police stop and search powers. Simon Brown LJ expressly gives an example from just that context. This is potentially very damaging to race relations law going beyond what may have been perceived to be the problem in the Roma case itself.'

I am in respectful agreement with this analysis. In my view the majority was wrong. Laws LJ was right.

38. I agree with the conclusion of Baroness Hale of Richmond that the system operated by immigration officers at Prague Airport was inherently and systemically discriminatory on racial grounds against Roma, contrary to section 1(1)(a) of the Race Relations Act.

Baroness Hale of Richmond
72. [The] issue is whether the operation at Prague Airport was carried out in an unlawfully discriminatory manner, in that would-be travellers of Roma origin were treated less favourably than non-Roma were. In particular, it is alleged that they were subjected to longer and more intrusive questioning, they were required to provide proof of matters which were taken on trust from non-Roma, and far more of them were refused leave to enter than were non-Roma. The appellants seek a declaration to that effect.

73. Since 1968, it has been unlawful for providers of employment, education, housing, goods and other services to discriminate against individuals on racial grounds. The current law is contained in the Race Relations Act 1976, which in most respects is parallel to the Sex Discrimination Act 1975. The principles are well known and simple enough to state although they may be difficult to apply in practice. The underlying concept in both race and sex discrimination laws is that individuals of each sex and all races are entitled to be treated equally. Thus it is just as discriminatory to treat men less favourably than women as it is to treat women less favourably than men; and it is just as discriminatory to treat whites less favourably than blacks as it is to treat blacks less favourably than whites. The ingredients of unlawful discrimination are (i) a difference in treatment between one person and another person (real or hypothetical) from a different sex or racial group; (ii) that the treatment is less favourable to one; (iii) that their relevant circumstances are the same or not materially different; and (iv) that the difference in treatment is on sex or racial grounds. However, because people rarely advertise their prejudices and may not even be aware of them, discrimination has normally to be proved by inference rather than direct evidence. Once treatment less favourable than that of a comparable person (ingredients (i), (ii) and (iii)) is shown, the court will look to the alleged discriminator for an explanation. The explanation must, of course, be unrelated to the race or sex of the complainant. If there is no, or no satisfactory explanation, it is legitimate to infer that the less favourable treatment was on racial grounds: see *Glasgow City Council* v. *Zafar* [1997] 1 WLR 1659, approving *King* v. *Great Britain-China Centre* [1992] ICR 516. If the difference is on racial grounds, the reasons or motive behind it are irrelevant: see, for example, *Nagarajan* v. *London Regional Transport* [2000] 1 AC 501.

74. If direct discrimination of this sort is shown, that is that. Save for some very limited exceptions, there is no defence of objective justification. The whole point of the law is to require

suppliers to treat each person as an individual, not as a member of a group. The individual should not be assumed to hold the characteristics which the supplier associates with the group, whether or not most members of the group do indeed have such characteristics, a process sometimes referred to as stereotyping. Even if, for example, most women are less strong than most men, it must not be assumed that the individual woman who has applied for the job does not have the strength to do it. Nor, for that matter, should it be assumed that an individual man does have that strength. If strength is a qualification, all applicants should be required to demonstrate that they qualify.

75. The complaint in this case is of direct discrimination against the Roma. Indirect discrimination arises where an employer or supplier treats everyone in the same way, but he applies to them all a requirement or condition which members of one sex or racial group are much less likely to be able to meet than members of another: for example, a test of heavy lifting which men would be much more likely to pass than women. This is only unlawful if the requirement is one which cannot be justified independently of the sex or race of those involved; in the example given, this would depend upon whether the job did or did not require heavy lifting. But it is the requirement or condition that may be justified, not the discrimination. This sort of justification should not be confused with the possibility that there may be an objective justification for discriminatory treatment which would otherwise fall foul of article 14 of the European Convention on Human Rights.

76. Discrimination law has always applied to public authority providers of employment, education and housing, and other services, as long as these services are of a similar kind to those which may be supplied by private persons. But a majority of this House held, in *R* v. *Entry Clearance Officer, Bombay, Ex p Amin* [1983] 2 AC 818, that it did not apply to acts done on behalf of the Crown which were of an entirely different kind from any act that would ever be done by a private person, in that case to the application of immigration controls. This is still the case for sex discrimination, but the race discrimination law was changed in response to the Macpherson Report into the Stephen Lawrence case. It is now unlawful for a public authority to discriminate on racial grounds in carrying out any of its functions. There are, however, a few exceptions and qualifications, one of which [insofar as it relates to the carrying out of immigration and nationality functions] is relevant to this case ...

78. The effect [of the said exception] is to exempt an immigration officer from the requirement not to discriminate if he was acting under a relevant authorisation, that is a requirement or express authorisation given by a Minister of the Crown acting personally (or by the law itself, but that does not arise here). Shortly before the Prague operation began on 18 July 2001, the Minister had made the Race Relations (Immigration and Asylum) (No 2) Authorisation 2001, which came into force in April 2001, at the same time as the 2000 Act amendments. [This Authorisation allowed for the screening of people of Roma origin.] ...

80. When these proceedings were begun on 18 October 2001, the claimants assumed that the immigration officers in Prague were operating under this Authorisation. The claim form therefore attacked the validity of the Authorisation. However, it is and has always been the respondents' case that the Authorisation did not apply to the Prague operation. Their case is not that the officers were discriminating lawfully but that they were not discriminating at all. Burton J accepted that they were not. Some individual differences in treatment were explicable, not by ethnic difference, but by more suspicious behaviour. There were too few instances of inexplicable differences in treatment to justify a general conclusion. The difference between the proportion

of Roma and non-Roma refused entry was explicable by reference to the proportions of Roma and non-Roma who were likely to seek asylum.

81. The Court of Appeal accepted that the judge was entitled to find that the immigration officers tried to give both Roma and non-Roma a fair and equal opportunity to satisfy them that they were coming to the United Kingdom for a permitted purpose and not to claim asylum once here. But they considered it 'wholly inevitable' that, being aware that Roma have a much greater incentive to claim asylum and that the vast majority, if not all, of those seeking asylum from the Czech Republic are Roma, immigration officers will treat their answers with greater scepticism, will be less easily persuaded that they are coming for a permitted purpose, and that 'generally, therefore, Roma are questioned for longer and more intensively than non-Roma and are more likely to be refused leave to enter than non-Roma' (Simon Brown LJ, paras 66–67). Laws LJ referred to the last of these propositions as 'plainly true on the facts of this case' (para 102). Simon Brown LJ, with whom Mantell LJ agreed, held that nevertheless this was not less favourable treatment, or if it was, it was not on racial grounds. The Roma were not being treated differently qua Roma but qua potential asylum-seekers. Laws LJ considered it 'inescapable' that this was less favourable treatment (para 102). He also concluded (para 109) that this was discrimination:

'One asks Lord Steyn's question [in *Nagarajan* v. *London Regional Transport* [2000] 1 A.C. 501, 521–2]: why did he treat the Roma less favourably? It may be said that there are two possible answers: (1) because he is Roma; (2) because he is more likely to be advancing a false application for leave to enter as a visitor. But it seems to me inescapable that the reality is that the officer treated the Roma less favourably because Roma are (for very well understood reasons) more likely to wish to seek asylum and thus, more likely to put forward a false claim to enter as a visitor. The officer has applied a stereotype; though one which may very likely be true. That is not permissible. More pointedly, he has an entirely proper reason (or motive) for treating the Roma less favourably on racial grounds: his duty to refuse those without a claim under the Rules, manifestly including covert asylum-seekers, and his knowledge that the Roma is more likely to be a covert asylum-seeker. But that is irrelevant to the claim under s 1(1)(a) of the 1976 Act.'

82. On the factual premises adopted by the Court of Appeal, this conclusion must be correct as a matter of law. The Roma were being treated more sceptically than the non-Roma. There was a good reason for this. How did the immigration officers know to treat them more sceptically? Because they were Roma. That is acting on racial grounds. If a person acts on racial grounds, the reason why he does so is irrelevant: see Lord Nicholls of Birkenhead in *Nagarajan* at p 511. The law reports are full of examples of obviously discriminatory treatment which was in no way motivated by racism or sexism and often brought about by pressures beyond the discriminators' control: the council which sacked a black road sweeper to whom the union objected in order to avoid industrial action (*R* v. *Commission for Racial Equality, Ex p Westminster City Council* [1985] ICR 827); the council which for historical reasons provided fewer selective school places for girls than for boys (*R* v. *Birmingham City Council, Ex p Equal Opportunities Commission* [1989] AC 1155). But it goes further than this. The person may be acting on belief or assumptions about members of the sex or racial group involved which are often true and which if true would provide a good reason for the less favourable treatment in question. But 'what may be true of a group may not be true of a significant number of individuals within that group' (see Hartmann J in *Equal Opportunities Commission* v. *Director of Education* [2001] 2 HKLRD 690, para 86, High

Court of Hong Kong). The object of the legislation is to ensure that each person is treated as an individual and not assumed to be like other members of the group. As Laws LJ observed, at para 108: 'The mistake that might arise in relation to stereotyping would be a supposition that the stereotype is only vicious if it is untrue. But that cannot be right. If it were, it would imply that direct discrimination can be justified ...'

83. As we have seen, the legislation draws a clear distinction between direct and indirect discrimination and makes no reference at all to justification in relation to direct discrimination. Nor, strictly, does it allow indirect discrimination to be justified. It accepts that a requirement or condition may be justified independently of its discriminatory effect.

84. The question for us, therefore, is whether the factual premise is made out. The appellants mount essentially the same argument before us as they did before both Burton J and the Court of Appeal. But, greatly to their credit, the respondents have made a further search and produced further evidence which casts a rather different light upon the case than was cast by their evidence in the courts below.

85. The appellants' case is, first, that the Prague operation carried with it a very high risk of racial discrimination. Its avowed object was to prevent people travelling from the Czech Republic to this country in order to seek asylum or otherwise overstay the limits of their leave to be here. The vast majority of those who have done this in the past are Roma. Many Roma have good reason to want to leave. For some, this may amount to persecution within the meaning of the Refugee Convention. The operation was targeting all potential asylum seekers, with or without a good claim. The object was not only to prevent the would-be travellers at the airport. It was also to deter others from even getting that far. Given the high degree of congruence between the object of the exercise and a particular ethnic group, which was recognised in public statements by the Czech Prime Minister and his deputy, the risk that the operation would be carried out in a racially discriminatory manner was very high.

86. That risk was exacerbated by the very existence of the Authorisation. This sanctioned discriminatory treatment of the very ethnic group to which the vast majority of the people against whom the Prague operation was targeted belonged. The evidence is that the immigration authorities responsible for the operation did not intend the officers in Prague to act on the Authorisation: its main object was to speed up processing at ports of entry to the United Kingdom when particular problems arose. So there was no instruction to the Prague officers to implement it. Nor do the records of individual cases give any indication that the officers thought that they were operating it. But the Authorisation was annexed to the Immigration Directorate's Instructions, chapter 1, section 11 of which is headed 'Race Relations (General)'. This seeks to explain the effect of this Authorisation, dealing with discrimination on grounds of ethnic or national origin, and an earlier one, which authorised discrimination on grounds of nationality if there was statistical or intelligence information of breach of immigration laws by persons of that nationality. Having set out the various ways in which officers might discriminate under either Authorisation, it contains the following passage about the later one with which we are concerned: 'The fact that a passenger belongs to one of these ethnic or national groups will be sufficient to justify discrimination – without reference to additional statistical or intelligence information – if an immigration officer considers such discrimination is warranted.'

87. This is under the heading of 'Examination of passengers', which relates to people arriving at UK ports of entry; but under the heading 'Persons wishing to travel to the UK' the following

passage appears: 'From May 2001, immigration officers may also discriminate in similar ways in relation to persons wishing to travel to the UK on the grounds of ethnic or national origin but only in relation to the groups listed ... Additional statistical or intelligence evidence is not required as Ministers authorised the discrimination in respect of the listed groups.'

88. Also available now are the slides and accompanying briefing for the training which all staff received on the 2000 Act and the Ministerial Authorisations under it. These stress the importance of the Authorisations to the work of the Department, point out that discrimination against the listed groups is permissible without statistical or intelligence information, and advise of the need to be familiar with the list, to be able to identify passengers belonging to those groups, and to use their experience, knowledge of groups and local intelligence to assist in identification. They do point out that 'discrimination is likely to be exercised primarily in relation to specific port exercises', but do not suggest that these are the only circumstances in which it can be done. The briefing stresses that 'personnel need to be alert to the ways in which the integrity of the control function might be detrimentally affected if staff chose to disengage by not subjecting certain people/groups to extra scrutiny where appropriate.'

89. The combination of the objective of the whole Prague operation and a very recent ministerial authorisation of discrimination against Roma was, it is suggested, to create such a high risk that the Prague officers would consciously or unconsciously treat Roma less favourably than others that very specific instructions were needed to counteract this. Officers should have been told that the Directorate did not regard the operation as one which was covered by the Authorisation. They should therefore have been given careful instructions in how to treat all would-be passengers in the same way, only subjecting them to more intrusive questioning if there was specific reason to suspect their intentions from the answers they had given to standard questions which were put to everyone.

90. It is worth remembering that good equal opportunities practice may not come naturally. Many will think it contrary to common sense to approach all applicants with an equally open mind, irrespective of the very good reasons there may be to suspect some of them more than others. But that is what is required by a law which tries to ensure that individuals are not disadvantaged by the general characteristics of the group to which they belong. In 2001, when the operation with which we are concerned began, the race relations legislation had only just been extended to cover the activities of the immigration service. It would scarcely be surprising if officers acting under considerable pressure of time found it difficult to conform in all respects to procedures and expectations which employers have been struggling to get right for more than quarter of a century.

91. It is against this background that such evidence as there is of what happened on the ground at Prague Airport needs to be assessed. The officers did not make any record of the ethnic origin of the people they interviewed. The respondents cannot therefore provide us with figures of how many from each group were interviewed, for how long, and with what result. This, they suggest, makes it clear that the officers were not relying on the Authorisation: if they had been, they would only have had to record their view of the passenger's ethnicity. If correct, that would have been enough to justify refusal of leave. But what it also shows is that no formal steps were being taken to gather the information which might have helped ensure that this high-risk operation was not being conducted in a discriminatory manner. It also means that the only information available is that supplied by the claimants, and in particular the ERRC which was

attempting to monitor the operation. The respondents can cast doubt on the reliability of this, but they cannot contradict it or provide more reliable information themselves. Indeed the figures gathered were used by both sides before Burton J as a 'useful working basis' (Judgment, para 27).

92. Mr Vasil, a Czech Roma working for the ERRC, observed most flights leaving for the UK on 11 days in January, 13 days in February, 14 days in March and 13 days in April 2002. He was able to identify the Roma travellers by their physical appearance, manner of dress and other details which were recognisable to him as a Roma himself. His observations showed that 68 out of 78 Roma were turned away whereas only 14 out of 6170 non-Roma were rejected. Thus any individual Roma was 400 times more likely to be rejected than any individual non-Roma. The great majority of Roma were rejected. And only a tiny minority of non-Roma were rejected. It is, of course, entirely unsurprising that a far higher proportion of Roma were turned away. But if the officers began their work with a genuinely open mind, it is more surprising that so many of the Roma were refused. If all or almost all asylum seekers are Roma, it does not follow that all or almost all Roma are asylum seekers. It is even more surprising that so few of the non-Roma were refused. One might have expected that there would be more among them whose reasons for wanting to travel to the UK were also worthy of suspicion. The apparent ease with which non-Roma were accepted is quite consistent with the emphasis given in the Instructions and training materials to the sensible targeting of resources at busy times. The respondents have not put forward any positive explanation for the discrepancy.

93. Mr Vasil also observed that questioning of Roma travellers went on longer than that of non-Roma and that 80% of Roma were taken back to a secondary interview area compared with less than 1% of non-Roma. The observations of Ms Muhic-Dizdarevic, who was monitoring the operation on behalf of the Czech Helsinki Committee, were to much the same effect. She also points out that 'It was very obvious from their appearance which travellers were Roma and which were not. Firstly, at least 80% of the Roma could be readily identified by their darker skin and hair ...' Aspects of her evidence have been attacked but not this.

94. These general observations are borne out by the experience of the individuals whose stories were before the court. The ERRC conducted an experiment in which three people tried to travel to the UK for a short visit. Two were young women with similar incomes, intentions and amounts of money with them, one non-Roma, Ms Dedikova, and one Roma, Ms Grundzova; the third, Ms Polakova, was a mature professional married Roma woman working in the media. Ms Dedikova was allowed through after only five minutes' questioning, none of which she thought intrusive or irrelevant. Her story that she was going to visit a woman friend who was also a student was accepted without further probing. Ms Grundzova was refused leave after longer questioning which she found intrusive and requests for confirmation of matters which had been taken on trust from Ms Dedikova. Ms Polakova was questioned for what seemed to her like half an hour, was then told to wait in a separate room, and was eventually given leave to enter. She felt that the interview process was very different from that undergone by the non-Roma passengers travelling at the same time as her and that the only reason she was allowed to travel was that she had told them that she was a journalist interested in the rights of the Roma people. All three of these people were to some extent acting a part, in that their trips had been provoked and financed by the ERRC, but they were genuinely intending to pay a short visit to a friend or relatives living here. Czech television also conducted a similar experiment with a Roma man and a non-Roma woman wishing to pay a short visit to the UK. The non-Roma was given leave while

the Roma was refused after a much longer interview. Unlike the ERRC test, we have a transcript from which one can see what it was about the Roma's answers which might have made the official suspicious even if he had not been a Roma. But the question still remains whether a non-Roma who gave similar answers would have been treated the same. The tiny numbers of non-Roma refused may suggest otherwise.

95. Then there are the claimants in the case. Three of them made no secret of their intention to seek asylum on arrival in the UK. They do not therefore complain of discrimination, because their less favourable treatment was on grounds other than their ethnic origin. Two of the claimants also intended to claim asylum but pretended that they did not. It is difficult therefore for them to complain of more intensive questioning which revealed their true intentions. The last claimant, HM, was refused entry in circumstances which again invite the question whether a non-Roma in similar circumstances would have been refused. She was of obviously Roma appearance, aged 61 at the time, living with her husband and children, but travelling alone. Her husband was recovering from a heart attack and she was awaiting spinal surgery. Both were unemployed and living on social security because of ill health, which might not be thought surprising given their age. She planned to visit her grandson-in-law in England, and was carrying a sponsorship letter from him, together with a return ticket and £100 cash. These facts do not suggest someone who is planning to abandon her husband and five children and move to England. On the other hand, the file note records that the grandson-in-law states that he has been awarded refugee status but provides no evidence of this, is currently living on benefits though seeking employment, and makes no mention of the grand-daughter to whom he was presumably married.

96. These are judicial review proceedings, not a discrimination claim in the county court. No oral evidence has been heard or findings of fact in the individual cases made. The question is not whether HM was indeed intending to claim asylum on arrival, although it seems somewhat unlikely in the circumstances. The question is whether a non-Roma grandmother would have been treated in the same way. Again, the ERRC figures and the outcome of their test are some evidence that she would not.

97. It is not the object of these proceedings to make a finding of discrimination in any individual case. The object, as Burton J pointed out (Judgment, para 53(iv)), is to establish a case that the Prague operation was carried out in a discriminatory fashion. All the evidence before us, other than that of the intentions of those in charge of the operation, which intentions were not conveyed to the officers on the ground, supports the inference that Roma were, simply because they were Roma, routinely treated with more suspicion and subjected to more intensive and intrusive questioning than non-Roma. There is nothing surprising about this. Indeed, the Court of Appeal considered it 'wholly inevitable'. This may be going too far. But setting up an operation like this, prompted by an influx of asylum seekers who are overwhelmingly from one comparatively easily identifiable racial or ethnic group, requires enormous care if it is to be done without discrimination. That did not happen. The inevitable conclusion is that the operation was inherently and systemically discriminatory and unlawful.

98. In this respect it was not only unlawful in domestic law but also contrary to our obligations under customary international law and under international treaties to which the United Kingdom is a party. It is commonplace in international human rights instruments to declare that everyone is entitled to the rights and freedoms they set forth without distinction

of any kind such as race, colour, sex and the like: see, for example, the Universal Declaration of Human Rights 1948, article 2; the International Covenant on Civil and Political Rights 1966, article 2; the European Convention on Human Rights, article 14; and the Refugee Convention itself in article 3 provides: 'The Contracting States shall apply the provisions of this Convention to refugees without discrimination as to race, religion or country of origin.'

99. But the ICCPR goes further, in article 26: 'All persons are equal before the law and are entitled without any discrimination to the equal protection of the law. In this respect, the law shall prohibit any discrimination and guarantee to all persons equal and effective protection against discrimination on any ground such as race, colour, sex, language, religion, political or other opinion, national or social origin, property, birth or other status.'

100. The International Convention on the Elimination of all Forms of Racial Discrimination 1966 provides in article 2: '(1) States Parties condemn racial discrimination and undertake to pursue by all appropriate means and without delay a policy of eliminating racial discrimination in all its forms and promoting understanding among all races, and, to this end: (a) Each State Party undertakes to engage in no act or practice of racial discrimination against persons, groups of persons or institutions and to ensure that all public authorities and public institutions, national and local, shall act in conformity with this obligation.'

101. Racial discrimination is defined in article 1 in terms of distinctions which have the 'purpose or effect of nullifying or impairing the recognition, or enjoyment or exercise, on an equal footing, of human rights and fundamental freedoms in the political, economic, social, cultural or any other field of public life.' Article 1(2) states that the Convention does not apply to distinctions, exclusions, restrictions or preference made between citizens and non-citizens, but this certainly does not mean that States Parties can discriminate between non-citizens on racial grounds.

102. It was the existence of these and other instruments, some only in draft at the time, together with the principle of equality enshrined in the Charter of the United Nations and emphasised in numerous resolutions of the General Assembly, which led Judge Tanaka and the dissenting minority of the International Court of Justice in the South West Africa Cases (*Ethiopia* v. *South Africa*) (*Liberia* v. *South Africa*) (second phase) [1966] ICJ Rep 6, 293 to conclude that 'we consider that the norm of non-discrimination or non-separation on the basis of race has become a rule of customary international law ...'

103. The General Assembly has 'urged all States to review and where necessary revise their immigration laws, policies and practices so that they are free of racial discrimination and compatible with their obligations under international human rights instruments' (UNGA Resolution 57/195, para I.6, adopted 18 December 2002; see also UNGA Resolution 58/160 adopted on 22 December 2003). The UN Committee on the Elimination of Racial Discrimination has expressed its concern at the application of section 19D, which it considers 'incompatible with the very principle of non-discrimination' (UN doc CERD/C/63/CO/11, para 16, 10 December 2003). A scheme which is inherently discriminatory in practice is just as incompatible as is a law authorising discrimination.

104. As to remedy, the conclusion is that discrimination is inherent in the operation of the scheme itself. It is therefore more appropriate to make a general declaration, rather than the more specific one sought by appellants. The refusal of leave to enter to far more Roma than non-Roma is only objectionable if some Roma were wrongly refused or some non-Roma were wrongly

given leave. That we do not know. But the differential is further evidence of a general difference in approach between the two groups, which may have had other aspects than those to which our attention has specifically been drawn. Hence the following declaration meets the case: 'United Kingdom Immigration Officers operating under the authority of the Home Secretary at Prague Airport discriminated against Roma who were seeking to travel from that airport to the United Kingdom by treating them less favourably on racial grounds than they treated others who were seeking to travel from that airport to the United Kingdom, contrary to section 1(1)(a) of the Race Relations Act 1976.'

105. I would therefore allow the appeal on this ground and make the above declaration.

Box 7.2.

The question of 'ethnic profiling'

The 'Prague Airport' case presented above constitutes a clear example of 'ethnic profiling', i.e. the use of ethnic or religious background as a determining criterion for law-enforcement decisions (on the use of ethnic profiling in counter-terrorism, see Report of the Special Rapporteur on the promotion and protection of human rights and fundamental freedoms while countering terrorism, Martin Scheinin, 29 January 2007, A/HRC/4/26; see also more generally the General Policy Recommendation No. 11 on combating racism and racial discrimination in policing adopted on 29 June 2007 by the Council of Europe's European Commission against Racism and Intolerance (ECRI), which defines 'racial profiling' as 'the use by the police, with no objective and reasonable justification, of grounds such as race, colour, language, religion, nationality or national or ethnic origin in control, surveillance or investigation activities', and recommends that States define and explicitly prohibit racial profiling by law). Other well-known examples include the *Williams* case presented to the Human Rights Committee, the *Timishev* case presented to the European Court of Human Rights, or the *Rasterfahndung* data-mining operation led by the German authorities following the September 11, 2001, terrorist attacks on New York and Washington:

- In December 1992, Rosalind Williams, who was travelling with her husband and son, was stopped by a police officer on the platform of a train station in Valladolid, Spain, and told to produce her identity documents. When asked why she was the only person stopped, the police officer told her 'It's because you're black.' She filed a complaint against this treatment. This finally reached the Spanish Constitutional Court, which adopted a decision on 29 January 2001 rejecting the complaint: according to the Court, 'the police action used the racial criterion as merely indicative of a greater probability that the interested party was not Spanish. None of the circumstances that occurred in said intervention indicates that the conduct of the acting National Police officer was guided by racial prejudice or special bias against the members of a specific ethnic group, as alleged in the complaint. Thus, the police action took place in a place of travellers' transit, a railway station, in which, on the one hand, it is not illogical to think that there is a greater probability than in other places that persons who are selectively asked for identification may be foreigners; moreover, the inconveniences that any request for identification generates are minor and also reasonably assumable as burdens inherent to social life.' The Human Rights Committee disagreed. It concluded on 30 June 2009 that Ms Williams had been a victim of discrimination prohibited under the ICCPR: while finding that 'it is generally legitimate to carry out identity checks for the purposes of protecting public safety and crime prevention or to control illegal immigration', the Committee noted that 'when the authorities carry out these checks, the physical or ethnic characteristics of the persons targeted should not be considered as indicative of their possibly illegal situation in the country. Nor should identity checks be carried out so that only people with certain physical characteristics or ethnic backgrounds are targeted. This would not only adversely affect the dignity of those affected, but also contribute to the spread of xenophobic attitudes among the general population; it would also be inconsistent with an effective policy to combat racial discrimination' (*Rosalind Williams* v. *Spain* (Communication No. 1493/2006), UN doc. CCPR/C/96/D/1493/2006 (17 August 2009)).

- In 1999, Mr Timishev, a Chechen lawyer living in Nalchik in the Kabardino-Balkaria Republic of the Russian Federation, travelled by car from the Ingushetia Republic to Nalchik. When reaching the administrative border of the Kabardino-Balkaria Republic, his car was stopped at a checkpoint and entry was refused to him: traffic police officers had received an oral instruction from the Ministry of the Interior of Kabardino-Balkaria Republic not to admit persons of Chechen ethnic origin. The Nalchik Town Court dismissed Mr Timishev's complaint that this was discriminatory: in its view, the order was aimed at preventing persons with terrorist or antisocial aspirations from penetrating towns and villages. Five years after Mr Timishev filed an application against Russia, the European Court of Human Rights found that Russian officers had violated the non-discrimination provision of Article 14 ECHR in combination with the freedom of movement guaranteed in Article 2 of Protocol No. 4. The order, which barred passage to any person of Chechen ethnicity or perceived as such, 'represented a clear inequality of treatment in the enjoyment of the right to liberty of movement on account of one's ethnic origin'. (Eur. Ct. H.R. (2nd section), *Timishev* v. *Russia* (Appl. Nos. 55762/00 and 55974/00), judgment of 13 December 2005 (final on 13 March 2006), §54).

- In the wake of September 11, 2001 terrorist attacks against New York and Washington, the German authorities, in an attempt to identify 'sleepers' of terrorist organizations, decided to resort to the so-called *Rasterfahndung* method, i.e. the screening by the police of personal data banks of public or private bodies in order to track individuals with suspects' characteristics. The criteria established at the national level for this operation included being male, Muslim, national of or born in one of twenty-six listed countries with predominantly Muslim population, current or former student, and legal resident in Germany. Numerous institutions, including universities, employers, health and social insurance agencies, were required to provide the police with the personal records of all individuals corresponding to the defined profile. Yet the operation did not result in any arrest or criminal charge for terrorism-related offences (D. Moeckli, 'Discrimination Profiles: Law Enforcement After 9/11 and 7/7', *European Human Rights Law Review*, 5 (2005), 517). On 4 April 2006, the Federal Constitutional Court ruled that the *Rasterfahndung* was in breach of the individual's fundamental right of self-determination over personal information (Arts. 2(1) and 1 of the German

Constitution *(Grundgesetz)*) and therefore was unconstitutional (Decision of 4 April 2006 (1 BvR 518/02) (2006) 59 *Neue Juristische Wochenschrift* 1939).

As this last example illustrates, data protection legislation (and particularly, the restrictions imposed on the processing of 'sensitive' personal data relating, *inter alia*, to race or ethnicity, national origin or religion) may protect from ethnic profiling, when it is formalized and takes the form of the processing of data. Yet, if interpreted too broadly, data protection legislation may also create an obstacle to the identification of ethnic profiling: where it is practised informally, ethnic profiling can only be documented by monitoring the impact on certain groups of the practices of law enforcement officers, which requires some form of processing of data relating to the victims of such practices in order to assign them to specific groups. Thus, if it is to be effectively consistent with combating discrimination in the form of ethnic profiling, data protection legislation should focus, not only on the more or less sensitive nature of the data which are processed, but also and perhaps primarily on the objective of the processing of personal data and the proportionality of the means of processing. For a discussion of these issues, see O. De Schutter and J. Ringelheim, 'Ethnic Profiling: a Rising Challenge for European Human Rights Law', *Modern Law Review*, 71 (2008), 358–84.

7.3. Question for discussion: different faces of ethnic profiling

Which similarities and differences are relevant between the four cases referred to above – the *'Prague Airport'* case presented to the House of Lords, the *Williams* case presented to the Human Rights Committee, the *Timishev* case before the European Court of Human Rights, and the *Rasterfahndung* operation practised by the German authorities after 9/11? From the point of view of the search for solutions to combat ethnic profiling, does it matter whether these different forms of ethnic profiling are either formalized or informal? Whether they proceed by automated means or not?

2.2 Equal protection of the law

The second norm contained in Article 26 ICCPR requires that the law does not create any discrimination, either by making distinctions which cannot be reasonably and objectively justified (direct discrimination), or by treating equally situations which require a differentiated treatment (indirect discrimination). This norm is addressed, not at law enforcement authorities, but at the lawmaker. It is clearly a norm distinct from the one examined in the previous section. This is made clear by the rejection, in the preparatory works of the Covenant, of an amendment proposed by Brazil inserting the expression 'therefore' between the two guarantees stipulated in the first sentence of Article 26, which would have resulted in a formulation ('All persons are equal before the law and are *therefore* entitled without any discrimination to the equal protection of the law') negating this distinction (for the discussion before the third committee of the UN General Assembly in 1961, see A/C.3/L.945; and for further developments, M. Nowak, *UN Covenant on Civil and Political Rights. CCPR Commentary*, cited above, at 606–7). The following cases offer illustrations of the obligation to provide for the equal protection of the law. They relate respectively to discrimination on grounds of sex, religious or philosophical conviction, sexual orientation and nationality.

(a) Sex

Human Rights Committee, *M. A. Müller and I. Engelhard* v. *Namibia*, Communication No. 919/2000 (CCPR/C/74/D/919/2000 (2002)), final views of 26 March 2002:

[Mr Müller, a German citizen, married Ms Engelhard, a Namibian citizen, on 25 October 1996. The couple wished to adopt Ms Engelhard's surname. However, under the applicable Namibian legislation, whereas a wife could assume her husband's surname without any formalities, a husband had to apply to change his surname: section 9, para. 1 of the Aliens Act No. 1 of 1937 as amended states that it is an offence to change one's surname without authorization following a certain procedure, unless one of the listed exceptions apply; among the listed exceptions in the Aliens Act is when a woman on her marriage assumes the surname of her husband (section 9, para. 1(a)). Mr Müller claims that he is the victim of a violation of Article 26 of the [ICCPR], as the Aliens Act section 9, para. 1(a) prevents Mr Müller from assuming his wife's surname without following a described procedure of application to a government service, whereas women wanting to assume their husbands' surname may do so without following this procedure. Likewise, Ms Engelhard claims that her surname may not be used as the family surname without complying with these same procedures, in violation of Article 26. They submit that this section of the law clearly differentiates in a discriminatory way between men and women, in that women automatically may assume the surnames of their husbands on marriage, whereas men have to go through specified procedures of application.]

6.7 With regard to the authors' claim under article 26 of the Covenant, the Committee notes the fact, undisputed by the parties to the case; that section 9, paragraph 1, of the Aliens Act differentiates on the basis of sex, in relation to the right of male or female persons to assume the surname of the other spouse on marriage. The Committee reiterates its constant jurisprudence that the right to equality before the law and to the equal protection of the law without any discrimination does not make all differences of treatment discriminatory. A differentiation based on reasonable and objective criteria does not amount to prohibited discrimination within the meaning of article 26 [see views adopted in *Danning* v. *Netherlands*, Communication No. 180/1984]. A different treatment based on one of the specific grounds enumerated in article 26, clause 2 of the Covenant, however, places a heavy burden on the State party to explain the reason for the differentiation. The Committee, therefore, has to consider whether the reasons underlying the differentiation on the basis of gender, as embodied in section 9, paragraph 1, remove this provision from the verdict of being discriminatory.

6.8 The Committee notes the State party's argument that the purpose of Aliens Act section 9, paragraph 1, is to fulfil legitimate social and legal aims, in particular to create legal security.

The Committee further notes the States party's submission that the distinction made in section 9 of the Aliens Act is based on a long-standing tradition for women in Namibia to assume their husbands' surname, while in practice men so far never have wished to assume their wives' surname; thus the law, dealing with the normal state of affairs, is merely reflecting a generally accepted situation in Namibian society. The unusual wish of a couple to assume as family name the surname of the wife could easily be taken into account by applying for a change of surname in accordance with the procedures set out in the Aliens Act. The Committee, however, fails to see why the sex-based approach taken by section 9, paragraph 1, of the Aliens Act may serve the purpose of creating legal security, since the choice of the wife's surname can be registered as well as the choice of the husband's surname. In view of the importance of the principle of equality between men and women, the argument of a long-standing tradition cannot be maintained as a general justification for different treatment of men and women, which is contrary to the Covenant. To subject the possibility of choosing the wife's surname as family name to stricter and much more cumbersome conditions than the alternative (choice of husband's surname) cannot be judged to be reasonable; at any rate the reason for the distinction has no sufficient importance in order to outweigh the generally excluded gender-based approach. Accordingly, the Committee finds that the authors have been the victims of discrimination and violation of article 26 of the Covenant.

(b) Religious or philosophical conviction

Human Rights Committee, *F. Foin* v. *France*, Communication No. 666/1995 (CCPR/C/67/D/666/1995), final views of 9 November 1999:

[The author, a recognized conscientious objector to military service, was assigned to civilian service duty in the national nature reserve of Camargue in December 1988. On 23 December 1989, after exactly one year of civilian service, he left his duty station; he invoked the allegedly discriminatory character of Article 116, para. 6, of the National Service Code (*Code du service national*), pursuant to which recognized conscientious objectors were required to perform civilian national service duties for a period of two years, whereas military service did not exceed one year. As a result of his action, Mr Foin was charged with desertion in peacetime, and was given a six-month suspended prison sentence.]

10.2 The Committee has noted the State party's argument that the author is not a victim of any violation, because he was not convicted for his personal beliefs, but for deserting the service freely chosen by him. The Committee notes, however, that during the proceedings before the courts, the author raised the right to equality of treatment between conscientious objectors and military conscripts as a defence justifying his desertion and that the courts' decisions refer to such claim. It also notes that the author contends that, as a conscientious objector to military service, he had no free choice in the service that he had to perform. The Committee therefore considers that the author qualifies as a victim for purposes of the Optional Protocol.

10.3 The issue before the Committee is whether the specific conditions under which alternative service had to be performed by the author constitute a violation of the Covenant.

The Committee observes that under article 8 of the Covenant, States parties may require service of a military character and, in case of conscientious objection, alternative national service, provided that such service is not discriminatory. The author has claimed that the requirement, under French law, of a length of 24 months for national alternative service, rather than 12 months for military service, is discriminatory and violates the principle of equality before the law and equal protection of the law set forth in article 26 of the Covenant. The Committee reiterates its position that article 26 does not prohibit all differences of treatment. Any differentiation, as the Committee has had the opportunity to state repeatedly, must however be based on reasonable and objective criteria. In this context, the Committee recognizes that the law and practice may establish differences between military and national alternative service and that such differences may, in a particular case, justify a longer period of service, provided that the differentiation is based on reasonable and objective criteria, such as the nature of the specific service concerned or the need for a special training in order to accomplish that service. In the present case, however, the reasons forwarded by the State party do not refer to such criteria or refer to criteria in general terms without specific reference to the author's case, and are rather based on the argument that doubling the length of service was the only way to test the sincerity of an individual's convictions. In the Committee's view, such argument does not satisfy the requirement that the difference in treatment involved in the present case was based on reasonable and objective criteria. In the circumstances, the Committee finds that a violation of article 26 occurred, since the author was discriminated against on the basis of his conviction of conscience.

Separate, dissenting, opinion of members Nisuke Ando, Eckart Klein and David Kretzmer

1. We agree with the Committee's approach that article 26 of the Covenant does not prohibit all differences in treatment, but that any differentiation must be based on reasonable and objective criteria. (See, also, the Committee's General Comment No. 18.) However, we are unable to agree with the Committee's view that the differentiation in treatment in the present case between the author and those who were conscripted for military service was not based on such criteria.

2. Article 8 of the Covenant, that prohibits forced and compulsory labour, provides that the prohibition does not include 'any service of a military character and, in countries where conscientious objection is recognized, any national service required by law of conscientious objectors'. It is implicit in this provision that a State party may restrict the exemption from compulsory military service to conscientious objectors. It may refuse to grant such an exemption to all other categories of persons who would prefer not to do military service, whether the reasons are personal, economic or political.

3. As the exemption from military service may be restricted to conscientious objectors, it would also seem obvious that a State party may adopt reasonable mechanisms for distinguishing between those who wish to avoid military service on grounds of conscience, and those who wish to do so for other, unacceptable, reasons. One such mechanism may be establishment of a decision-making body, which examines applications for exemption from military service and decides whether the application for exemption on grounds of conscience is genuine. Such decision-making bodies are highly problematical, as they may involve intrusion into matters of privacy and conscience. It would therefore seem perfectly reasonable

for a State party to adopt an alternative mechanism, such as demanding somewhat longer service from those who apply for exemption (see the Committee's Views in Communication No. 295/1988, *Järvinen* v. *Finland*). The object of such an approach is to reduce the chance that the conscientious objection exemption will be exploited for reasons of convenience. However, even if such an approach is adopted the extra service demanded of conscientious objectors should not be punitive. It should not create a situation in which a real conscientious objector may be forced to forego his or her objection.

4. In the present case the military service was 12 months, while the service demanded of conscientious objectors was 24 months. Had the only reason advanced by the State party for the extra service been the selection mechanism, we would have tended to hold that the extra time was excessive and could be regarded as punitive. However, in order to assess whether the differentiation in treatment between the author and those who served in the military was based on reasonable and objective criteria all the relevant facts have to be taken into account. The Committee has neglected to do this.

5. The State party has argued that the conditions of alternative service differ from the conditions of military service ... While soldiers were assigned to positions without any choice, the conscientious objectors had a wide choice of posts. They could propose their own employers and could do service within their own professional fields. Furthermore, they received higher remuneration than people servicing in the armed forces. To this should be added that military service, by its very essence, carries with it burdens that are not imposed on those doing alternative service, such as military discipline, day and night, and the risks of being injured or even killed during military manoeuvers or military action. The author has not refuted the arguments relating to the differences between military service and alternative service, but has simply argued that people doing other civil service also enjoyed special conditions. This argument is not relevant in the present case, as the author's service was carried out before the system of civil service was instituted.

6. In light of all the circumstances of this case, the argument that the difference of twelve months between military service and the service required of conscientious objectors amounts to discrimination is unconvincing. The differentiation between those serving in the military and conscientious objectors was based on reasonable and objective criteria and does not amount to discrimination. We were therefore unable to join the Committee in finding a violation of article 26 of the Covenant in the present case.

At the time it was adopted, this decision constituted a clear overruling from the previous case law of the Committee (see Communication No. 295/1988, *Järvinen* v. *Finland*, final views of 25 July 1990, CCPR/C/39/D/295/1988 (1990)). Since then, however, it has been reaffirmed on a number of occasions, over the consistent dissents of certain individual members of the Committee (see Communication No. 689/1996, *Maille* v. *France*, final views of 10 July 2000, CCPR/C/69/D/689/1996 (2000) (with a joint individual opinion (dissenting) of members Ando, Klein, Kretzmer et Zakhia); Communication No. 690 and 691/1996, *Venier and Nicolas* v. *France*, final views of 10 July 2000, CCPR/C/69/D/690/1996 (2000) (same)); in the Concluding Observations the Human Rights Committee adopted concerning Finland on 2 December 2004 (CCPR/CO/82/FIN), the

Committee 'regrets that the right to conscientious objection is acknowledged only in peacetime, and that the civilian alternative to military service is punitively long' (para. 14, referring to Articles 18 (freedom of religion) and 26 of the Covenant).

(c) Sexual orientation

Human Rights Committee, *X. v. Colombia*, Communication No. 1361/2005 (CCPR/C/89/D/1361/2005), final views of 30 March 2007:

[On 27 July 1993, the author's life partner Mr Y died after a relationship of twenty-two years, during which they lived together for seven years. The author, who was economically dependent on his late partner, lodged an application with the Social Welfare Fund of the Colombian Congress, Division of Economic Benefits (the Fund), seeking a pension transfer. The request was rejected, however, on the grounds that the law did not permit the transfer of a pension to a person of the same sex. Although, according to Regulatory Decree No. 1160 of 1989, 'for the purposes of pension transfers, the person who shared married life with the deceased during the year immediately preceding the death of the deceased or during the period stipulated in the special arrangements shall be recognized as the permanent partner of the deceased', this provision is not considered to apply to same-sex partners, since Act No. 54 of 1990 provides that 'for all civil law purposes, the man and the woman who form part of the de facto marital union shall be termed permanent partners'.]

7.1 The author claims that the refusal of the Colombian courts to grant him a pension on the grounds of his sexual orientation violates his rights under article 26 of the Covenant. The Committee takes note of the State party's argument that a variety of social and legal factors were taken into account by the drafters of the law, and not only the mere question of whether a couple live together, and that the State party has no obligation to establish a property regime similar to that established in Act No. 54 of 1990 for all the different kinds of couples and social groups, who may or may not be bound by sexual or emotional ties. It also takes note of the State party's claim that the purpose of the rules governing this regime was simply to protect heterosexual unions, not to undermine other unions or cause them any detriment or harm.

7.2 The Committee notes that the author was not recognized as the permanent partner of Mr Y for pension purposes because court rulings based on Act No. 54 of 1990 found that the right to receive pension benefits was limited to members of a heterosexual de facto marital union. The Committee recalls its earlier jurisprudence that the prohibition against discrimination under article 26 comprises also discrimination based on sexual orientation [Communication No. 941/2000, *Young* v. *Australia*, Views of 6 August 2003, para. 10.4.]. It also recalls that in previous communications the Committee found that differences in benefit entitlements between married couples and heterosexual unmarried couples were reasonable and objective, as the couples in question had the choice to marry or not, with all the ensuing consequences [Communication Nos. 180/1984, *Danning* v. *Netherlands*, Views of 9 April 1987, para. 14, and 976/2001, *Derksen and Bakker* v. *Netherlands*, Views of 1 April 2004, para. 9.2.]. The Committee also notes that, while it was not open to the author to enter into marriage with his same-sex permanent partner, the Act does not make a distinction between married and unmarried couples but between homosexual and heterosexual couples. The Committee finds that the State party has put forward no argument that might demonstrate that such a distinction between same-sex partners, who are not entitled to pension benefits, and unmarried heterosexual partners, who are so entitled, is reasonable and objective. Nor has the State party adduced any evidence of the existence of factors that might justify making such a distinction. In this context, the Committee finds that the State party has violated article 26 of the Covenant by denying the author's right to his life partner's pension on the basis of his sexual orientation.

[It would seem that the Constitutional Court brought Colombian law into compliance with the ICCPR even before the Human Rights Committee's decision. See *Sentencia* (Judgment) C-075/07, 7 February 2007.]

Separate opinion by Mr Abdelfattah Amor and Mr Ahmed Tawfik Khalil (dissenting)
Provisions of the Covenant cannot be interpreted in isolation from one another, especially when the link between them is one that cannot reasonably be ignored, let alone denied. Thus the question of 'discrimination on grounds of sex or sexual orientation' cannot be raised under article 26 in the context of positive benefits without taking account of article 23 of the Covenant, which stipulates that 'the family is the natural and fundamental group unit of society' and that 'the right of men and women of marriageable age to marry and found a family shall be recognized'. That is to say, a couple of the same sex does not constitute a family within the meaning of the Covenant and cannot claim benefits that are based on a conception of the family as comprising individuals of different sexes.

What additional explanations must the State provide? What other evidence must it submit in order to demonstrate that the distinction drawn between a same-sex couple and a mixed-sex couple is reasonable and objective? The line of argument adopted by the Committee is in fact highly contentious. It starts from the premise that all couples, regardless of sex, are the same and are entitled to the same protection in respect of positive benefits. The consequence of this is that it falls to the State, and not to the author, to explain, justify and present evidence, as if this was some established and undisputed rule, which is far from being the case. We take the view that in this area, where positive benefits are concerned, situations that are widespread can be presumed to be lawful – absent arbitrary decisions or manifest errors of assessment – and situations that depart from the norm must be shown to be lawful by those who so claim ...

On the other hand, there is no doubt that article 17, which prohibits interference with privacy, is violated by discrimination on grounds of sexual orientation. The Committee, both in its final comments on States parties' reports and in its Views on individual communications, has rightly and repeatedly found that protection against arbitrary or unlawful interference with privacy precludes prosecution and punishment for homosexual relations between consenting adults. Article 26, in conjunction with article 17, is fully applicable here because the aim in this case is precisely to combat discrimination, not to create new rights; but the same article cannot normally be applied in matters relating to benefits such as a survivor's pension for someone who has lost their same-sex partner. The situation of a homosexual couple in respect of survivor's pension, unless the problem is viewed from a cultural standpoint – and cultures are diverse and even, as regards certain social issues, opposed – is neither the same as nor similar to the situation of a heterosexual couple.

European Court of Human Rights (1st sect.), *Karner* v. *Austria* (Appl. No. 40016/98), judgment of 24 July 2003:

[The applicant lived with Mr W., with whom he had a homosexual relationship, in a flat in Vienna, which W. had rented a year earlier. They shared the expenses on the flat. In 1994 Mr W. died after designating the applicant as his heir. After the landlord of the flat brought proceedings against the applicant for termination of the tenancy, the lower courts dismissed the action, taking the view that section 14(3) of the Rent Act (*Mietrechtsgesetz*), which provided that family members (including 'life companions') had a right to succeed to a tenancy, was intended to protect persons who had lived together for a long time without being married against sudden homelessness, and thus applied to homosexuals as well as to persons of opposite sex. On 5 December 1996 the Supreme Court (*Oberster Gerichtshof*) adopted the opposite view. It granted the landlord's appeal and terminated the lease, finding that the notion of 'life companion' (*Lebensgefährte*) in section 14(3) of the Rent Act was to be interpreted as at the time it was enacted, and the legislature's intention in 1974 was not to include persons of the same sex.]

37. The Court reiterates that, for the purposes of Article 14, a difference in treatment is discriminatory if it has no objective and reasonable justification, that is, if it does not pursue a legitimate aim or if there is not a reasonable relationship of proportionality between the means employed and the aim sought to be realised ... Furthermore, very weighty reasons would have to be put forward before the Court could regard a difference in treatment based exclusively on the ground of sex as compatible with the Convention (see *Burghartz* v. *Switzerland*, judgment of 22 February 1994, Series A No. 280–B, p. 29, §27; *Karlheinz Schmidt* v. *Germany*, judgment of 18 July 1994, Series A No. 291–B, pp. 32–33, §24; *Salgueiro da Silva Mouta* v. *Portugal*, No. 33290/96, §29, ECHR 1999IX; *Smith and Grady* v. United Kingdom, nos. 33985/96 and 33986/96, §94, ECHR 1999–VI; *Fretté* v. *France*, No. 36515/97, §§34 and 40, ECHR 2002-I; and *S.L.* v. *Austria*, No. 45330/99, §36, ECHR 2003–I). Just like differences based on sex, differences based on sexual orientation require particularly serious reasons by way of justification (see *Smith and Grady*, cited above, §90, and *S.L.* v. *Austria*, cited above, §37).

38. In the present case, after Mr W.'s death, the applicant sought to avail himself of the right under section 14(3) of the Rent Act, which he asserted entitled him as a surviving partner to succeed to the tenancy. The court of first instance dismissed an action by the landlord for termination of the tenancy and the Vienna Regional Court dismissed the appeal. It found that the provision in issue protected persons who had been living together for a long time without being married against sudden homelessness and applied to homosexuals as well as to heterosexuals.

39. The Supreme Court, which ultimately granted the landlord's action for termination of the tenancy, did not argue that there were important reasons for restricting the right to succeed to a tenancy to heterosexual couples. It stated instead that it had not been the intention of the legislature when enacting section 14(3) of the Rent Act in 1974 to include protection for couples of the same sex. The Government now submit that the aim of the provision in issue was the protection of the traditional family unit.

40. The Court can accept that protection of the family in the traditional sense is, in principle, a weighty and legitimate reason which might justify a difference in treatment (see *Mata Estevez* v. *Spain* (dec.), No. 56501/00, ECHR 2001–VI, with further references). It remains to be ascertained whether, in the circumstances of the case, the principle of proportionality has been respected.

41. The aim of protecting the family in the traditional sense is rather abstract and a broad variety of concrete measures may be used to implement it. In cases in which the margin of appreciation afforded to States is narrow, as is the position where there is a difference in treatment based on sex or sexual orientation, the principle of proportionality does not merely require that the measure chosen is in principle suited for realising the aim sought. It must also be shown that it was necessary in order to achieve that aim to exclude certain categories of people – in this instance persons living in a homosexual relationship – from the scope of application of section 14 of the Rent Act. The Court cannot see that the Government have advanced any arguments that would allow such a conclusion.

42. Accordingly, the Court finds that the Government have not offered convincing and weighty reasons justifying the narrow interpretation of section 14(3) of the Rent Act that prevented a surviving partner of a couple of the same sex from relying on that provision.

43. Thus, there has been a violation of Article 14 of the Convention taken in conjunction with Article 8.

As illustrated by the two decisions above, the existing international law of human rights views differences in treatment between heterosexual couples (whether married or forming a '*de facto* marital union') and same-sex couples as a direct discrimination on grounds of sexual orientation. At the same time, the failure to extend to same-sex couples advantages recognized to married heterosexual couples where the institution of marriage is reserved to the latter is sometimes not considered to constitute a form of prohibited discrimination (Eur. Ct. H.R. (4th sect.), *Mata Estevez* v. *Spain* (Appl. No. 56501/00), decision (inadmissibility) of 10 May 2001, Rep. 2001–VI). This view is increasingly challenged, however. The two decisions reproduced above illustrate a tendency in the case law of human rights expert bodies to acknowledge that the sexual orientation of a person should not result in an impossibility for that person to live with another individual, in conditions which ensure that both will benefit from a certain level of security against the risks entailed by the illness or death of one partner, or by the separation of the couple when one of the partners is economically dependent on the other. Indeed, the Parliamentary Assembly of the Council of Europe requested Member States to introduce registered partnerships in their national laws, precisely in order to achieve this objective (Recommendation 1474 (2000) of 26 September 2000, para. 11 (iii), (i)).

In the case of *Joslin* v. *New Zealand* presented to the United Nations Human Rights Committee, the Committee refused in its final views adopted on 30 July 2002 to interpret Article 23(2) of the International Covenant on Civil and Political Rights as imposing on the States parties an obligation to recognize the right to marry to same-sex partners (Communication No. 902/1999, CCPR/C/75/D/902/1999). However, two members of the Committee, Messrs Lallah and Scheinin, underlined in their concurring opinion that this conclusion 'should not be read as a general statement that differential treatment between married couples and same-sex couples not allowed under the law to marry would never amount to a violation of article 26. On the contrary, the

Committee's jurisprudence supports the position that such differentiation may very well, depending on the circumstances of a concrete case, amount to prohibited discrimination ... [When] the Committee has held that certain differences in the treatment of married couples and unmarried heterosexual couples were based on reasonable and objective criteria and hence not discriminatory, the rationale of this approach was in the ability of the couples in question to choose whether to marry or not to marry, with all the entailing consequences (*Danning* v. *Netherlands*, Communication No. 180/1984). No such possibility of choice exists for same-sex couples in countries where the law does not allow for same-sex marriage or other type of recognized same-sex partnership with consequences similar to or identical with those of marriage. Therefore, a denial of certain rights or benefits to same-sex couples that are available to married couples may amount to discrimination prohibited under article 26, unless otherwise justified on reasonable and objective criteria.' Whether this trend in the international case law will be developed in the future remains to be seen.

(d) Nationality

The Universal Declaration on Human Rights prohibits any discrimination on grounds 'such as race, colour, sex, language, religion, political or other opinion, national or social origin, property, birth or other status'. In contrast to these classical grounds of prohibited discrimination, sexual orientation or disability have emerged more recently as 'suspect' in international human rights law, thus exhibiting a shift in social expectations about the kind of treatment of certain groups that is acceptable. The case of nationality is slightly different. While discrimination on grounds of 'national origin' has traditionally been prohibited, it is only recently that the use of the criterion of nationality (or citizenship) in the allocation of social goods has been seen with suspicion, as a result of developments in the case law of human rights bodies. In its General Recommendation 30 on 'Discrimination against Non-citizens', the UN Committee on the Elimination of Racial Discrimination recalls that, although some fundamental rights such as the right to participate in elections, to vote and to stand for election, may be confined to citizens, 'human rights are, in principle, to be enjoyed by all persons'. States parties to the International Convention on the Elimination of All Forms of Racial Discrimination therefore 'are under an obligation to guarantee equality between citizens and non-citizens in the enjoyment of these rights to the extent recognized under international law' (General Recommendation 30 adopted at the sixty-fourth session of the Committee on the Elimination of Racial Discrimination (CERD/C/64/Misc.11/rev.3) (1 October 2004), para. 5). In the view of the Committee, differential treatment based on nationality and national or ethnic origin constitutes discrimination if the criteria for such differentiation, judged in the light of the objectives and purposes of the Convention, are not applied pursuant to a legitimate aim, and are not proportional to the achievement of this aim. The prohibition of such discrimination extends to indirect discrimination on grounds of nationality, for instance when regulations are directed to newly established residents in a country even without explicitly targeting foreigners. In its 2006 Concluding Observations relating to Denmark, the Committee thus expressed its concern that under Act No. 361 of June 2002, social benefits for persons newly arrived in Denmark are reduced in order to entice them to seek employment, a policy which 'has reportedly created social marginalization, poverty and greater dependence on the social welfare system for those who have not become self-sufficient'. The Committee acknowledged that the new regulation applies to both citizens and non-citizens, yet it noted 'with concern that it is foreign nationals who are mainly affected by this policy' (Committee on the Elimination of Racial Discrimination, Concluding Observations: Denmark, UN Doc. CERD/C/DEN/CO/17, 19 October 2006, para. 18).

The Human Rights Committee adopts a similar view under the ICCPR. In its General Comment No. 15, *The Position of Aliens under the Covenant*, which it adopted in 1986, the Committee notes that 'in general, the rights set forth in the Covenant apply to everyone, irrespective of reciprocity, and irrespective of his or her nationality or statelessness. Thus, the general rule is that each one of the rights of the Covenant must be guaranteed without discrimination between citizens and aliens. Aliens receive the benefit of the general requirement of non-discrimination in respect of the rights guaranteed in the Covenant, as provided for in Article 2 thereof. This guarantee applies to aliens and citizens alike.' While Article 2 of the Covenant only prohibits discrimination in the enjoyment of other substantive rights of freedoms guaranteed by this instrument, Article 26 prohibits discrimination in all fields, whether or not covered by other substantive Covenant provisions. This also applies to discrimination on grounds of nationality. In the case of *Ibrahima Gueye and others* v. *France* (Communication No. 196/1985 (CCPR/C/35/D/196/1985 (1989))), the Human Rights Committee was asked to find whether France had violated its obligations under the Covenant after retired soldiers of Senegalese nationality who served in the French Army prior to Senegal's independence in 1960 were denied the pension rights which French nationals in the same situation were benefiting from, in accordance with a law enacted in December 1974 introducing a distinction between the retired members of the French Army on grounds of nationality. The Committee considered that differences of treatment on grounds of nationality could, in principle, be prohibited by Article 26 of the Covenant, since this provision prohibits differences in treatment on any grounds '*such as* race, colour, sex, language, religion, political or other opinion, national or social origin, property, birth *or other status*' (emphasis added). The Committee concluded that the difference in treatment of the authors of the communication is not based on reasonable and objective criteria and constitutes discrimination prohibited by the Covenant, since 'it was not the question of nationality which determined the granting of pensions to the authors but the services rendered by them in the past. They had served in the French Armed Forces under the same conditions as French citizens; for 14 years subsequent to the independence of Senegal they were treated in the same way as their French counterparts for the purpose of pension rights, although their nationality was not French but Senegalese' (para. 9.5). Since this decision the French administrative courts have aligned themselves with the position of the Human Rights Committee (see *Conseil d'Etat*, 30 November 2002, Nos. 212179 and 212211, Diop).

The Human Rights Committee adopted further decisions finding discrimination on grounds of nationality or on grounds of the status of permanent resident (see, e.g. Communication No. 516/1992, *Simunek* v. *Czech Republic*, final views of 19 July 1995, CCPR/C/54/D/516/1992; Communication No. 586/1994, *Adam* v. *Czech Republic*, final views of 23 July 1996, CCPR/C/57/D/586/1994). In the case of *Karakurt* v. *Austria* (Communication No. 965/2000, final views of 4 April 2002, CCPR/C/74/D/965/2000), the author of the communication complained that, because of his Turkish nationality, he could not stand for election to work-councils in Austria, since section 53(1) of the Industrial Relations Act (*Arbeitsverfassungsgesetz*) limited the entitlement to be eligible for election to such work-councils to Austrian nationals or members of the European Economic Area (EEA). The Committee concluded that this difference in treatment between, on the one hand, Austrians and nationals of EU Member States or EEA Member States, and nationals of other countries on the other hand, constituted a discrimination prohibited under Article 26 of the International Covenant on Civil and Political Rights: 'the State party has granted the author, a non-Austrian/EEA national, the right to work in its territory for an open-ended period. The question therefore is whether there are reasonable and objective grounds justifying exclusion of the author from a close and natural incident of employment in the State party otherwise available to EEA nationals, namely the right to stand for election to the relevant work-council, on the basis of his citizenship alone ... With regard to the case at hand, the Committee has to take into account the function of a member of a work council, i.e. to promote staff interests and to supervise compliance with work conditions ... In view of this, it is not reasonable to base a distinction between aliens concerning their capacity to stand for election for a work council solely on their different nationality' (para. 8.4.).

Of course, the difference in treatment which Mr Karakurt complained of had its source in the obligation imposed on Austria by EC law and by the Agreement on the European Economic Area not to establish any discrimination on grounds of nationality between Austrian nationals, on the one hand, and nationals of other EU Member States or EEA Member States, on the other hand. But this, in the view of the Committee, did not preclude it from finding discrimination. Although its earlier case law seemed to suggest that the existence of an international agreement that confers preferential treatment to nationals of a State party to that agreement might constitute an objective and reasonable ground for differentiation (see Communication No. 658/1995, *Jacob and Jantina Hendrika van Oord* v. *Netherlands*, final views of 23 July 1997 (CCPR/C/60/D/658/1995)), it stated in *Karakurt* that 'there is no general rule to the effect that such an agreement in itself constitutes a sufficient ground with regard to the requirements of article 26 of the Covenant. Rather, it is necessary to judge every case on its own facts.' It follows that differences in treatment between nationals of EU Member States, on the one hand, and third country nationals, on the other hand, may be considered discriminatory, despite the fact that they are the result of the establishment of a new legal order by the EU treaties and that they take the form of the creation of a citizenship of the Union.

A similar evolution took place before regional courts. Since the 1990s, differences in treatment on grounds of nationality have been increasingly treated as suspect in the case law of the European Court of Human Rights. In the case of *Gaygusuz* v. *Austria* (Appl. No. 17371/90, judgment of 16 September 1996, Reports 1996–IV), the applicant, a Turkish national who had worked in Austria, with certain interruptions, from 1973 until October 1984, was denied an advance on his pension in the form of emergency assistance after his entitlement to unemployment benefits expired in 1987. He complained before the European Court of Human Rights of the Austrian authorities' refusal to grant him emergency assistance on the ground that he did not have Austrian nationality, which was one of the conditions laid down in section 33(2)(a) of the 1977 Unemployment Insurance Act for entitlement to an allowance of that type. He claimed to be a victim of discrimination based on national origin, contrary to Article 14 of the Convention taken in conjunction with Article 1 of Protocol No. 1 to the Convention, which guarantees the right to property ('Every natural or legal person is entitled to the peaceful enjoyment of his possessions').

The Court agreed. It noted in the first place that 'Mr Gaygusuz was legally resident in Austria and worked there at certain times ... paying contributions to the unemployment insurance fund in the same capacity and on the same basis as Austrian nationals.' It observed therefore that the Austrian authorities' refusal to grant him emergency assistance was based exclusively on the fact that he did not have Austrian nationality as required by section 33(2)(a) of the 1977 Unemployment Insurance Act, since 'it has not been argued that the applicant failed to satisfy the other statutory conditions for the award of the social benefit in question. He was accordingly in a like situation to Austrian nationals as regards his entitlement thereto.' The Court concluded that 'the difference in treatment between Austrians and non-Austrians as regards entitlement to emergency assistance, of which Mr Gaygusuz was a victim, is not based on any "objective and reasonable justification"', and that it is therefore discriminatory (paras. 46–51).

In *Gaygusuz*, the Court had formulated its doctrine thus: 'a difference of treatment is discriminatory, for the purposes of Article 14, if it "has no objective and reasonable justification", that is if it does not pursue a "legitimate aim" or if there is not a "reasonable relationship of proportionality between the means employed and the aim sought to be realised". Moreover the Contracting States enjoy a certain margin of appreciation in assessing whether and to what extent differences in otherwise similar situations justify a different treatment. However, very weighty reasons would have to be put forward before the Court could regard a difference of treatment based exclusively on the ground of nationality as compatible with the Convention' (para. 42). In other terms, like birth out of wedlock (Eur. Ct. H.R., *Inze* v. *Austria*, judgment of 28 October 1987, Series A No. 126, §41; Eur. Ct. H.R. (3rd sect.), *Mazurek* v. *France* (Appl. No. 34406/97), judgment of 1 February 2000, §49; Eur. Ct H.R. (GC), *Sommerfeld* v. *Germany* (Appl. No. 31871/96), judgment of 8 July 2003, §93), sex (Eur. Ct. H.R., *Burghartz* v. *Switzerland*, judgment of 22 February 1994, Series A No. 280–B, p. 29, §27; *Karlheinz Schmidt* v. *Germany*, judgment of 18 July 1994, Series A No. 291–B, pp. 32–3, §24; *Petrovic* v.

Austria, judgment of 27 March 1998, *Reports of Judgments and Decisions* 1998–II, p. 587, §37), or sexual orientation (Eur. Ct. H.R., *Smith and Grady* v. *United Kingdom*, cited above; *Lustig-Prean and Beckett* v. *United Kingdom* (Appl. Nos. 31417/96 and 32377/96), judgment of 27 September 1999; and Eur. Ct. H.R. (3rd sect.), *A.D.T.* v. *United Kingdom* (Appl. No. 35765/97), judgment of 31 July 2000, E.C.H.R. 2000–IX, §37; Eur. Ct. H.R. (1st sect.), *L. and V.* v. *Austria* (Appl. Nos. 39392/98 and 39829/98), judgment of 9 January 2003, §45; Eur. Ct. H.R., *S.L.* v. *Austria* (Appl. No. 45330/99), judgment of 9 January 2003, §36; Eur. Ct. H.R. (1st sect.), *Karner* v. *Austria* (Appl. No. 40016/98), judgment of 24 July 2003, §37), nationality is considered to constitute a 'suspect' ground, requiring that any difference of treatment grounded on nationality be justified by particularly strong reasons and that it be strictly necessary to achieve the objectives pursued.

This was confirmed in the case of *Koua Poirrez* v. *France* (Eur. Ct. H.R. (3rd sect.), *Koua Poirrez* v. *France* (Appl. No. 40892/98), judgment of 30 September 2003). The applicant, a national of the Ivory Coast who had failed to obtain French nationality because he had applied after his eighteenth birthday, had been physically disabled since the age of seven. He had been adopted by Mr Bernard Poirrez, a French national. In May 1990 he applied for an 'allowance for disabled adults' (*allocation aux adultes handicapés* – AAH), stating in support of his application that he was a French resident of Ivory Coast nationality and the adopted son of a French national residing and working in France. His application was rejected on the ground that, as he was neither a French national nor a national of a country which had entered into a reciprocity agreement with France in respect of the AAH, he did not satisfy the relevant conditions laid down in Article L. 821–1 of the Social Security Code. The Court found this to constitute discrimination on grounds of nationality. It reiterated that 'very weighty reasons would have to be put forward before the Court could regard a difference of treatment based exclusively on the ground of nationality as compatible with the Convention' (para. 46).

In *Andrejeva* v. *Latvia* (Eur. Ct. H.R. (GC), *Andrejeva* v. *Latvia* (Appl. No. 55707/00), judgment of 18 February 2009), the Court found Latvia to have committed a discrimination against Ms Natālija Andrejeva, a 'permanently resident non-citizen' of Latvia who was previously a national of the former USSR. Because she did not have Latvian citizenship, Ms Andrejeva was denied pension rights since, in her case, the fact she had worked for an entity established outside Latvia despite having been physically in Latvian territory did not constitute 'employment within the territory of Latvia' within the meaning of the State Pensions Act. In finding that a discimination had occured, the Court dismissed the argument of the Latvian Government that the applicant could have applied to become a Latvian citizen by a naturalization process, in order to avoid being treated differently as a 'non-citizen permanent resident' in Latvia and to receive the full amount of the pension claimed. The Court said: 'The prohibition of discrimination enshrined in Article 14 of the Convention is meaningful only if, in each particular case, the applicant's personal situation in relation to the criteria listed in that provision is taken into account exactly as it stands. To proceed otherwise in dismissing the victim's claims on the ground that he or she could have avoided the discrimination by altering one of the factors in question – for example, by acquiring a nationality – would render Article 14 devoid of substance' (para. 91).

In the case of *The Girls Yean and Bosico* v. *Dominican Republic*, the Inter-American Court of Human Rights was required to determine whether rules applicable to late registrations of birth resulted in a discrimination on grounds of foreign descent.

Inter-American Court of Human Rights, case of *The Girls Yean and Bosico* v. *Dominican Republic*, judgment of September 8, 2005 [preliminary objections, merits, reparations and costs], Series C No. 130:

[The Girls, Dilcia Yean and Violeta Bosico, Haitian descendants born in the Dominican Republic, were denied birth registration by public authorities on the ground that they failed to comply with certain legal requirements. Under Dominican Law, the age of the person requesting birth registration was the only criterion to define the requirements and procedure to be followed. The requirements imposed on the petitioners were far more demanding than those applied to other children under the age of thirteen. The denial of a birth certificate entailed the denial of the Dominican nationality and rendered the petitioners stateless.]

171. Considering that it is the State's obligation to grant nationality to those born on its territory [under the *jus soli* principle embodied in the Dominican Constitution], the Dominican Republic must adopt all necessary positive measures to guarantee that Dilcia Yean and Violeta Bosico, as Dominican children of Haitian origin, can access the late registration procedure in conditions of equality and nondiscrimination and fully exercise and enjoy their right to Dominican nationality. The requirements needed to prove birth on Dominican territory should be reasonable and not represent an obstacle for acceding to the right to nationality.

172. The Court finds that, owing to the discriminatory treatment applied to the children, the State denied their nationality and left them stateless, which, in turn, placed them in a situation of continuing vulnerability that lasted until September 25, 2001; in other words, after the date on which the Dominican Republic accepted the Court's contentious jurisdiction.

173. The Court considers that the Dominican Republic failed to comply with its obligation to guarantee the rights embodied in the American Convention, which implies not only that the State shall respect them (negative obligation), but also that it must adopt all appropriate measures to guarantee them (positive obligation), owing to the situation of extreme vulnerability in which the State placed the Yean and Bosico children, because it denied them their right to nationality for discriminatory reasons, and placed them in the impossibility of receiving protection from the State and having access to the benefits due to them, and since they lived in fear of being expelled by the State of which they were nationals and separated from their families owing to the absence of a birth certificate.

174. The Court finds that for discriminatory reasons, and contrary to the pertinent domestic norms, the State failed to grant nationality to the children, which constituted an arbitrary deprivation of their nationality, and left them stateless for more than four years and four months, in violation of Articles 20 and 24 of the American Convention [respectively guaranteeing a right to a nationality and stipulating a principle of equality], in relation to Article 19 thereof [on the rights of the child], and also in relation to Article 1(1) of the Convention, to the detriment of the children Dilcia Yean and Violeta Bosico ...

178. A stateless person, *ex definitione*, does not have recognized juridical personality, because he has not established a juridical and political connection with any State; thus nationality is a prerequisite for recognition of juridical personality.

179. The Court considers that the failure to recognize juridical personality harms human dignity, because it denies absolutely an individual's condition of being a subject of rights and renders him vulnerable to non-observance of his rights by the State or other individuals.

180. In this specific case, the State maintained the Yean and Bosico children in a legal limbo in which, even though the children existed and were inserted into a particular social context, their existence was not recognized juridically; in other words they did not have juridical personality ...

190. In this regard, the Court considers that the domestic norms establishing the requirements for late birth registration must be coherent with the right to nationality in the Dominican Republic and with the terms of the American Convention and other international instruments; namely, they must accredit that the person was born on the State's territory.

191. In accordance with the obligation arising from Article 2 of the American Convention, the Court considers that the requirements for obtaining nationality must be clearly and objectively established previously by the competent authority. Likewise, the law should not provide the State officials applying it with broad discretionary powers, because this creates opportunities for discriminatory acts.

192. The requirements for late declaration of birth cannot be an obstacle for enjoying the right to nationality, particularly for Dominicans of Haitian origin, who belong to a vulnerable sector of the population in the Dominican Republic.

7.4. Question for discussion: the hierarchy of grounds in anti-discrimination law

Applying the Equal Protection Clause of the Bill of Rights appended to the United States Constitution (Fourteenth Amendment), the US Supreme Court applies a three-tiered approach when asked to decide whether the clause has been violated. Most classifications adopted by the legislator are subjected to a mere rationality review, requiring only that the classification be rationally related to a legitimate end. Other classifications are subjected to an intermediate form of scrutiny, requiring that the challenged classification serves an important State interest and that the classification is at least substantially related to serving that interest. Classifications on the basis of gender fall under this category (see *Craig* v. *Boren*, 429 U.S. 190 (1976), although more recent cases, beginning with *Mississippi University for Women* v. *Hogan*, 458 U.S. 718 (1982), added the requirement that, to be valid, a sex-based classification requires an 'exceedingly persuasive justification', bringing the test applied for sex-based classifications closer to strict scrutiny: see *United States* v. *Virginia*, 518 U.S. 515 (1996) and *J.E.B.* v. *Alabama*, 511 U.S. 127 (1994)); so do classifications on grounds of illegitimacy (*Caban* v. *Mohammed*, 441 U.S. 380 (1979)). Finally, some classifications, whether they relate to a 'suspect' ground such as race, national origin (see *Korematsu* v. *United States*, 323 U.S. 214 (1944)), religion (see *Sherbert* v. *Verner*, 374 U.S. 398 (1963)) or, arguably, alienage (*Gonzales* v. *O Centro Espirita Beneficente Uniao do Vegetal*, 546 U.S. 418 (2006)), or whether they burden fundamental rights (including denial or dilution of vote, interstate migration, or access to the courts), are subjected to the strictest form of scrutiny: the Government must show that the challenged classification serves a compelling state interest and that the classification is necessary to serve that interest.

It has sometimes been suggested that this approach, based on more clearly delineated variations in the strictness of scrutiny, should also be adopted by international or regional human rights bodies (see for instance, in the context of the European Convention on Human Rights, where the case law seems to be moving in such a direction, O. M. Arnadóttir, *Equality and Non-Discrimination under the European Convention on Human Rights*, International Studies in Human Rights No. 74 (The Hague: Martinus Nijhoff, 2003); and J. Gerards, 'Intensity of Judicial Review in Equal Treatment Cases', *Netherlands International Law Review* (2004), 135–83). Do you agree? What are the arguments for and against the establishment of such a 'hierarchy of grounds'? On the basis of which considerations should such a hierarchy be developed?

2.3 The legal prohibition of discrimination

The second sentence of Article 26 ICCPR (see box 7.1.) stipulates that the law should prohibit discrimination. This imposes a positive obligation on the legislator: whether they are committed by State agents or by private actors, discriminatory acts should be prohibited and subject to effective legal sanctions. As regards racial discrimination, this obligation already follows from Article 2(1)(d) of the International Convention on the Elimination of All Forms of Racial Discrimination, which provides that the States parties 'shall prohibit and bring to an end, by all appropriate means, including legislation as required by circumstances, racial discrimination by any persons, group or organization'. The Convention on the Elimination of All Forms of Discrimination against Women also imposes an obligation on States to 'adopt appropriate legislative and other measures, including sanctions where appropriate, prohibiting all discrimination against women'; to 'establish legal protection of the rights of women on an equal basis with men and to ensure through competent national tribunals and other public institutions the effective protection of women against any act of discrimination'; and to 'take all appropriate measures to eliminate discrimination against women by any person, organization or enterprise' (Art. 2(b), (c) and (e)). Under the ICCPR itself, Articles 2(1) and 3, which prohibit any discrimination in the enjoyment of the rights of the Covenant and guarantee the equal right of men and women to the enjoyment of all civil and political rights set forth in the Covenant, have been interpreted to require that the States parties 'take all steps necessary, including the prohibition of discrimination on the ground of sex, to put an end to discriminatory actions, both in the public and the private sector, which impair the equal enjoyment of rights' (Human Rights Committee, General Comment No. 28, *Equality of Rights between Men and Women* (Art. 3) (29 March 2000) (CCPR/C/21/Rev.1/Add. 10), para. 4). In addition, the Human Rights Committee notes that:

> **Human Rights Committee, General Comment No. 28, *Equality of Rights between Men and Women* (Art. 3) (29 March 2000) (CCPR/C/21/Rev.1/Add. 10), para. 31:**
>
> The right to equality before the law and freedom from discrimination, protected by article 26, requires States to act against discrimination by public and private agencies in all fields. Discrimination against women in areas such as social security laws (Communications Nos. 172/84, *Broeks* v. *Netherlands*, Views of 9 April 1987; 182/84, *Zwaan de Vries* v. *Netherlands*, Views of 9 April 1987; 218/1986, *Vos* v. *Netherlands*, Views of 29 March 1989) as well as in the area of citizenship or rights of non-citizens in a country (Communication No. 035/1978, *Aumeeruddy-Cziffra et al.* v. *Mauritius*, Views adopted 9 April 1981) violates article 26. The commission of so-called 'honour crimes' which remain unpunished constitutes a serious violation of the Covenant and in particular of articles 6, 14 and 26. Laws which impose more severe penalties on women than on men for adultery or other offences also violate the requirement of equal treatment. The Committee has also often observed in reviewing States parties reports that a large proportion of women are employed in areas which are not protected by labour laws and that prevailing customs and traditions discriminate against women, particularly with regard to access to better paid employment and to equal pay for work of equal value. States parties should review their legislation and practices and take the lead in implementing all measures necessary to eliminate discrimination against women in all fields, for example by prohibiting discrimination by private actors in areas such as employment, education, political activities and the provision of accommodation, goods and services. States parties should report on all these measures and provide information on the remedies available to victims of such discrimination.

The main difficulty which may arise in the implementation of this norm concerns the scope of the positive obligation it imposes. Article 1(1) of the International Convention on the Elimination of All Forms of Racial Discrimination defines the term 'racial discrimination' as meaning 'any distinction, exclusion, restriction or preference based on race, colour, descent, or national or ethnic origin which has the purpose or effect of nullifying or impairing the recognition, enjoyment or exercise, on an equal footing, of human rights and fundamental freedoms *in the political, economic, social, cultural or any other field of public life*' (emphasis added), thus apparently not extending the obligation to prohibit discrimination to private life narrowly understood as the sphere of family or intimate relationships.

A similar question of interpretation arose when Protocol No. 12 to the European Convention on Human Rights was adopted in 2000 (see above, section 1.2.). Article 1 of Protocol No. 12 imposes direct obligations only on public authorities (whether they belong to the executive, the legislative or the judicial branches). However, the States may have to adopt measures in order to prohibit discrimination by private parties, in situations where the failure to adopt such measures would be clearly unreasonable and result in depriving persons from the enjoyment of rights set forth by law. The Explanatory Report to Protocol No. 12 mentions that 'a failure to provide protection from discrimination in [relations between private persons] might be so clear-cut and grave that it might engage clearly the responsibility of the State and then Article 1 of the Protocol could come into play' (Explanatory Report to Protocol No. 12, para. 26). Although certain positive obligations may thus be imposed on States to protect from discrimination in the relationships between private parties, States parties may not, under the pretext of protecting from discrimination, commit disproportionate interferences with the right to respect for private or family life, as guaranteed by Article 8 ECHR.

> **Explanatory Report to Protocol No. 12 to the Convention for the Protection of Human Rights and Fundamental Freedoms (ETS No. 177), para. 28:**
>
> [A]ny positive obligation in the area of relations between private persons would concern, at the most, relations in the public sphere normally regulated by law, for which the state has a certain responsibility (for example, arbitrary denial of access to work, access to restaurants, or to services which private persons may make available to the public such as medical care or utilities such as water and electricity, etc). The precise form of the response which the state should take will vary according to the circumstances. It is understood that purely private matters would not be affected. Regulation of such matters would also be likely to interfere with the individual's right to respect for his private and family life, his home and his correspondence, as guaranteed by Article 8 of the Convention.

Therefore, a tripartite division is required, between three kinds of legal relations: in the interactions between the public authorities and private individuals, the former are prohibited from discriminating against the latter; in the interactions between private individuals occurring in the context of market relationships (in spheres such as employment, education, housing, or services accessible to the public), the State authorities may be under an obligation to intervene in order to prevent the most flagrant cases of discrimination and offer remedies to the victims thereof; finally, in the interactions between private individuals which concern the private sphere, in the original meaning of private and family life which restricts this notion to the sphere of intimacy, the public authorities shall be prohibited from intervening, even if their objective in doing so is to better protect from discriminatory acts. It is in the intermediate or semi-public sphere where the obligations of the State are the least clearly defined: there, discriminatory behaviour may be regulated in order to outlaw discrimination, but whether or not this is an obligation under Article 1 of Protocol No. 12 ECHR may in certain cases be debated.

This position is not unique to Protocol No. 12 ECHR. Thus for instance, within the EU, the European Court of Justice has concluded (albeit without making any reference to the ICCPR or, indeed, to international human rights law generally) that the United Kingdom could legitimately exclude from the prohibition of discrimination on grounds of sex (as imposed under European Union Law) employment in a private household: it took the view that this exception, provided in section 6(3) of the UK Sex Discrimination Act 1975, 'is intended … to reconcile the principle of equality of treatment with the principle of respect for private life, which is also fundamental' (Case

165/82, *Commission* v. *United Kingdom* [1983] E.C.R. 3431 (judgment of 8 November 1983), para. 13).

Indeed, the right to respect for private or family life may not be the sole relevant consideration where the legal prohibition of discrimination is extended to private relationships: other competing rights, such as the freedom of association of certain groups seeking to exclude individuals on the basis of criteria discriminatory on their face, may also come into play. This question was presented to the United States Supreme Court in the following case.

United States Supreme Court, *Boy Scouts of America et al.* v. *Dale*, 530 U.S. 640 (2000):

[The Boy Scouts of America (BSA) revoked assistant scoutmaster James Dale's membership when, following an interview with Dale published in a local newspaper, the officials of the organization discovered that he was a homosexual and a gay rights activist. In 1992, Dale filed suit against BSA, alleging that they had violated the New Jersey's public accommodations statute and its common law by revoking Dale's membership based solely on his sexual orientation. New Jersey's public accommodations statute prohibits, among other things, discrimination on the basis of sexual orientation in places of public accommodation. The BSA, a private, not-for-profit organization, asserted that homosexual conduct was inconsistent with the values it was attempting to instil in young people. The New Jersey Superior Court held that New Jersey's public accommodations law was inapplicable because the Boy Scouts was not a place of public accommodation. The Court also concluded that the Boy Scouts' First Amendment freedom of expressive association prevented the Government from forcing the Boy Scouts to accept Dale as an adult leader. On appeal however, the Court's Appellate Division held that New Jersey's public accommodations law applied to the Boy Scouts because of its broad-based membership solicitation and its connections with various public entities, and that the Boy Scouts violated it by revoking Dale's membership based on his homosexuality; it also rejected the Boy Scouts' federal constitutional claims. The New Jersey Supreme Court affirmed. The Court held that application of New Jersey's public accommodations law did not violate the Boy Scouts' First Amendment right of expressive association because Dale's inclusion would not significantly affect members' abilities to carry out their purpose: the Court said it was 'not persuaded ... that a shared goal of Boy Scout members is to associate in order to preserve the view that homosexuality is immoral' (160 N. J. 562 at 613 (1999)). With respect to the right to intimate association, the court concluded that the Boy Scouts' 'large size, nonselectivity, inclusive rather than exclusive purpose, and practice of inviting or allowing nonmembers to attend meetings, establish that the organization is not "sufficiently personal or private to warrant constitutional protection" under the freedom of intimate association.' (160 N. J. 562 at 608–9 (1999))]

Opinion of the Court by Chief Justice Rehnquist:
In *Roberts* v. *United States Jaycees*, 468 U.S. 609, 622 (1984), we observed that 'implicit in the right to engage in activities protected by the First Amendment' is 'a corresponding right to associate with others in pursuit of a wide variety of political, social, economic, educational, religious, and cultural ends'. This right is crucial in preventing the majority from imposing its views on groups that would rather express other, perhaps unpopular, ideas. See *ibid.* (stating that

protection of the right to expressive association is 'especially important in preserving political and cultural diversity and in shielding dissident expression from suppression by the majority'). Government actions that may unconstitutionally burden this freedom may take many forms, one of which is 'intrusion into the internal structure or affairs of an association' like a 'regulation that forces the group to accept members it does not desire'. *Id.*, at 623. Forcing a group to accept certain members may impair the ability of the group to express those views, and only those views, that it intends to express. Thus, '[f]reedom of association … plainly presupposes a freedom not to associate'. Ibid.

The forced inclusion of an unwanted person in a group infringes the group's freedom of expressive association if the presence of that person affects in a significant way the group's ability to advocate public or private viewpoints. *New York State Club Assn., Inc.* v. *City of New York*, 487 U.S. 1, 13 (1988). But the freedom of expressive association, like many freedoms, is not absolute. We have held that the freedom could be overridden 'by regulations adopted to serve compelling state interests, unrelated to the suppression of ideas, that cannot be achieved through means significantly less restrictive of associational freedoms'. *Roberts, supra*, at 623.

To determine whether a group is protected by the First Amendment's expressive associational right, we must determine whether the group engages in 'expressive association'. The First Amendment's protection of expressive association is not reserved for advocacy groups. But to come within its ambit, a group must engage in some form of expression, whether it be public or private.

[Having found that the general mission of the BSA is to 'instill values into young people', the Court concludes that they do engage in expressive activity, and that they have always in the past sought to convey the message that homosexual conduct was not consistent with those values. It further notes that 'the presence of Dale as an assistant scoutmaster would … interfere with the Boy Scout's choice not to propound a point of view contrary to its beliefs'.]

Having determined that the Boy Scouts is an expressive association and that the forced inclusion of Dale would significantly affect its expression, we inquire whether the application of New Jersey's public accommodations law to require that the Boy Scouts accept Dale as an assistant scoutmaster runs afoul of the Scouts' freedom of expressive association. We conclude that it does.

State public accommodations laws were originally enacted to prevent discrimination in traditional places of public accommodation – like inns and trains … Over time, the public accommodations laws have expanded to cover more places. New Jersey's statutory definition of '"[a] place of public accommodation"' is extremely broad. The term is said to 'include, but not be limited to', a list of over 50 types of places. N. J. Stat. Ann. §10:5 – 5(l) (West Supp. 2000) … Many on the list are what one would expect to be places where the public is invited. For example, the statute includes as places of public accommodation taverns, restaurants, retail shops, and public libraries. But the statute also includes places that often may not carry with them open invitations to the public, like summer camps and roof gardens. In this case, the New Jersey Supreme Court went a step further and applied its public accommodations law to a private entity without even attempting to tie the term 'place' to a physical location. As the definition of 'public accommodation' has expanded from clearly commercial entities, such as restaurants, bars, and hotels, to membership organizations such as the Boy Scouts, the potential for conflict between state public accommodations laws and the First Amendment rights of organizations has increased.

We recognized in cases such as *Roberts* and *Duarte* that States have a compelling interest in eliminating discrimination against women in public accommodations. But in each of these cases we went on to conclude that the enforcement of these statutes would not materially interfere with the ideas that the organization sought to express. In *Roberts*, we said '[i]ndeed, the Jaycees has failed to demonstrate ... any serious burden on the male members' freedom of expressive association' 468 U.S., at 626. In [*Board of Directors of Rotary Inter'l* v. *Rotary Club of Duarte*, 481 U.S. 537 (1987)], we said: '[I]mpediments to the exercise of one's right to choose one's associates can violate the right of association protected by the First Amendment. In this case, however, the evidence fails to demonstrate that admitting women to Rotary Clubs will affect in any significant way the existing members' ability to carry out their various purposes.' 481 U.S., at 548 (internal quotation marks and citations omitted).

We thereupon concluded in each of these cases that the organizations' First Amendment rights were not violated by the application of the States' public accommodations laws.

In [*Hurley* v. *Irish-American Gay, Lesbian and Bisexual Group of Boston, Inc.*, 515 U.S. 557 (1995)], we said that public accommodations laws 'are well within the State's usual power to enact when a legislature has reason to believe that a given group is the target of discrimination, and they do not, as a general matter, violate the First or Fourteenth Amendments'. 515 U.S., at 572. But we went on to note that in that case 'the Massachusetts [public accommodations] law has been applied in a peculiar way' because 'any contingent of protected individuals with a message would have the right to participate in petitioners' speech, so that the communication produced by the private organizers would be shaped by all those protected by the law who wish to join in with some expressive demonstration of their own'. *Id.*, at 572–573. And in the associational freedom cases such as *Roberts*, *Duarte*, and [*New York State Club Assn., Inc.* v. *City of New York*, 487 U.S. 1 (1988)], after finding a compelling state interest, the Court went on to examine whether or not the application of the state law would impose any 'serious burden' on the organization's rights of expressive association. So in these cases, the associational interest in freedom of expression has been set on one side of the scale, and the State's interest on the other.

Dale contends that we should apply the intermediate standard of review enunciated in *United States* v. *O'Brien*, 391 U.S. 367 (1968), to evaluate the competing interests. There the Court enunciated a four-part test for review of a governmental regulation that has only an incidental effect on protected speech – in that case the symbolic burning of a draft card. A law prohibiting the destruction of draft cards only incidentally affects the free speech rights of those who happen to use a violation of that law as a symbol of protest. But New Jersey's public accommodations law directly and immediately affects associational rights, in this case associational rights that enjoy First Amendment protection. Thus, *O'Brien* is inapplicable.

In *Hurley*, we applied traditional First Amendment analysis to hold that the application of the Massachusetts public accommodations law to a parade violated the First Amendment rights of the parade organizers. Although we did not explicitly deem the parade in *Hurley* an expressive association, the analysis we applied there is similar to the analysis we apply here. We have already concluded that a state requirement that the Boy Scouts retain Dale as an assistant scoutmaster would significantly burden the organization's right to oppose or disfavor homosexual conduct. The state interests embodied in New Jersey's public accommodations law do not justify such a severe intrusion on the Boy Scouts' rights to freedom of expressive association. That being the case, we hold that the First Amendment prohibits the State from imposing such a requirement through the application of its public accommodations law ...

We are not, as we must not be, guided by our views of whether the Boy Scouts' teachings with respect to homosexual conduct are right or wrong; public or judicial disapproval of a tenet of an organization's expression does not justify the State's effort to compel the organization to accept members where such acceptance would derogate from the organization's expressive message. 'While the law is free to promote all sorts of conduct in place of harmful behavior, it is not free to interfere with speech for no better reason than promoting an approved message or discouraging a disfavored one, however enlightened either purpose may strike the government.' *Hurley*, 515 U.S., at 579.

This position may be contrasted with the judgment adopted on 18 August 2008 by the California Supreme Court in a case involving a lesbian woman, Ms Benitez, who sought to become pregnant but was confronted with the refusal of the qualified physicians to treat her on the basis of religious objection.

California Supreme Court, *North Coast Women's Care Medical Care Group, Inc., et al.* v. *San Diego County Superior Court (Guadalupe T. Benitez)*, Case S142892, judgment of 18 August 2008:

Do the rights of religious freedom and free speech, as guaranteed in both the federal and the California Constitutions, exempt a medical clinic's physicians from complying with the California Unruh Civil Rights Act's prohibition against discrimination based on a person's sexual orientation? Our answer is no.

... Plaintiff Guadalupe T. Benitez is a lesbian who lives with her partner, Joanne Clark, in San Diego County. They wanted Benitez to become pregnant ... In August 1999, Benitez and Clark first met with defendant Christine Brody, an obstetrician and gynecologist employed by defendant North Coast. Benitez mentioned that she was a lesbian. Dr. Brody explained that at some point intrauterine insemination (IUI) might have to be considered ... Dr. Brody said that if IUI became necessary, her religious beliefs would preclude her from performing the procedure for Benitez ... [Similarly, Dr Fenton, another North Coast physician,] refused to prepare donated fresh sperm for Benitez because of his religious objection. Two of his colleagues, Drs. Charles Stoopack and Ross Langley, had no such religious objection, but unlike Dr. Fenton, they were not licensed to prepare fresh sperm. Dr. Fenton then referred Benitez to a physician outside North Coast's medical practice, Dr. Michael Kettle [who ultimately performed in vitro fertilization, making Ms Benitez pregnant].

In August 2001, Benitez sued North Coast and its physicians, Brody and Fenton, seeking damages and injunctive relief on several theories, notably sexual orientation discrimination in violation of California's Unruh Civil Rights Act. [The Defendants argued that their] 'alleged misconduct, if any' was protected by the rights of free speech and freedom of religion set forth in the federal and state Constitutions ...

[Part III of the opinion, which discusses the reliance of the defendants on the First Amendment to the Federal Constitution, is reproduced in full below. Parts IV and V, which discuss the Californian Constitution and procedural issues, are not reproduced here.]

The First Amendment to the federal Constitution states that 'Congress shall make no law respecting an establishment of religion, or prohibiting the free exercise thereof; or abridging the freedom of speech ...' (US Const., 1st Amend.) This provision applies not only to Congress but also to the states because of its incorporation into the Fourteenth Amendment. (See *Employment Div., Ore. Dept. of Human Resources* v. *Smith* (1990) 494 U.S. 872, 876–877 (*Smith*).) With respect to the free exercise of religion, the First Amendment 'first and foremost' protects 'the right to believe and profess whatever religious doctrine one desires'. (*Smith, supra*, at p. 877.) Thus, it 'obviously excludes all "government regulation of religious beliefs as such".' (*Ibid.*) Below, we discuss pertinent decisions of the high court construing the First Amendment's guarantee of the free exercise of religion.

Sherbert v. *Verner* (1963) 374 U.S. 398 (*Sherbert*) involved South Carolina's denial of unemployment benefits to a Seventh-day Adventist who refused on religious grounds to work on Saturdays. The high court held that restricting unemployment benefit eligibility to those who could work on Saturdays was a 'substantial infringement' of the claimant's First Amendment rights, and it declared the state law unconstitutional because it lacked a 'compelling [governmental] interest'. (*Id.* at pp. 406–407.)

Nine years later, the United States Supreme Court reiterated that test in *Wisconsin* v. *Yoder* (1972) 406 U.S. 205 (*Yoder*). At issue there was a Wisconsin law that required all children ages seven to 16 to attend school. Members of the Old Order Amish religion and the Conservative Amish Mennonite Church, however, kept their children out of school once they completed the eighth grade. (*Id.* at pp. 208–209.) Yoder held that under the First Amendment's clause guaranteeing the free exercise of religion, the Amish were exempt from obeying the state law in question because their 'objection to formal education beyond the eighth grade [was] firmly grounded' in their religious beliefs, and the State of Wisconsin lacked a compelling interest in applying the compulsory education law to Amish children. (*Id.* at p. 210; see *id.* at pp. 214, 219, 234.)

But then in 1990, in *Smith, supra*, 494 U.S 872, the high court repudiated the compelling state interest test it had used in *Sherbert, supra*, 374 U.S. 398, and in *Yoder, supra*, 406 U.S. 205. Instead, it announced that the First Amendment's right to the free exercise of religion 'does not relieve an individual of the obligation to comply with a "valid and neutral law of general applicability on the ground that the law proscribes (or prescribes) conduct that his religion prescribes (or proscribes)".' (*Smith, supra*, at p. 879.) Three years later, the court reiterated that holding in *Church of Lukumi Babalu Aye, Inc.* v. *Hialeah* (1993) 508 U.S. 520, 531 (*Lukumi*), stating that 'a law that is neutral and of general applicability need not be justified by a compelling governmental interest even if the law has the incidental effect of burdening a particular religious practice'.

Thus, under the United States Supreme Court's most recent holdings, a religious objector has no federal constitutional right to an exemption from a neutral and valid law of general applicability on the ground that compliance with that law is contrary to the objector's religious beliefs.

Just four years ago, in *Catholic Charities of Sacramento, Inc.* v. *Superior Court* (2004) 32 Cal.4th 527 (*Catholic Charities*), we considered the claim of a nonprofit entity affiliated with the Roman Catholic Church (Catholic Charities) that the First Amendment's guarantee of free exercise of religion exempted it from complying with a California law, the Women's Contraception Equity Act (WCEA), which required employers that provide prescription drug insurance coverage for their employees to include coverage for prescription contraceptives.

In rejecting that claim, we applied the test the United States Supreme Court had adopted in its 1990 decision in *Smith, supra*, 494 U.S. 872. We explained: 'The WCEA's requirements apply neutrally and generally to all employers, regardless of religious affiliation, except to those few who satisfy the statute's strict requirements for exemption on religious grounds. The act also addresses a matter the state is free to regulate; it regulates the content of insurance policies for the purpose of eliminating a form of gender discrimination in health benefits. The act conflicts with Catholic Charities' religious beliefs only incidentally, because those beliefs happen to make prescription contraceptives sinful.' (*Catholic Charities, supra*, at p. 549.)

In this case, too, with respect to defendants' reliance on the First Amendment, we apply the high court's *Smith* test. California's Unruh Civil Rights Act, from which defendant physicians seek religious exemption, is 'a valid and neutral law of general applicability' (*Smith, supra*, 494 U.S. at p. 879). As relevant in this case, it requires business establishments to provide 'full and equal accommodations, advantages, facilities, privileges, or services' to all persons notwithstanding their sexual orientation. (Civ. Code, §51, subds. (a) & (b).) Accordingly, the First Amendment's right to the free exercise of religion does not exempt defendant physicians here from conforming their conduct to the Act's antidiscrimination requirements even if compliance poses an incidental conflict with defendants' religious beliefs. (*Lukumi, supra*, 508 U.S. at p. 531; *Smith*, supra, at p. 879.)

Defendant physicians, however, insist that the high court's decision in *Smith, supra*, 494 U.S. 872, has language on 'hybrid rights' that lends support to their argument that under the First Amendment they are exempt from complying with the antidiscrimination provisions of California's Unruh Civil Rights Act. The pertinent passage in *Smith* states: 'The only decisions in which we have held that the First Amendment bars application of a neutral, generally applicable law to religiously motivated action have involved not the Free Exercise Clause alone, but the Free Exercise Clause in conjunction with other constitutional protections ...' (*Smith*, at p. 881.) But the facts in *Smith*, the court explained, did 'not present such a hybrid situation'. (*Id.* at p. 882.) Defendants here contend that they do have a hybrid claim, because compliance on their part with the state's Act interferes with a combination of their First Amendment rights to free speech and to freely exercise their religion. We rejected a similar hybrid claim in *Catholic Charities, supra*, 32 Cal.4th 527.

In that case, we explained that '[t]he high court has not, since the decision in *Smith, supra*, 494 U.S. 872, determined whether the hybrid rights theory is valid or invoked it to justify applying strict scrutiny to a free exercise claim.' (*Catholic Charities, supra*, 32 Cal.4th at p. 557.) We added, however, that Justice Souter's concurring opinion in *Lukumi, supra*, 508 U.S. 520, 567, was critical of the idea that hybrid rights would give rise to a stricter level of scrutiny: '"[I]f a hybrid claim is simply one in which another constitutional right is implicated, then the hybrid exception would probably be so vast as to swallow the Smith rule ..."' (*Catholic Charities, supra*, at pp. 557–558, quoting *Lukumi, supra*, at p. 567 (conc. opn. of Souter, J.).) We also noted that the federal Court of Appeals for the Sixth Circuit had rejected as '"completely illogical"' the proposition that "the legal standard [of review] under the Free Exercise Clause depends on whether a free exercise claim is coupled with other constitutional rights." (*Kissinger* v. *Board of Trustees* [(1993)] 5 F.3d 177, 180 & fn. 1.)' (*Catholic Charities, supra*, at p. 558.) Nonetheless, after assuming for argument's sake that 'the hybrid rights theory is not merely a misreading of *Smith, supra*, 494 U.S. 872', we concluded that *Catholic Charities* had 'not alleged a meritorious' claim under that theory. (*Ibid.*) We also rejected the contention by Catholic Charities that requiring it to provide prescription contraceptive coverage to its employees would violate its First Amendment right to free speech 'by requiring the organization to engage in symbolic speech it finds objectionable'. (*Ibid.*) As we explained, 'compliance with a law regulating health care benefits is not speech'. (*Ibid.*)

Here, defendant physicians contend that exposing them to liability for refusing to perform the IUI medical procedure for plaintiff infringes upon their First Amendment rights to free speech and free exercise of religion. Not so. As we noted earlier, California's Unruh Civil Rights Act imposes on business establishments certain antidiscrimination obligations, thus precluding any such establishment or its agents from telling patrons that it will not comply with the Act. Notwithstanding these statutory obligations, defendant physicians remain free to voice their objections, religious or otherwise, to the Act's prohibition against sexual orientation discrimination. 'For purposes of the free speech clause, simple obedience to a law that does not require one to convey a verbal or symbolic message cannot reasonably be seen as a statement of support for the law or its purpose. Such a rule would, in effect, permit each individual to choose which laws he would obey merely by declaring his agreement or opposition.' (*Catholic Charities, supra*, 32 Cal.4th at pp. 558–559.)

Defendant physicians also perceive a form of free speech infringement flowing from plaintiff's purported efforts 'to silence the doctors at trial'. But the First Amendment prohibits government abridgment of free speech. Here, plaintiff is a private citizen. Therefore, her conduct as complained of by defendants does not fall within the ambit of the First Amendment.

Plaintiff's motion in the trial court for summary adjudication of defendant physicians' affirmative defense claiming a religious exemption from liability under California's Unruh Civil Rights Act merely sought to preclude the presentation at trial of a defense lacking any constitutional basis. In ruling on the motion, the trial court granted summary adjudication of the defense only insofar as it applied to plaintiff's claim of sexual orientation discrimination as prohibited by the Act. (See p. 17, *post.*) Nothing in that ruling precludes defendants from later at trial offering evidence, if relevant, that their denial of the medical treatment at issue was prompted by their religious beliefs for reasons other than plaintiff's sexual orientation.

7.5. Question for discussion: conflicts between equality requirements and other human rights

How far should anti-discrimination legislation reach, when it conflicts with other rights such as the right to respect for private or family life, freedom of religion, or freedom of association? Is this kind of conflict specific, or is it simply one example of conflicting fundamental rights? Should it matter which forms of discrimination are at stake, in particular on which grounds the disputed classification is made?

The requirement of a legal prohibition of discrimination requires more than simply that a law exists to impose such a prohibition. Effective enforcement is also required. In the case of *Simone André Diniz* v. *Brazil*, the Inter-American Commission on Human Rights dealt with the issue of the lack of an effective prohibition of racial discrimination, and in particular the State's failure to establish appropriate judicial remedies:

Inter-American Commission on Human Rights, *Simone André Diniz* v. *Brazil*, **Case 12.001, Decision on the merits of 21 October 2006, Report No. 66/06:**

[In the present case, an employer published an advertisement in a regional newspaper offering domestic employment, with preference to white persons. An Afro-Brazilian job-seeker, after calling the employer and being turned down for her colour, brought charges of racism against the employer. After a brief investigation, the public prosecutor decided not to press charges alleging that the impugned behaviour – publication of an advertisement expressing racial preferences – did not constitute the crime of racism. The decision to classify was upheld by the judge. After acknowledging the important progress made by Brazil in establishing a legal framework – including criminal law provisions – for the punishment of racism, the Inter-American Commission noted that these norms remained largely ineffective. It then suggested three causes for the law's inefficiency: the difficulty of satisfying the procedural requirement to prove racial hatred or the intent to discriminate; the existence of institutional racism; and the non-existence of a hate-speech crime, all cases being treated under general laws of slander. In its analysis of the specific circumstances of the petition, the Commission observed:]

97. The Commission already held that every victim of a human rights violation must be assured of a diligent and impartial investigation, and, if there are indicia as to who committed the crime, the pertinent action should be initiated so that a judge with jurisdiction, in the context of a fair trial, can determine whether the crime occurred, as with every crime brought to the attention of the authorities.

98. As this has not happened with the complaints of racial discrimination lodged by Afrodescendants in Brazil, the Brazilian State has flagrantly violated the principle of equality enshrined in the American Declaration and the American Convention, which it undertook to respect, and which dictates that all persons are equal before the law and have the right to equal protection of the law, without discrimination.

99. First, the Commission understands that excluding a person from access to the labor market on grounds of race is an act of racial discrimination ...

100. The IACHR understands that Article 24 of the American Convention is violated, in conjunction with Article 1(1), if the State allows such conduct to remain in impunity, validating it implicitly or giving its acquiescence. Equal protection before the law requires that any expression of racist practices be dealt with diligently by the judicial authorities.

101. In the specific case of Simone André Diniz, there was an ad that excluded her, based on her racial status, from a job. When she lodged a complaint with the judicial authorities they proceeded to archive the case, even though the perpetrator herself verified that she had the ad published.

102. The archiving of the case was not an isolated event in the Brazilian justice system; rather, the Commission has shown that it reflects a purposeful and explicit pattern of conduct on the part of the Brazilian authorities, when they receive a complaint of racism.

103. In addition, the automatic archiving of racism complaints keeps the judiciary from considering whether there was malicious or deceitful intent (*dolo*). As shown above, the absence of racial motivation has led to the non-enforcement of Law 7716/89, either by the automatic archiving of complaints in the inquiry phase or by judgments of acquittal. In the instant case it was by archiving the police inquiry. The fact that Gisela Silva had told the police inquiry that she had no intent to discriminate racially, or that she had reasons for preferring a white domestic employee, did not justify archiving; the defense of no racial motivation should have been argued before and analyzed by the judge, in the context of a regular criminal proceeding ...

107. The Commission emphasizes to the Brazilian government that the failure of the public authorities to go forward diligently and adequately with the criminal prosecution of the perpetrators of racial discrimination and racism creates the risk of producing not only institutional racism, in which the judiciary is seen by the Afrodescendant community as a racist branch of government, but is also grave because of the impact on society, insofar as impunity encourages racist practices.

108. The Commission would like to conclude saying that it is of fundamental importance to foster a legal awareness capable of making the effort to combat racial discrimination and racism effectively, for the judiciary should respond effectively insofar as it's an essential tool for controlling and fighting racial discrimination and racism.

109. In view of the unequal treatment the Brazilian authorities accorded the complaint of racism and racial discrimination lodged by Simone André Diniz, which reveals a widespread discriminatory practice in the analysis of these crimes, the Commission concludes that the Brazilian State violated Article 24 of the American Convention in respect of Simone André Diniz.

2.4 The guarantee of an effective protection against discrimination

According to the fourth norm contained in Article 26 ICCPR (see box 7.1.), States parties must 'guarantee to all persons *equal and effective protection against discrimination* on any ground such as race, colour, sex, language, religion, political or other opinion, national or social origin, property, birth or other status' (emphasis added). This positive obligation goes beyond the mere legal prohibition of individual acts of discrimination. It requires that States effectively combat instances of structural or systemic discrimination, by the adoption of positive measures ensuring that no group is permanently disadvantaged or excluded from the community. The Human Rights Committee requests that States parties include in their reports information about 'any problems of discrimination in fact, which may be practised either by public authorities, by the community, or by private persons or bodies', and wishes to be informed about 'legal provisions and administrative measures directed at diminishing or eliminating such discrimination'. The Committee also notes that positive action may in certain cases be required.

Human Rights Committee, General Comment No. 18, *Non-discrimination* (1989) (HRI/GEN/1/Rev.7, at 146), paras. 9–10:

[T]he principle of equality sometimes requires States parties to take affirmative action in order to diminish or eliminate conditions which cause or help to perpetuate discrimination prohibited by the Covenant. For example, in a State where the general conditions of a certain part of the population prevent or impair their enjoyment of human rights, the State should take specific action to correct those conditions. Such action may involve granting for a time to the part of the population concerned certain preferential treatment in specific matters as compared with the rest of the population. However, as long as such action is needed to correct discrimination in fact, it is a case of legitimate differentiation under the Covenant.

We return to the question of positive action measures hereunder (section 3.3.). We may note here, however, that similar positive duties have also been identified under the American Convention on Human Rights. In the above-mentioned *Simone André Diniz* v. *Brazil* case (section 2.3.), the Commission established that institutional racism and structural and historical causes were responsible for the inefficiency of the anti-discrimination legal framework, which led the Commission to recommend that Brazil 'adopt and implement measures to educate court and police officials to avoid actions that involve discrimination in investigations, proceedings or in civil or criminal conviction for complaints of racial discrimination and racism'. Furthermore, in the *Yean and Bosico* case, which concerned discrimination on grounds of foreign descent (section 2.2.), the Inter-American Court of Human Rights took the view that there was a positive obligation to adopt legislative, administrative and other measures in order to remedy structural discrimination. This is expressed even more clearly in the following advisory opinion, requested by Mexico:

Inter-American Court of Human Rights, Advisory Opinion OC-18/03 of 17 September 2003, requested by the United Mexican States on the *Juridical Condition and Rights of the Undocumented Migrants*, paras. 112–19:

112. Migrants are generally in a vulnerable situation as subjects of human rights; they are in an individual situation of absence or difference of power with regard to non-migrants (nationals or residents). This situation of vulnerability has an ideological dimension and occurs in a historical context that is distinct for each State and is maintained by *de jure* (inequalities between nationals and aliens in the laws) and *de facto* (structural inequalities) situations. This leads to the establishment of differences in their access to the public resources administered by the State.

113. Cultural prejudices about migrants also exist that lead to reproduction of the situation of vulnerability; these include ethnic prejudices, xenophobia and racism, which make it difficult for migrants to integrate into society and lead to their human rights being violated with impunity ...

118. We should mention that the regular situation of a person in a State is not a prerequisite for that State to respect and ensure the principle of equality and nondiscrimination, because,

as mentioned above, this principle is of a fundamental nature and all States must guarantee it to their citizens and to all aliens who are in their territory. This does not mean that they cannot take any action against migrants who do not comply with national laws. However, it is important that, when taking the corresponding measures, States should respect human rights and ensure their exercise and enjoyment to all persons who are in their territory, without any discrimination owing to their regular or irregular residence, or their nationality, race, gender or any other reason.

119. Consequently, States may not discriminate or tolerate discriminatory situations that prejudice migrants. However, the State may grant a distinct treatment to documented migrants with respect to undocumented migrants, or between migrants and nationals, provided that this differential treatment is reasonable, objective, proportionate and does not harm human rights. For example, distinctions may be made between migrants and nationals regarding ownership of some political rights. States may also establish mechanisms to control the entry into and departure from their territory of undocumented migrants, which must always be applied with strict regard for the guarantees of due process and respect for human dignity.

3 THE NOTION OF DISCRIMINATION

Discrimination is a multi-pronged notion. The vocabulary used refers to notions such as *de facto* discrimination, institutional discrimination, real or substantive equality, positive or affirmative action. The precise meaning of these concepts may differ between treaties and jurisdictions. In this section, the different dimensions of the non-discrimination requirement are explored and illustrated through representative cases. We examine the notions of direct and indirect discrimination (section 3.1.); of reasonable accommodation (section 3.2.); and of positive action (section 3.3.). Finally, these different understandings of the requirement of non-discrimination are related to the four rules explained in section 2 above: together, these two dimensions provide a full matrix of the implications of the principle of equal treatment.

3.1 Direct and indirect discrimination

Cases such as *Müller and Engelhard* v. *Namibia* or *Foin* v. *France*, both discussed above, present us with relatively easy situations where the impugned difference in treatment was practised openly – and indeed, was written into the legislation whose compatibility with the requirements of non-discrimination was challenged before the Human Rights Committee. In certain cases, practices too will openly differentiate on the basis of a ground which may lack a reasonable and objective justification. However, discrimination may also result from the use of apparently neutral criteria, procedures, or practices, the effect of which will be similar to that of direct discrimination: it is then referred to as indirect discrimination. Such criteria, procedures or practices, which result in *de facto* discrimination, may be calculated in order to exclude the members of a certain category. Alternatively, even in the absence of any intention to discriminate, they may have a discriminatory impact because they are the result of established and unchecked routines, and fail to take into account the specific situation of certain groups. The notion of indirect discrimination serves, thus, two distinct ends: first, to unmask instances of conscious discrimination which hide behind the use of apparently neutral criteria, in order to arrive at the same result as would follow from the explicit use of prohibited differentiation criteria; second, to challenge certain rules or practices which, although not calculated to produce such effect, impose a specific disadvantage on certain groups, or have a disproportionate impact on such groups, without there being a justification for such disadvantage or such an impact. In this second conception, indirect discrimination may be completely detached from any kind of intention to discriminate, and it is best seen as a tool to revise permanently institutionalized habits and procedures, in order to make them more hospitable to difference. This is made possible by the use of statistical data, in order to measure the 'disparate (or disproportionate) impact' of apparently neutral measures on certain groups. There are advantages associated to this understanding of indirect discrimination, but also potential difficulties (see box 7.3.).

One famous example of 'disparate impact' discrimination is the case of *Griggs* v. *Duke Power Co*, which the US Supreme Court decided in 1971. This is generally seen as the first 'disparate impact' decision adopted under the Employment Title (Title VII) of the Civil Rights Act 1964 (see D. A. Strauss, 'Discriminatory Intent and the Taming of Brown', *University of Chicago Law Review*, 56 (1989), 935; or T. Eisenberg, 'Disproportionate Impact and Illicit Motive: Theories of Constitutional Adjudication', 52 *New York University Law Review*, vol. 36 (1977)). This class action, filed on behalf of the African-American employees of the Duke Power Company, challenged the defendant's 'inside' transfer policy, which required employees who wanted to work in all but the company's lowest paying Labour Department to register a minimum score on two separate aptitude tests in addition to having a high school education. The Court considered that this policy was in violation of the applicable provision of the Civil Rights Act. At the material time, section 703 of the Civil Rights Act 1964 provided that '(a) It shall be an unlawful employment practice for an employer ... (2) to limit, segregate, or classify his employees in any way which would deprive or tend to deprive any individual of employment opportunities or otherwise adversely affect his status as an employee, because of such individual's race, colour, religion, sex, or national origin ... (h) Notwithstanding any other provision of this title, it shall not be an unlawful employment practice for an employer ... to give and to act upon the results of any professionally developed ability test provided that such test, its administration or action upon the results is not designed, intended or used to discriminate because of race, colour, religion, sex or national origin ...' (78 Stat. 255, 42 U.S.C. 2000e-2). There was evidence that, under this policy, far more whites would accede to the other departments than African-Americans: in North Carolina, 1960 census statistics showed that, while 34 per cent of white males had completed high school, only 12 per cent of African-American males had done so; and with respect to standardized tests, the Employment Equal Opportunities Commission (EEOC) had found that use of a battery of tests, including the Wonderlic and Bennett tests used by the company in the instant case,

Box 7.3. **The promises and methodological difficulties associated with 'disparate impact' discrimination**

The reach of 'disparate impact' discrimination is potentially much broader than indirect discrimination construed as discrimination resulting from the adoption of a measure which is 'suspect' on its face. Although they do not overtly rely on a classification on a suspect ground, suspect measures must appear as if calculated to exclude the members of a certain category. Disparate impact discrimination, on the other hand, may be identified even in measures whose content, as such, is not in any way suspect. Wherever a particular measure produces a disparate impact on the members of certain protected categories, it will have to be justified, even where that measure, apart from this statistically proven impact, would not appear to be potentially discriminatory. This advantage is clear especially in situations where the challenged practice is opaque or informal, thus making it difficult to anticipate its impact. In the 1989 case of *Danfoss* for instance, as an undertaking had a pay policy which was characterized by a total lack of transparency, the European Court of Justice considered that 'it is for the employer to prove that his practice in the matter of wages is not discriminatory, if a female worker establishes, in relation to a relatively large number of employees, that the average pay for women is less than that for men' (Case 109/88, *Handels- og Kontorfunktionærernes Forbund I Danmark* v. *Dansk Arbejdsgiverforening, acting on behalf of Danfoss* [1989] E.C.R. 3199 (judgment of 17 October 1989), para. 16). A similar reasoning could be made where an employer bases a recruitment process on the use of criteria or procedures which either are opaque (for instance, psychotechnical tests or job interviews), or more generally, whose potentially discriminatory impact may only be identified by the use of statistics (for instance, where preference is given to candidates residing in a particular geographical area, where certain ethnic minorities are located primarily in other neighbourhoods and are thus disproportionately affected by the use of such a criterion).

The disadvantage of this method however, is that it requires reliance on a specific methodology, based on the collection and analysis of statistical data, which may be particularly burdensome or even unavailable to victims of discrimination. Disparate impact analysis requires a comparison between the representation of different categories of persons (say, women and men, or different ethnic groups) within a 'departure group' and their representation in the 'arrival group', after an apparently neutral measure has been applied: the existence of a discrimination shall be presumed where the impact of that measure appears 'disproportionate', that is, where the representation of one category (say, women, or persons of a certain ethnic origin) is significantly lower in the 'group of arrival' than in the 'departure group'. However, apart from the question of what constitutes a disproportionate impact for the purposes of this analysis, the implementation of such a methodology requires that we define with precision the boundaries of the 'departure group' on the basis of which the impact of the provision, criterion or practice may be calculated. In the context of employment, for instance, the delimitation of the 'departure group' raises the question which minimum level of qualifications may be required in order to delineate the 'pool' of candidates to a job between whom the selection is to be made. Thus for instance, it may not be justified to presume that a recruitment process is indirectly discriminatory where, although only 10 per cent of workers are of a certain ethnic origin in a region where 25 per cent of the active population is of that ethnic group, only 5 per cent of those having completed their secondary education are members of that group. If we consider that having completed high school is an essential requirement for being employed in the undertaking concerned (more plausibly: within a particular occupation in that undertaking), the recruitment process is in fact favourable to persons of that ethnic group, although they still are under-represented in that undertaking in comparison to their representation in the overall active population of the area (see, e.g. for situations where the definition of the relevant 'pool' has been discussed within the case law of the US Supreme Court, in the context of Title VII of the Civil Rights Act 1964: *Johnson* v. *Transportation Agency, Santa Clara County, Calif., et al.*, 107 S. Ct. 1442 at 1452 (1987) ('When a job requires special training ... the comparison should be with those in the labour force *who possess the relevant qualifications*'); *Mayor of Philadelphia* v. *Educational Equality League*, 415 U.S. 605 at 620 (1974) (noting that the Court is not dealing with a situation where 'it can be assumed that all citizens are *fungible* for purposes of determining whether members of a particular class have been unlawfully excluded'); *Hazelwood School District* v. *United States*, 433 U.S. 299 (1977) (in order to address the allegation that a procedure for the recruitment of schoolteachers is indirectly discriminatory on the basis of race, the percentage of black schoolteachers recruited in a particular county should be compared with 'the percentage of *qualified black teachers in the labour force*'); *City of Richmond* v. *J. A. Croson Co*, 488 U.S. 469 (1989) ('where special qualifications are necessary, the relevant statistical pool for purposes of demonstrating discriminatory exclusion must be *the number of minorities qualified to undertake the particular task*') (emphasis added)).

In the employment context, this first difficulty does not arise where the job offered requires no qualifications or only minimal qualifications, or may be acquired by the training which the employer will provide (see, e.g. *Teamsters* v. *United States*, 431 U.S. 324 (1977); *United Steelworkers of America* v. *Weber*, 443 U.S. 193 (1979) (stating that it should put an end to the affirmative action programme set up within the undertaking for access to training 'as soon as the percentage of black skilled craftworkers in the ... plant approximates *the percentage of blacks in the local labour force*') (emphasis added)). But there are other difficulties. For instance, which role could the 'preferences' expressed by potential applicants play? Should we allow such 'preferences' to be taken into account in determining the relevant 'pool', although such preferences are always suspect of being tainted by the existence of institutional discrimination or, indeed, by the very fact of under-representation of certain groups within certain sectors or at certain levels of the professional ladder? Moreover, the assessment of the impact of such measure requires that we define the representation of the different categories within both the 'departure group' and the 'arrival group' where, in many cases, such data may be inexistent or where there may even be legal obstacles to the collection of such data.

resulted in 58 per cent of whites passing the tests, as compared with only 6 per cent of the blacks. This prompted the following remarks by the Court:

United States Supreme Court, *Griggs* v. *Duke Power Co*, 401 U.S. 424 (1971), 429–36 (opinion for the Court by CJ Burger):

The objective of Congress in the enactment of Title VII [of the Civil Rights Act] was to achieve equality of employment opportunities and remove barriers that have operated in the past to favor an identifiable group of white employees over other employees. Under the Act, practices, procedures, or tests neutral on their face, and even neutral in terms of intent, cannot be maintained if they operate to 'freeze' the status quo of prior discriminatory employment practices.

The [fact that 'whites register far better on the Company's alternative requirements'] than members of the African-American community] would appear to be directly traceable to race. Basic intelligence must have the means of articulation to manifest itself fairly in a testing process. Because they are Negroes, petitioners have long received inferior education in segregated schools and this Court expressly recognized these differences in *Gaston County* v. *United States*, 395 U.S. 285 (1969). There, because of the inferior education received by Negroes in North Carolina, this Court barred the institution of a literacy test for voter registration on the ground that the test would abridge the right to vote indirectly on account of race. Congress did not intend by Title VII, however, to guarantee a job to every person regardless of qualifications. In short, the Act does not command that any person be hired simply because he was formerly the subject of discrimination, or because he is a member of a minority group. Discriminatory preference for any group, minority or majority, is precisely and only what Congress has proscribed. What is required by Congress is the removal of artificial, arbitrary, and unnecessary barriers to employment when the barriers operate invidiously to discriminate on the basis of racial or other impermissible classification.

Congress has now provided that tests or criteria for employment or promotion may not provide equality of opportunity merely in the sense of the fabled offer of milk to the stork and the fox. On the contrary, Congress has now required that the posture and condition of the job-seeker be taken into account. It has – to resort again to the fable – provided that the vessel in which the milk is proffered be one all seekers can use. The Act proscribes not only overt discrimination but also practices that are fair in form, but discriminatory in operation. The touchstone is business necessity. If an employment practice which operates to exclude Negroes cannot be shown to be related to job performance, the practice is prohibited.

On the record before us, neither the high school completion requirement nor the general intelligence test is shown to bear a demonstrable relationship to successful performance of the jobs for which it was used. Both were adopted ... without meaningful study of their relationship to job-performance ability. Rather, a vice president of the Company testified, the requirements were instituted on the Company's judgment that they generally would improve the overall quality of the work force.

The evidence, however, shows that employees who have not completed high school or taken the tests have continued to perform satisfactorily and make progress in departments for which the high school and test criteria are now used. The promotion record of present employees who would not be able to meet the new criteria thus suggests the possibility that the requirements may not be needed even for the limited purpose of preserving the avowed policy of advancement within the Company. In the context of this case, it is unnecessary to reach the question whether testing requirements that take into account capability for the next succeeding position or related future promotion might be utilized upon a showing that such long-range requirements fulfill a genuine business need. In the present case the Company has made no such showing.

The Court of Appeals held that the Company had adopted the diploma and test requirements without any 'intention to discriminate against Negro employees'. We do not suggest that either the District Court or the Court of Appeals erred in examining the employer's intent; but good intent or absence of discriminatory intent does not redeem employment procedures or testing mechanisms that operate as 'built-in headwinds' for minority groups and are unrelated to measuring job capability.

The Company's lack of discriminatory intent is suggested by special efforts to help the undereducated employees through Company financing of two-thirds the cost of tuition for high school training. But Congress directed the thrust of the Act to the consequences of employment practices, not simply the motivation. More than that, Congress has placed on the employer the burden of showing that any given requirement must have a manifest relationship to the employment in question.

The facts of this case demonstrate the inadequacy of broad and general testing devices as well as the infirmity of using diplomas or degrees as fixed measures of capability. History is filled with examples of men and women who rendered highly effective performance without the conventional badges of accomplishment in terms of certificates, diplomas, or degrees. Diplomas and tests are useful servants, but Congress has mandated the commonsense proposition that they are not to become masters of reality.

The Company contends that its general intelligence tests are specifically permitted by 703(h) of the Act. That section authorizes the use of 'any professionally developed ability test' that is not 'designed, intended or used to discriminate because of race ...'

Section 703(h) was not contained in the House version of the Civil Rights Act but was added in the Senate during extended debate. For a period, debate revolved around claims that the bill as proposed would prohibit all testing and force employers to hire unqualified persons simply because they were part of a group formerly subject to job discrimination. Proponents of Title VII sought throughout the debate to assure the critics that the Act would have no effect on job-related tests. Senators Case of New Jersey and Clark of Pennsylvania, comanagers of the bill on the Senate floor, issued a memorandum explaining that the proposed Title VII 'expressly protects the employer's right to insist that any prospective applicant, Negro or white, must meet the applicable job qualifications. Indeed, the very purpose of title VII is to promote hiring on the basis of job qualifications, rather than on the basis of race or color.' 110 Cong. Rec. 7247. Despite these assurances, Senator Tower of Texas introduced an amendment authorizing 'professionally developed ability tests'. Proponents of Title VII opposed the amendment because, as written, it would permit an employer to give any test, 'whether it was a good test or not, so long as it was professionally designed. Discrimination could actually exist under the guise of compliance with the statute.' 110 Cong. Rec. 13504 (remarks of Sen. Case).

The amendment was defeated and two days later Senator Tower offered a substitute amendment which was adopted verbatim and is now the testing provision of 703(h). Speaking for the supporters of Title VII, Senator Humphrey, who had vigorously opposed the first amendment, endorsed the substitute amendment, stating: 'Senators on both sides of the aisle who were deeply interested in title VII have examined the text of this amendment and have found it to be in accord with the intent and purpose of that title.' 110 Cong. Rec. 13724. The amendment was then adopted. From the sum of the legislative history relevant in this case, the conclusion is inescapable that the [reading of the Employment Equal Opportunities Commission, acccording to which] 703(h) [requires] that employment tests be job related comports with congressional intent.

Nothing in the Act precludes the use of testing or measuring procedures; obviously they are useful. What Congress has forbidden is giving these devices and mechanisms controlling force unless they are demonstrably a reasonable measure of job performance. Congress has not commanded that the less qualified be preferred over the better qualified simply because of minority origins. Far from disparaging job qualifications as such, Congress has made such qualifications the controlling factor, so that race, religion, nationality, and sex become irrelevant. What Congress has commanded is that any tests used must measure the person for the job and not the person in the abstract.

The point to be emphasized here is that, without data indicating the percentage of African-Americans and whites respectively having completed high school in North Carolina, and indicating the disproportionate impact of so-called 'aptitude tests' on African-American applicants, these practices would not have been considered suspect and presumptively discriminatory. In fact, without breaking down the workforce of the Duke Power Company into ethnic groups, those requirements would most probably have gone unnoticed: even though upon closer examination they may have been found to impose disproportionate requirements on applicants, they would not appear, on their face at least, to impose a particular disadvantage on the African-American workers. In contrast, in the decision below, the Human Rights Committee uses a very different understanding of 'indirect discrimination', one which is not dependent on the use of statistics and instead takes as its departure point that certain measures shall, by their very nature, affect certain groups defined, for instance, by the religious affiliation of their members:

Human Rights Committee, *Karnel Singh Bhinder* v. *Canada*, Communication No. 208/1986 (CCPR/C/37/D/208/1986), final views of 9 November 1989:

[The author of the communication, Mr Singh Bhinder, is a naturalized Canadian citizen who was born in India. A Sikh by religion, he wears a turban in his daily life and refuses to wear safety headgear during his work. This resulted in the termination of his employment contract. Mr Singh Bhinder claims to be a victim of a violation by Canada of Article 18 of the International Covenant on Civil and Political Rights (freedom of religion). The State party on the other side submits that the author was not discharged from his employment because of his religion as such but rather because of his refusal to wear a hard hat, and contends that a neutral legal requirement, imposed for legitimate reasons and applied to all members of the relevant work force without aiming at any religious group, cannot violate Art. 18 ICCPR.]

6.2 Whether one approaches the issue from the perspective of article 18 or article 26, in the view of the Committee the same conclusion must be reached. If the requirement that a hard hat be worn is regarded as raising issues under article 18, then it is a limitation that is justified by reference to the grounds laid down in article 18, paragraph 3 [according to which the freedom to manifest one's religion or beliefs may be subject only to such limitations as are prescribed by law and are necessary to protect public safety, order, health, or morals or the fundamental rights and freedoms of others]. If the requirement that a hard hat be worn is seen as a discrimination *de facto* against persons of the Sikh religion under article 26, then, applying criteria now well established in the jurisprudence of the Committee, the legislation requiring that workers in federal employment be protected from injury and electric shock by the wearing of hard hats is to be regarded as reasonable and directed towards objective purposes that are compatible with the Covenant.

Human Rights Committee, *C. Derksen* v. *Netherlands*, Communication No. 976/2001 (CCPR/C/80/D/976/2001), final views of 1 March 2004:

[The author, Cecilia Derksen, shared a household with her partner Marcel Bakker from August 1991 to February 1995, when Mr Bakker died. In April 1995, Ms Derksen gave birth to a child, Kaya Marcelle Bakker, which Mr Bakker had recognized as his during the pregnancy. On 6 July 1995, Ms Derksen requested benefits under the General Widows and Orphans Law (AWW, *Algemene Weduwen en Wezen Wet*). Her request was rejected, however, because she had not been married to Mr Bakker and therefore could not be recognized as a widow under the AWW. On 1 July 1996, the Surviving Dependants Act (ANW, *Algemene Nabestaanden Wet*) replaced the AWW. Under the ANW, unmarried partners are also entitled to benefit. On 26 November 1996 Ms Derksen applied for benefit under the ANW. However, her application was rejected because the ANW was considered not to apply retrospectively, i.e. to those who became widows prior to 1 July 1996 and were not, at the time of the entry into effect of the ANW, covered by the AWW. In her communication to the Committee, Ms Derksen alleges that it constitutes a violation of Article 26 of the Covenant to distinguish between half-orphans whose parents were married and those whose parents were not married, since such a distinction cannot be justified on objective and reasonable grounds.]

9.2 The first question before the Committee is whether the author of the communication is a victim of a violation of article 26 of the Covenant, because the new legislation which provides for equal benefits to married and unmarried dependants whose partner has died is not applied to cases where the unmarried partner has died before the effective date of the new law. The Committee recalls its jurisprudence concerning earlier claims of discrimination against the Netherlands in relation to social security legislation. The Committee reiterates that not every distinction amounts to prohibited discrimination under the Covenant, as long as it is based on reasonable and objective criteria. The Committee recalls that it has earlier found that a differentiation between married and unmarried couples does not amount to a violation of article 26 of the Covenant, since married and unmarried couples are subject to different legal regimes and the decision whether or not to enter into a legal status by marriage lies entirely with the cohabiting persons. By enacting the new legislation the State party has provided equal treatment to both married and unmarried cohabitants for purposes of surviving dependants' benefits. Taking into account that the past practice of distinguishing between married and unmarried couples did not constitute prohibited discrimination, the Committee is of the opinion that the State party was under no obligation to make the amendment retroactive. The Committee considers that the application of the legislation to new cases only does not constitute a violation of article 26 of the Covenant.

9.3 The second question before the Committee is whether the refusal of benefits for the author's daughter constitutes prohibited discrimination under article 26 of the Covenant. The State party has explained that it is not the status of the child that determines the allowance of benefits, but the status of the surviving parent of the child, and that the benefits are not granted to the child but to the parent. The author, however, has argued that, even if the distinction between married and unmarried couples does not constitute discrimination because different legal regimes apply and the choice lies entirely with the partners whether to marry or not, the decision not to marry cannot affect the parents' obligations towards the child and the child has no influence on the parents' decision. The Committee recalls that article 26 prohibits both direct and indirect discrimination, the latter notion being related to a rule or measure that may be neutral on its face without any intent to discriminate but which nevertheless results in discrimination because of its exclusive or disproportionate adverse effect on a certain category of persons. Yet, a distinction only constitutes prohibited discrimination in the meaning of article 26 of the Covenant if it is not based on objective and reasonable criteria. In the circumstances of the present case, the Committee observes that under the earlier AWW the children's benefits depended on the status of the parents, so that if the parents were unmarried, the children were not eligible for the benefits. However, under the new ANW, benefits are being denied to children born to unmarried parents before 1 July 1996 while granted in respect of similarly situated children born after that date. The Committee considers that the distinction between children born, on the one hand, either in wedlock or after 1 July 1996 out of wedlock, and, on the other hand, out of wedlock prior to 1 July 1996, is not based on reasonable grounds. In making this conclusion the Committee emphasizes that the authorities were well aware of the discriminatory effect of the AWW when they decided to enact the new law aimed at remedying the situation, and that they could have easily terminated the discrimination in respect of children born out of wedlock prior to 1 July 1996 by extending the application of the new law to them. The termination of ongoing discrimination in respect of children who had had no say in whether their parents chose to marry or not, could have taken place with or without retroactive effect. However, as the communication has been declared admissible only in respect of the period after 1 July 1996, the Committee merely addresses the failure of the State party to terminate the discrimination from that day onwards which, in the Committee's view, constitutes a violation of article 26 in regard of Kaya Marcelle Bakker in respect of whom half orphan's benefits through her mother was denied under the ANW ...

Individual opinion of Committee member, Mr Nisuke Ando (dissenting)

... It is unfortunate that the new law affects her as well as her daughter unfavourably in the present case. However, in interpreting and applying article 26, the Human Rights Committee must take into account the following three factors: First, the codification history of the Universal Declaration of Human Rights makes it clear that only those rights contained in the International Covenant on Civil and Political Rights are justiciable and the Optional Protocol is attached to that Covenant, while the rights contained in the International Covenant on Economic, Social and

Cultural Rights are not justiciable. Second, while the principle of non-discrimination enshrined in article 26 of the former Covenant may be applicable to any field regulated and protected by public authorities, the latter Covenant obligates its States parties to realize rights contained therein only progressively. Third, the right to social security, the very right at issue in the present case, is provided not in the former Covenant but in the latter Covenant and the latter Covenant has its own provision on non-discriminatory implementation of the rights it contains.

Consequently, the Human Rights Committee needs to be especially prudent in applying its article 26 to cases involving economic and social rights, which States parties to the International Covenant on Economic, Social and Cultural Rights are to realize without discrimination but step-by-step through available means. In my opinion, the State party in the present case is attempting to treat married couples and unmarried partners equally but progressively, thus making the application of ANW not retroactive. To tell the State party that it is violating article 26 unless it treats all married couples and unmarried partners exactly on the same footing at once sounds like telling the State party not to start putting water in an empty cup it if cannot fill the cup all at once!

Individual of Committee member, Sir Nigel Rodley (dissenting):
I do not consider that the Committee's finding of a violation in respect of Kaya Marcelle Bakker, the author's daughter (paragraph 9.3), withstands analysis. To comply with the Committee's interpretation of the Covenant, the State Party would have had to make the ANW retroactive. Indeed, it is the very absence of retroactivity that, according to the Committee, constitutes the violation. Since most legislation has the effect of varying people's rights as compared with the situation prior to the adoption of the legislation, the Committee's logic would imply that all legislation granting a new benefit must be retroactive if it is to avoid discriminating against those whose rights fall to be determined under the previous legislation ...

The notion of indirect discrimination was slow to emerge in the case law of the European Court of Human Rights. The first explicit acknowledgement of the notion by the Court occurred in the case of *Thlimmenos* v. *Greece*, decided in 2000. A Jehovah's Witness had been denied the right to register as a chartered accountant, due to his criminal record following a conviction for having refused to do his military service. The Court noted that the Greek authorities should have taken into account that the conviction was based on behaviour motivated by the religious beliefs of Mr Thlimmenos, rather than on behaviour raising doubts about his morality or trustworthiness, which would justify the rationale behind the rule excluding from the profession of chartered accountants all persons with a criminal record. In arriving at the conclusion that Article 14 ECHR had been violated, taken in combination with Article 9 ECHR (freedom of religion), the Court noted that 'the right under Article 14 [of the European Convention on Human Rights] not to be discriminated against in the enjoyment of the rights guaranteed under the Convention is violated when States treat differently persons in analogous situations without providing an objective and reasonable justification ... However, ... the right not to be discriminated against in the enjoyment of the rights guaranteed under the Convention is also violated when States without an objective and reasonable justification fail to treat differently persons whose situations are significantly different' (Eur. Ct. H.R. (GC), *Thlimmenos* v. *Greece* (Appl. No. 34369/97), judgment of 6 April 2000, §42). But the notion has progressed further in recent case law.

European Court of Human Rights (GC), *D.H. and others* v. *Czech Republic* (Appl. No. 57325/00), judgment of 13 November 2007:

[The applicants are eighteen Czech nationals of Roma origin who were born between 1985 and 1991 and live in the Ostrava region (Czech Republic). Between 1996 and 1999 they were placed in special schools for children with learning difficulties who were unable to follow the ordinary school curriculum. Under the law, the decision to place a child in a special school was taken by the head teacher on the basis of the results of tests to measure the child's intellectual capacity carried out in an educational psychology centre, and required the consent of the child's legal representative. Fourteen of the applicants sought a review of their situation by the Ostrava Education Authority on the grounds that the tests were unreliable and their parents had not been sufficiently informed of the consequences of giving consent. The Authority found that the placements had been made in accordance with the statutory rules. Twelve of the applicants appealed to the Constitutional Court. They argued that their placement in special schools amounted to a general practice that had resulted in segregation and racial discrimination through the co-existence of two autonomous educational systems, namely special schools for the Roma and 'ordinary' primary schools for the majority of the population. Their appeal was dismissed on 20 October 1999. They then turned to the European Court of Human Rights, arguing that, as a result of their Roma origin, they were assigned to special schools. On 7 February 2006 a Chamber held by six votes to one that there had been no violation of Article 14 of the Convention (non-discrimination), read in conjunction with Article 2 of Protocol No. 1 (right to education). In its view, the Government had established that the system of special schools in the Czech Republic had not been introduced solely to cater for Roma children and that considerable efforts had been made in those schools to help certain categories of pupils to acquire a basic education. In that connection, the Chamber had observed that the rules governing children's placement in special schools did not refer to the pupils' ethnic origin, but pursued the legitimate aim of adapting the education system to the needs, aptitudes and disabilities of the children.

Following the judgment delivered by the Chamber, the applicants then requested that the case be referred to the Grand Chamber.]

182. The Court notes that as a result of their turbulent history and constant uprooting the Roma have become a specific type of disadvantaged and vulnerable minority ... As the Court has noted in previous cases, they therefore require special protection ... As is attested by the activities of numerous European and international organisations and the recommendations of the Council of Europe bodies ..., this protection also extends to the sphere of education. The present case therefore warrants particular attention, especially as when the applications were lodged with the Court the applicants were minor children for whom the right to education was of paramount importance.

183. The applicants' allegation in the present case is not that they were in a different situation from non-Roma children that called for different treatment or that the respondent State had failed to take affirmative action to correct factual inequalities or differences between them

[*Thlimmenos* v. *Greece* [GC], No. 34369/97, §44, E.C.H.R. 2000–IV; and *Stec and others* v. *United Kingdom* [GC], No. 65731/01, §51]. In their submission, all that has to be established is that, without objective and reasonable justification, they were treated less favourably than non-Roma children in a comparable situation and that this amounted in their case to indirect discrimination.

184. The Court has already accepted in previous cases that a difference in treatment may take the form of disproportionately prejudicial effects of a general policy or measure which, though couched in neutral terms, discriminates against a group [*Hugh Jordan* v. *United Kingdom*, No. 24746/94, 4 May 2001, §154; and *Hoogendijk* v. *Netherlands* (dec.), No. 58461/00, 6 January 2005]. In accordance with, for instance, Council Directives 97/80/EC and 2000/43/EC ... and the definition provided by ECRI ..., such a situation may amount to 'indirect discrimination', which does not necessarily require a discriminatory intent.

(a) Whether a presumption of indirect discrimination arises in the instant case 185. It was common ground that the impugned difference in treatment did not result from the wording of the statutory provisions on placements in special schools in force at the material time. Accordingly, the issue in the instant case is whether the manner in which the legislation was applied in practice resulted in a disproportionate number of Roma children – including the applicants – being placed in special schools without justification, and whether such children were thereby placed at a significant disadvantage.

186. As mentioned above, the Court has noted in previous cases that applicants may have difficulty in proving discriminatory treatment (*Nachova and others* v. *Bulgaria* [GC] [judgment of 6 July 2005] Nos. 43577/98 and 43579/98, §145, ECHR 2005–VII, §§147 and 157). In order to guarantee those concerned the effective protection of their rights, less strict evidential rules should apply in cases of alleged indirect discrimination.

187. On this point, the Court observes that Council Directives 97/80/EC and 2000/43/EC stipulate that persons who consider themselves wronged because the principle of equal treatment has not been applied to them may establish, before a domestic authority, by any means, including on the basis of statistical evidence, facts from which it may be presumed that there has been discrimination ... The recent case law of the Court of Justice of the European Communities ... shows that it permits claimants to rely on statistical evidence and the national courts to take such evidence into account where it is valid and significant.

The Grand Chamber further notes the information furnished by the third-party interveners that the courts of many countries and the supervisory bodies of the United Nations treaties habitually accept statistics as evidence of indirect discrimination in order to facilitate the victims' task of adducing prima facie evidence.

The Court also recognised the importance of official statistics in [*Hoogendijk*] and has shown that it is prepared to accept and take into consideration various types of evidence (*Nachova and others*, cited above, §147).

188. In these circumstances, the Court considers that when it comes to assessing the impact of a measure or practice on an individual or group, statistics which appear on critical examination to be reliable and significant will be sufficient to constitute the prima facie evidence the applicant is required to produce. This does not, however, mean that indirect discrimination cannot be proved without statistical evidence.

189. Where an applicant alleging indirect discrimination thus establishes a rebuttable presumption that the effect of a measure or practice is discriminatory, the burden then shifts to the respondent State, which must show that the difference in treatment is not discriminatory

(see, *mutatis mutandis, Nachova and others*, cited above, §157). Regard being had in particular to the specificity of the facts and the nature of the allegations made in this type of case (*ibid.*, §147), it would be extremely difficult in practice for applicants to prove indirect discrimination without such a shift in the burden of proof.

190. In the present case, the statistical data submitted by the applicants was obtained from questionnaires that were sent out to the head teachers of special and primary schools in the town of Ostrava in 1999. It indicates that at the time 56% of all pupils placed in special schools in Ostrava were Roma. Conversely, Roma represented only 2.26% of the total number of pupils attending primary school in Ostrava. Further, whereas only 1.8% of non-Roma pupils were placed in special schools, the proportion of Roma pupils in Ostrava assigned to special schools was 50.3%. According to the Government, these figures are not sufficiently conclusive as they merely reflect the subjective opinions of the head teachers. The Government also noted that no official information on the ethnic origin of the pupils existed and that the Ostrava region had one of the largest Roma populations.

191. The Grand Chamber observes that these figures are not disputed by the Government and that they have not produced any alternative statistical evidence. In view of their comment that no official information on the ethnic origin of the pupils exists, the Court accepts that the statistics submitted by the applicants may not be entirely reliable. It nevertheless considers that these figures reveal a dominant trend that has been confirmed both by the respondent State and the independent supervisory bodies which have looked into the question.

192. In their reports submitted in accordance with Article 25 §1 of the Framework Convention for the Protection of National Minorities, the Czech authorities accepted that in 1999 Roma pupils made up between 80% and 90% of the total number of pupils in some special schools ... and that in 2004 'large numbers' of Roma children were still being placed in special schools ... The Advisory Committee on the Framework Convention observed in its report of 26 October 2005 that according to unofficial estimates Roma accounted for up to 70% of pupils enrolled in special schools. According to the report published by ECRI in 2000, Roma children were 'vastly overrepresented' in special schools. The Committee on the Elimination of Racial Discrimination noted in its concluding observations of 30 March 1998 that a disproportionately large number of Roma children were placed in special schools ... Lastly, according to the figures supplied by the European Monitoring Centre on Racism and Xenophobia, more than half of Roma children in the Czech Republic attended special school.

193. In the Court's view, the latter figures, which do not relate solely to the Ostrava region and therefore provide a more general picture, show that, even if the exact percentage of Roma children in special schools at the material time remains difficult to establish, their number was disproportionately high. Moreover, Roma pupils formed a majority of the pupils in special schools. Despite being couched in neutral terms, the relevant statutory provisions therefore had considerably more impact in practice on Roma children than on non-Roma children and resulted in statistically disproportionate numbers of placements of the former in special schools.

194. Where it has been shown that legislation produces such a discriminatory effect, the Grand Chamber considers that, as with cases concerning employment or the provision of services, it is not necessary in cases in the educational sphere (see, *mutatis mutandis, Nachova and others*, cited above, §157) to prove any discriminatory intent on the part of the relevant authorities (see paragraph 184 above).

195. In these circumstances, the evidence submitted by the applicants can be regarded as sufficiently reliable and significant to give rise to a strong presumption of indirect discrimination. The burden of proof must therefore shift to the Government, which must show that the difference in the impact of the legislation was the result of objective factors unrelated to ethnic origin.

(b) Objective and reasonable justification 196. The Court reiterates that a difference in treatment is discriminatory if 'it has no objective and reasonable justification', that is, if it does not pursue a 'legitimate aim' or if there is not a 'reasonable relationship of proportionality' between the means employed and the aim sought to be realised (see, among many other authorities, *Larkos* v. *Cyprus* [GC], No. 29515/95, §29, ECHR 1999–I; and *Stec and others*, cited above, §51). Where the difference in treatment is based on race, colour or ethnic origin, the notion of objective and reasonable justification must be interpreted as strictly as possible.

197. In the instant case, the Government sought to explain the difference in treatment between Roma children and non-Roma children by the need to adapt the education system to the capacity of children with special needs. In the Government's submission, the applicants were placed in special schools on account of their specific educational needs, essentially as a result of their low intellectual capacity measured with the aid of psychological tests in educational psychology centres. After the centres had made their recommendations regarding the type of school in which the applicants should be placed, the final decision had lain with the applicants' parents and they had consented to the placements. The argument that the applicants were placed in special schools on account of their ethnic origin was therefore unsustainable.

For their part, the applicants strenuously contested the suggestion that the disproportionately high number of Roma children in special schools could be explained by the results of the intellectual capacity tests or be justified by parental consent.

198. The Court accepts that the Government's decision to retain the special-school system was motivated by the desire to find a solution for children with special educational needs. However, it shares the disquiet of the other Council of Europe institutions who have expressed concerns about the more basic curriculum followed in these schools and, in particular, the segregation the system causes.

199. The Grand Chamber observes, further, that the tests used to assess the children's learning abilities or difficulties have given rise to controversy and continue to be the subject of scientific debate and research. While accepting that it is not its role to judge the validity of such tests, various factors in the instant case nevertheless lead the Grand Chamber to conclude that the results of the tests carried out at the material time were not capable of constituting objective and reasonable justification for the purposes of Article 14 of the Convention.

200. In the first place, it was common ground that all the children who were examined sat the same tests, irrespective of their ethnic origin. The Czech authorities themselves acknowledged in 1999 that 'Romany children with average or above-average intellect' were often placed in such schools on the basis of the results of psychological tests and that the tests were conceived for the majority population and did not take Roma specifics into consideration ... As a result, they had revised the tests and methods used with a view to ensuring that they 'were not misused to the detriment of Roma children' ...

In addition, various independent bodies have expressed doubts over the adequacy of the tests. Thus, the Advisory Committee on the Framework Convention for the Protection of National

Minorities observed that children who were not mentally handicapped were frequently placed in these schools '[owing] to real or perceived language and cultural differences between Roma and the majority'. It also stressed the need for the tests to be 'consistent, objective and comprehensive' ... ECRI noted that the channelling of Roma children to special schools for the mentally-retarded was reportedly often 'quasi-automatic' and needed to be examined to ensure that any testing used was 'fair' and that the true abilities of each child were 'properly evaluated' ... The Council of Europe Commissioner for Human Rights noted that Roma children were frequently placed in classes for children with special needs 'without an adequate psychological or pedagogical assessment, the real criteria clearly being their ethnic origin' ...

Lastly, in the submission of some of the third-party interveners, placements following the results of the psychological tests reflected the racial prejudices of the society concerned.

201. The Court considers that, at the very least, there is a danger that the tests were biased and that the results were not analysed in the light of the particularities and special characteristics of the Roma children who sat them. In these circumstances, the tests in question cannot serve as justification for the impugned difference in treatment.

[For the discussion of the relevance of parental consent, see chapter 4 (section 2.4.) above.]

(c) Conclusion 205. As is apparent from the documentation produced by ECRI and the report of the Commissioner for Human Rights of the Council of Europe, the Czech Republic is not alone in having encountered difficulties in providing schooling for Roma children: other European States have had similar difficulties. The Court is gratified to note that, unlike some countries, the Czech Republic has sought to tackle the problem and acknowledges that, in its attempts to achieve the social and educational integration of the disadvantaged group which the Roma form, it has had to contend with numerous difficulties as a result of, *inter alia*, the cultural specificities of that minority and a degree of hostility on the part of the parents of non-Roma children ... [T]he choice between a single school for everyone, highly specialised structures and unified structures with specialised sections is not an easy one. It entails a difficult balancing exercise between the competing interests. As to the setting and planning of the curriculum, this mainly involves questions of expediency on which it is not for the Court to rule (*Valsamis* v. *Greece*, judgment of 18 December 1996, *Reports* 1996–VI, §28).

206. Nevertheless, whenever discretion capable of interfering with the enjoyment of a Convention right is conferred on national authorities, the procedural safeguards available to the individual will be especially material in determining whether the respondent State has, when fixing the regulatory framework, remained within its margin of appreciation (see *Buckley* v. *United Kingdom*, judgment of 25 September 1996, *Reports* 1996–IV, §76; and *Connors* v. *United Kingdom*, judgment cited above, §83).

207. The facts of the instant case indicate that the schooling arrangements for Roma children were not attended by safeguards that would ensure that, in the exercise of its margin of appreciation in the education sphere, the State took into account their special needs as members of a disadvantaged class ... Furthermore, as a result of the arrangements the applicants were placed in schools for children with mental disabilities where a more basic curriculum was followed than in ordinary schools and where they were isolated from pupils from the wider population. As a result, they received an education which compounded their difficulties and compromised their subsequent personal development instead of tackling their real problems or

helping them to integrate into the ordinary schools and develop the skills that would facilitate life among the majority population. Indeed, the Government have implicitly admitted that job opportunities are more limited for pupils from special schools.

208. In these circumstances and while recognising the efforts made by the Czech authorities to ensure that Roma children receive schooling, the Court is not satisfied that the difference in treatment between Roma children and non-Roma children was objectively and reasonably justified and that there existed a reasonable relationship of proportionality between the means used and the aim pursued. In that connection, it notes with interest that the new legislation has abolished special schools and provides for children with special educational needs, including socially disadvantaged children, to be educated in ordinary schools.

209. Lastly, since it has been established that the relevant legislation as applied in practice at the material time had a disproportionately prejudicial effect on the Roma community, the Court considers that the applicants as members of that community necessarily suffered the same discriminatory treatment. Accordingly, it does not need to examine their individual cases.

210. Consequently, there has been a violation in the instant case of Article 14 of the Convention, read in conjunction with Article 2 of Protocol No. 1, as regards each of the applicants.

7.6. **Questions for discussion: defining indirect discrimination**

1. In its General Comment No. 20, *Non-discrimination* (2009), the Committee on Economic, Social and Cultural Rights defines indirect discrimination as referring to 'laws, policies or practices which appear neutral at face value, but have a disproportionate impact on the exercise of Covenant rights as distinguished by prohibited grounds of discrimination. For instance, requiring a birth registration certificate for school enrolment may discriminate against ethnic minorities or non-nationals who do not possess, or have been denied, such certificates' (para. 10). Do you agree that this is an adequate definition of indirect discrimination?

2. What are the respective advantages and limitations of each of the two understandings of indirect discrimination discussed above – the 'disparate impact' model and the 'suspect measure' model? Does one of these models include the other and therefore is more encompassing, or should we rather see them as complementary? Is one model more suitable for certain grounds of prohibited discrimination, such as gender or race, and one model more appropriate for other grounds, such as religion or sexual orientation?

3.2 Reasonable accommodation

The notion of reasonable accommodation was already briefly referred to above, in the presentation of the State's obligation to respect human rights: there, the reference to the Canadian Supreme Court cases of *Eldridge* v. *British Columbia* [1997] 3 S.C.R. 624 and *Multani* v. *Commission scolaire Marguerite-Bourgeoys* [2006] 1 S.C.R. 256 served to illustrate the point that certain rules, while adequately justified as general measures, may nevertheless be questioned as they apply to specific individual cases, for which certain exceptions may have to be provided in order to restrict any interference with the rights of individuals to the minimum inevitable (see chapter 3, section 3.5.).

The notion of reasonable accommodation is particularly important in the context of non-discrimination, where it fulfils a similar function. The 2006 Convention on the Rights of Persons with Disabilities (CRPD) recognizes that the refusal to provide reasonable accommodation may constitute a specific form of discrimination. The notions of equality and non-discrimination are defined as follows in this instrument:

Convention on the Rights of Persons with Disabilities (2006)

Article 5 – Equality and non-discrimination

1. States Parties recognize that all persons are equal before and under the law and are entitled without any discrimination to the equal protection and equal benefit of the law.
2. States Parties shall prohibit all discrimination on the basis of disability and guarantee to persons with disabilities equal and effective legal protection against discrimination on all grounds.
3. In order to promote equality and eliminate discrimination, States Parties shall take all appropriate steps to ensure that reasonable accommodation is provided.
4. Specific measures which are necessary to accelerate or achieve de facto equality of persons with disabilities shall not be considered discrimination under the terms of the present Convention.

Reasonable accommodation serves to designate the obligation for private parties or public services to adopt certain measures, on an individualized basis, that accommodate the specific needs of the individual with a disability, without imposing a disproportionate burden on the other party – i.e. one which it would be unable to afford. Article 2 CRPD defines 'reasonable accommodation' as 'necessary and appropriate modification and adjustments not imposing a disproportionate or undue burden, where needed in a particular case, to ensure to persons with disabilities the enjoyment or exercise on an equal basis with others of all human rights and fundamental freedoms'. The notion seems to be increasingly influencing jurisdictions confronted with allegations of discrimination on grounds of disability. In a judgment of 30 April 2009 in the case of *Glor* v. *Switzerland* (Appl. No. 13444/04), the European Court of Human Rights held that the Swiss Government had violated Mr Glor's rights under Article 14 (prohibition of discrimination) in conjunction with Article 8 (right to private and family life) ECHR. Mr Glor had diabetes and, because of his medical condition, could not carry out compulsory military service, as he was deemed medically unfit. His condition, according to the Swiss authorities, posed a problem on account of the particular restrictions related to military service including limited access to medical care and medication, the significant physical efforts required and psychological pressure exerted. However, the authorities decided that Mr Glor's diabetes was not severe enough to relieve him from paying a non-negligible military service exemption tax on his annual earnings for several years to come: they thus levied a tax for exemption from military service. Although Mr Glor wanted to do his military service, he was thus prohibited both from doing so and from carrying out alternative civil service, this being available only to conscientious objectors. Invoking Article 14 together with Article 8 ECHR, Mr Glor argued that he had been subjected to discrimination on the basis of his disability because he had been prohibited from carrying out his military service, and was obliged to pay the exemption tax as his disability was judged not to be severe enough for him to forgo the tax. The Court condemns the Swiss authorities for failing to provide reasonable accommodation to Mr Glor in finding a solution which responds to his individual circumstances. It takes note of the fact reasonable accommodation could have been provided by, for example, filling posts in the armed forces which require less physical effort by persons with disabilities. In highlighting the failure of the Swiss authorities, the Court points to legislation in other countries which ensure the recruitment of persons with disabilities to posts which are adapted to both the person's (dis)ability and to the person's professional skills (para. 94).

The notion of reasonable accommodation is particularly well suited to the situation of persons with disabilities. As illustrated by *Multani*, however, the usefulness of the notion is not limited to the integration of persons with disabilities. Consider also the following case:

Supreme Court of Canada, *Central Okanagan School District No. 23* v. *Renaud* [1992] 2 S.C.R. 970:

[Larry Renaud, a Seventh-Day Adventist, was a unionized custodian working a Monday to Friday job for the respondent school board (Board of School Trustees, School District No. 23 (Central Okanagan)). The work schedule, which formed part of the collective agreement, included a Friday afternoon shift from 3.00 p.m. until 11.00 p.m. during which only one custodian was on duty. Renaud's religion, however, prevented his working on his Sabbath, which began on sundown Friday to end on sundown Saturday. Renaud was reluctant to accept a further alternative, that he work a four-day week, as this would result in a substantial loss of pay. Although he proposed the creation of a Sunday to Thursday shift, something which would have been agreeable to his employer, such an accommodation involved an exception to the collective agreement and required union consent, which the union would not give. After further unsuccessful attempts to accommodate the appellant, the school board eventually terminated his employment when he refused to complete his regular Friday night shift. The appellant filed a complaint pursuant to section 8 of the British Columbia Human Rights Act against the school board and pursuant to section 9 against the union.]

The judgment of the Court was delivered by Sopinka, J.

The duty resting on an employer to accommodate the religious beliefs and practices of employees extends to require an employer to take reasonable measures short of undue hardship. In [*Ontario Human Rights Commission and O'Malley* v. *Simpsons-Sears Ltd* [1985] 2 S.C.R. 536], McIntyre J. explained that the words 'short of undue hardship' import a limitation on the employer's obligation so that measures that occasion undue interference with the employer's business or undue expense are not required.

The respondents [the school board and the union] submitted that we should adopt the definition of undue hardship articulated by the Supreme Court of the United States in *Trans World Airlines, Inc.* v. *Hardison*, 432 U.S. 63 (1977). In that case, the court stated at pp. 84–85: 'To require TWA to bear more than a de minimis cost in order to give Hardison Saturdays off is an undue hardship ... to require TWA to bear additional costs when no such costs are incurred to give other employees the days off that they want would involve unequal treatment of employees on the basis of their religion. By suggesting that TWA should incur certain costs in order to give Hardison Saturdays off ... would in effect require TWA to finance an additional Saturday off and then to choose the employee who will enjoy it on the basis of his religious beliefs. While incurring extra costs to secure a replacement for Hardison might remove the necessity of compelling another employee to work involuntarily in Hardison's place, it would not change the fact that the privilege of having Saturdays off would be allocated according to religious beliefs'.

This definition is in direct conflict with the explanation of undue hardship in *O'Malley*. This Court reviewed the American authorities in that case and referred specifically to Hardison but did not adopt the 'de minimis' test which it propounded.

Furthermore there is good reason not to adopt the 'de minimis' test in Canada. *Hardison* was argued on the basis of the establishment clause of the First Amendment of the U.S. Constitution and its prohibition against the establishment of religion. This aspect of the *Hardison* decision was thus decided within an entirely different legal context. The case law of this Court has approached the issue of accommodation in a more purposive manner, attempting to provide equal access to the workforce to people who would otherwise encounter serious barriers to entry. The approach of Canadian courts is thus quite different from the approach taken in U.S. cases such as *Hardison* and more recently *Ansonia Board of Education v. Philbrook*, 479 U.S. 60 (1986).

The *Hardison* 'de minimis' test virtually removes the duty to accommodate and seems particularly inappropriate in the Canadian context. More than mere negligible effort is required to satisfy the duty to accommodate. The use of the term 'undue' infers that some hardship is acceptable; it is only 'undue' hardship that satisfies this test. The extent to which the discriminator must go to accommodate is limited by the words 'reasonable' and 'short of undue hardship'. These are not independent criteria but are alternate ways of expressing the same concept. What constitutes reasonable measures is a question of fact and will vary with the circumstances of the case. Wilson J., in *Central Alberta Dairy Pool* v. *Alberta (Human Rights Commission)*, [1990] 2 S.C.R. 489, at p. 521, listed factors that could be relevant to an appraisal of what amount of hardship was undue as: '... financial cost, disruption of a collective agreement, problems of morale of other employees, interchangeability of work force and facilities. The size of the employer's operation may influence the assessment of whether a given financial cost is undue or the ease with which the work force and facilities can be adapted to the circumstances. Where safety is at issue both the magnitude of the risk and the identity of those who bear it are relevant considerations'. She went on to explain at p. 521 that '[t]his list is not intended to be exhaustive and the results which will obtain from a balancing of these factors against the right of the employee to be free from discrimination will necessarily vary from case to case'.

The concern for the impact on other employees which prompted the court in *Hardison* to adopt the 'de minimis' test is a factor to be considered in determining whether the interference with the operation of the employer's business would be undue. However, more than minor inconvenience must be shown before the complainant's right to accommodation can be defeated. The employer must establish that actual interference with the rights of other employees, which is not trivial but substantial, will result from the adoption of the accommodating measures. Minor interference or inconvenience is the price to be paid for religious freedom in a multicultural society.

[The risks of hostile reactions or reprisals from other employees] The reaction of employees may be a factor in deciding whether accommodating measures would constitute undue interference in the operation of the employer's business. In *Central Alberta Dairy Pool*, Wilson J. referred to employee morale as one of the factors to be taken into account. It is a factor that must be applied with caution. The objection of employees based on well-grounded concerns that their rights will be affected must be considered. On the other hand, objections based on attitudes inconsistent with human rights are an irrelevant consideration. I would include in this category objections based on the view that the integrity of a collective agreement is to be preserved irrespective of its discriminatory effect on an individual employee on religious grounds. The contrary view would effectively enable an employer to contract out of human rights legislation provided the employees were ad idem with their employer. It was in this context that Wilson J. referred to employee morale as a factor in determining what constitutes undue hardship.

There is no evidence in the record before the Court that the rights of other employees would likely have been affected by an accommodation of the appellant. The fact that the appellant would be assigned to a special shift may have required the adjustment of the schedule of some other employee but this might have been done with the consent of the employee or employees affected. The respondents apparently did not canvass this possibility. The union objected to the proposed accommodation on the basis that the integrity of the collective agreement would be compromised and not that any individual employee objected on the basis of interference with his or her right. In my opinion, the member designate came to the right conclusion with respect to this issue.

[The duty of the complainant] The search for accommodation is a multi-party inquiry. Along with the employer and the union, there is also a duty on the complainant to assist in securing an appropriate accommodation. The inclusion of the complainant in the search for accommodation was recognized by this Court in *O'Malley.* At page 555, McIntyre J. stated: 'Where such reasonable steps, however, do not fully reach the desired end, the complainant, in the absence of some accommodating steps on his own part such as an acceptance in this case of part-time work, must either sacrifice his religious principles or his employment.'

To facilitate the search for an accommodation, the complainant must do his or her part as well. Concomitant with a search for reasonable accommodation is a duty to facilitate the search for such an accommodation. Thus in determining whether the duty of accommodation has been fulfilled the conduct of the complainant must be considered.

This does not mean that, in addition to bringing to the attention of the employer the facts relating to discrimination, the complainant has a duty to originate a solution. While the complainant may be in a position to make suggestions, the employer is in the best position to determine how the complainant can be accommodated without undue interference in the operation of the employer's business. When an employer has initiated a proposal that is reasonable and would, if implemented, fulfil the duty to accommodate, the complainant has a duty to facilitate the implementation of the proposal. If failure to take reasonable steps on the part of the complainant causes the proposal to founder, the complaint will be dismissed. The other aspect of this duty is the obligation to accept reasonable accommodation. This is the aspect referred to by McIntyre J. in *O'Malley*. The complainant cannot expect a perfect solution. If a proposal that would be reasonable in all the circumstances is turned down, the employer's duty is discharged.

[The Court concludes that the appellant Renaud was victim of discrimination and unlawful dismissal.]

7.7. Questions for discussion

1. Should the 'burden' imposed on employers, as a result of an obligation to offer reasonable accommodation, vary in accordance of the size of the undertaking, or according to whether the organization is private or public?
2. How should reasonable accommodation be conceived for persons with mental disabilities?
3. Could reliance on an understanding of the non-discrimination requirement as including an obligation to provide reasonable accommodation have changed the result in the case of *Karnel Singh Bhinder* v. *Canada*, presented to the Human Rights Committee (above, section 3.1.)?

3.3 Positive action

(a) The notion of positive action or 'temporary special measures'

In his 2002 study on the concept of affirmative action prepared at the request of the UN Sub-Commission on the Promotion and Protection of Human Rights, the Special Rapporteur Bossuyt defines 'affirmative action' as consisting in 'a coherent packet of measures, of a temporary character, aimed specifically at correcting the position of members of a target group in one or more aspects of their social life, in order to obtain effective equality' ('The concept and practice of affirmative action', Final report submitted by Mr Marc Bossuyt, Special Rapporteur, in accordance with Resolution 1998/5 of the Sub-Commission for the Promotion and Protection of Human Rights, UN Doc. E/CN.4/Sub.2/2002/21, 17 June 2002, para. 6). In general, the distinctive feature of such measures is that they seek to promote *de facto* equality between different categories of persons, by granting specific treatment to the disadvantaged category (treatment often referred to as 'preferential'), in order to compensate for existing inequalities or to counter their effects. The legal technique of positive action is thus based on an explicit recognition that, in order to ensure effective equality, the mere prohibition of individual acts of discrimination, combined with the guarantee of formal equal treatment (equal protection of the law, in the meaning referred to above in section 2.2.), may not be sufficient. In certain cases, however, positive action measures may be adopted without any reference to pre-existing inequalities, and rather with the explicit aim of achieving diversity in certain settings where it matters that all segments of the population are represented.

In the international law of human rights, the expression 'temporary special measures' is usually preferred: it appears in Article 1(4) of the 1965 Convention on the Elimination of All Forms of Racial Discrimination and in Article 4(1) of the 1979 International Convention on the Elimination of All Forms of Discrimination against Women, and the Committee on the Elimination of Discrimination against Women has advocated reliance on this expression. As conveyed by the expression 'temporary special measures', a clear distinction should be made between such measures that seek to accelerate the achievement of *de facto* equality by treating differently the members of certain disadvantaged or under-represented groups (often referred to as 'positive action'), on the one hand, and measures which improve the situation of such groups by transforming the environment which they inhabit, but which do not imply differential treatment – although they do imply the recognition of the specific needs of the members of those groups. For instance, after stating in Article 4(1) that 'Adoption by States Parties of temporary special measures aimed at accelerating *de facto* equality between men and women shall not be considered discrimination as defined in the present Convention, but shall in no way entail as a consequence the maintenance of unequal or separate standards; these measures shall be discontinued when the objectives of equality of opportunity and treatment have been achieved', the Convention on the Elimination of All Forms of Discrimination against Women adds that 'Adoption by States Parties of special measures, including those measures contained in the present Convention, aimed at protecting maternity shall not be considered discriminatory' (Art. 4(2)). The Committee on the Elimination of Discrimination against Women described the relationship between the two provisions thus:

Committee on the Elimination of Discrimination against Women, General Recommendation No. 25, *Article 4, paragraph 1, of the Convention (Temporary Special Measures)*, adopted at the thirtieth session of the Committee (2004) (HRI/GEN/1/Rev.7, 12 May 2004, at 282), paras. 15–16:

There is a clear difference between the purpose of the 'special measures' under article 4, paragraph 1, and those of paragraph 2. The purpose of article 4, paragraph 1, is to accelerate the improvement of the position of women to achieve their *de facto* or substantive equality with men, and to effect the structural, social and cultural changes necessary to correct past and current forms and effects of discrimination against women, as well as to provide them with compensation. These measures are of a temporary nature.

Article 4, paragraph 2, provides for non-identical treatment of women and men due to their biological differences. These measures are of a permanent nature, at least until such time as the scientific and technological knowledge ... would warrant a review.

Similarly, the 1995 Council of Europe Framework Convention for the Protection of National Minorities guarantees to persons belonging to national minorities the right of equality before the law and of equal protection of the law and prohibits any discrimination based on belonging to a national minority (Art. 4(1)). It adds that the States parties 'undertake to adopt, where necessary, adequate measures in order to promote, in all areas of economic, social, political and cultural life, full and effective equality between persons belonging to a national minority and those belonging to the majority. In this respect, they shall take due account of the specific conditions of the persons belonging to national minorities' (Art. 4(2)), and makes clear that the measures adopted in accordance with this latter provision shall not be considered to be an act of discrimination (Art. 4(3)). The positive action measures thus deemed allowable under the Convention should, however, not be confused with the prohibition imposed on the States parties to aim at the forced assimilation of persons belonging to national minorities. The identity (religious, ethnic or linguistic) of national minorities must be fully respected at all times: under Article 5(1), the States parties are to 'undertake to promote the conditions necessary for persons belonging to national minorities to maintain and develop their culture, and to preserve the essential elements of their identity, namely their religion, language, traditions and cultural heritage'. The special measures referred to in Article 4(2) will only be acceptable insofar as they are 'adequate', that is 'in conformity with the proportionality principle, in order to avoid violation of the rights of others as well as discrimination against others', and provided they 'do not extend, in time or in scope, beyond what is necessary in order to achieve the aim of full and effective equality' (para. 39 of the Explanatory Report); instead, the prohibition of assimilation of members of national minorities against their will is permanent, and not subject to this limitation.

In contrast, in its General Comment No. 20 on *Non-discrimination*, the Committee on Economic, Social and Cultural Rights notes that '[e]liminating discrimination in practice requires paying sufficient attention to groups of individuals which suffer historical or persistent prejudice instead of merely comparing the formal treatment of individuals in similar situations'. It then goes on to state:

Committee on Economic, Social and Cultural Rights, General Comment No. 20, *Non-discrimination in Economic, Social and Cultural Rights* (Art. 2, para. 2, of the International Covenant on Economic, Social and Cultural Rights) (E/C.12/GC/20, 2 July 2009), para. 9:

In order to eliminate substantive discrimination, States parties may be, and in some cases are, under an obligation to adopt special measures to attenuate or suppress conditions that perpetuate discrimination. Such measures are legitimate to the extent that they represent reasonable, objective and proportional means to redress *de facto* discrimination and are discontinued when substantive equality has been sustainably achieved. Such positive measures may exceptionally, however, need to be of a permanent nature, such as interpretation services for linguistic minorities and reasonable accommodation of persons with sensory impairments in accessing health-care facilities.

This presentation is misleading, however. It confuses the prohibition of adopting or maintaining measures which, although apparently neutral, may result in indirectly discriminating against certain groups, in particular in the absence of reasonable accommodation, with positive action; these are measures aimed at improving the situation of certain groups by temporary measures which are justified by the need to ensure equitable representation or to overcome legacies of inequality, rather than by the need to respect the specific characteristics of such groups or individuals. In contrast, the Committee on the Elimination of Discrimination against Women emphasizes the difference between the two categories of measures:

Committee on the Elimination of Discrimination against Women, General Recommendation No. 5, *Temporary Special Measures*, adopted at the seventh session of the Committee (1988), in Compilation of the General Comments or General Recommendations adopted by Human Rights Treaty Bodies, UN Doc. HRI/GEN/1/Rev.7, 12 May 2004, at p. 235, para. 19:

States parties should clearly distinguish between temporary special measures taken under article 4, paragraph 1, to accelerate the achievement of a concrete goal for women of *de facto* or substantive equality, and other general social policies adopted to improve the situation of women and the girl child. Not all measures that potentially are, or will be, favourable to women are temporary special measures. The provision of general conditions in order to guarantee the civil, political, economic, social and cultural rights of women and the girl child, designed to ensure for them a life of dignity and non-discrimination, cannot be called temporary special measures.

The remainder of this section examines the contribution of positive action (or 'temporary special measures') to the promotion of equality (b), as well as the limits that are imposed to this tool by the requirements of formal equality (c). It relies on the views adopted on these issues by the UN human rights treaty bodies, but also on the position of judicial and quasi-judicial bodies at regional level.

(b) The contribution of temporary special measures to the promotion of equality
Both the Convention for the Elimination of All Forms of Racial Discrimination (CERD) and the Convention for the Elimination of All Forms of Discrimination Against Women (CEDAW) allow for the adoption of affirmative action, under certain

conditions. The International Convention for the Elimination of All Forms of Racial Discrimination defines in Article 1(1) 'racial discrimination' as 'any distinction, exclusion, restriction or preference based on race, colour, descent, or national or ethnic origin which has the purpose or effect of nullifying or impairing the recognition, enjoyment or exercise, on an equal footing, of human rights and fundamental freedoms in the political, economic, social, cultural or any other field of public life'. However, Article 1(4) adds:

> Special measures taken for the sole purpose of securing adequate advancement of certain racial or ethnic groups or individuals requiring such protection as may be necessary in order to ensure such groups or individuals equal enjoyment or exercise of human rights and fundamental freedoms shall not be deemed racial discrimination, provided, however, that such measures do not, as a consequence, lead to the maintenance of separate rights for different racial groups and that they shall not be continued after the objectives for which they were taken have been achieved.

While this provision appears to allow for the adoption of certain positive action measures by the States parties to ICERD, Article 2(2) adds that the adoption of such measures may be required under certain conditions:

> States Parties shall, when the circumstances so warrant, take, in the social, economic, cultural and other fields, special and concrete measures to ensure the adequate development and protection of certain racial groups or individuals belonging to them, for the purpose of guaranteeing them the full and equal enjoyment of human rights and fundamental freedoms. These measures shall in no case entail as a consequence the maintenance of unequal or separate rights for different racial groups after the objectives for which they were taken have been achieved.

In its General Recommendation XXVII on discrimination against Roma adopted in 2000, the Committee for the Elimination of Racial Discrimination, although not making explicit reference to Article 2(2) CERD, encourages the States parties to 'take special measures to promote the employment of Roma in the public administration and institutions, as well as in private companies', and to 'adopt and implement, whenever possible, at the central or local level, special measures in favour of Roma in public employment such as public contracting and other activities undertaken or funded by the Government, or training Roma in various skills and professions' (paras. 28–9). Similarly, in its General Recommendation XXIX on Article 1, para. 1, of the Convention (Descent), adopted in 2002, the CERD Committee recommends the adoption of 'special measures in favour of descent-based groups and communities in order to ensure their enjoyment of human rights and fundamental freedoms, in particular concerning access to public functions, employment and education', as well as to 'educate the general public on the importance of affirmative action programmes to address the situation of victims of descent-based discrimination' and to take 'special measures to promote the employment of members of affected communities in the public and private sectors' (paras. 1(f) and (h), and 7(jj)).

Similar provisions are contained in the Convention for the Elimination of All Forms of Discrimination against Women. Article 4(1) CEDAW states:

> Adoption by States Parties of temporary special measures aimed at accelerating *de facto* equality between men and women shall not be considered discrimination as defined in the present Convention, but shall in no way entail as a consequence the maintenance of unequal or separate standards; these measures shall be discontinued when the objectives of equality of opportunity and treatment have been achieved.

As we have seen, the purpose of this provision is to 'accelerate the improvement of the position of women to achieve their *de facto* or substantive equality with men, and to effect the structural, social and cultural changes necessary to correct past and current forms and effects of discrimination against women, as well as to provide them with compensation' (General Recommendation No. 25, Article 4, paragraph 1, of the Convention (temporary special measures) (2004), para. 15). In its fifth General Recommendation adopted in 1988, the Committee on the Elimination of Discrimination against Women encouraged States parties to 'make more use of temporary special measures such as positive action, preferential treatment or quota systems to advance women's integration into education, the economy, politics and employment' (General Recommendation No. 5, *Temporary Special Measures*, adopted at the seventh session of the Committee (1988)). In the specific context of participation of women in public and political life, the CEDAW Committee noted the following:

Committee on the Elimination of Discrimination against Women, General Recommendation No. 5, *Temporary Special Measures*, adopted at the seventh session of the Committee (1988) (HRI/GEN/1/Rev.7, 12 May 2004, at p. 235), para. 15:

While removal of *de jure* barriers is necessary, it is not sufficient. Failure to achieve full and equal participation of women can be unintentional and the result of outmoded practices and procedures which inadvertently promote men. Under article 4, the Convention encourages the use of temporary special measures in order to give full effect to articles 7 [relating to the elimination of discrimination against women in political and public life] and 8 [concerning the opportunity women must be provided to represent their Governments at the international level and to participate in the work of international organizations]. Where countries have developed effective temporary strategies in an attempt to achieve equality of participation, a wide range of measures has been implemented, including recruiting, financially assisting and training women candidates, amending electoral procedures, developing campaigns directed at equal participation, setting numerical goals and quotas and targeting women for appointment to public positions such as the judiciary or other professional groups that play an essential part in the everyday life of all societies. The formal removal of barriers and the introduction of temporary special measures to encourage the equal participation of both men and women in the public life of their societies are essential prerequisites to true equality in political life. In order, however, to overcome centuries of male domination of the public sphere, women also require the encouragement and support of all sectors of society to achieve full and effective participation, encouragement which must be led by States parties to the Convention, as well as by political parties and public officials. States parties have an obligation to ensure that temporary special measures are clearly designed to support the principle of equality and therefore comply with constitutional principles which guarantee equality to all citizens.

Three characteristics of the Convention for the Elimination of All Forms of Discrimination against Women encourage the shift from the possibility to adopt positive action measures without this being considered discriminatory to an obligation, in certain instances, to adopt such measures in the name of real and effective equality. First, CEDAW does not simply prohibit discrimination on grounds of sex: it is aimed specifically at the protection of women. Other equality clauses such as, in particular, Article 26 of the International Covenant on Civil and Political Rights (ICCPR) or Article 2(2) of the International Covenant on Economic, Social and Cultural Rights (ICESCR) – the latter, in the enjoyment of the rights guaranteed under the ICESCR – ensure a symmetrical protection of equality between women and men; in contrast, CEDAW focuses on discrimination against women, thus 'emphasizing that women have suffered, and continue to suffer from various forms of discrimination because they are women' (Committee on the Elimination of Discrimination against Women, General Recommendation No. 25, Article 4, paragraph 1, of the Convention (temporary special measures) (2004), para. 5). Second, Article 24 CEDAW imposes on the States Parties to 'adopt all necessary measures at the national level aimed at achieving the full realization of the rights recognized in the present Convention'. Third, a number of specific articles of the Convention also mention that States are to 'take all appropriate measures' in order to fulfil the rights guaranteed. On the basis of these arguments, as well as a dynamic interpretation of the Convention for the Elimination of All Forms of Discrimination against Women, the CEDAW Committee concludes in the General Recommendation it adopted in 2004 on Article 4, para. 1 of the Convention, that the adoption of certain positive action measures may be required under that instrument: 'States parties' obligation is to improve the *de facto* position of women through concrete and effective policies and programmes ... Pursuit of the goal of substantive equality also calls for an effective strategy aimed at overcoming underrepresentation of women and a redistribution of resources and power between men and women' (paras. 7–8). Indeed, States parties may have to 'provide adequate explanations with regard to any failure to adopt temporary special measures. Such failures may not be justified simply by averring powerlessness, or by explaining inaction through predominant market or political forces, such as those inherent in the private sector, private organizations, or political parties' (para. 29).

Typically, positive action measures granting special (or 'preferential') treatment to the members of certain groups who have been historically discriminated against or are in a position of structural disadvantage, are seen as an exception to the principle of formal equality: such measures are therefore only allowed under well-defined circumstances, and they must be limited to what is necessary, both in scope and in time. However, positive action measures may also be seen as a contribution to the promotion of substantive equality. This is the view of the Committee on the Elimination of Discrimination against Women under the CEDAW:

Committee on the Elimination of Discrimination against Women, General Recommendation No. 5, *Temporary Special Measures*, adopted at the seventh session of the Committee (1988) (HRI/GEN/1/Rev.7, 12 May 2004, at p. 235), paras. 14 and 18:

14. The Convention targets discriminatory dimensions of past and current societal and cultural contexts which impede women's enjoyment of their human rights and fundamental freedoms. It aims at the elimination of all forms of discrimination against women, including the elimination of the causes and consequences of their *de facto* or substantive inequality. Therefore, the application of temporary special measures in accordance with the Convention is one of the means to realize *de facto* or substantive equality for women, rather than an exception to the norms of non-discrimination and equality.

18. Measures taken under article 4, paragraph 1, by States parties should aim to accelerate the equal participation of women in the political, economic, social, cultural, civil or any other field. The Committee views the application of these measures not as an exception to the norm of non-discrimination, but rather as an emphasis that temporary special measures are part of a necessary strategy by States parties directed towards the achievement of *de facto* or substantive equality of women with men in the enjoyment of their human rights and fundamental freedoms. While the application of temporary special measures often remedies the effects of past discrimination against women, the obligation of States parties under the Convention to improve the position of women to one of *de facto* or substantive equality with men exists irrespective of any proof of past discrimination. The Committee considers that States parties that adopt and implement such measures under the Convention do not discriminate against men.

The view according to which, in certain circumstances, the adoption by a State of positive action measures may be not only acceptable, but even obligatory, is shared by the Human Rights Committee, under the ICCPR (General Comment No. 18, *Non-discrimination* (1989), para. 10), and by the Committee on Economic, Social and Cultural Rights, under the ICESCR (General Comment No. 20, *Non-discriminaiton in the Enjoyment of Economic, Social and Cultural Rights* (2009), para. 9). Indeed, the Committee on Economic, Social and Cultural Rights already took the view in its first General Comment that 'special attention [should] be given to any worse-off regions or areas and to any specific groups or subgroups which appear to be particularly vulnerable or disadvantaged' (General Comment No. 1, *Reporting by States Parties* (1989), para. 3). In its General Comment No. 5, *The Rights of Persons with Disabilities*, adopted in 1994, the Committee noted that 'appropriate measures [may] need to be taken to undo existing discrimination and to establish equitable opportunities for persons with disabilities', and considered that 'such actions should not be considered discriminatory in the sense of article 2(2) of the International Covenant on Economic, Social and Cultural Rights as long as they are based on the principle of equality and are employed only to the extent necessary to achieve that objective' (para. 18). It also noted:

Committee on Economic, Social and Cultural Rights, General Comment No. 5, *The Rights of Persons with Disabilities* (1994) (HRI/GEN/1/Rev.7, 12 May 2004, at p. 25), para. 9:

The obligation of States parties to the Covenant to promote progressive realization of the relevant rights to the maximum of their available resources clearly requires Governments to do much more than merely abstain from taking measures which might have a negative impact on persons with disabilities. The obligation in the case of such a vulnerable and disadvantaged group is to take positive action to reduce structural disadvantages and to give appropriate preferential treatment to people with disabilities in order to achieve the objectives of full participation and equality within society for all persons with disabilities. This almost invariably means that additional resources will need to be made available for this purpose and that a wide range of specially tailored measures will be required.

Other examples could be given in the doctrine of the Committee on Economic, Social and Cultural Rights (see, e.g. General Comment No. 4, *The Right to Adequate Housing* (Art. 11(1) of the Covenant) (1991), para. 11; see, generally, M. Craven, *The International Covenant on Economic, Social and Cultural Rights, a Perspective on its Development* (Oxford: Clarendon Press, 1995), p. 126 (emphasizing the obligation of States to focus their efforts on the most vulnerable and disadvantaged groups in society, which may include preferential treatment in favour of the members of these disadvantaged groups)). For instance, it noted in its General Comment No. 13, *The Right to Education* (Art. 13), that the adoption of 'temporary special measures intended to bring about *de facto* equality for men and women and for disadvantaged groups' is not a violation of the right to non–discrimination with regard to education, 'so long as such measures do not lead to the maintenance of unequal or separate standards for different groups, and provided they are not continued after the objectives for which they were taken have been achieved' (para. 32). It therefore considered – citing in this respect Article 2 of the UNESCO Convention against Discrimination in Education of 14 December 1960 – that separate educational systems or institutions for groups defined by the grounds listed in Article 2(2) of the Covenant shall be deemed not to constitute a breach of that instrument.

7.8. Question for discussion: temporary special measures and separate educational facilities

Is the reference made by the Committee on Economic, Social and Cultural Rights to Article 2 of the UNESCO Convention against Discrimination in Education of 14 December 1960 appropriate?

In its relevant part, this provision states that '[t]he establishment or maintenance, for religious or linguistic reasons, of separate educational systems or institutions offering an education which is in keeping with the wishes of the pupil's parents or legal guardians [shall not constitute discrimination in the meaning of the Convention], if participation in such systems or attendance at such institutions is optional and if the education provided conforms to such standards as may be laid down or approved by the competent authorities, in particular for education of the same level' (Art. 2(b)). Marc Bossuyt argues that this provision 'does not refer to special measures, but only determines when separate educational systems will not be deemed to constitute discrimination' ('The concept and practice of affirmative action', Final report submitted by Mr Marc Bossuyt, Special Rapporteur, in accordance with Resolution 1998/5 of the Sub-Commission for the Promotion and Protection of Human Rights, UN Doc. E/CN.4/Sub.2/2002/21, 17 June 2002, para. 56).

In the conclusions to his report, Marc Bossuyt notes that 'a persistent policy in the past of systematic discrimination of certain groups of the population may justify – *and in some cases may even require* – special measures intended to overcome the sequels of a condition of inferiority which still affects members belonging to such groups' ('The concept and practice of affirmative action', Final report submitted by Mr Marc Bossuyt, Special Rapporteur, in accordance with Resolution 1998/5 of the Sub-Commission for the Promotion and Protection of Human Rights, UN Doc. E/CN.4/Sub.2/2002/21, 17 June 2002, para. 101 (emphasis added)). At the same time, while the principle seems to be agreed that positive action measures may be required from the State in order to ensure real and effective equality under its jurisdiction, it will be typically difficult for any individual seeking to benefit from such scheme to impose on the State to take an initiative in this regard, considering the broad margin of appreciation which the State authorities have available as regards the choice of means through which to achieve substantive equality and the broad panoply of measures they have at their disposal. It is significant in this regard that, when they adopted Additional Protocol No. 12 to the ECHR (see above, section 1.2.), the signatories reaffirmed that 'the principle of non-discrimination does not prevent States Parties from taking measures in order to promote full and effective equality, provided that there is an objective and reasonable justification for those measures', but added:

Explanatory Report of Protocol No. 12 to the Convention for the Protection of Human Rights and Fundamental Freedoms, H (2000) 11 prov., 29 August 2000, para. 16:

The fact that there are certain groups or categories of persons who are disadvantaged, or the existence of *de facto* inequalities, may constitute justifications for adopting measures providing for specific advantages in order to promote equality, provided that the proportionality principle is respected ... However, the present Protocol does not impose any obligation to adopt such measures. Such a programmatic obligation would sit ill with the whole nature of the Convention and its control system which are based on the collective guarantee of individual rights which are formulated in terms sufficiently specific to be justifiable.

A deepening of the debate on the notion of 'structural discrimination' might serve in the future to clarify the conditions under which, under the international law of human rights, a State may be obliged to adopt positive action measures (for a detailed exploration of this notion, see C. McCrudden, 'Institutional Discrimination', *Oxford Journal of Legal Studies*, 2(3) (1982), 303–67). In the meaning attached to this notion here, structural discrimination is not simply a particularly serious form of discrimination. Instead, its defining characteristic would be that it cuts across different spheres (education, employment, housing and, in particular, access to health care), resulting in a situation where the prohibition of discrimination in any one of these spheres or, indeed, in all of them, will not suffice to ensure effective equality. For instance, it will not be sufficient to prohibit discrimination in employment if inequalities persist in access to education or vocational training, thus leading to a situation of under-representation of the group concerned in employment, in spite of the effective prohibition of (direct or indirect) discrimination in that sphere. And it will not be sufficient to prohibit discrimination in education if, due to segregated housing, the children of one particular minority community are disproportionately represented in certain educational establishments and never or almost never have access to other establishments attended by children from the majority group (for instance due to the lack of public transportation enabling these minority children to travel from their neighbourhood to the mainstream schools). Structural discrimination should be understood as a situation where, due to the extent of the discrimination faced by a particular segment of society, more is required in order to achieve effective equality than to outlaw direct and indirect discrimination.

7.9. Question for discussion: tackling structural discrimination

According to which modalities could we define an obligation to adopt positive action measures (or 'temporary special measures') in order to promote substantive equality and overcome historical legacies of discrimination or existing inequalities? For example, could a mechanism be devised according to which, where certain statistical imbalances are found in defined domains (such as at certain levels of the educational system or of the professional hierarchy), special measures will be taken to improve the position of under-represented groups?

The idea according to which temporary special measures may be obligatory under well-defined conditions, and that such measures should be seen as contributing to the promotion of the principle of equality rather than as mere derogations to the rule of formal equality, is also expressed in other contexts. In its General Comment No. 20

on *Non-discrimination in the Enjoyment of Economic, Social and Cultural Rights*, the Committee on Economic, Social and Cultural Rights states that:

Committee on Economic, Social and Cultural Rights, General Comment No. 20, *Non-discrimination in Economic, Social and Cultural Rights* (Art. 2, para. 2, of the International Covenant on Economic, Social and Cultural Rights) (E/C.12/ GC/20, 2 July 2009), para. 39:

States parties must adopt an active approach to eliminating systemic discrimination and segregation in practice. Tackling such discrimination will usually require a comprehensive approach with a range of laws, policies and programmes, including temporary special measures. States parties should consider using incentives to encourage public and private actors to change their attitudes and behaviour in relation to individuals and groups of individuals facing systemic discrimination, or penalize them in case of non-compliance. Public leadership and programmes to raise awareness about systemic discrimination and the adoption of strict measures against incitement to discrimination are often necessary. Eliminating systemic discrimination will frequently require devoting greater resources to traditionally neglected groups. Given the persistent hostility towards some groups, particular attention will need to be given to ensuring that laws and policies are implemented by officials and others in practice.

Another illustration is provided, in a regional context, by the European Social Charter. Article 1 para. 2 of the European Social Charter of 1961 imposes on the States parties an obligation to 'protect effectively the right of the worker to earn his living in an occupation freely entered upon'. This, according to the European Committee on Social Rights, requires the elimination in practice of all discrimination in employment: 'although a necessary requirement, appropriate domestic legislation that is in conformity with the Charter is not sufficient to ensure the principles laid down in the Charter are actually applied in practice. It is not sufficient therefore merely to enact legislation prohibiting discrimination ... as regards access to employment; such discrimination must also be eliminated in practice' (Concl. XVI–1, vol. 2 (Spain), pp. 602–6). Where the employment situation of women or certain minorities remains unsatisfactory, the Committee considers that this demonstrates that the measures taken to date are not sufficient. Indeed, as the ECSR examines on the basis of that provision of the Charter not only the adequacy of the *legal framework* prohibiting discrimination, but also the *results* which are achieved in the integration of certain target groups traditionally excluded from the employment market, providing training and education to the members of those groups constitutes a means for the States parties to comply with their obligations under that provision (see, with respect to the need to provide training and education to the Roma population, under-represented in the employment market, Concl. XVI–1, vol. 1, pp. 125–9). This insistence on the effectiveness of measures ensuring the integration of certain traditionally disadvantaged groups has been reiterated under Article E of the 1996 Revised European Social Charter:

European Committee of Social Rights, Collective Complaint No. 13/2002,
Autisme-Europe **v.** *France*, **decision (merits) of 4 November 2003:**

[The complainant non-governmental organization alleged before the Committee that France had violated Article 15 para. 1 (obligation to take the necessary measures to provide persons with disabilities with guidance, education and vocational training in the framework of general schemes whenever possible) and Article 17 para. 1 (right to education by the provision of sufficient and adequate institutions and services) of the revised European Social Charter, either alone or in combination with Article E (non-discrimination), because the proportion of children with autism being educated in either general or specialist schools is much lower than in the case of other children, whether or not disabled, and because of the chronic shortage of care and support facilities for autistic adults. The Committee cited the judgment of the European Court of Human Rights in *Thlimmenos* v. *Greece* to the effect that the principle of non-discrimination 'is also violated when States without an objective and reasonable justification fail to treat differently persons whose situations are significantly different', and continued:]

52. ... In other words, human difference in a democratic society should not only be viewed positively but should be responded to with discernment in order to ensure real and effective equality.

In this regard, the Committee considers that Article E not only prohibits direct discrimination but also all forms of indirect discrimination. Such indirect discrimination may arise by failing to take due and positive account of all relevant differences or by failing to take adequate steps to ensure that the rights and collective advantages that are open to all are genuinely accessible by and to all.

53. The Committee recalls, as stated in its decision relative to Complaint No. 1/1998 (*International Commission of Jurists* v. *Portugal*, §32), that the implementation of the Charter requires the State Parties to take not merely legal action but also practical action to give full effect to the rights recognised in the Charter. When the achievement of one of the rights in question is exceptionally complex and particularly expensive to resolve, a State Party must take measures that allows it to achieve the objectives of the Charter within a reasonable time, with measurable progress and to an extent consistent with the maximum use of available resources. States Parties must be particularly mindful of the impact that their choices will have for groups with heightened vulnerabilities as well as for others persons affected including, especially, their families on whom falls the heaviest burden in the event of institutional shortcomings.

54. In the light of the afore-mentioned, the Committee notes that in the case of autistic children and adults, notwithstanding a national debate going back more than twenty years about the number of persons concerned and the relevant strategies required, and even after the enactment of the Disabled Persons Policy Act of 30 June 1975, France has failed to achieve sufficient progress in advancing the provision of education for persons with autism. It specifically notes that most of the French official documents, in particular those submitted during the procedure, still use a more restrictive definition of autism than that adopted by the World Heath Organisation and that there are still insufficient official statistics with which to rationally measure progress through time. The Committee considers that the fact that the establishments specialising in the education and care of disabled children (particularly those with autism) are not in general financed from the same budget as normal schools, does not

in itself amount to discrimination, since it is primarily for States themselves to decide on the modalities of funding.

Nevertheless, it considers, as the authorities themselves acknowledge, and whether a broad or narrow definition of autism is adopted, that the proportion of children with autism being educated in either general or specialist schools is much lower than in the case of other children, whether or not disabled. It is also established, and not contested by the authorities, that there is a chronic shortage of care and support facilities for autistic adults.

For these reasons, the Committee concludes by 11 votes to 2 that the situation constitutes a violation of Articles 15§1 and 17§1 whether alone or read in combination with Article E of the revised European Social Charter.

This decision illustrates how the requirement of non-discrimination may provide guidance for the realization of socio-economic rights such as the right to education by identifying the categories which, because of their particular vulnerability, deserve special attention. It also shows how the shift from the prohibition of indirect discrimination (understood, as in the case of *Thlimmenos*, as a failure to take due account of relevant differences) to the obligation to adopt positive action measures (i.e. to take into account the need to redress or compensate for the situation of the most vulnerable or disadvantaged segments of society) may be more gradual than radical.

Similar positive obligations to adopt measures in the face of entrenched inequalities may be derived from the Council of Europe Framework Convention on the Protection of National Minorities, which entered into force in 1998. As already noted, under Article 4 of the Framework Convention, States parties are to adopt 'adequate measures in order to promote, in all areas of economic, social, political and cultural life, full and effective equality between persons belonging to a national minority and those belonging to the majority', taking due account in this respect of 'the specific conditions of the persons belonging to national minorities' (Art. 4(2)); such measures are specifically designated as not being discriminatory in character (Art. 4(3)). The Advisory Committee of the Framework Convention encourages the introduction of positive measures in favour of members of minorities, which are particularly disadvantaged (see, e.g. Opinion on Azerbaijan, 22 May 2003, ACFC/OP/I(2004)001, para. 28; Opinion on Ukraine, 1 March 2002, ACFC/OP/I(2002)010, para. 27; Opinion on Serbia and Montenegro, 27 November 2003, ACFC/OP/I(2004)002, para. 38). Thus, in an Opinion on Croatia, the Advisory Committee 'considers that one key to reaching full and effective equality for persons belonging to national minorities is the launching of additional positive measures in the field of employment and it supports efforts to seek financing for such measures. In this regard, the situation of persons belonging to the Serb minority merits particular attention, taking into account the past discriminatory measures, stirred by the 1991–1995 conflict, aimed at curtailing their number in various fields of employment, ranging from law-enforcement to education' (Opinion on Croatia, 6 February 2002, ACFC/INF/OP/I(2002)003, para. 26). In an Opinion on the Czech Republic, the Advisory Committee 'notes with deep concern that many Roma in the Czech Republic face considerable socio-economic difficulties in comparison to both the majority and other minorities, in particular in the fields of education, employment and housing ... The situation calls for the preparation and implementation of specific measures to realise full and effective equality between Roma and persons belonging to the majority as well as to other minorities' (Opinion on the Czech Republic, 25 January 2002, ACFC/INF/OP/I(2002)002, para. 29). A very similar observation was made with respect to the situation of the Roma in Hungary.

Advisory Committee on the Protection of National Minorities (Council of Europe), Opinion on Hungary adopted on 22 September 2000, (ACFC/INF/OP/I(2001)004), at paras. 18–19:

[The Advisory Committee] notes with concern, that, as the Government openly recognises, the Roma/Gypsies in Hungary face a broad range of serious problems to a disproportionate degree, be it in comparison to the majority or in comparison to other minorities. This state of affairs certainly justifies that specific measures be designed and implemented to tackle these problems. [Therefore the Advisory Committee welcomes the decision of the Hungarian authorities to develop medium and long-term plans of action towards improving the living conditions of the Roma/Gypsy minority and is encouraged by] the determination of the Government to resolve the problems of the Roma/Gypsy minority and considers that this gives rise to high expectations. The Advisory Committee stresses that the commitment to long term approaches should not lead to a delay in achieving improvements that can be secured in a short or medium term. Furthermore, a long-term approach requires that a consistent and sustained policy is designed, implemented and evaluated throughout this period and that appropriate resources are made available and maintained, even where there may be setbacks and disappointments. In the view of the Advisory Committee the Hungarian Government is to be commended and to be taken seriously for its initiative and its intentions. It is only consistent with this view that the future results of Hungary are to be evaluated in the light of the standards it has committed itself to. Finally, the Advisory Committee underlines that, when implementing special measures, particular attention should be paid to the situation of Romany women.

The Opinion it adopted on Ireland on 22 May 2003 offers another example of the Advisory Committee's insistence on combating identified instances of structural discrimination through positive action measures – in this case, in order to improve the situation of the Travellers' community:

Advisory Committee on the Protection of National Minorities (Council of Europe), Opinion on Ireland, 22 May 2003, ACFC/INF/OP/I (2004)003:

34. The Advisory Committee notes ... that progress in the area of legislation and institution building has not always been matched by implementation in practice. A number of important concerns remain, notably in relation to the Traveller community. Travellers continue to suffer discrimination in a wide range of societal settings including education (see under Article 12

below), employment, health care, accommodation (see under Article 5 below) and access to certain goods and services, including access to places of entertainment.

35. The Advisory Committee is particularly concerned about the high level of unemployment of persons belonging to the Traveller community. Travellers have also seen their traditional areas of economic livelihood (scrap metal, horse trading, market trading, etc.) hit by changing economic and social climates. They consider that certain aspects of changes in legislation (such as in the Control of Horses Act (1996) and the Casual Trading Act (1995)) unduly hinder their ability to earn a living. In view of the impact that this legislation has had on Travellers, the Advisory Committee considers that the Government should examine how to promote further both traditional and new economic activities of Travellers.

36. Notwithstanding the efforts made by the authorities to support the entrance of Travellers into the labour market, the Advisory Committee considers that more needs to be done in order to improve the situation. It is clear that the lack of statistics on Traveller employment makes it difficult to monitor the situation, and that such statistics are essential to the design, implementation and monitoring in this field ...

37. Concerning employment in the public service, the Advisory Committee supports the recommendations in this field made by the Committee to Monitor and Co-ordinate the Implementation of the Recommendations of the Task Force on the Travelling Community and in particular the need for setting targets to include Travellers in general recruitment strategies.

These statements by the Advisory Committee established under the Framework Convention for the Protection of National Minorities and by the European Committee of Social Rights monitoring the European Social Charter remain unclear as to the precise conditions under which the adoption of positive action measures may constitute an obligation for the States parties to these instruments. In this respect, the Council of Europe bodies have not gone further than the human rights treaty bodies established within the United Nations. Insofar as these bodies primarily seek to facilitate the adoption of States of adequate strategies for the implementation of their international obligations, in a spirit of co-operation with those States, this may not be particularly problematic. It may become an impairment, however, when these bodies assume quasi-judicial functions, as when the United Nations human rights treaty bodies receive individual communications or when the European Committee of Social Rights acts under the mechanism allowing non-governmental organizations or unions to file collective complaints.

The attitude of the bodies of the American Convention on Human Rights towards positive action is similar to that of the human rights bodies discussed above. The Inter-American Court, in its advisory opinion on the *Status of Undocumented Migrants* (OC-18/03) established an obligation to adopt positive measures to counter persistent patterns of discrimination:

104. ... States are obliged to take affirmative action to reverse or change discriminatory situations that exist in their societies to the detriment of a specific group of persons. This

implies the special obligation to protect that the State must exercise with regard to acts and practices of third parties who, with its tolerance or acquiescence, create, maintain or promote discriminatory situations.

The opinion decided unanimously:

1. That States have the general obligation to respect and ensure the fundamental rights. To this end, they must take affirmative action, avoid taking measures that limit or infringe a fundamental right, and eliminate measures and practices that restrict or violate a fundamental right.
2. That non-compliance by the State with the general obligation to respect and ensure human rights, owing to any discriminatory treatment, gives rise to international responsibility.

In 1999, the Inter-American Commission on Human Rights adopted a set of *Considerations Regarding the Compatibility of Affirmative Action Measures Designed to Promote the Political Participation of Women with the Principles of Equality and Non-discrimination*:

Inter-American Commission on Human Rights, *Considerations Regarding the Compatibility of Affirmative Action Measures Designed to Promote the Political Participation of Women with the Principles of Equality and Non-discrimination*, 1999 Annual Report (OEA/Ser.L/V/II.106, Doc. 6 rev., April 13, 1999):

In principle, examining the compatibility of special measures of affirmative action designed to promote the political participation of women with the principles of equality and non-discrimination set forth in the American Convention and Declaration requires analyzing a series of questions. Three questions are of central importance. First, does the measure bring about a difference in treatment that falls within the sphere of application of the American Convention or Declaration, respectively? Second, assuming that it does, does that difference in treatment pursue a legitimate aim? This analysis looks to the interest the state seeks to serve and the objectives sought to be accomplished. Third, are the means employed proportional to the end sought? In other words, is there a reasonable balance of interests between the end sought and any restriction of rights imposed? If there is a restriction involved, is it the least restrictive measure possible to accomplish the objective sought? Is the treatment involved arbitrary or unfair in any case? The evaluation of these questions must take into account that a distinction based on status, such as sex, gives rise to heightened scrutiny.

As a general matter, the regional and international communities have recognized that, while the existence of formal *de jure* equality is a fundamental prerequisite for overcoming discrimination, it does not necessarily lead to equality in practice. To the contrary, while the constitutions of our region guarantee equality between women and men, women remain severely under-represented in virtually all aspects of political life. Nor is it the case that apparently gender-neutral legislation and policies necessarily produce gender-neutral outcomes.

Consequently, instruments and policies adopted at both the regional and universal levels require the adoption of special measures where necessary to promote the equal access of women to participation in public life. The goal of bringing about the effective equal access of women to participation in public life is clearly, in and of itself, a legitimate and necessary goal. As referred to above, the regional and international human rights obligations of states must be made effective at the national level through domestic legislation and practice. Accordingly, where discrimination in law or in fact constrains women from fully exercising their right to participate in the government and public affairs of their country, that inconformity must be addressed through concrete action. One of the concrete ways the duty to respect and ensure the rights at issue can be realized is through the adoption of measures of affirmative measures to promote the participation of women in this sphere.

How this goal of promoting the equal access of women to political participation is pursued and implemented is, at first instance, necessarily a function of national law and policymaking, and integrally related to the specific situation and history in the country. The considerations reviewed above provide general guidance in examining the compatibility of a particular measure of affirmative action adopted by an OAS member state with the obligations of equality and non-discrimination. The specific measure must then be analyzed in light of those considerations, its precise characteristics, and the national context. In particular, the regional and international dispositions calling for and/or requiring the adoption of special measures of affirmative action to promote the political participation of women contemplate that the need for and appropriateness of such measures will be evaluated in relation to the actual existence of discriminatory treatment. They are, moreover, intended to be temporary, in the sense that, once equality of access and outcome are achieved, such measures are no longer required. These elements of analysis are, by definition, inextricably linked to the national context.

[Conclusion]

In principle, affirmative measures are fully in compliance with the principle of non-discrimination and the applicable provisions of human rights law; in fact, such measures may well be required to bring about substantive equality of opportunity. Achieving the free and full participation of women in political life is a priority for our hemisphere ...

The under-representation of women in government throughout the Americas demonstrates the need for further state action, in conjunction with initiatives of civil society, to bring about true respect for the right of women to participate in political life in compliance with international norms. As the regional and international communities have recognized, achieving the free and full participation of women in all spheres of public life is an obligation which may well require the adoption of special measures of affirmative action designed to effectuate equality of opportunity for women and men.

(c) The compatibility of temporary special measures with the non-discrimination requirement

It is still the dominant view that positive action measures shall only be compatible with the non-discrimination requirement under certain well-defined conditions. In the following communication, the author complained of the preferential treatment, regarding reinstatement to the public service, of former public officials who had previously been unfairly dismissed on ideological, political or trade union grounds. The author complained that this preferential treatment unfairly prejudiced his own chances of gaining a public-service job. The Human Rights Committee, however, found the alleged discrimination to be permissible affirmative action in favour of a formerly disadvantaged group.

Human Rights Committee, *R. D. Stalla Costa* v. *Uruguay*, Communication No. 198/1985 (Supp. No. 40 (A/42/40) at 170 (1987)), final views of 9 July 1987:

The main question before the Committee is whether the author of the communication is a victim of a violation of article 25(c) of the Covenant because, as he alleges, he has not been permitted to have access to public service on general terms of equality. Taking into account the social and political situation in Uruguay during the years of military rule, in particular the dismissal of many public servants pursuant to Institutional Act No. 7, the Committee understands the enactment of Act No. 15.737 of 22 March 1985 by the new democratic Government of Uruguay as a measure of redress. Indeed, the Committee observes that Uruguayan public officials dismissed on ideological, political or trade-union grounds were victims of violations of article 25 of the Covenant and as such are entitled to have an effective remedy under article 2, paragraph 3 (a), of the Covenant. The Act should be looked upon as such a remedy. The implementation of the Act, therefore, cannot be regarded as incompatible with the reference to 'general terms of equality' in article 25 (c) of the Covenant. Neither can the implementation of the Act be regarded as an invidious distinction under article 2, paragraph 1, or as prohibited discrimination within the terms of article 26 of the Covenant.

This generally favourable attitude towards positive action was made even more explicit in the later case law of the Human Rights Committee:

Human Rights Committee, *Guido Jacobs* v. *Belgium*, Communication No. 943/2000 (CCPR/C/81/D/943/2000 (2004)), final views of 7 July 2004:

[Under the Belgian Act of 22 December 1998 amending certain provisions of part two of the Judicial Code concerning the High Council of Justice, the nomination and appointment of magistrates and the introduction of an evaluation system, the High Council of Justice is to comprise forty-four members of Belgian nationality, divided into one twenty-two-member Dutch-speaking college and one twenty-two-member French-speaking college. Each college comprises eleven justices and eleven non-justices. It is also provided that the group of non-justices in each college shall have no fewer than four members of each sex (Art. 259*bis*-1, para. 3 of the Judicial Code). The author of the communication had applied to be elected as a non-justice to the High Council of Justice, but failed to be elected, following a second call for applications, since the first call had not led to a sufficient number of women applying. Mr Jacobs claims that the introduction of a gender requirement, namely that four non-justice seats in each college be reserved for women and four for men, makes it impossible to carry out the required comparison of the qualifications of candidates for the High Council of Justice, and that, since such a condition means that candidates with better qualifications may be rejected in favour of others whose only merit is that they meet the gender requirement, it constitutes a form of discrimination on grounds of sex, in violation of Articles 25(c) and 26 of the International Covenant on Civil and Political Rights. According to Article 25 ICCPR: 'Every citizen shall have the right and the opportunity, without any of the distinctions mentioned in article 2 and without unreasonable restrictions: ... (c) To have access, on general terms of equality, to public service in his country.' Article 26 contains a general requirement of non-discrimination. The claim based on these provisions is rejected by the Human Rights Committee.]

9.3 The Committee recalls that, under article 25(c) of the Covenant, every citizen shall have the right and opportunity, without any of the distinctions mentioned in article 2 and without unreasonable restrictions, to have access, on general terms of equality, to public service in his or her country. In order to ensure access on general terms of equality, the criteria and processes for appointment must be objective and reasonable. State parties may take measures in order to ensure that the law guarantees to women the rights contained in article 25 on equal terms with men. The Committee must therefore determine whether, in the case before it, the introduction of a gender requirement constitutes a violation of article 25 of the Covenant by virtue of its discriminatory nature, or of other provisions of the Covenant concerning discrimination, notably articles 2 and 3 of the Covenant, as invoked by the author, or whether such a requirement is objectively and reasonably justifiable. The question in this case is whether there is any valid justification for the distinction made between candidates on the grounds that they belong to a particular sex.

9.4 In the first place, the Committee notes that the gender requirement was introduced by Parliament under the terms of the Act of 20 July 1990 on the promotion of a balance between men and women on advisory bodies. The aim in this case is to increase the representation of and participation by women in the various advisory bodies in view of the very low numbers of women found there. On this point, the Committee finds the author's assertion that the insufficient number of female applicants in response to the first call proves there is no inequality between men and women to be unpersuasive in the present case; such a situation may, on the contrary, reveal a need to encourage women to apply for public service on bodies such as the High Council of Justice, and the need for taking measures in this regard. In the present case, it appears to the Committee that a body such as the High Council of Justice could legitimately be perceived as requiring the incorporation of perspectives beyond one of juridical expertise only. Indeed, given the responsibilities of the judiciary, the promotion of an awareness of gender-relevant issues relating to the application of law, could well be understood as requiring that perspective to be included in a body involved in judicial appointments. Accordingly, the Committee cannot conclude that the requirement is not objective and reasonably justifiable.

9.5 Secondly, the Committee notes that the gender clause requires there to be at least four applicants of each sex among the 11 non-justices appointed, which is to say just over one third of the candidates selected. In the Committee's view, such a requirement does not in this case amount to a disproportionate restriction of candidates' right of access, on general terms of equality, to public office. Furthermore, and contrary to the author's contention, the gender requirement does not make qualifications irrelevant, since it is specified that all non-justice applicants must have at least 10 years' experience. With regard to the author's argument that the gender requirement could give rise to discrimination between the three categories within the group of non-justices as a result, for example, of only men being appointed in one category, the Committee considers that in that event there would be three possibilities: either the female applicants were better qualified than the male, in which case they could justifiably be appointed; or the female and male applicants were equally well qualified, in which case the priority given to women would not be discriminatory in view of the aims of the law on the promotion of equality between men and women, as yet still lacking; or the female candidates were less well qualified than the male, in which case the Senate would be obliged to issue a second call for candidates in order to reconcile the two aims of the law, namely, qualifications and gender balance, neither of which may preclude the other. On that basis, there would appear to be no legal impediment to reopening applications. Lastly, the Committee finds that a reasonable proportionality is maintained between the purpose of the gender requirement, namely to promote equality between men and women in consultative bodies; the means applied and its modalities, as described above; and one of the principal aims of the law, which is to establish a High Council made up of qualified individuals. Consequently, the Committee finds that paragraph 3 of article 295*bis*-1 of the Act of 22 December 1998 meets the requirements of objective and reasonable justification.

Although this is not cited by the Human Rights Committee, it is probable that the conclusion which it arrives at in the case of *Jacobs* has been influenced by the position of the Committee on the Elimination of Discrimination against Women, which, in its 1997 General Recommendation No. 23, *Political and Public Life*, recommends to the States parties 'the adoption of a rule that neither sex should constitute less than 40 per cent of the members of a public body'. Any other conclusion by the Human Rights Committee in *Jacobs* would have potentially placed Belgium before two conflicting requirements, at least if we consider the general recommendations adopted by the CEDAW Committee as authoritative for the States parties to the Convention on the Elimination of All Forms of Discrimination against Women.

The position adopted by the Human Rights Committee in *Jacobs* v. *Belgium* is premised, arguably, on two considerations: (1) in employment matters, the principle of meritocracy (or 'qualifications') constitutes the baseline, and any departure from this principle requires a special justification; (2) positive action in favour of a disadvantaged group is only acceptable to the extent that it is strictly tailored to the need to combat existing inequalities, since it constitutes a derogation from the principle of formal equality, requiring that decisions are made only based on individual merit, rather than on characteristics such as the sex, race or ethnic origin, or age of the individual concerned. These are also the premises underlying the position of the European Court of Justice in the large number of judgments it has delivered on this issue. Box 7.4 provides a brief recapitulation of this case law.

A judgment delivered by the European Free Trade Association (EFTA) Court on this issue, on the basis of the same provisions of EU law as those referred to in box 7.4., offers an excellent summary of the ECJ's position on the issue. The EFTA Surveillance Authority considered that Norway was in violation of its obligations under the EEA

Box 7.4.	'Positive action' in the case law of the European Court of Justice on equal treatment between women and men

When it was initially adopted, Council Directive 76/207/EEC of 9 February 1976 on the implementation of the principle of equal treatment for men and women as regards access to employment, vocational training and promotion, and working conditions (O.J. 1976 L39/40), after defining the principle of equal treatment as the absence of any discrimination on grounds of sex, whether direct or indirect, provided in Article 2(4) that the Directive 'shall be without prejudice to measures to promote equal opportunity for men and women, in particular by removing existing inequalities which affect women's opportunities'. Moreover, on 13 December 1984, the Council adopted Recommendation 84/635/EEC on the promotion of positive action for women. Emphasizing that 'existing legal provisions on equal treatment, which are designed to afford rights to individuals, are inadequate for the elimination of all existing inequalities unless parallel action is taken by governments, both sides of industry and other bodies concerned, to counteract the prejudicial effects on women in employment which arise from social attitudes, behaviour and structures', this Recommendation encouraged the Member States to 'adopt a positive action policy designed to eliminate existing inequalities affecting women in working life and to promote a better balance between the sexes in employment' (O.J. 1984 L331/34).

Nevertheless, when it was confronted with affirmative action policies adopted by the Member States, the European Court of Justice considered that 'as a derogation from an individual right laid down in the Directive, Article 2(4) must be interpreted strictly' (Case C-450/93, *Kalanke* v. *Freie Hansestadt Bremen* [1995] E.C.R. I–3051). In *Kalanke*, its first judgment on this issue, delivered on 17 October 1995, the Court arrived at the conclusion that the provision of the 1990 Bremen Law on Equal Treatment for Men and Women in the Public Service which provided that women who have the same qualifications as men applying for the same post are to be given priority in sectors where they are under-represented, went beyond what was authorized by Article 2(4) of Directive 76/207/EEC. 'National rules which guarantee women absolute and unconditional priority for appointment or promotion', said the Court, 'go beyond promoting equal opportunities and overstep the limits of the exception in Article 2(4) of the Directive', and furthermore 'in so far as it seeks to achieve equal representation of men and women in all grades and levels within a department, … [the Bremen Law] substitutes for equality of opportunity as envisaged in Article 2(4) the result which is only to be arrived at by providing such equality of opportunity' (paras. 23–4).

The tension was manifest between, on the one hand, the limitations to positive action imposed by the Court's reading of Directive 76/207/EEC and, on the other hand, continued political support for positive action as a tool to encourage the professional integration of women. Following the judgment, the Governments of the Member States considered that there was a need to reaffirm the freedom of the national authorities to adopt positive action schemes, despite the limits imposed by the *Kalanke* case law. In 1997, the Treaty of Amsterdam amended Article 119 EEC (Art. 141 EC, now Art. 157 TFEU), introducing a new para. 4 providing that 'With a view to ensuring full equality in practice between men and women in working life, the principle of equal treatment shall not prevent any Member State from maintaining or adopting measures providing for specific advantages in order to make it easier for the underrepresented sex to pursue a vocational activity or to prevent or compensate for disadvantages in professional careers.' While the language used is symmetrical, applying identically to both women and men, Declaration No. 28 on Article 141(4) of the Treaty establishing the European Community, annexed to the Treaty of Amsterdam, states: 'When adopting measures referred to in Article 141(4) of the Treaty establishing the European Community, Member States should, in the first instance, aim at improving the situation of women in working life.'

This made little difference, however. Although the Court considered that the insertion of this provision in the Treaty of Rome might in principle lead to finding compatible with EU law a provision in the national law of a Member State which would conflict with Article 2(1) of Directive 76/207/EEC and would not be protected by Article 2(4) of that Directive (Case C-158/97, *Badeck and others* [2000] E.C.R. I-1875, para. 14), in practice, and despite the differences in wording between the two provisions until the original text of the Directive was modified in 2002, they have been interpreted similarly by the Court of Justice (see Case C-407/98, *Abrahamsson and Anderson* [2000] E.C.R. I-5539, paras. 54-5; Case C-319/03, *Briheche* [2004] E.C.R. I-8807, para. 31). Directive 76/207/EEC and the formulation in Article 141(4) EC (now 157 TFEU) have now been fully reconciled, as the Directive has been amended to refer to that provision of the Treaty. Indeed, after the 1976 Equal Treatment Directive was first amended in 2002 in order to make a direct reference to Article 141(4) of the Treaty, Directive 2006/54/EC of the European Parliament and of the Council of 5 July 2006 on the implementation of the principle of equal opportunities and equal treatment of men and women in matters of employment and occupation (recast) (O.J. 2006 L204/23) now states in Article 3 that 'Member States may maintain or adopt measures within the meaning of Article 141(4) of the Treaty with a view to ensuring full equality in practice between men and women'.

The strong signal sent by the Treaty of Amsterdam may have influenced the Court of Justice in the case of *Marschall*, which it delivered on 11 November 1997 (Case C-409/95, *Marschall v. Land Nordrhein-Westfalen* [1997] E.C.R. I-6363). In this second affirmative action case, the Court distinguished *Kalanke*, on the basis that the challenged provision contained a 'savings clause' (*Öffnungsklausel*), to the effect that women are not to be given priority in promotion if reasons specific to an individual male candidate tilt the balance in his favour (para. 24). Indeed, the 1981 Law on Civil Servants of the Land of Nordrhein-Westfalen, as last amended in 1995, provided that 'Where, in the sector of the authority responsible for promotion, there are fewer women than men in the particular higher grade post in the career bracket, women are to be given priority for promotion in the event of equal suitability, competence and professional performance, *unless reasons specific to an individual [male] candidate tilt the balance in his favour*' (emphasis added), a decisive element in the view of the Court, since the advantage conferred to women was neither 'automatic' nor 'unconditional', as it was (in its reading) in the previous *Kalanke* case. The judgment also illustrated the willingness of the Court to adopt a less formalistic stance towards the situation of women in the employment market and the virtues of equality of opportunities. It recognized that 'even where male and female candidates are equally qualified, male candidates tend to be promoted in preference to female candidates particularly because of prejudices and stereotypes concerning the role and capacities of women in working life and the fear, for example, that women will interrupt their careers more frequently, that owing to household and family duties they will be less flexible in their working hours, or that they will be absent from work more frequently because of pregnancy, childbirth and breastfeeding. For these reasons, the mere fact that a male candidate and a female candidate are equally qualified does not mean that they have the same chances' (para. 33).

The approach of the ECJ remains based on the idea that positive action in favour of women aimed at achieving equal 'opportunity' for men and women, cannot go beyond this objective and pursue equal 'results'. The latter objective would be contrary to the principle of equal treatment whereby each person has the right not to be disadvantaged on grounds of his/ her sex. According to the interpretation given by the Court, this limit is exceeded when affirmative action gives preference to women in the acquisition of a *result* (access to employment, obtaining a promotion) which has an *absolute* character, that is to say, which does not allow the rejected male candidate to bring forward the arguments that are likely to tilt the balance in his favour. Absolute preference in this sense would be considered discriminatory, since it establishes a non-rebuttable presumption in favour of women in cases where the candidates from both sexes are equally qualified, unless it is based on an 'actual fact' such as the proportion of men and women among the persons with such a qualification. On the other hand, the preferential treatment that is accorded to women in terms of access to certain *opportunities* (vocational training, calls to job interviews) will be considered with less severity: even when absolute, such preferential treatment is aimed at achieving equal opportunity for men and women, and on this account should be considered as covered by the exception provided for in Article 2(4) of Directive 76/207/EEC (now, Article 3 of the Gender (Recast) Directive 2006/54/EC).

The ECJ's suspicion of rules guaranteeing preferential treatment to women which are absolute and unconditional, i.e. which do not provide for the possibility to assess objectively all competing candidates in order to take into account their specific personal circumstances, leads it to insist that any affirmative action measure seeking to eliminate or reduce actual instances of inequality should be strictly proportionate to that end. Consistent with this view, the Court did not object to a national rule for the public service which, in trained occupations in which women are under-represented and for which the State does not have a monopoly of training, allocates at least half the training places to women, on the basis that 'the quota applies only to training places for which the State does not have a monopoly, and therefore concerns training for which places are also available in the private sector, [so that] no male candidate is definitively excluded from training' (Case C-158/97, *Badeck and others* [2000] E.C.R. I–1875, para.53). The requirement of proportionality imposed by the Court thus appears to be interpreted to ensure that the positive action measures developed by the Member States do not sacrifice individual justice (the right of each individual to be treated on the basis of his/her personal situation) in the name of group justice (the automatic and absolute preference given to the members of one group, e.g. women, simply because of that membership).

Agreement, Annex XVIII of which identifies the EU rules relating to equal treatment between men and women among the obligations of the Parties. Article 30(3) of the Norwegian Act No. 22 of 12 May 1995 relating to Universities and Colleges (the University Act) stipulated that 'If one sex is clearly under-represented in the category of post in the subject area in question, applications [for academic posts] from members of that sex shall be specifically invited. Importance shall be attached to considerations of equality when the appointment is made. The Board can decide that a post shall be advertised as only open to members of the underrepresented sex.' On the basis of this provision, a number of permanent and temporary academic positions were earmarked for women either by direction of the Norwegian Government or by the University of Oslo. The Norwegian Government in 1998 allocated forty so-called post-doctoral research grants, funded through the national budget, to universities and university colleges, twenty of which were assigned to the University of Oslo. Although such scholarships are designed to be a temporary position with a maximum duration of four years, they are intended to improve the recruitment base for high-level academic positions. Pursuant to Article 30(3) of the University Act, the University earmarked all of these positions for women. Moreover, of the 179 post-doctoral appointments at the University 1998–2001, 29 were earmarked for women. Of the 227 permanent academic appointments during that period, 4 were earmarked for women. And under the University's Plan for Equal Treatment 2000–4, another ten post-doctoral positions and twelve permanent academic positions were to be earmarked for women. According to the Plan, the University intended to allocate the permanent positions to the faculties by way of an evaluation of, *inter alia*, academic fields where women in permanent academic positions are considerably under-represented, giving priority to fields with less than 10 per cent female academics; and academic fields where women in permanent academic positions are under-represented as compared to the number of female students. Excerpts of the judgment delivered on 24 January 2003 follow:

European Free Trade Association (EFTA) Court, Case E–1/02, *EFTA Surveillance Authority* v. *Kingdom of Norway*, judgment of 24 January 2003:

[Pursuant to the positive action provision of the Norwegian Act No. 22 of 12 May 1995 relating to Universities and Colleges, a number of permanent and temporary academic positions are earmarked for women either by direction of the Norwegian Government or by the University of Oslo. The EFTA Surveillance Authority challenges the compatibility of this policy with the requirements of Council Directive 76/207/EEC, made applicable to Norway by point 18 of Annex XVIII to the EFTA Agreement. The Court holds that, by maintaining in force a rule which permits the reservation of a number of academic posts exclusively for members of the under-represented gender, Norway has failed to fulfil its obligations as defined by Articles 2(1), (4) and 3(1) of Directive 76/207/EEC of 9 February 1976 on the implementation of the principle of equal treatment for men and women as regards access to employment, vocational training and promotion, and working conditions as referred to in point 18 of Annex XVIII to the EEA Agreement:]

37 The Court of Justice of the European Communities has ... consistently held that Article 2(4) of the Directive permits measures that although discriminatory in appearance, are in fact intended to eliminate or reduce actual instances of inequality that may exist in the reality of social life. Measures relating to access to employment, including promotion, that give a specific advantage to women with a view to improving their ability to compete on the labour market and to pursue a career on an equal footing with men come within the scope of Article 2(4) of the Directive (Case 312/86 *Commission* v. *France* [1988] ECR 6315, at paragraph 15; C-450/93 *Kalanke* v. *Freie Hansestadt Bremen,* [1995] ECR I-3051, at paragraphs 18–19; C-409/95 *Marschall* v. *Land Nordrhein-Westfalen* [1997] ECR I-6363, at paragraphs 26–27; [Case C-158/97, *Badeck and others* [2000] E.C.R. I-1875] cited above, at paragraph 19 ...]. In *Kalanke* however, the Court of Justice of the European Communities found that Article 2(4), as a derogation from an individual right, had to be interpreted strictly and that the national rules at issue guaranteeing women in the case of equal qualifications absolute and unconditional priority for appointment or promotion in the public service were incompatible with the Directive. The Court, following the Opinion of Advocate General Tesauro, found that such measures went beyond promoting equal opportunities and substituted equality of representation for equality of opportunity (*Kalanke*, cited above, at paragraphs 21–23).

38 In *Marschall*, the Court of Justice of the European Communities considered the impact of prejudices and stereotypes concerning the role and capacities of women in working life and found that the mere fact that a male and a female candidate are equally qualified does not mean that they have the same chances (see *Marschall*, cited above, at paragraphs 29–30). Preferential treatment of female candidates in sectors where they are under-represented could therefore fall within the scope of Article 2(4) of the Directive if such preferential treatment was capable of counteracting the prejudicial effects on female candidates of societal attitudes and behaviour and reducing actual instances of inequality. However, such a measure may not guarantee absolute and unconditional priority for women in promotion, but should be subject to a savings clause (flexibility clause), guaranteeing an objective assessment of all candidates, taking into account their individual circumstances. Such an assessment, which should not be based on criteria that discriminate against women, could then override the priority accorded to women if the assessment tilted the balance in favour of the male candidate (*Marschall*, cited above, at paragraph 35; see also *Badeck*, cited above, at paragraph 23).

39 At issue in *Badeck* was national legislation where binding targets were set for the proportion of women in appointments and promotions. The Court of Justice of the European Communities found that such a rule that gave priority to equally qualified women in a sector where women are under-represented, if no reasons of greater legal weight were opposed, and subject to an objective assessment of all candidates, fell within the scope of Article 2(4) of the Directive. The Court of Justice of the European Communities further indicated that in assessing the qualifications of candidates, certain positive and negative criteria could be used, which, while formulated in gender neutral terms, were intended to reduce gender inequalities that occur in practice in social life. Among such criteria were capabilities and experiences acquired by carrying out family work. Negative criteria that should not detract from assessment of qualifications included parttime work, leaves and delays as a result of family work. Family status and partner's income should be viewed as immaterial and seniority, age and date of last promotion should not be given undue weight (*Badeck*, cited above, at paragraphs 31–32).

40 In *Badeck*, the Court of Justice of the European Communities held that a regime prescribing that posts in the academic service are to be filled with at least the same proportion of women as the proportion of women among the graduates and the holders of higher degrees in the discipline in question is compatible with the Directive. The Court of Justice of the European Communities thereby followed Advocate General Saggio's Opinion according to which such a system does not fix an absolute ceiling, but fixes one by reference to the number of persons who have received appropriate training, which amounts to using an actual fact as a quantitative criterion for giving preference to women (*Badeck*, cited above, at paragraphs 42–43; Opinion of Advocate General Saggio in *Badeck*, point 39).

41 In *Badeck*, the Court of Justice of the European Communities further accepted a rule according to which women are to be taken into account to the extent of at least one half in allocating training places in trained occupations in which women are under-represented. The Court of Justice of the European Communities found that the allocation of training places to women did not entail total inflexibility. The state did not have a monopoly on training places, as they were also available in the private sector. No male was therefore definitely excluded (*Badeck*, cited above, at paragraphs 51and 53).

42 In [Case C-407/98, *Abrahamsson* [2000] E.C.R. I-5539], the Court of Justice of the European Communities considered a Swedish statutory provision under which a candidate for a professorship who belongs to the under-represented gender and possesses sufficient qualifications for that post may be chosen in preference to a candidate of the opposite gender who would otherwise have been appointed, where this would be necessary to secure the appointment of a candidate of the under-represented gender, and the difference between the respective merits of the candidates would not be so great as to give rise to a breach of the requirement of objectivity in making appointments. It was found that this provision was incompatible with Article 2(1) and (4) of the Directive. The portent of the savings clause relating to the requirement of objectivity could not be precisely determined, implying that the selection would ultimately be based on the mere fact of belonging to the underrepresented gender.

43 As the case law outlined above shows, the Court of Justice of the European Communities has accepted as legitimate certain measures that promote substantive equality under Article 2(4) of the Directive. In determining the scope of a derogation from an individual right, such as the right to equal treatment of men and women laid down by the Directive, regard must, however, be had to the principle of proportionality, which requires that derogations remain within the limits of what is appropriate and necessary in order to achieve the aim in view and that the principle of equal treatment be reconciled as far as possible with the requirements of the aim pursued ...

44 The Court will now deal with the invocation of the case law of the Court of Justice of the European Communities as it applies to the arguments of the Defendant.

45 In the light of the homogeneity objective underlying the EEA Agreement, the Court cannot accept the invitation to redefine the concept of discrimination on grounds of gender in the way the Defendant has suggested. The Directive is based on the recognition of the right to equal treatment as a fundamental right of the individual. National rules and practices derogating from that right can only be permissible when they show sufficient flexibility to allow a balance between the need for the promotion of the under-represented gender and the opportunity for candidates of the opposite gender to have their situation objectively assessed. There must, as a matter of principle, be a possibility that the best-qualified candidate obtains the post. In this context the Court notes that it appears from the Defendant's answer to a written question from

the Court that it cannot be excluded that posts may be awarded to women applicants with inadequate qualifications, if there is not a sufficient number of qualified women candidates.

46 The Defendant's submission to the effect that Article 2(2) of the Directive applies in the present case, as gender constitutes a genuine occupational qualification to ensure the quality of the occupational activity and thus constitutes a determining factor for carrying out the activities in question, cannot be accepted. Such an interpretation does not find support in the wording of the Directive nor in the case law of the Court of Justice of the European Communities. The provision, which allows Member States to exclude from the field of the Directive certain occupational activities has primarily been applied in instances where public security calls for the reservation of certain policing or military activities for men only (see, for instance, Cases 222/84 *Johnston* v. *Chief Constable of the Royal Ulster Constabulary* [1986] ECR 1651; C-273/97 *Sirdar* [1999] ECR I-7403) ...

49 The Defendant has highlighted the training aspects of the contested post-doctoral positions. These positions, which are limited in time, are intended to offer holders of doctoral degrees the possibility to qualify for permanent academic posts and develop the necessary competence to compete for higher academic positions. The postdoctoral positions are further described as research posts, where teaching and administrative obligations are at a minimum. The Defendant has in this respect sought to rely on the principles developed by the Court of Justice of the European Communities in *Badeck*.

50 As the Commission of the European Communities has emphasized, the Court of Justice of the European Communities has drawn a distinction between training for employment and actual places in employment. With regard to training positions, it has relied on a restricted concept of equality of opportunity allowing the reservation of positions for women, with a view to obtaining qualifications necessary for subsequent access to trained occupations in the public service (*Badeck*, cited above, at paragraphs 52 and 55). The Court finds that even for training positions, the law requires a system that is not totally inflexible. Moreover, alternatives for postdoctoral positions in the private sector appear to be rather limited.

51 In the Court's view, the Norwegian rule goes further than the Swedish legislation in *Abrahamsson*, where a selection procedure, involving an assessment of all candidates was foreseen at least in principle. Since that Swedish rule was held by the Court of Justice of the European Communities to be in violation of the principle of equal treatment of women and men, the Norwegian rule must fall foul of that principle *a fortiori*.

52 It has been argued that the positions in question are new posts and that male applicants are not in a more difficult position with respect to career advancement than they would be without the earmarking scheme. The Court notes, however, that it is unlikely that newly created professorship posts would be allocated to specific disciplines, subjects or institutions without an evaluation of already existing posts, or without regard to future needs and expected consequential adjustments of teaching or research staff. It therefore appears that the earmarking scheme will have an impact on the number of future vacancies open to male applicants in any field in which it has been applied. The Defendant has not even alleged that in the case at hand the situation could be different.

53 The argument that the permanent professorships set up and earmarked for women are temporary in nature since they will lapse at the latest when such a professor retires cannot be accepted.

54 On the principles laid down in the foregoing, the Norwegian legislation in question must be regarded as going beyond the scope of Article 2(4) of the Directive, insofar as it permits earmarking of certain positions for persons of the under-represented gender. The last sentence of Article 30(3) of the University Act as applied by the University of Oslo gives absolute and unconditional priority to female candidates. There is no provision for flexibility, and the outcome is determined automatically in favour of a female candidate. The Defendant has argued that the criteria of unconditional and automatic priority do not exhaust the scope of the proportionality principle. The Court notes, in this respect, that other aspects of the Norwegian policy on gender equality in academia – including target measures for new professorship posts, priority in allocation of positions to fields with less than 10 percent female academics and in fields with high proportion of female students and graduates – have not been challenged by the EFTA Surveillance Authority, except with regard to the earmarking of positions exclusively for female candidates ...

56 The Court notes ... that since the entry into force of the Directive substantial changes have occurred in the legal framework of the Community, providing *inter alia* for increased Community competences in matters relating to gender equality. Under Article 2 EC the Community shall have as its task to promote equality between men and women. Article 3(2) EC states that the Community shall, in carrying out the activities referred to in the first paragraph of that provision, aim to eliminate inequalities and to promote equality between men and women. Article 13 EC gives the Council the competence to take appropriate action to combat discrimination based on sex. According to Article 141(4) EC, the principle of equal treatment shall, with a view to ensuring full equality in practice between men and women in working life, not prevent Member States from maintaining or adopting measures providing for specific advantages in order to make it easier for the under-represented sex to pursue a vocational activity or to prevent or compensate for disadvantages in professional careers. Inevitably, the interpretation of the Directive will reflect both the evolving legal and societal context in which it operates.

57 Under the present state of the law, the criteria for assessing the qualifications of candidates are essential. In such an assessment, there appears to be scope for considering those factors that, on empirical experience, tend to place female candidates in a disadvantaged position in comparison with male candidates. Directing awareness to such factors could reduce actual instances of gender inequality. Furthermore, giving weight to the possibility that in numerous academic disciplines female life experience may be relevant to the determination of the suitability and capability for, and performance in, higher academic positions, could enhance the equality of men and women, which concern lies at the core of the Directive.

58 The Defendant cannot justify the measures in question by reference to its obligations under international law. CEDAW, which has been invoked by the Defendant, was in force for Community Member States at the time when the Court of Justice of the European Communities rendered the relevant judgments concerning the Directive. Moreover, the provisions of international conventions dealing with affirmative action measures in various circumstances are clearly permissive rather than mandatory. Therefore they cannot be relied on for derogations from obligations under EEA law.

59 Based on the foregoing, the Court holds that by maintaining in force a rule which permits the reservation of a number of academic posts exclusively for members of the under-represented gender, Norway has failed to fulfil its obligations under ... Articles 2(1), 2(4)

and 3(1) of Directive 76/207/EEC of 9 February on the implementation of the principle of equal treatment for men and women as regards access to employment, vocational training and promotion, and working conditions as referred to in point 18 of Annex XVIII to the EEA Agreement.

7.10. Question for discussion: the relationship between positive action (temporary special measures) and the principle of equality

While certain jurisdictions, such as the ECJ in the field of gender equality law, conceptualize positive action as measures that derogate from the principle of (formal) equality and thus as exceptions to an individual right to equal treatment that must comply with strictly defined conditions, other bodies instead see positive action (or temporary special measures) as implementing the principle of equality, albeit in a substantive rather than in a formal sense. But how much does it really matter how we frame the issue? Are we not in both cases bound to seek a balance between the individual right of the person who is negatively impacted by a positive action scheme, and the broader social aim of substantive equality, which may correspond to the fulfilment of the rights of the members of the group benefiting from the scheme? In which respect precisely does the understanding of positive action as contributing to the promotion of substantive equality differ from an understanding which sees it as an exception to the principle of equal treatment?

4 SYSTEMATIZING ANTI-DISCRIMINATION LAW

In section 2 of this chapter, taking Article 26 ICCPR as a departure point, we have seen that the requirement of non-discrimination in fact imposes on States four separate obligations. They should (1) guarantee equality before the law, by ensuring that law enforcement authorities shall treat all people without discrimination; (2) guarantee the equal protection of the law, by removing any discriminatory provision from applicable laws and regulations; (3) prohibit any discrimination in private relationships; and (4) guarantee to all persons equal and effective protection against discrimination, if necessary, by the adoption of positive action measures in response to situations of structural discrimination. These four obligations may be combined with the different understandings of discrimination described in section 3, in order to describe the full content of the non-discrimination requirement.

This table also helps to understand the reasons why the collection of data relating to the situation of different categories of persons, for instance women or racial, ethnic or religious minorities, may constitute an essential tool in the adoption of effective anti-discrimination laws or policies. Such data primarily serve to build and improve

	Direct discrimination	Indirect discrimination resulting from the adoption of suspect measures	Indirect discrimination highlighted by statistics (disparate impact)	Discrimination as a failure to provide for reasonable accommodation	Structural discrimination
Equality before the law					
Equal protection of the law					
Prohibition of discrimination in private relationships					
Positive action in order to acheive substantive (real) equality					

anti-discrimination policies on the basis of an adequate mapping of the groups exposed to discrimination, the areas in which discrimination occurs as well as the nature and scale of discrimination. But the collection and processing of such data also have a potentially important role to play in the implementation of anti-discrimination law, particularly under the third and the fifth columns of the table presented above. Third, they may contribute to private or public organizations monitoring the impact of their practices, for instance their recruitment or promotion policies or their allocation of subsidies, on different categories: they may thus determine which remedial measures can be taken in order to correct manifest imbalances. Indeed, the collection of data relating to the membership of specific individuals in certain categories, such as racial, ethnic, or religious minorities, may be required for the implementation of equality schemes aimed at remedying imbalances. This may take the form of positive action measures implying preferential treatment of certain individuals: 'Whether or not they are linked to measures encouraging self-assessment of practices (in particular in the employment sector), positive action schemes granting preferential treatment to individuals in order to improve the representation of under-represented groups require the collection and processing of data, linking specific individuals to the relevant categories.' Fourth, 'statistical data may be crucial to enable victims to prove discrimination in legal proceedings, in legal systems which treat "disparate impact" as a form of prohibited discrimination' (J. Ringelheim and O. De Schutter, *Ethnic Monitoring. The Processing of Racial and Ethnic Data in Anti-discrimination Policies: Reconciling the Promotion of Equality with Privacy Rights* (Brussels: Bruylant, 2009).

The Durban Declaration and Plan of Action adopted by the World Conference against Racism, Racial Discrimination, Xenophobia and Related Intolerance (September 2001), urges States to collect, analyse and disseminate reliable statistical data to assess regularly the situation of individuals and groups victims of racial discrimination (Durban Declaration and Plan of Action, para. 92). Indeed, a number of human rights bodies have called upon States to collect data regularly in order to improve their anti-discrimination policies and to strengthen the effectiveness of their equality legislation. Referring to its previous general comments on specific rights of the International Covenant on Economic, Social and Cultural Rights, the Committee on Economic, Social and Cultural Rights notes for instance:

Committee on Economic, Social and Cultural Rights, General Comment No. 20, *Non-discrimination in Economic, Social and Cultural Rights* (Art. 2, para. 2 of the Covenant) (E/C.12/GC/20, 2 July 2009), para. 41:

States parties are obliged to monitor effectively the implementation of measures to comply with article 2, paragraph 2, of the Covenant. Monitoring should assess both the steps taken and the results achieved in the elimination of discrimination. National strategies, policies and plans should use appropriate indicators and benchmarks, disaggregated on the basis of the prohibited grounds of discrimination.

The same requirements are being imposed in regional settings. In its general policy Recommendation No. 1 on combating racism, xenophobia, anti-Semitism and intolerance, the European Commission against Racism and Intolerance (ECRI), an expert body of the Council of Europe, recommends that governments 'collect, in accordance with European laws, regulations and recommendations on data-protection and protection of privacy, where and when appropriate, data which will assist in assessing and evaluating the situation and experiences of groups which are particularly vulnerable to racism, xenophobia, anti-Semitism and intolerance' (4 October 1996, CRI (96) 43 rev.). The Advisory Committee on the Council of Europe Framework Convention on the Protection of National Minorities expects States to provide 'factual information ... such as statistics and the result of surveys' in their reports, adding that 'where complete statistics are not available, governments may supply data or estimates based on *ad hoc* studies, specialized or sample surveys, or other scientifically valid methods, whenever they consider the information so collected to be useful' (Outline for reports to be submitted pursuant to Art. 25 para. 1 of the Framework Convention for the Protection of National Minorities, adopted by the Committee of Ministers on 30 September 1998 at the 642nd meeting of the Ministers' Deputies; see also, *inter alia*, the second Opinion of the Advisory Committee on Denmark, 9 December 2004, ACFC/INF/OP/II(2004)005, para. 60 and its first Opinion on Spain, 27 November 2003, ACFC/INF/OP/I(2004)004).

However, this may be in conflict with the requirements of the right to respect for private life, both because of the restrictions imposed on the processing of sensitive personal data (such as data relating to the race or ethnicity, or to religion), and because of the requirement of 'self-identification', according to which – as stated by the UN Committee on the Elimination of Racial Discrimination – the identification of individuals as being members of a particular racial or ethnic group 'shall, if no justification exists to the contrary, be based upon self-identification by the individual concerned' (General Recommendation VIII, thirty-eighth session, 1990 (A/45/18 at 79 (1991)); see also, for instance, Committee on Economic, Social and Cultural Rights, General Comment No. 20, *Non-discrimination in Economic, Social and Cultural Rights*, para. 16).

This latter rule is emerging as a general requirement. It can be derived from the Council of Europe Framework Convention on the Protection of National Minorities (1995), which lays down that every individual shall have the right freely to choose to be treated or not to be treated as belonging to a national minority and that no disadvantage shall result from this choice (Art. 3(1)). Accordingly, States cannot in principle treat individuals against their will as members of a national minority group (H.-J. Heinze, 'Article 3' in M. Weller (ed.), *The Rights of Minorities in Europe – a Commentary on the European Framework Convention for the Protection of National Minorities* (Oxford University Press, 2005), pp. 107–37 at p. 119). In the view of the Advisory Committee for the Framework Convention, the right not to be treated as a person belonging to a national minority extends to census situations and entails that questions on one's ethnicity cannot be made mandatory (see, e.g. Opinion of the Advisory Committee of the Framework Convention on Estonia, 14 September 2001, ACFC/INF/OP/I(2002)005, para. 19 and Opinion on Poland, 27 November 2003, ACFC/INF/OP/I(2004)005, para. 24). The European Commission against Racism and Intolerance (ECRI) has consistently recommended, in its General Policy Recommendations and country reports, that ethnic data be collected in accordance with three principles: confidentiality, informed consent and voluntary self-identification (ECRI, Seminar with national specialized bodies to combat racism and racial discrimination on the issue of ethnic data collection (Strasbourg, 17–18 February 2005), Report, CRI(2005)14 at 4). Likewise, the 2001 Durban Declaration and Plan of Action states that information documenting racism, racial discrimination, xenophobia and related intolerance shall be collected with the explicit consent of the victims and be based on their self-identification: such information, it stated, shall be collected 'with the explicit consent of the victims, based on their self-identification and in accordance with provisions on human rights and fundamental freedoms, such as data protection regulations and privacy guarantees' (Durban Declaration and Plan of Action, para. 92(a)).

However, reliance on self-identification creates a risk of manipulation, which in practice may make this inapplicable and put in jeopardy the very possibility of strategies aiming at correcting imbalances between groups. Positive action schemes in particular are adopted in order to substitute a notion of group justice to a notion of individual justice. The efficacy of such schemes can hardly be reconciled with the possibility, for each individual potentially concerned, not to be classified for instance according to race or ethnicity, or to religion – whether that individual belongs to the traditionally disadvantaged group which the scheme intends to benefit, or whether he/ she belongs to the traditionally advantaged group, whose members will bear the cost of the positive action scheme. In box 7.5., the dilemma this creates for policy-makers is illustrated in the context of the Northern Ireland employment equality legislation.

Box 7.5.

Determining community affiliation in Northern Ireland

A controversy followed a proposal to include, in the Bill of Rights for Northern Ireland then under discussion, a provision identical to Article 3(1) of the Council of Europe Framework Convention for the Protection of National Minorities. That provision states that every person shall have the right freely to choose to be treated or not to be treated as belonging to a national minority and that no disadvantage shall result from this choice. The effect of the insertion of such a clause in the Northern Ireland Bill of Rights would have been to render inapplicable the implementation in Northern Ireland of the Fair Employment and Treatment (Northern Ireland) Order 1998 (FETO), legislation adopted as part of the Belfast (or 'Good Friday') Agreement of the same year that sought to put an end to the strife between the Protestant and Roman Catholic communities in Northern Ireland. The FETO aimed at improving the representation of the under-represented group in employment, by obliging employers to send 'monitoring returns' to the Equality Commission, breaking down the workforce according to the community affiliation of its members. While, in principle, the community affiliation is to be determined by each individual in answer to a direct question of the employer, a 'residuary method' applies where the answer is not determinative: the employer may then use any information transmitted to him by the employee (such as the surname and other names; address; educational background or training; leisure activities; the clubs, societies or other organizations to which he/she belongs; or the occupation as a clergyman or minister of a particular religious denomination or as a teacher in a particular school, of any referee nominated by the employee when he/she applied for the job), in order to determine whether the employee should be treated as a member of the Protestant or the Roman Catholic community. That determination is notified to the employee, however, who has seven days to object to the information received; if he/she does object, the monitoring return sent to the Equality Commission should reflect that response.

This arrangement was largely supported as one of the key elements resulting from the 1998 Belfast Agreement. It worked satisfactorily in practice. Whether it could be considered compatible with the requirement of Article 3(1) of the Council of Europe Framework Convention for the Protection of National Minorities, however, was intensely debated when the Northern Ireland Human Rights Commission proposed to include in the draft Bill of Rights for Northern Ireland a provision incorporating the substance of Article 3(1) of the Framework Convention. The Council of Europe was asked to provide an opinion on the issue. An ad hoc group of experts was set up for that purpose. It delivered an opinion where they stated that 'the inclusion of such a clause could open the way for challenges to be made to current equality provisions that would undermine recent gains in equality over past years'. They continued:

Aalt W. Heringa, Giorgio Malinverni, Josef Marko, 'Comments by the Council of Europe experts on certain aspects of a future Bill of Rights for Northern Ireland', Council of Europe, DG II (2004) 4 (3 February 2004):

64. Notwithstanding that the experts see that there may be an issue concerning the compatibility of certain equality provisions with the right to self-identification, they consider that this is not a matter that should be definitively solved in a bill of rights, but rather be addressed in ordinary legislation.

65. ...[A] bill of rights should be the product of a broad societal consensus. From the discussions held in Belfast it is clear that there is no such broad societal consensus concerning the inclusion of this provision. Furthermore, it can be said that it is rare for a bill of rights or for a constitution to treat such matters ...

66. The experts consider that it is important to note that the issue does not disappear if it is not specifically included in the Bill of Rights. The right remains to be implemented in the context of the application of Article 3 of the Framework Convention for the Protection of National Minorities. Furthermore, it can be argued that aspects of the right to self-identification may also be linked to Article 8 (right to privacy) of the ECHR for which redress procedures are already available under the Human Rights Act and under the ECHR itself ...

67. The experts note that if a review of the legislation is to take place, it will require an examination of the application of positive measures to ensure equality as this is a central element of the issue in question. It can be noted that there could well be a clash of rights, for example between the right of self-identification on the one hand and the need to ensure equality on the other.

68. The experts consider that this issue could be better and more fully discussed or advanced, *inter alia*, in the context of discussions concerning the reform of the equality legislation and proposals to have a single equality act. There may also be other forums in which this matter can be raised, including the Advisory Committee on the Framework Convention during the second monitoring cycle under the Framework Convention for the Protection of National Minorities.

69. The experts are therefore of the view that the issue of self-identification should not be examined in the context of the Bill of Rights project, but rather outside of the project in a more appropriate forum.

The recognition that the principle of self-identification to a national minority might jeopardize the implementation of equality schemes aimed at achieving social cohesion is an important one. It should also be read in the light of the comment contained in the Explanatory Protocol to the Council of Europe Framework Convention on the Protection of National Minorities, which states that Article 3(1) of this instrument 'does not imply a right for an individual to choose arbitrarily to belong to any national minority. The individual's subjective choice is inseparably linked to objective criteria relevant to the person's identity.' Precisely because reliance on the 'subjective' criterion of self-identification could make the implementation of equality legislation difficult if not impossible, the position of the Council of Europe experts seems to be that certain restrictions to the right to self-identification should be allowable. In the second Opinion it adopted on the United Kingdom, the Advisory Committee on the Framework Convention for the Protection of National Minorities seemed to endorse this view. It stated:

Council of Europe Advisory Committee on the Framework Convention for the Protection of National Minorities, second Opinion on the United Kingdom (ACFC/ OP/II(2007)003) (adopted on 6 June 2007 and made public, alongside the response by the UK Government, on 26 October 2007), at paras. 47–8:

The Advisory Committee takes note of the duties placed on employers by Northern Ireland's fair employment legislation as regards work force monitoring (see also comments under Article 4 below). Under this legislation, employers are required to submit annually a monitoring return giving details of the 'community background' of their employees, trainees and applicants, meaning their affiliation to the Protestant or Roman Catholic community in Northern Ireland. Whereas the principal method for collecting this data relies on the free self-identification of each employee, trainee or applicant, where the latter do not respond to a direct question on their 'community background', employers are encouraged to make such a determination themselves based on written information supplied by the person concerned. Persons belonging to minority ethnic groups are also subject to these monitoring requirements and have the option of indicating that they are not a member of either community.

The Advisory Committee notes that the data collected under the fair employment legislation remain anonymous and may be used purely for statistical purposes, in order to determine whether members of each community are enjoying fair participation in employment and, if not, to identify additional measures that could be adopted to secure fair participation. The Advisory Committee reminds the Government that restrictions on the right to free self-identification by persons belonging to national minorities are not consistent with Article 3 of the Framework Convention. However, the Advisory Committee considers that, in the specific context of Northern Ireland, and at this particular moment in time, the determination by employers of the community background of their employees, trainees and applicants may be relevant in order to secure the fair participation of under-represented groups.

The Advisory Committee did recommend that the Government regularly review the authorization given to employers in Northern Ireland to make a determination of the 'community background' of employees, trainees and applicants, when the latter do not provide this information, in order to ensure its continuing relevance to the objective of securing equality in the field of employment.

5 SELF-DETERMINATION AND MINORITY RIGHTS

This section explores the relationship between the prohibition of discrimination and rights which, while distinct, are sufficiently inter-related with this prohibition to justify their exposition here. These are the right to self-determination of peoples and the rights of minorities. Although the right to self-determination is mentioned in the Charter of the United Nations, both that right and minority rights were ignored in the drafting of the Universal Declaration of Human Rights: while attempts were made to include a reference to the right to self-determination, these efforts foundered both on the United States' and France's views about assimilation – both being hostile to the recognition of separate group rights – and on the idea that the Declaration should include only rights of the individual, and not group rights such as rights of minorities or of peoples (see M. A. Glendon, *A World Made New. Eleanor Roosevelt and the Universal Declaration of Human Rights* (New York: Random House, 2001), pp. 119–20).

5.1 The right to self-determination

(a) General principles

The era of decolonization in the 1960s and the insistence of newly independent, developing countries, particularly in the 1970s, on reclaiming not only their political, but also their economic sovereignty, led to the right to self-determination being revived in the instruments adopted during that period (see, among the most important contributions on this right, A. Cassese, *Self-determination of Peoples: a Legal Reappraisal* (Cambridge University Press, 1995); A. Cassese, 'The Self-determination of Peoples' in L. Henkin (ed.), *The International Bill of Rights. The Covenant on Civil and Political Rights* (New York: Columbia University Press, 1981), p. 92; B. Kingsbury, 'Claims by Non-State Groups in International Law', *Cornell International Law Journal*, 25 (1992), 481; R. McCorquodale, 'Self-determination: a Human Rights Approach', *International and Comparative Law Quarterly*, 43 (1994), 857; C. Tomuschat (ed.), *Modern Law of Self-determination* (Dordrecht: Martinus Nijhoff, 1993)).

International Covenant on Civil and Political Rights and International Covenant on Economic, Social and Cultural Rights, Article 1:

1. All peoples have the right of self-determination. By virtue of that right they freely determine their political status and freely pursue their economic, social and cultural development.

2. All peoples may, for their own ends, freely dispose of their natural wealth and resources without prejudice to any obligations arising out of international economic co-operation, based upon the principle of mutual benefit, and international law. In no case may a people be deprived of its own means of subsistence.

3. The States Parties to the present Covenant, including those having responsibility for the administration of Non-Self-Governing and Trust Territories, shall promote the realization of the right of self-determination, and shall respect that right, in conformity with the provisions of the Charter of the United Nations.

Declaration on Principles of International Law concerning Friendly Relations and Co-operation among States in accordance with the Charter of the United Nations, GA Res. 2625, Annex, 25 UN GAOR, Supp. (No. 28), UN Doc. A/5217 at 121 (1970):

[This Declaration lists in its annex a number of principles, the codification and development of which, according to the Declaration, should contribute to promote the realization of the purposes of the United Nations. The listed principles are: (a) the principle that States shall refrain in their international relations from the threat or use of force against the territorial integrity or political independence of any State, or in any other manner inconsistent with the purposes of the United Nations; (b) the principle that States shall settle their international disputes by peaceful means in such a manner that international peace and security and justice are not endangered; (c) the duty not to intervene in matters within the domestic jurisdiction of any State, in accordance with the Charter; (d) the duty of States to co-operate with one another in accordance with the Charter; (e) the principle of equal rights and self-determination of peoples; (f) the principle of sovereign equality of States; (g) the principle that States shall fulfil in good faith the obligations assumed by them in accordance with the Charter. The principle of self-determination is explained as follows:]

By virtue of the principle of equal rights and self-determination of peoples enshrined in the Charter of the United Nations, all peoples have the right freely to determine, without external interference, their political status and to pursue their economic, social and cultural development, and every State has the duty to respect this right in accordance with the provisions of the Charter.

Every State has the duty to promote, through joint and separate action, realization of the principle of equal rights and self-determination of peoples, in accordance with the provisions of the Charter, and to render assistance to the United Nations in carrying out the responsibilities entrusted to it by the Charter regarding the implementation of the principle, in order:

(a) To promote friendly relations and co-operation among States; and
(b) To bring a speedy end to colonialism, having due regard to the freely expressed will of the peoples concerned;

and bearing in mind that subjection of peoples to alien subjugation, domination and exploitation constitutes a violation of the principle, as well as a denial of fundamental human rights, and is contrary to the Charter.

Every State has the duty to promote through joint and separate action universal respect for and observance of human rights and fundamental freedoms in accordance with the Charter.

The establishment of a sovereign and independent State, the free association or integration with an independent State or the emergence into any other political status freely determined by a people constitute modes of implementing the right of self-determination by that people.

Every State has the duty to refrain from any forcible action which deprives peoples referred to above in the elaboration of the present principle of their right to self-determination and freedom and independence. In their actions against, and resistance to, such forcible action in pursuit of the exercise of their right to self-determination, such peoples are entitled to seek and to receive support in accordance with the purposes and principles of the Charter.

The territory of a colony or other Non-Self-Governing Territory has, under the Charter, a status separate and distinct from the territory of the State administering it; and such separate and distinct status under the Charter shall exist until the people of the colony or Non-Self-Governing Territory have exercised their right of self-determination in accordance with the Charter, and particularly its purposes and principles.

Nothing in the foregoing paragraphs shall be construed as authorizing or encouraging any action which would dismember or impair, totally or in part, the territorial integrity or political unity of sovereign and independent States conducting themselves in compliance with the principle of equal rights and self-determination of peoples as described above and thus possessed of a government representing the whole people belonging to the territory without distinction as to race, creed or colour.

Every State shall refrain from any action aimed at the partial or total disruption of the national unity and territorial integrity of any other State or country.

Human Rights Committee, General Comment No. 12, *The Right to Self-determination of Peoples* (Art. 1) (13 March 1984):

4. With regard to paragraph 1 of article 1 [of the ICCPR, quoted above in this section], States parties should describe [in their reports to the Human Rights Committee] the constitutional and political processes which in practice allow the exercise of this right.

5. Paragraph 2 affirms a particular aspect of the economic content of the right of self-determination, namely the right of peoples, for their own ends, freely to 'dispose of their natural wealth and resources without prejudice to any obligations arising out of international economic cooperation, based upon the principle of mutual benefit, and international law. In no case may a people be deprived of its own means of subsistence.' This right entails corresponding duties for all States and the international community. States should indicate any factors or difficulties which prevent the free disposal of their natural wealth and resources contrary to the provisions of this paragraph and to what extent that affects the enjoyment of other rights set forth in the Covenant.

6. Paragraph 3, in the Committee's opinion, is particularly important in that it imposes specific obligations on States parties, not only in relation to their own peoples but *vis-à-vis* all peoples which have not been able to exercise or have been deprived of the possibility of exercising their right to self-determination ... The obligations exist irrespective of whether a people entitled to self-determination depends on a State party to the Covenant or not. It follows that all States parties to the Covenant should take positive action to facilitate realization of and respect for the right of peoples to self-determination. Such positive action must be consistent with the States' obligations under the Charter of the United Nations and under international law: in particular, States must refrain from interfering in the internal affairs of other States and thereby adversely affecting the exercise of the right to self-determination. The reports should contain information on the performance of these obligations and the measures taken to that end.

7. In connection with article 1 of the Covenant, the Committee refers to other international instruments concerning the right of all peoples to self-determination, in particular the

Declaration on Principles of International Law concerning Friendly Relations and Co-operation among States in accordance with the Charter of the United Nations, adopted by the General Assembly on 24 October 1970 (General Assembly resolution 2625 (XXV)).

8. The Committee considers that history has proved that the realization of and respect for the right of self-determination of peoples contributes to the establishment of friendly relations and cooperation between States and to strengthening international peace and understanding.

Vienna Declaration and Programme of Action, as adopted by the World Conference on Human Rights on 25 June 1993 (A/CONF.157/23, 12 July 1993):

2. All peoples have the right of self-determination. By virtue of that right they freely determine their political status, and freely pursue their economic, social and cultural development.

Taking into account the particular situation of peoples under colonial or other forms of alien domination or foreign occupation, the World Conference on Human Rights recognizes the right of peoples to take any legitimate action, in accordance with the Charter of the United Nations, to realize their inalienable right of self-determination. The World Conference on Human Rights considers the denial of the right of self-determination as a violation of human rights and underlines the importance of the effective realization of this right.

In accordance with the Declaration on Principles of International Law concerning Friendly Relations and Cooperation Among States in accordance with the Charter of the United Nations, this shall not be construed as authorizing or encouraging any action which would dismember or impair, totally or in part, the territorial integrity or political unity of sovereign and independent States conducting themselves in compliance with the principle of equal rights and self-determination of peoples and thus possessed of a Government representing the whole people belonging to the territory without distinction of any kind.

International Court of Justice, Advisory Opinion of 9 July 2004, *Legal Consequences of the Construction of a Wall in the Occupied Palestinian Territory*, paras. 88, 119–22, and 159:

88. The Court would recall that in 1971 it emphasized that current developments in 'international law in regard to non-self-governing territories, as enshrined in the Charter of the United Nations, made the principle of self-determination applicable to all [such territories]'. The Court went on to state that 'These developments leave little doubt that the ultimate objective of the sacred trust' referred to in Article 22, paragraph 1, of the Covenant of the League of Nations 'was the self-determination ... of the peoples concerned' *(Legal Consequences for States of the Continued Presence of South Africa in Namibia (South West Africa) notwithstanding Security Council Resolution 276 (1970), Advisory Opinion, I.C.J. Reports 1971*, p. 31, paras. 52–53). The Court has referred to this principle on a number of occasions in its jurisprudence *(ibid.*; see also *Western Sahara, Advisory Opinion, I.C.J. Reports 1975*, p. 68, para. 162). The Court indeed made it

clear that the right of peoples to self-determination is today a right *erga omnes* (see *East Timor (Portugal* v. *Australia), judgment, I.C.J. Reports 1995,* p. 102, para. 29) ...

119. The Court notes that the route of the wall as fixed by the Israeli Government includes within the 'Closed Area' ... some 80 per cent of the settlers living in the Occupied Palestinian Territory. Moreover, it is apparent ... that the wall's sinuous route has been traced in such a way as to include within that area the great majority of the Israeli settlements in the occupied Palestinian Territory (including East Jerusalem).

120. As regards these settlements, the Court notes that Article 49, paragraph 6, of the Fourth Geneva Convention provides: 'The Occupying Power shall not deport or transfer parts of its own civilian population into the territory it occupies.' That provision prohibits not only deportations or forced transfers of population such as those carried out during the Second World War, but also any measures taken by an occupying Power in order to organize or encourage transfers of parts of its own population into the occupied territory.

In this respect, the information provided to the Court shows that, since 1977, Israel has conducted a policy and developed practices involving the establishment of Settlements in the Occupied Palestinian Territory, contrary to the terms of Article 49, paragraph 6, just cited. The Security Council has thus taken the view that such policy and practices 'have no legal validity'. It has also called upon 'Israel, as the occupying Power, to abide scrupulously' by the Fourth Geneva Convention and: 'to rescind its previous measures and to desist from taking any action which would result in changing the legal status and geographical nature and materially affecting the demographic composition of the Arab territories occupied since 1967, including Jerusalem, and, in particular, not to transfer parts of its own civilian population into the occupied Arab territories' (resolution 446 (1979) of 22 March 1979).

The Council reaffirmed its position in resolutions 452 (1979) of 20 July 1979 and 465 (1980) of 1 March 1980. Indeed, in the latter case it described 'Israel's policy and practices of settling parts of its population and new immigrants in [the occupied] territories' as a 'flagrant violation' of the Fourth Geneva Convention.

The Court concludes that the Israeli settlements in the Occupied Palestinian Territories (including East Jerusalem) have been established in breach of international law.

121. Whilst the Court notes the assurance given by Israel that the construction of the wall does not amount to annexation and that the wall is of a temporary nature ..., it nevertheless cannot remain indifferent to certain fears expressed to it that the route of the wall will prejudge the future frontier between Israel and Palestine, and the fear that Israel may integrate the settlements and their means of access. The Court considers that the construction of the wall and its associated régime create a 'fait accompli' on the ground that could well become permanent, in which case, and notwithstanding the formal characterization of the wall by Israel, it would be tantamount to *de facto* annexation.

122. The Court recalls moreover that, according to the report of the Secretary-General, the planned route would incorporate in the area between the Green line and the wall more than 16 per cent of the territory of the West Bank. Around 80 per cent of the settlers living in the Occupied Palestinian Territory, that is 320,000 individuals, would reside in that area, as well as 237,000 Palestinians. Moreover, as a result of the construction of the wall, around 160,000 other Palestinians would reside in almost completely encircled communities ...

In other terms, the route chosen for the wall gives expression in *loco* to the illegal measures taken by Israel with regard to Jerusalem and the settlements, as deplored by the

Security Council ... There is also a risk of further alterations to the demographic composition of the Occupied Palestinian Territory resulting from the construction of the wall inasmuch as it is contributing ... to the departure of Palestinian populations from certain areas. That construction, along with measures taken previously, thus severely impedes the exercise by the Palestinian people of its right to self-determination, and is therefore a breach of Israel's obligation to respect that right ...

159. Given the character and the importance of the rights and obligations involved, the Court is of the view that all States are under an obligation not to recognize the illegal situation resulting from the construction of the wall in the Occupied Palestinian Territory, including in and around East Jerusalem. They are also under an obligation not to render aid or assistance in maintaining the situation created by such construction. It is also for all States, while respecting the United Nations Charter and international law, to see to it that any impediment, resulting from the construction of the wall, to the exercise by the Palestinian people of its right to self-determination is brought to an end.

[Although the conclusion that Israel has acted in violation of international law by erecting the wall was reached by fourteen votes to one – with only Judge Buergenthal dissociating himself from the majority – six members of the Court attached separate concurring opinions to the Court's position. In his separate concurring opinion, Judge Koroma stressed that in its Opinion, the Court 'held that the right of self-determination as an established and recognized right under international law applies to the territory and to the Palestinian people. Accordingly, the exercise of such right entitles the Palestinian people to a State of their own as originally envisaged in resolution 181 (II) and subsequently confirmed. The Court has found that the construction of the wall in the Palestinian territory will prevent the realization of such a right and is therefore a violation of it.' By contrast, Judge Kooijmans expressed the view that the violation of the right to self-determination of the Palestinian should be examined in a wider context than that of the Opinion, and that the construction of the Wall, *per se*, should not be seen to constitute the sole or determining factor. Judge Rosalyn Higgins expressed her 'puzzlement' at the application by the Court of the principle of self-determination. While she stated her support for the 'post-colonial view of self-determination' which the Court espouses, she did not consider that the construction of the Wall, as such, violates the right of the Palestinian people to self-determination, when that right is continuously violated by Israeli occupation and the absence of a peace settlement:]

Separate concurring opinion of Judge Higgins:
30. ... Self-determination is the right of 'All peoples ... freely [to] determine their political status and freely pursue their economic, social and cultural development' (Art. 1(1), International Covenant on Civil and Political Rights and also International Covenant on Economic, Social and Cultural Rights). As this Opinion observes (para. 118), it is now accepted that the Palestinian people are a 'peoples' for purposes of self-determination. But it seems to me quite detached from reality for the Court to find that it is the wall that presents a 'serious impediment' to the exercise of this right. The real impediment is the apparent inability and/or unwillingness of both Israel and Palestine to move in parallel to secure the necessary conditions – that is, at one and the same time, for Israel to withdraw from Arab occupied territory and for Palestine to provide the conditions to allow Israel to feel secure in so doing. The simple point is underscored by the fact that if the wall had never been built, the Palestinians would still not yet have exercised their right

to self-determination. It seems to me both unrealistic and unbalanced for the Court to find that the wall (rather than 'the larger problem', which is beyond the question put to the Court for an opinion) is a serious obstacle to self-determination.

31. Nor is this finding any more persuasive when looked at from a territorial perspective. As the Court states in paragraph 121, the wall does not at the present time constitute, *per se*, a *de facto* annexation. 'Peoples' necessarily exercise their right to self-determination within their own territory. Whatever may be the detail of any finally negotiated boundary, there can be no doubt ..., that Israel is in occupation of Palestinian territory. That territory is no more, or less, under occupation because a wall has been built that runs through it. And to bring to an end that circumstance, it is necessary that both sides, simultaneously, accept their responsibilities under international law.

(b) The internal and external dimensions of self-determination

The right to self-determination has both an external and an internal dimension: it implies both that peoples under colonial or other forms of alien domination or foreign occupation have a right to resist against such domination or occupation, and to be supported by the international community in this regard, although within the limits imposed by international law; and that the population has a right to a government representative of all the groups within the population. This second dimension is illustrated by the interpretation of Article 20 of the African Charter on Human and Peoples' Rights in the *Gambian coup* case, where the African Commission held that the coup of 11 November 1994, that brought into power a military government, deprived the 'Gambian people' of their right to 'freely determine their political status', as required by Article 20(1) (Joined Communications 147/95 and 149/96, *Jawara* v. *The Gambia*, (2000) A.H.R.L.R. 107 (ACHPR 2000) (Thirteenth Annual Activity Report), para. 73). There is a link between the two dimensions: although, in principle, the right to self-determination only may be interpreted as a right to seek independence in cases of colonial or foreign occupation, and should not otherwise justify questioning the territorial integrity of the State, a different interpretation may prevail if and when a group of the population, located within one portion of the territory, is denied the right to take part on the basis of the principle of non-discrimination in the political life of the country (see, on this issue, J. Brossard, 'Le droit du peuple québécois de disposer de lui-même au regard du droit international', *Canadian Yearbook of International Law*, 15 (1977), 84; J. Crawford, 'State Practice and International Law in Relation to Secession', *British Yearbook of International Law*, 69 (1998), 85 (which is the slightly amended version of a brief prepared for *amici curiae* intervening in the *Secession of Quebec* case examined below); J. Crawford, 'The Right to Self-determination in International Law: its Development and Future' in P. Alston (ed.), *Peoples' Rights* (Oxford University Press, 2001), p. 7; D. Murswief, 'The Issue of a Right to Secession Reconsidered' in C. Tomuschat (ed.), *Modern Law of Self-determination* (Dordrecht: Martinus Nijhoff, 1993), p. 21)). Consider, arguably opening the door to this interpretation, the position of the African Commission on Human and Peoples' Rights in the *Katangese Secession* case:

African Commission on Human and Peoples' Rights, Communication 75/92, *Katangese Peoples' Congress* v. *Zaire* (2000) A.H.R.L.R. 72 (ACHPR 1995) (Eighth Annual Activity Report):

1. The communication was submitted in 1992 by Mr Gerard Moke, President of the Katangese Peoples' Congress requesting the African Commission on Human and Peoples' Rights to: recognise the Katangese Peoples' Congress as a liberation movement entitled to support in the achievement of independence for Katanga; – recognise the independence of Katanga; – help secure the evacuation of Zaire from Katanga.

The Law

2. The claim is brought under Article 20(1) of the African Charter on Human Rights. There are no allegations of specific breaches of other human rights apart from the claim of the denial of self-determination.

3. All peoples have a right to self-determination. There may however be controversy as to the definition of peoples and the content of the right. The issue in the case is not self-determination for all Zaireoise as a people but specifically for the Katangese. Whether the Katangese consist of one or more ethnic groups is, for this purpose immaterial and no evidence has been adduced to that effect.

4. The Commission believes that self-determination may be exercised in any of the following ways: independence, self-government, local government, federalism, confederalism, unitarism or any other form of relations that accords with the wishes of the people but fully cognisant of other recognised principles such as sovereignty and territorial integrity.

5. The Commission is obligated to uphold the sovereignty and territorial integrity of Zaire, member of the OAU and a party to the African Charter on Human and Peoples' Rights

6. In the absence of concrete evidence of violations of human rights to the point that the territorial integrity of Zaire should be called to question and in the absence of evidence that the people of Katanga are denied the right to participate in Government as guaranteed by Article 13(1) of the African Charter, the Commission holds the view that Katanga is obliged to exercise a variant of self-determination that is compatible with the sovereignty and territorial integrity of Zaire.

For the above reasons, the Commission

Declares that the case holds no evidence of violations of any rights under the African Charter. There quest for independence for Katanga therefore has no merit under the African Charter on Human and Peoples' Rights.

The position adopted by the Supreme Court of Canada a few years later seems to apply the same principle, refusing to identify a 'right to secede' in the internal dimension of the right to self-determination, although not excluding that, in certain cases of manifest oppression of a 'people' within a State, such a right might exist:

Supreme Court of Canada, *Reference re Secession of Quebec* [1998] 2 S.C.R. 217:

[The Supreme Court of Canada was referred three questions, pursuant to section 53 of the Supreme Court Act which allows the Governor in Council to refer to the Court any important question of law or fact. Among those questions was this one: 'Does international law give the National Assembly, legislature or government of Quebec the right to effect the secession of Quebec from Canada unilaterally? In this regard, is there a right to self-determination under international law that would give the National Assembly, legislature or government of Quebec the right to effect the secession of Quebec from Canada unilaterally?' The Court answers as follows:]

(1) Secession at International Law

111 It is clear that international law does not specifically grant component parts of sovereign states the legal right to secede unilaterally from their 'parent' state ... Given the lack of specific authorization for unilateral secession, proponents of the existence of such a right at international law are therefore left to attempt to found their argument (i) on the proposition that unilateral secession is not specifically prohibited and that what is not specifically prohibited is inferentially permitted; or (ii) on the implied duty of states to recognize the legitimacy of secession brought about by the exercise of the well-established international law right of 'a people' to self-determination. The *amicus curiae* addressed the right of self-determination, but submitted that it was not applicable to the circumstances of Quebec within the Canadian federation, irrespective of the existence or non-existence of a referendum result in favour of secession. We agree on this point with the *amicus curiae*, for reasons that we will briefly develop.

(a) Absence of a Specific Prohibition 112 International law contains neither a right of unilateral secession nor the explicit denial of such a right, although such a denial is, to some extent, implicit in the exceptional circumstances required for secession to be permitted under the right of a people to self-determination, e.g. the right of secession that arises in the exceptional situation of an oppressed or colonial people, discussed below. As will be seen, international law places great importance on the territorial integrity of nation states and, by and large, leaves the creation of a new state to be determined by the domestic law of the existing state of which the seceding entity presently forms a part (R. Y. Jennings, *The Acquisition of Territory in International Law* (1963), at pp. 8–9). Where, as here, unilateral secession would be incompatible with the domestic Constitution, international law is likely to accept that conclusion subject to the right of peoples to self-determination, a topic to which we now turn.

(b) The Right of a People to Self-determination 113 While international law generally regulates the conduct of nation states, it does, in some specific circumstances, also recognize the 'rights' of entities other than nation states – such as the right of a *people* to self-determination.

114 The existence of the right of a people to self-determination is now so widely recognized in international conventions that the principle has acquired a status beyond 'convention' and is considered a general principle of international law. (A. Cassese, *Self-determination of peoples: A legal reappraisal* (1995), at pp. 171–72; K. Doehring, 'Self-determination', in B. Simma, ed., *The Charter of the United Nations: A Commentary* (1994), at p. 70.) ...

122 As will be seen, international law expects that the right to self-determination will be exercised by peoples within the framework of existing sovereign states and consistently with the maintenance of the territorial integrity of those states. Where this is not possible, in the exceptional circumstances discussed below, a right of secession may arise.

(i) Defining 'Peoples' 123 International law grants the right to self-determination to 'peoples'. Accordingly, access to the right requires the threshold step of characterizing as a people the group seeking self-determination. However, as the right to self-determination has developed by virtue of a combination of international agreements and conventions, coupled with state practice, with little formal elaboration of the definition of 'peoples', the result has been that the precise meaning of the term 'people' remains somewhat uncertain.

124 It is clear that 'a people' may include only a portion of the population of an existing state. The right to self-determination has developed largely as a human right, and is generally used in documents that simultaneously contain references to 'nation' and 'state'. The juxtaposition of these terms is indicative that the reference to 'people' does not necessarily mean the entirety of a state's population. To restrict the definition of the term to the population of existing states would render the granting of a right to self-determination largely duplicative, given the parallel emphasis within the majority of the source documents on the need to protect the territorial integrity of existing states, and would frustrate its remedial purpose.

125 While much of the Quebec population certainly shares many of the characteristics (such as a common language and culture) that would be considered in determining whether a specific group is a 'people', as do other groups within Quebec and/or Canada, it is not necessary to explore this legal characterization to resolve Question 2 appropriately. Similarly, it is not necessary for the Court to determine whether, should a Quebec people exist within the definition of public international law, such a people encompasses the entirety of the provincial population or just a portion thereof. Nor is it necessary to examine the position of the aboriginal population within Quebec. As the following discussion of the scope of the right to self-determination will make clear, whatever be the correct application of the definition of people(s) in this context, their right of self-determination cannot in the present circumstances be said to ground a right to unilateral secession.

(ii) Scope of the Right to Self-determination 126 The recognized sources of international law establish that the right to self-determination of a people is normally fulfilled through *internal* self-determination – a people's pursuit of its political, economic, social and cultural development within the framework of an existing state. A right to *external* self-determination (which in this case potentially takes the form of the assertion of a right to unilateral secession) arises in only the most extreme of cases and, even then, under carefully defined circumstances. *External* self-determination can be defined as in the following statement from the *Declaration on Friendly Relations* as '[t]he establishment of a sovereign and independent State, the free association or integration with an independent State or the emergence into any other political status freely determined by a *people* constitute modes of implementing the right of self-determination by *that people*.' [Emphasis added by the court.]

127 The international law principle of self-determination has evolved within a framework of respect for the territorial integrity of existing states. The various international documents that support the existence of a people's right to self-determination also contain parallel statements supportive of the conclusion that the exercise of such a right must be sufficiently limited to prevent threats to an existing state's territorial integrity or the stability of relations between sovereign states.

128 The *Declaration on Friendly Relations*, the *Vienna Declaration* and the *Declaration on the Occasion of the Fiftieth Anniversary of the United Nations* are specific. They state, immediately after affirming a people's right to determine political, economic, social and cultural issues, that such rights are *not* to 'be construed as authorizing or encouraging any action that would dismember or *impair, totally or in part, the territorial integrity or political unity of sovereign and independent States conducting themselves in compliance with the principle of equal rights and self-determination of peoples* and thus possessed of a Government representing the whole people belonging to the territory without distinction ...' [Emphasis added by the court.] ...

130 While the *International Covenant on Economic, Social and Cultural Rights* and the *International Covenant on Civil and Political Rights* do not specifically refer to the protection of territorial integrity, they both define the ambit of the right to self-determination in terms that are normally attainable within the framework of an existing state. There is no necessary incompatibility between the maintenance of the territorial integrity of existing states, including Canada, and the right of a 'people' to achieve a full measure of self-determination. A state whose government represents the whole of the people or peoples resident within its territory, on a basis of equality and without discrimination, and respects the principles of self-determination in its own internal arrangements, is entitled to the protection under international law of its territorial integrity.

(iii) Colonial and Oppressed Peoples 131 Accordingly, the general state of international law with respect to the right to self-determination is that the right operates within the overriding protection granted to the territorial integrity of 'parent' states. However, as noted by Cassese, *supra*, at p. 334, there are certain defined contexts within which the right to the self-determination of peoples does allow that right to be exercised 'externally', which, in the context of this Reference, would potentially mean secession: '... the right to external self-determination, which entails the possibility of choosing (or restoring) independence, has only been bestowed upon two classes of peoples (those under colonial rule or foreign occupation), based upon the assumption that both classes make up entities that are inherently distinct from the colonialist Power and the occupant Power and that their "territorial integrity", all but destroyed by the colonialist or occupying Power, should be fully restored ...'

132 The right of colonial peoples to exercise their right to self-determination by breaking away from the 'imperial' power is now undisputed, but is irrelevant to this Reference.

133 The other clear case where a right to external self-determination accrues is where a people is subject to alien subjugation, domination or exploitation outside a colonial context. This recognition finds its roots in the *Declaration on Friendly Relations* [quoted above in this section].

134 A number of commentators have further asserted that the right to self-determination may ground a right to unilateral secession in a third circumstance. Although this third circumstance has been described in several ways, the underlying proposition is that, when a people is blocked from the meaningful exercise of its right to self-determination internally, it is entitled, as a last resort, to exercise it by secession. The *Vienna Declaration* requirement that governments represent 'the whole people belonging to the territory without distinction of any kind' adds credence to the assertion that such a complete blockage may potentially give rise to a right of secession.

135 Clearly, such a circumstance parallels the other two recognized situations in that the ability of a people to exercise its right to self-determination internally is somehow being totally frustrated. While it remains unclear whether this third proposition actually reflects an established international law standard, it is unnecessary for present purposes to make that determination. Even assuming that the third circumstance is sufficient to create a right to unilateral secession under international law, the current Quebec context cannot be said to approach such a threshold ...

136 The population of Quebec cannot plausibly be said to be denied access to government. Quebecers occupy prominent positions within the government of Canada. Residents of the province freely make political choices and pursue economic, social and cultural development within Quebec, across Canada, and throughout the world. The population of Quebec is equitably represented in legislative, executive and judicial institutions. In short, to reflect the phraseology of the international documents that address the right to self-determination of peoples, Canada is a 'sovereign and independent state conducting itself in compliance with the principle of equal rights and self-determination of peoples and thus possessed of a government representing the whole people belonging to the territory without distinction'.

137 The continuing failure to reach agreement on amendments to the Constitution, while a matter of concern, does not amount to a denial of self-determination. In the absence of amendments to the Canadian Constitution, we must look at the constitutional arrangements presently in effect, and we cannot conclude under current circumstances that those arrangements place Quebecers in a disadvantaged position within the scope of the international law rule.

138 In summary, the international law right to self-determination only generates, at best, a right to external self-determination in situations of former colonies; where a people is oppressed, as for example under foreign military occupation; or where a definable group is denied meaningful access to government to pursue their political, economic, social and cultural development. In all three situations, the people in question are entitled to a right to external self-determination because they have been denied the ability to exert internally their right to self-determination. Such exceptional circumstances are manifestly inapplicable to Quebec under existing conditions. Accordingly, neither the population of the province of Quebec, even if characterized in terms of 'people' or 'peoples', nor its representative institutions, the National Assembly, the legislature or government of Quebec, possess a right, under international law, to secede unilaterally from Canada.

The two dimensions – external and internal – of the right to self-determination are made explicit by the Committee on the Elimination of Racial Discrimination:

Committee on the Elimination of Racial Discrimination, General Recommendation No. 21, *Right to Self-determination* (adopted at the forty-eighth session, on 23 August 1996):

4. In respect of the self-determination of peoples two aspects have to be distinguished. The right to self-determination of peoples has an internal aspect, that is to say, the rights of all peoples

to pursue freely their economic, social and cultural development without outside interference. In that respect there exists a link with the right of every citizen to take part in the conduct of public affairs at any level, as referred to in article 5(c) of the International Convention on the Elimination of All Forms of Racial Discrimination. In consequence, Governments are to represent the whole population without distinction as to race, colour, descent or national or ethnic origin. The external aspect of self-determination implies that all peoples have the right to determine freely their political status and their place in the international community based upon the principle of equal rights and exemplified by the liberation of peoples from colonialism and by the prohibition to subject peoples to alien subjugation, domination and exploitation.

5. In order to respect fully the rights of all peoples within a State, Governments are again called upon to adhere to and implement fully the international human rights instruments and in particular the International Convention on the Elimination of All Forms of Racial Discrimination. Concern for the protection of individual rights without discrimination on racial, ethnic, tribal, religious or other grounds must guide the policies of Governments. In accordance with article 2 of the International Convention on the Elimination of All Forms of Racial Discrimination and other relevant international documents, Governments should be sensitive towards the rights of persons belonging to ethnic groups, particularly their right to lead lives of dignity, to preserve their culture, to share equitably in the fruits of national growth and to play their part in the Government of the country of which they are citizens. Also, Governments should consider, within their respective constitutional frameworks, vesting persons belonging to ethnic or linguistic groups comprised of their citizens, where appropriate, with the right to engage in activities which are particularly relevant to the preservation of the identity of such persons or groups.

6. The Committee emphasizes that, in accordance with the Declaration on Friendly Relations, none of the Committee's actions shall be construed as authorizing or encouraging any action which would dismember or impair, totally or in part, the territorial integrity or political unity of sovereign and independent States conducting themselves in compliance with the principle of equal rights and self-determination of peoples and possessing a Government representing the whole people belonging to the territory, without distinction as to race, creed or colour ... [I]nternational law has not recognized a general right of peoples unilaterally to declare secession from a State. In this respect, the Committee follows the views expressed in [the report of the UN Secretary-General of 17 June 1992 (A/47/277-S/2411) *An Agenda for Peace, Preventive Diplomacy, Peacemaking and Peace-keeping*] (paras. 17 and following), namely, that a fragmentation of States may be detrimental to the protection of human rights, as well as to the preservation of peace and security. This does not, however, exclude the possibility of arrangements reached by free agreements of all parties concerned.

The insistence of the Committee for the Elimination of Racial Discrimination on the need to have 'a Government representing the whole people belonging to the territory, without distinction as to race, creed or colour' illustrates the link between the right to self-determination of peoples, considered in its internal dimension, and the protection of minority rights. This link also clearly appears from the views adopted by the Human Rights Committee in the case of *Kitok* v. *Sweden*, presented below, as well as from the recent Concluding Observations adopted by the Committee on the implementation of the ICCPR in Canada in which the Committee, 'while noting with interest Canada's undertakings towards the establishment of alternative policies to extinguishment of inherent aboriginal rights in modern treaties, remains concerned that these alternatives may in practice amount to extinguishment of aboriginal rights' (CCPR/C/CAN/CO/5, 20 April 2006, para. 8 – see below, section 5.2., a)). *Kitok* is also significant, however, in another respect: it excludes the use of the individual communications procedure in order to raise an issue under Article 1 ICCPR, since the right-holder of the right to self-determination is the 'people', rather than any individual victim.

(c) The lack of justiciability of the right to self-determination in the context of individual communications

Human Rights Committee, *Ivan Kitok* v. *Sweden*, Communication No. 197/1985 (CCPR/C/33/D/197/1985), final views of 27 July 1988:

[The author of the communication is a Swedish citizen of Sami ethnic origin, who belongs to a Sami family which has been active in reindeer breeding for over one hundred years. He claims to have been denied the right to reindeer breeding inherited from his forefathers as well as the rights to land and water in Sörkaitum Sami Village, after having lost his membership in the Sami village. Indeed, in an attempt to reduce the number of reindeer breeders, the Swedish authorities have insisted that, if a Sami engages in any other profession for a period of three years, he loses his status and his name is removed from the rolls of the village, which he cannot re-enter unless by special permission: as a result, having become a non-member of the village, he cannot exercise Sami rights to land and water. Thus it is claimed that the Crown arbitrarily denies the immemorial rights of the Sami minority and that the author of the communication is the victim of such denial of rights. Ivan Kitok claims to be the victim of violations by the Government of Sweden of articles 1 and 27 of the Covenant.]

6.3 With regard to the State party's submission that the communication should be declared inadmissible as incompatible with article 3 of the Optional Protocol or as 'manifestly ill-founded', the Committee observed that the author, as an individual, could not claim to be the victim of a violation of the right of self-determination enshrined in article 1 of the Covenant. Whereas the Optional Protocol provides a recourse procedure for individuals claiming that their rights have been violated, article 1 of the Covenant deals with rights conferred upon peoples, as such. However, with regard to article 27 of the Covenant, the Committee observed that the author had made a reasonable effort to substantiate his allegations that he was the victim of a violation of his right to enjoy the same rights enjoyed by other members of the Sami community. Therefore, it decided that the issues before it, in particular the scope of article 27, should be examined with the merits of the case ...

9.1 The main question before the Committee is whether the author of the communication is the victim of a violation of article 27 of the Covenant because, as he alleges, he is arbitrarily denied immemorial rights granted to the Sami community, in particular, the right to membership of the Sami community and the right to carry out reindeer husbandry. In deciding whether or not the author of the communication has been denied the right to 'enjoy [his] own culture', as provided for in article 27 of the Covenant, and whether section 12, paragraph 2, of the 1971 Reindeer Husbandry Act, under which an appeal against a decision of a Sami community to refuse membership may only be granted if there are special reasons for allowing such membership, violates article 27 of the Covenant, the Committee bases its findings on the following considerations.

9.2 The regulation of an economic activity is normally a matter for the State alone. However, where that activity is an essential element in the culture of an ethnic community, its application to an individual may fall under article 27 of the Covenant, which provides: 'In those States in which ethnic, religious or linguistic minorities exist, persons belonging to such minorities shall not be denied the right, in community with the other members of their group, to enjoy their own culture, to profess and practise their own religion, or to use their own language.'

9.3 The Committee observes in this context that the right to enjoy one's own culture in community with the other members of the group cannot be determined in abstract but has to be placed in context. The Committee is thus called upon to consider statutory restrictions affecting the right of an ethnic Sami to membership of a Sami village.

9.4 With regard to the State party's argument that the conflict in the present case is not so much a conflict between the author as a Sami and the State party but rather between the author and the Sami community ..., the Committee observes that the State party's responsibility has been engaged, by virtue of the adoption of the Reindeer Husbandry Act of 1971, and that it is therefore State action that has been challenged. As the State party itself points out, an appeal against a decision of the Sami community to refuse membership can only be granted if there are Special reasons for allowing such membership; furthermore, the State party acknowledges that the right of the County Administrative Board to grant such an appeal should be exercised very restrictively.

9.5 According to the State party, the purposes of the Reindeer Husbandry Act are to restrict the number of reinder breeders for economic and ecological reasons and to secure the preservation and well-being of the Sami minority. Both parties agree that effective measures are required to ensure the future of reindeer breeding and the livelihood of those for whom reindeer farming is the primary source of income. The method selected by the State party to secure these objectives is the limitation of the right to engage in reindeer breeding to members of the Sami villages. The Committee is of the opinion that all these objectives and measures are reasonable and consistent with article 27 of the Covenant.

9.6 The Committee has none the less had grave doubts as to whether certain provisions of the Reindeer Husbandry Act, and their application to the author, are compatible with article 27 of the Covenant. Section 11 of the Reindeer' Husbandry Act provides that: 'A member of a Sami community is: 1. A person entitled to engage in reindeer husbandry who participates in reindeer husbandry within the pasture area of the community. 2. A person entitled to engage in reindeer husbandry who has participated in reindeer husbandry within the pasture area of the village and who has had this as his permanent occupation and has not gone over to any other main economic activity. 3. A person entitled to engage in reindeer husbandry who is the husband or child living at home of a member as qualified in subsection 1 or 2 or who is the surviving husband or minor child of a deceased member.' Section 12 of the Act provides that: 'A Sami community may accept as a member a person entitled to engage in reindeer husbandry other than as specified in section 11, if he intends to carry on reindeer husbandry with his own reindeer within the pasture area of the community. If the applicant should be refused membership, the County Administrative Board may grant him membership, if special reasons should exist.'

9.7 It can thus be seen that the Act provides certain criteria for participation in the life of an ethnic minority whereby a person who is ethnically a Sami can be held not to be a Sami for the purposes of the Act. The Committee has been concerned that the ignoring of objective ethnic criteria in determining membership of a minority, and the application to Mr Kitok of the designated rules, may have been disproportionate to the legitimate ends sought by the legislation. It has further noted that Mr Kitok has always retained some links with the Sami community, always living on Sami lands and seeking to return to full-time reindeer farming as soon as it became financially possible, in his particular circumstances, for him to do so.

9.8 In resolving this problem, in which there is an apparent conflict between the legislation, which seems to protect the rights of the minority as a whole, and its application to a single member of that minority, the Committee has been guided by the *ratio decidendi* in the *Lovelace* case (No. 24/1977, *Lovelace* v. *Canada*), namely, that a restriction upon the right of an individual member of a minority must be shown to have a reasonable and objective justification and to be necessary for the continued viability and welfare of the minority as a whole. After a careful review of all the elements involved in this case, the Committee is of the view that there is no violation of article 27 by the State party. In this context, the Committee notes that Mr Kitok is permitted, albeit not as of right, to graze and farm his reindeer, to hunt and to fish.

The view according to which Article 1 ICCPR is not justiciable in the context of individual communications has since been confirmed by the Human Rights Committee on a number of occasions. One of these was the case of *Diergaardt* v. *Namibia*, which also raised an issue under Article 25 ICCPR, which guarantees a right to effective political participation.

Human Rights Committee, *Diergaardt et al.* v. *Namibia*, Communication No. 760/1997 (CCPR/C/69/D/760/1997), final views of 25 July 2000:

[The applicants are representatives and members of the Rehoboth Baster Community, which numbers 35,000 persons. The Basters are the descendants of indigenous Khoi and Afrikaans settlers who originally lived in the Cape, but moved to an area of Namibia (south of Windhoek) in 1872. In this area they developed their own society, culture, language and economy, with which they largely sustained their own institutions, such as schools and community centres. They submit that the Namibian Government has confiscated the assets of the Rehoboth Basters, and that, more generally, the assimilation policy of the government endangers the traditional existence of the community as a collective of mainly cattle-raising farmers. The counsel explains that in times of drought the community needs communal land, on which pasture rights are given to members of the community on a rotating basis. The expropriation of the communal land and the consequential privatization of it, as well as the overuse of the land by inexperienced newcomers to the area, has led to bankruptcy for many community farmers, who have had to slaughter their animals. As a consequence, they cannot pay their interests on loans granted to them by the Rehoboth Development Corporation (which used to be communal property but has now been seized by the Government), their houses are then sold to the banks and they find themselves homeless. Counsel emphasizes that the confiscation of all property collectively owned by the community robbed the community of the basis of its economic livelihood, which in turn was the basis of its cultural, social and ethnic identity. This is said to constitute a violation of Article 27 ICCPR.

The authors also claim to be victims of a violation by the Government of Namibia of Article 1 of the Covenant. They claim that their right to self-determination inside the Republic of Namibia (so-called internal self-determination) has been violated, since they are not allowed to pursue their economic social and cultural development, nor are they allowed to dispose freely of their community's national wealth and resources. By enactment of the Law on Regional Government 1996, the 124-year long existence of Rehoboth as a continuously organized territory was brought to an end. The territory is now divided over two regions, thus preventing the Basters from effectively participating in public life on a regional basis, since they are a minority in both new districts. Counsel claims that this constitutes a violation of Article 25 of the Covenant.

In addition, the authors further claim a violation of Article 14 ICCPR, since they were forced to use English throughout the court proceedings, a language they do not normally use and in which they are not fluent. Moreover, they had to provide sworn translations of all documents supporting their claims (which were in Afrikaans) at very high cost. They claim therefore that their right to equality before the Courts was violated, since the Court rules favour English speaking citizens. While Article 3 of the Constitution declares English to be the only official language in Namibia, para. 3 of this article allows for the use of other languages on the basis of legislation by Parliament. But such a law has still not been passed, and this, in the view of the authors, constitutes discrimination against non-English speakers. According to counsel, attempts by the opposition to have such legislation enacted have been thwarted by the Government which declared having no intention to take any legislative action in this matter. In this connection, counsel refers to the 1991 census, according to which only 0.8 per cent of the Namibian population uses English as its mother tongue. This situation is said to be a violation of their rights under Articles 26 and 27 ICCPR.]

10.3 The authors have alleged that the termination of their self-government violates article 1 of the Covenant. The Committee recalls that while all peoples have the right of self determination and the right freely to determine their political status, pursue their economic, social and cultural development and dispose of their natural wealth and resources, as stipulated in article 1 of the Covenant, the question whether the community to which the authors belong is a 'people' is not an issue for the Committee to address under the Optional Protocol to the Covenant. The Optional Protocol provides a procedure under which individuals can claim that their individual rights have been violated. These rights are set out in part III of the Covenant, articles 6 to 27, inclusive (4) (5). As shown by the Committee's jurisprudence, there is no objection to a group of individuals, who claim to be commonly affected, to submit a communication about alleged breaches of these rights. Furthermore, the provisions of article 1 may be relevant in the interpretation of other rights protected by the Covenant, in particular articles 25, 26 and 27.

10.4 The authors have made available to the Committee the judgement which the Supreme Court gave on 14 May 1996 on appeal from the High Court which had pronounced on the claim of the Baster community to communal property. Those courts made a number of findings of fact in the light of the evidence which they assessed and gave certain interpretations of the applicable domestic law. The authors have alleged that the land of their community has been expropriated and that, as a consequence, their rights as a minority are being violated since their culture is bound up with the use of communal land exclusive to members of their community. This is said to constitute a violation of Article 27 of the Covenant.

10.5 The authors state that, although the land passed to the Rehoboth Government before 20 March 1976, that land reverted to the community by operation of law after that date. According to the judgement, initially the Basters acquired for and on behalf of the community land from the Wartbooi Tribe but there evolved a custom of issuing papers (*papieren*) to evidence the granting of land to private owners and much of the land passed into private ownership. However, the remainder of the land remained communal land until the passing of the Rehoboth Self-Government Act No. 56 of 1976 by virtue of which ownership or control of the land passed from the community and became vested in the Rehoboth Government. The Baster Community had asked for it. Self-Government was granted on the basis of proposals made by the Baster Advisory Council of Rehoboth. Elections were held under this Act and the Rehoboth area was governed in terms of the Act until 1989 when the powers granted under the Act were transferred by law to the Administrator General of Namibia in anticipation and in preparation for the independence of Namibia which followed on 21 March 1990. And in terms of the Constitution of Namibia, all property or control over property by various public institutions, including the Government of South West Africa, became vested in, or came under the control, of the Government of Namibia. The Court further stated:

'In 1976 the Baster Community, through its leaders, made a decision opting for Self-Government. The community freely decided to transfer its communal land to the new Government. Clearly it saw advantage in doing so. Then in 1989, the community, through the political party to which its leaders were affiliated, subscribed to the Constitution of an independent Namibia. No doubt, once again, the Community saw advantage in doing so. It wished to be part of the new unified nation which the Constitution created ... One aim of the Constitution was to unify a nation previously divided under the system of apartheid. Fragmented self-governments had no place in the new constitutional scheme. The years of divide and rule were over.'

10.6 To conclude on this aspect of the complaint, the Committee observes that it is for the domestic courts to find the facts in the context of, and in accordance with, the interpretation of domestic laws. On the facts found, if 'expropriation' there was, it took place in 1976, or in any event before the entry into force of the Covenant and the Optional Protocol for Namibia on 28 February 1995. As to the related issue of the use of land, the authors have claimed a violation of article 27 in that a part of the lands traditionally used by members of the Rehoboth community for the grazing of cattle no longer is in the *de facto* exclusive use of the members of the community. Cattle raising is said to be an essential element in the culture of the community. As the earlier case law by the Committee illustrates, the right of members of a minority to enjoy their culture under article 27 includes protection to a particular way of life associated with the use of land resources through economic activities, such as hunting and fishing, especially in the case of indigenous peoples. However, in the present case the Committee is unable to find that the authors can rely on article 27 to support their claim for exclusive use of the pastoral lands in question. This conclusion is based on the Committee's assessment of the relationship between the authors' way of life and the lands covered by their claims. Although the link of the Rehoboth community to the lands in question dates back some 125 years, it is not the result of a relationship that would have given rise to a distinctive culture. Furthermore, although the Rehoboth community bears distinctive properties as to the historical forms of self-government, the authors have failed to demonstrate how these factors would be based on their way of raising cattle. The Committee therefore finds that there has been no violation of article 27 of the Covenant in the present case.

10.7 The Committee further considers that the authors have not substantiated any claim under article 17 that would raise separate issues from their claim under article 27 with regard to their exclusion from the lands that their community used to own.

10.8 The authors have also claimed that the termination of self-government for their community and the division of the land into two districts which were themselves amalgamated in larger regions have split up the Baster community and turned it into a minority with an adverse impact on the rights under Article 25(a) and (c) of the Covenant. The right under Article 25(a) is a right to take part in the conduct of public affairs directly or through freely chosen representatives and the right under Article 25(c) is a right to have equal access, on general terms of equality, to public service in one's country. These are individual rights. Although it may very well be that the influence of the Baster community, as a community, on public life has been affected by the merger of their region with other regions when Namibia became sovereign, the claim that this has had an adverse effect on the enjoyment by individual members of the community of the right to take part in the conduct of public affairs or to have access, on general terms of equality with other citizens of their country, to public service has not been substantiated. The Committee finds therefore that the facts before it do not show that there has been a violation of article 25 in this regard.

10.9 The authors have claimed that they were forced to use English during the proceedings in court, although this is not their mother tongue. In the instant case, the Committee considers that the authors have not shown how the use of English during the court proceedings has affected their right to a fair hearing. The Committee is therefore of the opinion that the facts before it do not reveal a violation of article 14, paragraph 1.

10.10 The authors have also claimed that the lack of language legislation in Namibia has had as a consequence that they have been denied the use of their mother tongue in administration, justice, education and public life. The Committee notes that the authors have shown that the State party has instructed civil servants not to reply to the authors' written or oral communications with the authorities in the Afrikaans language, even when they are perfectly capable of doing so. These instructions barring the use of Afrikaans do not relate merely to the issuing of public documents but even to telephone conversations. In the absence of any response from the State party the Committee must give due weight to the allegation of the authors that the circular in question is intentionally targeted against the possibility to use Afrikaans when dealing with public authorities. Consequently, the Committee finds that the authors, as Afrikaans speakers, are victims of a violation of article 26 of the Covenant.

11. The Human Rights Committee, acting under article 5, paragraph 4, of the Optional Protocol to the International Covenant on Civil and Political rights, is of the view that the facts before it disclose a violation of article 26 of the Covenant.

Individual opinion of Abdalfattah Amor (dissenting):

I cannot subscribe to the Committee's finding of a violation of article 26 of the Covenant, for the following reasons:

1. In article 3 of its Constitution, Namibia, which had declared its independence on 21 March 1991, made English the country's official language out of a legitimate concern to improve the

chances of integration. It was thought that granting any privilege or particular status to one of the many other minority or tribal languages in the country would be likely to encourage discrimination and be an obstacle to the building of the nation. Since then, all languages other than English have been on an equal footing under the Constitution: no privileges, and no discrimination. It is the same for all languages, including Afrikaans, the introduction of which into Namibia was tied up with the history of colonization and which, in any case, ceased to be used as an official language on 21 March 1991.

2. Article 3(3) of the Constitution of Namibia permits the use of other languages in accordance with legislation adopted by Parliament. No such legislation, which in any case could have no effect on the use of English as the official language, has yet been adopted. The guarantees it might have provided or the restrictions it might have introduced have not been decreed and as the situation is the same for everyone, no distinction could have been established legislatively in either a positive or a negative sense. Naturally this also applies to the Afrikaans language.

3. The use of minority languages as such has not been limited, far less questioned, at any level other than the official level. In their personal relationships, among themselves or with others, people speaking the same language are able to use that language without interference – which would be difficult to imagine anyway – from the authorities. In other words, there is nothing to limit the use of Afrikaans as the language of choice of the Basters in their relations between themselves or with others who know the language and agree to communicate with them in that language.

4. Whatever legislative weaknesses there may have been so far, the right to use one's mother tongue cannot take precedence, in relations with official institutions, over the official language of the country, which is, or which is intended to be, the language of all and the common denominator for all citizens. The State may impose the use of the common language on everyone; it is entitled to refuse to allow a few people to lay down the law. In other words, everyone is equal in relation to the official language and any linguistic privileges – unless they apply to all, in which case they would no longer be privileges – would be unjustifiable and discriminatory. The Basters complain that they are not able to use their mother tongue for administrative purposes or in the courts. However, they are not the only ones in this situation. The situation is exactly the same for everyone speaking the other minority languages. In support of their complaint, the Basters provide a copy of a circular issued by the Regional Commissioner of the Central Region of Rehoboth dated 4 March 1992, in which, according to their counsel, 'the use of Afrikaans during telephone conversations with regional public authorities is explicitly excluded'. This circular, although not very skillfully drafted, actually says something else and, in any case, certainly says more than that. [It] refers to the fact that on 21 March 1992 Afrikaans ceased to be the official language and that since then English has been the official language of Namibia. As a result, Afrikaans has the same official status as the other tribal languages, of which there are many. [The circular also bans] the continuing use by State officials of Afrikaans in their replies, in the exercise of their official duties, to telephone calls and letters; [and it requires] that all telephone calls and official correspondence should be carried out exclusively in English, the official language of Namibia.

In other words, State services must use English, and English only, and refrain from giving privileged status to any unofficial language. From this point of view, Afrikaans is neither more nor less important than the other tribal languages. This means that minority languages must be treated without discrimination. Consequently, there is no justification, unless one wishes to discriminate against the other minority languages and disregard article 3 of the Constitution of Namibia, for continuing to deal with the linguistic problem in a selective manner by favouring one particular language, Afrikaans, at the expense of the others. In that respect, the Regional Commissioner's circular does not reveal any violation of the principle of equality and certainly not of the provisions of article 26 of the Covenant ...

Other dissenting opinions

[The views expressed by Mr Amor were shared by five other members of the Committee. Mr Nisuke Ando filed a separate dissenting opinion on the matter. In their joint dissenting opinion, P. N. Bhagwati, Lord Colville, and Maxwell Yalden noted the following:]

The circular is clearly intended to provide that all official phone calls and correspondence should be treated exclusively in English, which is the official language of the State. That is the thrust, the basic object and purpose of the circular and it is in pursuance of this object and purpose that the circular directs that the Government officials should refrain from using Afrikaans when responding to official phone calls and correspondence. The circular refers specifically only to Afrikaans and seeks to prohibit its use by Government officials in official phone calls and correspondence, because the problem was only in regard to Afrikaans which was at one time, until replaced by English, the official language and which continued to be used by Government officials in official phone calls and correspondence, though it had been ceased to be the official language of the State. There was apparently no problem in regard to the tribal languages because they were at no time used in administration or for official business. But Afrikaans was being used earlier for official purposes and hence it became necessary for the State to issue the circular prohibiting the use of Afrikaans in official phone calls and correspondence. That is why the circular specifically referred only to Afrikaans and not to the other languages. This is also evident from the statement in the circular that Afrikaans now enjoys the same status as other tribal languages. It is therefore not correct to say that the circular singled out Afrikaans for unfavourable treatment as against other languages in that there was hostile discrimination against Afrikaans. We consequently hold that there was no violation of the principle of equality and non-discrimination enshrined in article 26.

[In his dissenting opinion, Rajsoomer Lallah noted:]

The real complaint of the authors with regard to Article 26, when seen in the context of their other complaints, would suggest that they still hanker after the privileged and exclusive status they previously enjoyed in matters of occupation of land, self-government and use of language under a system of fragmented self-governments which apartheid permitted. Such a system no longer avails under the unified nation which the Constitution of their country has created.

The cases of *Kitok* and *Diergaardt* may be usefully contrasted with the approach adopted by the African Commission on Human and Peoples' Rights under Article 21 of the African Charter on Human and Peoples' Rights, in the context of the *actio popularis* recognized under the Charter.

African Commission on Human and Peoples' Rights, *The Social and Economic Rights Action Center and the Center for Economic and Social Rights* v. *Nigeria*, Comm. No. 155/96 (2001):

[This case was already examined in chapter 3, section 1. It will be recalled that this communication alleges that the military government of Nigeria has been directly involved in oil production through the State oil company, the Nigerian National Petroleum Company (NNPC), the majority shareholder in a consortium with Shell Petroleum Development Corporation (SPDC), and that these operations have caused environmental degradation and health problems resulting from the contamination of the environment among the Ogoni People. The complainants invoked, among other provisions, Article 21 of the African Charter of Human and Peoples' Rights:]

55. The Complainants ... allege that the Military government of Nigeria was involved in oil production and thus did not monitor or regulate the operations of the oil companies and in so doing paved a way for the Oil Consortiums to exploit oil reserves in Ogoniland. Furthermore, in all their dealings with the Oil Consortiums, the government did not involve the Ogoni Communities in the decisions that affected the development of Ogoniland. The destructive and selfish role played by oil development in Ogoniland, closely tied with repressive tactics of the Nigerian Government, and the lack of material benefits accruing to the local population, may well be said to constitute a violation of Article 21.

Article 21 provides:

1. All peoples shall freely dispose of their wealth and natural resources. This right shall be exercised in the exclusive interest of the people. In no case shall a people be deprived of it.
2. In case of spoliation the dispossessed people shall have the right to the lawful recovery of its property as well as to an adequate compensation.
3. The free disposal of wealth and natural resources shall be exercised without prejudice to the obligation of promoting international economic co-operation based on mutual respect, equitable exchange and the principles of international law.
4. States parties to the present Charter shall individually and collectively exercise the right to free disposal of their wealth and natural resources with a view to strengthening African unity and solidarity.
5. States Parties to the present Charter shall undertake to eliminate all forms of foreign economic exploitation particularly that practised by international monopolies so as to enable their peoples to fully benefit from the advantages derived from their national resources.

56. The origin of this provision may be traced to colonialism, during which the human and material resources of Africa were largely exploited for the benefit of outside powers, creating tragedy for Africans themselves, depriving them of their birthright and alienating them from the land. The aftermath of colonial exploitation has left Africa's precious resources and people still vulnerable to foreign misappropriation. The drafters of the Charter obviously wanted to remind African governments of the continent's painful legacy and restore co-operative economic development to its traditional place at the heart of African Society.

57. Governments have a duty to protect their citizens, not only through appropriate legislation and effective enforcement but also by protecting them from damaging acts that may be perpetrated by private parties (see *Union des Jeunes Avocats/Chad* [Communication 74/92]).

This duty calls for positive action on part of governments in fulfilling their obligation under human rights instruments. The practice before other tribunals also enhances this requirement as is evidenced in the case *Velàsquez Rodríguez* v. *Honduras* [Inter-American Court of Human Rights, *Velàsquez Rodríguez* case, judgment of 19 July 1988, Series C, No. 4]. In this landmark judgment, the Inter-American Court of Human Rights held that when a State allows private persons or groups to act freely and with impunity to the detriment of the rights recognised, it would be in clear violation of its obligations to protect the human rights of its citizens. Similarly, this obligation of the State is further emphasised in the practice of the European Court of Human Rights, in *X and Y* v. *Netherlands* [26 March 1985: see chapter 4, section 1.2.]. In that case, the Court pronounced that there was an obligation on authorities to take steps to make sure that the enjoyment of the rights is not interfered with by any other private person.

58. The Commission notes that in the present case, despite its obligation to protect persons against interferences in the enjoyment of their rights, the Government of Nigeria facilitated the destruction of the Ogoniland. Contrary to its Charter obligations and despite such internationally established principles, the Nigerian Government has given the green light to private actors, and the oil Companies in particular, to devastatingly affect the well-being of the Ogonis. By any measure of standards, its practice falls short of the minimum conduct expected of governments, and therefore, is in violation of Article 21 of the African Charter.

5.2 Minority rights

There are three ways, arguably, through which minority rights can be protected under human rights instruments (for further discussions about the relationship between human rights and minority rights, see M. Scheinin and R. Toivanen (eds.), *Rethinking Non-Discrimination and Minority Rights* (Turko/Abo: Institute for Human Rights of Abo Akamedi University and Berlin: German Institute for Human Rights, 2004); and J. Ringelheim, *Diversité culturelle et droits de l'homme* (Brussels: Bruylant, 2006)). First, minorities – whether they are ethnic, linguistic, religious, or cultural – can be protected through the general prohibition of non-discrimination. Second, minorities can be protected through other human rights provisions, such as freedom of religion, freedom of association, or the right to respect for private life. Third and finally, the right of minorities 'to enjoy their own culture, to profess and practise their own religion, or to use their own language', can be protected as such, under Article 27 of the International Covenant on Civil and Political Rights: although this provision refers to the 'persons belonging to minorities' as the rights-holders, it nevertheless begins with the recognition that such rights matter because of the existence of minorities under the State's jurisdiction. This latter form of protection may be called 'direct', since it refers explicitly to the rights of minorities rather than 'indirectly' allowing for members of minority groups to exercise their individual rights collectively. The boundaries between these different techniques of protection are sometimes blurred: for instance, as we shall see below, the right to respect for private life has occasionally been read as providing, in substance, a protection similar to that of Article 27 ICCPR.

These approaches may of course be combined, as they are under the ICCPR. Similarly, under the Council of Europe Framework Convention for the Protection of National Minorities adopted in 1995, the parties not only undertake to 'promote the conditions necessary for persons belonging to national minorities to maintain and develop their culture, and to preserve the essential elements of their identity, namely their religion, language, traditions and cultural heritage' and to 'refrain from policies or practices aimed at assimilation of persons belonging to national minorities against their will and shall protect these persons from any action aimed at such assimilation' (Art. 5), they also commit to 'guarantee to persons belonging to national minorities the right of equality before the law and of equal protection of the law' and to prohibit discrimination (Art. 4(1)) as well as to 'ensure respect for the right of every person belonging to a national minority to freedom of peaceful assembly, freedom of association, freedom of expression, and freedom of thought, conscience and religion' (Art. 7).

The potential of the non-discrimination provisions contained in international human rights instruments has been explored above. Here, we review the two other routes through which the rights of minorities – or of persons belonging to minorities – can be protected, beginning with the 'direct' approach.

(a) The direct route: the explicit protection of rights of minorities

According to Article 27 ICCPR, 'In those States in which ethnic, religious or linguistic minorities exist, persons belonging to such minorities shall not be denied the right, in community with the other members of their group, to enjoy their own culture, to profess and practise their own religion, or to use their own language'. As a number of the cases above illustrate, claims based on the right to self-determination may occasionally also raise issues which concern the protection of minority rights. This link is recognized by the Human Rights Committee:

Human Rights Committee, Concluding Observations: Canada (CCPR/C/CAN/CO/5, 20 April 2006), paras. 8–10:

8. The Committee, while noting with interest Canada's undertakings towards the establishment of alternative policies to extinguishment of inherent aboriginal rights in modern treaties, remains concerned that these alternatives may in practice amount to extinguishment of aboriginal rights (arts. 1 and 27).

The State party should re-examine its policy and practices to ensure they do not result in extinguishment of inherent aboriginal rights. The Committee would also like to receive more detailed information on the comprehensive land claims agreement that Canada is currently negotiating with the Innu people of Quebec and Labrador, in particular regarding its compliance with the Covenant.

9. The Committee is concerned that land claim negotiations between the Government of Canada and the Lubicon Lake Band are currently at an impasse. It is also concerned about information that the land of the Band continues to be compromised by logging and large-scale oil and gas extraction, and regrets that the State party has not provided information on this specific issue (arts. 1 and 27).

The State party should make every effort to resume negotiations with the Lubicon Lake Band, with a view to finding a solution which respects the rights of the Band under the Covenant, as already found by the Committee. It should consult with the Band before granting licences for economic exploitation of the disputed land, and ensure that in no case such exploitation jeopardizes the rights recognized under the Covenant.

10. The Committee, while noting the responses provided by the State party in relation to the preservation, revitalization and promotion of Aboriginal languages and cultures, remains concerned about the reported decline of Aboriginal languages in Canada (art. 27). The State party should increase its efforts for the protection and promotion of Aboriginal languages and cultures. It should provide the Committee with statistical data or an assessment of the current situation, as well as with information on action taken in the future to implement the recommendations of the Task Force on Aboriginal Languages and on concrete results achieved.

Human Rights Committee, *Chief Bernard Ominayak and the Lubicon Lake Band* v. *Canada*, Communication No. 167/1984 (UN Doc. Supp. No. 40 (A/45/40) at 1), final views of 26 March 1990:

[Chief Ominayak is the leader and representative of the Lubicon Lake Band, a Cree Indian band living within the borders of Canada in the Province of Alberta, which are subject to the jurisdiction of the Federal Government of Canada. The Lubicon Lake Band is a self-identified, relatively autonomous, socio-cultural and economic group. Its members have continuously inhabited, hunted, trapped and fished in a large area encompassing approximately 10,000 square kilometres in northern Alberta since time immemorial. Since their territory is relatively inaccessible, they have, until recently, had little contact with non-Indian society. Band members speak Cree as their primary language. Many do not speak, read or write English. The Band continues to maintain its traditional culture, religion, political structure and subsistence economy. It is claimed that the Canadian Government, despite the Indian Act of 1970 and Treaty 8 of 21 June 1899 (concerning aboriginal land rights in northern Alberta), which recognized the right of the original inhabitants of that area to continue their traditional way of life, has allowed the provincial Government of Alberta to expropriate the territory of the Lubicon Lake Band for the benefit of private corporate interests (e.g. leases for oil and gas exploration). The author alleges violations by the Government of Canada of the Lubicon Lake Band's right of self-determination and by virtue of that right to determine freely its political status and pursue its economic, social and cultural development, as well as the right to dispose freely of its natural wealth and resources and not to be deprived of its own means of subsistence. These violations allegedly contravene Canada's obligations under article 1, paras. 1–3, of the International Covenant on Civil and Political Rights.]

29.1 At the outset, the author's claim, although set against a complex background, concerned basically the alleged denial of the right of self-determination and the right of the members of the Lubicon Lake Band to dispose freely of their natural wealth and resources. It was claimed that, although the Government of Canada, through the Indian Act of 1970 and Treaty 8 of 1899, had recognized the right of the Lubicon Lake Band to continue its traditional way of life, its land (approximately 10,000 square kilometres) had been expropriated for commercial interest (oil and gas exploration) and destroyed, thus depriving the Lubicon Lake Band of its means of subsistence and enjoyment of the right of self-determination. It was claimed that the rapid destruction of the Band's economic base and aboriginal way of life had already caused irreparable injury. It was further claimed that the Government of Canada had deliberately used the domestic political and legal processes to thwart and delay all the Band's efforts to seek redress, so that the industrial development in the area, accompanied by the destruction of the environmental and economic base of the Band, would make it impossible for the Band to survive as a people. The author has stated that the Lubicon Lake Band is not seeking from the Committee a territorial rights decision, but only that the Committee assist it in attempting to convince the Government of Canada: (a) that the Band's existence is seriously threatened; and (b) that Canada is responsible for the current state of affairs.

29.2 From the outset, the State party has denied the allegations that the existence of the Lubicon Lake Band has been threatened and has maintained that continued resource development would not cause irreparable injury to the traditional way of life of the Band. It submitted that the Band's claim to certain lands in northern Alberta was part of a complex situation that involved a number of competing claims from several other native communications in the area, that effective redress in respect of the Band's claims was still available, both through the courts and through negotiations, that the Government had made an ex gratia payment to the Band of $C1.5 million to cover legal costs and that, at any rate, article 1 of the Covenant, concerning the rights of people, could not be invoked under the Optional Protocol, which provides for the consideration of alleged violations of individual rights, but not collective rights conferred upon peoples.

29.3 This was the state of affairs when the Committee decided in July 1987 that the communication was admissible 'in so far as it may raise issues under article 27 or other articles of the Covenant'. In view of the seriousness of the author's allegations that the Lubicon Lake Band was at the verge of extinction, the Committee requested the State party, under rule 86 of the rules of procedure 'to take interim measures of protection to avoid irreparable damage to [the author of the communication] and other members of the Lubicon Lake Band'.

29.4 Insisting that no irreparable damage to the traditional way of life of the Lubicon Lake Band had occurred and that there was no imminent threat of such harm, and further that both a trial on the merits of the Band's claims and the negotiation process constitute effective and viable alternatives to the interim relief which the Band had unsuccessfully sought in the courts, the State party, in October 1987, requested the Committee, under rule 93, paragraph 4, of the rules of procedure, to review its decision on admissibility, in so far as it concerns the requirement of exhaustion of domestic remedies. The State party stressed in this connection that delays in the judicial proceedings initiated by the Band were largely attributable to the Band's own inaction. The State party further explained its long-standing policy to seek the resolutions of valid, outstanding land claims by Indian bands through negotiations.

29.5 Since October 1987, the parties have made a number of submissions, refuting each other's statements as factually misleading or wrong. The author has accused the State party of creating a situation that has directly or indirectly led to the death of many Band members and is threatening the lives of all other members of the Lubicon community, that miscarriages and stillbirths have skyrocketed and abnormal births have risen from zero to near 100 per cent, all in violation of article 6 of the Covenant; that the devastation wrought on the community constitutes cruel, inhuman and degrading treatment in violation of article 7; that the bias of the Canadian courts has frustrated the Band's efforts to protect its land, community and livelihood, and that several of the judges have had clear economic and personal ties to the parties opposing the Band in the court actions, all in violation of articles 14, paragraph 1, and 26; that the State party has permitted the destruction of the families and homes of the Band members in violation of articles 17 and 23, paragraph 1; that the Band members have been 'robbed of the physical realm to which their religion attaches' in violation of article 18, paragraph 1; and that all of the above also constitutes violations of article 2, paragraphs 1 to 3, of the Covenant.

29.6 The State party has categorically rejected the above allegations as unfounded and unsubstantiated and as constituting an abuse of the right of submission. It submits that serious and genuine efforts continued in early 1988 to engage representatives of the Lubicon Lake Band in negotiations in respect of the Band's claims. These efforts, which included an interim offer to set aside 25.4 square miles as reserve land for the Band, without prejudice to negotiations or any court actions, failed. According to the author, all but the 25.4 square miles of the Band's traditional lands had been leased out, in defiance of the Committee's request for interim measures of protection, in conjunction with a pulp mill to be constructed by the Daishowa Canada Company Ltd near Peace River, Alberta, and that the Daishowa project frustrated any hopes of the continuation of some traditional activity by Band members.

29.7 Accepting its obligation to provide the Lubicon Lake Band with reserve land under Treaty 8, and after further unsuccessful discussions, the Federal Government, in May 1988, initiated legal proceedings against the Province of Alberta and the Lubicon Lake Band, in an effort to provide a common jurisdiction and thus to enable it to meet its lawful obligations to the Band under Treaty 8. In the author's opinion, however, this initiative was designated for the sole purpose of delaying indefinitely the resolution of the Lubicon land issues and, on 6 October 1988 (30 September, according to the State party), the Lubicon Lake Band asserted jurisdiction over its territory and declared that it had ceased to recognize the jurisdiction of the Canadian courts. The author further accused the State party of 'practicing deceit in the media and dismissing advisors who recommend any resolution favourable to the Lubicon people'.

29.8 Following an agreement between the provincial government of Alberta and the Lubicon Lake Band in November 1988 to set aside 95 square miles of land for a reserve, negotiations started between the federal Government and the Band on the modalities of the land transfer and related issues. According to the State party, consensus had been reached on the majority of issues, including Band membership, size of the reserve, community construction and delivery of programmes and services, but not on cash compensation, when the Band withdrew from the negotiations on 24 January 1989. The formal offer presented at that time by the federal Government amounted to approximately $C45 million in benefits and programmes, in addition to the 95 square mile reserve.

29.9 The author, on the other hand, states that the above information from the State party is not only misleading but virtually entirely untrue and that there had been no serious attempt by the Government to reach a settlement. He describes the Government's offer as an exercise in public relations, 'which committed the Federal Government to virtually nothing', and states that no agreement or consensus had been reached on any issue. The author further accused the State party of sending agents into communities surrounding the traditional Lubicon territory to induce other natives to make competing claims for traditional Lubicon land.

29.10 The State party rejects the allegation that it negotiated in bad faith or engaged in improper behaviour to the detriment of the interests of the Lubicon Lake Band. It concedes that the Lubicon Lake Band has suffered a historical inequity, but maintains that its formal offer would, if accepted, enable the Band to maintain its culture, control its way of life and achieve economic self-sufficiency and, thus, constitute an effective remedy. On the basis of a total of 500 Band members, the package worth $C45 million would amount to almost $C500,000 for each family of five. It states that a number of the Band's demands, including an indoor ice arena or a swimming pool, had been refused. The major remaining point of contention, the State party submits, is a request for $C167 million in compensation for economic and other losses allegedly suffered. That claim, it submits, could be pursued in the courts, irrespective of the acceptance of the formal offer. It reiterates that its offer to the Band stands.

29.11 Further submissions from both parties have, *inter alia*, dealt with the impact of the Daishowa pulp mill on the traditional way of life of the Lubicon Lake Band. While the author states that the impact would be devastating, the State party maintains that it would have no serious adverse consequences, pointing out that the pulp mill, located about 80 kilometres away from the land set aside for the reserve, is not within the Band's claimed traditional territory and that the area to be cut annually, outside the proposed reserve, involves less than 1 per cent of the area specified in the forest management agreement.

30. The Human Rights Committee has considered the present communication in the light of the information made available by the parties, as provided for in articles 5, paragraph 1, of the Optional Protocol. In so doing, the Committee observes that the persistent disagreement between the parties as to what constitutes the factual setting for the dispute at issue has made the consideration of the claims on the merits most difficult ...

Articles of the Covenant alleged to have been violated

32.1 The question has arisen of whether any claim under article 1 of the Covenant remains, the Committee's decision on admissibility notwithstanding. While all peoples have the right of self-determination and the right freely to determine their political status, pursue their economic, social and cultural development and dispose of their natural wealth and resources, as stipulated in article 1 of the Covenant, the question whether the Lubicon Lake Band constitutes a 'people' is not an issue for the Committee to address under the Optional Protocol to the Covenant. The Optional Protocol provides a procedure under which individuals can claim that their individual rights have been violated. These rights are set out in part III of the Covenant, articles 6 to 27, inclusive. There is, however, no objection to a group of individuals, who claim to be similarly affected, collectively to submit a communication about alleged breaches of their rights.

32.2 Although initially couched in terms of alleged breaches of the provisions of article 1 of the Covenant, there is no doubt that many of the claims presented raise issues under article 27. The Committee recognizes that the rights protected by article 27, include the right of persons, in community with others, to engage in economic and social activities which are part of the culture of the community to which they belong. Sweeping allegations concerning extremely serious breaches of other articles of the Covenant (6, 7, 14, para. 1, and 26), made after the communication was declared admissible, have not been substantiated to the extent that they would deserve serious consideration. The allegations concerning breaches of articles 17 and 23, paragraph 1, are similarly of a sweeping nature and will not be taken into account except in so far as they may be considered subsumed under the allegations which, generally, raise issues under article 27.

32.3 The most recent allegations that the State party has conspired to create an artificial band, the Woodland Cree Band, said to have competing claims to traditional Lubicon land, are dismissed as an abuse of the right of submission within the meaning of article 3 of the Optional Protocol.

Violations and the remedy offered

33. Historical inequities, to which the State party refers, and certain more recent developments threaten the way of life and culture of the Lubicon Lake Band, and constitute a violation of article 27 so long as they continue. The State party proposes to rectify the situation by a remedy that the Committee deems appropriate within the meaning of article 2 of the Covenant.

Human Rights Committee, *Ballantyne, Davidson, McIntyre* v. *Canada*, Communications Nos. 359/1989 and 385/1989 (CCPR/C/47/D/359/1989 and 385/1989/Rev.1 (1993)), final views of 31 March 1993:

[The authors of the communications are Canadian citizens residing in the Province of Quebec. The authors, one a painter, the second a designer and the third an undertaker by profession, have their businesses in Sutton and Huntingdon, Quebec. Their mother tongue is English, as is that of many of their clients. They allege to be victims of violations of Articles 2, 19, 26 and 27 of the International Covenant on Civil and Political Rights by the Federal Government of Canada and by the Province of Quebec, because they are forbidden to use English for advertising purposes, e.g. on commercial signs outside the business premises, or in the name of the firm. Indeed, Bill No. 178 enacted by the Provincial Government of Quebec on 22 December 1988 intends to ensure that only French may be used in public billposting and in commercial advertising outdoors. It stipulates that this rule shall also apply inside means of public transport and certain establishments, including shopping centres.]

11.2 As to article 27, the Committee observes that this provision refers to minorities in States; this refers, as do all references to the 'State' or to 'States' in the provisions of the Covenant, to ratifying States. Further, article 50 of the Covenant provides that its provisions extend to all parts of Federal States without any limitations or exceptions. Accordingly, the minorities referred to in article 27 are minorities within such a State, and not minorities within any province. A group may constitute a majority in a province but still be a minority in a State and thus be entitled to the benefits of article 27. English speaking citizens of Canada cannot be considered a linguistic minority. The authors therefore have no claim under article 27 of the Covenant.

11.3 Under article 19 of the Covenant, everyone shall have the right to freedom of expression; this right may be subjected to restrictions, conditions for which are set out in article 19, paragraph 3. The Government of Quebec has asserted that commercial activity such as outdoor advertising does not fall within the ambit of article 19. The Committee does not share this opinion. Article 19, paragraph 2, must be interpreted as encompassing every form of subjective ideas and opinions capable of transmission to others, which are compatible with article 20 of the Covenant, of news and information, of commercial expression and advertising, of works of art, etc.; it should not be confined to means of political, cultural or artistic expression. In the Committee's opinion, the commercial element in an expression taking the form of outdoor advertising cannot have the effect of removing this expression from the scope of protected freedom. The Committee does not agree either that any of the above forms of expression can be subjected to varying degrees of limitation, with the result that some forms of expression may suffer broader restrictions than others.

11.4 Any restriction of the freedom of expression must cumulatively meet the following conditions: it must be provided for by law, it must address one of the aims enumerated in paragraph 3(a) and (b) of article 19, and must be necessary to achieve the legitimate purpose. While the restrictions on outdoor advertising are indeed provided for by law, the issue to be addressed is whether they are necessary for the respect of the rights of others. The rights of others could only be the rights of the francophone minority within Canada under article 27. This is the right to use their own language, which is not jeopardized by the freedom of others to advertise in other than the French language. Nor does the Committee have reason to believe that public order would be jeopardized by commercial advertising outdoors in a language other than French. The Committee notes that the State party does not seek to defend Bill 178 on these grounds. Any constraints under paragraphs 3(a) and 3(b) of article 19 would in any event have to be shown to be necessary. The Committee believes that it is not necessary, in order to protect the vulnerable position in Canada of the francophone group, to prohibit commercial advertising in English. This protection may be achieved in other ways that do not preclude the freedom of expression, in a language of their choice, of those engaged in such fields as trade. For example, the law could have required that advertising be in both French and English. A State may choose one or more official languages, but it may not exclude, outside the spheres of public life, the freedom to express oneself in a language of one's choice. The Committee accordingly concludes that there has been a violation of article 19, paragraph 2.

11.5 The authors have claimed a violation of their right, under article 26, to equality before the law; the Government of Quebec has contended that Sections 1 and 6 of Bill 178 are general measures applicable to all those engaged in trade, regardless of their language. The Committee notes that Sections 1 and 6 of Bill 178 operate to prohibit the use of commercial advertising outdoors in other than the French language. This prohibition applies to French speakers as well as English speakers, so that a French speaking person wishing to advertise in English, in order to reach those of his or her clientele who are English speaking, may not do so. Accordingly, the Committee finds that the authors have not been discriminated against on the ground of their language, and concludes that there has been no violation of article 26 of the Covenant.

12. The Human Rights Committee ... is of the view that the facts before it reveal a violation of article 19, paragraph 2, of the Covenant.

Human Rights Committee, General Comment No. 23, *The Rights of Minorities* (Art. 27) (CCPR/C/21/Rev.1/Add. 5) (8 April 1994):

1. Article 27 of the Covenant provides that, in those States in which ethnic, religious or linguistic minorities exist, persons belonging to these minorities shall not be denied the right, in community with the other members of their group, to enjoy their own culture, to profess and practise their own religion, or to use their own language. The Committee observes that this

article establishes and recognizes a right which is conferred on individuals belonging to minority groups and which is distinct from, and additional to, all the other rights which, as individuals in common with everyone else, they are already entitled to enjoy under the Covenant ...

3.1. The Covenant draws a distinction between the right to self-determination and the rights protected under article 27. The former is expressed to be a right belonging to peoples and is dealt with in a separate part (Part I) of the Covenant. Self-determination is not a right cognizable under the Optional Protocol. Article 27, on the other hand, relates to rights conferred on individuals as such and is included, like the articles relating to other personal rights conferred on individuals, in Part III of the Covenant and is cognizable under the Optional Protocol.

3.2. The enjoyment of the rights to which article 27 relates does not prejudice the sovereignty and territorial integrity of a State party. At the same time, one or other aspect of the rights of individuals protected under that article – for example, to enjoy a particular culture – may consist in a way of life which is closely associated with territory and use of its resources. This may particularly be true of members of indigenous communities constituting a minority.

4. The Covenant also distinguishes the rights protected under article 27 from the guarantees under articles 2.1 and 26. The entitlement, under article 2.1, to enjoy the rights under the Covenant without discrimination applies to all individuals within the territory or under the jurisdiction of the State whether or not those persons belong to a minority. In addition, there is a distinct right provided under article 26 for equality before the law, equal protection of the law, and non-discrimination in respect of rights granted and obligations imposed by the States. It governs the exercise of all rights, whether protected under the Covenant or not, which the State party confers by law on individuals within its territory or under its jurisdiction, irrespective of whether they belong to the minorities specified in article 27 or not. Some States parties who claim that they do not discriminate on grounds of ethnicity, language or religion, wrongly contend, on that basis alone, that they have no minorities.

5.1. The terms used in article 27 indicate that the persons designed to be protected are those who belong to a group and who share in common a culture, a religion and/or a language. Those terms also indicate that the individuals designed to be protected need not be citizens of the State party. In this regard, the obligations deriving from article 2.1 are also relevant, since a State party is required under that article to ensure that the rights protected under the Covenant are available to all individuals within its territory and subject to its jurisdiction, except rights which are expressly made to apply to citizens, for example, political rights under article 25. A State party may not, therefore, restrict the rights under article 27 to its citizens alone.

5.2. Article 27 confers rights on persons belonging to minorities which 'exist' in a State party. Given the nature and scope of the rights envisaged under that article, it is not relevant to determine the degree of permanence that the term 'exist' connotes. Those rights simply are that individuals belonging to those minorities should not be denied the right, in community with members of their group, to enjoy their own culture, to practise their religion and speak their language. Just as they need not be nationals or citizens, they need not be permanent residents. Thus, migrant workers or even visitors in a State party constituting such minorities are entitled not to be denied the exercise of those rights. As any other individual in the territory of the State party, they would, also for this purpose, have the general rights, for example, to freedom of association, of assembly, and of expression. The existence of an ethnic, religious or linguistic minority in a given State party does not depend upon a decision by that State party but requires to be established by objective criteria.

5.3. The right of individuals belonging to a linguistic minority to use their language among themselves, in private or in public, is distinct from other language rights protected under the Covenant. In particular, it should be distinguished from the general right to freedom of expression protected under article 19. The latter right is available to all persons, irrespective of whether they belong to minorities or not. Further, the right protected under article 27 should be distinguished from the particular right which article 14.3(f) of the Covenant confers on accused persons to interpretation where they cannot understand or speak the language used in the courts. Article 14.3(f) does not, in any other circumstances, confer on accused persons the right to use or speak the language of their choice in court proceedings.

6.1. Although article 27 is expressed in negative terms, that article, nevertheless, does recognize the existence of a 'right' and requires that it shall not be denied. Consequently, a State party is under an obligation to ensure that the existence and the exercise of this right are protected against their denial or violation. Positive measures of protection are, therefore, required not only against the acts of the State party itself, whether through its legislative, judicial or administrative authorities, but also against the acts of other persons within the State party.

6.2. Although the rights protected under article 27 are individual rights, they depend in turn on the ability of the minority group to maintain its culture, language or religion. Accordingly, positive measures by States may also be necessary to protect the identity of a minority and the rights of its members to enjoy and develop their culture and language and to practise their religion, in community with the other members of the group. In this connection, it has to be observed that such positive measures must respect the provisions of articles 2.1 and 26 of the Covenant both as regards the treatment between different minorities and the treatment between the persons belonging to them and the remaining part of the population. However, as long as those measures are aimed at correcting conditions which prevent or impair the enjoyment of the rights guaranteed under article 27, they may constitute a legitimate differentiation under the Covenant, provided that they are based on reasonable and objective criteria.

7. With regard to the exercise of the cultural rights protected under article 27, the Committee observes that culture manifests itself in many forms, including a particular way of life associated with the use of land resources, especially in the case of indigenous peoples. That right may include such traditional activities as fishing or hunting and the right to live in reserves protected by law. The enjoyment of those rights may require positive legal measures of protection and measures to ensure the effective participation of members of minority communities in decisions which affect them.

8. The Committee observes that none of the rights protected under article 27 of the Covenant may be legitimately exercised in a manner or to an extent inconsistent with the other provisions of the Covenant.

9. The Committee concludes that article 27 relates to rights whose protection imposes specific obligations on States parties. The protection of these rights is directed towards ensuring the survival and continued development of the cultural, religious and social identity of the minorities concerned, thus enriching the fabric of society as a whole. Accordingly, the Committee observes that these rights must be protected as such and should not be confused with other personal rights conferred on one and all under the Covenant. States parties, therefore, have an obligation to ensure that the exercise of these rights is fully protected and they should indicate in their reports the measures they have adopted to this end.

The definition of minorities in international law

One obstacle to the protection of the rights of minorities in international law, whether under Article 27 ICCPR or under other instruments such as the Council of Europe Framework Convention for the Protection of National Minorities (FCNM), may reside in the absence of a generally agreed upon definition of 'minorities' which should benefit from this protection. The attempts to arrive at an authorized definition have failed. When asked to prepare a comment on the protection of the rights of minorities in the European Union, the EU Network of Independent Experts on Fundamental Rights – a group of independent experts charged with preparing reports and opinions on the basis of the EU Charter of Fundamental Rights, to inform the work of the European Commission and the European Parliament – remarked:

EU Network of Independent Experts on Fundamental Rights, Thematic Comment No. 3, *The Protection of Minorities in the European Union* (25 April 2005), para. 1.1.:

Several definitions of 'minorities' or 'national minorities' have been proposed within international organisations. Mr Francesco Capotorti drafted a study in 1977 for the UN Sub-Commission on the Prevention of Discrimination and the Protection of Minorities [F. Capotorti, *Study on the Rights of Persons belonging to Ethnic, Religious and Linguistic Minorities* (New York: United Nations, 1991)]. Mr Jules Deschênes was charged in 1985 by the same body with the study of the question of the definition of minorities [J. Deschênes, *Proposal concerning the Definition of the Term 'Minority'*, E/CN.4/Sub.2/1985/31, 14 May 1985] ... Although these definitions are not legally binding, they serve as a reference to determine the meaning of the notion of a 'minority' in international law. Indeed, although States are recognized a margin of appreciation in identifying the 'minorities' which exist under their jurisdiction, they may not use this margin of appreciation in order to evade their obligations under international law. Thus, international bodies have been led to note that the qualification of 'minority' is a matter of fact and not of law [Permanent Court of International Justice, Advisory opinion regarding Greco-Bulgarian communities, 31 July 1930, *P.C.J. Reports, Series B* No. 17]: a group has to be recognised as a 'minority' in the sense of international law when it possesses all the characteristics, independent of whether it is recognised as such by national law. In its General Comment on Article 27 ICCPR, the UN Human Rights Committee states: 'The existence of an ethnic, religious or linguistic minority in a given State party does not depend upon a decision by that State party but requires to be established by objective criteria.' [Human Rights Committee, General Comment on Article 27 ICCPR, para.5.2. See also the Advisory Committee of the Framework Convention for the Protection of National Minorities: '[T]he applicability of the Framework Convention does not necessarily mean that the authorities should in their domestic legislation and practice use the term "national minority" to describe the group concerned.' (Opinion on Norway, 12 September 2002, ACFC/INF/OP/I (2002)003, para.19); and Parliamentary Assembly of the Council of Europe, Recommendation 1623 (2003), para. 6.]

In the absence however of a consensus among states on the definition of a minority, neither the FCNM, nor any other legally binding international instrument contains such a definition [see the Explanatory Report of the FCNM: 'It was decided to adopt a pragmatic approach, based on the recognition that at this stage, it is impossible to arrive at a definition capable of mustering general support of all Council of Europe member States.' (para.12)]. The [Advisory Committee on the Framework Convention] recognises that the states parties have a margin of appreciation to determine the personal scope of application of the FCNM in order to take the specific circumstances prevailing in their country into account. However, it notes ... that this margin of appreciation 'must be exercised in accordance with general principles of international law and the fundamental principles set out in Article 3 of the Framework Convention. In particular, it stresses that the implementation of the Framework Convention should not be a source of arbitrary or unjustified distinctions.' [See, e.g. Opinion on Albania, (ACFC/INF/OP/I(2003)004), 12 September 2002, para.18; Opinion on Croatia, (ACFC/INF/OP/I(2002)003), 6 April 2001, para.15; Opinion on Italy, (ACFC/INF/OP/I(2002)007), 14 September 2001, para.14.]

[I]t is this latter requirement which is crucial. Where certain specific rights or protections are granted only to groups who are recognized as 'minorities', or to individuals under the condition that they are considered members of 'minorities', the definition relied upon by the States should not lead to arbitrary distinctions being introduced, which would be the source of discrimination. For instance, a State defining 'minorities' under its jurisdiction as a group of persons who reside on the territory of a State and are citizens thereof, display distinctive ethnic, cultural, religious or linguistic characteristics, are smaller in number than the rest of the population of that state or of a region of that state, and are motivated by a concern to preserve together that which constitutes their common identity, including their culture, their traditions, their religion or their language, although it would be resorting to a definition which appears dominant in Europe, should not be allowed to rely on that definition to exclude non-citizens from a full range of protections granted to its own nationals, even where these protections contribute to the preservation of 'minority rights'. As recalled by the UN Committee on the Elimination of Racial Discrimination in its General Recommendation 30 on 'Discrimination against non-citizens', although some fundamental rights 'such as the right to participate in elections, to vote and to stand for election, may be confined to citizens, *human rights are, in principle, to be enjoyed by all persons.* States parties are under an obligation to guarantee equality between citizens and non-citizens in the enjoyment of these rights to the extent recognized under international law' [General Recommendation 30 adopted at the sixty-fourth session of the Committee on the Elimination of Racial Discrimination (CERD/C/64/Misc.11/rev.3), para. 5 (emphasis added)]. Nor should such a State be allowed to use such a definition in order to reserve to the category of citizens certain rights, while imposing excessive barriers to the access to nationality for persons who are under its jurisdiction and have strong and permanent links to the State.

(b) The indirect route: the protection of the rights of minorities and the right to respect for private and family life

As illustrated by the decisions below, a broad understanding of the requirements of the right to respect for private life have allowed human rights bodies to protect minority rights even where a State denies that minorities exist under its jurisdiction, or in the absence of a specific clause relating to such rights. In the decision it adopted in the *Hopu and Bessert* case, the Human Rights Committee – while accepting that it is not competent to assess whether France has complied with Article 27 ICCPR, due to a declaration by France that this provision did not apply to it – protects the rights of indigeneous peoples by relying on the definition of 'family' it offered in its General Comment No. 16 (1988) where it stated that 'Regarding the term "family" [which appears in Article 17 ICCPR], the objectives of the Covenant require that for purposes of article 17 this term be given a broad interpretation to include all those comprising the family as understood in the society of the State party concerned' (para. 5).

Human Rights Committee, *Hopu and Bessert* v. *France*, Communication No. 549/1993 (CCPR/C/60/D/549/1993/Rev.1), final views of 29 July 1997:

[The authors are the descendants of the owners of a land tract (approximately 4.5 hectares) called Tetaitapu, in Nuuroa, on the island of Tahiti. They argue that their ancestors were dispossessed of their property by a judgment of the *Tribunal civil* of Papeete on 6 October 1961, awarding the ownership of the land to the Société hôtelière du Pacifique sud (SHPS), and as a result of which construction work has begun on a luxury hotel complex on the site. The authors and other descendants of the owners of the land contend that the land and the lagoon bordering it represent an important place in their history, their culture and their life. They add that the land encompasses the site of a pre-European burial ground and that the lagoon remains a traditional fishing ground and provides the means of subsistence for some thirty families living next to the lagoon. Although the authors claimed, *inter alia*, a violation of article 27 of the Covenant, since they are denied the right to enjoy their own culture, the Committee recalled in respect to that claim that 'France, upon acceding to the Covenant, had declared that "in the light of article 2 of the Constitution of the French Republic, … article 27 is not applicable as far as the Republic is concerned"'. The Committee confirmed its previous jurisprudence that the French 'declaration' on article 27 operated as a reservation and, accordingly, concluded that it was not competent to consider complaints directed against France under article 27 of the Covenant.]

10.3 The authors claim that the construction of the hotel complex on the contested site would destroy their ancestral burial grounds, which represent an important place in their history, culture and life, and would arbitrarily interfere with their privacy and their family lives, in violation of articles 17 and 23. They also claim that members of their family are buried on the site. The Committee observes that the objectives of the Covenant require that the term 'family' be given a broad interpretation so as to include all those comprising the family as understood in the society in question. It follows that cultural traditions should be taken into account when defining the term 'family' in a specific situation. It transpires from the authors' claims that they consider the relationship to their ancestors to be an essential element of their identity and to play an important role in their family life. This has not been challenged by the State party; nor has the State party contested the argument that the burial grounds in question play an important role in the authors' history, culture and life. The State party has disputed the authors' claim only on the basis that they have failed to establish a kinship link between the remains discovered in the burial grounds and themselves. The Committee considers that the authors' failure to establish a direct kinship link cannot be held against them in the circumstances of the communication, where the burial grounds in question pre-date the arrival of European settlers and are recognized as including the forbears of the present Polynesian inhabitants of Tahiti. The Committee therefore concludes that the construction of a hotel complex on the authors' ancestral burial grounds did interfere with their right to family and privacy. The State party has not shown that this interference was reasonable in the circumstances, and nothing in the information before the Committee shows that the State party duly took into account the importance of the burial grounds for the authors, when it decided to lease the site for the building of a hotel complex. The Committee concludes that there has been an arbitrary interference with the authors' right to family and privacy, in violation of articles 17, paragraph 1, and 23, paragraph 1.

[This generous reading of Article 17 ICCPR was challenged by four members of the Committee. Committee members David Kretzmer and Thomas Buergenthal wrote the following dissenting individual opinion, co-signed by Nisuke Ando and Lord Colville:]

4. In reaching the conclusion that the facts in the instant case do not give rise to an interference with the authors' family and privacy, we do not reject the view, expressed in the Committee's General Comment 16 on article 17 of the Covenant, that the term 'family' should 'be given a broad interpretation to include all those comprising the family as understood in the society of the State party concerned'. Thus, the term 'family', when applied to the local population in French Polynesia, might well include relatives, who would not be included in a family, as this term is understood in other societies, including metropolitan France. However, even when the term 'family' is extended, it does have a discrete meaning. It does not include all members of one's ethnic or cultural group. Nor does it necessarily include all one's ancestors, going back to time immemorial. The claim that a certain site is an ancestral burial ground of an ethnic or cultural group, does not, as such, imply that it is the burial ground of members of the authors' family. The authors have provided no evidence that the burial ground is one that is connected to their family, rather than to the whole of the indigenous population of the area. The general claim that members of their families are buried there, without specifying in any way the nature of the relationship between themselves and the persons buried there, is insufficient to support their claim, even on the assumption that the notion of family is different from notions that prevail in other societies. We therefore cannot accept the Committee's view that the authors have substantiated their claim that allowing building on the burial ground amounted to interference with their family.

5. The Committee mentions the authors' claim 'that they consider the relationship to their ancestors to be an essential element of their identity and to play an important role in their family life'. Relying on the fact that the State party has challenged neither this claim nor the authors' argument that the burial grounds play an important part in their history, culture and life, the Committee concludes that the construction of the hotel complex on the burial grounds interferes with the authors' right to family and privacy. The reference by the Committee to the authors' history, culture and life, is revealing. For it shows that the values that are being protected are not the family, or privacy, but cultural values. We share the concern of the Committee for these values. These values, however, are protected under article 27 of the Covenant and not the provisions relied on by the Committee. We regret that the Committee is prevented from applying article 27 in the instant case.

6. Contrary to the Committee, we cannot accept that the authors' claim of an interference with their right to privacy has been substantiated. The only reasoning provided to support the Committee's conclusion in this matter is the authors' claim that their connection with their ancestors plays an important role in their identity. The notion of privacy revolves around protection of those aspects of a person's life, or relationships with others, which one chooses to keep from the public eye, or from outside intrusion. It does not include access to public property,

whatever the nature of that property, or the purpose of the access. Furthermore, the mere fact that visits to a certain site play an important role in one's identity, does not transform such visits into part of one's right to privacy. One can think of many activities, such as participation in public worship or in cultural activities, that play important roles in persons' identities in different societies. While interference with such activities may involve violations of articles 18 or 27, it does not constitute interference with one's privacy.

7. We reach the conclusion that there has been no violation of the authors' rights under the Covenant in the present communication with some reluctance. Like the Committee we too are concerned with the failure of the State party to respect a site that has obvious importance in the cultural heritage of the indigenous population of French Polynesia. We believe, however, that this concern does not justify distorting the meaning of the terms family and privacy beyond their ordinary and generally accepted meaning.

An early decision of the European Court of Human Rights was *Noack and others* v. *Germany* (Appl. No. 46346/99, decision (inadmissibility) of 25 May 2000), which concerned the transfer – scheduled to take place at the end of 2002 – of the inhabitants of Horno, a village in the *Land* of Brandenburg near the Polish border. Horno has a population of 350, approximately a third of whom are from the Sorbian minority, of Slav origin. Approximately 20,000 Sorbs (*Sorben*) live in the *Land* of Brandenburg. They have their own language and culture. The inhabitants of Horno were to be transferred to a town some twenty kilometres away because of an expansion of lignite-mining operations in the area. The Court noted that 'for the purposes of Article 8 of the Convention, a minority's way of life is, in principle, entitled to the protection guaranteed for an individual's private life, family life and home (see, among other authorities, *G. and E.* v. *Norway*, applications nos. 9278/81 and 9415/81, decision of the Commission of 3 October 1983, DR 35, p. 30; and *Buckley* v. *United Kingdom*, application no. 20348/92, report of the Commission of 11 January 1995, §64; and *Chapman* v. *United Kingdom*, application no. 27238/95, report of the Commission of 25 October 1999, §65). Independently of the issue of the protection of minority rights – those of the Sorbs in this instance – the Court considers that transferring the population of a village raises a problem under Article 8 of the Convention, since it directly concerns the private lives and homes of the people concerned.' The position according to which Article 8 ECHR protects the rights of minorities was made explicit the following year:

European Court of Human Rights (GC), *Chapman* v. *United Kingdom* (Appl. No. 27238/95), judgment of 18 January 2001:

[The applicant is a Gypsy by birth. Since her birth she has travelled constantly with her family in search of work. When she married, the applicant and her husband continued to live in caravans, stopping for as long as possible on temporary or unofficial sites while he found work as a landscape gardener. They were on the waiting list for a permanent site but were never offered a place. They were constantly moved from place to place by the police and representatives of local authorities. Their four children's education was constantly interrupted because they had to move about. Due to harassment while she led a travelling life, which was detrimental to the health of the family and the education of the children, the applicant bought a piece of land in 1985 with the intention of living on it in a mobile home. The applicant and her family moved on to the land and applied for planning permission. This was to enable the children to attend school immediately. The District Council refused the application for planning permission on 11 September 1986 and served enforcement notices. The appeals lodged against the notices were unsuccessful. There are no local authority sites or private authorized sites in the Three Rivers district, which is defined as a Green Belt area. However, the Government submit that there are local authority and authorized private sites elsewhere in the same county of Hertfordshire, which contains 12 local authority sites which can accommodate 377 caravans. Figures on Gypsy caravans in England from 2000 disclosed that of 13,134 caravans counted, 6,118 were stationed on local authority pitches, 4,500 on privately owned sites and 2,516 on unauthorized sites. Of the latter, 684 Gypsy caravans were being tolerated on land owned by non-Gypsies (mainly local authority land) and 299 Gypsy caravans tolerated on land owned by Gypsies themselves. Of these figures, about 1,500 caravans were therefore on unauthorized and untolerated sites while over 80 per cent of caravans were stationed on authorized sites. The applicant complained that the refusal of planning permission to station caravans on her land and the enforcement measures implemented in respect of her occupation of her land disclosed a violation of Article 8 of the Convention.]

73. The Court considers that the applicant's occupation of her caravan is an integral part of her ethnic identity as a Gypsy, reflecting the long tradition of that minority of following a travelling lifestyle. This is the case even though, under the pressure of development and diverse policies or by their own choice, many Gypsies no longer live a wholly nomadic existence and increasingly settle for long periods in one place in order to facilitate, for example, the education of their children. Measures affecting the applicant's stationing of her caravans therefore have an impact going beyond the right to respect for her home. They also affect her ability to maintain her identity as a Gypsy and to lead her private and family life in accordance with that tradition.

74. The Court finds, therefore, that the applicant's right to respect for her private life, family life and home is in issue in the present case …

78. Having regard to the facts of this case, it finds that the decisions of the planning authorities refusing to allow the applicant to remain on her land in her caravans and the measures of enforcement taken in respect of her continued occupation constituted an interference with her right to respect for her private life, family life and home within the meaning of Article 8 §1 of the Convention. It will therefore examine below whether this interference was justified under paragraph 2 of Article 8 as being 'in accordance with the law', pursuing a legitimate aim or aims and as being 'necessary in a democratic society' in pursuit of that aim or aims …

82. The Court notes that the Government have not put forward any details concerning the aims allegedly pursued in this case and that they rely on a general assertion. It is also apparent that the reasons given for the interference in the planning procedures in this case were expressed primarily in terms of environmental policy. In these circumstances, the Court finds that the measures pursued the legitimate aim of protecting the 'rights of others' through preservation of the environment. It does not find it necessary to determine whether any other aims were involved …

90. An interference will be considered 'necessary in a democratic society' for a legitimate aim if it answers a 'pressing social need' and, in particular, if it is proportionate to the legitimate aim pursued. While it is for the national authorities to make the initial assessment of necessity, the final evaluation as to whether the reasons cited for the interference are relevant and sufficient remains subject to review by the Court for conformity with the requirements of the Convention ...

91. In this regard, a margin of appreciation must, inevitably, be left to the national authorities, who by reason of their direct and continuous contact with the vital forces of their countries are in principle better placed than an international court to evaluate local needs and conditions. This margin will vary according to the nature of the Convention right in issue, its importance for the individual and the nature of the activities restricted, as well as the nature of the aim pursued by the restrictions ...

92. The judgment by the national authorities in any particular case that there are legitimate planning objections to a particular use of a site is one which the Court is not well equipped to challenge. It cannot visit each site to assess the impact of a particular proposal on a particular area in terms of beauty, traffic conditions, sewerage and water facilities, educational facilities, medical facilities, employment opportunities and so on. Because planning inspectors visit the site, hear the arguments on all sides and allow the examination of witnesses, they are better placed than the Court to weigh the arguments. Hence, as the Court observed in *Buckley* (*Buckley* v. *United Kingdom* (judgment of 25 September 1996, *Reports of Judgments and Decisions* 1996–IV), p. 1292, §75 *in fine*), '[i]n so far as the exercise of discretion involving a multitude of local factors is inherent in the choice and implementation of planning policies, the national authorities in principle enjoy a wide margin of appreciation', although it remains open to the Court to conclude that there has been a manifest error of appreciation by the national authorities. In these circumstances, the procedural safeguards available to the individual will be especially material in determining whether the respondent State has, when fixing the regulatory framework, remained within its margin of appreciation. In particular, the Court must examine whether the decision-making process leading to measures of interference was fair and such as to afford due respect to the interests safeguarded to the individual by Article 8 (see *Buckley*, pp. 1292–93, §76).

93. The applicant urged the Court to take into account recent international developments, in particular the Framework Convention for the Protection of National Minorities, in reducing the margin of appreciation accorded to States in light of the recognition of the problems of vulnerable groups, such as Gypsies. The Court observes that there may be said to be an emerging international consensus amongst the Contracting States of the Council of Europe recognising the special needs of minorities and an obligation to protect their security, identity and lifestyle ..., not only for the purpose of safeguarding the interests of the minorities themselves but to preserve a cultural diversity of value to the whole community.

94. However, the Court is not persuaded that the consensus is sufficiently concrete for it to derive any guidance as to the conduct or standards which Contracting States consider desirable in any particular situation. The framework convention, for example, sets out general principles and goals but the signatory States were unable to agree on means of implementation. This reinforces the Court's view that the complexity and sensitivity of the issues involved in policies balancing the interests of the general population, in particular with regard to environmental

protection, and the interests of a minority with possibly conflicting requirements renders the Court's role a strictly supervisory one.

95. Moreover, to accord to a Gypsy who has unlawfully stationed a caravan site at a particular place different treatment from that accorded to non-Gypsies who have established a caravan site at that place or from that accorded to any individual who has established a house in that particular place would raise substantial problems under Article 14 of the Convention.

96. Nonetheless, although the fact of belonging to a minority with a traditional lifestyle different from that of the majority does not confer an immunity from general laws intended to safeguard the assets of the community as a whole, such as the environment, it may have an incidence on the manner in which such laws are to be implemented. As intimated in *Buckley*, the vulnerable position of Gypsies as a minority means that some special consideration should be given to their needs and their different lifestyle both in the relevant regulatory planning framework and in reaching decisions in particular cases (judgment cited above, pp. 1292–95, §§76, 80 and 84). To this extent, there is thus a positive obligation imposed on the Contracting States by virtue of Article 8 to facilitate the Gypsy way of life (see, *mutatis mutandis, Marckx* v. *Belgium*, judgment of 13 June 1979, Series A No. 31, p. 15, §31; *Keegan* v. *Ireland*, judgment of 26 May 1994, Series A No. 290, p. 19, §49; and *Kroon and Others* v. *Netherlands*, judgment of 27 October 1994, Series A No. 297–C, p. 56, §31).

97. It is important to appreciate that, in principle, Gypsies are at liberty to camp on any caravan site which has planning permission; there has been no suggestion that permissions exclude Gypsies as a group. They are not treated worse than any non-Gypsy who wants to live in a caravan and finds it disagreeable to live in a house. However, it appears from the material placed before the Court, including judgments of the English courts, that the provision of an adequate number of sites which the Gypsies find acceptable and on which they can lawfully place their caravans at a price which they can afford is something which has not been achieved.

98. The Court does not, however, accept the argument that, because statistically the number of Gypsies is greater than the number of places available on authorised Gypsy sites, the decision not to allow the applicant Gypsy family to occupy land where they wished in order to install their caravan in itself, and without more, constituted a violation of Article 8. This would be tantamount to imposing on the United Kingdom, as on all the other Contracting States, an obligation by virtue of Article 8 to make available to the Gypsy community an adequate number of suitably equipped sites. The Court is not convinced, despite the undoubted evolution that has taken place in both international law, as evidenced by the framework convention, and domestic legislations in regard to protection of minorities, that Article 8 can be interpreted as implying for States such a far-reaching positive obligation of general social policy (see paragraphs 93–94 above).

99. It is important to recall that Article 8 does not in terms recognise a right to be provided with a home. Nor does any of the jurisprudence of the Court acknowledge such a right. While it is clearly desirable that every human being have a place where he or she can live in dignity and which he or she can call home, there are unfortunately in the Contracting States many persons who have no home. Whether the State provides funds to enable everyone to have a home is a matter for political not judicial decision.

100. In sum, the issue to be determined by the Court in the present case is not the acceptability or not of a general situation, however deplorable, in the United Kingdom in the light

of the United Kingdom's undertakings in international law, but the narrower one of whether the particular circumstances of the case disclose a violation of the applicant's – Mrs Chapman's – right to respect for her home under Article 8 of the Convention.

101. In this connection, the legal and social context in which the impugned measure of expulsion was taken against the applicant is, however, a relevant factor.

102. Where a dwelling has been established without the planning permission which is needed under the national law, there is a conflict of interest between the right of the individual under Article 8 of the Convention to respect for his or her home and the right of others in the community to environmental protection (see paragraph 81 above). When considering whether a requirement that the individual leave his or her home is proportionate to the legitimate aim pursued, it is highly relevant whether or not the home was established unlawfully. If the home was lawfully established, this factor would self-evidently be something which would weigh against the legitimacy of requiring the individual to move. Conversely, if the establishment of the home in a particular place was unlawful, the position of the individual objecting to an order to move is less strong. The Court will be slow to grant protection to those who, in conscious defiance of the prohibitions of the law, establish a home on an environmentally protected site. For the Court to do otherwise would be to encourage illegal action to the detriment of the protection of the environmental rights of other people in the community.

103. A further relevant consideration, to be taken into account in the first place by the national authorities, is that if no alternative accommodation is available the interference is more serious than where such accommodation is available. The more suitable the alternative accommodation is, the less serious is the interference constituted by moving the applicant from his or her existing accommodation.

104. The evaluation of the suitability of alternative accommodation will involve a consideration of, on the one hand, the particular needs of the person concerned – his or her family requirements and financial resources – and, on the other hand, the rights of the local community to environmental protection. This is a task in respect of which it is appropriate to give a wide margin of appreciation to national authorities, who are evidently better placed to make the requisite assessment.

105. The seriousness of what is at stake for the applicant is demonstrated by the facts of this case. The applicant followed an itinerant lifestyle for many years, stopping on temporary or unofficial sites. She took up residence on her own land by way of finding a long-term and secure place to station her caravans. Planning permission for this was refused, however, and she was required to leave. The applicant was fined twice. She left her land, but returned as she had been moved on constantly from place to place. It would appear that the applicant does not in fact wish to pursue an itinerant lifestyle. She was resident on the site from 1986 to 1990, and between 1992 and these proceedings. Thus, the present case is not concerned as such with the traditional itinerant Gypsy lifestyle.

106. It is evident that individuals affected by an enforcement notice have in principle, and this applicant had in practice, a full and fair opportunity to put before the planning inspectors any material which they regard as relevant to their case and in particular their personal financial and other circumstances, their views as to the suitability of alternative sites and the length of time needed to find a suitable alternative site.

107. The Court recalls that the applicant moved on to her land in her caravans without obtaining the prior planning permission which she knew was necessary to render that occupation lawful. In accordance with the applicable procedures, the applicant's appeals against refusal of planning permission and enforcement notices were conducted in two public inquiries by inspectors who were qualified independent experts. In both appeals, the inspectors visited the site themselves and considered the applicant's representations. As is evidenced by the extension of the time-limit for compliance ..., some notice was taken of the points which the applicant advanced.

108. The first inspector had regard to the location of the site in the Metropolitan Green Belt and found that the planning considerations, both national and local, outweighed the needs of the applicant ... The second inspector considered that the use of the site for the stationing of caravans was seriously detrimental to the environment, and would 'detract significantly from the quiet rural character' of the site, which was both in a Green Belt and an Area of Great Landscape Value. He concluded that development of the site would frustrate the purpose of the Green Belt in protecting the countryside from encroachment. The arguments of the applicant did not in his judgment justify overriding these important interests ...

109. Consideration was given to the applicant's arguments, both concerning the work that she had done on the site by tidying and planting and concerning the difficulties of finding other sites in the area. However, both inspectors weighed those factors against the general interest of preserving the rural character of the countryside and found that the latter prevailed.

110. It is clear from the inspectors' reports ... that there were strong, environmental reasons for the refusal of planning permission and that the applicant's personal circumstances had been taken into account in the decision-making process. The Court also notes that appeal to the High Court was available in so far as the applicant felt that the inspectors, or the Secretary of State, had not taken into account a relevant consideration or had based the contested decision on irrelevant considerations.

111. The Court observes that during the planning procedures it was acknowledged that there were no vacant sites immediately available for the applicant to go to, either in the district or in the county as a whole. The Government have pointed out that other sites elsewhere in the county do exist and that the applicant was free to seek sites outside the county. Notwithstanding that the statistics show that there is a shortfall of local authority sites available for Gypsies in the country as a whole, it may be noted that many Gypsy families still live an itinerant life without recourse to official sites and it cannot be doubted that vacancies on official sites arise periodically.

112. Moreover, given that there are many caravan sites with planning permission, whether suitable sites were available to the applicant during the long period of grace given to her was dependent upon what was required of a site to make it suitable. In this context, the cost of a site compared with the applicant's assets, and its location compared with the applicant's desires are clearly relevant. Since how much the applicant has by way of assets, what expenses need to be met by her, what locational requirements are essential for her and why are factors exclusively within the knowledge of the applicant, it is for the applicant to adduce evidence on these matters. She has not placed before the Court any information as to her financial situation or as to the qualities a site must have before it will be locationally suitable for her. Nor does the Court have any information as to the efforts she has made to find alternative sites.

113. The Court is therefore not persuaded that there were no alternatives available to the applicant besides remaining in occupation on land without planning permission in a Green Belt area. As stated in *Buckley*, Article 8 does not necessarily go so far as to allow individuals' preferences as to their place of residence to override the general interest (judgment cited above, p. 1294, §81). If the applicant's problem arises through lack of money, then she is in the same unfortunate position as many others who are not able to afford to continue to reside on sites or in houses attractive to them.

114. In the circumstances, the Court considers that proper regard was had to the applicant's predicament both under the terms of the regulatory framework, which contained adequate procedural safeguards protecting her interests under Article 8 and by the responsible planning authorities when exercising their discretion in relation to the particular circumstances of her case. The decisions were reached by those authorities after weighing in the balance the various competing interests. It is not for this Court to sit in appeal on the merits of those decisions, which were based on reasons which were relevant and sufficient, for the purposes of Article 8, to justify the interferences with the exercise of the applicant's rights.

115. The humanitarian considerations which might have supported another outcome at national level cannot be used as the basis for a finding by the Court which would be tantamount to exempting the applicant from the implementation of the national planning laws and obliging governments to ensure that every Gypsy family has available for its use accommodation appropriate to its needs. Furthermore, the effect of these decisions cannot on the facts of this case be regarded as disproportionate to the legitimate aim pursued.

116. In conclusion, there has been no violation of Article 8 of the Convention.

7.11. Questions for discussion: self-determination, minority rights, and multicultural societies

1. According to the principles exposed above concerning the relationship between internal and external self-determination, were the Kosovars entitled to claim secession from Serbia in 2008? Consider the following view:

Dajena Kumbaro, *The Kosovo Crisis in an International Law Perspective: Self-determination, Territorial Integrity and the NATO Intervention*, prepared for the NATO Office of Information and Press, 16 June 2001, pp. 47–8:

The Kosovo Albanians as a group are entitled to the right to self-determination for the reason that they traditionally lived and continue to do so in a distinct territory with clearly defined borders. They have persistently cultivated and preserved their own ethnic identity through the development of their language, customs and traditions, and by practising their religion, in defiance of the systematic repression consistently exerted by the Serbian authorities.

For almost a decade, the Kosovo Albanians truly believed and advocated for a peaceful solution of the crisis in conformity with their right to self-determination, while continuously and steadily being subject to Serbian authorities' ethnic oppression. The outbreak of the war in

Kosovo completely destroyed this delusive equilibrium, and triggered the urgent need for a political settlement of the crisis.

The recent state practice has demonstrated and confirmed that peaceful changes of borders are already a possibility, such as the dissolution of Soviet Union, or Czechoslovakia. On the other hand, state practice has also recognised the legitimacy of secessionist movements performed through violent attempts to gain effective control over a territory, such as the cases of the secession of Eritrea from Ethiopia, the dissolution of Yugoslavia, and the relative success of the secessionist movement in Chechnya.

The fear that the recognition of a right to secession of Kosovo Albanians would open a Pandora's Box of problems related to other secessionist claims, could not be an argument *per se* against the Kosovo Albanians claim for independence. Each secessionist claim has its individuality and distinct features. Furthermore, the complete inconsistent state practice with regard to secession, even if the Kosovar Albanians claim is upheld and subsequently recognised, is genuinely not very encouraging. The support of the Kosovo Albanians right to self-determination, is relied upon the interpretation of the Saving Clause of the Declaration on Friendly Relations that, at a last resort, though debated, recognises a right to external self-determination if a people is completely denied from meaningfully exerting the right to self-determination internally. The exercise of the right to self-determination of the Kosovo Albanians grounds in the establishment of an occupation like situation in Kosovo featured by a long period of oppression by the Serbian regime. It encompassed the infliction of systematic and gross human rights violations against the ethnic Albanians, their complete expulsion from Kosovo's public life, the thorough frustration of their political, economic, social and cultural development. In addition, the attacks against their physical existence amounting to the performance of ethnic cleansing practices through indiscriminate and deliberate violence exerted by the Serb forces against ethnic Albanian civilians ...

2. Has the absence of a generally agreed upon definition of 'minorities' in international law constituted an obstacle, in practice, to the protection of the rights of minorities or of the persons belonging to minorities? Is the approach proposed by the EU Network of Independent Experts on Fundamental Rights plausible?

3. The debates about the desirability of recognizing the existence of minorities with distinct rights to the preservation of their identity against the pressure to integrate have often revolved around the opposition between liberalism and communitarianism. For communitarians such as Alasdair MacIntyre, Michael Sandel, Michael Walzer or Charles Taylor, individualist views of society are wrong to postulate a fictitious 'unencumbered self', detached from community affiliations; and the procedural approaches to justice that liberals put forward – essentially, that liberal societies should develop procedures that can be neutral towards competing views of the 'good life' – are simply implausible, since we cannot simply shed off the values we inherit and the universe of social norms we inhabit. For instance, while John Rawls, an early and prominent representative of the liberal view, posits an 'ignorance veil' at the basis of his political philosophy, stating that any just society should be built upon principles that we would arrive at should we ignore the position we would occupy within that society (J. Rawls, *A Theory of Justice* (Cambridge,

Mass.: Harvard University Press, 1971)), Walzer remarks: 'Even if they are committed to impartiality, the question most likely to arise in the minds of the members of a political community is not, "What should rational individuals choose under universalizing conditions of such-and-such a sort?" but rather "What would individuals like us choose, who are situated as we are, who share a culture and are determined to go on sharing it?" And this is a question that is readily transformed into "What choices have we already made in the course of our common life? What understandings do we (really) share?" Justice is a human construction, and it is doubtful that it can be made only one way' (M. Walzer, *Spheres of Justice. A Defence of Pluralism and Equality* (Oxford: Martin Robertson, 1983), p 5). On the other side of the debate, the liberals retort that a communitarian approach risks either locking individuals into a fixed identity, or justifying the imposition of the norms of the majority on the historically marginalized groups.

3.1. In your view, on which side of the debate between liberals and communitarians could a human rights approach be situated? Do human rights serve to protect collective identities forged by cultural, religious or moral norms, or do they instead put such norms into question, by imposing that they pass the test of human rights? If they do both, could you argue that human rights are neutral towards different cultures, or instead favour one culture over the other? Relate this to the examples seen in chapter 3, section 3.5., where the issue of restrictions to religious freedom through vestimentary codes was examined. Consider also the view expressed by W. Kymlicka, who writes in the vein of multiculturalism, and attempts to move beyond the liberal/communitarian debate: 'Government decisions on languages, internal boundaries, public holidays, and state symbols unavoidably involve recognizing, accommodating, and supporting the needs and identities of particular ethnic and national groups. The state unavoidably promotes certain cultural identities, and thereby disadvantages others' (W. Kymlicka, *Multicultural Citizenship. A Liberal Theory of Minority Rights* (Oxford: Clarendon Press, 1995), p. 108).

3.2. Some writers have proposed 'critical multiculturalism' as a way to accommodate difference in liberal societies: 'Critical multiculturalism seeks to use cultural diversity as a basis for challenging, revising, and relativizing basic notions and principles common to dominant and minority cultures alike, so as to construct a more vital, open, and democratic common culture' (T. Turner, 'Anthropology and Multiculturalism: What is Anthropology that Multiculturalists Should be Mindful of It?', *Cultural Anthropology*, 8, No. 4 (1993), 411). Do you agree? Are human rights an asset or a liability in the promotion of a 'critical multiculturalism' thus conceived?

4.1. As we have seen in chapter 7, the requirement of non-discrimination has a number of ramifications, from the prohibition of direct discrimination to the imposition of positive action. Keeping in mind the meaning of the requirement of non-discrimination, how do you evaluate the views expressed by the Human Rights Committee in *Ballantyne, Davidson, McIntyre* v. *Canada*? Is the decision defensible as a means to ensure that the francophone minority in Canada shall be able to preserve its linguistic identity?

4.2. Could you relate the previous question to the question of self-determination as discussed by the Canadian Supreme Court in the *Secession of Quebec* case? Consider the following view: 'there is growing acceptance that, for real equality to be achieved for [groups that are ethnically or culturally distinct within the State], measures of a collective kind may be necessary. These can include measures of local autonomy, provisions for separate representation in legislative and executive bodies at central or regional level, land rights (especially in the case of indigenous groups with historical links to areas of land) and so on. The state's acknowledged interest in territorial integrity does not require the subjection of distinct groups within the state to a unitary government dominated by an ethnically defined majority. On the contrary, "arithmetical" equality in such cases may involved a denial to a minority group of any adequate way of life other than that of assimilation into the majority group – in effect, a denial of their right to respect' (J. Crawford, 'The Right to Self-determination in International Law: Its Development and Future' in P. Alston (ed), *Peoples' Rights* (Oxford University Press, 2001), p. 7 at p. 65).

5. Is there a difference between protecting the rights of minorities and protecting the rights of the (individual) members of minorities? Can the latter be achieved without the former? Consider in this respect para. 6.2. of the Human Rights Committee's General Comment No. 23 on *The Rights of Minorities*. Consider also Article 3 of the Framework Convention for the Protection of National Minorities, that states that 'Every person belonging to a national minority shall have the right freely to choose to be treated or not to be treated as such and no disadvantage shall result from this choice or from the exercise of the rights which are connected to that choice' (para. 1) and adds that 'Persons belonging to national minorities may exercise the rights and enjoy the freedoms flowing from the principles enshrined in the present framework Convention individually as well as in community with others' (para. 2). The Explanatory Report states that 'no collective rights of national minorities are envisaged' (para. 31), and that the wording of Article 3 should not be interpreted otherwise. What are the implications of this distinction?

PART III

The Mechanisms of Protection

8

Ensuring Compliance with International Human Rights Law: The Role of National Authorities

INTRODUCTION

Since the general framework of international human rights law has been built in the 1960s to the 1980s, a new generation of questions has arisen, which focuses more on the effectiveness of that framework and, particularly, on its impact at national level. The role of national authorities is vital in this respect. International human rights can only be effective on the ground, where they really matter, if national courts, parliaments, and governments rely on them, and if civil society mobilizes in order to hold authorities accountable on that basis (see, e.g. D. Beyleveld, 'The Concept of a Human Right and Incorporation of the European Convention on Human Rights', (1995) *Public Law*, 577; C. Heyns and F. Viljoen, *The Impact of the United Nations Human Rights Treaties on the Domestic Level* (The Hague: Kluwer Law International, 2002); O. Schachter, 'The Obligation to Implement the Covenant in Domestic Law' in L. Henkin (ed.), *The International Bill of Rights. The Covenant on Civil and Political Rights* (New York: Columbia University Press, 1981), p. 311; on the role of national courts in applying international human rights, see B. Conforti and F. Francioni (eds.), *Enforcing International Human Rights in Domestic Courts* (The Hague: Martinus Nijhoff, 1997)).

Pressure from below is especially important since neither foreign governments, nor international actors, can substitute for the role of local actors. As we have seen, international human rights treaties are specific in that they are concluded not in the interest of the parties, but for the benefit of the population under the jurisdiction of the parties. As noted by Louis Henkin, the implication is that 'the principal element of horizontal deterrence is missing': 'the threat that "if you violate the human rights of your inhabitants, we will violate the human rights of our inhabitants" hardly serves as a deterrent' (L. Henkin, 'International Law: Politics, Values and Functions', *Recueil des cours*, 216 (1989), at 253). Or, as Oona Hathaway puts it: '... a nation's actions against its own citizens do not directly threaten or harm other states. Human rights law thus stands out as an area of international law in which countries have little incentive to police non-compliance with treaties or norms' (O. A. Hathaway, 'Do Human Rights Treaties Make a Difference', *Yale Law Journal*, 111 (2002), 1935 at 1938). Nor are other international actors, such as foreign non-governmental organizations or international organizations, in a position to compel compliance effectively, either because they lack the incentives to do so, or because they cannot access the information they would require to act effectively. Indeed, Hathaway argues that the ratification of human rights treaties essentially serves a symbolic – or expressive – function, sending a message that the State concerned wishes to be considered a trustworthy partner, but that it otherwise makes no difference in the reality of the lives of people living on the territory of that State. Thus, internalization is essential: it can compensate for the weaknesses of the international regime in bringing about compliance with the international obligations a State has agreed to upon ratifying a treaty.

This chapter examines how the national authorities can contribute to the implementation of the obligations imposed under international human rights law. A first section examines the measures which States may adopt, and in certain cases are obliged to adopt, in order to ensure that they will not violate international human rights treaties to which they are parties. Their basic obligation in this regard is to provide effective remedies to victims of human rights violations (see, generally, D. Shelton, *Remedies in International Human Rights Law*, second edn (Oxford University Press, 2005), particularly chapter 2 on remedies before national courts). While the principle of this obligation is relatively uncontested, its extension to economic and social rights – those enumerated, for instance, in the International Covenant on Economic, Social and Cultural Rights (ICESCR), in the European Social Charter (ESC), or in the Additional (San Salvador) Protocol to the American Convention on Human Rights on Economic, Social and Cultural Rights (ACHR) – still remains controversial, as illustrated by the current debates on the 'justiciability' of rights belonging to this category (see, in particular, opposing the justiciability of economic and social rights, A. Neier, 'Social and Economic Rights: a Critique', *Human Rights Brief* 13-2 (2006), 1–3; G. Rosenberg, *The Hollow Hope: Can Courts Bring About Social Change?* (University of Chicago Press, 1991); C. Tomuschat, 'An Optional Protocol for the International Covenant on Economic, Social and Cultural Rights?' in *Weltinnenrecht. Liber amicorum Jost Delbrück* (Berlin: Duncker & Humblot, 2005), pp. 815–834). The first section offers a number of illustrations of the tools national courts may use in order to ensure the justiciability of economic and social rights.

However, even where they also benefit economic and social rights, remedies provided to victims of violations may not be sufficient. First, it would not be acceptable for States to avoid having their international responsibility engaged simply by providing, on a case-by-case basis, a reparation to victims, without removing the structural causes of such violations and, thus, adopting the necessary measures to avoid their repetition. Second, there are a number of weaknesses inherent in litigation as a means of ensuring that human rights violations will not be committed. Courts are dependent on the applications they receive. Therefore, in certain cases, for example where the violations are widespread but only minimally affect each individual concerned, where they are committed without the individuals ever being aware of them – as in the case of the imposition of secret surveillance measures – or where individuals have reasons to fear reprisals if they file an application before a court, judicial mechanisms may prove ineffective. In addition, courts are ill-equipped to deal with general issues, which concern a collectivity of individuals or general policies: the case they are presented with may not be representative of the full range of situations concerned by the same problem; the impact of any particular decision on other individuals, in a situation similar or not to that of the private litigant, may be difficult to anticipate; jurisdictions may have neither the expertise nor the legitimacy to deal with issues which, for instance, raise questions about how the public budgets are spent, or how choices are made between conflicting priorities. For both these reasons, judicial remedies may have to be complemented by other, non-judicial mechanisms, which will ensure that the law- and policy-making in a State will comply with its obligations under the human rights treaties to which it is a party. The second section of this chapter, therefore, examines which non-judicial tools States should put in place in order to ensure the effective protection of human rights.

1 JUDICIAL REMEDIES

1.1 The general requirement to provide effective remedies

It is a general requirement that States provide effective remedies to individuals whose rights have been violated. Under Article 2 para. 3 of the International Covenant for Civil and Polticial Rights (ICCPR) for instance,

Each State Party to the present Covenant undertakes:

(a) To ensure that any person whose rights or freedoms as herein recognized are violated shall have an effective remedy, notwithstanding that the violation has been committed by persons acting in an official capacity;

(b) To ensure that any person claiming such a remedy shall have his right thereto determined by competent judicial, administrative or legislative authorities, or by any other competent authority provided for by the legal system of the State, and to develop the possibilities of judicial remedy;

(c) To ensure that the competent authorities shall enforce such remedies when granted.

The implications of this provision have been described as follows by the Human Rights Committee:

Human Rights Committee, General Comment No. 31, *The Nature of the General Legal Obligation Imposed on States Parties to the Covenant* (29 March 2004):

15. Article 2, paragraph 3, requires that in addition to effective protection of Covenant rights States Parties must ensure that individuals also have accessible and effective remedies to

vindicate those rights. Such remedies should be appropriately adapted so as to take account of the special vulnerability of certain categories of persons, including in particular children. The Committee attaches importance to States Parties establishing appropriate judicial and administrative mechanisms for addressing claims of rights violations under domestic law. The Committee notes that the enjoyment of the rights recognized under the Covenant can be effectively assured by the judiciary in many different ways, including direct applicability of the Covenant, application of comparable constitutional or other provisions of law, or the interpretive effect of the Covenant in the application of national law. Administrative mechanisms are particularly required to give effect to the general obligation to investigate allegations of violations promptly, thoroughly and effectively through independent and impartial bodies. National human rights institutions, endowed with appropriate powers, can contribute to this end. A failure by a State Party to investigate allegations of violations could in and of itself give rise to a separate breach of the Covenant. Cessation of an ongoing violation is an essential element of the right to an effective remedy.

16. Article 2, paragraph 3, requires that States Parties make reparation to individuals whose Covenant rights have been violated. Without reparation to individuals whose Covenant rights have been violated, the obligation to provide an effective remedy, which is central to the efficacy of article 2, paragraph 3, is not discharged. In addition to the explicit reparation required by articles 9, paragraph 5, and 14, paragraph 6, the Committee considers that the Covenant generally entails appropriate compensation. The Committee notes that, where appropriate, reparation can involve restitution, rehabilitation and measures of satisfaction, such as public apologies, public memorials, guarantees of non-repetition and changes in relevant laws and practices, as well as bringing to justice the perpetrators of human rights violations.

Despite the absence of a clause similar to Article 2 para. 3 ICCPR in the Convention on the Rights of the Child, the Committee on the Rights of the Child stated:

Committee on the Rights of the Child, General Comment No. 5 (2003), *General Measures of Implementation of the Convention on the Rights of the Child* (Arts. 4, 42 and 44, para. 6) (CRC/GC/2003/5, 27 November 2003), paras. 24–5:

For rights to have meaning, effective remedies must be available to redress violations. This requirement is implicit in the Convention and consistently referred to in the other six major international human rights treaties. Children's special and dependent status creates real difficulties for them in pursuing remedies for breaches of their rights. So States need to give particular attention to ensuring that there are effective, child-sensitive procedures available to children and their representatives. These should include the provision of child-friendly information, advice, advocacy, including support for self-advocacy, and access to independent complaints procedures and to the courts with necessary legal and other assistance. Where rights are found to have been breached, there should be appropriate reparation, including compensation, and, where needed, measures to promote physical and psychological recovery, rehabilitation and reintegration, as required by article 39 [CRC] ..., the Committee emphasizes that economic, social and cultural rights, as well as civil and political rights, must be regarded as justiciable. It is essential that domestic law sets out entitlements in sufficient detail to enable remedies for non-compliance to be effective.

The requirement to provide effective remedies to victims of human rights violations is also stipulated in regional human rights instruments, but with certain variations. Although its wording is otherwise very close to that of Article 2(3) ICCPR, Article 25 ACHR goes much further. It guarantees a right to an effective judicial remedy to the individual whose fundamental rights are violated, not only under the ACHR, but also under the domestic constitution: 'Everyone has the right to simple and prompt recourse, or any other effective recourse, to a competent court or tribunal for protection against acts that violate his fundamental rights recognized by the constitution or laws of the state concerned or by this Convention, even though such violation may have been committed by persons acting in the course of their official duties' (Art. 25 para. 1 ACHR). This autonomous right to an effective remedy where fundamental rights are violated complements specific guarantees under the habeas corpus clause of Article 7 para. 6 ACHR (see generally E. Davidson, 'Remedies for Violations of the American Convention on Human Rights', *International and Comparative Law Quarterly* (1995), 405; on the case below see P. Macklem and E. Morgan, 'Indigenous Rights in the Inter-American System: the Amicus Brief of the Assembly of First Nations in *Awas Tingni* v. *Republic of Nicaragua*', *Human Rights Quarterly*, 22, No. 2 (2000), 569). The following case illustrates how the requirement of an effective remedy is interpreted, in line with the broader obligations of the States parties to the ACHR under Articles 1 and 2:

Inter-American Court of Human Rights, *Mayagna (Sumo) Awas Tingni Community* v. *Nicaragua*, judgment of 31 August 2001 [2001] I.A.C.H.R. Petition No. 11,577:

[The Mayagna Awas Tingni Community (the Community) of the North Atlantic Autonomous Region filed a petition against Nicaragua under the American Convention on Human Rights with the Inter-American Commission on Human Rights in October 1995. According to the petition, the State was about to grant Sol del Caribe, SA (SOLCARSA), a Korean company, a concession to commence logging on Awas Tingni communal lands. In parallel proceedings, the Community brought its claims before the Nicaraguan courts. This resulted in a judgment by the Constitutional Court of the Supreme Court of Justice, ordering the logging to be stopped. The logging, however, continued despite the judgment.

In November 1997, the petitioners further stated to the Commission that the central element of the petition was Nicaragua's lack of protection of the rights of the community to its ancestral lands, and that this situation still persisted. Furthermore, they requested that the Commission issue a report in accordance with Article 50 of the Convention, which allows the Commission to state its conclusions when settlement cannot be reached and sets the stage for referral to the Inter-American Court of Human Rights (the Court).

The Commission concluded in favour of the Community. It made an application to the Court in June 1998 on the grounds that Nicaragua had not acted to demarcate the Community's land and to compensate it for lost resources. The Commission further stated that Nicaragua had not adopted effective measures to ensure the property rights of the Community to its ancestral lands and natural resources and that the State did not ensure an effective remedy in response to the Community's protests regarding its property rights. The Commission requested from the Court declarations that the State must establish a legal procedure to allow rapid demarcation and official recognition of the property rights of the Community, and must abstain from granting or considering the granting of any concessions used and occupied by the Community until the issue of land tenure has been resolved. The Commission also requested that the State be required to pay equitable compensation for damages suffered by the Community, as well as costs incurred in prosecuting the case under domestic jurisdiction and before the inter-American system.]

111. The Court has noted that article 25 of the Convention has established, in broad terms: 'the obligation of the States to offer, to all persons under their jurisdiction, effective legal remedy against acts that violate their fundamental rights. It also establishes that the right protected therein applies not only to rights included in the Convention, but also to those recognized by the Constitution or the law' [see Judicial Guarantees in States of Emergency (Arts 27.2, 25 and 8 ACHR) Advisory Opinion OC–9/87 of 6 October 1987, Series A No. 9, para 23].

112. The Court has also reiterated that the right of every person to simple and rapid remedy or to any other effective remedy before the competent judges or courts, to protect them against acts which violate their fundamental rights, 'is one of the basic mainstays, not only of the American Convention, but also of the Rule of Law in a democratic society, in the sense set forth in the Convention' [see *Bámaca Velásquez* case, judgment of 25 November 2000, Series C No. 70, para 191].

113. The Court has also pointed out that the inexistence of an effective recourse against the violation of the rights recognized by the Convention constitutes a transgression of the Convention by the State Party in which such a situation occurs. In that respect, it should be emphasized that, for such a recourse to exist, it is not enough that it is established in the Constitution or in the law or that it should be formally admissible, but it must be truly appropriate to establish whether there has been a violation of human rights and to provide everything necessary to remedy it [*Cantoral Benavides* case, judgment of 18 August 2000, Series C No. 69, para 164].

114. This Court has further stated that for the State to comply with the provisions of the aforementioned article, it is not enough for the remedies to exist formally, since they must also be effective [*Cesti Hurtado* case, judgment of 29 September 1999, Series C No. 56, para 125] ...

135. Furthermore, the Court has already said that article 25 of the Convention is closely linked to the general obligation of article 1(1) of the Convention, which assigns protective functions to domestic law in the States Party, and therefore the State has the responsibility to designate an effective remedy and to reflect it in norms, as well as to ensure due application of that remedy by its judicial authorities.

136. Along these same lines, the Court has expressed that '[t]he general duty under article 2 of the American Convention involves adopting protective measures in two directions. On the one hand, suppressing norms and practices of any type that carry with them the violation

of guarantees set forth in the convention. On the other hand, issuing norms and developing practices which are conducive to effective respect for such guarantees.'

137. As stated before, in this case Nicaragua has not adopted the adequate domestic legal measures to allow delimitation, demarcation, and titling of Indigenous community lands, nor did it process the amparo [alleging a violation of fundamental rights] remedy filed by members of the Awas Tingni Community within a reasonable time.

Article 13 of the European Convention on Human Rights is narrower in scope than Article 25 ACHR. It states that 'Everyone whose rights and freedoms as set forth in this Convention are violated shall have an effective remedy before a national authority notwithstanding that the violation has been committed by persons acting in an official capacity.' The European Court of Human Rights considers that 'where an individual has an arguable claim to be a victim of a violation of the rights set forth in the Convention, he should have a remedy before a national authority in order both to have his claim decided and, if appropriate, to obtain redress' (Eur. Ct. H.R., *Silver and others* v. *United Kingdom*, judgment of 25 March 1983, Series A No. 61, §113; Eur. Ct. H.R., *Leander* v. *Sweden*, judgment of 26 March 1987, Series A No. 116, §77). Since the claim needs to be 'arguable', not every grievance based on the Convention requires access to a remedy in domestic law, however unmeritorious; on the other hand, the requirement of an effective remedy has an autonomous function to fulfil, and it may be violated even if no other substantive right appears violated: the right to an effective remedy must be understood as a right of the individual to have access to a procedure for the determination of the merits of the claim made under the Convention, unless the allegation of violation is totally without any plausible foundation. The right to an effective remedy does not guarantee a remedy allowing a Contracting State's laws as such to be challenged before a national authority on the ground of being contrary to the Convention or equivalent domestic norms (Eur. Ct. H.R., *James and others* v. *United Kingdom*, judgment of 21 February 1986, Series A No. 98, §85); nor does it require access to a *judicial* remedy, since other remedies may present the required effectiveness, provided the authority before which they are filed has the competence to put an end to the violation and provided it is independent from the author of the measure that is allegedly causing the violation. The Court summarizes its interpretation of the requirement of an effective remedy as follows:

European Court of Human Rights (3rd sect.), *Čonka* v. *Belgium* (Appl. No. 51564/99) judgment of 5 February 2002, para. 75:

Article 13 of the Convention guarantees the availability at national level of a remedy to enforce the substance of the Convention rights and freedoms in whatever form they may happen to be secured in the domestic legal order. The effect of Article 13 is thus to require the provision of a domestic remedy to deal with the substance of an 'arguable complaint' under the Convention and to grant appropriate relief. The scope of the Contracting States' obligations under Article 13 varies depending on the nature of the applicant's complaint; however, the remedy required by Article 13 must be 'effective' in practice as well as in law. The 'effectiveness' of a 'remedy' within the meaning of Article 13 does not depend on the certainty of a favourable outcome for the applicant. Nor does the 'authority' referred to in that provision necessarily have to be a judicial authority; but if it is not, its powers and the guarantees which it affords are relevant in determining whether the remedy before it is effective. Also, even if a single remedy does not by itself entirely satisfy the requirements of Article 13, the aggregate of remedies provided for under domestic law may do so.

Effective remedies at domestic level should ensure that human rights violations find their solution at that level, without it being necessary to rely on the European machinery of protection: thus, only in exceptional cases – where the national authorities, in particular courts, fail to understand their obligations under the Convention or to act accordingly – should the European Court of Human Rights be called upon to intervene. The provision of effective remedies thus has a crucial function to fulfil in a system that emphasizes subsidiarity, according to which the primary responsibility for implementing and enforcing the guaranteed rights and freedoms is laid on the national authorities (Eur. Ct. H.R. (GC), *Kudła* v. *Poland* (Appl. No. 30210/96), judgment of 26 October 2000, §152). The need to strengthen effective remedies at national level is thus particularly important in a context in which, as under the ECHR, the international judicial supervisory mechanism is overburdened. The Committee of Ministers of the Council of Europe has therefore sought to build on the case law of the European Court of Human Rights to address the following recommendation to the Council of Europe Member States:

Committee of Ministers of the Council of Europe, Recommendation Rec(2004)6 of the Committee of Ministers to Member States on the improvement of domestic remedies (adopted by the Committee of Ministers on 12 May 2004, at its 114th session):

The Committee of Ministers, [r]ecalling the subsidiary character of the supervision mechanism set up by the Convention, which implies, in accordance with its Article 1, that the rights and freedoms guaranteed by the Convention be protected in the first place at national level and applied by national authorities;

Welcoming in this context that the Convention has now become an integral part of the domestic legal order of all states parties;

Emphasising that, as required by Article 13 of the Convention, member states undertake to ensure that any individual who has an arguable complaint concerning the violation of his rights and freedoms as set forth in the Convention has an effective remedy before a national authority;

Recalling that in addition to the obligation of ascertaining the existence of such effective remedies in the light of the case law of the European Court of Human Rights (hereinafter referred to as 'the Court'), states have the general obligation to solve the problems underlying violations found;

Emphasising that it is for member states to ensure that domestic remedies are effective in law and in practice, and that they can result in a decision on the merits of a complaint and adequate redress for any violation found;

Noting that the nature and the number of applications lodged with the Court and the judgments it delivers show that it is more than ever necessary for the member states to ascertain efficiently and regularly that such remedies do exist in all circumstances, in particular in cases of unreasonable length of judicial proceedings;

Considering that the availability of effective domestic remedies for all arguable claims of violation of the Convention should permit a reduction in the Court's workload as a result, on the one hand, of the decreasing number of cases reaching it and, on the other hand, of the fact that the detailed treatment of the cases at national level would make their later examination by the Court easier;

Emphasising that the improvement of remedies at national level, particularly in respect of repetitive cases, should also contribute to reducing the workload of the Court;

Recommends that member states, taking into account the examples of good practice appearing in the appendix:

I. ascertain, through constant review, in the light of case law of the Court, that domestic remedies exist for anyone with an arguable complaint of a violation of the Convention, and that these remedies are effective, in that they can result in a decision on the merits of the complaint and adequate redress for any violation found;

II. review, following Court judgments which point to structural or general deficiencies in national law or practice, the effectiveness of the existing domestic remedies and, where necessary, set up effective remedies, in order to avoid repetitive cases being brought before the Court;

III. pay particular attention, in respect of aforementioned items I and II, to the existence of effective remedies in cases of an arguable complaint concerning the excessive length of judicial proceedings ...

Appendix to Recommendation Rec(2004)6
Introduction

1. [It] is states parties who are primarily responsible for ensuring that the rights and freedoms laid down in the Convention are observed and that they must provide the legal instruments needed to prevent violations and, where necessary, to redress them. This necessitates, in particular, the setting-up of effective domestic remedies for all violations of the Convention, in accordance with its Article 13. The case law of the European Court of Human Rights has clarified the scope of this obligation which is incumbent on the states parties to the Convention by indicating notably that:

   – Article 13 guarantees the availability in domestic law of a remedy to secure the rights and freedoms as set forth by the Convention.
   – this article has the effect of requiring a remedy to deal with the substance of any 'arguable claim' under the Convention and to grant appropriate redress. The scope of this obligation

varies depending on the nature of the complaint. However, the remedy required must be 'effective' in law as well as in practice;

– this notably requires that it be able to prevent the execution of measures which are contrary to the Convention and whose effects are potentially irreversible;

– the 'authority' referred to in Article 13 does not necessarily have to be a judicial authority, but if it is not, its powers and the guarantees which it affords are relevant in determining whether the remedy it provides is indeed effective;

– the 'effectiveness' of a 'remedy' within the meaning of Article 13 does not depend on the certainty of a favourable outcome for the applicant; but it implies a certain minimum requirement of speediness.

2. In the recent past, the importance of having such remedies with regard to unreasonably long proceedings has been particularly emphasised, as this problem is at the origin of a great number of applications before the Court, though it is not the only problem.

3. The Court is confronted with an ever-increasing number of applications. This situation jeopardises the long-term effectiveness of the system and therefore calls for a strong reaction from contracting parties. It is precisely within this context that the availability of effective domestic remedies becomes particularly important. The improvement of available domestic remedies will most probably have quantitative and qualitative effects on the workload of the Court:

– on the one hand, the volume of applications to be examined ought to be reduced: fewer applicants would feel compelled to bring the case before the Court if the examination of their complaints before the domestic authorities was sufficiently thorough;

– on the other hand, the examination of applications by the Court will be facilitated if an examination of the merits of cases has been carried out beforehand by a domestic authority, thanks to the improvement of domestic remedies.

4. This recommendation therefore encourages member states to examine their respective legal systems in the light of the case law of the Court and to take, if need be, the necessary and appropriate measures to ensure, through legislation or case law, effective remedies as secured by Article 13. The examination may take place regularly or following a judgment by the Court.

5. The governments of member states might, initially, request that experts carry out a study of the effectiveness of existing domestic remedies in specific areas with a view to proposing improvements. National institutions for the promotion and protection of human rights, as well as non-governmental organisations, might also usefully participate in this work. The availability and effectiveness of domestic remedies should be kept under constant review, and in particular should be examined when drafting legislation affecting Convention rights and freedoms. There is an obvious connection between this recommendation and the recommendation on the verification of the compatibility of draft laws, existing laws and administrative practice with the standards laid down in the Convention.

6. Within the framework of the above, the following considerations might be taken into account.

The Convention as an integral part of the domestic legal order

7. A primary requirement for an effective remedy to exist is that the Convention rights be secured within the national legal system. In this context, it is a welcome development that the Convention has now become an integral part of the domestic legal orders of all states parties.

This development has improved the availability of effective remedies. It is further assisted by the fact that courts and executive authorities increasingly respect the case law of the Court in the application of domestic law, and are conscious of their obligation to abide by judgments of the Court in cases directly concerning their state (see Article 46 of the Convention) ...

8. The improvement of domestic remedies also requires that additional action be taken so that, when applying national law, national authorities may take into account the requirements of the Convention ... This notably means improving the publication and dissemination of the Court's case law (where necessary by translating it into the national language(s) of the state concerned) and the training, with regard to these requirements, of judges and other state officials ...

Specific remedies and general remedy

9. Most domestic remedies for violations of the Convention have been set up with a targeted scope of application. If properly construed and implemented, experience shows that such systems of 'specific remedies' can be very efficient and limit both the number of complaints to the Court and the number of cases requiring a time-consuming examination.

10. Some states have also introduced a general remedy (for example before the Constitutional Court) which can be used to deal with complaints which cannot be dealt with through the specific remedies available. In some member states, this general remedy may also be exercised in parallel with or even before other legal remedies are exhausted ... [S]tates which have such a general remedy tend to have fewer cases before the Court.

11. This being said, it is for member states to decide which system is most suited to ensuring the necessary protection of Convention rights, taking into consideration their constitutional traditions and particular circumstances.

12. Whatever the choice, present experience testifies that there are still shortcomings in many member states concerning the availability and/or effectiveness of domestic remedies, and that consequently there is an increasing workload for the Court.

8.1. Questions for discussion: providing effective remedies before national authorities

1. In principle, international law only imposes obligations of result on States, rather than obligations of conduct: it leaves it to each State to designate which measures shall be taken, and by which organ, in order to implement its international obligations. Consistent with this principle, the obligation to provide effective remedies formulated under international human rights treaties is not generally interpreted as imposing on the States parties an obligation to recognize the provisions of those treaties as directly applicable by national courts, i.e. to implement their obligations by 'direct incorporation' of those provisions. Thus for example, the European Court of Human Rights considers that 'Article 13 of the Convention guarantees the availability at national level of a remedy to enforce the substance of the Convention rights and freedoms *in whatever form they may happen to be secured in the domestic legal order*'; and the Human Rights Committee states in its General Comment No. 31 that 'the enjoyment of the rights recognized

under the Covenant can be effectively assured by the judiciary *in many different ways, including direct applicability of the Covenant, application of comparable constitutional or other provisions of law, or the interpretive effect of the Covenant in the application of national law'*. Is this a mistake? Should direct incorporation of international human rights be seen as inherent in the right to an effective remedy?

2. The European Court of Human Rights considers that the notion of an effective remedy under Article 13 ECHR requires that the remedy may prevent the execution of measures that are contrary to the Convention and whose effects are potentially irreversible (Eur. Ct. H.R. (3rd sect.), *Conka* v. *Belgium* (Appl. No. 51564/99), judgment of 5 February 2002, para. 79). In those cases, it may be inconsistent with Article 13 for such measures to be executed before the national authorities have examined whether they are compatible with the Convention. In which circumstances should the execution of measures alleged to result in violations of the Convention be considered to produce 'irreversible' consequences? Should this be limited to instances where a foreigner is facing removal from the national territory, or should it apply to a much larger set of situations?

1.2 The question of the justiciability of economic and social rights

The main question regarding the provision of effective remedies concerns the justiciability of economic and social rights (for general studies, see F. Coomans (ed.), *Justiciability of Economic and Social Rights. Experiences from Domestic Systems* (Antwerp-Oxford: Intersentia-Hart, 2006); M. Langford (ed.), *Social Rights Jurisprudence: Emerging Trends in International and Comparative Law* (Cambridge University Press, 2009); F. Matscher (ed.), *The Implementation of Economic and Social Rights: National, International and Comparative Aspects* (Kehl am Rhein: N. P. Engel, 1991); and the contributions of M. Scheinin, 'Economic, Social and Cultural Rights as Legal Rights' and S. Liebenberg, 'The Protection of Economic and Social Rights in Domestic Legal Systems' in A. Eide, C. Krause and A. Rosas, *Economic, Social and Cultural Rights. A Textbook*, second edn (Leiden: Martinus Nijhoff, 2001), p. 29 and p. 55 respectively; for a set of materials illustrating the use of economic, social and cultural rights before courts, see B. G. Ramcharan (ed.), *Judicial Protection of Economic, Social and Cultural Rights* (Leiden: Martinus Nijhoff, 2005)).

(a) Challenges to the justiciability of social and economic rights

1. The justiciability of these rights has traditionally been contested on three distinct grounds. The classical argument, as formulated by Bossuyt and Vierdag, and recently revived by Dennis and Stewart, is that economic and social rights are indeterminate: they are not sufficiently well defined in order to lend themselves to be adjudicated, and the judge would necessarily act arbitrarily – making the law rather than applying it – by seeking to provide meaning to those rights. By adjudicating social and economic rights, jurisdictions would be exceeding their powers under a classical

understanding of separation of powers: courts should leave it to the legislature or to the executive to implement social and economic rights, since they have no legitimacy to make choices of social policy. In addition, since they require resources for their implementation, social and economic rights cannot be immediately applied, but can only be progressively realized; and international assistance and co-operation is required in order to achieve this (see E. W. Vierdag, 'The Legal Nature of the Rights Granted by the International Covenant on Economic, Social and Cultural Rights', *Netherlands Yearbook of International Law*, 9 (1978), 69, and M. Bossuyt, 'La distinction juridique entre les droits civils et politiques et les droits économiques, sociaux et culturels', *Revue des droits de l'homme*, 8 (1975), 783, and the answer by G. J. H. Van Hoof, 'The Legal Nature of Economic, Social and Cultural Rights: a Rebuttal of Some Traditional Views' in P. Alston and K. Tomasevski (eds.), *The Right to Food* (Dordrecht: Martinus Nijhoff, 1984), p. 97; although they focus on international procedures rather than on domestic litigation, the arguments of Dennis and Stewart are largely similar: M. J. Dennis and D. P. Stewart, 'Justiciability of Economic, Social, and Cultural Rights: Should there be an International Complaints Mechanism to Adjudicate the Rights to Food, Water, Housing, and Health?', *American Journal of International Law*, 98, No. 3 (2004), 462).

2. The argument of legitimacy is sometimes hardly distinguishable from the argument of competence. Courts, it is said, are ill equipped to deal with complex, multipolar issues, and the adjudicatory setting is inappropriate for the resolution of problems of social policy:

Stephen Holmes and Cass R. Sunstein, *The Cost of Rights. Why Liberty Depends on Taxes* (New York and London: W. W. Norton, 1999), p. 95:

How can judges, in deciding a single case, take account of annual ceilings on government spending? Unlike a legislature, a court is riveted at any one time to a particular case. Because they cannot survey a broad spectrum of conflicting social needs and then decide how much to allocate to each, judges are institutionally obstructed from considering the potentially serious distributive consequences of their decisions. And they cannot easily decide if the state made an error when concluding, before the fact, that its limited resources were more effectively devoted to cases A, B, and C, rather than to case D.

Holmes and Sunstein do not fully subscribe to the position they describe in this excerpt. They note however that 'Courts that decide on the enforceability of rights claims in specific cases will ... reason more intelligently and transparently if they candidly acknowledge the way costs affect the scope, intensity, and consistency of rights enforcement' (at p. 98).

3. A final argument is that the adjudication of social and economic rights would be narrowing the room for the exercice of democratic self-determination. The argument is presented as follows by Michael Walzer:

Michael Walzer, 'Philosophy and Democracy', *Political Theory*, 9 (1981), pp. 391–2:

The judicial enforcement of welfare rights would radically reduce the reach of democratic decision. Henceforth, the judges would decide, and as cases accumulated, they would decide in increasing detail, what the scope and character of the welfare system should be and what sorts of redistribution it required. Such decisions would clearly involve significant judicial control of the state budget and, indirectly at least, of the level of taxation – the very issues over which the democratic revolution was originally fought.

(b) Answers to these challenges

1. One tendency within the doctrine, in order to overcome these objections, has been to set aside as misguided the focus on the 'progressive realization' of economic and social rights, and instead to treat these rights following the 'violations approach', usually adopted in the area of civil and political rights. The 'violations approach' would achieve protection of social and economic rights by focusing on three categories of violations: (1) violations that result from measures adopted by governments that contravene the rights of the International Covenant on Economic, Social and Cultural Rights, or that create conditions inimical to the realization of these rights; (2) patterns of discrimination, taking into account the fact that, in the ICESCR, the requirement of non-discrimination is not subject to progressive realization but constitutes instead an immediate obligation; (3) failure to fulfil minimum core obligations (see A. R. Chapman, '"Violations Approach" for Monitoring the International Covenant on Economic, Social and Cultural Rights', *Human Rights Quarterly*, 18(1) (1996), 23–66). This, it is claimed, 'would provide a more feasible and appropriate methodology both for monitors on the ground and for reviewers evaluating the compliance of individual countries with international standards. One major advantage is that the monitoring of violations does not depend on access to extensive and comparable good quality statistical data. Further, the identification of violations in order to end and rectify abuses constitutes a higher priority than promoting progressive realisation for its own sake. The monitoring of human rights is not an academic exercise. It is intended to be a means of ameliorating the human suffering which results from serious violations of international standards' (A. R. Chapman and S. Russell, 'Introduction', in A. R. Chapman and S. Russell (eds), *Core Obligations: Building a Framework for Economic, Social and Cultural Rights* (Antwerp: Intersentia, 2002), pp. 3–19 at pp. 6–7).

2. Another riposte has been to uncover the premises on which the arguments above are based. For instance, where the requirements of the rights are vague, judges would not necessarily have to usurp the powers normally allocated to legislatures: a 'co-operative model' of the relations between different branches of government could develop, in which judges and other authorities interact in ways that favour a 'constitutional dialogue' as to how human rights should be implemented (C. Scott and J. Nedelsky, 'Constitutional Dialogue' in J. Bakan and D. Schneidermann (eds.), *Social Justice and*

the Constitution: Perspectives on a Social Union for Canada (Ottawa: Carleton University Press, 1992), p. 59). More generally, judges and other branches of government should be seen less as opposing one another – the power attributed to the ones meaning less power left to the others – than as complementing each other. Courts therefore should not have to choose between substituting themselves for the other authorities, or abdicating their responsibility to monitor compliance with economic and social rights: 'The courts can place a burden on the executive and the legislature to justify the reasonableness of their policy choices in the light of the constitutional commitment to economic and social rights. Should they fail to discharge this burden of justification, a court may issue a declaratory order to this effect. This can set the parameters for a constitutionally acceptable decision while still preserving sufficient "space" for the exercise of a choice of means by the legislature' (S. Liebenberg, 'The Protection of Economic and Social Rights in Domestic Legal Systems' in A. Eide, C. Krause and A. Rosas, *Economic, Social and Cultural Rights. A Textbook*, second edn (Leiden: Martinus Nijhoff, 2001), p. 55, at p. 60).

Consider also the counter-objection by Fabre to the claim by Walzer about the anti-democratic character of constitutionalizing social rights. This claim, she states:

Cécile Fabre, *Social Rights under the Constitution. Government and the Decent Life* (Oxford Univeristy Press, 2000), p. 146:

rests on two questionable assumptions. First, it assumes that enforcing social rights is always more expensive than enforcing civil rights. But this is not always the case ... Secondly, it assumes that the constitution specifies the duties which are grounded in social rights in such a way as to leave no scope for democratic decision-making. But ... this need not always be the case ... [For instance, the] constitution can simply specify which level of resources individuals should get, and make it very clear that it is up to the democratic majority to decide whether, for example, employers should pay a minimum wages to their employees, or whether the state should top up wages that are below the poverty threshold. It could also state that decent housing should be provided while leaving it to the government to decide whether rents should be controlled, or whether housing benefits should be given to the needy, or both.

In order to respond to the denunciation of the constitutionalization of social rights as anti-democratic, Fabre instead proposes to distinguish, among social rights, between those that indeed, at a conceptual level, may be seen as limiting democratic decision-making – such as, for instance, social rights to adequate minimum income, housing, and health care – and those which are 'democratic' – such as the right to adequate education – insofar as they promote effective political participation.

3. Of course, a third answer could be to emphasize the complementarity between direct justiciability of economic and social rights before courts and the role of the legislator in implementing social and economic rights, thus guiding the courts and clarifying the content of requirements expressed in broad terms in international treaties or in domestic constitutions (see F. Viljoen, 'National Legislation as a Source of Justiciable Socio-Economic

Rights', *Economic and Social Rights Review*, 6, No. 3 (2005), 6–9). Fons Coomans concludes from a comparative study of the application of economic and social rights by courts:

Fons Coomans, 'Some Introductory Remarks on the Justiciability of Economic and Social Rights in a Comparative Constitutional Context' in F. Coomans (ed.), *Justiciability of Economic and Social Rights. Experiences from Domestic Systems* (Antwerp–Oxford: Intersentia–Hart, 2006), p. 1 at pp. 7–8:

Almost all domestic systems demonstrate that constitutional provisions on economic and social rights are not sufficient for an effective realisation of these rights. There is a need for implementation through secondary and other (delegated) forms of legislation or executive and administrative action. This is also emphasised in Article 2(1) ICESCR. Such legislation and executive measures may also provide for remedies. For example, the South African Social Assistance Act and the Social Security Agency Act create statutory socio-economic rights that are enforceable through the courts. In India, statutes give effect to particular economic and social rights listed in the Directive Principles of State Policy, such as the National Rural Employment Guarantee Act of 2005. In Canada, jurisdictions at state level have adopted anti-discrimination legislation that also prohibits discrimination in education, employment, housing and the provision of goods and services.

8.2. Questions for discussion: doctrinal objections to the adjudication of social and economic rights

1. To what extent do the objections summarized above apply, not only to the adjudication of social and economic rights, but also to civil and political rights, such as freedom of expression and the right to respect for private and family life? Is there any reason for these critiques to be addressed specifically to the former category of rights?

2. To what extent are these objections pre-supposing a specific institutionalization of the adjudicatory function? Would changes in the working methods followed by courts or in their relationship to the other branches of government be sufficient to answer these objections?

3. Is the 'violations approach' to social and economic rights preferable to one seeking to achieve compliance with the obligation to 'progressively realize' the rights of the ICESCR, or does it risk sacrificing certain important dimensions of social and economic rights? In response to the claim that, as they put it, the 'violations approach' presented above 'would weaken the call for eventual full implementation of economic and social rights by concentrating on the most flagrant abuses', A. Chapman and S. Russell note: 'The premise is that by focusing on the negative goal of preventing or halting serious violations of these rights the positive goal of full implementation, realised over time, would be overshadowed. However, the violations approach is not meant to replace the ultimate goal of full implementation of the rights of the [ICESCR], but rather, to provide a simple and effective monitoring method' (A. R. Chapman and S. Russell, 'Introduction' in A. R. Chapman and S. Russell (eds.), *Core Obligations: Building a Framework for Economic, Social and Cultural Rights* (Antwerp: Intersentia, 2002), pp. 3–19 at pp. 7–8). How convincing is this answer to the critiques addressed at the 'violations approach'?

(c) The justiciability of economic, social and cultural rights: conceptual guidance

The documents below can be seen as answers to the challenges described in (a). They are presented in chronological order. The Limburg Principles on the Implementation of the International Covenant on Economic, Social and Cultural Rights were elaborated by a group of international law experts in 1986 only months after the Committee on Economic, Social and Cultural Rights was established by Resolution 17/1985 of the Economic and Social Council. The set of principles these experts adopted relate, in particular, to the justiciability of the rights of the Covenant. In 1990, the Committee on Economic, Social and Cultural Rights adopted its General Comment No. 3, on the nature of States parties' obligations under Article 2, para. 1, of the Covenant. This provision states: 'Each State Party to the present Covenant undertakes to take steps, individually and through international assistance and co-operation, especially economic and technical, to the maximum of its available resources, with a view to achieving progressively the full realization of the rights recognized in the present Covenant by all appropriate means, including particularly the adoption of legislative measures.' The General Comment is an attempt to clarify that this clause does not deprive the obligations stipulated under the Covenant from any immediate effect. Finally, in 1998 the Committee on Economic, Social and Cultural Rights adopted its General Comment No. 9 on the domestic application of the Covenant, where it describes, in particular, the importance of judicial remedies in implementing the Covenant, and bridges the gap between the ICCPR and the ICESCR.

Limburg Principles on the Implementation of the International Covenant on Economic, Social and Cultural Rights (1986):

3. As human rights and fundamental freedoms are indivisible and interdependent, equal attention and urgent consideration should be given to the implementation, promotion and protection of both civil and political, and economic, social and cultural rights.

4. The International Covenant on Economic, Social and Cultural Rights (hereafter the Covenant) should, in accordance with the Vienna Convention on the Law of Treaties (Vienna 1969), be interpreted in good faith, taking into account the object and purpose, the ordinary meaning, the preparatory work and the relevant practice ...

7. States parties must at all times act in good faith to fulfil the obligations they have accepted under the Covenant.

8. Although the full realization of the rights recognized in the Covenant is to be attained progressively, the application of some rights can be made justiciable immediately while other rights can become justiciable over time ...

10. States parties are accountable both to the international community and to their own people for their compliance with the obligations under the Covenant.

11. A concerted national effort to invoke the full participation of all sectors of society is, therefore, indispensable to achieving progress in realizing economic, social and cultural rights. Popular participation is required at all stages, including the formulation, application and review of national policies ...

13. All organs monitoring the Covenant should pay special attention to the principles of non-discrimination and equality before the law when assessing States parties' compliance with the Covenant.

14. Given the significance for development of the progressive realization of the rights set forth in the Covenant, particular attention should be given to measures to improve the standard of living of the poor and other disadvantaged groups, taking into account that special measures may be required to protect cultural rights of indigenous peoples and minorities.

15. Trends in international economic relations should be taken into account in assessing the efforts of the international community to achieve the Covenant's objectives.

Committee on Economic, Social and Cultural Rights, General Comment No. 3, *The Nature of States Parties' Obligations* (Art. 2, para. 1, of the Covenant) (1990):

5. Among the measures which might be considered appropriate [to satisfy the obligation to take steps to implement the International Covenant on Economic, Social and Cultural Rights, as stated in article 2(1) by 'all appropriate means, including particularly the adoption of legislative measures'], in addition to legislation, is the provision of judicial remedies with respect to rights which may, in accordance with the national legal system, be considered justiciable. The Committee notes, for example, that the enjoyment of the rights recognized, without discrimination, will often be appropriately promoted, in part, through the provision of judicial or other effective remedies. Indeed, those States parties which are also parties to the International Covenant on Civil and Political Rights are already obligated (by virtue of articles 2 (paras. 1 and 3), 3 and 26) of that Covenant to ensure that any person whose rights or freedoms (including the right to equality and non-discrimination) recognized in that Covenant are violated, 'shall have an effective remedy' (art. 2(3)(a)). In addition, there are a number of other provisions in the International Covenant on Economic, Social and Cultural Rights, including articles 3, 7(a)(i), 8, 10(3), 13(2)(a), (3) and (4) and 15(3) which would seem to be capable of immediate application by judicial and other organs in many national legal systems. Any suggestion that the provisions indicated are inherently non-self-executing would seem to be difficult to sustain.

6. Where specific policies aimed directly at the realization of the rights recognized in the Covenant have been adopted in legislative form, the Committee would wish to be informed, *inter alia*, as to whether such laws create any right of action on behalf of individuals or groups who feel that their rights are not being fully realized. In cases where constitutional recognition has been accorded to specific economic, social and cultural rights, or where the provisions of the Covenant have been incorporated directly into national law, the Committee would wish to receive information as to the extent to which these rights are considered to be justiciable (i.e. able to be invoked before the courts). The Committee would also wish to receive specific information as to any instances in which existing constitutional provisions relating to economic, social and cultural rights have been weakened or significantly changed.

7. Other measures which may also be considered 'appropriate' for the purposes of article 2(1) include, but are not limited to, administrative, financial, educational and social measures ...

9. The principal obligation of result reflected in article 2 (1) is to take steps 'with a view to achieving progressively the full realization of the rights recognized' in the Covenant. The term

'progressive realization' is often used to describe the intent of this phrase. The concept of progressive realization constitutes a recognition of the fact that full realization of all economic, social and cultural rights will generally not be able to be achieved in a short period of time. In this sense the obligation differs significantly from that contained in article 2 of the International Covenant on Civil and Political Rights which embodies an immediate obligation to respect and ensure all of the relevant rights. Nevertheless, the fact that realization over time, or in other words progressively, is foreseen under the Covenant should not be misinterpreted as depriving the obligation of all meaningful content. It is on the one hand a necessary flexibility device, reflecting the realities of the real world and the difficulties involved for any country in ensuring full realization of economic, social and cultural rights. On the other hand, the phrase must be read in the light of the overall objective, indeed the raison d'être, of the Covenant which is to establish clear obligations for States parties in respect of the full realization of the rights in question. It thus imposes an obligation to move as expeditiously and effectively as possible towards that goal. Moreover, any deliberately retrogressive measures in that regard would require the most careful consideration and would need to be fully justified by reference to the totality of the rights provided for in the Covenant and in the context of the full use of the maximum available resources.

10. On the basis of the extensive experience gained by the Committee, as well as by the body that preceded it, over a period of more than a decade of examining States parties' reports the Committee is of the view that a minimum core obligation to ensure the satisfaction of, at the very least, minimum essential levels of each of the rights is incumbent upon every State party. Thus, for example, a State party in which any significant number of individuals is deprived of essential foodstuffs, of essential primary health care, of basic shelter and housing, or of the most basic forms of education is, prima facie, failing to discharge its obligations under the Covenant. If the Covenant were to be read in such a way as not to establish such a minimum core obligation, it would be largely deprived of its raison d'être. By the same token, it must be noted that any assessment as to whether a State has discharged its minimum core obligation must also take account of resource constraints applying within the country concerned. Article 2(1) obligates each State party to take the necessary steps 'to the maximum of its available resources'. In order for a State party to be able to attribute its failure to meet at least its minimum core obligations to a lack of available resources it must demonstrate that every effort has been made to use all resources that are at its disposition in an effort to satisfy, as a matter of priority, those minimum obligations.

11. The Committee wishes to emphasize, however, that even where the available resources are demonstrably inadequate, the obligation remains for a State party to strive to ensure the widest possible enjoyment of the relevant rights under the prevailing circumstances. Moreover, the obligations to monitor the extent of the realization, or more especially of the non-realization, of economic, social and cultural rights, and to devise strategies and programmes for their promotion, are not in any way eliminated as a result of resource constraints [on this, see chapter 5, section 4.]

12. Similarly, the Committee underlines the fact that even in times of severe resources constraints whether caused by a process of adjustment, of economic recession, or by other factors the vulnerable members of society can and indeed must be protected by the adoption of relatively low-cost targeted programmes ...

Committee on Economic, Social and Cultural Rights, General Comment No. 9,
The Domestic Application of the Covenant **(E/1999/22) (1998):**

A. The duty to give effect to the Covenant in the domestic legal order

1. In its general comment No. 3 (1990) on the nature of States parties' obligations (article 2, paragraph 1, of the Covenant) the Committee addressed issues relating to the nature and scope of States parties' obligations. The present general comment seeks to elaborate further certain elements of the earlier statement. The central obligation in relation to the Covenant is for States parties to give effect to the rights recognized therein. By requiring Governments to do so 'by all appropriate means', the Covenant adopts a broad and flexible approach which enables the particularities of the legal and administrative systems of each State, as well as other relevant considerations, to be taken into account.

2. But this flexibility coexists with the obligation upon each State party to use all the means at its disposal to give effect to the rights recognized in the Covenant. In this respect, the fundamental requirements of international human rights law must be borne in mind. Thus the Covenant norms must be recognized in appropriate ways within the domestic legal order, appropriate means of redress, or remedies, must be available to any aggrieved individual or group, and appropriate means of ensuring governmental accountability must be put in place.

3. Questions relating to the domestic application of the Covenant must be considered in the light of two principles of international law. The first, as reflected in article 27 of the Vienna Convention on the Law of Treaties, is that '[A] party may not invoke the provisions of its internal law as justification for its failure to perform a treaty'. In other words, States should modify the domestic legal order as necessary in order to give effect to their treaty obligations. The second principle is reflected in article 8 of the Universal Declaration of Human Rights, according to which 'Everyone has the right to an effective remedy by the competent national tribunals for acts violating the fundamental rights granted him by the constitution or by law.' The International Covenant on Economic, Social and Cultural Rights contains no direct counterpart to article 2, paragraph 3(b), of the International Covenant on Civil and Political Rights, which obligates States parties to, *inter alia*, 'develop the possibilities of judicial remedy'. Nevertheless, a State party seeking to justify its failure to provide any domestic legal remedies for violations of economic, social and cultural rights would need to show either that such remedies are not 'appropriate means' within the terms of article 2, paragraph 1, of the International Covenant on Economic, Social and Cultural Rights or that, in view of the other means used, they are unnecessary. It will be difficult to show this and the Committee considers that, in many cases, the other means used could be rendered ineffective if they are not reinforced or complemented by judicial remedies.

B. The status of the Covenant in the domestic legal order

4. In general, legally binding international human rights standards should operate directly and immediately within the domestic legal system of each State party, thereby enabling individuals to seek enforcement of their rights before national courts and tribunals. The rule requiring the exhaustion of domestic remedies reinforces the primacy of national remedies in this respect. The existence and further development of international procedures for the pursuit of individual claims is important, but such procedures are ultimately only supplementary to effective national remedies.

5. The Covenant does not stipulate the specific means by which it is to be implemented in the national legal order. And there is no provision obligating its comprehensive incorporation or requiring it to be accorded any specific type of status in national law. Although the precise method by which Covenant rights are given effect in national law is a matter for each State party to decide, the means used should be appropriate in the sense of producing results which are consistent with the full discharge of its obligations by the State party. The means chosen are also subject to review as part of the Committee's examination of the State party's compliance with its obligations under the Covenant.

6. An analysis of State practice with respect to the Covenant shows that States have used a variety of approaches. Some States have failed to do anything specific at all. Of those that have taken measures, some States have transformed the Covenant into domestic law by supplementing or amending existing legislation, without invoking the specific terms of the Covenant. Others have adopted or incorporated it into domestic law, so that its terms are retained intact and given formal validity in the national legal order. This has often been done by means of constitutional provisions according priority to the provisions of international human rights treaties over any inconsistent domestic laws. The approach of States to the Covenant depends significantly upon the approach adopted to treaties in general in the domestic legal order.

7. But whatever the preferred methodology, several principles follow from the duty to give effect to the Covenant and must therefore be respected. First, the means of implementation chosen must be adequate to ensure fulfilment of the obligations under the Covenant. The need to ensure justiciability (see paragraph 10 below) is relevant when determining the best way to give domestic legal effect to the Covenant rights. Second, account should be taken of the means which have proved to be most effective in the country concerned in ensuring the protection of other human rights. Where the means used to give effect to the Covenant on Economic, Social and Cultural Rights differ significantly from those used in relation to other human rights treaties, there should be a compelling justification for this, taking account of the fact that the formulations used in the Covenant are, to a considerable extent, comparable to those used in treaties dealing with civil and political rights.

8. Third, while the Covenant does not formally oblige States to incorporate its provisions in domestic law, such an approach is desirable. Direct incorporation avoids problems that might arise in the translation of treaty obligations into national law, and provides a basis for the direct invocation of the Covenant rights by individuals in national courts. For these reasons, the Committee strongly encourages formal adoption or incorporation of the Covenant in national law.

C. The role of legal remedies
Legal or judicial remedies? 9. The right to an effective remedy need not be interpreted as always requiring a judicial remedy. Administrative remedies will, in many cases, be adequate and those living within the jurisdiction of a State party have a legitimate expectation, based on the principle of good faith, that all administrative authorities will take account of the requirements of the Covenant in their decision-making. Any such administrative remedies should be accessible, affordable, timely and effective. An ultimate right of judicial appeal from administrative procedures of this type would also often be appropriate. By the same token,

there are some obligations, such as (but by no means limited to) those concerning non–discrimination, in relation to which the provision of some form of judicial remedy would seem indispensable in order to satisfy the requirements of the Covenant. In other words, whenever a Covenant right cannot be made fully effective without some role for the judiciary, judicial remedies are necessary.

Justiciability 10. In relation to civil and political rights, it is generally taken for granted that judicial remedies for violations are essential. Regrettably, the contrary assumption is too often made in relation to economic, social and cultural rights. This discrepancy is not warranted either by the nature of the rights or by the relevant Covenant provisions. The Committee has already made clear that it considers many of the provisions in the Covenant to be capable of immediate implementation. Thus, in general comment No. 3 (1990) it cited, by way of example, articles 3; 7, paragraph (a)(i); 8; 10, paragraph 3; 13, paragraph 2(a); 13, paragraph 3; 13, paragraph 4; and 15, paragraph 3. It is important in this regard to distinguish between justiciability (which refers to those matters which are appropriately resolved by the courts) and norms which are self-executing (capable of being applied by courts without further elaboration). While the general approach of each legal system needs to be taken into account, there is no Covenant right which could not, in the great majority of systems, be considered to possess at least some significant justiciable dimensions. It is sometimes suggested that matters involving the allocation of resources should be left to the political authorities rather than the courts. While the respective competences of the various branches of government must be respected, it is appropriate to acknowledge that courts are generally already involved in a considerable range of matters which have important resource implications. The adoption of a rigid classification of economic, social and cultural rights which puts them, by definition, beyond the reach of the courts would thus be arbitrary and incompatible with the principle that the two sets of human rights are indivisible and interdependent. It would also drastically curtail the capacity of the courts to protect the rights of the most vulnerable and disadvantaged groups in society.

Self-executing 11. The Covenant does not negate the possibility that the rights it contains may be considered self-executing in systems where that option is provided for. Indeed, when it was being drafted, attempts to include a specific provision in the Covenant to the effect that it be considered 'non-self-executing' were strongly rejected. In most States, the determination of whether or not a treaty provision is self-executing will be a matter for the courts, not the executive or the legislature. In order to perform that function effectively, the relevant courts and tribunals must be made aware of the nature and implications of the Covenant and of the important role of judicial remedies in its implementation. Thus, for example, when Governments are involved in court proceedings, they should promote interpretations of domestic laws which give effect to their Covenant obligations. Similarly, judicial training should take full account of the justiciability of the Covenant. It is especially important to avoid any *a priori* assumption that the norms should be considered to be non-self-executing. In fact, many of them are stated in terms which are at least as clear and specific as those in other human rights treaties, the provisions of which are regularly deemed by courts to be self-executing.

D. The treatment of the Covenant in domestic courts

12. In the Committee's guidelines for States' reports, States are requested to provide information as to whether the provisions of the Covenant 'can be invoked before, and directly enforced by,

the Courts, other tribunals or administrative authorities' (see E/1991/23, annex IV, chapter A, paragraph 1(d)(iv)). Some States have provided such information, but greater importance should be attached to this element in future reports. In particular, the Committee requests that States parties provide details of any significant jurisprudence from their domestic courts that makes use of the provisions of the Covenant.

13. On the basis of available information, it is clear that State practice is mixed. The Committee notes that some courts have applied the provisions of the Covenant either directly or as interpretative standards. Other courts are willing to acknowledge, in principle, the relevance of the Covenant for interpreting domestic law, but in practice, the impact of the Covenant on the reasoning or outcome of cases is very limited. Still other courts have refused to give any degree of legal effect to the Covenant in cases in which individuals have sought to rely on it. There remains extensive scope for the courts in most countries to place greater reliance upon the Covenant.

14. Within the limits of the appropriate exercise of their functions of judicial review, courts should take account of Covenant rights where this is necessary to ensure that the State's conduct is consistent with its obligations under the Covenant. Neglect by the courts of this responsibility is incompatible with the principle of the rule of law, which must always be taken to include respect for international human rights obligations.

15. It is generally accepted that domestic law should be interpreted as far as possible in a way which conforms to a State's international legal obligations. Thus, when a domestic decision maker is faced with a choice between an interpretation of domestic law that would place the State in breach of the Covenant and one that would enable the State to comply with the Covenant, international law requires the choice of the latter. Guarantees of equality and non-discrimination should be interpreted, to the greatest extent possible, in ways which facilitate the full protection of economic, social and cultural rights

1.3 Social and economic rights before national courts

Probably the best answers to the objections to the justiciability of social and economic rights are those provided by courts, which through a variety of techniques manage to rely on provisions guaranteeing such rights in domestic constitutions or in international treaties, and to identify the implications in the concrete cases they are presented with. The following decisions illustrate how national courts have given effect to social and economic rights such as the right to housing, the right to education, or the right to food, on the basis of constitutional provisions framed in terms similar or identical to those of international instruments.

Constitutional Court of South Africa, Case CCT 11/00, *Government of the Republic of South Africa and others* v. *Grootboom and others*, 2000 (11) B.C.L.R. 1169, judgment of 4 October 2000 (leading judgment of Yacoob J.):

[As explained in the judgment of Yacoob J., in which the other justices of the Constitutional Court concurred, 'the group of people with whom [the Constitutional Court was] concerned in these proceedings lived in appalling conditions, decided to move out and illegally occupied someone else's land. They were evicted and left homeless. The root cause of their problems is the intolerable conditions under which they were living while waiting in the queue for their turn to be allocated low-cost housing.' The applicants, who included children, were squatters. They had moved into informal homes on a vacant private land earmarked for formal low-cost housing because the living conditions in Wallacedene, their original place of abode, were intolerable. As explained in the judgment: 'A quarter of the households of Wallacedene had no income at all, and more than two thirds earned less than R500 per month. About half the population were children; all lived in shacks. They had no water, sewage or refuse removal services and only 5% of the shacks had electricity. The area is partly waterlogged and lies dangerously close to a main thoroughfare. Mrs Grootboom lived with her family and her sister's family in a shack about twenty metres square.' The owner then obtained a court order to evict them from the private land. In the course of the eviction, their building structures and materials were demolished and totally destroyed. To camp on a sports field in the surrounding area was the only available option to the applicants. These circumstances prompted them to approach the Cape of Good Hope High Court for redress, asking that Government provide them with adequate basic shelter or housing until they secured permanent accommodation, or basic nutrition, shelter, healthcare and social services to the respondents who are children. They based their claim on section 26 of the Constitution which provides that everyone has the right of access to adequate housing (section 26(2) provides that the State 'must take reasonable legislative and other measures, within its available resources, to achieve the progressive realisation of this right'); and on section 28(1) (c) of the Constitution which provides that children have the right to shelter. Section 7(2) of the Constitution requires the State 'to respect, protect, promote and fulfil the rights in the Bill of Rights'. The applicants were granted relief on the basis of the right of children to shelter stated in section 28(1)(c), which, however, also benefited the childrens' parents since 'an order which enforces a child's right to shelter should take account of the need of the child to be accompanied by his or her parent': the judgment provisionally concluded that 'tents, portable latrines and a regular supply of water (albeit transported) would constitute the bare minimum'. The Government appealed against this judgment to the Constitutional Court.]

[The interpretation of section 26 of the Constitution]

[21] Like all the other rights in Chapter 2 of the Constitution (which contains the Bill of Rights), section 26 must be construed in its context. The section has been carefully crafted. It contains three subsections. The first confers a general right of access to adequate housing. The second establishes and delimits the scope of the positive obligation imposed upon the state to promote access to adequate housing and has three key elements. The state is obliged: (a) to take reasonable legislative and other measures; (b) within its available resources; (c) to achieve the progressive realisation of this right. These elements are discussed later. The third subsection provides protection against arbitrary evictions.

[22] Interpreting a right in its context requires the consideration of two types of context. On the one hand, rights must be understood in their textual setting. This will require a consideration of Chapter 2 and the Constitution as a whole. On the other hand, rights must also be understood in their social and historical context.

[23] Our Constitution entrenches both civil and political rights and social and economic rights. All the rights in our Bill of Rights are inter-related and mutually supporting. There can be

no doubt that human dignity, freedom and equality, the foundational values of our society, are denied those who have no food, clothing or shelter. Affording socio-economic rights to all people therefore enables them to enjoy the other rights enshrined in Chapter 2. The realisation of these rights is also key to the advancement of race and gender equality and the evolution of a society in which men and women are equally able to achieve their full potential.

[24] The right of access to adequate housing cannot be seen in isolation. There is a close relationship between it and the other socio-economic rights. Socio-economic rights must all be read together in the setting of the Constitution as a whole. The state is obliged to take positive action to meet the needs of those living in extreme conditions of poverty, homelessness or intolerable housing. Their interconnectedness needs to be taken into account in interpreting the socio-economic rights, and, in particular, in determining whether the state has met its obligations in terms of them.

[25] Rights also need to be interpreted and understood in their social and historical context. The right to be free from unfair discrimination, for example, must be understood against our legacy of deep social inequality. The context in which the Bill of Rights is to be interpreted was described by Chaskalson P in [*Soobramoney v. Minister of Health (Kwazulu-Natal)* (CCT 32/97) [1997] ZACC 17]:

'We live in a society in which there are great disparities in wealth. Millions of people are living in deplorable conditions and in great poverty. There is a high level of unemployment, inadequate social security, and many do not have access to clean water or to adequate health services. These conditions already existed when the Constitution was adopted and a commitment to address them, and to transform our society into one in which there will be human dignity, freedom and equality, lies at the heart of our new constitutional order. For as long as these conditions continue to exist that aspiration will have a hollow ring.'

[The impact of international law]
[Section 39 of the Constitution provides that: '(1) When interpreting the Bill of Rights, a court, tribunal or forum (a) must promote the values that underlie an open and democratic society based on human dignity, equality and freedom; (b) must consider international law; and (c) may consider foreign law.' Relying extensively on the materials submitted by the *amici curiae*, the Court examines in paras. 27–33 how the right to adequate housing has been interpreted by the Committee on Economic, Social and Cultural Rights, and whether this should influence the reading of section 26 of the Constitution, which guarantees the right to housing. This part of the analysis concludes by noting the difficulty of identifying what constitutes the 'minimum core content' of the right of access to adequate housing in the context of the Constitution, especially since the needs of different groups may vary.]

[34] [S]ection 26 [provides]:

(1) Everyone has the right to have access to adequate housing.
(2) The state must take reasonable legislative and other measures, within its available resources, to achieve the progressive realisation of this right.
(3) No one may be evicted from their home, or have their home demolished, without an order of court made after considering all the relevant circumstances. No legislation may permit arbitrary evictions.

Subsections (1) and (2) are related and must be read together. Subsection (1) aims at delineating the scope of the right. It is a right of everyone including children. Although the subsection does not expressly say so, there is, at the very least, a negative obligation placed upon the state and all other entities and persons to desist from preventing or impairing the right of access to adequate housing. The negative right is further spelt out in subsection (3) which prohibits arbitrary evictions. Access to housing could also be promoted if steps are taken to make the rural areas of our country more viable so as to limit the inexorable migration of people from rural to urban areas in search of jobs.

[35] The right delineated in section 26(1) is a right of 'access to adequate housing' as distinct from the right to adequate housing encapsulated in the Covenant. This difference is significant. It recognises that housing entails more than bricks and mortar. It requires available land, appropriate services such as the provision of water and the removal of sewage and the financing of all of these, including the building of the house itself. For a person to have access to adequate housing all of these conditions need to be met: there must be land, there must be services, there must be a dwelling. Access to land for the purpose of housing is therefore included in the right of access to adequate housing in section 26. A right of access to adequate housing also suggests that it is not only the state who is responsible for the provision of houses, but that other agents within our society, including individuals themselves, must be enabled by legislative and other measures to provide housing. The state must create the conditions for access to adequate housing for people at all economic levels of our society. State policy dealing with housing must therefore take account of different economic levels in our society.

[36] In this regard, there is a difference between the position of those who can afford to pay for housing, even if it is only basic though adequate housing, and those who cannot. For those who can afford to pay for adequate housing, the state's primary obligation lies in unlocking the system, providing access to housing stock and a legislative framework to facilitate self-built houses through planning laws and access to finance. Issues of development and social welfare are raised in respect of those who cannot afford to provide themselves with housing. State policy needs to address both these groups. The poor are particularly vulnerable and their needs require special attention. It is in this context that the relationship between sections 26 and 27 and the other socio-economic rights is most apparent. If under section 27 the state has in place programmes to provide adequate social assistance to those who are otherwise unable to support themselves and their dependants, that would be relevant to the state's obligations in respect of other socio-economic rights.

[37] The state's obligation to provide access to adequate housing depends on context, and may differ from province to province, from city to city, from rural to urban areas and from person to person. Some may need access to land and no more; some may need access to land and building materials; some may need access to finance; some may need access to services such as water, sewage, electricity and roads. What might be appropriate in a rural area where people live together in communities engaging in subsistence farming may not be appropriate in an urban area where people are looking for employment and a place to live.

[38] Subsection (2) speaks to the positive obligation imposed upon the state. It requires the state to devise a comprehensive and workable plan to meet its obligations in terms of the subsection. However subsection (2) also makes it clear that the obligation imposed upon the state is not an absolute or unqualified one. The extent of the state's obligation is defined by three key elements that are considered separately: (a) the obligation to 'take reasonable legislative and other measures'; (b) 'to achieve the progressive realisation' of the right; and (c) 'within available resources'.

Reasonable legislative and other measures

[39] What constitutes reasonable legislative and other measures must be determined in the light of the fact that the Constitution creates different spheres of government: national government, provincial government and local government ... The Constitution allocates powers and functions amongst these different spheres emphasising their obligation to co-operate with one another in carrying out their constitutional tasks. In the case of housing, it is a function shared by both national and provincial government. Local governments have an important obligation to ensure that services are provided in a sustainable manner to the communities they govern. A reasonable programme therefore must clearly allocate responsibilities and tasks to the different spheres of government and ensure that the appropriate financial and human resources are available.

[40] Thus, a co-ordinated state housing programme must be a comprehensive one determined by all three spheres of government in consultation with each other as contemplated by Chapter 3 of the Constitution. It may also require framework legislation at national level, a matter we need not consider further in this case as there is national framework legislation in place. Each sphere of government must accept responsibility for the implementation of particular parts of the programme but the national sphere of government must assume responsibility for ensuring that laws, policies, programmes and strategies are adequate to meet the state's section 26 obligations. In particular, the national framework, if there is one, must be designed so that these obligations can be met. It should be emphasised that national government bears an important responsibility in relation to the allocation of national revenue to the provinces and local government on an equitable basis. Furthermore, national and provincial government must ensure that executive obligations imposed by the housing legislation are met.

[41] The measures must establish a coherent public housing programme directed towards the progressive realisation of the right of access to adequate housing within the state's available means. The programme must be capable of facilitating the realisation of the right. The precise contours and content of the measures to be adopted are primarily a matter for the legislature and the executive. They must, however, ensure that the measures they adopt are reasonable. In any challenge based on section 26 in which it is argued that the state has failed to meet the positive obligations imposed upon it by section 26(2), the question will be whether the legislative and other measures taken by the state are reasonable. A court considering reasonableness will not enquire whether other more desirable or favourable measures could have been adopted, or whether public money could have been better spent. The question would be whether the measures that have been adopted are reasonable. It is necessary to recognise that a wide range of possible measures could be adopted by the state to meet its obligations. Many of these would meet the requirement of reasonableness. Once it is shown that the measures do so, this requirement is met.

[42] The state is required to take reasonable legislative and other measures. Legislative measures by themselves are not likely to constitute constitutional compliance. Mere legislation is not enough. The state is obliged to act to achieve the intended result, and the legislative measures will invariably have to be supported by appropriate, well-directed policies and programmes implemented by the executive. These policies and programmes must be reasonable both in their conception and their implementation. The formulation of a programme is only the first stage in meeting the state's obligations. The programme must also be reasonably implemented. An otherwise reasonable programme that is not implemented reasonably will not constitute compliance with the state's obligations.

[43] In determining whether a set of measures is reasonable, it will be necessary to consider housing problems in their social, economic and historical context and to consider the capacity of institutions responsible for implementing the programme. The programme must be balanced and flexible and make appropriate provision for attention to housing crises and to short, medium and long term needs. A programme that excludes a significant segment of society cannot be said to be reasonable. Conditions do not remain static and therefore the programme will require continuous review.

[44] Reasonableness must also be understood in the context of the Bill of Rights as a whole. The right of access to adequate housing is entrenched because we value human beings and want to ensure that they are afforded their basic human needs. A society must seek to ensure that the basic necessities of life are provided to all if it is to be a society based on human dignity, freedom and equality. To be reasonable, measures cannot leave out of account the degree and extent of the denial of the right they endeavour to realise. Those whose needs are the most urgent and whose ability to enjoy all rights therefore is most in peril, must not be ignored by the measures aimed at achieving realisation of the right. It may not be sufficient to meet the test of reasonableness to show that the measures are capable of achieving a statistical advance in the realisation of the right. Furthermore, the Constitution requires that everyone must be treated with care and concern. If the measures, though statistically successful, fail to respond to the needs of those most desperate, they may not pass the test.

Progressive realisation of the right

[45] The extent and content of the obligation consist in what must be achieved, that is, 'the progressive realisation of this right'. It links subsections (1) and (2) by making it quite clear that the right referred to is the right of access to adequate housing. The term 'progressive realisation' shows that it was contemplated that the right could not be realised immediately. But the goal of the Constitution is that the basic needs of all in our society be effectively met and the requirement of progressive realisation means that the state must take steps to achieve this goal. It means that accessibility should be progressively facilitated: legal, administrative, operational and financial hurdles should be examined and, where possible, lowered over time. Housing must be made more accessible not only to a larger number of people but to a wider range of people as time progresses. The phrase is taken from international law and Article 2.1 of the Covenant in particular. The committee has helpfully analysed this requirement in the context of housing as follows: 'Nevertheless, the fact that realization over time, or in other words progressively, is foreseen under the Covenant should not be misinterpreted as depriving the obligation of all meaningful content. It is on the one hand a necessary flexibility device, reflecting the realities of the real world and the difficulties involved for any country in ensuring full realization of economic, social and cultural rights. On the other hand, the phrase must be read in the light of the overall objective, indeed the raison d'être, of the Covenant which is to establish clear obligations for States parties in respect of the full realization of the rights in question. It thus imposes an obligation to move as expeditiously and effectively as possible towards that goal. Moreover, any deliberately retrogressive measures in that regard would require the most careful consideration and would need to be fully justified by reference to the totality of the rights provided for in the Covenant and in the context of the full use of the maximum available resources.'

Although the committee's analysis is intended to explain the scope of states parties' obligations under the Covenant, it is also helpful in plumbing the meaning of 'progressive realisation' in the context of our Constitution. The meaning ascribed to the phrase is in harmony with the context in which the phrase is used in our Constitution and there is no reason not to accept that it bears the same meaning in the Constitution as in the document from which it was so clearly derived.

Within available resources

[46] The third defining aspect of the obligation to take the requisite measures is that the obligation does not require the state to do more than its available resources permit. This means that both the content of the obligation in relation to the rate at which it is achieved as well as the reasonableness of the measures employed to achieve the result are governed by the availability of resources. Section 26 does not expect more of the state than is achievable within its available resources ... There is a balance between goal and means. The measures must be calculated to attain the goal expeditiously and effectively but the availability of resources is an important factor in determining what is reasonable.

[Paras. 47–53 of the judgment then examine the national Housing Act, which provides a framework which establishes the responsibilities and functions of each sphere of government with regard to housing, and other measures aimed at housing development. It concludes in this respect that the programme adopted by the public authorities 'is aimed at achieving the progressive realisation of the right of access to adequate housing'. It then continues:]

[54] A question that nevertheless must be answered is whether the measures adopted are reasonable within the meaning of section 26 of the Constitution. Allocation of responsibilities and functions has been coherently and comprehensively addressed. The programme is not haphazard but represents a systematic response to a pressing social need. It takes account of the housing shortage in South Africa by seeking to build a large number of homes for those in need of better housing. The programme applies throughout South Africa and although there have been difficulties of implementation in some areas, the evidence suggests that the state is actively seeking to combat these difficulties.

[55] Legislative measures have been taken at both the national and provincial levels. As we have seen, at the national level the Housing Act sets out the general principles applicable to housing development, defines the functions of the three spheres of government and addresses the financing of housing development. It thus provides a legislative framework within which the delivery of houses is to take place nationally. At the provincial level there is the Western Cape Housing Development Act, 1999. This statute also sets out the general principles applicable to housing development; the role of the provincial government; the role of local government; and other matters relating to housing development. Thus, like the Housing Act, this statute provides a legislative framework within which housing development at provincial level will take place. All of the measures described form part of the nationwide housing programme.

[56] This Court must decide whether the nationwide housing programme is sufficiently flexible to respond to those in desperate need in our society and to cater appropriately for immediate and short-term requirements. This must be done in the context of the scope of the housing problem that must be addressed. This case is concerned with the situation in the Cape Metro and the municipality and the circumstances that prevailed there are therefore presented.

[The judgment then describes the efforts made in Cape Metro to develop housing, and concludes this review by noting that the crucial element is whether enough is done for families in desperate need: 'the question is whether a housing programme that leaves out of account the immediate amelioration of the circumstances of those in crisis can meet the test of reasonableness established by [section 26 of the Constitution]'.]

[65] The absence of this component may have been acceptable if the nationwide housing programme would result in affordable houses for most people within a reasonably short time. However the scale of the problem is such that this simply cannot happen. Each individual housing project could be expected to take years and the provision of houses for all in the area of the municipality and in the Cape Metro is likely to take a long time indeed. The desperate will be consigned to their fate for the foreseeable future unless some temporary measures exist as an integral part of the nationwide housing programme. Housing authorities are understandably unable to say when housing will become available to these desperate people. The result is that people in desperate need are left without any form of assistance with no end in sight. Not only are the immediate crises not met. The consequent pressure on existing settlements inevitably results in land invasions by the desperate thereby frustrating the attainment of the medium and long term objectives of the nationwide housing programme. That is one of the main reasons why the Cape Metro land programme was adopted.

[66] The national government bears the overall responsibility for ensuring that the state complies with the obligations imposed upon it by section 26. The nationwide housing programme falls short of obligations imposed upon national government to the extent that it fails to recognise that the state must provide for relief for those in desperate need. They are not to be ignored in the interests of an overall programme focussed on medium and long-term objectives. It is essential that a reasonable part of the national housing budget be devoted to this, but the precise allocation is for national government to decide in the first instance.

[67] This case is concerned with the Cape Metro and the municipality. The former has realised that this need has not been fulfilled and has put in place its land programme in an effort to fulfil it. This programme, on the face of it, meets the obligation which the state has towards people in the position of the respondents in the Cape Metro. Indeed, the amicus accepted that this programme 'would cater precisely for the needs of people such as the respondents, and, in an appropriate and sustainable manner'. However, as with legislative measures, the existence of the programme is a starting point only. What remains is the implementation of the programme by taking all reasonable steps that are necessary to initiate and sustain it. And it must be implemented with due regard to the urgency of the situations it is intended to address.

[68] Effective implementation requires at least adequate budgetary support by national government. This, in turn, requires recognition of the obligation to meet immediate needs in the nationwide housing programme. Recognition of such needs in the nationwide housing programme requires it to plan, budget and monitor the fulfilment of immediate needs and the management of crises. This must ensure that a significant number of desperate people in need are afforded relief, though not all of them need receive it immediately. Such planning too will require proper co-operation between the different spheres of government.

[69] In conclusion it has been established in this case that as of the date of the launch of this application, the state was not meeting the obligation imposed upon it by section 26(2) of the Constitution in the area of the Cape Metro. In particular, the programmes adopted by the state

fell short of the requirements of section 26(2) in that no provision was made for relief to the categories of people in desperate need identified earlier.

[Section 28(1)(c) and the right to shelter]
[Examining then the meaning of section 28(1)(c) of the Constitution, the judgment notes that the High Court granted relief on the basis of the right of children to shelter. However, this produces an 'anomalous result', since:]

[71] People who have children have a direct and enforceable right to housing under section 28(1)(c), while others who have none or whose children are adult are not entitled to housing under that section, no matter how old, disabled or otherwise deserving they may be. The carefully constructed constitutional scheme for progressive realisation of socio-economic rights would make little sense if it could be trumped in every case by the rights of children to get shelter from the state on demand. Moreover, there is an obvious danger. Children could become stepping stones to housing for their parents instead of being valued for who they are.

[Evaluation of the conduct of the appellants towards the respondents]
[80] The final section of this judgment is concerned with whether the respondents are entitled to some relief in the form of temporary housing because of their special circumstances and because of the appellants' conduct towards them. This matter was raised in argument, and although not fully aired on the papers, it is appropriate to consider it. At first blush, the respondents' position was so acute and untenable when the High Court heard the case that simple humanity called for some form of immediate and urgent relief. They had left Wallacedene because of their intolerable circumstances, had been evicted in a way that left a great deal to be desired and, as a result, lived in desperate sub-human conditions on the Wallacedene soccer field or in the Wallacedene community hall. But we must also remember that the respondents are not alone in their desperation; hundreds of thousands (possibly millions) of South Africans live in appalling conditions throughout our country.

[81] Although the conditions in which the respondents lived in Wallacedene were admittedly intolerable and although it is difficult to level any criticism against them for leaving the Wallacedene shack settlement, it is a painful reality that their circumstances were no worse than those of thousands of other people, including young children, who remained at Wallacedene. It cannot be said, on the evidence before us, that the respondents moved out of the Wallacedene settlement and occupied the land earmarked for low-cost housing development as a deliberate strategy to gain preference in the allocation of housing resources over thousands of other people who remained in intolerable conditions and who were also in urgent need of housing relief. It must be borne in mind however, that the effect of any order that constitutes a special dispensation for the respondents on account of their extraordinary circumstances is to accord that preference.

[82] All levels of government must ensure that the housing programme is reasonably and appropriately implemented in the light of all the provisions in the Constitution. All implementation mechanisms, and all state action in relation to housing falls to be assessed against the requirements of section 26 of the Constitution. Every step at every level of government must be consistent with the constitutional obligation to take reasonable measures to provide adequate housing.

[83] But section 26 is not the only provision relevant to a decision as to whether state action at any particular level of government is reasonable and consistent with the Constitution. The proposition that rights are interrelated and are all equally important is not merely a theoretical postulate. The concept has immense human and practical significance in a society founded on human dignity, equality and freedom. It is fundamental to an evaluation of the reasonableness of state action that account be taken of the inherent dignity of human beings. The Constitution will be worth infinitely less than its paper if the reasonableness of state action concerned with housing is determined without regard to the fundamental constitutional value of human dignity. Section 26, read in the context of the Bill of Rights as a whole, must mean that the respondents have a right to reasonable action by the state in all circumstances and with particular regard to human dignity. In short, I emphasise that human beings are required to be treated as human beings. This is the backdrop against which the conduct of the respondents towards the appellants must be seen ...

[85] Consideration is now given to whether the state action (or inaction) in relation to the respondents met the required constitutional standard. It is a central feature of this judgment that the housing shortage in the area of the Cape Metro in general and Oostenberg in particular had reached crisis proportions. Wallacedene was obviously bursting and it was probable that people in desperation were going to find it difficult to resist the temptation to move out of the shack settlement onto unoccupied land in an effort to improve their position. This is what the respondents apparently did.

[86] Whether the conduct of Mrs Grootboom and the other respondents constituted a land invasion was disputed on the papers. There was no suggestion however that the respondents' circumstances before their move to New Rust was anything but desperate. There is nothing in the papers to indicate any plan by the municipality to deal with the occupation of vacant land if it occurred. If there had been such a plan the appellants might well have acted differently.

[87] The respondents began to move onto the New Rust Land during September 1998 and the number of people on this land continued to grow relentlessly. I would have expected officials of the municipality responsible for housing to engage with these people as soon as they became aware of the occupation. I would also have thought that some effort would have been made by the municipality to resolve the difficulty on a case-by-case basis after an investigation of their circumstances before the matter got out of hand. The municipality did nothing and the settlement grew by leaps and bounds.

[88] There is, however, no dispute that the municipality funded the eviction of the respondents. The magistrate who ordered the ejectment of the respondents directed a process of mediation in which the municipality was to be involved to identify some alternative land for the occupation for the New Rust residents. Although the reason for this is unclear from the papers, it is evident that no effective mediation took place. The state had an obligation to ensure, at the very least, that the eviction was humanely executed. However, the eviction was reminiscent of the past and inconsistent with the values of the Constitution. The respondents were evicted a day early and to make matters worse, their possessions and building materials were not merely removed, but destroyed and burnt. I have already said that the provisions of section 26(1) of the Constitution burdens the state with at least a negative obligation in relation to housing. The manner in which the eviction was carried out resulted in a breach of this obligation ...

[92] This judgment must not be understood as approving any practice of land invasion for the purpose of coercing a state structure into providing housing on a preferential basis to those who participate in any exercise of this kind. Land invasion is inimical to the systematic provision of adequate housing on a planned basis. It may well be that the decision of a state structure, faced with the difficulty of repeated land invasions, not to provide housing in response to those invasions, would be reasonable. Reasonableness must be determined on the facts of each case.

Summary and conclusion

[93] This case shows the desperation of hundreds of thousands of people living in deplorable conditions throughout the country. The Constitution obliges the state to act positively to ameliorate these conditions. The obligation is to provide access to housing, health-care, sufficient food and water, and social security to those unable to support themselves and their dependants. The state must also foster conditions to enable citizens to gain access to land on an equitable basis. Those in need have a corresponding right to demand that this be done.

[94] I am conscious that it is an extremely difficult task for the state to meet these obligations in the conditions that prevail in our country. This is recognised by the Constitution which expressly provides that the state is not obliged to go beyond available resources or to realise these rights immediately. I stress however, that despite all these qualifications, these are rights, and the Constitution obliges the state to give effect to them. This is an obligation that courts can, and in appropriate circumstances, must enforce.

[95] Neither section 26 nor section 28 entitles the respondents to claim shelter or housing immediately upon demand. The High Court order ought therefore not to have been made. However, section 26 does oblige the state to devise and implement a coherent, co-ordinated programme designed to meet its section 26 obligations. The programme that has been adopted and was in force in the Cape Metro at the time that this application was brought, fell short of the obligations imposed upon the state by section 26(2) in that it failed to provide for any form of relief to those desperately in need of access to housing.

[96] In the light of the conclusions I have reached, it is necessary and appropriate to make a declaratory order. The order requires the state to act to meet the obligation imposed upon it by section 26(2) of the Constitution. This includes the obligation to devise, fund, implement and supervise measures to provide relief to those in desperate need.

[97] The Human Rights Commission is an amicus in this case. Section 184(1)(c) of the Constitution places a duty on the Commission to 'monitor and assess the observance of human rights in the Republic'. Subsections (2)(a) and (b) give the Commission the power: '(a) to investigate and to report on the observance of human rights; (b) to take steps to secure appropriate redress where human right have been violated.'

Counsel for the Commission indicated during argument that the Commission had the duty and was prepared to monitor and report on the compliance by the state of its section 26 obligations. In the circumstances, the Commission will monitor and, if necessary, report in terms of these powers on the efforts made by the state to comply with its section 26 obligations in accordance with this judgment ...

The Order

[99] The following order is made:

1. The appeal is allowed in part.
2. The order of the Cape of Good Hope High Court is set aside and the following is substituted for it:

It is declared that:

(a) Section 26(2) of the Constitution requires the state to devise and implement within its available resources a comprehensive and coordinated programme progressively to realise the right of access to adequate housing.

(b) The programme must include reasonable measures such as, but not necessarily limited to, those contemplated in the Accelerated Managed Land Settlement Programme, to provide relief for people who have no access to land, no roof over their heads, and who are living in intolerable conditions or crisis situations.

(c) As at the date of the launch of this application, the state housing programme in the area of the Cape Metropolitan Council fell short of compliance with the requirements in paragraph (b), in that it failed to make reasonable provision within its available resources for people in the Cape Metropolitan area with no access to land, no roof over their heads, and who were living in intolerable conditions or crisis situations ...

Supreme Court of Israel (sitting as the High Court of Justice), *Yated – Non-Profit Organization for Parents of Children with Down Syndrome, and 54 Parents* v. *Ministry of Education* (HCJ 2599/00), judgment of 14 August 2002 by Justice D. Dorner (leading judgment):

This petition raises the following questions: Are children with special needs only entitled to free special education in a special education institution? Or is the State also under an obligation to provide free special education to children with special needs who have been integrated into the regular education system?

The Statutory Provisions

1. Section 4 of the Special Education Law, 1988 provides that '[t]he State is responsible to provide special education under this law'. Sections 3 and 7 of the statute regulate the placement of children with special needs in educational institutions ...

Facts, Procedure, and Claims

2. Yated, a registered non-profit organization, together with 54 parents of children with Downs syndrome, asks that we order the State to provide free special education to children who, though having special educational needs, have been found suitable for integration in regular educational institutions. Petitioners claim that the authorities are required by the Special Education Law to finance special education in any educational institution where a child is placed. They claim that the approach expressed in section 7(b) of the law [according to which the Placement Committee determining the eligibility of a child with special needs for special education and his placement in a special education institution should, in determining the placement of a child with special needs, prefer placement in a recognized educational institution which is not a special education institution] requires the Placement Committee to prefer the placement of children with special needs in a regular educational institution. Furthermore, pursuant to the policy of the Ministry of Education, children with special needs should, wherever possible, be placed in the regular educational system and also be given additional educational assistance. Petitioners explained

that the Ministry of Education, though it encourages such integration, does not provide financial aid. As such, the financial burden falls on the parents. As such, parents who are unable to bear these expenses are forced to transfer their children to special education institutions, despite the fact that these children have been found suitable for integration into the regular educational system ...

This was the background for petitioners' claim that the policy of the Ministry of Education violates the right to education – a fundamental right. They further alleged that this policy infringes the fundamental right to equality. This is because it discriminates between parents whose children's special education needs are paid by the Ministry of Education and between parents who are forced to bear these costs independently. Furthermore, they claim, the policy also discriminates between those children integrated into regular classes – as their parents can bear the expenses involved – and those children placed in special education institution solely due to their parents' inability to bear those expenses.

3. In its response, the State did not dispute the pedagogical advantages of integrating children with special needs into regular educational institutions, and that the policy of the Ministry of Education was to encourage such integration. As part of this policy, since 1996 the Ministry of Education has even implemented programs for children with special needs who have been integrated into the regular education system. The Minister of Education appointed a public committee in 2000, which noted the importance of giving preference to integration within the regular education system, as provided by the Special Education Law. The Committee also noted the inadequacy of the resources allocated towards such integration. Internal ministerial committees were appointed to implement the recommendations of the public committee. These determined that the regular education system should be granted monies for additional integration hours and personnel trained in special education. They further determined that those special education students studying within the regular education system should receive the services provided by the law, as available resources allow.

The State claims that, subject to budgetary pressures, significant resources are allocated towards integration. Even so, the State contended that the clear import of section 3 of the law is that the right to free special education, which is conferred by section 4 of the law, can only be realized in an institution for special education or in a special education class within a regular institution. The actual extent of assistance granted to children with special needs in the regular education system is subject to the discretion of the Placement committee. The State claimed, however, that the Placement Committee is not authorized to provide assistance for all 'special education', as per the broad definition of that term in the law. They further argued that, pursuant to section 7(b) of the law, the State is under no statutory obligation to provide such assistance. This is because the decisions of the Placement Committee are only recommendations; their realization is contingent upon the resources actually available to the State.

The Right to Education

4. The right to education has long been recognized as a basic human right. The right is anchored in the Universal Declaration of Human Rights of 1948. Article 26 of this Declaration provides that every person has the right to education and that education must be free, at least in the elementary and fundamental stages. The International Covenant on Economic, Social and Cultural Rights of 1966 was also ratified by Israel in 1991. This declared in article 13 that education should be directed to the full development of the human personality, and that it

should strengthen the respect for human rights and fundamental freedoms. It also determined that elementary education should be compulsory and freely available ... The right to education is also anchored in articles 28 and 29 of the Convention on the Rights of the Child, 1989 ...

The right to education is also anchored in numerous constitutions, such as the Belgian Constitution (article 24), the South African Constitution (article 29), the Constitution of Spain (article 27), and the Irish Constitution (article 42). The German Constitution and the constitutions of most of the states of the United States establish the government's responsibility to provide education for its citizens ...

6. Shortly after its establishment, with the enactment of the Compulsory Education Law, 1949, the State of Israel delineated the scope of its obligation to ensure the rights of its citizenry to education. This law sets out an arrangement for compulsory education for every boy and girl until the age of 15, as well as the State's responsibility to ensure the provision of such education. More recently, the right of children to education in Israel was anchored in the Rights of the Student Law, 2000. The purpose of this law is to determine the principles for the rights of the student in the spirit of human dignity and the principles of the United Nations Convention on the Rights of the Child.

Case law, too, recognized the right to education as a fundamental right. Justice Theodor Or made the following comments regarding the importance of this right: 'One cannot exaggerate the importance of education as a social tool. This is one of the most important functions fulfilled by the government and the State. Education is critical for the survival of a dynamic and free democratic society. It constitutes a necessary foundation for every individual's self-fulfillment. It is essential for the success and flourishing of every individual. It is crucial to the survival of society, in which people improve their individual well-being and thus contribute to the well-being of the entire community' (HCJ 7715, 1554/95 *Shoharei Gilat* v. *Minister of Education and Culture*, at 24).

The right to free education is also an expression of the principle of equality. It enables every child to realize their innate talent and potential, to integrate into society and to progress therein, irrespective of their parents' socio-economic status ...

Discrimination in the exercise of the right to education, if occasioned on the basis of group affiliation, may indeed be regarded as degradation that violates the right to human dignity ... By contrast, unequal treatment occasioned by political, administrative, or budgetary reasons is not degrading, and does not, therefore, violate human dignity. For our purposes, discrimination against children with special needs, though rooted in their group affiliation, is motivated by budgetary considerations. As such, the question of whether such discrimination violates human dignity is not unequivocal and I see no need to answer it. Petitioners did not claim that the law should be annulled because it violates the right to human dignity. Their claim was rather that the law should be interpreted and applied in light of the right to education. Indeed, the basic right to education, as established by statute, our case law, and international law, is of independent validity, and has no necessary connection to the right to human dignity prescribed by the Basic Law: Human Dignity and Liberty ...

The Right to Special Education

7. The right to special education is a derivative of the right to education. Children with special needs are not able to exercise their right to education unless they receive special education that addresses their needs. Accordingly, the signatory States to the Convention on the Rights

of the Child recognized the right of children who are physically or mentally disabled to enjoy full and decent lives in conditions that ensure dignity, promote self-reliance and facilitate their active participation in communal life. See section 23 of the Convention. In order to ensure the protection of these rights, the Convention provides:

Party States recognize the right of the disabled child to special care. Party States shall encourage and ensure the extension, subject to available resources, to the suitable child and those responsible for his or her care, of assistance for which application is made and which is appropriate to the child's condition and to the circumstances of the parents or others caring for the child.

Children with special needs are entitled to an education suitable for their needs; this right is recognized in most of the countries around the world ... Many States have also recognized the importance of integrating people with special needs generally and children in particular into regular frameworks, and have created statutory arrangements for such integration. Thus, the [United States] Disabilities Education Act provides, in section 1412(a), that preference shall be given to placing children with special needs in the regular education system: '[States must establish procedures to ensure] to the maximum extent appropriate, children with disabilities, including children in public or private institutions or other care facilities, are educated with children who are not disabled, and special classes, separate schooling, or other removal of children with disabilities from the regular educational environment occurs only when the nature or severity of the disability of a child is such that education in regular classes with the use of supplementary aids and services cannot be achieved satisfactorily' (see also *Oberti* v. *Board of Education*, 1204 F. Supp. 995 (2d Cir. 1993); *Daniel R.R.* v. *State Board of Education*, 874 F. Supp. 2d 1036, 1049 (5th Cir.1989)).

In a similar vein, section 6(a)(2) of the Equal Rights For People With Disabilities Law of 1998 provides that 'the exercise of right and the grant of services to a person with disabilities shall be carried out ... within the framework of the services granted and intended for the general public, after making such adjustments as may be required under the circumstances ...' We ourselves ruled that the integration of the handicapped in the regular fabric of community life is intended to protect the dignity and the liberty of such persons, by ensuring equality and participation in society. HCJ 7081/93 *Botzer* v. *Municipal Council of Maccabim-Reut*, at 19. This is the background for the interpretation of the Special Education Law.

Interpretation of the Law

8. As stated above, the questions raised by this petition are: Is the right to special education conferred by the Special Education Law limited to special education provided in separate institutions for special education (as argued by the State)? Alternatively, does this right extend also to special education provided to children studying in the regular education system (as argued by petitioners)?

Our presumption is that statutes are interpreted in a manner commensurate with the basic values of the legal system. As such, our interpretations must accord with the principle of equality ... Similarly, statutory interpretation must harmonize with the right to education, including the right to special education.

Another rule of interpretation is the presumption that the norms adopted by the State should be in accord with the norms of international law by which the State is bound. According to this presumption, all rules will, wherever possible, be interpreted in a manner consistent with the norms of international law ...

These interpretive presumptions may be rebutted only when the language of the statute, or its particular purpose as specified in the law, cannot be reconciled with the general values of the legal system or with the international norm ...

9. For our purposes, the Special Education Law is intended to provide special education free of charge to any child with special needs, in order to ensure that he fulfills his potential and that he integrates into society. See also the Explanatory Notes to the Special Education Law Bill, 1988. The notes point out that special education is intended to aid integration into society and ensure the full development of the innate potential – physical, intellectual, and emotional – of each student. This purpose conforms with and gives expression to the right to education, the principle of equality, and the international conventions ratified by the State of Israel.

Section 7 of the law, which discusses special education in a regular educational institution, does not specifically provide that such education must be funded by the State, as it provides in section 3 regarding special education in separate institutions and classes. However, in view of the rights to education and to equality, the principles of international law, as well as the purpose of the law as described above, the necessary conclusion is that the funding duty of the State also applies to the assistance required for a child with special needs integrated into a regular educational institution.

Until now, the State has been guided by a discriminatory interpretation, which leads to an unreasonable result. The Special Education Law prescribes two paths for the provision of special education. The first path is within the separate framework of special education. The second path is within the regular educational framework. In the latter path, children receive assistance as determined by the Placement Committee in accordance with their needs. It is implausible that the Knesset would have arbitrarily decided to limit the State's duty to provide free special education to only one of these statutory frameworks. This is especially true in light of the undisputed fact that the regular framework has substantial advantages.

Furthermore, it is unacceptable that parents of children with special needs should waive their children's right to integration within the framework of regular education solely due to financial difficulties. This would undermine the very heart of substantive equality. The aspiration for such equality is manifest in the goal to provide equal opportunities for every child in Israel. When children with special needs are sent to frameworks for special education rather than the regular education framework – solely due to financial reasons – these children are deprived of this equal opportunity. Such discrimination is unacceptable.

10. The State's claim – that the duty of assistance under section 7 of the law is narrower than the duty set out by the definition of special education – is unacceptable. The provision regarding the recommendation for separate assistance is the natural result of placing a child with special needs in a regular educational framework. In such a case, it is the Placement Committee's duty to determine the type of assistance the child requires. This determination is classified as a 'recommendation', not because the State is released from its duty to provide the assistance, but rather because flexibility is required in implementing the recommendation. This implementation must consider the evolving needs of the particular child.

The Remedy

11. A purposive interpretation of the law requires that the state implement it in accord with the principle of equality. Discharge of this duty requires an equal budgetary allocation for all the

frameworks providing special education. In this context, a distinction must be made between the current budget and future budgets, beginning with the next fiscal year.

As for the future: it is clear that it is incumbent upon the Ministry of Education, with the assistance of the Ministry of Finance, to allocate its budget in a manner that implements the law as interpreted by this judgment ... And as for the present year: the appropriate remedy when human rights are violated is to compel the authorities to undo this breach immediately, even if this involves amending the budget structure ...

This is the rule, but in the present case it would be inappropriate for us to issue a rigid order, one that applies to the current fiscal year. For we fear that, as a result of the current dire economic straits in which the State finds itself, a renewed budgetary allocation would adversely affect those children with special needs currently being educated in special education institutions. In many cases the situation of these children is more acute than that of those in regular educational institutions, and it is not appropriate that the realization of the rights of the latter be at the expense of the former. Even now, however, the State should, wherever possible and at least partially, attempt to provide funding for the education of children with special needs in the regular educational institutions.

I therefore propose that the petition be accepted in the sense that it will be declared that the State has not discharged its statutory duty to provide free special education for children placed in regular educational institutions; that it must quickly adopt the measures necessary for it to come into compliance with the statutory requirements; and that it must comply with these requirements no later than the preparatory stages of the budget for the coming fiscal year, all subject to the restrictions of section 7(e) of the law.

Supreme Court of India, *People's Union for Civil Liberties and another* v. *Union of India & others*, in the Supreme Court of India, Civil Original Jurisdiction, Writ Petition (Civil) No. 196 of 2001, judgment of 2 May 2003:

[The People's Union for Civil Liberties (PUCL) claimed that starvation deaths had occurred in the state of Rajasthan, despite excess grain being kept for official times of famine, and various schemes throughout India for food distribution were also not functioning. It petitioned the Court for enforcement of both the food schemes and the Famine Code, a code permitting the release of grain stocks in times of famine. They grounded their arguments on the right to food, deriving it from the right to life. Various interim orders were made by the Court over two years, but with meagre implementation by the national and State Governments. In 2003, the court issued a judgment which found the right to life was imperiled due to the failure of the schemes to reach the poor. The Court noted the paradox of food being available in granaries while the poor were starving and it refused to hear arguments concerning the non-availability of resources given the severity of the situation. The court ordered that: (1) the Famine Code be implemented for three months; (2) grain allocation for the food for work scheme be doubled and financial support for schemes be increased; (3) ration shop licensees must stay open and provide the grain to families below the poverty line at the set price; (4) publicity be given to the rights of families below the poverty line to grain; (5) all individuals without means of support (older persons, widows, disabled adults) are to be granted an Antyodaya Anna Yozana ration card for free grain; (6) and State Governments should progressively implement the mid-day meal scheme in schools. The following excerpts include the departure point used by the Court and its direction as regards (1) the effective implementation of the Famine Code.]

This Court in various orders passed in the last two years has expressed its deep concern and it has been observed, in one of the orders, that what is of utmost importance is to see that food is provided to the aged, infirm, disabled, destitute women, destitute men who are in danger of starvation, pregnant and lactating women and destitute children, especially in cases where they or members of their family do not have sufficient funds to provide food for them. In case of famine, there may be shortage of food, but here the situation is that amongst plenty there is scarcity. Plenty of food is available, but distribution of the same amongst the very poor and the destitute is scarce and non-existent leading to malnutrition, starvation and other related problems. The anxiety of the Court is to see that the poor and destitute and the weaker sections of society do not suffer from hunger and starvation. The prevention of the same is one of the prime responsibilities of the Government – whether Central or the State. Mere schemes without any implementation are of no use. What is important is that the food must reach the hungry.

Article 21 of the Constitution of India protects for every citizen a right to live with human dignity. Would the very existence of life of those families which are below poverty line not come under danger for want of appropriate schemes and implementation thereof, to provide requisite aid to such families? Reference can also be made to Article 47 which, *inter alia*, provides that the State shall regard the raising of the level of nutrition and the standard of living of its people and the improvement of public health among its primary duties.

In the light of the aforesaid, we are of the view that for the time being for the months of May, June and July 2003, it is necessary to issue certain directions so that some temporary relief is available to those, who deserve it the most.

Our attention has been drawn to the Famine Code ... That Famine Code, we are informed, is the one formulated by State of Rajasthan and similar Codes have been formulated by other States ... Under the circumstances, we direct the implementation of the Famine Code for the period May, June and July 2003, as and when and where the situation may call for it, subject to the condition that if in subsequent schemes the relief is to be provided and preventive measures to be undertaken, during famine and drought, are better than the one stipulated by the Famine Code, the same may be implemented instead of the Famine Code.

| Box 8.1. | The adjudication of economic and social rights by the European Committee on Social Rights |

Although this chapter examines the role of domestic courts in the implementation of international human rights law, and particularly their role in protecting economic and social rights, inspiration may also be sought from the practice of certain international judicial or quasi-judicial bodies that have been confronted with similar problems. For instance, the European Committee on Social Rights established under the European Social Charter (on the role of the Committee in the context of collective complaints, see further box 11.1.) relied on the non-discrimination clause in order to affirm the justiciable nature of social rights, although recognizing that these are in principle subject to progressive realization. This, as we have seen (chapter 7, section 3.3., b)), was exemplified by the decision on the merits of collective Complaint No. 13/2002 (*Autisme-Europe* v. *France*), where the European Committee of Social Rights concluded that France had violated the provisions of the Revised European Social Charter on the right of persons with disabilities to integration and on the right to education, whether alone or combined with the non-discrimination requirement, because it had failed to raise significantly the proportion of children with autism being educated in either general or specialist schools in comparison to other children.

The Committee cited the judgment of the European Court of Human Rights in *Thlimmenos* v. *Greece*, Appl. No. 34369/97, judgment of 6 April 2000) to the effect that the principle of non-discrimination 'is also violated when States without an objective and reasonable justification fail to treat differently persons whose situations are significantly different'. Indirect discrimination, the Committee noted, 'may arise by failing to take due and positive account of all relevant differences or by failing to take adequate steps to ensure that the rights and collective advantages that are open to all are genuinely accessible by and to all' (para. 52). While acknowledging that the realization of certain rights having important budgetary implications could require an effort in time, the ECSR considered that this could not justify a failure of the State to adopt clear timeframes for the realization of the rights at stake and to monitor progress. It was clearly inspired by the approach of the Committee on Economic, Social and Cultural Rights with respect to the obligations of the Covenant on Economic, Social and Cultural Rights which are to be progressively realized (see General Comment No. 5, *Persons with Disabilities*, adopted at the eleventh session of the Committee (1994) (UN Doc. E/1995/22), in *Compilation of General Comments and General Recommendations Adopted by Human Rights Treaty Bodies* (UN Doc. HRI/GEN/1/Rev.7, 12 May 2004), p. 26: 'since the Covenant's provisions apply fully to all members of society, persons with disabilities are clearly entitled to the full range of rights recognized in the Covenant. In addition, insofar as special treatment is necessary, States parties are required to take appropriate measures, to the maximum extent of their available resources, to enable such persons to seek to overcome any disadvantages, in terms of the enjoyment of the rights specified in the Covenant, flowing from their disability').

The *Autisme-Europe* v. *France* decision illustrates how the requirement of non-discrimination may provide the direction for the realization of socio-economic rights by identifying the categories which, because of their particular vulnerability, deserve special attention. While that decision concerned the right to education, other decisions concerned, for instance, the right to housing: in *ERRC* v. *Bulgaria*, the Committee confirmed its view that, while 'States enjoy a margin of appreciation in determining the steps to be taken to ensure compliance with the Charter' (para. 35), 'the measures taken must meet the following three criteria: (i) a reasonable timeframe, (ii) a measurable progress and (iii) a financing consistent with the maximum use of available resources' (*ERRC* v. *Bulgaria*, Complaint No. 31/2005, decision on the merits of 18 October 2006, para. 37). In that case, Bulgaria was found to have violated the Charter because 'notwithstanding the clear political will ... to improve the housing situation of Roma families, [the programmes adopted to improve the housing conditions of the Roma segment of the population] have not yet yelded (*sic*) the expected results' (para. 38).

8.3. Questions for discussion: implementing social and economic rights through domestic courts

1. How would you describe the relationship between the Constitutional Court and the other branches of government in the South African case of *Grootboom*? Is the Court usurping the competences of the legislative or the executive branches of government?

2. In the case of *Yated* concerning the implementation of the Special Education Law in Israel, Justice Dorner expresses his 'fear that … a renewed budgetary allocation [for the current fiscal year] would adversely affect those children with special needs currently being educated in special education institutions'. This recognizes what Fuller and Hart have called the problem of 'polycentricity', which is sometimes seen as an obstacle to the adjudication of claims related to rights that require significant resources (see L. Fuller, 'The Forms and Limits of Adjudication', *Harvard Law Review*, 92 (1978), 353; and previously 'Adjudication and the Rule of Law', *Proceedings of the American Society of International Law*, 54, 1 (1960); the notion of 'polycentricity', as a characteristic of problems which should not be solved by adjudication, is borrowed from M. Polanyi, *The Logic of Liberty. Reflections and Rejoinders* (London: Routledge and Kegan Paul, 1951), p. 170 *et seq.*; see also, in a perspective similar to Fuller's, H. Hart, 'The Supreme Court, 1958 Term – Foreword: The Time Chart of Justices', *Harvard Law Review*, 73 (1959), 84 (1959); and for a discussion, see J. W. F. Allison, 'Fuller's Analysis of Polycentric Disputes and the Limits of Adjudication', *Cambridge Law Journal*, 53 (1994), 367). Where an individual complaint presents the judge with a problem the solution of which will have a ripple effect elsewhere and perhaps only worsen the situation of many others, how can the judge take this collective dimension into account? Would the alternative be between either denying the complaint or transforming him/herself into a social engineer, ordering and perhaps supervising large-scale changes to ensure that the remedy will meet the true dimensions of the problem the judge is confronted with? What is Justice Doner's solution to that problem? Is this solution appropriate?

3. In the course of its various orders concerning the implementation of the right to food in India, the Indian Supreme Court established its own independent monitoring mechanism to track both hunger and the Government's performance across the country. It appointed independent Commissioners for that purpose to provide the Court with reports on the implementation of its orders. For instance, in their fifth report, the Commissioners note in the introduction: 'At the outset, we would like to place on record, the complete lack of seriousness shown by many state governments to the implementation of schemes under review. On more than one occasion as the report will show, many states have not implemented Supreme Court's directions on one pretext or the other, and repeated orders from the Court have been blatantly ignored with no proper justification. It is our strong recommendation that the Honorable Court may take note of these violations, especially by the States of Uttar Pradesh, Bihar, Jharkand, Madhya Pradesh and Delhi, and pass appropriate orders for time-bound implementation of its orders' (*Right to Food* (India: Human Rights Law Network, 2008), p. 158; for a description of the role of the Supreme Court of India, see also C. Gonsalves, 'From International to Domestic Law: the Case of the Indian Supreme Court in Response to ESC Rights and the Right to Food' in

W. B. Eide and U. Kracht (eds.), *Food and Human Rights in Development*, vol. II, *Evolving Issues and Emerging Applications* (Antwerp-Oxford: Intersentia-Hart, 2007), p. 215). The reports of the Commissioners are an extraordinary collection of the failures of different levels of government to implement adequately the various schemes that are adopted in order to combat hunger and extreme poverty. Note that, in the *Grootboom* case, the Human Rights Commission was appointed to supervise compliance with the judgment of the Constitutional Court. Does this demonstrate that classical separation of powers may be inappropriate to deal with the need to ensure accountability for the progressive realization of economic and social rights? Should such 'fourth branches' be generalized?

4. How valid are the analogies between the protection of economic and social rights by international bodies, of a judicial or quasi-judicial nature, and their protection by domestic courts? For instance, may the approach chosen by the European Committee of Social Rights in *Autism-Europe* v. *France*, referred to in box 8.1. above, serve as a source of inspiration for domestic courts, or are the institutional settings too different for such a comparison to be justified?

5. In the light of the decisions above concerning the right to housing, the right to education for children with disabilities, or the right to food, do the critiques directed towards the adjudication of social and economic rights appear justified?

2 NON-JUDICIAL MECHANISMS

For the reasons briefly explained above, the provision of *ex post* remedies, however important, should not be considered sufficient for the effective protection of human rights. Preventive mechanisms should complement the role of courts or other authorities providing remedies to victims of violations (see, generally, T. Van Boven, 'Prevention of Human Rights Violations' in A. Eide and J. Helgesen (eds.), *The Future of Human Rights Protection in a Changing World: Fifty Years since the Four Freedoms Address. Essays in Honour of Torkel Opsahl* (Oslo: Norwegian University Press, 1991), p. 183). This section discusses three such mechanisms, or tools. These may be seen as elements of a governance model best suited to ensure respect for, and protection and fulfilment of, human rights: they are human rights impact assessments; the establishment of national human rights institutions; and the mainstreaming of human rights.

These tools go clearly beyond the 'judicial-normative' model that sees human rights as norms to be enforced by judicial mechanisms (on the need to move beyond such an approach, see P. Alston and J. H. H. Weiler, 'An "Ever Closer Union" in Need of a Human Rights Policy: the European Union and Human Rights' in P. Alston, with M. Bustelo and J. Heenan (eds.), *The EU and Human Rights* (Oxford University Press, 1999), p. 3). While the adoption of human rights action plans can be seen as another such governance tool, and while indicators are instruments that can be used both in the adoption and implementation of action plans and in impact assessments, both action plans and indicators have been discussed above (see chapter 5, sections 2.2. and 3, respectively), and they are not further elaborated upon here (for a study, as 'non-judicial preventive tools', of national human rights institutions, human rights indicators, human rights impact assessments, and human rights action plans, see G. de Beco, *Non-judicial Mechanisms for the Implementation of Human Rights in European States* (Brussels: Bruylant, 2009)).

2.1 The role of preventive mechanisms in general

The Committee on the Rights of the Child has provided useful guidance about the kind of measures which could be adopted in order to complement a remedial, *post hoc* approach to human rights violations, by a preventive, *ex ante* approach:

Committee on the Rights of the Child, General Comment No. 5 (2003), *General Measures of Implementation of the Convention on the Rights of the Child* **(Arts. 4, 42 and 44, para. 6) (CRC/GC/2003/5, 27 November 2003), paras. 18 and 27–59, and 65:**

[Review of legislation *ex ante* and *ex post*]
The Committee believes a comprehensive review of all domestic legislation and related administrative guidance to ensure full compliance with the Convention is an obligation. Its experience in examining not only initial but now second and third periodic reports under the Convention suggests that the review process at the national level has, in most cases, been started, but needs to be more rigorous. The review needs to consider the Convention not only article by article, but also holistically, recognizing the interdependence and indivisibility of human rights. The review needs to be continuous rather than one-off, reviewing proposed as well as existing legislation. And while it is important that this review process should be built into the machinery of all relevant government departments, it is also advantageous to have independent review by, for example, parliamentary committees and hearings, national human rights institutions, NGOs, academics, affected children and young people and others.

[Monitoring implementation – the need for child impact assessment and evaluation]
Ensuring that the best interests of the child are a primary consideration in all actions concerning children (art. 3(1)), and that all the provisions of the Convention are respected in legislation and policy development and delivery at all levels of government demands a continuous process of child impact assessment (predicting the impact of any proposed law, policy or budgetary allocation which affects children and the enjoyment of their rights) and child impact evaluation (evaluating the actual impact of implementation). This process needs to be built into government at all levels and as early as possible in the development of policy.

Self-monitoring and evaluation is an obligation for Governments. But the Committee also regards as essential the independent monitoring of progress towards implementation by, for example, parliamentary committees, NGOs, academic institutions, professional associations, youth groups and independent human rights institutions ...

The Committee commends certain States which have adopted legislation requiring the preparation and presentation to parliament and/or the public of formal impact analysis statements. Every State should consider how it can ensure compliance with article 3(1) and do so in a way which further promotes the visible integration of children in policy-making and sensitivity to their rights.

[Making children visible in budgets]

In its reporting guidelines and in the consideration of States parties' reports, the Committee has paid much attention to the identification and analysis of resources for children in national and other budgets (General Guidelines Regarding the Form and Contents of Periodic Reports to be Submitted under Article 44, Paragraph 1(b), of the Convention on the Rights of the Child, CRC/C/58, 20 November 1996, para. 20). No State can tell whether it is fulfilling children's economic, social and cultural rights 'to the maximum extent of ... available resources', as it is required to do under article 4, unless it can identify the proportion of national and other budgets allocated to the social sector and, within that, to children, both directly and indirectly. Some States have claimed it is not possible to analyse national budgets in this way. But others have done it and publish annual 'children's budgets'. The Committee needs to know what steps are taken at all levels of Government to ensure that economic and social planning and decision-making and budgetary decisions are made with the best interests of children as a primary consideration and that children, including in particular marginalized and disadvantaged groups of children, are protected from the adverse effects of economic policies or financial downturns.

Emphasizing that economic policies are never neutral in their effect on children's rights, the Committee has been deeply concerned by the often negative effects on children of structural adjustment programmes and transition to a market economy. The implementation duties of article 4 and other provisions of the Convention demand rigorous monitoring of the effects of such changes and adjustment of policies to protect children's economic, social and cultural rights.

[Training and capacity-building]

The Committee emphasizes States' obligation to develop training and capacity-building for all those involved in the implementation process – government officials, parliamentarians and members of the judiciary – and for all those working with and for children. These include, for example, community and religious leaders, teachers, social workers and other professionals, including those working with children in institutions and places of detention, the police and armed forces, including peacekeeping forces, those working in the media and many others. Training needs to be systematic and ongoing – initial training and re-training. The purpose of training is to emphasize the status of the child as a holder of human rights, to increase knowledge and understanding of the Convention and to encourage active respect for all its provisions. The Committee expects to see the Convention reflected in professional training curricula, codes of conduct and educational curricula at all levels. Understanding and knowledge of human rights must, of course, be promoted among children themselves, through the school curriculum and in other ways ...

The Committee's guidelines for periodic reports mention many aspects of training, including specialist training, which are essential if all children are to enjoy their rights. The Convention highlights the importance of the family in its preamble and in many articles. It is particularly important that the promotion of children's rights should be integrated into preparation for parenthood and parenting education.

There should be periodic evaluation of the effectiveness of training, reviewing not only knowledge of the Convention and its provisions but also the extent to which it has contributed to developing attitudes and practice which actively promote enjoyment by children of their rights.

[Independent human rights institutions]

In its general comment No. 2 (2002) entitled 'The role of independent national human rights institutions in the protection and promotion of the rights of the child', the Committee notes that it 'considers the establishment of such bodies to fall within the commitment made by States parties upon ratification to ensure the implementation of the Convention and advance the universal realization of children's rights'. Independent human rights institutions are complementary to effective government structures for children; the essential element is independence: 'The role of national human rights institutions is to monitor independently the State's compliance and progress towards implementation and to do all it can to ensure full respect for children's rights. While this may require the institution to develop projects to enhance the promotion and protection of children's rights, it should not lead to the Government delegating its monitoring obligations to the national institution. It is essential that institutions remain entirely free to set their own agenda and determine their own activities' (HRI/GEN/1/Rev. 6, para. 25, p. 295).

One of the reasons why preventive mechanisms should be developed, in addition to remedial mechanisms, is because of the considerable burden imposed on courts by the flow of individual applications of victims of violations. This was also the concern which led the Committee of Ministers of the Council of Europe to formulate the following recommendation:

Committee of Ministers of the Council of Europe, Recommendation Rec(2004)5 of the Committee of Ministers to Member States on the verification of the compatibility of draft laws, existing laws and administrative practice with the standards laid down in the European Convention on Human Rights (adopted by the Committee of Ministers on 12 May 2004 at its 114th session):

The Committee of Ministers, [r]ecalling that, according to Article 46, paragraph 1, of the Convention, the high contracting parties undertake to abide by the final judgments of the European Court of Human Rights (hereinafter referred to as 'the Court') in any case to which they are parties;

Considering however, that further efforts should be made by member states to give full effect to the Convention, in particular through a continuous adaptation of national standards in accordance with those of the Convention, in the light of the case law of the Court;

Convinced that verifying the compatibility of draft laws, existing laws and administrative practice with the Convention is necessary to contribute towards preventing human rights violations and limiting the number of applications to the Court;

Stressing the importance of consulting different competent and independent bodies, including national institutions for the promotion and protection of human rights and non-governmental organisations;

Taking into account the diversity of practices in member states as regards the verification of compatibility;

Recommends that member states, taking into account the examples of good practice appearing in the appendix:

I. ensure that there are appropriate and effective mechanisms for systematically verifying the compatibility of draft laws with the Convention in the light of the case law of the Court;

II. ensure that there are such mechanisms for verifying, whenever necessary, the compatibility of existing laws and administrative practice, including as expressed in regulations, orders and circulars;

III. ensure the adaptation, as quickly as possible, of laws and administrative practice in order to prevent violations of the Convention;

Instructs the Secretary General of the Council of Europe to ensure that the necessary resources are made available for proper assistance to member states which request help in the implementation of this recommendation.

Appendix to Recommendation Rec(2004)5
Introduction 1. ... [T]he number of applications submitted to the European Court of Human Rights (hereinafter referred to as 'the Court') is increasing steadily, giving rise to considerable delays in the processing of cases.

2. ... [I]t should not be forgotten that it is the parties to the Convention, which, in accordance with the principle of subsidiarity, remain the prime guarantors of the rights laid down in the Convention. According to Article 1 of the Convention, 'The High Contracting Parties shall secure to everyone within their jurisdiction the rights and freedoms defined in Section I of this Convention.' It is thus at national level that the most effective and direct protection of the rights and freedoms guaranteed in the Convention should be ensured. This requirement concerns all state authorities, in particular the courts, the administration and the legislature.

3. The prerequisite for the Convention to protect human rights in Europe effectively is that states give effect to the Convention in their legal order, in the light of the case law of the Court. This implies, notably, that they should ensure that laws and administrative practice conform to it.

4. This recommendation encourages states to set up mechanisms allowing for the verification of compatibility with the Convention of both draft laws and existing legislation, as well as administrative practice. Examples of good practice are set out below. The implementation of the recommendation should thus contribute to the prevention of human rights violations in member states, and consequently help to contain the influx of cases reaching the Court.

Verification of the compatibility of draft laws 5. It is recommended that member states establish systematic verification of the compatibility with the Convention of draft laws, especially those which may affect the rights and freedoms protected by it. It is a crucial point: by adopting a law verified as being in conformity with the Convention, the state reduces the risk that a violation of the Convention has its origin in that law and that the Court will find such a violation. Moreover, the state thus imposes on its administration a framework in line with the Convention for the actions it undertakes *vis-à-vis* everyone within its jurisdiction.

6. Council of Europe assistance in carrying out this verification may be envisaged in certain cases. Such assistance is already available, particularly in respect of draft laws on freedom of religion, conscientious objection, freedom of information, freedom of association, etc. It is none the less for each state to decide whether or not to take into account the conclusions reached within this framework.

Verification of the compatibility of laws in force 7. Verification of compatibility should also be carried out, where appropriate, with respect to laws in force. The evolving case law of the Court may indeed have repercussions for a law which was initially compatible with the Convention or which had not been the subject of a compatibility check prior to adoption.

8. Such verification proves particularly important in respect of laws touching upon areas where experience shows that there is a particular risk of human rights violations, such as police activities, criminal proceedings, conditions of detention, rights of aliens, etc.

Verification of the compatibility of administrative practice 9. This recommendation also covers, wherever necessary, the compatibility of administrative regulations with the Convention, and therefore aims to ensure that human rights are respected in daily practice. It is indeed essential that bodies, notably those with powers enabling them to restrict the exercise of human rights, have all the necessary resources to ensure that their activity is compatible with the Convention.

10. It has to be made clear that the recommendation also covers administrative practice which is not attached to the text of a regulation. It is of utmost importance that states ensure verification of their compatibility with the Convention.

Procedures allowing follow-up of the verification undertaken 11. In order for verification to have practical effects and not merely lead to the statement that the provision concerned is incompatible with the Convention, it is vital that member states ensure follow-up to this kind of verification.

12. The recommendation emphasises the need for member states to act to achieve the objectives it sets down. Thus, after verification, member states should, when necessary, promptly take the steps required to modify their laws and administrative practice in order to make them compatible with the Convention. In order to do so, and where this proves necessary, they should improve or set up appropriate revision mechanisms which should systematically and promptly be used when a national provision is found to be incompatible. However, it should be pointed out that often it is enough to proceed to changes in case law and practice in order to ensure this compatibility. In certain member states compatibility may be ensured through the non-application of the offending legislative measures.

13. This capacity for adaptation should be facilitated and encouraged, particularly through the rapid and efficient dissemination of the judgments of the Court to all the authorities concerned with the violation in question, and appropriate training of the decision makers ...

14. When a court finds that it does not have the power to ensure the necessary adaptation because of the wording of the law at stake, certain states provide for an accelerated legislative procedure.

15. Within the framework of the above, the following possibilities could be considered.

Examples of good practice ... *I. Publication, translation and dissemination of, and training in, the human rights protection system*

17. As a preliminary remark, one should recall that effective verification first demands appropriate publication and dissemination at national level of the Convention and the relevant case law of the Court, in particular through electronic means and in the language(s) of the country concerned, and the development of university education and professional training programmes in human rights.

II. Verification of draft laws 18. Systematic supervision of draft laws is generally carried out both at the executive and at the parliamentary level, and independent bodies are also consulted.

By the executive

19. In general, verification of conformity with the Convention and its protocols starts within the ministry which initiated the draft law. In addition, in some member states, special responsibility is entrusted to certain ministries or departments, for example, the Chancellery, the Ministry of Justice and/or the Ministry of Foreign Affairs, to verify such conformity. Some member states entrust the agent of the government to the Court in Strasbourg, among other functions, with seeking to ensure that national laws are compatible with the provisions of the Convention. The agent is therefore empowered, on this basis, to submit proposals for the amendment of existing laws or of any new legislation which is envisaged.

20. The national law of numerous member states provides that when a draft text is forwarded to parliament, it should be accompanied by an extensive explanatory memorandum, which must also indicate and set out possible questions under the constitution and/or the Convention. In some member states, it should be accompanied by a formal statement of compatibility with the Convention. In one member state, the minister responsible for the draft text has to certify that, in his or her view, the provisions of the bill are compatible with the Convention, or to state that he or she is not in a position to make such a statement, but that he or she nevertheless wishes parliament to proceed with the bill.

By the parliament

21. In addition to verification by the executive, examination is also undertaken by the legal services of the parliament and/or its different parliamentary committees.

Other consultations

22. Other consultations to ensure compatibility with human rights standards can be envisaged at various stages of the legislative process. In some cases, consultation is optional. In others, notably if the draft law is likely to affect fundamental rights, consultation of a specific institution, for example the Conseil d'Etat in some member states, is compulsory as established by law. If the government has not consulted as required, the text will be tainted by procedural irregularity. If, after having consulted, it decides not to follow the opinion received, it accepts responsibility for the political and legal consequences that may result from such a decision.

23. Optional or compulsory consultation of non-judicial bodies competent in the field of human rights is also often foreseen. In particular these may be independent national institutions for the promotion and protection of human rights, the ombudspersons, or local or international non-governmental organisations, institutes or centres for human rights, or the Bar, etc.

24. Council of Europe experts or bodies, notably the European Commission for Democracy through Law ('the Venice Commission'), may be asked to give an opinion on the compatibility with the Convention of draft laws relating to human rights. This request for an opinion does not replace an internal examination of compatibility with the Convention.

III. Verification of existing laws and administrative practice 25. While member states cannot be asked to verify systematically all their existing laws, regulations and administrative practice, it may be necessary to engage in such an exercise, for example as a result of national experience in applying a law or regulation or following a new judgment by the Court against another member state. In the case of a judgment that concerns it directly, by virtue of Article 46 [of the European Convention on Human Rights], the state is under obligation to take the measures necessary to abide by it.

By the executive

26. In some member states, the ministry that initiates legislation is also responsible for verifying existing regulations and practices, which implies knowledge of the latest developments in the case law of the Court. In other member states, governmental agencies draw the attention of independent bodies, and particularly courts, to certain developments in the case law. This aspect highlights the importance of initial education and continuous training with regard to the Convention system. The competent organs of the state have to ensure that those responsible in local and central authorities take into account the Convention and the case law of the Court in order to avoid violations.

By the parliament

27. Requests for verification of compatibility may be made within the framework of parliamentary debates.

By judicial institutions

28. Verification may also take place within the framework of court proceedings brought by individuals with legal standing to act or even by state organs, persons or bodies not directly affected (for example before the Constitutional Court).

By independent non-judicial institutions

29. In addition to their other roles when seized by the government or the parliament, independent non-judicial institutions, and particularly national institutions for the promotion and protection of human rights, as well as ombudspersons, play an important role in the verification of how laws are applied and, notably, the Convention which is part of national law. In some countries, these institutions may also, under certain conditions, consider individual complaints and initiate enquiries on their own initiative. They strive to ensure that deficiencies in existing legislation are corrected, and may for this purpose send formal communications to the parliament or the government.

2.2 Human rights impact assessments

Human rights impact assessments are among the tools that could improve the prevention of human rights violations (see G. de Beco, 'Human Rights Impact Assessments', *Netherlands Quarterly of Human Rights*, 27, No. 2 (2009), 139; T. Landman, 'Human Rights Impact Assessments' in *Studying Human Rights* (London: Routledge, 2006)). They differ from, and go beyond, compatibility assessments that merely examine whether a particular policy or regulatory measure is, *on its face*, compliant with the human rights obligations of the State concerned. Such compatibility exercises are regularly performed, for instance, before parliamentary committees, by the legal services of ministerial departments, or by courts, as described in the Annex to the Recommendation Rec(2004)5 on the verification of the compatibility of draft laws, existing laws and administrative practice with the standards laid down in the European Convention on Human Rights, addressed by the Committee of Ministers of the Council of Europe to the Member States of the organization, and presented above (section 2.1.). In contrast, impact assessments seek to assess compatibility not only on the basis of a conceptual analysis, but also through a sociological examination of the impacts, both intended and unintended, that a measure could have on the enjoyment of human rights or on the ability of the State to protect and fulfil human rights. While impact assessments have been common for a number of years to measure the economic, environmental, or social impacts of specific measures, human rights impact assessments differ in significant respects from these more classical impact assessments:

Paul Hunt and Gillian MacNaughton, *Impact Assessments, Poverty and Human Rights: a Case Study Using the Right to the Highest Attainable Standard of Health* (UNESCO, 2006), pp. 12–15:

Human rights impact assessment offers added value for several inter-related reasons. First, human rights impact assessment is based on a framework of international legal obligations to which governments have agreed. Second, human rights impact assessment provides an opportunity to make government policy-making more coherent across departments as the framework applies to all divisions of the government. Third, human rights impact assessment will result in more effective policies because the policies will be more coherent, they will be backed up by legal obligations and they will be adopted through human-rights respecting processes.

1. Legal Obligations

International human rights legal obligations arise when a State voluntarily endorses a human rights treaty ... To comply with its international human rights obligations, a State must ensure, before it adopts any proposed law, policy, program or project, that it is consistent with its human rights, as well as other, legal obligations ... In response to reports submitted by States, the [United Nations human rights] treaty bodies have also urged individual States to perform impact assessments. For example, the Committee on the Rights of the Child urged the Government of the Netherlands 'to develop ways to establish a systematic assessment of the impact of budgetary allocations and macroeconomic policies on the implementation of children's rights and to collect and disseminate information in this regard'. Similarly, the Committee on Economic, Social and Cultural Rights, has recommended to States that human rights impact assessments 'be made an integral part of every proposed piece of legislation or policy initiative on a basis analogous to environmental impact assessments or statements'.

Thus, human rights impact assessments are highly recommended, perhaps even legally required, for States to comply with the international human rights obligations that they have undertaken. Further, the human rights legal framework for impact assessments adds legitimacy to demands for policy changes that are based on these assessments. The legal obligations also bring both monitoring and accountability to bear on policy-making. Policy-makers will be subject to scrutiny by human rights institutions, including the international treaty bodies, and people can hold their governments accountable for the adverse human rights impacts of policies, programs and projects.

In sum, the international legal obligations underlying the human rights framework for impact assessments gives States a strong incentive to do the impact assessments, a legitimate rationale for modifying proposals based on the assessments and a system to hold policy-makers to account for the impact of their decisions on human rights.

2. Coherence

The human rights framework for impact assessment also offers States the opportunity to enhance coherence in policy-making processes. Governmental departments are often disconnected and do not necessarily know what other departments are doing or have agreed to do. Thus, for example, one department may adopt a policy or program that adversely affects the people that another policy or program in another department is designed to help. However, a State's national and international human rights obligations apply to all divisions of the government, and thus human rights must be consistently and coherently applied across all national policy-making processes. In this manner, the human rights framework can bring coherence to policy making, helping to ensure that the same factors are considered in policy-making in all departments of the government.

3. Effectiveness

The underlying legal obligations and the increased coherence offered by a human rights framework for impact assessment will both contribute to rigorous policy-making as well as to adoption of policies, programs and projects that are more effective in improving the well-being of people, especially those who are marginalized. The human rights approach also brings a number of factors to the assessment process that generally will improve effectiveness in policy making such as disaggregation, participation, transparency and accountability.

For example, a human rights approach to impact assessment requires assessing the decision-making process to determine whether it encourages the people who are likely to be affected by the policy, program or project to participate in a meaningful manner. It asks: does the government consult the people likely to be affected in determining the likely consequences of a proposal, in generating ideas for modifications and alternatives to a proposal, in weighing priorities and in making final trade-offs and decisions? Participation by the people affected is more likely to result in a decision that will be better for them, a decision that they will accept and a decision that they can own. In this way, the human rights requirement of participation will enhance effectiveness of the policy, program or project.

Similarly, the human rights approach to impact assessment requires consideration of the distributional impact of reforms on the well-being of various groups, especially people living in poverty and other marginalized groups. Disaggregated information allows for the impact analysis to identify mitigating measures or alternatives that may not have been evident without this information and that will result in a more effective policy, especially in terms of its impact on the most vulnerable people.

Overall, the human rights framework for impact assessment adds value because human rights (1) are based on legal obligations to which governments have agreed to abide, (2) apply to all parts of the government encouraging coherence to policy-making and ensuring that policies reinforce each other; (3) require participation in policy making by the people affected, enhancing legitimacy and ownership of policy choices; (4) enhance effectiveness through factors such as disaggregation, participation and transparency; and (5) demand mechanisms through which policy makers can be held accountable.

2.3 The role of national human rights institutions

In the Vienna Declaration and Programme of Action of 25 June 1993, the World Conference on Human Rights reaffirmed 'the important and constructive role played by national institutions for the promotion and protection of human rights, in particular in their advisory capacity to the competent authorities, their role in remedying human rights violations, in the dissemination of human rights information, and education in human rights'. It also encouraged 'the establishment and strengthening of national institutions, having regard to the "Principles relating to the status of national institutions" and recognizing that it is the right of each State to choose the framework which is best suited to its particular needs at the national level' (Vienna Declaration and Programme of Action of 25 June 1993, UN Doc. A/CONF.157/23, at para. 36). The establishment of national human rights institutions (NHRI) has further been encouraged by recommendations adopted at regional level – such as the Recommendation No. R(97)14 of the Committee of Ministers of the Council of Europe on the establishment of independent national institutions for the promotion and protection of human rights, adopted on 30 September 1997 – or at universal level – such as the General Recommendation adopted by the Committee on the Elimination of Racial Discrimination on this issue (General Recommendation XVII (1993), Establishment of national institutions to facilitate implementation of the Convention), or similar general comments by the Committee on Economic, Social and Cultural Rights (General Comment No. 10 of the Committee on Economic, Social and Cultural Rights of 14 December 1998, *The Role of National Human Rights Institutions in the Protection of Economic, Social and Cultural Rights* (E/C.12/1998/25)) or by the Committee on the Rights of the Child (General Comment No. 2 (2002), *The Role of Independent National Human Rights Institutions in the Promotion and Protection of the Rights of the Child*, HRI/GEN/1/Rev.9 (vol. II), p. 391).

A national human rights institution is an officially established and State-funded national entity independent from the government, mandated to promote and protect international human rights standards at domestic level. Different models of human rights institutions co-exist, ranging from bodies with a large membership including a wide range of civil society organizations, often referred to as the 'Committee' model (such as the French Commission nationale consultative des droits de l'homme, established in 1947 as the first NHRI in the world), to much smaller expert bodies, such as the 'Commission' model of Australia, which usually have a very broad mandate ranging from investigation of human rights violations to education and public relations, and participation in judicial procedures. Other models include single-member *Defensores del Pueblo* in Latin America or ombudsman institutions in European Nordic countries, which usually act on the basis of complaints and have far-reaching investigation and information rights; or the 'Danish model' of an institute mostly focusing on human rights education, research and documentation (on national human rights institutions, see M. Kjaerum, 'National Human Rights Institutions Implementing Human Rights' in M. Bergsmo (ed.), *Human Rights and Criminal Justice for the Downtrodden: Essays in Honour of Asbjorn Eide* (Leiden: Martinus Nijhoff, 2003), p. 631; R. Murray, *The Role of National Human Rights Institutions at the International and Regional Levels* (Oxford: Hart Publishing, 2007); R. Murray, 'National Human Rights Institutions. Criteria and Factors for Assessing their Effectiveness', *Netherlands Quarterly of Human Rights*, 25, No. 2 (2007), 189; A.-E. Pohjolainen, *The Evolution of National Human*

Rights Institutions: the Role of the United Nations (Copenhagen: The Danish Institute for Human Rights, 2006)).

Yet, despite this diversity, a number of key principles apply to all NHRIs. They are defined as the 'Paris Principles', since – although endorsed by the UN General Assembly in 1993, following their approval by the Commission on Human Rights (Commission on Human Rights Resolution 1992/54 of 3 March 1992) – they were initially approved at a meeting convened in Paris in 1991 by the Commission nationale consultative des droits de l'homme in co-operation with the UN. The minimum standards established by the Paris Principles are applied by the International Co-ordinating Committee (ICC) that relies on the Principles to determine accreditation status of NHRIs. The ICC distinguishes between status A-institutions (in compliance with each of the Paris Principles and recognized full voting rights as members), status B (not in compliance with each of the Principles or insufficient information provided, and thus recognized only as observer status), and C (non-compliant with the Paris Principles and thus without status). By mid-2008, the ICC had accredited sixty-two entities.

Principles relating to the Status of National Institutions (The Paris Principles) adopted by General Assembly Resolution 48/134 of 20 December 1993:

Competence and responsibilities

1. A national institution shall be vested with competence to promote and protect human rights.
2. A national institution shall be given as broad a mandate as possible, which shall be clearly set forth in a constitutional or legislative text, specifying its composition and its sphere of competence.
3. A national institution shall, *inter alia*, have the following responsibilities:

(a) To submit to the Government, Parliament and any other competent body, on an advisory basis either at the request of the authorities concerned or through the exercise of its power to hear a matter without higher referral, opinions, recommendations, proposals and reports on any matters concerning the promotion and protection of human rights; the national institution may decide to publicize them; these opinions, recommendations, proposals and reports, as well as any prerogative of the national institution, shall relate to the following areas:

  (i) Any legislative or administrative provisions, as well as provisions relating to judicial organizations, intended to preserve and extend the protection of human rights; in that connection, the national institution shall examine the legislation and administrative provisions in force, as well as bills and proposals, and shall make such recommendations as it deems appropriate in order to ensure that these provisions conform to the fundamental principles of human rights; it shall, if necessary, recommend the adoption of new legislation, the amendment of legislation in force and the adoption or amendment of administrative measures;

  (ii) Any situation of violation of human rights which it decides to take up;

  (iii) The preparation of reports on the national situation with regard to human rights in general, and on more specific matters;

(iv) Drawing the attention of the Government to situations in any part of the country where human rights are violated and making proposals to it for initiatives to put an end to such situations and, where necessary, expressing an opinion on the positions and reactions of the Government;

(b) To promote and ensure the harmonization of national legislation, regulations and practices with the international human rights instruments to which the State is a party, and their effective implementation;

(c) To encourage ratification of the above-mentioned instruments or accession to those instruments, and to ensure their implementation;

(d) To contribute to the reports which States are required to submit to United Nations bodies and committees, and to regional institutions, pursuant to their treaty obligations and, where necessary, to express an opinion on the subject, with due respect for their independence;

(e) To cooperate with the United Nations and any other orgnization in the United Nations system, the regional institutions and the national institutions of other countries that are competent in the areas of the protection and promotion of human rights;

(f) To assist in the formulation of programmes for the teaching of, and research into, human rights and to take part in their execution in schools, universities and professional circles;

(g) To publicize human rights and efforts to combat all forms of discrimination, in particular racial discrimination, by increasing public awareness, especially through information and education and by making use of all press organs.

Composition and guarantees of independence and pluralism

1. The composition of the national institution and the appointment of its members, whether by means of an election or otherwise, shall be established in accordance with a procedure which affords all necessary guarantees to ensure the pluralist representation of the social forces (of civilian society) involved in the protection and promotion of human rights, particularly by powers which will enable effective cooperation to be established with, or through the presence of, representatives of:

(a) Non-governmental organizations responsible for human rights and efforts to combat racial discrimination, trade unions, concerned social and professional organizations, for example, associations of lawyers, doctors, journalists and eminent scientists;

(b) Trends in philosophical or religious thought;

(c) Universities and qualified experts;

(d) Parliament;

(e) Government departments (if these are included, their representatives should participate in the deliberations only in an advisory capacity).

2. The national institution shall have an infrastructure which is suited to the smooth conduct of its activities, in particular adequate funding. The purpose of this funding should be to enable it to have its own staff and premises, in order to be independent of the Government and not be subject to financial control which might affect its independence.

3. In order to ensure a stable mandate for the members of the national institution, without which there can be no real independence, their appointment shall be effected by an official act which shall establish the specific duration of the mandate. This mandate may be renewable, provided that the pluralism of the institution's membership is ensured.

Methods of operation

Within the framework of its operation, the national institution shall:

(a) Freely consider any questions falling within its competence, whether they are submitted by the Government or taken up by it without referral to a higher authority, on the proposal of its members or of any petitioner,

(b) Hear any person and obtain any information and any documents necessary for assessing situations falling within its competence;

(c) Address public opinion directly or through any press organ, particularly in order to publicize its opinions and recommendations;

(d) Meet on a regular basis and whenever necessary in the presence of all its members after they have been duly concerned;

(e) Establish working groups from among its members as necessary, and set up local or regional sections to assist it in discharging its functions;

(f) Maintain consultation with the other bodies, whether jurisdictional or otherwise, responsible for the promotion and protection of human rights (in particular, ombudsmen, mediators and similar institutions);

(g) In view of the fundamental role played by the non-governmental organizations in expanding the work of the national institutions, develop relations with the non-governmental organizations devoted to promoting and protecting human rights, to economic and social development, to combating racism, to protecting particularly vulnerable groups (especially children, migrant workers, refugees, physically and mentally disabled persons) or to specialized areas.

Additional principles concerning the status of commissions with quasi-jurisdictional competence

A national institution may be authorized to hear and consider complaints and petitions concerning individual situations. Cases may be brought before it by individuals, their representatives, third parties, non-governmental organizations, associations of trade unions or any other representative organizations. In such circumstances, and without prejudice to the principles stated above concerning the other powers of the commissions, the functions entrusted to them may be based on the following principles:

(a) Seeking an amicable settlement through conciliation or, within the limits prescribed by the law, through binding decisions or, where necessary, on the basis of confidentiality;

(b) Informing the party who filed the petition of his rights, in particular the remedies available to him, and promoting his access to them;

(c) Hearing any complaints or petitions or transmitting them to any other competent authority within the limits prescribed by the law;

(d) Making recommendations to the competent authorities, especially by proposing amendments or reforms of the laws, regulations and administrative practices, especially if they have created the difficulties encountered by the persons filing the petitions in order to assert their rights.

The Paris Principles provide that national human rights institutions shall have the power to adopt opinions on draft bills (para. 3(a)(i)). The extent to which human rights institutions should be involved in the legislative process, however, and whether they should be asked to screen draft laws or regulations before they enter into force, remain debated, not least because such an involvement creates the risk of narrowing down the political debate to questions of human rights compatibility. The following conclusions emerged from a study of the extent to which NHRIs were involved in the legislative process:

Olivier De Schutter, *The Role of National Human Rights Institutions in the Human Rights Proofing of Legislation*, 4th Roundtable of European National Human Rights Institutions and the Council of Europe Commissioner for Human Rights, CommDH/NHRI(2006)2, Strasbourg, 28 September 2006:

Where the consultation of the NHRI prior to the adoption of legislation is ... not compulsory ..., it is resorted to selectively. In order to ensure that the legislation or regulations they adopt will comply with the requirements of human rights, States rely preferably either on expertise within ministerial departments, or on the evaluation made in the course of the parliamentary procedure, quite frequently by specialist units or parliamentary committees. A number of [Council of Europe] States, moreover, ensure a systematic or quasi-systematic human rights proofing of draft legislation by an independent instance (such as in Belgium or in the Netherlands, the Council of State, whose consultation in many cases is obligatory).

What this seems to illustrate is that verification of compliance is perceived as a technical issue, not requiring input by an instance representative of a wide range of societal interests and, especially, of different segments of the civil society; and requiring a purely legalistic approach, rather than an approach informed by the grass-roots knowledge civil society organizations may provide. Another indicia of this is the very weak role played by human rights impact assessments in such pre-legislative scrutiny for compatibility of draft legislation with human rights.

However, there is no need to make a choice between these two approaches. On the contrary, it is their complementarity which should be stressed. While the appreciation of the compatibility with human rights of certain draft legislative proposals requires a legal scrutiny, to be performed, preferably, by experts, such an evaluation also should be informed by an understanding of the impact the implementation of such proposals could have, for instance, on certain communities or in certain local settings. Indeed, each of the different institutional devices for human rights proofing of legislation which have been reviewed present certain advantages. [I]deally, they should be combined with one another rather than a choice having to be made between these techniques [see the table presented on the next page]:

It is probably unrealistic to expect that all these devices will be used, at least on a systematic basis, in combination with one another. At the same time, it is important to note that the advantages of relying on each of these techniques may add up, where they are used in combination.

There are certain risks attached to the multiplication of fora where such human rights screening takes place. In particular, the authority of the findings made by each instance (for instance, by an independent body such as the legislative section of the Council of State in Belgium) may be threatened if another (such as, for instance, a NHRI or a parliamentary committee) arrives at a different conclusion as to the same question of compatibility.

Human rights proofing performed by	Advantages
Ministerial department taking the initiative of the proposal	Ensures a better understanding of human rights implications of their legislative proposals by public servants (serves the mainstreaming of human rights within public administration and the building of a culture based on human rights)
Specialized unit within the government	Ensures an expert approach to the human rights issues raised by the proposal, and an adequate use of the existing international and European standards
Parliamentary committee	Ensures a transparency in the evaluation and facilitates control by the public opinion and the media, facilitates societal debate Opens up the possibility of consultation of external experts, including NHRIs
Specialized, independent instance located outside both government and Parliament	Guarantees an independency in the evaluation and ensures that the evaluation will not be subordinated to the need to reach political compromises Insulates the evaluation from the pressure of public opinion
NHRI of equivalent institution	Ensures that the impact of the proposed legislation on a wide range of interests will be taken into account, and that the existing standards of international and European human rights law will be taken into account

Similarly, if various procedures coexist through which the human rights compatibility of a draft proposal can be vetted, the Executive may be tempted to 'forum shop', and choose the procedure which it considers the least potentially damaging to its proposal. However, while such a risk should not be underestimated, in most cases the advantages of multiplying procedures will by far compensate for any potential handicap such multiplication might imply. In fact, the most promising route may be not to organize simply the coexistence of these mechanisms, but to achieve their interaction, as when the opinion of a NHRI forms the basis for the work of a parliamentary committee or of a unit within government in charge of verifying compliance. What should be avoided in any case is to fall into the trap of thinking that the more one instance is consulted, the less any other instance will be influential in the debate concerning the compatibility with the requirements of fundamental rights of any legislative proposal: for instance, a parliamentary committee will be better equipped to deliver a robust position if this is based on an opinion sought from a NHRI; the explanatory memorandum attached to a governmental legislative proposal will be richer, better informed, and more convincing, if it provides answers to certain concerns raised in consultations, for instance of an independent institution for the promotion and protection of human rights.

In general, it has been found that NHRIs pay far greater attention to civil and political rights than to economic, social and cultural rights, even when their mandate covers both sets of rights (see C. Raj Kumar, 'National Human Rights Institutions and Economic, Social and Cultural Rights: Toward the Institutionalization and Developmentalization of Human Rights', *Human Rights Quarterly*, 28 (2006), 755). Yet, as noted by the Committee on Economic, Social and Cultural Rights, the value added of NHRIs may be significant in the area of economic, social and cultural rights:

Committee on Economic, Social and Cultural Rights, General Comment No. 10, *The Role of National Human Rights Institutions in the Protection of Economic, Social and Cultural Rights* (1998):

The following list is indicative of the types of activities that can be, and in some instances already have been, undertaken by national institutions in relation to these rights:

(a) The promotion of educational and information programmes designed to enhance awareness and understanding of economic, social and cultural rights, both within the population at large and among particular groups such as the public service, the judiciary, the private sector and the labour movement;

(b) The scrutinizing of existing laws and administrative acts, as well as draft bills and other proposals, to ensure that they are consistent with the requirements of the International Covenant on Economic, Social and Cultural Rights;

(c) Providing technical advice, or undertaking surveys in relation to economic, social and cultural rights, including at the request of the public authorities or other appropriate agencies;

(d) The identification of national-level benchmarks against which the realization of Covenant obligations can be measured;

(e) Conducting research and inquiries designed to ascertain the extent to which particular economic, social and cultural rights are being realized, either within the State as a whole or in areas or in relation to communities of particular vulnerability;

(f) Monitoring compliance with specific rights recognized under the Covenant and providing reports thereon to the public authorities and civil society; and

(g) Examining complaints alleging infringements of applicable economic, social and cultural rights standards within the State.

2.4 Mainstreaming human rights

The institutionalization of human rights through impact assessments and an enhanced role for NHRIs could be further strengthened by systematically integrating human rights into daily policy-making, even in areas which, on their surface, may seem to present little or no relationship to the fulfilment of human rights. This is what the concept of mainstreaming refers to. In the area of gender equality, for instance, mainstreaming has been defined as 'the reorganisation, improvement, development and evaluation of policy processes, so that a gender equality perspective is incorporated in all policies at all levels and at all stages, by the actors normally involved in policy-making'

(Council of Europe, Gender Mainstreaming: Conceptual Framework, Methodology and Presentation of Good Practices. Final Report of the Activities of the Group of Specialists on Mainstreaming (EG-S-MS (98)2), Strasbourg 1998, p. 6). Mainstreaming may serve a number of functions (see further O. De Schutter, 'Mainstreaming Human Rights in the European Union' in P. Alston and O. De Schutter (eds.), *Monitoring Fundamental Rights in the EU. The Contribution of the Fundamental Rights Agency* (Oxford: Hart Publishing, 2005), p. 37, on which the following paragraphs draw):

1. *Mainstreaming is an incentive to develop new policy instruments.* Mainstreaming displaces questions which were sectorialized from the vertical to the horizontal, from the policy margins to their centre. It therefore requires policy-makers to ask new questions about old themes. For instance, the mainstreaming of disability issues would oblige the policy-makers to identify how, in their particular sector, they could contribute to the social and professional integration of persons with disabilities: rather than remedying the exclusion from employment of persons with disabilities, mainstreaming seeks to combat such exclusion by tackling the phenomenon at its root, in the market mechanisms which produce it. An obligation imposed on all policy-makers to identify how they could facilitate the realization of the objective which is mainstreamed, in this sense, is a first step towards identifying means by which the mechanisms producing undesirable outcomes may be modified: it therefore is a lever for political imagination.

2. *Mainstreaming is a source of institutional learning.* To the extent that they must mainstream human rights into decision-making, policy-makers are obliged to identify issues which are present in the policies they pursue or the sectors these policies impact upon, but which would otherwise be obliterated and marginalized. As they get acquainted with the new tools mainstreaming requires, these actors will learn about these implications which previously may have gone unnoticed. They will gradually gain an expertise in the issues mainstreaming requires them to consider. The objective is that, in time, the institutional culture within the organization will evolve, and that both awareness to fundamental rights issues and the capacity to address them will augment.

3. *Mainstreaming improves the implication of civil society organizations in policy-making.* As decision-makers are obliged to identify the policies which best take human rights into account, although they have no specialized knowledge in the issue, they will be required to consult externally. They may of course limit that consultation to experts. But they may also be incentivized to consult more widely, within the community of stakeholders, in order not only better to evaluate the impact the proposed policies may have (as such an impact may be difficult to anticipate and often will be impossible to measure), but also to stimulate the formulation of alternative proposals, better suited to the conciliation of the different objectives pursued and, therefore, more satisfactory in a mainstreaming perspective.

4. *Mainstreaming improves transparency and accountability.* In formulating policies or legislative proposals, policy-makers will have to refer to the impact they may have on the realization of human rights. This will not only incentivize them to develop alternatives they may have had no good reason previously to consider, it will also

lead the proposals to be more richly justified, as the policy-maker will have to explain why a particular route was chosen and preferred above alternative possibilities, after having examined those possibilities and evaluated their potential impact. Most often, mainstreaming will therefore be combined with an assessment of the impact on human rights of the different routes available to the policy-maker (on human rights impact assessments, see above, section 2.2.), since only by measuring such impacts can an informed choice be made. In turn, this will equip the stakeholders participating with the informational resources they require for their participation to be effective.

5. *Mainstreaming improves co-ordination between different services.* The sectoralization of policies, although inevitable in any large organization, may lead to the development of policies effectively contradicting one another. For instance, States may be under an obligation to adopt regulations ensuring health and safety at work, while at the same time having to guarantee the principle of equal treatment with respect to person with disabilities in employment – although it is well documented that the two objectives may conflict with one another, and that some form of co-ordination between the two sets of rules may be therefore desirable. Similarly, States are encouraged to promote diversity in business, yet at the same time the rules relating to the protection of personal data may constitute an obstacle for employers seeking to develop such diversity policies by monitoring the representation of ethnic groups in the workforce (see chapter 7, section 4, and box 7.5.). Because it is transversal and creates horizontal bridges between vertical sectors, mainstreaming may serve to identify such tensions, in order to remedy them. It is a way to restore communication between different services or departments, as one of its tools may consist in the organization of common meetings with representatives from different services to compare the schemes they are proposing and identify potential conflicts or redundancies, or other failures in coherence.

6. *Mainstreaming aims at the causes of the problems identified rather than at their surface manifestations.* Mainstreaming addresses the definition of policies at their initial stages and throughout their implementation. Therefore its transformative character is much more powerful than that of *post hoc* monitoring, where the impact of policies is measured. Although, like mainstreaming, impact assessment may also operate *ex ante*, i.e. in the initial stages of policy-selection, mainstreaming goes one step further in that it imposes on authorities a positive duty to identify how they may contribute to achieving the objective pursued. It therefore obliges them not only to examine whether the policy they have been pursuing or which they intend to pursue adversely impacts upon human rights, but also to ask how they may positively contribute to the realization of human rights: the promotion and protection of human rights thus becomes part of the set of objectives that they are pursuing and which, in combination with other objectives, will dictate the shape of policies. Again, the mainstreaming of disability may serve to illustrate this: it is one thing to measure the impact of certain policies on persons with disabilities, and choose the policy which appears to have the least adverse impact on them – for instance, where policies are devised which seek to create incentives to work and therefore to raise the level of activity of the active segment of the population; it is quite another to consider

that employment policies should contribute actively to the professional integration of persons with disabilities, and that the absence of adverse impact on persons with disabilities – or the adoption of measures mitigating any adverse impact there may be – is therefore necessary, but not sufficient.

8.4. Questions for discussion: tools to prevent human rights violations

1. The Committee on the Rights of the Child took the view that 'every State needs an independent human rights institution with responsibility for promoting and protecting children's rights' (General Comment No. 2 (2002), *The Role of Independent National Human Rights Institutions in the Promotion and Protection of the Rights of the Child*, HRI/GEN/1/Rev.9 (vol. II), p. 391, para. 7). Similarly, the Committee on the Elimination of Racial Discrimination considers that States should establish NHRIs in order to facilitate the implementation of the Convention for the Elimination of All Forms of Racial Discrimination (General Recommendation XVII (1993), Establishment of national institutions to facilitate implementation of the Convention). What are the respective advantages of establishing NHRIs with a broad mandate, covering all human rights, and of establishing NHRIs with a mandate covering only a limited set of rights, or focusing on one category of rights-holders?

2. Which body is best placed to perform human rights impact assessments prior to the adoption of certain policies or regulatory measures? Should this be done by the competent decision-maker, or by an independent body?

3. Are there any risks associated with attempts to mainstream human rights in all sectoral policies? Would it be recommended, for instance, to include in debates about the penitentiary policy of the government considerations related to the right to work of the prison staff? In public procurement, would it be recommended to choose as a sub-contractor for public contracts the economic operator that has the best internal human rights policy in place, rather than the operator making the most economically advantageous offer? Is there a risk that mainstreaming human rights distorts public policy-making in a way that underestimates the weight of other considerations, competing with the need to promote human rights?

The United Nations Human Rights Treaties System

INTRODUCTION

This chapter offers an overview of the role of the expert bodies set up under the core UN human rights treaties (see generally G. Alfredsson *et al.* (eds), *International Human Rights Monitoring Mechanisms* (The Hague: Kluwer Law International, 2001); P. Alston and J. Crawford (eds.), *The Future of the UN Human Rights Treaty System* (Cambridge University Press, 2000); P. Alston (ed.), *The United Nations and Human Rights: a Critical Appraisal*, second edn (Oxford: Clarendon Press, 2004)). Seven such bodies are currently in operation. These are the Committee on the Elimination of Racial Discrimination (CERD), which has been functioning since 1969, the Human Rights Committee (CCPR) (1976), the Committee on Economic, Social and Cultural Rights (CESCR) (1987), the Committee on the Elimination of Discrimination Against Women (CEDAW) (1981), the Committee Against Torture (CAT) (1987), the Committee on the Rights of the Child (CRC) (1990), and the Committee on Migrant Workers (CMW) (2003). All but one of these expert bodies have their role and composition defined in the respective treaties with which they supervise compliance. The exception is the Committee on Economic, Social and Cultural Rights (CESCR), which was established by Resolution 1985/17 of the Economic and Social Council (Ecosoc) and which was modelled on the Human Rights Committee created by the International Covenant on Civil and Political Rights (ICCPR).

The main competence of these expert bodies is to receive State reports about the implementation of the human rights treaties they monitor, and to adopt Concluding Observations on the basis of this information. In addition, most of the human rights treaty bodies (as they are generally referred to) may receive individual communications from victims of violations of the said treaties. In general, the other powers of these bodies play a comparatively much minor or even insignificant role. These are the powers to receive inter-State communications (a possibility which has been dormant since the origins); to make enquiries into certain situations, which may comprise a visit on the territory of the State concerned with the latter's consent; or, in the case of the Subcommittee on Prevention established under the 2002 Optional Protocol to the Convention against Torture and Other Cruel, Inhuman or Degrading Treatment or Punishment (which entered into force on 22 June 2006), to visit places where persons are detained and to make recommendations concerning the protection of these persons against torture and other cruel, inhuman or degrading treatment or punishment, as well as to support the national preventive mechanisms which the States parties to the said Protocol have to set up. In addition, under the 2006 International Convention for the Protection of All Persons from Enforced Disappearance, the Committee on Enforced Disappearances may decide urgently to bring the matter to the attention of the General Assembly of the United Nations, if it receives information which appears to contain well-founded indications that enforced disappearance is being practised on a widespread or systematic basis in the territory under the jurisdiction of a State party (Art. 34).

The following table presents the different UN treaty bodies and the competences they have been attributed:

	State reports	Individual communications	Inter-State communications	Enquiries or other
ICERD	Art. 9	Art. 14 (optional declaration)	Arts. 11–13	
ICCPR	Art. 40	OP-1	Arts. 41–43 (optional declaration)	
ICESCR	Art. 16 (Ecosoc)	Optional Protocol	OP Art. 10 (optional declaration)	OP Art. 11 (optional declaration)
CEDAW	Art. 18	OP Art. 1–7	Art. 29 (arbitration or submission to the ICJ)	OP Arts. 8–9 (but opt-out possible)
CAT	Art. 19	Art. 22 (optional declaration)	Art. 21 (optional declaration)	Art. 20
CRC	Arts. 44–45			
CMW	Arts. 73–74	Art. 77 (optional declaration)	Art. 76 (optional declaration)	
CFD	Art. 29	Art. 30 (urgent requests) and Art. 31 (optional declaration)	Art. 32 (optional declaration)	Arts. 33 and 34 (visit and bring to the attention of the UN GA)
CRPD	Arts. 35–36	OP Arts. 1–5		OP Arts. 6–7 (but opt-out possible)

This chapter is divided into four sections. First, we examine the role of the UN human rights treaties expert bodies in receiving States' reports and commenting upon those reports. Second, we look at their role in the examination of individual communications. Third, we briefly examine the questions raised by the follow-up given by States to the findings or recommendations of the human rights treaty bodies, whether in the concluding observations adopted on the basis of State reports or in the views they express on individual communications. Fourth, we revisit the debate on the reform of the human rights treaty bodies. With the exception of the fourth section, this chapter focuses on the concluding observations the UN human rights treaty bodies adopt on States' reports and on the views they express on the individual communications they receive. In addition, the treaty bodies adopt General Comments (labelled 'General Recommendations' in the context of the International Convention on the Elimination of All Forms of Racial Discrimination (ICERD)), in which they clarify their understanding of the States' obligations under the treaties they supervise, thus facilitating compliance by the guidance they provide: while no specific section is dedicated to this function, such General Comments have been extensively relied on in the other chapters of this volume, and they shall therefore not be studied further (see P. Alston, 'The Historical Origins of the Concept of "General Comments" in Human Rights Law' in L. Boisson de Chazournes and V. Gowland Debbas (eds.), *The International Legal System in Quest of Equity and Universality:* Liber Amicorum *George Abi-Saab* (Leiden: Brill Academic Publishers, 2001), p. 763).

1 STATE REPORTING

1.1 The objectives of State reporting

All the UN human rights treaties provide that States parties submit reports about the measures adopted in order to implement their treaty obligations. The initial reports are to be submitted within one or two years from the entry into force of the treaty for the State concerned, and thereafter, generally, every four or five years. The State reports are to 'indicate the factors and difficulties, if any, affecting the implementation' of the treaty concerned (see *Manual on Human Rights Reporting* (Geneva: Office of the High Commissioner for Human Rights, 1997); and, for the most up-to-date compilation of the reporting guidelines issued by the human rights treaty bodies, HRI/GEN/2/Rev.5 (2008)). Indeed, the identification of such obstacles may guide the UN specialized agencies when they can assist States overcoming them. Article 40 para. 3 ICCPR thus states that the Secretary-General of the United Nations 'may, after consultation with the Committee, transmit to the specialized agencies concerned copies of such parts of the reports as may fall within their field of competence'. The International Covenant on Economic Social and Cultural Rights (ICESCR) provides, even more explicitly, that the Economic and Social Council – which, in the ICESCR, is identified as the addressee of the States' reports (Article 16 para. 2) – 'may bring to the attention of other organs of the United Nations, their subsidiary organs and specialized agencies concerned with furnishing technical assistance any matters arising out of the reports referred to in this part of the [International Covenant on Economic, Social and Cultural Rights] which may assist such bodies in deciding, each within its field of competence, on the advisability of international measures likely to contribute to the effective progressive implementation of the present Covenant' (Art. 22; see also Art. 16 para. 2(b)). On the basis of these reports, the expert committees prepare concluding observations, which identify both positive aspects and areas of concern. During the 1970s and 1980s, the 'observations' in fact consisted of disparate observations made by the members of the committees in their individual capacity. The practice of adopting concluding observations reflecting the position of the committee as a whole was pioneered in 1990 by the Committee on Economic, Social and Cultural Rights. The Human Rights Committee followed suit in 1992, and so did the Committee on the Elimination of Racial Discrimination in 1993. This is now the general practice.

In its first General Comment, the Committee on Economic, Social and Cultural Rights offered a useful list of the functions fulfilled by the reporting procedure:

Committee on Economic, Social and Cultural Rights, General Comment No. 1, *Reporting by States Parties* (1989) (E/1989/22):

1. The reporting obligations which are contained in part IV of [the International Covenant on Economic, Social and Cultural Rights] are designed principally to assist each State party in fulfilling its obligations under the Covenant and, in addition, to provide a basis on which the Council, assisted by the Committee, can discharge its responsibilities for monitoring States parties' compliance with their obligations and for facilitating the realization of economic, social and cultural rights in accordance with the provisions of the Covenant. The Committee considers that it would be incorrect to assume that reporting is essentially only a procedural matter designed solely to satisfy each State party's formal obligation to report to the appropriate international monitoring body. On the contrary, in accordance with the letter and spirit of the Covenant, the processes of preparation and submission of reports by States can, and indeed should, serve to achieve a variety of objectives.

2. A first objective, which is of particular relevance to the initial report required to be submitted within two years of the Covenant's entry into force for the State party concerned, is to ensure that a comprehensive review is undertaken with respect to national legislation, administrative rules and procedures, and practices in an effort to ensure the fullest possible conformity with the Covenant. Such a review might, for example, be undertaken in conjunction with each of the relevant national ministries or other authorities responsible for policy-making and implementation in the different fields covered by the Covenant.

3. A second objective is to ensure that the State party monitors the actual situation with respect to each of the rights on a regular basis and is thus aware of the extent to which the various rights are, or are not, being enjoyed by all individuals within its territory or under its jurisdiction. From the Committee's experience to date, it is clear that the fulfilment of this objective cannot be achieved only by the preparation of aggregate national statistics or estimates, but also requires that special attention be given to any worse-off regions or areas and to any specific groups or subgroups which appear to be particularly vulnerable or disadvantaged. Thus, the essential first step towards promoting the realization of economic, social and cultural rights is diagnosis and knowledge of the existing situation. The Committee is aware that this process of monitoring and gathering information is a potentially time-consuming and costly one and that international assistance and cooperation, as provided for in article 2, paragraph 1 and articles 22 and 23 of the Covenant, may well be required in order to enable some States parties to fulfil the relevant obligations. If that is the case, and the State party concludes that it does not have the capacity to undertake the monitoring process which is an integral part of any process designed to promote accepted goals of public policy and is indispensable to the effective

implementation of the Covenant, it may note this fact in its report to the Committee and indicate the nature and extent of any international assistance that it may need.

4. While monitoring is designed to give a detailed overview of the existing situation, the principal value of such an overview is to provide the basis for the elaboration of clearly stated and carefully targeted policies, including the establishment of priorities which reflect the provisions of the Covenant. Therefore, a third objective of the reporting process is to enable the Government to demonstrate that such principled policy-making has in fact been undertaken. While the Covenant makes this obligation explicit only in article 14 in cases where 'compulsory primary education, free of charge' has not yet been secured for all, a comparable obligation 'to work out and adopt a detailed plan of action for the progressive implementation' of each of the rights contained in the Covenant is clearly implied by the obligation in article 2, paragraph 1 'to take steps ... by all appropriate means ...'

5. A fourth objective of the reporting process it to facilitate public scrutiny of government policies with respect to economic, social and cultural rights and to encourage the involvement of the various economic, social and cultural sectors of society in the formulation, implementation and review of the relevant policies. In examining reports submitted to it to date, the Committee has welcomed the fact that a number of States parties, reflecting different political and economic systems, have encouraged inputs by such non-governmental groups into the preparation of their reports under the Covenant. Other States have ensured the widespread dissemination of their reports with a view to enabling comments to be made by the public at large. In these ways, the preparation of the report, and its consideration at the national level can come to be of at least as much value as the constructive dialogue conducted at the international level between the Committee and representatives of the reporting State.

6. A fifth objective is to provide a basis on which the State party itself, as well as the Committee, can effectively evaluate the extent to which progress has been made towards the realization of the obligations contained in the Covenant. For this purpose, it may be useful for States to identify specific benchmarks or goals against which their performance in a given area can be assessed. Thus, for example, it is generally agreed that it is important to set specific goals with respect to the reduction of infant mortality, the extent of vaccination of children, the intake of calories per person, the number of persons per health-care provider, etc. In many of these areas, global benchmarks are of limited use, whereas national or other more specific benchmarks can provide an extremely valuable indication of progress.

7. In this regard, the Committee wishes to note that the Covenant attaches particular importance to the concept of 'progressive realization' of the relevant rights and, for that reason, the Committee urges States parties to include in their periodic reports information which shows the progress over time, with respect to the effective realization of the relevant rights. By the same token, it is clear that qualitative, as well as quantitative, data are required in order for an adequate assessment of the situation to be made.

8. A sixth objective is to enable the State party itself to develop a better understanding of the problems and shortcomings encountered in efforts to realize progressively the full range of economic, social and cultural rights. For this reason, it is essential that States parties report in detail on the 'factors and difficulties' inhibiting such realization. This process of identification and recognition of the relevant difficulties then provides the framework within which more appropriate policies can be devised.

9. A seventh objective is to enable the Committee, and the States parties as a whole, to facilitate the exchange of information among States and to develop a better understanding of the common problems faced by States and a fuller appreciation of the type of measures which might be taken to promote effective realization of each of the rights contained in the Covenant. This part of the process also enables the Committee to identify the most appropriate means by which the international community might assist States, in accordance with articles 22 and 23 of the Covenant...

These views remain fully valid today. In 2005, the objectives of the reporting process were summarized in almost identical terms:

Harmonized Guidelines on Reporting under the International Human Rights Treaties, including Guidelines on a Common Core Document and treaty-specific targeted documents (HRI/MC/2005/3, 1 June 2005):

9. States parties should see the process of preparing their reports for the treaty bodies not only as the fulfilment of an international obligation, but also as an opportunity to take stock of the state of human rights protection within their jurisdiction for the purpose of policy planning and implementation. The report preparation process offers an occasion for each State party to:

(a) Conduct a comprehensive review of the measures it has taken to harmonize national law and policy with the provisions of the relevant international human rights treaties to which it is a party;

(b) Monitor progress made in promoting the enjoyment of the rights set forth in the treaties in the context of the promotion of human rights in general;

(c) Identify problems and shortcomings in its approach to the implementation of the treaties;

(d) Assess future needs and goals for more effective implementation of the treaties; and

(e) Plan and develop appropriate policies to achieve these goals.

10. The reporting process should encourage and facilitate, at the national level, popular participation, public scrutiny of government policies and constructive engagement with civil society conducted in a spirit of cooperation and mutual respect, with the aim of advancing the enjoyment by all of the rights protected by the relevant convention.

11. At the international level, the reporting process creates a framework for constructive dialogue between States and the treaty bodies. The treaty bodies, in providing these guidelines, wish to emphasize their supportive role in fostering effective implementation of the international human rights instruments and in encouraging international cooperation in the promotion and protection of human rights in general.

In addition to the objectives listed above, State reports should serve as an opportunity to review any reservations or declarations made by the State upon ratification, since States are requested to justify the maintenance of such reservations or declarations. Moreover, where there exists an individual communications mechanism before the expert committee concerned, the State report should provide an opportunity for the

State to explain which follow-up was given to any views adopted by the committee on the basis of such communications (on the follow-up to individual communications, see further section 3.2. in this chapter). Consider, for instance, the Consolidated Guidelines for State reports under the ICCPR, adopted in 2001 by the Human Rights Committee.

Human Rights Committee, Consolidated Guidelines for State Reports under the International Covenant on Civil and Political Rights (26 February 2001)(CCPR/C/66/GUI/Rev.2) (excerpts):

C. General guidance for contents of all reports

C.1 The articles and the Committee's general comments. The terms of the articles in Parts I, II and III of the Covenant must, together with general comments issued by the Committee on any such article, be taken into account in preparing the report.

C.2 Reservations and declarations. Any reservation to or declaration as to any article of the Covenant by the State party should be explained and its continued maintenance justified.

C.3 Derogations. The date, extent and effect of, and procedures for imposing and for lifting any derogation under article 4 should be fully explained in relation to every article of the Covenant affected by the derogation.

C.4 Factors and difficulties. Article 40 of the Covenant requires that factors and difficulties, if any, affecting the implementation of the Covenant should be indicated. A report should explain the nature and extent of, and reasons for every such factor and difficulty, if any such exist; and should give details of the steps being taken to overcome these.

C.5 Restrictions or limitations. Certain articles of the Covenant permit some defined restrictions or limitations on rights. Where these exist, their nature and extent should be set out.

C.6 Data and statistics. A report should include sufficient data and statistics to enable the Committee to assess progress in the enjoyment of Covenant rights, relevant to any appropriate article.

C.7 Article 3. The situation regarding the equal enjoyment of Covenant rights by men and women should be specifically addressed.

C.8 Core document. Where the State party has already prepared a core document (see HRI/CORR/1, 24 February 1992), this will be available to the Committee: it should be updated as necessary in the report, particularly as regards 'General legal framework' and 'Information and publicity' (see HRI/CORR/1, paras. 3 and 4).

D. The initial report

D.1 General This report is the State party's first opportunity to present to the Committee the extent to which its laws and practices comply with the Covenant which it has ratified. The report should:

– Establish the constitutional and legal framework for the implementation of Covenant rights;
– Explain the legal and practical measures adopted to give effect to Covenant rights;
– Demonstrate the progress made in ensuring enjoyment of Covenant rights by the people within the State party and subject to its jurisdiction.

D.2 Contents of the report D.2.1 A State party should deal specifically with every article in Parts I, II and III of the Covenant; legal norms should be described, but that is not sufficient: the factual situation and the practical availability, effect and implementation of remedies for violation of Covenant rights should be explained and exemplified.

D.2.2 The report should explain:

How article 2 of the Covenant is applied, setting out the principal legal measures which the State party has taken to give effect to Covenant rights; and the range of remedies available to persons whose rights may have been violated;

Whether the Covenant is incorporated into domestic law in such a manner as to be directly applicable;

If not, whether its provisions can be invoked before and given effect to by courts, tribunals and administrative authorities;

Whether the Covenant rights are guaranteed in a Constitution or other laws and to what extent; or

Whether Covenant rights must be enacted or reflected in domestic law by legislation so as to be enforceable.

D.2.3 Information should be given about the judicial, administrative and other competent authorities having jurisdiction to secure Covenant rights.

D.2.4 The report should include information about any national or official institution or machinery which exercises responsibility in implementing Covenant rights or in responding to complaints of violations of such rights, and give examples of their activities in this respect.

D.3 Annexes to the report

D.3.1 The report should be accompanied by copies of the relevant principal constitutional, legislative and other texts which guarantee and provide remedies in relation to Covenant rights. Such texts will not be copied or translated, but will be available to members of the Committee; it is important that the report itself contains sufficient quotations from or summaries of these texts so as to ensure that the report is clear and comprehensible without reference to the annexes.

E. Subsequent periodic reports

E.1 There should be two starting points for such reports:

The concluding observations (particularly 'Concerns' and 'Recommendations' on the previous report and summary records of the Committee's consideration) (insofar as these exist);

An examination by the State party of the progress made towards and the current situation concerning the enjoyment of Covenant rights by persons within its territory or jurisdiction.

E.2 Periodic reports should be structured so as to follow the articles of the Covenant. If there is nothing new to report under any article it should be so stated.

E.3 The State party should refer again to the guidance on initial reports and on annexes, insofar as these may also apply to a periodic report.

E.4 There may be circumstances where the following matters should be addressed, so as to elaborate a periodic report:

There may have occurred a fundamental change in the State party's political and legal approach affecting Covenant rights: in such a case a full article by article report may be required;

New legal or administrative measures may have been introduced which deserve the annexure of texts and judicial or other decisions.

F. Optional protocols

F.1 If the State party has ratified the Optional Protocol and the Committee has issued Views entailing provision of a remedy or expressing any other concern, relating to a communication received under that Protocol, a report should (unless the matter has been dealt with in a previous report) include information about the steps taken to provide a remedy, or meet such a concern, and to ensure that any circumstance thus criticized does not recur.

F.2 If the State party has abolished the death penalty the situation relating to the Second Optional Protocol should be explained.

G. The Committee's consideration of reports

G.1 General The Committee intends its consideration of a report to take the form of a constructive discussion with the delegation, the aim of which is to improve the situation pertaining to Covenant rights in the State.

G.2 List of issues On the basis of all information at its disposal, the Committee will supply in advance a list of issues which will form the basic agenda for consideration of the report. The delegation should come prepared to address the list of issues and to respond to further questions from members, with such updated information as may be necessary; and to do so within the time allocated for consideration of the report.

G.3 The State party's delegation The Committee wishes to ensure that it is able effectively to perform its functions under article 40 and that the reporting State party should obtain the maximum benefit from the reporting requirement. The State party's delegation should, therefore, include persons who, through their knowledge of and competence to explain the human rights situation in that State, are able to respond to the Committee's written and oral questions and comments concerning the whole range of Covenant rights.

G.4 Concluding observations Shortly after the consideration of the report, the Committee will publish its concluding observations on the report and the ensuing discussion with the delegation. These concluding observations will be included in the Committee's annual report to the General Assembly; the Committee expects the State party to disseminate these conclusions, in all appropriate languages, with a view to public information and discussion.

G.5 Extra information G.5.1 Following the submission of any report, subsequent revisions or updating may only be submitted:

(a) No later than 10 weeks prior to the date set for the Committee's consideration of the report (the minimum time required by the United Nations translation services); or,
(b) after that date, provided that the text has been translated by the State party into the working languages of the Committee (currently English, Spanish and French).

If one or other of these courses is not complied with, the Committee will not be able to take an addendum into account. This, however, does not apply to updated annexes or statistics.

G.5.2 In the course of the consideration of a report, the Committee may request or the delegation may offer further information; the secretariat will keep a note of such matters which should be dealt with in the next report.

1.2 The role of non-governmental organizations

Non-governmental organizations play a key role in the reporting process, by providing the Committee members with first-hand information, in the form of 'shadow reports' which are now often as well or even better documented than the official State report. The system thus becomes increasingly triangular, shifting from a dialogue between the Committee members and the State's delegation to an exchange during which the Committee members confront the State with information obtained from other sources that may contradict the presentation made in the official report. The Committee on the Rights of the Child has been particularly eager to encourage the involvement of non-governmental organizations in the reporting process:

Committee on the Rights of the Child, General Comment No. 5 (2003), *General Measures of Implementation of the Convention on the Rights of the Child* **(Arts. 4, 42 and 44, para. 6) (CRC/GC/2003/5, 27 November 2003):**

The Committee welcomes the development of NGO coalitions and alliances committed to promoting, protecting and monitoring children's human rights and urges Governments to give them non-directive support and to develop positive formal as well as informal relationships with them. The engagement of NGOs in the reporting process under the Convention, coming within the definition of 'competent bodies' under article 45(a), has in many cases given a real impetus to the process of implementation as well as reporting. The NGO Group for the Convention on the Rights of the Child has a very welcome, strong and supportive impact on the reporting process and other aspects of the Committee's work. The Committee underlines in its reporting guidelines that the process of preparing a report 'should encourage and facilitate popular participation and public scrutiny of government policies' (para. 3). The media can be valuable partners in the process of implementation.

The Rules of Procedure of the human rights treaty bodies may specify what role non-governmental organizations may play in the reporting process. Consider for instance the Rules of Procedure of the Committee on Economic, Social and Cultural Rights, as initially adopted in 1989 and since revised on a number of occasions:

Committee on Economic, Social and Cultural Rights, Rules of the procedure of the Committee (provisional rules of procedure adopted by the Committee at its third session (1989), embodying amendments adopted by the Committee at its fourth (1990) and eighth (1993) sessions) (E/C.12/1990/4/Rev.1, 1 September 1993):

Rule 69. Submission of information, documentation and written statements
1. Non-governmental organizations in consultative status with the Council may submit to the Committee written statements that might contribute to full and universal recognition and realization of the rights contained in the Covenant.
2. In addition to the receipt of written information, a short period of time will be made available at the beginning of each session of the Committee's pre-sessional working group to provide NGOs with an opportunity to submit relevant oral information to the members of the working group.
3. Furthermore, the Committee will set aside part of the first afternoon at each of its sessions to enable it to receive oral information provided by NGOs. Such information should: (a) focus

specifically on the provisions of the Covenant on Economic, Scocial and Cultural Rights; (b) be of direct relevance to matters under consideration by the Committee; (c) be reliable, and (d) not be abusive. The relevant meeting will be open and will be provided with interpretation services, but will not be covered by summary records.

4. The Committee may recommend to the Council to invite United Nations bodies concerned and regional intergovernmental organizations to submit to it information, documentation and written statements, as appropriate, relevant to its activities under the Covenant.

1.3 The problem of overdue or lacking reports

States have regularly been late in submitting their reports to the human rights treaties expert bodies (see the concerns expressed by the Human Rights Committee in its General Comment No. 1, *Reporting Obligation* (27 July 1981)). The problem of overdue reporting or even lack of reporting by States has been plaguing the system, since its origins in the 1980s. 'As of 31 January 2004, 185 initial reports of States parties required under the various treaties were overdue, of which 114 had been overdue for more than five years. Furthermore, a total of 660 periodic reports from States parties were overdue' (*Effective Functioning of Human Rights Mechanisms Treaty Bodies. Note by the Office of the United Nations High Commissioner for Human Rights*, E/CN.4/2004/98, 11 February 2004, para. 10). Already in 1996, remarking that the 'present supervisory system can function only because of the large-scale delinquency of States which either do not report at all, or report long after the due date', Philip Alston commented on this in the following terms:

Effective functioning of bodies established pursuant to United Nations human rights instruments. Final report on enhancing the long-term effectiveness of the United Nations human rights treaty system, by Mr Philip Alston, independent expert (E/CN.4/1997/74, 27 March 1996):

43. Broadly stated, there are two reasons why States do not report: administrative incapacity including a lack of specialist expertise or lack of political will, or a combination of both. In the first situation, repeated appeals are, almost by definition, unlikely to bear fruit. Instead, the solution lies in a more serious, more expert and more carefully targeted advisory services programme in relation to reporting ...

44. In the second situation, a lack of political will translates essentially into a calculation by the State concerned that the consequences, both domestic and international, of a failure to report are less important than the costs, administrative and political, of complying with reporting obligations. In that case, the only viable approach on the part of the treaty bodies and/or the political organs is to seek to raise the 'costs' of non-compliance. A failure to devise appropriate responses of this nature has ramifications which extend well beyond the consequences for any individual State party. Large-scale non-reporting makes a mockery of the reporting system as a whole. It leads to a situation in which many States are effectively rewarded for violating their obligations while others are penalized for complying (in the sense

of subjecting themselves to scrutiny by the treaty bodies), and it will lead to a situation in which a diminishing number of States will report very regularly and others will almost never do so.

45. The key question, however, is what types of measures designed to raise the costs of non-compliance might be appropriate, potentially productive in terms of upholding the integrity of the system, consistent with the legal framework of the relevant treaty, and politically and otherwise acceptable. Various palliatives are available ... They include: the elimination of reporting and its replacement by detailed questions to which answers must be given; the preparation of a single consolidated report to satisfy several different requirements; and the much wider use of a more professional advisory services programme designed to assist in the preparation of reports. Ultimately, however, none of these might make a difference in hard-core cases. Under those circumstances the only viable option open to the treaty bodies is to proceed with an examination of the situation in a State party in the absence of a report. This has been done for a number of years by the Committee on Economic, Social and Cultural Rights and the Committee on the Elimination of Racial Discrimination has adopted a very similar approach. The situation has not yet become chronic for either the Committee on the Rights of the Child, because it is still much younger than the others, or for the Committee against Torture which has many fewer States parties than the other committees. And the Committee on the Elimination of Discrimination against Women has had so little meeting time, until very recently, that it was unlikely to take any steps that would increase its workload.

46. It seems inevitable, however, that each of these committees, and certainly the Human Rights Committee, will have to contemplate taking such a step sooner or later. While the precise legal basis for such measures will need to be rooted in the text of each of the relevant treaties, the principal foundation is to be found in a teleological approach to interpretation which acknowledges that any other outcome is absurd in that it enables a delinquent State party to defeat the object and purpose of the implementation provisions. In that regard, it is pertinent to recall that the General Assembly, in its resolution 51/87, specifically 'encourage[d] the efforts of the human rights treaty bodies to examine the progress made in achieving the fulfilment of human rights treaty undertakings by all States parties, without exception' ...

47. In implementing such an approach, the experience of the Committee on Economic, Social and Cultural Rights is instructive. Ample notice has been given to the States concerned and, in a majority of the cases taken up so far, reports which had been dramatically overdue have suddenly materialized. For the rest, it is particularly important that the Committee is in a position to undertake detailed research work and to be able to base its examination upon a wide range of sources of information. The resulting 'concluding observations' must be detailed, accurate and comprehensive. If they are not, States can again be rewarded for a failure to report by a routine or mechanistic response which fails to establish genuine accountability in any way. In this respect it is not clear that the conclusions adopted to date in such cases by the Committee on the Elimination of Racial Discrimination meet such criteria.

The delinquency of States as regards the submission of their reports has led the committees concerned to react, in line with what was proposed in para. 45 of the 1996 report by the independent expert Philip Alston:

Human Rights Committee, Consolidated Guidelines for State Reports under the International Covenant on Civil and Political Rights (26 February 2001) (CCPR/C/66/GUI/Rev.2):

G.6.1 The Committee may, in a case where there has been a long-term failure by a State party, despite reminders, to submit an initial or a periodic report, announce its intention to examine the extent of compliance with Covenant rights in that State party at a specified future session. Prior to that session it will transmit to the State party appropriate material in its possession. The State party may send a delegation to the specified session, which may contribute to the Committee's discussion, but in any event the Committee may issue provisional concluding observations and set a date for the submission by the State party of a report of a nature to be specified.

G.6.2 In a case where a State party, having submitted a report which has been scheduled at a session for examination, informs the Committee, at a time when it is impossible to schedule the examination of another State party report, that its delegation will not attend the session, the Committee may examine the report on the basis of the list of issues either at that session or at another to be specified. In the absence of a Delegation, it may decide either to reach provisional concluding observations, or to consider the report and other material and follow the course in para. G4 above.

Human Rights Committee, General Comment No. 30, *Reporting Obligations of States Parties under Article 40 of the Covenant* (16 July 2002):

1. States parties have undertaken to submit reports in accordance with article 40 of the Covenant within one year of its entry into force for the States parties concerned and, thereafter, whenever the Committee so requests.
2. The Committee notes, as appears from its annual reports, that only a small number of States have submitted their reports on time. Most of them have been submitted with delays ranging from a few months to several years and some States parties are still in default, despite repeated reminders by the Committee.
3. Other States have announced that they would appear before the Committee but have not done so on the scheduled date.
4. To remedy such situations, the Committee has adopted new rules:
   (a) If a State party has submitted a report but does not send a delegation to the Committee, the Committee may notify the State party of the date on which it intends to consider the report or may proceed to consider the report at the meeting that had been initially scheduled;
   (b) When the State party has not presented a report, the Committee may, at its discretion, notify the State party of the date on which the Committee proposes to examine the measures taken by the State party to implement the rights guaranteed under the Covenant:
      (i) If the State party is represented by a delegation, the Committee will, in presence of the delegation, proceed with the examination on the date assigned;
      (ii) If the State party is not represented, the Committee may, at its discretion, either decide to proceed to consider the measures taken by the State party to implement the guarantees of the Covenant at the initial date or notify a new date to the State party.

For the purposes of the application of these procedures, the Committee shall hold its meetings in public session if a delegation is present, and in private if a delegation is not present, and shall follow the modalities set forth in the reporting guidelines and in the rules of procedure of the Committee.

5. After the Committee has adopted concluding observations, a follow-up procedure shall be employed in order to establish, maintain or restore a dialogue with the State party. For this purpose and in order to enable the Committee to take further action, the Committee shall appoint a Special Rapporteur, who will report to the Committee [on the follow-up to concluding observations, see further, section 3.1. in this chapter].

6. In the light of the report of the Special Rapporteur, the Committee shall assess the position adopted by the State party and, if necessary, set a new date for the State party to submit its next report.

It is clear that part of the answer resides in the building of the adequate institutional framework at national level.

Harmonized Guidelines on Reporting under the International Human Rights Treaties, including Guidelines on a Common Core Document and treaty-specific targeted documents (HRI/MC/2005/3, 1 June 2005):

12. All States are parties to at least one of the main international human rights treaties, and more than seventy-five per cent are party to four or more. As a consequence, all States have considerable reporting obligations to fulfil and should benefit from adopting a coordinated approach to their reporting for all treaty bodies.

13. The treaty bodies recommend that States consider setting up an appropriate institutional framework for the preparation of their reports. These institutional structures – which could include an inter-ministerial drafting committee and/or focal points on reporting within each relevant government department – should support all of the State's reporting obligations under the international human rights instruments and related international treaties (for example Conventions of the International Labour Organization and the United Nations Educational, Scientific and Cultural Organization), and should provide an effective mechanism to coordinate follow-up to the concluding observations of the treaty bodies. They should allow for the involvement of sub-national entities where these exist and should be established on a permanent basis.

14. These institutional structures should develop an efficient system – supported by modern technologies – for the collection (from the relevant ministries and government statistical offices) of all statistical and other data relevant to the implementation of human rights, in a comprehensive and continuous manner. Technical assistance is available from the Office of the United Nations High Commissioner for Human Rights (OHCHR) in collaboration with the Division for the Advancement of Women (DAW), and from relevant United Nations agencies.

15. Permanent institutional structures of this nature could support States in meeting other reporting commitments, for example to follow up on international conferences and summits, monitor implementation of the Millennium Development Goals, etc. Much of the information collected and collated for such reports may be useful in the preparation of States' reports to the treaty bodies.

9.1. Questions for discussion: State reporting

1. The Paris Principles relating to the Status of the national institutions for the promotion and the protection of human rights adopted by General Assembly Resolution 48/134 of 20 December 1993 (see chapter 8, section 2.3.) provide that one of the missions of the national human rights institution should be to 'contribute to the reports which States are required to submit to United Nations bodies and committees, and to regional institutions, pursuant to their treaty obligations and, where necessary, to express an opinion on the subject, with due respect for their independence' (para. 3(d)). The Committee on the Elimination of Racial Discrimination also takes the view that, where national institutions have been established in accordance with the Paris Principles in order to contribute to the implementation of the International Convention for the Elimination of All Forms of Racial Discrimination, 'they should be associated with the preparation of reports and possibly included in government delegations in order to intensify the dialogue between the Committee and the State party concerned' (General Recommendation XVII (1993), establishment of national institutions to facilitate implementation of the Convention). In your view what role should national human rights institutions play in the preparation of States' reports before the UN human rights treaty bodies?

2. Non-governmental organizations have an important role to fulfil in the reporting procedure, by providing the independent experts sitting on the human rights treaty bodies with information which the government may have preferred to suppress or which it ignored. On the other hand, the human rights treaty bodies encourage the wide participation of civil society in the preparation of the reports and in the discussion of its content. Are these contradictory roles? To what extent should the report be owned by the government, or be the result of a consensus between the State authorities and civil society?

2 INDIVIDUAL COMMUNICATIONS

The Human Rights Committee (HRC), the Committee on the Elimination of Racial Discrimination (CERD), the Committee against Torture (CAT), the Committee on the Elimination of Discrimination against Women (CEDAW), and the Committee on Migrant Workers (CMW), all may receive communications from individuals claiming to be victims of violations under the respective treaties which they monitor. Such a competence has also been attributed to the Committee on Economic, Social and Cultural Rights (CESCR), under the Optional Protocol to the International Covenant on Economic, Social and Cultural Rights, adopted by the UN General Assembly on 10 December 2008 (A/RES/63/117). The admissibility of such communications, however, is subject to a number of conditions: the violation must not have taken place prior to the entry into force of the treaty concerned as regards the State against which the communication is addressed; the author of the communication must be a 'victim' of the violation he/she denounces; he/she must have exhausted the local remedies available; the communication may not be anonymous, nor may it constitute an abuse of the right to communication; the same matter must not have been examined under another procedure of international investigation or settlement or, at least – in the more flexible wording of the Optional Protocol to the International Covenant on Civil and Political Rights – it must not be under examination under such procedure at the time of the communication. Four of these conditions warrant further consideration. This will be done here primarily on the basis of the jurisprudence of the Human Rights Committee.

Box 9.1. **Who may file communications?**

The Optional Protocol to the ICESCR (OP-ICESCR), adopted in 2008, enables the Committee on Economic, Social and Cultural Rights to examine individual communications, thus aligning the competences of this committee with those of the Human Rights Committee under the ICCPR (for significant contributions on this issue and the process leading up to the adoption of this new instrument, see P. Alston, 'Establishing a Right to Petition under the Covenant on Economic, Social and Cultural Rights' in *Collected Courses of the Academy of European Law: the Protection of Human Rights in Europe* (Florence: European University Institute, 1993), vol. IV, book 2, p. 115; W. Vandenhole, 'Completing the UN Complaint Mechanisms for Human Rights Violations Step by Step: Towards a Complaints Procedure Complementing the International Covenant on Economic, Social and Cultural Rights', *Netherlands Quarterly of Human Rights*, 21, No. 3 (2003), 423; O. De Schutter, 'Le Protocole facultatif au Pacte international relatif aux droits économiques, sociaux et culturels', *Revue belge de droit international* (2006), 1; M. Scheinin, 'The Proposed Optional Protocol to the Covenant on Economic, Social and Cultural Rights: a Blueprint for UN Human Rights Treaty Body Reform – Without Amending the Existing Treaties', *Human Rights Law Review*, 6 (2006), 131; C. Mahon, 'Progress at the Front: the Draft Optional Protocol to the International Covenant on Economic, Social and Cultural Rights', *Human Rights Law Review*, 8 (2008), 617).

Under Article 2 of OP-ICESCR, such communications may be submitted 'by or on behalf of individuals or groups of individuals, under the jurisdiction of a State Party, claiming to be victims of a violation of any of the economic, social and cultural rights set forth in the Covenant by that State Party. Where a communication is submitted on behalf of individuals or groups of individuals, this shall be with their consent unless the author can justify acting on their behalf without such consent.' This formulation is identical to the one in Article 2 of the Optional Protocol to the International Convention on the Elimination of All Forms of Discrimination against Women, and it also corresponds to what is provided for under the CERD and, in the HRC's Rules of Procedure, under the ICCPR. In contrast, Article 1, para. 1 of the Optional Protocol to the Convention on the Rights of Persons with Disabilities (OP-CRPD) provides that the Committee on the Rights of Persons with Disabilities may receive communications 'from or on behalf of individuals or groups of individuals subject to its jurisdiction who claim to be victims of a violation by that State Party of the provisions of the Convention'.

The choice made in the OP-ICESCR goes further than the possibility provided for under the OP-CRPD, since non-governmental organizations, in particular, will have the option of filing communications on behalf of groups of individuals whose economic, social and cultural rights under the ICESCR have been violated but are unable to take action – for instance due to a fear of reprisals, or because of the material conditions in which they find themselves. At the same time, the initial proposal made by the Portuguese Catarina de Albuquerque, Chairperson of the Intergovernmental Open-Ended Working Group on the OP-ICESCR – the group within which the OP-ICESCR was prepared between February 2004 and June 2008 – went further. The first draft OP-ICESCR submitted by the Chairperson provided for the possibility of collective complaints filed by NGOs (see A/HRC/6/WG.4/2, 23 April 2007). In her revised proposal of December 2007, the Chairperson suggested the insertion of a provision according to which 'Where appropriate, the Committee may receive and consider communications from non-governmental organizations with relevant expertise and interest, alleging a violation of any of the rights set forth in the Covenant' (proposed Art. 1*ter*, in the Revised Draft Optional Protocol to the International Covenant on Economic, Social and Cultural Rights, A/HRC/8/WG.4/2, 24 December 2007). These proposals were inspired by the collective complaints mechanisms established in 1998 under the Council of Europe European Social Charter, which allows the European Committee on Social Rights to receive complaints from non-governmental organizations or unions, about the alleged incompatibility of certain measures or policies with the undertakings of the State concerned under the European Social Charter (on this procedure, see in chapter 11, box 11.1.). Yet, the idea of collective communications was not retained, despite the insistence of certain States that the ICESCR contained certain rights which, due to their collective nature – trade union rights in particular – would only be enforceable if organizations had the standing to file communications with the Committee on Economic, Social and Cultural Rights.

9.2. Questions for discussion: standing to file communications

How would you weigh the pros and the cons of allowing non-governmental organizations to file communications to denounce human rights violations, without having to prove that they are acting on behalf of direct victims of violations (or that the victims are unable to act directly)? Consider the following arguments in favour of the idea of allowing such collective communications:

1. Certain rights, particularly among social and economic rights, are of a collective nature, and can only be effectively enforced through communications if these can be filed by organizations, such as trade unions.

2. The expertise of non-governmental organizations will ensure that communications filed by them will be better prepared than communications filed by direct (individual) victims.

3. Allowing non-governmental organizations to file communications directly ensures that communications will be filed even where direct victims of violations face obstacles to their filing of individual communications.

4. Collective communications will improve the involvement of non-governmental organizations in the UN human rights system.

5. Collective communications will ensure that the human rights bodies concerned will not be overwhelmed by a flood of individual communications concerning the same issue, when the violation stems from a general measure or policy affecting a wide range of people.

6. Collective communications will ensure that, when the violation stems from a general measure or policy affecting a wide range of people, a problem of collective action will be solved: in the absence of standing for organisations, no single individual victim may have a sufficient incentive to act for the benefit of all the individuals aggrieved.

Consider also the arguments against the introduction of a mechanism allowing for collective communications:

1. Allowing non-governmental organizations to file communications alleging violations of human rights treaties may not be workable, since it cannot be reconciled with the obligation to exhaust domestic remedies prior to filing an international claim.

2. Allowing non-governmental organizations to file communications alleging violations of human rights treaties will deprive victims of their right to choose whether or not to denounce a particular violation affecting them.

3. Allowing non-governmental organizations to file communications alleging violations of human rights treaties will lead to human rights treaty bodies being flooded with communications, often motivated by political purposes.

4. Collective communications would only be feasible if the NGOs allowed to file them were selected, on the basis of objective criteria ensuring that they have the required expertise and/or representativity. However, it is very delicate to apply such criteria, or to draw up a list of such NGOs, and this would infringe upon the independence of NGOs.

2.1 The '*ratione temporis*' rule

Claims may be brought against States parties to human rights treaties only when they relate to violations alleged to have occurred after the entry into force of the treaty on the basis of which the communication is filed (for instance, the Optional Protocol to the International Covenant on Civil and Political Rights) as regards the defending State. This does not exclude the possibility of human rights treaty bodies examining 'continuing violations', i.e. violations which, while they have begun prior to the entry into force of the treaty on which the complaint is based, have continued after that date. Article 2(f) of the Optional Protocol to the Convention on the Rights of Persons with Disabilities makes this doctrine explicit, by providing that the Committee on the Rights of Persons with Disabilities shall consider a communication inadmissible when 'The facts that are the subject of the communication occurred prior to the entry into force of the present Protocol for the State Party concerned unless those facts continued after that date.' This rule is not always easy to apply, however, since the distinction between 'continuing violations' and violations whose effects have not been erased may be contested. The following cases illustrate the difficulty.

Human Rights Committee, *J. L.* v. *Australia*, Communication No. 491/1992 (final views of 28 July 1992) (CCPR/C/45/D/491/1992 (1994)):

[The author is a solicitor. In the State of Victoria, the practice of law is regulated by the Legal Profession Practice Act of 1958, section 83(1) of which provides that no one may practise law unless he/she is duly qualified and holds a certificate issued by the Law Institute of Victoria. In 1986, after he was denied such certificate due to his refusal to pay the required insurance premium, J. L. was prohibited by a judicial injunction from continuing to practise. Since he continued to practise, he was fined for contempt of court, and then imprisoned between September and November 1991 for having refused to pay the fine. The Optional Protocol entered into force for Australia on 25 December 1991. However, when J. L. complained to the Human Rights Committee that he had been denied proceedings before an independent and impartial tribunal, in violation of Article 14 of the Covenant on Civil and Political Rights, he claimed that this violation has continuing effects, in that he remained struck off the roll of solicitors of the Supreme Court, without any prospect of being reinstated. Although finding the application inadmissible on other grounds, the Human Rights Committee agreed with the author on this point.]

4.2 The Committee has noted the author's claim that his detention between 1 September and 29 November 1991 was unlawful. It observes that this event occurred prior to the entry into force of the Optional Protocol for Australia (25 December 1991), and that it does not have consequences which in themselves constitute a violation of any of the provisions of the Covenant. Accordingly, this part of the communication is inadmissible *ratione temporis*. As to the author's contention that he was denied a fair and impartial hearing, the Committee notes that although the relevant court hearings took place before 25 December 1991, the effects of the decisions taken by the Supreme Court continue until the present time. Accordingly, complaints about violations of the author's rights allegedly ensuing from these decisions are not in principle excluded *ratione temporis*.

This may be contrasted with the following case:

Human Rights Committee, *E. and A. Könye* v. *Hungary*, Communication No. 520/1992 (final views of 7 April 1994) (UN Doc. CCPR/C/50/D/520/1992 (1994)):

[The authors' property was expropriated in 1984, after the municipal police of Budapest declared Mr and Mrs K. to be citizens staying abroad unlawfully, since the author's work permit allowing him to be employed abroad (he was a public servant for the ILO) expired on 30 June 1984. On the basis of this decision, the administration of the Budapest City Council confiscated the authors' apartment property as well as the family home and took them into State ownership. The authors were denied compensation. Their subsequent appeals were rejected by the City Council of Budapest, acting as an Administrative Court, on the grounds that under the then applicable rules and regulations, property of individuals found to be unlawfully staying or residing abroad had to be taken into State ownership. The Optional Protocol entered into force for Hungary on 7 December 1988. In January 1990, the authors requested the newly appointed Minister of Justice to reopen their case. The Minister's reply was negative. Towards the end of 1991, the authors wrote to the Secretariat for Rehabilitation attached to the Prime Minister's Office and asked that their case be reconsidered. Although the Secretariat's reply presented an apology on behalf of the new Government and promised assistance with respect to the recovery of the authors' property, and although the authors' passports were returned to them, there was no subsequent follow-up on the property issue. The authors sought to exercise remedies before the Hungarian courts in 1990–2, but neither the Constitutional Court, which declared itself incompetent, nor the Budapest Central District Court, which dismissed the petition on 15 January 1992 without summoning any of the parties, nor the Court of Appeal, accepted to entertain the case.

The authors state before the Human Rights Committee that they did not get a fair and public hearing before an independent and impartial tribunal, whether under the former communist regime or under the present democratically elected Government. Until the change of Government in 1989, the judicial decisions were handed down 'without a public hearing and by incompetent administrative authorities'. The decisions of these authorities were final, and the authors allegedly did not have any possibility of appealing against them. Under the new Government, in 1990–1, the authors' request for reopening of the matter was again rejected in proceedings which did not include a public hearing. This again is said to constitute an on-going and continuing violation of Article 14 of the International Covenant on Civil and Political Rights. Instead, the Government points out to the Committee that the events complained of occurred prior to 7 December 1988, the date of entry into force of the Optional Protocol for the State party. It therefore considers the case inadmissible *ratione temporis*.]

6.4 The Committee begins by noting that the State party's obligations under the Covenant apply as of the date of its entry into force for the State party. There is, however, a different issue as to when the Committee's competence to consider complaints about alleged violations of the Covenant under the Optional Protocol is engaged. In its jurisprudence under the Optional Protocol, the Committee has held that it cannot consider alleged violations of the Covenant which occurred before the entry into force of the Optional Protocol for the State party, unless the violations complained of continue after the entry into force of the Optional Protocol. A continuing violation is to be interpreted as an affirmation, after the entry into force of the Optional Protocol, by act or by clear implication, of the previous violations of the State party.

6.5 In the present case, it is not possible to speak of such a continuing affirmation, by the Hungarian authorities, of the acts committed by the State party prior to 7 December 1988. For one, the authors' passports have been returned to them, and such harassment as they may have been subjected to prior to 7 December 1988 has stopped.

6.6 The only remaining issue, which might arise in relation to article 17 [right to respect for private and family life], is whether there are continuing effects by virtue of the State party's failure to compensate the authors for the confiscation of their family home or apartment. However, the Committee recalls that there is no autonomous right to compensation under the Covenant (see decision of 26 March 1990 on case No. 275/1988, *S. E.* v. *Argentina*); and a failure to compensate after the entry into force of the Optional Protocol does not thereby constitute an affirmation of a prior violation by the State party.

7. In the light of the above, the Human Rights Committee considers that the authors' claims are inadmissible *ratione temporis*.

[One member of the Committee, Ms Christine Chanet, filed the following individual opinion, dissenting from the majority:]

The authors' allegations under article 14 [fair trial] referred to procedure that took place during a period subsequent to the entry into force of the Optional Protocol, since they were contesting the procedure followed by the Central District Court in 1991, while the Optional Protocol entered into force for Hungary in December 1988.

The Committee could certainly have found that the allegations were not sufficiently supported, but not that article 14 could not be invoked because of the *ratione temporis* rule.

With respect to article 14, the contents of the case submitted to the national court can be evaluated by the Committee only in terms of the criteria listed in the text itself, i.e. in this particular case, rights and obligations in a suit at law.

With the exception of this criterion relating to substance, article 14 refers to the conditions under which the procedure is conducted, and it is the dates on which the various procedural acts took place that should be taken into consideration when analysing the communication *ratione temporis*. The dates relating to the substance of the case brought before the national court should not be taken into consideration when applying the *ratione temporis* rule.

Finally, it is my view that when the Committee considers a communication under the Optional Protocol, its decisions should be guided only by the legal principles found in the provisions of the Covenant itself, and not by political considerations, even of a general nature, or the fear of a flood of communications from countries that have changed their system of Government.

The following decision is distinguishable from *Köyne* v. *Hungary* since, in this latter case, the procedural defects of the remedies exercised by the authors were denounced under Article 14 ICCPR. In the following case, the complaint is based on the continuing effects of what are alleged to be past violations of the rights protected under the Covenant:

Human Rights Committee, *Kurowski* v. *Poland*, Communication No. 872/1999 (CCPR/C/77/D/872/1999 (2003)), final views of 18 March 2003:

[On 31 July 1990, E. Kurowski was dismissed pursuant to the State Protection Office Act of 6 April 1990, apparently because he was a member of the Polish United Workers' Party. Reinstatement could take place only after a regional qualifying commission issued a positive assessment or through an appeal to the Central Qualifying Commission in Warsaw. However, on 22 July 1990, the Bielsko-Biala Qualifying Commission declared that the author did not meet the requirements for officers or employees of the Ministry of Internal Affairs, and it again confirmed this opinion, on appeal from the author, in September 1990. The Optional Protocol to the International Covenant on Civil and Political Rights entered into force for Poland on 7 February 1992. On 25 April 1995, the author requested the Minister of Internal Affairs to overturn the decisions of the qualifying commissions and to reinstate him in the police force, but the Minister replied that he had no authority to alter decisions by the qualifying commissions or to recruit anyone who did not receive a positive assessment from them. An appeal lodged with the Central Administrative Court was equally unsuccessful, since the Court considered that it was not competent to give a ruling on decisions taken by the qualifying commissions.]

6.3 The Committee notes that the State party claims that the communication is inadmissible *ratione temporis*, since the qualification proceedings for the author ended on 5 September 1990, that is, before the Optional Protocol entered into force for Poland on 7 February 1992. The author challenges that argument and replies that the State was party to the Covenant since June 1977, that the Optional Protocol entered into force in 1992 and that he did not take legal action against his dismissal until 1995 (after the Optional Protocol had come into force).

6.4 The Committee recalls that the obligations that the State party assumed when it signed the Covenant took effect on the date on which the Covenant entered into force for the State party. Following its jurisprudence, the Committee considers that it cannot consider violations that took place before the Optional Protocol entered into force for the State party, unless such violations persisted after the entry into force of the Optional Protocol. A persistent violation is understood to mean the continuation of violations which the State party committed previously, either through actions or implicitly.

6.5 In the present case, the author was dismissed from his post in 1990, under the law in force at the time, and the same year he presented himself as a candidate, without success, before one of the regional qualifying commissions in order to determine whether he satisfied the new statutory criteria for employment in the restructured Ministry of Internal Affairs. The fact that he did not win his case during the proceedings which he initiated in 1995, after the Optional Protocol came into force, does not in itself constitute a potential violation of the Covenant. The Committee is unable to conclude that a violation occurred prior to the entry into force of the Optional Protocol for the State party and continued thereafter. Consequently, the Committee declares the communication inadmissible ratione temporis, in accordance with article 1 of the Optional Protocol.

By contrast, both this decision and the preceding one are difficult to reconcile with the following:

Human Rights Committee, *Aduayom et al.* v. *Togo*, Communications Nos. 422/1990, 423/1990 and 424/1990 (final views of 12 July 1996) (UN Doc. CCPR/C/51/D/422/1990, 423/1990 and 424/1990):

[The three authors were arrested in September and December 1985 for transparently political reasons; they were released in April and July 1986. Their wages were suspended under administrative procedures after their arrest, on the ground that they had unjustifiably deserted their posts. The authors claim that both their arrest and their detention were contrary to Article 9, para. 1 ICCPR. They further contend that the State party has violated Article 19 in respect to them, because they were persecuted for having carried, read or disseminated documents that contained no more than an assessment of Togolese politics, either at the domestic or foreign policy level. The Committee stated that the communications were not inadmissible *ratione temporis*, although the Optional Protocol to the International Covenant on Civil and Political Rights only entered into force for Togo on 30 June 1988:]

6.2 The Committee noted the authors' claims under article 9 and observed that their arrest and detention occurred prior to the entry into force of the Optional Protocol for Togo (30 June 1988). It further noted that the alleged violations had continuing effects after the entry into force of the Optional Protocol for Togo, in that the authors were denied reinstatement in their posts until 27 May and 1 July 1991 respectively, and that no payment of salary arrears or other forms of compensation had been effected. The Committee considered that these continuing effects could be seen as an affirmation of the previous violations allegedly committed by the State party. It therefore concluded that it was not precluded *ratione temporis* from examining the communications and considered that they might raise issues under articles 9, paragraph 5; 19; and 25(c), of the Covenant.

2.2 The 'victim' requirement

In principle, individual communications must be presented to the human rights treaty expert bodies by those who have been directly affected by the violations complained of. Challenges in the abstract to the laws or practices of a State, by individuals or groups which pretend to act in the public interest by filing an *actio popularis*, are not allowed. The most recent instruments, however, have taken into account the difficulties which certain individual victims may be facing due to this requirement, if it is interpreted too strictly. For example, as we have seen (box 9.1. above), Article 2 of the 1999 Optional Protocol to the Convention on the Elimination of Discrimination against Women, which entered into force on 22 December 2000, provides that

> Communications may be submitted by or on behalf of individuals or groups of individuals, under the jurisdiction of a State Party, claiming to be victims of a violation of any of the rights set forth in the Convention by that State Party. Where a communication is submitted on behalf of individuals or groups of individuals, this shall be with their consent unless the author can justify acting on their behalf without such consent.

A problem may result from the fact that, in order to be a 'victim', and thus to possess the required standing in the context of individual communications, the complainants may have to make serious sacrifices and accept, temporarily, a violation of their rights. In the case of *Tadman* v. *Canada*, the authors were non-Catholics complaining that the Roman Catholic schools were the only non-secular schools receiving full and direct public funding. Their communication was considered inadmissible by the Committee, since – although they belonged to different religious denominations, i.e. United Church of Canada, Lutheran Church, Serbian Orthodox Church and Humanist – their children were attending public secular schools, which are funded like Catholic schools. But the implication is that, in order to challenge the Canadian legislation on this point, the authors of the complaint in *Tadman* would have had to place their children in non-public, non-Roman Catholic schools, with the financial implications this would have entailed for them.

Human Rights Committee, *Tadman et al.* v. *Canada*, Communication No. 816/1998 (final views of 4 November 1999) (UN Doc. CCPR/C/67/D/816/1998):

6.2 The State party has challenged the admissibility of the communication on the basis that the authors cannot claim to be victims of a violation of the Covenant. In this context, the Committee notes that the authors while claiming to be victims of discrimination, do not seek publicly funded religious schools for their children, but on the contrary seek the removal of the public funding to Roman Catholic separate schools. Thus, if this were to happen, the authors' personal situation in respect of funding for religious education would not be improved. The authors have not sufficiently substantiated how the public funding given to the Roman Catholic separate schools at present causes them any disadvantage or affects them adversely. In the circumstances, the Committee considers that they cannot claim to be victims of the alleged discrimination, within the meaning of article 1 of the Optional Protocol.

[Four Committee members (P. Bhagwati, E. Evatt, L. Henkin and C. Medina Quiroga) disagreed with the majority:]

The situation is that the Province of Ontario provides a benefit to the Catholic community by incorporating their religious schools into the public school system and funding them in full. This benefit is discriminatory in nature as it prefers one group in the community on the ground of religion. Those whose religious schools are not funded in this way are clearly victims of this discrimination (as in the *Waldman* case [see chapter 7, section 1.1.]).

But that does not exhaust the scope of those who may claim to be victims. Parents who desire religious education for their children and are not provided with it within the school system and who have to meet the cost of such education themselves may also be considered as victims. The applicants in this case include such persons, and the claims of at least those persons should, in my view, be considered admissible.

The limits of the views adopted by the majority in *Tadman* v. *Canada* become clear if we compare this with its decision in *Toonen* v. *Australia*. There, the author complained about two provisions of the Tasmanian Criminal Code, namely sections 122(a) and (c) and 123, which criminalize various forms of sexual contacts between men, including all forms of sexual contacts between consenting adult homosexual men in private. Mr Toonen, an activist for the promotion of the rights of homosexuals in Tasmania, agreed that 'in practice the Tasmanian police has not charged anyone either with "unnatural sexual intercourse" or "intercourse against nature" (section 122) nor with "indecent practice between male persons" (section 123) for several years'. However, he argued that 'because of his long-term relationship with another man, his active lobbying of Tasmanian politicians and the reports about his activities in the local media, and because of his activities as a gay rights activist and gay HIV/AIDS worker, his private life and his liberty are threatened by the continued existence of sections 122(a), (c) and 123 of the Criminal Code'. The Committee agreed that he could be considered a victim of the alleged violation of Article 17 ICCPR although the challenged provisions had not been applied to him:

Human Rights Committee, *Toonen* v. *Australia*, Communication No. 488/1992 (final views of 31 March 1994) (UN Doc. CCPR/C/50/D/488/1992 (1994)):

5.1 [T]he Committee considered the admissibility of the communication. As to whether the author could be deemed a 'victim' within the meaning of article 1 of the Optional

Protocol, it noted that the legislative provisions challenged by the author had not been enforced by the judicial authorities of Tasmania for a number of years. It considered, however, that the author had made reasonable efforts to demonstrate that the threat of enforcement and the pervasive impact of the continued existence of these provisions on administrative practices and public opinion had affected him and continued to affect him personally, and that they could raise issues under articles 17 and 26 of the Covenant. Accordingly, the Committee was satisfied that the author could be deemed a victim within the meaning of article 1 of the Optional Protocol, and that his claims were admissible *ratione temporis*.

8.2 Inasmuch as article 17 is concerned, it is undisputed that adult consensual sexual activity in private is covered by the concept of 'privacy', and that Mr Toonen is actually and currently affected by the continued existence of the Tasmanian laws. The Committee considers that sections 122(a), (c) and 123 of the Tasmanian Criminal Code 'interfere' with the author's privacy, even if these provisions have not been enforced for a decade. In this context, it notes that the policy of the Department of Public Prosecutions not to initiate criminal proceedings in respect of private homosexual conduct does not amount to a guarantee that no actions will be brought against homosexuals in the future, particularly in the light of undisputed statements of the Director of Public Prosecutions of Tasmania in 1988 and those of members of the Tasmanian Parliament. The continued existence of the challenged provisions therefore continuously and directly 'interferes' with the author's privacy.

Thus, the chilling effect created by the existence of legislation which could be applied in order to repress the exercise of certain fundamental rights suffices to establish the quality of 'victim', even where the said legislation has not been effectively applied to the person concerned.

The 'victim' requirement would be easy to circumvent if non-governmental organizations were authorized to claim that they are victims of violations which they have chosen to denounce, by defining their activities as aiming to combat such violations. In the following case presented to the Committee on the Elimination of Racial Discrimination, the applicant was a non-governmental organization, represented by the head of its board of trustees. The NGO alleged that the State party had violated its obligations under Articles 4 and 6 of the Convention on the Elimination of All Forms of Racial Discrimination, as it failed to investigate whether a job advertisement constituted an act of racial discrimination. It argued that it 'should be recognized as having status of victim under article 14 of the Convention [on the Elimination of All Forms of Racial Discrimination], since it represents "a large group of persons of non-Danish origin discriminated against by the job advertisement in question"'. They noted in support of this claim 'that both the police and the Regional Public Prosecutor have accepted it as a party to domestic proceedings'.

Committee on the Elimination of Racial Discrimination, *Documentation and Advisory Centre on Racial Discrimination* **v.** *Denmark***, Communication No. 28/2003, U.N. Doc. CERD/C/63/D/28/2003 (2003):**

6.4 The Committee does not exclude the possibility that a group of persons representing, for example, the interests of a racial or ethnic group, may submit an individual communication, provided that it is able to prove that it has been an alleged victim of a violation of the Convention or that one of its members has been a victim, and if it is able at the same time to provide due authorization to this effect.

6.5 The Committee notes that, according to the petitioner, no member of the board of trustees applied for the job. Moreover, the petitioner has not argued that any of the members of the board, or any other identifiable person whom the petitioner would be authorized to represent, had a genuine interest in, or showed the necessary qualifications for, the vacancy.

6.6 While Section 5 of Act No. 459 [of 12 June 1996 on prohibition against discrimination in respect of employment and occupation etc. in the employment market] prohibits discrimination of all persons of non-Danish origin in job advertisements, whether they apply for a vacancy or not, it does not automatically follow that persons not directly and personally affected by such discrimination may claim to be victims of a violation of any of the rights guaranteed in the Convention. Any other conclusion would open the door for popular actions (*actio popularis*) against the relevant legislation of States parties.

6.7 In the absence of any identifiable victims personally affected by the allegedly discriminatory job advertisement, whom the petitioner would be authorized to represent, the Committee concludes that the petitioner has failed to substantiate, for purposes of article 14, paragraph 1, its claim that it constitutes or represents a group of individuals claiming to be the victim of a violation by Denmark of articles 2, paragraph 1(d), 4, 5 and 6 of the Convention.

There are two important exceptions to the requirement that communications may only be filed by the 'direct' victims, however. First, where the direct victim is unable to act, the complaint may be filed by a person who has sufficiently close links to him/her, so that it may be presumed that the wishes of the victim are adequately taken into account and that, if he/she could have done so, the victim would have consented to being represented. This will allow the relatives of the victim, in particular, to represent the latter, by filing a claim on their behalf. As illustrated by the case of *Mbenge* v. *Zaire* decided by the Human Rights Committee, an extension beyond the family circle will be difficult to justify, even in situations where the other persons on behalf of which a complainant seeks to act have been victims of a similar treatment, linked to the same string of facts on which the complaint is based (Human Rights Committee, *Mbenge* v. *Zaire*, Communication No. 16/1977 (final views of 25 March 1983) (UN Doc. Supp. No. 40 (A/38/40) at 134 (1983))). Second, where the violation has not occured yet but may be considered both imminent and sufficiently certain – where the violation would be the foreseeable and necessary consequence of the challenged measure, in the words of the Human Rights Committee – a communication may be filed in anticipation of the violation which is about to occur.

Human Rights Committee, *Cox* v. *Canada*, Communication No. 539/1993 (CCPR/C/52/D/539/1993 (1994)), final views of 31 October 1994:

2.1 On 27 February 1991, the author was arrested at Laval, Quebec, for theft, a charge to which he pleaded guilty. While in custody, the judicial authorities received from the United States a request for his extradition, pursuant to the 1976 Extradition Treaty between Canada and the United States. The author is wanted in the State of Pennsylvania on two charges of first-degree murder, relating to an incident that took place in Philadelphia in 1988. If convicted, the author could face the death penalty, although the two other accomplices were tried and sentenced to life terms ...

3. The author claims that the order to extradite him violates articles 6, 14 and 26 of the Covenant [ICCPR]; he alleges that the way death penalties are pronounced in the United States generally discriminates against black people. He further alleges a violation of article 7 of the Covenant, in that he, if extradited and sentenced to death, would be exposed to 'the death row phenomenon', i.e. years of detention under harsh conditions, awaiting execution ...

10.4 With regard to the allegations that, if extradited, Mr Cox would be exposed to a real and present danger of a violation of articles 14 and 26 of the Covenant in the United States, the Committee observed [in its decision of 3 November 1993 on the admissibility of the communication] that the evidence submitted did not substantiate, for purposes of admissibility, that such violations would be a foreseeable and necessary consequence of extradition. It does not suffice to assert before the Committee that the criminal justice system in the United States is incompatible with the Covenant. In this connection, the Committee recalled its jurisprudence that, under the Optional Protocol procedure, it cannot examine *in abstracto* the compatibility with the Covenant of the laws and practice of a State. [Views in Communication No. 61/1979, *Leo Hertzberg et al.* v. *Finland*, para. 9.3.] For purposes of admissibility, the author has to substantiate that in the specific circumstances of his case, the Courts in Pennsylvania would be likely to violate his rights under articles 14 and 26, and that he would not have a genuine opportunity to challenge such violations in United States courts. The author has failed to do so. This part of the communication is therefore inadmissible under article 2 of the Optional Protocol.

10.5 The Committee considered that the remaining claim, that Canada violated the Covenant by deciding to extradite Mr Cox without seeking assurances that the death penalty would not be imposed, or if imposed, would not be carried out, may raise issues under articles 6 and 7 of the Covenant which should be examined on the merits.

[Canada questioned, however, whether Mr Cox did satisfy the criterion of being a 'victim' within the meaning of article 1 of the Optional Protocol:]

12.4. ... Firstly, it has not been alleged that the author has already suffered any violation of his Covenant rights; secondly, it is not reasonably foreseeable that he would become a victim after extradition to the United States. The State party cites statistics from the Pennsylvania District Attorney's Office and indicates that since 1976, when Pennsylvania's current death penalty law was enacted, no one has been put to death; moreover, the Pennsylvania legal system allows for several appeals. But not only has Mr Cox not been tried, he has not been convicted, nor sentenced to death. In this connection the State party notes that the two other individuals who were alleged to have committed the crimes together with Mr Cox were not given death sentences but are serving life sentences. Moreover, the death penalty is not sought in all murder cases. Even if sought, it cannot be imposed in the absence of aggravating factors which must outweigh any mitigating factors. Referring to the Committee's jurisprudence in the *Aumeeruddy-*

Cziffra case that the alleged victim's risk be 'more than a theoretical possibility', the State party states that no evidence has been submitted to the Canadian courts or to the Committee which would indicate a real risk of his becoming a victim. The evidence submitted by Mr Cox is either not relevant to him or does not support the view that his rights would be violated in a way that he could not properly challenge in the courts of Pennsylvania and of the United States. The State party concludes that since Mr Cox has failed to substantiate, for purposes of admissibility, his allegations, the communication should be declared inadmissible under article 2 of the Optional Protocol.

[This argument failed to convince the majority of the members of the Committee to review their decision on the admissibility of the communication. However, six members of the Committee dissented from the decision on admissibility, stating (individual opinion by Mrs Rosalyn Higgins, co-signed by Messrs Laurel Francis, Kurt Herndl, Andreas Mavrommatis, Birame Ndiaye and Waleed Sadi (dissenting); a similar opinion was filed by Ms Elisabeth Evatt):]

... it is not always necessary that a violation already have occurred for an action to come within the scope of article 1. But the violation that will affect him personally must be a 'necessary and foreseeable consequence' of the action of the defendant State.

It is clear that in the case of Mr Cox, unlike in the case of Mr Kindler, this test is not met. Mr Kindler had, at the time of the Canadian decision to extradite him, been tried in the United States for murder, found guilty as charged and recommended to the death sentence by the jury. Mr Cox, by contrast, has not yet been tried and *a fortiori* has not been found guilty or recommended to the death penalty. Already it is clear that his extradition would not entail the possibility of a 'necessary and foreseeable consequence of a violation of his rights' that would require examination on the merits. This failure to meet the test of 'prospective victim' within the meaning of article 1 of the Optional Protocol is emphasized by the fact that Mr Cox's two co-defendants in the case in which he has been charged have already been tried in the State of Pennsylvania, and sentenced not to death but to a term of life imprisonment. The fact that the Committee – and rightly so in our view – found that Kindler raised issues that needed to be considered on their merits, and that the admissibility criteria were there met, does not mean that every extradition case of this nature is necessarily admissible. In every case, the tests relevant to articles 1, 2, 3 and 5, paragraph 2, of the Optional Protocol must be applied to the particular facts of the case.

The Committee has not at all addressed the requirements of article 1 of the Optional Protocol, that is, whether Mr Cox may be considered a 'victim' by reference to his claims under articles 14, 26, 6 or 7 of the Covenant.

We therefore believe that Mr Cox was not a 'victim' within the meaning of article 1 of the Optional Protocol, and that his communication to the Human Rights Committee is inadmissible.

The duty to address carefully the requirements for admissibility under the Optional Protocol is not made the less necessary because capital punishment is somehow involved in a complaint.

9.3. Questions for discussion: the 'victim' requirement under the International Covenant on Civil and Political Rights

1. Is the decision adopted by the Human Rights Committee in *Tadman et al.* v. *Canada* consistent with its approach in *Waldman* v. *Canada*? The latter case was examined in chapter 7,

section 1.1.: Waldman enrolled his children in a private Jewish day school, and complained that in the province of Ontario, Roman Catholic schools are the only non-secular schools receiving full and direct public funding. The Committee found a violation of the non-discrimination requirement, noting that 'the Committee observes that the Covenant does not oblige States parties to fund schools which are established on a religious basis. However, if a State party chooses to provide public funding to religious schools, it should make this funding available without discrimination' (para. 10.6. of its final views, adopted on 5 November 1999). Would Waldman's situation be improved if Canada were to cut off funding for the Roman Catholic schools, in order not to discriminate against other faiths?

2. Is the understanding the Human Rights Committee offers of the notion of 'victim' of a violation of the ICCPR in *Toonen* v. *Australia* compatible with its position in the case of *Tadman et al.* v. *Canada*?

2.3 The exhaustion of local remedies

Complainants filing individual communications before human rights treaty bodies are required to demonstrate that they have unsuccessfully sought remedies before the national authorities, prior to filing their claim at international level. The requirement is that they invoke, at least in substance, the violation of the rights recognized in the international human rights treaty concerned, and that they thus provide the national authorities with an opportunity to address the claim before it is presented to a human rights treaty expert body. Only remedies which have a reasonable chance of success, however, must be exhausted. In addition, remedies which are not effective, because they will not provide a protection before irreparable harm is caused, do not have to be exercised, as illustrated in the following case:

Human Rights Committee, *Chief Bernard Ominayak and the Lubicon Lake Band* v. *Canada*, Communication No. 167/1984 (Supp. No. 40 (A/45/40) at 1 (1990)), final views of 26 March 1990:

[A summary of the context of this case is offered above (chapter 7, section 5.2.). Chief Ominayak is the leader and representative of the Lubicon Lake Band, a Cree Indian band living within the borders of Canada in the Province of Alberta. They allege that the Provincial Government of Alberta has been allowed to expropriate the territory of the Lubicon Lake Band for the benefit of private corporate interests and that this violates the Lubicon Lake Band's right of self-determination. One of the questions raised in the procedure before the Committee was whether pending litigation and negotiation for a settlement of the case constituted an effective remedy available to the applicants and whether, therefore, the communication was not filed prior to the exhaustion of local remedies. As will be seen below, the Human Rights Committee takes the view that in such a situation, only interim measures may be considered to constitute an effective remedy, which must be exhausted as a condition of admissibility of the Communication before the Committee. It is, however, noteworthy that, while finding that Article 27 ICCPR is violated, the Committee concludes by stating that 'The State party proposes to rectify the situation by a remedy that the Committee deems appropriate within the meaning of article 2 of the Covenant.']

15. [Canada] requests the Committee to review its decision on admissibility, submitting that effective domestic remedies have not been exhausted by the Band. It observes that the Committee's decision appears to be based on the assumption that an interim injunction would be the only effective remedy to address the alleged breach of the Lubicon Lake Band's rights. This assumption, in its opinion, does not withstand close scrutiny. The State party submits that, based on the evidence of the Alberta Court of Queen's Bench and the Court of Appeal – the two courts which had had to deal with the Band's request for interim relief – as well as the socio-economic conditions of the Band, its way of life, livelihood and means of subsistence have not been irreparably damaged, nor are they under imminent threat. Accordingly, it is submitted that an interim injunction is not the only effective remedy available to the Band, and that a trial on the merits and the negotiation process proposed by the Federal Government constitute both effective and viable alternatives. The State party reaffirms its position that it has a right, pursuant to article 5, paragraph 2(b), of the Optional Protocol, to insist that domestic redress be exhausted before the Committee considers the matter. It claims that the terms 'domestic remedies', in accordance with relevant principles of international law, must be understood as applying to all established local procedures of redress. As long as there has not been a final judicial determination of the Band's rights under Canadian law, there is no basis in fact or under international law for concluding that domestic redress is ineffective, nor for declaring the communication admissible under the Optional Protocol. In support of its claims, the State party provides a detailed review of the proceedings before the Alberta Court of Queen's Bench and explains its long-standing policy to seek the resolution of valid, outstanding land claims by Indian Bands through negotiation.

16.5 With respect to the requirement of exhaustion of domestic remedies, the author rejects the State party's assertion that a trial on the merits would offer the Band an effective recourse against the Federal Government and redress for the loss of its economy and its way of life. First, this assertion rests upon the assumption that past human rights violations can be rectified through compensatory payments; secondly, it is obvious that the Band's economy and way of life have suffered irreparable harm. Furthermore, it is submitted that a trial on the merits is no longer available against the Federal Government of Canada since, in October 1986, the Supreme Court of Canada held that aboriginal land rights within provincial boundaries involve provincial land rights and must therefore be adjudicated before the provincial courts. It was for that reason that, on 30 March 1987, the Lubicon Lake Band applied to the Alberta Court of Queen's Bench for leave to amend its statement of claim before that court so as to be able to add the Federal Government as a defendant. On 22 October 1987, the Court of Queen's Bench denied the application. Therefore, despite the fact that the Canadian Constitution vests exclusive jurisdiction for all matters concerning Indians and Indian lands in Canada with the Federal Government, it is submitted that the Band cannot avail itself of any recourse against the Federal Government on issues pertaining to these very questions ...

17.2 With respect to the effectiveness of available domestic remedies, the State party takes issue with the author's submission detailed in paragraph 16.5 above, which it claims seriously misrepresents the legal situation as it relates to the Band and the Federal and Provincial Governments. It reiterates that the Band has instituted two legal actions, both of which remain pending: one in the Federal Court of Canada against the federal Government; the other in the Alberta Court of Queen's Bench against the province and certain private corporations. To the extent that the author's claim for land is based on aboriginal title, as opposed to treaty entitlement, it is established case law that a court action must be brought against the province and not the Federal Government.

17.3 The State party adds that in the action brought before the Alberta Court of Queen's Bench: 'The communicant sought leave to add the Federal Government as a party to the legal proceedings in the Alberta Court of Queen's Bench. The Court there held that, based on existing case law, a provincial court is without jurisdiction to hear a claim for relief against the Federal Government; rather, this is a matter properly brought before the Federal Court of Canada. The plaintiff has in fact done this and the action is, as already indicated, currently pending. Therefore, recourse against the Government of Canada is still available to the Band, as it has always been, in the Federal Court of Canada. Moreover, the communicant has appealed the decision of the Court of Queen's Bench to the Alberta Court of Appeal.' ...

27.1 In his comments of 2 October 1989 on the State party's reply to the Committee's interim decision, the author contends ... that no domestic remedy exists which could restore the Lubicon Lake Band's traditional economy or way of life, which 'has been destroyed as a direct result of both the negligence of the Canadian Government and its deliberate actions'. The author submits that from the legal point of view, the situation of the Band is consistent with the Committee's decision in the case of *Munoz* v. *Peru* [Communication No. 203/1986, UN Doc. Supp. No. 40 (A/44/40) at 200 (1988), final views of 4 November 1988], in which it was held that the concept of a fair hearing within the meaning of article 14, paragraph 1, of the Covenant necessarily entails that justice be rendered without undue delay. In that case, the Committee had considered a delay of seven years in the domestic proceedings to be unreasonably prolonged. In the case of the Band, the author states, domestic proceedings were initiated in 1975. Furthermore, although the Band petitioned the Federal Government for a reserve for the first time in 1933, the matter remains unsettled. According to the Band, it was forced to bring 14 years of litigation to an end, primarily because of two decisions that effectively deny the Band an opportunity to maintain aboriginal rights claim against the Federal Government ...

27.2 As to the State party's reference to a negotiated settlement, the author submits that the offer is neither equitable nor does it address the needs of the Lubicon community, since it would leave virtually all items of any significance to future discussions, decisions by Canada, or applications by the Band; and that the Band would be required to abandon all rights to present any future domestic and international claims against the State party, including its communication to the Human Rights Committee. The author further submits that the agreement of October 1988 between the Band and the Province of Alberta does not in the least solve the Band's aboriginal land claims, and that the State party's characterization of the agreement has been 'deceptive'. In this context, the author argues that, contrary to its earlier representations, the State party has not offered to implement the October 1988 agreement and that if it were willing to honour its provisions, several issues including the question of just compensation would have to be settled ...

29.4 Insisting that no irreparable damage to the traditional way of life of the Lubicon Lake Band had occurred and that there was no imminent threat of such harm, and further that both a trial on the merits of the Band's claims and the negotiation process constitute effective and viable alternatives to the interim relief which the Band had unsuccessfully sought in the courts, the State party, in October 1987, requested the Committee, under rule 93, paragraph 4, of the rules of procedure, to review its decision on admissibility, in so far as it concerns the requirement of exhaustion of domestic remedies. The State party stressed in this connection that delays in the judicial proceedings initiated by the Band were largely attributable to the Band's own inaction. The State party further explained its long-standing policy to seek the resolutions of valid, outstanding land claims by Indian bands through negotiations...

29.7 Accepting its obligation to provide the Lubicon Lake Band with reserve land under Treaty 8, and after further unsuccessful discussions, the Federal Government, in May 1988, initiated legal proceedings against the Province of Alberta and the Lubicon Lake Band, in an effort to provide a common jurisdiction and thus to enable it to meet its lawful obligations to the Band under Treaty 8. In the author's opinion, however, this initiative was designated for the sole purpose of delaying indefinitely the resolution of the Lubicon land issues and, on 6 October 1988 (30 September, according to the State party), the Lubicon Lake Band asserted jurisdiction over its territory and declared that it had ceased to recognize the jurisdiction of the Canadian courts. The author further accused the State party of 'practicing deceit in the media and dismissing advisors who recommend any resolution favourable to the Lubicon people'.

29.8 Following an agreement between the Provincial Government of Alberta and the Lubicon Lake Band in November 1988 to set aside 95 square miles of land for a reserve, negotiations started between the Federal Government and the Band on the modalities of the land transfer and related issues. According to the State party, consensus had been reached on the majority of issues, including Band membership, size of the reserve, community construction and delivery of programmes and services, but not on cash compensation, when the Band withdrew from the negotiations on 24 January 1989. The formal offer presented at that time by the Federal Government amounted to approximately $C45 million in benefits and programmes, in addition to the 95 square mile reserve.

29.9 The author, on the other hand, states that the above information from the State party is not only misleading but virtually entirely untrue and that there had been no serious attempt by the Government to reach a settlement. He describes the Government's offer as an exercise in public relations, 'which committed the Federal Government to virtually nothing', and states that no agreement or consensus had been reached on any issue. The author further accused the State party of sending agents into communities surrounding the traditional Lubicon territory to induce other natives to make competing claims for traditional Lubicon land.

29.10 The State party rejects the allegation that it negotiated in bad faith or engaged in improper behaviour to the detriment of the interests of the Lubicon Lake Band. It concedes that the Lubicon Lake Band has suffered a historical inequity, but maintains that its formal offer would, if accepted, enable the Band to maintain its culture, control its way of life and achieve economic self-sufficiency and, thus, constitute an effective remedy. On the basis of a total of 500 Band members, the package worth $C45 million would amount to almost $C500,000 for each family of five. It states that a number of the Band's demands, including an indoor ice arena or a swimming pool, had been refused. The major remaining point of contention, the State party submits, is a request for $C167 million in compensation for economic and other losses allegedly suffered. That claim, it submits, could be pursued in the courts, irrespective of the acceptance of the formal offer. It reiterates that its offer to the Band stands...

31.1 The Committee has seriously considered the State party's request that it review its decision declaring the communication admissible under the Optional Protocol 'in so far as it may raise issues under article 27 or other articles of the Covenant'. In the light of the information now before it, the Committee notes that the State party has argued convincingly that, by actively pursuing matters before the appropriate courts, delays, which appeared to be unreasonably prolonged, could have been reduced by the Lubicon Lake Band. At issue, however, is the question of whether the road of litigation would have represented an effective method of saving or restoring the traditional or cultural livelihood of the Lubicon Lake Band, which, at the material time, was allegedly at the brink of collapse. The Committee is not persuaded that that would have constituted an effective remedy within the meaning of article 5, paragraph 2(b), of the Optional Protocol. In the circumstances, the Committee upholds its earlier decision on admissibility.

Individual opinion submitted by Mr Bertil Wennergren:
The rationale behind the general rule of international law that domestic remedies should be exhausted before a claim is submitted to an instance of international investigation or settlement is primarily to give a respondent State an opportunity to redress, by its own means within the framework of its domestic legal system, the wrongs alleged to have been suffered by the individual. In my opinion, this rationale implies that, in a case such as the present one, an international instance shall not examine a matter pending before a court of the respondent State. To my mind, it is not compatible with international law that an international instance considers issues which, concurrently, are pending before a national court. An instance of international investigation or settlement must, in my opinion, refrain from considering any issue pending before a national court until such time as the matter has been adjudicated upon by the national courts. As that is not the case here, I find the communication inadmissible at this point in time.

It has also been recognized that remedies which are inaccessible in practice because of the absence of legal aid do not have to be exhausted:

Human Rights Committee, *Henry* v. *Jamaica*, Communication No. 230/1987 (CCPR/C/43/D/230/1987 (1991)), final views of 1 November 1991:

[The author is awaiting execution at a prison in Jamaica. He claims to be the victim of a violation by Jamaica of his rights under Article 14 of the International Covenant on Civil and Political Rights. The State party argues that the Communication is inadmissible on the ground of non-exhaustion of domestic remedies, since the author failed to take action under the Jamaican Constitution to seek enforcement of his right, under section 20 of the Constitution, to a fair trial and legal representation.]

6.4 In respect of the absence of legal aid for the filing of constitutional motions, the State party submits that nothing in the Optional Protocol or in customary international law would support the contention that an individual is relieved of the obligation to exhaust domestic remedies on the grounds that there is no provision for legal aid and that his indigence has prevented him from resorting to an available remedy. In this connection, the State party observes that the Covenant only imposes a duty to provide legal aid in respect of criminal offenses (article 14, paragraph 3(d)). Furthermore, international conventions dealing with economic, social and cultural rights do not impose an unqualified obligation on States to implement such rights: article 2 of the International Covenant on Economic, Social and Cultural Rights, for instance, provides for the progressive realization of economic rights and relates to the 'capacity of implementation' of States. In the circumstances, the State party argues that it is incorrect to infer from the author's indigence and the absence of legal aid in respect of the right to apply for constitutional redress that the remedy is necessarily nonexistent or unavailable. Accordingly, the State party requests the Committee to review its decision on admissibility ...

7.3 The Committee recalls that by submission of 10 October 1991 in a different case, the State party indicated that legal aid is not provided for constitutional motions. In the view of the Committee, this supports the finding made in its decision on admissibility, that a constitutional motion is not an available remedy which must be exhausted for purposes of the Optional Protocol. In this context, the Committee observes that it is not the author's indigence which absolves him from pursuing constitutional remedies, but the State party's unwillingness or inability to provide legal aid for this purpose.

7.4 The State party claims that it has no obligation under the Covenant to make legal aid available in respect of constitutional motions, as such motions do not involve the determination of a criminal charge, as required by article 14, paragraph 3(d), of the Covenant. But the issue before the Committee has not been raised in the context of article 14, paragraph 3(d), but only in the context of whether domestic remedies have been exhausted.

Although the individual filing a communication should have exhausted all available domestic remedies, Article 5, para. 2(b), of the Optional Protocol to the ICCPR adds that 'This shall not be the rule where the application of the remedies is unreasonably prolonged.'

Human Rights Committee, *Hendriks* v. *Netherlands*, Communication No. 201/1985 (27 July 1988), UN Doc. Supp. No. 40 (A/43/40) at 230 (1988):

[Article 23, para. 4 ICCPR provides that 'States Parties ... shall take appropriate steps to ensure equality of rights and responsibilities of spouses as to marriage ... and at its dissolution. In the case of dissolution, provision shall be made for the necessary protection of any children.' Mr Hendriks claims that this article has been violated by the courts of the Netherlands which granted exclusive custody of his son, Wim Hendriks, Jr., born in 1971, to the mother without ensuring the father's right of access to the child. The author claims that his son's rights have been and are being violated by his subjection to one-sided custody; moreover, the author maintains that his rights as a father have been and are being violated and that he has been deprived of his responsibilities *vis-à-vis* his son without any reason other than the unilateral opposition of the mother. The marriage was dissolved in September 1974 by decision of the Amsterdam District Court, without settling the questions of guardianship and visiting rights. After six years of procedures, the arrangement according to which Wim Hendriks, Jr. would remain with his mother was confirmed. The Dutch courts considered that 'a number of years have passed since the parents were divorced, both have remarried, but there is still serious conflict between the parents', and that 'in such a case, it is likely that an access order will lead to tension in the family of the parent who has custody of the child and that the child can easily develop a conflict of loyalties', so that it would not be in the best interests of the child to grant access rights to his father. Challenging the admissibility of the Communication for failure to exhaust local remedies, the Netherlands submitted that 'there is nothing to prevent the author from once again requesting the Netherlands courts to issue an access order, basing his request on "changed circumstances", since Wim Hendriks, Jr. is now over 12 years old, and, in accordance with the new article 902(b) of the Code of Civil Procedure which came into force on 5 July 1982, Wim Hendriks, Jr. would have to be heard by the Court in person before a judgement could be made'. The Committee rejected this argument:]

6.3 Article 5, paragraph 2(b), of the Optional Protocol precludes the Committee from considering a communication unless domestic remedies have been exhausted. In that connection, the Committee noted that, in its submission of 9 July 1986, the State party had informed the Committee that nothing would prevent Mr Hendriks from once again requesting the Netherlands courts to issue an access order. The Committee observed, however, that Mr Hendriks' claim, initiated before the Netherlands courts 12 years earlier, had been adjudicated by the Supreme Court in 1980. Taking into account the provision of article 5, paragraph 2(b), *in fine* of the Optional Protocol regarding unreasonably prolonged remedies, the author could not be expected to continue to request the same courts to issue an access order on the basis of 'changed circumstances', notwithstanding the procedural change in domestic law (enacted in 1982) which would now require Hendriks, Jr. to be heard. The Committee observed that, although in family law disputes, such as custody cases of that nature, changed circumstances might often justify new proceedings, it was satisfied that the requirement of exhaustion of domestic remedies had been met in the case before it.

9.4. Question for discussion: the exhaustion of domestic remedies under the International Covenant on Civil and Political Rights

Should the position of the Human Rights Committee in *Chief Bernard Ominayak and the Lubicon Lake Band* v. *Canada* be interpreted as meaning that, in order to be effective – and thus as having to be exercised for the purposes of the rule on the prior exhaustion of domestic remedies – a remedy should provide interim protection to the individual?

2.4 Non-duplication with other international procedures

There exists a notable difference of wording between the (First) Optional Protocol to the International Covenant on Civil and Political Rights and other international human rights instruments as regards the requirement that, in order for a communication to be admissible, it must not have been examined already under another international procedure. Article 5, para. 2(a), of the OP-ICCPR provides that 'The Committee shall not consider any communication from an individual unless it has ascertained that: (a) The same matter *is not being examined* under another procedure of international investigation or settlement.' In contrast, the other UN human rights treaties that refer to this condition provide that the expert bodies they establish shall not consider individual communications unless they have ascertained that 'the same matter *has not been, and is not being examined* under another procedure of international investigation or settlement' (emphasis added: see, e.g. Art. 22, para. 5(1) CAT; Art. 4, para. 2(a) OP-CEDAW; Art. 2(b) OP-CPRD). Hence, in principle, this admissibility condition is formulated in the OP-ICCPR in terms that are significantly less restrictive than in these other treaties. However, most States parties to the European Convention on Human Rights, and a number of other States, have included one reservation on that point, upon ratifying the OP-ICCPR, stating in the reservation that the competence of the Human Rights Committee does not extend to communications which have already been considered under another procedure of international investigation or settlement, even if the proceedings under that procedure are definitively closed. It is therefore primarily on the basis of these reservations, which it considers acceptable as they do not run counter to the object and purpose of the Covenant or the procedure of individual communications, that the Human Rights Committee has interpreted the meaning of the expression 'same matter'.

In the case of *Sánchez López* v. *Spain* (Communication No. 777/1997 (CCPR/C/67/D/777/1997) (final views of 25 November 1999)), the Human Rights Committee had taken the view that 'The words "the same matter", within the meaning of article 5, paragraph 2(a), of the Optional Protocol, must be understood as referring to one and the same claim concerning the same individual, as submitted by that individual, or by some other person empowered to act on his behalf, to the other international body.' It confirmed this reading in the following case, even extending it further.

Human Rights Committee, *Leirvåg* v. *Norway*, Communication No. 1155/2003 (CCPR/C/82/D/1155/2003), final views of 23 November 2004:

[The authors complain of the introduction by the Norwegian Government, in August 1997, of a new mandatory religious subject in the Norwegian school system, entitled 'Christian Knowledge and Religious and Ethical Education', which only provides for exemption from certain limited segments of the teaching. The newly introduced subject is to be based on the schools' Christian object clause and it should provide 'thorough knowledge of the Bible and Christianity as a cultural heritage and Evangelical-Lutheran Faith'. The Leirvåg and the other authors of the Communication have a non-religious humanist life stance and do not wish to see their daughter participate in such classes. In the challenge brought against the new scheme before the national courts, the authors were joining with the Norwegian Humanist Association as well as with other parents, three of whom presented their claim to the European Court of Human Rights following a rejection of their action by the Norwegian courts. The following excerpts focus exclusively on the question of admissibility raised by the Norwegian Government.]

8.1 On 3 July 2003, the State party commented on the admissibility of the complaint. It challenges the admissibility on the basis that the same matter is already being examined under another procedure of international investigation or settlement, for non-exhaustion of domestic remedies and for non-substantiation of their claims.

8.2 The State party notes that before the Norwegian courts, the authors' claims of exemption from the school subject named 'Christian Knowledge and Religious and Ethical Education'

[CKREE subject] were adjudicated in a single case, along with identical claims from three other sets of parents. The different parties were all represented by the same lawyer (the identical to counsel in this case), and their identical claims were adjudicated as one. No attempts were made to individualize the cases of the different parties. The domestic courts passed a single judgment concerning all the parties, and none of the courts differentiated between the parties. Despite having pleaded their case jointly before the domestic courts, the parties opted to send complaints both to the European Court of Human Rights (ECHR) and to the Human Rights Committee. Four sets of parents lodged their communications with the Human Rights Committee, and three others with the ECHR on 20 February 2002. The communications to the Human Rights Committee and to the ECHR are to a large extent identical. Thus it appears that the authors stand together, but that they are seeking a review by both international bodies of what is essentially one case.

8.3 While the State party acknowledges the Committee's findings on communication 777/1997, it submits that the present case should be held inadmissible because the same matter is being examined by the ECHR. It contends that the present case differs from the case of Sanchez Lopez in that the authors in that case argued that 'although the complaint submitted to the European Commission of Human Rights relates to the same matter, [they differ] in that the complaint, the offence, the victim and, of course, the Spanish judicial decisions, including the relevant application for amparo, were not the same'. In the present case the same judgment by the Norwegian Supreme Court is being challenged before both bodies. The Norwegian Supreme Court judgment concerned an issue of principle, whether or not the CKREE subject violated international human rights standards.

8.4 If the communication is deemed admissible, the international bodies will need to take a general approach, i.e. they have to ask whether or not the subject as such, in the absence of the right to a full exemption, is in violation of the right to freedom of religion. As the primary objective of article 5, paragraph 2(a), of the Optional Protocol is to prevent a duplication of examination by international bodies of the same case, such duplication is exactly what the different parties to the case adjudicated by Norwegian courts are operating.

[The Committee responded as follows:]

13.3 The State party has contested the admissibility also on the ground that the 'same matter' is already being examined by the ECHR as three other sets of parents have lodged a similar complaint with the ECHR and that before the Norwegian courts, the authors' claims for full exemption from the CKREE subject were adjudicated in a single case, along with identical claims from these three other sets of parents. The Committee reiterates its jurisprudence that the words 'the same matter' within the meaning of article 5, paragraph 2(a), of the Optional Protocol, must be understood as referring to one and the same claim concerning the same individual, as submitted by that individual, or by some other person empowered to act on his behalf, to the other international body. That the authors' claims were joined with the claims of another set of individuals before the domestic courts does not obviate or change the interpretation of the Optional Protocol. The authors have demonstrated that they are individuals distinct from those of the three sets of parents that filed a complaint with the ECHR. The authors in the present communication chose not to submit their cases to the ECHR. The Committee, therefore, considers that it is not precluded under article 5, paragraph 2(a), of the Optional Protocol from considering the communication.

Human Rights Committee, *Karakurt* v. *Austria*, Communication No. 965/2000 (CCPR/C/74/D/965/2000 (2002)), final views of 4 April 2002:

[The author, a Turkish national, alleges to be a victim of a breach by the Republic of Austria of Article 26 ICCPR. Indeed, although he was elected to one of the two positions open in the work council (*Betriebsrat*) of the Association for the Support of Foreigners in Linz, where he is employed, section 53(1) of the Industrial Relations Act (*Arbeitsverfassungsgesetz*) limited the entitlement to stand for election to such work councils to Austrian nationals or members of the European Economic Area (EEA). Accordingly, the author, satisfying neither criteria, was excluded from standing for the work council. After having failed in his remedies before the Austrian courts, Mr Karakurt applied to the European Court of Human Rights. On 14 September 1999, the Third Chamber of the Court, by a majority, found application 32441/96 manifestly ill founded and accordingly inadmissible. The Court held that the work council, as an elected body exercising functions of staff participation, could not be considered an 'association' within the meaning of Article 11 ECHR, and that the statutory provisions in question did not interfere with any such rights under this article. Like a number of Member States of the Council of Europe who have also ratified the ICCPR, Austria had made a reservation upon entering the Covenant on 10 December 1987, under the terms of which: 'further to the provisions of article 5(2) of the Protocol, the Committee provided for in Article 28 of the Covenant shall not consider any communication from an individual unless it has been ascertained that the same matter has not been examined by the European Commission on Human Rights established by the European Convention for the Protection of Human Rights and Fundamental Freedoms.']

5.4. As to the State party's contention that its reservation to article 5 of the Optional Protocol excludes the Committee's competence to consider the communication, the Committee notes that the concept of the 'same matter' within the meaning of article 5(2)(a) of the Optional Protocol must be understood as referring to one and the same claim of the violation of a particular right concerning the same individual. In this case, the author is advancing free-standing claims of discrimination and equality before the law, which were not, and indeed could not have been, made before the European organs. Accordingly, the Committee does not consider itself precluded by the State party's reservation to the Optional Protocol from considering the communication.

[The Committee concludes in this case that Austria is in violation of Article 26 ICCPR, since nationals of the EEA Member States are not excluded from sitting in work councils and 'it is not reasonable to base a distinction between aliens concerning their capacity to stand for election for a work council solely on their different nationality'.]

The same reservation made by Austria upon entering the ICCPR was discussed in the case of *Kollar* v. *Austria* (Communication No. 989/2001 (CCPR/C/78/DR/989/2001), final views of 30 July 2003). In the views it adopted in that case, the Human Rights Committee made it clear that it would be reluctant to examine a case already considered by the European Court of Human Rights insofar as the provisions of the ICCPR and those of the ECHR invoked by the alleged victim converge, even though certain differences of interpretation may exist between the Human Rights Committee and the European Court of Human Rights respectively: as regards the right to a fair trial invoked by the author of the communication, for instance, the Committee notes that 'despite certain differences in the interpretation of article 6, paragraph 1, of the European Convention and article 14, paragraph 1, of the Covenant by the competent organs, both the content and scope of these provisions largely converge. In the light of the great similarities between the two provisions, and on the basis of the State party's reservation, the Committee considers itself precluded from reviewing a finding of the European Court on the applicability of article 6, paragraph 1, of the European Convention by substituting its jurisprudence under article 14, paragraph 1, of the Covenant' (para. 8.6.). The Committee also confirmed that, although the non-discrimination requirement of Article 26 ICCPR possessed a free-standing quality Article 14 ECHR did not possess, it would not consider admissible communications based on Article 26 ICCPR for that sole reason, where Article 14 ECHR could be invoked before the European Court of Human Rights in combination with another right of the Convention.

9.5. Questions for discussion: the 'same matter' examined under another procedure of international investigation or settlement

1. Consider the position of the Human Rights Committee in *Leirvåg* v. *Norway*. Is this position defensible from a legal point of view? Is it opportune, from a pragmatic point of view? Will it result in human rights bodies being put in competition with one another, by victims gaming on differences in approaches adopted by the various bodies concerned? In *Leirvåg*, the Committee went on to find that Article 18(4) ICCPR had been violated. The European Court of Human Rights arrived at the same conclusion in the parallel application it was presented with, on the basis of Article 2 of Protocol No. 1 to the ECHR which guarantees the parents' right to ensure that their children's education will be in conformity with their own religious and philosophical convictions (Eur. Ct. H.R. (GC), *Folgerø and others* v. *Norway* (Appl. No. 15472/02), judgment of 26 June 2007). In its admissibility decision of 14 February 2006, the Court found that the complaints made respectively to the European Court of Human Rights and to the Human Rights Committee 'concerned substantially the same matters ... The essential parts of their complaints were the same, word by word.' It held nevertheless that the application was admissible, since 'notwithstanding the common features between the application lodged under the Convention in Strasbourg and the communication filed under the UN Covenant in Geneva', the two groups of families were different: therefore, the rule regarding inadmissibility of any application to the European Court of Human Rights that 'has already been submitted to another procedure of international investigation or settlement and contains no relevant new information' (Article 35 para. 2(b) of the Convention) did not apply. This position of the Court was criticized by two members of the Court, Messrs Zupančič and Borrego Borrego, in a separate opinion to the judgment of 26 June 2007. They stated:

'Both the Human Rights Committee (without a prior decision of the ECHR) and the European Court of Human Rights (aware of the Human Rights Committee's decision) came to the conclusion that the key issue was not whether there had been a single set of domestic proceedings, or whether the single judgment had been examined by two different international bodies, or whether the facts submitted before the two organs were identical. No. What really mattered was the fact that, as the applicants were a group of individuals, some of them had opted to petition the Human Rights Committee and some of them had submitted an application to the European Court of Human Rights. To put it briefly, different applicants of the same party had addressed different international bodies. International litispendence exists if the case concerns "the same matter", "the same judgment", "the same complaint", "the same party" and the like. In this case, according to the interpretation given by the majority, international litispendence ceases to exist when different individuals of the original group of applicants decide to separate in two groups to submit the same matter before different international organs.

Nevertheless, the risk of contradictory decisions, in which international litispendence has its origin, does exist. This is an example of what the Convention and the Optional Protocol tried to avoid. Unfortunately, their subsequent interpretation by the competent international organs has deprived them of their original sense.'

2. Is the position of the Human Rights Committee in *Kollar* v. *Austria* compatible with the refusal of the Committee to follow the interpretation of the European Court of Human Rights, even where the rights of the ECHR are drafted in essentially the same terms as the equivalent provision of the ICCPR? Consider for instance the case of *Carlos Correia de Matos* v. *Portugal* (Communication No. 1123/2002 (CCPR/C/86/D/1123/2002), final views of 18 April 2006). Here, the author complained before the Committee that he was not permitted to defend himself in person. This, he considered to be in contravention of Article 14, para. 3(d), of the Covenant, which provides that everyone accused of a criminal charge shall be entitled 'to defend himself in person or through legal assistance of his own choosing'. He had made a similar argument before the European Court of Human Rights on the basis of Article 6, para. 3(c) ECHR – which is worded in similar terms – and had failed. Yet, the Human Rights Committee agreed to examine the merits of the application, because Portugal had entered no reservation to Article 5, para. 2(a), of the Optional Protocol, and the Committee thus was not precluded from examining a case already examined under another international procedure provided the examination has been completed. The Committee went on to find a violation of Article 14, para. 3(d), of the Covenant, by interpreting this provision in a way that totally contradicts the view adopted on the equivalent provision of the ECHR, leading three members of the Committee to regret that 'two international instances, instead of trying to reconcile their jurisprudence with one another, come to different conclusions when applying exactly the same provisions to the same facts'. However, if Portugal had filed a reservation concerning the competence of the Committee to examine communications when 'the same matter has been, or is being examined under another procedure of international investigation or settlement', the Committee would have refused to examine the application of Mr Correia de Matos, consistent with its position in *Kollar* v. *Austria* (see C. Phuong, 'The Relationship Between the European Court of Human Rights and the Human Rights Committee: Has the "Same Matter" Already Been "Examined"?', *Human Rights Law Review*, 7 (2007), 385). Is this consistent? Or rather does that reveal an uncertain and ambivalent relationship between the Human Rights Committee and the European Court of Human Rights?

3. The positions adopted by the Human Rights Committee in *Leirvåg* v. *Norway* and *Carlos Correia de Matos* v. *Portugal*, taken together, show a willingness of the Committee both to entertain communications that are identical, or pose identical questions, to the European Court of Human

Rights, and yet not to align itself with the interpretation of the European Court of Human Rights. What are the consequences? Should forum-shopping by victims of human rights violations, including the successive submission of petitions in various forums, be discouraged? It has been suggested that the interest of 'forum shopping, and successive petition forum shopping in particular, lies in reducing the chances of ... divergences and conflicts by providing jurists with a structured setting in which to communicate with each other about common legal questions. When the same factual allegations are submitted before two different tribunals consecutively, the second set of jurists cannot ignore the fact that another tribunal is wrestling with issues that they too must consider in their own treaty regimes. In exercising their discretion to decide whether to dismiss the petition or hear it on the merits, these jurists can benefit enormously from the first tribunal's reasoning and conclusions. The second tribunal can use them either to confirm similarities in the two treaties, or as a point of departure from which to justify a divergent approach based on the differing text, structures, or objectives of the two agreements. By adopting an openly deliberative approach and candidly weighing the persuasive value of decisions from outside their own treaty regime, jurists can fashion a forum shopping policy that not only does justice between the parties, but also builds a more fully informed and coherent human rights jurisprudence' (L. R. Helfer, 'Forum Shopping for Human Rights', *University of Pennsylvania Law Review*, 148 (1999), 285 at 398). Do you agree?

4. If improved co-ordination between the approaches of various human rights bodies, at both UN and regional levels, is desirable, how could this be achieved? Consider the proposals made in 1993 by Philip Alston (*Effective Implementation of International Instruments on Human Rights, Including Reporting Obligations under International Instruments on Human Rights*, UN GAOR World Conference on Human Rights Preparatory Committee, fourth session, Annex, Agenda Item 5, paras. 139–55, A/CONF.157/PC/62/Add. 11/Rev.1 (1993)). He suggested (a) preparing a 'programme of action designed solely to ensure that the United Nations treaty bodies and the relevant regional bodies are kept reasonably well informed of one another's activities'; (b) strengthening 'exchanges between the United Nations and regional intergovernmental organisations dealing with human rights', at the initiative of the UN Secretary-General; (c) convening regular meetings between the members of UN human rights treaty bodies and their counterparts in bodies established in regional organizations; (d) developing legal databases to facilitate mutual information and ensure that the jurisprudence developed by each body is accessible and known to the others. Are these proposals desirable, and can they achieve the desired outcome? What obstacles or disadvantages do they present?

3 THE IMPLEMENTATION OF FINDINGS OF UN HUMAN RIGHTS TREATY BODIES

The UN human rights treaty bodies adopt concluding observations, views (on the basis of individual communications), and general comments (or general recommendations). Even where civil society organizations and the public authorities, including the judiciary, have a good knowledge of the standards contained in the treaties to which the State concerned is a party, the findings of the treaty bodies themselves are often ignored. These findings, however, do serve to clarify the normative content of the requirements stipulated in the treaties; and a better understanding of these requirements would greatly facilitate an improved compliance, in the future, with those international obligations of the State. States may thus be expected to translate the findings concerning them into their national language; to disseminate these findings widely; to organize a public debate on the implementation measures which they call for; and, on that basis, to adopt the measures required to ensure compliance.

3.1 The follow-up of Concluding Observations

Human Rights Committee, Concluding Observations: Canada (CCPR/C/CAN/CO/5, 20 April 2006), para. 6:

6. The Committee notes with concern that many of the recommendations it addressed to the State party in 1999 remain unimplemented. It also regrets that the Committee's previous concluding observations have not been distributed to members of Parliament and that no parliamentary committee has held hearings on issues arising from the Committee's observations, as anticipated by the delegation in 1999 (art. 2).

The State party should establish procedures, by which oversight of the implementation of the Covenant is ensured, with a view, in particular, to reporting publicly on any deficiencies. Such procedures should operate in a transparent and accountable manner, and guarantee the full participation of all levels of government and of civil society, including indigenous peoples.

The view thus expressed by the Human Rights Committee has been adopted on a number of occasions, not only by that Committee, but also by other UN human rights treaty bodies (see, e.g. Concluding Observations of the Human Rights Committee on: Australia (A/55/40, paras. 498–528, para. 528); Canada (CCPR/C/79/Add. 105 (1999)), para. 21; Czech Republic (CCPR/CO/72/CZE (2001)), para. 26; Finland (CCPR/C/79/Add. 91 (1998)), para. 22; Sweden, (CCPR/CO/74/SWE (2002)), para. 16; Concluding Observations of the Committee against Torture on: Czech Republic (A/56/44, paras. 106–14, para. 114(h)); Spain (CAT/C/CR/29/3 (2002)), para. 18; Sweden (CAT/C/CR/28/6 (2002)), para. 9; Concluding Observations of the Committee on the Elimination of All Forms of Racial Discrimination on: Australia (A/49/18, paras. 535–51, para. 550 and CERD/C/304/Add. 10 (2000), para. 19); Canada (A/57/18, paras. 315–43, para. 342); Czech Republic (CERD/C/304/Add. 47 (1998), para. 25, and CERD/C/304/Add.109 (2001), para. 17); Sweden (CERD/C/304/Add. 37 (1997), para. 21, and CERD/C/304/Add. 103 (2001), para. 19); Concluding Observations of the Committee on Economic, Social and Cultural Rights on: Australia (E/C.12/1993/9 (1993), para. 15, and E/C.12/1/Add. 50 (2000), para. 37); Canada (E/C.12/1/Add. 31 (1998), para. 60); Spain (E/C.12/1/Add. 2 (1996), para. 19); Concluding Observations of the Committee on the Rights of the Child on Canada (CRC/C/15/Add. 37 (1995)), para. 27). The reasons for this are obvious: adequate implementation of the Concluding Observations adopted by the UN human rights treaty bodies will only occur if not only the parliamentarians, but also civil society organizations and the media have full knowledge of the content of these observations, and thus are able to put pressure on the public authorities, including both the Government and Parliament, to take them into account. And indeed, the Optional Protocol to the CEDAW includes a provision under which 'Each State Party undertakes to make widely known and to give publicity to the Convention and the present Protocol and to facilitate access to information about the views and recommendations of the Committee, in particular, on matters involving the State Party'; Article 36(4) of the Convention on the Rights of Persons with Disabilities provides that 'States Parties shall make their reports widely available to the public in their own countries and facilitate access to the suggestions and general recommendations relating to these reports.' In addition, as we have seen in section 1, the treaty bodies suggest that States set up an inter-departmentmental taskforce to prepare the State report, and that this structure, if established on a permanent basis, 'should provide an effective mechanism to coordinate follow-up to the concluding observations of the treaty bodies' (Harmonized Guidelines on Reporting under the International Human Rights Treaties, including Guidelines on a Common Core Document and treaty-specific targeted documents (HRI/MC/2005/3, 1 June 2005), para. 13).

In order to improve the follow-up to their Concluding Observations adopted on the basis of States' reports, the human rights treaty bodies have developed 'follow-up activities', which seek to create incentives for States to co-operate in the implementation of the recommendations. Thus, Rule 71, para. 5 of the Rules of Procedure of the Human Rights Committee provide that: 'The Committee may request the State party to give priority to such aspects of its concluding observations as it may specify.' Rule 72 in turn states that where the Committee has thus specified that priority should be given to certain aspects of its Concluding Observations on a State party's report, 'it shall establish a procedure for considering replies by the State party on those aspects and deciding what consequent action, including the date set for the next periodic report, may be appropriate'.

Human Rights Committee, Annual Report to the UN General Assembly, A/63/40 (2008):

Follow-up to Concluding Observations
196. For all reports of States parties examined by the Committee under article 40 of the Covenant [in 2007], the Committee has identified, according to its developing practice, a limited number of priority concerns, with respect to which it seeks the State party's response, within a period of a year, on the measures taken to give effect to its recommendations. The Committee welcomes the extent and depth of cooperation under this procedure by States parties ... Over the reporting period, since 1 August 2007, 11 States parties (Bosnia and Herzegovina, Brazil, Hong Kong Special Administrative Region (China), Mali, Paraguay, Republic of Korea, Sri Lanka, Suriname, Togo, United States of America and Ukraine), as well as the United Nations Interim

Administration Mission in Kosovo (UNMIK), have submitted information to the Committee under the follow-up procedure. Since the follow-up procedure was instituted in March 2001, 10 States parties (Barbados, Central African Republic, Chile, Democratic Republic of the Congo, Equatorial Guinea, Gambia, Honduras, Madagascar, Namibia and Yemen) have failed to supply follow-up information that has fallen due. The Committee reiterates that it views this procedure as a constructive mechanism by which the dialogue initiated with the examination of a report can be continued, and which serves to simplify the process of the next periodic report on the part of the State party ...

198. The Committee emphasizes that certain States parties have failed to cooperate with it in the performance of its functions under Part IV of the Covenant, thereby violating their obligations (Gambia, Equatorial Guinea).

In order to increase the quality of follow-up on its conclusions and recommendations addressed to the States parties to the Convention against Torture, the Committee against Torture established the post of Rapporteur for follow-up to conclusions and recommendations adopted under Article 19 of the Convention against Torture. The following excerpts of the 2008 Annual Report of the Committee against Torture describe this development:

Committee against Torture, Annual Report to the UN General Assembly, A/63/44 (2008):

49. The Rapporteur has emphasized that the follow-up procedure aims 'to make more effective the struggle against torture and other cruel, inhuman and degrading treatment or punishment', as articulated in the preamble to the Convention. At the conclusion of the Committee's review of each State party report, the Committee identifies concerns and recommends specific actions designed to enhance each State party's ability to implement the measures necessary and appropriate to prevent acts of torture and cruel treatment, and thereby assists States parties in bringing their law and practice into full compliance with the obligations set forth in the Convention.

50. In its follow-up procedure, the Committee has identified a number of these recommendations as requiring additional information specifically for this procedure. Such follow-up recommendations are identified because they are serious, protective, and are considered able to be accomplished within one year. The States parties are asked to provide within one year information on the measures taken to give effect to its follow-up recommendations which are specifically noted in a paragraph near the end of the conclusions and recommendations on the review of the States parties' reports under article 19.

51. Since the procedure was established at the thirtieth session in May 2003, through the end of the fortieth session in May 2008, the Committee has reviewed 67 States for which it has identified follow-up recommendations. Of the 53 States parties that were due to have submitted their follow-up reports to the Committee by 16 May 2008, 33 had completed this requirement (Albania, Argentina, Austria, Azerbaijan, Bahrain, Bosnia and Herzegovina, Canada, Chile, Czech Republic, Colombia, Croatia, Ecuador, Finland, France, Georgia, Germany, Greece, Guatemala, Hungary, Republic of Korea, Latvia, Lithuania, Monaco, Morocco, Nepal, New Zealand, Qatar,

Russian Federation, Sri Lanka, Switzerland, United Kingdom of Great Britain and Northern Ireland, United States of America and Yemen). As of 16 May, 20 States had not yet supplied follow-up information that had fallen due (Bulgaria, Burundi, Cambodia, Cameroon, Democratic Republic of the Congo, Denmark, Guyana, Italy, Japan, Luxembourg, Mexico, Moldova, the Netherlands, Peru, Poland, South Africa, Tajikistan, Togo, Uganda and Ukraine). In March 2008, the Rapporteur sent a reminder requesting the outstanding information to each of the States whose follow-up information was due in November 2007, but had not yet been submitted, and who had not previously been sent a reminder.

52. The Rapporteur noted that 14 follow-up reports had fallen due since the previous annual report. However, only 2 (Hungary and the Russian Federation) of these 14 States had submitted the follow-up information in a timely manner. Despite this, she expressed the view that the follow-up procedure had been remarkably successful in eliciting valuable additional information from States on protective measures taken during the immediate follow-up to the review of the periodic reports. While comparatively few States had replied precisely on time, 25 of the 33 respondents had submitted the information on time or within a matter of one to four months following the due date. Reminders seemed to help elicit many of these responses. The Rapporteur also expressed appreciation to non-governmental organizations, many of whom had also encouraged States parties to submit follow-up information in a timely way.

53. Through this procedure, the Committee seeks to advance the Convention's requirement that 'each State party shall take effective legislative, administrative, judicial or other measures to prevent acts of torture ...' (art. 2, para. 1) and the undertaking 'to prevent ... other acts of cruel, inhuman and degrading treatment or punishment ...' (art. 16).

54. The Rapporteur expressed appreciation for the information provided by States parties regarding those measures taken to implement their obligations under the Convention. In addition, she has assessed the responses received as to whether all the items designated by the Committee for follow-up (normally between three and six recommendations) have been addressed, whether the information provided responds to the Committee's concern, and whether further information is required. Each letter responds specifically and in detail to the information presented by the State party. Where further information has been needed, she has written to the concerned State party with specific requests for further clarification. With regard to States that have not supplied the follow-up information at all, she requests the outstanding information.

55. At its thirty-eighth session in May 2007, the Committee decided to make public the Rapporteur's letters to the States parties. These would be placed on the web page of the Committee ...

56. Since the recommendations to each State party are crafted to reflect the specific situation in that country, the follow-up responses from the States parties and letters from the Rapporteur requesting further clarification address a wide array of topics. Among those addressed in the letters sent to States parties requesting further information have been a number of precise matters seen as essential to the implementation of the recommendation in question. A number of issues have been highlighted to reflect not only the information provided, but also the issues that have not been addressed but which are deemed essential to the Committee's ongoing work, in order to be effective in taking preventive and protective measures to eliminate torture and ill-treatment.

A similar procedure exists, for instance, under Article 65 of the Rules of Procedure of the Committee for the Elimination of Racial Discrimination, which since 2006 provides that the Committee may appoint a 'follow-up coordinator', for a period of two years, charged with following up on the requests of the Committee for further reports or information from the State party. This is part of a broader strategy to improve the follow-up to the Concluding Observations adopted by the Committee on the basis of States' reports:

Committee on the Elimination of Racial Discrimination, Guidelines to follow-up on concluding observations and recommendations (CERD/C/68/Misc.5/Rev.1, 5 March 2006):

1. Dissemination of the concluding observations
The Committee encourages the State party to disseminate the concluding observations as widely as possible. It is recommended that the concluding observations and recommendations be translated into local languages and in particular languages of concerned minorities to facilitate their participation in the implementation of the Convention on the Elimination of All Forms of Racial Discrimination (the Convention) and the concluding observations of the Committee .

2. Coordination of implementation efforts and designation of a focal point/liaison person
The Committee acknowledges that its concluding observations touch on a wide range of issues and that their implementation will involve the active engagement and commitment of various ministries, departments and other stakeholders. There may consequently be a need to establish or strengthen existing mechanisms within the State party for the effective coordination of all activities related to the implementation of the Convention.

The State party is invited to designate a representative to act as focal point and who would be in charge of liaising with the Follow-up Coordinator or the alternate. This would greatly facilitate the task of the coordinator and communication between the State party and the Committee.

3. Regular reporting on progress
The State party is required to submit comprehensive reports on the general fulfilment of its obligations under the Convention on a regular basis. The periodic reports should contain information on measures taken to implement the recommendations of the Committee, as requested in the reporting guidelines of the Committee. In addition, the Committee may, in accordance with article 9, paragraph 1 of the Convention, request information from the State party at any time and may, in its concluding observations, request States to provide information within a year on follow-up to some of its recommendations. The Committee would welcome receiving information between the regular reporting sessions on concrete steps taken by the State party to implement these recommendations.

4. Cooperation with national human rights institutions and non-governmental organisations
The Committee invites the State party to involve national human rights institutions, non-governmental organisations and other stakeholders in the process of implementation of the Convention and of its concluding observations. This can be done by convening roundtables and

workshops on a regular basis with the aim of assessing the progress in the implementation of the concluding observations and recommendations.

5. Concluding observations and recommendations and national action plans.
In the Programme of Action adopted at the World Conference Against Racism, Racial Discrimination, Xenophobia and Related Intolerance, States were called upon to elaborate action plans in order to combat racism, racial discrimination, xenophobia and related intolerance. In States where such plans or human rights plans of action have been developed, the concluding observations and recommendations can serve as key qualitative and quantitative indicators of progress made in the implementation of the Convention. In this way the concluding observations and recommendations become an integrated part of domestic human rights strategies.

6. Assistance to follow-up activities
The Follow-up Coordinator or in his/her place the alternate is available to meet with representatives of the State party to discuss the implementation of the concluding observations and recommendations.

The State party may request technical assistance from the Office of the High Commissioner for Human Rights to assist in the implementation of the concluding observations and recommendations.

Should any further initiatives be taken, in order to develop the Concluding Observations adopted by human rights treaty bodies on the basis of State reports into statements binding upon the States concerned? Consider the following view:

Michael O'Flaherty, 'The Concluding Observations of United Nations Human Rights Treaty Bodies', *Human Rights Law Review,* **6, No. 1 (2006), 27:**

Any [further effort] at the articulation of any form of obligation which may arise from concluding observations would be unhelpful and inappropriate. Concluding observations emerge from a process of dialogue, notable for its non-adversarial nature. The according of a compulsive quality to the subsequent findings by the treaty body would be inconsistent with this model and is likely to meet with the resistance of states and their further unwillingness to participate in the reporting process. In any case, much of the content of concluding observations simply does not lend itself to normative expression. Apart from the elements which have nothing to do with the treaties themselves, a considerable proportion of the analysis and recommendations may have a hortatory quality. It is also commonplace for recommendations to propose approaches which are either very case-specific or are of an experimental or untried nature – approaches of a type which may change radically over time or according to regional specificities that are hardly the stuff of law.

Heli Niemi has sought to examine the national implementation of UN treaty body findings, including final views, concluding observations, and general comments, in Australia, Canada, the Czech Republic, Finland, Spain and Sweden. The conclusions are the following:

Heli Niemi, *National Implementation of Findings by United Nations Human Rights Treaty Bodies. A Comparative Study* (Institute for Human Rights, Abo Akademi University, December 2003):

The functioning of the treaty body system and the quality of treaty body output certainly leave room for improvement, but in the end it is the strength of states' domestic institutions that determines the degree of compliance. The ... existence and strength of domestic 'institutions' in the field of national implementation of treaty body findings is one positive indicator of a state's commitment to implement treaties to which it is a party. Consequently, developing and strengthening such institutions is a way to improve state compliance ...

As a first step in the implementation process, governments should disseminate concluding observations, views and general comments both 'internally' (that is, distribute copies of them within relevant parts of administration and to the legislature, judiciary and other state institutions dealing with human rights), among NGOs and to the general public. There will be no national implementation of treaty body findings unless relevant actors have knowledge of them. Moreover, such knowledge will enable the media and civil society to better monitor governments' response to the Committees' views and recommendations and to pressure governments towards better compliance with the treaties. Indeed, the treaty bodies usually recommend in their concluding observations (and the Human Rights Committee does so in its final views) that governments should disseminate these documents.

In this context one should not ignore the question of translation of treaty body findings into local language(s); the impact of dissemination will suffer if no translation is available ... [As regards dissemination *per se*,] one can observe a clear trend towards an increasing use of governmental websites for the purpose of disseminating both reports and concluding observations soon after their submission (reports) or release (concluding observations). Such development is very welcome, for it is not enough that country reports and concluding observations are published on the OHCHR website alone. It is clear that governments carry the main responsibility for translating and disseminating concluding observations, and Internet is an easy, economic and efficient way to increase awareness of the treaty body output at the domestic level. Placing reports and concluding observations on a governmental website in citizens' mother language(s) renders these documents more accessible, as one does not have to be able to speak foreign languages or be familiar with the complexities of the UN system in order to obtain them. Naturally, Internet should not replace the distribution of printed copies of concluding observations to relevant national and local actors and institutions (such as government policy-makers, civil servants, judges, parliamentarians, ombudsmen, human rights commissioners, NGOs) or the practice of informing the general public through electronic and/or print media.

In contrast, the practice of disseminating views and general comments appears to be less developed, possibly because of a lower incentive to translate and disseminate these documents which, owing to their more legal language, are less accessible to the general public than concluding observations. Nonetheless, when a Committee issues its final views on an individual communication in respect of a particular country, the government of that country should at least inform the media of the outcome of the case and place information about the views in question on its website (preferably the original document in its entirety accompanied by a translated summary if need be). Moreover, both views and general comments should be disseminated within relevant parts of national administration, including state institutions dealing with human rights, in parliament and among judges. The Australian government's practice of tabling in the federal parliament a brief description outlining the main allegations raised in each communication submitted against Australia and, subsequently, the views themselves and the government's responses, is a good one.

In general, it would be important to undertake the dissemination of all three categories of treaty body findings as quickly as possible in order to obtain the maximum amount of attention, both within state institutions, NGOs and public at large. In addition, regarding those institutions, bodies and officials that are responsible for the implementation of UN human treaties, mere dissemination is not necessarily enough but (multidisciplinary) workshops and seminars (if appropriate, with NGO participation) should be considered, in particular in relation to concluding observations ('dissemination with analysis'). The Canadian practice of holding a 'post-mortem' meeting in the week following the oral presentation of the country report between federal contributors to the report and members of the government delegation certainly qualifies as a best practice. It constitutes an effective opening of the subsequent implementation process in that the participants discuss the concluding observations and determine what, if any, follow-up and/or future action is required.

In addition to translating (if necessary) and disseminating concluding observations by the various means specified above, governments should study them carefully and use them (a) as the basis for improving the compatibility of national legislation and practices with international human rights treaties and (b) as the basis for the next country report. Both ways of using treaty body output, in particular concluding observations, is connected to governmental mechanisms for the implementation of UN human rights treaties in general and for the preparation of country reports in particular ... [S]ome sort of permanent inter-ministerial mechanism or structure for the implementation of concluding observations should be established in order to facilitate the process towards better compliance with international human rights standards. Preparation of reports may well function as a national follow-up mechanism, but a more proactive process focusing on how to implement concluding observations is needed to accompany reporting within the overall framework of treaty implementation. One has to remember that UN human rights conventions are 'multidisciplinary' or 'inter-departmental/ministerial', so the need for governmental co-ordination, co-operation and monitoring is evident. Also, different levels of government have powers in the field of human rights, so both horizontal and vertical mechanisms or structures should exist.

[In addition,] a comprehensive National Human Rights Action Plan [could be drafted] with a number of priority areas and an emphasis on co-ordination, co-operation and monitoring. It could contain the following components relating to the national implementation of both concluding observations and other forms of treaty body output:

- use of concluding observations and final views to draft the Action Plan, in particular when defining priority areas, together with highlighting the Committees' views and recommendations in the text itself in relevant contexts;
- establishment of an inter-ministerial working group for human rights within an appropriate ministry ... to strengthen co-ordination and monitoring of the implementation of human rights treaties;
- mandating the inter-ministerial working group to integrate concluding observations in its activities;
- periodic submission of reports by the government on the internal human rights situation of [the country concerned] to Parliament within the framework of the follow-up of the Action Plan, taking into account the Committee's views and recommendations on [that country].

While the suggestions above are addressed primarily to the executive and the legislative, whose roles are indeed crucial in the implementation of the findings of the UN human rights treaty bodies, courts should also be encouraged to use those findings more frequently in their judgments, either in order to interpret national provisions (in particular constitutional provisions or provisions included in a Bill of Rights) in accordance with those findings; or in order to apply directly the provisions of the international human rights treaties concerned, since the authoritative interpretation provided to them may contribute to give them more concrete meaning and thus facilitate such application by national courts. The Committee on International Human Rights Law and Practice of the International Law Association attempted to assess the practice of national jurisdictions in this regard, and to identify which factors encouraged, or impeded, a more systematic reference to the findings of the UN human rights treaty bodies in their work. Excerpts from the final report which resulted follow.

Committee on International Human Rights Law and Practice of the International Law Association, Final Report on the Impact of the Work of the United Nations Human Rights Treaty Bodies on National Courts and Tribunals, adopted at the 2004 Berlin Conference (excerpt of the conclusions):

The material surveyed ... shows that treaty body output has become a relevant interpretive source for many national courts in the interpretation of constitutional and statutory guarantees of human rights, as well as in interpreting provisions which form part of domestic law, as well as for international tribunals. While national courts have generally not been prepared to accept that they are formally bound by committee interpretations of treaty provisions, most courts have recognised that, as expert bodies entrusted by the States parties with functions under the treaties, the treaty bodies' interpretations deserve to be given considerable weight in determining the meaning of a relevant right and the existence of a violation.

[The material surveyed] shows clear patterns both in the types of material cited by national courts and the committees whose material they cite. The overwhelming number of references documented in the two reports are to cases decided under individual communications procedures and to general comments or recommendations adopted by the treaty bodies; concluding observations, States parties' reports and other output has been referred to on a relatively small number of occasions. The Human Rights Committee has received the majority of references, both as regards cases and general comments. References to the other committees' work have been less frequent.

This pattern of citation reflects a number of factors, including the relative volume of the material produced by the Human Rights Committee so far as case law and general comments are concerned, the range of rights protected by the ICCPR, the fact that domestic courts have a clear preference for drawing on material that will help them to resolve a concrete case before them (thus the dominance of reference to cases), the fact that the Human Rights Committee's period of operation is the second longest of the treaty bodies, and a higher level of public awareness of the Committee and its work. For example, by comparison the Committee against Torture has heard far fewer cases – most of them relating to article 3 of the Torture Convention – and its output is cited at the domestic level almost exclusively in cases in which a challenge is made to a deportation or expulsion order by person.

One would reasonably expect that as time passes advocates and judges will become more familiar with the increasing jurisprudence emanating from other committees. However, given the factors mentioned above, it seems likely that the output of the Human Rights Committee will continue to be the predominant source cited.

Against this background, it is important to recall that the mode of citation of treaty body materials varies widely, from inconsequential references in passing, to more substantive references, to detailed analysis of a particular source that may be important in influencing or supporting a court's decision in a given case. The number of cases in which a treaty body finding is a significant factor in influencing the outcome of a decision is a small minority of the cases referred. This reflects the pertinence of the findings to the issue in the case, the detail and persuasiveness of the reasoning in the treaty body source, the particular norm that is being interpreted, and the receptiveness of the court to the international source material. The availability of other international or national material that deals with the issues in a more detailed manner also influences the use made of treaty body material, as does the membership of a regional organisation in which there exists an organ (such as the European or Inter-American Courts of Human Rights) which can deliver binding judgments.

[It] may be useful to make a few comments as to factors which at least in individual cases appear to have been conducive to the use of treaty body findings. They are partly those which help to explain why some national courts are more amenable to using international law in other contexts, and partly factors which are specific to the area of international human rights law. There appears to be no one critical factor that is determinative, other than perhaps an awareness on the part of advocates of the material and a preparedness on the part of judges to consider it with an open mind when it is placed before them. The fact that international law (including human rights treaties) forms part of domestic law under a country's constitution does appear to assist, although there are many common law countries (where treaties do not form part of domestic law) in which courts have made quite extensive use of treaty body products.

One factor which does seem to contribute to the use of treaty body output is a direct incorporation of provisions of a treaty in a domestic statute or constitution. A number of the common law jurisdictions referred to have adopted Bills of Rights which are an enactment of terms of one or both Covenants, or very similar; this has made reference to the output of the Human Rights Committee and the Committee on Economic, Social and Cultural Rights frequent. Another important factor appears to be the general awareness in the country concerned of the treaty bodies; in particular, public awareness of, and engagement in, the treaty reporting procedures may encourage knowledge of the work of the treaty bodies and the use of that output in advocacy before the courts and other national institutions. The availability of relevant treaty body findings in local languages would also appear to be a factor.

3.2 The implementation of decisions (views) adopted on the basis of individual communications

The implementation of decisions adopted on the basis of individual communications represents a specific challenge, since findings of violations should in principle lead to remedies being provided to the individual aggrieved, or compensation made to him/her; in addition, measures of a general nature, such as a change in legislation, may be required. According to the 2008 Annual Report of the Human Rights Committee to the UN General Assembly, 429 Views out of the 547 Views adopted since 1979 concluded that there had been a violation of the ICCPR. The question of whether and how the Human Rights Committee could monitor the follow-up given to its findings has been debated, particularly since the early 1990s. The following excerpt of the 1994 Annual Report to the UN General Assembly summarizes the initiatives the Committee has taken in this regard:

Human Rights Committee Annual Report to the UN General Assembly, A/49/40 vol. 1 (1994):

Remedies called for under the Committee's views

458. The Committee's decisions on the merits are referred to as 'views' in article 5, paragraph 4, of the Optional Protocol. After the Committee has made a finding of a violation of a provision of the Covenant, it proceeds to ask the State party to take appropriate steps to remedy the violation. For instance, in the period covered by the present report, the Committee, in a case concerning arbitrary detention and torture, found as follows: 'The Committee is of the view that Mr Mohammed Bashir El-Megreisi is entitled, under article 2, paragraph 3(a), of the Covenant, to an effective remedy. It urges the State party to take effective measures (a) to secure his immediate release; (b) to compensate Mr Mohammed El-Megreisi for the torture and cruel and inhuman treatment to which he has been subjected and (c) to ensure that similar violations do not occur in the future' ...

The Committee further stated that it would wish to receive information, within 90 days, on any relevant measures taken by the State party in respect of the Committee's views (Communication No. 440/1990, *El-Megreisi* v. *the Libyan Arab Jamahiriya*) (*ibid.*, para. 8).

Follow-up activities

459. From its seventh session, in 1979, to its fifty-first session, in July 1994, the Human Rights Committee has adopted 193 views on communications received and considered under the Optional Protocol. The Committee has found violations of the Covenant in 142 of them. During the years, however, the Committee was informed by States parties in only a relatively limited number of cases of any measures taken by them to give effect to the views adopted. Because of the lack of knowledge about State compliance with its decisions, the Committee sought to devise a mechanism that would enable it to evaluate State compliance with its views.

460. At its thirty-ninth session (July 1990), following a thorough debate on the Committee's competence to engage in follow-up activities, the Committee set up a procedure which allows it to monitor the follow-up to its views adopted pursuant to article 5, paragraph 4, of the Optional Protocol. The Committee also established the mandate of a Special Rapporteur for follow-up on views ... During its fifty-first session, the Committee adopted a new rule of procedure, rule 95 [now Rule 101, under the current version of the Rules of Procedure (CCPR/C/3/Rev.8)], which spells out the mandate of the Special Rapporteur for follow-up on views. [This rule provides that the Committee designates a Special Rapporteur for follow-up on views adopted under Article 5, para. 4, of the Optional Protocol, 'for the purpose of ascertaining the measures taken by States parties to give effect to the Committee's views'. The Special Rapporteur 'may make such contacts and take such action as appropriate for the due performance of the follow-up mandate. The

Special Rapporteur shall make such recommendations for further action by the Committee as may be necessary.' It also provides that the Committee shall include information on follow-up activities in its annual report.]

461. In accordance with his mandate, the Special Rapporteur has been requesting follow-up information from States parties since the autumn of 1990. Follow-up information has been requested in respect of all views with a finding of a violation of the Covenant. At the beginning of the Committee's fifty-first session, follow-up information had been received in respect of 65 views; no information had been received in respect of 55 views. It is to be noted that in many instances, the secretariat has also received information from authors to the effect that the Committee's views have not been implemented.

462. While it is obviously difficult to categorize follow-up replies, it appears that a little over one fourth of the replies received thus far are fully satisfactory, in that they display a willingness on the part of the State party concerned to implement the Committee's views or to offer the applicant a remedy. A little over one third of the replies cannot be considered satisfactory, as they either do not address the Committee's recommendations at all, merely relate to one aspect thereof or indicate that the State party is not willing to grant the remedy recommended by the Committee. A number of replies have explicitly challenged the Committee's findings, either on factual or on legal grounds. The remaining replies are either couched in general terms, promise an investigation of the matter considered by the Committee or reiterate the State party's position during the proceedings.

463. While the overall results of the first four years of experience with the follow-up procedure are encouraging, they cannot be termed fully satisfactory. Some States parties have indeed replied that they are implementing the Committee's recommendations, for example, by releasing from detention victims of human rights violations, by granting them compensation for the violations suffered, by amending legislation found incompatible with the provisions of the Covenant or by offering the complainants different remedies. In a number of cases, States parties have indicated that compensatory payments to victims were made *ex gratia*, notably where the domestic legal system does not provide for compensation in a different manner. The Committee is aware that the absence of specific enabling legislation is a key factor that often stands in the way of monetary compensation to victims of violations of the Covenant, and commends those States which have compensated victims of violation of the Covenant; it encourages States parties to consider the adoption of such specific enabling legislation.

464. The Committee has carefully examined and analysed the information gathered through the follow-up procedure. Between the thirty-ninth and fiftieth sessions, it considered follow-up information on a confidential basis. Periodic reports on follow-up activities were not made public, and debates on follow-up matters took place in closed meetings.

465. At the same time, however, the Committee recognized that publicity for follow-up activities would be an appropriate means for making the procedure more effective. Thus, publicity for follow-up activities would not only be in the interest of victims of violations of provisions of the Covenant, but could also serve to enhance the authority of the Committee's views and provide an incentive for States parties to implement them.

466. Thus, during its forty-seventh session, in March-April 1993, the Committee agreed in principle that information on follow-up activities should be made public. [I]n March 1994, the Committee formally adopted a number of decisions concerning the effectiveness and publicity of the follow-up procedure. Those decisions were as follows:

(a) Every form of publicity will be given to follow-up activities;

(b) Future annual reports will include a separate and highly visible section on follow-up activities under the Optional Protocol. This should clearly convey to the public which States parties have cooperated and which States parties (hitherto) have failed to cooperate with the Special Rapporteur for the follow-up on views ... Reminders will be sent to all those States which have failed to provide follow-up information;

(c) Press communiqués will be issued once a year after the Committee's summer session, highlighting both positive and negative developments concerning the Committee's and the Special Rapporteur's follow-up activities;

(d) The Committee will welcome any information which non-governmental organizations might wish to submit as to what measures States parties have taken, or failed to take, in respect of the implementation of the Committee's views;

(e) The Special Rapporteur and members of the Committee should, as appropriate, establish contacts with particular Governments and Permanent Missions to the United Nations to further inquire about the implementation of the Committee's views;

(f) The Committee should draw the attention of States parties, at their biannual meetings, to the failure of certain States to implement the Committee's views and to cooperate with the Special Rapporteur in providing information on the implementation of views.

467. The Committee notes with concern that a number of countries have either not provided any follow-up information or have not replied to requests from the Special Rapporteur for follow-up on views. Those States which have not replied to at least four requests are, in alphabetical order, Jamaica, Madagascar, Suriname and Zaire.

468. The Committee decided to anchor firmly the publicity of the follow-up procedure in its rules of procedure, by adopting a new rule (Rule 99) to this effect. [This rule – Rule 103 under the current Rules of Procedure of the Committee – provides that: 'Information furnished by the parties within the framework of follow-up to the Committee's Views is not subject to confidentiality, unless the Committee decides otherwise. Decisions of the Committee relating to follow-up activities are equally not subject to confidentiality, unless the Committee decides otherwise.'] It also decided to keep the functioning of the follow-up procedure under constant review.

Committee against Torture, Annual Report to the UN General Assembly, A/63/44 (2008):

93. At its twenty-eighth session, in May 2002, the Committee against Torture revised its rules of procedure and established the function of a Rapporteur for follow-up of decisions on complaints submitted under article 22. [I]n 16 May 2002, the Committee decided that the Rapporteur shall engage, *inter alia*, in the following activities: monitoring compliance with the Committee's decisions by sending *notes verbales* to States parties enquiring about measures adopted pursuant to the Committee's decisions; recommending to the Committee appropriate action upon the receipt of responses from States parties, in situations of non-response, and upon the receipt henceforth of all letters from complainants concerning non-implementation of the Committee's decisions; meeting with representatives of the permanent missions of States parties

to encourage compliance and to determine whether advisory services or technical assistance by the Office of the United Nations High Commissioner for Human Rights would be appropriate or desirable; conducting with the approval of the Committee follow-up visits to States parties; preparing periodic reports for the Committee on his/her activities.

94. During its thirty-fourth session, the Committee, through its Special Rapporteur on follow-up to decisions, decided that in cases in which it had found violations of the Convention, including Decisions made by the Committee prior to the establishment of the follow-up procedure, the States parties should be requested to provide information on all measures taken by them to implement the Committee's recommendations made in the Decisions. To date, the following countries have not yet responded to these requests. [A list of countries found to have violated the CAT in specific cases follows.]

95. Action taken by the States parties in the following cases complied fully with the Committee's Decisions and no further action will be taken under the follow-up procedure. [A list of cases follows.]

96. In the following cases, the Committee considered that for various reasons no further action should be taken under the follow-up procedure. [A list of cases follows.] In one case, the Committee deplored the State party's failure to abide by its obligations under article 3 having deported the complainant, despite the Committee's finding that there were substantial grounds for believing that he would be in danger of being tortured: *Dadar* v. *Canada* (No. 258/2004).

97. In the following cases, either further information is awaited from the States parties or the complainants and/or the dialogue with the State party is ongoing. [A list of cases follows.]

98. During the thirty-ninth and fortieth sessions, the Special Rapporteur on follow-up to decisions presented new follow-up information that had been received since the last annual report with respect to the following cases. [A list of cases follows.]

4 THE REFORM OF THE UN HUMAN RIGHTS TREATIES SYSTEM

In his final report on enhancing the long-term effectiveness of the UN human rights treaty system, Philip Alston evoked the probable scenario of wide-scale delays and lack of reporting by States, combined with the overburdening of the expert bodies which, given the increasing number of ratifications of human rights treaties, can barely deal with the reports which are submitted to them within the narrow limits of their resources. He commented as follows on the possible reactions to such a scenario:

Effective functioning of bodies established pursuant to United Nations human rights instruments. Final report on enhancing the long-term effectiveness of the United Nations human rights treaty system, by Mr Philip Alston, independent expert (UN Doc. E/CN.4/1997/74, 27 March 1996):

C. A review of options
85. In essence, there would seem to be four options available to States in dealing with [the scenario described above]. The first is to dismiss the concern as alarmist and misplaced on

the ground that the situation will not in fact evolve in this way. States will not move towards universal ratification; they will continue to be chronically overdue in reporting; and they will become increasingly blasé in their dealings with the treaty bodies. The response by the latter will remain essentially as it is today and, somehow, existing resources will be used more efficiently in order to enable the maintenance of the status quo. The number of complaints procedures will not increase and the number of communications will stabilize. And the migrant workers convention will not enter into force. Over time, this option will lead to a reporting system that will have become little more than a costly charade, since it will be unable to cope in any meaningful way with the various functions entrusted to it.

86. The second option would amount to the fulfilment of the dreams of some reformers and of most budget-cutters: the treaty bodies will undertake far-reaching reforms of their existing procedures, and will manage from within existing resources. Extensive authority will be delegated to the Secretariat to undertake preliminary report processing. The latter will be staffed largely by interns, junior professional officers (JPOs) paid for on a voluntary basis by the industrialized countries, and by individuals from other countries sponsored by foundations or their own Governments. Individual committee members will be responsible for drafting assessments which will be reviewed in small working groups and, except in especially controversial cases, will be rapidly endorsed in plenary. Any 'dialogue' will take place largely in writing. No report would be considered in plenary for more than one or two hours and each expert would be limited to five minutes' speaking time (thus making a total of 90 minutes in the case of the two Covenant-related committees, for example). Communications will be processed in a similar manner. Summary records will be dispensed with, and translation will only be available for the final products of the committees. Interpretation will be available only for plenary sessions and the remaining work will be done by heterogeneous language groups working overwhelmingly in English.

87. Apart from the difficulty of achieving any of these reforms, the main problem with this option is that it would require a radical change in many of the assumptions on the basis of which the current system has been developed. For the most part, States have shown no preparedness to make such changes. Moreover, the quality of the resulting outcomes, as well as their ability to command respect and generate the desired domestic responses, is unlikely to be high.

88. The third option is the provision of greatly enhanced budgetary resources to support all aspects of the procedures with a view to more or less maintaining the status quo. Funding would be provided for increased Secretariat staffing, translation and interpretation facilities, and a large technical cooperation budget would be allocated to fund an extensive array of advisory services designed to enable States to meet their extensive reporting obligations. Even leaving aside the question of whether this would be a workable approach in practice, current as well as foreseeable future budget trends would seem to be moving in the opposite direction to that required.

89. The fourth option is a more complex one, drawing on elements of the other options, and based primarily upon the adoption of some or all of the reforms canvassed below.

D. Consolidated reports

90. The interim report by the independent expert outlined a proposal for the preparation of a single consolidated report by each State party, which would then be submitted in satisfaction of the requirements under each of the treaties to which the State is a party. That proposal is for individual States to consider and act upon. It does not require endorsement or other formal action by any United Nations body or the treaty bodies. The detailed analytical study called for

by the General Assembly in resolution 51/87 will, when completed, assist in the preparation of any such consolidated reports. Ultimately, the questions and concerns that have been raised can only be answered definitively on the basis of concrete efforts to produce and work on the basis of such reports.

E. Elimination of comprehensive periodic reports in their present form

91. Another proposal, previously foreshadowed by the independent expert but not developed in any detail, would be to eliminate the requirement that States parties' periodic reports should be comprehensive. Such an approach would clearly not be appropriate in relation to initial reports. Similarly, it might be better suited to the situation of some treaty bodies than others, and might not be applied in all cases. The broader the scope of a treaty, the more appropriate it would seem to be to seek to limit the range of issues which must be addressed in a report. In effect, the reporting guidelines would be tailored to each State's individual situation. In many respects, it is a logical extension of an approach followed by the Human Rights Committee since 1989.

92. Since there are various formulas which might be adopted, the following process is only indicative. It would begin with a decision by the committee at session A to draw up a list of questions at session B. In the intervening period it would invite submissions of information from all relevant sources and would request the Secretariat to prepare a country analysis. The pre-sessional working group could then meet, perhaps immediately before or during session B, and draft a specific and limited list of questions. After endorsement by the Committee at session B the list would be forwarded immediately to the State party with a request for a written report to be submitted in advance (in sufficient time to enable translation) of session C or D. Such a procedure would: focus the dialogue on a limited range of issues; entirely eliminate the need to produce a lengthy report covering many issues of little particular import in relation to the country concerned; ensure that issues of current importance are the principal focus; guarantee that a report would be examined on schedule; enable individuals with expertise in the matters under review to participate in the delegation; reduce the number of ministries directly involved in report preparation; enhance the capacity of expert members of the committees to be well prepared for the dialogue; and provide a strong foundation for more detailed and clearly focused concluding observations.

93. It is therefore recommended that each committee should consider the extent to which all or some of its principal supervisory functions could be conducted on the basis not of general reports based on universally applicable reporting guidelines but of more limited and specially tailored requests for reports as described above.

F. Towards a consolidation of the treaty bodies

94. Some of the arguments for and against this reform have already been explored in the independent expert's 1989 report (A/44/668, paras. 182–183) [where Philip Alston adopted a balanced view of this proposal, noting the risks implicated by such a massive overhaul of the system, which could weaken further certain fragile, but promising, aspects of the current system]. For that reason, they will not be repeated here. Given the limitations of space it must suffice to note in this context that while the legal and procedural problems inherent in such an initiative would not be negligible, the prior issue is whether there is the political will to begin exploring in any detail the contours of such a reform. If that will were manifest, the technical challenges would be resolvable. It is therefore recommended that consideration be given to the convening of a small expert group, with an appropriate emphasis upon international legal expertise, to prepare a report on the modalities that might be considered in this respect.

G. The desirability of additional proactive measures

95. In addition to examining the possibility of steps to reduce the existing number of treaty bodies, it is important for United Nations organs which are involved in the design of new procedures to bear in mind the desirability of limiting the number of additional bodies to be created. Viewed in isolation, and on their individual merits, proposals to establish new, and improved, mechanisms are inevitably attractive. This attraction should, however, be balanced against the impact on the system as a whole of new bodies competing for scarce resources and perhaps, in some respects at least, unnecessarily duplicating the demands upon States parties. At least two current endeavours might be relevant in this respect.

96. The first concerns a procedure which has already been finalized and enshrined in a treaty. Article 72 of the International Convention on the Protection of the Rights of All Migrant Workers and Members of Their Families provides for the election of a Committee on the Protection of the Rights of All Migrant Workers and Members of Their Families within six months of the Convention's entry into force. This occurs when there are 20 States parties. Although it was adopted six years ago (in December 1990), as at 1 November 1996 there were only seven States parties. By acting now to amend the treaty so as to provide that the supervisory functions which the Convention entrusts to a new committee would instead be performed by one of the existing committees (presumably either the Committee on Economic, Social and Cultural Rights or the Human Rights Committee) the United Nations could avoid the expense of establishing an entire new supervisory apparatus, States parties could avoid increasing the number of committees to which they must report and the number of occasions on which reports must be presented and evaluated, and the number of States which would have to ratify the amendment would be minimal. A failure to act now will only result in exacerbating a situation that most States already consider to be unwieldy. Moreover, one of the major obstacles to reform in all such matters is the resistance of those (including experts, Secretariat officials, Governments, NGOs, etc.) with a vested interest in the maintenance of the status quo. Action taken at this stage would encounter comparatively very little resistance from such sources. But if delayed, it will probably become impossible.

97. The second example concerns the draft optional protocol to the Convention against Torture and Other Cruel, Inhuman or Degrading Treatment or Punishment, the drafting of which is currently being undertaken by a working group of the Commission on Human Rights. The protocol would, *inter alia*, provide for visits to places of detention by an expert body entrusted with that function. At its most recent session the working group took note of two different views as to the relationship, on the one hand between the new instrument and the existing Convention, and on the other hand between the proposed new sub-committee and the existing Committee against Torture. Persuasive arguments were put forward in favour of the instrument being kept quite separate from the Convention and of the sub-committee being entirely independent of the Committee (see E/CN.4/1997/33, paras. 14, 16, 19). But whatever the undoubted merits of those proposals, they would contribute very significantly to the further proliferation of instruments and committees, while doing nothing to ameliorate the present situation. A more appropriate solution would seem to be to arrive at a formula by which States which accepted the new procedures would be exempted from most, if not all, of their reporting obligations under the Convention and to explore all possible formulas by which the members of the Committee could serve on the new mechanism as well. This would seem to be a case in which the Secretariat should be requested to prepare an analytical paper exploring different options in a creative rather than mechanistic fashion.

H. Amending the treaties

98. Since the submission of the first report on treaty body reform, in 1989, amendments to three of the six treaties have been approved by the respective Meetings of the States Parties and endorsed by the General Assembly. They seek to ensure that the activities of both the Committee on the Elimination of Racial Discrimination and the Committee against Torture are financed from the regular budget of the United Nations (rather than wholly or partly by the States parties as currently provided for in the respective treaties) and to permit the Committee on the Elimination of Discrimination against Women to meet for longer than the two weeks annually specified in the Convention. A fourth proposed amendment would expand the membership of the Committee on the Rights of the Child from 10 to 18. The fact that both the respective Meetings of States Parties, as well as the General Assembly, have approved these amendments is an indication of the need for reform and of the preparedness of Governments to endorse such reforms.

99. Despite this clear consensus none of the amendments has yet entered into force and the prospects that they will do so in the foreseeable future must be considered slight. Thus, for example, over a period of four years only 20 of the 148 (as at 19 February 1997) States parties to the International Convention on the Elimination of All Forms of Racial Discrimination had accepted the amendments. In the case of the Convention against Torture and Other Cruel, Inhuman or Degrading Treatment or Punishment 20 of 101 States parties had done so (see E/CN.4/1997/73, para. 7). The problem is not that States parties are opposed to the amendment or that they are reluctant to see them brought into force. This is illustrated by the fact that every State party stands to gain financially from the amendments, since the costs involved will then be spread among the entire membership of the United Nations, rather than falling only on the parties to the relevant treaty. It is thus the non-States parties that would have a financial incentive to oppose such amendments, but they have chosen not to do so when called upon to vote in the General Assembly. Rather, the problem lies in the process of satisfying all of the domestic legal and political requirements needed to approve an amendment to a treaty. It is apparent that they are considered by many Governments, all of whom are confronted with an ever-increasing volume of international agreements to 'process', to be too time-consuming and cumbersome to be worth the effort.

100. To the extent possible, the General Assembly has, in each instance, authorized temporary measures to ameliorate the situation in the intervening period. Such flexibility is indispensable, even though it might have the unintended consequence of further discouraging States parties from taking the domestic steps required to effect their legal acceptance of the amendments.

101. Several recommendations emerge from this situation:

(a) All future human rights treaties should provide for a simplified process to be followed in order to amend the relevant procedural provisions. While the specific endorsement of this proposal by the Commission on Human Rights could not be binding in the context of any future negotiations it would constitute a clear policy guideline and help to facilitate the adoption of such flexibility in the future;

(b) A report should be requested from the Legal Counsel which would explore the feasibility of devising more innovative approaches in dealing with existing and future amendments to the human rights treaties;

(c) The General Assembly should request the Meetings of the States Parties to the relevant treaties to discuss means by which the States concerned might be encouraged to attach a higher priority to ratification of the amendments already approved;

(d) Consideration should be given immediately to amending the International Convention on the Protection of the Rights of All Migrant Workers and Members of Their Families in line with the recommendation made [above, in para. 96] ...

Against the background of growing delayed reporting or non-reporting by States parties to human rights treaty bodies, as well as the difficult demands reporting to six committees imposes on States parties, the UN Secretary-General suggested in his report 'Strengthening of the United Nations: an Agenda for Further Change', (a) that the committees craft a more co-ordinated approach to their activities; and (b) that they standardize their varied reporting requirements (see UN Doc. A/57/387 (9 September 2002), chapter II, section B, and Corr. 1). The report also specifically recommended that 'each State should be allowed to produce a single report summarizing its adherence to the full range of international human rights treaties to which it is a party' (para. 54). Consultations among the chairpersons of the human rights treaty bodies and within inter-committee meetings, however, showed a consensus in favour of one core document being prepared by each State, rather than one single, consolidated, report, to be presented to all human rights treaty bodies concerned. The result has been the preparation of Harmonized Guidelines on Reporting under the International Human Rights Treaties, including Guidelines on a Common Core Document and treaty-specific targeted documents (HRI/MC/2005/3, 1 June 2005).

Under the new Harmonized Guidelines on Reporting under the International Human Rights Treaties, each State report consists of 'two complementary documents: an up-to-date common core document and a targeted treaty-specific document. The common core document will be submitted to all treaty bodies in conjunction with a targeted report specific to the relevant treaty' (para. 26). The common core document 'should contain information relating to the implementation of each of the treaties to which the reporting State is party and which may be of relevance to all or several of the treaty bodies monitoring the implementation of those treaties. The aim is to avoid reproducing the same information in several reports produced in accordance with the provisions of different treaties. It also allows each committee to view the implementation of its treaty in the wider context of the protection of human rights in the State in question' (para. 27). This document shall contain general factual and statistical information about the reporting State (including demographic, economic, social and cultural characteristics of the State, and the constitutional, political and legal structure of the State); a description of the general framework for the protection and promotion of human rights; a summary of the acceptance of international human rights norms; a description of the general legal framework within which human rights are protected and promoted at the national level; a description of the reporting process in promoting human rights at the national level (for example, concerning the participation of non-governmental organizations, national human rights institutions, or the organization of a public debate); and other related human rights information, particularly the follow-up given to international conferences. In addition, the common core document would also discuss the implementation of substantive human rights provisions common to all or several treaties, in particular the non-discrimination and equality provisions thereof.

The purpose of these Harmonized Guidelines is best explained in paras. 3–4 of this document:

Harmonized Guidelines on Reporting under the International Human Rights Treaties, including Guidelines on a Common Core Document and treaty-specific targeted documents (HRI/MC/2005/3, 1 June 2005):

3. Reports presented in accordance with the present common guidelines will enable each treaty body and the State party to obtain a complete picture of progress made in the implementation of the relevant treaties, set within the wider context of the State's international human rights obligations, and provide a uniform framework within which each committee, in collaboration with the other treaty bodies, can work.

4. Compliance with these guidelines will:

(a) Avoid unnecessary duplication of information already submitted to other treaty bodies;

(b) Minimize the possibility that reports may be considered inadequate in scope and insufficient in detail to allow the treaty bodies to fulfil their mandates;

(c) Reduce the need for a committee to request supplementary information before considering a report;

(d) Enable a consistent approach by all committees in considering the reports presented to them; and

(e) Help each committee to consider the situation regarding human rights in every State party on an equal basis.

At the same time, the case has been made for a unified standing treaty body, resulting from the merger of all existing human rights treaty bodies. This, it has been argued, would enhance the effectiveness of the system and correspond to what is required for a 'holistic', i.e. integrated, approach to the human rights obligations of States (see also on this debate M. Bowman, 'Towards a Unified Treaty Body for Monitoring Compliance with UN Human Rights Conventions? Legal Mechanisms for Treaty Reform', *Human Rights Law Review*, 7, No. 1 (2007), 225; M. O'Flaherty and C. O'Brien, 'Reform of UN Human Rights Treaty Monitoring Bodies: a Critique of the Concept Paper on the High Commissioner's Proposal for a Unified Standing Treaty Body', *Human Rights Law Review*, 7, No. 1 (2007), 141; see also the summary of an international meeting of experts on the theme of treaty body reform, held at Triesenberg, Liechtenstein, 14–16 July 2006 (Malbun II), A/HRC/2/G/5, 25 September 2006, Annex). Others have proposed the establishment of a World Court of Human Rights, to the jurisdiction of which States could decide to submit on an optional basis, to remedy the lack of effectiveness and gaps in the current system (see M. Nowak, 'The Need for a World Court of Human Rights', *Human Rights Law Review*, 7, No. 1 (2007), 251; S. Trechsel, 'A World Court for Human Rights', *Northwestern University Journal of International Human Rights*, 1 (2004), 3). As High Commissioner for Human Rights (2005–8), Louise Arbour sought, unsuccessfully, to push forward the idea of a standing and unified treaty body:

Concept paper on the High Commissioner's proposal for a unified standing treaty body. Report by the Secretariat (HRI/MC/2006/2, 22 March 2006):

27. The proposal of a unified standing treaty body is based on the premise that, unless the international human rights treaty system functions and is perceived as a unified, single entity responsible for monitoring the implementation of all international human rights obligations, with a single, accessible entry point for rights-holders, the lack of visibility, authority and access which affects the current system will persist. The proposal is also based on the recognition that, as currently constituted, the system is approaching the limits of its performance, and that, while steps can be taken to improve its functioning in the short and medium term, more fundamental, structural change will be required in order to guarantee its effectiveness in the long term. Unlike the current system of seven part-time Committees, a unified standing treaty body comprised of permanent, full-time professionals is more likely to produce consistent and authoritative jurisprudence. A unified standing treaty body would be available to victims on a permanent basis and could respond rapidly to grave violations. As a permanent body, it would have the flexibility to develop innovative working methods and approaches to human rights protection and be able to develop clear modalities for the participation of United Nations partners and civil society, which build on the good practices of the current system. It would also be able to develop a strong capacity to assist States parties in their implementation of human rights obligations, including through follow-up activities and the country engagement strategies envisaged by the High Commissioner in her Plan of Action. Also in line with the Plan of Action, the Secretariat would be significantly strengthened to provide the expert support and advice required by a unified standing treaty body, as well as that required to strengthen national capacity and partnerships to allow full engagement in the treaty implementation process ...

28. As States implement human rights obligations in an integrated rather than treaty-specific way, and individuals and groups do not enjoy their human rights or experience violations along treaty lines, a unified standing treaty body would provide a framework for a comprehensive, cross-cutting and holistic approach to implementation of the treaties. In contrast to the current system of seven treaty bodies which consider reports which are submitted in accordance with different periodicities, a unified standing treaty body could introduce flexible and creative measures to encourage reporting, and maximize the effectiveness and impact of monitoring. For example, a single cycle for reporting by each State party on implementation of all treaty obligations could be introduced, which would occur once every three to five years, providing States parties and partners with the opportunity to carry out in-depth, holistic, comprehensive and cross-cutting assessments and analysis of a State's human rights performance against all relevant obligations. A single reporting cycle monitored by a unified standing treaty body would provide a framework for prioritization of action needed at the country level to comply with human rights obligations. Reporting could be aligned with national processes and systems such as the development and implementation of national human rights action plans and other reporting obligations of the State party. As a result of comprehensive examination of a State party's implementation of all its treaty obligations, reporting to a unified standing treaty body would stimulate more effective mainstreaming of the rights of specific groups or issues in the interpretation and implementation of all human rights treaty obligations, thereby making these

more visible and central. At the same time, the current specialized expertise of treaty bodies and their focused attention on specific rights and rights-holders would be safeguarded and built upon.

29. A comprehensive and holistic assessment of a State's human rights performance against all relevant obligations by the unified standing treaty body resulting in a single document containing all key concerns and recommendations would facilitate States parties' and other national stakeholders' consideration of the whole range of relevant human rights concerns and legislative, policy and programme measures required. By providing a complete picture of the human rights priorities, this holistic approach would also facilitate the work of stakeholders, such as NGOs, NHRIs and other parts of civil society at the country level, and make it easier for them to integrate these recommendations into their country programming. Partners would benefit from their different areas of human rights expertise and develop a common approach to human rights issues and requirements at the national level.

30. A unified standing treaty body would ensure a consistent approach to the interpretation of provisions in the treaties which are similar or overlap substantively. Complainants would also have the opportunity to invoke substantively overlapping or similar provisions of more than one instrument, thereby enhancing consistence and coherence in the interpretation of substantively similar provisions in the different instruments. A unified standing treaty body would also guarantee consistency and clarity of General Comments/Recommendations and, in that way, strengthen the interpretation of treaty provisions. The output of a unified standing treaty body would strengthen appreciation of the indivisibility of human rights obligations and the importance of a holistic, cross-cutting and comprehensive approach to implementation.

31. A unified standing treaty body could extend the period of the dialogue with individual States parties from the current average of one day per treaty body to, for example, up to five days, depending on factors such as the number of treaties ratified. By combining the seven dialogues currently operating independently into one, in-depth session with one monitoring counterpart rather than seven, the dialogue would be transformed into a strategic and continuous tool for monitoring human rights performance against all obligations. States parties would be encouraged to send expert delegations including all Government ministries having responsibility for the full range of human rights to respond to detailed questions and benefit from the expertise of Committee members. An extension of the period of dialogue would provide new opportunities for stakeholders to contribute information and exchange views with the Committee. Enhanced participation, information and exchange of views on all human rights obligations would result in an overall package of more precise, clear and practical recommendations. Improved dialogue, engagement and output would encourage greater participation of civil society and other actors, thereby facilitating implementation at the national level.

32. Members of the unified standing treaty body would be available on a permanent basis. This would allow them to build on the current achievements of the system to develop strong, coherent, innovative and flexible approaches to monitoring implementation of the treaties. As members would be permanent pending individual complaints would be adjudicated expeditiously, which would heighten the impact of views adopted in the context of complaints procedures, and encourage their wider use by rights-holders. Similarly, a unified standing treaty body would allow for a strengthening of follow-up capacity, by increasing the potential and feasibility for follow-up missions by the experts, given the permanent nature of their work.

33. A unified standing treaty body would inevitably be more visible than the existing treaty bodies, and would be able to make its procedures, recommendations and decisions better known at the national level. Enhanced visibility, in tandem with open and transparent procedures, would also

arouse media interest, and conclusions and recommendations adopted by a unified standing treaty body on the overall human rights situation in a country are likely to attract more media attention than conclusions and recommendations adopted on the implementation of a single treaty.

34. In comparison to the current system of seven part-time bodies, as a standing body, the unified standing treaty body would be more flexible than the current bodies in respect of the timing and venue of its sessions. It would be able to group the consideration of the reports of several States parties from one region over the course of a few weeks, thereby enhancing regional peer pressure to engage with the system. It would also be available to convene sessions in regions, thereby strengthening the visibility of the system and ensuring its accessibility. It could also develop a regular pattern of missions relating to follow-up or capacity building.

35. A unified standing treaty body could also absorb new standards. It would be easier to integrate the monitoring of a new instrument into a unified monitoring structure already dealing with several treaties rather than incorporating new monitoring functions into the mandate of an existing treaty body, an option which has previously been rejected in the cases of CAT and the draft International Convention for the Protection of All Persons from Enforced Disappearance.

36. The permanent availability and functioning of a unified standing treaty body would allow for the establishment of stronger links with other human rights bodies, such as the special procedures mechanisms or regional human rights systems, to coordinate activities and complement action in accordance with the respective mandates. A unified standing treaty body would also be able to establish links with political bodies more readily than seven part-time bodies. A comprehensive, overall assessment of the implementation of international legal obligations under human rights treaties for countries in one single document, rather than in seven separate documents, would be more likely to attract heightened attention from political bodies such as [the] Human Rights Council or the Security Council.

9.6. Question for discussion: the virtues of specialized human rights bodies v. the benefits of consolidation

Apart from the resistance this proposal may meet from States or current members of existing human right treaty bodies, is the consolidation of the UN human rights treaty bodies into one single, standing body, desirable? Consider the following view: 'it is debatable whether a single tribunal will actually enhance, rather than diminish, the jurists' expertise to address the enormous range of human rights issues in a comprehensive way. This question is of particular concern to those parties championing historically underrepresented human rights perspectives such as children's rights, gender discrimination, and economic, social, and cultural rights. Such parties might fear that centralization would privilege a dominant interpretive position that marginalizes these issues. In addition, amending the existing treaty system raises the disquieting prospect that some States would use the opportunity to press for a 'least common denominator' approach. This approach would favor adopting for the new tribunal the least rights-protective petition procedures found among the ... existing treaty bodies' (L. R. Helfer, 'Forum Shopping for Human Rights', *University of Pennsylvania Law Review*, 148 (1999), 285 at 396).

10

The United Nations Charter-Based Monitoring of Human Rights

INTRODUCTION

The United Nations Charter-based system of human rights monitoring has been through major changes in 2006–7. Acting under Article 68 of the UN Charter, the Economic and Social Council (Ecosoc) had established the Commission on Human Rights as an inter-governmental body initially composed of eighteen Member States. The membership of the Commission on Human Rights was progressively expanded to fifty-three members in 2006 to take account of the more diverse membership of the United Nations. The Commission was assisted in its work by the UN Sub-Commission for the Promotion and Protection of Human Rights, until 1999 called the Sub-Commission on Prevention of Discrimination and Protection of Minorities. Despite major achievements, the system thus developed was considered to be overpoliticized, and to lack credibility due, in particular, to the selective approach to the human rights records of governments. In its place, it was decided in 2005 to establish a Human Rights Council, as a subsidiary organ of the UN General Assembly, whereas the former Commission on Human Rights was one of a number of subsidiary bodies of the Ecosoc.

This chapter examines how this change came about, and which tools the Human Rights Council has at its disposal to promote and protect human rights (for useful presentations, see P. Alston, 'Reconceiving the UN Human Rights Regime: Challenges Confronting the New Human Rights Council', *Melbourne Journal of International Law*, 7 (2006), 185; K. Boyle (ed.), *New Institutions for Human Rights Protection* (Oxford University Press, 2009), chapters 1–3; G. Luca Burci, The United Nations Human Rights Council' in *Italian Yearbook of International Law*, XV (2005), 25: F. D. Gaer, 'A Voice Not an Echo: Universal Periodic Review and the UN Treaty Body System', *Human Rights Law Review*, 7, No. 1 (2007), 109; N. Ghanea, 'From UN Commission on Human Rights to UN Human Rights Council: One Step Forwards or Two Steps Sideways', *International and Comparative Law Quarterly*, 55, No. 3 (2006), 695; F. Hampson, 'An Overview of the Reform of the UN Human Rights Machinery', *Human Rights Law Review*, 7, No. 1 (2007), 7; P. G. Lauren, '"To Preserve and Build on Its Achievements and to Redress Its Shortcomings": the Journey from the Commission on Human Rights to the Human

Rights Council', *Human Rights Quarterly*, 29 (2007), 307). The materials collected present, first, the background to the overhaul of the UN Charter-based system of human rights protection (section 1). Next, they review the three tools at the Human Rights Council's disposal: complaints related to 'a consistent pattern of gross and reliably attested violations of human rights' (section 2); the universal periodic review (section 3); and the so-called 'special procedures' established initially by the Commission on Human Rights and now contributing to the work of the Council (section 4).

1 THE ESTABLISHMENT OF THE HUMAN RIGHTS COUNCIL

Against the background briefly referred to in the introduction to this chapter, the following excerpt explains the objectives behind replacing the Commission on Human Rights by a Human Rights Council. In 2003, faced with new threats to multilateralism as a result of the policies of the United States under the Bush Administration, and with strong criticism from the US Congress directed against the effectiveness of the United Nations as an organization, the Secretary-General, Koffi Annan, decided to convene a high-level panel of eminent persons to provide him with proposals for reform. The High-level Panel on Threats, Challenges and Change was chaired by Anand Panyarachun, the former Prime Minister of Thailand. It had the following to say on the reform of the UN human rights machinery:

A More Secure World: Our Shared Responsibility, Report of the High-level Panel on Threats, Challenges and Change transmitted to the UN Secretary-General (A/59/565, 1 December 2004, Annex) (bold characters in the original):

283. In recent years, the [UN Human Rights] Commission's capacity to perform its tasks has been undermined by eroding credibility and professionalism. Standard-setting to reinforce human rights cannot be performed by States that lack a demonstrated commitment to their promotion and protection. We are concerned that in recent years States have sought membership of the Commission not to strengthen human rights but to protect themselves against criticism or to criticize others. The Commission cannot be credible if it is seen to be maintaining double standards in addressing human rights concerns.

284. Reform of this body is therefore necessary to make the human rights system perform effectively and ensure that it better fulfils its mandate and functions. We support the recent efforts of the Secretary-General and the United Nations High Commissioner for Human Rights to ensure that human rights are integrated throughout the work of the United Nations, and to support the development of strong domestic human rights institutions, especially in countries emerging from conflict and in the fight against terrorism. Member States should provide full support to the Secretary General and the High Commissioner in these efforts.

285. In many ways, the most difficult and sensitive issue relating to the Commission on Human Rights is that of membership. In recent years, the issue of which States are elected to the Commission has become a source of heated international tension, with no positive impact on human rights and a negative impact on the work of the Commission. Proposals for membership

criteria have little chance of changing these dynamics and indeed risk further politicizing the issue.

Rather, **we recommend that the membership of the Commission on Human Rights be expanded to universal membership.** This would underscore that all members are committed by the Charter to the promotion of human rights, and might help to focus attention back on to substantive issues rather than who is debating and voting on them.

286. In the first half of its history, the Commission was composed of heads of delegation who were key players in the human rights arena and who had the professional qualifications and experience necessary for human rights work. Since then this practice has lapsed. We believe it should be restored, and we propose that **all members of the Commission on Human Rights designate prominent and experienced human rights figures as the heads of their delegations.**

287. In addition, we propose that **the Commission on Human Rights be supported in its work by an advisory council or panel.** This council or panel would consist of some 15 individuals, independent experts (say, three per region), appointed for their skills for a period of three years, renewable once. They would be appointed by the Commission on the joint proposal of the Secretary-General and the High Commissioner. In addition to advising on country-specific issues, the council or panel could give advice on the rationalization of some of the thematic mandates and could itself carry out some of the current mandates dealing with research, standard-setting and definitions.

288. **We recommend that the High Commissioner be called upon to prepare an annual report on the situation of human rights worldwide.** This could then serve as a basis for a comprehensive discussion with the Commission. The report should focus on the implementation of all human rights in all countries, based on information stemming from the work of treaty bodies, special mechanisms and any other sources deemed appropriate by the High Commissioner.

289. The Security Council should also more actively involve the High Commissioner in its deliberations, including on peace operations mandates. We also welcome the fact that the Security Council has, with increasing frequency, invited the High Commissioner to brief it on country-specific situations. We believe that this should become a general rule and that **the Security Council and the Peacebuilding Commission should request the High Commissioner to report to them regularly about the implementation of all human rights–related provisions of Security Council resolutions, thus enabling focused, effective monitoring of these provisions.**

290. More also needs to be done with respect to the funding situation of the Office of the High Commissioner. We see a clear contradiction between a regular budget allocation of 2 per cent for this Office and the obligation under the Charter of the United Nations to make the promotion and protection of human rights one of the principal objectives of the Organization. There is also a need to redress the limited funding available for human rights capacity-building. Member States should seriously review the inadequate funding of this Office and its activities.

291. In the longer term, Member States should consider upgrading the Commission to become a 'Human Rights Council' that is no longer subsidiary to the Economic and Social Council but a Charter body standing alongside it and the Security Council, and reflecting in the process the weight given to human rights, alongside security and economic issues, in the Preamble of the Charter.

Although only presented by the High-level Panel on Threats, Challenges and Change as one option to consider for the future, the replacement of the Commission on Human Rights by a Human Rights Council was proposed by the UN Secretary-General, Kofi Annan, in the following terms:

In Larger Freedom: Towards Development, Security and Human Rights for All. Report of the Secretary-General (A/59/2005, 21 March 2005):

165. Its founders endowed the United Nations with three Councils, each having major responsibilities in its own area: the Security Council, the Economic and Social Council and the Trusteeship Council. Over time, the division of responsibilities between them has become less and less balanced: the Security Council has increasingly asserted its authority and, especially since the end of the cold war, has enjoyed greater unity of purpose among its permanent members but has seen that authority questioned on the grounds that its composition is anachronistic or insufficiently representative; the Economic and Social Council has been too often relegated to the margins of global economic and social governance; and the Trusteeship Council, having successfully carried out its functions, is now reduced to a purely formal existence.

166. I believe we need to restore the balance, with three Councils covering respectively, (a) international peace and security, (b) economic and social issues, and (c) human rights, the promotion of which has been one of the purposes of the Organization from its beginnings but now clearly requires more effective operational structures. These Councils together should have the task of driving forward the agenda that emerges from summit and other conferences of Member States, and should be the global forms in which the issues of security, development and justice can be properly addressed. The first two Councils, of course, already exist but need to be strengthened. The third requires a far-reaching overhaul and upgrading of our existing human rights machinery ...

181. The Commission on Human Rights has given the international community a universal human rights framework, comprising the Universal Declaration on Human Rights, the two International Covenants and other core human rights treaties. During its annual session, the Commission draws public attention to human rights issues and debates, provides a forum for the development of United Nations human rights policy and establishes a unique system of independent and expert special procedures to observe and analyse human rights compliance by theme and by country. The Commission's close engagement with hundreds of civil society organizations provides an opportunity for working with civil society that does not exist elsewhere.

182. Yet the Commission's capacity to perform its tasks has been increasingly undermined by its declining credibility and professionalism. In particular, States have sought membership of the Commission not to strengthen human rights but to protect themselves against criticism or to criticize others. As a result, a credibility deficit has developed, which casts a shadow on the reputation of the United Nations system as a whole.

183. If the United Nations is to meet the expectations of men and women everywhere – and indeed, if the Organization is to take the cause of human rights as seriously as those of security and development – then Member States should agree to replace the Commission on Human Rights with a smaller standing Human Rights Council. Member States would need to decide if they want the Human Rights Council to be a principal organ of the United Nations or a subsidiary

body of the General Assembly, but in either case its members would be elected directly by the General Assembly by a two-thirds majority of members present and voting. The creation of the Council would accord human rights a more authoritative position, corresponding to the primacy of human rights in the Charter of the United Nations. Member States should determine the composition of the Council and the term of office of its members. Those elected to the Council should undertake to abide by the highest human rights standards.

Addendum to the Report (A/59/2005/Add. 1, 23 May 2005):
The Human Rights Council would be a standing body, able to meet regularly and at any time to deal with imminent crises and allow for timely and in-depth consideration of human rights issues. Moving human rights discussions beyond the politically charged six-week session [during which the Commission on Human Rights convened in March–April on an annual basis] would also allow more time for substantive follow-up on the implementation of decisions and resolutions. Being elected by the entire membership of the General Assembly would make members more accountable and the body more representative. And being elected directly by the General Assembly – the principal United Nations legislative body – would also have greater authority than the Commission, which is a subsidiary body of the Economic and Social Council. Indeed, according to the Charter, responsibility for discharging the functions under the Economic and Social Council, including the promotion of human rights, is ultimately vested in the General Assembly. A smaller membership would allow the Human Rights Council to have more focused debate and discussions.

On 15 March 2006, following up on the suggestion made in the 'In Larger Freedom' Report, the General Assembly adopted Resolution A/RES/60/251 to establish the Human Rights Council. The Resolution created the Human Rights Council to replace the Commission on Human Rights, as a subsidiary organ of the General Assembly. It read further:

UN General Assembly, Resolution 60/251. Human Rights Council (A/RES/60/251, 15 March 2006):

3. [The General Assembly decides also] that the Council should address situations of violations of human rights, including gross and systematic violations, and make recommendations thereon. It should also promote the effective coordination and the mainstreaming of human rights within the United Nations system;

4. Decides further that the work of the Council shall be guided by the principles of universality, impartiality, objectivity and non-selectivity, constructive international dialogue and cooperation, with a view to enhancing the promotion and protection of all human rights, civil, political, economic, social and cultural rights, including the right to development;

5. Decides that the Council shall, *inter alia*:

(a) Promote human rights education and learning as well as advisory services, technical assistance and capacity-building, to be provided in consultation with and with the consent of Member States concerned;

(b) Serve as a forum for dialogue on thematic issues on all human rights;

(c) Make recommendations to the General Assembly for the further development of international law in the field of human rights;

(d) Promote the full implementation of human rights obligations undertaken by States and follow-up to the goals and commitments related to the promotion and protection of human rights emanating from United Nations conferences and summits;

(e) Undertake a universal periodic review, based on objective and reliable information, of the fulfilment by each State of its human rights obligations and commitments in a manner which ensures universality of coverage and equal treatment with respect to all States; the review shall be a cooperative mechanism, based on an interactive dialogue, with the full involvement of the country concerned and with consideration given to its capacity-building needs; such a mechanism shall complement and not duplicate the work of treaty bodies; the Council shall develop the modalities and necessary time allocation for the universal periodic review mechanism within one year after the holding of its first session;

(f) Contribute, through dialogue and cooperation, towards the prevention of human rights violations and respond promptly to human rights emergencies;

(g) Assume the role and responsibilities of the Commission on Human Rights relating to the work of the Office of the United Nations High Commissioner for Human Rights, as decided by the General Assembly in its resolution 48/141 of 20 December 1993;

(h) Work in close cooperation in the field of human rights with Governments, regional organizations, national human rights institutions and civil society;

(i) Make recommendations with regard to the promotion and protection of human rights;

(j) Submit an annual report to the General Assembly;

6. Decides also that the Council shall assume, review and, where necessary, improve and rationalize all mandates, mechanisms, functions and responsibilities of the Commission on Human Rights in order to maintain a system of special procedures, expert advice and a complaint procedure; the Council shall complete this review within one year after the holding of its first session;

7. Decides further that the Council shall consist of forty-seven Member States, which shall be elected directly and individually by secret ballot by the majority of the members of the General Assembly; the membership shall be based on equitable geographical distribution, and seats shall be distributed as follows among regional groups: Group of African States, thirteen; Group of Asian States, thirteen; Group of Eastern European States, six; Group of Latin American and Caribbean States, eight; and Group of Western European and other States, seven [these 'other' States of the WEOG group are Australia, Canada and New Zealand; while formally not a member of any geographical group, the United States is considered a member of WEOG for election purposes, and Israel has an 'observer' status within WEOG]; the members of the Council shall serve for a period of three years and shall not be eligible for immediate re-election after two consecutive terms;

8. Decides that the membership in the Council shall be open to all States Members of the United Nations; when electing members of the Council, Member States shall take into account the contribution of candidates to the promotion and protection of human rights and their voluntary pledges and commitments made thereto; the General Assembly, by a two-thirds majority of the members present and voting, may suspend the rights of membership in the Council of a member of the Council that commits gross and systematic violations of human rights;

9. Decides also that members elected to the Council shall uphold the highest standards in the promotion and protection of human rights, shall fully cooperate with the Council and be reviewed under the universal periodic review mechanism during their term of membership;

10. Decides further that the Council shall meet regularly throughout the year and schedule no fewer than three sessions per year, including a main session, for a total duration of no less than ten weeks, and shall be able to hold special sessions, when needed, at the request of a member of the Council with the support of one third of the membership of the Council;

The Resolution was the result of a broad consensus, although the United States, the Marshall Islands, Palau, and Israel voted against it. Belarus, Iran, and Venezuela abstained. The United States explained their vote as follows:

Explanation of Vote by Ambassador John R. Bolton, US Permanent Representative to the United Nations, on the Human Rights Council Draft Resolution, in the General Assembly, March 15, 2006:

UN Secretary General Kofi Annan established ambitious but appropriate goals for the effort to reform the Commission on Human Rights. Though all of us recognized that the Commission on Human Rights needed changing, it was the Secretary General who framed the discussion by saying that 'the Commission's capacity to perform its tasks has been increasingly undermined by its declining credibility and professionalism', which 'casts a shadow on the reputation of the United Nations system as a whole'.

To help the Member States move forward, he made a number of proposals to improve the body, as did the United States and other Member States. We appreciate UNGA President Jan Eliasson's efforts to create an effective human rights body, as well as the efforts of Ambassador Kumalo and Ambassador Arias. Through their leadership, some of these goals were achieved with this text, and there are provisions that make improvements over the existing Commission on Human Rights. But on too many issues the current text is not sufficiently improved.

In focusing on the membership of the body, the United States was in excellent company. The Secretary-General had targeted this as the fundamental problem with the Commission, noting, 'states have sought membership of the Commission not to strengthen human rights but to protect themselves against criticism or to criticize others'. We strongly agreed with the Secretary-General, and our preeminent concern was always about the credibility of the body's membership.

The Secretary-General also proposed a strong tool to fix this – he proposed that the Council elect its members by a two-thirds majority. This proposal is not included in the resolution before us today, and it should be. The higher hurdle for membership would have made it harder for countries that are not demonstrably committed to human rights to win seats on the Council. It would have helped to prevent the election of countries that only seek to undermine the new body from within.

The United States also proposed an exclusionary criteria to keep gross abusers of human rights off the Council. This proposal would have excluded Member States against which measures are in effect under Chapter VII of the UN Charter related to human rights abuses or acts of terrorism. We also expressed a willingness to consider alternatives to satisfy the need for a strong mechanism to exclude the worst human rights violators.

Sadly, these suggestions were not included in the new text. The resolution before us merely requires Member States to 'take into account' a candidate's human rights record when voting. And the provision for the General Assembly to suspend an elected member of the Council requires a two-thirds vote, a standard higher than that for electing members.

Our position on the need for a strong, credible membership is one of principle, and one we know that others here today share. We extend our appreciation to those Member States that agreed with our assertion that there should be no place on the new Council for countries where there is objective evidence of systematic and gross violations of human rights, or where United Nations sanctions have been applied for human rights violations. Some Member States have signed letters and plan to make statements to this effect. Although these commitments could not ultimately change our position on this draft resolution, they represent a welcome and appropriate effort on behalf of many dedicated Member States.

We had a historic opportunity to create a primary human rights organ in the UN poised to help those most in need and offer a hand to governments to build what the Charter calls 'fundamental freedoms'. The Council that is created will be our legacy. We must not let the victims of human rights abuses throughout the world think that UN Member States were willing to settle for 'good enough'. We must not let history remember us as the architects of a Council that was a 'compromise' and merely 'the best we could do' rather than one that ensured doing 'all we could do' to promote human rights.

Mr President, absent stronger mechanisms for maintaining credible membership, the United States could not join consensus on this resolution. We did not have sufficient confidence in this text to be able to say that the HRC would be better than its predecessor.

Despite the reservations thus expressed by the United States, one important difference between the Human Rights Council and the former Commission on Human Rights resides in the mechanism for the election of its members. The Ecosoc formerly elected the members of the Commission on Human Rights. In contrast, the members of the Human Rights Council are elected by the 192 members of the General Assembly 'directly and individually' by secret ballot, although in order to ensure equitable geographical representation, each group of States (divided along geographical lines into groups that have remained unchanged since 1963) is allocated a predefined number of seats (see para. 7 of UN General Assembly Resolution 60/251). During the discussions preceding the adoption of Resolution 60/251 on the Human Rights Council, there were proposals to ensure that only candidates with a clean human rights record should be allowed to stand as candidates for membership in the Council. While this proposal was not retained – a major factor explaining the negative vote of the United States – para. 8 of Resolution 60/251 nevertheless refers to the need to 'take into account the contribution of candidates to the promotion and protection of human rights and their voluntary pledges and commitments made thereto'. Thus, when presenting their candidacy to the Council, governments describe their record in the field of human rights. They also make certain pledges that may play a role, subsequently, under the universal periodic review process (see below, section 3). For instance, in her letter to the President of the UN General Assembly announcing that the United States (now under the Administration of President Obama) were a candidate for membership to the Human Rights Council for the term 2009–12, the Ambassador of the United States of America to the United Nations, Ms Susan Rice, attached a list of 'human rights commitments and pledges', excerpts of which are presented below:

Human rights commitments and pledges of the United States of America – Annex to the letter dated 22 April 2009 from the Permanent Representative of the United States of America to the United Nations addressed to the President of the General Assembly:

Commitment to advancing human rights in the United Nations system

1. The United States commits to continuing its efforts in the United Nations system to be a strong advocate for all people around the world who suffer from abuse and oppression, and to be a stalwart defender of courageous individuals across the globe who work, often at great personal risk, on behalf of the rights of others.

2. The United States commits to working with principled determination for a balanced, credible and effective United Nations Human Rights Council to advance the purpose of the Universal Declaration of Human Rights. To that same end, in partnership with the international community, we fully intend to promote universality, transparency and objectivity in all of the Council's endeavours. The United States commits to participating fully in the universal periodic review process and looks forward to the review in 2010 of its own record in promoting and protecting human rights and fundamental freedoms in the United States.

3. The United States is committed to advancing the promotion and protection of human rights and fundamental freedoms in the General Assembly and the Third Committee, and in this vein intends to actively participate in the 2011 review by the General Assembly of the work of the Human Rights Council.

4. The United States is also committed to the promotion and protection of human rights through regional organizations ...

5. The United States recognizes and upholds the vital role of civil society and human rights defenders in the promotion and protection of human rights and commits to promoting the effective involvement of non-governmental organizations in the work of the United Nations, including the Human Rights Council, and other international organizations.

6. As part of our commitment to the principle of universality of human rights, the United States commits to working with our international partners in the spirit of openness, consultation and respect and reaffirms that expressions of concern about the human rights situation in any country, our own included, are appropriate matters for international discussion.

Commitment to continue providing support to human rights activities in the United Nations system

1. The United States is committed to continuing its support for the Office of the United Nations High Commissioner for Human Rights. In 2009, the United States intends to pledge $8 million to the Office of the United Nations High Commissioner for Human Rights and its efforts to address violations of human rights worldwide, as well as an additional $1.4 million to the

United Nations Voluntary Fund for Technical Cooperation in the Field of Human Rights, and more than $7 million to other funds.

2. The United States is also committed to continuing its support of other United Nations bodies whose work contributes to the promotion of human rights. In 2008–2009, the United States has contributed funding to support human rights efforts, inter alia, through the United Nations Children's Fund (UNICEF) ($130 million), the United Nations Democracy Fund ($7.9 million) and the United Nations Development Fund for Women (UNIFEM) ($4.5 million). The United States also supports the United Nations Population Fund (UNFPA) and is contributing $50 million for fiscal year 2009.

Commitment to advancing human rights, fundamental freedoms, and human dignity and prosperity internationally

1. The United States commits to continuing to support States in their implementation of human rights obligations, as appropriate, through human rights dialogue, exchange of experts, technical and interregional cooperation, and programmatic support of the work of non-governmental organizations.
2. The United States commits to continuing its efforts to strengthen mechanisms in the international system established to advance the rights, protection and empowerment of women.

Commitment to advancing human rights, fundamental freedoms, and human dignity and prosperity internationally

1. The United States commits to continuing to support States in their implementation of human rights obligations, as appropriate, through human rights dialogue, exchange of experts, technical and interregional cooperation, and programmatic support of the work of non-governmental organizations.
2. The United States commits to continuing its efforts to strengthen mechanisms in the international system established to advance the rights, protection and empowerment of women ...
3. The United States commits to continuing to promote respect for workers' rights worldwide, including by working with other Governments and the International Labour Organization (ILO) to adopt and enforce regulations and laws that promote respect for internationally recognized worker rights and by providing funding for technical assistance projects designed to build the capacity of worker organizations, employers and Governments to address labour issues, including forced labour and the worst forms of child labour, such as child soldiering, workplace discrimination, and sweatshop and exploitative working conditions.
4. The United States commits to continuing to advocate a victim-centred and multidisciplinary approach to combating all forms of trafficking in persons and to restoring the dignity, human rights and fundamental freedoms of human trafficking victims.
5. The United States commits to continuing to promote freedom of religion for individuals of all beliefs, particularly members of minority and vulnerable religious groups, through dedicated outreach, advocacy, training and programmatic efforts.
6. The United States is committed to continuing to promote human rights in the fight against HIV/AIDS in a variety of ways, including through promoting the rights of people living with HIV/AIDS, fighting against stigma and discrimination, and supporting women's rights. The United States is committed to preventing suffering and saving lives by confronting global health challenges through improving the quality, availability and use of essential health services.

7. The United States is committed to continuing its leadership role in promoting voluntary corporate social responsibility and business and human rights initiatives globally ...

8. Recognizing the essential contributions of independent media in promoting the fundamental freedom of expression, exposing human rights abuses and promoting accountability and transparency in governance, the United States commits to continuing to champion freedom of expression and to promote media freedom and the protection of journalists worldwide.

9. We are dedicated to combating both overt and subtle forms of racism and discrimination internationally.

Commitment to advancing human rights and fundamental freedoms in the United States

1. The United States executive branch is committed to working with its legislative branch to consider the possible ratification of human rights treaties, including but not limited to the Convention on the Elimination of All Forms of Discrimination against Women and ILO Convention No. 111 concerning Discrimination in Respect of Employment and Occupation.

2. The United States is committed to meeting its United Nations treaty obligations and participating in a meaningful dialogue with treaty body members.

3. The United States is committed to cooperating with the human rights mechanisms of the United Nations, as well as the Inter-American Commission on Human Rights and other regional human rights bodies, by responding to inquiries, engaging in dialogues and hosting visits.

4. The United States is also strongly committed to fighting racism and discrimination, and acts of violence committed because of racial or ethnic hatred. Despite the achievements of the civil rights movement and many years of striving to achieve equal rights for all, racism still exists in our country and we continue to fight it.

5. The United States is committed to continuing to promote human prosperity and human rights and fundamental freedoms of all persons within the United States, including through enforcement of the Americans with Disabilities Act and its amendments, engaging religious and community leaders in upholding religious freedom and pluralism, and encouraging the members of the private sector to serve as good corporate citizens both in the United States and overseas.

The newly established Human Rights Council held its inaugural session in Geneva, 9–30 June 2006. On 18 June 2007, acting in accordance with para. 6 of UN General Assembly Resolution 60/251, the Human Rights Council adopted the President text entitled 'UN Human Rights Council: Institution Building' (Institution-building of the United Nations Human Rights Council, A/HRC/Res/5/1, 18 June 2007). The Resolution establishes a new complaints procedure in order to address consistent patterns of gross and reliably attested violations of all human rights and all fundamental freedoms occurring in any part of the world and under any circumstances. It outlines the functioning of the universal periodic review (UPR). It describes the way mandate-holders of special procedures will be appointed, and how they are expected to fulfil their mandate; and it sets up the Human Rights Council Advisory Committee, the successor to the Sub-Commission for the Promotion and Protection of Human Rights. The following sections of this chapter review the three tools the Council has at its disposal.

Box 10.1.	**The Advisory Committee of the Human Rights Council**

The Advisory Committee is composed of eighteen experts serving in their personal capacity, elected by the Human Rights Council (the Sub-Commission on the Promotion and Protection of Human Rights, which the Advisory Committee replaced, comprised twenty-six independent experts). The geographical balance is ensured by the following distribution: five members shall originate from African States; five from Asian States; two from Eastern European States; three from Latin American and Carribean States; and three from Western European and other States. The experts must have a recognized competence and experience in the field of human rights; they must be of high moral standing; and they must be independent and impartial, which implies that individuals holding decision-making positions in Government or any other organization which might give rise to a conflict of interest with responsibilities inherent to the mandate may not be elected (Decision 6/102 of the Human Rights Council, Follow-up to Human Rights Council Resolution 5/1).

The Advisory Committee will 'function as a think-tank for the Council and work at its direction', providing it with the necessary expertise (Human Rights Council Resolution 5/1, para. 65). The 'Institution-building' Resolution of the Council makes it clear that the Advisory Committee should serve the agenda of the Council, and not take initiatives of its own as did the former Sub-Commission on the Promotion and Protection of Human Rights: 'The function of the Advisory Committee is to provide expertise to the Council in the manner and form requested by the Council, focusing mainly on studies and research-based advice. Further, such expertise shall be rendered only upon the latter's request, in compliance with its resolutions and under its guidance' (Human Rights Council Resolution 5/1, para. 68). However, although the Advisory Committee is explicitly prohibited from adopting resolutions or decisions, it 'may propose within the scope of the work set out by the Council, for the latter's consideration and approval, suggestions for further enhancing its procedural efficiency, as well as further research proposals within the scope of the work set out by the Council' (para. 69).

The Advisory Committee shall convene up to two sessions for a maximum of ten working days per year, although additional sessions may be scheduled on an ad hoc basis with prior approval of the Council. Its inaugural session was held on 4–15 August 2008 in Geneva.

2 THE COMPLAINTS MECHANISM

When the Human Rights Council was established, it was decided that its mandate would include addressing 'situations of violations of human rights, including gross and systematic violations, and make recommendations thereon' (UN General Assembly Resolution 60/251, para. 3). The idea was to build on the procedures developed over time by the Commission on Human Rights. Although it initially declined to examine the complaints about human rights violations sent to the United Nations, the Commission gradually adopted a bolder stance at the initiative of developing countries seeking to challenge apartheid in South Africa and other issues related to racial discrimination or to the self-determination of peoples. The Economic and Social Council adopted Resolution 1235 (1967) (Ecosoc Res. 1235(XLII) of 6 June 1967) authorizing the Commission on Human Rights to examine information relevant to gross violations of human rights and fundamental freedoms. It later adopted Resolution 1503 (1970), establishing a procedure for dealing with communications relating to violations of human rights and fundamental freedoms (Ecosoc Res. 1503(XLVIII) of 27 May 1970, revised by Ecosoc Res. 2000/3 of 9 June 2000). The resulting system, which involved the Sub-Commission on the Promotion and Protection of Human Rights prior to any complaint being transmitted to the Commission on Human Rights, was to a large extent reproduced when the Human Rights Council was established, to be placed in the hands of the Council in co-operation with its Advisory Committee:

Human Rights Council, Resolution 5/1: Institution building (18 June 2007): Complaint Procedure

A. Objective and scope

85. A complaint procedure is being established to address consistent patterns of gross and reliably attested violations of all human rights and all fundamental freedoms occurring in any part of the world and under any circumstances.

86. Economic and Social Council resolution 1503 (XLVIII) of 27 May 1970 as revised by resolution 2000/3 of 19 June 2000 served as a working basis and was improved where necessary, so as to ensure that the complaint procedure is impartial, objective, efficient, victims-oriented and conducted in a timely manner. The procedure will retain its confidential nature, with a view to enhancing cooperation with the State concerned.

B. Admissibility criteria for communications

87. A communication related to a violation of human rights and fundamental freedoms, for the purpose of this procedure, shall be admissible, provided that:

(a) It is not manifestly politically motivated and its object is consistent with the Charter of the United Nations, the Universal Declaration of Human Rights and other applicable instruments in the field of human rights law;

(b) It gives a factual description of the alleged violations, including the rights which are alleged to be violated;

(c) Its language is not abusive. However, such a communication may be considered if it meets the other criteria for admissibility after deletion of the abusive language;

(d) It is submitted by a person or a group of persons claiming to be the victims of violations of human rights and fundamental freedoms, or by any person or group of persons, including non-governmental organizations, acting in good faith in accordance with the principles of human rights, not resorting to politically motivated stands contrary to the provisions of the Charter of the United Nations and claiming to have direct and reliable knowledge of the violations concerned. Nonetheless, reliably attested communications shall not be inadmissible solely because the knowledge of the individual authors is second-hand, provided that they are accompanied by clear evidence;

(e) It is not exclusively based on reports disseminated by mass media;

(f) It does not refer to a case that appears to reveal a consistent pattern of gross and reliably attested violations of human rights already being dealt with by a special procedure, a treaty body or other United Nations or similar regional complaints procedure in the field of human rights;

(g) Domestic remedies have been exhausted, unless it appears that such remedies would be ineffective or unreasonably prolonged.

88. National human rights institutions, established and operating under the Principles Relating to the Status of National Institutions (the Paris Principles), in particular in regard to quasi-judicial competence, may serve as effective means of addressing individual human rights violations.

C. Working groups

89. Two distinct working groups shall be established with the mandate to examine the communications and to bring to the attention of the Council consistent patterns of gross and reliably attested violations of human rights and fundamental freedoms.

90. Both working groups shall, to the greatest possible extent, work on the basis of consensus. In the absence of consensus, decisions shall be taken by simple majority of the votes. They may establish their own rules of procedure.

1. Working Group on Communications: composition, mandate and powers 91. The Human Rights Council Advisory Committee shall appoint five of its members, one from each Regional Group, with due consideration to gender balance, to constitute the Working Group on Communications.

92. In case of a vacancy, the Advisory Committee shall appoint an independent and highly qualified expert of the same Regional Group from the Advisory Committee.

93. Since there is a need for independent expertise and continuity with regard to the examination and assessment of communications received, the independent and highly qualified experts of the Working Group on Communications shall be appointed for three years. Their mandate is renewable only once.

94. The Chairperson of the Working Group on Communications is requested, together with the secretariat, to undertake an initial screening of communications received, based on the admissibility criteria, before transmitting them to the States concerned. Manifestly ill-founded or anonymous communications shall be screened out by the Chairperson and shall therefore not be transmitted to the State concerned. In a perspective of accountability and transparency, the Chairperson of the Working Group on Communications shall provide all its members with a list of all communications rejected after initial screening. This list should indicate the grounds of all decisions resulting in the rejection of a communication. All other communications, which have not been screened out, shall be transmitted to the State concerned, so as to obtain the views of the latter on the allegations of violations.

95. The members of the Working Group on Communications shall decide on the admissibility of a communication and assess the merits of the allegations of violations, including whether the communication alone or in combination with other communications appear to reveal a consistent pattern of gross and reliably attested violations of human rights and fundamental freedoms. The Working Group on Communications shall provide the Working Group on Situations with a file containing all admissible communications as well as recommendations thereon. When the Working Group on Communications requires further consideration or additional information,

it may keep a case under review until its next session and request such information from the State concerned. The Working Group on Communications may decide to dismiss a case. All decisions of the Working Group on Communications shall be based on a rigorous application of the admissibility criteria and duly justified.

2. Working Group on Situations: composition, mandate and powers 96. Each Regional Group shall appoint a representative of a member State of the Council, with due consideration to gender balance, to serve on the Working Group on Situations. Members shall be appointed for one year. Their mandate may be renewed once, if the State concerned is a member of the Council.

97. Members of the Working Group on Situations shall serve in their personal capacity. In order to fill a vacancy, the respective Regional Group to which the vacancy belongs, shall appoint a representative from member States of the same Regional Group.

98. The Working Group on Situations is requested, on the basis of the information and recommendations provided by the Working Group on Communications, to present the Council with a report on consistent patterns of gross and reliably attested violations of human rights and fundamental freedoms and to make recommendations to the Council on the course of action to take, normally in the form of a draft resolution or decision with respect to the situations referred to it. When the Working Group on Situations requires further consideration or additional information, its members may keep a case under review until its next session. The Working Group on Situations may also decide to dismiss a case.

99. All decisions of the Working Group on Situations shall be duly justified and indicate why the consideration of a situation has been discontinued or action recommended thereon. Decisions to discontinue should be taken by consensus; if that is not possible, by simple majority of the votes.

D. Working modalities and confidentiality

100. Since the complaint procedure is to be, *inter alia*, victims-oriented and conducted in a confidential and timely manner, both Working Groups shall meet at least twice a year for five working days each session, in order to promptly examine the communications received, including replies of States thereon, and the situations of which the Council is already seized under the complaint procedure.

101. The State concerned shall cooperate with the complaint procedure and make every effort to provide substantive replies in one of the United Nations official languages to any of the requests of the Working Groups or the Council. The State concerned shall also make every effort to provide a reply not later than three months after the request has been made. If necessary, this deadline may however be extended at the request of the State concerned.

102. The Secretariat is requested to make the confidential files available to all members of the Council, at least two weeks in advance, so as to allow sufficient time for the consideration of the files.

103. The Council shall consider consistent patterns of gross and reliably attested violations of human rights and fundamental freedoms brought to its attention by the Working Group on Situations as frequently as needed, but at least once a year.

104. The reports of the Working Group on Situations referred to the Council shall be examined in a confidential manner, unless the Council decides otherwise. When the Working

Group on Situations recommends to the Council that it consider a situation in a public meeting, in particular in the case of manifest and unequivocal lack of cooperation, the Council shall consider such recommendation on a priority basis at its next session.

105. So as to ensure that the complaint procedure is victims-oriented, efficient and conducted in a timely manner, the period of time between the transmission of the complaint to the State concerned and consideration by the Council shall not, in principle, exceed 24 months.

E. Involvement of the complainant and of the State concerned

106. The complaint procedure shall ensure that both the author of a communication and the State concerned are informed of the proceedings at the following key stages:

(a) When a communication is deemed inadmissible by the Working Group on Communications or when it is taken up for consideration by the Working Group on Situations; or when a communication is kept pending by one of the Working Groups or by the Council;
(b) At the final outcome.

107. In addition, the complainant shall be informed when his/her communication is registered by the complaint procedure.

108. Should the complainant request that his/her identity be kept confidential, it will not be transmitted to the State concerned.

F. Measures

109. In accordance with established practice the action taken in respect of a particular situation should be one of the following options:

(a) To discontinue considering the situation when further consideration or action is not warranted;
(b) To keep the situation under review and request the State concerned to provide further information within a reasonable period of time;
(c) To keep the situation under review and appoint an independent and highly qualified expert to monitor the situation and report back to the Council;
(d) To discontinue reviewing the matter under the confidential complaint procedure in order to take up public consideration of the same;
(e) To recommend to OHCHR to provide technical cooperation, capacity-building assistance or advisory services to the State concerned.

3 THE UNIVERSAL PERIODIC REVIEW

The universal periodic review (UPR) envisaged in operative para. 5(e) of the UN General Assembly Resolution 60/251 was initially presented in an address of the UN Secretary-General to the Commission on Human Rights in April 2005:

> [The Human Rights Council] should have an explicitly defined function as a chamber of peer review. Its main task would be to evaluate the fulfilment by all States of all their human rights obligations. This would give concrete expression to the principle that human rights are universal and indivisible. Equal attention will have to be given to civil, political, economic, social and cultural rights, as well as

the right to development. And it should be equipped to give technical assistance to States and policy advice to States and United Nations bodies alike. Under such a system, every Member State could come up for review on a periodic basis. Any such rotation should not, however, impede the Council from dealing with any massive and gross violations that might occur. Indeed, the Council will have to be able to bring urgent crises to the attention of the world community.

The Addendum to the Report 'In Larger Freedom' provides the following elaboration:

In Larger Freedom: Towards Development, Security and Human Rights for All. Report of the Secretary-General, Addendum (A/59/2005/Add. 1, 23 May 2005):

7. The peer review mechanism would complement but would not replace reporting procedures under human rights treaties. The latter arise from legal commitments and involve close scrutiny of law, regulations and practice with regard to specific provisions of those treaties by independent expert panels. They result in specific and authoritative recommendations for action. Peer review would be a process whereby States voluntarily enter into discussion regarding human rights issues in their respective countries, and would be based on the obligations and responsibilities to promote and protect those rights arising under the Charter and as given expression in the Universal Declaration of Human Rights. Implementation of findings should be developed as a cooperative venture, with assistance given to States in developing their capacities.

8. Crucial to peer review is the notion of universal scrutiny, that is, that the performance of all Member States in regard to all human rights commitments should be subject to assessment by other States. The peer review would help avoid, to the extent possible, the politicization and selectivity that are hallmarks of the Commission's existing system. It should touch upon the entire spectrum of human rights, namely, civil, political, economic, social and cultural rights. The Human Rights Council will need to ensure that it develops a system of peer review that is fair, transparent and workable, whereby States are reviewed against the same criteria. A fair system will require agreement on the quality and quantity of information used as the reference point for the review. In that regard, the Office of the High Commissioner could play a central role in compiling such information and ensuring a comprehensive and balanced approach to all human rights. The findings of the peer reviews of the Human Rights Council would help the international community better provide technical assistance and policy advice. Furthermore, it would help keep elected members accountable for their human rights commitments.

The appendix to the Human Rights Council Resolution 5/1 'Institution-building of the United Nations Human Rights Council' (18 June 2007) describes the UPR in the following terms:

Human Rights Council, Resolution 5/1: Institution-building (18 June 2007):

A. Basis of the review

1. The basis of the review is:
   (a) The Charter of the United Nations;

(b) The Universal Declaration of Human Rights;

(c) Human rights instruments to which a State is party;

(d) Voluntary pledges and commitments made by States, including those undertaken when presenting their candidatures for election to the Human Rights Council (hereinafter 'the Council').

2. In addition to the above and given the complementary and mutually interrelated nature of international human rights law and international humanitarian law, the review shall take into account applicable international humanitarian law.

B. Principles and objectives

1. Principles

3. The universal periodic review should:

(a) Promote the universality, interdependence, indivisibility and interrelatedness of all human rights;

(b) Be a cooperative mechanism based on objective and reliable information and on interactive dialogue;

(c) Ensure universal coverage and equal treatment of all States;

(d) Be an intergovernmental process, United Nations Member-driven and action-oriented;

(e) Fully involve the country under review;

(f) Complement and not duplicate other human rights mechanisms, thus representing an added value;

(g) Be conducted in an objective, transparent, non-selective, constructive, non-confrontational and non-politicized manner;

(h) Not be overly burdensome to the concerned State or to the agenda of the Council;

(i) Not be overly long; it should be realistic and not absorb a disproportionate amount of time, human and financial resources;

(j) Not diminish the Council's capacity to respond to urgent human rights situations;

(k) Fully integrate a gender perspective;

(l) Without prejudice to the obligations contained in the elements provided for in the basis of review, take into account the level of development and specificities of countries;

(m) Ensure the participation of all relevant stakeholders, including non-governmental organizations and national human rights institutions, in accordance with General Assembly resolution 60/251 of 15 March 2006 and Economic and Social Council resolution 1996/31 of 25 July 1996, as well as any decisions that the Council may take in this regard.

2. Objectives

4. The objectives of the review are:

(a) The improvement of the human rights situation on the ground;

(b) The fulfilment of the State's human rights obligations and commitments and assessment of positive developments and challenges faced by the State;

(c) The enhancement of the State's capacity and of technical assistance, in consultation with, and with the consent of, the State concerned;

(d) The sharing of best practice among States and other stakeholders;

(e) Support for cooperation in the promotion and protection of human rights;

(f) The encouragement of full cooperation and engagement with the Council, other human rights bodies and the Office of the United Nations High Commissioner for Human Rights.

C. Periodicity and order of the review

5. The review begins after the adoption of the universal periodic review mechanism by the Council.

6. The order of review should reflect the principles of universality and equal treatment.

7. The order of the review should be established as soon as possible in order to allow States to prepare adequately.

8. All member States of the Council shall be reviewed during their term of membership.

9. The initial members of the Council, especially those elected for one or two-year terms, should be reviewed first.

10. A mix of member and observer States of the Council should be reviewed.

11. Equitable geographic distribution should be respected in the selection of countries for review.

12. The first member and observer States to be reviewed will be chosen by the drawing of lots from each Regional Group in such a way as to ensure full respect for equitable geographic distribution. Alphabetical order will then be applied beginning with those countries thus selected, unless other countries volunteer to be reviewed.

13. The period between review cycles should be reasonable so as to take into account the capacity of States to prepare for, and the capacity of other stakeholders to respond to, the requests arising from the review.

14. The periodicity of the review for the first cycle will be of four years. This will imply the consideration of 48 States per year during three sessions of the working group of two weeks each.

D. Process and modalities of the review

1. Documentation

15. The documents on which the review would be based are:

(a) Information prepared by the State concerned, which can take the form of a national report, on the basis of general guidelines to be adopted by the Council at its sixth session (first session of the second cycle), and any other information considered relevant by the State concerned, which could be presented either orally or in writing, provided that the written presentation summarizing the information will not exceed 20 pages, to guarantee equal treatment to all States and not to overburden the mechanism. States are encouraged to prepare the information through a broad consultation process at the national level with all relevant stakeholders;

(b) Additionally a compilation prepared by the Office of the High Commissioner for Human Rights of the information contained in the reports of treaty bodies, special procedures, including observations and comments by the State concerned, and other relevant official United Nations documents, which shall not exceed 10 pages;

(c) Additional, credible and reliable information provided by other relevant stakeholders to the universal periodic review which should also be taken into consideration by the

Council in the review. The Office of the High Commissioner for Human Rights will prepare a summary of such information which shall not exceed 10 pages.

16. The documents prepared by the Office of the High Commissioner for Human Rights should be elaborated following the structure of the general guidelines adopted by the Council regarding the information prepared by the State concerned.

17. Both the State's written presentation and the summaries prepared by the Office of the High Commissioner for Human Rights shall be ready six weeks prior to the review by the working group to ensure the distribution of documents simultaneously in the six official languages of the United Nations, in accordance with General Assembly resolution 53/208 of 14 January 1999.

2. Modalities

18. The modalities of the review shall be as follows:

    (a) The review will be conducted in one working group, chaired by the President of the Council and composed of the 47 member States of the Council. Each member State will decide on the composition of its delegation;

    (b) Observer States may participate in the review, including in the interactive dialogue;

    (c) Other relevant stakeholders may attend the review in the Working Group;

    (d) A group of three rapporteurs, selected by the drawing of lots among the members of the Council and from different Regional Groups (troika) will be formed to facilitate each review, including the preparation of the report of the working group. The Office of the High Commissioner for Human Rights will provide the necessary assistance and expertise to the rapporteurs.

19. The country concerned may request that one of the rapporteurs be from its own Regional Group and may also request the substitution of a rapporteur on only one occasion.

20. A rapporteur may request to be excused from participation in a specific review process.

21. Interactive dialogue between the country under review and the Council will take place in the working group. The rapporteurs may collate issues or questions to be transmitted to the State under review to facilitate its preparation and focus the interactive dialogue, while guaranteeing fairness and transparency.

22. The duration of the review will be three hours for each country in the working group. Additional time of up to one hour will be allocated for the consideration of the outcome by the plenary of the Council.

23. Half an hour will be allocated for the adoption of the report of each country under review in the working group.

24. A reasonable time frame should be allocated between the review and the adoption of the report of each State in the working group.

25. The final outcome will be adopted by the plenary of the Council.

E. Outcome of the review

1. Format of the outcome

26. The format of the outcome of the review will be a report consisting of a summary of the proceedings of the review process; conclusions and/or recommendations, and the voluntary commitments of the State concerned.

2. Content of the outcome

27. The universal periodic review is a cooperative mechanism. Its outcome may include, *inter alia*:

    (a) An assessment undertaken in an objective and transparent manner of the human rights situation in the country under review, including positive developments and the challenges faced by the country;

    (b) Sharing of best practices;

    (c) An emphasis on enhancing cooperation for the promotion and protection of human rights;

    (d) The provision of technical assistance and capacity-building in consultation with, and with the consent of, the country concerned;

    (e) Voluntary commitments and pledges made by the country under review.

3. Adoption of the outcome

28. The country under review should be fully involved in the outcome.

29. Before the adoption of the outcome by the plenary of the Council, the State concerned should be offered the opportunity to present replies to questions or issues that were not sufficiently addressed during the interactive dialogue.

30. The State concerned and the member States of the Council, as well as observer States, will be given the opportunity to express their views on the outcome of the review before the plenary takes action on it.

31. Other relevant stakeholders will have the opportunity to make general comments before the adoption of the outcome by the plenary.

32. Recommendations that enjoy the support of the State concerned will be identified as such. Other recommendations, together with the comments of the State concerned thereon, will be noted. Both will be included in the outcome report to be adopted by the Council.

F. Follow-up to the review

33. The outcome of the universal periodic review, as a cooperative mechanism, should be implemented primarily by the State concerned and, as appropriate, by other relevant stakeholders.

34. The subsequent review should focus, *inter alia*, on the implementation of the preceding outcome.

35. The Council should have a standing item on its agenda devoted to the universal periodic review.

36. The international community will assist in implementing the recommendations and conclusions regarding capacity-building and technical assistance, in consultation with, and with the consent of, the country concerned.

37. In considering the outcome of the universal periodic review, the Council will decide if and when any specific follow-up is necessary.

38. After exhausting all efforts to encourage a State to cooperate with the universal periodic review mechanism, the Council will address, as appropriate, cases of persistent non-cooperation with the mechanism.

Human Rights Council, Decision 6/102. Follow-up to Human Rights Council Resolution 5/1 (27 September 2007) – General Guidelines for the Preparation of Information under the Universal Periodic Review:

[The report prepared by States for the universal periodic review should contain the following information:]

A. Description of the methodology and the broad consultation process followed for the preparation of information provided under the universal periodic review;

B. Background of the country under review and framework, particularly normative and institutional framework, for the promotion and protection of human rights: constitution, legislation, policy measures, national jurisprudence, human rights infrastructure including national human rights institutions and scope of international obligations identified in the 'basis of review' in resolution 5/1, annex, section IA;

C. Promotion and protection of human rights on the ground: implementation of international human rights obligations identified in the 'basis of review' in resolution 5/1, annex, section IA, national legislation and voluntary commitments, national human rights institutions activities, public awareness of human rights, cooperation with human rights mechanisms ...;

D. Identification of achievements, best practices, challenges and constraints;

E. Key national priorities, initiatives and commitments that the State concerned intends to undertake to overcome those challenges and constraints and improve human rights situations on the ground;

F. Expectations of the State concerned in terms of capacity-building and requests, if any, for technical assistance;

G. Presentation by the State concerned of the follow-up to the previous review.

In order to illustrate the functioning of the UPR in practice, the following are excerpts of three of the documents pertaining to the review of the United Kingdom in 2008. The first excerpt is the full list of conclusions and recommendations made by the members of the Human Rights Council (Working Group on the Universal Periodic Review), upon examining the situation of the United Kingdom on the basis of the three documents submitted to them – the State report, the compilation by the Office of the High Commissioner for Human Rights of findings of treaty bodies and special procedures, and the compilation of information received from other sources. The second document is the decision of the Human Rights Council on the outcome of the UPR regarding the United Kingdom. The third document lists the responses of the United Kingdom to certain recommendations made in the course of the UPR. While for reasons of space the full set of responses could not be reproduced, the sample presented is representative of the type of questions addressed, and the kind of justification offered when a recommendation is not accepted.

Human Rights Council, Report of the Working Group on the Universal Periodic Review: United Kingdom of Great Britain and Northern Ireland (A/HRC/8/25, 23 May 2008)

Conclusions and/or Recommendations

56. In the course of the discussion, the following recommendations were made to the United Kingdom of Great Britain and Northern Ireland:

1. To set up a strategic oversight body, such as a commission on violence against women, to ensure greater coherence and more effective protection for women. (India)
2. To address the high incarceration rate of children, ensure that the privacy of children is protected and put an end to the so-called 'painful techniques' applied to children. (Algeria)
3. To consider further measures in order to address the problem of violence against children, including corporal punishment. (Italy)
4. To reconsider its position about the continued legality of corporal punishment against children. (Sweden)
5. To consider going beyond current legislation and to ban corporal punishment, also in the private sector and in its Overseas Territories. (France)
6. To continue to review all counter-terrorism legislation and ensure that it complies with the highest human rights standards. (Cuba, Ghana and the Netherlands)
7. To harmonize its legislation with its human rights obligations towards individual protesters exercising their freedom of expression and opinion and to curtail excessive pretrial detention. (Algeria)
8. To enshrine in legislation the right of access of detainees to a lawyer immediately after detention, and not after 48 hours. (Russian Federation)
9. To strengthen guarantees for detained persons, and not to extend but to shorten the length of time of pretrial detentions. (Switzerland)
10. To introduce strict time limits on pre-charge detention of those suspected of terrorism, and provide information about so-called 'secret flights'. (Russian Federation)
11. To consider that any person detained by its armed forces is under its jurisdiction and respect its obligations concerning the human rights of such individuals. (Switzerland)
12. To elaborate specific policies and programmes aimed at ensuring that its applicable human rights obligations are not violated in situations of armed conflict. (Egypt)
13. To elaborate a national programme to combat the problem of overcrowding of prisons. (Russian Federation)
14. To facilitate the access of the International Committee of the Red Cross (ICRC) to its prisons. (Algeria)
15. To enhance the programmes aimed at addressing socio-economic inequalities, from a human rights perspective in fulfilment of its obligations under the International Covenant on Economic, Social and Cultural Rights. (Egypt)
16. To provide further information with regard to efforts to reduce poverty among children in half by 2010. (France)
17. To provide more care and attention to the rights of the elderly. (Canada)

18. To follow the Council of the European Union 'Asylum Qualification Directive' in future cases with regard to sexual orientation as a ground for asylum-seeking. (Canada)

19. To consider holding a referendum on the desirability or otherwise of a written constitution, preferably republican, which includes a bill of rights. (Sri Lanka)

20. That the example of the United Kingdom in issuing, in principle, a specific law dealing with incitement to racial and religious hatred, be emulated as a good practice in countries which have not done so, in implementation of article 20(2) of ICCPR and its stipulated purpose. (Egypt)

21. To protect the children and families of migrants and refugees (Algeria, Ecuador) and to accede to the International Convention on Protection of the Rights of All Migrant Workers and Members of their Families. (Algeria, Ecuador and Egypt)

22. To reflect upon and consider setting a date for signing the International Convention on the Protection of All Persons from Enforced Disappearance. (France)

23. To withdraw its interpretative statement with respect to article 4 of the International Convention on the Elimination of All Forms of Racial Discrimination [ICERD]. (Egypt) [Upon signing the International Convention on the Elimination of All Forms of Racial Discrimination, the United Kingdom stated its understanding that, although it imposes the criminalization of speech or activities promoting the idea of racial superiority or racial discrimination, Article 4 ICERD could only be implemented by the United Kingdom 'with due regard to the principles embodied in the Universal Declaration of Human Rights and the rights expressly set forth in article 5 of the Convention (in particular the right to freedom of opinion and expression and the right to freedom of peaceful assembly and association)'.]

24. To study, with a view to withdraw, its reservation to article 4 of the International Convention on the Elimination of All Forms of Racial Discrimination. (Cuba)

25. To withdraw its reservation to the Convention on the Rights of the Child, concerning the provision that detained children be separated from adults while in detention, as well as the reservation concerning refugee and asylum-seeking children. (Indonesia)

26. To consider removal of its reservations to the Convention on the Rights of the Child and the Optional Protocol on the involvement of children in armed conflict. (Russian Federation)

27. To accept the full and unrestricted implementation of the provisions of the Convention against Torture and the International Covenant on Civil and Political Rights in overseas territories under its control. (Algeria)

28. To integrate fully a gender perspective in the next stages of the UPR review, including the outcome of the review. (Slovenia)

57. The response of the United Kingdom to these recommendations will be included in the outcome report adopted by the Human Rights Council at its eighth session.

Human Rights Council, Decision 8/107. Outcome of the universal periodic review: United Kingdom of Great Britain and Northern Ireland (10 June 2008):

The Human Rights Council,
Acting in compliance with the mandate entrusted to it by the General Assembly in its resolution 60/251 of 15 March 2006 and Council resolution 5/1 of 18 June 2007, and in

accordance with the President's statement PRST/8/1 on modalities and practices for the universal periodic review process of 9 April 2008;

Having conducted the review of the United Kingdom of Great Britain and Northern Ireland on 10 April in conformity with all the relevant provisions contained in Council resolution 5/1;

Adopts the outcome of the universal periodic review on the United Kingdom of Great Britain and Northern Ireland which is constituted of the report of the Working Group on the review of the United Kingdom of Great Britain and Northern Ireland (A/HRC/8/25), together with the views of the United Kingdom of Great Britain and Northern Ireland concerning the recommendations and/or conclusions, as well as its voluntary commitments and its replies presented before the adoption of the outcome by the plenary to questions or issues that were not sufficiently addressed during the interactive dialogue in the Working Group (A/HRC/8/52 chap. VI and A/HRC/8/25/Add. 1).

Human Rights Council, Report of the Working Group on the Universal Periodic Review: United Kingdom of Great Britain and Northern Ireland. Views on conclusions and/or recommendations, voluntary commitments and replies presented by the State under review (A/HRC/8/25/Add. 1, 13 August 2008):

The Government of the United Kingdom welcomed the recommendations made in the course of its Universal Periodic Review on 10 April 2008. It has given them careful consideration, and its responses are as follows:

1. Elaborate a national programme to combat the problem of overcrowding in prisons. (Russian Federation)

The United Kingdom **accepts** the recommendation and will implement it immediately. Lord Carter's review of prisons in England & Wales, which was published on 5 December 2007, looked at demand for prison places over the long and medium term. In response to his recommendations, the UK Government has announced a series of measures that will create an additional 10,500 prison places by 2014.

7. Study, with a view to withdrawing, its interpretative statement to Article 4 of the International Convention on the Elimination of All Forms of Racial Discrimination (ICERD). (Cuba and Egypt)

The United Kingdom **does not accept** the recommendation. The United Kingdom has a long tradition of freedom of speech which allows individuals to hold and express views which may well be contrary to those of the majority of the population, and which many may find distasteful or even offensive. The UK maintains its view that individuals have the right to express such views so long as they are not expressed violently or do not incite violence or hatred against others. The Government believes that this strikes the right balance between maintaining the right to freedom of speech and protecting individuals from violence and hatred.

8. Continue to review all counter-terrorism legislation and ensure that it complies with the highest human rights standards. (Cuba, Ghana and the Netherlands)

The United Kingdom **accepts** the recommendation, and has already implemented it. The UK's counter-terrorism legislation is already subject to annual independent review. The independent reviewer of counter-terrorism legislation is required to produce an annual report for the Home Secretary on the operation of the Terrorism Act 2000, the Prevention of Terrorism Act 2005 (control orders) and Part 1 of the Terrorism Act 2006. This report must then also be laid before Parliament. It will continue to be the case that all of the UK's anti-terrorism measures have to be set in the context of the UK's general commitment to human rights and the protection of individual freedoms.

16. Consider that any person detained by its armed forces is under its jurisdiction and respect its obligations concerning the human rights of such individuals. (Switzerland)
The United Kingdom **accepts** the recommendation that the UK should respect its obligations concerning the human rights of detained persons but **does not accept** that any person detained by our armed forces is under our jurisdiction.

To the extent that the UK has human rights obligations in respect of persons detained by the armed forces, we comply fully with them. However, the House of Lords, the UK's highest court, has held that those detained by UK Forces operating overseas fall within UK jurisdiction for the purposes of the European Convention on Human Rights only in very limited circumstances. Other international human rights treaty obligations may also be applicable in limited circumstances.

While the effectiveness of the UPR still has to be evaluated, the initial appraisals have been reassuring. Using the review of the United Kingdom as an example, Kevin Boyle concludes:

Kevin Boyle, 'The United Nations Human Rights Council: Origins, Antecedents, and Prospects', in K. Boyle (ed.), *New Institutions for Human Rights Protection* (Oxford University Press, 2009), p. 11 at p. 36:

States under review and Council members in the three hours of interactive dialogue have made serious efforts to give the process meaning and depth. The atmosphere has been constructive and the issues raised for scrutiny have addressed both strengths and weaknesses of the countries in question. What is most interesting and of longer term significance, has been the extent to which countries under review have been both self-critical and have accepted recommendations made by other states for positive action, including the ratification of international instruments. The frankness with which some countries accepted that they have human rights problems and agreed to address them is genuinely new and encouraging.

When the UPR was proposed, certain fears were expressed that this would undermine the human rights treaty bodies' authority, or that of the special procedures established by the Human Rights Council (see Sir N. Rodley, 'The United Nations Human Rights Council, Its Special Procedures, and Its Relationship with the Treaty Bodies: Complementarity or Competition?' in K. Boyle (ed.), *New Institutions for Human Rights Protection* (Oxford University Press, 2009), p. 49). In 2009, however, the Office of the High Commissioner for Human Rights was reassuring on that point. It noted for instance:

> **Office of the High Commissioner for Human Rights, Special Procedures Facts and Figures 2008 (2009):**
>
> A notable development in 2008 was the emergence of new synergies between the Special procedures and the new Universal Periodic Review (UPR). States under review have now invited special procedures mandate holders to visit their countries; three States under review issued standing invitations, bringing to 63 the total number of standing invitations. Increasingly, States under review are addressing issues of concern to special procedures in the interactive dialogue that forms part of the review process, and these issues also typically feature in the recommendations of the UPR Working Group.

4 THE SPECIAL PROCEDURES

4.1 The origins and diversity of the special procedures of the Human Rights Council

'Special procedures' are mechanisms established by the Commission on Human Rights, and now assumed by the Human Rights Council, to address either specific country situations or thematic issues in all parts of the world. The origin of special procedures resides in the establishment by the Commission on Human Rights, at the request of the newly independent African States and the broader non-aligned movement, of an ad hoc Working Group on South Africa, with the mandate of investigating and reporting back on allegations of torture and ill-treatment by the South African police (E/CN4/Res/2 (XXIII), 6 March 1967). It was only in 1980, however, that the Commission created its first thematic mechanism, the Working Group on Enforced or Voluntary Disappearances. Special Procedures then developed in the 1980s and 1990s, with little consistency across the different mandates.

Special procedures are either an individual (called 'Special Rapporteur', 'Special Representative of the Secretary-General', 'Representative of the Secretary-General' or 'Independent Expert') or a working group usually composed of five members (one from each region). The mandate-holders of the Human Rights Council are unpaid individual experts who act in their personal capacity, and who contribute both to developing the understanding of human rights norms and to protecting human rights by using the various tools at their disposal. Depending on which special procedure is concerned, these tools include the preparation of reports to the Human Rights Council or to the Third Committee of the General Assembly; addressing communications to States, in the form either of letters of allegations or urgent appeals; and carrying out country missions, with the consent of the State concerned, in order to assess the situation of human rights there. One mechanism, the Working Group on Arbitrary Detention, receives complaints and issues 'opinions' on individual cases, as well as 'deliberations' on general matters (for general studies on special procedures, see I. Nifosi, *The UN Special Procedures in the Field of Human Rights* (Antwerp-Oxford: Intersentia-Hart, 2005); J. Gutter, *Thematic*

Procedures of the United Nations Commission on Human Rights and International Law: in Search of a Sense of Community (Antwerp-Oxford: Intersentia-Hart, 2006); J. Gutter, 'Special Procedures and the Human Rights Council: Achievements and Challenges Ahead', *Human Rights Law Review*, 7, No. 1 (2007), 93; M. Lempinen, *Challenges Facing the System of Special Procedures of the United Nations Commission on Human Rights* (Turku/Abo: Institute for Human Rights, Abo Akademi University, 2001)).

In June 2009, there were thirty-one thematic and nine country mandates, working with the support of the Office of the High Commissioner for Human Rights. The thematic mandates were established on the following themes: enforced or involuntary disappearances (established in 1980), extra-judicial, summary or arbitrary executions (1982), torture (1985), freedom of religion or belief (1986), sale of children, child prostitution and child pornography (1990), arbitrary detention (1991), freedom of opinion and expression (1993), racism, racial discrimination (1993), independence of judges and lawyers (1994), violence against women (1994), toxic wastes (1995), right to education (1998), extreme poverty (1998), migrants (1999), right to food (2000), adequate housing (2000), human rights defenders (2000), effects of foreign debt and other related international financial obligations of States on the full enjoyment of human rights (2000), indigenous people (2001), people of African descent (2002), physical and mental health (2002), internally displaced persons (2004), trafficking in persons (2004), mercenaries (2005), minority issues (2005), international solidarity (2005), countering terrorism (2005), transnational corporations (2005), contemporary forms of slavery (2007), right to water (2008), and cultural rights (2009). Country-specific mandates were established on Myanmar (1992), Cambodia (1993), Palestinian Occupied Territories (1993), Somalia (1993), Haiti (1995), Liberia (2003), Burundi (2004), Democratic People's Republic of Korea (2004), Sudan (2005). When the Human Rights Council was established, it was tasked with the 'review and rationalization' of the existing mandates, and many observers expressed the fear that the Special Procedures – despite or maybe precisely because of the important role they had come to play in the UN human rights system – would be significantly cut back as a result. In fact, although two country mandates were abolished immediately after the Council was set up (these were the country rapporteurs for Cuba and Belarus), all the other special procedures were preserved.

Manual of Operations of the Human Rights Council Special Procedures (August 2008), paras. 4–5:

4. Thematic Special Procedures are mandated by the HRC to investigate the situation of human rights in all parts of the world, irrespective of whether a particular government is a party to any of the relevant human rights treaties. This requires them to take the measures necessary to monitor and respond quickly to allegations of human rights violations against individuals or groups, either globally or in a specific country or territory, and to report on their activities. In the case of country mandates, mandate-holders are called upon to take full account of all human rights (civil, cultural, economic, political and social) unless directed otherwise. In carrying out their activities, mandate holders are accountable to the Council.

5. The principal functions of Special Procedures include to:

- **analyze** the relevant thematic issue or country situation, including undertaking on-site missions,;
- **advise** on the measures which should be taken by the Government(s) concerned and other relevant actors;
- **alert** United Nations organs and agencies, in particular, the HRC, and the international community in general to the need to address specific situations and issues. In this regard they have a role in providing 'early warning' and encouraging preventive measures;
- **advocate** on behalf of the victims of violations through measures such as requesting urgent action by relevant States and calling upon Governments to respond to specific allegations of human rights violations and provide redress;
- **activate** and mobilize the international and national communities, and the HRC to address particular human rights issues and to encourage cooperation among Governments, civil society and inter-governmental organizations.
- **Follow-up to recommendations**

The only powers of the special procedures are of a persuasive nature: while they may put pressure on governments by making public statements or in their submissions to the Human Rights Council or the Third Committee of the General Assembly, they are ultimately dependent on the willingness of States to co-operate with them. The Commission on Human Rights did refer to a State obligation in this regard:

Commission on Human Rights, Resolution 2004/76, Human Rights and Special Procedures (21 April 2004):

The Commission on Human Rights, ...
Considering that special procedures duly established by the Commission with regard to the consideration of questions relating to the promotion and protection of economic, social and cultural and civil and political rights represent a major achievement and an essential element of United Nations efforts to promote and protect internationally recognized human rights, ...

Urges all Governments to cooperate with the Commission through the pertinent Special Procedures, including by:

(a) Responding without undue delay to requests for information made to them through the Special Procedures, so that the procedures may carry out their mandates effectively;
(b) Considering Special Procedures to visit their countries and considering favourably accepting visits from Special Procedures when requested;
(c) Facilitating follow-up visits as appropriate in order to help to contribute to the effective implementation of recommendations by the Special Procedures concerned;

3. *Calls upon* the Governments concerned to study carefully the recommendations addressed to them by Special Procedures and to keep the relevant mechanisms informed without undue delay on the progress made towards their implementation;

4. *Calls upon* all States to protect individuals, organizations or groups of persons who provide information to, meet with, or otherwise cooperate with the Special Procedures from any type of violence, coercion, harassment, or other form of intimidation or reprisal ...

4.2 The selection of mandate-holders of special procedures of the Human Rights Council

Human Rights Council, Resolution 5/1: Institution-building, Appendix (18 June 2007):

[Selection and appointment of mandate-holders]

39. The following general criteria will be of paramount importance while nominating, selecting and appointing mandate-holders: (a) expertise; (b) experience in the field of the mandate; (c) independence; (d) impartiality; (e) personal integrity; and (f) objectivity.

40. Due consideration should be given to gender balance and equitable geographic representation, as well as to an appropriate representation of different legal systems.

41. Technical and objective requirements for eligible candidates for mandate-holders will be approved by the Council at its sixth session (first session of the second cycle), in order to ensure that eligible candidates are highly qualified individuals who possess established competence, relevant expertise and extensive professional experience in the field of human rights.

42. The following entities may nominate candidates as special procedures mandate-holders: (a) Governments; (b) Regional Groups operating within the United Nations human rights system; (c) international organizations or their offices (e.g. the Office of the High Commissioner for Human Rights); (d) non-governmental organizations; (e) other human rights bodies; (f) individual nominations.

43. The Office of the High Commissioner for Human Rights shall immediately prepare, maintain and periodically update a public list of eligible candidates in a standardized format, which shall include personal data, areas of expertise and professional experience. Upcoming vacancies of mandates shall be publicized.

44. The principle of non-accumulation of human rights functions at a time shall be respected.

45. A mandate-holder's tenure in a given function, whether a thematic or country mandate, will be no longer than six years (two terms of three years for thematic mandate-holders).

46. Individuals holding decision-making positions in Government or in any other organization or entity which may give rise to a conflict of interest with the responsibilities inherent to the mandate shall be excluded. Mandate-holders will act in their personal capacity.

47. A consultative group would be established to propose to the President, at least one month before the beginning of the session in which the Council would consider the selection of mandate-holders, a list of candidates who possess the highest qualifications for the mandates in question and meet the general criteria and particular requirements.

48. The consultative group shall also give due consideration to the exclusion of nominated candidates from the public list of eligible candidates brought to its attention.

49. At the beginning of the annual cycle of the Council, Regional Groups would be invited to appoint a member of the consultative group, who would serve in his/her personal capacity. The Group will be assisted by the Office of the High Commissioner for Human Rights.

50. The consultative group will consider candidates included in the public list; however, under exceptional circumstances and if a particular post justifies it, the Group may consider additional nominations with equal or more suitable qualifications for the post. Recommendations to the President shall be public and substantiated.

51. The consultative group should take into account, as appropriate, the views of stakeholders, including the current or outgoing mandate-holders, in determining the necessary expertise, experience, skills, and other relevant requirements for each mandate.

52. On the basis of the recommendations of the consultative group and following broad consultations, in particular through the regional coordinators, the President of the Council will identify an appropriate candidate for each vacancy. The President will present to member States and observers a list of candidates to be proposed at least two weeks prior to the beginning of the session in which the Council will consider the appointments.

53. If necessary, the President will conduct further consultations to ensure the endorsement of the proposed candidates. The appointment of the special procedures mandate-holders will be completed upon the subsequent approval of the Council. Mandate-holders shall be appointed before the end of the session.

The criteria which mandate-holders should meet according to HRC Resolution 5/1 were clarified as follows in Decision 6/102 of the Human Rights Council:

Human Rights Council, Decision 6/102. Follow-up to Human Rights Council Resolution 5/1 (27 September 2007):

1. Qualifications: relevant educational qualifications or equivalent professional experience in the field of human rights. Good communication skills in one of the UN languages.
2. Relevant expertise: knowledge of international human rights instruments, norms and principles; as well as knowledge of institutional mandates related to the United Nations or other international or regional organizations work in the area of human rights; proven work experience in the field of human rights.
3. Established competence: nationally, regionally or internationally recognized competence related to human rights.
4. Flexibility/readiness and availability of time to perform effectively the functions of the mandate and to respond to its requirements, including attending Human Rights Council sessions.

4.3 The code of conduct for special procedures of the Human Rights Council

Because of their independence and the flexibility with which they fulfil their mandate, as well as their ability to react immediately in urgent situations, particularly when they are an individual rather than a working group, the special procedures have not been popular with all States. Country-specific mandates in particular have created bitter feelings among States which have been subject to such monitoring. When the Human Rights Council was established, certain governments considered that the work of special procedures should be better codified, particularly in order to ensure that they remain within the limits set by the terms of the mandate. On 18 June 2007, acting on the basis of a proposal initially submitted by Algeria on behalf of the African Group, the Human Rights Council adopted Resolution 5/2, Code of Conduct for Special Procedures Mandate-holders of the Human Rights Council. The Code of Conduct purports to define 'the standards of ethical behaviour and professional conduct that special procedures mandate-holders of the Human Rights Council ... shall observe whilst discharging their mandates'. It recalls the principles of independence, truthfulness, loyalty and impartiality inherent in their mandate. Certain provisions of the Code of Conduct have been discussed intensively. Although the Code of Conduct confirms that the mandate-holders are entitled to privileges and immunities as provided for under relevant international instruments, including section 22 of Article VI of the Convention on the Privileges and Immunities of the United Nations, it also stipulates that 'the mandate-holders shall carry out their mandate while fully respecting the national legislation and regulations of the country wherein they are exercising their mission' (Article 4, para. 3). Under the Code of Conduct mandate-holders are also requested to 'give representatives of the concerned State the opportunity of commenting on mandate-holders' assessment and of responding to the allegations made against this State, and annex the State's written summary responses to their reports' (Article 8(d)); in addition, in presenting their views in public, they are expected to 'indicate fairly what responses were given by the concerned State'. Under Article 12 of the Code of Conduct, mandate-holders shall '(a) bear in mind the need to ensure that their personal political opinions are without prejudice to the execution of their mission, and base their conclusions and recommendations on objective assessments of human rights situations; (b) in implementing their mandate, therefore, show restraint, moderation and discretion so as not to undermine the recognition of the independent nature of their mandate or the environment necessary to properly discharge the said mandate'.

In the course of the discussions leading to the adoption of the Code of Conduct, the Co-ordination Committee of the Special Procedures presented a Note (dated 13 April 2007) in which it offered its views about the proposed code. The Note questioned the usefulness of the initiative of adopting a code of conduct. It also remarked that, if the objective of the Code of Conduct were to enhance the effectiveness of the special procedures, it would then be 'indispensable' to 'also address the responsibilities of Governments in terms of their cooperation with the Special Procedures system. This necessary balance [between the obligations of mandate-holders and those of governments] would best be achieved through the addition of an extra section' in the code identifying such responsibilities. The Note contained other, more detailed comments. For instance, as regards the obligation of mandate-holders to respect the national legislation of the countries in which they effectuate their missions, it proposed to add 'to the extent that these laws and regulations are consistent with human rights and the effective performance of the mandate holder's official functions'. Particular concern was expressed about the provisions, in a draft version of the Code of Conduct, which referred to the need to verify facts before relying on them:

Note by the Special Procedures' Co-ordination Committee in Response to Discussions on a Code of Conduct and Annex: Possible Elements of a Code of Conduct (13 April 2007):

The reference to verification of facts ... by mandate-holders is inappropriate in various respects. First, the primary task of mandate-holders is to identify situations of concern, rather than to act as judges who are able to verify facts. The role of the mandate-holder is to ensure a dialogue with the Government in relation to alleged violations. The act of verification or denial is one for the Government or for the courts of the relevant State, or for regional or UN human rights courts or treaty bodies. Second, the role of mandate-holders is generally described in the relevant resolutions as being humanitarian, rather than judicial, in nature. A requirement that every fact be 'verified' in any formal sense would ensure that almost no allegations, however well substantiated, could be relied upon by the mandate-holder. It would establish a higher standard of proof than applies even in criminal proceedings in the vast majority of countries. In essence, the use of the term 'verify' confuses the obligations of the Government with that of the mandate-holder. The provision should instead require mandate-holders to 'establish the facts, based on information which they believe to be objective and reliable'.

Article 8 of the Code of Conduct as adopted by the Human Rights Council takes into account this latter concern:

Human Rights Council, Resolution 5/2, Code of Conduct for Special Procedures Mandate-holders of the Human Rights Council (18 June 2007, Art. 8):

In their information-gathering activities the mandate-holders shall:

(a) Be guided by the principles of discretion, transparency, impartiality, and even-handedness;
(b) Preserve the confidentiality of sources of testimonies if their divulgation could cause harm to individuals involved;
(c) Rely on objective and dependable facts based on evidentiary standards that are appropriate to the non-judicial character of the reports and conclusions they are called upon to draw up;
(d) Give representatives of the concerned State the opportunity of commenting on mandate-holders' assessment and of responding to the allegations made against this State, and annex the State's written summary responses to their reports.

Following a number of instances in which individual mandate-holders of the Human Rights Council were accused, sometimes explicitly, of not complying with the Code of Conduct – concerns were expressed particularly by the non-aligned movement (NAM) and from the African Group – certain members of the Human Rights Council considered it necessary to strenghen their ability to ensure full respect for the Code of Conduct.

A first step was taken on 18 June 2008, when the Council adopted a Statement by its President entitled Terms in Office of Special Procedure Mandate-holders, in which it was announced that the President of the Human Rights Council would henceforth convey to the Council information brought to his/her attention including, *inter alia*, by States and/or by the Co-ordination Committee of Special Procedures, concerning cases of persistent non-compliance by a mandate-holder with the provisions of the HRC Resolution 5/2, especially prior to the renewal of mandate-holders in office. The Statement noted that, on the basis of such information, the Council would act upon it as appropriate; in the absence of such information, the terms in office of the mandate-holders shall be extended for a second three-year term by the Council.

Further tensions linked to specific mandate-holders and, particularly, to the role of country-specific rapporteurs or independent experts, led the Human Rights Council to adopt Resolution L.8 on 12 June 2009 (A/HRC/11/L.8). In that Resolution, the Human Rights Council 'reaffirms that the Code of Conduct for special procedures mandate holders is aimed at strengthening the capacity of mandate holders to exercise their functions while enhancing their moral authority and credibility, and that it requires supportive action by all stakeholders'. The Resolution 'recalls that it is incumbent on special procedures mandate holders to exercise their functions in full respect for and strict observance of their mandates, as outlined in the relevant Council resolutions establishing such mandates, without challenging or questioning them, as well as to comply fully with the provisions of the Code of Conduct, and that it is incumbent on the Office of the United Nations High Commissioner for Human Rights to further assist special procedures in that regard'. This followed attacks made in particular on the Special Rapporteur on extrajudicial, summary or arbitrary executions, Mr Philip Alston. Mr Alston conducted a mission to Kenya on 16–25 February 2009. Upon returning, he held a press conference, summarized as follows by the UN News Service:

UN News Service – UN rights expert calls on Kenya to confront 'widespread' police killings (25 February 2009):

A United Nations independent human rights expert today called on the President of Kenya to acknowledge, and take steps to end, what he called 'systematic, widespread and carefully planned' police killings in the East African country.

'Effective leadership on this issue can only come from the very top, and sweeping reforms to the policing sector should begin with the immediate dismissal of the Police Commissioner', Philip Alston, the UN Special Rapporteur on extrajudicial executions, said in a press statement released at the conclusion of a ten-day fact-finding mission.

'Further, given his role in encouraging the impunity that exists in Kenya, the Attorney General should resign so that the integrity of the office can be restored', he added.

Mr Alston, ... who reports to the UN Human Rights Council in an independent, unpaid capacity, concluded that police killings 'are committed at will and with utter impunity', after travelling the country and conducting interviews with over 100 victims and witnesses.

He concluded that death squads were set up upon the orders of senior police officials to exterminate the Mungiki, an underground religious sect reported by media to be responsible for a range of criminality in the capital, Nairobi.

He said he also found compelling evidence that the police and military committed organised torture and extrajudicial executions against civilians during a 2008 operation to flush out a militia known as the Sabaot Land Defence Force (SLDF).

'For two years, the SLDF militia terrorized the population and the Government did far too little. And when the Government did finally act, they responded with their own form of terror and brutality, killing over 200 people', he said, advocating for an independent investigation.

With respect to accountability for violence that followed disputed elections at the beginning of 2008, the Special Rapporteur stated that the Special Tribunal for Kenya was 'absolutely indispensable to ensure that Kenya does not again descend into chaos during the 2012 elections'.

He called on civil society and the international community to take a firm stand on the tribunal's establishment, adding that the International Criminal Court (ICC) should take up the case concurrently, on a parallel track.

Among other recommendations, Mr Alston called for the establishment of a civilian police oversight body, the centralization of records of police killings, and the payment of compensation for the victims of those unlawfully killed.

In addition to victims and witnesses, the Special Rapporteur also met during his visit with senior Government officials and representatives of the Kenya National Commission on Human Rights and independent national human rights institutions.

Ten days after these statements were made, on 5 March 2009, Oscar Kamau King'ara and John Paul Oulu were assassinated in Nairobi by people believed to be police officers. Both were witnesses the Special Rapporteur had spoken to during his recent mission. The Kenyan civil society organizations linked the killing of the two activists to the information they had given to Mr Alston.

At the interactive dialogue which took place at the Human Rights Council when the Special Rapporteur presented his report on Kenya, the Egyptian Ambassador, speaking on behalf of the African Group, accused Mr Alston of violating the Code of Conduct. On 10 June 2009, Mr Alston addressed the following letter to the President of the Human Rights Council:

Letter to the President of the Human Rights Council from the UN Special Rapporteur on extrajudicial, summary or arbitrary executions, Mr Philip Alston (10 June 2009):

Excellency,

I would like to take this opportunity to respond to the statement made on 8 June by the representative of Egypt on behalf of the African Group regarding alleged violations of the Code of Conduct in relation to my report on Kenya.

In its official statement to the Council on 3 June 2009, in response to my report, the Government of Kenya did not raise any issues concerning the Code of Conduct. Instead, it expressed its support for the process. In relation to my report, as well as those of other Special Procedures, it stated: 'We have found most of the recommendations contained in these reports on Kenya constructive and useful, and remain committed to fulfilling our obligations under the international instruments which we are party to.'

In the same statement, it added: 'It is intended that in the constitutional review process some of the concerns raised by Prof Alston ... will be addressed.'

However, at the end of a subsequent ministerial statement the Government did raise Code objections. These were then taken up in the African Group statement presented to the Council on 8 June. It is my understanding that the alleged violations of the Code of Conduct focused on the following concerns:

(a) It was stated that a press conference was held at the end of the mission without first consulting with the Government. The African Union statement also accuses me of announcing my report publicly before 'sharing it with the Government of Kenya'. These statements are factually wrong. My report states clearly in para. 2: 'A briefing on the contents of my preliminary findings was provided in person to the [then] Minister of Justice and a copy of the conclusions and recommendations presented at the press conference was provided well in advance to both the principal liaison officer for the mission, at the Ministry of Justice, as well as to the Ministry of Foreign Affairs.'

I would like to highlight that the holding of a Press Conference at the end of a mission is absolutely standard practice for all Special Rapporteurs and is not at all 'unprecedented', as claimed by the Government of Kenya.

(b) It was stated that I had not cooperated with the Kenyan Government during the mission. There was no such concern expressed to me by the Government at any stage during the mission. The allegation was only raised after the receipt of my final report in which I thanked the Government for its overall cooperation, but indicated that I did not consider that the police had cooperated in a meaningful way with my fact-finding endeavours, as required by my mandate.

(c) It has been stated that my recommendation that the Police Commissioner should be replaced, and that the Attorney General should resign, were 'illegal'. The African Group statement indicates that the Code of Conduct does not allow any Special Procedure 'to interfere in the appointment of public officials, let alone constitutional ones, in any country'. The Code of Conduct does not in fact address this issue. Where strong evidence provided to the Special Rapporteur indicates that a Police Commissioner is found to have presided over death squads with direct responsibility for the extrajudicial executions of at least several hundred persons, it would seem appropriate to recommend such a course of action to the Government of the day. This is not, however, to 'interfere in the appointment of public officials'. The recommendation is one for the Government itself to accept or reject.

(d) The Spokesman for Police Commissioner accused me of not writing my own report but instead using a text provided to me by the Kenyan National Commission on Human Rights (KNCHR). This statement is taken further by the African Group which says that my report is 'identical' to one written by the KNCHR and that, at a side event in Geneva on June 4, I 'admitted' that my own report had been given to me by the KNCHR. These claims are completely unfounded. There is not a single sentence in my report which has been plagiarized from the many reports prepared by the KNCHR. The members of that organization never provided me with as much as a single phrase or a paragraph which they wished to see included in my report. If they had, I would have rejected it as an interference with my independence. And the suggestion that I admitted such plagiarism at the side event is entirely false. I did no such thing.

I trust that the above will be of assistance in clarifying the actual manner in which my report was prepared in consultation with the concerned country.

Please accept, Excellency, the assurances of my sincere consideration.

[signed] Philip Alston

4.4 The tools used by the special procedures of the Human Rights Council

Although the tools used by the special procedures of the Human Rights Council are diverse and, because of their variety, defy systematization, three tools are relied upon most frequently by the special procedures established as individual mandates, particularly Special Rapporteurs and Independent Experts. These are communications sent to countries; country missions; and annual reports submitted to the Human Rights Council and, for some mandate-holders, to the General Assembly, where they are then presented before the Third Committee.

(a) Communications

When mandate-holders receive credible information about human rights violations or about the risk of violations, they may correspond with the government concerned to seek clarification about such allegations. This takes the form of a letter addressed to the State's permanent mission to the UN in Geneva, through the Office of the High Commissioner for Human Rights that supports the work of the special procedures. In principle, mandate-holders do not disclose from whom the information was received, which constitutes a protection from retaliation or reprisals. Victims of alleged violations or individuals or organizations having a direct knowledge of the alleged violations may correspond with the mandate-holder concerned, without there being an obligation to exhaust any domestic remedies available: the communications procedure is not a quasi-judicial procedure, rather it is a means to provide immediate protection to the victims, by drawing the attention of the government to certain situations.

Such communications may take the form either of urgent appeals or of letters of allegation. Urgent appeals are made 'in cases where the alleged violations are time-sensitive in terms of involving loss of life, life-threatening situations or either (*sic*) imminent or ongoing damage of a very grave nature to victims that cannot be addressed in a timely manner by the procedure under letters of allegation' (*Manual of Operations of the Human Rights Council Special Procedures* (August 2008), para. 43). Letters of allegation are used to communicate information about violations that are said to have already occurred and whose impact on the alleged victim can no longer be changed.

Whereas urgent appeals normally require a substantive response within thirty days – although in certain circumstances the mandate-holder may make a public statement prior to receiving that response – governments generally have two months to respond to letters of allegation. Each mandate-holder submits to the Human Rights Council, with his/her annual report, a report on the communications with governments; it is now envisaged that a joint report on communications will be prepared, which should facilitate the identification of patterns related to the co-operation (or lack thereof) of certain countries with the Special Procedures of the Human Rights Council. In 2008, letters of allegation represented 22 per cent of the total number of communications sent to governments by the special procedures; joint letters of allegation represented 23 per cent of that total; urgent appeals represented 12 per cent; and joint urgent appeals, 43 per cent.

Manual of Operations of the Human Rights Council Special Procedures (August 2008), paras. 28–37:

28. Most Special Procedures provide for the relevant mandate-holders to receive information from different sources and to act on credible information by sending a communication to the relevant Government(s). Such communications are sent through diplomatic channels, unless agreed otherwise between individual Governments and the Office of the High Commissioner for Human Rights, in relation to any actual or anticipated human rights violations which fall within the scope of their mandate.

29. Communications may deal with cases concerning individuals, groups or communities, with general trends and patterns of human rights violations in a particular country or more generally, or with the content of existing or draft legislation considered to be a matter of concern. Communications related to adopted or draft legislation may be formulated in various ways, as required by the specificities of each mandate.

30. Communications do not imply any kind of value judgment on the part of the Special Procedure concerned and are thus not per se accusatory. They are not intended as a substitute for judicial or other proceedings at the national level. Their main purpose is to obtain clarification in response to allegations of violations and to promote measures designed to protect human rights ...

36. In light of information received in response from the Government concerned, or of further information from sources, the mandate-holder will determine how best to proceed. This might include the initiation of further inquiries, the elaboration of recommendations or observations to be published in the relevant report, or other appropriate steps designed to achieve the objectives of the mandate.

37. The text of all communications sent and responses received thereon is confidential until such time as they are published in relevant reports of mandate-holders or mandate-holders determine that the specific circumstances require action to be taken before that time. Periodic reports issued by the Special Procedures should reflect the communications sent by mandate-holders and annex the governments' responses thereto. They may also contain observations of the mandate-holders in relation to the outcome of the dialogue with the Government. The names of alleged victims are normally reflected in the reports, although

exceptions may be made in relation to children and other victims of violence in relation to whom publication of names would be problematic.

Office of the High Commissioner for Human Rights, Special Procedures Facts and Figures 2008 (2009):

The decision to intervene is at the discretion of the special procedure mandate holder and depends on criteria established by him or her, as well as the criteria laid out in the Code of Conduct adopted by the Human Rights Council (Resolution 5/2 of 18 June 2007). Criteria generally relate to the reliability of the source and the credibility of information; the details provided; and the scope of the mandate itself. Further information is frequently requested from sources. Communications should not be politically motivated, abusive or based solely on media reports. Mandate holders may send joint communications when the case falls within the scope of more than one mandate. The OHCHR's Special Procedures Division Quick Response Desk coordinates communications and keeps relevant databases updated.

(b) Country visits

Although the mandate-holders of the Human Rights Council routinely travel abroad to hold consultations or take part in seminars or other public events, they may also conduct official missions in order to examine the situation of human rights (as related to their mandate) at national level. Such missions request the consent of the State in which they take place, and they lead to a report being prepared on the country, which is presented to the Human Rights Council after the government concerned has been provided an opportunity to comment. Mandate-holders typically ask to be invited to the country on official mission, although occasionally a government may take the initiative of inviting a mandate-holder to visit the country. A number of countries (sixty-three on 31 December 2008) have issued standing invitations to Special Procedures – increasingly as a result of pledges made when presenting a candidacy to be elected to the Human Rights Council – but even concerning those countries, the dates of the visit must be agreed with the authorities before they can take place. In 2008, special procedures mandate-holders conducted fifty-three fact-finding missions to forty-eight countries.

Office of the High Commissioner for Human Rights, Special Procedures Facts and Figures 2008 (2009):

During such missions, the experts assess the general human rights situation in a given country, as well as the specific institutional, legal, judicial, administrative and *de facto* situation under their respective mandates. During the country visit the experts will meet with national and local authorities, including members of the judiciary and parliamentarians; members of the national human rights institution, if applicable; non-governmental organizations, civil society organizations and victims of human rights violations; the UN and other inter-governmental agencies; and the press when giving a press-conference at the end of the mission. After their visits, special procedures' mandate-holders issue a mission report to the Human Rights Council including their findings and recommendations.

Terms of Reference for Fact-finding Missions by Special Rapporteurs/ Representatives of the Commission on Human Rights (Appendix V, E/CN.4/1998/45):

During fact-finding missions, special rapporteurs or representatives of the Commission on Human Rights, as well as United Nations staff accompanying them, should be given the following guarantees and facilities by the Government that invited them to visit its country:

(a) Freedom of movement in the whole country, including facilitation of transport, in particular to restricted areas;
(b) Freedom of inquiry, in particular as regards:

(i) Access to all prisons, detention centres and places of interrogation;
(ii) Contacts with central and local authorities of all branches of government;
(iii) Contacts with representatives of non-governmental organizations, other private institutions and the media;
(iv) Confidential and unsupervised contact with witnesses and other private persons, including persons deprived of their liberty, considered necessary to fulfil the mandate of the special rapporteur; and
(v) Full access to all documentary material relevant to the mandate;

(c) Assurance by the Government that no persons, official or private individuals who have been in contact with the special rapporteur/representative in relation to the mandate will for this reason suffer threats, harassment or punishment or be subjected to judicial proceedings;
(d) Appropriate security arrangements without, however, restricting the freedom of movement and inquiry referred to above;
(e) Extension of the same guarantees and facilities mentioned above to the appropriate United Nations staff who will assist the special rapporteur/representative before, during and after the visit.

(c) Annual reports

Probably the most visible contribution of special procedures at international level are the reports they submit, at least on an annual basis, to the Human Rights Council, and – for some, but not all special procedures – to the General Assembly (Third Committee).

In 2008, the special procedures' mandate-holders submitted 135 reports to the Human Rights Council (120 by thematic mandate-holders), including 79 annual reports and 56 country visits reports, and 19 reports to the General Assembly. The annual reports contain an overview of the activities conducted by the mandate-holder in fulfilment of his/her mandate, and a set of recommendations addressed to governments or, occasionally, to other actors, including to the UN agencies. The reports are discussed in an 'interactive dialogue' with the delegates to the Human Rights Council or the Third Committee of the General Assembly. This interactive dialogue is based on an initial presentation by the mandate-holders, followed by the observations of the governments, and final remarks by the mandate-holder.

Manual of Operations of the Human Rights Council Special Procedures (August 2008), paras. 84–6:

84. Mandate-holders report on their activities on a regular basis to the relevant United Nations bodies, and particularly the HRC and the GA. With regard to the recommendations contained in their reports, mandate holders should ensure that they recommendations do not exceed their mandate or the mandate of the HRC. Recommendations may also serve to bring to the attention of the Council any suggestions of the mandate holder which will enhance his or her capacity to fulfill the mandate ...

86. An inter-active dialogue constitutes an important element in the presentation of reports by mandate-holders. Mandate holders present their reports to the HRC, and in some cases to the GA, and States are given the opportunity to respond to the contents of the reports and to pose questions to the mandate holders. Such dialogues are considered to be an integral part of cooperation between mandate holders and States.

10.1. Questions for discussion: the UN Charter-based mechanisms

1. When they present their candidacy to the Human Rights Council, States make 'pledges', which then may be relied upon in the context of the Universal Periodic Review. To what extent does this ensure that the Human Rights Council will be composed only of States dedicated to the promotion and protection of human rights? Consider the pledges made by the United States when applying for membership of the Council in April 2009. Are such pledges a significant progress?

2. How significant is the risk of overlap between the role of the Human Rights Council and that of the UN human rights treaty bodies and the special procedures established by the Human Rights Council? Which safeguards should be put in place to ensure that the UPR does not develop into an appeals chamber for States unwilling to recognize the authority of the findings of independent human rights experts? Consider the following summary of how the risk of overlap and, hence, competition, could be avoided:

Sir Nigel Rodley, 'The United Nations Human Rights Council, Its Special Procedures, and Its Relationship with the Treaty Bodies: Complementarity or Competition?' in K. Boyle (ed.), *New Institutions for Human Rights Protection* (Oxford University Press, 2009), p. 49 at p. 55:

One [suggestion], considered but not retained during the discussions leading to the institution-building package, would have focused UPR on the extent to which states had actually implemented recommendations of the treaty bodies and special procedures ... Another suggestion ... would have been for UPR to avoid reviewing an issue covered by a treaty obligation with regard to which the state is up to date with its reporting obligations, limiting such a consideration to the activities of the state to give effect to the recommendations. Yet a further variation ... would have been for the outcome to avoid arriving at 'conclusions' in respect of the treaty obligations just mentioned, restricting the outcome to recommendations. This was based on the probability that competing assessments of human rights performance as could be expected to be reflected in 'conclusions' could be more harmful to the promotion of human rights than would non-identical recommendations on how to address a specific human rights problem.

3. Does the UPR serve to undermine the human rights obligations of States rather than to strengthen them? Consider the response of the United Kingdom to the suggestion by Switzerland that they should accept that any person detained by their armed forces is under UK jurisdiction (Recommendation 16). The United Kingdom states that it does not accept this recommendation, although it corresponds, arguably, to an obligation under international human rights law (see chapter 2). How serious is this difficulty?

4. Could the emergence of the UPR be interpreted as a shift from a 'vertical' supervision of human rights, as performed by independent expert bodies, to a 'horizontal' supervision of human rights, by the States themselves? To what extent is the UPR evidence of such a shift occurring? How significant is it, for instance, that a number of the recommendations addressed to States undergoing the UPR relate to the reservations they have made to the human rights treaties they have ratified, whereas it is precisely because of the failure of the States to monitor effectively the reservations entered by other parties to multilateral treaties that the Human Rights Committee took the view that it could assess the validity of the reservations to the International Covenant on Civil and Political Rights?

5 According to Resolution 60/251 of the General Assembly, the Human Rights Council shall be reviewed within five years of its establishment, and the Council itself is directed to undertake a review of its work in 2011 or 2012. Which benchmarks should such a review rely upon? How should the effectiveness of the Council in fulfilling its functions be evaluated? Could you propose indicators for such an evaluation?

11

Regional Mechanisms of Protection

INTRODUCTION

This chapter reviews a number of questions raised by the protection of human rights at a regional level. It does not offer a systematic treatment of how the Universal Declaration of Human Rights has been implemented in the regional context; nor does it examine in detail the working methods or case law of regional human rights courts or expert bodies established at regional level. This case law has been presented in chapters 3–7, which examined the content of States' obligations to respect, protect and fulfil human rights without discrimination. In those chapters, the contribution of regional courts or non-judicial bodies has been analysed alongside that of bodies established at the international level, in order to describe the content of the emerging *jus commune* in the field of human rights. As to the overall context, it has been briefly recalled in chapter 1, section 2, which discussed the role of human rights in the Council of Europe, the Organization of American States, and the African Union.

Instead, this chapter aims to review a set of core questions raised at regional level, that remained unaddressed in the previous chapters. It is divided into three sections, corresponding respectively to the Council of Europe, the Organization of American States, and the African Union (formerly Organization of African Unity). The materials presented seek to identify some of the challenges that regional courts have been facing. They address the role of these jurisdictions in the development of the *jus commune* of human rights, as well as the solutions these courts have developed to ensure the effective implementation of their judgments. In addition, the section on the Council of Europe provides a presentation of the role of the European Committee on Social Rights (ECSR), established under the European Social Charter. The ECSR is chosen as an illustration of one expert body established at regional level, operating roughly along the lines of the UN human rights treaty bodies: the discussion addresses the relationship between the function of the Committee in receiving reports from the States parties to the Charter and its function in receiving collective complaints, and the nature of the collective complaints mechanism itself.

The European Court of Human Rights and the Inter-American Court of Human Rights constitute the two most mature and well-developed systems of judicial protection of human rights at regional level (among the most useful recent textbooks on the European Convention on Human Rights and the contribution of the European Court of Human Rights, see S. Greer, *The European Convention on Human Rights. Achievements, Problems and Prospects* (Cambridge University Press, 2006); D. Harris, M. O'Boyle, E. Bates and C. Buckley, *Law of the European Convention on Human Rights*, second edn (Oxford University Press, 2009); and P. van Dijk, F. van Hoof, A. van Rijn and L. Zwaak (eds.), *Theory and Practice of the European Convention on Human Rights*, fourth edn (Antwerp: Intersentia, 2006); for important studies on the Inter-American human rights system, see T. Buergenthal and D. Shelton (eds.), *Protecting Human Rights in the Americas: Cases and Materials*, fourth edn (Kehl am Rhein: N. P. Engel, 1995); T. Buergenthal, *La protección de los derechos humanos en las Américas* (Madrid: Instituto Interamericano de Derechos Humanos, 1990); S. Davidson, *The Inter-American Court of Human Rights* (Aldershot: Dartmouth, 1992); S. Davidson, *The Inter-American Human Rights System* (Aldershot: Dartmouth, 1997); D. Harris and S. Livingstone (eds.), *The Inter-American System of Human Rights* (Oxford: Oxford University Press and Clarendon Press, 1998); L. Hennebel, *La Convention américaine des droits de l'homme. Mécanismes de protection et étendue des droits et libertés* (Brussels: Bruylant, 2007); C. Medina Ortega, *The Battle of Human Rights: Gross Systematic Violations and the Inter-American System* (Leiden: Martinus Nijhoff, 1988)). Both the European and Inter-American courts have a long and largely successful record behind them: the European Court of Human Rights delivered its first judgment on the merits in 1961, while the first judgment of the Inter-American Court of Human Rights intervened in 1989. For these two Courts, as we shall see, the questions of effective implementation of their judgments and their ability to function effectively in the context of an exponential increase in the number of applications they receive have become of vital importance.

In contrast, the African Court of Human and Peoples' Rights is still in its infancy: the Protocol to the African Charter on Human and Peoples' Rights on the African Court of Human and Peoples' Rights (Ouagadougou Protocol) was signed in 1998, and entered into force on 25 January 2004; the first judges to sit on the Court were elected in 2006, but at the time of writing, the Court had only delivered one judgment, on 15 December 2009, on a communication filed in August 2008. As to the African Commission on Human and Peoples' Rights, although it was established in 1987 following the entry into force, on 21 October 1986, of the 1981 African Charter on Human and Peoples' Rights (Banjul Charter), its powers are limited under the Charter and its visibility has remained relatively low (for the most significant studies on the development of the African Charter of Human and Peoples' Rights, see E. A. Ankumah, *The African Commission: Practice and Procedures* (The Hague: Martinus Nijhoff, 1996); M. Evans and R. Murray (eds.), *The African Charter on Human and Peoples' Rights: the System in Practice 1986–2000* (Cambridge University Press, 2002); R. Murray, *Human Rights in Africa: From the OAU to the African Union* (Cambridge University Press, 2004); M. Mubiala, *Le système régional africain de protection des droits de l'homme* (Brussels: Bruylant, 2005); N. S. Rembe, *Africa and Regional Protection of Human Rights: a Study of the African Charter on Human and Peoples' Rights. Its Effectiveness and Impact on the African States* (Rome: Leoni editore, 1985); K. M'Baye, *Les droits de l'homme en Afrique* (Paris: CIJ, Pedone, 1992); O. C. Eze, *Human Rights in Africa: Some Selected Problems* (Lagos: Nigerian Institute of International Affairs, Macmillan Nigeria Publishers, 1984); F. Viljoen, *International Human Rights Law in Africa* (Oxford University Press, 2007); and F. Viljoen, 'The African Regional Human Rights System' in C. Krause and M. Scheinin (eds.), *International Protection of Human Rights: a Textbook* (Turku: Åbo Akademi University Institute for Human Rights, 2009, p. 503)).

1 THE EUROPEAN SYSTEM OF PROTECTION OF HUMAN RIGHTS

1.1 The original system: before Protocol No. 11 restructuring the control machinery of the European Convention on Human Rights

In its original version as adopted on 4 November 1950 within the framework of the newly established Council of Europe (for the context in which the Convention was adopted, see chapter 1, section 2.1.), the European Convention on Human Rights (ECHR) established both the European Commission and the European Court of Human Rights. The Commission's competence was to receive applications submitted either by alleged victims of violations of the Convention or, more rarely, by States, and to examine their admissibility, including whether they were 'manifestly ill-founded', i.e. obviously lacking merit. If it considered the application admissible, the Commission then prepared a report in which it stated its opinion as to whether the Convention had been violated, and it directed the case either to a political body, the Committee of Ministers of the Council of Europe, or to the European Court of Human Rights.

The procedure thus established was revolutionary at the time for two reasons. First, inter-State applications were allowed, making it possible for each State party to the Convention to file an application against another State party, even when the violation alleged does not affect its nationals (as in the classic case of diplomatic protection), and without having to show otherwise that it has been prejudiced by the alleged violation: thus, a form of *actio popularis* was instituted in favour of the States parties to the Convention, leading the European Court on Human Rights to remark that 'the Convention comprises more than mere reciprocal engagements between Contracting States' since it 'creates, over and above a network of mutual, bilateral undertakings, objective obligations which ... benefit from a "collective enforcement"' (Eur. Ct. H.R., *Ireland v. United Kingdom* judgment of 18 January 1978, Series A No. 25, p. 90). Second, for the first time, individuals had access to a remedy before an international procedure, although they were not initially allowed to file a direct application with the Court (that was the sole prerogative of the European Commission, who played a role similar to that of an Advocate General before the Court), and although initially both the possibility for individuals to file applications before the Commission and the jurisdiction of the Court were optional. Under Article 32 ECHR, when the State concerned had not recognized the jurisdiction of the Court, or when, three months after the notification of the report submitted by the Commission on the merits, the case had not been transmitted to the Court for resolution (both the Commission and the State party concerned could choose to bring the case before the Court), the Committee of Ministers of the Council of Europe (thus a political organ) was allowed to take a decision as to whether or not the Convention had been violated. The considerations that guided the adoption of this compromise in the original text of the ECHR have been summarized as follows:

Explanatory Report to Protocol No. 11 to the Convention for the Protection of Human Rights and Fundamental Freedoms, restructuring the control machinery established thereby (1994):

6. The idea of a European Convention on Human Rights to be implemented by a Court to which individuals would have access can be traced back to the Congress of Europe, convened by the International Committee of Movements for European Unity and held at The Hague from 8 to 10 May 1948. In their 'Message to Europeans' adopted at the final plenary session, the Congress delegates pledged *inter alia*:

'2. We desire a Charter of Human Rights guaranteeing liberty of thought, assembly and expression as well as the right to form a political opposition;

3. We desire a Court of Justice with adequate sanctions for the implementation of this Charter;'

The Resolution adopted by the Congress on the proposal of its Political Committee should also be noted:

'The Congress –

6. Is convinced that in the interest of human values and human liberty, the [proposed] Assembly should make proposals for the establishment of a Court of Justice with adequate sanctions for the implementation of this Charter [of Human Rights], and to this end any citizen of the associated countries shall have redress before the Court, at any time and with the least possible delay, of any violation of his rights as formulated in the Charter.'

7. The idea of a Human Rights Charter and a Court of Justice was subsequently examined in depth by the European Movement, which on 12 July 1949 submitted the text of a draft European Convention on Human Rights to the Committee of Ministers. This text notably made provision not only for a Court but also for a Human Rights Commission, to which litigants would first have to submit their case. It was foreseen that this body would be empowered to reject without investigation petitions from individuals who had failed to exhaust domestic remedies and that, moreover, its authorisation would be required for an individual to initiate proceedings before the Court.

The proposal for a Human Rights Commission, in addition to a Court, was made to counter the criticism that the latter would be inundated with frivolous litigation and its facilities exploited for political ends. The subsequent debates in the Consultative (now renamed 'Parliamentary') Assembly and the bodies established by the Committee of Ministers to draw up the Convention confirmed that these fears were deeply felt.

8. The creation of a European Commission of Human Rights was in fact not a contentious issue during the drafting of the Convention. On the other hand, there was considerable opposition to the creation of a Court, it being argued that it would not correspond to a real need of the member States. Articles 46 and 48 of the Convention [providing that the jurisdiction of the Court is optional] represented a compromise between this position and that of those States which felt the creation of a Court was essential (the controversy over whether individuals should have the right to address petitions to the Commission was, of course, settled in a similar way).

9. The net result was the tripartite structure, which entered into force on 3 September 1953: the Commission – to consider the admissibility of petitions, to establish the facts, to promote friendly settlements and, if appropriate, to give an opinion as to whether or not the petitions reveal a violation of the Convention; the Court – to give a final and binding judgment on cases referred to it by the Commission or by a Contracting Party concerned; the Committee of Ministers – to give a final and binding decision on cases which cannot be referred to the Court or which, for one reason or another, are not referred to it.

1.2 The system reformed: Protocol No. 11 restructuring the control machinery of the European Convention on Human Rights

Significant changes were made to the Convention in recent years. In 1994, with the entry into force of Protocol No. 9, individuals were authorized to refer a case directly to the Court, at least insofar as their application was filed against a State party to the Protocol. On 1 November 1998, Protocol No. 11 to the Convention for the Protection of Human Rights and Fundamental Freedoms, restructuring the control machinery established thereby, entered into force, bringing about fundamental changes to the supervisory system. One single and permanent Court was established, taking over the responsibilities previously assumed by the Commission, although one of the functions of the latter – to provide the Court with an independent opinion on the case pending before it, in the manner of an Advocate General – was abandoned. In contrast with the earlier system, but consistent with what had become the general practice among the States parties to the Convention (which, by the time Protocol No. 11 was adopted, had all made a declaration accepting the filing of individual communications and the jurisdiction of the Court), both the jurisdiction of the Court and its competence to receive individual applications became compulsory for all the States parties to the Convention. While the Committee of Ministers preserved its role in supervising compliance with the judgments of the Court – now under Article 46(2) ECHR – it was deprived of the quasi-judicial function it had previously exercised under Article 32 of the original Convention.

(a) The admissibility phase

Under the current system, then, individual applications are filed directly with the Court. Any victim of the violation alleged may file an application: the victim may be an individual, a non-governmental organization, or a group of individuals, but only the individual(s) or organization directly aggrieved shall have access to the Court. Thus, although in some exceptional cases the family members of the victim may act on his/her behalf, no form of *actio popularis* is admitted (Art. 34 ECHR). In addition, although this occurs comparatively much more rarely, inter-State applications are allowed (Art. 33 ECHR). The admissibility criteria are set out in Article 35 of the Convention:

European Convention on Human Rights, Article 35 – Admissibility criteria

1. The Court may only deal with the matter after all domestic remedies have been exhausted, according to the generally recognised rules of international law, and within a period of six months from the date on which the final decision was taken.

2. The Court shall not deal with any application submitted under Article 34 that:

- is anonymous; or
- is substantially the same as a matter that has already been examined by the Court or has already been submitted to another procedure of international investigation or settlement and contains no relevant new information.

3. The Court shall declare inadmissible any individual application submitted under Article 34 if it considers that:

a. the application is incompatible with the provisions of the Convention or the Protocols thereto, manifestly ill-founded, or an abuse of the right of individual application; or

b. the applicant has not suffered a significant disadvantage, unless respect for human rights as defined in the Convention and the Protocols thereto requires an examination of the application on the merits and provided that no case may be rejected on this ground which has not been duly considered by a domestic tribunal.

4. The Court shall reject any application which it considers inadmissible under this Article. It may do so at any stage of the proceedings.

The condition according to which the local remedies available should be exhausted prior to the filing of an application before an international court corresponds to a general principle of international law (on this rule in international law, see C. F. Amerasinghe, *Local Remedies in International Law* (Cambridge University Press, 1990); A. A. Cançado Trindade, *The Application of the Rule of Exhaustion of Local Remedies. Its Rationale in the International Protection of Human Rights* (Cambridge University Press, 1983)). Whether or not the alleged victim should have used a particulary remedy available before domestic authorities, however, depends on whether such remedy is effective. There exists, thus, a complementarity between the requirement imposed on the State to provide an effective remedy and the rule requiring the exhaustion of local remedies prior to the filing of an application before the Court. This complementarity clearly expresses the principle of subsidiarity of international judicial supervision, which the European Court of Human Rights often refers to. It has been made explicit by the European Court of Human Rights, for instance, in the 2000 judgment of *Kudła* v. *Poland*.

The background to the *Kudła* v. *Poland* case may be described as follows. The ECHR contains both a provision containing a number of guarantees related to the right to a fair trial, that applies to all criminal accusations and disputes relating to civil rights or obligations (Art. 6 ECHR), and a provision guaranteeing access to an effective remedy for any person making an arguable claim that he/she is a victim of a violation of the rights established in the Convention (Art. 13 ECHR) (on the right to an effective remedy, see chapter 8, section 1.1.). In its earlier case law, the European Court of Human Rights considered that, since Article 6 ECHR (fair trial) is more detailed than the right to an effective remedy of Article 13 ECHR, the guarantees afforded by the latter provision are 'absorbed' by those stipulated in the former, in situations where both provisions are equally applicable – i.e. in criminal procedures or in procedures relating to civil rights and obligations that arguably also may result in violations of the ECHR. The implication, the Court considered, was that in those cases only Article 6 ECHR should apply: any invocation of Article 13 ECHR would be redundant, as it could not offer the individual a higher degree of protection. Revisiting its previous doctrine on the subject, the Court in *Kudła* holds instead that, where the requirement that trials be conducted within a reasonable time (stipulated in Article 6 ECHR as part of broader fair trial guarantees) is allegedly not complied with, the individual should be guaranteed access to an 'effective remedy' under Article 13 ECHR: the 'effective remedy' clause thus complements the protection afforded under Article 6 ECHR, as far as the 'reasonable time' requirement is concerned. The Court explains its decision by the contribution that access to effective domestic remedies can make to alleviating the workload of the Court, in accordance with the principle of subsidiarity underlying the relationship between national authorities and international judicial supervision in the Convention.

European Court of Human Rights (GC), *Kudła* v. *Poland* (Appl. No. 30210/96) judgment of 26 October 2000, para. 152:

[T]he place of Article 13 in the scheme of human rights protection set up by the Convention would argue in favour of implied restrictions of Article 13 being kept to a minimum.

By virtue of Article 1 (which provides: 'The High Contracting Parties shall secure to everyone within their jurisdiction the rights and freedoms defined in Section I of this Convention'), the primary responsibility for implementing and enforcing the guaranteed rights and freedoms is laid on the national authorities. The machinery of complaint to the Court is thus subsidiary to national systems safeguarding human rights. This subsidiary character is articulated in Articles 13 and 35 §1 of the Convention.

The purpose of Article 35 §1, which sets out the rule on exhaustion of domestic remedies, is to afford the Contracting States the opportunity of preventing or putting right the violations alleged against them before those allegations are submitted to the Court (see, as a recent authority, *Selmouni* v. *France* [GC], No. 25803/94, §74, ECHR 1999-V). The rule in Article 35 §1 is based on the assumption, reflected in Article 13 (with which it has a close affinity), that there is an effective domestic remedy available in respect of the alleged breach of an individual's Convention rights (*ibid.*).

In that way, Article 13, giving direct expression to the States' obligation to protect human rights first and foremost within their own legal system, establishes an additional guarantee for an individual in order to ensure that he or she effectively enjoys those rights. The object of Article 13, as emerges from the *travaux préparatoires* (see the *Collected Edition of the 'Travaux Préparatoires' of the European Convention on Human Rights*, vol. II, pp. 485 and 490, and vol. III, p. 651), is to provide a means whereby individuals can obtain relief at national level for violations of their Convention rights before having to set in motion the international machinery of complaint before the Court.

(b) The merits phase and the supervision of the execution of judgments

In practice, a large percentage of applications filed with the Court (above 90 per cent in a typical year) are rejected at the admissibility stage. In the new system established in 1998 by Protocol No. 11, the decision finding an application inadmissible may be adopted either by a Chamber of seven judges, or by a committee of three judges, if they are unanimous, and without justification. In addition, since the entry into force on 1 June 2010 of Protocol No. 14 (CETS No. 194), it is possible for a single judge, assisted by rapporteurs who are members of the Court's registry, to declare cases inadmissible, including if 'the applicant has not suffered a significant disadvantage, unless respect for human rights as defined in the Convention and the Protocols thereto requires an examination of the application on the merits and provided that no case may be rejected on this ground which has not been duly considered by a domestic tribunal' (Art. 35, para. 3, b)). If an application is found admissible, a judgment on the merits may be adopted by a Chamber or, if the question of interpretation or application of the Convention is one that is already the subject of a well-established case law of the Court, a committee of three judges, in the revised system introduced by Protocol No. 14. After a judgment on the merits is delivered by a Chamber, a period of three months is open, during which any party may request that the case be referred to a Grand Chamber of seventeen judges; the request for a referral is examined by a panel of five judges, who are directed by the Convention to accept the request 'if the case raises a serious question affecting the interpretation or application of the Convention or the protocols thereto, or a serious issue of general importance' (Art. 43(2) ECHR). In practice, few requests for referral are accepted. The judgments delivered by the Court thus become final either (1) if it is adopted by a committee of three judges acting unanimously, or (2) three months after the delivery of the judgment by a Chamber, unless a party has requested a referral to the Grand Chamber, or (3) if the request for a referral is rejected, or (4) if the judgment is delivered by the Grand Chamber.

In cases where the Court arrives at the conclusion that the Convention has been violated, the supervision of the execution of the judgments is left to the Council of Europe Committee of Ministers. Before adopting a resolution which closes the file, the Committee examines whether the State had paid the amount awarded by the Court as a 'just satisfaction' to the victim, or whether the victim has been replaced in the situation he/she would have found him/herself in the absence of a violation of the Convention (*restitutio in integrum*). In addition, it examines whether the State has taken general measures to ensure that new, similar violations of the Convention will not recur in the future.

Committee of Ministers of the Council of Europe, Supervision of the execution of judgments of the European Court of Human Rights, second annual report, April 2009:

16. The scope of the execution measures required is defined in each case primarily on the basis of the conclusions of the [European Court of Human Rights – ECtHR] in its judgment and relevant information about the domestic situation. In certain situations, it may be necessary to await further decisions by the ECtHR clarifying outstanding issues (e.g. decisions declaring new,

similar complaints inadmissible as general reforms adopted are found to be effective or decisions concluding that the applicant continues to suffer the violation established or its consequences).

17. As regards the payment of just satisfaction, the execution conditions are usually laid down with considerable detail in the ECtHR's judgments (deadline, recipient, currency, default interest, etc.) ...

18. As regards the nature and scope of other execution measures, whether individual or general, the judgments usually remain silent. These measures have thus in principle, as has been stressed also by the ECtHR on numerous occasions, to be identified by the state itself under the supervision of the [Committee of Ministers of the Council of Europe – CM]. Besides the different considerations enumerated in the preceding paragraph, national authorities may find additional guidance *inter alia* in the rich practice of other states as developed over the years, and in relevant CM recommendations (e.g. Recommendation (2000)2 on the re-examination or reopening [of certain cases at domestic level following judgments of the European Court of Human Rights] or (2004)6 on the improvement of domestic remedies [for this Recommendation, see chapter 8, section 1.1.]).

19. This situation is explained by the principle of subsidiarity, by virtue of which respondent states have freedom of choice as regards the means to be employed in order to meet their obligations under the ECHR. However this freedom goes hand-in-hand with the CM's control so that in the course of its supervision of execution the CM may also, where appropriate, adopt decisions or interim resolutions to express concern, encourage and/or make suggestions with respect to the execution.

20. In certain circumstances, however, it might happen that the ECtHR in its judgment provide itself guidance as to relevant execution measures. The ECtHR has thus recently provided recommendations as to individual or even general measures it considered as appropriate. Furthermore, sometimes the ECtHR directly orders the taking of the relevant measure. The first cases of this kind were decided by the ECtHR in 2004–2005: in both the ECtHR ordered the release of applicants who were being arbitrarily detained [see *Assanidze* v. *Georgia*, judgment of 8 April 2004 and *Ilascu* v. *Moldova and the Russian Federation*, judgment of 13 May 2005. The Court had previously developed some practice in this direction in certain property cases by indicating in the operative provisions that States could choose between restitution and compensation – see e.g. the *Papamichalopoulos and others* v. *Greece* judgment of 31 October 1995 (Art. 50)]. Moreover, in the context of the 'pilot' judgment procedure the ECtHR examines more in detail the causes of certain systemic problems likely to lead to, or having already led to, a massive influx of new applications and provides certain recommendations as to general measures, most importantly as regards the necessity of setting up efficient domestic remedies. The ECtHR has in certain 'pilot' judgments [see, for instance, *Broniowski* v. *Poland* (Appl. No. 31443/96; Grand Chamber judgment of 22 June 2004 – pilot judgment procedure brought to an end on 6 October 2008 (see below in this section)); *Hutten-Czapska* v. *Poland* (Appl. No. 35014/97, Grand Chamber judgment of 19 June 2006 and Grand Chamber friendly settlement of 28 April 2008)] also ordered that such remedies be set up and has 'frozen' its examination of all pending applications while waiting that the remedies start to function.

With the increase over the last decade of the number of applications to the Court, the supervisory role of the Committee of Ministers has become a heavy burden. According to the second annual report of the Committee of Ministers on the supervision of the execution of judgments of the European Court of Human Rights, in 2008, 1,384 new judgments finding violations of the Convention on Human Rights were brought before the Committee for supervision of their execution. This brought the number of pending cases to 6,614. The compensation awarded to the victims in these new judgments amounted to some €55.5 million.

One particularly delicate issue in recent years has been whether, in order to execute the judgments of the European Court of Human Rights faithfully, States should allow a derogation to the principle of *res judicata*, and agree to reopen a case closed at domestic level. For example, where a person has been sentenced to a term in prison following a trial found by the European Court of Human Rights to have been held under unfair conditions, in violation of Article 6 ECHR, should a new trial be held? Where divorce proceedings have been conducted under rules found by the Court to be discriminatory, should those proceedings be reopened? The Committee of Ministers adopted the following recommendation on this issue:

Recommendation No. R (2000) 2 of the Committee of Ministers to Member States on the re-examination or reopening of certain cases at domestic level following judgments of the European Court of Human Rights (adopted by the Committee of Ministers on 19 January 2000 at the 694th meeting of the Ministers' Deputies):

The Committee of Ministers, ... [n]oting that under Article 46 of the Convention on Human Rights and Fundamental Freedoms the Contracting Parties have accepted the obligation to abide by the final judgment of the European Court of Human Rights in any case to which they are parties and that the Committee of Ministers shall supervise its execution;

Bearing in mind that in certain circumstances the above-mentioned obligation may entail the adoption of measures, other than just satisfaction awarded by the Court in accordance with Article 41 of the Convention and/or general measures, which ensure that the injured party is put, as far as possible, in the same situation as he or she enjoyed prior to the violation of the Convention (*restitutio in integrum*);

Noting that it is for the competent authorities of the respondent State to decide what measures are most appropriate to achieve *restitutio in integrum*, taking into account the means available under the national legal system;

Bearing in mind, however, that the practice of the Committee of Ministers in supervising the execution of the Court's judgments shows that in exceptional circumstances the re-examination of a case or a reopening of proceedings has proved the most efficient, if not the only, means of achieving *restitutio in integrum*;

I. Invites, in the light of these considerations the Contracting Parties to ensure that there exist at national level adequate possibilities to achieve, as far as possible, *restitutio in integrum*;

II. Encourages the Contracting Parties, in particular, to examine their national legal systems with a view to ensuring that there exist adequate possibilities of re-examination of the case, including reopening of proceedings, in instances where the Court has found a violation of the Convention, especially where: (i) the injured party continues to suffer very serious negative consequences because of the outcome of the domestic decision at issue, which are not adequately remedied by the just satisfaction and cannot be rectified except by re-examination or reopening, and (ii) the judgment of the Court leads to the conclusion that (a) the impugned domestic decision is on the merits contrary to the Convention, or (b) the violation found is based on procedural errors or shortcomings of such gravity that a serious doubt is cast on the outcome of the domestic proceedings complained of.

In order to encourage swift and full compliance with the judgments of the Court, the Committee of Ministers has recommended that the Council of Europe Member States establish a national 'co-ordinator' to ensure appropriate follow-up and co-ordination of all relevant actors at domestic level, including parliaments:

Recommendation CM/Rec(2008)2 of the Committee of Ministers to Member States on efficient domestic capacity for rapid execution of judgments of the European Court of Human Rights (adopted by the Committee of Ministers on 6 February 2008 at the 1,017th meeting of the Ministers' Deputies):

The Committee of Ministers, ...

b. Reiterating that judgments in which the Court finds a violation impose on the High Contracting Parties an obligation to:

  - pay any sums awarded by the Court by way of just satisfaction;
  - adopt, where appropriate, individual measures to put an end to the violation found by the Court and to redress, as far as possible, its effects;– adopt, where appropriate, the general measures needed to put an end to similar violations or prevent them.

c. Recalling also that, under the Committee of Ministers' supervision, the respondent state remains free to choose the means by which it will discharge its legal obligation under Article 46 of the Convention to abide by the final judgments of the Court;

d. Convinced that rapid and effective execution of the Court's judgments contributes to enhancing the protection of human rights in member states and to the long-term effectiveness of the European human rights protection system; ...

g. Noting ... that there is a need to reinforce domestic capacity to execute the Court's judgments;

h. Underlining the importance of early information and effective co-ordination of all state actors involved in the execution process and noting also the importance of ensuring within national systems, where necessary at high level, the effectiveness of the domestic execution process; ...

Recommends that member states:

1. designate a co-ordinator – individual or body – of execution of judgments at the national level, with reference contacts in the relevant national authorities involved in the execution process. This co-ordinator should have the necessary powers and authority to:
  - acquire relevant information;
  - liaise with persons or bodies responsible at the national level for deciding on the measures necessary to execute the judgment; and

- if need be, take or initiate relevant measures to accelerate the execution process;

2. ensure, whether through their Permanent Representation or otherwise, the existence of appropriate mechanisms for effective dialogue and transmission of relevant information between the co-ordinator and the Committee of Ministers;

3. take the necessary steps to ensure that all judgments to be executed, as well as all relevant decisions and resolutions of the Committee of Ministers related to those judgments, are duly and rapidly disseminated, where necessary in translation, to relevant actors in the execution process;

4. identify as early as possible the measures which may be required in order to ensure rapid execution;

5. facilitate the adoption of any useful measures to develop effective synergies between relevant actors in the execution process at the national level either generally or in response to a specific judgment, and to identify their respective competences;

6. rapidly prepare, where appropriate, action plans on the measures envisaged to execute judgments, if possible including an indicative timetable;

7. take the necessary steps to ensure that relevant actors in the execution process are sufficiently acquainted with the Court's case law as well as with the relevant Committee of Ministers' recommendations and practice;

8. disseminate the vademecum prepared by the Council of Europe on the execution process to relevant actors and encourage its use, as well as that of the database of the Council of Europe with information on the state of execution in all cases pending before the Committee of Ministers;

9. as appropriate, keep their parliaments informed of the situation concerning execution of judgments and the measures being taken in this regard;

10. where required by a significant persistent problem in the execution process, ensure that all necessary remedial action be taken at high level, political if need be.

(c) Treating large-scale violations: the 'pilot' judgments

The difficulties raised at the level of the execution of judgments, however, are simply one indicator of the much broader problem facing the system of the European Convention on Human Rights, as a result of the increase in the number of applications it receives. This increase is particularly marked since the entry into force of Protocol No. 11 on 1 November 1998: more than 90 per cent of the Court's judgments since it was set up in 1959 have been delivered between 1998 and 2008, although this figure should be put in perspective since there are important differences between the States parties – more than half the judgments delivered by the Court between 1998 and 2008 concerned four of the Council of Europe's forty-seven Member States (Turkey takes the lead (1,857 judgments), followed by Italy (1,789 judgments), France (613 judgments) and Poland (601 judgments)) (*The European Court of Human Rights. Some Facts and Figures, 1998–2008* (Strasbourg: Council of Europe, 2008)). On 31 August 2009, 113,850 applications were pending before the Court; it is estimated that the backlog increases by about 1,000 applications each month. One of the answers to this problem was to develop the practice of 'pilot judgments', when an individual application appears to raise an issue of general importance, concerning potentially a large number of individuals. This technique was applied for the first time in the 2004 case of *Broniowski* v. *Poland*:

European Court of Human Rights (GC), *Broniowski* v. *Poland* **(Appl. No. 31443/96) judgment of 22 June 2004:**

[The case originates in Poland's failure to implement compensatory measures in respect of persons repatriated from the 'territories beyond the Bug River' in the aftermath of the Second World War who had had to abandon their property. According to the Polish Government, the anticipated total number of people entitled to such measures is nearly 80,000. One of them is the applicant, whose grandmother owned property in what was formerly part of Poland, but became part of Ukraine after Poland's eastern border had been redrawn along the Bug River (other parts of those eastern provinces went to Belarus and to what is now Lithuania). Although Poland had undertaken to compensate those who had been 'repatriated' from the 'territories beyond the Bug River' and had had to abandon their properties, and since 1946 had allowed for compensation in kind, the entry into force of the Local Government Act of 10 May 1990 and the enactment of further laws reduced the pool of State property available to the Bug River claimants – in particular, by excluding the possibility of enforcing their claims against State agricultural and military property. As a result, the State Treasury has been unable to fulfil its obligation to meet the compensation claims: the land available was insufficient to meet the demand. In addition, Bug River claimants have frequently been either excluded from auctions of State property or have had their participation subjected to various conditions.

On 19 December 2002 the Polish Constitutional Court declared the provisions that excluded the possibility of enforcing the Bug River claims against State agricultural and military property unconstitutional. However, following this judgment, the State agencies administering State agricultural and military property suspended all auctions, considering that further legislation was required to deal with the implementation of the judgment. The Law of 12 December 2003 was subsequently adopted (it entered into force on 30 January 2004). Under this new legislation, the Polish State's obligations towards the applicant, and all other Bug River claimants who had ever obtained any compensatory property under the previous legislation, was deemed to have been discharged. Claimants who had never received any such compensation were awarded 15 per cent of their original entitlement, subject to a ceiling of 50,000 Polish zlotys.

In its judgment, the Court expressly draws attention to the existence of a systemic problem underlying the violation of the European Convention of Human Rights in the applicant's case. As this problem is seen as likely to generate large numbers of similar cases, the Court calls upon the Polish authorities to take the necessary measures to secure the property right in question in respect of the remaining Bug River claimants. Thus, while holding, unanimously, that there had been a violation of Article 1 of Protocol No. 1 (protection of property) to the Convention, the Court also notes that the violation originates in a systemic problem connected with the malfunctioning of Polish legislation and practice caused by the failure to set up an effective mechanism to implement the 'right to credit' of Bug River claimants. It emphasizes that Poland should take appropriate legal measures and administrative practices, in order to secure the implementation of the property right in question in respect of the remaining Bug River claimants or provide them with equivalent redress in lieu.]

189. It is inherent in the Court's findings that the violation of the applicant's right guaranteed by Article 1 of Protocol No. 1 originated in a widespread problem which resulted from a malfunctioning of Polish legislation and administrative practice and which has affected and remains capable of affecting a large number of persons. The unjustified hindrance on the applicant's 'peaceful enjoyment of his possessions' was neither prompted by an isolated incident nor attributable to the particular turn of events in his case, but was rather the consequence of administrative and regulatory conduct on the part of the authorities towards an identifiable class of citizens, namely the Bug River claimants.

The existence and the systemic nature of that problem have already been recognised by the Polish judicial authorities ... Thus, in its judgment of 19 December 2002 the Constitutional Court described the Bug River legislative scheme as 'caus[ing] an inadmissible systemic dysfunction' ... Endorsing that assessment, the Court concludes that the facts of the case disclose the existence, within the Polish legal order, of a shortcoming as a consequence of which a whole class of individuals have been or are still denied the peaceful enjoyment of their possessions. It also finds that the deficiencies in national law and practice identified in the applicant's individual case may give rise to numerous subsequent well-founded applications.

190. As part of a package of measures to guarantee the effectiveness of the Convention machinery, the Committee of Ministers of the Council of Europe adopted on 12 May 2004 a Resolution (Res(2004)3) on judgments revealing an underlying systemic problem, in which, after emphasising the interest in helping the State concerned to identify the underlying problems and the necessary execution measures (seventh paragraph of the preamble), it invited the Court 'to identify in its judgments finding a violation of the Convention what it considers to be an underlying systemic problem and the source of that problem, in particular when it is likely to give rise to numerous applications, so as to assist States in finding the appropriate solution and the Committee of Ministers in supervising the execution of judgments' (paragraph I of the resolution). That resolution has to be seen in the context of the growth in the Court's caseload, particularly as a result of series of cases deriving from the same structural or systemic cause.

191. In the same context, the Court would draw attention to the Committee of Ministers' Recommendation of 12 May 2004 (Rec(2004)6) on the improvement of domestic remedies, in which it is emphasised that, in addition to the obligation under Article 13 of the Convention to provide an individual who has an arguable claim with an effective remedy before a national authority, States have a general obligation to solve the problems underlying the violations found [see below, immediately following this judgment]. Mindful that the improvement of remedies at the national level, particularly in respect of repetitive cases, should also contribute to reducing the workload of the Court, the Committee of Ministers recommended that the Contracting States, following Court judgments which point to structural or general deficiencies in national law or practice, review and, 'where necessary, set up effective remedies, in order to avoid repetitive cases being brought before the Court'.

192. Before examining the applicant's individual claims for just satisfaction under Article 41 of the Convention, in view of the circumstances of the instant case and having regard also to the evolution of its caseload, the Court wishes to consider what consequences may be drawn for the respondent State from Article 46 of the Convention. It reiterates that by virtue of Article 46 the High Contracting Parties have undertaken to abide by the final judgments of the Court in any case to which they are parties, execution being supervised by the Committee of Ministers. It follows, *inter alia*, that a judgment in which the Court finds a breach imposes on the

respondent State a legal obligation not just to pay those concerned the sums awarded by way of just satisfaction under Article 41, but also to select, subject to supervision by the Committee of Ministers, the general and/or, if appropriate, individual measures to be adopted in their domestic legal order to put an end to the violation found by the Court and to redress so far as possible the effects. Subject to monitoring by the Committee of Ministers, the respondent State remains free to choose the means by which it will discharge its legal obligation under Article 46 of the Convention, provided that such means are compatible with the conclusions set out in the Court's judgment (see *Scozzari and Giunta* v. *Italy* [GC], Nos. 39221/98 and 41963/98, §249, ECHR 2000–VIII).

193. The Court has already noted that the violation which it has found in the present case has as its cause a situation concerning large numbers of people. The failure to implement in a manner compatible with Article 1 of Protocol No. 1 the chosen mechanism for settling the Bug River claims has affected nearly 80,000 people ... There are moreover already 167 applications pending before the Court brought by Bug River claimants. This is not only an aggravating factor as regards the State's responsibility under the Convention for an existing or past state of affairs, but also represents a threat to the future effectiveness of the Convention machinery.

Although it is in principle not for the Court to determine what remedial measures may be appropriate to satisfy the respondent State's obligations under Article 46 of the Convention, in view of the systemic situation which it has identified, the Court would observe that general measures at national level are undoubtedly called for in execution of the present judgment, measures which must take into account the many people affected. Above all, the measures adopted must be such as to remedy the systemic defect underlying the Court's finding of a violation so as not to overburden the Convention system with large numbers of applications deriving from the same cause. Such measures should therefore include a scheme which offers to those affected redress for the Convention violation identified in the instant judgment in relation to the present applicant. In this context the Court's concern is to facilitate the most speedy and effective resolution of a dysfunction established in national human rights protection. Once such a defect has been identified, it falls to the national authorities, under the supervision of the Committee of Ministers, to take, retroactively if appropriate (see *Bottazzi* v. *Italy* [GC], No. 34884/97, §22, ECHR 1999–V, *Di Mauro* v. *Italy* [GC], No. 34256/96, §23, ECHR 1999–V, and the Committee of Ministers' Interim Resolution ResDH(2000)135 of 25 October 2000 (Excessive length of judicial proceedings in Italy: general measures); see also *Brusco* v. *Italy* (dec.), No. 69789/01, ECHR 2001–IX, and *Giacometti and others* v. *Italy* (dec.), No. 34939/97, ECHR 2001–XII), the necessary remedial measures in accordance with the subsidiary character of the Convention, so that the Court does not have to repeat its finding in a lengthy series of comparable cases.

194. With a view to assisting the respondent State in fulfilling its obligations under Article 46, the Court has sought to indicate the type of measure that might be taken by the Polish State in order to put an end to the systemic situation identified in the present case. The Court is not in a position to assess whether the December 2003 Act ... can be treated as an adequate measure in this connection since no practice of its implementation has been established as yet. In any event, this Act does not cover persons who – like Mr Broniowski – had already received partial compensation, irrespective of the amount of such compensation. Thus, it is clear that for this group of Bug River claimants the Act cannot be regarded as a measure capable of putting an end to the systemic situation identified in the present judgment as adversely affecting them.

Nevertheless, as regards general measures to be taken, the Court considers that the respondent State must, primarily, either remove any hindrance to the implementation of the right of the numerous persons affected by the situation found, in respect of the applicant, to have been in breach of the Convention, or provide equivalent redress in lieu. As to the former option, the respondent State should, therefore, through appropriate legal and administrative measures, secure the effective and expeditious realisation of the entitlement in question in respect of the remaining Bug River claimants, in accordance with the principles for the protection of property rights laid down in Article 1 of Protocol No. 1, having particular regard to the principles relating to compensation ...

Committee of Ministers of the Council of Europe, Recommendation Rec(2004)6 of the Committee of Ministers to Member States on the improvement of domestic remedies (adopted by the Committee of Ministers on 12 May 2004, at its 114th session) (Appendix) [see also excerpts of this Recommendation in chapter 8, section 1.1.]:

Remedies following a 'pilot' judgment

13. When a judgment which points to structural or general deficiencies in national law or practice ('pilot case') has been delivered and a large number of applications to the Court concerning the same problem ('repetitive cases') are pending or likely to be lodged, the respondent state should ensure that potential applicants have, where appropriate, an effective remedy allowing them to apply to a competent national authority, which may also apply to current applicants. Such a rapid and effective remedy would enable them to obtain redress at national level, in line with the principle of subsidiarity of the Convention system.

14. The introduction of such a domestic remedy could also significantly reduce the Court's workload. While prompt execution of the pilot judgment remains essential for solving the structural problem and thus for preventing future applications on the same matter, there may exist a category of people who have already been affected by this problem prior to its resolution. The existence of a remedy aimed at providing redress at national level for this category of people might allow the Court to invite them to have recourse to the new remedy and, if appropriate, declare their applications inadmissible.

15. Several options with this objective are possible, depending, among other things, on the nature of the structural problem in question and on whether the person affected by this problem has applied to the Court or not.

16. In particular, further to a pilot judgment in which a specific structural problem has been found, one alternative might be to adopt an ad hoc approach, whereby the state concerned would assess the appropriateness of introducing a specific remedy or widening an existing remedy by legislation or by judicial interpretation.

17. Within the framework of this case-by-case examination, states might envisage, if this is deemed advisable, the possibility of reopening proceedings similar to those of a pilot case which has established a violation of the Convention, with a view to saving the Court from dealing with these cases and where appropriate to providing speedier redress for the person concerned. The criteria laid out in Recommendation Rec(2000)2 of the Committee of Ministers might serve as a source of inspiration in this regard.

18. When specific remedies are set up following a pilot case, governments should speedily inform the Court so that it can take them into account in its treatment of subsequent repetitive cases.

19. However, it would not be necessary or appropriate to create new remedies, or give existing remedies a certain retroactive effect, following every case in which a Court judgment has identified a structural problem. In certain circumstances, it may be preferable to leave the cases to the examination of the Court, particularly to avoid compelling the applicant to bear the further burden of having once again to exhaust domestic remedies, which, moreover, would not be in place until the adoption of legislative changes.

Another illustration of the 'pilot judgment' procedure involves the failure to enforce the judgments of domestic courts in Russia. This was the issue at stake in *Burdov* v. *Russia (No. 2)*. The judgment states in its operative part:

European Court of Human Rights, *Burdov* v. *Russia (No. 2)* (Appl. No. 33509/04), judgment of 15 January 2009:

6. [The Court] *Holds* that the respondent State must set up ... an effective domestic remedy or combination of such remedies which secures adequate and sufficient redress for non-enforcement or delayed enforcement of domestic judgments in line with the Convention principles as established in the Court's case law;

7. *Holds* that the respondent State must grant such redress, within one year from the date on which the judgment becomes final, to all victims of non-payment or unreasonably delayed payment by State authorities of a judgment debt in their favour who lodged their applications with the Court before the delivery of the present judgment and whose applications were communicated to the Government ...;

8. *Holds* that pending the adoption of the above measures, the Court will adjourn, for one year from the date on which the judgment becomes final, the proceedings in all cases concerning solely the non-enforcement and/or delayed enforcement of domestic judgments ordering monetary payments by the State authorities.

(d) Co-operation in the execution of judgments

The implementation of the judgments of the Court would be greatly encouraged if the States parties were provided positive incentives to move towards implementing the reforms the findings of violation seem to require. An encouraging development in this regard is described in the following terms in the second annual report of the Committee of Ministers on the supervision of the execution of judgments of the Court:

Committee of Ministers of the Council of Europe, Supervision of the execution of judgments of the European Court of Human Rights, second annual report, April 2009:

3. The 2008 tendency has been to increase the importance attached to co-operation activities. Such activities, involving permanent representations and national authorities on the one side

and the Secretariat of the Council of Europe, in particular the Department for the execution of the judgments of the ECtHR, on the other have thus increased considerably. The aim is to catalyse the execution process so that fewer problems, requiring in depth CM [Committee of Ministers of the Council of Europe] attention arise. In addition, in case of problems, the improved preparation of cases which results from these co-operation activities facilitates the debates in the Committee and the adoption of adequate responses.

4. This new approach notably includes increased efforts to propose to states, wherever needed, different forms of assistance in defining and/or implementing the necessary execution measures, notably taking into account interesting practices of other states. Whereas such activities were previously only undertaken on an infrequent ad hoc basis, such activities have now become a more regular feature of the supervision of execution. Activities may be limited to the respondent state, but may also encompass groups of states with similar problems. The CM has allowed a special budget for this purpose starting in 2007, clearly signalling its increased importance: the 2007 expenses were just over 52000 euros, the 2008 totalled almost 66000. This increase is, of course, reflected in the number of activities, which also increased by over 20 per cent from 2007 to 2008. The 2009 budget totals 90000 euros. Activities include, in particular, high level discussions with competent authorities, expert opinions on legislation and training sessions either in the country concerned or in Strasbourg.

5. In addition, a most important development is the new Human Rights Trust Fund set up in 2008 whose mission, inter alia, is to assist in ensuring full and timely execution of judgments of the ECtHR. The Fund, a Norwegian initiative, has approved its first projects. The Assembly of the Fund's Contributors has recently allocated almost 785000 euros to the financing of execution-related activities in certain key areas: the non-execution of domestic court judgments in six countries and the responses to violations of the ECHR by security forces in Chechnyan Republic.

| Box 11.1. | The monitoring of social rights under the European Social Charter |

The original European Social Charter. When it was initially adopted in 1961 (C.E.T.S. No. 35; 529 U.N.T.S. 89; entered into force on 26 February 1965), the European Social Charter (ESC) was intended to be the counterpart in the field of economic and social rights to the European Convention on Human Rights, the major achievement of the Council of Europe in the field of human rights. Yet, the ESC has been largely overshadowed by the Convention, and largely ignored, even within specialized circles, until the mid 1990s. The conclusions adopted by the Committee of Independent Experts tasked with supervising compliance with the Charter were relatively obscure and hardly publicized. The Committee of Independent Experts also remained largely subordinated to the Governmental Committee of the Social Charter and, ultimately, to the Committee of Ministers of the Council of Europe, resulting in an ambiguous mechanism of control, neither fully judicial nor purely political. The system provided neither for individual nor for collective complaints, relying solely instead on the reports the States parties were to submit on their implementation of the Charter. The Charter also presented certain characteristics which seemed definitively to set it apart from other human rights instruments implementing the Universal Declaration of Human Rights: it had a scope of application *ratione personae* limited to the nationals of the States parties; it adopted an à la carte approach, allowing each State, within certain limits, to select the provisions of the Charter which it will accept to be bound by, upon acceding to the Charter; and certain of its guarantees were considered to be satisfied if the great majority of the intended beneficiaries were protected, even though some might not be.

The 'revitalization' of the European Social Charter. Much of this changed in the 1990s, following the 'revitalization' of the Charter through the formation of an ad hoc committee (CHARTE-REL) (see particularly D. Harris, 'A Fresh Impetus for the European Social Charter', *International and Comparative Law Quarterly*, 41 (1992), 659; and D. Harris and J. Darcy, *The European Social Charter*, second edn (New York: Transnational Publishers, 2001)). The CHARTE-REL Committee first prepared a Protocol Amending the European Social Charter, which was opened for signature in Turin on 21 October 1991 (Protocol amending the European Social Charter (C.E.T.S., No. 142); see M. Mohr, 'The Turin Protocol of 22 October 1991: a Major Contribution to Revitalizing the European Social Charter', *European Journal of International Law*, 3 (1992), 362). Although the Turin Protocol has never entered into force (since it did not secure all the ratifications required), the clarifications it intended to bring to the relations between the Committee of Independent Experts and the Governmental Committee – reserving to the former, in effect, the exclusive competence to interpret and apply the Charter – have in fact been implemented in practice, to the extent that this did not necessarily require an amendment of the Charter, but rather an understanding, by each of these bodies, of its role in the supervisory system of the Charter. Other changes to the supervisory system proposed under the Turin Protocol, including the increase in the number of members of the Committee of Independent Experts, the abolition of the role of the Parliamentary Assembly of the Council of Europe in the supervision of the Charter, the changes in the Committee of Ministers' voting rules for recommendations addressed to the States parties, or the improved role of social partners and non-governmental organizations in the supervisory system, were also implemented in practice.

In 1995, also as part of the 'revitalization' process, an Additional Protocol to the European Social Charter Providing for a System of Collective Complaints was adopted (C.E.T.S. No. 158, opened for signature in Strasbourg on 9 November 1995; see M. Jaeger, 'The Additional Protocol to the European Social Charter Providing for a System of Collective Complaints', *Leiden Journal of International Law*, 10 (1997), 69, and for an evaluation of the first years of functioning, see R. Churchill and U. Khaliq, 'The Collective Complaints System of the European Social Charter: an Effective Mechanism for Ensuring Compliance with Economic and Social Rights?', *European Journal of International Law*, 15 (2004), 417). This instrument allows non-governmental organizations and organizations of employers and of workers to seek a declaration that certain laws and policies of the States parties are not compatible with their commitments under the Charter, without having to exhaust any local remedies which may be available to those aggrieved by such measures. Despite its many innovative features, the Protocol gathered the five ratifications it needed to enter into force on 1 July 1998; on 1 September 2009 it had attracted twelve ratifications.

Finally, in 1996, agreement was reached on a Revised European Social Charter (C.E.T.S. No. 163, opened for signature in Strasbourg on 3 May 1996; entered into force on 1 July 1999). The Revised Charter does not bring changes to the control mechanism of the original Charter, but it enriches the list of the rights protected, and includes rights such as the right to protection against poverty and social exclusion (Art. 30) and the right to housing (Art. 31), clearly placing the Revised European Social Charter at the forefront of instruments protecting economic and social rights in international law. On 1 September 2009, twenty-eight Member States of the Council of Europe had ratified the Revised European Social Charter.

The reporting procedure. The reporting under the European Social Charter relies mainly on the European Committee of Social Rights (ECSR), which the Charter refers to as the Committee of Independent Experts. The Committee now comprises fifteen members. These are 'experts of the highest integrity and of recognised competence in national and international social questions' (Art. 25(2) of the 1961 Charter, as amended by the Turin Protocol) elected by the Committee of Ministers of the Council of Europe. From 2007, States are to submit one annual report on 31 October of each year, covering in turn employment, training and equal opportunities (group 1 of the provisions of the Charter: Arts. 1, 9, 10, 15, 18, 20, 24 and 25); health, social security and social protection (group 2: Arts. 3, 11, 12, 13, 14, 23 and 30); labour rights (group 3: Arts. 2, 4, 5, 6, 21, 22, 26, 28 and 29); and children, families, migrants (group 4: Arts. 7, 8, 16, 17, 19, 27 and 31). This ensures that each provision of the Charter will be reported on once every four years.

The ECSR adopts conclusions on the reports submitted by States parties to the Charter on the implementation of the provisions they have accepted, often also relying on sources other than those of the State reports and the comments made on those reports by organizations of workers and employers, including in particular information from the International Labour Organization. The conclusions of the ECSR are to provide an assessment 'from a legal standpoint [of] the compliance of national law and practice with the obligations arising from the Charter for the Contracting Parties concerned' (Art. 24(2) of the 1961 Charter, as revised by the Turin Protocol). These conclusions in turn are submitted to the Governmental Committee. This body is composed of representatives of each of the States parties, although representatives of international organizations of employers and workers (presently the European Trade Union Confederation (ETUC), the International Organization of Employers (IOE) and the Union of the Confederations of Industry and Employers of Europe (UNICE)) attend their meetings in a consultative capacity and take an active part in the discussions. The role of the Governmental Committee is, not to overrule the assessment of the ECSR, but to 'select, giving reasons for its choice, on the basis of social, economic and other policy considerations, the situations which should, in its view, be the subject of recommendations to each Contracting Party concerned' by the Committee of Ministers (Art. 27(3) of the 1961 Charter, as revised by the Turin Protocol). Neither the ECSR nor the Governmental Committee are full-time bodies: the ECSR meets eight to ten times a year for one-week sessions, and the Governmental Committee at even less regular intervals. Finally, the Committee of Ministers of the Council of Europe receives the report of the Governmental Committee. On that basis, it votes, by a two-thirds majority of the votes cast – the vote being reserved to the States parties to the Charter – 'a resolution covering the entire supervision cycle and containing individual recommendations to the Contracting Parties concerned' (Art. 28(1) of the 1961 Charter, as revised by the Turin Protocol). Recommendations addressed to individual States for failure to comply with the

Charter remain very exceptional in practice: only three such recommendations were adopted between 2002 and 2008 (concerning Turkey, the United Kingdom, and Ireland).

The Collective Complaints Protocol. The 1995 Additional Protocol to the European Social Charter Providing for a System of Collective Complaints (CCP) provides for the possibility for social partners and non-governmental organizations to file complaints alleging the unsatisfactory application of the Charter. According to Article 1 CCP, the organizations which may use this mechanism are: (a) international organizations of employers and trade unions (the ETUC, the UNICE and the IOE); (b) other international non-governmental organizations which have consultative status with the Council of Europe and have been put on a list established for this purpose by the Governmental Committee, comprising at present sixty-seven organizations; and (c) 'representative' national organizations of employers and trade unions within the jurisdiction of the Contracting Party against which they have lodged a complaint, such 'representativeness' being determined by the ECSR, 'in the absence of any criteria on a national level, [on the basis of] factors such as the number of members and the organisation's actual role in national negotiations' (Explanatory Report to the CCP, para. 23). In addition, States parties to the CCP may declare that they recognize the right of any other representative national non-governmental organization within their jurisdiction which has particular competence in the matters governed by the Charter, to lodge complaints against them in the area in which they have such competence (Art. 2 CCP).

Remarkably, and in contrast to most similar procedures for the settlement of disputes between private parties and States, the CCP does not require that the local remedies available to the complainant organization be exhausted before a collective complaint is filed with the ECSR. The explanation is that the collective complaints procedure – which is modelled on the procedure established within the International Labour Organization (ILO) before the Freedom of Association Committee – is not meant to address specific (or individual) instances of violation of the European Social Charter. Instead, 'complaints may only raise questions concerning non-compliance of a state's law or practice with one of the provisions of the Charter. Individual situations may not be submitted' (Explanatory Report to the CCP, para. 31): it is to this feature, and not to the nature of the organizations authorized to file a complaint, that the adjective 'collective' refers. For the same reason, a complaint may be declared admissible 'even if a similar case has already been submitted to another national or international body'; and 'the fact that the substance of a complaint has been examined as part of the "normal" government reports procedure does not in itself constitute an impediment to the complaint's admissibility' (*ibid.*). This has been confirmed in the admissibility decision adopted on the first collective complaint to have been filed under the CCP, where the ECSR noted:

European Committee on Social Rights, *International Commission of Jurists* v. Portugal, Complaint No. 1/1998, decision on the admissibility of 10 March 1999, para. 10:

The object of [the collective complaints] procedure, which is different in nature from the procedure of examining national reports, is to allow the Committee to make a legal assessment of the situation of a state in the light of the information supplied by the complaint and the adversarial procedure to which it gives rise. Neither the fact that the Committee has already examined this situation in the framework of the reporting system, nor the fact that it will examine it again during subsequent supervision cycles do not [*sic*] in themselves imply the inadmissibility of a collective complaint concerning the same provision of the Charter and the same Contracting Party.

Following the decision on admissibility, the ECSR examines the evidence and arguments presented by the complainant organization and the defending State, taking also into account any observations submitted by other States parties to the Protocol or by the ETUC, the UNICE or the IOE. The Committee then adopts a report containing its conclusions as to whether or not the State concerned has complied with the Charter. This report is transmitted to the Committee of Ministers and made public either when the Committee of Ministers adopts a resolution on the basis of the report, or no more than four months following the transmission of the report. The resolution of the Committee of Ministers based on the report drawn up by the ECSR is adopted by a majority of the States parties to the Charter voting. While the Committee of Ministers must act on the basis of the determinations of the ECSR concerning the merits of the complaint, the resolution 'may be based on social and economic policy considerations' (Explanatory Report, para. 46). In addition, Article 9(1) of the CCP provides that if the ECSR finds that the Charter has not been complied with, 'the Committee of Ministers shall adopt, by a majority of two-thirds of those voting, a recommendation addressed to the Contracting Party concerned'. In fact, and despite this clear wording, only once did the Committee of Ministers adopt an individual recommendation following a finding of non-compliance with the Charter based on a collective complaint. The compliance rate with the decisions adopted by the ECSR is nevertheless quite high, in large part thanks to the complementarity between the collective complaints procedure and the periodical State-reporting mechanism described above: the States whose legislation or policies are found to have violated to Charter are to provide information on the measures taken to comply with the recommendation of the Committee of Ministers in their next periodical report submitted under Article 21 of the Charter.

The decision adopted on the merits in the case of *International Commission of Jurists* v. *Portugal* sheds some light on the distinct approach adopted by the ECSR upon receiving collective complaints. This approach contrasts with its more cautious attitude in the context of the examination of State reports, when efforts over long periods of time seem to be required from States in order to implement fully the requirements of the Charter (see, however, the approach followed in case of *Autism-Europe* v. *France*, Collective Complaint No. 13/2002, presented in chapter 7, section 3.3., b)). Article 7 para. 1 of the European Social Charter provides that, 'with a view to ensuring the effective exercise of the right of children and young persons to protection, the Contracting Parties undertake: 1. to provide that the minimum age of admission to employment shall be 15 years, subject to exceptions for children employed in prescribed light work without harm to their health, morals or education'. The International Commission of Jurists (ICJ) alleged in its complaint that Portugal was in violation of this obligation, since despite the prohibition of child labour in Portuguese legislation, 'a large number of children under the age of 15 years continue to work illegally in many economic sectors, especially in the north of the country'. Portugal on the other hand questioned ICJ's interpretation of Article 7 para. 1 of the Charter, and affirmed in particular that 'although some instances of child labour still exist within the state, it would be unfair to conclude that the situation in Portugal fails to comply with Article 7 para. 1 in the light of the measures implemented to eradicate this problem'. The ECSR took the view that well-intended efforts were not enough, however. It suggested that, at least in the context of collective complaints, it would consider the obligations imposed under the Charter as obligations of result, and not of means:

European Committee of Social Rights, *International Commission of Jurists* v. *Portugal,* Complaint No. 1/1998, decision on the merits, 9 September 1999:

33. [The] Committee notes first that, according to the information provided by the Government and mentioned by the Committee in Conclusions XIII-5, in Portugal only young people who are already aged fifteen (as of 1 January 1997) and who have completed compulsory schooling of nine years may be employed in light work. Accordingly, any work, including light work, performed by a child under the age of fifteen is illegal. The statutory measures adopted in Portugal to implement Article 7 para. 1 are rigorous, which the Committee can only welcome.

34. However, the Committee observes from the evidence contained in the file that in Portugal, children under the age of fifteen actually perform work. It notes that the Government does not dispute this. In order to seek to establish the exact dimensions of this problem and its characteristics, it may take account of all information submitted by the parties, whatever the period it relates to. In the present case, it considers it sufficient to rely on the results of the 1998 survey which provides the most recent evidence and the validity of which is not disputed by the International Commission of Jurists, even if its interpretation of the results differs from that given by the Government.

35. It emerges from this survey that in September 1998 several thousand children under the age of fifteen years performed work in breach of the requirements of Article 7 para. 1 of the Charter and Portuguese law. The Committee considers in particular that the 25,000 children who, out of an estimated total of 27,500, performed unpaid work as part of helping out the family must be taken into account under Article 7 para. 1.

36. The Committee notes further that, according to the survey, a not insignificant number of children under the age of fifteen years who declared that they performed an economic activity work in the agricultural (66%), manufacturing (7.1%) and construction (2.7%) sectors. These sectors may, by their very natures, give rise to certain types of work which may have negative consequences on the children's health as well as on their development.

37. The Committee observes lastly that, taking all sectors together, the duration of work declared exceeds that which may be considered compatible with children's health or schooling: 31.6% of the children concerned worked on average for more than 4 hours per day across all sectors. This percentage is particularly high in the construction sector and the manufacturing sector where, respectively, 66.6% and 42% of the children concerned worked on average for more than four hours per day. The Committee notes that among the children aged between 6 and 14 years who performed paid work, just 68% attended school.

38. With particular regard to child labour as part of helping the family out, which occurs mainly in agriculture and the restaurant sector, according to the Government, the Committee has no reason to presume that by its nature or the conditions in which it is performed (duration, working hours) it can in all cases be considered light work within the meaning of Article 7 para. 1.

39. The Committee then considers whether the measures taken by the Government rectify the situation criticised.

40. It acknowledges that the Government, especially in recent years, has taken many legal and practical measures to combat child labour, tackling its many diverse and complex causes. These measures have brought about a progressive reduction in the number of children working illegally, an improvement which is not in dispute. However, it is clear that the problem has not been resolved.

41. The Committee acknowledges that many measures have been taken by the Government to increase the efficiency of the Labour Inspectorate. It observes that in 1997 labour inspectors carried out 1,462 visits in enterprises and found 167 children under the age of 16 years working illegally there. In 1998, they carried out 2,475 visits in enterprises and found 191 cases of children under the age of 16 working illegally. The Committee considers that, in the light of the results of the 1998 survey and the fact that the existing legislation and rules cover family businesses, these figures are modest.

42. As regards the allegation of the ICJ that the Labour Inspectorate is corrupt, which is vigorously disputed by the Government, it is not supported by evidence.

43. Finally, as the Government recognises, efforts must be maintained to increase the effectiveness of supervision of children's work within the family and in private dwellings. The Committee is aware of the difficulty of this task, which involves the Labour Inspectorate or the educational and social services as appropriate ...

45. The Committee concludes that the situation in Portugal is not in conformity with Article 7 para. 1.

Dissenting opinion of Mr Alfredo Bruto da Costa:

By adopting a conclusion focused on the 'situation in Portugal', the Committee did not respond to what is demanded from it in Article 8 of the Additional Protocol. The article refers to a conclusion 'as to whether or not the Contracting Party concerned has ensured the satisfactory application of the provision', which relates more to the performance of the Contracting Party than to the actual situation. Furthermore, the term 'satisfactory' admits a certain flexibility that the assessment of the compliance in terms of 'yes or no' does not.

The Committee adopts a static and narrow concept of 'legality', ignoring the natural and unavoidable viscosity of social changes, and the need of taking account of the dynamic aspect of social problems. Hence the fact that the progress achieved in the area (child work) in Portugal is mentioned but is not properly evaluated by the Committee.

Indeed, of all information on the quantitative dimension of the problem mentioned in the 'various documents' provided by the ICJ, the Committee only quotes the number of 200 000 working children in 1992. On the other hand, it refers to the number of 27 500 working children that, according to a survey undertaken by the Portuguese Government, existed in 1998. The Committee did not take sufficient account of the dramatic fall from 200 000 to 27 500 working children (a decrease of around 86%) over a period of 6 years in terms of assessing whether or not the Contracting Party has ensured a 'satisfactory application of the provision'. Rather, the conclusion seems to go no further than observing that 'the problem has not been solved' and, therefore, that the situation is not in conformity with the article concerned.

2 THE INTER-AMERICAN SYSTEM OF PROTECTION OF HUMAN RIGHTS

2.1 The powers of the Inter-American Commission on Human Rights

The Inter-American system for the protection of human rights was first institutionalized with the establishment of the Inter-American Commission on Human Rights (IACHR) in 1959, by Resolution VIII adopted at the Fifth Meeting of Consultation of Ministers of Foreign Affairs of the Organization of American States (for the broader context in which human rights were integrated within the work of the OAS, see chapter 1, section 2.2.). The Commission was created as a body of seven independent members, tasked with the furtherance of respect for human rights in the OAS Member States. The Statute of the IACHR, which was adopted the following year (OEA/Ser. L.5/VI.4, 1 December 1960), provided that the IACHR would make recommendations to the Governments of the OAS Member States for the adoption of appropriate measures to further observance of human rights, and that it should receive information from the Member States in order to allow it to exercise this function. The IACHR was conceived as an advisory body to the OAS, whose main role should consist in the preparation of reports and studies for the promotion of human rights. However, despite a relatively fragile basis in its original Statute, the IACHR soon developed into an enquiry mechanism, based on the reports submitted to the Commission by the Member States and on the petitions it received. At the time, the Commission could only base itself on the American Declaration of the Rights and Duties of Man, adopted at Bogota in 1948 alongside the Charter of the Organization of American States. Yet, the Commission soon added references to the other international human rights treaties to which the OAS Member States were parties. Reports on the situation of human rights in specific countries were particularly frequent during the 1970s and 1980s, confronting the OAS political organs with human rights violations which, the Commission hoped, they would react to – which in fact they seldom did.

The powers of the Commission were significantly enhanced in 1965 when it received the competence to examine individual communications, and to prepare on that basis a report containing its opinion as to whether or not the State concerned had violated its human rights obligations. This power remains of significance today, since it allows the Commission to adopt opinions on alleged violations committed by OAS Member States that (such as the United States or Canada) are not parties to the American Convention on Human Rights. The enlargement of the powers of the Commission significantly raised the stakes of the debate about whether or not the Declaration should be treated as having a binding status. The Inter-American Court of Human Rights addressed the issue at the request of the Government of Colombia which asked whether the Court could render advisory opinions regarding the interpretation of the American Declaration of the Rights and Duties of Man. Article 64(1) of the 1969 American Convention on Human Rights provides that the Court may be consulted 'regarding the interpretation of this Convention or of other treaties concerning the protection of human rights in the American states'. In its request for an Advisory Opinion, Colombia submitted that it 'understands, of course, that the Declaration is not a treaty. But this conclusion does not automatically answer the question. It is perfectly reasonable to assume that the interpretation of the human rights provisions contained in the Charter of the OAS, as revised by the Protocol of Buenos Aires, involves, in principle, an analysis of the rights and duties of man proclaimed by the Declaration, and thus requires the determination of the normative status of the Declaration within the legal framework of the inter-American system for the protection of human rights.' This position was opposed, in particular, by the United States. The Court answered in convoluted terms:

Inter-American Court of Human Rights, Interpretation of the American Declaration of the Rights and Duties of Man within the Framework of Article 64 of the American Convention on Human Rights, Advisory Opinion OC–10/89, 14 July 1989, Series A, No. 10 (1989):

34. [It] must be recalled that the American Declaration was adopted by the Ninth International Conference of American States (Bogotá, 1948) through a resolution adopted by the Conference itself. It was neither conceived nor drafted as a treaty. Resolution XL of the Inter-American Conference on the Problems of War and Peace (Chapultepec, 1945) expressed the belief that in order to achieve the international protection of human rights, the latter should be listed and defined 'in a Declaration adopted as a Convention by the States'. In the subsequent phase of preparation of the draft Declaration by the Inter-American Juridical Committee and the Ninth Conference, this initial approach was abandoned and the Declaration was adopted as a declaration, without provision for any procedure by which it might become a treaty (Novena Conferencia Internacional Americana, 1948, Actas y Documentos. Bogotá: Ministerio de Relaciones Exteriores de Colombia, 1953, vol. I, pp. 235–236). Despite profound differences, in the Sixth Committee of the Conference the position prevailed that the text to be approved should be a declaration and not a treaty (see the report of the Rapporteur of the Sixth Committee, Novena Conferencia Internacional Americana, 1948, Actas y Documentos. Bogotá: Ministerio de Relaciones Exteriores de Colombia, 1953, vol. V, p. 512).

In order to obtain a consensus, the Declaration was conceived as 'the initial system of protection considered by the American states as being suited to the present social and juridical conditions, not without a recognition on their part that they should increasingly strengthen that system in the international field as conditions become more favorable (American Declaration, Fourth Considerandum)'.

This same principle was confirmed on September 26, 1949, by the Inter-American Committee of Jurisconsults, when it said: 'It is evident that the Declaration of Bogotá does not create a contractual juridical obligation, but it is also clear that it demonstrates a well-defined orientation toward the international protection of the fundamental rights of the human person (C.J.I., Recomendaciones e informes, 1949–1953 (1955), p. 107. See also US Department of State, Report of the Delegation of the United States to the Ninth International Conference of American States, Bogotá, Colombia, March 30–May 2, 1948, at 35–36 (Publ. No. 3263, 1948)).'

35. The mere fact that the Declaration is not a treaty does not necessarily compel the conclusion that the Court lacks the power to render an advisory opinion containing an interpretation of the American Declaration.

36. In fact, the American Convention refers to the Declaration in paragraph three of its Preamble which reads as follows: 'Considering that these principles have been set forth in the Charter of the Organization of the American States, in the American Declaration of the Rights and Duties of Man, and in the Universal Declaration of Human Rights, and that they have been reaffirmed and refined in other international instruments, worldwide as well as regional in scope.'

And in Article 29(d) which indicates [that]: 'No provision of this convention shall be interpreted as: d. excluding or limiting the effect that the American Declaration of the Rights and Duties of Man and other international acts of the same nature may have.'

From the foregoing, it follows that, in interpreting the Convention in the exercise of its advisory jurisdiction, the Court may have to interpret the Declaration.

37. The American Declaration has its basis in the idea that 'the international protection of the rights of man should be the principal guide of an evolving American law' (Third Considerandum). This American law has evolved from 1948 to the present; international protective measures, subsidiary and complementary to national ones, have been shaped by new instruments. As the International Court of Justice said: 'an international instrument must be interpreted and applied within the overall framework of the juridical system in force at the time of the interpretation' (*Legal Consequences for States of the Continued Presence of South Africa in Namibia (South West Africa) notwithstanding Security Council Resolution 276 (1970)*, Advisory Opinion, I.C.J. Reports 1971, p. 16 ad 31). That is why the Court finds it necessary to point out that to determine the legal status of the American Declaration it is appropriate to look to the inter-American system of today in the light of the evolution it has undergone since the adoption of the Declaration, rather than to examine the normative value and significance which that instrument was believed to have had in 1948.

38. The evolution of the here relevant 'inter-American law' mirrors on the regional level the developments in contemporary international law and especially in human rights law, which distinguished that law from classical international law to a significant extent. That is the case, for example, with the duty to respect certain essential human rights, which is today considered to be an *erga omnes* obligation (*Barcelona Traction, Light and Power Company, Limited*, Second Phase, Judgment, I.C.J. Reports 1970, p. 3. For an analysis following the same line of thought see also Legal Consequences for States of the Continued Presence of South Africa in Namibia (South West Africa) notwithstanding Security Council Resolution 276 (1970) *supra* 37, p. 16 ad 57; cfr. *United States Diplomatic and Consular Staff in Tehran*, I.C.J. Reports 1980, p. 3 ad 42).

39. The Charter of the Organization refers to the fundamental rights of man in its Preamble (paragraph three) and in Arts. 3(j), 16, 43, 47, 51, 112 and 150; Preamble (paragraph four), Arts. 3(k), 16, 44, 48, 52, 111 and 150 of the Charter revised by the Protocol of Cartagena de Indias), but it does not list or define them. The member states of the Organization have, through its diverse organs, given specificity to the human rights mentioned in the Charter and to which the Declaration refers.

40. This is the case of Article 112 of the Charter (Art. 111 of the Charter as amended by the Protocol of Cartagena de Indias) which reads as follows: 'There shall be an Inter-American Commission on Human Rights, whose principal function shall be to promote the observance and protection of human rights and to serve as a consultative organ of the Organization in these matters. An inter-American convention on human rights shall determine the structure, competence, and procedure of this Commission, as well as those of other organs responsible for these matters.'

Article 150 of the Charter provides as follows: 'Until the inter-American convention on human rights, referred to in Chapter XVIII (Chapter XVI of the Charter as amended by the Protocol of Cartagena de Indias), enters into force, the present Inter-American Commission on Human Rights shall keep vigilance over the observance of human rights.'

41. These norms authorize the Inter-American Commission to protect human rights. These rights are none other than those enunciated and defined in the American Declaration. That conclusion results from Article 1 of the Commission's Statute, which was approved by Resolution No. 447, adopted by the General Assembly of the OAS at its Ninth Regular Period of Sessions, held in La Paz, Bolivia, in October, 1979. That Article reads as follows: '1. The Inter-American Commission on Human Rights is an organ of the Organization of the American States, created to promote the observance and defense of human rights and to serve as consultative organ of the Organization in this matter. 2. For the purposes of the present Statute, human rights are understood to be: a. The rights set forth in the American Convention on Human Rights, in relation to the States Parties thereto; b. The rights set forth in the American Declaration of the Rights and Duties of Man, in relation to the other member states.' ...

42. The General Assembly of the Organization has also repeatedly recognized that the American Declaration is a source of international obligations for the member states of the OAS. For example, in Resolution 314 (VII-O/77) of June 22, 1977, it charged the Inter-American Commission with the preparation of a study to 'set forth their obligation to carry out the commitments assumed in the American Declaration of the Rights and Duties of Man.' In Resolution 371 (VIII-O/78) of July 1, 1978, the General Assembly reaffirmed 'its commitment to promote the observance of the American Declaration of the Rights and Duties of Man', and in Resolution 370 (VIII-O/78) of July 1, 1978, it referred to the 'international commitments' of a member state of the Organization to respect the rights of man 'recognized in the American Declaration of the Rights and Duties of Man'. The Preamble of the American Convention to Prevent and Punish Torture, adopted and signed at the Fifteenth Regular Session of the General Assembly in Cartagena de Indias (December, 1985), reads as follows: 'Reaffirming that all acts of torture or any other cruel, inhuman, or degrading treatment or punishment constitute an offense against human dignity and a denial of the principles set forth in the Charter of the Organization of American States and in the Charter of the United Nations and are violations of the fundamental human rights and freedoms proclaimed in the American Declaration of the Rights and Duties of Man and the Universal Declaration of Human Rights.'

43. Hence it may be said that by means of an authoritative interpretation, the member states of the Organization have signaled their agreement that the Declaration contains and defines the fundamental human rights referred to in the Charter. Thus the Charter of the Organization cannot be interpreted and applied as far as human rights are concerned without relating its norms, consistent with the practice of the organs of the OAS, to the corresponding provisions of the Declaration.

44. In view of the fact that the Charter of the Organization and the American Convention are treaties with respect to which the Court has advisory jurisdiction by virtue of Article 64(1), it follows that the Court is authorized, within the framework and limits of its competence, to interpret the American Declaration and to render an advisory opinion relating to it whenever it is necessary to do so in interpreting those instruments.

45. For the member states of the Organization, the Declaration is the text that defines the human rights referred to in the Charter. Moreover, Articles 1(2)(b) and 20 of the Commission's

Statute define the competence of that body with respect to the human rights enunciated in the Declaration, with the result that to this extent the American Declaration is for these States a source of international obligations related to the Charter of the Organization.

46. For the States Parties to the Convention, the specific source of their obligations with respect to the protection of human rights is, in principle, the Convention itself. It must be remembered, however, that, given the provisions of Article 29(d), these States cannot escape the obligations they have as members of the OAS under the Declaration, notwithstanding the fact that the Convention is the governing instrument for the States Parties thereto.

47. That the Declaration is not a treaty does not, then, lead to the conclusion that it does not have legal effect, nor that the Court lacks the power to interpret it within the framework of the principles set out above.

However important the functions of the Inter-American Commission on Human Rights *vis-à-vis* all the OAS Member States, it is only with the adoption of the American Convention on Human Rights (sometimes referred to as the Pact of San José, Costa Rica) on 22 November 1969 and with its entry into force on 18 July 1978 that the Inter-American system truly provided for a jurisdictional system of control of the human rights obligations of the OAS Member States, although of course only for the parties to the Convention. Although the ACHR establishes a new body, the Inter-American Court of Human Rights, the IACHR also has a role under this instrument. Its Statute as currently in force describes in the following terms the functions of the Inter-American Commission on Human Rights: while Article 19 describes its role under the ACHR (also referred to in Arts. 44–51 of the ACHR), and thus only applies to States parties to the Convention, Articles 18 and 20 describe the powers of the Commission *vis-à-vis* OAS Member States that are not parties to the ACHR, and this includes a competence to examine individual communications:

Statute of the Inter-American Commission on Human Rights, approved by Resolution No. 447 taken by the General Assembly of the OAS at its ninth regular session, held in La Paz, Bolivia, October 1979:

Article 18

The Commission shall have the following powers with respect to the member states of the Organization of American States:

a. to develop an awareness of human rights among the peoples of the Americas;
b. to make recommendations to the governments of the states on the adoption of progressive measures in favor of human rights in the framework of their legislation, constitutional provisions and international commitments, as well as appropriate measures to further observance of those rights;
c. to prepare such studies or reports as it considers advisable for the performance of its duties;
d. to request that the governments of the states provide it with reports on measures they adopt in matters of human rights;

e. to respond to inquiries made by any member state through the General Secretariat of the Organization on matters related to human rights in the state and, within its possibilities, to provide those states with the advisory services they request;

f. to submit an annual report to the General Assembly of the Organization, in which due account shall be taken of the legal regime applicable to those States Parties to the American Convention on Human Rights and of that system applicable to those that are not Parties;

g. to conduct on-site observations in a state, with the consent or at the invitation of the government in question; and

h. to submit the program-budget of the Commission to the Secretary General, so that he may present it to the General Assembly.

Article 19

With respect to the States Parties to the American Convention on Human Rights, the Commission shall discharge its duties in conformity with the powers granted under the Convention and in the present Statute, and shall have the following powers in addition to those designated in Article 18:

a. to act on petitions and other communications, pursuant to the provisions of Articles 44 to 51 of the Convention;

b. to appear before the Inter-American Court of Human Rights in cases provided for in the Convention;

c. to request the Inter-American Court of Human Rights to take such provisional measures as it considers appropriate in serious and urgent cases which have not yet been submitted to it for consideration, whenever this becomes necessary to prevent irreparable injury to persons;

d. to consult the Court on the interpretation of the American Convention on Human Rights or of other treaties concerning the protection of human rights in the American states;

e. to submit additional draft protocols to the American Convention on Human Rights to the General Assembly, in order to progressively include other rights and freedoms under the system of protection of the Convention, and

f. to submit to the General Assembly, through the Secretary General, proposed amendments to the American Convention on Human Rights, for such action as the General Assembly deems appropriate.

Article 20

In relation to those member states of the Organization that are not parties to the American Convention on Human Rights, the Commission shall have the following powers, in addition to those designated in Article 18:

a. to pay particular attention to the observance of the human rights referred to in Articles I, II, III, IV, XVIII, XXV, and XXVI of the American Declaration of the Rights and Duties of Man;

b. to examine communications submitted to it and any other available information, to address the government of any member state not a Party to the Convention for information deemed pertinent by this Commission, and to make recommendations to it, when it finds this appropriate, in order to bring about more effective observance of fundamental human rights; and,

c. to verify, as a prior condition to the exercise of the powers granted under subparagraph b. above, whether the domestic legal procedures and remedies of each member state not a Party to the Convention have been duly applied and exhausted.

In order to fulfil its duties under Article 18 of its Statute, the Inter-American Commission on Human Rights also decided to appoint a number of Rapporteurs, on issues such as the rights of indigenous peoples and the rights of women, the rights of children, or the rights of Afro-descendants and against racial discrimination.

2.2 The powers of the Inter-American Court of Human Rights

The Inter-American Court of Human Rights was established as a jurisdiction composed of seven members, elected by the States Parties to the ACHR, in the General Assembly of the OAS, from a panel of candidates proposed by those states (Art. 53 ACHR). It has two functions.

(a) The advisory function

One function of the Court is to deliver advisory opinions 'regarding the interpretation of [the ACHR] or of other treaties concerning the protection of human rights in the American states', at the request of the OAS Member States or of the organs established under the OAS Charter (Art. 64(1) ACHR); the Court may also provide any OAS Member State, at its request, with 'opinions regarding the compatibility of any of its domestic laws with the aforesaid international instruments' (Art. 64(2) ACHR). In practice, this advisory competence has proved of great importance, as illustrated by the references made in this volume to a number of advisory opinions delivered by the Inter-American Court. In the following opinion, the Court describes the raison d'être of its advisory function:

> **Inter-American Court of Human Rights, Restrictions to the Death Penalty (Art. 4(2) and (4) of the American Convention on Human Rights), Advisory Opinion OC-3/83, 8 September 1983, Inter-Am. Ct. H.R. (Ser. A) No. 3 (1983):**
>
> [Guatemala objected to the Inter-American Court of Human Rights agreeing to deliver an advisory opinion at the request of the Inter-American Commission on Human Rights, since the request concerned questions of interpretation that were in dispute between that country and the Commission. Guatemala contended that, although the Commission may in principle seek an advisory opinion from the Court regarding the interpretation of any article of the Convention as provided in Article 64(1) of the Convention, if that opinion were to concern a given State directly, the Court could not render the opinion unless the State in question has accepted the tribunal's jurisdiction pursuant to Article 62(1) of the Convention. The Court disagreed:]
>
> 31. The Convention distinguishes very clearly between two types of proceedings: so-called adjudicator or contentious cases and advisory opinions. The former are governed by the provisions of Articles 61, 62 and 63 of the Convention; the latter by Article 64 ...
>
> 32. In contentious proceedings, the Court must not only interpret the applicable norms, determine the truth of the acts denounced and decide whether they are a violation of the Convention imputable to a State Party; it may also rule 'that the injured party be ensured the enjoyment of his right or freedom that was violated' [Art. 63(1) ACHR]. The States Parties to such proceeding are, moreover, legally bound to comply with the decisions of the Court in contentious cases [Art. 68(1) ACHR]. On the other hand, in advisory opinion proceedings the

Court does not exercise any fact-finding functions; instead, it is called upon to render opinions interpreting legal norms. Here the Court fulfills a consultative function through opinions that 'lack the same binding force that attaches to decisions in contentious cases' (I/A Court H.R., 'Other Treaties' Subject to the Advisory Jurisdiction of the Court (Art. 64 American Convention on Human Rights), Advisory Opinion OC-1/82 of 24 September 1982. Series A No. 1, para. 51; *cf.* Interpretation of Peace Treaties, 1950 I.C.J. 65).

33. The provisions applicable to contentious cases differ very significantly from those of Article 64, which govern advisory opinions. Thus, for example, Article 61(2) speaks of 'case' and declares that 'in order for the Court to hear a *case*, it is necessary that the procedures set forth in Articles 48 to 50 shall have been completed (emphasis added).' These procedures apply exclusively to 'a petition or communication alleging violation of any of the rights protected by this Convention' [Art. 48(1) ACHR]. Here the word 'case' is used in its technical sense to describe a contentious case within the meaning of the Convention, that is, a dispute arising as a result of a claim initiated by an individual (Art. 44) or State Party (Art. 45), charging that a State Party has violated the human rights guaranteed by the Convention.

34. One encounters the same technical use of the word 'case' in connection with the question as to who may initiate a contentious case before the Court, which contrasts with those provisions of the Convention that deal with the same issue in the consultative area. Article 61(1) provides that 'only States Parties and the Commission shall have a right to submit a case to the Court'. On the other hand, not only 'States Parties and the Commission', but also all of the 'Member States of the Organization' and the 'organs listed in Chapter X of the Charter of the Organization of American States' may request advisory opinions from the Court [Art. 64(1) ACHR]. There is yet another difference with respect to the subject matter that the Court might consider. While Article 62(1) refers to 'all matters relating to the interpretation and application of this Convention', Article 64 authorizes advisory opinions relating not only to the interpretation of the Convention but also to 'other treaties concerning the protection of human rights in the American states'. It is obvious, therefore, that what is involved here are very different matters, and that there is no reason in principle to apply the requirements contained in Articles 61, 62 and 63 to the consultative function of the Court, which is spelled out in Article 64.

35. Article 62(3) of the Convention – the provision Guatemala claims governs the application of Article 64 – reads as follows: 'The jurisdiction of the Court shall comprise all *cases* concerning the interpretation and application of the provisions of this Convention that are submitted to it, provided that the States Parties to the *case* recognize or have recognized such jurisdiction, whether by special declaration pursuant to the preceding paragraphs, or by a special agreement (emphasis added).'

It is impossible to read this provision without concluding that it, as does Article 61, uses the words 'case' or 'cases' in their technical sense.

36. The Court has already indicated that situations might arise when it would deem itself compelled to decline to comply with a request for an advisory opinion. In Other Treaties (cited above, para. 32), the Court acknowledged that resort to the advisory opinion route might in certain situations interfere with the proper functioning of the system of protection spelled out in the Convention or that it might adversely affect the interests of the victim of human rights violations. The Court addressed this problem in the following terms: 'The advisory jurisdiction of the Court is closely related to the purposes of the Convention. This jurisdiction is intended to assist the American States in fulfilling their international human rights obligations and to assist

the different organs of the inter-American system to carry out the functions assigned to them in this field. It is obvious that any request for an advisory opinion which has another purpose would weaken the system established by the Convention and would distort the advisory jurisdiction of the Court (*ibid.*, para. 25)'.

37. The instant request of the Commission does not fall within the category of advisory opinion requests that need to be rejected on those grounds because nothing in it can be deemed to interfere with the proper functioning of the system or might be deemed to have an adverse effect on the interests of a victim. The Court has merely been asked to interpret a provision of the Convention in order to assist the Commission in the discharge of the obligation it has as an OAS Charter organ 'to promote the observance and protection of human rights and to serve as a consultative organ of the Organization in these matters' (OAS Charter, Art. 112).

38. The powers conferred on the Commission require it to apply the Convention or other human rights treaties. In order to discharge fully its obligations, the Commission may find it necessary or appropriate to consult the Court regarding the meaning of certain provisions whether or not at the given moment in time there exists a difference between a government and the Commission concerning an interpretation, which might justify the request for an advisory opinion. If the Commission were to be barred from seeking an advisory opinion merely because one or more governments are involved in a controversy with the Commission over the interpretation of a disputed provision, the Commission would seldom, if ever, be able to avail itself of the Court's advisory jurisdiction. Not only would this be true of the Commission, but the OAS General Assembly, for example, would be in a similar position were it to seek an advisory opinion from the Court in the course of the Assembly's consideration of a draft resolution calling on a Member State to comply with its international human rights obligations.

39. The right to seek advisory opinions under Article 64 was conferred on OAS organs for requests falling 'within their spheres of competence'. This suggests that the right was also conferred to assist with the resolution of disputed legal issues arising in the context of the activities of an organ, be it the Assembly, the Commission, or any of the others referred to in Chapter X of the OAS Charter. It is clear, therefore, that the mere fact that there exists a dispute between the Commission and the Government of Guatemala regarding the meaning of Article 4 of the Convention does not justify the Court to decline to exercise its advisory jurisdiction in the instant proceeding.

40. This conclusion of the Court finds ample support in the jurisprudence of the International Court of Justice. That tribunal has consistently rejected requests that it decline to exercise its advisory jurisdiction in situations in which it was alleged that because the issue involved was in dispute the Court was being asked to decide a disguised contentious case (see, e.g. *Interpretation of Peace Treaties, supra* para. 32; *Reservations to the Convention on Genocide*, 1951 I.C.J. 15; *Legal Consequences for States of the Continued Presence of South Africa in Namibia (South West Africa) notwithstanding Security Council Resolution 276 (1970)*, 1971 I.C.J. 16; *Western Sahara, supra* 25). In doing so, the Hague Court has acknowledged that the advisory opinion might affect the interests of States which have not consented to its contentious jurisdiction and which are not willing to litigate the matter. The critical question has always been whether the requesting organ has a legitimate interest to obtain the opinion for the purpose of guiding its future actions (*Western Sahara, supra* para. 25, p. 27).

41. The Commission, as an organ charged with the responsibility of recommending measures designed to promote the observance and protection of human rights (OAS Charter, Art. 112; Convention, Art. 41; Statute of the Commission, Arts. 1 and 18), has a legitimate institutional

interest in the interpretation of Article 4 of the Convention. The mere fact that this provision may also have been invoked before the Commission in petitions and communications filed under Articles 44 and 45 of the Convention does not affect this conclusion. Given the nature of advisory opinions, the opinion of the Court in interpreting Article 4 cannot be deemed to be an adjudication of those petitions and communications.

42. ... [T]he Commission enjoys, in general, a pervasive legitimate institutional interest in questions bearing on the promotion and protection of human rights in the inter-American system, which could be deemed to confer on it, as a practical matter, 'an absolute right to request advisory opinions within the framework of Article 64(1) of the Convention' (*ibid.*, para. 16). Viewed in this light, the instant request certainly concerns an issue in which the Commission has a legitimate institutional interest.

43. The advisory jurisdiction conferred on the Court by Article 64 of the Convention is unique in contemporary international law. As this Court already had occasion to explain, neither the International Court of Justice nor the European Court of Human Rights has been granted the extensive advisory jurisdiction which the Convention confers on the Inter-American Court (Other Treaties, *supra* para. 32, paras. 15 and 16). Here it is relevant merely to emphasize that the Convention, by permitting Member States and OAS organs to seek advisory opinions, creates a parallel system to that provided for under Article 62 and offers an alternate judicial method of a consultative nature, which is designed to assist states and organs to comply with and to apply human rights treaties without subjecting them to the formalism and the sanctions associated with the contentious judicial process. It would therefore be inconsistent with the object and purpose of the Convention and the relevant individual provisions, to adopt an interpretation of Article 64 that would apply to it the jurisdictional requirements of Article 62 and thus rob it of its intended utility merely because of the possible existence of a dispute regarding the meaning of the provision at issue in the request.

(b) Individual petitions

The Court may adopt judgments on cases submitted to it either by a State party to the ACHR, or by the Inter-American Commission of Human Rights, provided the defending State party has recognized the jurisdiction of the Court – which, at the time of writing, all States parties to the Convention had done. According to Article 44 ACHR, 'Any person or group of persons, or any nongovernmental entity legally recognized in one or more member states of the Organization, may lodge petitions with the Commission containing denunciations or complaints of violation of this Convention by a State Party.' This provision thus allows for a form of *actio popularis* to denounce violations of the ACHR to the Commission. Upon receiving such a petition, the Commission may decide that the case raises a situation of extreme gravity and urgency, in which case it may request the Inter-American Court of Human Rights to adopt any provisional measures 'when necessary to avoid irreparable damage to persons' (Art. 63(2) ACHR). The procedure is divided in two phases.

The admissibility phase

The Commission shall first determine whether the petition is admissible. Article 46 ACHR provides that a petition shall only be considered admissible by the Commission if 'the remedies under domestic law have been pursued and exhausted in accordance with generally recognized principles of international law', although under Article 46(2) this requirement does not apply when (a) 'the domestic legislation of the state concerned does not afford due process of law for the protection of the right or rights that have allegedly been violated'; (b) 'the party alleging violation of his rights has been denied access to the remedies under domestic law or has been prevented from exhausting them'; or (c) 'there has been unwarranted delay in rendering a final judgment under the aforementioned remedies'. The Inter-American Court of Human Rights has recalled that the rule of prior exhaustion of local remedies is 'a prerequisite established in favor of the State, which may waive its right, even tacitly, and this occurs, inter alia, when it is not timely invoked' (*Fairén Garbi and Solís Corrales* case, judgment of 15 March 1989, Series C No. 6, para. 109). Therefore, when a State does not invoke the failure to exhaust local remedies before the Commission, it is estopped from raising the same objection before the Court. This is in accordance with the understanding of the function of the rule of prior exhaustion of local remedies in human rights instruments, as noted by Judge A. A. Cançado Trindade in his concurring opinion:

Inter-American Court of Human Rights, *Gangaram Panday* case, Preliminary Objections, judgment of 4 December 1991, (Ser. C) No. 12 (1994):

38. This requirement [to exhaust local remedies] 'allows the state to resolve the problem under its internal law before being confronted with an international proceeding. This is particularly true in the international jurisdiction of human rights, because the latter reinforces or complements the domestic jurisdiction' (American Convention, Preamble) (*Velásquez Rodríguez* Case, Judgment of July 29, 1988. Series C No. 4, para. 61; *Godínez Cruz* Case, Judgment of January 20, 1989, Series C No. 5, para. 64; *Fairén Garbi and Solís Corrales* Case, Judgment of March 15, 1989. Series C No. 6, para. 85).

The Court has stated that: 'Generally recognized principles of international law indicate, first, that this is a rule that may be waived, either expressly or by implication, by the State having the right to invoke it, as this Court has already recognized (see *Viviana Gallardo et al.*, Judgment of November 13, 1981, No. G 101/81. Series A, para. 26). Second, the objection asserting the non-exhaustion of domestic remedies, to be timely, must be made at an early stage of the proceedings by the State entitled to make it, lest a waiver of the requirement be presumed. Third, the State claiming non-exhaustion has an obligation to prove that domestic remedies remain to be exhausted and that they are effective' (*Velásquez Rodríguez* Case, Preliminary Objections, *supra* 18, para. 88; *Fairén Garbi and Solís Corrales* Case, Preliminary Objections, *supra* 18, para. 87; *Godínez Cruz* Case, Preliminary Objections, *supra* 38, para. 90. See also *In the Matter of Viviana Gallardo et al.*, No. G 101/81. Series A) ...

39. The Court notes that the Government did not interpose the objection of non-exhaustion of domestic remedies before the Commission ... This constitutes a tacit waiver of the objection. The Government also failed to indicate in a timely fashion the domestic remedies that, in its opinion, should have been exhausted or how they would be effective.

40. Consequently, the Court considers that the Government is untimely when it now seeks to invoke the objection of non-exhaustion of domestic remedies that it should have interposed before the Commission but did not.

Concurring opinion of Judge Antônio Augusto Cançado Trindade:

11. The specificity or special character of human rights treaties and instruments, the nature and gravity of certain human rights violations and the imperatives of protection of the human person stress the need to avoid unfair consequences and to secure to this end a necessarily distinct (more flexible and equitable) application of the local remedies rule in the particular context of the international protection of human rights. This has accounted for, in the present domain of protection, the application of the principles of good faith and estoppel in the safeguard of due process and of the rights of the alleged victims, the distribution of the burden of proof as to exhaustion of local remedies between the alleged victim and the respondent Government with a heavier burden upon the latter. This comes to acknowledge that generally recognized principles of international law, referred to in the formulation of the local remedies rule in human rights treaties and instruments, necessarily undergo some degree of adaptation or adjustment when enshrined in those treaties and instruments, given the specificity of these latter and the special character of their ultimate object and purpose.

In its Advisory Opinion OC-11/90, the Inter-American Court had already adopted a generous reading of the requirement of prior exhaustion of domestic remedies. The Commission had submitted two questions to the Court. One was whether the requirement of the exhaustion of domestic legal remedies applies to an indigent, who because of economic circumstances is unable to avail himself of the legal remedies within a country. Another one was whether the same requirement applied where a person is unable to retain representation due to a general fear in the legal community, and therefore cannot avail himself of the legal remedies provided by law in a country. The Advisory Opinion usefully highlights the link between the obligation of the State to provide effective remedies and the application of the requirement to exhaust local remedies:

Inter-American Court of Human Rights, *Exceptions to the Exhaustion of Domestic Remedies (Art. 46(1), 46(2)(a) and 46(2)(b) American Convention on Human Rights)*, Advisory Opinion OC-11/90 of 10 August 1990 requested by the Inter-American Commission on Human Rights:

18. Article 46(2) makes no specific reference to indigents, the subject of the first question, nor to those situations in which a person has been unable to obtain legal representation because of a generalized fear in the legal community to take such cases, which the second question addresses.

19. The answers to the questions presented by the Commission thus depend on a determination of whether a person's failure to exhaust domestic remedies in the circumstances posited falls under one or the other exception spelled out in Article 46(2). That is, whether or under what circumstances a person's indigency or inability to obtain legal representation because of a generalized fear among the legal community will exempt him from the requirement to exhaust domestic remedies.

20. In addressing the issue of indigency, the Court must emphasize that merely because a person is indigent does not, standing alone, mean that he does not have to exhaust domestic

remedies, for the provision contained in Article 46(1) is of a general nature. The language of Article 46(2) suggests that whether or not an indigent has to exhaust domestic remedies will depend on whether the law or the circumstances permit him to do so.

21. In analyzing these issues, the Court must bear in mind the provisions contained in Articles 1(1), 24 and the relevant parts of Article 8 of the Convention [concerning respectively the obligation to respect the rights of the Convention without discrimnation, *inter alia*, on grounds of economic status; the right to equal protection; and the right to a fair trial].

22. The final section of Article 1(1) prohibits a state from discriminating on a variety of grounds, among them 'economic status'. The meaning of the term 'discrimination' employed by Article 24 must, then, be interpreted by reference to the list enumerated in Article 1(1). If a person who is seeking the protection of the law in order to assert rights which the Convention guarantees finds that his economic status (in this case, his indigency), prevents him from so doing because he cannot afford either the necessary legal counsel or the costs of the proceedings, that person is being discriminated against by reason of his economic status and, hence, is not receiving equal protection before the law.

23. '[P]rotection of the law' consists, fundamentally, of the remedies the law provides for the protection of the rights guaranteed by the Convention. The obligation to respect and guarantee such rights, which Article 1(1) imposes on the States Parties, implies, as the Court has already stated, 'the duty of the States Parties to organize the governmental apparatus and, in general, all the structures through which public power is exercised, so that they are capable of juridically ensuring the free and full enjoyment of human rights (*Velásquez Rodríguez* Case, Judgment of July 29, 1988, Series C No. 4, para. 166; *Godínez Cruz* Case, Judgment of January 20, 1989, Series C. No. 5, para. 175)'.

24. Insofar as the right to legal counsel is concerned, this duty to organize the governmental apparatus and to create the structures necessary to guarantee human rights is related to the provisions of Article 8 of the Convention. That article distinguishes between 'accusations[s] of a criminal nature' and procedures 'of a civil, labor, fiscal, or any other nature'. Although it provides that '[e]very person has the right to a hearing, with due guarantees ... by a ... tribunal' in both types of proceedings, it spells out in addition certain 'minimum guarantees' for those accused of a criminal offense. Thus, the concept of a fair hearing in criminal proceedings also embraces, at the very least, those 'minimum guarantees'. By labeling these guarantees as '*minimum guarantees*', the Convention assumes that other, additional guarantees may be necessary in specific circumstances to ensure a fair hearing.

25. Sub-paragraphs(d) and (e) of Article 8(2) indicate that the accused has a right 'to defend himself personally or to be assisted by legal counsel of his own choosing' and that, if he should choose not to do so, he has 'the inalienable right to be assisted by counsel provided by the state, paid or not as the domestic law provides ...' Thus, a defendant may defend himself personally, but it is important to bear in mind that this would only be possible where permitted under domestic law. If a person refuses or is unable to defend himself personally, he has the right to be assisted by counsel of his own choosing. In cases where the accused neither defends himself nor engages his own counsel within the time period established by law, he has the right to be assisted by counsel provided by the state, paid or not as the domestic law provides. To that extent the Convention guarantees the right to counsel in criminal proceedings. But since it does not stipulate that legal counsel be provided free of charge when required, an indigent would suffer discrimination for reason of his *economic status* if, when in need of legal counsel, the state were not to provide it to him free of charge.

26. Article 8 must, then, be read to require legal counsel only when that is necessary for a fair hearing. Any state that does not provide indigents with such counsel free of charge cannot, therefore, later assert that appropriate remedies existed but were not exhausted.

27. Even in those cases in which the accused is forced to defend himself because he cannot afford legal counsel, a violation of Article 8 of the Convention could be said to exist if it can be proved that the lack of legal counsel affected the right to a fair hearing to which he is entitled under that Article.

28. For cases which concern the determination of a person's 'rights and obligations of a civil, labor, fiscal, or any other nature', Article 8 does not specify any 'minimum guarantees' similar to those provided in Article 8(2) for criminal proceedings. It does, however, provide for 'due guarantees'; consequently, the individual here also has the right to the fair hearing provided for in criminal cases. It is important to note here that the circumstances of a particular case or proceeding – its significance, its legal character, and its context in a particular legal system – are among the factors that bear on the determination of whether legal representation is or is not necessary for a fair hearing.

29. Lack of legal counsel is not, of course, the only factor that could prevent an indigent from exhausting domestic remedies. It could even happen that the state might provide legal counsel free of charge but neglect to cover the costs that might be required to ensure the fair hearing that Article 8 prescribes. In such cases, the exceptions to Article 46(1) would apply. Here again, the circumstances of each case and each particular legal system must be kept in mind.

30. In its advisory opinion request, the Commission states that it 'has received certain petitions in which the victim alleges that he has not been able to comply with the requirement of the exhaustion of remedies set forth in the domestic legislation because he cannot afford legal assistance or, in some cases, the obligatory filing fees'. Upon applying the foregoing analysis to the examples set forth by the Commission, it must be concluded that if legal services are required either as a matter of law or fact in order for a right guaranteed by the Convention to be recognized and a person is unable to obtain such services because of his indigency, then that person would be exempted from the requirement to exhaust domestic remedies. The same would be true of cases requiring the payment of a filing fee. That is to say, if it is impossible for an indigent to deposit such a fee, he cannot be required to exhaust domestic remedies unless the state provides some alternative mechanism.

31. Thus, the first question presented to the Court by the Commission is not whether the Convention guarantees the right to legal counsel as such or as a result of the prohibition of discrimination for reason of economic status (Art. 1(1)). Rather, the question is whether an indigent may appeal directly to the Commission to protect a right guaranteed in the Convention without first exhausting the applicable domestic remedies. The answer to this question given what has been said above, is that if it can be shown that an indigent needs legal counsel to effectively protect a right which the Convention guarantees and his indigency prevents him from obtaining such counsel, he does not have to exhaust the relevant domestic remedies. That is the meaning for the language of Article 46(2) read in conjunction with Articles 1(1), 24 and 8.

32. The Court will now turn to the second question. It concerns the exhaustion of domestic remedies in situations where an individual is unable to obtain the necessary legal representation due to a general fear in the legal community of a given country. The Commission explains that, according to what some complainants have alleged, '[t]his situation has occured where an atmosphere of fear prevails and lawyers do not accept cases which they believe could place their own lives and those of their families in jeopardy'.

33. In general, the same basic principles govern this question as those which the Court has deemed applicable to the first question. That is to say, if a person, for a reason such as the one stated above, is prevented from availing himself of the domestic legal remedies necessary to assert a right which the Convention guarantees, he cannot be required to exhaust those remedies. The state's obligation to guarantee such remedies, is, of course, unaffected by this conclusion ...

35. It follows therefrom that where an individual requires legal representation and a generalized fear in the legal community prevents him from obtaining such representation, the exception set out in Article 46(2)(b) is fully applicable and the individual is exempted from the requirement to exhaust domestic remedies.

36. The Court is of the opinion that, in the cases posited by the Commission, it is the considerations outlined that render the remedies adequate and effective in accordance with generally recognized principles of international law to which Article 46(1) refers; namely, remedies 'suitable to address an infringement of a legal right and capable of producing the result for which [they were] designed' (*Velásquez Rodríguez* Case, *supra* 23, paras. 64 and 66; *Godínez Cruz* Case, *supra* 23, paras. 67 and 69, and *Fairén Garbi and Solís Corrales* Case, *supra* 34, paras. 88 and 91).

The merits phase

Once the Inter-American Commission on Human Rights has determined that the petition is admissible, it may seek to reach a friendly settlement between the parties. If that fails or if there is no room for such a friendly settlement, the case proceeds to the merits stage. The Commission investigates whether the violation alleged in the petition existed, and if it arrives at the conclusion that such a violation has indeed occurred, it shall 'draw up a report setting forth the facts and stating its conclusions' (Art. 50 ACHR). This report contains the proposals and recommendations of the Commission. It is transmitted to the parties. This may lead to the issue being solved, either because a friendly settlement is reached on the basis of the Commission's report, or because the State agrees with the conclusions and follows the recommendations of the Commission. If not, the case may be transmitted to the Inter-American Court, either by the Commission or by the State concerned, if this State is a party to the Convention. If the case is not presented to Court, the Commission publishes a second report, as provided for in Article 51 ACHR:

American Convention on Human Rights, Article 51:

1. If, within a period of three months from the date of the transmittal of the report of the Commission to the states concerned, the matter has not either been settled or submitted by the Commission or by the state concerned to the Court and its jurisdiction accepted, the Commission may, by the vote of an absolute majority of its members, set forth its opinion and conclusions concerning the question submitted for its consideration.
2. Where appropriate, the Commission shall make pertinent recommendations and shall prescribe a period within which the state is to take the measures that are incumbent upon it to remedy the situation examined.

3. When the prescribed period has expired, the Commission shall decide by the vote of an absolute majority of its members whether the state has taken adequate measures and whether to publish its report.

If the case is transmitted to the Court, the Court shall receive memorials from the Commission, the representatives of the petitioner, and the State, all of which also take part in the hearings. Article 63(1) ACHR describes the effect of a Court judgment finding that the Convention has been violated:

American Convention on Human Rights, Article 63(1):

If the Court finds that there has been a violation of a right or freedom protected by this Convention, the Court shall rule that the injured party be ensured the enjoyment of his right or freedom that was violated. It shall also rule, if appropriate, that the consequences of the measure or situation that constituted the breach of such right or freedom be remedied and that fair compensation be paid to the injured party.

The supervision of compliance with the judgments of the Inter-American Court of Human Rights

Apart from the compensatory damages it may award, the Court has no means under the ACHR to enforce its judgments. It nevertheless took the initiative of requesting States to report back about the measures taken to implement the judgments. Its power to do so was occasionally challenged. In the *Baena Ricardo et al.* case *(270 Workers v. Panama)*, the Comité Panameño por los Derechos Humanos denounced the State of Panama before the Inter-American Commission on Human Rights for having laid off 270 public officials and union leaders who had taken part in several rallies against the administration's policies and to defend their labour rights, and were alleged by the Government to have collaborated with a military uprising. After the employees were dismissed, a law was passed under which any actions started by the workers to challenge their dismissal had to be lodged with courts dealing with administrative matters – instead of labour courts, as normally required by the applicable law. The actions filed with the Supreme Court of Panama failed. After examining the petition and having found it admissible, the Inter-American Commission of Human Rights transmitted the case to the Inter-American Court of Human Rights. In a judgment of 2 February 2001, the Court concluded the State of Panama had violated the rights of freedom of association, judicial guarantees and judicial protection, as well as the principles of legality and freedom from *ex post facto* laws in detriment of the 270 workers. The Court also stated that minimum due process guarantees set forth in Article 8(2) ACHR must be observed in the course of an administrative procedure, as well as in any other procedure leading to a decision that may affect the rights of persons. The Court decided that the State had to reassign the workers to their previous positions and pay them the outstanding wages.

Following its initial judgment on the merits, the Court adopted a series of decisions on the measures adopted by Panama to comply with the judgment. However, Panama soon took the view that by seeking to monitor compliance with its own judgment, the Court 'ha[d] interpreted its own judgment', and that the stage of monitoring compliance with judgment was 'a post-judgment stage ... that did not fall within the judicial sphere of the Court, but strictly within the political sphere'. The Court felt compelled to justify its practice of monitoring compliance with its judgments. It adopted the following judgment on its competence:

Inter-American Court of Human Rights, *Baena Ricardo et al.* case (270 *Workers* v. *Panama*), judgment on competence, 28 November 2003:

58. Panama has been a State Party to the Convention since June 22, 1978, and, in accordance with Article 62 of this treaty, it accepted the contentious jurisdiction of the Court on May 9, 1990. On February 2, 2001, the Court delivered judgment on merits, and the reparations and costs.

59. Given that this is the first time that a State Party in a case before the Inter-American Court questions the competence of the Court to monitor compliance with its judgments, a function carried out in all the cases on which judgment has been passed and invariably respected by the States Parties, this Court considers it necessary to refer to the obligation of the States to comply with the decisions of the Court in any case to which they are parties, and to the competence of the Inter-American Court to monitor compliance with its decisions and issue instructions and orders on compliance with the measures of reparations it has ordered.

60. When the Court has ruled on the merits and the reparations and costs in a case submitted to its consideration, the State must observe the norms of the Convention that refer to compliance with that judgment or those judgments. In accordance with the provisions of Article 67 of the American Convention, the State must comply with the judgments of the Court promptly and fully. Moreover, Article 68(1) of the American Convention stipulates that '[t]he States parties to the Convention undertake to comply with the judgment of the Court in any case to which they are parties'. The treaty obligation of the States Parties to comply promptly with the Court's decisions binds all the State's powers and bodies.

(A) State obligations

(a) Pacta sunt servanda 61. The obligation to comply with the provisions of the Court's decisions corresponds to a basic principle of the law on the international responsibility of the State, which is supported by international case law; according to this, a State must comply with its international treaty obligations in good faith (pacta sunt servanda) and ... as established in Article 27 of the 1969 Vienna Convention on the Law of Treaties, a party may not invoke the provisions of its internal law as justification for its failure to perform a treaty. As regards execution of the reparations ordered by the Court in the sphere of domestic law, the responsible State may not modify or fail to comply with them by invoking the provisions of domestic law.

(b) Obligation to repair 62. The obligation to repair, all aspects of which (scope, nature, methods and determination of the beneficiaries) are regulated by international law, may not be modified or not complied with by the State which has this obligation, by invoking provisions or difficulties of domestic law ...

64. Article 63(1) ACHR [cited above] grants the Inter-American Court a wide margin of judicial discretion to determine the measures that all the consequences of the violation to be repaired.

65. As the Court has stated, Article 63.1 of the Convention reproduces the text of a customary law norm that is one of the fundamental principles of the law of the international responsibility of States. And that is how this Court has applied it. When an unlawful act occurs that may be attributed to the State, this entails the latter's international responsibility for violating an international norm. Based on this responsibility, a new juridical relationship is born for the State consisting in the obligation to make reparation.

(c) Scope of 'effet utile' 66. The States Parties to the Convention must guarantee compliance with treaty provisions and their effects (*effet utile*) at the level of their respective domestic laws. This principle is applicable not only with regard to the substantive norms of the human rights treaties (namely, those that contain provisions on protected rights), but also with regard to the procedural norms, such as those referring to compliance with the decisions of the Court (Articles 67 and 68(1) of the Convention). The provisions contained in the said articles must be interpreted and applied so as to ensure that the protected guarantee is truly practical and effective, recalling the special nature of human rights treaties and their collective implementation.

67. Regarding the said principle of *effet utile*, in the *Corfu Channel* case, the International Court of Justice reiterated what the Permanent Court of International Justice had said, to the effect that: '... regarding the specific question on the competence pending decision, it may be sufficient to observe that, when determining the nature and scope of a measure, the Court must observe its practical effect instead of the predominant motive that it is believed inspired it' [*Corfu Channel* case, judgment of 9 April 1949: I.C.J. Reports 1949, p. 24; and P.C.I.J, Advisory Opinion No. 13 of July 23rd, 1926, Series B, No. 13, p. 19].

(B) Scope of the competence of the Court to determine its own competence
68. The Court, as any body with jurisdictional functions, has the authority inherent in its attributions to determine the scope of its own competence (*compétence de la compétence/ Kompetenz-Kompetenz*). The instruments accepting the optional clause on obligatory jurisdiction (Article 62(1) of the Convention) assume that the States submitting them accept the Court's right to settle any dispute relative to its jurisdiction, such as the dispute in this case on the function of monitoring compliance with its judgments. An objection or any other action of the State intended to affect the competence of the Court has no consequence, because, in all circumstances, the Court retains the *compétence de la compétence*, as it is master of its own jurisdiction ...

70. The Court cannot abdicate the prerogative to determine the scope of its own jurisdiction, which is also an obligation imposed upon it by the American Convention in order to exercise its functions according to Article 62(3) thereof. That provision reads as follows: 'The jurisdiction of the Court shall comprise all cases concerning the interpretation and application of the provisions of th[e] Convention that are submitted to it, provided that the States Parties to the case recognize or have recognized such jurisdiction, whether by special declaration ... or by a special agreement.'

71. As the Courts has stated in its constant case law, acceptance of the contentious jurisdiction of the Court is a binding clause that does not admit limitations that are not included

expressly in Articles 62(1) and 62(2) of the American Convention. Given the fundamental importance of this clause for the operation of the Convention's system of protection, it cannot be subject to unanticipated limitations invoked by States Parties for reasons of domestic policy.

(C) Effectiveness of decisions on reparations

72. When it has determined the international responsibility of the State for violation of the American Convention, the Court proceeds to order measures designed to remedy this violation. Its jurisdiction includes the authority to administer justice; it is not restricted to stating the law, but also encompasses monitoring compliance with what has been decided. It is therefore necessary to establish and implement mechanisms or procedures for monitoring compliance with the judicial decisions, an activity that is inherent in the jurisdictional function. Monitoring compliance with judgments is one of the elements that comprises jurisdiction. To maintain otherwise, would mean affirming that the judgments delivered by the Court are merely declaratory and not effective. Compliance with the reparations ordered by the Court in its decisions is the materialization of justice for the specific case and, ultimately, of jurisdiction; to the contrary, the *raison d'être* for the functioning of the Court would be imperiled.

73. The effectiveness of judgments depends on their execution. The process should lead to the materialization of the protection of the right recognized in the judicial ruling, by the proper application of this ruling.

74. Compliance with judgment is strongly related to the right to access to justice, which is embodied in Articles 8 (Right to a Fair Trial) and 25 (Judicial Protection) of the American Convention ...

77. The Court has established that the formal existence of remedies is not sufficient; these must be effective; in other words, they must provide results or responses to the violations of rights included in the Convention. In this respect, the Court has stated that: '... those remedies that, owing to the general conditions of the country or even the particular circumstances of a case, are illusory cannot be considered effective. This may occur, for example, when their uselessness has been shown in practice, because the jurisdictional body lacks the necessary independence to decide impartially or because the means to execute its decisions are lacking; owing to any other situation that establishes a situation of denial of justice, as happens when there is unjustified delay in the decision.'

78. '[T]he safeguard of the individual in the face of the arbitrary exercise of the power of the State is the primary purpose of the international protection of human rights'; such protection must be genuine and *effective*.

79. States have the responsibility to embody in their legislation and ensure due application of effective remedies and guarantees of due process of law before the competent authorities, which protect all persons subject to their jurisdiction from acts that violate their fundamental rights or which lead to the determination of the latter's rights and obligations. However, State responsibility does not end when the competent authorities issue the decision or judgment. The State must also guarantee the means to execute the said final decisions.

80. In this respect, the Inter–American Court declared the violation of Article 25 of the Convention in '*Five Pensioners*' v. *Peru*, when it stated that the defendant State did not execute the judgments issued by the domestic courts for a long period of time.

81. Likewise, when considering the violation of Article 6 of the European Convention for the Protection of Human Rights and Fundamental Freedoms (hereinafter 'the European Convention'), which embodies the right to a fair trial, the European Court established in *Hornsby* v. *Greece*,

that: '... that right would be illusory if a Contracting State's domestic legal system allowed a final, binding judicial decision to remain inoperative to the detriment of one party ... *Execution of a judgment given by any court must therefore be regarded as an integral part of the "trial" ...*' (emphasis added).

82. In light of the above, this Court considers that, in order to comply with the right to access to justice, it is not sufficient that a final ruling be delivered during the respective proceeding or appeal, declaring rights and obligations, or providing protection to certain persons. It is also necessary that there are effective mechanisms to execute the decisions or judgments, so that the declared rights are protected effectively. The execution of such decisions and judgments should be considered an integral part of the right to access to justice, understood in its broadest sense, as also encompassing full compliance with the respective decision. The contrary would imply the denial of this right.

83. The above-mentioned considerations are applicable to international proceedings before the inter-American system for the protection of human rights. In the judgments on merits and reparations and costs, the Inter-American Court decides whether the State is internationally responsible and, when it is, orders the adoption of a series of measures of reparation to make the consequences of the violation cease, guarantee the violated rights, and repair the pecuniary and non-pecuniary damage produced by the violations. As previously stated (*supra* paras. 61 and 62), the responsible States are obliged to comply with the provisions of the decisions of the Court and may not invoke provisions of domestic law in order not to execute them. If the responsible State does not execute the measures of reparations ordered by the Court at the domestic level, it is denying the right to access to international justice.

(D) Legal grounds for monitoring compliance with the decisions of the Court

... 88. The American Convention does not establish a specific body responsible for monitoring compliance with the judgments delivered by the Court, as provided for in the European Convention [in which Article 46(2) ECHR provides that the Committee of Ministers of the Council of Europe, composed of the Foreign Affairs Ministers of the Council of Europe Member States or their delegates, monitors the execution of the judgments of the European Court of Human Rights]. When the American Convention was drafted, the model adopted by the European Convention was followed as regards competent bodies and institutional mechanisms; however, it is clear that, when regulating monitoring compliance with the judgments of the Inter-American Court, it was not envisaged that the OAS General Assembly or the OAS Permanent Council would carry out a similar function to the Committee of Ministers in the European system.

... 90. [On the basis of the preparatory works of the American Convention on Human Rights, t]he Court considers that, when adopting the provisions of Article 65 of the Convention [according to which: 'To each regular session of the General Assembly of the Organization of American States the Court shall submit, for the Assembly's consideration, a report on its work during the previous year. It shall specify, in particular, the cases in which a state has not complied with its judgments, making any pertinent recommendations'], the intention of the States was to grant the Court the authority to monitor compliance with its decisions, and that the Court should be responsible for informing the OAS General Assembly, through its annual report, of the cases in which the decisions of the Court had not been complied with, because it is not possible to apply Article 65 of the Convention unless the Court monitors compliance with its decisions.

... 92. According to the provisions of Article 62(1) of the Convention, the Court has jurisdiction in all matters relating to the interpretation or application of the American Convention ...

93. From this, it is evident that, the matters relating to the application of the Convention encompass everything related to monitoring compliance with the judgments of the Court. It is obvious that, in the issues related with the application of the Convention, is included everything referring to the monitoring of the compliance of the judgments of the Court.

94. Article 31(1) of the 1969 Vienna Convention on the Law of Treaties states that: 'A treaty shall be interpreted in good faith in accordance with the ordinary meaning to be given to the terms of the treaty in their context and in the light of its object and purpose.'

95. Moreover, Article 29(a) of the American Convention establishes that no provision of the Convention shall be interpreted as permitting any State Party, group, or person to suppress the enjoyment or exercise of the rights and freedoms recognized in the Convention or to restrict them to a greater extent than is provided for therein. An interpretation of the American Convention that did not allow any body to monitor compliance with judgments by the responsible States would run counter to the goal and purpose of this treaty, which is the effective protection of human rights, and would deprive all the beneficiaries of the Convention of the guarantee of protection of those rights by the actions of its jurisdictional body, and the consequent execution of the latter's decisions. Allowing States to comply with the reparations ordered in the judgments without adequate monitoring would be equal to leaving the execution of the Court's decisions to their free will.

... 101. In order to comply with the mandate established in [the Convention] to monitor compliance with the commitment assumed by the States Parties to 'comply with the judgment of the Court in any case to which they are parties' (Article 68(1) of the Convention) and, in particular, to inform the OAS General Assembly of the cases in which 'a State has failed to comply with the Court's ruling', the Court must first know the degree of compliance with its decisions. To this end, the Court must monitor that the responsible States comply effectively with the reparations ordered by the Court, before advising the OAS General Assembly that they have failed to comply with a ruling.

102. Moreover, the Court's authority to monitor compliance with its judgments and the procedure adopted to this end, are also grounded in the constant and standard practice of the Court and in the resulting *opinio juris communis* of the States Parties to the Convention, with regard to whom the Court has issued various orders on compliance with judgment. The *opinio juris communis* means the expression of the universal juridical conscience through the observance, by most of the members of the international community, of a determined practice because it is obligatory. This *opinio juris communis* has been revealed because these States have shown a general and repeated attitude of accepting the monitoring function of the Court, which has been clearly and amply demonstrated by their presentation of the reports that the Court has asked for, and also their compliance with the decisions of the Court when giving them instructions or clarifying aspects on which there is a dispute between the parties regarding compliance with reparations.

103. Moreover, in all the cases before the Court, the Inter-American Commission and the victims or their legal representatives have accepted its monitoring function, have forwarded their comments on the reports submitted by the States to the Court, and have abided by the decisions of the Court regarding compliance with judgment. Thus, the activity of the Court and the conduct of both the States, and the Inter-American Commission and the victims or their legal representatives, have been complementary in relation to monitoring compliance with judgments, so that the Court has exercised the function of carrying out this monitoring and, in turn, the

States, the Inter-American Commission and the victims or their legal representatives have respected the decisions issued by the Court in the exercise of this supervisory function.

104. Contrary to what Panama has affirmed (*supra* para. 54(e)), as regards the lapse of time required in order to consider that constant practice exists, this Court considers that the important point is that the practice is observed without interruption and constantly, and that it is not essential that the conduct should be practiced over a specific period of time. This is how it has been understood by international legal writings and case law [*North Sea Continental Shelf*, judgment, I.C.J. Reports 1969, paras. 73 and 74; and *Free City of Danzig and International Labour Organization*, Advisory Opinion, 1930, P.C.I.J., Collection of Advisory Opinions, Series B–No. 18, pp. 12–13]. International case law has even recognized the existence of customary norms that were developed over very short periods [*Free City of Danzig and International Labour Organization*, cited above, pp. 12–13].

(E) Procedure applied to monitoring compliance with the decisions of the Court

105. Neither the American Convention, nor the Statute and Rules of Procedure of the Court indicate a procedure that should be observed for monitoring compliance with the judgments delivered by the Court, or with regard to other matters, such as urgent and provisional measures. The Court has carried out this monitoring using a written procedure, which consists in the responsible State presenting the reports that the Court requests, and the Inter-American Commission and the victims or their legal representatives forwarding comments on these reports. Likewise, with regard to the stage of monitoring compliance with judgments, the Court has adopted the constant practice of issuing orders or sending communications to the responsible State in order, *inter alia*, to express its concern in relation to aspects of the judgment pending compliance, to urge the State to comply with the Court's decisions, to request detailed information on the measures taken to comply with specific measures of reparation, and to provide instructions for compliance, as well as to clarify aspects relating to execution and implementation of the reparations about which there is a dispute between the parties.

106. This written procedure allows the Courts to monitor compliance with its judgments and guarantees respect for the adversarial principle, since both the State and the Inter-American Commission and the victims or their legal representatives are able to provide the Court with all the information they deem relevant concerning compliance with the Court's decisions. Hence, the Court does not issue an order or, through another act, consider the status of compliance with its judgment without first examining the reports presented by the State and the respective comments forwarded by the Commission and the victims or their legal representatives. However, it should be explained that, although the stage of monitoring compliance with judgment has been developed through this written procedure and a public hearing has never been convened during this stage, if, in the future, the Court considers it appropriate and necessary, it can convene the parties to a public hearing to listen to the arguments on compliance with the judgment. There is no provision in the Convention or in the Statute and the Rules of Procedure of the Court that requires the latter to hold public hearings to decide on the merits of a case and order reparations, so it may be inferred that neither is it necessary to hold hearings to consider compliance with judgments, unless the Court considers it essential.

107. Since it issued its first judgments on reparations in 1989, the Court has monitored compliance with the judgments delivered in the contentious cases through this written procedure constantly and without interruption – even in the cases in which the defendant States acknowledged their international responsibility – and, to this end, has issued communications

and orders on compliance with its judgments in all the cases, in order to ensure the full and effective implementation of its decisions ...

109. [A]nother example that reveals the acceptance by the States of the competence of the Court to monitor compliance with its decisions occurred when a State consulted the Court about whether filing the investigation into the facts that constituted the matter of the case at the domestic level relieved it of the responsibility established in the Court's judgment. In its reply to this State communication, the Court decided that the State must 'continue to investigate the facts and prosecute and punish those responsible; consequently, reopening the respective judicial proceeding'.

(F) Position of the OAS General Assembly on monitoring compliance with the decisions of the Court

110. [A]s of the very first cases heard by the Court, when presenting its annual report, the Court has informed the OAS General Assembly of the procedure followed to monitor compliance with judgments and their compliance status. If monitoring compliance with the judgments of the Court were the 'exclusive [competence] of the General Assembly of the Organization of American States' [as alleged by Panama], this political body would already have ruled in this respect, and this has not happened. It is not possible to suppose that, since 1989, the Court has been exercising a function that belongs to the maximum political body of the OAS and that the latter, knowing this, has allowed it ...

114. Consequently, the OAS General Assembly's position concerning monitoring compliance with the judgments of the Court has been to consider that this supervision falls under the authority of the Court and that the latter should indicate the cases in which a State has not complied with its judgments in its annual report ...

(G) Acceptance by the State of the authority of the Court to monitor compliance with its decisions

... 121. The Court observes that the State first questioned its competence to monitor compliance with its judgments more than two years after the Court had delivered the judgment on merits and reparations and costs – in which it stated that it would monitor compliance with the judgment. Since that judgment was rendered, Panama has presented 14 briefs on compliance with that decision to the Court ..., in which it has kept the Court informed about the different measures taken in order to comply with this judgment of the Court. Likewise, the State has manifested 'its intention to comply with the judgment of February 2, 2001'. After the Court had issued a second order, in which it referred to the general parameters that the State should respect when complying with the reparations ordered in this case, Panama questioned the Court's competence to monitor compliance with its decisions. However, it in no way questioned the first order issued by the Court.

122. Even though Panama submitted two briefs ... in which it contested the Court's competence to monitor compliance with its judgments, in these same briefs, the State informed the Court about different measures taken to comply with the decisions of the Court ...

124. Furthermore, Panama not only complied with its obligation to present reports to the Court and carry out acts that reveal its acknowledgment of the Court's monitoring function, but also it never mentioned its disagreement about the meaning or scope of the judgment delivered in this case; specifically with regard to the Court's competence to monitor compliance with this judgment and, accordingly, it abstained from filing a request for interpretation of judgment.

125. [A]ccording to Article 67 of the Convention: 'The judgment of the Court shall be final and not subject to appeal. In case of disagreement as to the meaning or scope of the judgment, the Court shall interpret it at the request of any of the parties, provided the request is made within ninety days from the date of notification of the judgment.' [I]n paragraph 213 of the judgment of February 2, 2001, the Court 'reserve[d] the power to supervise the overall compliance with th[e] judgment', and in the tenth operative paragraph of this judgment 'it decided[d] that it [would] supervise compliance with th[e] judgment ...'

126. After examining the measures taken by the State in its different briefs, the Court concludes the following: (a) although it had the authority to request an interpretation of the judgment, owing to disagreement on the meaning and scope of the provisions relating to the Court's competence to monitor compliance with the judgment, the State did not use the procedural measures established in Article 67 of the Convention; (b) the State presented numerous reports on compliance with the judgment; (c) the State did not contest the first order issued by the Court on compliance with the judgment of June 21, 2002 ...; (d) the constant conduct of the State implied a recognition of the Court's authority to monitor compliance with the judgment on merits and reparations and costs delivered in this case; (e) Panama only contested the Court's authority to monitor compliance with its judgments after the Court issued a second order on compliance with judgment on November 22, 2002. It is worth emphasizing that this occurred two years after delivery of the judgment on merits and reparations and costs in the case; and (f) despite questioning the Court's monitoring function, the State has continued to provide the Court with information on the measures taken to comply with its judgment, which reveals its recognition of the Court's competence to monitor compliance with its decisions.

127. In conclusion, the Court considers that there is no doubt that the State's conduct reveals that it recognized the Court's competence to monitor compliance with its decisions, and, in consequence, it has behaved thus during almost all the monitoring procedure.

IV Conclusions with regard to monitoring compliance with the decisions of the Court

128. The Court, like any body with jurisdictional functions, has the authority, inherent in its attributions, to determine the scope of its own competence, and also of its orders and judgments, and compliance with the latter cannot be left to the discretion of the parties, because it would be inadmissible to subordinate the mechanism established in the American Convention to restrictions that make the Court's function and, consequently, that of the human rights protection system embodied in the Convention inoperable.

129. Monitoring compliance with judgments is one of the elements of jurisdiction. The effectiveness of the judgments depends on compliance with them.

130. Likewise, compliance with the decisions and judgments should be considered an integral part of the right of access to justice, understood it is broadest sense. The contrary would presume the very denial of this right. If the responsible State does not execute the measures of reparation ordered by the Court at the national level, this would deny the right of access to international justice.

131. The Court has the authority inherent in its jurisdictional function to monitor compliance with its decisions. The States undertake to comply with 'the judgment of the Court in any case to which they are parties', according to Article 68(1) of the Convention. To this end, the State must ensure implementation at the national level of the Court's decisions in its judgments.

132. The Court has the authority inherent in its jurisdictional function to issue, at the request of a party or *motu proprio*, instructions for the compliance with and implementation of the

measures of reparation that it has ordered, so as to comply effectively with the function of supervising genuine compliance with its decisions. The decisions issued by the Court in the procedure for monitoring compliance relate directly to the reparations ordered by the Court, so that they do not modify its judgments, but clarify their scope in light of the State's conduct, and try to ensure that compliance and implementation of the reparations is carried out as indicated in the said decisions and so as to best protect human rights.

133. The legal grounds for the competence of the Inter-American Court to monitor compliance with its decisions are established in Articles 33, 62(1), 62(3) and 65 of the Convention, and also in Article 30 of the Statute of the Court. The Court must exercise the authority that is inherent and non-discretional in its attributions to monitor compliance with its decisions, in order to comply with the mandate established in the said norms of the American Convention, specifically in order to comply with the provisions of Article 65 of the Convention, in order to inform the General Assembly when a State fails to comply with its decisions.

134. Monitoring compliance with the orders of the Court implies, first, that the Court requests information from the State on the activities carried out to ensure this compliance, and also to receive the comments of the Commission and the victims or their legal representatives. When the Court has this information, it can assess whether its decisions have been complied with, guide the corresponding actions of the State, and comply with its obligation to inform the General Assembly in the terms of Article 65 of the Convention.

135. The position of the OAS General Assembly on the monitoring of compliance with the judgments of the Court has been to consider that this monitoring is a function of the Court itself ...

137. The conduct of the Panamanian State implies recognition of the Court's authority to monitor compliance with its decisions, and the objection that the State now makes to this authority, to the detriment of the general principle of legal certainty, is inadmissible. Furthermore, the States Parties to the Convention with regard to whom the Court has issued orders on compliance with judgment have established an *opinio juris communis* by exhibiting a general and repeated attitude of acceptance of the Court's monitoring function (*supra* para. 102).

138. For the above reasons, this Court has the authority to continue monitoring full compliance with the judgment of February 2, 2001, in the *Baena Ricardo et al.* case.

2.3 The approach of the Inter–American Court of Human Rights

Perhaps the most remarkable feature of the Inter-American Court of Human Rights, however, resides in its original understanding of its role in the development of international human rights law, particularly under the influence of Judge Cançado Trindade, a member of the Court 1995–2008 and its President 1999–2004. The following excerpts of the case law offer a good exposition of this philosophy:

Inter-American Court of Human Rights, The Right to Information on Consular Assistance within the Framework of the Guarantees of Due Process of Law, Advisory Opinion OC-16/99 of 1 October 1999, Series A No. 16, para. 115:

The *corpus juris* of international human rights law comprises a set of international instruments of varied content and juridical effects (treaties, conventions, resolutions and declarations). Its dynamic evolution has had a positive impact on international law in affirming and building up the latter's faculty for regulating relations between States and the human beings within their respective jurisdictions. This Court, therefore, must adopt the proper approach to consider this question in the context of the evolution of the fundamental rights of the human person in contemporary international law.

Inter-American Court of Human Rights, Juridical Condition and Rights of the Undocumented Migrants, Advisory Opinion OC–18/03 of 17 September 2003, requested by the Union of Mexican States – concurring opinion of Judge Antônio Augusto Cançado Trindade:

[Mexico requested, in substance, whether an American State could establish in its labour legislation a differential treatment between legal residents or citizens, on the one hand, undocumented migrant workers, on the other hand, in the enjoyment of their labour rights. The request also questioned the Court about 'the status that the principles of legal equality, non-discrimination and equal and effective protection of the law have achieved in the context of the progressive development of international human rights law and its codification'. The Court concludes, unanimously, that 'the fundamental principle of equality and non-discrimination forms part of general international law, because it is applicable to all States, regardless of whether or not they are a party to a specific international treaty. At the current stage of the development of international law, the fundamental principle of equality and non-discrimination has entered the domain of *jus cogens*.' In addition, 'the fundamental principle of equality and non-discrimination, which is of a peremptory nature, entails obligations *erga omnes* of protection that bind all States and generate effects with regard to third parties, including individuals'. It takes the view that 'the migratory status of a person cannot constitute a justification to deprive him of the enjoyment and exercise of human rights, including those of a labor-related nature', and that the State is under an obligation to protect workers from discrimination. In the 'Epilogue' to his concurring opinion, the President of the Court, Judge Antônio Augusto Cançado Trindade, explains thus the underlying philosophy of the opinion:]

86. The fact that the concepts both of the *jus cogens* and of the obligations (and rights) *erga omnes* already integrate the conceptual universe of International Law discloses the reassuring and necessary opening of this latter, in the last decades, to certain superior and fundamental values. This significant evolution of the recognition and assertion of norms of *jus cogens* and *erga omnes* obligations of protection ought to be fostered, seeking to secure its full practical application, to the benefit of all human beings. Only thus shall we rescue the universalist vision of the founding fathers of the *droit des gens*, and shall we move closer to the plenitude of the international protection of the rights inherent to the human person. These new conceptions impose themselves in our days, and, of their faithful observance, in my view, will depend in great part the future evolution of the present domain of protection of the human person, as well as, ultimately, of the International Law itself as a whole.

87. It is not the function of the jurist simply to take note of what the States do, particularly the most powerful ones, which do not hesitate to seek formulas to impose their 'will', including in relation to the treatment to be dispensed to the persons under its jurisdiction. The function

of the jurist is to show and to tell what the Law is. In the present Advisory Opinion ..., the Inter-American Court of Human Rights has determined, firmly and with clarity, what the Law is. This latter does not emanate from the inscrutable 'will' of the States, but rather from human conscience. General or customary international law emanates not so much from the practice of States (not devoid of ambiguities and contradictions), but rather from the *opinio juris communis* of all the subjects of International Law (the States, the international organizations, and the human beings). Above the will is the conscience.

88. The fact that, despite all the sufferings of past generations, persist in our days new forms of exploitation of man by man, – such as the exploitation of the labour force of the undocumented migrants, forced prostitution, the traffic of children, forced and slave labour, amidst a proved increase of poverty and social exclusion and marginalization, the uprootedness and family disruption, – does not mean that 'regulation is lacking' or that Law does not exist. It rather means that Law is being ostensibly and flagrantly violated, from day to day, to the detriment of millions of human beings, among whom the undocumented migrants all over the world. In reacting against these generalized violations of the rights of the undocumented migrants, which affront the juridical conscience of humankind, the present Advisory Opinion of the Inter-American Court contributes to the current process of the necessary *humanization* of International Law.

89. In so doing, the Inter-American Court bears in mind the universality and unity of the human kind, which inspired, more than four and a half centuries ago, the historical process of formation of the *droit des gens*. In rescuing, in the present Advisory Opinion, the universalist vision which marked the origins of the best doctrine of International Law, the Inter-American Court contributes to the construction of the new *jus gentium* of the XXIst century, oriented by the general principles of law (among which the fundamental principle of equality and non-discrimination), characterized by the intangibility of the due process of law in its wide scope, crystallized in the recognition of *jus cogens* and instrumentalized by the consequent obligations *erga omnes* of protection, and erected, ultimately, on the full respect for, and guarantee of, the rights inherent to the human person.

3 THE AFRICAN SYSTEM OF PROTECTION OF HUMAN AND PEOPLES' RIGHTS

Although the African Union (AU) (until 2002 the Organization of African Unity) has other achievements in the area of human rights (see chapter 1, section 2.3.), the focus here will be on the African Charter on Human and Peoples' Rights and its Protocol on the Rights of Women in Africa (the latter, which entered into force in 2005, is subject to the same monitoring mechanisms as the Charter itself). The circumstances in which the Charter was adopted in 1981 have already been recalled. The Charter entered into force on 21 October 1986, and the African Commission on Human and Peoples' Rights began functioning in 1987. In 1998, the African system of human rights protection was further strengthened by the adoption of the Protocol to the African Charter on the Establishment of an African Court on Human and Peoples' Rights. The Protocol entered into force on

25 January 2004, but the setting up of the new Court proceeded slowly, in no small part because of discussions about the merger of the African Court on Human and Peoples' Rights and the Court of Justice established by the Constitutive Act of the African Union, the principle of which was agreed by the AU Assembly of Heads of State and Government in July of that same year: the 2008 Protocol on the Statute of the African Court of Justice and Human Rights provides for the merger, in the future, of the two judicial bodies.

3.1 The African Commission on Human and Peoples' Rights

The Commission comprises eleven commissioners, elected by the Assembly of Heads of State and Government for six-year terms and serving in their personal capacity (Arts. 31–32 of the Charter). They meet for two annual sessions of fifteen days each, in addition to which they have held extraordinary sessions on rare occasions (four such extraordinary sessions were held over twenty years, most recently in February 2008). The functions of the Commission may be described as falling under three categories, although these are not water-tight and a number of activities of the Commission serve simultaneously more than one of these functions.

(a) Promoting human and peoples' rights

The Commission has among its duties to 'promote Human and Peoples' Rights', a task which the Charter describes as comprising in particular:

African Charter on Human and Peoples' Rights (Banjul Charter) (1981), Art. 45(1):

(a) To collect documents, undertake studies and researches on African problems in the field of human and peoples' rights, organize seminars, symposia and conferences, disseminate information, encourage national and local institutions concerned with human and peoples' rights, and should the case arise, give its views or make recommendations to Governments.

(b) To formulate and lay down, principles and rules aimed at solving legal problems relating to human and peoples' rights and fundamental freedoms upon which African Governments may base their legislations.

(c) Co-operate with other African and international institutions concerned with the promotion and protection of human and peoples' rights.

The Commission has been inventive in fulfilling these promotional duties. It has, for instance, appointed thematic Special Rapporteurs, following the practice of the UN Commission on Human Rights or the Inter-American Commission on Human Rights, on issues such as prisons and conditions of detention in Africa, human rights defenders in Africa, refugees and displaced persons in Africa, or the rights of women in Africa. It has created thematic working groups such as the Working Group on Economic, Social and Cultural Rights in Africa, the Working Group on the Death Penalty, or the Working Group on the Situation of Indigenous Peoples/Communities in Africa. And it has adopted a number of resolutions, similar in kind to the general comments or recommendations adopted by the UN human rights treaty bodies, providing the States parties to the Charter with an authoritative reading of their obligations under this instrument. The low visibility of the African Commission, however, which stems to a large extent from the lack of publicity of its reports and decisions, has constituted a major obstacle not only to the enforcement of its recommendations to States, but also to the effectiveness of its promotional efforts (see M. Killander, 'Confidentiality versus Publicity: Intepreting Article 59 of the African Charter on Human and Peoples' Rights', *African Human Rights Law Journal*, 6, No. 2 (2006), 572).

(b) Providing an authoritative interpretation of the Charter

The Commission is also empowered under Article 45(3) of the Charter to provide an interpretation of the Charter 'at the request of a State party, an institution of the OAU [now the AU] or an African Organization recognized by the OAU'. Although this competence was used only on one occasion, the resulting Advisory Opinion, which concluded that the draft of the UN Declaration on the rights of indigenous peoples was compatible with the African Charter on Human and Peoples' Rights, is credited for having convinced the African Governments to support the Declaration towards which, initially, they were sceptical (see Advisory Opinion of the African Commission on Human and Peoples' Rights on the UN Declaration on the Rights of Indigenous Peoples, adopted by the African Commission on Human and Peoples' Rights at its forty-first ordinary session, Accra, Ghana, May 2007).

(c) Protecting human and peoples' rights

The Commission may also 'ensure the protection of human and peoples' rights', as stipulated by Article 45(2) of the Charter. It is the protective function of the Commission which it has exercised most effectively. The Commission has occasionally conducted fact-finding missions in countries after receiving allegations of serious human rights violations, in order to investigate such allegations, publishing recommendations addressed to the State concerned about how to improve the situation of human rights. As provided for by Article 62 of the African Charter, it also receives reports submitted by States every two years, on the basis of which it adopts concluding observations containing recommendations to the State concerned. This function has been gaining in importance over the years: according to one observer, 'States in Africa are now taking seriously the work of the African Commission, as is evident in the increasingly high-ranking state officials who personally present, thoroughly engage, and respond to queries as well as points of clarifications during state reporting' (G. M. Wachira, *African Court on Human and Peoples' Rights: Ten Years on and Still no Justice* (Minority Rights Group, African Centre for Democracy and Human Rights Studies, and Centre for Minority Rights Development, 2008, p. 10)).

The Commission also exercises its protective function by considering any communications submitted by individuals or non-governmental organizations or States. Indeed, quite remarkably, the Charter provides for the possibility of inter-State communications, without it being necessary for the State concerned to have made a separate declaration accepting this competence of the Commission (Arts. 47–53 of the Charter). As to individual communications, they may be filed not only by the direct victims of the violation denounced or by their duly mandated representatives, but by any individual or organization, without it being necessary to demonstrate that the victims directly affected are unable to file the complaint themselves. In practice therefore, most communications filed with the Commission were authored by non-governmental organizations, including, in a significant proportion of cases, northern-based international non-governmental organizations (such as the UK-based Interights). The Commission has thus adopted a broad reading of Article 56 of the Charter, which lists the conditions of admissibility of communications. This is also reflected in its interpretation of the condition according to which communications will only be admissible if they are sent 'after exhausting local remedies, if any, unless it is obvious that this procedure is unduly prolonged' (Art. 56(5) of the Charter).

African Commission on Human and Peoples' Rights, *Purohit and Moore* v. *Gambia*, Comm. No. 241/2001 (2003):

[The complainants are mental health advocates, submitting the communication on behalf of patients detained at Campama, a Psychiatric Unit of the Royal Victoria Hospital, and existing and 'future' mental health patients detained under the Mental Health Acts of the Republic of the Gambia. They allege that legislation governing mental health in the Gambia is outdated. Specifically, they allege that the Lunatics Detention Act (the instrument governing mental health) contains no definition of who is a lunatic, and that there are no provisions and requirements establishing safeguards during the diagnosis, certification and detention of the patient. They also allege that the Psychiatric Unit is overcrowded, that there is no requirement of consent to treatment or subsequent review of continued treatment, and that there exists no independent examination of administration, management and living conditions within the Unit itself. According to the complainants, there is no provision for legal aid and the Act does not make provision for a patient to seek compensation if his/her rights have been violated. The African Commission concludes that the communication is admissible, since the victims of the alleged violations do not have an effective remedy at their disposal. It takes into account the fact that those people represented in the communication 'are likely to be people picked up from the streets or people from poor backgrounds and as such it cannot be said that the remedies available in terms of the Constitution are realistic remedies for them in the absence of legal aid services':]

24. Article 56 of the African Charter governs admissibility of communications brought before the African Commission in accordance with Article 55 of the African Charter. All of the conditions of this Article are met by the present communication. Only Article 56(5), which requires that local remedies be exhausted, necessitates close scrutiny ...

25. The rule requiring exhaustion of local remedies as a condition of the presentation of a complaint before the African Commission is premised on the principle that the Respondent State must first have an opportunity to redress by its own means within the framework of its own domestic legal system, the wrong alleged to have been done to the individual.

26. The Complainants submit that they could not exhaust local remedies because there are no provisions in the national laws of the Gambia allowing for the Complainants to seek remedies where a violation has occurred.

27. The Respondent State concedes that the Lunatics Detention Act does not contain any provisions for the review or appeal against an order of detention or any remedy for detention made in error or wrong diagnosis or treatment. Neither do the patients have the legal right to challenge the two separate Medical Certificates, which constitute the legal basis of their detention.

28. The Respondent State submits that in practice patients found to be insane are informed that they have a right to ask for a review of their assessment. The Respondent State further states that there are legal provisions or procedures within the Gambia that such a vulnerable group of persons could have utilised for their protection. Section 7(d) of the Constitution of the Gambia recognises that Common Law forms part of the laws of the Gambia. As such, Respondent State argues, the Complainants could seek remedies by bringing an action in tort for false imprisonment or negligence where a patient held at Campama Psychiatric Unit is wrongly diagnosed.

29. The Respondent State further submits that patients detained under the Lunatics Detention Act have every right to challenge the Act in a Constitutional Court claiming that their detention under that Act deprives them of their right to freedom of movement and association as provided for under the Gambian Constitution.

30. The concern raised in the present communication is that in the Gambia, there are no review or appeal procedures against determination or certification of one's mental state for both involuntary and voluntary mental patients. Thus the legislation does not allow for the correction of an error assuming a wrong certification or wrong diagnosis has been made, which presents a problem in this particular case where examination of the said mental patients is done by general practitioners and not psychiatrists. So if an error is made and there is no avenue to appeal or review the medical practitioners' assessment, there is a great likelihood that a person could be wrongfully detained in a mental institution.

31. Furthermore, the Lunatics Detention Act does not lay out fixed periods of detention for those persons found to be of unsound mind, which, coupled with the absence of review or appeal procedures could lead into a situation where a mental patient is detained indefinitely.

32. The issue before the African Commission is whether or not there are domestic remedies available to the Complainants in this instance.

33. The Respondent State indicates that there are plans to amend the Lunatics Detention Act, which, in other words is an admission on part of the Respondent State that the Act is imperfect and would therefore not produce real substantive justice to the mental patients that would be detained.

34. The Respondent State further submits that even though the Act itself does not provide review or appeal procedures, there are legal procedures or provisions in terms of the constitution that the Complainants could have used and thus sought remedies in court. However, the Respondent State has informed the African Commission that no legal assistance or aid is availed to vulnerable groups to enable them access the legal procedures in the country. Only persons charged with Capital Offences get legal assistance in accordance with the Poor Persons Defence (Capital Charge) Act.

35. In the present matter, the African Commission cannot help but look at the nature of people that would be detained as voluntary or involuntary patients under the Lunatics Detention Act and ask itself whether or not these patients can access the legal procedures available (as stated by the Respondent State) without legal aid.

36. The African Commission believes that in this particular case, the general provisions in law that would permit anybody injured by another person's action are available to the wealthy and those that can afford the services of private counsel. However, it cannot be said that domestic remedies are absent as a general statement – the avenues for redress are there if you can afford it.

37. But the real question before this Commission is whether looking at this particular category of persons the existent remedies are realistic. The category of people being represented in the present communication are likely to be people picked up from the streets or people from poor backgrounds and as such it cannot be said that the remedies available in terms of the Constitution are realistic remedies for them in the absence of legal aid services.

38. If the African Commission were to literally interpret Article 56(5) of the African Charter, it might be more inclined to hold the communication inadmissible. However, the view is that, even as admitted by the Respondent State, the remedies in this particular instance are not realistic for this category of people and therefore not effective and for these reasons the African Commission declares the communication admissible.

[On the merits, the Commission finds the Gambia in violation of a number of provisions of the African Charter. It 'strongly urges' the Gambian Government to 'repeal the Lunatics Detention Act and replace it with a new legislative regime for mental health in the Gambia compatible with the African Charter on Human and Peoples' Rights and International Standards and Norms for the protection of mentally ill or disabled persons as soon as possible', and in the interim, to create 'an expert body to review the cases of all persons detained under the Lunatics Detention Act and make appropriate recommendations for their treatment or release'; and to 'provide adequate medical and material care for persons suffering from mental health problems in the territory of the Gambia'].

The Commission proceeds to examine the merits of the communications it receives having decided on their admissibility. The African Charter on Human and Peoples' Rights contains no provisions on the implementation of the findings of the Commission. Well-informed and perceptive commentators have identified this as a particularly weak aspect of the protective mandate of the Commission (F. Viljoen and L. Louw, 'The Status of the Findings of the African Commission: From Moral Persuasion to Legal Obligation', *Journal of African Law*, 48 No. 1 (2004), 1; F. Viljoen and L. Louw, 'State Compliance with the Recommendations of the African Commission on Human and Peoples' Rights, 1993– 2004', *American Journal of International* Law, 101 (2007), 1; F. Viljoen, 'The African Regional Human Rights System' in C. Krause and M. Scheinin (eds.), *International Protection of Human Rights: a Textbook* (Turku: Åbo Akademi University Institute for Human Rights, 2009), p. 503 at p. 512; and, for a proposal from two former employees of the African Commission, arguing in favour of a strengthened role of the AU's Assembly of Heads of State and Government or of the African Court in the enforcement of the decisions of the Commission, see G. M. Wachira and A. Ayinla, 'Twenty Years of Elusive Enforcement of the Recommendations of the African Commission on Human and Peoples' Rights: a Possible Remedy', *African Human Rights Law Journal*, 6, No. 2 (2006), 465). This is further compounded by the fact that the Commission examines communications in private sessions, and no information about the Commission's treatment of them may be made public before its annual report of activities is presented to the African Union's Assembly of Heads of State and Government: only after such presentation is the report published, so that at this point the procedure loses its confidential character.

In order to compensate for this liability as far as implementation is concerned, the Commission typically requests the States found to be in violation of their obligations under the Charter to provide information in their next periodic report (submitted in accordance with Art. 62 of the African Charter) on the measures taken to comply with the recommendations and directions of the African Commission in the decisions rendered against them. In 2006, it also adopted a Resolution on the Importance of the Implementation of the Recommendations of the African Commission on Human and Peoples' Rights (ACHPR/Res. 97(XXXX)06, 29 November 2006), in which it announced its decision to submit at every session of the AU Executive Council a report on the situation of the compliance with its recommendations by the State Parties, as an annex to its Annual Activity Report, and in which it requests all State parties to the African Charter on Human and Peoples' Rights to 'indicate the measures taken and/ or the obstacles in implementing the recommendations of the African Commission within a maximum period of ninety days starting from the date of notification of the recommendations'.

3.2 The African Court on Human and Peoples' Rights

The first eleven members of the African Court of Human and Peoples' Rights have been elected at the AU Summit held in Khartoum in January 2006, and they were sworn in in June of that year. Yet, its first communication reached the Court only on 11 August 2008, leading to the first ruling of the Court on 15 December 2009 in the *Matter of Michelot Yogogombaye* v. *Republic of Senegal* (Appl. No. 001/2008). The Court concluded it had no jurisdiction to hear the case: the applicant requested a suspension of the proceedings brought in Senegal against Hissène Habré, the former Head of State of Chad, but the Court dismissed the petition because Senegal had not entered a declaration accepting the Court's jurisdiction to hear individual petitions as required under Article 34(6) of the 1998 Protocol establishing the Court. It is therefore too early to assess its contribution to strengthening the protection of human rights on the African continent. It is already clear, however, that the jurisdiction of the Court shall be very wide-ranging: it shall extend to 'all cases and disputes submitted to it concerning the interpretation and application of the Charter, this Protocol and any other relevant Human Rights instrument ratified by the States concerned' (Art. 3 of the Protocol to the African Commission on Human and Peoples' Rights on the establishment of the African Court on Human and Peoples' Rights).

The Court has the competence to deliver advisory opinions at the request of any Member State of the AU, the AU or any of its organs, or any African organization recognized by the AU (Art. 4). The Court may receive complaints either from the Commission, from the State party which had lodged a complaint to the Commission, or from the State party against which the complaint has been lodged at the Commission;

the State party whose citizen is a victim of human rights violation and African inter-governmental organizations also have access to the Court (Art. 5). Individuals or non-governmental organizations shall have direct access to the Court only exceptionally, when the defending State has made a specific declaration to that effect, as provided for in Article 34(6) and Article 5(3) of the Protocol. The provisions of the Protocol on enforcement of judgments represent a clear step forward in comparison to the existing situation as regards the decisions of the African Commission: the AU's Executive Council, composed of the Foreign Affairs Ministers of the AU Member States or their delegates (still called the Council of Ministers in the Protocol) 'shall also be notified of the judgment and shall monitor its execution on behalf of the Assembly' (Art. 29(2)). This will significantly raise the political cost for a State refusing to comply with the judgment delivered in a case to which it is a party.

11.1. Questions for discussion: the effectiveness of regional systems of protection of human rights

1. Compare the supervision of the execution of judgments of the European Court of Human Rights and of the Inter-American Court of Human Rights, respectively. What advantages does the involvement of political organs, as in the European Convention on Human Rights' model of enforcement, present? Which problems do you see in such a model? Is the continued involvement of the Court in monitoring implementation, as in the *Baena Ricardo et al. (270 Workers* v. *Panama)* of the Inter-American Court of Human Rights, a more desirable alternative?

2. On 13 May 2004, Protocol No. 14 to the European Convention on Human Rights amending the control system of the Convention was concluded, in particular in order to improve the ability of the European Court of Human Rights to manage its increasing caseload. The Protocol is in force since 1 June 2010. One of the provisions of Protocol No. 14 amends Article 46 ECHR in order to provide in para. 3 that: 'If the Committee of Ministers considers that the supervision of the execution of a final judgment is hindered by a problem of interpretation of the judgment, it may refer the matter to the Court for a ruling on the question of interpretation.' Is this a recognition that entrusting a political organ with the task of monitoring the execution of judgments entails the risk of the monitoring becoming excessively politicized, and departing from the intent of the court? Note that, in its task of supervising the execution of the judgments of the Court, the Committee of Ministers of the Council of Europe is assisted by a special section of the Council of Europe's Secretariat, the Department for the Execution of Judgments of the European Court of Human Rights, that examines with great care whether the necessary execution measures have been taken, sometimes even seeming to go beyond what the judgment in fact seems to imply, according to the States concerned.

3. One influential theory of compliance in international law presents itself as 'managerial', as opposed to based on 'enforcement'. Its argument is essentially that, in an increasingly interdependent community of States, no State can afford to remain isolated: '... for all but a few self-isolated nations, sovereignty no longer consists in the freedom of states to act independently, in their perceived self-interest, but in membership in reasonably good standing in the

regimes that make up the substance of international life. To be a player, the state must submit to the pressures that international regulations impose. Its behavior in any single episode is likely to affect future relationships not only within a particular regime involved but in many others as well, and perhaps its position within the international system as a whole ... The need to be an accepted member in this complex web of international arrangements is itself a critical factor in ensuring acceptable compliance with regulatory agreements ... Sovereignty, in the end, is status – the vindication of the state's existence as a member of the international system' (A. Chayes and A. Handler Chayes, *The New Sovereignty. Compliance with International Regulatory Agreements* (Cambridge, Mass.: Harvard University Press, 1995), p. 27). If this is correct – if compliance really is reliant on the self-interest of the State in being an 'accepted member' of the international community, as a repeat-player in international relations – are regional systems of human rights protection, developed within political organizations such as the Council of Europe, the Organization of American States, or the African Union, more likely to succeed in ensuring compliance than human rights systems developed at broader, universal level? Or rather is it the opposite? Would it depend on which State is concerned?

Index of Keywords